The
Illustrated Dictionary of
Electronics

The Illustrated Dictionary of Electronics

Seventh Edition

Stan Gibilisco
Editor-in-Chief

McGraw-Hill

New York San Francisco Washington, D.C. Auckland Bogotá
Caracas Lisbon London Madrid Mexico City Milan
Montreal New Delhi San Juan Singapore
Sydney Tokyo Toronto

Library of Congress Cataloging-in-Publication Data

Gibilisco, Stan.
  The illustrated dictionary of electronics / Stan Gibilisco.—7th
ed.
    p.   cm.
  ISBN 0-07-024186-4 (pbk.)
  1. Electronics—Dictionaries. I. Title.
TK7804.G497 1997
621.381'03—dc21   97-9081
                                                        CIP

McGraw-Hill

A Division of The McGraw·Hill Companies

1 2 3 4 5 6 7 8 9 0   FGR/FGR   9 0 2 1 0 9 8 7

ISBN 0-07-024186-4

The sponsoring editor for this book was Scott Grillo, and the production supervisor
was Pamela Pelton. It was set in Bookman by Lisa Mellott through the services of
Barry E. Brown (Broker—Editing, Design and Production).

Printed and bound by Quebecor/Fairfield.

McGraw-Hill books are available at special quantity discounts to use as premiums
and sales promotions, or for use in corporate training programs. For more information, please write to the Director of Special Sales, McGraw-Hill, 11 West 19th
Street, New York, NY 10011. Or contact your local bookstore.

This book is printed on acid-free paper.

To Tony and Tim
from Uncle Stan

Introduction

The Illustrated Dictionary of Electronics—7th Edition has been thoroughly revised, clarified, and updated, reflecting technological advances of recent years. Many definitions contain cross-references (indicated in ALL CAPITALS); these provide recommended additional information or allow comparison with related terms. Expressions of special significance are printed in *italics*. Definitions are arranged in alphabetical order, ignoring internal spaces and punctuation. Many electronics abbreviations are included in the text; the full terms are stated as definitions.

Appendix A contains the standard symbols used in electrical and electronic diagrams. These symbols are used in illustrations throughout this dictionary.

Appendix B contains the following data tables:

1. Conversion between electrical systems
2. Greek alphabet
3. Mathematical functions and operations
4. Prefix multipliers
5. Resistor color code

Appendix C contains an alphabetical listing of hundreds of abbreviations commonly used in electronics and related industries.

Suggestions for future editions are welcome.

Stan Gibilisco
Editor-in-Chief

Acknowledgments

The new and updated art in this book was drawn using CorelDRAW graphics software. All clip art in new and updated illustrations is courtesy of Corel Corporation, 1600 Carling Avenue, Ottawa, Ontario, Canada K1Z 8R7.

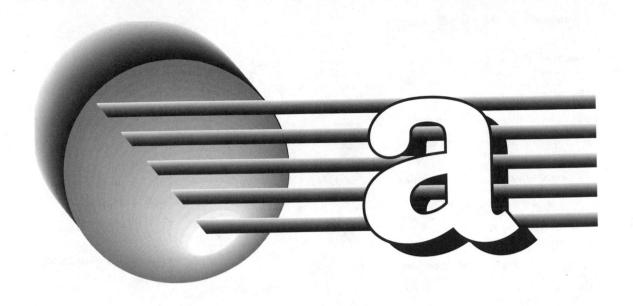

A **1.** Symbol for GAIN. **2.** Symbol for AREA. **3.** Symbol for AMPERE (SI unit for current).

A- Symbol for negative terminal of filament-voltage source in a vacuum-tube circuit.

A+ Symbol for positive terminal of filament-voltage source in a vacuum-tube circuit.

a **1.** Abbreviation of ATTO- (prefix). **2.** Abbreviation of AREA. **3.** Abbreviation of ACCELERATION. **4.** Abbreviation of ANODE. **5.** Obsolete abbreviation of cgs prefix AB-.

aA **1.** Abbreviation of *attoampere*. **2.** Obsolete for ABAMPERE.

AAAS Abbreviation for *American Association for the Advancement of Science*.

AAC Abbreviation of *automatic aperture control* (NASA).

AAS Abbreviation of *advanced antenna system* (NASA).

AASR Abbreviation of *airport and airways surveillance radar*.

AB Abbreviation of *acquisition beacon* (NASA).

A-B In sound and acoustics, the direct comparison of two sources of sound by alternately turning on one and the other.

ab- **1.** Prefix that transforms the name of a practical electrical unit to that of the equivalent electromagnetic cgs unit (e.g., ABAMPERE, ABOHM, ABVOLT). See individual entries of such cgs units. **2.** Abbreviation for ABSOLUTE.

abac A graphic device for the solution of electronics problems. Also see ALIGNMENT CHART.

abampere The unit of current in the cgs electromagnetic system. One abampere equals 10 amperes and corresponds to 1 abcoulomb per second.

Abbe condenser **1.** In microscopy, a special two-piece lens that has enhanced light-gathering power. **2.** A similar focusing device in an electromagnetic antenna.

abbreviated dialing In telephone systems, special circuits requiring fewer-than-normal dialing operations to connect subscribers.

abc **1.** Abbreviation of AUTOMATIC BASS COMPENSATION, a system for boosting the volume of bass sounds at low amplifier gain. **2.** Abbreviation of AUTOMATIC BIAS CONTROL. **3.** Abbreviation of AUTOMATIC BRIGHTNESS CONTROL. **4.** Abbreviation of AUTOMATIC BRIGHTNESS COMPENSATION.

abcoulomb The unit of electrical quantity in the cgs electromagnetic system. One abcoulomb equals 10 coulombs and is the quantity of electricity that flows past any point in a circuit in one second when the current is one abampere.

aberration **1.** Distortion from perfect shape in a lens or reflecting mirror or antenna dish. **2.** A small error in the determination of the direction of a source of electromagnetic energy, on account of the motion of the source and/or the detecting apparatus. **3.** A small displacement in the apparent positions of the stars from month to month on account of the earth's orbital motion.

ABETS Acronym for *airborne beacon electronic test set* (NASA).

abfarad The unit of capacitance in the cgs electromagnetic system. One abfarad equals 10^9 farads and is the capacitance across which a charge of 1 abcoulomb produces a potential of 1 abvolt.

abhenry The unit of inductance in the cgs electromagnetic system. One abhenry equals 10^{-9} henry and is the inductance across which a current that changes at the rate of 1 abampere per second induces a potential of 1 abvolt.

ABL Abbreviation of *Automated Biology Laboratory* (NASA).

abmho The obsolete unit of conductance and of conductivity in the cgs electromagnetic system. Replaced with ABSIEMENS.

abnormal dissipation Power dissipation higher or lower than the customary level, usually an overload.

abnormal oscillation **1.** Oscillation where none is desired or expected, as in an amplifier. **2.** Oscillation at two or more frequencies simultaneously when single-frequency operation is expected. **3.** Oscillation at an incorrect frequency. **4.** Parasitic oscillation.

abnormal propagation **1.** The chance shifting of the normal path of a radio wave, as by displacements in the ionosphere, so that reception is degraded. **2.** Unintentional radiation of energy from some point other than the transmitting antenna. **3.** Propagation over a path or in a direction not expected.

abnormal reflections Sharp, intense reflections at frequencies higher than the critical frequency of the ionosphere's ionized layer.

abnormal termination The shutdown of a running computer program or other process. Caused by the detection of an error by the associated hardware that indicates that some ongoing series of actions cannot be executed correctly.

abnormal triggering The false triggering or switching of a circuit or device, such as a flip-flop, by some undesirable source instead of the true trigger signal. Electrical noise pulses often cause abnormal triggering.

abohm The unit of resistance and of resistivity in the cgs electromagnetic system. One abohm equals 10^{-9} ohms and is the resistance across which a steady current of 1 abampere produces a potential difference of 1 abvolt.

abort To deliberately terminate an operation, experiment, process, or project before it has run its normal course.

AB power pack **1.** A portable dry-cell or wet-cell array containing both A and B batteries in one package. **2.** An ac-operated unit in one package for supplying A and B voltages to equipment normally operated from batteries.

abrasion machine An instrument for determining the abrasive resistance of a wire or cable.

abrasion resistance A measure of the ability of a wire or wire covering to resist mechanical damage.

ABS A basic programming abbreviation for the absolute value (of a number, variable, or expression).

abscissa **1.** The independent variable in a function. **2.** The axis (usually horizontal) on the graph of a function that indicates the independent variable.

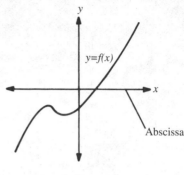

abscissa

absence-of-ground searching selector A rotary switch that searches for an ungrounded contact in a dial telephone system.

absiemens The unit of conductance or conductivity in the cgs electromagnetic system. One absiemens equals 10^9 siemens and is the conductance through which a potential of 1 abvolt forces a current of 1 abampere.

absolute **1.** A temperature scale in which zero represents the complete absence of heat. Units of measure are same as units on Celsius and Fahrenheit scales. See ABSOLUTE SCALE. **2.** Independent of any arbitrarily assigned units of measure or value.

absolute accuracy The full-scale accuracy of a meter with respect to a primary (absolute) standard.

absolute address In a digital computer program, the location of a word in memory, as opposed to location of the word in the program.

absolute code A computer code in which the exact address is given for storing or locating the reference operand.

absolute coding In computer practice, coding that uses absolute addresses.

absolute constant A mathematical constant that has the same value wherever it is used.

absolute delay The time elapsing between the transmission of two synchronized signals from the same station or from different stations, as in radio, radar, or loran. By extension, the time interval between two such signals from any source, as from a generator.

absolute digital position transducer A digital position transducer whose output signal indicates absolute position. (See ENCODER.)

absolute efficiency The ratio X_x/X_s, where X_x is the output of a given device, and X_s is the output of an ideal device of the same kind under the same operating conditions.

absolute encoder system A system that permits the encoding of any function (linear, nonlinear, continuous, step, and so on) and supplies a nonambiguous output.

absolute error The difference indicated by the approximate value of a quantity minus the actual value. This difference is positive when the approximate value is higher than the exact value, and it is negative when the approximate value is lower than the exact value. Compare RELATIVE ERROR.

absolute gain Antenna gain for a given orientation when the reference antenna is isolated in space and has no main axis of propagation.

absolute humidity The mass of water vapor per unit volume of air. Compare RELATIVE HUMIDITY.

absolute instruction A computer instruction that states explicitly and causes the execution of a specific operation.

absolute magnitude For a complex number quantity, the vector sum of the real and imaginary components (i.e., the square root of the sum of the squares of those components). Also see ABSOLUTE VALUE and IMPEDANCE.

absolute maximum rating The highest value a quantity can have before malfunction or damage occurs.

absolute maximum supply voltage The highest supply voltage that can be applied to a circuit without permanently altering its characteristics.

absolute measurement of current Measurement of a current directly in terms of defining quantities. **1.** TANGENT GALVANOMETER method: Current is proportional to the tangent of the angle of deflection of the needle of this instrument. Deflection depends on torque, resulting from the magnetic field produced by current in the galvanometer coil acting against the horizontal component of the earth's magnetic field. **2.** ELECTRODYNAMOMETER method: With this 2-coil instrument, current is determined from the observed deflection, the torque of the suspension fiber of the movable coil, and the coil dimensions.

absolute measurement of voltage Measurement of a voltage directly in terms of defining quantities. **1.** CALORIMETRIC method: A current-carrying coil immersed in water raises the temperature of the water. The difference of potential that forces the current through the coil then is determined in terms of the equivalent heat energy. **2.** Disk-electrometer method: In this setup, a metal disk attached to one end of a balance beam is attracted by a stationary disk mounted below it, the voltage being applied to the two disks. The other end of the beam carries a pan into which accurate weights are placed. At balance, the voltage is determined in terms of

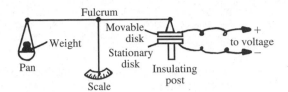

absolute measurement of voltage, 2

the weight required to restore balance, the upper-disk area, and the disk separation.

absolute minimum resistance The resistance between the wiper and the nearer terminal of a potentiometer, when the wiper is as close to that terminal as physically possible. All potentiometers have two such specifications, one for each end terminal.

absolute Peltier coefficient The product of the absolute Seebeck coefficient and absolute temperature of a material.

absolute pitch A tone in a standard scale, determined according to the rate of vibration, independent of other tones in the range of pitch.

absolute pressure Pressure (force per unit area) of a gas or liquid determined with respect to that of a vacuum (taken as zero).

absolute-pressure transducer A transducer actuated by pressure from the outputs of two different pressure sources, and whose own output is proportional to the difference between the two applied pressures.

absolute scale **1.** A scale in which the zero value indicates the lowest physically possible value that a parameter can attain. **2.** A standard scale for measurement of a quantity. **3.** A universally agreed-upon scale for the determination of a variable quantity. **4.** The Kelvin temperature scale. **5.** The Rankine temperature scale.

absolute Seebeck coefficient The quotient, as an integral from absolute zero to the given temperature, of the Thomson coefficient of a material divided by its absolute temperature.

absolute spectral response The frequency output or response of a device in absolute power units (such as milliwatts) as opposed to relative units (such as decibels).

absolute system of units A system of units in which the fundamental (ABSOLUTE) units are those expressing length (l), mass (m), charge (q), and time (t). All other physical units, including practical ones, are then derived from these absolute units.

absolute temperature Temperature measured on either the Kelvin or Rankine scales, where zero represents the total absence of heat energy.

absolute temperature scale **1.** The Kelvin temperature scale, in which the divisions are equal in size to 1° Celsius, and the zero point is absolute zero, the coldest possible temperature, approximately –273.16° Celsius. **2.** The Rankine temperature scale, in which the divisions are equal in size to 1° Fahrenheit, and the zero point is absolute zero or approximately –459.7° Fahrenheit.

absolute tolerance The value of a component as it deviates from the specified or nominal value. It is usually expressed as a percentage of the specified value.

absolute units Fundamental physical units (see ABSOLUTE SYSTEM OF UNITS) from which all others are derived. See, for example, AMPERE, OHM, VOLT, and WATT.

absolute value The magnitude of a quantity without regard to sign or direction. The absolute value of a is written $|a|$. The absolute value of a positive number is the number itself; thus, $|10|$ equals 10. The absolute value of a negative number is the number with its sign changed: $|-10|$ equals 10.

absolute-value circuit A circuit that produces a unipolar signal in response to a bipolar input and in proportion to the absolute value of the magnitude of the input.

absolute-value computer A computer in which data is processed in its absolute form; i.e., every variable maintains its full value. (Compare to INCREMENTAL COMPUTER.)

absolute-value device In computer practice, a device that delivers a constant-polarity output signal equal in amplitude to that of the input signal. Thus, the output signal always has the same sign.

absolute zero The temperature –273.16°C (-459.7°F and 0 Kelvin). The coldest possible temperature, representing the complete absence of heat energy.

absorbed wave A radio wave that dissipates in the ionosphere as a result of molecular agitation. This effect is most pronounced at low and medium frequencies.

absorptance The amount of radiant energy absorbed in a material; equal to 1 minus the transmittance.

absorption The taking up of one material or medium by another into itself, as by sucking or soaking up. Also, the retention of one medium (or a part of it) by another medium, through which the first one attempts to pass. See, for example, ABSORBED WAVE, ABSORPTION COEFFICIENT, DIELECTRIC ABSORPTION. Compare ADSORPTION.

absorption band See ABSORPTION SPECTRUM.

absorption circuit A circuit that absorbs energy from another circuit or from a signal source—especially a resonant circuit, such as a wavemeter or wavetrap.

absorption current In a capacitor, the current resulting from absorption of energy by the dielectric material.

absorption dynamometer A power-measuring instrument in which a brake absorbs energy from a revolving shaft or wheel.

absorption fading Fading of a radio wave, resulting from (usually) slow changes in the absorption of the wave in the line of propagation.

absorption frequency meter See WAVEMETER.

absorption line See ABSORPTION SPECTRUM.

absorption loss **1.** Transmission loss caused by dissipation of electrical energy, or conversion of it into heat or other forms of energy. **2.** Loss of all or part of a skywave because of absorption by the ionosphere. Also called *ionospheric absorption* or *atmospheric absorption.*

absorption marker A small blip introduced onto an oscilloscope trace to indicate a frequency point. It is so called because it is produced by the action of a frequency-calibrated tuned trap, similar to an absorption wavemeter.

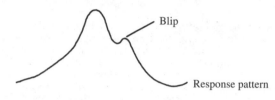

absorption marker

absorption modulation Amplitude modulation of a transmitter or oscillator by means of an audio-frequency-actuated absorber circuit. In its simplest form, the modulator consists of a few turns of wire coupled to the transmitter tank coil and connected to a carbon microphone. The arrangement absorbs energy from the transmitter at a varying rate as the microphone changes its resistance in accordance with the sound waves it receives.

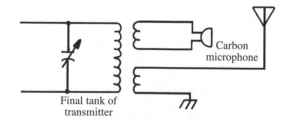

absorption modulation

absorption spectrum For electromagnetic waves, a plot of absorption coefficient (of the medium of

propagation) versus frequency. Also called EMIS-
SION SPECTRUM.

absorption trap　See WAVETRAP.

absorption wavemeter　A resonant-frequency indicating instrument that is inductively coupled
to the device under test.

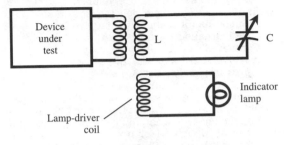

absorption wavemeter

absorptivity　In audio and microwave technologies, a measure of the energy absorbed by a
given volume of material.

A-B test　Comparison of two sounds by reproducing them in alternating succession.

abvolt　The unit of potential difference in the cgs
electromagnetic system. One abvolt equals 10^{-8}
V and is the difference of potential between any
two points when 1 erg of work is required to
move 1 abcoulomb of electricity between them.

abwatt　The unit of power in the cgs electromagnetic system. One abwatt equals 10^{-7} W and is
the power corresponding to 1 erg of work per
second.

ac　**1.** Abbreviation of ALTERNATING CURRENT.
2. Abbreviation of ATTITUDE CONTROL. **3.** Abbreviation of AERODYNAMIC CENTER. **4.** A suffix meaning AUTOMATIC CALCULATOR or
AUTOMATIC COMPUTER.

a/c　**1.** Abbreviation of AIRCRAFT. **2.** Abbreviation of AIR CONDITIONING.

Ac　Symbol for ACTINIUM.

ACA　Abbreviation of *automatic circuit analyzer.*

ac base current　Symbol, $I_{B(ac)}$. The ac component
of base current in a bipolar transistor.

ac base resistance　Symbol, $R_{B(ac)}$. The dynamic
base resistance in a bipolar transistor.

ac base voltage　Symbol, $V_{B(ac)}$. The ac component
of base voltage in a bipolar transistor. It is the
ac input signal voltage in a common-emitter
amplifier or emitter-follower amplifier.

ac bias　In a tape recorder, the high-frequency
current that passes through the recording head
to linearize operation.

acc　**1.** Abbreviation of AUTOMATIC CHROMI-
NANCE CONTROL. **2.** Abbreviation of AUTO-
MATIC COLOR COMPENSATION. **3.** Abbreviation
of ACCELERATION.

ac cathode current　Symbol, $I_{K(ac)}$. The ac component of cathode current in an electron tube.

ac cathode resistance　Symbol, $R_{K(ac)}$. The dynamic cathode resistance in an electron tube.
$R_{K(ac)}$ equals dV_K/dI_K for a constant value of V_G.

ac cathode voltage　Symbol, $V_{K(ac)}$. The ac component of cathode voltage in an electron tube. It is
the ac output signal voltage in cathode-follower
and grounded-grid amplifiers.

accelerated life test　A test program that simulates the effects of time on devices or apparatus,
by artificially speeding up the aging process.

accelerated service test　A service or bench test
in which equipment or a circuit is subjected to
an extreme condition in an attempt to simulate
the effects of average use over a long time.

accelerating conductor or relay　A conductor or
relay that prompts the operation of a succeeding device in a starting mode according to established conditions.

accelerating electrode　In a cathode-ray tube or
klystron, the electrode to which the accelerating
voltage is applied.

accelerating time　The elapsed time that starts
when voltage is applied to a motor, and ends
when the motor shaft reaches maximum speed.

accelerating voltage　A positive high voltage applied to the accelerating electrode of a cathode-
ray tube to increase the velocity of electrons in
the beam.

acceleration at stall　The angular acceleration of
a servomotor at stall, determined from the stall
torque and the moment of inertia of the motor's
rotor.

acceleration derivative　Acceleration (*a*) expressed as the second derivative of distance (*s*)
with respect to time (*t*): *a* equals d^2s/dt^2.

acceleration potential　See ACCELERATING
VOLTAGE.

acceleration switch　A switch that operates automatically when the acceleration of a body to
which it is attached exceeds a predetermined
rate in a given direction.

acceleration time　The time required by a computer to take in or deliver information after interpreting instructions. Compare ACCESS TIME.

acceleration torque　During the accelerating period of a motor, the difference between the
torque demanded and the torque actually produced by the motor.

acceleration voltage　The potential between accelerating elements in a vacuum tube, the value
of which determines average electron velocity.

accelerator　**1.** A type of atom smasher: a machine
or device in which charged particles, such as
protons or electrons, are given high velocity for
use in atomic disintegration and kindred processes. **2.** A substance that speeds up a chemical
reaction (e.g., the catalyst used with certain
resins for encapsulating electronic equipment).

accelerometer A transducer whose output voltage is proportional to the acceleration of the moving body to which it is attached.

accentuation The emphasis of a desired band of frequencies, usually in the audio-frequency spectrum.

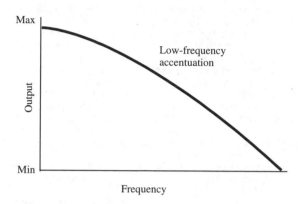

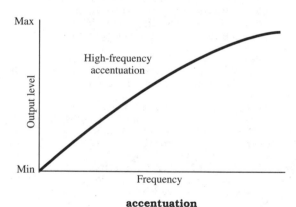

accentuation

accentuator A circuit or device, such as a filter, tone control, or equalizer, used to emphasize a band of frequencies, usually in the audio-frequency spectrum. Also see ACCENTUATION.

acceptable-environmental-range test A test to disclose the environmental conditions that equipment can endure while maintaining at least the minimum desired reliability.

acceptable quality level Abbreviation, AQL. A percentage that represents an acceptable average of defective components allowable for a process, or the lowest quality that a supplier is permitted to regularly present for acceptance.

acceptance sampling plan A probabilistic method of sampling a quantity of units from a lot, and determining from the sample whether to accept the lot, reject the lot, or perform another sampling.

acceptance test A test performed on incoming equipment or on submitted samples to determine if they meet tester's or supplier's specifications.

acceptor **1.** Any device or circuit, such as a series-resonant circuit, that provides relatively easy transmission of a signal, in effect accepting the signal. **2.** A hole-rich impurity added to a semiconductor to make the latter p-type. It is so called because its holes can accept electrons. Compare DONOR.

acceptor circuit See ACCEPTOR, **1.**

acceptor impurity See ACCEPTOR, **2.**

access **1.** To gain entrance to something, such as the interior of the cabinet of a high-fidelity amplifier. **2.** In a computer, the action of going to a specific memory location for the purpose of data retrieval. **3.** A port or opening into a piece of equipment, placed there to make the equipment easy to maintain and repair.

access arm A mechanical device that positions the read/write mechanism in a computer storage unit.

access control register A register that is part of a computer protection system that prevents interference between different software modules.

access method A method of transferring information or data from main storage to an input/output unit.

access right The access status given to computer system users that indicates the method of access permitted (e.g., read a file only or write to a file).

access time The time required by a computer to begin delivering information after the memory or storage has been interrogated.

accidental error An unintentional error committed by a person making measurements and recording data.

accidental triggering The undesired chance operation of a flip-flop or other switching circuit caused by a noise pulse or other extraneous signal.

ac collector current Symbol, $I_{C(ac)}$. The ac component of collector current in a bipolar transistor.

ac collector resistance Symbol, $R_{C(ac)}$. The dynamic collector resistance of a bipolar transistor. $R_{C(ac)}$ equals dV_C/dI_C for a constant value of base current I_B (in a common-emitter circuit) or emitter current I_E (in a common-base circuit).

ac collector voltage Symbol, $V_{C(ac)}$. The ac component of collector voltage in a bipolar transistor. The ac output signal voltage in a common-emitter or common-base amplifier.

accompanying audio channel The RF signal that supplies television sound. Also called *Cochannnel sound frequency.*

ac component In a complex wave (i.e., one containing both ac and dc), the alternating, fluctuating, or pulsating part of the combination. Compare DC COMPONENT.

accordion A printed-circuit connector contact with a Z-shaped spring that allows high deflection with low fatigue.

ac-coupled flip-flop A flip-flop that is operated by the rise or fall of a clock pulse.

ac coupling Transformer coupling or capacitive coupling, which transmit ac, but not dc. Compare DIRECT COUPLING.

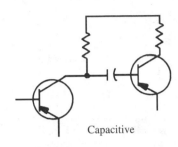

Capacitive

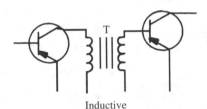

Inductive

ac coupling

accumulator 1. In a digital computer, a circuit or register device that receives numbers, totals them, and stores them. 2. Storage battery.

accuracy 1. Precision in the measurement of quantities and in the statement of physical characteristics. 2. Degree of precision. Usually expressed, in terms of error, as a percentage of the specified value (e.g., 10 V plus or minus 1%), as a percentage of a range (e.g., 2% of full scale), or as parts (e.g., 100 parts per million).

accuracy rating The maximum error in an instrument, given as a percentage of the full-scale value.

accw Abbreviation of ALTERNATING-CURRENT CONTINUOUS WAVE.

ac/dc Abbreviation of ALTERNATING CURRENT/DIRECT CURRENT. Pertains to equipment that will operate from either ac utility power or a dc power source. A notebook computer is a good example.

ac directional overcurrent relay A relay that works on a specific value of alternating overcurrent that is rectified for a desired polarity.

ac drain current Symbol, $I_{D(ac)}$. The ac component of drain current in a field-effect transistor.

ac drain resistance Symbol, $R_{D(ac)}$. The dynamic drain resistance in a field-effect transistor; $R_{D(ac)}$ equals dV_D/dI_D for a constant value of gate voltage V_G.

ac drain voltage Symbol, $V_{D(ac)}$. The ac component of drain voltage in a field-effect transistor. The ac output signal voltage in a common-source FET amplifier.

ac dump The removal of all ac power from a system or component.

ac emitter current Symbol, $I_{E(ac)}$. The ac component of emitter current in a bipolar transistor.

ac emitter resistance Symbol, $R_{E(ac)}$. The dynamic emitter resistance of a bipolar transistor; $R_{E(ac)}$ equals dV_E/dI_E for a constant value of base current I_B (in an emitter-follower circuit) or collector voltage V_{CC} (in a common-base circuit).

ac emitter voltage Symbol, $V_{E(ac)}$. The ac component of emitter voltage in a bipolar transistor. The ac input signal voltage in a common-base amplifier; the ac output signal voltage in an emitter-follower amplifier.

ac equipment An apparatus designed for operation from an ac power source only. Compare DC EQUIPMENT and AC/DC.

ac erasing In tape recording, the technique of using an alternating magnetic field to erase material already recorded on the tape.

ac erasing head Also called *ac erase head*. In tape and wire recording, a head that carries alternating current to erase material already recorded on the tape or wire. Also see AC ERASING.

acetate Cellulose acetate, a tough thermoplastic material that is an acetic acid ester of cellulose. It is used as a dielectric and in the manufacture of photographic films.

acetate base 1. The cellulose acetate film that served as the base for the magnetic oxide coating in early recording tape. Most such tapes today are of polyester base. 2. The cellulose acetate substrate onto which certain photosensitive materials are deposited for lithographic reproduction. Also see ACETATE and ANCHORAGE.

acetate tape Recording tape consisting of a magnetic oxide coating on a cellulose acetate film. Also see ACETATE BASE.

ac gate voltage Symbol, $V_{G(ac)}$. The ac component of gate voltage in a field-effect transistor. The ac input signal voltage.

ac generator 1. A rotating electromagnetic machine that produces alternating current (e.g., a dynamo or alternator). 2. An oscillator or combination of an oscillator and an output amplifier.

ac grid voltage Symbol, $V_{G(ac)}$. The ac component of control grid voltage in an electron tube. The ac input signal voltage in a common-cathode amplifier or cathode follower.

A channel The left channel of a two-channel stereo system.

achieved reliability A statement of reliability based on the performance of mass-produced parts or systems under similar environmental conditions. Also called OPERATIONAL RELIABILITY.

achromatic **1.** Without color. In a TV image, the tones from black through gray to white. The term occasionally refers to black-and-white television, although MONOCHROMATIC is more often used in this sense.

achromatic locus Also called *achromatic region*. An area on a chromaticity diagram that contains all points, representing acceptable reference white standards.

achromatic scale A musical scale without accidentals.

ACIA Abbreviation of *asynchronous communications interface adapter*.

acicular Pertaining to the shape of magnetic particles on recording tape. Under magnification, these particles look like thin rods.

acid A substance that dissociates in water solution and forms hydrogen (H) ions (e.g., sulfuric acid). Compare BASE, **2.**

acid depolarizer Also called *acidic depolarizer*. An acid, in addition to the electrolyte, used in some primary cells to slow the process of polarization.

ac line A power line that delivers alternating current only.

ac line filter A filter designed to remove extraneous signals or electrical noise from an ac power line, while causing virtually no reduction of the power-line voltage or power.

ac line voltage The voltage commonly delivered by the commercial power line to consumers. In the United States, the two standards are 117 V and 234 V (~ about 5 percent). The lower voltage is used by most appliances; the higher voltage is intended for appliances and equipment that draws high power, such as electric ovens, cooking ranges, clothes dryers, and amateur-radio amplifiers. In Europe, 220 V is the common standard.

aclinic line Also called *magnetic equator*. An imaginary line drawn on a map of the world or of an area that connects points of zero inclination (dip) of the needle of a magnetic compass.

ACM Abbreviation for *Association for Computing Machinery*.

ac magnetic bias See AC BIAS.

ac meter A meter that is intended to work only on alternating current or voltage. Such meters include iron-vane and rectifier types.

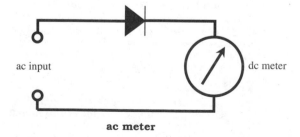

ac meter

ac noise **1.** Electromagnetic interference originating in the ac power lines. **2.** Electrical noise of a rapidly alternating or pulsating nature.

ac noise immunity In computer practice, the ability of a logic circuit to maintain its state, despite excitation by ac noise.

acous Abbreviation for ACOUSTIC.

acoustic Pertaining to audible sound disturbances, usually in air (versus audio-frequency currents or voltages).

acoustic absorption The assimilation of energy from sound waves passing through or reflected by a given medium.

acoustic absorption loss That portion of sound energy lost (as by dissipation in the form of heat) because of ACOUSTIC ABSORPTION.

acoustic absorptivity The ratio of sound energy absorbed by a material to sound energy striking the surface of the material.

acoustic attenuation constant The real-number component of the complex acoustical propagation constant, expressed in nepers per unit distance.

acoustic burglar alarm An alarm that receives the noise made by an intruder. The alarm device responds to the impulses from concealed microphones.

acoustic capacitance The acoustic equivalent of electrical capacitance.

acoustic clarifier In a loudspeaker system, a set of cones attached to the baffle that vibrate to absorb and suppress sound energy during loud bursts.

acoustic communication Communications by means of sound waves. This can be through the atmosphere, or it can be through solids or liquids, such as a taut wire, a body of water, or the earth.

acoustic compliance COMPLIANCE in acoustic transducers, especially loudspeakers. It is equivalent to electrical capacitive reactance.

acoustic coupling Data transfer via a sound link between a telephone and a pickup/reproducer. Was once common in computer terminals and facsimile machines. This scheme has been largely replaced by hard wiring and optical coupling.

acoustic damping The deadening or reduction of the vibration of a body to eliminate (or cause to die out quickly) sound waves arising from it.

acoustic delay line Any equivalent of a special transmission line that introduces a useful time delay between input and output signals. In one form, it consists of a crystal block or bar with an input transducer at one end and an output transducer at the other. An electrical input signal in the first transducer sets up sound waves that travel through the interior of the crystal; the piezoelectric reaction of the crystal to sound vibrations sets up an output voltage in the second transducer. The delay is caused by the time required for the acoustic energy to travel the length of the crystal bar.

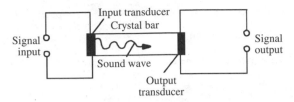

acoustic delay line

acoustic depth finder A direct-reading device for determining the depth of a body of water, or for locating underwater objects via sonic or ultrasonic waves transmitted downward and reflected back to the instrument.

acoustic dispersion Variation of the velocity of sound waves, depending on their frequency.

acoustic elasticity **1.** In a loudspeaker enclosure, the compressibility of air behind the vibrating cone of the speaker. **2.** In general, the compressibility of any medium through which sound passes.

acoustic electric transducer A transducer, such as a microphone or hydrophone, that converts sound energy into electrical energy. Compare ELECTRICAL/ACOUSTIC TRANSDUCER. Also see ACOUSTIC TRANSDUCER.

acoustic feedback A usually undesirable effect that occurs when sound waves from a loudspeaker (or other reproducer) reach a microphone (or other input transducer) in the same system. This can cause an amplifier to oscillate, with a resultant rumbling, howling, or whistling.

acoustic filter Any sound-absorbing or transmitting arrangement, or combination of the two, that transmits sound waves of desired frequency while attenuating or eliminating others.

acoustic frequency response The sound-frequency range as a function of sound intensity. A means of describing the performance of an acoustic device.

acoustic generator A device that produces sound waves of a desired frequency and/or intensity. Examples are electrical devices (headphones or loudspeakers operated from a suitable oscillator, buzzer, bell, or flame) and mechanical devices (tuning forks, bells, string, or whistles).

acoustic grating A set of bars or slits that are parallel to one another and arranged a fixed distance apart so that an interference pattern forms as sound passes through. Used to determine the wavelength of acoustic waves.

acoustic homing system **1.** A system that uses a sound signal for guidance purposes. **2.** A guidance method in which a missile homes in on noise generated by a target.

acoustic horn A tapered tube (round or rectangular, but generally funnel-shaped) that directs sound and, to some extent, amplifies it. So called to distinguish it from a microwave horn.

acoustic howl See ACOUSTIC FEEDBACK.

acoustician **1.** A person skilled in acoustics (an acoustics technician). **2.** An AUDIOLOGIST.

acoustic impedance Unit, ACOUSTIC OHM. The acoustic equivalent of electrical impedance. Like the latter, acoustic impedance is the total opposition encountered by acoustic force. Also like electrical impedance, acoustic impedance has resistive and reactive components: ACOUSTIC RESISTANCE and ACOUSTIC REACTANCE.

acoustic inductance Also called *inertance*. The acoustic equivalent of electrical inductance.

acoustic inertance See ACOUSTIC INDUCTANCE.

acoustic inhibition See AUDITORY INHIBITION.

acoustic intensity See SOUND INTENSITY.

acoustic interferometer An instrument that evaluates the frequency and velocity of sound waves in a liquid or gas, in terms of a standing wave set up by a transducer and reflector as the frequency or transducer-to-reflector distance varies.

acoustic labyrinth A loudspeaker enclosure whose internal partitions form a maze-like path or "tube" lined with sound-absorbing material. The tube effectively runs from the back of the speaker down to where it terminates in a MOUTH or PORT that opens at the front of the enclosure. The labyrinth provides an extremely efficient reproduction system because of its excellent acoustic impedance-matching capability.

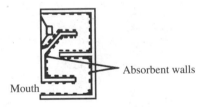

acoustic labyrinth

acoustic lens A system of barriers that refracts sound waves the way that an optical lens does with light waves.

acoustic line Baffles or other such structures within a speaker that act as the mechanical equivalent of an electrical transmission line to enhance the reproduction of very low bass frequencies.

acoustic load A device that serves simultaneously as the output load of an amplifier and as a transducer of electrical energy into acoustic energy (e.g., headphones or a loudspeaker).

acoustic memory In a computer, a volatile memory element employing an acoustic delay line, often incorporating quartz or mercury as the transmission and delay element.

acoustic mirage A type of sound distortion in which the listener experiences the illusion of two sound sources when there is only one. The phenomenon is caused by the effect of a large temperature gradient in the air or water through which the sound passes.

acoustic mode Crystal-lattice vibration without producing an oscillating dipole.

acoustic noise Interferential (usually disagreeable) sounds carried by the air (or other propagation medium) to the ear or to an acoustic transducer. This is in contrast to electrical noise, which consists of extraneous current or voltage impulses and is inaudible until converted into sound.

acoustic ohm The unit of acoustic resistance, reactance, or impedance. One acoustic ohm equals the volume velocity of 1 cm/s produced by a sound pressure of 1 microbar (0.1 Pa). Also called *acoustical ohm*.

acoustic phase constant The imaginary-number component of the complex acoustic propagation constant expressed in radians per second or radians per unit distance.

acoustic phase inverter A bass reflex loudspeaker enclosure.

acoustic pressure **1.** The acoustic equivalent of electromotive force, expressed in dynes per square centimeter; also called *acoustical pressure*. **2.** Sound pressure level.

acoustic propagation The transmission of sound waves, or subaudible or ultrasonic waves, as a disturbance in a medium, rather than as an electric current or electromagnetic field.

acoustic radiator A device that emits sound waves. Examples are the cone of a loudspeaker, the diaphragm of a headphone, and the vibrating reed of a buzzer.

acoustic radiometer An instrument for measuring the intensity of a sound wave (see SOUND INTENSITY) in terms of the unidirectional steady-state pressure exerted at a boundary as a result of absorption or reflection of the wave.

acoustic reactance Unit, ACOUSTIC OHM. The imaginary-number component of ACOUSTIC IMPEDANCE. It can take the form of ACOUSTIC CAPACITANCE or ACOUSTIC INDUCTANCE.

acoustic reflectivity The ratio F_r/F_i, where F_r is the rate of flow of sound energy reflected from a surface and F_i is the rate of flow of sound energy incident to the surface.

acoustic refraction The deflection of sound waves being transferred obliquely between media that transmit sound at different speeds.

acoustic regeneration See ACOUSTIC FEEDBACK.

acoustic resistance Unit, ACOUSTIC OHM. The real-number component of ACOUSTIC IMPEDANCE. The opposing force that causes acous-

tic energy to be dissipated in the form of heat. It is attributed to molecular friction in the medium through which sound passes. See ACOUSTIC OHM.

acoustic resonance Intensification of sound because of peak response of a reproducer or acoustic filter at a particular frequency or narrow band of frequencies, or to the coincidence of two or more sound waves in phase. Also see ACOUSTIC FEEDBACK.

acoustic resonator **1.** A chamber, such as a box, cylinder, or pipe, in which an air column resonates at a particular frequency. **2.** A piezoelectric, magnetostrictive, or electrostrictive body that vibrates at a resonant audio frequency that is governed by the mechanical dimensions of the body when an audio voltage at that frequency is applied.

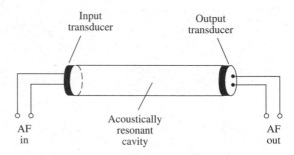

acoustic resonator, 1

acoustics **1.** The physics of sound. The study and applications of acoustic phenomena. **2.** The qualities of an enclosure or sound chamber (room, auditorium, or box) that describe how sound waves behave in it.

acoustic scattering The spreading of a sound wave in many directions as a result of diffraction, reflection, or refraction.

acoustic suspension A loudspeaker design that allows exceptional low-frequency reproduction for a fairly small physical size. An airtight enclosure is used to increase the tension on the speaker cone.

acoustic system **1.** A coordinated array of acoustic components (e.g., acoustic filters, resonators, etc.) that responds to sound energy in a predetermined manner. **2.** An audio-frequency system in which sound energy is converted into electrical energy, processed, and then reconverted into sound energy for a clearly defined purpose.

acoustic telegraph A telegraph that gives audible signals, as opposed to visual signals or printed messages.

acoustic transducer **1.** Any device, such as headphones or a loudspeaker, for converting audio-frequency electrical signals into sound waves. **2.** Any device, such as a microphone, for converting sound waves into alternating, pulsating, or fluctuating currents.

acoustic transmission The direct transmission of sound energy without the intermediary of electric currents.

acoustic transmission system A set of components designed to generate acoustic waves.

acoustic transmissivity Also called *acoustic transmittivity*. The ratio e_t/e_i, where e_t is the sound energy transmitted by a medium, and e_i is the incident sound energy reaching the surface of the medium. Acoustic transmissivity is proportional to the angle of incidence.

acoustic treatment Application of sound-absorbing materials to the interior of an enclosure or room to control reverberation.

acoustic wave The traveling vibration, consisting of molecular motion, via which sound is transmitted through a gas, liquid or solid. Usually refers to sound waves in air.

acoustic wave filter See ACOUSTIC FILTER.

acoustoelectric effect The generation of a voltage across the faces of a crystal by sound waves traveling longitudinally through the crystal.

acoustoelectronics A branch of electronics concerned with the interaction of sound energy and electrical energy in devices, such as surface-wave filters and amplifiers. In such devices, electrically induced acoustic waves travel along the surface of a piezoelectric chip and generate electrical energy. Also called *praetersonics* and *microwave acoustics*.

ac plate current Symbol, $I_{P(ac)}$. The ac component of plate current in a vacuum tube.

ac plate resistance Symbol, $R_{P(ac)}$. The dynamic plate resistance of an electron tube. $R_{P(ac)}$ equals dE_P/dI_P, where E_P is the plate voltage and I_P is the plate current, for a constant value for grid voltage E_G.

ac plate voltage Symbol, $E_{P(ac)}$. The ac component of plate voltage in an electron tube. The ac output-signal voltage in a common-cathode amplifier.

ac power Symbol, P_{ac}. Unit, watt (W). The power acting in an ac circuit, P_{ac} equals $EI \cos q$, where E is in volts, I in amperes, and q is the phase angle. Compare DC POWER. Also see POWER.

ac power supply A power unit that supplies ac only (e.g., ac generator, vibrator-transformer, oscillator, or inverter). Compare DC POWER SUPPLY.

acquisition **1.** The gathering of data from transducers or a computer. **2.** Locating the path of an orbiting body for purposes of collecting telemetered data. **3.** Orienting an antenna for optimum pickup of telemetered data.

acquisition and tracking radar An airborne or ground radar, which locks in on a strong signal and tracks the body that reflects (or transmits) the signal.

acquisition radar A radar that spots an oncoming target and supplies position data regarding the target to a fire-control or missile-guidance radar, which then tracks the target.

acr **1.** Abbreviation of AUDIO CASSETTE RECORDER. **2.** Abbreviation of AUDIO CASSETTE RECORDING SYSTEM.

ac reclosing relay The controlling component in an alternating-current circuit breaker. It causes the breaker to reset after a specified period of time.

ac relay A relay designed to operate on alternating current without chattering or vibrating.

ac resistance Pure resistance in an ac circuit. Unlike reactance and impedance, which are also forms of opposition to the flow of current, ac resistance introduces no phase shift.

acronym A word formed from letters or syllables taken from other applicable words of a multi-word term. Acronyms are convenient for naming new devices and processes in electronics. Usually, a term is considered an acronym only when it is spelled in all-capital letters; once the term is accepted and popularized, it is written as a conventional word and is no longer thought of as an acronym. For example, *LASER* was once an acronym for light amplification by the stimulated emission of radiation. By the popularization process, the acronym became a conventional word from which other terms (such as the verb "lase") were derived.

acrylic resin A synthetic resin used as a dielectric and in electronic encapsulations. It is made from acrylic acid or one of its derivatives.

ACS Abbreviation of *automatic control system*.

ac source current Symbol, $I_{S(ac)}$. The ac component of source current in a field-effect transistor.

ac source resistance Symbol, $R_{S(ac)}$. The dynamic source resistance in a field-effect transistor; $R_{S(ac)}$ equals dV_S/dI_S for a constant value of V_G.

ac source voltage Symbol, $V_{S(ac)}$. The ac component of source voltage in a field-effect transistor. The ac output-signal voltage in a source-follower (grounded-drain) FET amplifier.

acss Abbreviation of *analog computer subsystem*.

ac time overcurrent relay A device with a certain time characteristic, which breaks a circuit when the current exceeds a certain level.

actinic rays Short-wavelength light rays in the violet and ultraviolet portion of the spectrum that give conspicuous photochemical action.

actinism The property whereby radiant energy (such as visible and ultraviolet light, X-rays, etc.) causes chemical reactions.

actinium Symbol, Ac. A radioactive metallic element. Atomic number, 89. Atomic weight, 227.

actinodielectric Exhibiting a temporary rise in electrical conductivity during exposure to light.

actinoelectric effect The property whereby certain materials (such as selenium, cadmium sulfide, germanium, and silicon) change their electrical resistance or generate a voltage on exposure to light. Also see ACTINODIELECTRIC.

actinometer An instrument for measuring the direct heating power of the sun's rays or the actinic power of a light source.

action 1. A chemical process (e.g., LOCAL ACTION on the plate of a battery cell, electrolytic action in marine corrosion, or galvanic action in cells). 2. A unique electronic phenomenon (e.g., photoelectric action, transistor action, tunneling action, antenna action, or switching action). 3. A performance (e.g., abortive action or initiating action).

action current A small transient current that flows in a nerve in the human body as a result of stimulation.

activate To start an operation, usually by applying an appropriate enabling signal.

activation 1. Supplying electrolyte to a battery cell to prepare the cell for operation. 2. Causing the acceleration of a chemical reaction.

activation time In the activation of a battery cell (see ACTIVATION, 1), the interval between addition of the electrolyte and attainment of full cell voltage.

activator A substance added to an accelerator (see ACCELERATOR, 3) to speed the action of the accelerator.

active Pertaining to a circuit or device that requires a power supply for its operation. This differs from a passive circuit or device, which operates with no external source of power.

active antenna An antenna that uses a small whip, loop, or ferrite loopstick with a high-gain amplifier for receiving at very-low, low, medium, and high radio frequencies (approximately 9 kHz to 30 MHz).

active area The forward-current-carrying portion of the rectifying junction of a metallic rectifier.

active arm See ACTIVE LEG.

active balance In telephone repeater operation, the sum of return currents at a terminal network balanced against the local circuit or drop resistance.

active chord mechanism Abbreviation, ACM. In robots, an electromechanical gripper capable of conforming to irregular objects. It has a structure similar to the human spine, with numerous small, rigid links connected by hinges.

active communications satellite A satellite containing receivers (which pick up beamed electromagnetic signals from a ground point and amplify them) and transmitters (which send signals back to the surface of the earth). Also called *active comsat*. Compare PASSIVE COMMUNICATIONS SATELLITE.

active component 1. A device capable of some dynamic function (such as amplification, oscillation, or signal control) that usually requires a power supply for its operation. Examples include bipolar transistors, field-effect transistors, and integrated circuits. Compare PASSIVE COMPONENT. 2. In an ac circuit, a quantity that contains no reactance so that the current is in phase with the voltage.

active component of current See ACTIVE CURRENT.

active computer A computer in an installation or network that is processing data.

active comsat See ACTIVE COMMUNICATIONS SATELLITE.

active control system A device or circuit that compensates for irregularities in the operating environment.

active current In an ac circuit, the current component that is in phase with the voltage. This is in contrast to reactive current, which is not in phase with the voltage, and is "inactive," with respect to power in the circuit. The active current is equal to the average power divided by the effective voltage.

active decoder An automatic ground-station device that gives the number or letter designation of a received radio beacon reply code.

active device 1. An electronic component, such as a transistor that needs a power supply, and/or that is capable of amplifying. 2. Broadly, any device (including electromechanical relays) that can switch (or amplify) by application of low-level signals.

active electric network A network containing one or more active devices or components, usually amplifiers or generators, in addition to passive devices or components.

active element The driven or RF-excited element in a multielement antenna or antenna array.

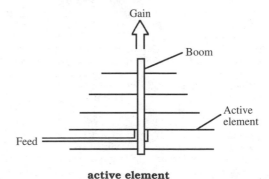

active element

active file A computer file in use (i.e., one that is being updated or referred to).

active filter A bandpass, bandstop, highpass or lowpass filter, consisting of resistors, capacitors, and operational amplifiers, arranged to

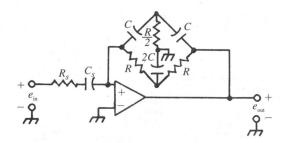

active filter

pass a desired frequency response. Commonly used at audio frequencies.

active infrared detection Detection of infrared rays reflected from a target to which they were beamed.

active ingredient In a chemical mixture, a component that is responsible for, or that contributes to, desired behavior of the mixture. This is in contrast to an *inert ingredient*, which serves only as a supporting vehicle to hold the mixture together.

active jamming Transmission or retransmission of signals for the purpose of disrupting communications.

active junction A pn junction in a semiconductor device that has been created by a diffusion process.

active leg An element within a transducer that changes one or more of its electrical characteristics in response to the input signal of the transducer. Also called *active arm*.

active lines In a U.S. television picture, the lines (approximately 488) that make up the picture. The remaining 37 of the 525 available lines are blanked and are called INACTIVE LINES.

active material **1.** In a storage cell, the chemical material in the plates that provides the electrical action of the cell, as distinguished from the supporting material of the plates themselves. **2.** A radioactive substance. **3.** The phosphor coating of a cathode-ray tube screen. **4.** The material used to coat an electron-tube cathode.

active mixer A signal mixer using one or more active components, such as transistors or integrated circuits. An active circuit provides amplification, input-output isolation, and high input impedance, in addition to the mixing action. Compare PASSIVE MIXER.

active modulator A modulator using one or more active components, such as transistors or integrated circuits. An active circuit provides gain, input-output isolation, and high input impedance, in addition to modulation. Compare PASSIVE MODULATOR.

active network See ACTIVE ELECTRIC NETWORK.

active pressure The electromotive pressure that produces a current in an ac circuit.

active pull-up An arrangement using a transistor as a pull-up resistor replacement in an integrated circuit, providing low output impedance and low power consumption.

active RC network **1.** A resistance-capacitance (RC) circuit that contains active components (transistors or integrated circuits), as well as passive components (capacitors and resistors). **2.** An RC network in which some or all of the resistors and capacitors are simulated by the action of active components.

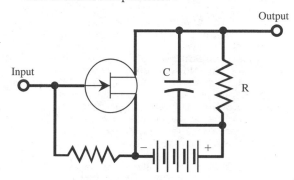

active RC network

active repair time The time during which maintenance is done on a system and the system is out of operation.

active satellite See ACTIVE COMMUNICATIONS SATELLITE.

active sensor In an electronic security system, a transducer that generates an electromagnetic field or acoustic-wave field, and detects changes in the field resulting from the presence or movement of objects in the vicinity.

active substrate In an integrated circuit, a substrate consisting of single-crystal semiconductor material into which the components are formed; it acts as some or all of the components. This is in contrast to a substrate consisting of a dielectric, where the components are deposited on the surface.

active system A radio and/or radar system that requires transmitting equipment to be carried in a vehicle.

active tracking system A system in which a transponder or responder on board a vehicle retransmits information to tracking equipment (e.g., *azusa, secor*).

active transducer **1.** A transducer that contains an active device, such as a transistor or integrated circuit, for immediate amplification of the sensed quantity. **2.** A transducer that is itself an active device.

active wire In the armature of a generator, a wire experiencing induction and, therefore, is delivering voltage.

activity **1.** Intensity of, as well as readiness for, oscillation in a piezoelectric crystal. **2.** Radioactive intensity. **3.** Intensity of thermal agitation. **4.** Thermionic emission of electrons.

activity ratio The ratio of active to inactive records in a computer file.

ac transducer A transducer that either requires an ac supply voltage or delivers an ac output signal—even when operated from a dc supply.

ac transmission The use of an alternating voltage to transfer power from one point to another, usually from generators to a distribution center, and generally over a considerable distance.

actual ground The ground as "seen" by an antenna. The actual ground surface is not necessarily in the same physical location as the true ground surface (i.e., the earth itself). An actual ground can be an artificial ground plane, such as that provided in some antenna structures. Actual ground can also be modified by nearby rooftops, buildings, guy wiring, and utility wiring.

actual height The highest altitude where radio wave refraction actually occurs.

actual power Also called active or AVERAGE POWER. Symbol, P_{avg}. In a resistive circuit under sine-wave conditions, average power is the product of the rms voltage and the rms current. It is also equal to half the product of the maximum current and maximum voltage.

actuating device A device or component that operates electrical contacts to affect signal transmission.

actuating system **1.** An automatic or manually operated system that starts, modifies, or stops an operation. **2.** A system that supplies energy for ACTUATION.

actuating time Also called *actuation time*. The time interval between generation of a control signal, or the mechanical operation of a control device, and the resulting ACTUATION.

actuation **1.** The starting, modification, or termination of an operation or process. **2.** Activation of a mechanical or electromechanical switching device.

actuator An electromechanical device that uses electromagnetism to produce a longitudinal or rotary thrust for mechanical work. It is often the end (load) device of a servosystem.

ACU Abbreviation of *automatic calling unit*.

ac voltage A voltage, the average value of which is zero, that periodically changes its polarity. In one cycle, an ac voltage starts at zero, rises to a maximum positive value, returns to zero, rises to a maximum negative value, and finally returns to zero. The number of such cycles per second is termed the *ac frequency*.

ac voltmeter See AC METER.

acyclic machine Also called ACYCLIC GENERATOR. A dc generator in which voltage induced in the active wires of the armature is always of the same polarity.

A/D Abbreviation for ANALOG-TO-DIGITAL. See ANALOG-TO-DIGITAL CONVERSION.

Ada A microcomputer language designed primarily for use in multi-computer systems, where each small computer communicates with the others, providing some of the advantages of a larger computer.

Adam A communications code word sometimes used for phonetic verbalizing of the letter A. More commonly, ALPHA is used.

adapter **1.** A fitting used to change either the terminal scheme or the size of a jack, plug, or socket to that of another. **2.** A fitting used to provide a transition from one type or style of conductor to another (e.g., waveguide to coaxial line). **3.** An auxiliary system or unit used to extend the operation of another system (e.g., a citizens-band adapter for a broadcast receiver).

UG-212C/U

adapter

adaptive communication A method of communication that adjusts itself according to the particular requirements of a given time.

adaptive suspension vehicle Abbreviation, ASV. A specialized robot that moves on mechanical legs, rather than on wheels. It generally has six legs and resembles an insect. It is designed to move over extremely irregular or rocky terrain, and to carry a human passenger.

adaptivity The ability of a system to respond to its environment by changing its performance characteristics.

adc Abbreviation of ANALOG-TO-DIGITAL CONVERTER.

Adcock antenna A directional antenna system consisting of two vertical antennas, spaced in

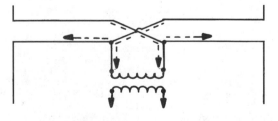

Adcock antenna

such a way that the whole array behaves like a loop antenna. Its members are connected and positioned so that it discriminates against horizontally polarized waves, and delivers output that is proportional to the vector difference of signal voltages induced in the two vertical arms.

Adcock direction finder A radio direction-finding system based on the directivity of the ADCOCK ANTENNA.

Adcock radio range A radio range system with four ADCOCK ANTENNAS situated at the corners of a square, and a fifth antenna at the center of the square.

add-and-subtract relay A stepping relay that can be switched either uprange (add) or downrange (subtract).

addend In a calculation, any number to be added to another. Compare AUGEND.

addend register In a digital computer, the register that stores the addend.

adder 1. In a digital computer, the device or circuit that performs binary addition. A HALF ADDER is a two-input circuit that can produce a sum output and a carry output, but it cannot accommodate a carry signal from another adder. A FULL ADDER can accommodate a carry input, as well as two binary signals to be added. Also see ANALOG ADDER. 2. A circuit in a color TV receiver that amplifies the receiver primary matrix signal.

additive 1. The character or characters added to a code to encipher it. 2. In a calculation, an item that is to be added. 3. An ingredient, usually in a small quantity, added to another material to improve the latter in quality or performance.

additive color A color formed by combining the rays from two or three primary-colored lights onto a single neutral surface. For example, by projecting a red and a green beam onto a neutral screen, a yellow additive color results.

additive primaries Primary colors that form other colors in a mixing of light (see ADDITIVE COLOR), but are not themselves formed by mixing other additive primaries. For example, red, green, and blue are the additive primaries used in color television. Through appropriate mixing, these colors can be used to generate an unlimited variety of other colors. Compare SUBTRACTIVE PRIMARIES, which form the color spectrum by mixing pigments rather than lights. In additive systems, each superimposed primary color increases the total light output from the reflecting (viewing) surface; in subtractive systems, each superimposed primary decreases the total reflectivity. Thus, equal combination of additive primaries produces gray or white, and equal combination of subtractive primaries produces gray or black.

addition record An extra data store created in a computer during processing.

address 1. In computer operations, a usually numerical expression designating the location of material within the memory or the destination of such material. 2. The accurately stated location of information within a computer; a data point within a grid, matrix, or table; a station within a network. 3. In computer operations, to select the location of stored information.

address comparator A device that ensures that the address being read is correct.

address computation In digital computer operations, the technique of producing or modifying only the address part of an instruction.

address field In a computer, the part of the instruction that gives the address of a bit of data (or a word) in the memory.

address generation The programmed generation of numbers or symbols used to retrieve records from a randomly stored direct-access file.

address indirect An address that specifies a storage location that contains another address.

address memory The memory sections in a digital computer that contain each individual register.

address modification In computer operations, altering only the address portion of an instruction; if the command or instruction routine is then repeated, the computer will go to the new address.

address part In a digital computer instruction, the part of an expression that specifies the location. Also called ADDRESS FIELD.

address register In a computer, a register in which an address is stored.

add/subtract time In a computer, the time required to perform addition or subtraction, excluding the time required to get the quantities from storage and to enter the sum or difference into storage.

add time In computer operations, the time required to perform addition, excluding the time required to get the quantities from storage and to enter the sum into storage.

a/d converter A device that changes an analog quantity into a digital signal. See ANALOG-TO-DIGITAL CONVERSION.

ADF Abbreviation of AUTOMATIC DIRECTION FINDER.

ADI Abbreviation of ALTERNATE DIGIT INVERSION.

adiabatic damping In an accelerator (see ACCELERATOR, 1), reduction of beam size as beam energy is increased.

adiabatic demagnetization A technique using a magnetic field to keep a substance at a low temperature, sometimes within a fraction of a degree of absolute zero.

adjacency A character-recognition condition in which the spacing reference lines of two characters printed consecutively in line are closer than specified.

adjacent- and alternate-channel selectivity The selectivity of a receiver or radio-frequency (RF) amplifier, with respect to adjacent-channel and

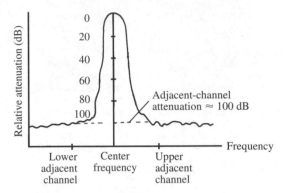

adjacent-channel attenuation

alternate-channel signals. That is, the extent to which a desired signal is passed, and nearby unwanted signals are rejected.

adjacent audio channel See ADJACENT SOUND CHANNEL.

adjacent channel The channel (frequency band) immediately above or below the channel of interest.

adjacent-channel attenuation The reciprocal of the *selectivity ratio* of a radio receiver. The selectivity ratio is the ratio of the sensitivity of a receiver (tuned to a given channel) to its sensitivity in an adjacent channel or on a specified number of channels removed from the original.

adjacent-channel interference In television or radio reception, the interference from stations on adjacent channels. A common form arises from the picture signal in the next higher channel and the sound signal in the next lower channel.

adjacent-channel selectivity The extent to which a receiver or tuned circuit can receive on one channel and reject signals from the nearest outlying channels.

adjacent sound channel In television, the radio-frequency (RF) channel containing the sound modulation of the next lower channel.

adjacent video carrier In television, the radio-frequency (RF) carrier containing the picture modulation of the next higher channel.

adjustable component Any circuit component whose main electrical value can be varied at will (e.g., a variable capacitor, inductor, resistor, or load).

adjustable instrument **1.** An instrument whose sensitivity, range, or response can be varied at will (e.g., multirange meter or wideband generator). **2.** An instrument that requires adjustment or manipulation to measure a quantity (e.g., bridge, potentiometer, or attenuator).

adjustable motor tuning An arrangement that allows the motor tuning of a receiver to be confined to a portion of the frequency spectrum.

adjustable resistor A wirewound resistor in which the resistance wire is partially exposed to allow varying the component's value.

adjustable voltage divider A wirewound resistor with terminals that slide on exposed resistance wire to produce various voltage values.

adjusted circuit A circuit in which leads that are normally connected to a circuit breaker are shunted so that current can be measured under short-circuit conditions without breaker tripping.

adjusted decibels Noise level (in decibels) above a reference noise level (designated arbitrarily as zero decibels) measured at any point in a system with a noise meter that has previously been adjusted for zero (at reference), according to specifications.

admittance Symbol, Y. Unit, siemens (formerly mho). The property denoting the comparative ease with which an alternating current flows through a circuit or device. Admittance is the reciprocal of impedance (Z): $Y = 1/Z$.

adp **1.** Abbreviation of AMMONIUM DIHYDROGEN PHOSPHATE, a piezoelectric compound used for sonar crystals. **2.** Abbreviation of AUTOMATIC DATA PROCESSING.

adsorption Adhesion of a thin layer of molecules of one substance to the surface of another without absorption. An example is adsorption of water to the surface of a dielectric. This term is often confused with ABSORPTION because the spellings of the two words are almost identical. Compare ABSORPTION.

adu Abbreviation of *automatic dialing unit.*

advanced-class license An amateur-radio license conveying all operating privileges, except for a few small bands that are allocated to extra-class licensees. The second-highest class of amateur license.

advance information Data published prior to the actual production or availability of a manufactured component, circuit, or system. Advance information is often only an approximate reflection of the expected characteristics of a device.

advance wire A resistance wire used in thermocouples and precision applications. It is an alloy of copper and nickel, which has high resistivity and a negligible temperature coefficient of resistance.

aeolight A glow lamp using a cold cathode and a mixture of inert gases. Because its illumination can be regulated with an applied signal voltage, it is sometimes used as a modulation indicator for motion-picture sound recording.

aerial See ANTENNA.

aerial cable A wire or cable run through the air, using support structures, such as towers or poles.

aerodiscone antenna A miniature discone antenna designed for use on aircraft.

aerodynamics The science dealing with forces exerted by air and other gases in motion—especially upon bodies (such as aircraft) moving through these gases.

aerogram See RADIOGRAM.

aeromagnetic Pertaining to terrestrial magnetism, as surveyed from a flying aircraft.

aeronautical advisory station A civil defense and advisory communications station in service for the use of private aircraft stations.

aeronautical broadcasting service The special service that broadcasts information regarding air navigation and meteorological data pertinent to aircraft operation.

aeronautical broadcast station A station of the aeronautical broadcasting service.

aeronautical fixed service A fixed radio service that transmits information regarding air navigation and flight safety.

aeronautical fixed service station A station that operates in the aeronautical fixed service.

aeronautical ground station A land station that provides communication between aircraft and ground stations.

aeronautical marker-beacon signal A distinctive signal that designates a small area above a beacon transmitting station for aircraft navigation.

aeronautical marker-beacon station A land station that transmits an aeronautical marker-beacon signal.

aeronautical mobile service A radio service consisting of communications between aircraft, and between aircraft and ground stations.

aeronautical radio-beacon station An aeronautical radio-navigation land station that transmits signals used by aircraft and other vehicles to determine their position.

aeronautical radionavigation services Services provided by stations transmitting signals used in the navigation of aircraft.

aeronautical radio service A service that encompasses aircraft-to-aircraft, aircraft-to-ground, and ground-to-aircraft communications important to the operation of aircraft.

aeronautical station A station on land, and occasionally aboard ship, operating in the aeronautical mobile service.

Aeronautical Telecommunication Agency The agency that administers the operation of stations in the aeronautical radio service.

aeronautical telecommunications Collectively, all of the electronic and nonelectronic communications used in the aeronautical service.

aeronautical utility land station A ground station in an airport control tower that provides communications having to do with the control of aircraft and other vehicles on the ground.

aeronautical utility mobile station At an airport, a mobile station that communicates with aeronautical utility land stations and with aircraft and other vehicles on the ground.

aerophare See RADIO BEACON.

aerospace 1. The region encompassing the earth's atmosphere and extraterrestrial space. 2. Pertaining to transport and travel in the earth's atmosphere and in outer space. This includes aircraft, orbiting space vessels, and interplanetary spacecraft.

AES Abbreviation for *Audio Engineering Society.*

AEW Abbreviation of *airborne (or aircraft) early warning.*

aF Abbreviation of ATTOFARAD.

AF Abbreviation of AUDIO FREQUENCY.

AFC 1. Abbreviation of AUTOMATIC FREQUENCY CONTROL. 2. Abbreviation of AUDIO-FREQUENCY CHOKE.

affirmative In voice communications, a word often used for "yes"—especially when interference is present or signals are weak.

AFIPS Acronym for *American Federation of Information Processing Societies.*

afpc Abbreviation of *automatic frequency/phase control.*

AFSK Abbreviation of AUDIO-FREQUENCY-SHIFT KEYING.

afterglow The tendency of the phosphor of a cathode-ray-tube screen to glow for a certain time after the cathode-ray beam has passed. Also see PERSISTENCE.

afterpulse An extraneous pulse in a multiplier phototube (photomultiplier), induced by a preceding pulse.

a/g Abbreviation of AIR-TO-GROUND.

AGC Abbreviation of AUTOMATIC GAIN CONTROL.

AGE Abbreviation of AEROSPACE GROUND EQUIPMENT.

agenda A schedule of the major procedural operations for a solution or computer run; a group of programs used to manipulate a problem matrix in linear programming.

agendum call card In linear programming, a card punched to represent an item of an agenda.

agent An active force, condition, mechanism, or substance that produces or sustains an effect. Thus, a sudden voltage rise is a triggering agent in certain bistable circuits; arsenic is a doping agent in semiconductor processing; the slow cooling of a heated metal to improve ductility is an ANNEALING AGENT.

aging 1. An initial run of a component or circuit over a certain period of time shortly after manufacture to stabilize its characteristics and performance. 2. The changing of electrical characteristics or of chemical properties over a protracted period of time.

agonic line An imaginary line connecting points on the earth's surface at which a magnetic needle shows zero declination (i.e., points to true geographic north).

AGREE Acronym for *Advisory Group on Reliability of Electronics Equipment.*

Ah Abbreviation of AMPERE-HOUR. Depending on the standard used, the abbreviation can be amp-hr, a-h, a-hr, or A-h.

aH Abbreviation of ATTOHENRY.

aided tracking In radar and fire control, a system in which manual correction of target tracking error automatically corrects the rate of movement of the tracking mechanism.

AIEE   Abbreviation for *American Institute of Electrical Engineers*, now consolidated with the IRE, forming the IEEE.

AIP   Abbreviation for *American Institute of Physics*.

air   The mixture of gases that constitutes the earth's atmosphere and figures prominently in the manufacture and operation of numerous electronic devices. By volume, air contains about 21 percent oxygen, 78 percent nitrogen, and lesser amounts of argon, carbon dioxide, helium, hydrogen, krypton, neon, and xenon. It also contains varying amounts of water vapor, and in smoggy areas, carbon monoxide and the oxides of sulfur and nitrogen.

airborne intercept radar   A type of short-range radar used aboard fighter and interceptor aircraft for tracking their targets.

airborne long-range input   Equipment aboard aircraft, for the purpose of facilitating the use of long-range missiles.

airborne noise   See ACOUSTIC NOISE.

airborne radar platform   Surveillance and altitude-finding radar used aboard aircraft.

air capacitor   A capacitor in which air is the dielectric between two sets of conductive plates. Also called *air-dielectric capacitor*.

aircarrier aircraft station   On an aircraft, a radio station that is involved in carrying people for hire or in transporting cargo.

air cell   A primary electrochemical cell in which the positive electrode is depolarized by reduced oxygen in the air.

air cleaner   See DUST PRECIPITATOR.

air column   The open space inside an acoustic chamber, pipe, or horn.

air-cooled component   A component, such as a power transistor, that is cooled by circulating air, compared with one cooled by a circulating liquid, such as water or oil.

air-cooled transistor   A transistor (particularly a power transistor) from which the heat of operation is drawn away, through radiation and convection, into the surrounding air. The transistor is usually mounted on a heatsink or fitted with fins.

air-cooled tube   An electron tube from which heat is drawn away, mainly via convection, into the surrounding air. A device called a *chimney* can be placed around the tube, through which air is blown by a fan. Cool air enters through the bottom of the assembly, and hot air escapes from the top.

air-core coil   An inductor with no magnetic core material, so called because the only material at the center of the coil is air.

air-core transformer   A transformer without a ferromagnetic core, so called because air is the only material at the center of (and immediately surrounding) the transformer coils.

aircraft bonding   The practice of solidly connecting, for electrical purposes, the metal parts of an aircraft, including the engine.

aircraft flutter   Rapid, repetitive fading and intensifying of a received radio or television signal, resulting from reflections of the signal by passing aircraft.

aircraft station   A nonautomatic radio communications station installed on an aircraft.

air-dielectric coax   A special type of COAXIAL CABLE designed to have minimum loss. The space between inner and outer conductors is mostly empty (i.e., air-filled). Some such cables are sealed and filled with an inert gas. The inner conductor is held away from the inner wall of the outer conductor by beads, washers, or a spiral-wound filament of high-grade dielectric material, such as polyethylene.

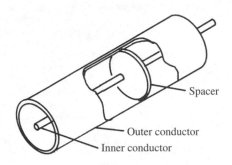

air-dielectric coax

air environment   Pertaining to communications equipment aboard aircraft.

airflow   The path or movement of air in, through, or around an electronic device or piece of equipment—especially pertaining to an AIR-COOLED COMPONENT.

air gap   **1.** A narrow space between two parts of a magnetic circuit (e.g., the gap in the core of a filter choke). Often, this gap is filled with a nonmagnetic material, such as plastic, for mechanical support. **2.** The space between two or more magnetically coupled or electrostatically coupled components. **3.** A device that gets its name from the narrow gap between two small metal balls, needle points, or blunt rod tips therein. When an applied voltage is sufficiently high, a spark discharges across the gap.

air/ground control radio station   A station for aeronautical telecommunications related to the operation and control of local aircraft.

air-insulated line   **1.** An open-wire feeder or transmission line. Typically, the line consists of two parallel wires held apart by separators (bars or rods of high-grade dielectric material) situated at wide intervals. **2.** AIR-DIELECTRIC COAX.

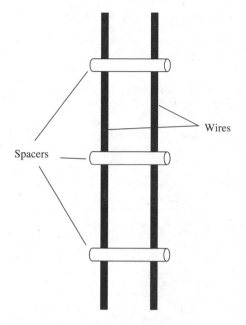

air-insulated line, 1

air-moving device   A mechanical device, such as a specially designed fan or blower, used to facilitate air cooling of electronic components.

airport beacon   A radio or light beacon that marks the location of an airport.

airport control station   A station that provides communications between an airport control tower and aircraft in the vicinity.

airport surveillance radar   An air-traffic-control radar that scans the airspace within about 60 miles (approximately 100 kilometers) of an airport, and displays in the control tower the location of all aircraft below a certain altitude and all obstructions in the vicinity.

air-position indicator   An airborne computer system that, using airspeed, aircraft heading, and elapsed time, furnishes a continuous indication of the position of the aircraft. The indication is affected by high-altitude winds. Compare GROUND-POSITION INDICATOR.

air-to-air communication   Radio transmission from one aircraft to another in flight. Compare AIR-TO-GROUND COMMUNICATION and GROUND-TO-AIR COMMUNICATION.

air-to-ground communication   Radio transmission from an aircraft in flight to a station located on the ground. Compare AIR-TO-AIR COMMUNICATION and GROUND-TO-AIR COMMUNICATION.

air-to-ground radio frequency   The carrier frequency, or band of such frequencies, allocated for transmissions from an aircraft to a ground station.

airwaves   **1.** Radio waves. The term is slang, but is widely used. It probably came from the public's mistaken notion that radio signals are propagated by the air. **2.** Skywaves.

Al   Symbol for ALUMINUM.

alabamine   See ASTATINE.

alacratized switch   A mercury switch in which the tendency of the mercury to stick to the parts has been reduced.

alarm   **1.** An electronic security system. **2.** A silent and/or audible alert signal transmitted by an electronic security system when an intrusion occurs. **3.** A silent and/or audible signal that informs personnel of the occurrence of an equipment malfunction.

alarm circuit   A circuit that alerts personnel to a system malfunction, a detected condition, or an intruder.

alarm condition   **1.** An intrusion or equipment malfunction that triggers an alarm circuit. **2.** The operation of an alarm circuit that occurs in response to an intrusion or equipment malfunction.

alarm hold   A device that keeps an alarm sounding once it has been actuated.

alarm output   The signal sent from an alarm circuit to a siren, buzzer, computer, or other external device to alert personnel to an ALARM CONDITION.

alarm relay   A relay that is actuated by an alarm device.

A-law   A form of companding law frequently used in European electronics (the mu-law is more often used in North America). A nonlinear transfer characteristic in companding circuits. It can be continuous, or can be a piecewise linear approximation of a continuous function.

A-law companded   Companding by means of an 8-bit binary code following the A-LAW, a specific companding function.

albedo   For an unpolished surface, the ratio of reflected light to incident light. It can vary from 0.0 to 1.0, or from 0 to 100 percent.

albedograph   An instrument for measuring the albedo of planets.

ALC   Abbreviation of AUTOMATIC LEVEL CONTROL.

alerting device   An audible alarm that includes a self-contained solid-state audio oscillator. Powered from the ac line or a battery, the device produces a raucous noise when actuated.

Alexanderson antenna   A very-low-frequency (VLF) and low-frequency (LF) vertically polarized antenna, designed to minimize ground losses in structures of manageable height. It usually consists of several wires, each quarter-wave resonant with a loading coil, and all connected together at the apex of a tower. The antenna is fed between the ground and the base of one of the wires.

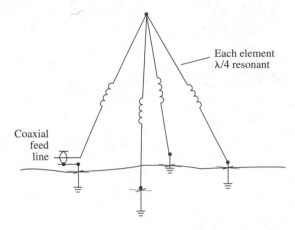

Each element
λ/4 resonant

Coaxial
feed
line

Alexanderson antenna

Alford antenna A loop antenna, in a square configuration, with the corners bent toward the center to lower the impedance at the current nodes.

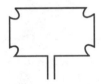

Alford antenna

algebraic adder In computer operations, an adder that provides the algebraic sum, rather than the arithmetic sum, of the entered quantities.

algebraic operation A form of electronic calculator operation, in which the keystrokes proceed in an intuitive sequence, following the way in which the calculation is written down. Compare REVERSE POLISH NOTATION.

algebraic sum The sum of two or more quantities with consideration of their signs. Compare ARITHMETIC SUM.

ALGOL Acronym for *algorithmic language*. A problem-oriented, high-level computer programming language that uses algebraic notation to express information and follows the rules of Boolean algebra.

algorithm A step-by-step procedure for solving a problem, (e.g., the procedure for finding the square root of a number). It can be expressed in a line-by-line instruction set or as a flowchart.

algorithmic language A computer language used to describe a numeral or algebraic process.

alias A label that is an alternate term for items of the same type; a label and several aliases can identify the same data element in a computer program.

aliasing **1.** In analog-to-digital (A/D) conversion, a false output signal that results from a sampling rate that is too slow. Ideally, the sampling rate is at least twice the highest input signal frequency. **2.** Sawtooth-like irregularities, also called *jaggies*, which are sometimes introduced into a bit-mapped computer image when it is changed in size.

aliasing noise A form of signal distortion caused by a signal with an excessive bandwidth.

align **1.** To adjust (i.e., to preset) the circuits of an electronic system, such as a receiver, transmitter, or test instrument, for predetermined response. **2.** To arrange elements in a certain precise orientation and spacing, relative to each other, as in a Yagi antenna. **3.** To orient antennas so that they are in line of sight, with respect to each other.

alignment The process of ensuring that equipment, components, or systems are adjusted, both physically and electronically, for the most efficient possible performance.

alignment chart A line chart for the simple solution of electronic problems. It is so called because its use involves aligning numerical values on various scales, the lines intersecting at the solution on another scale. Also called *nomograph*.

alignment pin A pin or protruding key, usually in the base of a removable or plug-in component, to ensure that the latter will be inserted correctly into a circuit. Often, the pin mates with a keyway, notch, or slot.

alignment tool A specialized screwdriver or wrench (usually nonmagnetic) used to adjust padder or trimmer capacitors or inductor cores.

alive See LIVE.

alkali See BASE, 2.

alkali metals Metals whose hydroxides are bases (alkalis). The group includes cesium, francium, lithium, potassium, rubidium, and sodium.

alkaline battery **1.** A battery composed of alkaline cells and characterized by a relatively flat discharge curve under load.

alkaline cell **1.** A primary cell in which the negative electrode is granular zinc mixed with a potassium hydroxide (alkaline) electrolyte; the positive electrode is a polarizer in electrical contact with the outer metal can of the cell. A porous separator divides the electrodes. This type of cell delivers a terminal potential of 1.5 V, but has much higher energy-storage capacity than a 1.5-V carbon-zinc cell. **2.** See EDISON BATTERY.

alkaline-earth metals The elemental metals barium, calcium, strontium, and sometimes beryllium, magnesium, and radium, some of which are used in vacuum tubes.

alkaline earths Substances that are oxides of the alkaline-earth metals. Some of these materials are used in vacuum tubes.

all-diffused A type of INTEGRATED CIRCUIT in which both active and passive elements have been fabricated by diffusion and related processes.

Allen screw A screw fitted with a six-sided (hexagonal) hole.

Allen wrench A tool used to tighten or loosen an Allen screw. It is a hexagonal rod and is available in various sizes.

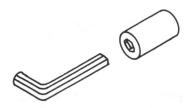

Allen screw and wrench

alligator clip A spring-loaded clip with jagged teeth, designed to be used for temporary electrical connections.

allocate 1. To assign (especially through legislation) operating frequencies or other facilities or conditions needed for scientific or technical activity; see, for example, ALLOCATION OF FREQUENCIES. 2. In computer practice, to assign locations in the memory or registers for routines and subroutines.

allocated channel A frequency channel assigned to an individual or group.

allocated-use circuit 1. A circuit in which one or more channels have been authorized for the exclusive use of one or more services. 2. A communications link assigned to users needing it.

allocation of frequencies See RADIO SPECTRUM.

allocator A telephone system distributor associated with the finder control group relay assembly. It reserves an inactive line-finder for another call.

alloter relay A telephone system line-finder relay that reserves an inactive line-finder for the next incoming call from the line.

allotropic Pertaining to a substance existing in two forms.

alloy A metal that is a mixture of several other metals (e.g., brass from copper and zinc), or of a metal and a nonmetal.

alloy deposition In semiconductor manufacture, depositing an alloy on a substrate.

alloy-diffused transistor A transistor in which the base is diffused and the emitter is alloyed. The collector is provided by the semiconductor substrate into which alloying and diffusion are affected. Compare ALLOY TRANSISTOR and DIFFUSE TRANSISTOR.

alloy diode A junction-type semiconductor diode in which a suitable substance (such as p-type) is alloyed into a chip of the opposite type (such as n-type) to form the junction. Also called *alloy-junction diode*.

alloy junction In a semiconductor device, a positive/negative (pn) junction formed by alloying a suitable material (such as indium) with the semiconductor (silicon or germanium).

alloy transistor A transistor whose junctions are created by alloying. Also see ALLOY JUNCTION.

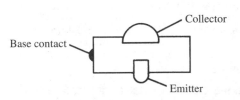

alloy transistor

all-pass filter Also called *all-pass network*. A filter that (ideally) introduces a desired phase shift or time delay, but has zero attenuation at all frequencies.

all-relay central office In telephone service, an automatic central-office switchboard that uses relay circuits to make line interconnections.

all-wave Pertaining to a wide operating-frequency range. Few systems are literally all-wave. For example, a so-called "all-wave radio receiver" might cover 500 kHz to 30 MHz only.

all-wave antenna An antenna that can be operated over a wide frequency range with reasonable efficiency and preferably without needing readjustment. Examples are the DISCONE ANTENNA and the LOG-PERIODIC ANTENNA.

all-wave generator A signal generator that will supply output over a wide range of frequencies.

all-wave receiver A radio receiver that can be tuned over a very wide range of frequencies, such as 10 kHz to 70 MHz.

allyl plastics Plastics, sometimes used as dielectrics or for other purposes in electronics, based on resins made by polymerization of monomers (such as diallyl phthalate) that contain allyl groups.

alnico Coined from the words aluminum, nickel, and cobalt. An alloy used in strong permanent magnets, it contains the constituents noted plus (sometimes) copper or titanium.

alpha 1. Symbol, α. The current gain of a common-base-connected bipolar transistor. It is the ratio of the differential of collector current to the differential of emitter current; $\alpha = dI_C/dI_E$. For a junction transistor, alpha is always less than unity, but very close to it. 2. In voice communications, the phonetic representation of the letter A.

alphabet The set of all characters in a natural language.

alphabetic coding In computer practice, an abbreviation system for coding information to be fed into the computer. The coding contains letters, words, and numbers.

alphabetic-numeric Also called *alphabetical-numerical* and *alphanumeric.* In computer operations, pertaining to letters of the alphabet and special characters, and to numerical digits.

alpha cutoff frequency The frequency at which the ALPHA of a common-base-connected bipolar transistor falls to 70.7 percent of its value at some specified lower frequency, usually 1 kHz.

alpha decay The decay of a substance in which the nuclei of the atoms emit alpha particles, resulting in a change of the atomic number and atomic weight of the substance over a period of time.

alphanumeric See ALPHABETIC-NUMERIC.

alphanumeric code In computer operations or in communications, a code composed of, or using, both letters and numbers.

alphanumeric readout A type of digital readout that displays both letters and numerals.

alpha particle A nuclear particle bearing a positive charge. Consisting of two protons and two neutrons, it is given off by certain radioactive substances. Compare BETA RAYS and GAMMA RAYS.

alpha system An alphabetic code-signaling system.

alphatron An ionizing device in which the radiation source is an emitter of alpha particles.

alteration An inclusive-OR operation.

alternate channel In communications, a channel situated two channels higher or lower than a given channel. Compare ADJACENT CHANNEL.

alternate-channel interference Interference caused by a transmitter operating in the channel beyond an adjacent channel. Compare ADJACENT-CHANNEL INTERFERENCE.

alternate digit inversion In multiplex equipment, a method of switching the binary signals to the opposite state, in accordance with A-law companding.

alternate frequency A frequency allocated as an alternative to a main assigned frequency and used under certain specified conditions.

alternate-mark inversion signal A signal that conveys bits in which the successive signals are of opposite polarity (positive, then negative, then positive, etc.). They are equal in absolute value amplitude.

alternate mode The technique of displaying several signals on an oscilloscope screen by rapidly switching the signals in sequence at the end of each sweep.

alternate routing A secondary, or backup, communications path, used when primary (normal) routing is impossible.

alternating-charge characteristic In a nonlinear capacitor, the relationship between the instantaneous charge and the instantaneous value of an alternating voltage.

alternating current Abbreviation, ac. A current that periodically reverses its direction of flow. In one cycle, an alternation starts at zero, rises to a maximum positive level, returns to zero, rises to a maximum negative level, and again returns to zero. The number of such cycles completed per second is termed the *ac frequency.* Also see CURRENT.

alternating-current continuous wave An amplitude-modulated signal resulting from the operation of an oscillator or RF amplifier with raw ac voltage.

alternating current/direct current See AC/DC.

alternating-current erasing head See AC ERASING HEAD.

alternating-current pulse A short-duration ac wave.

alternating-current transmission 1. The propagation of alternating currents along a length of conductor—especially for power-transfer purposes. 2. A means of picture transmission in which a given signal strength produces a constant value of brightness for a very short time.

alternating voltage Also called *alternating-current voltage.* See AC VOLTAGE.

alternation In ac practice, a half cycle. In a complete cycle, there are two alternations, one in the positive direction and one in the negative direction.

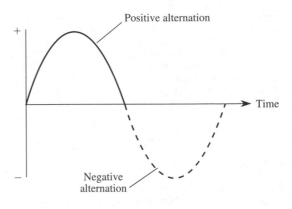

alternation

alternative denial A NOT-AND operation.

alternator Any mechanically driven machine for generating ac power. Sometimes specifically one having a permanent-magnet rotor, such as a *magneto.*

altimeter station An airborne transmitter whose signals are used to determine the altitude of aircraft.

altitude **1.** The vertical distance of an object above sea level. **2.** The vertical distance of an object above the earth's surface. **3.** The angle, measured in degrees, with respect to the horizon, at which a highly directional antenna is pointed.

altitude delay In a plan-position-indicating type of radar, the sync delay introduced between transmission of the pulse and start of the trace on the indicator screen to eliminate the altitude circle in the display.

ALU Abbreviation of ARITHMETIC AND LOGIC UNIT.

alumel An alloy used in the construction of one type of THERMOCOUPLE. It is composed of nickel (three parts) and aluminum (one part).

alumina An aluminum-oxide ceramic used in electron tube insulators and as a substrate in the fabrication of thin-film circuits.

aluminum Symbol, Al. An elemental metal. Atomic number, 13. Atomic weight, 26.98. Aluminum is widely used in electronics, familiar instances being chassis, wire, shields, semiconductor doping, and electrolytic-capacitor plates.

aluminum antimonide Formula, AlSb. A crystalline compound useful as a semiconductor dopant.

aluminized screen A television picture-tube screen with a thin layer of aluminum deposited on its back to brighten the image and reduce ion-spot formation.

Am Symbol for AMERICIUM.

A/m Abbreviation of *ampere per meter:* the SI unit of magnetic field strength.

AM **1.** Abbreviation of *amplitude modulator.* **2.** Abbreviation of AMPLITUDE MODULATION.

amalgam An alloy of a metal and mercury. Loosely, any combination of metals.

amateur **1.** A nonprofessional, usually noncommercial devotee of any technology (i.e., a hobbyist). **2.** A licensed radio operator legally authorized to operate a station in the AMATEUR SERVICE.

amateur band Any band of radio frequencies assigned for noncommercial use by licensed radio amateurs (see AMATEUR, **2**). In the United States, numerous such bands are above 1.8 MHz (160 meters). Also see AMATEUR SERVICE and AMATEUR STATION.

amateur call letters Call letters assigned by a government licensing authority—especially to amateur stations. Call-letter combinations consist of a letter prefix denoting the country in which the station is situated, plus a number designating the location within the country, and two or more letters identifying the particular station. For example: W6ABC: W (or K) = United States, 6 = California, and ABC = identification of individual licensee (issued alphabetically, except under special circumstances).

amateur callsign See AMATEUR CALL LETTERS.

amateur extra-class license The highest class of amateur-radio operator license in the United States. It conveys all operating privileges.

amateur radio **1.** A general term, referring to the practice of operation, experimentation, and other work in and related to the amateur service. **2.** The hardware that comprises an amateur radio station. **3.** A radio receiver, transmitter, or transceiver that is specifically designed for operation in the amateur bands.

amateur radio operator Also called *radio ham* or *ham radio operator.* An individual licensed to transmit radio signals in the amateur service.

amateur service A two-way radio service, existing purely for hobby purposes (i.e., without pecuniary interest).

amateur station A radio station licensed in the AMATEUR SERVICE.

amauroscope An electronic aid to the blind, in which photocells in a pair of goggles receive light images. Electric pulses proportional to the light are impressed upon the visual receptors of the brain through electrodes in contact with nerves above each eye.

amber A yellow or brown fossil resin that is historically important in electronics. It is the first material reported to be capable of electrification by rubbing (Thales, 600 BC). Also, the words *electricity, electron,* and *electronics* are derived from the Greek name for amber, *elektron.*

ambience The acoustic characteristic of a room, in terms of the total amount of sound reaching a listener from all directions.

ambient An adjective meaning "surrounding." Often used as a noun in place of the adjective-noun combination (thus, "10 degrees above ambient," instead of "10 degrees above ambient temperature").

ambient humidity The amount of moisture in the air at the time of measurement or operations in which dampness must be accounted for.

ambient level The amplitude of all interference (acoustic noise, electrical noise, illumination, etc.) emitted from sources other than that of a signal of interest.

ambient light Also called *ambient illumination.* Room light or outdoor light incident to a location at the time of measurement or operations.

ambient-light filter In a television receiver, a filter mounted in front of a picture-tube screen to minimize the amount of ambient light reaching the screen.

ambient noise **1.** In electrical measurements and operation, background electrical noise. **2.** In acoustical measurements and operations, audible background noise.

ambient pressure Surrounding atmospheric pressure.

ambient temperature The temperature surrounding apparatus and equipment (e.g., room temperature).

ambient-temperature range   1. The range over which ambient temperature varies at a given location. **2.** The range of ambient temperature that will cause no malfunction of, or damage to, a circuit or device.

ambiguity   1. Any unclear, illogical, or incorrect indication or result. **2.** The seeking of a false null by a servo. **3.** In digital computer operations, an error resulting from improper design of logic.

ambiguous count   In digital counters, a clearly incorrect count. See ACCIDENTAL TRIGGERING.

ambisonic reproduction   A close approximation of the actual directional characteristics of a sound in a given environment. The reproduced sound almost exactly duplicates the sound in the actual environment in which it was recorded.

American Morse code   (Samuel F. B. Morse, 1791-1872). Also called *Railroad Morse*. A telegraph code, at one time used on wire telegraph lines in the United States. It differs from the *Continental code*, also called the *International Morse Code*, which is used in radiotelegraphy. Compare CONTINENTAL CODE.

American National Standards Institute   Acronym, ANSI. An industrial group in the United States that encourages companies to manufacture devices and equipment in accordance with certain standards. The objective is to minimize hardware incompatibility problems.

American Radio Relay League   A worldwide organization of amateur radio operators, headquartered in Newington, Connecticut. The official publications are the monthly magazines, *QST* and *QEX*. They also publish numerous books and other educational materials.

American Standards Association   Abbreviation, ASA. At one time, the name of the national association in the U.S. devoted to the formation and dissemination of voluntary standards of dimensions, performance, terminology, etc. See ANSI.

American wire gauge   Abbreviation, AWG. Also called *Brown and Sharpe gauge* or *B & S gauge*. The standard American method of designating wire sizes. Wire is listed according to gauge number from 0000 (460 mils diameter) to 40 (3.145 mils diameter).

americium   Symbol, Am. A radioactive elemental metal first produced artificially in the 1940s. Atomic number, 95. Atomic weight, 243.

AM/FM receiver   A radio set that can receive either amplitude-modulated or frequency-modulated signals. Usually, a band switch incorporates the demodulation-selection circuitry so that as the frequency range is changed, the appropriate detector is accessed.

AM/FM transmitter   A radio transmitter whose output signal can be frequency- or amplitude-modulated by a panel selector switch.

AM/FM tuner   A compact radio receiver unit that can handle either amplitude- or frequency-mod-

Character	Symbol	Character	Symbol
A	· —	U	· · —
B	— · · ·	V	· · · —
C	· · ·	W	· — —
D	— · ·	X	· — · ·
E	·	Y	· · · ·
F	· — ·	Z	· · · ·
G	— — ·	1	· — — ·
H	· · · ·	2	· · — · ·
I	· ·	3	· · · — ·
J	— · — ·	4	· · · · —
K	— · —	5	— — —
L	——	6	· · · · · ·
M	— —	7	— · · —
N	— ·	8	— · · ·
O	· ·	9	— · · —
P	· · · · ·	0	——
Q	· · — ·	period	· · — — · ·
R	· · ·	comma	· — · — ·
S	· · ·	question mark	— · · — ·
T	—		

American Morse Code

AWG	Dia. (mm)	AWG	Dia. (mm)
1	7.35	21	0.723
2	6.54	22	0.644
3	5.83	23	0.573
4	5.19	24	0.511
5	4.62	25	0.455
6	4.12	26	0.405
7	3.67	27	0.361
8	3.26	28	0.321
9	2.91	29	0.286
10	2.59	30	0.255
11	2.31	31	0.227
12	2.05	32	0.202
13	1.83	33	0.180
14	1.63	34	0.160
15	1.45	35	0.143
16	1.29	36	0.127
17	1.15	37	0.113
18	1.02	38	0.101
19	0.912	39	0.090
20	0.812	40	0.080

American wire gauge equivalents

ulated signals, and delivers low-amplitude output to a high-fidelity audio power amplifier. Compare AM TUNER and FM TUNER.

AMI   See ALTERNATE-MARK INVERSION SIGNAL.

A-minus   Also, A-. The negative terminal of an A battery, or pertaining to the part of a circuit connected to that terminal.

ammeter   An instrument used to measure the amount of current (in amperes) flowing in a circuit.

ammeter shunt A resistor connected in parallel with an ammeter to increase its current range. Also see AYRTON-MATHER GALVANOMETER SHUNT.

ammeter-voltmeter method The determination of resistance or power values from the measurement of voltage (E) and current (I). For resistance, $R = E/I$; for power, $P = EI$.

ammonium chloride Formula, NH_4Cl. The electrolyte in the carbon-zinc type of primary cell. Also called SAL AMMONIAC.

AMNL Abbreviation of AMPLITUDE-MODULATION NOISE LEVEL.

amortisseur winding **1.** A winding that acts against pulsation of the magnetic field in an electric motor. **2.** A winding that acts to prevent oscillation in a synchronous motor.

amorphous substance A noncrystalline material.

amp **1.** Slang for AMPERE. **2.** Slang for AMPLIFIER—especially in audio high-fidelity applications.

ampacity Current-carrying capacity expressed in amperes.

amperage The strength of an electric current (i.e., the number of amperes).

ampere (Andre Marie Ampere, 1775-1836). Abbreviations, A (preferred), a, amp. The SI base unit of current intensity (I). The ampere is the constant current that, if maintained in two straight parallel conductors of infinite length and of negligible circular cross section and placed 1 meter apart in a vacuum, would produce between the conductors a force of 2×10^{-7} newton per meter. One ampere flows through a 1-ohm resistance when a potential of 1 volt is applied; thus $I = E/R$. Also see MICROAMPERE, MILLIAMPERE, NANOAMPERE, and PICOAMPERE.

ampere balance A device consisting of two conductors in which the force between them (caused by current) is balanced against the gravitational force exerted on an object in the gravitational field of the earth. Used for the precise determination of current of large dimension, or of the size of the ampere.

ampere-hour Abbreviations: Ah, amp-hr. The quantity of electricity that passes through a circuit in one hour when the rate of flow is one ampere. Also see BATTERY CAPACITY.

ampere-hour meter An instrument for measuring ampere-hours. It contains a small motor driven by the current being measured and which moves a point on an ampere-hour scale. The motor speed is proportional to the current. The position of the pointer is proportional to current and elapsed time.

Ampere's law Current flowing in a wire generates a magnetic flux that encircles the wire in the clockwise direction when the current is moving away from the observer.

ampere-turn Symbol, NI. A unit of magnetomotive force equal to 1 ampere flowing in a single-turn coil. The ampere-turns value for any coil is obtained by multiplying the current (in amperes) by the number of turns in the coil.

Amperian whirl The stream of electrons in a single-turn, current-conducting wire loop acting as an elementary electromagnet.

amp-hr One style of abbreviating AMPERE-HOUR. Also, Ah.

amplidyne A dynamo-like rotating dc machine that can act as a power amplifier because the response of the output voltage to changes in field excitation is quite rapid. Used in servo systems.

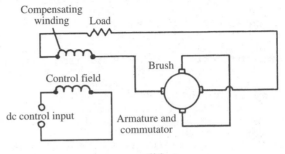

amplidyne

amplification **1.** The process of increasing the magnitude of a signal. This entails an input signal controlling a local power supply to produce a larger output signal. Depending on the kind of input and output signals, amplification can be categorized as CURRENT, VOLTAGE, POWER, or some combination of these. **2.** The qualitative signal increase resulting from the process in **1**. **3.** The quantitative signal increase (resulting from the process in **1**), expressed as a factor (such as 100) or in terms of *decibels* (dB). See AMPLIFICATION FACTOR and DECIBEL.

amplification factor **1.** The ratio of the output voltage, current, or power to the input voltage, current, or power of an AMPLIFIER circuit. For voltage or current, this ratio has meaning only when the input and output impedances are identical. **2.** The number of decibels by which an AMPLIFIER circuit increases the amplitude of a signal. For voltage or current, this figure has meaning only when the input and output impedances are identical. See DECIBEL. **3.** The ALPHA or BETA of a bipolar transistor. **4.** In the operation of an electron tube, the ratio of the derivative (instantaneous rate of change) of the plate voltage to the derivative of the grid voltage, for zero change in plate current.

amplified ALC Abbreviation, AALC. An automatic-level-control (ALC) system that uses the amplification of the fed-back control signal. It is used in RF power amplifiers, particularly single-sideband (SSB) linear amplifiers, to prevent overmodulation and nonlinearity.

amplified back bias A declining voltage developed across a fast-time-constant circuit in an amplifier stage and fed back into a preceding stage.

amplifier Any device that increases the magnitude of an applied signal. It receives an input signal and delivers a larger output signal that, in addition to its increased amplitude, is a replica of the input signal. Also see CURRENT AMPLIFIER, POWER AMPLIFIER, and VOLTAGE AMPLIFIER.

amplifier diode Any semiconductor that can provide amplification in a suitable circuit or microwave system. See DIODE AMPLIFIER.

amplifier distortion A change in the waveform of a signal, arising within an amplifier that is operated in compliance with specified conditions.

amplifier input 1. The terminals and section of an amplifier that receive the signal to be amplified. 2. The signal to be amplified.

amplifier noise Collectively, all extraneous signals present in the output of an amplifier when no working signal is applied to the amplifier input terminals.

amplifier nonlinearity A condition in which the amplifier output signal does not exhibit a linear relationship to the corresponding input signal. Some amplifiers are designed to operate in a linear manner at all times, but many amplifier types need not function in this manner to be effective. Also see AMPLIFIER DISTORTION and LINEAR AMPLIFIER.

amplifier output 1. The terminals and section of an amplifier that deliver the amplified signal for external use. 2. The amplified signal.

amplifier power The power level of the output signal delivered by an amplifier (also called OUTPUT POWER), or the extent to which the amplifier increases the power of the input signal (also called POWER AMPLIFICATION).

amplifier response The performance of an amplifier throughout a specified frequency band. Factors usually included are gain, distortion, amplitude versus frequency, and power output.

amplify To perform the functions of amplification (see AMPLIFICATION, 1).

amplifying delay line A delay line that causes amplification of signals in a circuit intended for pulse compression.

amplistat A self-saturating magnetic amplifier.

amplitron A backward-wave amplifier used in microwave circuits.

amplitude The extent to which an alternating or pulsating current or voltage swings, positively and negatively, from zero or from a mean value.

amplitude-controlled rectifier A thyratron- or thyristor-based rectifier circuit.

amplitude density distribution A mathematical function giving the probability that, at a given instant in time, a fluctuating voltage has a certain value.

amplitude distortion In an amplifier or network, the condition in which the output-signal amplitude exhibits a nonlinear relationship to the input-signal amplitude.

amplitude error 1. The error in measuring the amplitude of a signal, normally expressed as a percentage of signal amplitude or as a percentage of full scale. 2. The frequency at which the output amplitude of a signal is in error by 1% with amplitude at 10% of full scale.

amplitude factor For an ac wave, the ratio of the peak value to the rms value. The amplitude factor of a sine wave is equal to the square root of $2 = 1.4142136$.

amplitude fading In the propagation of electromagnetic waves, a condition in which the amplitudes of all components of the signal (i.e., carrier and sidebands) increase and decrease uniformly. Compare SELECTIVE FADING.

amplitude/frequency response Performance of an amplifier throughout a specified range, as exhibited by a plot of output-signal amplitude versus frequency for a constant-amplitude input signal.

amplitude gate A transducer that transmits only those portions of an input wave that lie within two close-spaced amplitude boundaries; also called *slicer*.

amplitude limiter A circuit, usually with automatic gain control (AGC), that keeps an amplifier output signal from exceeding a certain level, despite large variations in input-signal amplitude. A dc-biased diode performs passive limiting action via *clipping*.

amplitude-modulated generator A signal generator whose output is amplitude modulated. Usually, this instrument is an RF generator that is modulated at an audio frequency.

amplitude-modulated transmitter A radio-frequency transmitter whose carrier is varied in amplitude, according to the rate of change of some data-containing signal (such as voice, music, facsimile, television pictures, control signals, or instrument readings).

amplitude modulation A method of conveying information, in which a usually analog low-frequency signal (such as audio or video) is impressed on a carrier, producing sidebands at frequencies above and below that of the carrier, without changing the instantaneous frequency of the carrier itself. Compare FREQUENCY MODULATION.

amplitude-modulation noise Spurious amplitude modulation of a carrier wave by extraneous signals and random impulses, rather than by the intended data-containing signal.

amplitude noise In radar, amplitude fluctuations of an echo returned by a target. This noise limits the precision of the system.

amplitude of noise The level of random noise in a system. The amplitude of noise is measured in the same way that signal amplitude is measured.

amplitude range The maximum-to-minimum amplitude variation of a signal. It can be expressed as a direct numerical ratio or in decibels.

amplitude response The maximum output obtainable at various frequencies over the range of an instrument operating under rated conditions.

amplitude selection The selection of a signal, according to its correspondence to a predetermined amplitude or amplitude range.

amplitude separator In a television receiver, a circuit that separates the control pulses from the composite video signal.

amplitude suppression ratio The ratio of an undesired output of a frequency-modulated (FM) receiver to the desired output, when the test signal is amplitude modulated and frequency modulated simultaneously.

amplitude-versus-frequency distortion Distortion resulting from varying gain or attenuation of an amplifier or network, with respect to signal frequency.

AMTOR A form of amateur-radio data communications, in which the accuracy of a group of characters in a message is checked periodically by the receiving station. If an error appears likely, then the receiving station sends an instruction to the transmitting station to retransmit that particular group of characters. Characters are sent in bunches with pauses for possible inquiries from the receiving station.

AM tuner A compact radio receiver unit that handles amplitude-modulated signals and delivers low-amplitude audio output to a high-fidelity amplifier. Compare AM/FM TUNER and FM TUNER.

amu Abbreviation of *atomic mass unit*.

amusement robot An electromechanical robot, often computer-controlled, that is intended for use as a toy.

AN- A prefix designator used by American military services to indicate commonality.

anacoustic Pertaining to the lack of sound or absence of reverberation or transmission of sonic waves.

analog **1.** A quantity that corresponds, point for point or value for value, to an otherwise unrelated quantity. Thus, voltage is the analog of water pressure, and current is the analog of water flow. **2.** Varying over a continuous range and, therefore, capable of attaining an infinite number of values or levels. Compare DIGITAL.

analog adder An analog circuit or device that receives two or more inputs and delivers an output equal to their sum.

analog adder/subtracter An analog circuit or device that receives two or more inputs and delivers an output equal to their sum or difference (in any combination), as desired.

analog channel In an ANALOG COMPUTER, an information channel in which the extreme limits of data magnitude are fixed, and the data can have any value between the limits.

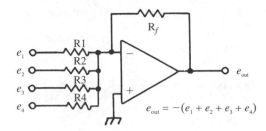

**analog adder
(inverting)**

analog communications Any form of communications in which a carrier, generally an electromagnetic wave or high-frequency current, is varied in a continuous and controlled way by a data-containing signal. See ANALOG, **2.**

analog computer A computer in which input and output quantities are represented as points on continuous (or small-increment) scales. To represent these quantities, the computer uses voltages or resistances that are proportional to the numbers to be worked on. When the quantities are nonelectrical (such as pressure or velocity), they are made analogous by proportional voltages or resistances.

analog data **1.** Data represented in a quantitatively analogous way. Examples are the deflection of a movable-coil meter, the positioning of a slider on a slide rule, and the setting of a variable resistor to represent the value of a nonelectrical quantity. Also see ANALOG. **2.** Data displayed along a smooth scale of continuous values (as by a movable-coil meter), rather than in discrete steps (as by a digital meter).

analog differentiator An analog circuit or device whose output waveform is the derivative of the input-signal waveform, with respect to time.

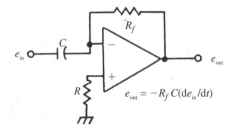

analog differentiator

analog divider An analog circuit or device that receives two inputs and delivers an output equal to their quotient.

analog electronics Electronic techniques and equipment that is based on uniformly changing signals, such as sine waves, and often having continuous-scale indicators, such as D'Arsonval meters. Compare DIGITAL ELECTRONICS.

analog information Approximate numerical information, as opposed to digital information, which is assumed to be exact.

analog integrator An analog circuit or device whose output waveform is the integral of the input signal waveform, with respect to time.

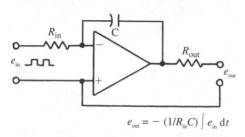

$$e_{out} = - (1/R_{in}C) \int e_{in}\, dt$$

analog integrator

analog inverting adder An analog adder that delivers a sum with the opposite sign to that of the input quantities.

analog meter An indicating instrument that uses a movable-coil arrangement or the equivalent, causing a rotating pointer to indicate a particular value on a graduated printed scale. Compare DIGITAL METER.

analog meter

analog multiplexer 1. A multiplexer used with analog signals (see MULTIPLEXER). 2. An analog time-sharing circuit.

analog multiplier An analog circuit or device that receives two or more inputs and delivers an output equal to their product.

analog network A circuit that permits mathematical relationships to be shown directly by electric or electronic means.

analogous pole In a PYROELECTRIC MATERIAL, the end or face having the positive electric charge.

analog output An output quantity that varies smoothly over a continuous range of values, rather than in discrete steps.

analog record Also called *analog recording*. A record or recording method in which some property of the recorded material, such as displacement or magnetization, varies over a continuous range that is relative to time and/or physical position.

analog recorder Any recorder, such as a recording oscillograph, potentiometric recorder, electroencephalograph, electrocardiograph, or lie detector, that produces an analog record. The counterpart is a digital recorder, which produces a readout in discrete numbers (printed or visually displayed).

analog representation Representation of information within a smooth, continuous range, rather than as separate (discrete) steps or points.

analog signal A signal that attains an infinite number of different amplitude levels, as opposed to one that can attain only a finite number of levels as a function of time.

analog subtracter An analog circuit or device that receives two inputs and delivers an output equal to their difference.

analog summer See ANALOG ADDER.

analog switch A switching device that will only pass signals that are faithful analogs of transducer parameters.

analog-to-digital conversion 1. A process in which an analog signal (such as a voice waveform) is changed into a digital or binary signal that conveys the same information. This process is commonly used in digital computers to encode sounds and images. It is also used in communications systems to improve efficiency, minimize the necessary bandwidth, and optimize the signal-to-noise ratio. 2. A process in which continuous mechanical motion is encoded into a digital or binary electronic signal.

analog-to-digital converter Any circuit or device that performs ANALOG-TO-DIGITAL CONVERSION.

analysis 1. The rigorous determination of the constants and modes of operation for electronic equipment. Compare SYNTHESIS. 2. A branch of mathematics dealing with point sets, relations, and functions.

analytical engine A primitive mechanical calculating machine, invented in 1833 by Charles Babbage.

analyzer 1. Any instrument that permits analysis through close measurements and tests (e.g., distortion analyzer, WAVE ANALYZER, or gas analyzer). 2. A computer program used for debugging purposes; it analyzes other programs and summarizes references to storage locations. 3. An analysis interface to an oscilloscope.

anastigmatic yoke   Also called *full-focus yoke*. In a television (TV) receiver, a deflection yoke with a cosine winding for better focus at the edges of the picture.

anchorage   In plastic recording tape, the adhesion of the magnetic oxide coating to the surface of the tape.

ancillary equipment   Equipment that does not directly enter into the operation of a central system. Examples are input/output components of a computer and test instruments attached to a system.

AND circuit   In digital systems and other switching circuits, a logic gate whose output is high (logic 1) only when all input signals are high. Otherwise the output is low (logic 0). Compare OR CIRCUIT.

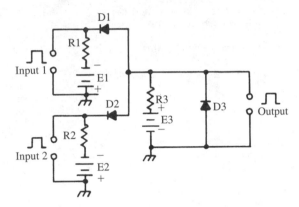

AND circuit

Anderson bridge   An ac bridge circuit with six impedances, permitting the value of an un-

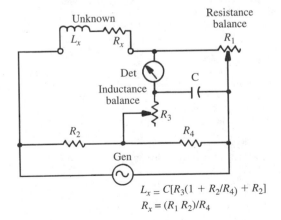

$$L_x = C[R_3(1 + R_2/R_4) + R_2]$$
$$R_x = (R_1 R_2)/R_4$$

Anderson bridge

known inductance to be determined in terms of a standard capacitance.

AND gate   **1.** AND circuit. **2.** In a TV receiver, an AND circuit that holds the keyed-AGC signal off until a positive horizontal flyback pulse and a horizontal sync pulse appear simultaneously at the input.

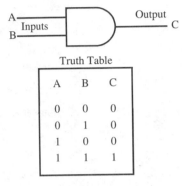

Truth Table

A	B	C
0	0	0
0	1	0
1	0	0
1	1	1

AND gate

android   A sophisticated robot built in humanoid form. Usually, it propels itself by rolling on wheels or on a track drive. A rotatable head contains position sensors, a machine vision system, and/or a machine hearing system. Mechanical arms are equipped with end effectors to perform various tasks. The most advanced androids have self-contained computer control systems.

anechoic   Pertaining to the absence of echoes. Examples: ANECHOIC CHAMBER, *anechoic enclosure*, or *anechoic room*.

anechoic chamber   An enclosure that does not reflect sound waves that approach its walls. Such a chamber is used to test certain audio devices.

anemograph   An electromechanical device that produces a recording of wind speed versus time. Generally, it consists of an ANEMOMETER connected to a PEN-AND-INK RECORDER via a suitable electronic interface.

anemometer   An instrument that measures or indicates wind speed, or speed and direction (velocity).

angel   **1.** An extraneous image, usually of short duration, on a cathode-ray-tube (CRT) display. The term applies particularly to anomalies in a radar image caused by low-atmospheric reflection, birds, or other mobile objects. **2.** Air-deployed metallic debris, also known as *chaff*, designed to create radar echoes as a decoy or diversion tactic.

angle jamming   A radar jamming technique in which the return echo is jammed with a signal containing improper azimuth or elevation angle components.

angle modulation   Variation of the angle of a sine-wave carrier in response to the modulating source, as in FREQUENCY MODULATION and PHASE MODULATION.

angle noise   In radar reception, the interference resulting from variations in the angle at which an echo arrives from the target.

angle of arrival   The angle which the line of propagation of an incoming radio wave makes with the surface of the earth. Compare ANGLE OF DEPARTURE.

angle of azimuth   The horizontal angle between the viewer and object or target, usually measured clockwise from north.

angle of beam   The angle enclosing most of the transmitted energy in the radiation from a directional antenna. It is usually measured between the *half-power points* in the main lobe of the directional pattern. This angle can be measured in the horizontal (azimuth) plane or in the vertical (elevation) plane.

angle of conduction   **1.** Also called *angle of flow*. The number of degrees of an excitation-signal cycle during which output (drain, collector or plate) current flows in an amplifier circuit. **2.** The number of degrees of any sine wave at which conduction of a device (e.g., a diode) begins.

angle of convergence   **1.** In any graphical representation, the angle formed by any two lines or plots that come together at a point. **2.** The angle formed by the light paths of two photocells focused on the same object.

angle of declination   The angle between the horizon and a descending line. Compare ANGLE OF ELEVATION.

angle of deflection   In a cathode-ray tube, the angle between the electron beam at rest and a new position resulting from deflection.

angle of departure   The angle, relative to the horizon, made by the line of propagation of a transmitted radio wave. Compare ANGLE OF ARRIVAL.

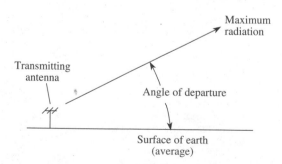

angle of departure

angle of depression   See ANGLE OF DECLINATION.

angle of divergence   In a cathode-ray tube, the angle formed by the spreading of an undeflected electron beam as it extends from the gun to the screen.

angle of elevation   The angle that an ascending line subtends, with respect to the horizon. Compare ANGLE OF DECLINATION.

angle of flow   See ANGLE OF CONDUCTION.

angle of incidence   The angle, measured relative to the perpendicular (orthogonal) to a surface or boundary, subtended by an approaching ray. Compare ANGLE OF REFLECTION and ANGLE OF REFRACTION.

angle of lag   The phase difference (in degrees or radians) whereby one component follows another in time, both components being of the same frequency. Compare ANGLE OF LEAD. Also see PHASE ANGLE.

angle of lead   The phase difference (in degrees or radians) whereby one component precedes another in time, both components being of the same frequency. Compare ANGLE OF LAG. Also see PHASE ANGLE.

angle of radiation   **1.** The angle, measured with respect to the horizon, at which the principal lobe of an electromagnetic wave leaves a transmitting antenna. **2.** The angle, measured relative to the horizon, of a receiving or transmitting antenna's optimum sensitivity.

angle of reflection   The angle, measured relative to the perpendicular (orthogonal) to a surface, subtended by a ray leaving the surface after having been reflected from it. Compare ANGLE OF INCIDENCE.

angle of refraction   The angle, measured relative to the perpendicular (orthogonal) to a boundary between two different media, subtended by a ray leaving the boundary after having been refracted thereat. Compare ANGLE OF INCIDENCE.

angle tracking noise   Noise in a servo system that results in a tracking error.

angstrom   (Anders J. Angstrom, 1814-1874). A unit of length used to describe certain extremely short waves and microscopic dimensions; 1 angstrom equals 10^{-4} microns (10^{-10} meters).

angular deviation loss   The ratio of microphone or loudspeaker response on the principal axis of response to the response at a designated angle from that axis. Expressed in decibels.

angular difference   See PHASE ANGLE.

angular displacement   In an ac circuit, the separation, in degrees, between two waves. See PHASE ANGLE.

angular frequency   The frequency of an ac signal, expressed in *radians per second (rad/sec)* and approximately equal to $6.28f$, where f is the frequency in Hertz.

angular length   Length, as along the horizontal axis of an ac wave or along the standing-wave pattern on an antenna, expressed as the product of radians and wavelength.

angular-mode keys On a calculator or computer, the DEG, RAD, and GRAD keys for expressing or converting angles in DEGREES, RADIANS, and GRADS, respectively.

angular phase difference For two sinusoidal waves, the phase difference, expressed in degrees or radians.

angular rate In navigation, the rate of bearing change, expressed in degrees or radians.

angular resolution The ability of a radar to distinguish between two targets by angular measurement.

angus pen recorder An instrument that makes a permanent record of the time whenever a channel is used.

anharmonic oscillator An oscillating device in which the force toward the balance point is not linear, with respect to displacement.

anhysteresis The magnetization of a material by a unidirectional field containing an alternating field component of gradually decreasing amplitude.

anhysteretic state The condition of a substance after it has been subjected to a strong magnetic field, the intensity of which alternates in direction and diminishes gradually to zero.

animism A belief or philosophy, held especially in Eastern civilizations, such as Japan, that all things contain an essence of life. This theory renders irrelevant the question of whether or not machines, such as computers and robots can be "alive."

anion A negative ion. Also see ION.

anisotropic Pertaining to the tendency of some materials to display different magnetic and other physical properties along different axes.

ANL Abbreviation of AUTOMATIC NOISE LIMITER.

anneal To heat a metal to a predetermined temperature and let it cool slowly. The operation prevents brittleness and often stabilizes electrical characteristics.

annealed laminations Core laminations for transformers or choke coils that have been annealed.

annealed shield A magnetic shield for cathode-ray tubes, that has been processed by annealing.

annealed wire Soft-drawn wire that has been subjected to annealing.

annotations **1.** Marking on copies of original engineering-installation documents to show changes made during the installation. **2.** Any set of comments or notes accompanying a program, an equipment or system, or a process.

annular **1.** Pertaining to the region between two concentric circles that lie in the same plane; ring-shaped. **2.** Pertaining to two or more concentric circles that lie in a common plane.

annular conductor A number of wires stranded in three concentric layers of alternating twists around a hemp core.

annular transistor A mesa transistor in which the base and collector take the form of concentric rings around a central emitter.

annulling network A subcircuit that shunts a filter to cancel reactive impedance at the extreme ends of the pass band of the filter.

annunciation relay A relay that indicates whether or not a circuit is carrying current.

annunciator A device that produces loud sound and/or conspicuous light to attract attention (e.g., the electronic siren in an automotive security system).

anode **1.** The positive electrode of a vacuum tube or solid-state device (i.e., the electrode toward which electrons move during current flow). **2.** In an electrochemical cell, the electrode that loses electrons by oxidation. This is usually the negative electrode.

anode balancing coil Mutually coupled windings used to maintain equal currents in parallel anodes operating from a common transformer terminal.

anode current Current flowing in the anode circuit of a device.

anode efficiency Also called *plate efficiency*. In a power amplifier using an electron tube, the ratio P_o/P_i, where P_o is the output power in watts and P_i is the dc anode power input in volt-amperes.

anode power input Symbol, $P_{A(input)}$. The product of anode current and anode voltage.

anode power supply The ac or positive dc power supply unit that delivers current and voltage to the anode of a device.

anode saturation The point beyond which a further increase in anode voltage does not produce an increase in anode current.

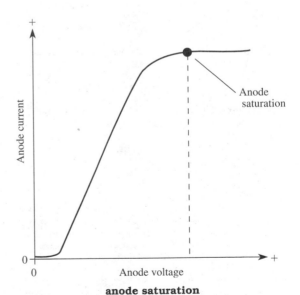

anode saturation

anode strap In a multicavity magnetron, a metal strap connecting the anodes.

anode terminal **1.** In a diode, the terminal to which a positive dc voltage must be applied for forward bias. Compare CATHODE TERMINAL. **2.** In a diode, the terminal at which a negative dc voltage appears when the device is used as an ac rectifier. Compare CATHODE TERMINAL. **3.** The terminal that is connected internally to the anodic element of any device.

anode voltage Symbol, E_A or V_A. The difference in potential between the anode and cathode of a device.

anodic Pertaining to the anode of a device, or to anode-like effects.

anodizing An electrolytic process in which a protective oxide film is deposited on the surface of a metallic body acting temporarily as the anode of the electrolytic cell.

anomalous dispersion Dispersion of electromagnetic radiation that is characterized by a decrease in refractive index with increase in frequency.

anomalous propagation **1.** The low-attenuation propagation of UHF or microwave signals through atmospheric layers. **2.** Unusual, bizarre, or unexplainable electromagnetic-wave propagation (e.g., apparent F-layer ionospheric effects in the FM broadcast band). **3.** Rapid fluctuation of a sonar echo because of variations in propagation.

anoxemia toximeter An electronic instrument for measuring or alerting against the onset of anoxemia (deficiency of oxygen in the blood)—especially in airplane pilots.

AN radio range A navigational facility entailing four zones of equal signal strength. When the aircraft deviates from course, an aural Morse-code signal, A (DIT DAH) or N (DAH DIT) is heard; but when the aircraft is on course, a continuous tone is heard.

ANSI Acronym for *American National Standards Institute.*

AN signal The signal provided by an AN radio range to apprise aircraft pilots of course deviation.

answerback The automatic response of a terminal station to a remote-control signal.

answer cord In a telephone system, the cord used for answering subscribers' calls and incoming trunk calls.

answering machine A device that automatically answers a telephone and records an audio message from the caller.

answer lamp A telephone switchboard lamp that lights when an answer cord is plugged into a line jack; it switches off when the telephone answers and lights when the call is completed.

ant Abbreviation of ANTENNA.

antenna In a communications system, a specialized transducer that converts incoming electromagnetic fields into alternating electric currents having the same frequencies (*receiving antenna*), or converts an alternating current at a specific frequency into an outgoing electromagnetic field at the same frequency (*transmitting antenna*). An antenna can be a simple wire or rod, or a complicated structure. Thousands of geometries and specifications are possible. The optimum antenna type for a given situation depends on the communications frequency, the distance to be covered, and various other factors.

antenna ammeter An RF ammeter, usually of the thermocouple type, employed to measure current flowing to a transmitting antenna.

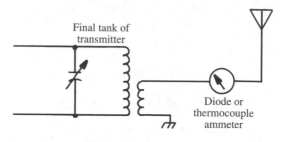

antenna ammeter

antenna amplifier **1.** A radio-frequency amplifier, often installed at the antenna, used to boost signals before they reach a receiver (also called an *RF preamplifier*). **2.** Occasionally, the first RF amplifier stage of a receiver, also known as the *front end.*

antenna array See ARRAY.

antenna bandwidth The frequency range throughout which an antenna will operate at a specified efficiency without needing alteration or adjustment.

antenna beamwidth A measure of the extent to which a directional antenna focuses a transmitted electromagnetic field, or focuses its response to incoming electromagnetic fields. Expressed as the angle in degrees between opposite *half-power points* in the main lobe of the directional pattern. Usually determined in the horizontal plane, but occasionally in the vertical plane.

antenna coil The primary coil of the input RF transformer of a receiver, or the secondary coil of the output RF transformer of a transmitter.

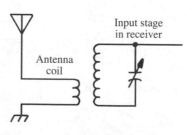

antenna coil

antenna coincidence The condition in which two directional antennas are pointed directly toward each other.

antenna-conducted interference Extraneous signals generated in a transmitter or receiver and presented to the antenna, from which they are radiated.

antenna core A ferrite rod or slab around which a coil of wire is wound to act as a self-contained antenna, usually in a miniature receiver.

antenna coupler A device consisting of an inductor, RF transformer, or a combination of inductor(s) and capacitor(s), used to match the impedance of an antenna to that of a transmitter or receiver. Also known as a *transmatch* or *antenna tuner*.

antenna coupling Inductive and/or capacitive coupling used to optimize the transfer of energy from an antenna to a receiver, or from a transmitter to an antenna.

antenna current **1.** Radio-frequency current flowing from a transmitter into an antenna. **2.** Radio-frequency current flowing from a receiving antenna into a receiver.

antenna detector A circuit that warns aircraft personnel that they are being observed by radar. It picks up the radar pulses and actuates a warning light or other device.

antenna diplexer A coupling device that permits several transmitters to share one antenna without troublesome interaction. Compare ANTENNA DUPLEXER.

antenna directivity The directional characteristics of a transmitting or receiving antenna, usually expressed qualitatively (e.g., *omnidirectional*, *bidirectional*, or *unidirectional*). A more precise expression is ANTENNA BEAMWIDTH.

antenna director In a directional antenna, a PARASITIC ELEMENT situated in front of the radiator and separated from it by an appropriate fraction of a wavelength. Its function is to intensify radiation in the direction of transmission. Compare ANTENNA RADIATOR and ANTENNA REFLECTOR.

antenna duplexer A circuit or device permitting one antenna to be shared by two transmitters without undesirable interaction.

antenna effect The tendency of wires or metallic bodies to act as antennas (i.e., to radiate or receive radio waves).

antenna efficiency The ratio between the radio-frequency power applied to an antenna and the power actually radiated into space. Usually expressed as a percentage.

antenna factor A factor (in decibels) added to an RF voltmeter reading to find the true open-circuit voltage induced in an antenna.

antenna field The electromagnetic field immediately surrounding an antenna.

antennafier Low-profile antenna/amplifier device, sometimes used with portable communications systems. Also called an *active antenna*.

antenna front-to-back ratio For a directional antenna, the ratio of field strength in front of the antenna (i.e., directly forward in the line of maximum directivity) to field strength in back of the antenna (i.e., 180 degrees from the front), as measured at a fixed distance from the radiator. It is usually specified in decibels.

antenna gain For a given antenna, the ratio of signal strength (received or transmitted) to that obtained with a comparison antenna, such as a simple dipole. Generally specified in decibels.

antenna ground system The earth, counterpoise, guy wires, radials, and/or various conducting objects in the vicinity of an antenna which, taken together, form the radio-frequency (RF) ground system against which the antenna operates. Some antennas require an extensive ground system to function efficiently; others need no ground system.

antenna/ground system An arrangement embodying both an antenna and a low-resistance connection to the earth, as opposed to an antenna system that involves no connection to earth.

antenna height **1.** The height of an antenna above the surface of the earth immediately beneath the driven element(s). **2.** The height of an antenna above the effective radio-frequency (RF) ground immediately beneath the driven element(s). **3.** The height of an antenna above average terrain, determined against the mean altitude of a number of points on the earth's surface that lie within a certain radius of the antenna structure. Also called *height above average terrain (HAAT)*.

antenna impedance The complex-number impedance that an antenna presents to a transmission line. It can vary over a tremendous range, and depends on the antenna type, antenna size, antenna height, operating frequency, and various other factors.

antenna-induced potential Also called *antenna-induced microvolts*. The voltage across the open-circuited terminals of an antenna.

antenna lens Also called *lens antenna*. A radiator designed to focus microwave energy in much the same manner that an optical lens focuses light rays. Lens antennas are made from dielectric materials and/or metals.

antenna lobe A well-defined region in the radiation pattern of an antenna in which radiation is most intense, or in which reception is strongest. Also see ANTENNA PATTERN.

antenna matching The technique of establishing a satisfactory relationship between the antenna impedance and the transmission-line or transmitter-output impedance, for maximum transfer of power into the antenna. Also, the matching of antenna impedance to receiver-input impedance, for delivery of maximum energy to the receiver.

antennamitter   An antenna/oscillator combination that serves as a low-power transmitter.

antenna pattern   A polar plot of antenna performance that shows field strength versus angle of azimuth, with the antenna at the center. It is usually specified in the horizontal plane.

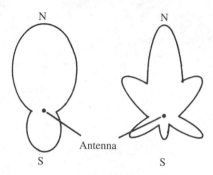

antenna patterns

antenna polarization   The orientation of electric lines of flux, with respect to the surface of the earth, for which an antenna is most efficient. A vertical antenna radiates and receives vertically polarized waves. A horizontal antenna radiates and receives horizontally polarized waves broadside to itself, and vertically polarized waves at high elevation angles off its ends. In other directions, the polarization is slanted at various angles.

antenna power   Symbol, P_{ant}. The RF power developed in an antenna by a transmitter; P_{ant} equals I^2R, where I is the antenna current and R is the antenna resistance at point I is measured.

antenna power gain   The ratio of the power required to produce a selected field strength from an antenna of interest to the power required for the same field strength (at the same test location) from a reference antenna, such as a dipole.

antenna preamplifier   A highly sensitive amplifier used to enhance the gain of a receiver. It is usually used at the very high frequencies and above.

antenna radiation   The propagation of radio waves by a transmitting antenna.

antenna radiator   The element of an antenna that receives RF energy from the transmitter and radiates waves into space. Also known as the *driven element*. Compare ANTENNA DIRECTOR and ANTENNA REFLECTOR.

antenna range   1. The frequency band, communication distance characteristically covered, or other continuum of values that specify the operating limits of an antenna. 2. The region immediately surrounding an antenna in which tests and measurements usually are made. Sometimes called ANTENNA FIELD.

antenna reflector   In a directional antenna, a PARASITIC ELEMENT situated behind the radiator and separated from the latter by an appropriate fraction of a wavelength. Its function is to intensify radiation in the direction of transmission. Compare ANTENNA DIRECTOR and ANTENNA RADIATOR.

antenna relay   In a radio station, a low-loss, heavy-duty relay that enables the antenna to be switched between transmitter and receiver.

antenna resistance   The resistive component of ANTENNA IMPEDANCE.

antenna resonant frequency   The frequency, or narrow band of frequencies, at which an antenna's impedance appears resistive.

antenna stage   1. The first RF amplifier stage of a receiver. 2. Occasionally, the final RF amplifier of a transmitter.

antenna switch   In a radio station, a low-loss, heavy-duty switch that enables the antenna to be connected to transmitter, receiver, or safety ground.

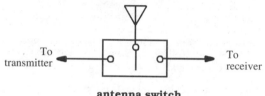

antenna switch
(single-pole, double-throw)

antenna system   Collectively, an antenna and all of the auxiliary electrical and mechanical devices needed for its efficient operation, including couplers, tuners, transmission lines, supports, insulators, and rotator.

antenna terminals   1. The points at which a transmission line is attached to an antenna. 2. The signal input terminals of a receiver. 3. The signal output terminals of a transmitter.

antennaverter   An antenna and converter combined into a single circuit, intended for connection to the antenna terminals of a receiver to allow operation on frequencies outside the band for which the receiver has been designed.

antenna wire   1. The radiator element of a wire-type antenna. 2. A strong solid or stranded wire (e.g., hard-drawn copper, copper-clad steel, or phosphor-bronze) used for antennas.

anthropomorphism   The perception, by people, of machines as having human qualities. This can lead to emotional attachment to hardware, such as computers and robots. The more sophisticated the apparatus, in general, the more powerful this perception can become.

antialiasing filter   A low-pass or bandpass filter that limits the bandwidth of an input signal to prevent *aliasing* and its effects. See ALIASING, **1**.

anticapacitance switch   A switch whose members are thin blades and stiff wires widely separated to minimize capacitance between them.

anticathode   The target electrode of an X-ray tube.

Anticipatory Sciences   A group of *futurists*, people who attempt to predict the course of technology. Some futurists believe that progress will continue until, for example, homes become fully automated and artificial intelligence reaches a level comparable to human intelligence. Other futurists believe that such things are highly improbable.

anticlutter circuit   A supplementary circuit in a radar receiver that minimizes the effect of extraneous reflections that would obscure the image of the target.

anticlutter gain control   In a radar receiver, a circuit that automatically raises the gain of the receiver slowly to maximum after each transmitter pulse to reduce the effect of clutter-producing echoes.

anticoincidence   Noncoincidental occurrence of two or more signals. Compare COINCIDENCE.

anticoincidence circuit   In computers and control systems, a circuit that delivers an output signal only when two or more input signals are not received simultaneously. Compare COINCIDENCE CIRCUIT. Also see NAND CIRCUIT.

anticoincidence operation   An exclusive-OR operation.

anticollision radar   A vehicular radar system that is used to minimize the probability of a collision with another vehicle, whether or not that other vehicle has a similar system.

antiferroelectric   **1.** Pertaining to the property wherein the polarization curve of certain crystalline materials shows two regions of symmetry. **2.** A material that exhibits the aforementioned property.

antiferromagnetic   Pertaining to the behavior of materials in which, at low temperatures, the magnetic moments of adjacent atoms point in opposite directions.

antihunt   The condition in which *hunting* is counteracted, usually by removing overcorrection in automatic control or compensation systems.

antihunt circuit   **1.** A circuit that minimizes or eliminates hunting. Also see ANTIHUNT. **2.** In a television (TV) receiver, a circuit that stabilizes an automatic frequency control (afc) system.

antijamming   Pertaining to communications systems that are resistant to, or that counteract, the effects of *jamming*.

antilogarithm   Abbreviated, antilog or log^{-1}. The number corresponding to a given logarithm. For example, log 10,000 = log 10^4 = 4, and thus antilog 4 = 10^4 = 10,000.

antilogous pole   In a PYROELECTRIC MATERIAL, the end that becomes negatively charged as the temperature rises.

antimagnetic   Pertaining to materials having extremely low RETENTIVITY.

antimatter   Pertaining to particles that are the counterparts of conventional particles (i.e., positrons instead of electrons, antineutrons instead of neutrons, and antiprotons instead of protons). When a particle meets its antiparticle, the two annihilate, releasing energy. Also see ANTIPARTICLE.

antimicrophonic   See NONMICROPHONIC.

antimony   Symbol, Sb. A metalloidal element. Atomic number, 51. Atomic weight, 121.76. Often used as n-type dopant in semiconductor manufacture.

antineutrino   The antiparticle of the NEUTRINO, emitted as a result of radioactive decay.

antineutron   An uncharged particle with a mass equal to that of the neutron, but with a magnetic moment in the direction opposite that of the neutron.

antinode   A point of maximum amplitude in a standing wave.

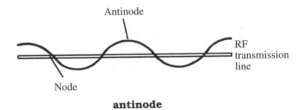

antinode

antinoise carrier-operated circuit   A circuit that cuts off the audio output of a receiver while the station transmitter is in use. This can be accomplished in the automatic-gain-control (AGC) circuit of the receiver, or in the speaker or audio line. The circuit is actuated by energy from the transmitted signal.

antinoise microphone   Any microphone that discriminates against acoustic noise (e.g., a *lip microphone* or *throat microphone*).

antinucleon   A particle with the mass of a nucleon, but with the opposite electrical charge and direction of magnetic moment. Compare NUCLEON.

antioxidant   A material, such as a lacquer coat or an inactive oxide layer, that prevents or slows oxidation of a material exposed to air.

antiparticle   A subatomic particle opposite in character to conventional particles, such as electrons, neutrons, protons. Antiparticles constitute *antimatter*. Also see ANTINEUTRINO, ANTINEUTRON, ANTINUCLEON, ANTIPROTON, and POSITRON.

antiphase The property of being in phase opposition (180 degrees out of phase).

antipincushioning magnets In some television (TV) receivers, a pair of corrective magnets in the deflection assembly on the picture tube that eliminate *pincushion distortion* (disfigurement of the raster so that it resembles a pincushion—a rectangle with its sides bowed in).

antiproton A subatomic particle with a mass equal to that of the proton, but with opposite electrical charge.

antiquark An ANTIPARTICLE of a QUARK.

antirad substance A material that protects against damage caused by atomic radiation.

antiresonance 1. Parallel resonance. **2.** The condition of being detuned from a resonant frequency.

antiresonant circuit See PARALLEL-RESONANT CIRCUIT.

antiresonant frequency 1. The resonant frequency of a parallel-resonant circuit. **2.** In a piezoelectric crystal, the frequency at which impedance is maximum (as in a parallel-resonant circuit).

antisidetone Pertaining to the elimination in telephone circuits of interference between the microphone and earphone of the same telephone.

antistickoff voltage The low voltage applied to the coarse synchro control transformer rotor winding in a dual-speed servo system to eliminate ambiguous behavior in the system.

antitransmit/receive switch Abbreviated *ATR*. In a radar installation, an automatic device to prevent interaction between transmitter and receiver.

antivirus program A computer program or utility designed to detect and eliminate viruses and Trojan horses in a computer system.

antivoice-operated transmission Radio communications that use a voice-activated circuit as a transmitter interlock during reception on the companion receiver.

apc 1. Abbreviation of *automatic picture control*. **2.** Abbreviation of AUTOMATIC PHASE CONTROL.

aperiodic Characterized by a lack of predictable repetitive behavior. For example, the *sferics* or "static" electromagnetic interference caused by lightning.

aperiodic current The unidirectional current that follows an electromagnetic disturbance in an LCR circuit, in which R is equal to or higher than the critical circuit resistance.

aperiodic damping Damping of such a high degree that the damped system, after disturbance, comes to rest without oscillation or hunting.

aperiodic discharge A discharge in which current flowing in an LCR circuit is unidirectional, rather than oscillatory. For this condition, $1/LC$ is less than or equal to $R^2/4L^2$.

aperiodic function A nonrepetitive function (e.g., a hyperbolic trigonometric function).

aperture 1. The larger, normally open end of a horn antenna or horn loudspeaker. **2.** An opening in an opaque disk or mask that passes a predetermined amount of light or other radiant energy. **3.** The portion of a directional antenna through which most of the radiated energy passes.

aperture angle For an antenna or telescope or microscope, the half angle formed by the radius of the detecting instrument, as viewed from the source.

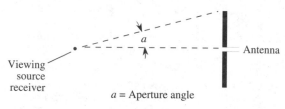

a = Aperture angle

aperture angle

aperture antenna An antenna whose beamwidth depends on the size of a horn, reflector, or lens.

aperture compensation In a television (TV) camera, the minimizing of APERTURE DISTORTION by widening the video-amplifier passband.

aperture distortion In a television (TV) camera tube, a form of distortion that occurs when the scanning beam covers several mosaic elements simultaneously. This condition, caused by excessive beam thickness, results in poor image resolution.

aperture mask In a three-gun color picture tube, a thin, perforated sheet mounted behind the viewing screen to ensure that a particular color phosphor will be excited only by the beam for that color. Also called *shadow mask*.

aperture synthesis In telescopes, a method of obtaining high resolution using several small antennas separated by great distances. The small antennas are moved around to simulate the resolving power of a much larger antenna that would, in practice, be impossible or impractical to construct.

APL Abbreviation for *A Programming Language*. A high-level computer language designed for ease of use, and characterized by the requirement for a special character set.

apl 1. Abbreviation of *average picture level*. **2.** Abbreviation of *automatic phase lock*.

A plus Also, A+. The positive terminal of an A battery. Also, pertaining to the part of a circuit connected to that terminal.

A power supply A term sometimes used to denote the unit that supplies energy to a vacuum-tube filament. Compare B POWER SUPPLY.

apparent bearing   In radio-direction finding, the uncorrected direction from which a signal appears to arrive.

apparent power   In an ac circuit, the power value obtained by multiplying the current by voltage (P equals IE), with no consideration of the effects of phase angle. Compare TRUE POWER.

apparent power loss   The loss in an ammeter or voltmeter, caused by the imperfection of the instrument. At full scale, the ammeter has a certain voltage across its terminals; the apparent power loss is the current multiplied by this voltage. A voltmeter carries a small current; the apparent power loss is the product of the current and the indicated voltage.

appearance potential   The potential through which an electron must move to produce a certain ion from the atom with which it is associated.

applause meter   An instrument consisting essentially of a microphone, audio amplifier, and indicating meter (reading directly in sound level). It is so called because of its familiar use in measuring audience response, as indicated by loudness of applause.

Applegate diagram   For a velocity-modulated tube, a plot of the positions of electron bunches in the drift space versus time.

Appleton layer   Collectively, the F1 and F2 layers of the ionosphere, at a height between 150 and 400 kilometers above the surface of the earth.

apple tube   A color picture tube, used in television, with the red, blue, and green phosphor in vertical strips.

appliance   Electrical equipment in general. This might include any home-operated device.

application   A task or job for which an electronic device or system is used. It especially pertains to personal-computer software that has practical usefulness.

application factor   A factor involved in determining the failure rate of a circuit or system affected by unusual operating conditions.

application schematic diagram   A diagram of pictorial symbols and lines that illustrate the interrelationship of functional circuit blocks in a specific program mode.

applicators   **1.** In dielectric heating, the electrodes between which the dielectric body is placed and the electrostatic field developed. **2.** In medical electronics, the electrodes applied to a patient undergoing diathermy or ultrasonic therapy.

applied voltage   The voltage presented to a circuit point or system input, as opposed to the voltage drop resulting from current flow through an element.

applique circuit   A circuit for adapting equipment to a specialized job.

approach-control radar   A radar installation serving a ground-controlled approach (GCA) system.

approximate data   **1.** Data obtained through physical measurements. Such data can never be exact; all measurements are subject to error. **2.** Loosely estimated data or imprecise calculations.

AQL   Abbreviation of ACCEPTABLE QUALITY LEVEL. A statistically defined quality level, defined in terms of percent defective, accepted on an average of 95 percent of the time.

Aquadag   A tradename for a material that consists of a slurry of fine particles of graphite. Aquadag forms a conductive coating on the inside and outside walls of some cathode-ray tubes.

aqua pura   Pure water; in most instances, distilled water. Formula, H_2O. Pure water is a nonconductor with a dielectric constant of about 81.

Ar   Symbol for ARGON.

arbitrary function fitter   A circuit or device, such as a potentiometer, curve changer, or analog computer element, providing an output current or voltage that is some preselected function of the input current or voltage.

arc   **1.** A luminous sustained discharge between two electrodes. Because it is sustained, rather than intermittent, an arc is distinguished from a spark discharge, the latter being a series of discharges (sparks)—even when it appears continuous. **2.** In graphical presentations, a section of curved line, as of a circle.

arc angle   The angle in degrees traced out by a circular arc if the center point of the circle is considered to be the vertex of an angle formed by two rays intersecting the arc at designated points.

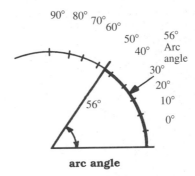

arc angle

arc cosecant   Abbreviated arc csc or $\csc^{-1}$. **1.** The inverse of the *cosecant* function. **2.** The angle, in radians or degrees, corresponding to a given cosecant.

arc cosine   Abbreviated arc cos or $\cos^{-1}$. **1.** The inverse of the *cosine* function. **2.** The angle, in radians or degrees, corresponding to a given cosine.

arc cotangent   Abbreviated arc cot or $\cot^{-1}$. **1.** The inverse of the *cotangent* function. **2.** The angle, in radians or degrees, corresponding to a given cotangent.

arc failure   **1.** Damage to, and/or failure of, insulation or a dielectric as a result of ARCOVER. **2.** Failure of make-and-break contacts through damage caused by arcover.

arc function   An *inverse trigonometric function.* See ARC COSECANT, ARC COSINE, ARC COTANGENT, ARC SECANT, ARC SINE, and ARC TANGENT.

arc furnace   A high-temperature electric furnace in which heat is produced by one or more electrical arcs.

architecture   The functional design elements of a computer—especially the components of the *central processing unit (CPU)* and the manner in which these elements interact.

archived file   A computer file stored on some backup medium, such as magnetic tape, diskette, or CD-ROM (compact disk, read-only memory), rather than being held on the hard disk. Such a file will be apart from the operating system's catalog of current files, but can be reconstituted as needed.

archives   A complete, periodically updated set of ARCHIVED FILES.

arcing   See ARCOVER.

arcing contacts   Make-and-break contacts between which an arc occurs when they are separated.

arcing ring   A metal ring placed around an insulator in a high-voltage electrical system. This keeps an arc from charring or breaking the insulator.

arcing time   The elapsed time between the breaking of contacts and the end of the arc between the contacts.

arc lamp   An electric lamp in which a brilliant arc jumps between the tips of two rods (originally carbon).

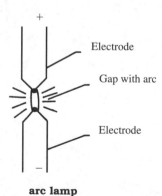

arc lamp

arc length   The length along a given arc, usually a part of the circumference of a circle. If the circle has circumference C and the arc measures x degrees, then the arc length is $Cx/360$ units.

arc minute   See MINUTE.

arc oscillation   Oscillations that can occur when opening relay contacts arc.

arcover   The occurrence of an electrical ARC between electrodes, contacts, or capacitive plates.

arcover voltage   The voltage at which disruptive discharge occurs, typically accompanied by an arc.

arc resistance   The ability of a material, usually a dielectric, to resist damage from arcing. This property is commonly expressed as the length of time between the start of the arc and the establishment of a conductive path through the material.

arc secant   Abbreviated arc sec or $\sec^{-1}$. **1.** The inverse of the *secant* function. **2.** The angle, in radians or degrees, that corresponds to a given secant.

arc second   See SECOND.

arc sensor   A device for detecting visible arcs and excessive reflected power in microwave systems.

arc sine   Abbreviated arc sin or $\sin^{-1}$. **1.** The inverse of the *sine* function. **2.** The angle, in radians or degrees, that corresponds to a given sine.

arc suppression   Extinguishing an arc discharge. Disruptive arcs in electronic circuits are suppressed by means of auxiliary diodes or resistor-capacitor networks.

arc-suppressor diode   A semiconductor diode used to prevent arcing between make-and-break contacts.

arc tangent   Abbreviated arc tan or $\tan^{-1}$. **1.** The inverse of the *tangent* function. **2.** The angle, in radians or degrees, corresponding to a given tangent.

arcthrough   The puncturing of a material by an arc.

area code   In the United States, a three-digit number that indicates the location, according to specified assigned districts, of a telephone subscriber. When making a long-distance call, the area code of the desired station must be given in addition to the seven-digit telephone number.

area protection   Coverage of a defined region, in terms of area or volume, by an alarm system.

area redistribution   A scheme to determine the effective duration of an irregularly shaped pulse. A rectangle is constructed whose height is equal to the peak height of the pulse, as displayed on an oscilloscope. The rectangle width is adjusted until the area of the rectangle is the same as the area under the curve representing the pulse. The width of the rectangle then represents the effective duration of the pulse.

area search   The scanning of a large group of computer records for those of a major category or class.

area sensor   A transducer, used with an alarm system, that protects a defined region or volume, such as an office or bedroom.

Argand diagram Named after Jean Robert Argand, (1768-1822) of Geneva, for his work on the graphical representation of complex numbers. A graphical illustration of a complex number in the form $A + jB$, where the real-number (A) axis is perpendicular to the imaginary-number (jB) axis. The value j is the square root of -1, the unit imaginary number. The axes are perpendicular, usually with the A axis horizontal. The length of the line from the point (0,0) to the point (A,jB) is the amplitude of the vector $\mathbf{X} = A + jB$. The direction is specified as the angle, in degrees or radians, of the vector measured counterclockwise from the A axis.

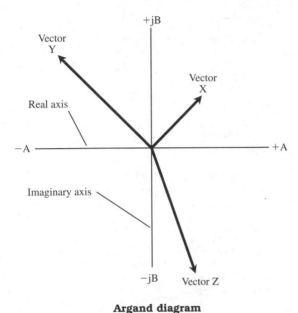

Argand diagram

argon Symbol, Ar. An inert gaseous element. Atomic number, 18. Atomic weight, 39.94. Argon, present in small amounts in the earth's atmosphere, is used in various specialized devices, such as lasers.

argon laser A laser whose tube is filled with argon gas. It generates coherent light at specific wavelengths that are characteristic of elemental argon.

argument **1.** The direction angle of a polar vector. **2.** An independent variable whose value determines the value of a function.

arithmetic address An address obtained by performing an arithmetic operation on another address.

arithmetic and logic unit Abbreviation, ALU. The part of a digital computer containing the circuits that perform calculations and logic operations; distinguished from mass storage, input/output, and peripheral units.

arithmetic circuit Also called *arithmetic element.* In a digital computer, a circuit that is involved in the execution of calculations. Included are adders, storage registers, accumulators, subtracters, and multipliers.

arithmetic mean The average of a group of quantities, obtained by dividing their sum by the number of quantities.

arithmetic operation In digital computer practice, a numerical process performed: addition, subtraction, multiplication, division, comparison.

arithmetic progression A mathematical series in which each term following the first is obtained by adding a constant quantity to the preceding one. For example, $S = 1, 2, 3, 4, \ldots n$. Compare GEOMETRIC PROGRESSION.

arithmetic shift In a digital computer, the multiplication or division of a quantity by a power of the base used in the notation.

arithmetic sum The sum of two or more quantities disregarding their signs. Compare ALGEBRAIC SUM.

arithmetic symmetry A filter response that is exactly symmetrical about the center frequency when the frequency scale is linear.

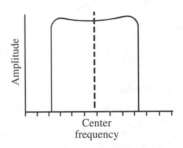

arithmetic symmetry

arm **1.** Any of the distinct branches of a circuit or network. Also called *leg.* **2.** A movable element in a device, usually containing a contact for switching.

armature **1.** The rotating member of a motor. **2.** The rotating member of some types of electromechanical generator. **3.** The movable member of a relay, bell, buzzer, or gong. **4.** The movable member of an actuator. **5.** The soft-iron *keeper* placed across the poles of a permanent magnet to conserve power.

armature coil A coil of insulated wire wound on a ferromagnetic core to provide the electromagnetic properties of an armature. In a motor or generator, the armature coil is distinguished from the FIELD COIL.

armature core The ferromagnetic core upon which the armature coil of a motor or generator is wound.

armature gap **1.** In a motor or generator, the space between an armature core and the pole of a field magnet. **2.** In a relay, the space between the armature and the relay-coil core.

armature hesitation A momentary delay in the movement of a relay.

armature-hesitation contact chatter Undesired (usually rapid, repetitive) making and breaking of relay contacts. Generally caused by armature hesitation.

armature-impact contact chatter Undesired (usually rapid, repetitive) making and breaking of relay contacts, caused by *contact bounce* when the armature strikes the relay core (closure) or backstop (opening).

armature relay A relay that uses an electromagnet to pull a lever toward or away from a set of fixed contacts.

armature travel The distance traveled by an armature during relay operation.

armor A protective metal cable covering.

Armstrong FM system (Edwin H. Armstrong, 1890-1954). A phase-shift method of frequency modulation. See PHASE MODULATION.

armature voltage control A means of controlling motor speed by changing the applied armature winding voltage.

armchair copy An amateur radio term for reception of exceptionally clear signals.

arming the oscilloscope sweep Enabling an oscilloscope to trigger on the next pulse by closing a switch.

Armstrong oscillator (Edwin H. Armstrong, 1890-1954). An oscillator circuit that uses inductive feedback between the output and input. Either the output coil or the input coil can be tuned to set the oscillator frequency. The amount of positive feedback is controlled by varying the coupling between the coils.

Armstrong superheterodyne circuit See SUPERHETERODYNE CIRCUIT.

Armstrong superregenerative circuit See SUPERREGENERATIVE CIRCUIT.

ARPA Acronym for *Advanced Research Projects Agency*, a subsidiary of the U.S. Department of Defense.

array **1.** A directive antenna that consists of an assembly of properly dimensioned and spaced elements, such as radiators, directors, and reflectors. **2.** A coordinated group or matrix of components, such as diodes, resistors, memory cells, etc., often enclosed in one capsule. **3.** Subscripted variables representing data arranged so that a program can examine the array and extract data relevant to a particular subscript.

array device A group of similar or identical components that are connected together in a certain fashion, to perform a specific task.

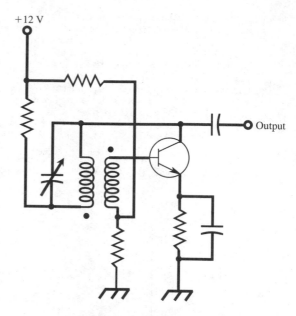

+12 V

Output

Armstrong oscillator

arrester **1.** A device used to protect an installation from lightning. It consists of a varistor or an air gap connected between an antenna or power line and an earth ground. The device passes little or no current under ordinary conditions, but passes heavy current to ground during a lightning stroke. Also called LIGHTNING ARRESTER. **2.** A self-restoring protective device used to reduce voltage surges on power lines.

ARRL Abbreviation for *American Radio Relay League.*

arrowhead A wideband, log-periodic antenna with linear polarization.

ARS Abbreviation of *Amateur Radio Service.*

arsenic Symbol, As. A metalloidal element. Atomic number, 33. Atomic weight, 74.91. Arsenic is familiar as an n-type dopant in semiconductor processing.

ARSR Abbreviation of *air route surveillance radar.*

articulation A measure of the effectiveness of voice communications, expressed as the percentage of speech units understood by the listener when the effect of context is negligible.

artificial antenna See DUMMY ANTENNA.

artificial ear A microphone-type sensor, equivalent to the human ear, used to measure sound pressures.

artificial echo **1.** In radar practice, the reflections of a transmitted pulse returned by an artificial target. **2.** A signal from a pulsed radio-frequency (RF) generator, delayed to simulate an echo.

artificial ground The effective ground provided by the radials or disk of a ground-plane antenna, as opposed to actual ground (the earth itself). Compare TRUE GROUND.

artificial horizon In aircraft instrumentation, a device that displays lines showing the position of the aircraft in flight, with reference to the horizon.

artificial intelligence Abbreviation, AI. **1.** A specialized field of computer science overlapping with electronics, biology, physiology, and other sciences, concerning attempts to develop advanced computer systems that can emulate the processes of the human mind. **2.** The ability of a computer to learn from its mistakes, refine its own processes, and perhaps ultimately reason in a humanlike manner.

artificial ionization An artificial reflecting layer that is created in the atmosphere to provide a skip condition.

artificial language A language that is not commonly used, but has been devised for efficiency in a particular situation—especially in a computer system.

artificial life **1.** The ultimate endpoint of ARTIFICIAL INTELLIGENCE, wherein machines acquire qualities, such as wisdom and the capability to feel emotions. The state of the art is currently nowhere near this point. **2.** A hypothetical machine or set of machines with lifelike qualities, including human-level intelligence, wisdom, and emotion.

artificial stimulus An electronic method of robot guidance and navigation using radar, sonar, vision systems, edge detection, and/or beacons.

artificial transmission line A network of capacitors and inductors with characteristics similar to those of the more bulky transmission line it replaces in tests and measurements. It also serves as a time-delay or phase-shift device and as a pulse-forming network.

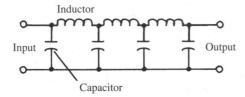

artificial transmission line

artificial voice A device used to test and calibrate noise-canceling microphones, consisting essentially of a small loudspeaker that has a baffle whose acoustical properties simulate those of the human head.

artos stripper A machine that cuts and strips wire for the fabrication of multiconductor cables.

artwork **1.** In the manufacture of printed circuits, the scaled drawings from which the mask or etch pattern is obtained photographically. **2.** Collectively, the illustrations depicting an electronic circuit, device, or system.

As Symbol for ARSENIC.

ASA Abbreviation of AMERICAN STANDARDS ASSOCIATION.

asbestos A nonflammable fibrous material consisting of calcium and magnesium silicates that is used for high-temperature insulation.

A-scan A radar-screen presentation in which the horizontal time axis displays distance or range, and the vertical axis displays the amplitude of signal pulse and echo pulses.

ASCII Acronym (pronounced "*ask-*ee") for *American Standard Code for Information Interchange.*

Speed rates for the ASCII code

Baud rate	Length of pulse, ms	WPM
110	9.09	110
150	6.67	150
300	3.33	300
600	1.67	600
1200	0.833	1200
1800	0.556	1800
2400	0.417	2400
4800	0.208	4800
9600	0.104	9600
19,200	0.052	19,200

ASI Abbreviation for *American Standards Institute.*

A-scope A radar system that displays an A-SCAN.

Askarel A synthetic, nonflammable liquid dielectric.

aspect ratio The width-to-height ratio of a video image, generally three units high by four units wide.

asperities On the surface of an electrode, tiny points at which the electric field is intensified and from which discharge is highly probable.

ASR **1.** Abbreviation of AIRBORNE (or AIRPORT) surveillance radar. **2.** Abbreviation of AUTOMATIC SEND/ RECEIVE.

ASRA Acronym for *automatic stereophonic recording amplifier.*

assemble **1.** To gather subprograms into a complete digital computer program. **2.** To translate a symbolic program language into a machine (binary) language program by substituting operation codes and addresses.

assembly **1.** A finished unit that can be either a practical working model or a dummy, a prototype, or a final model; an integrated aggregation

Symbols for ASCII teleprinter code

First four signals	Last three signals							
signals	000	001	010	011	100	101	110	111
0000	NUL	DLE	SPC	0		P	/	p
0001	SOH	DC1	!	1	A	Q	a	q
0010	STX	DC2	"	2	B	R	b	r
0011	ETX	DC3	#	3	C	S	c	s
0100	EOT	DC4	$	4	D	T	d	t
0101	ENQ	NAK	%	5	E	U	e	u
0110	ACK	SYN	&	6	F	V	f	v
0111	BEL	ETB	'	7	G	W	g	w
1000	BS	CAN	(	8	H	X	h	x
1001	HT	EM	)	9	I	Y	i	y
1010	LF	SUB	*	:	J	Z	j	z
1011	VT	ESC	+	;	K	[	k	{
1100	FF	FS	,	<	L	/	l	/
1101	CR	GS	–	=	M	]	m	}
1110	SO	RS	.	>	N		n	~
1111	SI	US			?	O	–	o	DEL

ACK: acknowledge
BEL: bell
BS: back space
CAN: cancel
CR: carriage return
DC1: device control no. 1
DC2: device control no. 2
DC3: device control no. 3
DC4: device control no. 4
DEL: delete
DLE: data link escape
ENQ: enquiry
EM: end of medium
EOT: end of transmission
ESC: escape
ETB: end of transmission block
ETX: end of text

FF: form feed
FS: file separator
GS: group separator
HT: horizontal tab
LF: line feed
NAK: do not acknowledge
NUL: null
RS: record separator
SI: shift in
SO: shift out
SOH: start of heading
SPC: space
STX: start of text
SUB: substitute
SYN: synchronous idle
US: unit separator
VT: vertical tab

of subunits. **2.** A low-level computer source-code language that uses crude mnemonics that are easier to remember than the *machine-language* equivalents.

assembly language A source code that uses mnemonic instructions. (See ASSEMBLY, **2.**)

assembly program The program that operates on a symbolic-language program to produce a machine language program in the process of assembly. Also called *assembler*.

assembly robot A form of *industrial robot* that puts hardware together. Such a robot is gener-

ally a component of an *automated integrated manufacturing system (AIMS)*. The robot can do repetitive work at high speed and precision for long periods of time.

assign To reserve part of a computing system for a specific purpose, normally for the duration of a program run.

assigned frequency The radio carrier frequency or band of frequencies designated for a transmitting station by a licensing authority. Also see RADIO SPECTRUM.

associative memory Computer memory in which locations are identified by content, rather than by specific address.

assumed decimal point A decimal point that does not occupy an actual computer storage space, but is used by the computer to align values for calculation; the decimal point is assumed to be at the right unless otherwise specified.

astable Having two temporary states; BISTABLE.

astable circuit A circuit that has two unstable states, and whose operation is characterized by alternation between those states at a frequency determined by the circuit constants.

astable multivibrator A free-running multivibrator. The common circuit uses two bipolar or field-effect transistors, their inputs and outputs being cross coupled. Conduction switches alternately between the two.

astatic **1.** Without fixed position or direction. **2.** In a state of neutral equilibrium.

astatic galvanometer A galvanometer with a movable element consisting of two identical magnetized needles mounted nonparallel on the same suspension. Each needle is surrounded by a coil. The coils are wound in opposite directions, and are connected in series to the current source. A large permanent magnet provides the field against which the needle assembly rotates. The instrument functions independently of the geomagnetic field.

astatine Symbol, At. A radioactive elemental halogen produced from radioactive decay. Atomic number, 85. Atomic weight, 210. Formerly called *alabamine*.

A station One of the two stations in the transmitting system of LORAN (long-range navigation).

astigmatism A focusing fault in a cathode-ray tube (CRT), in which electrons in different axial planes focus at different points.

ASTM Abbreviation for *American Society for Testing and Materials*.

astrionics The design, production, and application of electronic devices and systems for use in space vehicles and space navigation.

astronomical unit Abbreviation, AU. A unit of distance equal to 1.496×10^8 kilometers (9.296×10^7 miles). Approximately equal to the mean distance between the earth and the sun.

A supply See A POWER SUPPLY.

asymmetrical cell A photocell exhibiting ASYMMETRICAL CONDUCTIVITY.

asymmetrical conductivity   A condition in which a device conducts well in one direction, but poorly in the other direction. A rectifier diode is a common example of a component that exhibits this effect.

asymmetrical distortion   In a binary system, lengthening or shortening of one of the states, by comparison to the theoretical or ideal duration.

asymmetrical FET   A FIELD-EFFECT TRANSISTOR in which the source and drain cannot be interchanged without degrading performance.

asymmetrical multivibrator   An unbalanced multivibrator (i.e., one in which the circuit halves are not identical). If the time constants of the halves are different, the output pulses will be short and widely separated.

asymmetrical sideband   See VESTIGIAL SIDEBAND.

asymmetrical sideband transmission   See VESTIGIAL SIDEBAND TRANSMISSION.

asymmetrical wave   A wave whose upper (positive half-cycle) and lower (negative half-cycle) portions have different amplitudes or shapes. Also called *asymmetric wave.*

asymmetry control   An adjustment in a device intended for measuring the pH (acidity/alkalinity). This corrects the inaccuracies that results from the differences between the electrodes.

asymptote   In analytical geometry, a fixed straight line or ray L with a special relationship to a curve or part of a curve K that recedes to infinity. As the distance from the origin (0,0) increases without limit, the separation between K and L approaches zero, but K and L never actually meet.

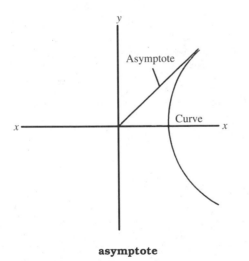

asymptote

asymptotic breakdown voltage   A voltage that will cause *dielectric breakdown* if applied continuously for a sufficiently long time.

asymptotic expression   An expression having a very small error in terms of percentage.

asynchronous   **1.** Not synchronous, i.e., nonrecurrent (as in out-of-phase waves). **2.** A mode of computer operation in which the completion of one operation starts another.

asynchronous device   A device not regulated by the system in which it is used, as far as its operating frequency or rate is concerned.

asynchronous input   In digital circuitry, any flip-flop input at which a pulse can affect the output independently of the clock.

asychronous motor   An ac motor whose speed is not proportional to the supply frequency.

asynchronous transmission   Data transmission in which each character or symbol begins with a start signal and ends with a stop signal. This eliminates the need for the data to be sent at a uniform speed.

asynchronous vibrator   In a vibrator-type portable power supply, a vibrator that only makes and breaks the primary circuit of the step-up transformer. This is in contrast to the synchronous vibrator, which also makes and breaks the secondary circuit in synchronism with the primary. Also called NONSYNCHRONOUS VIBRATOR.

AT   A quartz crystal cut wherein the angle between the x-axis and the crystal face is 35 degrees.

At   Symbol for astatine.

AT-cut crystal   A piezoelectric crystal cut at a 35-degree angle, with respect to the optical axis of the quartz. The frequency of such a crystal does not appreciably change with variations in temperature.

atmosphere   **1.** The gas surrounding a planet, particularly the air sheathing the earth. **2.** Abbreviation, atm. A unit of pressure equal to 1.013×10^6 dynes per square centimeter (about 14.7 pounds per square inch).

atmospheric absorption   **1.** The conversion of electromagnetic energy into heat, with resulting loss, as the energy passes through the earth's atmosphere. The extent of this effect depends on the wavelength. **2.** See ABSORPTION LOSS, **2.**

atmospheric absorption noise   Noise, principally above 1 GHz, resulting from atmospheric absorption (see ABSORPTION LOSS, **2**).

atmospheric bending   The refraction or reflection of electromagnetic waves by the troposphere or ionosphere. See ATMOSPHERIC REFLECTION.

atmospheric duct   A tropospheric stratum, often associated with temperature inversions, lake effects, or weather fronts, through which electromagnetic energy at ultra-high and microwave frequencies is efficiently propagated for long distances.

atmospheric electricity   Static electricity present in the atmosphere, which evidences itself in disturbance of radio communications and in displays of lightning.

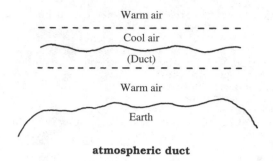

atmospheric duct

atmospheric noise Receiver noise resulting from ATMOSPHERIC ELECTRICITY. Also called *sferics* or *static*.

atmospheric pressure Abbreviation, atm press. **1.** The pressure exerted by the earth's atmosphere, as indicated by a barometer at sea level; normally between 29 and 31 inches of mercury. **2.** A pressure of 1.013×10^6 dynes per square centimeter. See ATMOSPHERE, **2.**

atmospheric radio wave See SKYWAVE.

atmospheric radio window The band of frequencies (approximately 10 MHz to 10 GHz), including radio waves that can penetrate the earth's troposphere and ionosphere.

atmospheric reflection The return of a radio wave to earth, resulting from reflection by an ionized portion of the atmosphere.

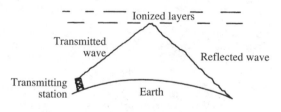

atmospheric reflection

atmospheric refraction **1.** Downward bending of radio waves as a result of variations in the dielectric constant of the troposphere. **2.**

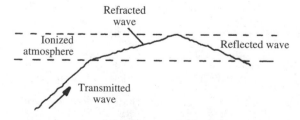

atmospheric refraction

Downward bending of radio waves in the ionosphere, resulting in long-range propagation at high frequencies.

atmospheric scatter **1.** The scattering of very-high frequency (VHF) and ultra-high frequency (UHF) radio waves by the lower atmosphere. **2.** Communication via scattering of VHF and UHF radio waves in the lower atmosphere.

atmospherics See ATMOSPHERIC NOISE.

atom **1.** The smallest material particle that displays the unique characteristics and properties of an element. Atoms consist of a dense, positively charged central nucleus, around which less-massive, negatively charged electrons "swarm" at definite levels called *shells*. Also see BOHR ATOM and RUTHERFORD ATOM. **2.** In a computer-compiling operation, an operator or operand.

atomechanics The physics of electron movement.

atomic battery A battery in which atomic energy is converted into electrical energy.

atomic charge The electrification (i.e., the electron charge) exhibited by an ion.

atomic clock Also called *atomic time standard*. A highly accurate electronic clock, driven by the characteristic oscillations of certain atoms.

atomic energy Energy released by the FUSION or FISSION of atomic nuclei. Also see ATOMIC POWER.

atomic fission See FISSION.

atomic frequency The natural vibration frequency of an atom.

atomic fusion See FUSION.

atomic pile See REACTOR, **2.**

atomic mass unit Abbreviated amu. A unit that expresses the relative mass of an elemental *isotope*. One amu is equal to $\frac{1}{12}$ of the atomic mass of carbon 12 (C12). A neutron has a mass of roughly one amu.

atomic migration The transfer or "wandering" of a valence electron between or among atoms in a single molecule.

atomic number The number of protons in the nucleus of an atom. Also, the number of electrons if the atom is electrically neutral. For example, the atomic number for copper is 29, indicating 29 protons in the nucleus. An electrically neutral atom of copper has 29 electrons. The atomic number uniquely identifies an element.

atomic radiation The emission of radiant energy by radioactive substances.

atomic reactor See REACTOR, **2.**

atomic theory The scientific theory that all matter is composed ultimately of *atoms*, which are the smallest particles retaining the identity of an element. Atoms combine to form *molecules*, the smallest particles that retain the identity of a compound. Atoms themselves contain minute *subatomic particles*, some of which carry electric charges. See BOHR ATOM and RUTHERFORD ATOM.

atomic time **1.** A means of time determination that makes use of the resonant vibrations of certain substances, such as cesium. **2.** Synchronized astronomical time, as determined by an ATOMIC CLOCK.

atomic unit of energy In a hydrogen atom, the potential energy of the electron in the lowest-energy shell, as averaged over a certain length of time. The shell represents the mean energy of the electron.

atomic weight **1.** The mass of a particular atom in ATOMIC MASS UNITS (amu). **2.** A number characterizing the average mass of individual atoms for a specific isotope of an element. Thus, carbon 12 (C12) has an atomic weight of 12, oxygen 16 (O16) has an atomic weight of approximately 16, and uranium 238 (U238) has an atomic weight of about 238.

atomistics The science of the atom and atomic energy. Also called *atomics*.

attack **1.** The rise of a pulse from zero to maximum amplitude. **2.** The time required for a pulse to rise from zero to maximum amplitude. **3.** The initialization of a circuit voltage or current for a certain purpose, such as an automatic gain control. **4.** The rise of a musical note from zero to full volume.

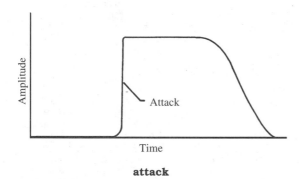

attack

attack time The time required for an applied signal that suddenly increases in amplitude to reach 63.2 percent of its final, stable value.

attemperator An automatic temperature-controlling device; a *thermostat*.

attention display A computer-generated chart or graph, displayed as an alert signal concerning a particular situation.

attenuate To reduce in amplitude.

attenuation A reduction of signal amplitude.

attenuation characteristic Also called *attenuation constant*. **1.** In an amplifier, network, or component, the decrease in signal amplitude as a function of frequency, usually expressed in decibels per octave. **2.** In a transmission line, the decrease in signal amplitude per unit length.

Usually expressed in decibels per 100 feet, decibels per mile, or decibels per kilometer.

attenuation constant See ATTENUATION CHARACTERISTIC.

attenuation distortion A type of distortion characterized by variation of attenuation with frequency within a given frequency range.

attenuation equalizer An equalizer that stabilizes the transfer impedance between two ports at all frequencies within a specified frequency band.

attenuation-frequency distortion Distortion characterized by the attenuation of the frequency components in a complex waveform. Frequency-sensitive RC networks (such as a Wien bridge) exhibit this type of distortion when they attenuate a fundamental and each harmonic unequally.

attenuation network A combination of components (R, C, or L singly or in any necessary combination) that provide constant signal attenuation with negligible phase shift throughout a frequency band.

attenuation ratio The ratio indicating a relative current, voltage, power or energy decrease. For example, for voltage, $E_{input}/E_{output} = 6/2 = 3:1 = 3$.

attenuator A device for reducing signal amplitude in precise, predetermined steps, or smoothly over a continuous range. A network of resistors, capacitors, or both. The simplest attenuator consists of one or more noninductive resistors.

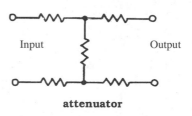

attenuator

attitude The position of an aircraft or space vehicle relative to a (usually terrestrial) reference point, often determined with electronic instruments.

atto- Abbreviated, a. A prefix meaning 10^{-18} or multiplication by 10^{-18}.

attofarad Abbreviation, aF. An extremely small unit of low capacitance; 1 aF equals 10^{-18} F.

attracted-disk electrometer A device to measure potential difference consisting of two parallel metal disks—one of which is connected to a tension spring. The force between the disks indicates the magnitude of the electric field.

attraction The drawing together or pulling toward, as in the attraction between electric charges or magnetic poles. Dissimilar charges and poles attract each other (electric plus to minus, magnetic north to south). Compare REPULSION.

ATV Abbreviation of *amateur television*, used in the Amateur Radio Service.

AU Abbreviation of ASTRONOMICAL UNIT.

Au Symbol for GOLD.

audibility The quality of being detectable by the human ear. In a healthy listener, the *threshold of audibility* is extremely low; at the threshold, the pressure of a sound wave varies from normal by approximately 10^{-4} pascal. The frequency range of human audibility extends roughly from 20 Hz to 20 kHz.

Sound	Audibility (dB)
Threshold of hearing	0
Whisper	10–20
Electric fan at 10 feet	30–40
Running water at 10 feet	40–60
Speech at 5 feet	60–70
Vacuum cleaner at 10 feet	70–80
Passing train at 50 feet	80–90
Jet at 1000 feet altitude	90–100
Rock band on stage	110–120
Air hammer at 5 feet	130–140

audibility table

audibility curve A graph (such as the *Fletcher-Munson curve*) that depicts the range of human hearing in terms of frequency versus the sound pressure at the threshold of AUDIBILITY.

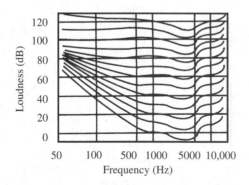

audibility curves

audible Detectable by the human ear.

audible alarm device An ANNUNCIATOR that produces an easily identifiable sound in response to an ALARM CONDITION in a security system.

audible frequency See AUDIO FREQUENCY.

audible tone A vibration of air molecules that can be detected by the human ear, and with periodic properties, such as a sine-wave vibration.

audio 1. Pertaining to the spectrum of frequencies corresponding to the human hearing range (about 20 Hz to 20 kHz), or to equipment or performance associated with that spectrum. 2. Any disturbance, such as a current or compression wave, falling within the range of about 20 Hz to 20 kHz. 3. AUDIO FREQUENCY.

audio amplifier See AUDIO-FREQUENCY AMPLIFIER.

audio band The range (band) of audio frequencies.

audio channel 1. The portion of a complex signal or waveform used to convey audio information exclusively. 2. The audio-frequency section of a transmitter or receiver (as opposed to the radio-frequency section). 3. A radio channel of fixed frequency that is reserved for voice communications.

audio component The audio-frequency portion of any wave or signal.

audio converter A circuit in which a received radio-frequency (RF) signal is heterodyned with a local RF oscillator signal to produce an audio-frequency (AF) beat-note output. The beat note is then amplified by an AF amplifier. It is used especially by amateur radio operators in the reception of continuous-wave (CW) radiotelegraphy, radioteletype, and packet radio at high frequencies.

audio frequency A frequency lying within the audible spectrum. Abbreviated AF. See AUDIO-FREQUENCY SPECTRUM.

audio-frequency amplifier An amplifier that operates in part or all of the frequency range 20 Hz to 20 kHz. High-fidelity amplifiers function over a somewhat wider range (e.g., 10 Hz to 50 kHz).

audio-frequency choke An inductor (usually having a ferromagnetic core) that blocks audio-frequency current, but passes direct current.

audio-frequency feedback 1. Electrical FEEDBACK (positive and/or negative) that affects audio-frequency circuits. 2. ACOUSTIC FEEDBACK.

audio-frequency filter A filter of any type that operates on any part of the frequency range 20 Hz to 20 kHz.

audio-frequency meter An instrument to measure frequencies in the audio-frequency spectrum (approximately 20 Hz to 20 kHz). Three types are commonly used:

- *Analog* Gives direct indications of frequency on the scale of a D'Arsonval meter; the usual range is 20 Hz to 100 kHz.

- *Digital* Gives direct indications of frequency by means of readout lamps; the usual range is 1 Hz to 15 MHz. This instrument is useful also as a radio-frequency meter.

• **Bridge** Consists of a frequency-sensitive bridge, such as a Wien bridge, with a null-indicating meter. The operator balances the bridge and reads the unknown frequency from the dial of the balance control.

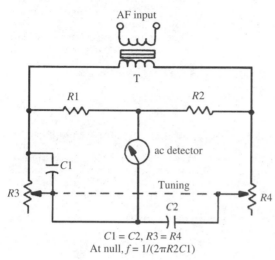

AF input

T

R1   R2

ac detector

C1

R3   Tuning   R4

C2

C1 = C2, R3 = R4
At null, $f = 1/(2\pi R2C1)$

audio-frequency meter

audio-frequency noise Any electrical noise signal causing interference within the audio-frequency spectrum.

audio-frequency oscillator See AUDIO OSCILLATOR.

audio-frequency peak limiter Any circuit or device, such as a biased diode, that performs the function of audio limiting.

audio frequency-shift keying Abbreviation, AFSK. A type of radio-frequency (RF) emission in which the carrier is continuously modulated by a tone (e.g., 1200 Hz); keying is accomplished by changing the tone to another frequency (e.g., 2200 Hz). Used in facsimile, packet, and radioteletype communications.

audio-frequency-shift modulator A modulator for audio-frequency-shift keying of a signal.

audio-frequency spectrum The band of frequencies extending from roughly 20 Hz to 20 kHz. High-fidelity component specifications extend this range somewhat in both directions (e.g., from 10 Hz to 50 kHz).

audio-frequency transformer A transformer designed for operation in the audio-frequency spectrum. A high-quality AF transformer is characterized by high-efficiency core material, low-capacitance windings, low leakage reactance, and excellent magnetic shielding.

audio-frequency transistor A transistor that is usually used only at audio frequencies.

audiogram A graph used to rate hearing, used by audiologists and audiometrists.

audio image In a direct-conversion receiver, a response to a signal on one side of (above or below) the local-oscillator (LO) frequency, when the operator is listening to a signal on the other side of the LO frequency. These responses are reduced or eliminated in single-signal receivers.

audio-level meter An ac meter for monitoring signal amplitude in an audio-frequency system. It can indicate in volts, decibels, volume units (VU), or arbitrary units, and is often permanently connected in the circuit.

audio limiter A limiter or clipper operated in the audio-frequency (AF) channel of a receiver or transmitter to hold the output-signal amplitude constant, or to minimize the effect of noise peaks.

audiologist A person skilled in testing hearing (i.e., in using audiometers and other electronic instruments) and evaluating their indications for the fitting of hearing aids.

audiometer An instrument used for hearing tests, which consists of a specialized audio-frequency (AF) amplifier with calibrated attenuators, output meter, and signal source.

audiometrist A person skilled in the use of audiometers and other electronic instruments that measure sound and human hearing, and who deals with attendant health and behavior problems. Compare ACOUSTICIAN and AUDIOLOGIST.

audio mixer An amplifier circuit for blending two or more audio-frequency (AF) signals, such as those delivered by microphones or receivers.

audio oscillator 1. An oscillator that delivers an output signal in the frequency range 20 Hz to 20 kHz. 2. An audio-frequency (AF) signal generator. Some instruments of this type operate above and below the limits of the common audio-frequency spectrum (e.g., 1 Hz to 1 MHz).

audio output The output of an audio-frequency oscillator or amplifier. It can be measured in terms of peak or rms volts, amperes, or watts.

audiophile A sound-reproduction hobbyist.

audio power Alternating-current power at frequencies roughly between 20 Hz and 20 kHz. When used in connection with transmitters and other modulated radio-frequency (RF) equipment, the term refers to modulator power output.

audio response unit A device that links digitized responses, held in computer storage, to a telephone set or line to answer incoming calls and inquiries.

audio signal generator See AUDIO OSCILLATOR, 2.

audio spectrum The range of sine-wave frequencies detectable by the human ear when they occur as acoustic vibrations. This range is about 20 Hz to 20 kHz.

audio squelch A squelch circuit that operates only on the audio channel of a receiver.

audio system **1.** The portion of any electronic assembly that is used to process sound. **2.** Special computer equipment capable of storing and processing digitized audio-frequency (AF) data.

audiotape Magnetic tape for the recording and reproduction of data in the audio-frequency (AF) range.

audio taper In potentiometers, a semilogarithmic variation of resistance versus rotation. Used in volume and tone controls for audio circuits. At midposition (the halfway point), the counterclockwise portion of the device has about ⅒ the resistance of the clockwise portion. A listener will hear sound at half-volume because of the logarithmic nature of the human audibility curve.

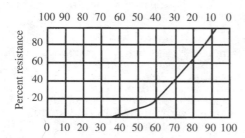

audio taper

audio-visual Pertaining to a combination of sound and sight (e.g., television and sound motion pictures).

auditory backward inhibition A subjective phenomenon, in which a sound is erased from the memory of a listener by a second sound arriving about 60 milliseconds later.

auditory inhibition The tendency of sound waves to be partially or totally canceled by the ears/mind of a listener, depending on the waves' intensity, relative phase, and/or direction of impact.

auditory mirage See ACOUSTIC MIRAGE.

audit trail A history of the processes relating to a record, transaction, or file in a computer system. Created during the routine processing of data, the trail is stored as a file. The audit trail allows auditing of the system or the subsequent recreation of files.

augend In a calculation, the number to which another is to be added. Compare ADDEND.

augend register In a digital computer, the register that stores the augend. Compare ADDEND REGISTER.

aural Pertaining to sound actually heard, as opposed to sound that exists only as audio-frequency currents or waves.

aurora A phenomenon sometimes called the *northern lights* or *southern lights*, as seen in the night sky. In the Northern Hemisphere, it is known as *Aurora Borealis*; in the Southern Hemisphere, it is called *Aurora Australis*. It generally occurs a few hours after a solar flare, when charged particles, emitted from the sun, arrive at the earth, and are accelerated in the vicinity of the the geomagnetic poles.

auroral absorption Radio wave absorption by an aurora.

auroral flutter Rapid fading of a signal at high or very high frequencies, so-called because it often imparts a fluttering quality to the signal that is caused by phase distortion and Doppler shift when the waves are reflected from the aurora.

auroral interference **1.** Interference to high-frequency radio propagation and also occasionally to medium-frequency and low-frequency propagation, caused by the activity of the aurora. **2.** Auroral flutter on a signal.

auroral opening A condition in which radio communication becomes possible via AURORAL PROPAGATION. It can occur when communication between two points is normally impossible at a certain frequency. Auroral openings allow long-distance communication well into the very-high-frequency (VHF) spectrum.

auroral propagation Reflection of radio waves by the aurora. The reflection generally occurs between about 15 MHz and 150 MHz, and makes communication possible at times, although the signals generally contain "flutter" caused by phase distortion.

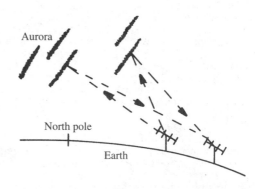

auroral propagation

auroral reflection The return of electromagnetic waves that have been beamed toward an aurora. Most often observed between 15 MHz and 150 MHz.

authorized access switch   A device that disables a security system in a defined region or volume so that authorized personnel can enter without triggering an alarm condition.

authorized channel   The carrier frequency or band assigned to a transmitting station by a licensing authority. Also see RADIO SPECTRUM.

autoalarm   A device that is actuated from a received signal to alert a radio or computer network operator to the existence of a message.

autobaud   **1.** In digital communications, a function that allows the equipment to adjust itself to the speed of the terminal. **2.** Any digital communications equipment capable of automatically adjusting to the speed of the terminal.

autocondensation   The application of radio-frequency (RF) energy to the human body for medical purposes. The living organs serve as an impedance or load, across which the RF is applied.

autoconduction   The application of radio-frequency (RF) currents into the body, by placing the living organ inside a coil and supplying the coil with RF. Used for medical purposes.

autocorrelation function   A measure of the similarity between delayed and undelayed versions of a signal, expressed as a delay function.

autodyne reception   Radio reception of cw signals by means of an oscillating detector. This is in contrast to heterodyne reception, in which a local oscillator (LO) generates an audio beat note with the cw signal in a separate detector.

autoionization   A two-phase process of atomic ionization. The atom is excited beyond its ionization potential, and then it is allowed to deionize, causing the emission of an electron. The result is a positively charged atom (positive ion).

automated communications   The transfer of data without the use of operating personnel; generally done with computers connected to communications equipment.

automated guided vehicle   Abbreviation, AGV. A robot cart that runs without a driver. It uses an electric engine and is guided by the magnetic field produced by a current-carrying wire embedded in the floor or pavement. Alternatively, the robot can run on a track.

automated home   A residence in which many, or most, of the routine chores are done by computers and/or robots. Examples of such tasks are dishwashing, doing the laundry, mowing the lawn, blowing snow, and vacuuming the floors.

automated integrated manufacturing system   Acronym, AIMS. An assembly line or factory that uses robots, often controlled by one or more computers, to perform specific tasks that result in the production of various hardware items.

automatic   Self-regulating, independent of human intervention. Some periodic adjustment might be needed.

automatic base bias   A method of obtaining base bias in a bipolar transistor, where a resistor develops a voltage drop because of the current flowing through it. The resistor is usually placed in the emitter circuit, raising the emitter above ground potential.

automatic bass compensation   Also called *bass boost.* In audio high-fidelity systems, a resistor-capacitor (RC) network that increases the relative amplitude of the bass at low volume levels. This compensates for the ear's inefficiency at low frequencies. The function can be automatically actuated by the setting of the volume control, or it can be switched manually on and off.

automatic bias   In an amplifier, dc base/gate/grid bias obtained from the voltage drop produced by collector/drain/plate current flowing through a resistor common to the input and output. This resistor is usually shunted by a capacitor and placed in the emitter/source/cathode circuit.

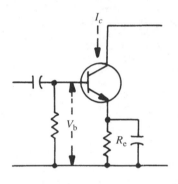

automatic bias

automatic brightness control   A circuit that uses the same principles used in AUTOMATIC GAIN CONTROL (AGC) to hold steady the average brightness of a television (TV) picture.

automatic carriage   Typewriters, automatic key punches, and other devices that can control automatically the spacing and feeding of paper, cards, and forms.

automatic check   **1.** In a digital computer, the automatic inspection of operation and performance by a self-contained subsystem. **2.** The circuit or device for performing this inspection.

automatic chrominance control   In a color television (TV) receiver, a subcircuit that controls the gain of the chrominance bandpass amplifier by automatically adjusting its bias.

automatic circuit breaker   Any device that opens a circuit automatically when the flow of current becomes excessive. The breaker generally resets automatically after a specified length of time, or after power has been temporarily removed from the circuit.

automatic coding   The use of a computer to determine the steps for solving a problem, before the actual program for the problem is written. This can help software engineers develop long and/or complex computer programs.

automatic contrast control   A circuit that automatically adjusts the gain of the video IF and RF stages of a television (TV) receiver to preserve good picture contrast.

automatic controller   In servo systems, any of several circuits or devices that samples a variable signal, compares it with a standard (reference) signal, and delivers a control or correction signal to an actuator.

automatic crossover   1. Current limiting in a power supply. **2.** A device that switches a circuit from one operating mode to another automatically when conditions change in a predetermined manner.

automatic current limiter   A circuit or device for holding the output current of a power supply to a safe value during overload.

automatic current regulator   A circuit or device that holds the output current of a generator or power supply to a predetermined value, in spite of wide variations in load resistance.

automatic cutout   A device that shuts down a circuit or system when the safe limits of operation are exceeded. A circuit breaker is an example of such a device, as is a thermostat in a power amplifier.

automatic data processing   Abbreviation, ADP. The use of computers and accessories for calculations and tabulations using data gathered automatically by the system.

automatic degausser   A system for automatically demagnetizing the picture tube in a color television (TV) receiver.

automatic dialing unit   Abbreviated, ADU. A device that automatically generates dialing digits. Many telephone sets have these devices, some of which can be programmed for several different telephone numbers, including country codes and area codes.

automatic dictionary   A computer system component that substitutes codes for words and phrases in information retrieval systems. In language-translating systems, it provides word-for-word substitutions.

automatic direction finder   Abbreviated ADF. A specialized receiver/antenna combination for automatically showing the direction from which a signal arrives.

automatic error correction   A technique of correcting transmission errors using error-detecting and error-correcting codes and, usually, automatic retransmission.

automatic exchange   A transmission exchange in which interterminal communications are accomplished without operators.

automatic focusing   A method of focusing a picture tube automatically, in which a resistor connects the focusing anode to the cathode; thus, no external focusing voltage is necessary.

automatic frequency control   Abbreviation, AFC. A system that keeps a circuit automatically tuned to a desired signal frequency. A detector (such as a discriminator) operated from the tuned circuit delivers a dc output voltage only when the circuit is operating above or below the signal frequency; otherwise, it has zero dc output. The dc output, when present, alters the capacitance of a varactor in the tuned circuit to retune the stage to the desired frequency.

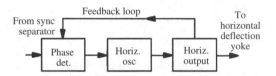

**automatic frequency control
(used in typical TV receiver)**

automatic gain control   Abbreviated AGC. A system that holds the output of a receiver or amplifier substantially constant despite input-signal amplitude fluctuations. A rectifier samples the ac signal output and delivers a dc signal proportional to that output. The dc signal is filtered, and the smoothed-out voltage is applied in correct polarity as bias to one or more preceding stages to reduce their gain. The stronger the signal entering the system, the greater the reduction in gain. As a result, weak signals are amplified much more than strong ones. Various forms of this scheme are used in many types of amplifiers and communications systems.

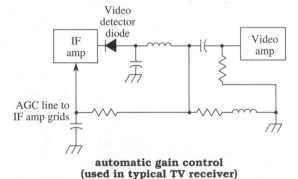

**automatic gain control
(used in typical TV receiver)**

automatic gate bias   A method of obtaining gate bias in a FET, where a resistor develops a voltage drop because of the current flowing through it.

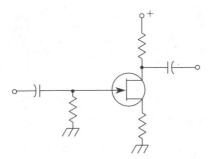

automatic gate bias

The resistor is usually placed in the source circuit, raising the source above ground potential.

automatic hardware dump The assignment of data from memory to a peripheral, caused by a system error. It is used to provide diagnostic information (e.g., concerning the condition of an instruction code process). The information dumped goes to a medium that allows convenient analysis.

automatic height control In a television (TV) receiver, a system that automatically maintains the height of the picture, despite signal-amplitude fluctuations, power-line voltage changes, and gain variations.

automatic intercept A telephone answering machine. It allows messages to be recorded when the subscriber is not able to answer the telephone.

automatic interrupt A program interruption caused by hardware or software acting in response to some event independent of the program.

automatic level compensation See AUTOMATIC GAIN CONTROL.

automatic level control Abbreviation, ALC. **1.** A circuit that adjusts the input gain of a magnetic-tape recording device to compensate for changes in the loudness of the sound reaching the microphone. **2.** A form of AUTOMATIC GAIN CONTROL used in single-sideband (SSB) radio transmitters to maintain linearity while increasing the level of the average power relative to the peak power.

automatic line feed In the digital transmission of printed matter, the automatic insertion of a line feed (LF) character immediately following every carriage return (CR) character.

automatic modulation control Abbreviation, AMC. In a frequency-modulated (FM) radio transmitter, a form of AUTOMATIC GAIN CONTROL that regulates the gain of the audio amplifiers to compensate for fluctuating audio input amplitude. This prevents overdeviation while optimizing signal intelligibility.

automatic noise limiter Abbreviation, ANL. Any of several circuits for clipping noise peaks exceeding a predetermined maximum received-signal amplitude.

automatic phase control In a color television (TV) receiver, a circuit that synchronizes the burst signal with the 3.58-MHz color oscillator.

automatic pilot An electronic device, often computer-controlled, that automatically keeps a ship, airplane, or space vehicle on course.

automatic polarity In an electronic metering device, a means of automatically switching the input polarity of the instrument when the input signal polarity is shifted. Also called *bipolar operation.*

automatic programming See AUTOMATIC CODING.

automatic protective device A circuit or device (such as a fuse, circuit breaker, limiter, or regulator) that protects another circuit or device by automatically removing, reducing, or increasing the current or voltage during overload or underload.

automatic radio compass See AUTOMATIC DIRECTION FINDER.

automatic ranging In a metering device, the automatic adjustment or optimization of the full-scale range to compensate for large changes in the input parameter.

automatic regulation **1.** *Voltage regulation.* In a power supply, the automatic holding of the output voltage to a constant value, despite variations in the input voltage or load resistance. **2.** *Current regulation.* In a power supply, the automatic holding of the output current to a constant value, despite variations in the input voltage or load resistance.

automatic relay The relaying of messages automatically from one station to another via intermediate points, without the need for human operators.

automatic repeater station A station that receives signals and simultaneously retransmits them, usually on a different frequency.

automatic reset **1.** The self-actuated restoration of a circuit or device to a given state (e.g., the state of rest). **2.** A circuit or device that restores another circuit or device to a given state.

automatic scanning **1.** The automatic (usually repetitive) tuning or adjustment of a circuit or system throughout a given frequency range. In a radio receiver, the system can be programmed to pause or stop at occupied channels, passing over vacant ones; or it can be programmed to pause or stop at vacant channels, passing over occupied ones. **2.** The repetitive sweep of a cathode-ray-tube (CRT) electron beam.

automatic scanning receiver Also called PANORAMIC RECEIVER. A radio receiver that is automatically tuned (usually repetitively) over a frequency band. Such a receiver either homes in on a signal when one is found, or displays on a cathode-ray-tube (CRT) screen the distribution of signals in the band.

automatic secure voice communications A wideband and narrowband voice-digitizing application to a security network that provides encoded voice communications.

automatic send/receive set A teletypewriter or terminal that is capable of receiving and transmitting.

automatic sensitivity control 1. A self-actuating circuit using principles similar to those used in AUTOMATIC GAIN CONTROL. It varies the sensitivity of the radio-frequency (RF) and intermediate-frequency (IF) sections of a receiver in inverse proportion to the strength of a received signal. 2. In a bridge null detector, a circuit similar to the one described in 1, which operates ahead of the detector, varying the sensitivity of the latter automatically.

automatic sequencing The ability of a digital computer to perform successive operations without additional instructions from the operator.

automatic short-circuiter A device that automatically short-circuits the commutator bias in some single-phase commutator motors.

automatic short-circuit protection A circuit that allows the output of a power supply to be short-circuited without damage to the components in the supply. It usually consists of a current-limiting device.

automatic shutoff A switching arrangement that automatically shuts off a device or circuit under certain specified conditions.

automatic switch center A telephone-switching network that routes calls to their destinations without the need for a human operator.

automatic target control For a vidicon television camera tube, a circuit that automatically adjusts the target voltage in proportion to brightness of the scene.

automatic telegraph reception Telegraph reception providing a direct printout of the received information, without intervention by an operator.

automatic telegraph transmission Telegraph transmission originating from tapes, disks, or other records, rather than from a hand-operated key.

automatic telegraphy Communications that utilize automatic telegraph transmission and reception.

automatic time switch A time-dependent circuit or device that opens or closes another circuit at the end of a predetermined time interval.

automatic tracking A method of keeping a radar beam automatically fixed on a target.

automatic trip A circuit breaker that automatically opens a circuit.

automatic tuning A process whereby a circuit tunes itself to a predetermined frequency upon receiving a command signal.

automatic voltage regulator A circuit that keeps the output of a power supply constant, despite the load resistance or input voltage to the supply.

automatic volume control Abbreviated AVC. The use of AUTOMATIC GAIN CONTROL in an audio amplifier system.

automatic zero In an electronic meter, a means of automatically setting the indicator to zero in the absence of an input signal.

automation 1. The control of machines or processes by self-correcting electronic systems. See ROBOT. 2. The use of robots and/or computers, rather than human beings, to perform repetitive tasks. 3. The use of robots and/or computers to assist human beings in industrial, office, governmental, and educational work.

automaton A simple robot that performs a task or set of tasks without artificial intelligence (AI). These machines have existed for decades. Compare ANDROID.

automonitor In digital computer operations, to require the machine to supply a record of its information-handling operations. Also, the program for such instructions.

autonomous robot A self-contained robot with an independent computerized control system. It moves under its own power, usually by rolling on wheels or a track drive. Compare INSECT ROBOT.

autopatch A remotely controllable device that interconnects a radio-communications system into a telephone network.

autopilot A self-correcting control and guidance device for the automatic management of an aircraft or missile.

autoranging See AUTOMATIC RANGING.

autosyn A device or system that operates on the principle of the synchronous ac motor, in which the position of the rotor in one motor (the transmitter) is assumed by the rotor in a distant motor (the receiver) to which the first is connected.

auto tracking A method of controlling the output voltages of many different power supplies simultaneously.

autotransducter A type of magnetic amplifier whose power windings serve also as control windings.

autotransformer A single-winding transformer in which the primary coil is a fraction of the entire winding for voltage step-up, or the secondary coil is a fraction of the entire winding for voltage step-down.

auxiliary circuit A circuit that is supplementary to the main system.

auxiliary contacts In switches and relays, contacts that are supplementary to the main contacts and are usually actuated with them.

auxiliary equipment 1. Also known as *peripherals*. An apparatus not directly governed by the central processing unit of a digital computer,

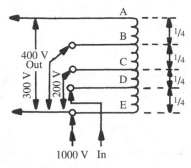

autotransformer

such as a printer or personal robot. **2.** Peripheral equipment in any system. **3.** Backup equipment.

auxiliary memory In a digital computer, a unit that is supplementary to the main memory, which it augments.

auxiliary receiver Also called *standby receiver.* In a radio communications system, a receiver that is available for use if the main receiver fails.

auxiliary relay **1.** A standby relay. **2.** A relay whose operation supports that of another relay. **3.** A relay that is actuated by the operation of another relay.

auxiliary switch **1.** A standby switch. **2.** A switch wired in series or parallel with another switch. **3.** A switch that is operated by another switch.

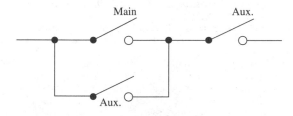

auxiliary switch, 2

auxiliary transmitter Also called *standby transmitter.* In a radio communications system, a transmitter that is available for use if the main transmitter fails.

a/v Abbreviation of AUDIO-VISUAL.

aV Abbreviation of *attovolt.*

availability The proportion of time during which an apparatus is operating correctly. It is usually given as a percentage.

available conversion gain The ratio of the input power to the output power of a transducer or converter. It is generally given in decibels.

available gain The ratio P_o/P_i, where P_i is the available power at the input of a circuit and P_o is the available power at the output.

available line The percentage of the length of a facsimile scanning line that is usable for picture signals.

available power The mean square of the open-circuit terminal voltage of a linear source divided by four, times the resistive component of the source impedance. The available power is the maximum power delivered to a load impedance, equal to the conjugate of the internal impedance of the power source.

available power gain In a power transistor, the ratio of available transistor output power to the power available from the generator. It depends on the generator resistance, but not on the transistor load resistance.

available signal-to-noise ratio The ratio P_s/P_n, where P_s is the available signal power at a given point in a system and P_n is the available random-noise power at that point.

available time **1.** The time during which a computer is available and ready for immediate use. **2.** The amount of time a computer is available to an individual.

avalanche The phenomenon in semiconductors operated at high reverse bias voltage, whereby carriers acquire sufficient energy to produce new electron-hole pairs as they collide with atoms. The action causes the reverse current to increase sharply.

avalanche breakdown In a reverse-biased semiconductor, the sudden, marked increase of reverse current at the bias voltage at which AVALANCHE begins. The action resembles a breakdown, but it is nondestructive when the current is limited by external means.

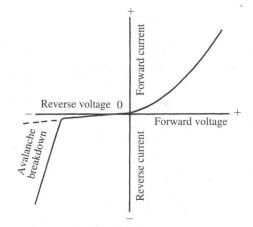

avalanche breakdown

avalanche conduction In a semiconductor junction, the enhanced reverse-bias conduction caused by a condition of AVALANCHE.

avalanche current The high current that flows through a semiconductor junction when AVALANCHE occurs.

avalanche diode   See ZENER DIODE.

avalanche impedance   The reduced impedance of a diode during avalanche.

avalanche noise   Electrical noise generated in a junction diode operated at the point at which avalanche just begins.

avalanche transistor   A transistor that operates at a high value of reverse-bias voltage, causing the pn junction between the emitter and base to conduct because of avalanche breakdown.

avalanche voltage   The reverse voltage at which AVALANCHE occurs in a semiconductor junction.

AVC   Abbreviation of *automatic volume control.*

avdp   Abbreviation for *Avoirdupois,* a weight-measurement scheme that is used in English-speaking countries and is based on the pound.

average absolute pulse amplitude   The average (disregarding algebraic sign) of the absolute amplitudes of a pulse, taken over the duration of the pulse.

average brightness   The average brilliance of a television (TV) picture, cathode-ray-tube (CRT) computer display, or oscilloscope image.

average calculating operation   The operating time considered typical for a computer calculation (i.e., one that is longer than an addition and shorter than a multiplication); it is frequently taken as the average of nine additions and one multiplication.

average current   Abbreviation, I_{avg}. The average value of alternating current flowing in a circuit. Taking polarity into account, this value is zero for a pure sine wave. For other waveforms, it can vary. When polarity is not considered, the sine-wave value of I_{avg} is equal to 0.637 times I_{pk}, the peak value of current; $I_{avg} = 0.637\ I_{pk}$.

average life   See MEAN LIFE.

average noise figure   The ratio of the total noise output from a circuit to the thermal noise output at 290 degrees Kelvin. It is usually expressed in decibels, with the noise taken at all frequencies.

average power   The average value of power in an ac circuit. In a resistive circuit, it is the square of the effective (rms) current times the resistance; $P_{avg} = (I_{rms})^2 R$ (for sine waves).

average pulse amplitude   Also called *effective pulse amplitude.* The value obtained by integrating the pulse amplitude, with respect to time, from the start of the pulse to its end, then dividing this integral by the pulse duration.

average rectified current   Abbreviation, I_{avg}. The average value of rectifier output current before filtering. For a full-wave rectifier with a sine wave input and a resistive load, I_{avg} is equal to the maximum current I_m multiplied by 0.637.

average rectified voltage   Abbreviation, E_{avg}. The average value of rectifier output voltage before filtering. For a full-wave rectifier with a sine-wave input and a resistive load, E_{avg} is maximum voltage E_m multiplied by 0.637.

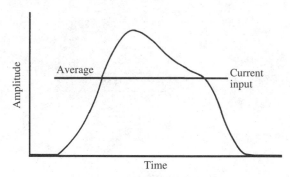

average pulse amplitude

average value   **1.** The *arithmetic mean* of two or more quantities. **2.** The *geometric mean* of two or more quantities. **3.** The *harmonic mean* of two or more quantities. **4.** In ac operation, the average current, voltage, or power.

average voltage   Abbreviation, E_{avg}. The average value of ac voltage in a circuit. Taking polarity into account, this value is zero for a pure sine wave. For other waveforms, it can vary. When polarity is not considered, the sine-wave value of E_{avg} is equal to 0.637 times E_{pk}, the peak value of voltage.

avg   Abbreviation of *average.*

aviation channels   Frequency channels assigned to the AVIATION SERVICES.

Aviation services   The radio-communication services used by aeronautical-mobile and radio navigation personnel.

avigation   Acronym for *aviation navigation.* Aircraft navigation by means of electronic equipment.

avionics   Acronym for *aviation electronics.* The design, production, and application of electronic devices and systems for use in aviation, navigation, and astronautics.

Avogadro's constant   (Amedeo Avogadro, 1776-1856.) Symbol, NA. The number of molecules in a kilogram-molecular weight of any substance; NA equals 6.025×10^{26} (kg-mole)$^{-1}$.

A voltage   The filament voltage in a vacuum-tube circuit.

aW   Abbreviation of *attowatt.*

AWG   Abbreviation of AMERICAN WIRE GAUGE.

AX.25   A signal format used in some digital communications systems, notably amateur *packet radio.*

axial leads   The centrally located leads emanating from the ends of cylindrical components, such as resistors and diodes.

axial ratio   The ratio of the minor to major axes of a waveguide's polarization ellipse.

axis   **1.** A coordinate in a graphical presentation or display (e.g., horizontal and vertical axes in a rectangular coordinate system). **2.** The real or imaginary straight line around which a body rotates, or the line that passes through the center of a symmetrical arrangement (line of symmetry).

axis of abscissas The horizontal axis (x-axis) of a rectangular-coordinate graph or screen. Compare AXIS OF ORDINATES.

axis of imaginaries The vertical axis of the complex plane in which rectangular vectors lie. Compare AXIS OF REALS.

axis of ordinates The vertical (y-axis) of a rectangular-coordinate graph or screen. Compare AXIS OF ABSCISSAS.

axis of reals The horizontal axis of the complex plane in which rectangular vectors lie. Compare AXIS OF IMAGINARIES.

Ayrton-Mather galvanometer shunt A step-adjustable universal shunt resistor for varying the sensitivity of a galvanometer. It has the virtue of keeping the galvanometer critically damped. The shunt is also useful in multirange milliammeters, microammeters, and ammeters. The sensitive meter movement is never without a shunting resistor during range switching.

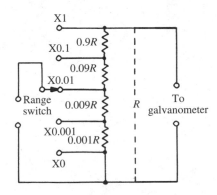

Ayrton-Mather galvanometer shunt

Ayrton-Perry winding A noninductive winding comprising two inductors conducting current in opposite directions; the opposing flow cancels the magnetic field.

azel display A plan-position display that incorporates two different radar traces on a single cathode-ray tube (CRT), one giving bearing, the other elevation.

azimuth Also called *compass direction*. Angular measurement in the horizontal plane, clockwise from north. It is important in radio and television communications, navigation, direction finding, land surveying, and radar.

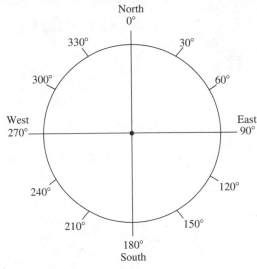

azimuth

azimuth alignment In a tape recorder, the alignment of record and playback head gaps so that their centerlines are parallel.

azimuth blanking In a radar system, blacking-out of the image as the antenna sweeps across a specified range of azimuth angles. Effectively eliminates nuisance echoes from stationary, permanent objects (such as tall buildings or communications towers).

azimuth resolution In a radar system, the minimum azimuth separation of two targets whose range (distance from the station) are equal that is required for the system to show two echoes, rather than one. It is generally measured in degrees.

azusa An electronic tracking system, in which a single station provides slant range and two direction cosines for a distant airborne object. This accurately defines the coordinates of the distant object in three-dimensional space.

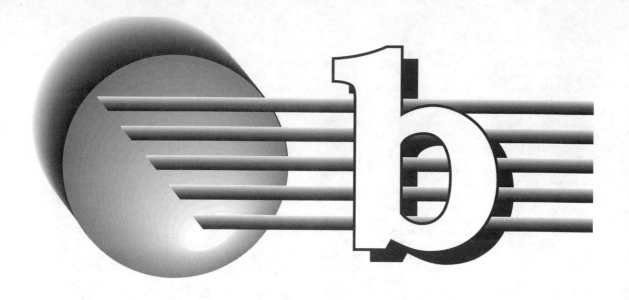

B 1. Symbol for SUSCEPTANCE. **2.** Symbol for FLUX DENSITY. **3.** Abbreviation of BATTERY. **4.** Symbol for BORON. **5.** Symbol for base of transistor (see BASE, 1). **6.** Abbreviation of BASS. **7.** Abbreviation of BEL. **8.** Anode voltage or main operating voltage in any circuit (when used with sign). Also see B VOLTAGE.

b 1. Symbol for SUSCEPTANCE. **2.** Symbol for base of transistor (see BASE, 1). **3.** Abbreviation of BASS. **4.** Symbol for BARN.

B&S See AMERICAN WIRE GAUGE.

B5-cut crystal A piezoelectric plate cut from a quartz crystal in such a way that the face of the plate is at an angle, with respect to the z-axis of the crystal. This type of crystal has good frequency stability under conditions of changing temperature.

BA Abbreviation of BATTERY. Also see B and BAT.

Ba Symbol for BARIUM.

babbit A relatively soft, tin-base alloy of various compositions. One composition contains 7.4% antimony, 3.7% copper, and 88.9% tin.

babble Interference caused by *crosstalk* from a number of channels.

babble signal A jamming signal containing babble components. See BABBLE and JAMMING.

BABS Abbreviation of BLIND-APPROACH BEACON SYSTEM.

back bias **1.** A feedback signal (negative or positive). **2.** Reverse bias (also see BIAS). **3.** A reverse bias voltage, obtained from a voltage divider connected between a voltage source and ground.

backbone A form of transmission line with capacitive connections between the generator and the load.

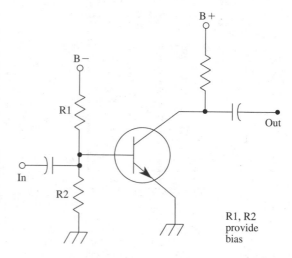

back bias, 3

back conduction Conduction of current in the reverse direction, as across a semiconductor junction that is reverse-biased.

back contact A contact that closes a circuit when a relay, switch, or jack is in its normal rest position.

back current Symbol, I_b. The normally small current flowing through a reverse-biased pn semiconductor junction. Also called *reverse current* and *inverse current*. Compare FORWARD CURRENT.

back diode   A semiconductor diode that is normally back-biased (reverse-biased).

back echo   An echo resulting from the rear lobe of an antenna radiation pattern.

back emf   See BACK VOLTAGE.

Back-Goudsmit effect   See ZEEMAN EFFECT.

background   **1.** The context or supporting area of a picture (e.g., the background of a television picture). **2.** Background noise.

background control   In a color television receiver, a potentiometer used to set the dc level of the color signal at one input of the three-gun picture tube.

background count   Residual response of a radioactivity counter in an environment as free as practicable of radioactivity. This background is caused largely by cosmic rays and inherent radioactivity of surrounding buildings and other bodies.

background job   A low-priority, relatively long-running computer program that can be interrupted so that a higher-priority program can be run.

background noise   Electrical noise inherent to a particular circuit, system, or device that remains when no other signal is present.

background processing   In a computer, the running of programs having low priority.

background radiation   Nuclear radiation from materials in the environment. Also see BACKGROUND COUNT.

background response   The response of a radiation detector to background radiation.

backing store   In a computer, a device that stores large amounts of information. In most small computers, this is done via MAGNETIC DISK and/or MAGNETIC TAPE. A backing store can also be an optical storage medium, such as CD-ROM (compact disk, read-only memory).

backlash   **1.** Slack or lag in action of moving parts. Example: delay between initial application of a force (such as that required to turn a knob) and movement of a part or device (e.g., a potentiometer or variable capacitor). **2.** On a mechanical analog tuning dial, an arc within which slack or lag is discernible.

backloaded horn   A loudspeaker enclosure in which the front of the speaker cone feeds sound directly into the listening area, and the rear of the cone feeds sound into the same area through a folded horn.

backloading   In a cascaded series of amplifiers, the tendency of loading effects to be passed to earlier stages. A change in the output impedance of a final amplifier circuit, for example, could also result in a change in the output impedance of the driver circuit, and perhaps even in a change in the output impedance of the predriver.

back lobe   In the pattern of a directional antenna, the lobe directly opposite the major lobe, representing the radiation or response in or from a direction 180 degrees from that in which the gain is greatest.

backplate   A flat electrode in a television (TV) camera tube that receives the stored-charge image via capacitive coupling.

back porch   In a television (TV) horizontal sync pulse, the time interval between the end of the rise of the blanking pedestal and the beginning of the rise of the sync pulse. That portion of the flat top of the blanking pedestal behind the sync pulse. Compare FRONT PORCH.

back-porch effect   In transistor operation, the continuation of collector-current flow for a short time after the input signal has fallen to zero.

back-porch tilt   The departure of the top edge of a back porch from true horizontal.

back pressure sensor   A device that detects and measures the torque that a motor is applying, and produces a signal whose amplitude is proportional to the torque. This signal can be used for various purposes. In a robotic device, for example, the sensor output can be fed back to the motor control to limit the applied force.

back resistance   Symbol, R_b. The resistance of a reverse-biased pn semiconductor junction. Also called REVERSE RESISTANCE.

back scatter   Scattering of a wave back toward a radio transmitter from points beyond the skip zone. This phenomenon is caused by ionospheric reflection. Compare FORWARD SCATTER.

backstop   A contact or barrier (such as a screw or post) that serves to limit the BACKSWING of the armature of a relay.

backswing   **1.** The tendency of a pulse to overshoot, or reverse direction after completion. Backswing is measured in terms of the overshoot amplitude as a percentage of the maximum amplitude of the pulse. **2.** The extent to which a relay armature moves back from a contact when the relay contacts are open.

back-to-back connection   The connection of diodes or rectifiers in reverse parallel (i.e., the anode of one to the cathode of the other) across a signal line to pass both half cycles of ac in certain control circuits.

back-to-back sawtooth   A symmetrical sawtooth wave in which the rise slope is equal to the fall slope. Also called *triangular wave* and *pyramidal wave*.

backup   **1.** An element, such as a circuit component, that is used to replace a main component, in case of main-component failure. **2.** Any process or scheme that serves to maintain operation of a system in case of main-component failure. **3.** A battery that maintains volatile memory data stored in one or more integrated circuits. **4.** A computer file, or set of files, stored in a nonvolatile medium, such as diskettes or magnetic tape, to prevent catastrophic data loss in the event of hard-disk failure. **5.** A battery or alternative power source that keeps an alarm system operational in the event of a utility power failure.

backup battery   1. In a computer or microcomputer-controlled electronic device, a source of voltage to preserve volatile memory data if the power is removed. **2.** A battery used for powering a system in the event that the main power source should fail.

backup facility   In an electrical or communications system, a facility that is intended for use when the primary, or main, facility is not operational.

back voltage   1. Voltage induced in an inductor by the flow of current through the inductor, so called because its polarity is opposite to that of the applied voltage. Also called *counter emf*. **2.** A voltage used to obtain bucking action (e.g., the voltage used to zero the meter in an electronic voltmeter circuit). **3.** Reverse voltage applied to a semiconductor junction.

backwall   In a pot core, the plate or disk that connects the sleeve and center post to close the magnetic circuit.

backward diode   A semiconductor diode manufactured in such a way that its high-current flow occurs when the junction is reverse biased. Such a diode is also a negative-resistance device.

backward-wave oscillator   Abbreviation, BWO. A microwave oscillator tube similar to the *traveling-wave tube*. Like the traveling-wave tube, the BWO contains a helical transmission line. In the electron beam, electron bunching results from interaction between the beam and the electromagnetic field, and reflection occurs at the collector. The wave moves backward from collector to cathode, and oscillation is sustained because the backward wave is in phase with the input. Output is taken from the cathode end of the helix.

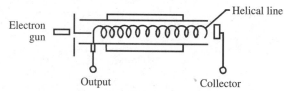

backward-wave oscillator

back wave   The oscillator signal present in an amplifier-keyed, continuous-wave (CW), Morse-code transmitter. Normally, this signal is at the same frequency as the transmitter output, but is not sufficiently strong to be radiated over the air.

back-wave radiation   The condition wherein a back wave is strong enough to be heard on a continuous-wave (CW) keyed signal at the receiving station. This results from ineffective amplifier keying.

baffle   A board on which a loudspeaker is mounted to separate acoustic radiation from the back of the cone from radiation emanating from the front. The baffle improves bass response by increasing the wavelength (lowering the frequency) at which phase cancellation occurs.

baffle plate   1. See BAFFLE. **2.** A metal plate mounted in a waveguide to reduce the cross-sectional area.

bail   A wire loop or chain that holds one member of a two-member assembly to prevent loss (e.g., the short chain holding the dust cap of a jack).

Bakelite   The trade name for a specialized plastic dielectric material. Its chemical composition is *phenol-formaldehyde* resin.

baker   An obsolete phonetic alphabet code word for letter B. BRAVO is commonly used instead.

baking-out   In the process of evacuating a system, the procedure of heating the system to a high temperature to drive out gases occluded in the glass and metal parts.

balance   1. See BRIDGE. **2.** To null a bridge or similar circuit. **3.** To equalize loads, voltages, or signals between two circuits or components. **4.** In a high-fidelity stereo sound system, a control or set of controls that adjusts the relative loudness of the left and right channels. **5.** Alignment of a *balanced modulator* for minimum carrier output amplitude. **6.** A condition in which two branches of a circuit have identical impedances, relative to ground.

balance coil   1. A type of autotransformer that enables a three-wire ac circuit to be supplied from a two-wire line. A series of taps around the center of the winding enables the circuit to be compensated for unequal loads. **2.** See BALANCING COIL.

balance control   A variable component, such as a potentiometer or variable capacitor, that is used to balance bridges, null circuits, or loudspeakers.

balanced   Having identical impedances, with respect to ground.

balanced amplifier   Any amplifier with two branches that have identical impedances, with respect to ground. Usually, the two branches are in phase opposition (180 degrees out of phase).

balanced antenna   An antenna system where two halves are exact replicas of each other, geometrically and electrically. Such an antenna normally must either be fed with a balanced transmission line or with a coaxial cable and balun.

balanced antenna system   A balanced antenna, fed with a balanced transmission line, that has currents of equal magnitude in each side. An example is a half-wave dipole at uniform height above electrical ground, fed at the center with parallel-wire line. It is important that the transmission line runs away from the antenna at a right angle for at least ¼ wavelength, preferably ½ wavelength or more, to prevent line imbalance caused by currents induced from the radiated field.

balanced bridge   Any four-leg bridge circuit in which all legs are identical in all electrical respects.

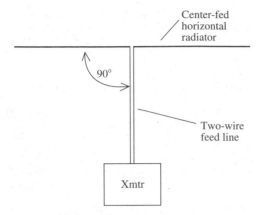

balanced antenna system

balanced circuit 1. A circuit that has its electrical midpoint grounded, as opposed to the *single-ended circuit*, which has one side grounded. **2.** A bridge circuit in the condition of null.

balanced converter See BALUN.

balanced currents Currents with the same value. In the two conductors of a balanced transmission line, these currents are equal in amplitude and opposite in phase at every point along the line.

balanced delta A set of coils or generators in a three-phase system, connected so that the currents in any two coils differ in phase by 120 degrees.

balanced detector A symmetrical demodulator, such as a full-wave diode detector or a discriminator.

balanced electronic voltmeter An electronic voltmeter circuit in which two matched transistors are connected in a four-arm bridge arrangement. The drift in one half of the circuit opposes that in the other half; the resulting drift of the zero point is virtually eliminated.

balanced filter A filter consisting of two identical sections, one in each branch of a balanced system, such as a parallel-wire transmission line.

balanced input An input circuit whose electrical midpoint is grounded. Compare SINGLE-ENDED INPUT.

balanced input transformer An input transformer in which the center tap of the primary winding is grounded.

balanced line A pair of parallel wires that possesses a uniform characteristic impedance. The two conductors are of the same material and have identical diameters. The distance between them is constant. In a balanced two-wire line, the currents in the two conductors are of equal amplitude and opposite phase.

balanced lines In high-fidelity audio systems, a cable that consists of two parallel conductors surrounded by a single braid. The parallel wires carry the audio-frequency (AF) signals, and the braid is grounded for shielding.

balanced loop antenna A loop antenna with a grounded electrical midpoint, determined by the junction of two identical series-connected capacitors shunting the loop.

balanced low-pass filter A low-pass filter used in a balanced system or balanced transmission line.

balanced method A system of instrumentation in which a zero-center scale is used. The reading can be either side of the zero reading.

balanced modulator A symmetrical modulator circuit using bipolar transistors, field-effect transistors, an integrated circuit, or diodes as principal components, that delivers an output signal containing the sidebands, but not the carrier. It is commonly used to generate a double-sideband (DSB) signal that can be filtered to obtain a single-sideband (SSB) signal.

balanced multivibrator A switching oscillator circuit in which the two halves are identical in configuration, and as nearly identical as practicable in performance.

balanced network Any network intended to be used with a balanced system or balanced transmission line. It is characterized by a pair of terminals, each of which shows the same impedance with respect to ground.

balanced oscillator A PUSH-PULL OSCILLATOR.

balanced output Output balanced against ground (e.g., where the electrical midpoint of the output circuit is grounded).

balanced output transformer 1. A push-pull output transformer with a center-tapped primary winding. **2.** An output transformer with a grounded center tap on its secondary winding.

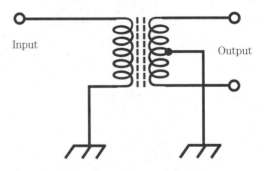

balanced output transformer, 2.

balanced probe A probe, such as one for an electronic voltmeter or oscilloscope, that has a balanced input and (usually) a single-ended output.

balanced-tee trap A wavetrap constructed in a T configuration, with a resonant section in each conductor of a balanced transmission line.

balanced telephone line A telephone transmission line that has two sides, similar to a balanced radio-frequency transmission line. Either side has the same impedance, with respect to ground.

balanced termination A load device (or the practice of using such a device) in which the sections provide identical termination for each of the sections or conductors of a balanced system, such as a balanced line.

balanced-to-unbalanced transformer See BALUN.

balanced transmission line See BALANCED LINE.

balanced varactor tuning A two-varactor, back-to-back circuit for adjusting the value of a capacitor using an applied dc voltage. This arrangement has an advantage over a single-varactor (unbalanced) circuit, because high-tuned-circuit Q is maintained and harmonic generation is reduced.

balanced voltages In any symmetrical system, such as a balanced line or push-pull circuit, two or more input or output voltages that are adjusted to have the same amplitude and (usually) opposite phase.

balanced-wire circuit A circuit or conductor system with identical halves that are symmetrical, with respect to ground and to other conductors.

balancing circuit See BUCKING CIRCUIT.

balancing coil In a receiver, a center-tapped antenna coil that is balanced to ground to eliminate MARCONI EFFECT.

ballast **1.** A component that is used to stabilize the current flow through, or operation of, a circuit, stage, or device. **2.** An iron-core choke connected in series with one of the electrodes in a fluorescent or other gas-discharge lamp.

ballast resistor **1.** A nonlinear inductive power resistor whose voltage-current (EI) characteristic is such that current through the resistor is independent of voltage over a useful range. This feature enables the ballast resistor to act as an automatic voltage regulator when it is simply connected in series with a power supply and load. **2.** A small (usually high-resistance) resistor operated in series with a glow lamp, such as a neon lamp, to prevent overload.

ballast transformer A misnomer often used in place of BALLAST, **2.**

ballistic galvanometer An undamped galvanometer that is used particularly to observe electric charges by noting the single throw resulting from the momentary flow of current through the galvanometer coil.

ballistics The electronics-supported science concerned with the motion of projectiles and similar bodies in air or space.

balloon antenna A vertical antenna consisting of a wire or wires held aloft by a captive balloon. Occasionally, used by radio amateurs and shortwave listeners at low and medium frequen-cies. A potentially dangerous antenna because of large static-electric buildup, a tendency to attract lightning, the possibility of its breaking loose, and the risk of accidental contact with high-voltage power lines.

balop Contraction of BALOPTICON.

balopticon An opaque-picture projecting system in which the picture is viewed by a television (TV) camera, such as a vidicon, and displayed by a picture tube. Also called *balop.*

balun A specialized impedance-matching radio-frequency (RF) transformer. It is a wideband device, usually providing a 1:1 or 1:4 impedance ratio and available in several different forms. It is so called because it has an unbalanced input suitable for coaxial transmission lines, and a balanced output suitable for dipole, Yagi, and quad antennas.

banana jack The female half of a two-part quick-connector combination. Splicing of a circuit is completed by inserting a BANANA PLUG into this jack.

banana plug The male half of a two-part quick-connector combination, with sides usually composed of flat springs that ensure contact with the female BANANA JACK into which it is inserted.

banana jack and plug

band **1.** A continuous range of radio or television communications frequencies or wavelengths, usually designated by the lowest and highest frequencies, or the approximate wavelength (e.g., the 20-meter amateur radio band). **2.** A set of discrete radio or television frequency channels within a specified range (e.g., the standard AM broadcast band). **3.** A range of wavelengths for infrared, visible, ultraviolet, X-ray, or gamma-ray energy. **4.** A range of energy levels. **5.** A colored stripe on a resistor or capacitor that forms part of the code that indicates component value and tolerance.

band center **1.** In a given radio or television communications band, the arithmetic mean of the lowest and highest frequencies. **2.** In a given band, the geometric mean of the longest and shortest wavelengths.

band-elimination filter See BAND-REJECTION FILTER.

band gap In any atom, the difference in electron energy between the conduction and valence bands.

bandpass **1.** The frequency limits between which a BANDPASS FILTER or BANDPASS AMPLIFIER transmits ac energy with negligible loss. **2.** The ability to allow passage of signals at a given frequency or band of frequencies while blocking other signals. Compare BANDSTOP.

bandpass amplifier   An amplifier that is tuned to pass only those frequencies between preset limits.

bandpass coupling   A coupling circuit with a flat-topped frequency response so that a band of frequencies, rather than a single frequency, is coupled into a succeeding circuit. Also see BANDPASS, **1.**

bandpass filter   A filter designed to transmit a specific band of frequencies with negligible loss while rejecting all other frequencies. Compare BAND-REJECTION FILTER.

bandpass flatness   The degree to which a bandpass device's attenuation-versus-frequency curve is a straight line with zero slope within the passband.

band pressure level   The net acoustic pressure of a sound source within a specified frequency range (band).

band-rejection filter   Also called *bandstop filter.* A circuit or device that blocks signals within a specific range (band) of frequencies, while passing signals at frequencies outside that band.

band selector   Any switch or relay that facilitates switching the frequency of a radio transmitter, receiver, or transceiver among various bands.

bandset capacitor   In some older communications receivers, a variable capacitor is used to preset the tuning range in each band to correspond to graduations on the tuning dial. This capacitor is a trimmer or padder operated in conjunction with the main tuning capacitor.

bandspreading   In some older communications receivers, the process of widening the tuning range within a given frequency band to cover the entire dial. Otherwise, the band would occupy only a portion of the dial, and tuning would be difficult. It is usually accomplished with a BANDSPREAD TUNING CONTROL whose range is preset via the main tuning control and/or a BANDSET CAPACITOR.

bandspread tuning control   An analog adjustment in some older communications receivers that allows continuous tuning over a desired band of frequencies. This control is separate from the main tuning control.

bandstop   **1.** The frequency limits between which a BAND-REJECTION FILTER blocks, or greatly attenuates, ac energy. **2.** The ability to suppress or block signals of a given frequency or band of frequencies, while allowing signals of other frequencies to pass with little or no attenuation. Compare BANDPASS.

bandstop filter   See BAND-REJECTION FILTER.

band suppression   **1.** The property of blocking, or greatly attenuating, signals within a specific frequency band. **2.** The frequency limits between which a device or circuit rejects or blocks ac energy, while passing energy at other frequencies with negligible loss.

band-suppression filter   See BAND-REJECTION FILTER.

bandswitch   A low-reactance selector switch (usually rotary) that facilitates changing the tuning range of a radio receiver, transmitter or transceiver from one band of frequencies to another.

bandswitching   In a receiver, transmitter, or test instrument, the process of switching self-contained tuned circuits to change from one frequency spectrum to another within the range of the device's intended operation.

bandwidth   **1.** For a communications or data signal, a measure of the amount of spectrum space the signal occupies. Usually, it is given as the difference between the frequencies at which the signal amplitude is nominally 3 dB down with respect to the amplitude at the center frequency. These frequencies represent the half-power points of the amplitude-versus-frequency function. In general, the bandwidth increases as the data rate (in bits per second, baud, or words per minute) increases. **2.** Also called NECESSARY BANDWIDTH. The minimum amount of spectrum space normally required for effective transmission and reception of a communications or data signal. **3.** See BANDPASS, **1.**

bank   A collection of usually similar components used in conjunction with each other, usually in a parallel configuration. Some examples are resistor bank, lamp bank, and transformer bank.

banked transformers   Parallel-operated transformers.

bankwound coil   A coil wound in such a way that most of its turns are not side by side, thus reducing the inherent distributed capacitance.

bar   **1.** Abbreviation, b. The cgs unit of pressure, in which $1 \, b = 10^5$ pascals per square centimeter. **2.** A horizontal or vertical line produced on a television (TV) screen by a bar generator and used to check linearity. **3.** A thick plate of piezoelectric crystal. **4.** A solid metal conductor, usually uninsulated, of any cross section. **5.** A silicon ingot from which semiconductor devices can be fabricated.

BAR   Abbreviation of BUFFER ADDRESS REGISTER.

bar code   A printed pattern that contains data that can be recovered by laser scanning. It is commonly used for the pricing and identification of store merchandise. It can also be used by an assembly or maintenance robot as an aid to identifying tools.

bar-code reader   A laser scanning device that recovers the data from a tag that contains a BAR CODE. The laser beam moves across the tag. The beam is reflected from the white regions between the lines, but is absorbed by the dark lines themselves. This produces modulation of the reflected beam by the data contained in the tag.

bare conductor A conductor with no insulating covering, a common example being bare copper wire.

bar generator A special type of radio-frequency signal generator that produces horizontal or vertical bars on the screen of a television receiver. It is used in adjustment of horizontal and vertical linearity.

bar graph A graphical presentation of data, in which numerical values are represented by horizontal bars of width that correspond to the values. This type of graph is nonstandard in the sense that the ordinate is horizontal, whereas it is usually vertical. Compare COLUMNAR GRAPH.

bar-graph meter See BAR METER.

barium Symbol, Ba. An elemental metal of the alkaline-earth group. Atomic number, 56. Atomic weight, 137.36. It is present in some compounds used as dielectrics (e.g., barium titanate).

barium-strontium oxides The combined oxides of barium and strontium used as coatings of vacuum-tube cathodes to increase electron emission at relatively low temperatures.

barium strontium titanate A compound of barium, strontium, oxygen, and titanium that is used as a ceramic dielectric material. It exhibits ferroelectric properties and is characterized by a high dielectric constant.

barium titanate Formula, $BaTiO_2$. A ceramic used as the dielectric in ceramic capacitors. It exhibits high dielectric constant and some degree of ferroelectricity.

Barkhausen effect The occurrence of minute jumps in the magnetization of a ferromagnetic substance as the magnetic force is increased or decreased over a continuous range.

Barkhausen interference Interference that results from oscillation because of the BARKHAUSEN EFFECT.

bar magnet A relatively long permanent magnet in the shape of a bar with a rectangular or square cross section.

bar meter A digital meter that displays a quantity, such as signal strength, incrementally, using a set of LEDs or LCDs arranged in a straight line. Its main advantage is that it has no moving parts, yet (unlike direct-readout digital meters) gives the viewer some impression of the way a rapidly fluctuating quantity changes. Its chief

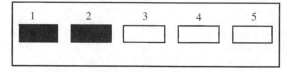

bar meter

disadvantage is that it does not provide a precise indication.

barn Symbol, b. A non-SI unit of nuclear cross section equal to 100 square femtometers or 10^{-24} square centimeters. This unit is approved as compatible with SI (International System of Units).

Barnett effect The development of a small amount of magnetization in a long iron cylinder that is rotated rapidly about its longitudinal axis.

barograph A recording barometer, using either a drum recorder (pen recorder) or a computer to store the data as a function of atmospheric pressure versus time.

barometer An instrument for measuring atmospheric pressure.

barometer effect A relation that appears to exist between the intensity of *cosmic rays* and the atmospheric pressure. It is an inverse relation; that is, increasing pressure seems to correlate with reduced intensity of cosmic rays. It is said to be approximately to 1 or 2% per centimeter of mercury.

barometric pressure The atmospheric pressure, usually given in inches of mercury. The average barometric pressure at the surface of the earth is just under 30 inches of mercury.

bar pattern A series of spaced lines or bars (horizontal, vertical, or both) produced on a television picture screen by means of a BAR GENERATOR. It is useful in adjusting horizontal and vertical linearity of the picture.

barrage array An antenna array in which a string of collinear elements are vertically stacked. The end quarter wavelength of each string is bent in to meet the end quarter wavelength of the opposite radiator to improve balance.

barrage jamming The jamming of many frequencies, or an entire band, at the same time.

barrell distortion Television picture distortion consisting of horizontal and vertical bulging.

barrier 1. The carrier-free space-charge region in a semiconductor pn junction. 2. An insulating partition placed between two conductors or terminals to lengthen the dielectric path.

barrier balance The state of near equilibrium in a semiconductor pn junction (after initial junction forming), entailing a balance of majority and minority charge carrier currents.

barrier capacitance 1. The capacitance in a bipolar transistor between the emitter and collector. It varies with changes in applied voltage, and also with the junction temperature. 2. The capacitance across any pn junction that is reverse-biased.

barrier height The difference in voltage between opposite sides of a barrier in a semiconductor material.

barrier layer See BARRIER, 1.

barrier-layer cell A photovoltaic cell, such as the copper oxide or selenium type, in which photons striking the barrier layer produce the potential difference.

barrier potential   The apparent internal dc potential across the barrier (see BARRIER, **1**) in a pn junction.

barrier strip   A terminal strip having a barrier (see BARRIER, **2**) between each pair of terminals.

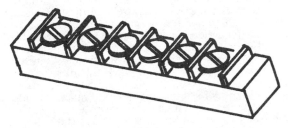

barrier strip

barrier voltage   The voltage required for the initiation of current flow through a pn junction.

Bartlett force   See EXCHANGE FORCE.

baryon   A subatomic particle made up of three quarks.

base   **1.** In a bipolar transistor, the intermediate region between the emitter and collector, which usually serves as the input or controlling element of transistor operation. **2.** A substance that dissociates in water solution and forms hydroxyl (OH) ions. For example, sodium hydroxide. **3.** The constant figure upon which logarithms are computed (10 for common logs, 2.71828 for natural logs). **4.** The radix of a number system (e.g., base 10 for the decimal system, base 8 for the octal system, base 16 for the hexadecimal system, and base 2 for the binary system). **5.** A fixed nonportable radio communications installation.

base address   The number in a computer address that serves as the reference for subsequent address numbers.

baseband   The frequency band of the modulating signal in a communications, broadcast, or data transmitter. For voice communications, this is generally the range of voice frequencies necessary for intelligible transmission. For high-fidelity music broadcasting, it is approximately the range of human hearing. For fast-scan television, it ranges up to several megahertz. It can be restricted or expanded, depending on the nature of the transmitted signal. See BASEBAND FREQUENCY RESPONSE.

baseband frequency response   **1.** The amplitude-versus-frequency characteristic of the audio-frequency (AF) or composite video section of a transmitter that defines the BASEBAND, or range of modulating frequencies. **2.** The range of frequencies over which a radio transmitter can be modulated to convey information. For

single sideband (SSB), it is approximately 300 Hz to 3 kHz; for high-fidelity, frequency-modulated (FM) music transmission, it is about 10 Hz to 20 kHz or 30 kHz; for fast-scan television, it consists of frequencies up to several megahertz. This range is determined by bandpass and/or lowpass filters in the AF or composite video section of the transmitter.

base bias   The steady dc voltage applied to the base electrode of a transistor to determine the operating point along the transistor characteristic curve.

base-bulk resistance   The resistance of the semiconductor material in the base layer of a bipolar transistor.

base-charging capacitance   In the common-emitter connection of a bipolar transistor, the internal capacitance of the base-emitter junction.

base current   Symbol, I_B. Current flowing through the base electrode of a bipolar transistor. Also see AC BASE CURRENT and DC BASE CURRENT.

base electrode   See BASE, **1.** Also called *base element*.

base element   **1.** Base electrode. **2.** One of the basic metals, such as iron or tin, that are not generally considered precious (as opposed to NOBLE).

base-e logarithm   See NAPIERIAN LOGARITHM.

base film   The plastic substrate of a magnetic recording tape.

base frequency   **1.** The frequency of the principal, or strongest, component in a complex signal or waveform; also called *basic frequency*. **2.** The frequency of operation of a base-station transmitter when the receiver is tuned to a second channel.

base-input circuit   A common-collector circuit, common-emitter circuit, or emitter follower.

base insulator   A stout dielectric insulator, used to support a heavy conducting element and keep the conductor isolated from other possible conductors or conductive paths.

base line   In visual alignment procedures involving an oscilloscope and radio-frequency (RF) sweep generator, a zero-voltage reference line developed by the generator as a horizontal trace on the oscilloscope screen.

baseline stabilizer   A clamping circuit that holds the reference voltage of a waveform to a predetermined value. Also called DC RESTORER.

base-loaded antenna   A usually vertical antenna or radiating element, the electrical length of which is adjusted by means of a loading coil or tuned circuit in series with, and positioned at the bottom of, the antenna or radiator.

base material   In printed circuits, the dielectric material used as a substrate for the metal pattern. Also called *base medium*.

base notation   The numbering or radix system used in any application (as octal, decimal, binary, or hexadecimal).

base number   See BASE, **4.**

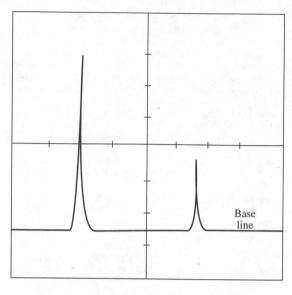

base line

base pin   One of the straight prong-like terminals on an electrical or electronic component; it is used to provide support for the device and to allow a physical connection between the socket terminal, into which it fits, and one of the internal electrodes of the device.

base plate   The chassis plate upon which components are mounted before wiring.

base potential   See BASE VOLTAGE.

base region   See BASE, 1.

base resistance   Symbol, R_B. Resistance associated with the base electrode of a bipolar transistor. Also see AC BASE RESISTANCE and DC BASE RESISTANCE.

base resistor   The external resistor connected to the base of a bipolar transistor. In the common-emitter circuit, the base resistor is analogous to the gate resistor of a field-effect transistor (FET) circuit.

base spreading resistance   Symbol, r_{BB}. In a bipolar transistor, the bulk-material resistance of the base region between the collector junction and emitter junction.

base station   The head station or fixed home station in a communication network.

base-10 logarithm   Abbreviation, $\log_{10}$. A logarithm based on the decimal number 10. If $\log_{10}(x) = y$, then $10^y = x$. Base-10 logarithms are commonly used in engineering. Compare NAPIERIAN LOGARITHM.

base voltage   Symbol, V_B. The voltage at the base electrode of a bipolar transistor. Also see AC BASE VOLTAGE and DC BASE VOLTAGE.

BASIC   Acronym for BEGINNER'S ALL-PURPOSE SYMBOLIC INSTRUCTION CODE, a relatively primitive, but versatile and easy-to-learn computer language developed at Dartmouth College.

basic frequency   1. The FUNDAMENTAL FREQUENCY of a signal, as opposed to one of its harmonics. 2. See BASE FREQUENCY, 1.

basic protection   Devices and procedures essential to minimize the risk of damage to electronic equipment, and/or injury or death to its operators, as a result of lightning. Hardware provisions include a substantial earth ground, heavy-gauge grounding wire, lightning arrestors for antennas, and transient suppressors for power connections. The safest procedure is to disconnect and ground all antennas, and unplug all equipment from utility outlets, during electrical storms and/or when the apparatus is not in use. Radio communications equipment with outdoor antennas, in particular, should not be operated during thunderstorms.

basket   The structure that supports the cone in an acoustic loudspeaker.

basket-weave coil   A type of single-layer inductor in which adjacent turns do not parallel each other around the circumference, but zigzag oppositely as a strand does in the woven pattern of a basket. This reduces distributed capacitance.

bass   Low audio frequencies (AF) corresponding to low-frequency musical notes or sounds.

bass boost   1. The special emphasis given to low audio frequencies (the bass notes) by selective circuits in audio systems. 2. The technique of increasing the loudness of the bass, relative to the higher audio frequencies, to render a more faithful reproduction of sound at low volume levels.

bass compensation   See BASS BOOST, 2.

bass control   1. A manually variable potentiometer for adjusting bass boost of an amplifier or sound system. 2. The arrangement of components that are required to achieve amplitude variation of bass in an audio signal.

bass port   In a loudspeaker, a hole in the cabinet that enhances the low-frequency (bass) sound output. Used in high-fidelity audio systems.

bass-reflex enclosure   A loudspeaker cabinet with a critically dimensioned duct or port that allows back waves to be radiated in phase with front waves, thus averting unwanted acoustic phase cancellation.

bass-reflex loudspeaker   A loudspeaker mounted in a bass reflex enclosure. Also see ACOUSTICAL PHASE INVERTER.

bass-resonant frequency   The low frequency at which a loudspeaker or its enclosure displays resonant vibration.

bass roll-off   1. The attenuation of the low-frequency (bass) component in a high-fidelity audio signal. 2. A control that allows adjustable attenuation of the low-frequency component in a high-fidelity audio signal.

bass suppression   In speech transmission, the removal of all frequencies below about 300 Hz, on the assumption that those frequencies contribute little to intelligibility. This suppression permits the speech level to be increased without overmodulating a transmitter. It also allows smaller audio transformers to be used because transformer core size must increase as the frequency it passes decreases.

bassy In audio and high-fidelity applications, a sound in which the low-frequency components, below about 500 Hz, are overly predominant.

BAT Abbreviation of BATTERY.

batch fabrication process The manufacture of devices in a single batch from materials of uniform grade. Particularly, the manufacture of a large number of semiconductor devices from one batch of semiconductor material by means of carefully controlled, identical processes.

batch processing In digital-computer operations, the processing of quantities of similar information during a single run.

bat-handle switch A toggle switch, the lever of which is relatively long and thick, and is shaped like a baseball bat.

bat-handle switch

bathtub capacitor A (usually oil-filled) capacitor housed in a metal can that looks like a miniature bathtub.

bathyconductorgraph An instrument that is used to measure the electrical conductivity of seawater.

bathythermograph An instrument that plots a graph of temperature versus depth in a body of water, such as a lake or an ocean.

batten Supporting bars or braces that hold a loudspeaker in place within its cabinet, and/or that hold the cabinet panels in place.

battery Abbreviations, B, BA. BAT. A device consisting of two or more interconnected electrochemical or photovoltaic cells that generate dc electricity. The cells can be connected in series to supply a desired voltage, in parallel to supply a desired current-delivering capability, or in series-parallel to obtain a desired voltage and cur-

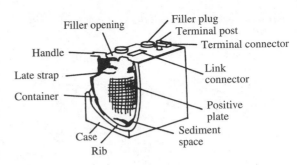

battery

rent-delivering capability. Also see CELL, EDISON BATTERY, LEAD-ACID BATTERY, PHOTOVOLTAIC CELL, PRIMARY BATTERY, and STORAGE BATTERY.

battery acid 1. A chemical acid, such as sulfuric acid, used as the electrolyte of a battery. 2. Colloquially, any cell or battery electrolyte, whether acid, base, or salt.

battery capacity The current-supplying capability of a battery, usually expressed in ampere-hours (Ah).

battery cell See CELL, 1.

battery charger 1. A specialized dc power supply, usually embodying a stepdown transformer, rectifier, and filter. It is used to charge a storage battery from an ac power line. 2. A motor-generator combination used to charge a storage battery from an ac power line. 3. A combination of solar cells, generators, or other voltaic transducers, that are used to charge a storage battery with dc obtained from a nonelectrical energy source.

battery clip 1. A heavy-duty metallic clamp that is used for quick, temporary connection to a large cell terminal, such as that of a lead-acid storage battery. 2. A small connector of the snap-fastener type, used for quick connection to a small power source, such as a transistor-radio battery.

battery eliminator A specialized dc power supply, usually embodying a transformer, rectifier, and filter, that permits battery-powered equipment to be operated from an ac power line.

battery holder 1. A case or container of any kind for holding a cell or battery. 2. A shelf for holding a cell or battery. 3. A small, metal bracket-type device for holding a cell or battery between two contacts.

battery life 1. The ampere-hour or watt-hour capacity of a battery. 2. The number of times that a rechargeable electrochemical battery can be cycled before it becomes unusable. 3. The nominal length of time (e.g., hours, days, or weeks) that an electrochemical battery will function effectively in a given application before it must be discarded or recharged.

battery receiver A usually portable radio or television receiver operated from self-contained batteries.

battery substitute See BATTERY ELIMINATOR.

bat wing On a television (TV) or frequency-modulation (FM) broadcast receiving antenna, a metallic element with a shape that resembles that of a bat's wing.

baud A unit of communications processing speed in telegraphy and digital data communications systems. Often confused with *bits per second* (bps). Baud refers to the number of times per second that a signal changes state. The speed in bps is generally higher than the speed in baud, sometimes by a factor of several times. Compare BITS PER SECOND.

Baudot code A machine communications code that uses five parallel binary digits of equal length, the interpretation of which depends on the history of the previous transmission or an additional case bit.

baud rate **1.** A colloquial expression for data speed in BAUD. **2.** Colloquial, and technically inaccurate, expression for data speed in BITS PER SECOND.

Baume (Antione Baume, 1728-1804). Abbreviation, Be. Pertaining to the *Baume scales* for hydrometers. The two such scales are for liquids heavier than water and for liquids lighter than water.

bay One of several sections of a directional antenna array.

bayonet base The insertable portion of a plug-in component (e.g., a lamp) that has a projecting pin that fits into a slot or keyway in the shell of the socket into which the component is inserted.

bayonet socket A socket with a suitably slotted shell for receiving the bayonet base of a plug-in component.

bazooka A linear BALUN, in which a quarter wavelength of metal sleeving surrounds a coaxial feeder, and is shorted to the outer conductor of the feeder to form a shorted quarter-wave section.

bb Abbreviation of BLACKBODY.

BBC Abbreviation of *British Broadcasting Corporation*.

BBM Abbreviation of BREAK BEFORE MAKE.

b-box The index register of a computer.

BC Abbreviation of BROADCAST.

BCD Abbreviation of BINARY-CODED DECIMAL.

BCFSK Abbreviation of BINARY CODE FREQUENCY-SHIFT KEYING.

B channel One of the channels of a two-channel stereophonic system. Compare A CHANNEL.

BCI Abbreviation of BROADCAST INTERFERENCE.

BCL Amateur radio abbreviation of BROADCAST LISTENER.

BCN Abbreviation of BEACON.

BCO Abbreviation of BINARY-CODED OCTAL.

BCST Abbreviation of BROADCAST.

BDC Abbreviation of BINARY DECIMAL COUNTER.

B display A radar display in which the target is represented by a bright spot on a rectangular-coordinate screen. Compare A DISPLAY and J DISPLAY.

Be Symbol for BERYLLIUM.

Be Abbreviation of BAUME.

beacon **1.** A beam of radio waves, or a radio signal, that is used for navigation and/or direction finding. **2.** A transmitter that radiates a beam of radio waves, or a radio signal, as an aid in navigation and/or direction finding. **3.** A signal transmitted continuously on a specific frequency, to help radio operators ascertain propagation conditions. **4.** A station or transmitter that generates and radiates a signal to help radio operators determine propagation conditions. **5.** In robotics, a device or system that aids in navigation. For example, tri-corner reflectors can be positioned in strategic locations, and a mobile robot equipped with a scanning infrared laser. The robot controller determines the distance to any given reflector by measuring the time required for the laser beam to return. In this way, two mirrors can allow the robot to locate its position in two dimensions; three mirrors can facilitate position determination in three-dimensional space.

beacon direction finder A direction finder using a signal received from a beacon station.

beacon receiver A receiver that is specially adapted for the reception of beacon signals (see BEACON, **1** and **3**).

beacon station **1.** A station broadcasting beacon signals (see BEACON, **1** and **3**) for direction finding, navigation, and/or determination of radio-wave propagation conditions. **2.** Sometimes, a radar transmitting station.

beacon transmitter A transmitter specially adapted for the transmission of beacon signals (see BEACON, **1** and **3**).

bead **1.** A small ferromagnetic ring that is used as a passive decoupling choke by slipping it over the input power leads of a circuit or stage, or around a coaxial transmission line. **2.** A magnetic memory element in a ferrite-core matrix.

beaded coax A low-loss, coaxial transmission line, in which the inner conductor is separated from the outer conductor by means of spaced dielectric beads.

beaded support A plastic or dielectric bead that is used to support the inner conductor of an air-insulated transmission line of coaxial construction.

bead thermistor A thermistor consisting essentially of a small bead of temperature-sensitive resistance material into which two leads are inserted.

beam **1.** The more-or-less narrow pattern of radiation from a directional antenna. **2.** A directional antenna—especially a YAGI ANTENNA. **3.** The stream or cloud of electrons emitted by the cathode in an electron tube—especially a BEAM POWER TUBE.

beam alignment   1. The lining-up of a directional transmitting antenna with a directional receiving antenna for maximum signal transfer. **2.** In a television (TV) camera tube, the lining-up of the electron beam so that it is perpendicular to the target. **3.** In a cathode-ray tube, the positioning of the electron rays so that they converge properly on the screen, regardless of the deflection path.

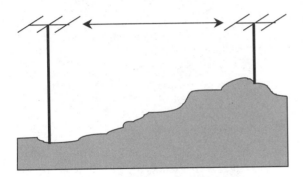

beam alignment

beam angle   In the radiation from an antenna, the direction of most intense radiation, the side limits of which are determined by the points at which the field strength drops to half the value in the principal direction.

beam antenna   1. A multielement directional antenna, consisting of a half-wave driven dipole and one or more parasitic elements. See YAGI ANTENNA. **2.** Any directional antenna used for transmitting and receiving radio-frequency (RF) signals.

beam bender   1. In a television (TV) picture tube, the ion-trap magnet. **2.** Deflection-plate correction device or circuit.

beam bending   Deflection of an electron beam by electric or magnetic fields.

beam blanking   See BLANK, **2.**

beam convergence   The meeting, at a shadow-mask opening, of the three electron beams in a three-color television picture tube. See BEAM ALIGNMENT, **3.**

beam coupling   A method of producing an alternating current between two electrodes by passing a density-modulated beam of electrons between the electrodes. This, in effect, demodulates the electron beam, recovering the information.

beam crossover   Either of the half-power points in the beam of a directional antenna, usually in the horizontal plane. The reference point is considered to be the direction of maximum radiation.

beam current   The current represented by the flow of electrons in the beam of a cathode-ray tube.

beam cutoff   In an oscilloscope or television picture tube, the complete interruption of the electron beam, usually as a result of highly negative control-grid bias.

beam deflector   A deflection plate in an oscilloscope tube.

beam efficiency   In a cathode-ray tube, the ratio of the number of electrons generated by the gun to the number reaching the screen. The efficiency is high in electromagnetic-deflection tubes and lower in electrostatic-deflection tubes.

beam lead   In an integrated circuit, a relatively thick and strong lead that is deposited in contact with portions of the thin-film circuit. It provides stouter connections than continuations of the thin film would provide.

beam-lead isolation   In an integrated circuit, reduction of distributed capacitance and other interaction through use of beam leads.

beam modulation   See INTENSITY MODULATION.

beam parametric amplifier   A PARAMETRIC AMPLIFIER in which the variable-reactance component is supplied by a modulated electron beam.

beam-positioning magnet   In a three-gun color television picture tube, a permanent magnet that is used to position one of the electron beams correctly, with respect to the other two.

beam power tube   A tetrode or pentode vacuum tube, in which special deflector plates concentrate the electrons into beams in their passage from cathode to plate. The beam action greatly increases plate current at a given plate voltage. It is used in some radio-frequency (RF) power amplifiers.

beam-rider control system   A missile-guidance system in which a control station sends a radio beam to a missile. The beam is moved in such a way that as the missile stays within the beam, it hits the target.

beam-rider guidance   1. An aircraft landing guidance system, in which the aircraft follows a radio beam in its glide path. **2.** The circuitry in a guided missile using a beam-rider control system.

beam splitter   A device used to divide a light beam (as by a transparent mirror) into two components, one transmitted and the other reflected; hence, a BEAM-SPLITTING MIRROR.

beam splitting   In radar, a method of calculating the mean azimuth of a target from the azimuth at which the target is first revealed by one scan, and the azimuth at which the target information ceases.

beam-splitting mirror   In an oscilloscope-camera system, a tilted, transparent mirror that allows rays to pass horizontally from the oscilloscope screen to the camera and to be reflected vertically to the viewer's eye.

beamwidth of antenna   The angular width of the main lobe of the pattern of radiation from a directional antenna. Generally, it is measured between the half-power points in the horizontal plane. Occasionally, it is measured in the vertical plane.

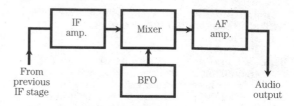

beat-frequency oscillator

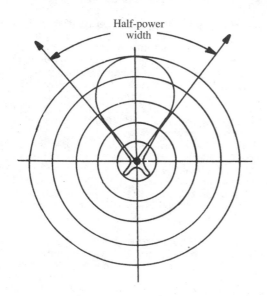

beamwidth of antenna

bearing   The direction of an object or point expressed in degrees within a 360° horizontal clockwise boundary, with the center of the circle serving as the observation point.

bearing resolution   In radar operations, the minimum horizontal separation of two targets, in degrees, that permits the individual targets to be displayed as two echoes, rather than one.

beat   Any one of the series of pulsations constituting a beat note, which results from heterodyning one signal against another.

beat frequency   Either of two frequencies f_{C1} and f_{C2} resulting from the mixing of two signals of different frequencies f_A and f_B. Frequency f_{C1} is the sum of the two input frequencies; $f_{C1} = f_A + f_B$. Frequency f_{C2} is the difference; $f_{C2} = f_A - f_B$ when f_A is the higher of the two input frequencies.

beat-frequency oscillator   Abbreviation, BFO. An oscillator used to set up audible beat frequencies with an incoming received signal and installed in the intermediate-frequency (IF) stages of a superheterodyne communications receiver. For single-sideband (SSB) reception, the BFO is set at the frequency of the received

suppressed carrier. In continuous-wave (CW) Morse code reception, the BFO is set at a frequency that differs from that of the incoming signal by about 400 to 1000 Hz. The resulting tone has an audio frequency equal to the difference between the BFO frequency and the received signal carrier frequency. For reception of frequency-shift-keyed (FSK) signals, the BFO is set to such a frequency that the resulting audio beat notes are appropriate for the mark and space inputs of a terminal unit or modem.

beating   **1.** Also called *heterodyning*. The combination of signals of different frequencies resulting in sum and difference frequencies. **2.** The fluttering noise heard when two audio tones, very close in frequency and very similar in amplitude, are emitted at the same time.

beat marker   In the visual (oscilloscopic) alignment of a tuned circuit, a marker pip that results from the beat note between the sweep-generator signal and the signal from a marker oscillator.

beat note   The sum or difference frequency that results from the heterodyning of two signals or, under some conditions, of more than two signals.

beat-note reception   **1.** Reception in which a radio-frequency carrier is made audible by heterodyning it with a beat-frequency oscillator (BFO) to produce an audible beat note. **2.** Superheterodyne reception (see SUPERHETERODYNE CIRCUIT).

beat tone   A beat note in which the frequency is within the range of hearing.

beaver tail   A flat or elongated radar beam, wide in the azimuth plane. Primarily used to determine the altitude of a target. The beam is moved up and down to find the target elevation.

Becquerel effect   A phenomenon in which a voltage is produced when radiant energy, such as infrared, visible light, ultraviolet, or X-rays, falls on one electrode in an electrolytic cell.

bedspring   A directional antenna consisting of a broadside array with a flat reflector and one or more helical driven elements.

beep   A test or control signal, usually of single tone and short duration.

beeper   **1.** A pocket- or hand-carried transceiver—especially one for maintaining two-way contact with personnel who are away from their base. **2.**

An acoustic transducer that produces a beep in response to an input signal.

beetle A urea formaldehyde plastic used as a dielectric material and as a container material.

bel Abbreviation, B. The basic logarithmic unit (named for Alexander Graham Bell) for expressing gain or loss ratios. One bel is equivalent to a power gain of 10. Also see DECIBEL.

bell An electric alarm device consisting of a metallic gong that emits a ringing sound when it is struck by an electrically vibrated clapper.

Bellini-Tosi direction finder A direction finder in which the sensing element consists of two triangular vertical antennas crossed at right angles, the antennas being open at the top and accordingly not acting as conventional coil antennas.

bell-shaped curve A statistical curve (so called from its characteristic shape) that exhibits a *normal distribution* of data. Typically, the curve describes the distribution of errors of measurement around the real value.

bell transformer A (usually inexpensive) step-down transformer that operates an electric bell or similar alarm or signaling device from the ac power line.

bell wire Insulated 18-gauge (AWG) solid copper wire, so called because of its principal early use in the wiring of electric-bell circuits.

belt generator Also known as a *Van de Graaff generator*. A very-high-voltage electrostatic generator, a principal part of which is a fast-traveling endless belt of dielectric material. At the lower end, charges of one sign are sprayed on the belt at 10 to 100 kV dc and are carried to the inside of a hollow metal sphere at the upper end, where they are removed and spread to the surface of the sphere, which they raise to a potential up to several million volts.

benchmark A test standard to measure product performance.

benchmark routine A routine designed to evaluate computer software and/or hardware, producing a good indication of how well the software or hardware will perform in real-life situations. In particular, tests *instructions per second* and *throughput*, thereby producing an indication of the overall computer power in applications, such as word processing, database, spreadsheet, graphics, animation, and mathematical calculations.

bench test An extensive checkout of a piece of equipment in the test laboratory—either to find an intermittent problem, or to check for reliability.

bend An angular shift in the lengthwise direction of a waveguide.

bending effect 1. The downward refraction of a radio wave by the ionosphere. 2. The low-atmosphere turning of a radio wave downward by temperature discontinuity and atmospheric inversions.

Benedick effect In a closed circuit, a voltage that results from temperature differences. The circuit consists of one metal in its purest possible form and free from strain, electric fields, and magnetic fields.

Benito A continuous-wave method of measuring the distance of an aircraft from the ground, involving the transmission of an audio-modulated signal from ground and the retransmission back to ground by the aircraft. The phase shift between the two signals is proportional to the distance to the aircraft.

bent antenna An antenna that has its driven element bent, usually near the ends and at right angles, to conserve space.

bent gun A television picture tube neck arrangement having an electron gun that is slanted to direct the undesired ion beam toward a positive electrode, but which allows the electron beam to pass to the screen. This prevents the ion beam from "burning" a permanent spot on the phosophor of the screen.

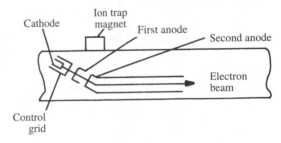

bent gun

BeO Formula for beryllium oxide. Also see BERYLLIA.

berkelium Symbol, Bk. A radioactive elemental metal produced artificially. Atomic number, 97. Atomic weight, 247.

beryllia Formula, BeO. Beryllium oxide, used in various forms as an insulator and structural element (as in resistor cores).

beryllium Symbol, Be. An elemental metal. Atomic number, 4. Atomic weight, 9.01218. Beryllium is present in various dielectrics and alloys used in electronic components.

Bessel functions Sophisticated mathematical functions for dealing with periodic electronic phenomena in which the waveform often displays decrement. Also called *cylindrical functions*.

beta Symbol, β. The current gain of a common-emitter bipolar transistor stage. It is the ratio of the induced change of collector current to the applied change of base current: $\beta = dI_C/dI_B$.

beta circuit The output-input feedback circuit in an amplifier.

beta cutoff frequency The frequency at which the current amplification of a bipolar transistor falls to 70.7% of its low-frequency value.

beta particles Minute radioactive subatomic bits identical to the electron or positron, and emitted by some radioactive materials. Also see BETA RAYS.

beta rays Rays emitted by the nuclei of radioactive substances, consisting of a stream of beta particles (i.e., electrons or positrons) that move at velocities up to 299.8 million meters per second. Compare ALPHA PARTICLE and GAMMA RAYS.

beta-to-alpha conversion For a bipolar transistor, the conversion of current amplification expressed as beta (β) to current amplification expressed as alpha (α): $\alpha = \beta/(\beta + 1)$.

betatron A particle accelerator in which injected electrons are given extreme velocity by being propelled in circular paths in a doughnut-shaped glass container. The term comes from the fact that high-speed electrons constitute BETA PARTICLES.

beta videocassette recorder The earliest scheme for videocassette recording, developed by Sony corporation in the 1970s. Compare *VHS videocassette recorder.*

beta zinc silicate phosphor Formula, $(ZnO + SiO_2):Mn$. A phosphorescent substance used to coat the screen of a cathode-ray tube. The fluorescence is green-yellow.

BeV Abbreviation of *billion electronvolts.* Also see ELECTRONVOLT, GEV, MEV, and MILLION ELECTRONVOLTS. This abbreviation has been supplanted by the SI (International System of Units) abbreviation GeV, for GIGAELECTRON-VOLTS.

bevatron An accelerator (see ACCELERATOR, **1**) similar to the synchrotron, which accelerates particles to levels greater than 10 GeV.

Beverage antenna (Harold H. Beverage.) A nonresonant, directional long-wire antenna, erected a few feet above ground and run in a straight line for one to several wavelengths. It is generally used for reception at low and medium frequencies, the best response is to vertically polarized signals arriving from one or both directions in line with the wire. It can be left unterminated for bidirectional response, or it can be terminated at its far end by a noninductive resistor of about 600 ohms for a unidirectional response.

beyond-the-horizon propagation See FORWARD SCATTER.

bezel A faceplate for an electronic instrument, usually having a fitted rim and cutouts for knobs, switches, jacks, etc.

BFO Abbreviation of BEAT-FREQUENCY OSCILLATOR.

BG Abbreviation of BIRMINGHAM WIRE GAUGE. Also abbreviated BWG.

B-H curve A plot showing the B and H properties of a magnetic material. Magnetizing force H is plotted along the horizontal axis, and flux density B is plotted along the vertical axis.

B-H loop See BOX-SHAPED LOOP.

B-H meter Any instrument for displaying or evaluating the hysteresis loop of a magnetic material.

bhp Abbreviation of *brake horsepower.*

Bi Symbol for BISMUTH.

bias **1.** Any parameter of which the value is set to a predetermined level to establish a threshold or operating point. Although it is common to think of bias currents and bias voltages, other parameters (e.g., capacitance, resistance, illumination, magnetic intensity, etc.) can serve as biases. **2.** In a high-fidelity audio system, a circuit in a tape recorder/player that optimizes performance for a particular type of recording tape.

bias current A steady, constant current that presets the operating threshold or operating point of a circuit or device, such as a transistor, diode, or magnetic amplifier. Compare BIAS VOLTAGE.

bias current drift The ratio of a change in input bias current to a change in ambient temperature, generally expressed in nanoamperes per degree Celsius.

bias distortion Distortion caused by operation of a tube or transistor with incorrect bias so that the response of the device is nonlinear.

biased diode A diode having a dc voltage applied in either forward or reverse polarity. Current flows readily through the forward-biased diode; the reverse-biased diode appears as an open circuit. The biased diode is the basis of clippers, limiters, slicers, and similar circuits.

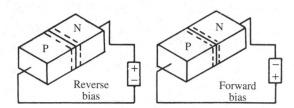

biased diodes

biased off In a circuit or device, the state of cutoff caused by application of a control-electrode bias. Examples include collector-current cutoff (when the dc base bias of a bipolar transistor reaches a critical value), and drain-current cutoff (when the dc gate bias reaches a critical value in a field-effect transistor).

biased search A scheme that a mobile robot can use to find its way to a destination or target, by deliberately searching off to the side and then homing in as the approach progresses. It is so called because the general nature of the initial error (bias) is known, although its exact extent need not be known.

bias oscillator In a magnetic recorder, an oscillator operated at a frequency in the 40-kHz to 100-kHz range to erase prerecorded material and bias the system magnetically for linear recording.

bias resistor A usually fixed resistor, such as the source resistor in a field-effect-transistor (FET) circuit or the emitter resistor in a bipolar-transistor circuit, across which a desired bias voltage is developed by current flowing through the resistor.

bias set A control, such as a potentiometer or variable autotransformer, that facilitates manual adjustment of the dc bias of a circuit.

bias stabilization **1.** The maintenance of a constant bias voltage, despite variations in load impedance or line voltage. It is usually accomplished by means of automatic voltage regulation. **2.** The stabilization of transistor dc bias voltage by means of resistance networks or through the use of barretters, diodes, or thermistors.

bias supply **1.** Batteries that provide bias voltage or current for bipolar or field-effect transistors. **2.** A line-operated unit for supplying dc bias and consisting of a transformer, rectifier, and high-grade filter.

bias voltage A steady voltage that presets the operating threshold or operating point of a circuit or device, such as a transistor. Compare BIAS CURRENT.

bias windings The dc control windings of a saturable reactor or magnetic amplifier.

biconical antenna A form of broadband antenna, consisting of two conical sections joined at the apexes. The cones are at least ¼ wavelength in diagonal height. The vertex angles of the cones can vary, although the apex angle is usually the same in each cone. The vertex angle affects the feed-point impedance. Such an antenna radiates, and responds optimally to, signals with polarization parallel to the axis of the cones.

biconical horn antenna A double-horn microwave antenna that radiates along relatively sharp front and back beams.

bidecal base The 20-pin base of a cathode-ray tube. Also see DIHEPTAL, DUODECAL, and MAGNAL.

bidirectional Radiating or receiving (usually equally) from opposite directions (e.g., front-and-back radiation from an antenna or loudspeaker, or front-and-back pickup with an antenna or microphone).

bidirectional antenna An antenna with a directional pattern that consists of maximum lobes 180 degrees apart.

bidirectional bus In computers, a data path over which both input and output signals are routed.

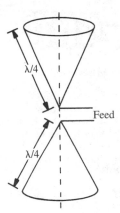

biconical antenna

bidirectional bus driver In a microcomputer, a signal-driving device that permits direct connection of a buffer-to-buffer arrangement on one end (the interface to I/O, memories, etc.) and data inputs and outputs on the other. This device permits bidirectional signals to pass and provides drive capability in both directions.

bidirectional counter A counter that can count consecutively up from a given number or down from that number. Also called UP-DOWN COUNTER.

bidirectional current A current that flows in both directions. Utility alternating current (ac) is a common example.

bidirectional loudspeaker A loudspeaker that delivers sound waves to the front and rear.

bidirectional microphone A microphone that picks up sound waves equally well from the front and rear.

bidirectional transistor A symmetrical transistor (i.e., one in which the two main current-carrying electrodes can be interchanged without influencing device performance). Some field-effect transistors (FETs) are of this type; the drain and the source can be interchanged.

bifilar electrometer An electrometer in which the sensitive element consists of two long platinized-quartz fibers. When an electric potential is applied, the fibers separate by a distance proportional to the voltage.

bifilar resistor A wirewound resistor with two oppositely wound filaments. The nature of the winding tends to cancel the inductance, making the device useful at a much higher frequency than an ordinary wirewound resistor.

bifilar transformer A transformer in which unity coupling is approached by interwinding the primary and secondary coils (i.e., the primary and secondary turns are wound side by side and in the same direction).

bifilar winding **1.** A method of winding a coil (such as a resistor coil) in the shape of a coiled

bifilar winding

hairpin so that the magnetic field is self-canceling and the inductance is minimized. **2.** A method of winding transformers to minimize leakage reactance.

bifurcated contact   A forked contact whose parts act as two contacts in parallel for increased reliability.

bilateral amplifier   An amplifier that transmits or receives in either direction equally well (i.e., the input and output can be exchanged at will).

bilateral antenna   A bidirectional antenna, such as a loop antenna or a half-wave dipole.

bilateral element   A circuit element or component (as a capacitor, resistor, or inductor) that transmits energy equally well in either direction. Compare UNILATERAL ELEMENTS.

bilateral network   A network, usually passive and either balanced or unbalanced, that has BILATERAL SYMMETRY. Thus, the input and output terminals can be exchanged without affecting the performance of the network in any way.

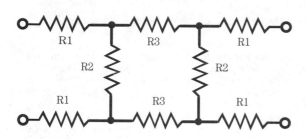

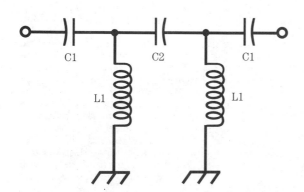

bilateral network

bilateral symmetry   **1.** Exhibiting symmetry, with respect to a vertical line or plane. **2.** For a network, having the property that if the input and output are reversed, the circuit behavior remains precisely the same. See BILATERAL NETWORK. **3.** For an amplitude-versus-frequency response curve, having the property that the right-hand and left-hand halves are mirror images of each other.

billboard antenna   A phased group of dipole antennas that lie in one plane. A reflector might be used behind the entire array.

bilobe pattern   An antenna radiation pattern consisting of two major lobes in a given plane, usually the horizontal plane. Often the lobes exist in opposite directions relative to each other, as in a half-wave dipole. But they can be at varying angles, as in a long-wire antenna.

bimetal   A union of two dissimilar metals—especially those having a different temperature coefficient of expansion. The two are usually welded together over their entire surface.

bimetallic element   A strip or disk of bimetal. When the element is heated, it bends in the direction of the metal that has the lower temperature coefficient of expansion; when cooled, it unbends. Usually, an electrical contact is made at one extreme or the other so that the element can serve as a thermostat.

bimetallic switch   A temperature-sensitive switch based on a bimetallic element.

bimetallic thermometer   A thermometer based on a bimetallic element that is mechanically coupled (as through a lever and gear system) to a pointer that moves over a temperature scale.

bimetallic thermostat   A thermostat in which a bimetallic element closes or opens a pair of switch contacts.

bimorphous cell   A piezoelectric transducer that consists of two crystal plates, such as Rochelle salt, bound intimately face to face. In a crystal microphone, vibration of the transducer results in a voltage output; in a crystal headphone, an ac signal voltage impressed on the transducer causes vibratory mechanical motion.

BiMOS   A combination of bipolar and MOSFET transistors in an integrated circuit. Thus, a typical BiMOS device can have MOSFET input for high impedance and bipolar output for low impedance.

binant electrometer   An electrometer in which a thin platinum vane ("the needle") is suspended within two halves of a metal pillbox-shaped container. The halves or binants are biased with a dc voltage of 1 to 12 V, and the unknown voltage is applied to the vane. It is also called DUANT ELECTROMETER and HOFFMAN ELECTROMETER.

binary   **1.** Pertaining to the base-2 number system. Thus, binary arithmetic uses two digits: 0 and 1. **2.** Pertaining to two-element chemical compounds.

binary arithmetic   Mathematical operations performed using only the digits 0 and 1.

binary cell   In a computer memory, an element that can display either of two stable states.

binary chain   A cascade of binary elements, such as flip-flops, each unit of which affects the stable state of the succeeding unit in sequence.

binary channel   Any channel whose use is limited to two symbols.

binary code   A system of numbers representing quantities by combinations of 1 and 0; a binary-number system.

binary-coded decimal notation   In digital computer operations, a system of notation in which each digit of a decimal number is represented by its binary equivalent. Thus, the decimal number 327 in BCD notation becomes 0011 0010 0111. (By contrast, in pure binary notation, 327 is 101000111.)

binary-coded octal notation   A method of numbering in which each base-8 digit is represented by a binary number from 000 to 111.

binary-controlled gate circuit   A gate circuit controlled by a binary stage. An example is a gating transistor that receives its on/off pulses from a flip-flop.

binary counter   A counter circuit consisting of a cascade of bistable stages. Each stage is a scale-of-two counter because its output is on for every second input pulse. At any instant, the total binary count in a multistage counter thus is shown by the on and off states of the various stages in sequence.

binary decoder   A device or stage that accepts binary signals on its input lines, and provides a usually exclusive output (representing a decimal digit, for example).

binary digit   See BIT.

binary number system   The base-two system of notation. This system uses only two symbols, 0 and 1, and accordingly is easily applied to two-position switches, relays, and flip-flops.

binary preset switch   In a binary counter or binary control circuit, a selector switch that allows the circuit to be preset to deliver an output pulse only after a predetermined number of input pulses.

binary relay   See BISTABLE RELAY.

binary scaler   In its simplest form, a single two-stage device, such as a flip-flop, which functions as a divide-by-two counter, because one output pulse results from every two input pulses. Higher-order scaling is obtained by cascading stages.

binary search   A system of search entailing the successive division of a set of items into two parts and the rejection of one of the two until all items of the sought-for kind are isolated.

binary signal   Any signal that can attain either of two states. Such a signal is always a digital signal.

binary-to-decimal conversion   **1.** The automatic conversion of a number represented by a series

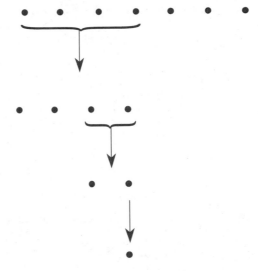

binary search

of binary pulses into the corresponding decimal number, which then is displayed by a readout device. **2.** The arithmetic operation of converting a binary number into a decimal number; this can be done by noting the powers of 2 represented by the various binary digits in a number, and then adding the decimal values of these powers.

binary word   A binary numeral that has a particular meaning, agreed upon by convention. For example, the letters A through Z can be represented by binary numbers 00001 through 11010; a word can be represented by several blocks of five digits.

binaural   Literally, two-eared. In sound recording and reproduction, the transcription of a broad sound source using two microphones spaced at approximately the distance between the ears on a human head, and played back using headphones to re-create the stereo effect. The technique evolved into multichannel stereophonic reproduction.

binaural machine hearing   Also called *stereo machine hearing.* The ability of a machine, such as a robot, to sense the direction and distance to a source of sound, using two acoustic transducers and a computer to process their output signals. The machine determines the location of the sound source by comparing the relative amplitude and phase of the signals from the two transducers. It functions according to the same principle as human hearing, in which a person can determine the general direction and distance to a sound source by subconsciously comparing the relative amplitude and phase of the sounds arriving at the left and right ears.

binaural sound   The equivalent of a listener hearing a concert through a pair of earholes; it takes earphones to reproduce the signal. If speakers are substituted for the earphones, the listener hears monophonically, as if standing back several feet from the earholes.

binder A material (such as lacquer) that acts as a holder and cohesive medium for the particles of another material. It is used in carbon resistors, ceramic dielectric bodies, powder cores, and resistive and metallic paints.

binding energy A property of the nucleus of an atom. The binding energy of a nucleus is equal to the difference between the nuclear weight and the sum of the weights of the lighter particles making up the nucleus. The nucleus is stable when the binding energy is high.

binding force Any one of the electrostatic forces that bind crystals together.

binding post A screw-type terminal of various styles, often having a hole into which a wire or tip can be inserted and gripped. It is used for temporary indoor connections only.

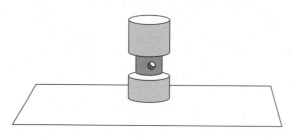

binding post

binistor A semiconductor switching device that exhibits two stable states and also negative resistance.

binocular machine vision Also called *stereoscopic machine vision*. The ability of a machine vision system to provide depth and perspective data. Uses two optical sensors spaced a fixed distance apart. The left sensor sees a slightly different image than the right sensor. These two images are combined and processed by a computer, allowing the machine (such as a mobile robot) to determine the distances to various objects in its environment. Functions on the same principle as stereoscopic human vision.

bin picking In robotics, the selection of a particular object from a container (bin) in which there are many objects. Can be done using object recognition, bar coding, or passive transponders. It requires a sensor, operating in conjunction with a computer that processes the sensed data and controls the movements of the robot.

binomial An algebraic expression containing two terms joined by a plus or minus sign. Examples: $a^2 + b^2$, $3x^3 - 6x$.

binomial theorem The theorem, proven by Isaac Newton, permits a binomial to be raised to any desired power without performing the multiplications. In electronics, *power series* are convenient for expressing such expressions.

biochemical cell A fuel-cell energy source in which electricity is generated chemically through the oxidation of biological substances. Also called *biochemical fuel cell.*

biochip **1.** A natural, living organism with a physical structure that in some way resembles that of an electronic *integrated circuit (IC)*. **2.** A theoretical possibility, according to some scientists, but not yet a practical reality: An IC manufactured by a laboratory process that mimics the way in which nature builds living organisms. A form of *artificial life*, harnessed for electronic and/or computing applications.

bioelectricity **1.** Electric currents in living tissues, generated by the organism and not applied by external means. **2.** The science or study of such currents.

bioelectrogenesis The study and application of electricity generated by living animals, including humans, in the powering and control of electronic devices.

bioelectronics Electronics in relation to the life sciences—especially the electronic instrumentation of biological experiments.

bioengineering **1.** The engineering of equipment, such as electron microscopes, electroencephalographs, centrifuges, irradiators, etc., for study and experimentation in the life sciences. **2.** The engineering of equipment, such as pacemakers, hearing aids, X-ray apparatus, shock-therapy units, etc., for aid or support-of-life processes.

biofeedback A technique in which changes in skin temperature and resistance are detected and displayed by an electronic device.

biofeedback monitor A system that provides an indication of skin temperature and resistance to a user. Because skin temperature and resistance are affected by emotions, such as fear, nervousness, anger, etc., these monitors might be of value to people who wish to gain improved control of their emotions, and thus perhaps minimize the physiological effects of stress.

biological robot Believed by some researchers to be possible, but not yet a practical reality: A living organism created by biological cloning, whose brain has been programmed exactly as a computer is programmed.

biological shield An absorbent shield that blocks or attenuates ionizing radiation to protect personnel working near radioactive materials.

bioluminescence **1.** The emission of light by a living organism. **2.** The light itself so produced by living organisms.

biomechanism An electromechanical device that simulates the workings of some part of a living being's body. Examples are electromechanical hands, arms, and legs. Such a device is often difficult to distinguish from its biological counterpart when obscured by clothing.

biomechatronics   A contraction of the words *biology*, *mechanics* and *electronics*. Research, development and manufacturing that encompasses aspects of all three fields. This is especially important in robotics.

biometrics   Mathematics, and in particular, statistics and probability, applied to biology.

bionics   The study, design, and application of microelectronic systems that simulate the functions of living organisms.

biotelemetry   The use of telemetry to collect data from living organisms or to direct their movement.

biotelescanner   An instrument that monitors body functions via radio, from a great distance.

Biot/Savart law   A principle of electromagnetism that expresses the intensity of magnetic field H in the vicinity of a long, straight wire carrying a steady current I. The basic formula is $H = 2I/r$, where H is in oersteds, I is in amperes, and r is the distance in centimeters from the wire.

bip   Abbreviation of *binary image processor*.

biphase half-wave rectifier   An alternative term for FULL-WAVE RECTIFIER; also, each leg of a two-diode full-wave rectifier.

BIPM   Abbreviation of *International Bureau of Weights and Measures*.

bipolar   The condition of possessing two pole sets. In a conventional (non-FET) transistor, one pole set exists between the base and collector, and another pole set exists between the base and emitter.

bipolar driving unit   A magnetic headphone or loudspeaker in which both poles (north and south) of a magnet actuate a diaphragm or lever.

bipolar operation   See AUTOMATIC POLARITY.

bipolar transistor   A two-junction transistor whose construction takes the form of a pnp or an npn "sandwich." Such devices are current-operated, compared with field-effect transistors, which are voltage-operated. The bipolar transistor (of which the familiar npn and pnp types are examples) uses both electron and hole conduction.

biquinary code   A variety of binary-coded-decimal notation in which seven bits are used to represent each decimal digit. A number is written in two groups of bits: a two-bit group followed by a five-bit group. The positional values are 5 and 0 for the two-bit group, and 4, 3, 2, 1, and 0 for the five-bit group.

biquinary decade   A decade counter that consists of a binary stage, followed by a quinary stage.

bird   **1.** Slang for orbiting SATELLITE. **2.** Slang for *guided missile*.

birdie   **1.** A spurious beat note in a superheterodyne receiver. So called because of the characteristic chirping sound it makes as the operator

tunes by the frequency on which it occurs. **2.** A parasitic oscillation in a radio transmitter, also called a *spurious emission* or *spur*.

Birmingham wire gauge   Abbreviation, BWG. Also called *Stubs gauge*. A method of designating the various sizes of solid wire. BWG diameters are somewhat larger than corresponding AMERICAN WIRE GAUGE diameters for a given wire-size designator.

bismuth   Symbol, Bi. A metallic element. Atomic number, 83. Atomic weight, 209.

bismuth flux meter   A flux meter in which the sensor contains a length of bismuth wire, which acts as a magnetoresistor.

bismuth thermocouple   A thermocouple that uses the junction between bismuth and antimony wires. Used in thermocouple-type meters.

bistable   Having two stable states.

bistable device   Any device, such as a flip-flop, the operation of which exhibits two stable states and which can be switched at will from one state to the other.

bistable multivibrator   A multivibrator, the operation of which exhibits two stable states. More commonly known as a FLIP-FLOP. These circuits are abundant in digital electronic equipment. Compare ASTABLE MULTIVIBRATOR and MONOSTABLE MULTIVIBRATOR.

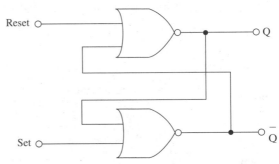

bistable multivibrator

bistable relay   A relay that has two stable states: open and closed. Successive actuating pulses open and close the relay, two consecutive pulses being required to return the relay to a given state. Also called *binary relay*, *relay flip-flop*, and *electromechanical flip-flop*.

bistatic radar   A radar set in which the transmitting and receiving antennas are separate.

bistate   Having two states. Example: the performance of a FLIP-FLOP.

bit   An acronym formed from the words *binary digit*. The smallest or elementary unit of data in digital electronics. Represented either by logic 0 (low) or logic 1 (high). These states can be represented by any dichotomy, such as off/on, false/true, minus/plus, dark/bright, red/green, etc.

BIT   Abbreviation of *built-in test.*

bit density   The number of digital bits per unit area or volume, as the number of bits per square centimeter of magnetic tape.

BITE   Abbreviation of built-in test equipment.

bit rate   The speed in BITS PER SECOND (bps) at which digital data bits are transmitted or handled.

bit-slice processor   A microprocessor whose word or byte capacity is achieved through the use of interrelated smaller capacity processors (e.g., a 16-bit unit derived from eight 2-bit "slices").

bits per second   Abbreviation, bps. An expression of digital data speed. Commonly used in computer communications. This unit is often confused with, and improperly called, the *baud.* There is generally a difference between the speed of a signal in baud, and the speed of the same signal in bps. Compare BAUD.

bitter pattern   A pattern produced in a suspension of ferromagnetic powder in the presence of an imperfection in a magnet. The pattern appears as an irregularity that is easy to see.

Bjerknes' equation   An expression for the total (primary plus secondary) decrement of a tuned circuit, based on measurements of the tank current at the resonant frequency and at a frequency near resonance.

BK   **1.** Radiotelegraph signal for BREAK. **2.** Abbreviation of BREAK-IN.

Bk   Symbol for BERKELIUM.

black-and-white   Also called *monochrome* and *gray-scale.* Any system of image reproduction, transmission, or reception in which the image is composed of opaque elements (black) and white or bright areas, as in noncolor television reception.

black area   An area in which there is only an encrypted signal.

blackboard system   A method via which computers can recognize, and to some extent determine the meaning of, spoken words and visual images. Incorporates machine vision and/or machine hearing in conjunction with artificial intelligence (AI). Incoming voices and/or images are digitized and entered into a large-capacity random-access memory (RAM). The data is evaluated by sophisticated software to determine the most logical or probable interpretations of the sounds and images.

blackbody   An ideal surface or object, that completely absorbs energy of any wavelength that strikes it. Such an object is a theoretically perfect radiator of energy at all wavelengths.

blackbody radiation   Electromagnetic radiation from a heated ideal BLACKBODY. This radiation is conceived as covering the entire ELECTRO-MAGNETIC FREQUENCY SPECTRUM. It can be expressed graphically as a characteristic curve with a peak at a wavelength that depends on the absolute temperature of the object. As the absolute temperature increases, the peak occurs at progressively shorter wavelengths (higher frequencies). This enables radio astronomers to get a reasonably good idea of the temperatures of distant celestial objects, such as planets.

black box   **1.** Any "box" or "block" that can be included in an analysis or synthesis based upon the BLACK-BOX CONCEPT. **2.** Any functional unit (such as a module) whose operating characteristics are known, and that can be inserted into a system in development or maintenance operations. **3.** Any subcircuit or stage that can be specified in total as required in a system, in terms of its known or prescribed performance, but whose internal structure need not be known.

black-box concept   A technique for development of equivalent circuits and of considering their operation. The "box" has a pair of input terminals and a pair of output terminals; one input terminal is often common to one output terminal. The contents of the box need not be known, but from the input and output current and voltage relationships, its nature can be determined. Moreover, from the available input signal and desired output signal, the internal circuit of the box can be specified. Integrated circuits (ICs) are often treated as black boxes by engineers designing complex electronic equipment.

black compression   Attenuation of the level of dark areas in a television picture.

blacker than black   The video-signal amplitude region above the level that just darkens the screen. Signal information (such as control pulses) in this region are therefore not seen.

black light   **1.** Ultraviolet radiation—especially when used to cause visible fluorescence in certain materials. **2.** A lamp that produces a principal portion of its radiation in the ultraviolet region, causing visible fluorescence of certain substances. Such lamps are used in some scientific experiments, and also for creating special effects at presentations or parties. It is hazardous to look directly at the output of such a lamp with unprotected eyes.

blackout   **1.** A complete interruption of ac utility power to numerous customers at the same time. **2.** A complete cessation of ionospheric radio-wave propagation, such as might be caused by a solar flare. **3.** Complete blanking of the screen of an oscilloscope or picture tube.

black reference   In a television signal, the blanking level of pulses, beyond which the sync pulse is in the *blacker-than-black* region.

black reference level   In a television signal, the voltage threshold of the BLACK REFERENCE (i.e., its level above zero volts).

black transmission   A system of picture or facsimile transmission in which the maximum copy darkness corresponds to the greatest amplitude (in an amplitude-modulated transmitter) or the lowest instantaneous frequency (in a frequency-modulated transmitter). Compare WHITE TRANSMISSION.

blank **1.** A piezoelectric plate cut from a quartz crystal, but not yet finished to operate at a desired frequency. **2.** To obscure or interrupt a signal or electron beam (usually momentarily), as in z-axis blanking in an oscilloscope. **3.** A silicon wafer cut from a large slab, containing dopants only. **4.** A magnetic diskette or tape on which nothing is recorded. **5.** An optical diskette on which nothing is recorded. **6.** A location (such as a symbol or space) that is used to verify proper data character grouping and values.

blanketing A form of radio interference accompanied by severe degradation of reception, virtually unaffected by tuning, over a wide range of frequencies. An example is ac line noise caused by an arcing power transformer or electrical appliance in the vicinity of a receiving antenna. It tends to occur most often at low, medium, and high frequencies.

blanking Obscuring or momentary elimination of a signal (see BLANK, **2**).

blanking interval The short period during which the electron beam of a cathode-ray tube is cut off so that the beam can return to its start position without creating a trace on the screen.

blanking level The discrete, predetermined level (usually a threshold voltage) at which BLANKING occurs.

blanking pedestal In the horizontal pulse of a television signal, the lower portion between zero volts and the blanking level.

blanking pulse A pulse that produces momentary blanking (see BLANK, **2**).

blanking time The time interval during which the electron beam of a cathode-ray tube is interrupted by a blanking signal.

blank tape **1.** Magnetic tape that has never been subjected to the recording process and that is substantially free from noise. **2.** Magnetic tape from which all preexisting information has been erased.

blasting **1.** Severe overloading of a sound system, usually caused by setting the volume control at or near maximum and then applying a significant input signal to the amplifier. Accompanied by distortion, in its worst form, it can cause damage to speakers and/or headsets. **2.** In a communications receiver, the result of a strong signal coming in unexpectedly when the automatic gain control (AGC) has been switched off, and the audio-frequency (AF) and radio-frequency (RF) gain controls are set high for reception of weak signals.

bleeder A resistor or group of resistors, used permanently to drain current from charged capacitors. It establishes the predetermined initial load level for a power supply or signal source, and it serves as a safety device in high-voltage power supplies.

bleeder current The current normally flowing through a bleeder.

bleeder divider A network of resistors, series-strung across the output of a power supply or its regulator. As a load resistor, the bleeder improves regulation and protects against no-load voltage surges. The resistor junctions allow various voltages to be drawn from the supply.

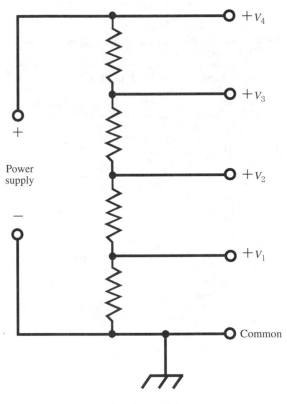

bleeder divider

bleeder power Power dissipated as heat in a bleeder.

bleeder resistor See BLEEDER.

bleeder temperature The operating temperature in a bleeder. It is generally high because of power dissipation in the form of heat.

bleeding whites A flowing of the white areas of a television picture into the black areas; an overload condition.

blemish See BURN.

blind flight The flying of aircraft entirely by means of instruments and electronic communications.

blind landing Landing of an aircraft entirely by means of instruments and electronic commnications.

blind zone **1.** In radar operations, an area that gives no echoes. **2.** Skip zone (see ZONE OF SILENCE).

blip **1.** The pulse-like figure on a radar scan, indicating the transmission or reflection (see A-SCAN and J-SCAN). Also called PIP. **2.** In visual alignment of a tuned circuit using a sweep generator and marker generator, the pulse or dot produced on the response curve by the marker signal. **3.** A short, momentary signal pulse, such as a single Morse dot.

BLIP Abbreviation for *background-limited infrared photoconductor.*

blip-scan ratio The number of radar scans necessary to show a visible blip, or echo, on a radar screen.

Bloch functions Solutions of the *Schrodinger wave equation* for a single electron surrounded by an electric field. The field varies periodically with distance from the source.

Bloch wall The transition layer between adjacent ferromagnetic domains (see DOMAIN).

block **1.** A group of data words or digits. **2.** A group of memory storage spaces. **3.** A circuit that operates as an identifiable unit. **4.** The symbol for a circuit, stage, unit, or device in a BLOCK DIAGRAM.

block diagram A simplified diagram of an electronic system, in which circuits, stages, units, or devices are shown as two-dimensional boxes with the internal wiring and detail circuitry omitted. This makes it possible to clearly show the interconnection among circuits, stages, units or devices. It also provides a concise rendition of the overall functional concept of the system.

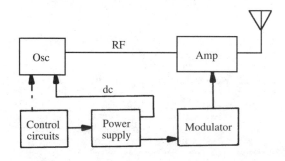

**block diagram
(of a radio transmitter)**

blocked impedance The input impedance of a transducer, whose output load is a theoretically infinite impedance.

blockette In a computer, the subdivision of a character block that is handled as a unit during data transfer.

blocking action Obstruction of circuit action, usually abrupt, through internal action or by the application of an external signal. Thus, the operation of an amplifier can be blocked (output reduced to zero) by an input signal or by excessive feedback, either of which overloads the input.

blocking capacitor A capacitor inserted into a circuit to prevent the passage of direct current while easily passing alternating current.

blocking choke Any inductor, such as a choke coil, that is used to prevent the flow of an alternating current while allowing direct current to pass with little resistance.

blocking interference Radio interference from signals strong enough to reduce the receiver output through blocking action.

blocking oscillator An oscillator that turns itself off after one or more cycles. It does this as a result of an accumulation of negative charge on its input electrode (base of a bipolar transistor or gate of a field-effect transistor). The action is repetitive. In the self-pulsing type of blocking oscillator, a series of pulses consisting of trains of sine waves with intervening spaces is generated. In the single-swing type of blocking oscillator, the output consists of a series of single cycles with long intervals between them.

blocking oscillator synchronization **1.** In the BLOCKING OSCILLATOR used in the vertical deflection circuit of a television receiver, the oscillator is synchronized with vertical sync pulses arriving in the video signal. **2.** Synchronization of the repetition rate of any blocking oscillator with a suitable external control signal.

blocking system In a telephone system, a method of dealing with the condition of having more subscribers than connection paths. Allocation is made on a demand basis. If all channels are in use, it is impossible to make new calls. This prevents excessive degradation of the quality of existing connections.

block length The number of characters, bits, or words that compose a defined unit word or character group.

block transfer The conveyance of a word or character grouping in a computer register to another register or a peripheral device.

blooming On a cathode-ray-tube (CRT) screen, an enlargement of the electron-beam spot, caused by poor focusing. This results in poor image resolution.

blooper **1.** A radio receiver that is in oscillation, and is transmitting a signal that causes interference. **2.** A parasitic oscillation in a radio transmitter. **3.** In broadcasting, a statement in which a radio or television announcer makes an embarrassing error or breach of etiquette.

blow   The opening of a fuse or circuit breaker as a result of excessive current.

blower   A fan used to remove heat from electronic circuits. These are often used in tube-type radio-frequency (RF) power amplifiers, where much heat is generated, and in computers to cool the microprocessor and surrounding components.

blowout   **1.** An alternate term for BURNOUT. **2.** The forceful opening of a circuit breaker. **3.** The extinguishing of an arc.

blowout coil   An electromagnet that provides a field to extinguish an arc.

blowout magnet   A permanent magnet that provides a field to extinguish an arc.

blst   Abbreviation of *ballast.*

blue-beam magnet   In a color television picture-tube assembly using three electron guns, a small permanent magnet to adjust the static convergence of the beam for blue phosphor dots.

blue box   An accessory device (sometimes unlawfully used) that generates tones that switch a telephone circuit in the placing of calls.

blue glow   **1.** In a neon lamp, a bluish light that results from high-voltage arcing. 2. The normal color of the gas discharge in an argon glow lamp. **3.** The bluish glow between anode and cathode of a gassy vacuum tube. **4.** The normal color of the discharge that fills a mercury-vapor tube.

blue gun   The electron in a three-gun color picture tube, the beam from which strikes the blue phosphor dots.

blueprint   **1.** A type of contact-print reproduction in which a sheet of sensitized paper is exposed to an image on a translucent or transparent film, under strong light, and is then developed and fixed. Although this process is still used to reproduce electronic illustrations and type-scripts, it has been superseded largely by other (dry) processes. **2.** Loosely, any plan or design for the development of a system.

blue restorer   In a three-gun color television circuit, the dc restorer in the blue channel.

blue ribbon program   A computer program that has been hand-prepared and debugged completely before its first computer run.

blue video voltage   The signal voltage presented to the grid of the blue gun of a three-gun color picture tube.

blurring   **1.** BLOOMING. **2.** A defocusing of a television picture or oscilloscope trace. **3.** An obscuring of a signal by echoes or trailing (e.g., the slow decrement of a Morse code signal element).

B-minus   Also called *B-negative.* The negative terminal of a B-power supply.

BNC   Abbreviation of *bayonet Neill-Concelman.* A type of coaxial connector that can be quickly connected and disconnected. It is commonly used with test equipment.

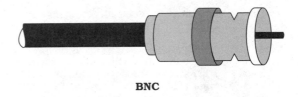

BNC

B-negative   Alternative expression for B-MINUS.

BNL   Abbreviation of *Brookhaven National Laboratory.*

BO   Abbreviation of *beat oscillator.* Also abbreviated BFO.

board   **1.** A panel containing patch jacks. **2.** A printed circuit.

boat   A type of crucible in which a semiconductor material is melted and sometimes processed. The material of which the boat is made (e.g., graphite) does not react with or contaminate the semiconductor material.

bobbin   **1.** A usually nonmetallic spool on which a coil is wound. **2.** The form onto which the voice coil of a loudspeaker is wound.

Bode plot   A pair of curves plotted to the same frequency axis, one showing the gain of a network or amplifier and the other showing its phase shift. Phase and amplitude of active and passive networks can be exhibited. Also called *Bode curve* and *Bode diagram.*

body-antenna effect   The tendency of the human body to act as a receiving antenna when a finger is touched to the antenna input terminal of a receiver or when a hand (or the whole body) is brought close enough to the circuit to provide capacitive coupling.

body capacitance   Capacitance between the body of the operator (as one plate of an equivalent capacitor) and a piece of electronic equipment (as the other plate). This phantom capacitance is often the cause of detuning and of the injection of interfering signals and noise because the body acts as a pickup antenna.

body electrode   **1.** An electrode attached to the human body (or to the body of a laboratory animal) to conduct body-generated currents to an instrument, as in cardiography, electroencephalography, and myography. **2.** An electrode attached to the human body (or to the body of a laboratory animal) to conduct currents into the body, as in shock therapy and skin-resistance measurement.

body leakage   Leakage of current through the bulk or body of a dielectric material, as opposed to SURFACE LEAKAGE.

body temperature   In a thermistor, a rating that represents the temperature measured on the surface of the device. It is any combination of ambient temperature, power dissipation, and operation of the internal heater element (if the thermistor has one).

bof   Abbreviation of *barium oxide ferrite.*

boffle A loudspeaker enclosure consisting of stretched screens that are sound absorbing and elastic.

bogie Also called *bogey*. **1.** The exact value of a specified characteristic. Thus, if resistance is given as 1 kΩ ±0.5%, the bogie value is 1 kΩ. **2.** The average value (i.e., the ARITHMETIC MEAN). **3.** A false or unidentified echo on a radar screen.

Bohr atom The concept of the nature of the atom, proposed by Niels Bohr in 1913 partly to explain why the electrons in the Rutherford atom do not fly off into space or fall into the nucleus. The Bohr theory places the electrons in permissible orbits where they cannot radiate energy (see BOHR RADIUS). They can radiate or absorb energy, however, if they go to a lower orbit or to a higher orbit, respectively. Compare RUTHERFORD ATOM.

Bohr radius Symbol, a_0. A physical constant whose value is approximately 5.291772×10^{-11} meter.

boiling point Abbreviation, bp. The temperature at which a liquid vaporizes. The boiling point of water in air at a pressure of one atmosphere is 100°C or 212°F.

bolometer Any device that is essentially a small, nonrectifying, temperature-sensitive resistor that can be used for heat sensing, radio-frequency power measurement, curve changing, demodulation, circuit protection, etc. Included in this category are the BARRETTER, the THERMISTOR, and the wire-type FUSE.

bolometer bridge A dc bridge in which a bolometer is one of the four arms. The bridge is balanced first with the bolometer cold. The bolometer then is excited with a radio-frequency (RF) current, whereupon the resultant heating changes the bolometer resistance. The bridge is rebalanced for the new resistance. The RF power driving the bolometer is determined according to a predetermined function of bridge settings versus RF input power.

Boltzmann constant Symbol, k. A figure that enters into the calculation of thermionic emission and of thermal noise factor. It represents the temperature equivalent of work function, in electron volts per Kelvin (eV/K) or joules per Kelvin (J/K). The values are approximately:

$$k = 8.617 \times 10^{-5} \text{ eV/K} = 1.38 \times 10^{-23} \text{ J/K}$$

Boltzmann's principle A description of the statistical distribution of large numbers of tiny particles under the influence of a force, such as an electric or magnetic field. When the system is in statistical equilibrium, the number of particles in any portion of the field is given by:

$$N_E = N_0 e^{-E/kT}$$

where E is the potential energy of a particle in the observed area, N_0 is the number of particles per unit volume in a part of the field where E is zero, k is the BOLTZMANN CONSTANT, T is the absolute temperature of the system of particles, and e is approximately equal to 2.718.

bombardment The usually forceful striking of a target with rays or a stream of particles.

bond **1.** An area in which two or more items are securely and intimately joined. **2.** The attractive force that holds an atomic or subatomic particle or particle group together.

bonded-barrier transistor A bipolar transistor in which the connection at the base region is alloyed.

bonded negative-resistance diode A diode that displays a negative-resistance characteristic over part of its current curve. This results from avalanche breakdown.

bond energy In a molecule, the energy necessary to break an atomic bond.

bonding **1.** The formation of bonds between adjacent atoms in a crystalline material, such as a semiconductor. See specifically COVALENT BINDING FORCES, IONIC BINDING FORCES, and METALLIC BINDING FORCES. **2.** The secure fastening together of conducting surfaces, as by soldering or brazing, to produce a high-conductance, leak-free continuum.

bond strength The minimum stress required to separate a material from another to which it is bonded.

bone-conduction transducer A device used in place of the earphone in a hearing aid to convey sound energy to the bone structure of the head.

Bongard problem A method of evaluating how well a machine vision system can differentiate among patterns. Similarities and differences are noted between objects in two sets of boxes. It was developed for object-recognition systems, mainly for use in intelligent robots.

book capacitor A variable capacitor in which the metal plates are bonded along one edge and separated from each other by means of mica sheets. The capacitance is varied by opening and closing the assembly book fashion. It is used as a padder or trimmer.

Boolean algebra A system of symbolic logic. Statements are represented as symbols, usually variables such as x, y, and z. The logical AND operation is represented by multiplication; the logical inclusive OR operation is represented by addition; the logical NOT operation is repre-

Boolean truth table

x	y	AND xy	NOT x	OR $x + y$
0	0	0	1	0
0	1	0	1	1
1	0	0	0	1
1	1	1	0	1

sented by a minus sign or a line over the element symbol. The system has rules, definitions and axioms via which *theorems* can be derived. Used by engineers in the design of digital electronic circuits.

Boolean function   In mathematical logic, a function that makes use of BOOLEAN ALGEBRA.

Boolean theorems

1. $x + 0 = x$ (additive identity)
2. $x1 = x$ (multiplicative identity)
3. $x + 1 = 1$
4. $x0 = 0$
5. $x + x = x$
6. $xx = x$
7. $(x')' = x$ (double negation)
8. $x + x' = 1$
9. $x'x = 0$
10. $x + y = y + x$ (commutativity of addition)
11. $xy = yx$ (commutativity of multiplication)
12. $x + xy = x$
13. $xy' + y = x + y$
14. $x + y + z = (x + y) + z = x + (y + z)$
    (associativity of addition)
15. $xyz = (xy)z = x(yz)$ (associativity of multiplication)
16. $x(y + z) = xy + xz$ (distributivity)
17. $(x + w)(y + z) = xy + xz + wy + wz$ (distributivity)

boom   **1.** A horizontal support for a microphone, enabling the microphone to be suspended over a sound source, but out of the sight of a camera. **2.** A horizontal support for a small antenna that is undergoing tests or sampling the field of another antenna. **3.** The supporting element in a Yagi, quad, or log-periodic antenna. It establishes the center of gravity and directional axis of the radiation pattern. The driven element(s) and parasitic element(s) are attached, usually at right angles.

boost capacitor   In the damper circuit of a television receiver, the capacitor that is used to boost the B-plus voltage. Also called *booster capacitor*.

boost charge   A high-current, short-interval charge used to revitalize a storage battery quickly. Also called *booster charge*.

booster   **1.** Any device used to increase the amplitude of a signal (e.g., as an amplifier or preamplifier) or of an energy source (e.g., to boost the output of a power supply). **2.** A radio-frequency preamplifier used ahead of a television receiver.

booster battery   **1.** A battery used to forward bias a diode detector into a favorable region of its conduction curve, or to bias a bolometer into the square-law region of its response. **2.** A battery supplying power to a booster.

booster gain   The amplification (usually in terms of voltage gain) provided by a booster (see especially BOOSTER, **2**).

boot   **1.** The powering-up routine in a digital computer, in which the machine executes a series of programs to get itself ready for use. **2.** The resetting of a computer, by pressing certain keyboard keys (e.g., CTRL-ALT-DEL), pressing a reset button, or by powering-down, waiting about two minutes, and then powering-up again. **3.** To install a computer diskette and instruct the computer to execute one or more programs on the diskette. **4.** A usually flexible protective nipple or jacket pulled over a cable or connector, so called from its resemblance to a foot boot.

boot loader   A form of computer program that operates on the BOOTSTRAP ROUTINE.

bootstrap   A technique for making a device or process achieve a condition through its own actions; see BOOTSTRAP CIRCUIT, for example.

bootstrap circuit   A specialized form of follower circuit that presents very high input impedance. Its chief feature is the return of the control-element resistor to a tap on the source or emitter resistor. The technique takes its name from the figurative notion that such a circuit "lifts its input impedance by its own bootstraps."

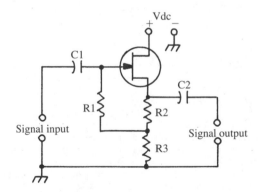

bootstrap circuit
(with junction-type field-effect transistor)

bootstrap routine   **1.** Also called *bootstrap program.* In a digital computer, and especially in a personal computer, the routine that the machine follows when first powered-up. See BOOT, **1. 2.** In a digital computer, a routine in which the first few instructions put in storage are later used to complete the routine, as supplemented by some operator instruction. **3.** A portion of a computer program that is used to establish an alternate version of the program.

borax-aluminum cell   An electrolytic cell that consists essentially of an aluminum electrode and a lead electrode in a saturated solution of sodium tetraborate (borax). After electroforming, such a cell can be used either as a rectifier or as an electrolytic capacitor.

boric acid   Formula, H_3BO_3. A compound used variously in electronics—especially as the electrolyte in electrolytic capacitors.

bornite   Formula, Cu_5FeS_4. A natural mineral that is a sulfide of copper and iron. Its crystalline structure made it important in early semiconductor diodes (crystal detectors).

boron   Symbol, B. A metalloidal element. Atomic number, 5. Atomic weight, 10.82. It is used as a dopant in semiconductor processing.

bot   **1.** Abbreviation for *beginning of tape.* **2.** Abbreviation of *bottom.*

bottoming   Excessive movement of the cone of a loudspeaker or the diaphragm of a headphone so that the magnet or supporting structure is struck by the moving-coil piston assembly. It produces a clapping sound, particularly on bass (low-frequency) audio peaks.

bounce   **1.** The springback or vibration of the armature of a relay on closure. **2.** An abnormal, abrupt change in the brightness of the image in a television receiver or cathode-ray-tube (CRT) computer monitor.

boundary   **1.** In a polycrystalline substance, the area of contact between adjacent crystals. **2.** The area of meeting of two regions (such as n and p) in a semiconductor.

boundary defect   A condition in which a piezoelectric crystal has two regions, intersecting in a plane, with different polarizations.

boundary effect   In audio systems, a phenomenon in which the proximity of an acoustic transducer to a flat surface enhances the pickup and/or transmission of sound. Occurs because of reflection of acoustic waves from the surface.

bound charge   The portion of the electric charge on a conductor that does not escape to ground when the conductor is grounded. This occurs because of induction from neighboring charge carriers. Compare FREE CHARGE.

bound electron   An electron held tightly in its orbit within an atom so that it is not ordinarily free to drift between atoms and contribute to electric current flow.

bow-tie antenna   A center-fed antenna in which the two horizontal halves of the radiator are triangular plates that resemble a bow tie. A flat reflector consisting of closely spaced horizontal wires is mounted behind the triangles.

bow-tie test   An oscilloscope-display checkout of a single-sideband (SSB) signal, in which the appearance of the display indicates the signal quality. The transmitter output signal is fed to the vertical deflection plates of the oscilloscope. The exciter audio output is fed to the horizontal sweep input of the scope.

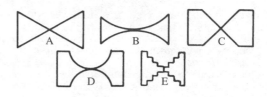

bow-tie test

boxcars   Long pulses with short separating spaces between them.

box-shaped loop   The characteristic square-loop hysteresis curve (B-H loop) that result when a sine wave of current is used to magnetize a sample of magnetic material. In this plot, which covers all four quadrants, the horizontal axis (H) displays magnetizing force, and the vertical axis (B) displays magnetization. Also see HYSTERESIS.

Boys radiomicrometer   A detector for radiant energy. The device consists of a thermocouple and a galvanometer. When energy falls on the thermocouple, a voltage is produced, and this is measured by the galvanometer.

bp   **1.** Abbreviation of BOILING POINT. **2.** Abbreviation of BANDPASS.

bpi   Abbreviation of *bits per inch.*

B-plus   Also called *b-positive.* **1.** Symbol, B+. The positive dc voltage required for certain electrodes of vacuum tubes, transistors, etc. **2.** The positive terminal of a B power supply.

B positive   See B-PLUS.

B power supply   A name used sometimes for the unit that supplies high-voltage dc energy to a vacuum tube plate or screen circuit.

bps   Abbreviation of BITS PER SECOND.

Br   Symbol for BROMINE.

bracketing   A troubleshooting routine characterized by isolating progressively smaller areas in a circuit or chain of stages until the defective subcircuit or stage is located.

Bradley detector   A locked-oscillator circuit that was once used as an FM detector.

braid   **1.** A woven network of fine metal wires used for grounding purposes. It is usually made of fine copper conductors. The increased surface-area-to-volume ratio improves the conductivity, at radio frequencies, over a single conductor that has the same cross-sectional area. Braid can be tinned (saturated with solder) to retard corrosion. **2.** It is also called a *shield.* The outer conductor in prefabricated coaxial cable.

braided wire   A length of braid. Used for grounding or shielding purposes.

brain waves   Alternating or pulsating voltages that are caused by electrical activity in the brain of an animal or human being. The voltages can be picked up by electrodes attached to the scalp, and amplified to be viewed on a cathode-ray-tube

(CRT) screen, heard by headphones or speakers, or traced by an electroencephalograph.

branch **1.** Any one of the separate paths of a circuit. With respect to the layout of its components, a branch can be series, parallel, series-parallel, parallel-series, or any combination of these. It is also called a LEG. **2.** See BRANCH CIRCUIT.

branch circuit In electrical wiring, a group of outlets served through a single cutout from a source of power-line ac voltage. The source can be a distribution center, subdistribution center, main, or submain. Interior lighting circuits are usually branch circuits because many lights are connected to one circuit controlled by a single fuse or circuit breaker.

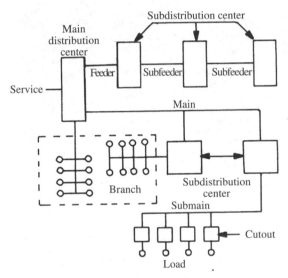

**branch circuit
(enclosed in broken lines)**

branch current Current flowing through a branch of a circuit, whose magnitude, with respect to the total current of the circuit depends on the nature of the branch.

branched In molecular polymers, the condition of side chains being attached to the main chain.

branched windings Forked windings of a polyphase transformer.

branching In robotics and artificial intelligence (AI), a set of routines or programs containing points at which a computer must select from among two or more alternatives. Such routines are used in critical processes, such as the manufacture of precision equipment.

branch point See JUNCTION POINT.

branch voltage The voltage, or voltage drop, across a branch of a circuit.

brass **1.** An alloy of copper and zinc that is widely used in electronics. Compared to annealed cop-

per, this metal has four times the resistivity (or ¼ the conductivity), half the temperature coefficient, more than twice the tensile strength, and a lower melting point (900°C). **2.** A colloquialism for an old-fashioned, straight telegraph key.

brass pounder **1.** Colloquialism for telegraph operator or radiotelegraph operator. **2.** A radio amateur who handles large amounts of message traffic, particularly via Morse code. **3.** A radio amateur proficient in Morse code operation.

Braun electroscope An electroscope consisting essentially of a fixed metal vane to which a movable needle is fastened at a pivot. The repulsion between the two, when an electric charge is applied, causes the needle to move over a calibrated scale.

bravo Phonetic representation of the letter B.

brazing The joining of two metal (usually iron or steel) parts together with a suitable melted copper-alloy metal. Compare SOLDERING.

breadboard **1.** A perforated board, a chassis, or any basic framework on which electronic components can be mounted and quickly wired for the preliminary test of a circuit. It is so called because the first such foundation units of this sort actually were wooden breadboards. **2.** Any preproduction electronic prototype circuit. **3.** To set up a circuit on a breadboard.

breadboard model **1.** The preliminary model of an electronic device, often built on a breadboard (see BREADBOARD, 1). **2.** Loosely, any prototype.

break **1.** An open circuit. **2.** To open a circuit. **3.** In communications, a word indicating a desire to transmit on a wavelength already occupied by radio traffic. **4.** See BREAK-IN, 1.

break-before-make contacts Contacts, especially in a rotary selector switch, that open one circuit before closing the next one.

breakdown **1.** Failure of a circuit or device, caused mainly by excessive voltage, current, or power. A sudden high current, however, does not always indicate failure. **2.** AVALANCHE BREAKDOWN. **3.** The separation of an electronics problem or project into its constituent parts for an easier solution.

breakdown diode See ZENER DIODE.

breakdown region The region, in a pn junction, in which avalanche breakdown occurs.

breakdown strength See DIELECTRIC STRENGTH.

breakdown voltage **1.** The voltage at which current suddenly passes in destructive amounts through a dielectric. **2.** The voltage at which a gas suddenly ionizes, as in a gas tube. **3.** The voltage at which the reverse current of a semiconductor junction suddenly rises to a high value (nondestructive if the current is limited). See AVALANCHE BREAKDOWN.

break-in **1.** A technique of radio communication in which one station interrupts a transmission from another station, rather than waiting until the end of the latter's transmission. **2.** Also called *full break-in.* In a radio communications transceiver or transmitter/receiver combination, extremely rapid transmit/receive switching, approaching *full duplex* communications. Every pause in transmission, even of only a few milliseconds, creates a "receive window" allowing reception between spoken words or Morse code elements. **3.** BURN-IN.

breaking current   The momentary current that flows when the contacts of a switch or relay are broken.

break-in keying   A system of radiotelegraph keying in which the receiver is in operation whenever the key is open. See BREAK-IN, **2.**

break-in operation   In radiotelegraph or single-sideband (SSB) communications, the practice of interrupting at any time to "talk back" to the other transmitting station. This operation is made possible by high-speed transmit/receive switching. See BREAK-IN, **2.**

break-in relay   An electromechanical or solid-state relay that enables break-in operation. Largely supplanted by solid-state switching devices.

breakover point   In a silicon-controlled rectifier, the source-voltage value at which the load current is suddenly triggered to its steep climb. Also called TRIGGERING POINT.

breakover voltage   In a silicon-controlled rectifier with open gate circuit, the anode voltage at which anode current is initiated.

breakpoint   A point in a computer program when, for the purpose of obtaining information for the program's analysis, the sequence of operations is interrupted by an operator or a monitor program.

breakpoint frequencies   The upper- and lower-frequency points at which the gain-versus-frequency response of an amplifier or network departs from flatness.

breakpoint instruction   An instruction that stops a computer.

breakthrough   **1.** A new discovery, insight, or solution to a problem that results in an advancement in the state of the art. **2.** See PUNCHTHROUGH. **3.** See BREAKDOWN, **1. 4.** See AVALANCHE BREAKDOWN.

break time   The time taken for a relay to drop out completely or a switch to open. Compare MAKE TIME.

breathing   Slow, rhythmic pulsations of a quantity, such as current, voltage, brightness, beat note, etc.

breezeway   In a sync pulse in NTSC color television, the part of the back porch between the trailing edge of the pulse and the color burst.

B-register   An index register in a computer for storing words that are used to change an instruction before it is executed by the program.

Bremsstrahlung radiation   The radiation emitted by a charged particle whose speed is altered when it passes through the electric field in the vicinity of an atomic nucleus.

brevity code   A code not intended to conceal information, but to shorten the number of characters in a message or data file. The Q SIGNALS are an example of a brevity code used in communications. In computer data transfer and communications, brevity codes allow compression, speeding up the transfer rate and reducing the storage space for a given amount of data.

Brewster angle   From BREWSTER'S LAW, the polarizing angle at which the reflected and refracted rays of incident light are perpendicular to each other.

Brewster's law   (Sir David Brewster, 1781-1868). For any dielectric reflector, the relationship in which the refractive index is equal to the tangent of the polarizing angle.

bridge   **1.** A network, usually consisting of four branches, connected so that an input signal can be applied between two opposite points and the output taken between the other two opposite points. When the component values are in a certain ratio, the voltage between the output points is zero and the bridge is said to be *balanced* or *set to null.* **2.** A circuit, such as that described in **1,** used for electrical measurements. **3.** An audio or servo amplification system in which the load is driven from two oppositely polarized outputs, neither of which are at ground potential.

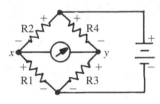

bridge, 1

bridge balance control   A potentiometer, variable capacitor, or variable inductor that is used to adjust a bridge circuit to balance.

bridge-connected amplifier   **1.** A dc amplifier stage in which the transistors and resistors are connected in a four-arm bridge circuit, with respect to dc. When the bridge is initially balanced, all dc is eliminated in the output load. The input signal unbalances the bridge, which results in an amplified output signal in the load. **2.** An amplifier pair having opposing outputs across which a load can be bridged to obtain twice the power output of either amplifier alone.

bridged differentiator   See HALL NETWORK.

bridge detector   The output-indicating device (e.g., meter, oscilloscope, or headphones) that indicates whether a bridge is balanced or unbalanced. Also called *null detector* or *null indicator.*

bridged integrator A null network that consists of a two-stage resistance-capacitance (RC) integrator circuit bridged by a capacitor. This network produces a shallow null at a single frequency determined by the R and C values in the integrator. Compare HALL NETWORK.

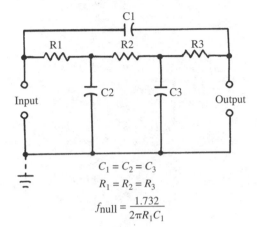

$$C_1 = C_2 = C_3$$
$$R_1 = R_2 = R_3$$
$$f_{null} = \frac{1.732}{2\pi R_1 C_1}$$

bridged integrator

bridged-tee attenuator An attenuator consisting of a tee section, between the input and output of which is bridged a single-series arm.

bridged-tee circuit Any circuit (of resistors, capacitors, inductors, or a combination of these) that consists of a tee section, bridged by a single-series section, from input to output.

bridged-tee null network A bridged-tee circuit of resistance (R) and capacitance (C), proportioned so that at some setting of the R and C values, the output of the circuit is zero.

bridged-tee oscillator A low-distortion oscillator circuit whose frequency is determined by a bridged-tee null network inserted into the negative-feedback path of the circuit.

bridge feedback A combination of current feedback and voltage feedback around an amplifier circuit. It is so called because, in the feedback circuit, the resistors and the output resistance of the amplifier form a four-arm bridge.

bridge generator The power source (e.g., a battery or oscillator) that supplies the signal to a BRIDGE used for electrical measurements.

bridge indicator See BRIDGE DETECTOR.

bridge oscillator See BRIDGE GENERATOR.

bridge rectifier A full-wave rectifier circuit in which four rectifying diodes are connected in a bridge configuration. Each half-cycle of ac input is rectified by a pair of diodes in opposite quarters of the bridge and in series with each other. The bridge does not require a transformer with

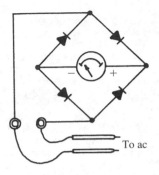

bridge rectifier

a center-tapped secondary, as does the FULL-WAVE, CENTER-TAP RECTIFIER circuit.

bridge source See BRIDGE GENERATOR.

bridge-type meter A frequency-sensitive bridge (such as the Wien bridge) that can be used to measure audio frequency. Because the bridge can be balanced at only one frequency at a time, its adjustable arm can be calibrated to read the frequency directly.

bridge-type impedance meter An impedance-measuring circuit in which unknown impedance Z is connected in series with a calibrated variable resistor R. An ac voltage is applied to the series circuit. The separate voltage drops across the resistor and impedance are measured successively as the value of R is varied. When the two voltage drops are identical, Z equals R, and the impedance can be read from a calibrated dial on the variable-resistor control.

bridge-type oscillator A resistance-capacitance (RC) tuned oscillator in which a Wien bridge is used as the frequency-determining circuit in the feedback loop.

bridge-type power meter **1.** See BOLOMETER BRIDGE. **2.** A four-arm bridge specially designed to operate at radio frequencies. At null, the impedance of the unknown is read directly from the balancing dial or calculated from bridge constants. This instrument is used to measure the impedance of circuit components, antennas, and transmission lines.

bridge-type SWR meter A four-arm bridge that is specially designed to operate at radio frequencies. At null, the standing-wave ratio (SWR) is calculated from the bridge resistance values or read from a direct-reading scale on the null-indicating meter.

bridging amplifier An amplifier whose input impedance is so high that it can be considered infinite for practical purposes. Thus, the amplifier can be connected across a load or line without significantly affecting the operation of the system.

bridging coupler A voltage-dependent resistor that permits an occasionally used device (such as a bell) to be connected permanently across a regularly used device (such as a telephone) without continuously short-circuiting the latter. Thus, the bridging coupler ordinarily has very high resistance; but when the line voltage is momentarily raised, the resistance lowers and the occasionally used device is actuated (e.g., the bell rings).

bridging gain   The gain of a bridging amplifier expressed as the ratio (in decibels) of the power developed in the amplifier load to the power in the load to which the input terminals of the amplifier are connected.

bridging loss   The loss that results from the shunting of a speaker, microphone, earphone, or other transducer by a resistor, capacitor, or inductor. Generally, the loss is expressed as a power ratio in decibels.

Briggsian logarithm   (Henry Briggs, 1556-1631). A base-10 logarithm, generally known as a COMMON LOGARITHM. Compare NAPIERIAN LOGARITHM.

brightness   SI unit, candela per square meter (cd/m^2); cgs unit, lambert (L). The quantity of light, per unit area, emitted or reflected perpendicular to a light-emitting surface.

brightness control   1. In a computer monitor, television receiver, or oscilloscope, a potentiometer that varies the negative bias voltage on the control grid of the cathode-ray tube (CRT). The brightness of the image is inversely proportional to this negative bias voltage. **2.** The control of the brightness of an illuminated area.

brilliance   See BRIGHTNESS.

brilliance control   1. The BRIGHTNESS CONTROL in a television receiver or computer monitor. **2.** The brightness control in a cathode-ray oscilloscope. **3.** A control for adjusting the level of the tweeter output in a speaker system.

British thermal unit   Abbreviation, Btu. The amount of heat required to raise the temperature of a pound of water by one degree Fahrenheit, in an ambient environment of slightly greater than 39°F.

broadband   Also called *wideband*. Possessing a characteristic wide bandwidth or range of operating frequencies. This term can be applied at audio frequencies (AF) or radio frequencies (RF), and is frequently used to describe the performance of oscillators, amplifiers, antennas, and various types of networks. The term can also be applied to describe the nature of electromagnetic emissions or noise. Examples are given in the following several definitions. Compare NARROWBAND.

broadband amplifier   An amplifier that has very wide frequency response, such as 10 Hz to 10 MHz. Examples are an instrument amplifier and a video amplifier.

broadband antenna   An antenna that operates satisfactorily over a comparatively wide band of

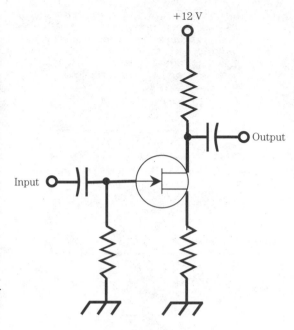

broadband amplifier

frequencies without requiring retuning at individual frequencies. Examples are the log-periodic and discone antennas.

broadband electrical noise   Electrical noise that is present over a wide frequency spectrum (e.g., 3 kHz to 30 MHz).

broadband I-F   An intermediate-frequency (IF) amplifier or amplifier chain. The wide frequency response is important when an increased bandpass is preferred to high selectivity, as in high-fidelity radio tuners.

broadband interference   Interference, other than noise, that is present over a wide band of frequencies. An example is over-the-horizon shortwave radar, recognizable by its characteristic "woodpecker" sound in communications receivers at high frequencies.

broadband Klystron   A Klystron oscillator with a broadbanded tuned circuit.

broadband tuning   Receiver tuning characterized by a selectivity curve having a pronounced flat top or broad nose that passes a wide band of frequencies. Also called *broadband response*.

broadcast   1. A radio-frequency transmission of an intelligence-bearing signal that is directed to numerous unspecified receiving stations. **2.** The transmission or dissemination of signals to a large, unspecified number of receiving stations.

broadcast band   Any band of frequencies allocated for broadcasting (see BROADCAST SERVICE, **1**), but particularly the U.S. standard amplitude-modulation (AM) and frequency-modulation (FM) radio broadcast bands at 535 to 1605 kHz (AM) and 88 to 108 MHz (FM).

broadcasting The dissemination of signals for reception by the general public, not for communications purposes.

broadcast interference Abbreviation, BCI. Interference to normal reception by broadcast receivers, usually arising from signals emitted by other stations.

broadcast receiver A receiver intended primarily to pick up standard broadcast stations. Also see BROADCAST BAND.

broadcast service **1.** Any radio transmitting service (including television) that exists for the purpose of sending out electromagnetic signals for general reception, rather than addressing them to specific receiving stations. **2.** The service provided by a station operating in the broadcast band.

broadcast station Any station in the broadcast service, but especially one assigned to operate in the standard U.S. broadcast bands. Also called *broadcasting station.*

broadcast transmitter A radio transmitter designed specifically for, and operated in, the broadcast service.

broad response Slow deflection of an indicator, such as a meter, over a relatively wide range of values of the input quantity.

broadside In a perpendicular direction; for example, broadside radiation from an antenna.

broadside array An antenna array so designed that maximum-signal radiation and response occur at right angles to the plane containing the antenna elements. Such an array can be unidirectional (main lobe in a single direction) or bidirectional (two main lobes in opposite directions).

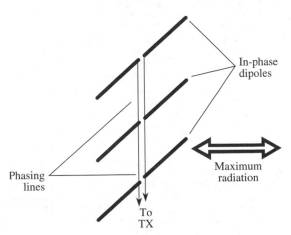

broadside array

broad tuning Tuning that is characterized by pronounced signal width, often resulting in ad-jacent-channel interference. A common cause of such impaired selectivity is low Q in the tuned circuit(s).

Broca galvanometer A device consisting of an astatic magnetic arrangement, with a coil enclosing central consequent poles. The device is characterized by fast response and high sensitivity.

bromine Symbol, Br. A nonmetallic element of the halogen family. Atomic number, 35. Atomic weight, 79.90.

bronze An alloy of copper and tin that has various uses in electronics. Also see PHOSPHOR BRONZE.

Brown and Sharpe gauge See AMERICAN WIRE GAUGE.

Brownian movement (Robert Brown, 1773-1858). Random movement of microscopic particles—especially in solutions. It occurs because of collisions of molecules with the particles. Einstein showed, in his early work, a connection between this movement and the *Boltzmann constant.*

brownout A deliberate lowering of line voltage by a power company to reduce load demands. Minor events of this type often pass unnoticed by the average consumer. More pronounced events produce observable effects, such as shrinkage of television and cathode-ray-tube (CRT) computer-display images.

Bruce antenna A vertical collinear array that consists of several resonant sections connected by short, rigid, parallel-conductor stubs. The currents in the radiating sections are in phase. Maximum radiation and response occur broadside to the antenna (omnidirectional in the horizontal plane). Polarization is vertical. The antenna produces gain at low radiation and response angles, and is commonly used in repeater installations and fixed communications stations at very-high frequencies (VHF) and ultra-high frequencies (UHF).

brush A usually metal or carbon strip, blade, or block, that slides in contact with another part, as in a motor commutator.

brush discharge Also called *Saint Elmo's fire.* A cloud of repelled ions around the tip of a pointed conductor charged to a high voltage. It often produces a visible glow in the air.

brush holder The housing for a brush in a motor, generator, rheostat, slip-ring junction in a rotating data-transmission system, etc.

brute force **1.** The transmission of a signal of excessive or unnecessary power. **2.** An inefficient approach to a problem, which might solve the problem, but requires far more energy, effort, or computer memory/storage space than the minimum needed to accomplish the same result.

brute-force filter A pi-type lowpass dc power supply filter, so called because of the extremely large inductances and capacitances that are generally used.

brute supply An unregulated power supply.

B-scope   A cathode-ray tube (CRT), used in radar, that presents a B DISPLAY.

B service   A teletype communication system operated by the Federal Aviation Administration (FAA).

B-supply   The dc power supply that provides anode operating voltages, such as plate and screen voltages in a vacuum-tube radio-frequency (RF) power amplifier.

BT-cut crystal   A piezoelectric plate cut from a quartz crystal at an angle of rotation (relative to the x-axis) of -49°. It has a zero temperature coefficient of frequency at approximately 25°C. Also see CRYSTAL AXES and CRYSTAL CUTS.

Btu   Abbreviation of BRITISH THERMAL UNIT.

BuAer   Abbreviation of *Bureau of Aeronautics*.

bubble memory   In digital-computer practice, a special type of static magnetic memory. The magnetic material is divided into regions that are magnetized in different directions. So called because the flux lines of the tiny magnetized regions are shaped somewhat like, and move around after the fashion of, bubbles on the surface of a glass of soda.

bubble shift register   A shift register that uses a magnetic bubble (see BUBBLE MEMORY) that can be moved sequentially from electrode to electrode on a wafer.

bubbling   See MOTORBOATING.

bucket   A computer memory or a designated location in such a memory.

bucking   The process of counteracting one quantity, such as a current or voltage, via series or parallel application of a similar quantity that has opposite polarity (180 degrees out of phase).

bucking circuit   **1.** A circuit used to obtain bucking action. The simplest form is a battery and potentiometer that supply a variable voltage of polarity opposite to that of the voltage to be bucked. A more sophisticated form is an ac transformer, the secondary of which is connected in series and out of phase with the ac utility line. **2.** The zero-set circuit in an electronic voltmeter.

bucking coil   A coil placed and positioned so that its magnetic field partially or completely cancels the field of another coil. Troublesome hum fields sometimes are neutralized with such a coil.

bucking voltage   See BACK VOLTAGE, **2.**

buckling   The warping of storage-battery plates, usually resulting from excessive charge or discharge.

buckshot   In an amplitude-modulated (AM) or single-sideband (SSB) radio transmission, broadband signal splatter caused by excessive modulation, or detuned multiplier circuits.

buffer   **1.** An amplifier used principally to match two dissimilar impedance points and isolate one stage from a succeeding one in a cascaded system, and thus to prevent undesirable interaction between the two. **2.** In a digital computer, a

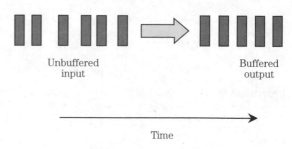

Unbuffered input

Buffered output

Time

buffer, 2.

storage site used temporarily during data transfers to compensate for differences in data flow rates. **3.** In digital-computer operations, a follower stage that is used to drive a number of gates without overloading the preceding stage.

buffer amplifier   See BUFFER, **1.**

buffer capacitor   A high-voltage fixed capacitor that is placed across a transformer secondary to suppress voltage spikes and sharp waveforms—especially when the input is a square wave.

buffer circuit   **1.** In a data system that uses a keyboard, an electronic circuit that allows the operator to type ahead of the data output. **2.** See BUFFER, **1, 2** and **3.**

buffered output   An output (power, signal, etc.) that is delivered from the generating device through an isolating stage, such as a buffer amplifier. This arrangement protects the device from variations in the external load. Compare UNBUFFERED OUTPUT.

buffer storage   **1.** A buffer that is used to interface between data systems with different rates of transmission. **2.** See BUFFER, **2.**

bug   **1.** Slang for WIRETAP, **1. 2.** Slang for circuit fault, **1. 3.** A semiautomatic key that some radiotelegraph operators use to send Morse code.

bug key   See BUG, **3.**

building-block technique   The process of assembling electronic equipment by quickly connecting together already completed stages (in the form of boxes or blocks) and supplying power and signals to the setup. Also called *modular technique* and *modular construction*.

building-out circuit   A short section of transmission line shunting another line; it is used for impedance matching. Also called *building-out section*.

buildup   **1.** The process whereby the voltage of a rotating generator starts at a point that is determined by the residual magnetism of the machine, and gradually increases to a voltage representing the point at which the resistance line crosses the magnetization curve. **2.** The (usually gradual) accumulation of a quantity (e.g., the buildup of charge in a capacitor).

bulb   A globe-like container having any of a number of characteristic shapes from spherical to tubular and usually evacuated, for enclosing the elements of an electron device, such as a vacuum tube, gas tube, photocell, or lamp.

bulge **1.** A nonlinear attenuation-versus-frequency curve in a transmission line. **2.** A localized non-linearity in a function.

bulk The body or mass of a semiconductor specimen, as opposed to junctions within the specimen. Current flows through a junction, but it can also flow, more or less, through the mass of semiconductor wafer into which the junction has been formed.

bulk effect An effect, such as current, resistance, or resistivity, observed in the overall body of a sample of material, as opposed to a region within the material or on its surface. Thus, a silicon diode can display junction resistance (i.e., resistance offered by a junction processed in a wafer of silicon), as well as bulk resistance (i.e., the effective resistance of all paths around the junction, through the mass of the wafer). Compare SURFACE EFFECT.

bulk-erased tape Recording tape whose signal content has been removed via a bulk eraser.

bulk-erase noise **1.** The residual magnetic impulses that remain on a magnetic tape after it has been bulk-erased. **2.** Noise generated by bulk-erased tape when the latter passes through deenergized record or erase heads in a tape machine.

bulk eraser A type of power-line-frequency degausser that erases an entire reel of magnetic tape without requiring that the tape be unreeled and passed continuously under an erase head. This saves considerable time, but often leaves some BULK-ERASE NOISE on the tape. Also called BULK DEGAUSSER.

bulletin board In personal computing or amateur packet communications, a system that allows subscribers to leave messages for each other for access via a *modem* or *terminal node controller.*

bulletin station A station intended for the transmission of bulletins of interest to certain parties, such as military personnel or amateur radio operators. An example is W1AW in Newington, Connecticut, an amateur radio station that transmits bulletins and code practice.

buncher In a Klystron, a cavity resonator that contains two grids mounted parallel to the electron stream. The electrostatic field of the grids alternately accelerates and retards the electrons, velocity-modulating the stream into bunches.

buncher grids In a Klystron, the closely spaced grids that velocity-modulate the electron beam into successive bunches.

buncher resonator In a velocity-modulated tube, such as a Klystron, the input cavity resonator.

buncher voltage The radio-frequency (RF) grid-to-grid voltage in the buncher resonator of a Klystron.

bunching The production of electron bunches in a velocity-modulated tube, such as a Klystron. Also see BUNCHER.

bunch stranding A technique for combining several thin wires into a single thick wire. Often used in guy wires and electrical conductors to improve tensile strength and flexibility. At radio frequencies, bunch stranding also improves electrical conductivity by increasing the ratio of surface area to cross-sectional area. This minimizes losses caused by *skin effect.*

Bunet's formula A formula for calculating the inductance of a multilayer air-core coil that has a diameter less than three times the length:

$$L = a^2 N^2 / (9a + 10l + 8.4c + 3.2cl/a)$$

where N is the number of turns, a is the average coil radius, c is the winding thickness, and l is the length of the coil.

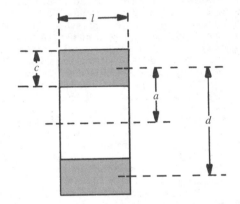

Bunet's formula

Bunsen cell A cell consisting of a zinc rod in a sulfuric acid solution contained in a porous pot, which is in a nitric acid solution. The zinc rod serves as the negative pole; the positive pole is a piece of hard carbon. The cell produces about 1.9 volts and delivers relatively high current.

burden See VOLTAGE BURDEN.

burn **1.** A blemish on the screen of a cathode-ray tube (CRT), caused by destruction of the phosphor there. This results from prolonged focusing of an intense electron beam in one spot. **2.** A blemish on the screen of a television picture tube, usually resulting from ions that reach the screen when the ion trap is not working correctly.

burn-in A long, thorough, carefully controlled preliminary test of a component, device, or system, to stabilize its electrical characteristics after manufacture and to ensure that it will function according to rated specifications. An important test for equipment whose reliability must be guaranteed, such as an emergency communciations transceiver.

burnout **1.** Failure of a conductor or component caused by overheating from excess current or voltage. **2.** The open-circuiting of a fuse. **3.** Electrical failure of any type.

burst **1.** The abrupt ionization of the gas in an ionization chamber by cosmic rays. **2.** An abrupt increase in the amplitude of a signal. Also, the type of signal that results from burst action. **3.** See COLOR BURST.

burst amplifier In a color-television receiver, the amplifier that separates the burst pulse from the video signals and amplifies the former. See COLOR BURST.

burst gate timing In a color-television receiver, the timing of the gating pulse with the input signal of the burst amplifier.

burst generator A signal generator delivering a burst output (see BURST, **2**) for testing various types of equipment. Its output is intermediate between sine waves and square waves, and is convenient for rapidly appraising the performance of such devices as amplifiers, filters, electronic switches, transducers, and loudspeakers.

burst transmission A short transmission at high speed. This method of transmission saves time, but increases the necessary bandwidth of a signal by the same factor as the ratio of the high speed to the original speed.

bus **1.** A main conductor in a circuit. A bus can be high in the sense that its potential is above or below ground, or it can be low or at ground reference. **2.** In computer operations, a common group of paths over which input and output signals are routed.

bus driver A buffering device designed to increase the driving capability of a microprocessor, which itself might be capable of driving no more than a single load.

business machine Any piece of electronic or electromechanical equipment used mainly, or entirely, for business purposes. Examples are photocopiers, facsimile (fax) machines, printers, and computers.

busing The parallel interconnection of circuits.

busy test A check conducted to find out whether or not a certain telephone subscriber line is in use.

busy tone Also called *busy signal.* An intermittent tone that indicates that the subscriber line being called is in use.

Butler oscillator An oscillator that consists of a two-stage amplifier with a quartz crystal in the positive-feedback path from output to input.

butterfly capacitor A plate-type variable capacitor that has two stator sections and a single rotor section common to the two stators. External connections are made to the stators only. Thus, no wiping contact is required to the rotor, and the troubles associated with such a contact are

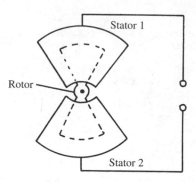

butterfly capacitor

avoided. The butterfly capacitor is actually two variable capacitors in series. The unit is so called from the shape of its rotor.

butterfly circuit A combination of a butterfly capacitor and a ring, of which the stator plates of the capacitor are an integral part. The resulting structure is a compact variable-frequency tuned circuit. The ring supplies the inductance, and the butterfly supplies the capacitance. It is also called *butterfly tank* and *butterfly resonator.*

Butterworth filter A high-pass, low-pass, band-pass or band-rejection filter, characterized by a flat passband (absence of passband ripple) and high attenuation at frequencies far removed from the passband.

Butterworth function A mathematical function that is used in the design of a BUTTERWORTH FILTER.

button **1.** Usually, a small switch that is actuated by finger pressure. It is also called pushbutton and pushbutton switch. Sometimes, the term is applied only to the insulated knob or pin which is pushed to operate the switch. **2.** A tiny lump of impurity material, placed on the surface of a semiconductor wafer for alloying with the wafer to form a junction. See ALLOY JUNCTION. **3.** The carbon element(s) in a BUTTON MICROPHONE.

button capacitor A button-shaped ceramic or silvered-mica fixed capacitor. Because of its disk shape and mode of terminal connection, it offers very low internal inductance.

button microphone A microphone in which a button-shaped carbon element is attached to a diaphragm, which is set into vibration by sound waves. This motion causes the button resistance to vary, modulating a direct current that passes through the button. A single-button microphone has only one button, whereas a double-button microphone has two—one mounted on each side of the center of the diaphragm.

buzz **1.** A low-pitched rough sound with high-frequency components, usually the result of elec-

Single button

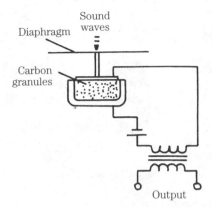

Double button

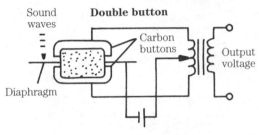

button microphone

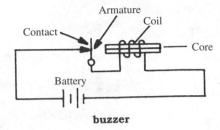

buzzer

trical interference from nonsinusoidal voltages generated by neighboring equipment or devices. **2.** The waveform associated with such a sound. **3.** Fastening two conducting surfaces by a KEL-LIE BOND.

buzzer A nonringing device used principally to generate sound other than that achievable with sine waves. In an electromechanical vibrating-reed buzzer, the reed acts as an armature, which is mounted close to the core of an electromagnet. At quiescence, the reed rests against a stationary contact. When voltage is applied to the electromagnet, the reed is attracted to the core, moving away from the contact; but this breaks the circuit, the magnetism ceases, and the reed springs back to the contact. The action is repeated continuously at a frequency that depends on the reed dimensions and its distance from the core.

BV Abbreviation of BREAKDOWN VOLTAGE.

B voltage The dc voltage required by certain electrodes of vacuum tubes and transistors. It especially pertains to voltages required by the plate and screen of a vacuum tube, as opposed to the filament voltage and control-grid voltage.

bw **1.** Abbreviation of *bandwidth*. **2.** Abbreviation of *black-and-white*.

BWA Abbreviation of *backward-wave amplifier*.

BWG Abbreviation of BIRMINGHAM WIRE GAUGE.

BWO Abbreviation of BACKWARD-WAVE OSCILLATOR.

BX Symbol and abbreviation for armored and insulated flexible electrical cable.

bypass A route (either intended or accidental) through which current easily flows around a component or circuit instead of through it.

bypass capacitor A capacitor that is used to conduct an alternating current around a component or group of components. Often the ac is removed from an ac/dc signal, the dc being free to pass through the bypassed component.

B-Y signal In a color television receiver, the color-difference signal which, when combined with a luminance (Y) signal, forms a blue primary signal for the three-gun picture tube.

byte In digital-computer and data-communications operations, a unit of data consisting of eight contiguous bits. In packet communications, the term *octet* is often used.

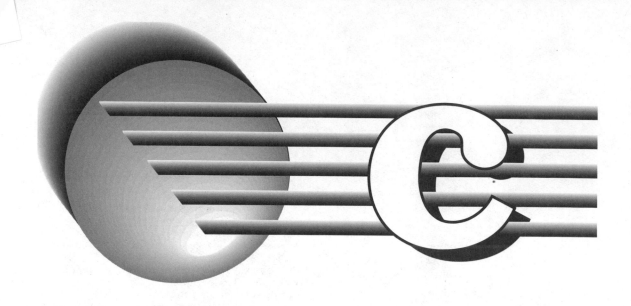

C 1. Abbreviation of CAPACITANCE. **2.** Symbol for COLLECTOR of a transistor. **3.** Symbol for CARBON. **4.** Abbreviation of CELSIUS. **5.** Symbol for COULOMB. **6.** Abbreviation of CALORIE.

c 1. Abbreviation of CENTI. **2.** Abbreviation of CENTS. **3.** Symbol for CAPACITANCE. **4.** Symbol for SPEED OF LIGHT in a vacuum.

Ca Symbol for CALCIUM.

cabinet An enclosure for a piece of apparatus. It might or might not incorporate electromagnetic shielding.

cable 1. A usually flexible (but sometimes rigid) medium, via which electrical power or signals are transferred. Although the term is occasionally applied to a single conductor, especially when it is a braid or weave of a number of wires, cable usually means a bundle of separate, insulated wires or strands of fiberoptic material. **2.** CABLEGRAM.

cable address A code word that specifies the recipient of a CABLEGRAM.

cable assembly A special-purpose cable with connectors.

cable attenuation Reduction of signal intensity along a cable, usually expressed in decibels per foot, hundred feet, mile, etc.

cable capacitance Capacitance between conductors in a cable or between conductors and the outer sheath of a cable. **2.** Sometimes, capacitance between a cable and earth.

cable clamp A support device for cable runs in equipment and systems.

cable communications Telegraphy or telegraphy via a (usually undersea) cable.

cable connector A connector, such as a coaxial fitting, that joins cable circuits or connects a cable to a device.

cabled wiring Insulated leads connecting circuit points; they are tied together with lacing cord or with spaced fasteners.

cablegram A (usually printed) message transmitted or received via undersea cable. Compare RADIOGRAM and TELEGRAM.

cable loss See CABLE ATTENUATION.

cable run The path taken by a cable.

cable splice 1. An electrical attachment between two sections of cable that has identical or similar construction, with or without the use of connectors. **2.** To electrically attach two sections of cable that have identical or similar construction, with or without the use of connectors.

cable tie A short piece of wire or plastic that holds wires or cables in a bundle.

cable TV See COMMUNITY-ANTENNA TELEVISION.

cache memory A short-term, high-speed, high-capacity computer memory. Similar to a scratch-pad or read-write memory.

CAD Acronym for *computer-aided design.*

CAD/CAM Acronym for *computer-aided design and manufacturing.*

cadmium Symbol, Cd. A metallic element. Atomic number, 48. Atomic weight, 112.41. Many electronic structures are cadmium plated for protection.

cadmium borate phosphor Formula, $(CdO + B_2O_3)$: Mn. A substance used as a phosphor coating on the screen of cathode-ray tubes. The characteristic fluorescence is green-orange.

cadmium cell Also called *Weston standard cell.* An electrochemical standard cell used as a reference voltage source. Produces 1.0186 volt at 20°C.

cadmium plating The process of coating a conductor or component with cadmium to increase its resistance to corrosion.

cadmium selenide photocell A photoconductive cell in which cadmium selenide is the light-sensitive material.

cadmium silicate phosphor Formula, $(CdO + SiO_2)$. A substance used as a phosphor coating on the screen of cathode-ray tubes; the characteristic fluorescence is orange-yellow.

cadmium standard cell See STANDARD CELL.

cadmium sulfide photocell A photoconductive cell in which cadmium sulfide is the light-sensitive material.

cadmium tungstate phosphor Formula, $CdO + WO_3$. A substance used as a phosphor coating on the screen of cathode-ray tubes; the characteristic fluorescence is light blue.

cage A completely shielded enclosure, such as a screen room, which is covered with a grounded fine-mesh conductive screen on all sides.

cage antenna An antenna, usually center-fed and balanced, that consists of multiple parallel conductors arranged in a cylindrical cage configuration. The cage results in a much broader bandwidth than is the case with an antenna made up of a single conductor. Cage antennas are typically used at frequencies between about 10 and 200 MHz.

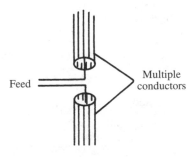

Feed / Multiple conductors

cage antenna

CAI Abbreviation for *computer-assisted instruction*.

CAL An acronym for *conversional algebraic language*, a general-purpose problem-oriented computer programming language used in time-sharing systems.

calcium Symbol, Ca. A metallic element of the alkaline-earth group. Atomic number, 20. Atomic weight, 40.08.

calcium phosphate phosphor Formula, $Ca_3(PO_4)_2$. A substance used as a phosphor coating on the screen of long-persistence cathode-ray tubes; the characteristic fluorescence is white, as is the phosphorescence.

calcium silicate phosphor Formula, $(CaO + SiO_2)$: Mn. A substance used as a phosphor coating on the screen of cathode-ray tubes; the characteristic fluorescence ranges from green to orange.

calcium tungstate phosphor Formula, $CaWO_4$. A substance used as a phosphor coating on the screen of short-persistence cathode-ray tubes; the characteristic fluorescence is blue, as is the phosphorescence.

calculate To perform the steps of an intricate mathematical operation. Compare COMPUTE.

calculating punch A data-processing peripheral that reads punched cards, makes calculations, and punches new data into those cards or new cards.

calculator A machine that performs mathematical operations, especially arithmetic. Typically, the device is a small box with buttons and a miniature numeric display. Used only in mathematical applications. In contrast, a COMPUTER can be used for a much wider variety of jobs, such as word processing, graphics, and database. Many personal computers have calculator programs; the "buttons" are actuated by pointing and clicking with a mouse.

calculus **1.** The symbology and rules comprising a system of logic, such as BOOLEAN ALGEBRA. **2.** A branch of mathematical analysis concerned with rates of change and accumulation. See DIFFERENTIAL CALCULUS and INTEGRAL CALCULUS.

calendar age The age of a piece of equipment, measured since the date of manufacture. Specified in years, months, and days. The actual manufacture date might alternatively be given.

calendar time The time available in a working period [i.e., a 40-hour work week represents a calendar time of 120 hours (five days times 24 hours per day)].

calibrate To compare and bring into agreement with a standard.

calibrated measurement **1.** A measurement made with an instrument that has been calibrated with a standard reference source. **2.** A measurement that is corrected for instrument error.

calibrated meter An analog or digital meter that has been adjusted to agree as closely as possible with a reference source.

calibrated scale **1.** A scale whose graduations have been carefully checked for accuracy (i.e., they correspond to the true values of the quantity that they represent). The scale is graduated to read directly in units of the quantity, such as milliamperes, kilohertz, volts, etc. **2.** A scale with fixed, plain numeric graduations (e.g., 0 to 100) that do not directly indicate the magnitude of a quantity, but that can be converted to various quantities via graphs, nomographs, tables, or charts. See CALIBRATION CURVE.

calibrated sweep In an oscilloscope, a sweep circuit calibrated to indicate sweep frequency or time at all control settings.

calibrated triggered sweep In an oscilloscope, a triggered sweep circuit calibrated in terms of sweep time or frequency.

calibration **1.** Determining the accuracy with which an instrument indicates a quantity. **2.**

Determining the degree to which the response of a circuit or device corresponds to desired performance. **3.** Marking a scale to show actual values of a quantity in the form of a direct readout. For example, the scale of an analog meter might be calibrated in milliamperes (mA) from 0 to 50 in increments of 1 mA.

calibration accuracy 1. A quantitative expression of the agreement between the value of a quantity, as indicated by an instrument, and the true value. Usually expressed as the maximum percentage of the true value by which the indicated value can be expected to deviate in either direction (e.g., ±0.5 percent). **2.** The precision of a direct-reading meter in terms of its full-scale deflection (e.g., ±2.0 percent of full scale).

calibration curve A graph showing the relation between the actual values of a quantity and the setting or indication of an instrument or component. Usually plotted in rectangular coordinates.

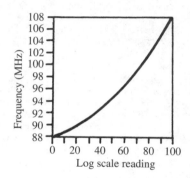

calibration curve

calibration marker A pip or blip, superimposed on a pattern displayed on a cathode-ray-tube (CRT) screen, to identify a point closely as to frequency, voltage, distance, or some similar term.

calibrator A device used to perform a calibration (e.g., a signal generator).

calibrator crystal A highly accurate and stable quartz crystal, used in an oscillator as a frequency standard. An example is the 100-kHz crystal oscillator and harmonic generator used in some communications receivers.

californium Symbol, Cf. A radioactive element produced artificially. Atomic number, 98. Atomic weight, 251.

call 1. In communications, a transmission by a station for the purpose of either alerting a particular receiving station for which there is a message, or alerting all receiving stations to prepare them for a general broadcast message. **2.** In a computer program, a branch to a closed subroutine; also, to branch to such a subroutine.

call direction code Abbreviation, CDC. In telegraph networks, a special code that, when transmitted to a terminal, causes the teleprinter to be automatically switched on.

calling sequence 1. Computer program instructions needed to establish the conditions for a call (see CALL, **2**). **2.** Subroutine instructions providing a link to the main program.

call instruction A computer program instruction that makes a program controller branch to a subroutine; it also locates and identifies the parameters needed for the subroutine's execution. Also known as *subroutine call*.

call letters Letters and/or numbers assigned to, and used to identify, licensed radio stations.

calorie Abbreviation, cal or C. The amount of heat energy, at a pressure of 1 atmosphere, that will raise the temperature of 1 gram of water by 1 degree Celsius.

calorimeter An instrument for measuring heat energy. By adaptation, a calorimeter can be used to measure radio-frequency (RF) power—especially at microwave frequencies (see CALORIMETRIC POWER METER).

calorimeter system See CALORIMETRIC POWER METER.

calorimetric power meter A specialized form of wattmeter, in which the power to be measured is dissipated in an oil or water bath that has a known and fixed mass. The wattage is determined indirectly, by measuring the extent to which the temperature of the liquid increases in a certain amount of time.

CAM 1. Abbreviation of *computer-aided manufacturing*. **2.** Abbreviation of *content-addressed memory*.

cambric Finely woven cotton or linen used for insulation. One type of spaghetti (conductor insulation), for example, is varnished cambric tubing.

camera cable A multiwire cable that conducts the video signal from a television camera to control equipment.

camera chain In television, the camera and the equipment immediately associated with it, excluding the transmitter and its peripherals.

camera signal The output signal delivered by a television camera.

camera tube Any video pickup tube, such as an iconoscope or orthicon, that converts light reflected by a scene into a corresponding television signal.

Campbell bridge A circuit that is used for comparing mutual inductance with capacitance.

camp-on In a telephone system, a method of engaging a line that is busy until it becomes available for use.

CAN Abbreviation of CANCEL CHARACTER.

can 1. A metal enclosure or container roughly resembling a tin can (though not necessarily cylindrical), used for shielding or potting components. **2.** Colloquial expression for HEADPHONE.

Canada balsam A transparent cement derived from the turpentine distilled from balsam fir resin. It is useful in optical technology and in certain areas of electro-optics.

Canadian Standards Association The Canadian equivalent of the *National Bureau of Standards* in the United States. An agency that publishes agreed-on standards for industries.

cancel character 1. IGNORE CHARACTER. 2. A control character indicating that the associated data is erroneous.

cancellation The elimination of one quantity by another, as when a voltage is reduced to zero by another voltage of equal magnitude and opposite sign.

candela Symbol, cd. The SI unit of luminous intensity; 1 cd represents $\frac{1}{60}$ of the radiating power of one square centimeter of a perfect radiator at the temperature of freezing platinum.

candle Abbreviation, c. Also called *international candle*. A unit of light intensity that is the value of emission by the flame of a sperm-whale-oil candle burning at the rate of 7.776 grams per hour.

candle power Abbreviation, cp. Luminous intensity in international candles: the luminous intensity resulting from the burning of a sperm-whale-oil candle at 7.776 grams per hour.

candoluminescence White light produced without extreme heat.

cannibalization The deliberate use of parts from operational equipment to temporarily repair or maintain other equipment: It is a last-resort, emergency measure.

cap 1. Abbreviation of CAPACITANCE. 2. Abbreviation of CAPACITOR.

capacimeter See CAPACITANCE METER.

capacitance Symbol, C. Unit, farad. The property exhibited by two conductors separated by a dielectric, whereby an electric charge becomes stored between the conductors. Capacitance is thought of as analogous to mechanical elasticity. Also see FARAD.

capacitance bridge A four-arm ac bridge for gauging capacitance against a standard capacitor. In its simplest form, it has a standard capacitor in one arm and resistors in the other three.

capacitance coupling The transfer of ac energy between two circuits or devices by a capacitor or capacitance effect. Also see COUPLING.

capacitance diode See VARACTOR.

capacitance divider An alternating-current voltage divider that uses capacitors, rather than resistors. It is used in certain oscillators, such as the Colpitts type.

capacitance filter A filter consisting of only a high-capacitance capacitor. Because the capacitor cannot discharge instantaneously, it tends to maintain its voltage and smooth out the ripples in the voltage applied to it.

capacitance-inductance bridge A combination ac bridge that can be used for either capacitance or inductance measurement. Both capacitance and inductance can be measured in terms of a standard capacitance; however, some of these bridges use standard inductors in the inductance-measuring mode.

capacitance meter A direct-reading meter for measuring capacitance. In most available types, a stable ac voltage is applied to the meter circuit, to which an unknown capacitor is connected in series; meter deflection is roughly proportional to the reactance of the capacitor. Also called MICROFARAD METER.

capacitance ratio In a variable capacitor, the ratio of maximum to minimum capacitance.

capacitance relay A relay circuit that operates from a small change in its own capacitance. It consists of an RF oscillator whose tank capacitance is very low. When a finger is brought near the circuit's short pickup antenna, the attendant increase in capacitance detunes the oscillator, activating the relay. Also called PROXIMITY RELAY and PROXIMITY SWITCH.

capacitance-resistance bridge A combination ac bridge that can be used for either capacitance or resistance measurement. The unknown resistance is measured against a standard resistor; the unknown capacitance against a standard capacitor.

capacitance sensor See CAPACITANCE TRANSDUCER.

capacitive amplifier See DIELECTRIC AMPLIFIER.

capacitive attenuator An ac attenuator whose elements are capacitors in any desired combination of fixed and/or variable units. The desired attenuation is afforded by the capacitance ratio.

capacitive coupling A means of coupling between circuits that uses a series capacitor for direct-current blocking. The signal passes through the capacitor, but the blocking effect allows different bias voltages to be applied to the two stages.

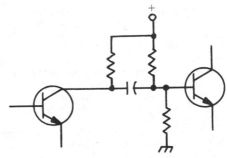

capacitive coupling

capacitive diaphragm A metal plate deliberately placed in a waveguide to introduce capacitive reactance and, thereby, cancel an inductive reactance.

capacitive-discharge ignition An electronic ignition system for automotive engines. Provides nearly constant high voltage, regardless of engine speed. A dc-to-dc step-up converter charges a large capacitor (typically to 300 volts) when the distributor breaker points are closed; when they are open, the capacitor discharges through the ignition coil, thereby generating an ignition pulse of several thousand volts.

capacitive division Reduction of an ac voltage by a capacitive voltage divider.

capacitive feedback Feeding energy back from the output to the input of an amplifier or oscillator through a capacitor.

capacitive-input filter A smoothing filter for ac power supplies, in which the element closest to the rectifier is a capacitor, regardless of the components or circuits placed subsequently.

capacitive load A load consisting of a capacitor or a predominantly capacitive circuit.

capacitive post A protrusion inside a waveguide for the purpose of introducing capacitive reactance to cancel an inductive reactance.

capacitive potentiometer See CAPACITIVE VOLTAGE DIVIDER.

capacitive proximity sensor A transducer used in mobile robots that detects the presence of certain kinds of objects. It consists of an oscillator whose frequency is determined by an inductance-capacitance (LC) circuit to which a metal plate is connected. When a conducting or partially conducting object comes near the plate, the mutual capacitance changes the oscillator frequency. This change is detected and sent to the robot controller.

capacitive reactance Symbol, X_C. Unit, ohm. The reactance exhibited by an ideal capacitor, considered as a negative pure-imaginary quantity; $X_C = -j/(6.28fC)$, where f is the frequency in hertz, C is the capacitance in farads, and j is the unit imaginary number (the square root of -1). Alternatively, f can be specified in megahertz and C in microfarads. In a pure capacitive reactance, current leads voltage by 90 degrees. Also see CAPACITANCE, CAPACITOR, and REACTANCE.

capacitive speaker See ELECTROSTATIC SPEAKER.

capacitive transducer A transducer consisting essentially of a refined variable capacitor whose value is varied by a quantity under test, such as pressure, temperature, liquid level, etc.

capacitive tuning Variable-capacitor tuning of a circuit.

capacitive voltage divider A capacitive attenuator usually consisting of two series-connected capacitors whose values are such that an applied ac voltage is divided across them in the desired ratio.

capacitive welding An electronic welding system in which energy stored in a capacitor is discharged through the joint to be welded. This develops the heat necessary for the operation.

capacitive window A pair of capacitive diaphragms used in a waveguide to introduce capacitive reactance.

capacitor A passive electronic-circuit component consisting of, in basic form, two metal electrodes or plates separated by a dielectric (insulator).

capacitor amplifier See DIELECTRIC AMPLIFIER.

capacitor antenna See CONDENSER ANTENNA.

capacitor bank A network of capacitors connected in combination, yielding a desired characteristic.

capacitor braking The connection of a capacitor to the winding of a motor after the removal of power, to speed up the process of braking.

capacitor color code See COLOR CODE.

capacitor decade See DECADE CAPACITOR.

capacitor-discharge ignition CAPACITIVE-DISCHARGE IGNITION.

capacitor filter In a direct-current power supply, a filter consisting simply of a capacitor connected in parallel with the rectifier output.

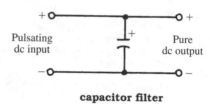

capacitor filter

capacitor-input filter A filter whose input component is a capacitor. The capacitor-input power-supply filter is distinguished by its relatively high dc output voltage, but somewhat poorer voltage regulation, compared with the CHOKE-INPUT FILTER.

capacitor leakage Direct current flowing through the dielectric of a capacitor. In a good nonelectrolytic capacitor, this current is normally less than 1 microampere. In an electrolytic capacitor, it can be up to several milliamperes, depending on the capacitance and the applied voltage.

capacitor loudspeaker See ELECTROSTATIC SPEAKER.

capacitor microphone See CONDENSER MICROPHONE.

capacitor motor An ac motor that uses a capacitor in series with an auxiliary field winding for starting purposes. Initially out-of-phase current in the auxiliary field (starting winding) causes a rotating field that turns the rotor. When the rotor reaches a safe speed, a centrifugal switch disconnects the capacitor and auxiliary field, and the motor continues running as an induction motor.

capacitor series resistance   The ohmic loss in a capacitor. It results partly from conductor losses, and partly from losses in the dielectric material.

capacitor substitution box   An enclosed assortment of selected-value capacitors arranged to be switched one at a time to a pair of terminals. In troubleshooting and circuit development, any of several useful fixed capacitance values can be thus obtained.

capacitor voltage   **1.** The voltage at the terminals of a capacitor. **2.** The maximum voltage rating of a capacitor.

capacitor voltmeter   See ELECTROSTATIC VOLT-METER.

capacity   **1.** A measure of a cell's or battery's ability to supply current during a given period. **2.** CAPACITANCE. **3.** The number of bits or bytes a computer storage device can hold. **4.** The limits of numbers that a register can process.

capacity lag   In an automatic control system, a delay caused by the storing of energy by the components. For example, in a heating system, capacity lag results from the time taken to heat the air or fluid after the thermostat turns on the heat.

capillary electrometer   A sensitive voltage indicator, consisting of a column of mercury in a transparent capillary tube, in which is suspended a small drop of acid. When a voltage is applied to both ends of the mercury column, the acid drop moves toward the low-potential end of the column over a distance proportional to the voltage.

capstan   The driven spindle or shaft of a magnetic tape recorder or transport.

capture area   The effective ability of a radio antenna to pick up electromagnetic signals. The larger the capture area, the greater the antenna gain.

capture effect   **1.** In frequency-modulation (FM) radio receivers, the effect of domination by the stronger of two signals, or by the strongest of several signals, on the same frequency. **2.** In an automatic-frequency-control system, the tendency of the receiver to move toward the strongest of several signals near a given frequency. **3.** In general, the tendency of one effect to totally predominate over other effects of lesser amplitude.

capture ratio   A measure of frequency-modulation (FM) tuner selectivity: The amplitude difference, in decibels, between unwanted signals and the one being tuned in.

carbon   Symbol, C. A nonmetallic element. Atomic number, 6. Atomic weight, 12.011. Carbon, besides being an invaluable material in electronics, is an important constituent of organic compounds.

carbon arc   The arc between two electrified pencils of carbon or, as in an arc converter, between a carbon pencil and a metal electrode.

carbon brush   A contact made of carbon or some mixture of carbon and another material, used in motors, generators, variable auto-transformers, rheostats, and potentiometers.

carbon-button amplifier   An audio-frequency amplifier having as the active component an earphone whose diaphragm is attached to a carbon microphone button. The input signal applied to the earphone makes its diaphragm vibrate. The vibrating button modulates a local direct current. Amplification results from the large ratio of modulated local current to input-signal current.

carbon/disk rheostat   A rheostat consisting of a stack of carbon disks or washers, arranged so that a controllable pressure can be exerted on the stack. As a knob is turned, a screw increases or decreases the pressure, varying the total resistance of the stack.

carbon-film resistor   A stable resistor whose resistance element is a film of carbon, vacuum-deposited on a substrate, such as a ceramic.

carbonization   The application of a coat of carbon onto an electrode, either by electroplating or by any other means.

carbon microphone   A microphone that includes one or two carbon buttons. See BUTTON MICROPHONE.

carbon-paper recorder   A recorder in which a signal-actuated stylus writes, by impression only, through a sheet of carbon paper onto a plain sheet underneath. This eliminates the need for an ink-carrying stylus.

carbon-pile regulator   A voltage regulator in which a stack of carbon disks or washers is in series with the shunt field. The pile resistance and field current depend on pressure applied to the pile by a wafer spring acting through a movable iron armature. Voltage drops increase the pressure and voltage rises decrease the pressure, thus regulating the generator with which it is associated.

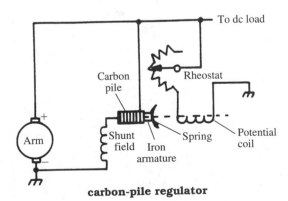

carbon-pile regulator

carbon-pile rheostat See CARBON-DISK RHEOSTAT.

carbon recording 1. A record made with a CARBON-PAPER RECORDER. 2. The use of a carbon-paper recorder in data acquisition, facsimile, communications, and similar applications.

carbon resistor A resistor made from carbon, graphite, or some composition that contains carbon.

carbon/silicon-carbide thermocouple A thermocouple that is a junction between carbon and silicon carbide.

carbon transfer recording A method of facsimile reception in which the image is reproduced by carbon particles sprayed on the paper, a process controlled by the received signal.

carbon-zinc cell See ZINC-CARBON CELL.

Carborundum Formula, SiC. Trade name for a synthetic silicon carbide used as a semiconductor, refractory, or abrasive. Also see SILICON CARBIDE.

Carborundum crystal Trade name for a characteristically superhard crystal of silicon carbide.

Carborundum varistor A voltage-dependent resistor made from Carborundum.

carcinotron A special kind of oscillator tube used at ultra-high and microwave frequencies.

card 1. A usually thin, rectangular board containing a PRINTED CIRCUIT, often equipped with an edge connector that makes it easy to install, remove, or replace. Common in electronic and computer equipment having modular construction. 2. The usually flat, thin insulating strip on which a resistor element is wound. 3. A thin (usually paper) board perforated with holes, according to a code, to store data (i.e., PUNCHED CARD).

card back The unprinted side of a punched card. Compare CARD FACE.

card bed In a punched-card machine, the device that holds the cards before they are punched or read.

card code The scheme whereby the holes in a punched card represent letters or numbers.

card column Punched card lines running parallel with the short edge; the columns that are punched with holes represent characters or numbers. Compare CARD ROW.

card face The printed side of a punched card.

card feed In a punched-card system, the mechanism that successively advances the cards.

card field The fixed columns on a punched card that contain the same type of information.

card fluff The paper burrs around the edges of holes in a punched card, often the cause of misfeeding or misreading.

card format A description of punched card content (usually specified by a program).

card image An exact, stored representation of all the characters (not holes) on a punched card. Compare BINARY IMAGE.

cardiac monitor An electronic device that displays or records electrical impulses from the heart for medical observation or diagnosis.

cardiac pacemaker An electrical cardiac stimulator that causes the heart to beat at certain intervals. Used when the patient has heart disease that prevents the heart from regulating itself.

cardiac stimulator An electronic device (sometimes implanted in the subject) that supplies electric pulses to stimulate heart action. Also called DEFIBRILLATOR and PACEMAKER.

card image In memory storage, the data contained on a single card.

cardiogram ELECTROCARDIOGRAM.

cardiograph ELECTROCARDIOGRAPH.

cardioid diagram A polar response curve in the shape of a cardioid pattern.

cardioid microphone A microphone with a (roughly) heart-shaped sound-field pickup pattern.

cardioid pattern A radiation/response pattern with one sharp null in the direction opposite the single main lobe. The lobe is extremely broad. In two dimensions, the curve is shaped somewhat like a "Valentine" heart.

cardiotachometer A device that indicates the pulse rate.

cardistimulator See CARDIAC STIMULATOR.

card jamming In a card reader, the accidental piling up of cards.

card loader A load routine for punched cards.

card machine A device that translates data into a punched-hole pattern on a card, or that reads the hole pattern on a previously punched card.

card pickup A photocell or feller contact that produces signals from holes in a punched card.

card-programmed Programmed (as a computer or instrument) by means of punched cards.

card punch A machine used to punch holes in (data) cards, according to a code, for the storage of data.

card punch buffer A temporary memory that holds card-punch control signals coming from a central processor.

card reader In a punched-card system, the device that picks up information from the holes in a punched card, and translates the data represented by the pattern of perforations into electrical pulses.

card reproducer An offline machine for duplicating punched cards.

card row On a punched card, a horizontal line of punching positions. Compare CARD COLUMN.

card sensing The conversion of card information into electrical impulses for use by a machine.

card stacker A machine that stacks punched cards in a deck after they have been punched or read.

card system A computer system in which the only input peripheral is a card reader and the only output peripherals are a card punch and printer.

card to card A method of punched-card duplication in which the duplicate is made at a terminal receiving the original card's data.

card-to-magnetic-tape converter A device that writes, as logical records on a magnetic tape, data it reads from punched cards.

card to tape **1.** The programmed transfer of punched-card data to magnetic tape. **2.** The programmed transfer of punched-card data to paper tape.

card track In a punched-card machine, the transport that carries cards from hopper to stacker (i.e., through reading and punching stations).

card verifier **1.** A punched-card machine that checks the accuracy of data on punched cards against a document containing the data; the process can be automatic or operator implemented. **2.** The human operator who checks card accuracy.

card wreck The jamming of punched cards being transported along the track in a punched-card machine.

Carey-Foster bridge A special version of the slide-wire bridge that is useful for measuring an unknown resistance, whose value is close to that of a standard resistance.

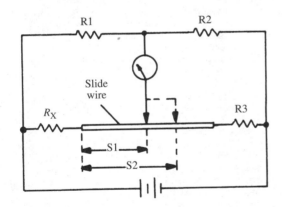

Carey-Foster bridge

Carey-Foster mutual inductance bridge An ac bridge that permits the measurement of mutual inductance in terms of a standard capacitor.

carnauba wax A wax obtained from the Brazilian wax palm. Used as an electrical insulator, and as the dielectric in some electrets.

Carnot theorem In thermodynamics, the proposition that in a reversible cycle, all available energy is converted into mechanical work. Also called *Carnot's principle.*

carrier **1.** See CARRIER WAVE. **2.** See CHARGE CARRIER.

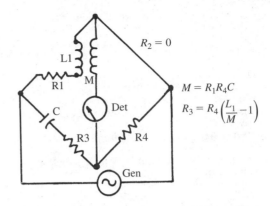

$$R_2 = 0$$
$$M = R_1 R_4 C$$
$$R_3 = R_4 \left(\frac{L_1}{M} - 1 \right)$$

Carey-Foster mutual inductance bridge

carrier amplifier See DIELECTRIC AMPLIFIER.

carrier beating **1.** The mixing of two radio-frequency carriers that are separated by a small amount of frequency, resulting in an audible tone in a receiver. **2.** A heterodyne in a facsimile or television signal, resulting in a pattern of cross hatches in the received image.

carrier choke A radio-frequency (RF) choke, inserted in a line to block a carrier component.

carrier chrominance signal For conveying color television information, sidebands of a modulated chrominance subcarrier.

carrier color signal For conveying color information in color television transmission, the sidebands of a modulated chrominance subcarrier (plus the unsuppressed chrominance subcarrier) added to the monochrome signal.

carrier concentration In a semiconductor material, the number of charge carriers per unit volume.

carrier control **1.** The modification, adjustment, or switching of a carrier wave. **2.** Adjustment of a circuit or device by means of a carrier wave.

carrier current The current component of a carrier wave, or the amplitude of that current. Compare CARRIER POWER and CARRIER VOLTAGE.

carrier-current communication See WIRED WIRELESS.

carrier-current control **1.** Control of the current component in a carrier wave. **2.** Remote control by means of wired wireless.

carrier-current receiver See WIRED-RADIO RECEIVER.

carrier-current relay A radio-frequency (RF) relay circuit, operated over a wire line by means of a transmitter.

carrier-current transmitter See WIRED-RADIO TRANSMITTER.

carrier deviation See CARRIER SWING.

carrier dispersion In a semiconductor, the spreading out of electrons and holes that leave the emitter simultaneously, but arrive at the collector at various times after following different paths.

carrier frequency   The center frequency of a CARRIER WAVE.

carrier-frequency pulse   A pulse that contains radio-frequency oscillation.

carrier-frequency range   The band of carrier frequencies over which a transmitter or signal generator can operate.

carrier injection   The apparent emission (injection) of electrons or holes into a semiconductor when a voltage is applied to the junction.

carrier leak   **1.** A point at which carrier-wave energy escapes a circuit or enclosure. **2.** The residual carrier voltage present in the output of a carrier-suppressing circuit.

carrier level   The amplitude of an unmodulated carrier wave.

carrier lifetime   In a semiconductor, the interval before an injected current carrier (see CARRIER INJECTION) recombines with an opposite carrier and ceases to be mobile.

carrier line   In carrier-current systems (see WIRED WIRELESS), the line or cable conducting the carrier-wave energy.

carrier mobility   Symbol, μ. In a semiconductor material, the average drift velocity of electrons and holes per unit electrostatic field.

carrier noise   Modulation of a carrier when there is no input from the modulator itself; unwanted modulation.

carrier noise level   The noise signal amplitude that results from unintentional fluctuations of an unmodulated carrier.

carrier-on-light transmission   A form of transmission in which many different signals are sent simultaneously by modulating a beam of light at multiple frequencies.

carrier-on-microwave transmission   A form of transmission in which many different signals are sent simultaneously by modulating a microwave signal at multiple lower frequencies.

carrier-on-wire transmission   A form of transmission in which many different signals are sent at the same time over a wire, by using radio-frequency carriers. Also called CARRIER-CURRENT COMMUNICATIONS or WIRED RADIO.

carrier oscillator   In a single-sideband receiver, the radio-frequency (RF) oscillator that supplies the missing CARRIER WAVE.

carrier power   The actual power represented by a radio-frequency (RF) carrier applied to an antenna, measured by either the direct or indirect method. The direct method involves determination of power according to the formula $P = I^2R$, where I is antenna current and R is antenna resistance at the point of current measurement. The indirect method involves determination of power according to the formula $P = EIF$, where E and I are antenna voltage and current, and F is

a factor less than 1.0, whose value depends on the type of modulation used.

carrier power-output rating   The power delivered by an unmodulated transmitter or generator to the normal load or its equivalent.

carrier shift   In an amplitude-modulated transmitter or generator, the undesired change of average carrier voltage during modulation.

carrier-shift indicator   An instrument for detecting carrier shift. It usually contains only a pickup coil, semiconductor diode, and dc milliammeter in series. Meter deflection is steady until carrier shift is detected; then, the needle fluctuates.

carrier signaling   In wire telephony, the use of carrier-wave signals to operate such functions as dialing, ringing, busy signal, etc.

carrier storage   In a semiconductor device, the tendency of mobile carriers to stay near a junction for a short time after the junction voltage has been removed or reversed in polarity.

carrier suppression   The elimination of the carrier in an amplitude-modulated signal so that only the sideband energy remains.

carrier swing   In frequency-modulated or phase-modulated transmission, the total deviation (lowest to highest instantaneous frequency) of the carrier wave.

carrier system   The transmission of many signals over one circuit, accomplished by modulating various different carriers at different frequencies. Different signals can use different modulation methods.

carrier telegraphy   **1.** Continuous-wave telegraphy by WIRED WIRELESS. **2.** Wired-wireless telegraphy in which a radio-frequency carrier is modulated by an audio-frequency keying wave.

carrier telephony   Telephone communication by WIRED WIRELESS.

carrier terminal   **1.** At each end of a carrier-current line or cable, the equipment for generating, modifying, or utilizing the carrier energy. **2.** In a balanced modulator, the point of carrier insertion.

carrier-to-noise ratio   The ratio of carrier amplitude to noise-voltage amplitude.

carrier transmission   Transport of information by a carrier, as by an amplitude-modulated radio wave that carries the low-frequency information as the AF modulation envelope and delivers it to the demodulator at the receiving station.

carrier-type dc amplifier   A high-frequency ac amplifier, ahead of which is operated a generator and transducer. A dc voltage applied to the transducer modulates the carrier supplied by the generator; the amplifier boosts the modulated wave, and the resultant output is rectified at a level higher than that of the dc input signal.

carrier voltage   The voltage component of a carrier wave; also, the amplitude of this component. Compare CARRIER CURRENT and CARRIER POWER.

carrier wave An electromagnetic wave that serves as the vehicle for the transmission of information via MODULATION.

carry **1.** In adding a column of figures, the digit added to the column at the left when the sum exceeds one less than the radix value. **2.** In digital computers and counters, a pulse that corresponds to the arithmetic operation in which a figure is carried to the next column in addition.

carrying capacity The ability of a conductor, such as copper wire, to carry current safely (expressed in maximum amperes).

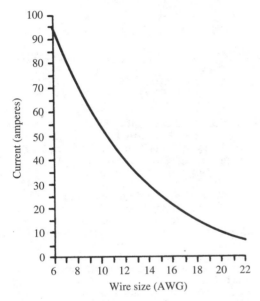

carrying capacity
(of some AWG sizes of copper wire)

carry-complete signal In an arithmetic computation by a computer, an adder-produced signal indicating that the pertinent carries have been generated.

carry system A communications system in which several carries occupy one circuit.

carry time The time taken for a digital computer or counter to perform a carry operation (See CARRY, **2**).

Cartesian coordinate geometry Also called *rectangular coordinate geometry*. In robotic systems, a movement scheme in two or three dimensions. The position of the robot arm is determined by linear coordinates, relative to an origin point. These coordinates are specified along linear axes—each of which is perpendicular to the others at the origin. See CARTESIAN COORDINATES, CARTESIAN PLANE, and CARTESIAN THREE-SPACE.

Cartesian coordinates Also called *rectangular coordinates*. A mathematical system that uniquely defines the position of a point on a plane, in space, or in general, in an *n*-dimensional hyperspace when *n* is a whole number greater than 3. There are *n* axes for *n* dimensions, each axis intersects all the others at a single point, called the origin. The axes are mutually perpendicular at this origin. The axes are scaled in units with the origin having coordinate values that are all equal to zero (usually). Positive values go along the axes in one direction; negative numbers go in the opposite direction for each axis. Usually, the axes are graduated in equal-sized units. The system gets its name from the mathematician Rene Descartes.

Cartesian plane A linear, two-dimensional coordinate plane commonly used for graphing equations in one variable.

Cartesian three-space A linear, three-dimensional graph-coordinate system used for rendering equations in one or two variables.

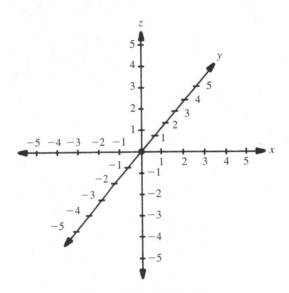

Cartesian three-space

Cartesian three-space graph A three-dimensional graph that shows an equation in one or two variables. Three-space graphs are often displayed more clearly by means of computer graphics, in which the entire display can be rotated to show the characteristics of the surface resulting from a given equation or function.

Cartesian n-space The coordinate space defined by a Cartesian system of *n* coordinates, where *n* is a whole number of 2 or greater.

cartridge **1.** The replaceable transducer assembly of a microphone. **2.** A magnetic-tape magazine. Also see TAPE CARTRIDGE. **3.** A removable computer mass-storage medium, containing a tape, magnetic diskette, or optical diskette. **4.** An insulating tube housing a fuse, semiconductor component, resistor, capacitor, or other part.

cartridge fuse A fuse consisting of a fusible wire enclosed in a cartridge, having a ferrule at each end for plug-in connection.

cascadable Capable of, or designed for, being connected in cascade with other similar or identical components.

cascade **1.** Components or stages connected and operated in sequence, as in a three-stage amplifier. The components or stages are often but not necessarily identical. **2.** To form a cascade.

cascade control **1.** In an automatic control system, a controller whose setting is varied by the output of another controller. **2.** An automatic control system in which the control units are connected in stages, so that one unit must operate before the next one can function.

cascaded amplifier A multistage amplifier in which the stages are forward-coupled in succession.

cascaded carry In digital computer practice, a system of performing the carry operation (see CARRY) in which the $n + 1$ place receives a carry pulse only when the nth place has received carry information to generate the pulse.

cascade thermoelectric device A thermoelectric component or circuit that consists of several cascaded sensors (see CASCADE, **1**).

cascade voltage doubler A voltage-doubler circuit (see VOLTAGE DOUBLER) consisting of two diode-capacitor combinations in cascade. Unlike the conventional voltage-doubler circuit with two capacitors in the output, the cascade voltage doubler has one in the input and one in the output.

cascode A high-gain, low-noise, high-input-impedance amplifier circuit, consisting of a grounded-emitter or grounded-source input stage coupled directly to a grounded-base or grounded-gate output stage.

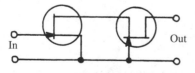

cascode
(field-effect transistor arrangement)

case temperature The temperature at a designated point on the outside surface of a component's case or housing.

Cassegrain antenna A dish antenna that uses CASSEGRAIN FEED.

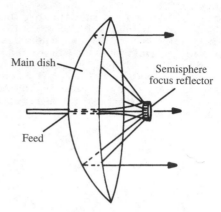

Cassegrain antenna

Cassegrain feed A dish-antenna feed system in which the feed point is located at the center of the dish itself. For transmission, the radio-frequency energy emerges from a waveguide and is directed to a small convex reflector at the focal point of the dish. The small reflector directs the signal back to the dish, spreading the energy out to cover the entire surface of the dish. The dish reflects the energy again and collimates it in the desired direction of propagation. For reception, the process is reversed; the dish focuses the energy on the small reflector, which propagates it back to the feed point.

cassette **1.** A holder (magazine) of reels of magnetic tape that is itself a mechanical subassembly, which can be easily inserted into and removed from a tape deck. **2.** A lightweight holder of photographic film or X-ray plates (before, during, and after exposure).

castor oil A viscous insulating oil extracted from castor beans. Highly refined castor oil is used as an impregnant in some oil-filled capacitors. Dielectric constant, 4.3 to 4.7. Dielectric strength, 380 V/mil.

CAT Abbreviation of COMPUTERIZED AXIAL TOMOGRAPHY.

catalysis The process whereby an agent, called a catalyst, enhances a chemical reaction without entering into the reaction. Catalysts are used in electronics, for example, to promote the setting of resins in potting and encapsulating operations.

catalytic agent A substance that accomplishes catalysis.

cataphoresis As caused by the influence of an electrostatic field, the migration toward the cathode of particles suspended in a liquid.

catastrophic failure **1.** Sudden, unexpected failure of a component or circuit. **2.** Failure that can result in the breakdown of an entire system. Also called *catastrophic breakdown*.

catcher In a Klystron, the second reentrant cavity. (See KLYSTRON).

catcher diode A diode that is connected to regulate the voltage at the output of a power supply. The cathode is connected to a source of reference voltage. If the anode, connected to the source to be regulated, becomes more positive than the cathode, the diode conducts and prevents the regulated voltage from rising more than 0.3 volt above the reference voltage (for germanium diodes) or 0.6 volt above the reference voltage (for silicon diodes).

catcher grids In a Klystron, the grids through which the bunched electrons pass on their way from the buncher to the collector. Catcher grids absorb energy from the bunched electrons and present it to the collector circuit.

category In a computer system, a group of magnetic disk volumes containing information related by a common application.

category storage A computer-file storage section that contains a number of categories and used by an operating system.

catenation See CONCATENATION.

cathode **1.** The negative electrode of a device (i.e., the electrode from which electrons move when a current passes through the device). **2.** In an electrochemical cell, the electrode that gains electrons. This is generally the positive electrode. **3.** In a vacuum tube, the electron-emitting electrode (filament or indirectly heated cathode sleeve).

cathode current Symbol I_K. The current flowing in the cathode circuit of a tube. Cathode current is the total of grid, plate, screen, and suppressor currents, and can have an ac and a dc component.

cathode dark current The electron emission from the photocathode of a camera tube when there is no illumination.

cathode element In a vacuum tube, an indirectly heated emitter of electrons. Also see CATHODE, **2.**

cathode emission **1.** The giving up of electrons by the cathode element of a device, such as a vacuum tube. Electrons can be emitted by either hot or cold cathodes, depending on the tube. **2.** Collectively, electrons released by a cathode.

cathode heating time The time required for the temperature of a tube cathode to increase from cold to its maximum specified operating temperature after the cathode current has been initiated. Also called cathode warmup time.

cathode luminous sensitivity For a photomultiplier tube, the cathode's sensitivity to light. This sensitivity figure is the ratio of photocathode current to incident light flux.

cathode-ray oscillograph An instrument that provides a permanent record, by photographic or other means, of the image on the screen of a cathode-ray tube.

cathode-ray oscilloscope See OSCILLOSCOPE.

cathode rays Invisible rays emanating from the cathode element of an evacuated tube operated with a high voltage between the anode and cathode. Cathode rays (electrons) cause certain substances, PHOSPHORS, to glow upon striking them.

cathode-ray scanning tube Any tube in which an electron beam is deflected horizontally and vertically to scan an area. These include oscilloscope tubes, some computer monitors, radar displays, and television camera tubes.

cathode-ray tube **1.** An evacuated tube containing an anode and cathode that generates cathode rays when operated at high voltage. **2.** An oscilloscope tube. **3.** A picture tube.

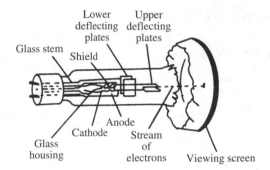

cathode-ray tube

cathode terminal **1.** In a diode (semiconductor or tube), the terminal to which a negative dc voltage must be applied for forward-biasing the diode. Compare ANODE TERMINAL. **2.** In a diode, the terminal at which a positive dc voltage appears when the diode acts as an ac rectifier. Compare ANODE TERMINAL. **3.** The terminal connected internally to the cathode element of device. **4.** In a vacuum tube, an indirectly heated electron emitter.

cathode voltage Symbol, E_K. The voltage between ground (or B-minus) and the cathode of a tube; it can have both ac and dc components.

cathodic protection A method of preventing corrosive galvanic action in underground metal pipes or the submerged hulls of ships. The part to be protected is used as the cathode of a circuit through which a direct current is passed in the direction opposite to that which caused the corrosion, thus counteracting it.

cathodofluorescence Fluorescence resulting from a material's exposure to cathode rays.

cathodoluminescence In a vacuum chamber in which a metal target is bombarded with high-velocity electrons (cathode rays), the emission of radiation of a wavelength characteristic of the metal.

cation A positive ion. Also see ION.

CAT scanner The X-ray apparatus for COMPUTERIZED AXIAL TOMOGRAPHY.

CATV Abbreviation of COMMUNITY-ANTENNA TELEVISION (usually cable television).

caustic soda electrolyte Symbol, NaOH. Sodium hydroxide solution, as used in some secondary cells and experimental devices.

cavitation The local formation of cavities in a fluid used in ultrasonic cleaning because of the reduction in pressure at those points.

cavitation noise In an ultrasonic cleaner, the noise resulting from the collapse of bubbles produced by cavitation.

cavity A metallic chamber (can) in which energy is allowed to reflect, sometimes resulting in resonance.

cavity filter A microwave (usually band rejection) filter consisting of a resonant cavity and associated coupling devices.

cavity frequency meter See CAVITY WAVEMETER.

cavity impedance The impedance across a cavity at a particular frequency. At resonance, the cavity impedance is purely resistive.

cavity magnetron A magnetron whose anode is a series of resonant cavities.

cavity oscillator An oscillator with a cavity-tuned circuit.

cavity radiation Energy radiated from a tiny hole in an otherwise sealed chamber. The radiation occurs at all electromagnetic wavelengths; the greater the temperature within the chamber, the greater the frequency at which the radiation has its maximum amplitude.

cavity resonance The phenomenon whereby a hollow cavity resonates; specifically, resonance in small metal cavities at microwave frequencies.

cavity resonator See RESONANT CAVITY.

cavity wavemeter An absorption wavemeter whose adjustable element is a tunable resonant cavity into which radio-frequency (RF) energy is injected through a wave-guide or coaxial cable. Such an instrument is useful at microwave frequencies.

CB Abbreviation of CITIZENS BAND.

Cb Symbol for COLUMBIUM.

C_B Symbol for BASE CAPACITANCE of a transistor.

C band The band of radio frequencies between 3.9 and 6.2 GHz.

C_c Symbol for collector capacitance of a transistor.

cc **1.** Alternative abbreviation of *cubic centimeter*. The International Organization for Standardization recommends cm³. **2.** Abbreviation of COTTON-COVERED.

CCA Abbreviation of CURRENT-CONTROLLED AMPLIFIER.

CCD Abbreviation of CHARGE-COUPLED DEVICE.

CCIS Abbreviation of COMMON-CHANNEL INTERFACE SIGNALING.

CCIR Abbreviation of *Comite Consultatif International des Radiocommunications (International Radio Consultative Committee)*.

CCIT Abbreviation of *Comite Consultatif International Telegrafique (International Telegraph Consultative Committee)*.

CCITT Abbreviation of *Comite Consultatif International Telegrafique et Telephonique (International Telegraph and Telephone Consultative Committee)*.

CCS **1.** Abbreviation of CONTINUOUS COMMERCIAL SERVICE. **2.** Abbreviation of *common-channel signaling*.

CCTV Abbreviation of CLOSED-CIRCUIT TELEVISION.

CCTV monitor A video monitor that receives a signal from a CCTV transmitter.

CCTV signal The picture signal in a CCTV system. It can be either a modulated radio-frequency signal or a composite video signal.

ccw Abbreviation of COUNTERCLOCKWISE.

CD Abbreviation of COMPACT DISK.

Cd Symbol for CADMIUM.

cd Abbreviation of CANDELA.

CD-4 A method of obtaining quadraphonic reproduction on a phonograph disk using modulated carriers with frequencies above the human hearing range.

CDI Abbreviation of CAPACITOR-DISCHARGE IGNITION.

C display A radar display showing the target as a dot whose coordinates represent the bearing (horizontal) and angle of elevation (vertical). Compare A DISPLAY, J DISPLAY, and K DISPLAY.

cd/m² Candelas per square meter, the SI unit of luminance.

CD-ROM Abbreviation of COMPACT-DISK READ-ONLY MEMORY.

Ce Symbol for CERIUM.

C_e Symbol for EMITTER CAPACITANCE of a transistor.

ceiling **1.** The maximum possible power output from a transmitter. **2.** The maximum possible current or voltage that a circuit can deliver. **3.** In aviation, the level of the cloud base.

ceilometer An instrument for measuring ceiling (cloud height).

cel In animated graphics, an individual image or frame.

cell **1.** A single (basic) unit for producing dc electricity by electrochemical or biochemical action, as in a battery (a group of connected cells). Also see PRIMARY CELL, STANDARD CELL, and STORAGE CELL. **2.** An addressable, one-word-capacity storage element in a computer memory. **3.** An electrostatic charge dipole in the atmosphere, usually occurring in or near thunderstorms. **4.** A thunderstorm.

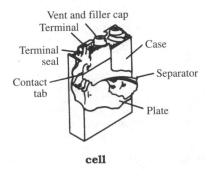

Vent and filler cap
Terminal
Terminal seal
Contact tab
Case
Separator
Plate

cell

cell constant The surface area of the electrodes in a cell divided by the distance between them. The basic linear units must be the same: for example, square centimeters for surface area and centimeters for distance.

cell counter A bioelectronic instrument used to count blood cells and other minute particles.

cell reversal A condition that can occur in some rechargeable electrochemical cells and batteries, such as *nickel-cadmium batteries.* It most often results from neglecting to recharge the cell or battery when it has become fully discharged.

cell-type enclosure A room designed to prevent the entrance or escape of radio-frequency (RF) electromagnetic fields, characterized by double-walled copper-mesh shielding.

cellular coil A coil having a crisscross (usually multilayer) winding. Examples: lattice-wound coil, honeycomb coil, basket-weave coil.

cellular communications A radio, telephone, or television communications network that makes use of numerous fixed repeaters. Subscribers use mobile or portable transceivers that are always within range of at least one repeater. The most common form is known as *cellular telephone* or *cellular mobile radio telephone.*

celluloid A thermoplastic dielectric material that is a blend of cellulose nitrate and camphor. Dielectric constant, 4 to 7. Dielectric strength, 250 to 780 V/mil.

cellulose acetate A plastic dielectric material used as a substrate for magnetic tapes, photographic film, and similar applications. Dielectric constant, 6 to 8. Dielectric strength, 300 V to 1 kV/mil. Also see ACETATE.

cellulose acetate base See ACETATE BASE.

cellulose acetate butyrate A thermoplastic dielectric material that is an acetic and butyric acid ester of cellulose.

cellulose acetate tape See ACETATE TAPE.

cellulose nitrate The nitric acid ester of cellulose, a plastic insulating material.

cellulose propionate A thermoplastic molding material that is a propionic acid ester of cellulose.

Celsius scale A temperature scale in which 0 degrees is the freezing point of water, and 100 degrees the boiling point of water. Also called CENTIGRADE SCALE. Compare ABSOLUTE SCALE, and FAHRENHEIT SCALE.

cent An audio-frequency interval of 0.01 ($\frac{1}{100}$) of a half step. A half step is the frequency difference between two immediately adjacent keys on a piano.

center channel In high-fidelity stereo, a phantom sound source that appears to exist midway between the left and right speakers or earpieces. The effect is caused by identical, or nearly identical, signals in the left and right channels.

center-fed antenna An antenna in which the feeders are connected to the center of the radiator.

center feed **1.** Attaching a feeder or transmission line to the center of the radiator of an antenna. **2.** Connection of signal-input terminals to the center of a coil. **3.** Descriptive of paper tape whose feed holes are aligned with character hole centers. Compare ADVANCE FEED TAPE.

center frequency **1.** The frequency, in a communications receiver, that is midway between the lower and upper 3-dB-down amplitude points. **2.** The average frequency of a modulated carrier. **3.** The carrier frequency of a modulated signal, whether or not the carrier is suppressed.

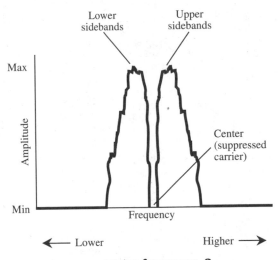

Lower sidebands
Upper sidebands
Max
Amplitude
Center (suppressed carrier)
Min
Frequency
← Lower   Higher →

center frequency, 3.

centering control In an oscilloscope circuit, a potentiometer used to position the image on the screen (particularly in the center). Separate controls are provided for horizontal and vertical centering.

center loading   In an inductively loaded antenna, placement of the loading coil(s) at or near a point or points midway between the feed point and the end(s) of the radiating element.

center of beam   1. In a directional antenna system, the direction, denoted by a straight ray, where the signal strength or response is the greatest. **2.** In a beam of visible light, the geometric center of the spot produced when the beam strikes a surface perpendicular to the beam. **3.** In a beam of visible light, the axis within the beam where the intensity is greatest.

center of channel   The frequency that is midway between the lowest and highest frequency components of a communications channel.

center of radiation   The point from which the energy radiated by an object appears to arrive.

center tap   A connection made to the centermost turn of a coil or to the center-value point of a resistor, filament, or capacitor pair.

center-tapped coil   See CENTER-TAPPED WINDING.

center-tapped filament   A tube or lamp filament that has a tap at its center.

center-tapped inductor   An inductor that has a tap at half the total number of turns (the physical center of the winding).

center-tapped potentiometer   A potentiometer that has a tap at half the total resistance of the resistance element.

center-tapped resistor   A fixed resistor that has a tap at half the total resistance.

center-tapped transformer   A transformer that has one or more center-tapped windings.

center-tapped winding   A winding that has a tap at half the total number of turns (the physical center of the winding).

center-tapped winding

center tracking frequency   In three-frequency alignment (tracking) of a circuit, the frequency between the upper and lower frequency limits (alignment or tracking points of the circuit).

center-zero meter   A meter that has its zero point at the center of the scale (e.g., a dc galvanometer).

centi-   Abbreviation, c. Prefix meaning hundredth(s) (10^{-2}).

centigrade scale   See CELSIUS SCALE.

centimeter   Abbreviation, cm. A unit of length equal to 10^{-2} meter, or 0.3937 inch.

centimeter-gram-second   system   Abbreviation, cgs. A system of units, now seldom used, in which the centimeter is the fundamental unit of length, the gram is the fundamental unit of mass, and the mean solar second is the fundamental unit of time. Electrical units in the cgs system fall into two categories: *electrostatic* and *electromagnetic*. The names of cgs electrostatic units have the prefix *stat-* (e.g., STATAMPERE, STATVOLT, etc.). Cgs electromagnetic units have the prefix *ab-* (e.g., ABAMPERE, ABVOLT, etc.).

centimetric waves   See MICROWAVES.

centipoise   A cgs measure of the dynamic viscosity of liquids. Equal to 10^{-2} poise.

central office   In telephone systems, a switching network at which numerous circuits or subscriber lines converge.

central processing unit   Abbreviation, CPU. In a digital computer, the section containing the arithmetic and logic unit (ALU), control circuits, and internal memory circuits. Also called *central processor*.

Central Radio Propagation Laboratory   A government laboratory that studies radio propagation and collects, correlates, and analyzes data for predicting propagation conditions. The organization also studies methods of measuring propagation.

centrifugation potential   An electric potential that occurs in a colloidal solution when the solution is centrifuged.

centrifugal switch   A switch actuated by rotational motion (e.g., the automatic disconnection switch in a capacitor motor).

centripetal force   The force that draws the mass of a rotating body toward the axis of rotation.

ceramal   See CERMET.

ceramet seal   See CERAMIC-TO-METAL SEAL.

ceramic-based microcircuit   A tiny circuit printed or deposited on a ceramic substrate.

ceramic capacitor   A capacitor that uses a ceramic dielectric, such as barium titanate or titanium dioxide. Such capacitors offer reasonably high capacitance in a small package.

ceramic dielectric   1. A ceramic used as a dielectric in capacitors. Examples: barium titanate, barium strontium titanate, and titanium dioxide. Ceramic dielectrics provide high dielectric constant. **2.** A ceramic used as an insulator. Examples: isolantite, porcelain, and steatite.

ceramic filter   A resonant filter similar to a crystal filter, but using a piezoelectric ceramic material.

ceramic magnet   A permanent magnet made of a magnetic ceramic material, such as mixtures of barium oxide and iron oxide.

ceramic microphone   A microphone that uses a CERAMIC PIEZOELEMENT to convert sound waves into electrical impulses.

ceramic piezoelement   A component that uses a piezoelectric ceramic material. Examples: ceramic filter, ceramic microphone, ceramic phono pickup, ceramic transducer, and electrostrictive transducer. Also called PIEZOELECTRIC CERAMIC.

ceramic resistor A carborundum resistor whose value is voltage-dependent. It usually displays a negative temperature coefficient of resistance (but a positive coefficient is available) and a negative voltage coefficient of resistance.

ceramics **1.** Clay-based materials used as dielectrics and insulators in electronics. Examples: barium titanate, titanium dioxide, porcelain, isolantite, and steatite. **2.** The science and art of using and developing ceramics.

ceramic-to-metal seal A bond in which ceramic and metal bodies are joined, for example, the bonding of a metal lead to a ceramic disk, through which it passes to provide a leak-proof seal. Also called *ceramet seal.*

ceramic transducer A transducer that uses a CERAMIC PIEZOELEMENT to translate such parameters as pressure and vibration into electrical pulses.

ceramic tube A high-temperature vacuum tube that uses a ceramic material, instead of glass, as the envelope; the tube offers low losses at high frequencies.

Cerenkov radiation Light emanating from a transparent material that is traversed by charged particles, whose speed is higher than the speed of light through the material.

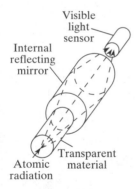

Cerenkov radiation

Cerenkov rebatron device An apparatus for generating radio-frequency energy by passing an electron beam through a piece of dielectric having a small aperture.

ceresin wax A yellow or white wax obtained by refining *ozocerite.* Used as an insulant and sealant against moisture. Dielectric constant, 2.5 to 2.6.

cerium Symbol, Ce. A metallic element of the rare-earth group. Atomic number, 58. Atomic weight, 140.13.

cerium metals A group of metals belonging to the rare-earth group: cerium, lanthanum, neodymium, praseodymium, promethium, and samarium.

cermet An alloy of a ceramic, such as titanium carbide, and nickel, a metal. A thin film of cermet is used as a resistive element in some microcircuits. Cermet is an acronym for *ceramic metal.*

certified tape A magnetic recording tape that has been thoroughly checked and found to have no flaws.

cesium Symbol, Cs. A metallic element of the alkali-metal group. Atomic number, 55. Atomic weight, 132.91. The oscillations of this element's atoms have been used as atomic time standards. The element is used in some phototubes as the light-sensitive material, and in some arc lamps.

cesium-vapor lamp A low-voltage arc lamp used as an infrared source.

Cf Symbol for CALIFORNIUM.

cgs Abbreviation of CENTIMETER-GRAM-SECOND.

chad The punched-out particle(s) constituting refuse from paper-tape punching.

chadded tape Punched paper tape in which the chad is left partially attached to the tape's punched holes.

chadless tape Punched paper tape without CHAD.

chafe **1.** An area that has been abraded by rubbing or scraping. **2.** To produce a chafe.

chaff Strips of metal foil used to create radar interference or ambiguity in locating a target by multiple reflections of the beam. Also called MIRROR.

chain broadcasting Simultaneous transmissions from a number of broadcast transmitters connected together in a network by wire line, coaxial cable, or microwave link.

chain calculation As performed by a calculator, a calculation that can be entered as it would normally be written (i.e., without the need for regrouping operands).

chain printer In the readout channel of a digital computer, a high-speed printer carrying printer's type on a revolving chain.

chain radar system A number of radar stations along a missile-flight path that are connected in a communications or control network.

chain reaction A reaction (as in nuclear fission) that is self-sustaining or self-repeating. Unless controlled from outside, such a reaction runs to destruction.

chain switch A switch that is actuated by pulling a light metal chain. Successive pulls turn the switch alternatively on and off.

change dump In computer operation (especially in debugging), the display of the names of locations that have changed following a specific event.

change file See TRANSACTION FILE.

chain switch

change of control In a sequence of computer records being processed, a logical break that initiates a predetermined action, after which processing continues.

changer In a high-fidelity disk player, a device that allows several disks to be played, one after the other, without the need for manually exchanging the disks.

change record A computer record that changes information in a related master record. Also called *transaction record.*

change tape See TRANSACTION TAPE.

channel 1. A frequency (or band of frequencies) assigned to a radio or television station. 2. See KEYWAY. 3. A subcircuit in a large system [e.g., the radio-frequency (RF) channel of a receiver, the vertical-amplifier channel of an oscilloscope, or the modulator channel of a radio transmitter]. 4. The end-to-end electrical path through the semiconductor body in a field-effect transistor. 5. One of the independent audio circuits in a stereo sound system (e.g., the left channel or the right channel).

channel analyzer A (usually multiband) continuously tunable instrument, similar to a tuned radio receiver, used in troubleshooting radio communications circuits by substituting a perfect channel for one that is out of order.

channel balance The state in which the apparent amplitude of two or more channels is identical.

channel bank In a transmission system, the terminal equipment used for the purpose of multiplexing the individual channels.

channel capacity The fullest extent to which a channel can accommodate the information (frequencies, bits, words, etc.) to be passed through it.

channel designator A name, number, or abbreviation given to a channel in a communications system.

channel effect The possible current flow through a high impedance between the collector and emitter in a bipolar transistor.

channel frequency The CENTER FREQUENCY of a communications channel.

channeling Multiplex transmission in which separate carriers within a sufficiently wide frequency band are used for simultaneous transmission.

channelizing The subdivision of a relatively wide frequency band into a number of separate subbands.

channel reliability 1. The proportion of time, usually expressed as a percentage, that a communications channel is useful for its intended purpose. 2. The relative ease with which communications can be carried out over a particular channel.

channel reversal In stereo reproduction, interchanging the left and right channels.

channel-reversing switch In a stereo system, a switch that allows channel reversal without the need for reorienting speaker cables or connectors.

channel sampling rate The rate at which individual channels are sampled. For example, in the electronic switching of an oscilloscope, the number of times per second each input-signal channel is switched to the instrument.

channel selector A switch or relay used to put any of a series of channels into functional status in a system.

channel separation 1. The spacing between communications channels, expressed in kilohertz. 2. In stereo reproduction, the degree to which the information on one channel is separate from the other; usually expressed in decibels.

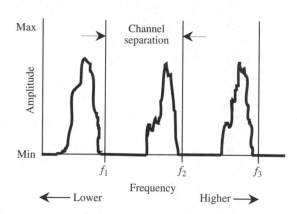

channel separation, 1.

channel slot On a carrier modulated by numerous signals, the position or frequency of a specific modulating signal.

channel shift The interchange of communications channels (e.g., the shift from a calling frequency to a working frequency).

channel strip A fixed-channel amplifier for a television receiver.

channel time slot In a frame of transmitted information, such as a television picture, a time interval designated to a channel for the transmission of a character signal or other information.

channel-to-channel connection A device, such as a channel adapter, used to transfer data rapidly between any two channels of two digital computers, at the data speed of the slower channel.

channel-utilization index An indication of the extent to which channel capacity is used. For a given channel, the index is the ratio of information rate to channel capacity, each expressed in units per second.

channel wave An acoustic wave that travels within a region or layer of a substance because of a physical difference between that layer and the surrounding material. An example of a channel wave is the propagation of sound over a still lake.

channel width In a frequency channel, the difference $f_2 - f_1$, where f_1 is the lower-frequency limit and f_2 is the upper-frequency limit of the channel.

chapter A self-contained computer program section.

character 1. One of the symbols in a code. 2. In computer operations, a digit, letter, or symbol used alone or in some combination to express information, data, or instructions.

character code In a communications or computer system, the combination of elements (e.g., bits) representing characters.

character crowding A reduction of the time interval between successive characters—especially those read from tape.

character density The number of characters that can be stored in a given length or surface area of a medium. On a magnetic tape, it might be specified in characters per millimeter; on a magnetic disk, it might be specified in characters per square millimeter.

character emitter A coded pulse generator in a digital computer.

character generator A device that converts coded information into readable alphanumeric characters.

characteristic 1. A quantity that characterizes (typifies) the operation of a device or circuit. Examples are emitter current, output power, and frequency deviation. 2. In floating point notation, the exponent.

characteristic curve A curve showing the relationship between an independent variable and a dependent variable, with respect to the parameter(s) for a device or circuit. Example: the collector voltage-collector current characteristic curve of a transistor.

characteristic distortion 1. In a digital signal, pulse distortion caused by the effects of the previous pulse or pulses. 2. Distortion in the characteristic curve of a component or device.

characteristic frequency The frequency peculiar to a given channel, service, or response.

characteristic impedance Symbol, Z_0. The impedance that would be simulated by a given two-conductor line of uniform construction, if that line were of infinite length. Characteristic impedance is determined by the materials used for the two conductors, the dielectric used to insulate the two conductors, the diameters of the conductors, and the spacing between them. The characteristic impedance of TV twinlead is 300 ohms; that of RG-8/U coaxial cable is 52 ohms. 2. The value of impedance that, if it terminates a transmission line, results in no reflections along the line.

characteristic overflow In floating-point arithmetic, the condition that occurs when a characteristic exceeds the upper limit specified by a program or computer.

characteristic spread The range of values over which a characteristic extends. For example, if an amplifier's output ranges from 15 W to 25 W, its characteristic spread is 10 W.

characteristic underflow In floating-point arithmetic, the condition that occurs when a characteristic exceeds the lower limit specified by a program or computer.

character modifier In address modification, a constant (compare VARIABLE) that refers to a specific character's location in memory.

character-oriented A computer in which character locations, rather than words, can be addressed.

character printer A computer output device that prints matter in the manner of a conventional typewriter.

character reader Also called an *optical scanner*. In a digital computer, an input device that can read printing and script directly.

character recognition The reading of a written or printed character by a computer, including its identification and encoding.

character sensing The detection of characters by a computer input device. This can be done galvanically, electrostatically, magnetically, or optically.

character set The set of characters in a complete language, or in a communications system.

character signal The set of elements or bits representing a character in a digital transmission system. The signal can also represent the quantizing value of a sample.

characters per minute An expression of the speed of transmission of a digital signal. The number of characters (on average) transmitted in a period of one minute. In Morse code (CW) transmission, this is generally taken as the number of times the word *paris* plus the subsequent space, multiplied by six (five letters and one space following), can be sent in one minute.

characters per second An expression of the speed of transmission of a digital signal. The number of characters (on average) transmitted in a period of one second.

character string A one-dimensional character array [i.e., a list of characters that, when printed or displayed, would appear in a row or column, but not both (as in a matrix)].

character subset   A classification of characters within a set.

Charactron   A cathode-ray readout tube that displays letters, numbers, and symbols on its screen. More commonly called a *monitor.*

charcoal tube   In a system for producing a high vacuum, a trap containing activated charcoal, which is heated to dull red, then cooled by liquid air to absorb air gases.

charge   1. A quantity of electricity associated with a space, particle, or body. 2. To electrify a space, particle, or body (i.e., to give an electric charge). 3. To store electricity, as in a storage battery or capacitor. Compare DISCHARGE.

charge carrier   1. An ELECTRON whose movement constitutes a flow of electric current. 2. An electron deficiency (HOLE) whose movement constitutes a flow of electric current. 3. Any particle, such as a charged atom (ION), PROTON, ALPHA PARTICLE, or BETA PARTICLE, whose movement constitutes a flow of electric current.

charge-coupled device   Abbreviation, CCD. A form of analog-to-digital converter that generates a digital signal output representing an analog image input. The transfer of stored charges provides the method of operation. Used in machine vision systems and in numerous scientific applications.

charge density   The degree of charge or current-carrier concentration in a region.

charged particle   1. See CHARGE CARRIER. 2. See ION.

charged voltage   1. The voltage across a fully charged capacitor. 2. The terminal voltage of a fully charged storage cell.

charge holding   See CHARGE RETENTION.

charge of electron   The negative electric charge carried by a single electron. Approximately equal to 1.602×10^{-19} coulombs.

charger   1. See BATTERY CHARGER. 2. Any device or circuit that charges a capacitor.

charge retention   1. The holding of an electric charge by a cell or battery when no current is being drawn from it. 2. A measure of the ability of a cell or battery to maintain an electric charge when no current is drawn from it. Often specified in terms of *shelf life.* 3. The holding of a charge by a capacitor.

charge-storage tube   A cathode-ray tube that holds a display of information on its screen until the operator removes it by pressing an erase button.

charge-to-mass   The ratio of the electric charge to the mass of a subatomic particle.

charge-to-mass ratio of electron   The ratio of the charge (e) of the electron to the mass (m_e) of the electron, in coulombs per kilogram (C/kg). For an electron at rest, e/m_e is approximately equal to 1.602×10^{-19} C divided by 9.11×10^{-31} kg = 1.76×10^{11} C/kg.

charge transfer   1. The switching of an electric charge from one capacitor to another. 2. The capture of an electron by a positive ion from a neutral atom of the same kind, resulting in the ion becoming a neutral atom, and the previously neutral atom becoming a positive ion.

charge transfer device   A semiconductor in which an electric charge is moved from location to location. Applications include delay lines, video signal processing, and signal storage.

charging   1. The process of storing electrical energy in a capacitor. 2. The process of storing electrochemical energy in a storage cell or battery.

charging current   1. The current flowing into a capacitor. 2. The current flowing into a previously discharged storage cell.

charging rate   1. The rate at which charging current flows into a storage cell or battery, expressed in amperes or milliamperes. For most cells and batteries, the rate is greatest initially, when the cell or battery is depleted or nearly depleted; the rate decreases as the cell or battery becomes charged. 2. The instantaneous rate at which charging current flows into a capacitor or capacitance-resistance circuit, expressed in amperes, milliamperes, or microamperes.

charged voltage   1. The voltage across a fully charged capacitor. 2. The terminal voltage of a fully charged storage cell.

Charlie   Phonetic alphabet code word for the letter C.

chassis   A (usually metal) foundation on which components are mounted and wired.

chassis ground   A ground connection made to the metal chassis on which the components of a circuit are mounted. When several ground connections are made to a single point on the chassis, a COMMON GROUND results.

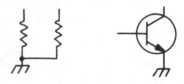

chassis ground

chatter   1. A rapidly repetitive signal, caused by interruption or variation of a current (usually interference). 2. Extraneous vibration, as of the armature in a relay.

chatter time   The interval between the instant that contacts close (for example, in a relay) and the instant at which chatter ends.

cheater cord   An extension cord used to conduct power to a piece of equipment (especially a television receiver) by temporarily bypassing the safety switch or interlock. Use of such a cord presents a potentially fatal shock hazard to personnel using, or working on, the equipment.

Chebyshev filter   Also spelled *Tschebyscheff* or *Tschebysheff*. A form of inductance-capacitance (LC) lowpass, highpass, bandpass, or band-rejection filter, characterized by an attenuation-versus-frequency curve with ripple in the passband.

check   **1.** A test generally made to verify condition, performance, state, or calculations; specifically, in computer operations, it applies to operands or results. **2.** The usually abrupt halting of an action.

check bit   A binary CHECK DIGIT.

check character   In a group of characters, one whose value depends on the other characters, which it checks when the group is stored or transferred.

check digit   Also called *check number*. In computer operations, a number added to a group of digits, forming a code that identifies entities in the system (including personnel) and can be used for verification. The check digit is the remainder when the number code (for example, 459) is divided by a fixed number (for example, 5); in this case, the check digit (the remainder of 459/5) is 4, and the amended code number is 4594.

check indicator   An indication, made via a video display, that something has been shown to be invalid according to a check.

checking program   Also called *checking routine*. For debugging purposes, a diagnostic computer program capable of detecting errors in another program.

checkout   A test routine that ascertains whether or not a circuit or system is functioning according to specifications.

checkout routine   A routine used by programmers to debug programs.

checkpoint   A point in a digital-computer program at which sufficient information has been stored to allow restarting the computation from that point.

checkpoint dump   The process of recording details of a computer program run. This process might be necessary in the event of a system failure that requires reconstruction of a program or programs.

checkpointing   The writing of a computer program in such a manner that, during a program run, information is frequently dumped as insurance against possible loss in the event of a system failure.

check problem   A presolved problem used to check the operation of a digital computer or program.

check register   In some digital computers, a register in which transferred information is stored so that it can be checked against the same information as it is received a second time.

check routine   A special program designed to ascertain if a program or computer is operating correctly. Also see CHECK PROBLEM.

checksum   Used as part of a summation check, a sum derived from the digits of a number. For example, the checksum of 23,335 is 16. Also called HASH TOTAL.

check symbol   For a specific data item, a digit or digits obtained by performing an arithmetic check on the item, which it then accompanies through processing stages for the purpose of checking it.

check total   See CONTROL TOTAL.

check word   A check symbol in the form of a word added to, and containing data from, a block of records.

chelate   Pertaining to cyclic molecular structure in which several atoms in a ring hold a central metallic ion in a COORDINATION COMPLEX.

chemical deposition   The coating of a surface with a substance resulting from *chemical reduction* of a solution. In mirror making, for example, formaldehyde reduces a solution of silver nitrate, and deposits metallic silver on the surface of polished glass. Also see CHEMICALLY DEPOSITED PRINTED CIRCUIT and CHEMICAL REDUCTION.

chemical detector   See ELECTROLYTIC DETECTOR.

chemical effect   An alteration in the chemical makeup of a substance or solution, resulting from the passage of an electric current through it. Examples include electrolysis, electroplating, and the reduction of ores.

chemical energy   Energy that is stored in the chemical bonds of a material or solution. An example is the stored energy in terms of watt hours in an electrolytic cell.

chemical load   An arrangement of a chemical material or device for the passage of electricity through it. Examples: electroplater, electrolytic cell for the production of hydrogen gas, and storage battery.

chemically deposited printed circuit   A printed circuit in which the pattern of metal lines and areas are chemically deposited on a substrate.

chemically pure   Abbreviation, CP. Free from impurities.

chemical rectifier   See ELECTROLYTIC CELL.

chemical reduction   The process of making a chemical compound (usually in solution) into a metal, by removing the nonmetallic component from the compound. For example, when copper oxide is heated in the presence of hydrogen (a reducing agent), the oxygen (the nonmetallic component) is driven out, and copper (along with some water) remains.

chemical resistor   See ELECTROLYTIC RESISTOR.

chemical switch   See ELECTROCHEMICAL SWITCH.

CHIL Abbreviation for *current-hogging injection logic*. A form of bipolar digital logic technology.

chip 1. An INTEGRATED CIRCUIT. **2.** A small slab, wafer, or die of dielectric or semiconductor material, on which a subminiature component or circuit is formed or deposited.

chip capacitor A subminiature capacitor formed on a chip.

chip resistor A subminiature resistor formed on a chip.

chip tray A chad receptacle located at a card or paper tape punching site.

Chireix-Mesny antenna A high-frequency (HF) beam antenna, in which each dipole section constitutes one side of a diamond. Cophased horizontal and vertical components of current flow in each of the diagonals, and radiation is broadside to the plane of the driven element.

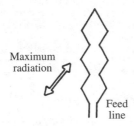

Chireix-Mesny antenna

chirp A rapid change in the frequency of a continuous-wave Morse-code signal. The chirp usually occurs at the beginning of each dot or dash, and can go up or down in frequency. Chirp occurs because of a change in the output impedance of an oscillator as it is keyed. Modern code transmitters do not exhibit significant chirp.

chirp modulation A form of modulation in which the frequency of a signal is deliberately changed in a systematic way. Used in some radar systems.

chirp radar A radar system that uses CHIRP MODULATION.

Chladni's plates Conducting plates that are used to evaluate the nature of a vibration in a solid material. The plates are clamped to the material, and sand is sprinkled on the surface. This produces patterns that indicate the nature of the vibrations.

chlorinated diphenyl A synthetic organic substance used as an impregnant in some oil-filled capacitors.

chlorinated naphthalene See HALOWAX.

chlorine Symbol, Cl. A gaseous element of the halogen family. Atomic number, 17. Atomic weight, 35.453.

choke 1. To restrict or curtail passage of a particular current or frequency by means of a discrete component, such as a choke coil. **2.** See CHOKE COIL.

choke air gap A fractional-inch opening in the iron core of a filter choke, usually filled with wood or plastic. The gap prevents saturation of the core when the choke coil carries maximum rated direct current.

choke coil 1. A large-value inductor that provides a high impedance to alternating current (ac), while offering virtually no opposition to direct current (dc). **2.** In radio-frequency (RF) applications, an inductor that provides a high impedance to RF signals while showing low impedance for audio-frequency (AF) signals and direct currents (dc).

choke-coupled modulation An amplitude-modulation (AM) scheme, in which the modulator is coupled to the radio-frequency (RF) amplifier through a shared iron-core choke coil.

choke flange At the end of a waveguide, a flange in which a groove forms a CHOKE JOINT.

choke-input filter A filter whose input component is an inductor (choke). The choke-input power-supply filter is distinguished by its superior voltage regulation, compared with the CAPACITOR-INPUT FILTER.

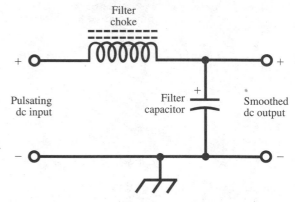

choke-input filter

choke joint A joint connecting two waveguide sections and permitting efficient energy transfer without requiring electrical contact with the inside wall of the waveguide.

chopped dc See INTERRUPTED DC.

chopped mode In a single-gun cathode-ray-tube (CRT) oscilloscope, a technique for sequentially displaying several signals that are not referenced to the oscilloscope sweep.

chopped signal An ac or dc signal that is periodically interrupted, as by means of a CHOPPER.

chopper A device or circuit that interrupts a direct current (dc) at some predetermined rate. Ideally, such a device is characterized by distinct on and off operation.

chopper amplifier   A circuit that amplifies the output of a CHOPPER. Used in conjunction with a CHOPPER CONVERTER in dc amplification.

chopper converter   A device that interrupts a direct current (dc), and changes it to a pulsating, rectangular-wave current or voltage that can be handled by a stable ac amplifier and rectified to supply amplified dc.

chopper stabilization   1. Stabilization of direct-current (dc) amplification by using a CHOPPER CONVERTER ahead of a stable ac amplifier, and rectifying the amplifier output. **2.** In a regulated power supply, use of a CHOPPER AMPLIFIER at the control-circuit input to improve regulation.

chopper-stabilized amplifier   See CHOPPER AMPLIFIER and CHOPPER STABILIZATION, **1.**

chopper transistor   A transistor that provides rapid and repeated on/off switching of direct current (dc), in the manner of an electromechanical interrupter. See CHOPPER.

chopping frequency   The frequency at which a chopper interrupts a signal.

chord   1. A harmonious mixture of musical tones of various frequencies. **2.** A straight line that joins two points on a curve (such as an arc of a circle). **3.** The width of an airfoil.

chord organ   An electronic organ that will sound a musical chord when a key is pressed (see CHORD, **1**).

choreographer program   A computer program similar to one originally written by Charles Lecht of Lecht Sciences, Inc. The computer operator gives commands that cause a human form, portrayed on the display screen, to make various movements. Used in animated computer graphics.

chorus   Signals at very low radio frequencies (VLF), natural in origin, that sweep upward in frequency. Believed to result from lightning-generated electromagnetic fields that circulate in the magnetosphere (earth's magnetic field). The term is derived from the sound the signals make in high-gain audio-frequency (AF) amplifiers connected directly to VLF receiving antennas.

Christiansen antenna   A radio-telescope antenna for obtaining high resolution. Two straight arrays are placed at an angle, intersecting approximately at their centers. The resulting interference pattern has extremely narrow lobes.

Christmas tree   A tree-like pattern on the screen of a television receiver, caused by loss of horizontal synchronization.

chroma   The quality of a color: *hue* and *saturation*.

chroma circuit   In color television, one of several circuits whose ultimate purpose is to produce a color component on the screen.

chroma-clear raster   In color television reception, the clear raster resulting from a white video signal, or from operation of the chroma circuits of the receiver (as if they were receiving a white transmission). Also called *white raster.*

chroma control   In a color television receiver, a rheostat or potentiometer that permits adjustment of color saturation through variation of the chrominance-signal amplitude before demodulation.

chromatic fidelity   See COLOR FIDELITY.

chromaticity   1. The state of being chromatic (see CHROMA). **2.** A quantitative assessment of a color in terms of dominant or complementary wavelength and purity.

chromaticity coordinate   For a color sample, the ratio of any one of the three tristimulus values (primary colors) to the sum of the three.

chromaticity diagram   A rectangular-coordinate graph in which one of the three CHROMATICITY COORDINATES of a three-color system is plotted against another coordinate.

chromaticity flicker   Flicker caused entirely by chromaticity fluctuation (see CHROMATICITY, **2**).

chromel   A nickel-chromium alloy with some iron content, used in thermocouples.

chromel-alumel junction   A thermocouple that uses wires of the alloys *chromel* and *alumel.*

chromel-constantan thermocouple   A thermocouple consisting of a junction between wires or strips of *chromel* and *constantan.* Typical output is 6.3 mV at 100°C.

chrome plating   The process of coating a metal with chromium. Generally protects against corrosion.

chrome recording tape   Also called *chrome tape* or *chromium tape.* Tape that is manufactured from the compound chromium dioxide. Noted for its ability to faithfully record and reproduce music.

chrominance   In color television, the difference between a reproduced color and a standard reference color of the same luminous intensity.

chrominance amplifier   In a color television circuit, the amplifier separating the chrominance signal from the total video signal.

chrominance cancellation   On a black-and-white picture tube screen, cancellation of the fluctuations in brightness caused by a chrominance signal.

chrominance-carrier reference   In color television, a continuous signal at the frequency of the chrominance subcarrier; it is in fixed phase with the color burst and provides modulation or demodulation phase reference for carrier-chrominance signals.

chrominance channel   In color television, a circuit devoted exclusively to the color function, as opposed to audio and general control channels.

chrominance component   In the NTSC color television systems, either of the components (I-signal or Q-signal) of the complete chrominance signal.

chrominance demodulator   In a color television receiver, a demodulator that extracts video-frequency chrominance components from the

chrominance signal, and a sine wave from the chrominance subcarrier oscillator.

chrominance gain control   A rheostat or potentiometer in the red, green, and blue matrix channels of a color television receiver, used to adjust the primary-signal amplitudes.

chrominance modulator   In a color television transmitter, a device that generates the chrominance signal from the I and Q components and the chrominance subcarrier.

chrominance primary   One of the transmission primaries (red, green, and blue) upon which the chrominance of a color depends.

chrominance signal   The signal component in color television that represents the hues and saturation levels of the colors in the picture.

chrominance subcarrier   In color television, the 3579.545-kHz signal that serves as a carrier for the I- and Q-signals.

chrominance-subcarrier oscillator   In a color television receiver, a crystal-controlled oscillator that generates the subcarrier signal (see CHROMINANCE SUBCARRIER).

chrominance video signals   Output signals from the red, green, and blue channels of a color television camera or receiver matrix.

chromium   Symbol, Cr. A metallic element. Atomic number, 24. Atomic weight, 51.996. Commonly used as a plating for metals to improve resistance to corrosion.

chronistor   An elapsed-time indicator in which current, flowing during a given time interval, electroplates an electrode. The duration of the interval is determined from the amount of deposit.

chronograph   **1.** An instrument that provides an accurate time base along the horizontal axis of its permanent record. **2.** Stopwatch.

chronometer   A precision clock. Electronic chronometers often use a highly accurate and stable crystal oscillator, followed by a string of multivibrators to reduce the crystal frequency to an audio frequency (such as 1 kHz) that drives the clock motor.

chronoscope   An instrument for precisely measuring small time intervals.

CHU   Call letters of the Canadian time-signal station whose primary frequency is 7.335 MHz.

Ci   Symbol for INPUT CAPACITANCE.

CIE   Abbreviation for *International Commission on Illumination.*

cinching   In a reel of magnetic tape, the slipping of tape as force is applied.

cinematograph   See KINEMATOGRAPH.

cipher   A code used for the purpose of preventing interception of a message by third parties.

circ   **1.** Abbreviation of *circuit.* **2.** Abbreviation of *circular.*

circle graph   Also called a *pie graph.* A representational device consisting of a disk subdivided into various triangular areas (radiating from the center of the circle), which are proportional to represented quantities.

circle of confusion   A circular image of a point source of light, resulting from an aberration in an optical system.

circle of declination   The graduated circular scale of a *declinometer.*

circlotron amplifier   A high-powered microwave amplifier of the one-port, cross-field, nonlinear type using a magnetron.

circuit   **1.** A closed path through which current flows from a generator, through various components, and back to the generator. (An electronic circuit is often a combination of interconnected subcircuits.) **2.** The wiring diagram of an electronic device or system.

circuit analysis   The careful determination of the nature and behavior of a circuit and its various parts. It can be theoretical, practical, or both. Compare CIRCUIT SYNTHESIS.

circuit analyzer   See CIRCUIT TESTER.

circuit board   A panel, plate, or card on which electronic components are mounted and interconnected to provide a functional unit.

circuit breaker   A resettable fuse-like device that is designed to protect a circuit against overloading. In a typical circuit breaker, the winding of an electromagnet is connected in series with the load circuit and with the switch contact points. Excessive current through the magnet winding causes the switch to be opened.

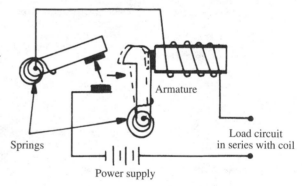

Armature

Load circuit in series with coil

Springs

Power supply

circuit breaker

circuit capacitance   The total capacitance (lumped, distributed, and stray) present in a circuit.

circuit capacity   **1.** The ability of a circuit to handle a quantity (such as current, voltage, frequency, power, etc.) safely and efficiently. **2.** The maximum value of some parameter at which a circuit can function safely and efficiently (e.g., a circuit capacity of 50 A). **3.** The number of channels that can be accommodated simultaneously by a circuit.

circuit component   **1.** Any of the electronic devices or parts (capacitors, resistors, transistors, etc.) that are connected through wiring to form a circuit. **2.** An electrical quantity required for, or arising from, circuit operation. Examples: input voltage, feedback current, stray capacitance, and circuit noise.

circuit diagram   A drawing in which symbols and lines represent the components and wiring of an electronic circuit. Also called CIRCUIT SCHEMATIC, SCHEMATIC DIAGRAM, and WIRING DIAGRAM.

circuit dropout   A momentary interruption of circuit operation, often caused by a break in the circuit.

circuit efficiency   A quantitative measure of the effectiveness of circuit operation, customarily expressed as the ratio of the useful output power to the total input power.

circuit element   See CIRCUIT COMPONENT, **1.**

circuit engineer   An electronics engineer who specializes in circuit analysis, circuit synthesis, or both.

circuit fault   **1.** Malfunction of a circuit. **2.** An error in circuit wiring.

circuit hole   A perforation within the conductive area of a printed-circuit board, for the insertion and connection of a pigtail, terminal, etc., or for connecting the conductors on one side of the board with those on the other.

circuit loading   Intentionally or unintentionally drawing power from a circuit.

circuit noise   **1.** Electrical noise generated by a circuit in the absence of an applied signal. **2.** In wire telephony, electrical noise as opposed to acoustic noise.

circuit noise level   The ratio of circuit-noise amplitude to reference-noise amplitude, expressed in decibels above the reference amplitude.

circuit-noise meter   A meter that measures the intensity of the noise generated within a circuit.

circuit parameter   See CIRCUIT COMPONENT, **2.**

circuit protection   Automatic safeguarding of a circuit from damage from overload, excessive drive, heat, vibration, etc. Protection is afforded by various devices and subcircuits, ranging from the common fuse to sophisticated limiters and breakers.

circuit reliability   A quantitative indication of the ability of a circuit to provide dependable operation as specified. See MEAN TIME BEFORE FAILURE and MEAN TIME BETWEEN FAILURES.

circuitry   **1.** Collectively, electronic and electrical circuits. **2.** A detailed plan of a circuit and its subcircuits. **3.** Collectively, the components of a circuit.

circuit schematic   See CIRCUIT DIAGRAM.

circuit simplification   **1.** In circuit analysis, the reduction of a complex circuit to its simplest representation to minimize labor and to promote clarity. Thus, through application of Kirchhoff's laws, a complicated circuit could theoretically be reduced to a single generator in series with a single impedance. **2.** In circuit synthesis, the arrangement of a circuit so as to provide desired performance with the fewest components and least-complex wiring.

circuit synthesis   The development of a circuit under the guidance of theoretical or practical knowledge of basic electronics principles and component parameters. Compare CIRCUIT ANALYSIS.

circuit tester   An instrument for checking the performance of electronic circuits. Often consists of a specialized continuity tester, but occasionally it includes a dynamic performance tester.

circuit tracking   The alignment and/or pretuning of circuits for identical or optimum response. It applies especially to cascaded circuits, whose variable elements, such as tuned inductance-capacitance (LC) networks, must follow each other in step when ganged together.

circular angle   The angle described by a radius vector as it rotates counterclockwise around a circle.

circular antenna   A half-wave horizontally polarized antenna, whose driven element is a rigid conductor bent into a circle with a break opposite the feed point. Also called *halo antenna*. Used primarily at very-high frequencies (VHF).

circular electric wave   An electromagnetic wave with circular electric lines of flux. An example is the field in the immediate vicinity of a CIRCULAR ANTENNA.

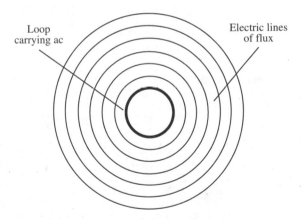

circular electric wave

circular functions   Trigonometric functions of the angle described by a vector rotating counterclockwise around a circle. Also see COSINE, COSECANT, COTANGENT, SECANT, SINE, and TANGENT.

circular magnet   See RING MAGNET.

circular magnetic wave   An electromagnetic wave in which the magnetic lines of flux are circular. An example is the field in the immediate vicinity of a straight-conductor antenna.

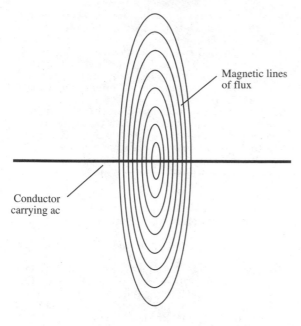

Magnetic lines
of flux

Conductor
carrying ac

circular magnetic wave

circular mil   A unit of cross-sectional area equivalent to 0.785 millionths of a square inch, or the area of a circle having a diameter of 0.001 inch. Generally, the circular mil is used to specify the cross-sectional area of a conductor, such as wire.

circular mil foot   A unit of volume in which the length is 1 foot and the cross-sectional area is 1 circular mil.

circular polarization   A form of electromagnetic-wave polarization in which the orientation of the electric flux rotates continuously and uniformly as the wave propagates through space. Circular polarization can occur in either a clockwise or counterclockwise sense.

circular radian   The angle enclosed by two radii of a unit circle and subtended by a unit arc. Equal to about 57.296 angular degrees.

circular scan   A radar scan in which the electron-beam spot describes a circle centered around the transmitting antenna.

circular sweep   In an oscilloscope, a sweep obtained when the horizontal and vertical sinusoidal deflecting voltages have the same amplitude and frequency, but are out of phase by 90 degrees (¼ cycle).

circular trace   An oscilloscope pattern consisting of a circle obtained with a circular sweep of the electron beam.

circular waveguide   A waveguide with a circular cross section.

circulating register   In a digital computer, a register in which digits are taken from locations at one end and returned to those at the other end.

circulating tank current   The alternating current that oscillates between the capacitor and inductor within a tank circuit.

circulator   A multi-terminal coupler in which microwave energy is transmitted in a particular direction from one terminal to the next.

circumvention   In a security or alarm system, the evasion of detection. Can be done by physically avoiding regions of coverage, or by defeating the system electronically.

cis   A prefix meaning "on this side of." For example, the *cislunar field* is the field on this side of the moon.

Citizen Band   Abbreviation, CB. A band of radio frequencies allocated for two-way communication between private citizens (apart from amateur and commercial services).

Citizens Radio Service   Two-way radio communication in a CITIZEN BAND. In the United States, the FCC licenses users of this service without requiring them to take an examination.

C/kg   Abbreviation of *coulombs per kilogram,* the unit for electron charge-to-mass ratio.

C/kmol   Abbreviation of *coulombs per kilomole,* the unit for the Faraday constant.

ckt   Abbreviation of CIRCUIT.

Cl   Symbol for CHLORINE.

cl   Abbreviation of CENTILITER.

cladding   The bonding of one metal to another to minimize or prevent corrosion. A common example is copper-clad steel wire, ideal for use in radio-frequency antenna systems. The copper provides excellent conduction, and the steel provides high tensile strength with a minimum of wire stretching.

clamper   A device that restricts a wave to a predetermined dc level. Also called DC RESTORER.

clamping   **1.** Fixing the operation of a device at a definite dc level. Also see CLAMPER. **2.** In television, establishing a fixed level for the picture signal at the start of each scanning line.

clamping circuit   See CLAMPER.

clamping diode   A diode used to fix the voltage level of a signal at a particular reference point.

clapper   In a bell, the ball or hammer that strikes the bell; in an electric bell, it is affixed to the vibrating armature.

Clapp-Gouriet oscillator   A *Colpitts oscillator* in which a capacitor is connected in series with the inductor. The circuit offers high frequency stability in the presence of input and output capacitance variations.

Clapp oscillator   A series-tuned hybrid *Colpitts oscillator,* having a tuning capacitor in series with the inductor, rather than in parallel with the inductor. The circuit allows the use of a smaller tuning capacitor, resulting in improved stability.

Clark cell   See ZINC STANDARD CELL.

class-A amplifier   An amplifier whose bias is set at approximately the midpoint of the characteristic curve. Output electrode current flows during the complete ac driving-voltage cycle. The

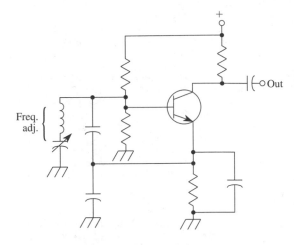

Clapp oscillator

input signal never drives the device into the nonlinear portion of the characteristic curve.

class-AB amplifier   Either a CLASS-AB$_1$ AMPLIFIER or a CLASS-AB$_2$ AMPLIFIER.

class-AB$_1$ amplifier   An amplifier whose bias is adjusted to a level between that of a class-A amplifier and that of a class-AB$_2$ amplifier. Output electrode current flows during the entire ac driving-voltage cycle. The input signal drives the device into the nonlinear portion of the characteristic curve during part of the cycle.

class-AB$_2$ amplifier   An amplifier whose bias is adjusted to a level between that of a class-AB$_1$ amplifier and that of a class-B amplifier. Output electrode current flows during more than 50 percent, but less than 100 percent, of the input signal cycle.

class-AB modulator   A modulator whose output stage is a class-AB$_1$ or class-AB$_2$ amplifier.

class-A modulator   A circuit for obtaining amplitude-modulated signals; essentially a class-A amplifier with two inputs, one for the carrier and the other for the modulating signal.

class-A operation   The operation of a transistor, field-effect transistor, or vacuum tube, in which the collector, drain, or plate current flows during the entire signal cycle.

class-B amplifier   An amplifier whose bias is adjusted to operate at the cutoff point in the characteristic curve. Output current flows during approximately 50 percent of the input signal cycle. Efficiency is higher than that of a class-A amplifier.

class-B modulator   A push-pull modulator whose output stage is a class-B amplifier.

class-B operation   The operation of a transistor, field-effect transistor, or vacuum tube, in which the collector, drain, or plate current flows for approximately half the signal cycle.

class-C amplifier   An amplifier whose input-electrode bias is adjusted for operation at a point considerably beyond cutoff. Output current flows during less than half of the input signal cycle. Such an amplifier requires comparatively high driving power, but is capable of excellent efficiency. Commonly used in continuous-wave (CW), amplitude-modulated (AM), and frequency-modulated (FM) radio transmitters.

class-C operation   The operation of a transistor, field-effect transistor, or vacuum tube, in which the collector, drain, or plate current flows for significantly less than half the signal cycle.

class-D telephone   A telephone restricted to use by emergency services, such as fire departments and guard alarm installations.

classical electron radius   Abbreviated r_e. The quantity expressed as $e^2/(m_e c^2)$, where e is the electron's charge in electrostatic units, m_e is its rest mass, and c is the speed of light. The value r_e is equal to approximately 2.82×10^{-13} cm or 2.82×10^{-15} m.

clean room   A room for the assembly or testing of critical electronic equipment. The term is derived from the extraordinary steps taken to remove dust and other contaminating agents. The personnel wear carefully cleaned garments (or disposable clothing), gloves, caps, and masks; in some situations, they are required to walk between ceiling and floor ducts of a vacuum system upon entering the room.

cleanup process   In the process of electron tube evacuation, a technique used to remove residual and occluded gases from the vacuum apparatus and from the device being evacuated.

clear   **1.** In computer operations, to restore a switching element (e.g., a flip-flop) or a memory element to its standard (e.g., zero) state. **2.** In computer practice, an asynchronous input.

clearance   The distance between two live terminals, or between one live terminal and ground.

clear band   In optical character recognition, the part of a document that must remain unprinted.

clear channel   **1.** A channel in the standard amplitude-modulation (AM) broadcast band that is designated to only one station within the area covered by the signal from that station. **2.** In television broadcasting, a channel for which there are no restrictions on the nature of the programming.

clear memory   A function in a calculator or small computer that erases the contents of the memory.

clear raster   The raster on the screen of a television picture tube in the absence of a signal, noise, or faulty beam deflection.

cleavage   In a crystalline substance, the quality of splitting along definite planes. Also, a fragment resulting from such a cleft.

click filter   See KEY-CLICK FILTER.

click method   An emergency technique for rendering an electric current audibly detectable, by making and breaking the circuit carrying the current to a headset or earphone. A single click results from each make and each break. Also see TIKKER.

click suppressor   See KEY-CLICK FILTER.

climate chamber   A test chamber that provides accurately controlled temperature, humidity, and/or barometric pressure, for evaluating the performance of electronic components and circuits. Also called ENVIRONMENTAL TEST CHAMBER.

climatometer   An instrument incorporating a hygrometer and bimetallic thermometer, whose dial pointers intersect to indicate comfort zones (best temperature-to-humidity ratio).

clinometer   An electromechanical device that measures the steepness of a slope. When the device is level (horizontal), the output voltage is zero. If the device is tipped in one direction, a negative voltage is produced; if it is tipped in the other direction, a positive voltage is produced. The output voltage is proportional to the angle at which the device is tipped. Used in mobile robots.

clip   A pinch-type connector whose jaws are normally held closed by a spring.

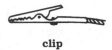

clip

clipped-noise modulation   Modulation of a jamming signal through clipping action to increase the sideband energy and resulting interference.

clipper   A circuit whose output voltage is fixed at a value for all input voltages higher than a predetermined value. Clippers can flat-top the positive, negative, or both positive and negative peaks of an input voltage.

clipper amplifier   An amplifier operated so that the positive, negative, or both positive and negative peaks are clipped in the output signal. The clipping action results from feeding a regular symmetric waveform into an amplifier so that on negative excursion extremes, the stage is cut off; on positive excursion extremes, the amplifier is driven into saturation.

clipper limiter   A device that delivers an output signal whose amplitude range corresponds to input-signal voltages between two predetermined limits. It can be used as a *noise limiter* with an element or elements that clip all pulses whose amplitudes are greater than the signal being processed.

clipping   1. Leveling off (flat-topping) a signal peak at a predetermined level. Also see CLIPPER. **2.** In audio practice, the loss of syllables or words because of cutoff periods in the operation

of the circuit (usually caused by overdriving a stage).

clock   In a digital computer or controller, the device or circuit that supplies timing pulses to pace the operation of the system.

clocked flip-flops   A master-slave arrangement of direct-coupled flip-flops. Information entered into the master unit when the input-trigger pulse amplitude is high is transferred to the slave unit when the amplitude is low.

clock frequency   In a digital computer or control, the reciprocal of the period of a single cycle, expressed in terms of the number of cycles occurring in one second of time (hertz, kilohertz, or megahertz).

clock generator   A test-signal generator that supplies a chain of pulses identical to those supplied by the clock of a digital computer.

clock module   A complete plug-in or wire-in digital unit whose readout indicates time of day or elapsed time. Connected to a suitable power supply, it serves as either a clock or timer.

clock pulse   A time-base pulse supplied by the clock of a digital computer, expressed as a period whose reciprocal is frequency.

clock rate   See CLOCK FREQUENCY.

clock track   On a magnetic tape or disk for data storage, a track containing read or write control (clock) pulses.

clockwise   Abbreviation, cw. Rotation in a right-hand direction around a circle, starting at the top. Compare COUNTERCLOCKWISE.

clockwise-polarized wave   An elliptically polarized electromagnetic wave whose electric-intensity vector rotates clockwise, as observed from the point of propagation. Compare COUNTERCLOCKWISE-POLARIZED WAVE.

clone   A machine manufactured by a relatively unknown company that performs all the same functions, in basically the same way, as another machine manufactured by a well-known, major corporation. The term is used especially in reference to computers and computer peripherals. If a device is compatible with a certain computer, then clones of that device are generally compatible with that computer. Also, the device is likely to be compatible with all clones of the computer.

close coupling   Also called *tight coupling.* In a transformer, the placement of the primary and secondary coils as close together as possible for maximum energy transfer. Compare LOOSE COUPLING.

closed capacitance   The value of a variable capacitor whose rotor plates are completely meshed with the stator plates. Compare OPEN CAPACITANCE.

closed circuit   A continuous unbroken circuit (i.e., one in which current can flow without interruption). Compare OPEN CIRCUIT.

closed-circuit cell A primary cell, such as the early gravity cell, designed for heavy and polarization-free service.

closed-circuit communication Communication between units only within a defined, hard-wired system, not extending to other units or systems.

closed-circuit security system An electronic security or alarm system, consisting of subsystems interconnected so that a disturbance anywhere in the circuit will result in an alarm signal pinpointing the location of the disturbance.

closed-circuit signaling Signaling accomplished by raising or lowering the level of a signaling current flowing continuously in a circuit.

closed-circuit television Abbreviation, CCTV. A usually in-plant television system, in which a transmitter feeds one or more receivers through a cable.

closed core A magnetic core generally constructed in an "O" or "D" configuration to confine the magnetic path to the core material. Compare OPEN CORE.

closed-core choke A choke coil wound on a CLOSED CORE. Also called CLOSED-CORE INDUCTOR.

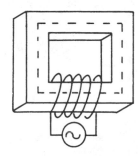

closed-core choke

closed-core transformer A transformer wound on a CLOSED CORE.

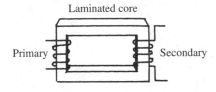

Laminated core

Primary   Secondary

closed-core transformer

closed loop **1.** The feedback path in a self-regulating control system. An oscillator, for example, is a closed-loop amplifier. **2.** A loop within a program that would continue indefinitely, except for an external exit command.

closed-loop bandwidth The frequency at which the gain of a closed-loop circuit (see CLOSED LOOP, **1**) drops 3 decibels from the direct-current or midband value.

closed-loop control system A control system in which self regulation is obtained by means of a feedback path (see CLOSED LOOP). An example is a voltage regulator, in which a rise in output voltage is fed back to the input. This changes the input voltage and reduces the output voltage to its correct value. Compare OPEN-LOOP CONTROL SYSTEM.

closed-loop input impedance The input impedance of an amplifier that has feedback.

closed-loop output impedance The output impedance of an amplifier that has feedback.

closed-loop voltage gain The voltage gain of an amplifier that has feedback.

closed magnetic circuit A magnetic circuit in which the flux is uninterrupted, as in a ferromagnetic core, which has no air gap. Also see CLOSED CORE.

closed subroutine In a digital computer program, a subroutine that can be accessed and left by branch instructions, such as GOSUB and RETURN in the high-level language BASIC.

close-spaced array A beam antenna in which the elements (radiator, director, and reflector) are spaced less than a quarter-wavelength apart.

close-talk microphone A microphone that must be placed close to the mouth. Such a microphone is less susceptible to background noises than an ordinary microphone, and is useful in environments where the ambient noise level is high.

closing rating A specification for closure conditions in a relay, including duty cycle and contact life (total guaranteed closures before contact failure).

closure **1.** The act of closing or being closed (e.g., *switch closure* or *relay closure*). **2.** Circuit completion (i.e., the elimination of all discontinuities).

cloud The mass of electrons constituting the space charge in a vacuum tube.

cloverleaf antenna An omnidirectional transmitting antenna in which numerous horizontal, four-element radiators (stacked vertically, a quarter-wavelength apart) are arranged in the shape of a four-leaf clover.

C/L ratio See LC RATIO.

clutter Extraneous echoes that interfere with the image on a radar display.

clutter gating In radar operations, a switching process that causes the normal video to be displayed in regions free of clutter, and the video indicating target movement to be displayed only in cluttered areas.

Cm Symbol for CURIUM.

cm Abbreviation of CENTIMETER.

c.m. Abbreviation of CIRCULAR MIL.

cm² Abbreviation of *square centimeter*.

cm³ Abbreviation of *cubic centimeter*.

C_max Abbreviation of *maximum capacitance*.

C meter See CAPACITANCE METER.

C_min Abbreviation of *minimum capacitance*.

CML Abbreviation of CURRENT-MODE LOGIC.

CMOS Abbreviation of COMPLEMENTARY METAL-OXIDE SEMICONDUCTOR.

CMR See COMMON-MODE REJECTION.

CMRR See COMMON-MODE REJECTION RATIO.

CMV See COMMON-MODE VOLTAGE.

C network A circuit with three impedances connected in series, the free leads being connected to a pair of terminals and the two internal junctions, to another pair of terminals.

Co Symbol for COBALT.

C_o Symbol for OUTPUT CAPACITANCE.

coalesce In computer operations, to create one file from several.

coarse adjustment Adjustment of a quantity in large increments. Compare FINE ADJUSTMENT.

coarse-chrominance primary See Q SIGNAL.

coastal bending A change in the horizontal direction of a line-of-sight radio wave when it crosses a coastline.

coast station In the Maritime Mobile Radio Service, a land station that communicates with shipboard stations.

coating **1.** The application of a substance to another substance by means of electroplating, electrophoresis, or similar process, for the purpose of protecting the material, isolating it from the environment, or improving the conductivity of an electrical connection to some other object. **2.** The magnetic material on a recording tape. **3.** In a computer system, the magnetic material on a magnetic diskette or hard disk.

coating thickness On magnetic tape or magnetic disks, the depth of the magnetic coating applied to the base.

coax Abbreviation of COAXIAL CABLE or COAXIAL LINE.

coaxial antenna A half-wave vertical antenna that is center-fed by coaxial cable. The cable runs upward through a ¼-wave section of tubing that composes the lower half of the antenna. The outer conductor of the cable is connected to this tubing through a shorting disk at the top. The inner conductor of the cable is connected to a ¼-wave vertical radiator that is insulated from, and that extends upward from the top of, the lower section.

coaxial cable An unbalanced cable consisting of two concentric conductors: an inner wire and an outer, braided sleeve. The inner and outer conductors are separated by a dielectric, usually solid or foamed polyethylene. The outer conductor is generally grounded while the inner conductor carries the signals. This cable is used in community-antenna television (CATV) networks, and as a transmission line connecting antennas to radio transmitters, receivers, and transceivers at low, medium, high, and very-high frequencies. It is also used in some high-fidelity sound systems—especially to connect microphones, compact-disc players, tape players, tuners, and speakers to audio amplifiers.

coaxial cable
(From left to right: insulating jacket, woven outer conductor, low-loss insulating sleeve, inner conductor.)

Characteristics of prefabricated coaxial transmission lines.

Type	Characteristic impedance, (ohms)	Velocity factor	Outside dia. (in.)	Picofarads per foot
RG-8/U	52	0.66	0.41	29.5
RG-9/U	51	0.66	0.42	30.0
RG-11/U	75	0.66	0.41	20.6
RG-17/U	52	0.66	0.87	29.5
RG-58/U	54	0.66	0.20	28.5
RG-59/U	73	0.66	0.24	21.0
RG-174/U	50	0.66	0.10	30.8
hard line	50	0.81	0.50	25.0
(½-inch)	75	0.81	0.50	16.7
hard line	50	0.81	0.75	25.0
(¾-inch)	75	0.81	0.75	16.7

coaxial cavity A cavity consisting of a cylindrical metal chamber housing a central rod. The cavity can be tuned to resonance by means of a piston.

coaxial connector A device used to splice coaxial line or to connect a coaxial line to a transmitter, receiver, or other piece of apparatus.

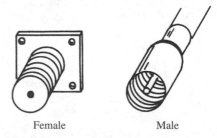

Female   Male

coaxial connector

coaxial diode A semiconductor diode housed in a cylindrical metal shell acting as one contact, and provided with a recessed, concentrically mounted end pin, which serves as the other contact.

coaxial driver See COAXIAL SPEAKER.

coaxial filter **1.** A filter that uses a coaxial cable as a tuned circuit. **2.** A filter designed to be used in a coaxial transmission line.

coaxial jack A female receptacle or connector, whose concentric terminals have the same spacing as a male coaxial-cable connector designed to fit it.

coaxial line A signal transmission line consisting of COAXIAL CABLE.

coaxial-line frequency meter A microwave absorption wavemeter (see WAVEMETER) with input and output receptacles for insertion into a coaxial line.

coaxial-line oscillator See CONCENTRIC-LINE OSCILLATOR.

coaxial loudspeaker See COAXIAL SPEAKER.

coaxial plug A male connector whose concentric terminals have the same spacing as a female coaxial cable connector designed to fit it.

coaxial receptacle A coaxial connector, such as a coaxial jack or plug. Receptacles are installed in equipment, whereas plugs are usually attached to the end of coaxial cables.

coaxial relay A relay designed to connect and disconnect, or to interchange, coaxial cables in a transmission line without disturbing the characteristic impedance of the line.

coaxial speaker Also called *coaxial driver* and *coaxial loudspeaker*. A large low-frequency speaker and a small high-frequency speaker mounted concentrically, the smaller within the larger. When used with a crossover network, this arrangement provides fairly good wide-range audio-frequency response, and saves physical space, compared with the use of separate speakers.

coaxial stub **1.** A length of coaxial cable acting as a branch to another coaxial cable. Commonly used for impedance matching. **2.** A length of coaxial cable, usually cut to ¼ or ½ wavelength, and connected across a coaxial transmission line to act as a WAVETRAP. Commonly used to reject strong interfering signals.

coaxial switch A switch designed to connect and disconnect, or to interchange, coaxial cables in a transmission line without disturbing the characteristic impedance of the line.

coaxial tank A tank circuit consisting of a rod within a cylinder. The tank is usually tuned by a small variable capacitor connected between the rod and cylinder at one end of the combination. Generally used at ultra-high frequencies (UHF).

coaxial-tank oscillator A stable, self-excited oscillator that uses a COAXIAL TANK. Also see CONCENTRIC-LINE OSCILLATOR.

coaxial transistor A transistor in which a semiconductor wafer is mounted centrally in a metal cylinder (the base connection) and is contacted on opposite faces by the emitter and collector whiskers, which are axially mounted.

coaxial transmission line A transmission line that is a COAXIAL CABLE.

coaxial wavemeter A type of absorption wavemeter in which the tunable element is a section of coaxial line (i.e., a metal cylinder surrounding a metal rod). An internal short-circuiting disk is moved along the cylinder to connect its inner wall to selected points along the rod's length, thereby varying the resonant frequency. The instrument is useful at microwave frequencies.

cobalt Symbol, Co. A metallic element. Atomic number, 27. Atomic weight, 58.94.

COBOL Acronym for *common business-oriented language*. A high-level computer programming language in a standard English form, used for business data processing. A COBOL compiler can interpret such statements as "If stock less than minimum, go to reorder."

cochannel interference Interference between similar signals transmitted on the same channel.

Cockcroft-Walton accelerator A proton accelerator in which nuclei of hydrogen atoms are given high velocity through a straight tube by a high dc voltage.

codan Any of several muting (SQUELCH) systems. In particular, a squelch circuit that suppresses noise in a sensitive receiver equipped with automatic gain control (AGC). The receiver is quiet until a carrier of predetermined strength is received. The name is an acronym for *carrier-operated device antinoise*.

codan lamp A lamp that alerts a radio operator that a signal of satisfactory strength is being received. Also see CODAN.

code **1.** A set of symbols for communications (e.g., the Morse code of radiotelegraphy and wire telegraphy in which dots and dashes correspond to letters, numbers, and marks of punctuation). **2.** In a computer program, symbolically represented instructions. **3.** ENCODE.

codec In encoding and decoding equipment, a *coder/decoder*, usually in a single package and operating at 8 kHz for an input signal with a passband of 3100 Hz (300 to 3400 Hz).

code character **1.** The representation of character in a particular code form. **2.** A sequence of dots and dashes in the Morse code.

code conversion The translation of a coded signal from one form of code to another.

coded decimal digit A number expressed in binary form (computer code), that is, in terms of zeros and ones only.

code-directing characters Characters added to a message to indicate how and where it is going.

coded program See PROGRAM.

coded signal **1.** A wire- or radiotelegraph signal in which secrecy is achieved by using letters in cipher groups, instead of straight language. **2.** SCRAMBLED SIGNAL.

coded stop   See PROGRAMMED HALT.

code elements   The smallest identifiable parts that compose a digital code. For example, in computer code, the elements are ones and zeroes (*high* and *low* logic states); in Morse code, they are *dots* and *dashes*.

code holes   In a punched card or tape, holes representing data.

code line   A written computer program instruction.

code machine   Any one of several devices for recording or reproducing code signals.

code position   The part of a data medium (e.g., card row) reserved for data.

code-practice oscillator   A simple keyed audio oscillator intended for practicing Morse code.

coder   1. In computer operations, a person who prepares instructions from flow charts and procedures devised by a programmer. **2.** A device that delivers coded signals.

code receiver   A radiotelegraph receiver.

code ringing   A method of ringing a telephone subscriber in a predetermined manner to convey a certain message.

code segment   The instruction part of computer storage associated with a process. Compare DATA SEGMENT and DUMP SEGMENT.

code set   The collection of codes representing all of the characters in a language.

code speed   See KEYING SPEED.

code transmitter   1. A radiotelegraph transmitter. **2.** A tape-operated keyer for wire telegraphy or radiotelegraphy.

code word   See PHONETIC ALPHABET CODE WORD.

coding   1. Performing the service of a CODER. **2.** Writing instructions for a digital computer; a part of programming.

coding check   A pencil-and-paper verification of a routine's validity.

coding sheet   A form on which program instructions are written prior to input.

codiphase radar   A radar system that uses beam forming, signal processing, and a phased-array antenna.

codistor   A voltage-regulating semiconductor device.

coefficient   1. A factor in an indicated product. Thus, in $4y$, 4 is the coefficient of y. **2.** A parameter that indicates a specific characteristic of some component or device (e.g., COEFFICIENT OF COUPLING or COEFFICIENT OF REFLECTION).

coefficient of coupling   Symbol k. The ratio of MUTUAL INDUCTANCE between two inductors to the maximum possible (theoretical) value of mutual inductance. This ratio is always greater than or equal to 0 (no coupling between inductors), and less than or equal to 1 (perfect coupling between inductors).

coefficient of current detection   See CURRENT-DETECTION COEFFICIENT.

coefficient of reflection   A measure of the amount of electromagnetic field reflected in a transmission line from the load feed point. The coefficient of reflection is equal to the square root of the reflected power divided by the forward power.

coercive force   The demagnetizing force required to remove residual magnetism from a material.

coercivity   See COERCIVE FORCE.

cogging   Nonuniform rotation of a motor armature. The velocity increases as an armature coil enters the magnetic field and decreases as it leaves the field.

coherence   In electromagnetic radiation, a condition in which all the wavefronts are in phase. This results in high energy concentration, and makes possible the long-distance transmission of infrared, visible light, and ultraviolet, because the rays are almost perfectly parallel. It also makes possible the extreme radiation intensity characteristic of some LASER devices.

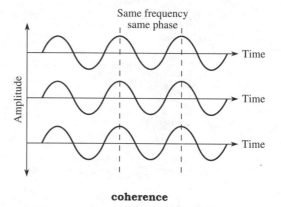

coherence

coherent bundle   A bundle of optical fibers, such that the individual fibers are in the same relative positions at either end of the bundle.

coherent carrier   A carrier that agrees in frequency and phase with a reference signal.

coherent electroluminescent device   See LASER DIODE.

coherent light   Visible light in which the phase relationship between successive waves is such that the beam consists of parallel rays that provide a high concentration of energy. Also see LASER.

coherent-light radar   See COLIDAR.

coherent oscillator   In a radar system, an oscillator that provides a COHERENT REFERENCE.

coherent-pulse operation   Pulse operation characterized by a fixed phase relationship between pulses.

coherent radiation   Radiation characterized by COHERENCE.

coherent reference   A stable reference frequency with which other signals are phase locked for coherence.

coherent transponder   A transponder in which the frequency and phase of the input and output signals have a fixed relationship.

coil   A long conductor or group of conductors wound into a tight helical package, often in several layers on a cylindrical form. This takes advantage of the resulting concentration of magnetic flux, maximizing the inductance that can be obtained in a component of limited physical size. Further increases in inductance can be realized by the use of ferromagnetic core materials. See also INDUCTOR.

coil antenna   See LOOP ANTENNA.

coil checker   An alternating-current (ac) meter or simple bridge for checking inductors. Such instruments usually only indicate inductance values, but some list readings of resistance or approximate inductor Q factor.

coil dissipation   The power wasted in a coil as heat. Generally, this dissipation or loss is proportional to the resistance of the coil, and to the square of the current passing through the coil.

coil form   The insulating support around which an air-core coil is wound.

coil loading   The insertion of one or more inductors into a transmission line or antenna element, for the purpose of impedance matching, alteration of the resonant frequency, or both.

coil magnification factor   The Q factor of an inductor. Generally given by the ratio X_L/R_L, where X_L is the inductive reactance of the coil in ohms, and R_L is the resistance of the coil in ohms.

coil neutralization   See INDUCTIVE NEUTRALIZATION.

coil resistance   The resistance of a coil (inductor), as distinct from its reactance. It is almost entirely the result of ohmic loss in the wire from which the coil is manufactured.

coilshield   A metal can designed to provide efficient electrostatic and electromagnetic shielding of a coil, preventing unwanted inductive coupling to other components.

coincidence   The simultaneous occurrence of two or more signals. Compare ANTICOINCIDENCE.

coincidence amplifier   An amplifier that delivers an output signal only when two or more input signals occur simultaneously.

coincidence circuit   See AND CIRCUIT.

coincidence counter   A circuit or device, such as a gate, that delivers an output pulse only when two or more input pulses occur simultaneously; the output pulses go to a device that counts them.

coincidence detector   See AND CIRCUIT.

coincidence gate   See AND GATE.

coincident-current selection   Selection of a magnetic core (in a core memory or similar device) by applying two or more currents simultaneously.

coin shooting   Searching for coins and similar small, buried metallic objects using a METAL LOCATOR.

coke   A porous material obtained from the destructive distillation of coal. It is valued for the production of carbon components for electronics, such as dry-cell electrodes and motor brushes.

cold   **1.** Pertaining to an electrical circuit, component, or terminal that is at ground potential. **2.** A term denoting a bad solder joint. **3.** Pertaining to an unheated electrode or element. See COLD CATHODE.

cold alignment   The alignment of a tracking system (especially of its tuned circuits) when the system is not in operation, as when transistor power is off. Also called QUIET ALIGNMENT.

cold cathode   **1.** In an electron tube, a cathode that emits electrons without being heated. **2.** A cathode electrode operated at a temperature below ambient temperature.

cold chamber   An enclosure in which electronic equipment can be tested at selected, precise low temperatures. Compare OVEN.

cold flow   The (usually gradual) change in the dimensions of a material, such as plastic in a molded part.

cold junction   In a thermocouple system, an auxiliary thermocouple connected in series with the hot thermocouple, and immersed in ice or operated at ambient temperature.

cold light   Light produced without significant heat, as from the ionization of a gas by a high voltage (as in neon bulbs and fluorescent lamps), or by electroluminescence, bioluminescence, cathodoluminescence, or a similar phenomenon.

cold pressure welding   Welding sometimes used in the fabrication of electronic equipment, in which the metal parts to be joined are pressed together tightly to the point of deformation, whereupon they become welded.

cold resistance   The resistance of an unheated electronic component. Compare HOT RESISTANCE.

cold rolling   A method of manufacturing an inductor core so that the magnetic grains are all arranged lengthwise.

cold solder joint   A solder joint in which insufficient heat has been applied, resulting in a bad connection.

cold spot   **1.** An area of a circuit or component whose temperature is ordinarily lower than that of the surrounding area. **2.** A node of current or voltage. Compare HOT SPOT.

cold weld   A welded joint produced by means of COLD PRESSURE WELDING.

colidar   An optical radar system using unmodulated, coherent (laser-produced) light. The term is an acronym for *coherent light detection and ranging.*

collate   In data processing, to produce an ordered set from two or more similarly ordered sets (as punched cards).

collator   In a punched-card system, a device that collates (see COLLATE) punched cards.

collector   **1.** In a bipolar transistor, the electrode toward which emitted current carriers travel. **2.** In a Klystron, the final electrode toward which electrons migrate after passing through the buncher and catcher. **3.** In an iconoscope, a cylindrical electrode around the circumference of the tube, which gathers and conducts away the electrons released by the mosaic. **4.** The final (target) electrode in a backward-wave or traveling-wave tube. **5.** A computer program segment that collates compiled segments so that they can be loaded into the computer.

collector capacitance   **1.** Symbol, C_C. The capacitance of the collector junction in a bipolar transistor. **2.** The capacitance of the collector electrode in a Klystron, iconoscope, backward-wave tube, or traveling-wave tube.

collector current   **1.** Symbol, I_C. The current flowing in the collector circuit of a bipolar transistor. Also see AC COLLECTOR CURRENT and DC COLLECTOR CURRENT. **2.** Current flowing in the collector circuit of a Klystron, iconoscope, backward-wave tube, or traveling-wave tube.

collector-current cutoff   See COLLECTOR CUTOFF.

collector cutoff   In a bipolar transistor, the condition in which the collector current is cut off (i.e., reduced to the residual value). Also see CUTOFF CURRENT.

collector cutoff current   See CUTOFF CURRENT.

collector-diffusion isolation   A method of making integrated circuits that contain bipolar transistors. Provides electrical separation of the transistors in a semiconductor integrated circuit.

collector dissipation   Symbol, P_C. In a bipolar transistor, the power dissipation of the collector electrode. The collector dc power dissipation is the product of collector current and collector voltage: $P_C = V_C I_C$.

collector efficiency   In a bipolar transistor circuit, the ratio of ac power output to dc collector-power input.

collector family   For a bipolar transistor, a group of collector current versus collector voltage curves. Each is plotted for a particular value of base current (common-emitter circuit) or emitter current (common-base circuit).

collector junction   In a bipolar transistor, the junction between collector and base layers.

collector mesh   In a cathode-ray storage tube, a flat, fine wire screen that attracts and conducts

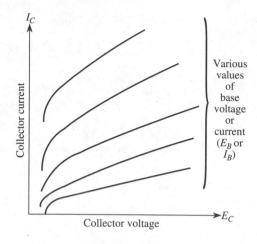

Various values of base voltage or current (E_B or I_B)

Collector current

Collector voltage

collector family

away the secondary electrons knocked out of the storage mesh by the electron beam.

collector multiplication   In a bipolar transistor, an increase in the number of electrons at the collector electrode, caused by a momentary alteration of the charge density of the collector junction by injected carriers reaching the junction.

collector resistance   In a bipolar transistor, the internal resistance of the collector junction. See AC COLLECTOR RESISTANCE and DC COLLECTOR RESISTANCE.

collector ring   **1.** A rotating, brush-contacted ring electrode connected to one end of a coil in an ac generator. **2.** A similar ring which, with a brush, serves as a connection to a rotating element, as in a signal-gathering system. **3.** The collector electrode in an iconoscope.

collector transition capacitance   The capacitance between the collector and base of a bipolar transistor under normal operating conditions. This capacitance has a limiting effect on the operating frequency of a bipolar device.

collector voltage   Symbol, V_C. In a bipolar transistor, the voltage on the collector electrode. See AC COLLECTOR VOLTAGE and DC COLLECTOR VOLTAGE.

collimated rays   Electromagnetic waves made parallel or nearly parallel. This can be done by means of a reflector, a lens, or a laser.

collimation   **1.** The process of rendering electromagnetic rays parallel. **2.** Adjustment of the line of sight of an instrument, such as a level or transit.

collimation equipment   Optical-alignment equipment.

collimator   A device for producing parallel rays of light or other radiation. In electronics, the most common example is a *dish antenna.*

collinear antenna A broadside directional antenna consisting of two or more half-wave radiators; the current is kept in phase in each section by quarter-wave stubs between each radiating section. The radiators are stacked end to end horizontally or vertically. Also called FRANKLIN ANTENNA.

Collins coupler A single-section, pi-filter circuit, used to match a radio transmitter to a wide range of antenna impedances. Also called *pi coupler* and *Collins network.*

collodion A viscous solution of pyroxylin and a solvent (such as acetone, alcohol, or ether) sometimes used as a binding agent for coils and other components.

cologarithm Abbreviation, colog. The logarithm of the reciprocal of a number; $\operatorname{colog} x = \log (1/x) = \log x^{-1} = -\log x$.

color A perceived characteristic, and a direct function, of visible-light wavelength. Seen by the human eye as a spectrum of hues, ranging from red at the longest visible wavelengths, through orange, yellow, green, blue, indigo, and finally violet at the shortest visible wavelengths. See HUE.

coloration In audio applications, a blending of sounds as a result of mixing among components at different frequencies. Sometimes this is done deliberately; in other instances, it is undesirable.

color balance In a color television receiver, adjustment of the beam intensities of the individual guns of a three-gun picture tube. Compensates for the difference in light emissivity of the red, green, and blue phosphors on the tube screen.

color bar-dot generator A radio-frequency (RF) signal generator that produces a bar or dot pattern on the screen of a color television picture tube. Used for testing and alignment.

color-bar pattern A color television test pattern of vertical bars—each of a different color.

color breakup A transient separation of a color television picture into its red, green, and blue components, as a result of a sudden disturbance of viewing conditions (blinking of eyes, moving of head, intermittent blocking of screen, etc.).

color burst As a phase reference for the 3.579545-MHz oscillator in a color television receiver, approximately nine cycles of the chrominance subcarrier added to the back porch of the horizontal blanking pedestal in the composite color signal.

color carrier See CHROMINANCE SUBCARRIER.

colorcast A color television broadcast.

color code 1. A system that uses colored stripes or dots to mark the nominal values and other characteristics on capacitors, resistors, and other components. 2. A code that represents the various frequencies being used by radio-control modelers in competition, and used on flags attached to transmitters, for example, as a safeguard against jamming.

color coder See COLOR ENCODER.

color contamination In a color television system, faulty color reproduction resulting from incomplete separation of the red, green, and blue channels.

color-coordinate transformation In a color television system, the computation (performed electrically in the system) of the tristimulus (primary) values with reference to one set of primaries, from the same colors derived from another set of primaries.

color depth An expression for the extent to which an image can accurately render color. Generally expressed in bits or in number of colors. Some systems can reproduce millions of different colors.

color-difference signal Designated B-Y, G-Y, and R-Y. The signal resulting from reducing the amplitude of a color signal by an amount equal to the luminance-signal amplitude. Also see B-Y SIGNAL, G-Y SIGNAL, and R-Y SIGNAL.

color dot 1. A phosphor spot on the screen of a color television picture tube. 2. One of the spots stamped on a capacitor, indicating the capacitance, voltage, and tolerance (see COLOR CODE, 1). 3. A spot stamped on a resistor, indicating the number of zeros to be added to the value indicated by the color bands.

color edging In a color television picture, an aberration consisting of false color at the boundaries between areas of different color.

color encoder In a color television transmitter, the circuit or channel in which the camera signals and the chrominance subcarrier are combined into the color-picture signal.

color equation A mathematical means of determining the resultant color obtained by adding primary colors in various proportions.

color fidelity The faithfulness with which a color television system, lens, or film reproduces the colors of a scene.

color filter A transparent plate or film that transmits light of a desired color, and eliminates or attenuates all other colors.

color flicker In a color television system, image instability that occurs when the luminance and chromaticity both fluctuate.

color fringing In a color television picture, false color around objects, sometimes causing them to appear separated into different colors.

color generator A special radio-frequency (RF) signal generator to adjust or troubleshoot a color television receiver. The color signals it delivers are identical to those produced by a broadcast station.

color graphics Computer graphics displayed in color on a cathode-ray tube (CRT) or liquid-crystal display (LCD).

colorimeter A device used to quantitatively measure the color intensity of a sample relative to a standard.

colorimetric   A characteristic of visible light, representing the wavelength concentration. Refers to the perceived color of a light beam.

colorimetry   The science and art of color measurement.

color killer   In a color television receiver, a circuit that, in the absence of a color signal, delivers a negative bias to cut off the bandpass amplifier.

color match   In photometry, the condition in which color agreement exists between the halves of an area. Also see COLOR MATCHING.

color matching   The art of selecting colors that are identical in hue, saturation, and brilliance. This can be done with the unaided eye or with the help of an instrument.

color media   Substances that transmit essentially one color of visible light while blocking other colors.

color meter   A photoelectric instrument for measuring color values, and comparing and matching colors.

color mixture   An additive combination of two or more colors. Thus, red + yellow = orange, blue + red = violet, red + blue + green = white, etc.

color oscillator   The oscillator in a color television receiver that coordinates the color response. This oscillator is operated at 3.579545 MHz, to within plus or minus 10 Hz.

color palette   In a color video image, the total number of possible colors that can be displayed.

color phase   In color television, the phase difference between an I or Q chrominance primary signal and the chrominance carrier reference.

color-phase diagram   In color television, a quadrant diagram showing (for each of the three primary and complementary colors) the difference in phase between the color-burst signal and the chrominance signal, as well as the peak amplitude of the chrominance signal. Also shown are the peak amplitude and polarity of both in-phase and quadrature components required for the chrominance signals. For color TV receiver adjustment, the color-phase diagram is displayed, in effect, by a VECTORSCOPE when a suitable signal from a color generator is applied to the receiver.

color picture signal   1. In color television and/or computer graphics, an electrical signal containing components corresponding to the hue, saturation, and brilliance of a fixed or changing visual image. 2. In color television, the combination of chrominance and luminance signals minus blanking and sync signals.

color picture tube   A specialized type of cathode-ray tube (CRT), used in color television receivers and computer displays. Three different images are produced: one in red, one in blue, and one in green. The three monochrome images are combined to form a complete color image.

color primaries   1. Also called *additive primaries* or *primary colors*. In color television, the hues red (R), green (G), and blue (B). When these colors are mixed in various ratios, any visual color can result. 2. Also called *subtractive primaries* or *primary pigments*. In color printing, the hues magenta (M), cyan (C), and yellow (Y). These roughly correspond to red (R), blue (B) and yellow (Y). Sometimes black (K) is also included. When these pigments are mixed in various ratios, any visual pigment can result.

color purity   The ratio of wanted to unwanted components in a color. In a pure color, there are no components other than those required to produce the color. Color, in this context, includes white, black, and all shades of gray.

color-purity magnet   A permanent magnet on the neck of a color television picture tube, used to help ensure color purity by maintaining proper displacement of the electron beam.

color registration   In color television reception, the precise superimposition of red, green, and blue so that the composite is free from COLOR EDGING.

color rendering index   A mathematical expression defining the effect of the color of a light source on an object. For example, in red light, a blue object appears nearly black.

color sampling rate   The number of times per second that each primary color is sampled in a color television receiver.

color saturation   A measure of the purity of a hue. The extent to which a hue is without a white component; 100% saturation indicates a complete absence of white.

color sensing   In machine vision systems, the ability to distinguish between light of different wavelengths. Usually done with red, green and blue color filters and three separate cameras.

color sensitivity   1. The degree of which a photosensitive device, such as a photocell or camera tube, responds to various colors of light. 2. The degree to which photographic film responds to various colors of light.

color signal   See COLOR PICTURE SIGNAL.

color spectrum   The band of electromagnetic energy containing visible light; it extends from red (at the longest wavelengths) to violet (at the shortest). Commonly measured in *nanometers (nm)*, where 1 nm = 10^{-9} m. Also expressed in *Angstroms*, where 1 Angstrom = 10^{-10} m = 0.1 nm. In order of decreasing wavelength, the colors are red at 750 to 700 nm (7500 to 7000 Angstroms), orange, yellow, green, blue, indigo, and violet at 410 to 390 nm (4100 to 3900 Angstroms).

color subcarrier   A modulated monochrome signal whose sidebands convey color information.

color-sync signal   See COLOR BURST.

color system   Also called *RGB color model*. A means of representing a color in terms of mathematical coordinates. This can be done in three dimensions because there are three COLOR

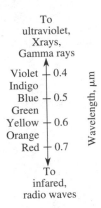

To
ultraviolet,
Xrays,
Gamma rays

Violet ┬ 0.4
Indigo
Blue ┼ 0.5
Green
Yellow ┼ 0.6
Orange
Red ┼ 0.7

Wavelength, μm

To
infared,
radio waves

color spectrum

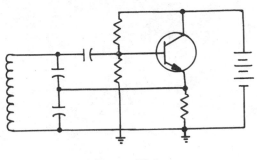

Colpitts oscillator

PRIMARIES. Each color primary is represented by an axis. Any COMPOSITE COLOR can be represented by a unique vector. The relative amount of each color primary is given by the length of the composite-color vector components along each axis.

color television Television in which the picture approximates natural color. It operates on the basis of mixing three primary colors (red, blue, and green) of phosphors on the picture tube screen.

color television receiver A television receiver designed to reproduce color pictures.

color television signal The signal transmitted by a color television transmitter, containing all of the information needed to reproduce a complete, full-color, moving image.

color transmission The television transmission of a picture in color.

color triad On the screen of a color picture tube, one of the color cells, each of which contains one of the three phosphor dots: red, green, and blue.

color triangle A triangle that can be inscribed on a chromaticity diagram to reveal the chromaticity range resulting from adding the three color primaries.

color TV signal The complete signal (video, color, and sync components) required for transmitting a picture in color.

color weather radar A computer-enhanced radar rendition of weather patterns, usually showing various intensities of precipitation as different colors. Commonly, areas of precipitation show up as violet, blue, green, yellow, orange, and red, in order of increasing intensity.

Colpitts oscillator A self-excited oscillator circuit in which the tank is divided into input and feedback portions by a capacitive voltage divider (two capacitors connected in series across the tank coil), rather than by a center tap on the coil.

columbium Symbol, Cb. The former name of the metallic element *niobium*. Atomic number, 41. Atomic weight, 92.9064.

column See CARD COLUMN.

columnar graph A graphical presentation of data, in which the ordinates are represented by vertical columns whose height depends on the value. Commonly used in *presentation graphics*, but less common in *analytical graphics*.

column binary Binary number representation on punched cards, wherein consecutive digits correspond to consecutive column punching positions.

column speaker An acoustic speaker with a long cabinet, so that a large column of air is used for resonating or reinforcing purposes. This type of speaker radiates over a wide azimuth angle, while providing a narrow beam in the elevation plane.

column split On a punched card machine, the device for reading, as two separate characters or codes, two parts of a single column.

COM 1. Abbreviation for *communications port*. 2. Abbreviation for *computer output on microfilm*.

coma An aberration that causes the beam spot on the screen of a cathode-ray tube to resemble a comet.

coma lobes An aberration in the radiation or response pattern of a dish antenna that occurs when the radiating element is not exactly at the focal point of the reflector. When the directional pattern is altered by moving the driven element, rather than turning the entire antenna, these lobes appear.

comb amplifier An arrangement of several sharply tuned bandpass amplifiers whose inputs are connected in parallel and whose outputs are separate; the amplifiers separate various frequencies from a multifrequency input signal. The name is derived from the comb-like appearance of the response pattern of various output peaks displayed along a frequency-base axis.

comb filter A selective device that passes several narrow bands of frequencies within a larger

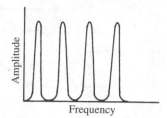

comb filter response

band, while rejecting frequencies in between the narrow bands. So called because its frequency-response curve resembles the teeth of a comb when observed on a spectrum analyzer. Also see COMB AMPLIFIER.

comb generator **1.** A signal generator that provides outputs at evenly spaced frequencies. So called because, on a spectrum analyzer, its output looks like the teeth of a comb. **2.** A transmitter with many spurious signals at its output.

combination **1.** A functional, usually stationary, installation consisting of two or more pieces of equipment. Examples: transmitter/receiver combination, motor/generator combination, and tuner/amplifier combination. **2.** In mathematics, a selection of several factors from a group, without regard to order. Thus, from the group ABC, the three possible combinations are AB, AC, and BC. Compare PERMUTATION.

combinational circuit Two or more basic logic circuits, combined in such a way that the output state depends entirely on the input states.

combination bridge A bridge that affords two or more classes of measurement, usually selectable by means of a function switch. Examples: capacitance-inductance bridge, and capacitance-resistance bridge.

combination cable A cable that has conductors grouped in pairs, threes, quads, or similar arrangements.

combination feedback See CURRENT-VOLTAGE FEEDBACK.

combination microphone Two or more microphones combined into one unit.

combination speaker Two or more loudspeakers combined into one (e.g., a COAXIAL SPEAKER).

combination tone An acoustic tone resulting from the combination of two other acoustic tones. If the original tones have frequencies f_1 and f_2 (where f_1 is higher than f_2), then the first-order combination frequencies are $f_1 + f_2$ and $f_1 - f_2$. Higher-order combination tones can result from mixing among the original tones and the first-order combination tones.

combinatorial logic A form of digital logic, in which the output states depend on the input states, but on no other factor.

combined head See READ-WRITE HEAD.

combined reactance The net reactance (X) in a circuit, obtained by vectorially adding the inductive reactance (X_L) and the capacitive reactance (X_C).

combiner A circuit or device for mixing various signals to form a new signal. Also see MIXER.

combiner circuit In a color television camera, the circuit that combines the chroma and luminance with the sync.

comeback A spurious response in a bandpass or band-rejection filter, at a frequency well above or below the passband or stopband.

command **1.** In computer operations, the group of selected pulses or other signals that cause the computer to execute a step in its program. **2.** Instruction.

command chain Part of a computer operation carried out independently as a series of input/output instructions.

command control In automation, electronic control, and computer operations, the performance of functions in response to a transmitted signal.

command destruct signal A signal for instigating the destruction of a missile in flight.

command guidance system A system in which a guided missile and its target are both tracked by radar.

command language A computer language made up of command operators.

command link In a command guidance system, the section that transmits missile-steering commands.

command network A radio communications network in which the chain of command is rigorously defined and followed.

command reference The current or voltage to which a feedback signal is referenced in a control system or servomechanism.

comment A statement written into a computer program for a documentation, rather than implementation (e.g., to describe the purpose of a step or subroutine).

comment field A record or file in which instructions or explanations are given.

commercial data processing A commercial (rather than industrial, scientific, or personal) application of data processing.

commercial killer A usually remote-controlled, electronic relay for disabling a radio or television receiver during advertisements.

commercial language A computer programming language for commercial applications (payroll, for example).

common **1.** Grounded. **2.** Pertaining to a connection shared by several different points in a circuit or system. **3.** See COMMON GROUND.

common area A computer storage area usable by several programs or segments within a program.

common-base circuit A bipolar transistor circuit in which the transistor base is the common (or grounded) electrode. Also called *grounded-base circuit.*

common battery **1.** A battery shared by two or more different circuits or pieces of equipment. **2.** In wire telephony, a central office battery that supplies the entire system.

common-battery office In wire telephony, a central office that provides a common battery.

common business-oriented language See COBOL.

common-capacitor coupling The process of coupling one tuned circuit to another by means of a capacitor that is common to both circuits.

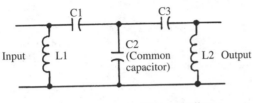

common-capacitor coupling

common-carrier fixed station A fixed radio station that provides public service.

common-cathode circuit A tube circuit in which the cathode is the common (or grounded) electrode. Also called *grounded-cathode circuit.*

common-channel interference Radio interference resulting from two stations transmitting on the same channel. It is characterized principally by beat-note (heterodyne whistle) generation, and suppression or capture of the weaker signal by the stronger one.

common-collector circuit A bipolar-transistor circuit in which the collector is the common (or grounded) electrode. Also called *grounded-collector circuit* and EMITTER FOLLOWER.

common communications carrier A communications company authorized by the licensing agency to furnish public communications.

common-component coupling See COMMON-CAPACITOR COUPLING, COMMON-INDUCTOR COUPLING, and COMMON-RESISTOR COUPLING.

common-drain circuit A field-effect transistor circuit in which the drain terminal is the common (or grounded) electrode. Also called *grounded-drain circuit* and SOURCE FOLLOWER.

common-emitter circuit A bipolar transistor circuit in which the emitter is the common (or grounded) electrode. Also called *grounded-emitter circuit.*

common-gate circuit A field-effect transistor circuit in which the gate is the common (or grounded) electrode. Also called *grounded-gate circuit.*

common-grid circuit A tube circuit in which the control grid is the common (or grounded) electrode. Also called *grounded-grid circuit.*

common ground A single ground-point connection shared by several portions of a circuit.

common impedance A single impedance shared by parts of a circuit. Because currents from the various parts flow through this impedance simultaneously, coupling (desired or undesired) can occur between them.

common-impedance coupling See COMMON-CAPACITOR COUPLING, COMMON-INDUCTOR COUPLING, and COMMON-RESISTOR COUPLING.

common-inductor coupling The process of coupling one tuned circuit to another by means of an inductor that is common to both circuits.

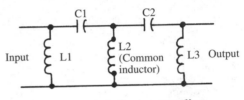

common-inductor coupling

common language A language recognized by all the equipment in a data processing system.

common logarithm Abbreviation, $\log_{10}$. Also called *base-10 logarithm.* A logarithm in which the base number is 10. Also see LOGARITHM.

common mode Pertaining to signals or signal components that are identical in amplitude and duration.

common-mode characteristics In an operational amplifier, characteristics denoting amplifier performance when a common signal is applied to inverting and noninverting inputs.

common-mode gain The voltage gain of a differential amplifier with a common-mode input.

common-mode impedance input The impedance between ground and one of the inputs of a differential amplifier. Compare COMMON-MODE INPUT IMPEDANCE.

common-mode input capacitance In a differential amplifier, the internal capacitance of the common-mode input circuit.

common-mode input circuit In a differential amplifier, the input circuit between ground and the inputs connected together.

common-mode input impedance In a differential amplifier, the open-loop impedance between ground and the inputs connected together. Compare COMMON-MODE IMPEDANCE INPUT.

common-mode input signal A signal applied to the common-mode input circuit of a differential amplifier (i.e., to both inputs connected together). Compare COMMON-MODE SIGNAL.

common-mode input voltage In a differential amplifier, the maximum voltage that can be applied safely between ground and the inputs connected together.

common-mode interference A form of interference that occurs across the terminals of a grounded system.

common-mode rejection The extent to which a differential amplifier will reject a signal presented simultaneously to both inputs in phase, or of two signals identical in amplitude, frequency, and phase applied separately to the two inputs. Also see COMMON-MODE REJECTION RATIO.

common-mode rejection ratio In a differential amplifier, the extent to which the amplifier cancels undesired signals. It is the ratio of the differential gain to the common-mode gain. Also see COMMON-MODE REJECTION.

common-mode signal The algebraic average of two signals applied simultaneously to the two ends of a balanced circuit, such as a differential amplifier. Compare COMMON-MODE INPUT SIGNAL.

common-mode voltage The part of the input that is common to both inputs of a differential amplifier circuit. It is quantitatively defined as the arithmetic mean of the voltages at the inputs.

common-mode voltage gain See COMMON-MODE GAIN.

common-mode voltage range The range limited by the maximum nonsaturating input voltage that can be applied to both inputs of an operational amplifier.

common pool An assigned memory store, utilized by two or more circuits or systems.

common-resistor coupling The process of coupling one circuit to another by means of a resistor that is common to both circuits.

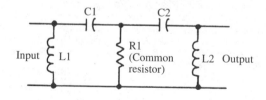

common-resistor coupling

common-source circuit A field-effect transistor circuit in which the source terminal is the common (or grounded) electrode. Also called *grounded-source circuit.*

common-user channels Communication channels open to all licensees in a particular service.

communication band A band of frequencies whose use is authorized expressly for communications, rather than for other services (such as broadcasting, education, remote control, etc.).

communication channel 1. In radio or wire service, a (usually auxiliary) channel for direct exchange of information between units of the service (e.g., a "talking circuit" between a broadcast studio and the transmitter house). 2. A data transmission channel between two points (e.g., a remote terminal and a central computer system).

communication link 1. Collectively, the equipment providing a communication channel between two transmitters. 2. Data terminal equipment.

communication protocol The specifications of a digital signal, including the speed in bits per second (bps) or bauds, the code type, the bit duration, the mark-to-space ratio, etc.

communications The science and art of using and developing electronic equipment and processes for the transmission and reception of information.

communications common carrier An organization licensed to provide public communication services.

communications network An organization of transmitting and receiving stations for the reliable exchange of intelligence. Also called *net.*

communications receiver A general-coverage or multiband radio receiver, designed primarily for listening to amateur, weather, or other nonbroadcast stations. Compare BROADCAST RECEIVER.

communications satellites Satellites in earth orbit that provide propagation paths (e.g., by reflection or retransmission) for radio waves between terrestrial transmitters and receivers. Also see ACTIVE COMMUNICATIONS SATELLITE and PASSIVE COMMUNICATIONS SATELLITE.

community-antenna television Abbreviation, CATV. A system in which an advantageously located receiving station receives television signals, amplifies them if necessary, and distributes them in the community served by the system. Commonly called *cable TV.*

commutating capacitor 1. In a flip-flop circuit, a capacitor connected in parallel with the cross-coupling resistor to accelerate the transition from one stable state to the other. Also called *speedup capacitor.* 2. A capacitor connected in parallel between silicon-controlled rectifier (SCR) stages to momentarily reverse the current going through the SCR, thereby causing the SCR to go into the cutoff condition.

commutation 1. In a direct-current (dc) generator, periodic reversal of the current in the armature coils as the coils alternately pass the north and south poles of the magnetic field. When the ends of each coil are connected to opposite bars of the commutator, the electrical polarity at the commutator brushes remains constant. 2. In a thyratron or silicon-controlled rectifier (SCR) circuit, momentarily reversing the polarity to cut the device off.

commutator   **1.** In a direct-current (dc) motor, generator, or rotating selector, an arrangement of parallel metal bars or strips on a rotating drum. As the drum turns, the bars contact one or more brushes that are in sliding contact with the commutator. **2.** An electronic circuit that switches a single input sequentially to a series of output terminals, or switches a number of inputs sequentially to a single pair of output terminals.

commutator ripple   The pulsating voltage superimposed on the direct-current (dc) voltage delivered by an unfiltered dc generator.

compact disc   Abbreviation, CD. A digital, high-density optical disc, used in high-fidelity stereo sound systems. Also used to store computer data. The information is encoded as tiny pits on the surface of the disc, and is recovered by a laser, a sensor and a digital-to-analog (D/A) converter. These disks have largely superseded magnetic tapes, and have rendered long-playing vinyl disks and turntables obsolete. See also COMPACT-DISK READ-ONLY MEMORY.

compact-disk read-only memory   Abbreviation, CD-ROM. A digital COMPACT DISC used for the long-term storage of computer data and/or software programs. Usually the same size as a high-fidelity stereo disk, it can hold over 600 megabytes of data. Although data can be read from the disk, it cannot be overwritten.

compander   Term for *compressor/expander*. In the transmission and reception of audio-frequency (AF) intelligence, a system that uses an amplitude compressor at the transmitter and an amplitude expander at the receiver. The compressor reduces the dynamic range before transmission, and the expander restores it after reception. Provides improved signal-to-noise ratio under marginal communications conditions. Also increases the ratio of average power to peak power. See COMPANDING.

companding   A process in which a signal is compressed at the transmitting end of a circuit and expanded at the receiving end, yielding a signal like the original at the receiver output. Signals are more efficiently transmitted when they are compressed because the average power increases, relative to the peak power. This improves the average signal-to-noise ratio for weak signals. See COMPANDER.

companding law   The mathematical function used for companding. It is an output-amplitude versus input-amplitude function for the compression at the transmitter, and the inverse of this function for the expansion at the receiver.

companion keyboard   An auxiliary keyboard connected to a regular keyboard and operated remotely.

companionship machine   A computer or robot with sufficient machine intelligence to provide entertainment and mental stimulation for humans.

comparator   **1.** An instrument for checking the condition of a component by comparing it directly with an identical component of known quality. Has a scale reading in percent deviation, or simply "GO/NO-GO." Examples: capacitor comparator, resistor comparator, and coil comparator. **2.** An operational amplifier whose halves are well balanced and without hysteresis; it is suitable for circuits in which two electrical quantities are compared. **3.** In a computer system, a device whose output signal depends on the result of its comparing two data items.

compare   In computer operations, a relational test performed on two quantities to determine their relative magnitude, including an indication of the test result and, sometimes, the taking of action. Example: the process and action resulting from execution of the statement "IF A > B THEN GO TO LINE 250."

comparison   **1.** An expression of the relationship between two voltages, currents, phase angles, component values, or other quantities in an electrical or electronic circuit or system. **2.** An examination of different data bits or items, which results in a conclusion about some aspect of their relationship.

comparison bridge   A bridge designed especially for the quick comparison of components (e.g., the comparison of resistors with a standard resistor, inductors with a standard inductor, and capacitors with a standard capacitor).

comparison measurement   A measurement in which a quantity or component is compared with a known, similar quantity or component value, rather than having the measurement displayed directly by a meter. Examples: bridge measurements, potentiometric measurements, and frequency matching.

compass   **1.** Any of several instruments for determining direction on the earth's surface [e.g., magnetic (mariner's) compass and gyrocompass]. **2.** A radio direction finder. **3.** An instrument for drawing circles.

compatibility   **1.** A desirable condition in which devices or systems can function efficiently together, without any modification of equipment. **2.** In computer operations, a desirable condition in which different computers can run the same software, without any modification of hardware or software.

compatible color television   A color-television system whose transmissions can be received in black and white by any ordinary monochromatic receiver.

compatible integrated circuit   A hybrid integrated circuit (IC) that has an active element inside the integrated structure and a passive element deposited on its insulated outer surface.

compensated amplifier A wideband amplifier whose frequency range is extended by special components and circuit modifications. Also see COMPENSATING CAPACITOR and COMPENSATING COIL.

compensated diode detector A diode detector in which a positive dc voltage from the automatic-gain-control (AGC) rectifier is applied to the diode anode. The voltage is always proportional to the signal carrier. The arrangement allows the diode to handle a heavily modulated AM signal without producing excessive distortion.

compensated-impurity resistor A resistor consisting of a diffused semiconductor material to which are added controlled amounts of n- or p-type dopants (impurities).

compensated-loop direction finder A direction finder whose loop antenna is complemented by another antenna for polarization-error compensation.

compensated semiconductor A doped semiconductor material in which the acceptor impurity cancels the effects of the donor impurity.

compensated volume control A combination volume-tone control that provides bass boost at low volume levels to compensate for the ear's deficiency at low frequencies.

compensating capacitor 1. A capacitor that has a temperature coefficient of capacitance numerically equal to, but having the opposite sign from, that of another capacitor in a tank or other circuit. When the capacitors are connected in parallel, a temperature-induced value change in the main capacitor is balanced by an equal and opposite change in the compensating capacitor; the net capacitance of the circuit does not change. This greatly reduces frequency drift. 2. In a video amplifier, a large capacitance connected between ground and a tap on the collector or drain resistor to boost low-frequency response. Compare COMPENSATION COIL. 3. A usually low-capacitance capacitor of known temperature coefficient, operated in combination with a main capacitor to reduce capacitance/temperature drift of the latter to zero or to some desired positive or negative value.

compensating diode A junction diode used to temperature-stabilize a transistor circuit. It is usually forward-biased in the base-bias network of the transistor.

compensating filter 1. A selective filter used for the purpose of eliminating some irregularity in the frequency distribution of received energy. 2. A filter used to change the wavelength distribution of electromagnetic energy.

compensating resistor 1. A low-value resistor of known temperature coefficient, connected in series with a main resistor to reduce the resistance/temperature drift to zero, or to some desired positive or negative value. 2. See TRIMMER RESISTOR.

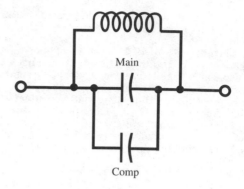

compensating capacitor, 1.

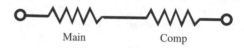

compensating resistor, 1.

compensation Adjusting a quantity, manually or automatically, to obtain precise values, or to counteract undesired variations. Example: temperature compensation of electronic components. For illustration, see COMPENSATING CAPACITOR, 1.

compensation coil In a video amplifier, an inductor connected in series with the collector or drain resistor, or in the coupling path between stages, or both, to boost high-frequency response.

compensation filter See COMPENSATING CAPACITOR, 2.

compensation signal A signal recorded on a tape track containing computer data, to ensure that the tape plays back at exactly the correct speed at all times.

compensation theorem An impedance (Z) in a network can be replaced by a generator having zero internal impedance, and whose generated voltage equals the instantaneous potential difference produced across Z by the current flowing through it. Compare MAXIMUM POWER TRANSFER THEOREM, NORTON'S THEOREM, RECIPROCITY THEOREM, SUPERPOSITION THEOREM, and THEVENIN'S THEOREM.

compensator A device or circuit that facilitates the adjustment of a quantity, manually or automatically, to obtain precise values, or to counteract undesired variations.

compilation time The period during which a program is compiled, as distinct from RUN TIME.

compile **1.** To unify computer subroutines into an all-encompassing program. **2.** To gather information or data together into a single file or file set.

compiler In computer operations, a program that changes a HIGH-LEVEL LANGUAGE, such as BASIC, C, C++, COBOL, or FORTRAN, into MACHINE LANGUAGE. A compiler must be written especially for the high-level language being used.

compiler language Any computer language that serves as an interface between the operator and the computer.

compiler program A program that converts compiler language into machine language.

compiling routine In digital computer operation, a routine permitting the computer itself to construct a program to solve a problem.

complement **1.** The difference between a number and the radix (modulus or base) of the number system. For example, the complement of 7 is equal to 3 (because 10 − 7 = 3) in the decimal (radix-10) number system. **2.** Also called *ones complement*. In computer operations, a representation of the negative value of a binary number. All the available digits are set to 1, and then the number in question is subtracted. For example, the complement of 101 is equal to 010 (because 111 - 101 = 010); the complement of 1001 is equal to 0110 (because 1111 - 1001 = 0110).

complementary A Boolean operation whose result is the same as that of another operation, but with the opposite sign; thus, OR and NOR operations are complementary.

complementary colors **1.** In the additive color system, two colors that produce light gray or white when combined. **2.** In the subtractive color system, two pigments that produce dark gray or black when combined. **3.** Colors or pigments that are opposite each other on the color wheel.

complementary constant-current logic A form of bipolar logic with high operating speed and high component density.

complementary metal-oxide semiconductor Also sometimes called *complementary metal-oxide silicon*. Acronym, CMOS (pronounced "seamoss"). A digital integrated-circuit (IC) technology, in which logic gates are formed by n-channel/p-channel pairs of metal-oxide-semiconductor field-effect transistors (MOSFETs) fabricated on a substrate. Noted for high speed and low current drain.

complementary operator The logical negation (NOT) operation.

complementary pushpull circuit See COMPLEMENTARY-SYMMETRY CIRCUIT.

complementary rectifier In the output circuit of a magnetic amplifier, nonsaturating half-wave rectifier elements.

complementary silicon-controlled rectifier A silicon-controlled rectifier that has polarity opposite from the usual silicon-controlled rectifier.

complementary-symmetry circuit A bipolar-transistor circuit that uses an npn and pnp transistor. The transistors conduct during opposite half-cycles of the input signal, the result being that push-pull output is provided with a single-ended input; no phase-splitting input circuit is required. The complementary-symmetry circuit offers very low output impedance, permitting a loudspeaker voice coil (or other low-impedance load) to be operated directly without a coupling transformer.

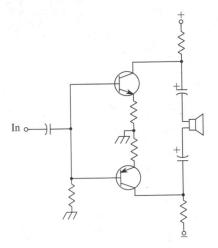

complementary-symmetry circuit

complementary tracking A control system in which several secondary (slave) devices are controlled by a primary (master) device.

complementary transistors A transistor pair of opposite polarity operated in a complementary-symmetry circuit or its equivalent.

complementary wave An electromagnetic wave in a transmission line that occurs as a result of reflection. Any impedance discontinuity will result in complementary waves.

complementer A logic circuit that provides an output pulse when there is no input pulse, and vice versa. Also called INVERTER and NOT CIRCUIT.

complement number In a base-n number system, for a given positive integer p less than n, the positive integer m such that $m + p = n$. For example, in the decimal (base-10) system, the complement of 4 is 6, the complement of 7 is 3, and the complement of 9 is 1. In the hexadecimal (base-16) number system, the complement of 4 is 12, the complement of 7 is 9, and the complement of 9 is 7.

complement-number handling   A computer system in which the operations are carried out via the complements of the input numbers.

complement-setting technique   A process of determining the number of pulses required to complete the switching of a counter circuit when it is started at some state higher than full zero. The number of pulses required for completion is equal to the number that represents the starting state's complement.

complete carry   In digital computer operation, a system permitting all carries to generate carries.

complete circuit   See CONTINUOUS CIRCUIT.

complete modulation   Modulation to the maximum extent possible while maintaining acceptable circuit or system operation.

complete operation   In computer operations, the condition in which the machine rigorously follows program instructions.

complete routine   A vendor-supplied computer program that is usable without modification.

complex function   1. A mathematical function of a complex-number variable. 2. An integrated circuit (IC) containing two or more subcircuits that perform an operation more complicated that of any one of the circuits alone.

complex notation   Notation taking into consideration both the real-number and imaginary-number components of a quantity. Thus, impedance (Z) is a complex quantity that includes a resistive (real) component (R) and a reactive (imaginary) component (jX). See COMPLEX NUMBER and COMPLEX OPERATOR.

complex number   A number expressed in complex notation (e.g., $a + jb$, where a and b are real numbers and j is the COMPLEX OPERATOR). Can also be expressed as a point or a vector in an ARGAND DIAGRAM.

complex operator   The unit imaginary number, represented as j by engineers and as i by mathematicians. This number is defined mathematically as the positive square root of -1.

complex parallel permeability   An expression of the permeability of an inductor core under actual operating conditions, assuming zero loss in the conductors of the coil winding. A parallel combination of reactance and resistance.

complex periodic wave   A periodic wave composed of a sine-wave fundamental and certain harmonics in specific proportions.

complex permeability   An expression of inductor-core permeability, obtained from the mathematical ratio of the magnitudes of the vectors representing the induction and electromagnetic field strength within the core.

complex plane   A Cartesian coordinate system with real numbers on the horizontal axis and imaginary numbers on the vertical axis. Used for vectorial representation of complex numbers. See ARGAND DIAGRAM.

complex quantity   A quantity containing both real and imaginary components. Example: Impedance (Z) is a complex combination of resistance R (a real component) and reactance jX (an imaginary component): $Z = R + jX$.

complex radar target   A radar target that is large enough in theory to be detected by radar, but, because of its geometry, cannot be detected. This effect is the result of phase combinations of signal components reflected from various surfaces on the target.

complex series permeability   An expression of complex permeability of an inductor core under actual operating conditions, assuming zero loss in the conductors of the coil winding. A series combination of reactance and resistance.

complex steady-state vibration   Periodic vibration with more than one sine-wave component.

complex tone   An audio tone made up of more than one sine-wave component.

complex variable   A variable having real and imaginary parts.

complex waveform   The shape of a COMPLEX PERIODIC WAVE. It is the resultant of the individual sine-wave components (i.e., of the fundamental and the harmonics).

complex-wave generator   A signal generator whose output signal is any of several selectable waveforms and frequencies (or repetition rates). Also see FUNCTION GENERATOR.

compliance   1. The ease with which a material can be flexed or bent, an important characteristic of transducers (such as loudspeakers). Expressed in cm/dyne, compliance is the reciprocal of stiffness, and is the acoustical or mechanical equivalent of capacitance. 2. A measure of the output impedance of a switched-current signal source. Generally given as maximum current for a certain change in the voltage.

compliance range   The voltage range required to maintain a constant current throughout a load-resistance range.

compliance voltage   The range over which the output voltage of a constant-current power supply must swing in order to maintain a steady current in a varying load.

compliance-voltage range   The output voltage range of a constant-current power supply.

component   1. A device or part used in a circuit to obtain some desired electrical action [e.g., a resistor (passive component) or an integrated circuit (active component)]. Also see ACTIVE COMPONENT and PASSIVE COMPONENT. 2. An attribute inherent in a device, circuit, or performance (e.g., the REACTIVE COMPONENT of an inductor). 3. A specified quantity or term (e.g., the WATTLESS COMPONENT of ac power). **4.** A piece of equipment in a high-fidelity sound system.

component density The number of components (see COMPONENT, **1**) in an electronic assembly of a given physical volume.

component failure rate **1.** The percentage of components, out of a specified group, that can be expected to fail within a specified length of time. **2.** The frequency with which a given component, in a certain application, can be expected to fail.

component layout The mechanical arrangement of components (see COMPONENT, **1**) in an electronic assembly.

component stress The electrical or mechanical strain to which a component is subjected. In general, the greater the stress, the higher the component failure rate.

composite cable A cable containing other cables of different types.

composite circuit A circuit handling telegraphy and telephony simultaneously without causing mutual interference.

composite color A color that is not one of the COLOR PRIMARIES, but instead, consists of a combination of the three color primaries.

composite color signal The complete color television signal, including all picture, color, and control components.

composite conductor A set of wires connected in parallel. The wires are often, but not necessarily, of identical size and constitution.

composite current A current having both alternating-current (ac) and direct-current (dc) components; an alternating current superimposed on a direct current. Also called *fluctuating current.*

composite curve A curve or pair of curves showing two modes of operation, as of biased and unbiased conditions.

composite filter A filter consisting of more than one section. The sections might be, but often are not, identical.

composite video signal The television picture signal containing picture information and sync pulses.

composite-video-signal distortion Distortion of the composite video signal as evidenced by overshooting, ringing, and sync-pulse shortening.

composite voltage A voltage having both alternating-current (ac) and direct-current (dc) components; an ac voltage superimposed on a dc voltage. Also called *fluctuating voltage.*

composite wave filter Two or more wave filters (not necessarily of the same type) operated in cascade.

composition resistor A resistor made from a mixture of materials, usually finely powdered carbon and a binder.

compound A substance in which the atoms of two or more elements have united chemically to form a molecule. For example, an atom of cadmium (Cd) and one of sulfur (S) combine to form a molecule of cadmium sulfide (CdS).

compound connection A direct connection of two transistors, the amplified output of the first being further amplified by the second. The connection provides extremely high current gain. Also called DARLINGTON PAIR.

compound generator A generator that has both series and shunt fields. Also called *compound-wound generator.*

compound horn A horn reflector used for transmission of microwave energy. The faces of the horn approach four geometric plane surfaces as the distance from the center increases.

compound modulation A system of successive modulation, the modulated wave from one step becoming the modulating wave in the next. Also called *multiple modulation.*

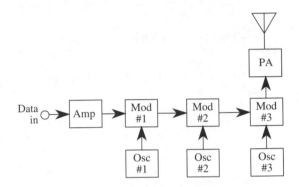

compound modulation

compound motor An electric motor having both series and shunt fields. Also called *compound-wound motor.*

compound transistor Two or more transistors directly coupled in the same envelope for increased amplification. Also see COMPOUND CONNECTION.

compound-wound generator See COMPOUND GENERATOR.

compound-wound motor See COMPOUND MOTOR.

compress **1.** In communications, to reduce or minimize the bandwidth of a signal. **2.** In communications, the processing of a signal to increase low-level components and thereby raise the average power level relative to the peak power level. **3.** In computer operations, to reduce or minimize the number of bits in a digital signal or file, while still retaining all the essential information. Compare EXPAND.

compressed-air capacitor A high voltage air-dielectric capacitor enclosed in a case in which the air pressure is held at several atmospheres.

The device exploits the dielectric strength of compressed air, which is higher than that of air at normal pressure.

compressed-air speaker A speaker that uses an airtight chamber to enhance the acoustic reproduction at certain frequencies.

compression 1. In communications, the reduction or minimization of signal bandwidth. **2.** In communications, the processing of a signal to increase low-level components and thereby raise the average power level relative to the peak power level. Usually, a logarithmic function. **3.** In computer operations, the reduction or minimization of the number of bits in a digital signal or file, while still retaining all the essential information. Compare EXPANSION.

compression ratio In a system using COMPRESSION, the ratio A_1/A_2, where A_1 is the gain (or transmission) at a reference-signal level and A_2 is the gain (or transmission) at a specified higher signal level.

compression wave A wave disturbance that travels via longitudinal motion of particles in a medium. Sound waves through air are the most common example.

compressor A circuit or device that limits the amplitude of its output signal to a predetermined value, despite wide variations in input signal amplitude.

compressor driver unit A loudspeaker that works into an air space connected by a throat to a horn, rather than by driving a diaphragm.

Compton diffusion An effect that occurs when a photon and electron collide. Some of the energy from the photon is transferred to the electron. On a large scale, such collisions result in diffusion of electromagnetic waves.

Compton effect The increase in wavelength (decrease in frequency) of X-rays scattered by the electrons of lighter atoms bombarded with the X-rays.

Compton shift See COMPTON EFFECT.

compute To perform a mathematical operation by means of a relatively simple process. Thus, a digital computer solves intricate problems using simple arithmetic steps. Compare CALCULATE.

computer A device or machine for performing mathematical operations on data, and producing the results as information or control signals. There are numerous types, the most common being the *digital computer.*

computer-aided design Abbreviation, CAD. The use of computers in conceiving, developing, and perfecting new products.

computer-aided manufacturing Abbreviation, CAM. The use of automated manufacturing systems, such as assembly lines, that are partially or totally controlled by computers.

computer antibody Also called *vaccine.* A small subprogram designed to eliminate viruses from computer systems.

computer-assisted instruction Abbreviation, CAI. The use of computers as teaching and training aids.

computer code See MACHINE LANGUAGE.

computer consciousness The degree to which a machine can be considered aware of its own existence. Until recently, this idea was considered ridiculous. But as microprocessor power continues to grow, some researchers now consider it worth thinking about.

computer-controlled catalytic converter A microprocessor-controlled system for automatically supervising gaseous emissions exhausted by a motor vehicle. An oxygen sensor monitors the exhaust stream, and the associated electronic system adjusts the air-to-fuel ratio of the carburetor to reduce smog-producing pollutants in the exhaust.

computer diode A semiconductor diode having low capacitance and fast RECOVERY TIME, thus suiting it to rapid switching in computer circuits and to very-high-frequency applications.

computer engineer A person skilled in the theory and application of computers, related equipment, and associated mathematics.

computer file See FILE.

computer game See VIDEO GAME.

computer graphics 1. The use of computers to assist in drawing and drafting, and in the processing of video images such as photographs. **2.** Broadly, any computer-generated or computer-processed image.

computer instruction See INSTRUCTION.

computer interfacing apparatus The equipment used to connect a computer to other systems, and to peripherals.

computerized axial tomography Abbreviation, CAT. A multiple X-ray system that enables the observer to obtain cross-sectional images of the internal organs of the body.

computer map A blueprint, used in conjunction with machine vision, sonar, radar or beacons, that a mobile robot can use as a navigational aid. One or more such blueprints are stored in the robot controller's main memory.

computer music 1. Music that is composed by a computer. **2.** See MUSICAL INSTRUMENT DIGITAL INTERFACE.

computer program See PROGRAM.

computer programmer A person skilled in devising and/or writing the routines that a digital computer uses to solve problems or process data.

computer storage tube A cathode-ray tube in which the electron beam scans and stores information in thousands of memory cells on a target. A cell "remembers" by acquiring and holding an electrostatic charge when it is struck by the beam from the writing gun. Information taken is read out of a cell by a second beam from the reading gun.

computer system A central processor and its associated online and offline peripherals, such as a monitor, modem, printer, optical scanner, magnetic disk drives, CD-ROM drive, and tape backup.

computer technician A professional skilled in building, repairing, and maintaining computers, and who, occasionally, designs them. Usually works under the supervision of a computer engineer.

computer terminal **1.** A teleprinter or video display unit and keyboard, used by human operator(s) of a computer. **2.** An interface between a computer and its human operator(s).

computer/TV interface A device or circuit for delivering the output of a digital computer to a standard television receiver so that the latter can serve as a GRAPHIC TERMINAL.

computer virus A deliberately created and disseminated subprogram or piece of programming code, that electronically spreads through computer systems and hinders operation. Usually diverts the computer(s) from intended functions; sometimes causes a catastrophic malfunction. Often exists undetected, being transferred from one computer to another by means of diskettes or software.

computer word See WORD.

computing amplifier See OPERATIONAL AMPLIFIER.

computing machine See COMPUTER.

concatenation **1.** A method of speed control for a 3-phase motor in which two induction motors are operated with their shafts coupled together. The stator of the first motor is connected to the 3-phase supply, and the slip rings of this motor are connected to the field of the second motor. The slip rings of the second motor are connected to the three ganged sections of a Y-rheostat used for adjusting the speed. **2.** Arrangement of a set into a series.

concentrated-arc lamp A brilliant low-voltage lamp, containing nonvaporizing electrodes in an inert-gas atmosphere. An arc across the electrodes creates the light source.

concentrated winding A coil winding that has a large number of turns in a small space.

concentration cell An electrolytic cell in which two electrodes are immersed in solutions of the same compound but having different combinations. The voltage is usually very small, 0.1 volt or less.

concentration gradient Between points in a semiconductor, the difference in electron or hole concentration.

concentric cable See COAXIAL CABLE.

concentric capacitor A fixed or variable capacitor whose plates are concentric cylinders. Also called *concentric-plate capacitor.*

concentric jack See COAXIAL JACK.

concentric line See COAXIAL LINE.

concentric-line oscillator A stable, self-excited oscillator whose frequency-determining tank consists principally of a section of concentric (coaxial) line. Used primarily at ultra-high frequencies (UHF).

concentric plug See COAXIAL PLUG.

concentric receptacle See COAXIAL RECEPTACLE.

concentric tank See COAXIAL TANK.

concentric-wound coil A combination of two or more coils wound on top of, and insulated from, each other.

conceptual modeling A technique for solving problems by devising a mathematical model based on the results of an experiment; experiments performed on the model are used to verify its validity.

concurrent conversion In computer operations, running conversion and conventional programs together. Also see CONVERSION PROGRAM.

concurrent processing See MULTIPROGRAMMING.

condenser **1.** An obsolete term for CAPACITOR. **2.** A mirror or lens for concentrating light (on an object, for example). **3.** Something that condenses a gas or vapor. **4.** See CONDENSER MICROPHONE.

condenser antenna A two-wire horizontal antenna system in which the radiator is a wire situated above a counterpoise.

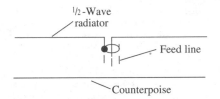

condenser antenna

condenser microphone Also called *capacitor microphone.* A microphone in which a tightly stretched metal diaphragm forms one plate of an air capacitor, and a closely situated metal plug forms the other plate. A dc bias voltage is applied to the arrangement. Impinging sound waves cause the diaphragm to vibrate, varying the capacitance and causing the output current to fluctuate accordingly.

condensing routine In computer operations, a program that compresses data. See COMPRESSION, **3.**

condensite A plastic insulating material whose base is phenol formaldehyde resin.

conditional Pertaining to a quantity or phenomenon that depends on some external factor, and is therefore subject to change.

conditional branch A point in a computer program where a relational test is performed, and the statement line in which the test is made is left so that an out-of-sequence instruction can be implemented. Such a branch might be made, for example, following a statement, such as "IF Z = Y THEN GO TO LINE 380."

conditional branch instruction The instruction in a computer program that causes a CONDITIONAL BRANCH.

conditional implication operation A Boolean operation in which the result of operand values X and Y are such that the output is high only if input X is high and input Y is low. Also called *inclusion* or *if-then operation.*

conditional jump See CONDITIONAL BRANCH.

conditional stop instruction In a computer program, an instruction that can cause a halt in the run, as dictated by some specified condition.

conditional transfer See CONDITIONAL BRANCH.

condition code A set of constraints for a computer program; sets limits on what can be done with the computer under certain circumstances.

conditioning **1.** The process of making equipment compatible for use with other equipment. Generally involves some design or installation changes. **2.** Interfacing.

Condor A continuous-wave navigational system that produces a cathode-ray-tube display for automatically determining the bearing and distance from a ground station.

conductance Symbol, *G*. Unit, siemens. The ability of a circuit, conductor, or device to conduct electricity. Conductance in siemens is the reciprocal of resistance: $G = 1/R$, where R is the resistance in ohms.

conducted heat Heat transferred by conduction through a material substance, as opposed to *convection* and *radiation.* A heatsink conducts dissipated energy away from a transistor, whereupon convection and radiation allow heat to escape from the sink.

conduction **1.** The propagation of energy through a medium, depending on the medium for its travel. **2.** The transfer of electrons through a wire. **3.** The transfer of holes through a P-type semiconductor material. **4.** Heat transfer through a material object (see CONDUCTED HEAT).

conduction angle See ANGLE OF CONDUCTION.

conduction band In the arrangement of energy levels within an atom, the band in which a free electron can exist; it is above the *valence band* in which electrons are bound to the atom. In a metallic atom, conduction and valence bands overlap; but in semiconductors and insulators, they are separated by an energy gap.

conduction current **1.** The electromagnetic-field flow that occurs in the direction of propagation. A measure of the ease with which the field is propagated. **2.** Current in a wire or other conductor.

conduction-current modulation In a microwave tube, cyclic variations in the conduction current; also, the method of producing such modulation.

conduction electron See FREE ELECTRON.

conduction error In a temperature-acutated transducer, error caused by conduction of heat between the sensor and the mounting.

conduction field An energy field that exists in the vicinity of an electric current.

conductive coating A conducting layer applied to the glass envelope of a cathode-ray tube, such as an oscilloscope tube or picture tube.

conductive coupling See DIRECT COUPLING.

conductive material See CONDUCTOR.

conductive pattern The pattern of conductive lines and areas in a printed circuit.

conductivity Unit, S/m (siemens per meter). An expression of conductance per unit length of a material; the reciprocal of *resistivity.*

conductivity meter A device for measuring electrical conductivity. Generally, such a device is calibrated in siemens.

conductivity modulation In a semiconductor, the variation in conductivity that results from a variation of charge-carrier density.

conductivity-modulation transistor A transistor in which the bulk resistivity of the semiconductor material is modulated by minority carriers.

conductor **1.** A material that allows charge carriers (usually electrons) to move with ease among atoms. Examples are metals, electrolytes, and ionized gases. Substances vary widely in their suitability as conductors; the conductivity of commercial copper, for example, is almost twice that of aluminum. Compare INSULATOR. **2.** An individual conducting wire in a cable, insulated or uninsulated.

conduit A hollow tube, made of plastic or metal, through which wires, cables, and other transmission media are fed.

cone The conical diaphragm of a (usually dynamic) loudspeaker.

cone antenna An antenna in which the radiator is a sheet-metal cone or a conical arrangement of rods or wires.

Conelrad An early amplitude-modulation (AM) broadcast protocol, intended for use in the event of a nuclear war. Now replaced by the EMERGENCY BROADCAST SYSTEM.

cone marker A UHF marker beacon whose conical energy lobe radiates vertically from a radio-range beacon station. Aircraft in flight use such markers to accurately locate the beacon station.

cone of protection The zone surrounding a lightning rod, in which the chances of a lightning strike are greatly reduced. The cone has an apex angle of 45°, relative to the rod. Objects en-

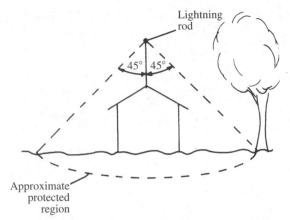

cone of protection

tirely within this cone are unlikely to be struck (although it is still possible).

cone of silence   A small zero-signal zone directly over a low-frequency radio-range beacon. The zone is the product of the combined directive properties of the beacon transmitting antenna and the antenna on an aircraft.

cone speaker   A loudspeaker having a sound-producing cone (diaphragm) made of specially treated paper or other material, as opposed to a loudspeaker having a flat diaphragm.

confetti   On a color TV screen, color spots caused by chrominance-amplifier noise.

confidence   The probability that a predicted result will occur.

confidence factor   Confidence, expressed either as a fraction (between 0 and 1) or as a percentage.

confidence interval   The range over which a parameter can vary so that a given confidence factor is maintained.

confidence level   See CONFIDENCE FACTOR.

confidence limitations   The maximum and minimum points of a confidence interval. Outside the confidence-limitation points, the confidence factor drops below the required minimum.

configuration   **1.** The characteristic arrangement of components in an electronic assembly, or of the equipment symbols in the corresponding circuit diagram. **2.** Computer system.

configuration state   In a computer system, an expression of the availability status of a device for a given application. A *configured-in* device is available; a *configured-out* device is available, but is restricted to certain users; a *configured-off* device is unavailable.

configuration table   Within a computer's operating system, a table that provides the configuration state for various system units.

configured-in   See CONFIGURATION STATE.
configured-off   See CONFIGURATION STATE.
configured-out   See CONFIGURATION STATE.

conformance   The degree to which a quantity or variable corresponds to a standard or to expectations.

conformance error   The extent (usually expressed as a percentage) to which conformance is lacking.

conical antenna   See CONE ANTENNA.

conical horn   A horn (antenna, loudspeaker, or sound pickup) having the general shape of a cone: the cross-sectional area varies directly as the square of the horn's axial length.

conical monopole antenna   An unbalanced broadband antenna that derives its name from its shape. It is usually constructed from wire and must be operated against a good radio-frequency (RF) ground.

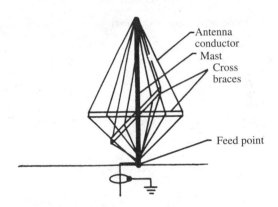

conical monopole antenna

conical scanning   In radar transmission, a method of scanning in which the beam describes a cone, at the apex of which is the antenna.

conic sections   The geometric plane figures that result from the intersection of a cone with a plane. These figures are the *circle*, the *ellipse*, the *parabola*, and the *hyperbola*.

conjugate   For a given complex number $A + jB$, the quantity $A - jB$. When complex conjugates are multiplied together, the result is $A^2 + B^2$.

conjugate branches   In a network, two branches of such a nature that a signal in one has no effect on the other.

conjugate bridge   A bridge in which the detector and generator occupy positions opposite to those in a conventional bridge of the same general type.

conjugate impedance   For a given complex impedance, $R + jX$, where R is the resistive component and jX is the reactive component, the impedance: $R - jX$. The resistance is identical; the reactance is of equal magnitude, but opposite sign (capacitive as opposed to inductive, or vice-versa).

conjunction   The logical AND operation.

connect   To provide an electrical path between two points.

connection   The point at which two conductors are physically joined.

connective   An operation symbol written between operands.

connector   **1.** A device that provides electrical connection. **2.** A fixture (either male or female) attached to a cable or chassis for quickly making and breaking one or more circuits. **3.** A symbol that connects points on a flowchart.

conoscope   A device that uses focused polarized light to examine crystals (as in checking the optical axis of a quartz crystal).

consequent poles   The poles of an equivalent single magnet that is formed when two magnets are aligned with their two identical poles together. Thus, when the two north poles are placed together, the consequent poles are a south pole at each end and a north pole at the center.

conservation of energy   **1.** The preservation of the potential for work by a given quantity of energy—even when it undergoes a change in form within a system. **2.** The *law of conservation of energy*, which states that energy can be neither created nor destroyed, but only changed in form.

console   **1.** The main station or position for the control of electronic and/or computer equipment. **2.** The equipment at a fixed location. **3.** An equipment-containing cabinet that stands on the floor. **4.** Equipment permitting communication with a computer. Also called *dumb terminal*.

consonance   **1.** Harmony between audio tones. **2.** Acoustical or electrical resonance between bodies or circuits that are not physically connected.

constant   **1.** A quantity whose value remains fixed, such as the speed of light in a vacuum. Compare VARIABLE. **2.** The value of a component specified for use in a particular electronic circuit. **3.** An electronic component, particularly a capacitance or inductance. **4.** In a computer program, data items that remain unchanged for each run.

constant-amplitude recording   In sound recording, the technique of holding the maximum amplitude of the signal steady as the frequency changes.

constantan   An alloy of copper and nickel used in some thermocouples and standard resistors.

constantan-platinum thermocouple   A thermocouple that uses the junction between constantan and platinum wires, which is contained in thermocouple-type meters.

constant area   As allocated by a computer program, an area of memory that holds constants.

constant bandwidth   In a broadband tuned circuit, bandwidth that does not change with frequency.

constant current   A current that undergoes no change in value as it flows through a changing resistance. Compare CONSTANT VOLTAGE.

constant-current characteristic   A condition in which the current through a circuit remains constant—even if the voltage across the circuit increases or decreases.

constant-current curve   A graph in which the dependent variable is an electric current that levels off at, or approaches, a specific maximum. An example is the collector-current versus collector-voltage curve for a bipolar transistor.

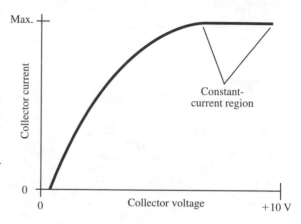

constant-current curve

constant-current drive   Driving power obtained from a constant-current source.

constant-current modulation   See CHOKE-COUPLED MODULATION.

constant-current power supply   See CONSTANT-CURRENT SOURCE.

constant-current sink   See CURRENT SINK.

constant-current source   A power supply whose current remains steady during variations in load resistance. Also called *constant-current supply* and *current-regulated supply*. Compare CONSTANT-VOLTAGE SOURCE.

constant-current supply   See CONSTANT-CURRENT SOURCE.

constant-current transformer   A transformer supplied from a constant-voltage source that automatically delivers a constant current to a varying secondary load.

constant-k filter   Also called a *Zobel filter*. A filter section in which Z_1Z_2 equals k^2 at all frequencies, where Z_1 is the impedance of the series element and Z_2 is the impedance of the shunt element.

constant-power dissipation line   A line connecting points on a family of current-voltage characteristic curves, the points corresponding to the maximum power that can safely be dissipated by the device to which the curves apply.

constant-resistance network   A circuit of resistors that, when terminated in a resistance load, presents a constant resistance to a driving source under various conditions of operation.

constant-speed motor **1.** Also called a *shunt motor.* A motor whose speed varies little, or not at all, with variations in the armature current. **2.** A motor that runs at an unvarying speed through the action of associated automatic electronic control circuitry.

constant voltage A voltage that does not change as the load resistance varies. Compare CONSTANT CURRENT.

constant-voltage, constant-current supply A combination current-regulated and voltage-regulated power supply; delivers constant current to low load resistances and constant voltage to high load resistances.

constant-voltage drive Driving power obtained from a CONSTANT-VOLTAGE SOURCE.

constant-voltage source A power supply whose output voltage remains steady during variations in load current. Also called *constant-voltage supply* and *voltage-regulated supply.*

constant-voltage transformer A special transformer used to reduce variations in power-line voltage. A capacitor in the device causes a winding to resonate at the line frequency (e.g., 60 Hz). This tends to maintain a more constant current than would be the case in an ordinary transformer.

construct A source (user's) computer program statement that, when implemented, produces a predetermined effect.

consumer reliability risk **1.** The chance a consumer takes when buying a component or piece of equipment that has not been subjected to quality-assurance/quality-control (QA/QC) testing. **2.** An expression of the failure rate for a consumer item.

contact **1.** A conducting body (such as a button, disk, or blade) that serves to close an electric circuit when pressed against another conductor. Example: switch contact and spring contact. **2.** The state of being touched together, as when two conductors are brought into contact to close a circuit.

contact arc The arc that initially occurs when current-carrying contacts are separated.

contact area **1.** The face of an electrical contact. **2.** The common area shared by two conductors in mutual contact.

contact bounce The springing apart or vibration of contacts upon making or breaking.

contact chatter The abnormal vibration of mating contacts, caused by contact bounce or by an extraneous alternating current.

contact-closure input The input circuit of a device, such as a control-system amplifier, that is actuated by the closing of switching contacts. Compare CONTACT-OPEN INPUT.

contact combination The set of contacts on a switch or electronic relay.

contact detector A rectifier or demodulator, composed of two dissimilar materials in contact with each other. Semiconductor diodes are of this general type. Some contact-detector action can be obtained with two dissimilar fine wires (such as copper and iron) by touching their tips lightly together.

contact EMF Short for *contact electromotive force*; also called *contact potential.* A low direct-current (dc) voltage that is sometimes generated by the contact of two dissimilar materials.

contact follow The tendency of relay contacts to follow the actuating signals.

contact force **1.** The force with which relay contacts close with a given amount of coil current. **2.** The force with which a pair of relay contacts are held together when current flows through the coil. **3.** In a mercury-wetted relay, the force exerted by the mercury on the contacts as the relay closes.

contact gap The distance between contacts when they are open.

contact load **1.** The power dissipated by a load that is connected to a power supply through a closed set of contacts. **2.** The current passing through a set of closed contacts.

contact microphone A microphone placed in direct contact with a vibrating surface for pickup. Actuated by the vibration of a solid, rather than by the movement of air molecules.

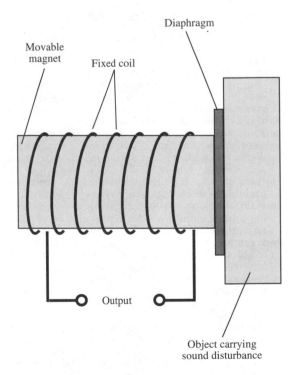

contact microphone

contact miss   1. The improper alignment of contacts in a switch or relay. **2.** The condition of relay contacts not lining up properly.

contact modulator   An electromechanical CHOPPER.

contact-open input   The input circuit of a device, such as a control-system amplifier, that is actuated by the opening of switching contacts. Compare CONTACT-CLOSURE INPUT.

contactor   A switch used for frequent opening or closing of a circuit. An example is a relay contactor used for keying a transmitter.

contactor noise   1. Electrical noise that is the product of make-and-break contact action or fluctuations in conduction when the contacts are closed. **2.** Sounds coming directly from contacts that are opening and closing.

contact potential   The small direct-current (dc) voltage that results from the bombardment of an electrode by electrons, when the electrode has no external voltage applied to it.

contact pressure   The pressure that holds contacts together.

contact protector   A component (such as a diode, capacitor, resistor, or combination of these) that serves to suppress contact arcing.

contact rating   The maximum current, voltage, and/or power specified for a given set of contacts.

contact rectifier   A rectifier consisting of two dissimilar materials in direct contact. Examples: copper and copper oxide, magnesium and copper sulfide, selenium and aluminum, and germanium and indium.

contact resistance   The resistance of the closed contacts of switches, relays, and other similar devices. Normally, this is a very small resistance.

contact separation   See CONTACT GAP.

contact strip   See TERMINAL STRIP.

contact switch   An electromechanical switch that uses contacts to make and break a circuit, as compared with an electronic switch that uses semiconductor devices.

contact travel   The distance over which a relay or switch contact must move to close a circuit.

contact wetting   The use of mercury (a conducting liquid) to improve the action of a relay contact or contacts.

contact wipe   A sliding motion between closed contacts. Helps to establish a good connection and to keep the contact surfaces clean.

container file   See CONTROLLING FILE.

contaminated material   1. A semiconductor material containing some undesired substance. **2.** A material unintentionally made radioactive.

contamination   1. The presence of an impurity in a substance. **2.** The addition of a radioactive material to a substance. **3.** In a coaxial cable, the tendency for the jacket material to bleed through the outer braid into the dielectric, resulting in increased loss.

content-addressed storage   In a computer, memory- or data-storage locations identified by content (see CONTENTS), instead of by address. Also called *associative storage.*

contention   The result of interference among more than one transmitting station on the same communications channel.

contents   1. The data in a computer random-access memory (RAM). **2.** The data in a specific storage location, such as on a hard disk, diskette, or CD-ROM.

context   1. The environment in which a word is used in a natural language (such as English, Spanish, or Russian). Important in speech recognition and speech synthesis. **2.** The environment in which a string of characters, composing a data unit or word, is used in a computer program.

Continental code   A version of the Morse code used internationally in radiotelegraphy. Also called *International Morse code* and *general service code.* Compare AMERICAN MORSE CODE.

continuity   A condition of being uninterrupted—especially pertaining to current flowing in an electrical or electronic circuit.

continuity test   A test of the completeness of an electrical path. Ideally, the only concern is whether the circuit is open or closed, but sometimes circuit resistance is also of interest.

continuity tester   A device (such as an ohmmeter, battery and buzzer, and battery and lamp) with which a continuity test can be made.

continuity writer   The person who prepares copy for a radio or television broadcaster.

continuous carrier   A medium (such as a radio-frequency wave) that will convey information (as when the carrier is modulated) with no disruption of the medium itself.

continuous circuit   An uninterrupted circuit.

Continuous Commercial Service   Abbreviation, CCS. A category in which safe operating parameters are listed for electronic components and communications equipment operated over long, uninterrupted periods. Compare INTERMITTENT COMMERCIAL AND AMATEUR SERVICE.

continuous duty   The requirement of a device to sustain a 100-percent duty cycle for a prolonged period of time.

continuous-duty rating   A maximum current, voltage, or power rating for equipment operated for extended periods at a 100-percent duty cycle.

continuous load   A load that requires a continuous feed for a prolonged period of time.

continuous memory   See NONVOLATILE MEMORY.

continuous-path motion   In robotics, machine movement that occurs in a smooth fashion, rather than in discrete steps. Allows precise positioning of a mechanical arm or gripper.

continuous power   The maximum sine-wave power that an amplifier can deliver for 30 seconds.

Character	Symbol
A	•—
B	—•••
C	—•—•
D	—••
E	•
F	••—•
G	——•
H	••••
I	••
J	•———
K	—•—
L	•—••
M	——
N	—•
O	———
P	•——•
Q	——•—
R	•—•
S	•••
T	—
U	••—
V	•••—
W	•——
X	—••—
Y	—•——
Z	——••
0	—————
1	•————
2	••———
3	•••——
4	••••—
5	•••••
6	—••••
7	——•••
8	———••
9	————•
Period	•—•—•—
Comma	——••——
Query	••——••
Slash	—••—•
Dash	—••••—
Break (pause)	—•••—
Semicolon	—•—•—•
Colon	———•••

continental code

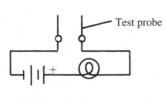

Test probe

continuity tester

continuous recorder An instrument that provides an uninterrupted recording.

continuous recording A record made on a continuous sheet or tape, instead of on separate sheets or tapes. An example is a continuous-playing tape used for repeated public announcements.

continuous spectrum **1.** The range of all electromagnetic frequencies between a specified lower limit f_1 and a specified upper limit f_2. **2.** A range of electromagnetic frequencies that exhibits similar behavior between its lower and upper limits.

continuous stationery Also called *fanfold paper*. The pack of paper a line printer uses. It consists of sheets connected by perforated or tear-off edges, folded in accordion fashion. It usually has tear-off perforated strips along either side to facilitate feed through the printer mechanism.

continuous variable A variable that can attain any value within a specific range of values. An example is a frequency within the 75- to 80-meter amateur radio band, from 3.5 to 4.0 MHz.

continuous wave Abbreviation, CW. **1.** A periodic wave, such as a radio-frequency (RF) carrier, that is not interrupted at any point between its normal start and termination, and that is unmodulated. **2.** An RF carrier that is interrupted digitally with a keying device according to some code (such as Morse), for the purpose of conveying information.

continuous-wave laser See CW LASER.

continuous-wave radar See CW RADAR.

contour A control on an audio reproduction system that increases the base and treble amplitudes at low levels to compensate for the ear's natural losses in these ranges. Alternatively, this control can attenuate signals in the 3-kHz region, where the human ear is most sensitive.

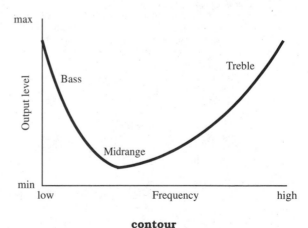

contour

contours of equal loudness See AUDIBILITY CURVES.

CONTRAN A computer language that requires no compiler, or translating, interface between the operator and the machine. The programming is done in a language similar to machine language.

contrast 1. In a video image, the degree to which adjacent areas of a picture are differentiated. Insufficient contrast makes for a "flat" picture; excessive contrast, a "hard" picture. **2.** In optical character recognition, the degree to which a character is distinguishable from its background.

contrast control A potentiometer for adjusting the gain of the video in a television receiver or cathode-ray-tube (CRT) computer display and, accordingly, the image contrast.

contrast range In an image or pattern, the brightness range from the lightest to the darkest parts.

contrast ratio In a video image, the ratio of maximum to minimum luminance.

control 1. An adjustable component, such as a rheostat, potentiometer, variable capacitor, or variable inductor, that allows some quantity to be varied at will. **2.** A test or experiment conducted simultaneously with another similar test conducted under conditions lacking the factor under consideration. Thus, if 100 resistors coated with a special varnish are tested at 120°F, 100 identical unvarnished resistors could be tested (as a control) under the same conditions; in this way, the effect of the varnish would be ascertainable. **3.** As a computer function, understanding and implementing instructions or carrying out tasks, according to specific conditions.

control ampere-turns The ampere-turns of the control winding in a magnetic amplifier.

control block A storage block for control information in a computer.

control bus In a digital computer, the electrical conductors linking the central-processing-unit (CPU) control register to the memory circuits.

control card A card that provides control information for a computer.

control character A character (bit group) used to start the control of a peripheral.

control characteristic A representation (such as a collector-current versus collector-voltage curve) depicting the extent to which the value of one quantity affects or controls the value of another.

control circuit 1. A circuit in which one signal or process is made to control another signal or process. **2.** In a digital computer, a circuit that handles and interprets instructions and commands, particularly in the arithmetic and logic unit (ALU).

control computer A computer that receives signals concerning the parameters in some process, and responds with signals that control those parameters.

control counter See CONTROL REGISTER.

control data 1. In a computer record having a key, information used to put the records in some sequence. **2.** Information affecting a routine's selection or modification.

control electrode An electrode to which an input signal can be applied to control an output signal. Common examples are the base of a bipolar transistor, the gate of a field-effect transistor, and the inputs of a logic gate.

control field 1. In direct-current generators of the amplifying type, an auxiliary field winding used for feedback and regulation, in contrast to the self-excited field winding (which is the conventional field winding of the generator). **2.** A computer record field containing control data.

control flux In an amplidyne, magnetic flux generated by current flowing through the control winding.

control grid See GRID, 1.

control-grid bias The negative dc voltage applied between ground and the control grid of a vacuum tube to establish the operating point.

control hole One of the holes in a punched card that specifies how other information on the card is to be handled. Also called FUNCTION HOLE.

control language Within the operating system of a computer, the command set that the operator or programmer uses to control the running of a program or the operation of peripherals. Also called *job control language* or *system control language*.

control language interpreter See CONTROL LANGUAGE and INTERPRETER.

controlled avalanche diode Also called *avalanche diode* or *Zener diode*. A diode that has a well-defined avalanche voltage. Used primarily for voltage regulation in power supplies.

controlled-carrier modulation See QUIESCENT CARRIER OPERATION.

controlled-carrier transmission See QUIESCENT CARRIER OPERATION.

controlled rectifier A rectifier whose dc output can be varied by adjusting the voltage or phase of a signal applied to the control element. See SILICON-CONTROLLED RECTIFIER.

controller 1. The control signal of an electronic control (or servo), system. **2.** A device, such as a specialized variable resistor, used to adjust current or voltage. **3.** A computer that oversees and controls the operation of a robot or fleet of robots.

controller function The control of the movements of a servo system.

controlling file A computer storage area encompassing several complete magnetic disk cylinders; its size can be changed to accommodate a number of files.

control loop See CONTROL TAPE.

control mark See TAPE MARK.

control panel 1. An accessible surface on which are mounted switches, buttons, potentiometers,

meters, digital indicators, monitoring devices, and other apparatus essential to regulating and supervising an electronic system. **2.** The console that a computer operator or programmer uses to communicate with the central processing unit (CPU).

control plate The metallic plate or disk that serves as the antenna of a CAPACITANCE RELAY or TOUCHPLATE RELAY.

control program A program that arranges computer-operation programs in a certain order. Puts information in the computer memory for later use.

control punching See CONTROL HOLE.

control rectifier A semiconductor diode device, used for the purpose of switching large currents. A small control signal can provide switching of high-power devices.

control register In a computer, the register that stores the address of the next instruction in the program being run.

control sequence The order in which instructions are executed in a digital computer.

control stack In a computer system, a unit of hardware having storage locations and used to perform arithmetic, assist in allocating memory to programs, and to control internal processes.

control statement In a programming language, an instruction that causes some action to be taken, as specified by a condition; it is also applicable to source program statements that affect the compiler's operation without modifying the machine code.

control tape Punched paper or plastic tape in the form of a closed loop and used to control printing devices. Also called *control loop*.

control total For a file or record group, a total derived during an operation; it is used to verify that all the records have been processed similarly.

control transfer The situation in which the control unit of a digital computer leaves the main sequence of instructions and takes its next instruction from an out-of-sequence address.

control transfer instruction See BRANCH INSTRUCTION.

control-voltage winding In a servomotor, the winding that receives a varying voltage of a phase different from that applied to the fixed-voltage windings.

control winding In a magnetic amplifier, the winding that conducts the control-signal current.

control word A word (a bit group) stored in a computer memory and used for a control function.

convection The flow of a gas or liquid that results in the transfer of heat from one location to another.

convection cooling The removal of excess heat from a component, such as a power vacuum tube or transistor, via upward movement of surrounding air that has been heated by the component.

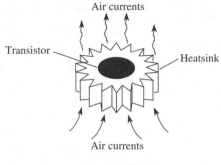

**convection
cooling**

convection current **1.** The motion of current carriers or a charge across the surface of a conductor or dielectric. **2.** Air currents rising above a heat source or heated body.

convective discharge The continuous high-voltage current discharge across a spark gap.

convectron A device that indicates the angle, with respect to the vertical, based on convection cooling of a straight wire. The temperature difference is greatest when the angle is 0 degrees (the wire is vertical); the temperature difference decreases as the angle increases, reaching a minimum at 90 degrees (when the wire is horizontal).

convenience outlet **1.** In North America, a wall outlet providing a nominal 117 volts alternating current (ac) at 60 Hz for common household appliances. **2.** An outlet in a laboratory that provides power for a certain application.

conventional current The notion that current flows from the positive pole to the negative pole in an electric circuit. This representation is used most often by physicists. Electron flow is opposite to conventional current flow; positively charged particles, such as holes, move in the same direction as the conventional current.

convergence **1.** The eventual meeting of values or bodies at some point (sometimes at infinity, as in certain mathematical series). **2.** The intersection point of the beams from separate electron guns in a cathode-ray tube (CRT).

convergence coil One of a pair of coils used in a color television receiver to produce dynamic beam convergence (see CONVERGENCE, 2).

convergence control In a color television receiver, a potentiometer in the high-voltage circuit for convergence adjustment (see CONVERGENCE, 2).

convergence electrode An electrode that provides an electrostatic field for converging electron beams. Compare CONVERGENCE MAGNET.

convergence frequency The frequency of the last member of a spectrum series.

convergence magnet   An assembly that provides a magnetic field to converge electron beams. Compare CONVERGENCE ELECTRODE.

convergence phase control   In a three-gun color picture tube, a variable resistor or variable inductor used to adjust the phase of the dynamic convergence voltage.

convergence plane   **1.** In a color picture tube, the plane in which the red, green, and blue beams all focus. **2.** In a cathode-ray tube, the plane in which the electron beam reaches its sharpest focus.

convergent series   A mathematical series that approaches a specific, finite numerical value as the number of terms increases. Thus, the series $0.3 + 0.03 + 0.003 + . . .$ approaches a limiting value of $\frac{1}{3}$. Compare DIVERGENT SERIES and INFINITE SERIES.

converging lens   A lens having a real focus for parallel rays; generally a *convex lens.*

conversational compiler   In computer operations, a compiler that, using the CONVERSATIONAL MODE of operation, shows the programmer whether or not each statement entered into the computer is valid, and whether or not to proceed with the next instruction.

conversational mode   High-level computer operation or programming, in which the computer gives responses to the operator's input.

conversion   **1.** The deliberate mixing of radio-frequency (RF) signals to produce signals at the sum and/or difference frequencies. **2.** The process of changing direct current (dc) to alternating current (ac). **3.** The process of changing low-voltage dc to high-voltage dc. **4.** The changing of a computer file to another format and, possibly, transferring it to a different storage medium (e.g., from tape to internal memory). **5.** The processing of a program or file written for one computer or application into a form suitable for another computer or application.

conversion efficiency   In a converter (see CONVERTER, **1**), the ratio of output-signal amplitude to input-signal amplitude. For example, in a superheterodyne converter, a large intermediate-frequency (IF) output for a low radio-frequency (RF) input indicates high conversion efficiency.

conversion equipment   In a computer system, an offline device for transferring data from one medium to another [e.g., a disk-to-tape converter (tape drive)]. Also called CONVERTER.

conversion exciter   An exciter for transmitters, in which an output signal of a desired frequency is obtained by beating the output of a variable-frequency self-excited oscillator with the output of a fixed-frequency oscillator (such as a crystal oscillator).

conversion gain   Amplification as a byproduct of conversion. See CONVERSION EFFICIENCY.

conversion loss   Conversion gain of less than 1.

conversion program   In computer operations, a program for data conversion (see CONVERSION, **4** and **5**).

conversion rate   Also called *sampling rate.* The number of samples per second taken by an ANALOG-TO-DIGITAL CONVERTER.

conversion time   In digital computer operation, the time required for the machine to read out all the digits in a coded word.

conversion transconductance   See CONVERSION EFFICIENCY.

convert   **1.** To perform frequency conversion (see CONVERSION, **1**). **2.** To perform voltage conversion (see CONVERSION, **2** and **3**). **3.** In computer operations, to change information from one number base to another. **4.** To perform data conversion (see CONVERSION, **4** and **5**).

converter   **1.** A heterodyne mixer in which two input signals of different frequency are mixed to yield a third (output) signal of yet a different frequency. **2.** A machine for converting direct current (dc) to alternating current (ac) (e.g., a chopper converter). **3.** A transistor circuit for converting a low-voltage dc to higher-voltage dc. **4.** Conversion equipment. **5.** A circuit or device that changes analog data to digital data or vice versa.

converter amplifier   See CHOPPER AMPLIFIER.

converter stage   A circuit used principally to mix two signals (such as a received signal and local-oscillator signal in a superheterodyne receiver), and deliver the resultant signal.

convexo-concave   Pertaining to a lens having a convex face of greater curvature than its concave face.

coolant   A liquid (often water or oil) used to remove heat from an electronic component.

Coolidge X-ray tube   An X-ray tube containing a heated filament (with focusing shield) and a slanting tungsten target embedded in a heavy copper anode.

cooling   Maintenance of the operating temperature of an electronic component or system at a safe level. Common devices for cooling are heatsinks, circulating or forced air, and circulating liquid.

coordinate bond   A covalent bond that consists of a pair of electrons supplied by only one of the atoms joined by the bond.

Coordinated Universal Time   Abbreviation, UTC. Astronomical time at the Greenwich meridian (zero degrees longitude). The UTC day begins at 0000 hours and ends at 2400 hours. Based on the mean, or average, synodic (sun-based) rotational period of the earth. The earth is slightly behind UTC near June 1, and is slightly ahead near October 1.

coordinate digitizer   A device or circuit that encodes a coordinate graph into digital signals for storage or transmission.

coordinate of chromaticity   See CHROMATICITY COORDINATE.

coordinates   A set of axes with points that can be uniquely defined or located on a line, in a plane, or in space. See CARTESIAN COORDINATES and POLAR COORDINATES.

coordinate system   A mathematical means of uniquely defining or locating a point on a line, in a plane, or in space. The most common coordinates are CARTESIAN COORDINATES (also called *rectangular coordinates*), consisting of numbered lines intersecting at right angles.

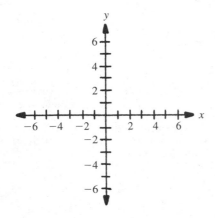

**coordinate system
(Cartesian)**

coordination complex   An ion or compound having a central (usually metallic) ion combined by coordinate bonds with a definite number of surrounding groups, ions, or molecules.

coplanar array   A set of antennas that lie in the same plane, and are fed by a common transmission line.

copper   Symbol, Cu. A metallic element. Atomic number, 29. Atomic weight, 63.546. An excellent conductor of electricity and heat, commonly used in the manufacture of wires and cables.

copper-clad wire   Iron or steel wire plated with copper.

copper-constantan thermocouple   A thermocouple consisting of a junction between wires or strips of copper and constantan. Typical output is 4.24 mV at 100°C.

copper loss   Power (I^2R) loss in copper wires, cables, and/or coils.

copper-oxide diode   A small diode in which the semiconductor material is copper oxide. Such diodes, widely used before the ready availability of selenium and silicon, are still occasionally found in meter-rectifier service.

copper-oxide modulator   An amplitude modulator whose action is derived from the nonlinear conduction characteristic of copper-oxide diodes.

copper-oxide photocell   A photoelectric cell in which the light-sensitive material is copper oxide.

copper-oxide rectifier   A rectifier in which the semiconductor material is copper oxide. Rectifiers of this type are suitable for low-voltage service; they were widely used before the advent of germanium, silicon, and selenium rectifiers.

copper pyrites   See CHALCOPYRITE.

copper-sulfide rectifier   A rectifier in which the unilateral junction is between copper-sulfide and magnesium elements. Like the copper-oxide rectifier, the copper-sulfide unit was once widely used in low-voltage applications.

copy   **1.** Also called *hard copy.* Printed or written text. **2.** In communications, a qualitative expression of the extent to which received data is intelligible (e.g., a radio operator's signal report, "You are solid (perfect) copy."). **3.** To duplicate data in a storage system, the original being in another system, or in a different location in the same system. **4.** An exact duplicate of data in any form.

copying telegraph   A descriptive term for a *facsimile* system.

CORAL   A high-level computer programming language for real-time applications.

Corbino disk   A variable resistor consisting of a semiconductor disk capable of exhibiting the CORBINO EFFECT. The disk is inserted into an adjustable magnetic field, which serves as the control medium.

Corbino effect   A phenomenon similar to the HALL EFFECT, in which a current flows around a disk carrying a radial current when the disk is inserted into a magnetic field whose lines of flux are perpendicular to the disk. Compare HALL EFFECT.

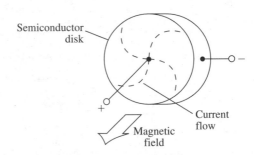

Corbino effect

cord   **1.** A length of flexible, insulated cable, usually having two or three conductors. **2.** Tough, insulating string (e.g., *dial cord* or *lacing cord*).

cordless   **1.** Descriptive of a plug without a flexible cord. **2.** Pertaining to radio-frequency (RF) or infrared short-range links for communications and control (e.g., a *cordless telephone* set).

cordwood   A type of construction in which electronic components are sandwiched perpendicularly between layers of components. So called because it looks somewhat like stacked cordwood.

cordwood module   A module containing discrete components mounted perpendicularly between two parallel printed circuits.

core   1. The body or form on which a coil or transformer is wound. Can be made of ferromagnetic or dielectric material. The properties depend on the application. 2. CORE MEMORY.

core dump   Dumping core memory content to an output peripheral. Also see DUMP.

coreless induction heater   An induction heater in which the body to be heated receives energy directly from the field of the energizing coil (there is no intervening core). Compare CORE-TYPE INDUCTION HEATER.

core loss   Loss of energy in a magnetic core, caused by eddy currents and hysteresis in the core material.

core memory   An older memory technology, consisting of a series of small ringshaped magnetic cores, into or out of which data can be written or read by changing the magnetization of the cores.

core plane   A usually flat assembly of special magnetic cores, through which pass associated current-conducting wires to provide a CORE MEMORY.

core saturation   The condition in which a core of magnetic material accommodates the maximum number of magnetic lines characteristic of that material. Increasing the magnetizing force produces no additional magnetization.

core shift register   A shift register that uses special magnetic cores as bistable components. See CORE MEMORY.

core storage   A high-speed magnetic core storage unit. Also see CORE MEMORY and CORE PLANE.

core transformer   A transformer whose coils are wound around a ferromagnetic core.

core wrapping   The placing of an insulating layer over an inductor or transformer core. This minimizes the chances of short-circuiting between the windings and the core material.

core-type induction heater   An induction heater in which the body to be heated is magnetically linked, by a core, to the energizing coil. Compare CORELESS INDUCTION HEATER.

corner   1. An abrupt turn in the axis of a waveguide. 2. The line, and the region in the vicinity thereof, at which two intersecting plane surfaces meet (e.g., the reflector screen of a CORNER-RE-FLECTION ANTENNA). The plane surfaces are usually perpendicular to each other. 3. The point, and the region in the vicinity thereof, at which three intersecting plane surfaces meet. Generally, the plane surfaces are mutually per-

pendicular. 4. The passband frequency limit(s) of a bandpass, band-rejection, high-pass, or low-pass filter. 5. A sharp bend in the attenuation-versus-frequency curve of a bandpass, band-rejection, high-pass, or low-pass filter, depicting the limit(s) of the passband.

corner diffraction   1. The bending of sound waves around a corner. 2. The bending of radio-frequency (RF) energy around an object, when the wavelength is great, compared with the size of the object.

corner effect   A rounding off of the frequency response of a filter at the corner(s) [i.e., at the limit(s) of the passband].

corner frequency   See CORNER, 4.

corner reflection   The reflection of a beam of light (or of microwave energy or other short-wavelength energy) from a corner reflector, so the beam leaves the reflector in exactly the opposite direction from which it approaches. See CORNER REFLECTOR, 2.

corner-reflection antenna   A directional antenna consisting of a dipole radiator situated at the apex formed by two nonparallel, flat reflecting sheets or a single folded sheet. See CORNER REFLECTOR, 1.

corner reflector   1. A set of two reflecting plane surfaces, joining along a common line, and usually perpendicular to each other. Used in some directional antenna systems, and also in some optical systems. 2. A set of three mutually perpendicular reflecting plane surfaces; causes a ray of energy to be turned by exactly 180 degrees.

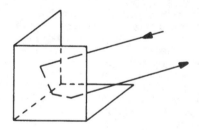

corner reflector, 2

corona   A luminous discharge in the space surrounding a high-voltage conductor; caused by ionization of the air. The discharge constitutes a loss of energy.

corona effect   The production of a luminous discharge, especially at the end of a pointed terminal, when the voltage gradient reaches a critical value.

corona failure   A form of high-voltage failure, resulting from the erosion of an object (such as an electrical insulator) by corona.

corona loss Loss caused by energy dissipation through a corona. It occurs as a result of the emission of electrons from the surface of electrical conductors at high potentials, and depends on the curvature of the conductor surface, with most emission occurring from sharp points and the least from surfaces with a large radius of curvature. It is often accompanied by a blue glow and a crackling or hissing sound.

corona resistance The length of time that an insulating material can withstand a specified level of field-intensified ionization before completely breaking down.

corona shield A shield surrounding a high-voltage point to prevent corona by redistributing the electric flux.

corona starting voltage The minimum voltage between two electrodes, or on a single electrode in free space, at which corona occurs.

corona voltmeter A voltmeter used to measure the peak value of a voltage in terms of corona discharge. It consists of a metal tube in which a central wire is mounted, the parts being connected to the voltage source. The air density in the tube is varied until corona occurs.

corpuscle A tiny particle. It was the name given to the ELECTRON by some early experimenters and theorists.

correction **1.** The addition of a factor that provides greater accuracy in a measurement. **2.** A change in the calibration of an instrument to increase the accuracy.

correction factor A percentage, or numerical factor, added to or subtracted from a reading to provide a greater degree of accuracy. Often used with instruments known to be inaccurate by a certain amount.

corrective feedback Feedback that is used to correct (bring to a prescribed level) a quantity constituting the input to a system.

corrective maintenance The repair of a circuit or system after it has malfunctioned or broken down.

corrective network A network that improves the performance of the circuit into which it is inserted.

corrective stub A combination tuning-matching stub used in some antenna systems. It matches the resistive component of the antenna impedance to the characteristic impedance of a feed line, and also eliminates any reactance that might be present at the antenna feed point.

correed relay A sealed reed relay used as a high-speed switching device in communications equipment.

correlation A statistical expression or measure of the degree to which two sets of data are related. Can be given qualitatively (high-positive, low-positive, zero, low-negative, or high-negative) or quantitatively (as a number between -1 and 1). Does not necessarily imply causation.

correlation detector A detector that compares a signal of interest with a standard signal at every point, delivering an output that is proportional to the correspondence between the two signals.

correlation distance The smallest distance between two antennas that results in fading of signals under conditions of tropospheric propagation. It is used at very-high frequencies (VHF) and above, to determine the maximum range over which communications can be carried out reliably.

correlation tracking A method of target tracking in which phase relationships are used to determine positions.

correspondence The ability of a binocular machine vision system to tell when both of its optical sensors are processing an image from the same object; also, the ability of the system to keep both sensors tracking the same object.

corrosion-resistant Pertaining to materials that are treated to be immune to corrosion by the elements. Such substances are preferable for use in marine or tropical environments, where corrosion is especially severe.

corruption The altering of data or a code as a result of a program error or machine fault.

COS Abbreviation of COMPLEMENTARY-SYMMETRY CIRCUIT.

cosecant Abbreviation, csc. A trigonometric function; $\csc q = c/a$, where c is the hypotenuse of a right triangle and a is the side opposite q. The cosecant is the reciprocal of sine: $\csc q = 1/\sin q$.

cosecant-squared antenna A radar antenna that radiates a COSECANT-SQUARED BEAM.

cosecant-squared beam A radar beam whose intensity varies directly with the square of the cosecant of the angle of elevation.

cosech Abbreviation of HYPERBOLIC COSECANT. Also abbreviated as csch.

cosh Abbreviation of HYPERBOLIC COSINE.

cosine Abbreviation, cos. A trigonometric function; $\cos q = b/c$, where b is the side adjacent to q and c is the hypotenuse of the right triangle.

cosine law The brightness in any direction from a perfectly diffusing surface is proportional to the cosine of the angle between the direction vector and a vector perpendicular to the surface.

cosine wave A periodic wave that follows the cosine of the phase angle. It has a shape identical with a SINE WAVE, but differs by 90 degrees of phase.

cosine yoke A magnetic-deflection yoke that has nonuniform windings for improved focus at the edges of a television picture. Also called *anastigmatic yoke* and *full-focus yoke*.

cosmic noise Radio noise produced by signals from extraterrestrial space.

cosmic rays Extremely penetrating rays consisting of streams of atomic nuclei entering the earth's atmosphere from outer space.

COS/MOS IC An integrated circuit (IC), such as an operational amplifier, utilizing metal-oxide-semiconductor (MOS) field-effect transistors in a complementary-symmetry (COS) arrangement.

cost analysis In a commercial or industrial organization, ascertaining the expense associated with a service, process, or job.

cot Abbreviation of COTANGENT.

cotangent Abbreviation, cot. A trigonometric function; cot $q = b/a$, where a is the side adjacent to q and b is the side opposite q (in a right triangle). Cotangent is the reciprocal of tangent: cot $q = 1/\tan q$.

coth Abbreviation of HYPERBOLIC COTANGENT.

Cotton-Mouton effect See KERR MAGNETO-OPTICAL EFFECT.

Cottrell process Dust precipitated by high voltage. Dust in the air is made to flow through a grounded metal chamber that contains a wire maintained at high voltage. The dust particles become charged and adhere to the chamber walls, from which they are later collected.

coul-cell A coulometer of the electrolytic-cell type.

coulomb (Charles Augustin Coulomb, 1736–1806). Abbreviation, C. The unit of electrical charge quantity, equal to the charge contained in 6.24×10^{18} electrons. A current of one ampere (1 A) represents 1 coulomb per second (C/s).

Coulomb's law The force between two electrically charged objects is directly proportional to the product of the charge quantities in coulombs, and inversely proportional to the square of the distance between the charge centers. This force is an attraction for opposite charges, and a repulsion for similar charges.

coulometer An instrument that measures electrical charge quantity in coulombs. A typical version keeps a cumulative count of coulombs (ampere-seconds) by integrating current, with respect to time. Also called *coulombmeter*.

Coulter counter See CELL COUNTER.

count **1.** The number of pulses tallied by a counting system in a given period of time. **2.** A single response by a radioactivity counter. **3.** A record of the number of times an instruction or subroutine in a computer program is executed (by increasing the value of a variable by one, as stated in a FOR-NEXT loop, for example).

countdown A decreasing count of time units remaining before an event or operation occurs showing time elapsed and time remaining.

counter **1.** A circuit, such as a cascade of flip-flops, that tracks the number of pulses applied to it and usually displays the total number of pulses. **2.** A mechanism, such as an electromechanical indicator, that tracks the number of impulses applied to it and displays the total. **3.** An electronic switching circuit, such as a flip-flop or stepping circuit, that responds to sequential input pulses applied to it, giving one output pulse after receiving a certain number of input pulses.

counter- Prefix meaning "opposite to" or "contrary to." Examples: *counter EMF, counterclockwise.*

counterclockwise Abbreviation, ccw. Pertaining to rotational motion in a sense opposite that of a typical analog clock. Movement is to the left at the top of the rotational circle, and to the right at the bottom of the circle. Compare CLOCKWISE.

counterclockwise-polarized wave An elliptically polarized electromagnetic wave whose electric-intensity vector rotates counterclockwise as observed from the point of propagation. Compare CLOCKWISE-POLARIZED WAVE.

counter efficiency The sensitivity of a radiation counter or scintillation counter to incident X-rays or gamma rays.

counterelectromotive cell A cell used to counteract a direct-current voltage.

counter EMF See BACK VOLTAGE and KICK-BACK.

counter-meter A radioactivity instrument, such as a Geiger counter, that indicates the number of radioactive particles per unit time.

counterpoise A means of obtaining a radio-frequency (RF) ground by using a grid of wires or tubing in a plane parallel to the earth's surface or to average terrain. The radius of the grid is usually at least 0.25 wavelength, but might be smaller if the feed-point impedance of the antenna is very high.

counterpoise ground system A counterpoise with a radius such that resonance is obtained with a quarter-wavelength antenna operated at a height of more than 0.25 wavelength above actual ground. Usually such a system consists of three or four radials measuring 0.25 wavelength each, and extending outward from the base of the antenna nearly parallel to the average terrain.

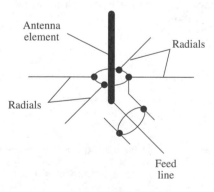

**counterpoise
ground system**

counter tube A tube, such as the Geiger-Meuller tube, in which a penetrating radioactive particle ionizes a gas and produces an output pulse.

counter voltage See BACK VOLTAGE and KICK-BACK.

counting-type frequency meter A direct-reading analog or digital frequency meter that indicates the number of pulses (or cycles) per second applied to it.

count-remaining technique See COMPLEMENT-SETTING TECHNIQUE.

couple Two dissimilar metals in contact with each other or immersed in an electrolyte.

coupled circuits Circuits between which energy is transferred electrostatically, electromagnetically, by some combination of the two, or by direct connection.

coupled impedance The impedance that a circuit "sees" when it is coupled to another circuit. Thus, when the secondary of a transformer is terminated with an impedance, the primary "sees" a combination of that impedance and its own.

coupler A device for transferring energy between two circuits and using capacitive coupling, direct coupling, inductive coupling, or some combination of these.

coupling **1.** Also called *electrostatic coupling* or *capacitive coupling*. The linking of two circuits or devices by electric flux. **2.** Also called *magnetic coupling* or *inductive coupling*. The linking of two circuits or devices by magnetic flux. **3.** Also called *direct coupling*. The linking of two circuits or devices by direct connection. **4.** Also called *resistive coupling*. The linking of two circuits or devices through a resistance. **5.** Also called *optical coupling*. The linking of two circuits or devices through an optoisolator.

coupling aperture A hole in a waveguide that is used to transmit energy to the waveguide, or receiving energy from outside the waveguide.

coupling capacitor A capacitor used to conduct ac energy from one circuit to another. Also see CAPACITIVE COUPLING.

coupling coefficient See COEFFICIENT OF COUPLING.

coupling diode A semiconductor diode connected between the stages of a direct-coupled amplifier. When the diode is connected in the correct polarity, it acts as a high resistance between stages when there is no signal, and does not pass the high dc operating voltage from one stage to the next. When a signal is present, the diode resistance decreases, and the signal gets through.

coupling efficiency A measure of the effectiveness of a coupling system (i.e., the degree to which it delivers an undistorted signal of correct amplitude and phase).

coupling loop **1.** A single turn of a coupling transformer. **2.** A small loop inserted into a waveguide to introduce microwave energy.

coupling probe A usually short, straight wire or pin protruding into a waveguide to electrostatically introduce microwave energy into the waveguide. It acts like a miniature whip antenna.

coupling transformer A transformer used primarily to transfer alternating-current (ac) energy electromagnetically into or out of a circuit.

covalent binding forces In a crystal, the binding forces resulting from the sharing of valence electrons by neighboring atoms.

covalent bonding The binding together of the atoms of a material as a result of shared electrons or holes.

coverage **1.** The area within which a broadcast or communication station can be reliably heard. **2.** The shielding effectiveness of a coaxial cable.

coversed sine Abbreviation, covers. The trigonometric functional equivalent of the *versed sine* of the complement of an angle [i.e., the difference between the sine of an angle and unity (1)]. Thus, covers $q = 1 - \sin q$.

CP Abbreviation of *chemically pure*.

cp **1.** Abbreviation of CANDLE POWER. **2.** Abbreviation of *central processor*.

cps **1.** Abbreviation of CYCLES PER SECOND. Cycles per second, to denote ac frequency, has been supplanted by HERTZ. **2.** Abbreviation of *characters per second*.

CPU Abbreviation of CENTRAL PROCESSING UNIT.

CQ A general call signal used in radio communication, especially by amateur stations, to invite a response from any station that hears it.

Cr Symbol for CHROMIUM.

cracked-carbon resistor A high-stability resistor in which the resistance material is particulate carbon.

cradle guard See GUARD WIRE.

cradlephone A telephone set in which the microphone and earphone are mounted on opposite ends of a handle. This handle, called the *receiver*, rests on the crossmember of a stand connected to a base containing the dial and ringing circuits. Also called *French phone, French telephone*, and *handset*.

crash **1.** A condition in which a computer or network server becomes inoperative because of a software or memory-management problem. **2.** In a computer hard disk or diskette drive, contact of the read/write head with the surface of a disk or platter. Usually, it is the result of excessive physical vibration or shock.

crate A foundation unit into which modules are plugged to establish a circuit.

crawl **1.** See CREEPING COMPONENT. **2.** The credits (names of staff and their contribution to content) superimposed and moving on a television picture at the end of a program.

crazing The formation of tiny cracks in materials, particularly in such dielectrics as plastic and ceramic.

creep See COLD FLOW.

creepage Current leakage across the surface of a dielectric.

creeping component A quantity, such as current, voltage, or frequency, that slowly changes in value with time.

crest factor See AMPLITUDE FACTOR.

crest value The maximum amplitude of a composite current or voltage.

crest voltmeter A peak-reading (or sometimes peak-responsive) voltmeter.

crippled mode The mode of operation for a computer or other hardware in which some of the components are inoperable. Compare GRACEFUL DEGRADATION.

crisscross neutralization See CROSS-CONNECTED NEUTRALIZATION.

crisscross rectifier circuit A conventional bridge rectifier circuit configured in such a way that two of the diodes are connected in crisscross fashion between the input and output terminals.

critical angle **1.** In radio communications, an angle of departure that a transmitted electromagnetic field subtends, with respect to the horizon at the transmitting (TX) point, below which the ionosphere will reliably return the signal to the earth, and above which the ionosphere will not reliably return the signal. This angle (shown by the double arc marked X in the drawing) depends on the frequency of the transmitted electromagnetic wave, and also on ionospheric conditions. **2.** For an electromagnetic wave or ray approaching a boundary at which the index of refraction abruptly decreases, the minimum angle of incidence (relative to a line perpendicular to a plane tangent to the boundary) at which the energy is totally reflected.

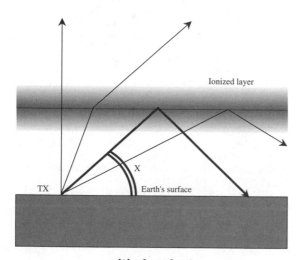

Ionized layer

X

TX   Earth's surface

critical angle, 1

critical characteristic A parameter that has a disproportionate effect on other variables. A small change in this characteristic can result in a large change in the operating conditions of a circuit or system.

critical component A component or part that is especially important in the operation of a circuit or system.

critical coupling The value of coupling at which maximum power transfer occurs. Increasing the extent of coupling beyond the critical value decreases power transfer.

critical damping The value of damping that yields the fastest transient response without overshoot.

critical dimension The cross-sectional size of a waveguide that determines its minimum usable frequency.

critical failure A component or circuit failure that results in shutdown of a system, or a malfunction that results in improper operation.

critical field The smallest magnetic-field intensity in a magnetron that keeps an electron, emitted from the cathode, from reaching the anode.

critical frequency For a particular layer of the ionosphere, the high frequency at which a vertically propagated wave is no longer reflected back to the earth.

critical inductance In a choke-input power-supply filter, the minimum inductance that will maintain a steady value of average load current.

critical potential The potential difference required for an electron to excite or ionize an atom with which it collides.

critical voltage The voltage at which a gas ionizes.

critical wavelength The wavelength that corresponds to CRITICAL FREQUENCY.

CRO Abbreviation of *cathode-ray oscilloscope.*

Crookes dark space In a glow-discharge tube, the narrow dark space next to the cathode. Also see CROOKES TUBE.

Crookes tube A glow-discharge tube containing an anode, cathode, and a small amount of gas under low pressure.

cross antenna An antenna in which two (usually equal-length) horizontal radiators cross each other at right angles and are connected together to a feeder at their point of intersection. It takes its name from its horizontal-cross shape.

cross assembler A program used with one computer to translate instructions for another computer.

crossband operation **1.** Communications in which two frequency bands are used. Station X, for example, might transmit on frequency f_A in band A and receive on frequency f_B in band B; station Y would then transmit on f_B and receive on f_A. **2.** In satellite communications, the use of two frequency bands to facilitate full-duplex operation and to allow the satellite transponder to effectively function. The transponder receives signals from the earth within a specific frequency band, and converts this entire band of signals to a set of signals that occupies an equal amount of spectrum space on another frequency band. The converted signals are then retransmitted back to earth.

crossbar switch A three-dimensional array of switch contacts in which a magnetic selector chooses individual contacts, according to their coordinates in the matrix.

cross bearings A method of radionavigation, in which directional readings are taken from a receiving station (such as a ship or aircraft) for two fixed transmitting stations whose locations are known. Lines are drawn on a map from the transmitting stations, in directions 180 degrees opposite the bearings obtained from the receiving station. The intersection point of these lines is the location of the receiving station.

cross beat A spurious frequency arising from CROSS MODULATION.

cross-check To compare the result of a calculation or computer routine with the result obtained by a different method.

cross color In the chrominance channel of a color television receiver, crosstalk interference caused by monochrome signals.

cross-connected neutralization Neutralization of a push-pull amplifier by feedback through two capacitors—each connected from the output circuit of one transistor to the input circuit of the other.

cross-coupled multivibrator A multivibrator circuit in which feedback is provided by a coupling capacitor between the output of the second stage and the input of the first stage; the stages are forward-coupled by a capacitor of the same value.

cross coupling **1.** The state of being cross-coupled (see, for example, CROSS-COUPLED MULTIVIBRATOR). **2.** Undesired coupling between two circuits.

cross current A current that flows in the opposite direction from some other current.

crossed-pointer indicator **1.** Also called *crossed-needle meter.* A combination of two analog metering instruments in one case. Each needle has its own independently calibrated scale. A third scale corresponds to the intersection point of the needles. Commonly used in directional wattmeters that simultaneously show forward power, reflected power, and standing-wave ratio (SWR). **2.** A two-pointer meter used in aircraft to show the position of the aircraft, relative to the glide path.

crossed-wire thermoelement Two wires or strips of dissimilar metals joined or twisted at a point that constitutes a thermoelectric junction. In usual operation, a high-frequency current is passed through one wire, and a proportional direct-current (dc) voltage, generated by thermoelectric action, appears at the other wire.

cross flux The magnetic flux component that is perpendicular to the flux produced by field magnets.

cross-hair pattern A television test pattern consisting of a single vertical line and a single horizontal line, which form a simple cross. The pattern resembles the cross hairs of an optical instrument.

crosshatch generator A modulated radio-frequency (RF) signal generator that produces a crosshatch pattern on a picture-tube screen.

crosshatch pattern A grid of horizontal and vertical lines produced on a picture-tube screen by a cross-hatch generator. It is used in checking horizontal and vertical linearity.

cross modulation **1.** A type of radio-frequency interference (RFI) between two strong stations that are close in frequency. The desired carrier is modulated by the interfering signal. **2.** The production of signals by rectifier junctions in pipes and wiring near a radio receiver. These objects pick up waves and deliver energy at a different frequency, which finds its way into the receiver. Also called *external cross modulation.* **3.** The interaction between signals of different frequency when they magnetize a core of nonlinear magnetic material. Also see CROSSTALK.

cross-modulation factor An expression of the amount of cross modulation (or crosstalk) present in a particular instance. It is equal to M_1/M_2, where M_1 is the modulation percentage that a modulated wave produces in a superimposed unmodulated wave, and M_2 is the modulation percentage of the modulated wave.

cross-neutralized circuit See CROSS-CONNECTED NEUTRALIZATION.

crossover **1.** In a circuit diagram, a point at which lines representing wires intersect, but are not connected. **2.** In a characteristic curve, point at which the plot crosses an axis or operating point. **3.** See CROSSOVER NETWORK.

crossover distortion Distortion of a characteristic at a crossover point (see CROSSOVER, **2**); for example, a bend in the curve where the plot of a waveform passes through zero.

crossover frequency The frequency at which a crossover network delivers equal power to the two circuits it supplies.

crossover network Following final amplification in a sound-reproduction system, an outboard filter circuit that facilitates delivery of the low and high audio frequency (AF) components to the correct speakers.

crossover point See CROSSOVER, **2**.

crossover S-curve The S-shaped image obtained on an oscilloscope screen during sweep-generator alignment of a frequency-modulation (FM) detector. In correct alignment, the exact center of the S-curve (the crossover point) coincides with the zero point on the screen.

cross product   Also called *vector product*. For vectors **A** and **B** having lengths A and B, respectively, and subtending an angle θ relative to each other, the cross product **A** × **B** points in a direction perpendicular to the plane containing both **A** and **B**. The length of **A** × **B** is equal to AB sin θ.

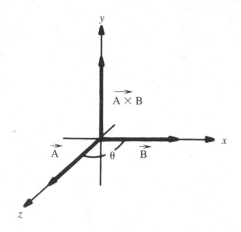

cross product

cross-sectional area   **1.** The surface area of a face of a conductor after cutting through it at a right angle. Specified in square inches, square millimeters, or circular mils. **2.** The total of the cross-sectional areas of all the wires in a stranded conductor.

cross-sectional testing   In quality assurance and quality control (QA/QC), a method of checking a large lot of units or components. Instead of testing every device, a fraction of the devices is tested. The sampling is taken uniformly from the group (e.g., every fifth unit).

crosstalk   Undesired transfer of signals between or among telephone lines, data lines, or system components. In computer operations, this effect places a practical limit on the lengths of parallel data cables.

crosstalk coupling   Undesired coupling between circuits, caused by crosstalk.

crosstalk factor   See CROSS-MODULATION FACTOR.

crosstalk level   The amplitude of crosstalk, usually expressed in decibels above a reference level.

crosstalk loss   Loss of energy caused by crosstalk.

crowbar   An action producing a high overload on a circuit protection device.

crowfoot   **1.** A pattern formed by the cracking or crazing of solid plastics of solidified encapsulating compounds, so called from its resemblance to a bird's footprint. **2.** In a gravity battery cell, the zinc electrode, so called from its resemblance to a bird's foot.

CRT   Abbreviation of CATHODE-RAY TUBE.

crud   **1.** Broadband electrical noise, originating inside and/or outside a system. **2.** Undesired signals that interfere with a desired signal.

cryogenic device   A device that exhibits unique electrical characteristics (such as superconductivity) at extremely low temperatures.

cryogenic motor   A motor designed for operation at extremely low temperatures.

cryoelectronics   The study of the behavior of electronic devices, circuits, and systems at extremely low temperatures.

cryogenics   The branch of physics dealing with the behavior of matter at temperatures approaching absolute zero. Also concerned with methods of obtaining such temperatures in controlled environments.

cryosar   A semiconductor switch utilizing low-temperature avalanche breakdown.

cryoscope   An instrument used to determine freezing point.

cryostat   A chamber for maintaining a very low temperature for cryogenic operations. Also see CRYOGENICS.

cryotron   A switching device consisting essentially of a straight tantalum wire, around which a single-layer control coil is wound. The magnetic field generated by control current flowing through the coil causes the tantalum wire to become superconductive at a temperature of approximately 4.4 degrees K.

cryotronics   Low-temperature electronics, concerned with such phenomena as superconductivity. The term is an acronym from cryogenics and electronics. Also see CRYOGENICS.

cryptanalysis   The breaking of ciphers.

crypto-   A prefix added to words, that implies encoding for the purpose of changing or hiding the meaning of a message or signal.

cryptography   The creating and writing of ciphers.

cryptology   The art and science of creating, writing, unscrambling, and breaking ciphers.

crystal   **1.** A material distinguished by the arrangement of its atoms into a redundant pattern called a *lattice* that presents, in fragments of various sizes, a characteristic polyhedral shape. Common shapes include cubes, parallelepipeds, and hexagonal prisms. **2.** A fragment of material as defined in (1). **3.** A plate or bar cut from a piece of piezoelectric material.

crystal amplifier   **1.** A semiconductor diode circuit using carrier storage. Transistor action and, accordingly, pulse amplification is obtained by alternately making one electrode of the diode an emitter or collector. **2.** Archaic term for TRANSISTOR.

crystal audio receiver   An audio radar receiver, consisting of a crystal detector and audio-amplifier stages.

crystal axes The imaginary lines traversing a piezoelectric crystal, along which (or perpendicular to which) plates are cut for oscillators, resonators, or transducers.

crystal calibrator A crystal oscillator used to generate harmonic checkpoints for frequency calibration. Common fundamental calibrator frequencies are 100 kHz and 1 MHz.

crystal capacitor See VARACTOR.

crystal control The control of the operating frequency of a circuit by means of a piezoelectric crystal.

crystal-controlled receiver A superheterodyne radio receiver whose local oscillator is crystal controlled.

crystal-controlled transmitter A radio transmitter whose master oscillator is crystal controlled.

crystal counter A device for counting the frequency of subatomic particles, based on their ability to change the conductivity of a crystal. The particles can be photons, electrons, protons, neutrons, or the nuclei of atoms.

crystal current Current flowing through a crystal; specifically, the radio-frequency (RF) current flowing through a quartz plate in a crystal-controlled oscillator.

crystal cuts The classification of piezoelectric plates according to the angle at which they were cut from a quartz crystal. Common cut designations are AT, BT, CT, DT, X, Y, and Z. Various cuts afford such complementary factors as frequency, temperature, and thickness. Also see CRYSTAL AXES.

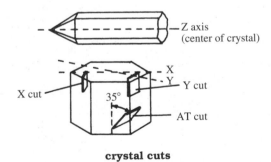

crystal cuts

crystal detector A rudimentary form of semiconductor diode consisting of a mounted lump of mineral (the crystal) in contact with a springy wire ("cat's whisker"). The point of the wire is moved to various points of contact on the crystal surface until the most-sensitive rectifying spot is found.

crystal diffraction The tendency of electromagnetic waves to be scattered when passing through a crystal material.

crystal diode Archaic term for SEMICONDUCTOR DIODE. Also see GALLIUM-ARSENIDE DIODE; GERMANIUM DIODE; JUNCTION DIODE; LASER DIODE; POINT-CONTACT DIODE; SELENIUM DIODE; SIGNAL DIODE; SILICON DIODE.

crystal earphone An earphone in which the transducer is a piezoelectric crystal. Electrical impulses applied to the crystal vary its shape and cause a vibration that is transmitted to a diaphragm; this in turn produces corresponding sound waves.

crystal filter See CRYSTAL RESONATOR.

crystal headphone See CRYSTAL EARPHONE.

crystal holder A fixture specially designed to hold a piezoelectric crystal; it ensures minimum distortion of crystal dimensions and minimum residual capacitance, inductance, and resistance.

crystal imperfection A flaw in the lattice structure of a crystal.

crystal lattice The orderly, redundant pattern of atoms and molecules within a crystalline material; it is a characteristic of a given material.

crystal-lattice filter A crystal resonator in which piezoelectric crystals are used to give a desired shape to the filter response curve.

crystalline material A material exhibiting the characteristic properties of a crystal (see CRYSTAL, **1**).

crystallogram An X-ray photograph or other record of crystal structure.

crystallography The science dealing with crystals and their properties (see CRYSTAL, **1**).

crystal loudspeaker A loudspeaker whose transducer is a piezoelectric crystal. Electrical impulses applied to the crystal vary its shape and cause vibrations that are transmitted to a diaphragm or cone, which produces corresponding sound waves.

crystal meter A rectifier-type ac meter using a semiconductor diode in series with a dc milliammeter or microammeter.

crystal microphone A microphone whose transducer is a natural or synthetic piezoelectric crystal. Sound waves striking the crystal (directly or via a diaphragm) vary its shape, making it produce an audio-frequency (AF) output voltage.

crystal mixer A mixer (converter) circuit utilizing the nonlinearity of a semiconductor diode to mix signals.

crystal operation 1. The characteristics of a piezoelectric crystal in a particular circuit. **2.** Crystal frequency control.

crystal oscillator An oscillator whose operating frequency is determined by the dimensions of an oscillating piezoelectric quartz-crystal plate. Compare SELF-EXCITED OSCILLATOR.

crystal oven A constant-temperature chamber for stabilizing the frequency of a quartz crystal by maintaining its operating temperature at a fixed point.

crystal photocell A photoelectric cell in which the light-sensitive material is a crystalline sub-

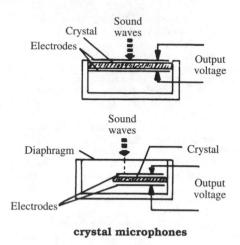

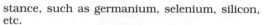

crystal microphones

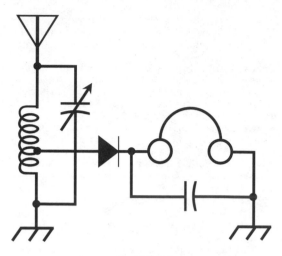

crystal set

stance, such as germanium, selenium, silicon, etc.

crystal pickup   A phonograph pickup whose transducer is a natural or synthetic piezoelectric crystal. The crystal is attached (either directly or through a mechanical linkage) to a stylus, whose movement in the disk groove varies the shape of the crystal. The resultant vibration generates a corresponding audio-frequency (AF) output voltage across the crystal.

crystal probe   A radio-frequency (RF) probe, whose rectifying element is a semiconductor diode.

crystal pulling   **1.** The extraction of a single crystal from a molten mass of crystalline material. Single crystals are used for high-quality semiconductor devices. Also see CZOCHRALSKI METHOD, SINGLE CRYSTAL, and SINGLE-CRYSTAL MATERIAL. **2.** The use of an inductor or capacitor in a crystal-controlled radio-frequency (RF) oscillator circuit to allow adjustment of the frequency over a small range.

crystal receiver   See CRYSTAL SET.

crystal rectifier   **1.** A semiconductor diode used for the purpose of rectifying alternating current (dc), usually in a power supply.

crystal resistor   A temperature-sensitive resistor made from silicon, and exhibiting a positive temperature coefficient of resistance.

crystal resonator   A highly selective resonant circuit in which the center frequency is the resonant frequency of a piezoelectric quartz-crystal plate.

crystal sensor   See CRYSTAL TRANSDUCER.

crystal set   A simple radio receiver that uses a tuned circuit, semiconductor-diode detector, and earphones.

crystal slab   See QUARTZ BAR.

crystal socket   **1.** A low-capacitance, low-loss socket for a piezoelectric crystal. **2.** A socket for a semiconductor diode.

crystal tester   **1.** An oscillator used to check quartz crystals. Most such units check only the crystal's ability to oscillate; more elaborate ones also check crystal current, frequency, temperature coefficient, activity, filter action, etc. **2.** An instrument for checking the electrical characteristics of semiconductor diodes. **3.** An instrument for checking the performance of piezoelectric ceramics.

crystal tetrode   A transistor having four elements: emitter, collector, and two bases.

crystal transducer   A transducer using a piezoelectric crystal as the sensitive element. Examples: crystal earphone, crystal loudspeaker, crystal microphone, and crystal pickup.

crystal triode   See TRANSISTOR.

Cs   Symbol for CESIUM.

CS   Abbreviation of COMPLEMENTARY SYMMETRY. Also COS.

C$_s$ **1.** Symbol for *standard capacitance*. **2.** Symbol for *source capacitance*.

csc   Abbreviation of COSECANT.

C scan   See C DISPLAY.

csch   Abbreviation of HYPERBOLIC COSECANT.

C scope   A cathode-ray tube used in radar to provide a C DISPLAY.

CT-cut crystal   A piezoelectric plate cut from a quartz crystal at an angle of rotation around the X-axis of +38°. Such a plate has a zero temperature coefficient of frequency at 25°C. Also see CRYSTAL AXES and CRYSTAL CUTS.

CTL   Abbreviation of *complementary-transistor logic*.

Cu   Symbol for COPPER.

cube   **1.** A regular polyhedron with six identical square faces and eight vertices. At each vertex, three edges converge at mutual right angles. **2.** The third power of a number; thus the cube of n is written n^3.

cube tap   An electrical adapter, in which a set of male prongs and three sets of female contacts are on the sides of a molded cube. Allows three appliances to be used with a single electrical socket.

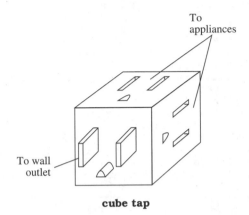

To appliances

To wall outlet

cube tap

cubical antenna   An antenna in which the elements form the outline of a geometric cube or rectangular prism. The most common example is the QUAD ANTENNA.

cubical quad antenna   See QUAD ANTENNA.

cubic equation   A polynomial equation of the third degree. Its general form is $ax^3 + bx^2 + cx + d = 0$.

cue   A condition or signal that alerts an operator, circuit or system to act in a specific manner.

cue circuit   A device for transmitting cues used in program control.

cueing receiver   1. A (usually miniature) radio receiver used to pick up cues. Example: a receiver carried by a technician, actor, or lecturer. 2. A receiver or other pickup circuit that receives a cuing pulse, which it uses to set another circuit.

cu ft   Abbreviation of *cubic foot* or *cubic feet*.

cu in   Abbreviation of *cubic inch* or *cubic inches*.

cumulative error   In a sum or other final value, the total error that has accumulated from the individual errors in the terms. Also called *systematic error*.

cup core   A coil core that also forms a magnetic shield around the coil.

cuprous-oxide rectifier   See COPPER-OXIDE RECTIFIER.

cur   Abbreviation of CURRENT.

curie   Abbreviation Ci. A unit of radioactivity; 1 curie is the amount of radiation from (or in equilibrium with) 1 gram of radium. Also equivalent to 3.7×10^{10} atomic breakdowns per second.

Curie point   1. The temperature above which a ferromagnetic material loses its magnetism or becomes paramagnetic. 2. The temperature at which the ferroelectric properties of a substance disappear.

curie temperature   As a magnetized substance is heated, the lowest temperature at which magnetization is lost. It is generally measured in degrees Celsius or degrees Kelvin. For iron, this temperature is 760 degrees Celsius; for nickel, it is 356 degrees Celsius.

Curie's law   For a paramagnetic substance, the ratio of the magnetization to the magnetizing force is inversely proportional to the absolute temperature.

Curie-Weiss law   Above the Curie point, the susceptibility of a paramagnetic material varies inversely as the excess of temperature above the Curie point increases. This law is invalid for applications at or below the Curie point.

curium   Symbol, Cm. A radioactive metallic element produced artificially. Atomic number, 96. Atomic weight, 247.

current   Symbol, I or i. The movement of charge carriers, such as electrons, holes, or ions. Also see AMPERE.

current amplification   1. An electronic process in which the instantaneous, average, or peak magnitude of a current is increased. 2. The extent to which a current increases in a circuit; the ratio (always greater than one) of output current to input current, I_{out}/I_{in}. Also called *current gain*.

current amplifier   An amplifier operated primarily to increase a signal current. Compare POWER AMPLIFIER and VOLTAGE AMPLIFIER.

current antinode   See CURRENT LOOP.

current attenuation   1. The reduction of current amplitude along a line. 2. The extent to which a current decreases in a line or circuit; the ratio (always less than one) of output current to input current, I_{out}/I_{in}.

current balance   An instrument for determining the size of the ampere. This is done by measuring the force between two current-carrying conductors.

current-balance switch   A switch or relay, operated by the existence of a difference between two currents.

current-carrying capacity   The maximum current (usually expressed in amperes) that a conductor or device can safely conduct.

current coil   The series coil in a nonelectronic wattmeter. Compare POTENTIAL COIL.

current-controlled amplifier   Abbreviation, CCA. An amplifier in which gain is controlled by means of a current applied to a control-input terminal.

current density   The current (usually expressed in amperes per square centimeter) passing through a cross-sectional area of a conductor.

current drain   1. The current supplied to a load by a generator or generator-equivalent. 2. The current required by a device for its operation;

also, the current taken by the device during standby periods.

current echo Reflected current in a transmission line that is not terminated in an impedance exactly matching its characteristic impedance.

current-fed antenna An antenna in which the transmission line is attached to the radiator at a current loop (voltage node). Compare VOLTAGE-FED ANTENNA.

current feed **1.** The delivery of power to a device or circuit at a point where current dominates. Compare VOLTAGE FEED. **2.** In an antenna, feeding it at a current maximum.

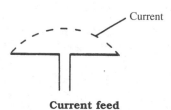

Current

Current feed

current feedback **1.** A feedback signal consisting of current fed from the output to the input circuit of an amplifier. **2.** A system or circuit for obtaining current feedback.

current-feedback pair A two-stage, direct-coupled transistor amplifier having direct-current shunt-series feedback.

current flow Charge carriers passing through a solid, liquid, gas, or vacuum. Also see CURRENT and CURRENT DENSITY.

current gain See CURRENT AMPLIFICATION.

current hogging **1.** An undesirable condition that sometimes takes place when two or more transistors are operated in parallel. One device tends to do all the work, taking all the current. The result can be destruction of that device. **2.** The tendency of one component in a group of identical parallel-connected components to dissipate most of the power.

current-hogging injection logic Acronym, CHIL. A form of bipolar digital logic, similar to current-hogging logic but having the greater density characteristic of injection logic.

current instruction register A register in which are held instructions ready for execution by a program controller.

current lag A circuit condition in which current variations are delayed by up to 180 degrees of phase relative to voltage variations. Compare CURRENT LEAD.

current lead A circuit condition in which current variations occur earlier than voltage variations by up to 180 degrees of phase. Compare CURRENT LAG.

current limiting The controlling of current so that it does not exceed a desired value.

current-limiting resistor A series resistor inserted into a circuit to limit the current to a prescribed value.

current loop A point on a transmission line or antenna radiator at which the current reaches a local maximum. Compare CURRENT NODE.

current meter A usually direct-reading instrument, such as an ammeter, milliammeter, or microammeter, used to measure current strength. Also see ELECTRONIC CURRENT METER.

current-meter operation The operation of a voltmeter as a current meter by connecting it to respond to the voltage drop across a resistor that carries the current of interest.

current-mode logic In computer operations, transistor logic in which the transistors operate in the unsaturated mode.

current node A point on a transmission line or antenna radiator at which the current reaches a local minimum. Compare CURRENT LOOP.

current noise Electrical noise produced by current flowing through a resistor.

current probe A transformer usually having a snap-around, one-turn coil that picks up energy from a conductor and couples it into an alternating-current ammeter.

current rating **1.** A specified value of operating current. **2.** See CURRENT-CARRYING CAPACITY.

current-regulated supply See CONSTANT-CURRENT SOURCE.

current regulation The stabilization of current at a predetermined level or value.

current regulator See BARRETTER.

current relay A relay actuated by specific values of pickup and dropout current.

current saturation In the operation of a device (such as a transistor, saturable reactor, or magnetic amplifier), the leveling off of current at a value beyond which no further increase occurs—even though an input parameter is further increased.

current sense amplifier An amplifier used to increase the sensitivity of, or to decrease the loading of, a current-sensing component.

current sensing Sampling a current (e.g., when the voltage drop across a series resistor is used as a proportional indication of the current flowing through the resistor).

current-sensing resistor A low-value resistor inserted into a circuit primarily for current sensing.

current sensitivity In a current meter or galvanometer, current (in amperes or fractions thereof) per scale division.

current-sheet inductance Symbol, L_S. The low-frequency inductance of a single-layer coil, calculated with the formula $L_S = (0.10028 \, a^2 N^2)/s$, where L_S is in microhenrys, a is the coil radius in inches, N is the total number of turns, and s is the coil length in inches.

current shunt **1.** A resistor connected in parallel with a voltmeter to convert it into an ammeter.

2. A resistor connected in parallel with the input of a voltage amplifier to make the response of the amplifier proportional to input-signal current.

current sink A circuit or device through which a constant current can be maintained.

current-sinking logic A form of bipolar digital logic. Current flows from one stage to the input of the stage immediately before.

current-squared meter An ammeter or milli-ammeter whose deflection is proportional to the square of the current.

current-stability factor In a common-base connected bipolar transistor, the ratio dI_E/dI_C, where I_E is the emitter current and I_C is the collector current.

current strength The magnitude of electric current (see CURRENT) (i.e., the number of carriers flowing past a given point per unit time, expressed in coulombs per second or in amperes).

current transformer **1.** A transformer used to increase or decrease current flow. A primary-to-secondary step-up turns ratio reduces the current; a primary-to-secondary step-down turns ratio increases the current. **2.** A particular transformer (as in 1) used to change the range of an alternating-current milliammeter or ammeter.

current vector In a vector diagram, a line with an arrowhead (vector) showing the magnitude and phase of a current. Compare VOLTAGE VECTOR.

current-voltage feedback In an amplifier or oscillator, the process of applying some of the output current and voltage to the input. This feedback might be in phase (positive) or out of phase (negative), with respect to the input.

cursor **1.** A marker that indicates the position where a character can be entered in a video alphanumeric display. Commonly used in computers and word processors. **2.** The sweeping line on a radar display. **3.** The movable marker on a slide rule.

curve trace **1.** A device that supplies a special variable test voltage to a component or circuit under test, at the same time supplying a sweep voltage to an oscilloscope. The component's output voltage is also presented to the oscilloscope. As a result, the response curve of the component appears on the oscilloscope screen. **2.** A device that produces a permanent record (photographic or graphic) of an electrical phenomenon. Also called OSCILLOGRAPH or RECORDER.

curvilinear trace A trace made on paper with curved vertical lines. The lines are curved to match the arc through which the recording pen swings.

cut-in angle In a semiconductor rectifier circuit, a phase angle slightly greater than zero degrees, at which current conduction begins. Compare CUT-OUT ANGLE.

Cutler antenna A parabolic-dish antenna, in which the driven element consists of a waveguide that has two apertures on opposite sides of a resonant cavity.

Cutler feed An aircraft antenna feed system in which radio-frequency (RF) energy is fed to the reflector by a resonant cavity at the end of a waveguide.

Cutler tone control A dual resistance-capacitance (RC) filter circuit of the general bridged-tee variety. Variation of the series leg provides adjustable treble boost; variation of the shunt leg provides adjustable bass boost.

cutoff **1.** The process of reducing some operating parameter, such as collector current, to zero by adjusting the bias at the input electrode. **2.** The point on the characteristic curve of an amplifying device, at which the output current drops to zero under no-signal conditions. **3.** The lowest frequency at which a waveguide will efficiently function. **4.** The frequency or frequencies corresponding to the point or points in a filter response, at which the attenuation is three decibels greater than the lowest attenuation within the passband. See also CUTOFF FREQUENCY.

cutoff attenuator A variable, nondissipating attenuator consisting of a variable length of waveguide used at a frequency below cutoff.

cutoff bias In a transistor or vacuum-tube circuit, the value of control-electrode bias that produces output current cutoff.

cutoff current Symbol, I_{co}. In a transistor, the small collector current that flows when the emitter current is zero (common-base circuit) or when the base current is zero (common-emitter circuit).

cutoff frequency **1.** Symbol, f_{co}. The high frequency at which the current-amplification factor of a transistor drops to 70.7% of its 1-kHz value. **2.** In a filter, amplifier, or transmission line, the frequency point(s) at which transmission loss or filter rejection begins. It is generally specified as the half-power point(s), or the point(s) at which the attenuation is three decibels, relative to the lowest attenuation. Examples: the high-frequency cutoff of an amplifier and the upper and lower cutoff points of a bandpass filter.

cutoff limiting Output-peak clipping that results from overdrive in an amplifying device. Compare SATURATION LIMITING.

cutoff potential See CUTOFF BIAS.

cutoff voltage See CUTOFF BIAS.

cutoff wavelength **1.** The wavelength corresponding to cutoff frequency. **2.** For a waveguide, the ratio of the velocity of electromagnetic waves in free space (3×10^8 meters per second) to the cutoff frequency of the waveguide in Hz. The result is thus expressed in meters.

cutout **1.** A device, such as a circuit breaker, that automatically disconnects a circuit, usually to prevent overload, but occasionally to prevent underload. **2.** Emergency switch. **3.** Fuse.

cut-out angle In a semiconductor rectifier circuit, a phase angle slightly less than 180 degrees at which current conduction ceases. Compare CUT-IN ANGLE.

cutout base A fuse block.

cut rate **1.** The speed at which a cutter moves across the surface of a blank vinyl disk during the recording process. **2.** The number of cut lines per inch in a vinyl disk recording.

CW **1.** Abbreviation of CONTINUOUS WAVE. **2.** Abbreviation of CLOCKWISE.

CW filter In a communications receiver, a highly selective filter in the intermediate-frequency (IF) or audio-frequency (AF) stage. The bandwidth is typically 200 Hz to 500 Hz; some audio filters can be set for bandwidths as low as about 50 Hz.

CW laser A laser that emits energy in an uninterrupted stream, rather than in pulses.

CW monitor See KEYING MONITOR.

CW oscillator **1.** In a radio receiver, a variable-frequency oscillator that heterodynes a radiotelegraph signal in the intermediate-frequency (IF) amplifier chain, to make audible the continuous-wave dits and dahs. **2.** Sometimes, an external variable-frequency radio-frequency (RF) oscillator, whose output beats against the actual carrier of a continuous-wave radiotelegraph signal, making it audible as dits and dahs. **3.** An unmodulated, unkeyed oscillator.

CW radar A radar system in which radio-frequency (RF) energy is transmitted continuously.

CW reference signal A sinusoidal radio-frequency (RF) signal, used to control the conduction time of a synchronous demodulator in color television.

C_x Symbol for UNKNOWN CAPACITANCE.

cyan Blue-green, one of the three primary pigments.

cyber- A prefix that indicates relevance to, or involvement with, computers, computer systems, and electronic control systems.

cybernetics The study of control system theory in terms of the relationship between animal and machine behavior.

Cyber Sapiens An expression for a computer or robot with artificial intelligence (AI) on the forefront of current technology.

cyberspace **1.** Alternative expression for INFORMATION SUPERHIGHWAY. **2.** Alternative expression for VIRTUAL REALITY.

cyborg Acronym of the words *cybernetic* and *organism*. **1.** A human being with at least one artificial body part, such as a *prosthesis* (artificial limb). **2.** A human being who is largely composed of robotic body parts.

cycle **1.** Abbreviation, c. One complete, 360-degree revolution of the current or voltage vector in an alternating-current (ac) wave. An ac frequency of 1 cycle per second is 1 Hz (see HERTZ). **2.** A complete sequence of operations.

cycle counter A device that totals the number of cycles of a phenomenon repeated during a given period.

cycle index The number of times that a particular cycle has been, or must be, iterated in a computer program.

cycle index counter A variable that indicates how often a cycle of computer program instructions has been executed. In a program, for example, this can be accomplished by increasing, through instruction, the value of a location's content every time a loop operation is performed.

cycle life The total number of charge-discharge cycles a rechargeable cell or battery can tolerate before becoming useless.

cycle reset To change the value of a cycle count (making it zero or some other value).

cycle shift See CYCLIC SHIFT.

cycles per second Abbreviation, cps. Archaic term for HERTZ.

cycle time Pertaining to an operation, the duration of a complete cycle.

cycle timer A timer that switches a circuit or device on and off, according to a predetermined cycle. Also called *programmed timer*.

cyclic code See GRAY CODE.

cyclic memory In computer operations, a memory whose locations can only be accessed points in a cycle, as of a magnetic diskette.

cyclic shift The moving of data out of one end of a storage register and reentering it character-by-character or bit-by-bit at the other end in a closed loop (e.g., 87654 cyclically shifted one place to the right becomes 48765).

cyclic variations Periodic changes in the features of the ionosphere, occurring on a daily, seasonal, or sunspot-related basis. These changes are fairly predictable.

cycling The tendency of a parameter to oscillate back and forth between two different values.

cyclogram A method of showing the relationship between two signals on an oscilloscope. The two signals must have a fixed phase relationship.

cyclotron A type of particle accelerator. An applied electromagnetic field, acting together with an intense applied magnetic field, cause

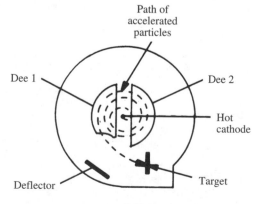

cyclotron

charged subatomic particles to travel with increasing velocity in a spiral path between two
semicircular metal boxes called *dees*. When
the particles go fast enough in the correct
path, they are expelled and strike a target in
their path.

cyclotron frequency The angular frequency of a
charged particle in a cyclotron. The cyclotron frequency depends on the number of times per second the magnetic field of the device is reversed.

cyclotron radiation An electromagnetic field produced by the circular movement of charged particles in a fluctuating magnetic field.

cylinder In computer operations, the combination of equal-radius tracks on the platters of a
hard disk.

cylinder magnet A permanent magnet in the
shape of a cylinder.

cylindrical capacitor See CONCENTRIC CAPAC-
ITOR.

cylindrical contour The most common curvature
of the face of a magnetic tape recording head; it
is a section of a cylinder having a constant radius of 0.5 inch to 1 inch.

cylindrical coordinate geometry A scheme for
robot-arm movement. There are three coordinates, called *reach, angle,* and *elevation*. It allows precise positioning of a robot end effector
within a region consisting of two concentric
cylinders and all the volume in between.

cylindrical coordinates A method of locating a
point in three-space in which height, distance,
and angle are used to uniquely define points.

cylindrical magnet See CYLINDER MAGNET.

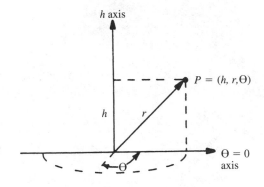

cylindrical coordinates

cylindrical wave An electromagnetic wave whose
field surfaces are nearly perfect cylinders.

cylindrical waveguide A waveguide resembling a
round pipe.

cylindrical winding A method of coil winding in
which the wire is formed into a helix. There
might be only one layer, or there might be several layers. The length of the coil is greater than
the diameter. Also called a *linear winding.*

Czochralski method A technique for obtaining a
relatively large single crystal from a substance,
such as the semiconductors germanium and
silicon. The method consists essentially of dipping a seed crystal into a molten mass of the
same substance, then slowly withdrawing it
while rotating it.

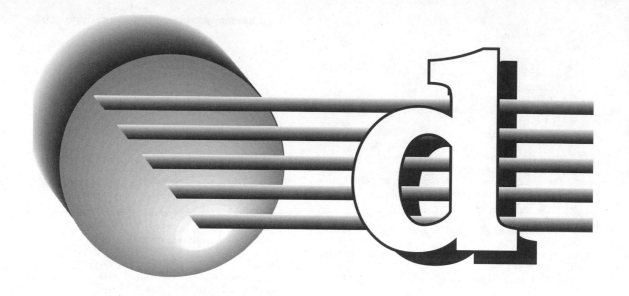

D **1.** Symbol for DEUTERIUM. **2.** Symbol for ELECTRIC DISPLACEMENT. **3.** Symbol for ELECTRIC FLUX DENSITY. **4.** Symbol for DISSIPATION FACTOR. **5.** Symbol for *drain* (see DRAIN, **3**). **6.** Abbreviation of DISSIPATION. **7.** Symbol for *determinant*. **8.** Symbol for DIFFUSION CONSTANT.

d **1.** Abbreviation of DECI. **2.** Symbol for DIFFERENTIAL. **3.** Symbol for distance. **4.** Symbol for DENSITY. **5.** Symbol for *drain* (see DRAIN, **3**). **6.** Abbreviation of DISSIPATION. **7.** Abbreviation of day. **8.** Abbreviation of DEGREE. **9.** Abbreviation of diameter. **10.** Abbreviation of DRIVE.

D/A Abbreviation of DIGITAL-TO-ANALOG. See DIGITAL-TO-ANALOG CONVERSION.

dA **1.** Symbol for DIFFERENTIAL OF AREA. **2.** Symbol for *differential of amplification*. **3.** Seldom-used abbreviation of *deciampere*.

da Abbreviation of DEKA.

DAC Abbreviation of DIGITAL-TO-ANALOG CONVERTER.

DACI Abbreviation of *direct adjacent-channel interference*.

DAGC Abbreviation of DELAYED AUTOMATIC GAIN CONTROL.

daisy chain A method of transferring a signal in a computer from one stage to the next.

daisy wheel A form of printing device consisting of a disk having several dozen radial spokes, each of which has a character molded on its face. The disk rotates to the proper position in the printing process, and a hammer strikes the spoke to press the molding against the ribbon and paper.

DAM Abbreviation of *data-addressed memory*.

Damon effect The change that the susceptibility of ferrite undergoes under the influence of high RF power.

damped galvanometer A galvanometer with a provision for overswing limiting or oscillation prevention.

damped loudspeaker A loudspeaker in which undesirable excursions are prevented by damping in the associated amplifier or speaker circuit.

damped meter **1.** A meter with a provision for overswing limiting or oscillation prevention. **2.** A meter that is protected during transport by a shorting bus between the two meter terminals.

damped natural frequency **1.** The frequency at which a damped system having one degree of freedom will oscillate after momentary application of a transient force. **2.** In the presence of damping, the rate at which a sensing element oscillates freely.

damped oscillations Oscillations in which the amplitude of each peak is lower than that of the preceding one; the oscillation eventually dies out (the amplitude becomes zero). Compare CONTINUOUS WAVE.

damped speaker See DAMPED LOUDSPEAKER.

damped wave A wave whose successive peaks decrease in amplitude (i.e., it decays), eventually reaching an amplitude of zero. Compare CONTINUOUS WAVE and UNDAMPED WAVE.

damped-wave decay See DECREMENT, **1**.

dampen To cause the amplitude of a signal to decay.

damper See DAMPING DIODE.

damper diode See DAMPING DIODE.

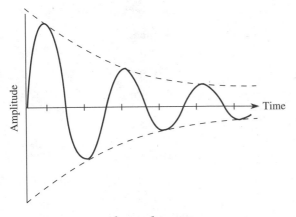

damped wave

damper winding A special short-circuited motor winding that opposes pulsation or rotation of the magnetic field.

damping 1. See DAMPING ACTION. 2. In a loudspeaker, sound-absorbent material used to minimize resonant effects within the enclosure.

damping action 1. Quenching action. 2. The prevention of overswing, dither, or flutter in a meter or loudspeaker (see DAMPED GALVANOMETER, DAMPED LOUDSPEAKER, DAMPED METER). 3. The prevention of oscillation or ringing in a circuit. 4. Inhibition of the vibration of an acoustic transducer to prevent ringing and other unwanted effects.

damping coefficient A figure expressing the ratio of the damping in a system to critical damping.

damping diode A diode used to prevent oscillation in an electric circuit (e.g., the diode that prevents ringing in the power supply of a television receiver). Also called *damper*.

damping factor 1. Symbol, a. For a coil of inductance L and RF resistance R in a damped-wave circuit, the value $R/2L$, where L is in henrys and R in ohms. 2. Abbreviation, F_o. For a torque motor, the ratio of the stall torque to the no-load rotational speed.

damping magnet A permanent magnet so situated, with respect to a moving conductor, disk, or plate, that the resulting field opposes the movement.

damping ratio See DAMPING COEFFICIENT.

damping resistance 1. The value of shunt resistance required to prevent ringing in a coil. 2. The value of resistance required for critical damping of a galvanometer.

damping resistor 1. A shunt across a coil to prevent ringing. 2. A resistor used to provide critical damping of a galvanometer.

Daniell cell A nonpolarizing primary wet cell with zinc (negative) and copper (positive) electrodes. The zinc plate is in a porous cup containing a weak zinc-sulfate solution with a little sulfuric acid; the cup is in a jar filled with a saturated copper-sulfate solution in which the copper electrode is immersed. Typical voltage for the cell is 1.1 V.

daraf The unit of ELASTANCE. Elastance in darafs is the reciprocal of capacitance in farads.

dark conduction The flow of dark current in a photoconductive or glow-discharge device.

dark current The usually tiny current flowing through a darkened photoconductive cell, phototransistor, or glow-discharge device.

dark discharge The occurrence of a discharge in a gas, without the production of visible light.

dark-spot signal A spurious signal generated by some camera tubes, arising from secondary-emission effects.

dark-trace tube An oscilloscope tube on whose white screen a long-persistence magenta image is traced by the electron beam. Illuminating the screen with bright light intensifies the image.

Darlington amplifier A high-gain amplifier that uses a COMPOUND CONNECTION of two bipolar transistors.

Darlington pair See COMPOUND CONNECTION.

D'Arsonval current A large, low-voltage, high-frequency current at one time thought to be therapeutic.

D'Arsonval meter A electromechanical analog meter, in which a coil turns on jeweled pivots between the poles of a strong magnet and against the force of spiral springs. A pointer is attached to the coil. The pointer moves over a calibrated scale.

D'Arsonval movement The mechanism of a D'Arsonval meter.

DART Abbreviation of *data analysis recording tape*.

dart leader A flow of electrons along a path traveled by a lightning stroke, preceding a second stroke. The dart leader, if any, occurs a few milliseconds after the first stroke. Several strokes could occur, each preceded by a dart leader, within less than 1 second.

dash The longer of the two characters (DOT and DASH) of the telegraph code. The duration of the dash is three times longer than that of a dot.

dashpot A delayed-action device in which the movement of a piston is slowed by air or a liquid in a closed cylinder.

dashpot relay A time-delay relay assembly in which the delay is obtained with a DASHPOT.

DAT 1. Abbreviation of DIGITAL AUDIO TAPE. 2. Abbreviation of *diffused-alloy transistor*.

data 1. A collection of digital bits (binary digits) with informational content (e.g., a computer file, a digital image, or a digital sound recording). 2. General expression for information, especially in encoded or written form.

data acquisition The reception and gathering of data (see DATA COLLECTION and DATA SYSTEM, 1).

data-acquisition system   A computer or dumb terminal used to gather data from one or more external points.

data analysis display unit   A video display peripheral for online data analysis.

data area   A computer memory area that holds data only (i.e., one that does not contain program instructions).

data bank   A data file stored in a direct-access storage device, which can be drawn from by many system users through remote terminals.

database   **1.** A computer file containing often-used information (e.g., names and addresses, or electronic part numbers). **2.** A popular form of computer software that allows users to create, maintain, and modify information.

data block   A set of data bits, comprising an identifiable item.

data bus   A conductor or medium over which digital data is transmitted from one place to another within a computer.

data carrier storage   A medium of data storage outside of a computer (e.g., a magnetic disk).

data code   A set of abbreviations or codes for data characters or words.

data collection   The pickup of signals representing test data and their transmission to a computer, data processor, or recorder. Also see DATA SYSTEM, **1.**

datacom   Acronym for DATA COMMUNICATION.

data communication   The transmission and reception of data signals between or among points in a system.

data communication terminal   A computer peripheral providing an input and output link to a central computer system, and that can be used offline for other functions.

data compression   **1.** The process of reducing the size of a data file by eliminating redundancies. **2.** The process of minimizing the length of a data transmission by eliminating redundancies. **3.** The process of reducing the bandwidth of a data transmission. **4.** The process of reducing the dynamic amplitude range of a data transmission.

data control   The automatic control of incoming and outgoing data in a data processing system.

data conversion   The process of changing data from one form to another, e.g., from analog to digital (A/D), digital to analog (D/A), parallel to serial, or serial to parallel.

data converter   **1.** A circuit or device for performing DATA CONVERSION. **2.** An analog-to-digital (A/D) converter. **3.** A digital-to-analog (D/A) converter. **4.** A parallel-to-serial converter. **5.** A serial-to-parallel converter.

data description   The description of a unit of data, as included in a computer source program.

data display   A device, such as a cathode-ray tube (CRT) or liquid-crystal display (LCD), that pre-sents data for visual examination. Compare DATA PRINTOUT.

data element   **1.** A component of a data signal (e.g., a number, letter, symbol, or the equivalent electrical pulses). **2.** A device or circuit for acquiring or processing data. **3.** A unit of data (e.g., a field in a file).

data-flow diagram   A block diagram showing the movement of data through a data-processing system.

data format   The form of data in a record or file (e.g., character format or numerical format).

data gathering   See DATA COLLECTION.

data-handling capacity   **1.** The amount of data that can be stored in a memory circuit. **2.** The amount of data that can be transmitted over a certain medium. **3.** The rate at which data can be transferred under certain conditions.

data-handling system   A system that gathers, routes, transmits, or receives data, but does not necessarily process it.

data item   A logical element (character, byte, or bit) describing a characteristic of a record used by a system for which there is a specific application.

data level   Descriptive, through a programming language, of the relative weight of logical elements (data items) in a computer record. Also called *data hierarchy*.

data link   The portion of a computer system that gathers data and, if necessary, converts it to a form acceptable by a computer.

data matrix   Variables and their possible values stored as a series of columns and rows of values in a computer memory.

data name   An operand specified in a computer source program.

data pickup   **1.** A transducer that collects data signals from a source; it converts nonelectrical data into corresponding electrical signals and delivers its output to a data processing system. **2.** Data acquisition.

data playback   The reproduction of data signals stored by some method of data recording.

data plotter   See X-Y PLOTTER.

data printout   **1.** A device that prints a record of data or the results of a computation. **2.** A permanent printed record, usually of a calculation or computation—especially the printed output of a computer peripheral device.

data processing   Work performed on acquired data, as in solving problems, making comparisons, classifying material, organizing files. Usually done by a computer.

data-processing equipment   A digital computer and the peripheral equipment needed to collate, store, analyze, and reduce data.

data-processing machine   A computer or system used to collate, store, analyze, and reduce data, as opposed to a computer or system used primarily to solve problems or perform routine tasks. Also called *data processor.*

data-processing system An electronic system for automatic data processing. It can be based on analog and/or digital techniques.

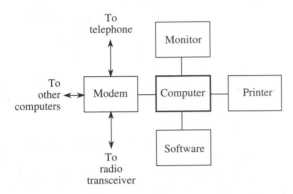

data-processing system

data processor See DATA-PROCESSING MACHINE.

data receiver At a particular point in a data-processing system, a circuit or device for receiving data from a data transmitter.

data reception Receiving data signals from some point within or outside a data-processing system.

data-reception system A data receiver and its associated equipment.

data record A computer-processed record containing a data unit.

data recorder A machine for storing data acquired in the form of electrical signals (see DATA RECORDING).

data recording **1.** The preservation of data signals by some process, such as magnetic-disk encoding, optical-disk encoding, or tape recording, for future use or as a backup. **2.** A record of data signals, as on magnetic tape.

data reduction The summarization of a mass of electronically gathered data.

data-reduction system A system used to minimize the amount of data necessary to convey given information.

data representation Values and data as described by numerals, symbols, and letters (e.g., computer program instructions).

data segment As related to a particular computer process, a subunit of allocated storage containing data only.

data selector/multiplexer A digital circuit that has several or many input signals, and feeds one of them onto a common line.

data set A device that connects a data processor to a telegraph or telephone line.

data signal **1.** A signal (such as one of binary bit combinations) that can represent data as numbers, letters, or symbols. **2.** A signal current or voltage proportional to some sampled quantity, and that can be used to actuate indicating instruments during tests or measurements.

data statement A computer source program statement identifying a data item and specifying its format.

data storage The preservation of data, particularly computer files, for long periods of time in nonvolatile form (no source of power is required to ensure that the data remains intact).

data storage media Hardware that preserves data, particularly computer files, for long periods of time in nonvolatile form (no source of power is required to ensure that the data remains intact). Common media include magnetic disks, magnetic tape, and optical disks.

data synchronizer A device used to synchronize data transmission within a computing or processing system.

data system **1.** An arrangement for collecting, recording, and routing data in the form of electrical signals. **2.** An arrangement for processing data (i.e., for correlating, computing, routing, storing, etc.).

data terminal A remote input/output device connected to a central computer.

data throughput In a computer system, the amount of data per unit time (bytes, kilobytes, megabytes, gigabytes, or terabytes per second or minute) that can be transferred from one place to another.

data transducer In tests and measurements, a transducer that converts a monitored phenomenon into electrical quantities that can be used for computer analysis or calculations.

data transmission Sending data signals from a pickup point or processing stage to another point within a data-processing system; also, sending such signals to points outside the system.

data-transmission system A data transmitter and its associated equipment.

data transmission utilization measure The ratio of the useful data output of a data-transmission system to the total data input.

data transmitter A circuit or device for sending data from point to point within or outside of a data-processing system.

data unit Characters in a group that are related in a way that makes them a meaningful whole (e.g., a text word, or an object such as a circle in vector graphics).

data value A measure of the amount of information contained in a certain number of data bits. The greater the ratio of the actual information to the number of bits, the higher the data value.

data words In digital computer operations, words (bit groups) representing data, rather than program instructions.

DAVC Abbreviation of DELAYED AUTOMATIC VOLUME CONTROL.

David Phonetic alphabet code word for letter D.

daylight effect The modification of transmission paths during the day because of ionization of the upper atmosphere by solar radiation.

daylight lamp An incandescent lamp whose filament is housed in a blue glass bulb, which absorbs some red radiation and transmits most of the green, blue, and violet. So called because the spectral output resembles that of typical daylight.

daylight range The distance over which signals from a given transmitter are consistently received during the day.

DB **1.** Abbreviation of DIFFUSED BASE of a transistor. **2.** Abbreviation of DOUBLE BREAK (relay).

dB **1.** Abbreviation of DECIBEL or *decibels*. **2.** Symbol for *differential of susceptance*.

dBa Abbreviation of ADJUSTED DECIBELS.

dBc Abbreviation of *decibels referred to the carrier*.

DBD Abbreviation of *double-base diode*.

dBd The power gain of an antenna in the direction of maximum radiation, compared to the radiation in the favored direction of a half-wave dipole in free space receiving the same amount of power. Expressed in decibels.

dBi The power gain of an antenna in the direction of maximum radiation, compared to the radiation from a theoretical isotropic antenna in free space receiving the same amount of power. Expressed in decibels.

dBj The level of an RF signal, in decibels, relative to 1 millivolt.

dBk Abbreviation of DECIBELS REFERRED TO 1 KILOWATT.

DBM Abbreviation of *database management*.

dBm Abbreviation of DECIBELS REFERRED TO 1 MILLIWATT.

dBm0 Signal level in dBm, referred to a zero-transmission level.

dBm0p Noise in dBm0, measured with set psophometric weighting.

dB meter A usually high-impedance ac voltmeter with a scale reading directly in decibels.

dBmp The level in dBm, measured with psophometric weighting. Generally equal to dBm - 2.5, for a noise level that is flat within the communications audio range.

dBmr Decibels measured with respect to zero transmission level.

dBmV Abbreviation of DECIBELS REFERRED TO 1 MILLIVOLT.

dBrap Abbreviation of DECIBELS ABOVE REFERENCE ACOUSTIC POWER (10^{-6} W).

dBrn Abbreviation for *decibels above reference noise*. A level of 0 dBrn is defined as noise power of 10^{-9} W (1 nanowatt).

dBrnc Noise power in dBrn for a circuit with message weighting c.

dBrnc0 Noise in dBrnc measured with respect to zero transmission level.

dBV Abbreviation of DECIBELS REFERRED TO 1 VOLT.

dBW Abbreviation of DECIBELS REFERRED TO 1 WATT.

dBx Abbreviation of DECIBELS ABOVE REFERENCE COUPLING.

dC Symbol for *differential of capacitance*.

dc **1.** Abbreviation of DIRECT CURRENT. **2.** Abbreviation of *direct-coupled*.

dc-ac converter A circuit that converts a dc input voltage into an ac output voltage, with or without step-up or step-down. Also called INVERTER.

dc alpha The current amplification factor (ALPHA) of a common-base transistor stage for a dc input (emitter) signal. Compare DC BETA.

dc amplifier **1.** A *direct-coupled amplifier*. **2.** An amplifier for boosting direct-current signals.

dc balance **1.** Adjustment of a circuit or device for dc stability or dc null. **2.** Adjustment of a circuit for dc stability during gain changes. **3.** A potentiometer or other variable component used to stabilize or null a dc circuit.

dc bar See DC BUS.

dc base current Symbol, $I_{B(dc)}$. The static direct current in the base element of a bipolar transistor.

dc base resistance Symbol, $R_{B(dc)}$. The static dc resistance of a bipolar transistor's base element; $R_{B(dc)} = V_B/I_B$.

dc base voltage Symbol, $V_{B(dc)}$. The static dc voltage at the base element of a bipolar transistor.

dc beta The current amplification factor (BETA) of a common-emitter-connected transistor for a dc input (base) signal. Compare DC ALPHA.

dc block A coaxial section that has a capacitance in series with the inner or outer conductor, or both, to block dc while passing RF. Compare DC SHORT.

dc bus A supply conductor carrying direct current only.

dcc Abbreviation of double cotton covered (wire).

dc cathode current Symbol, $I_{K(dc)}$. The static direct current in the cathode element of an electron tube.

dc cathode resistance Symbol, $R_{K(dc)}$. The static dc resistance of the cathode path of an electron tube.

dc cathode voltage Symbol, $V_{K(dc)}$. The static dc voltage at the cathode of an electron tube.

dc circuit breaker A circuit breaker operated by direct-current overload or underload, depending on its design and application.

dc collector current Symbol, $I_{C(dc)}$. The static direct current in the collector element of a bipolar transistor.

dc collector resistance Symbol, $R_{C(dc)}$. The static dc resistance of a bipolar transistor's collector element; $R_{C(dc)} = V_C/I_C$.

dc collector voltage Symbol, $V_{C(dc)}$. The static dc voltage at the collector element of a bipolar transistor.

dc component In a complex wave (i.e., one containing both ac and dc), the current component having an unchanging polarity. The dc component constitutes the mean (average) value around which the ac component alternates, pulsates, or fluctuates.

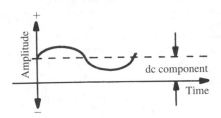

dc component

dc converter A dynamoelectric machine for converting low-voltage dc into higher-voltage dc. It is essentially a low-voltage dc motor coupled mechanically to a higher-voltage dc generator. Compare DC INVERTER.

dc coupling See DIRECT COUPLING.

dc drain current Symbol, $I_{D(dc)}$. The static direct current in the drain element of a field-effect transistor.

dc drain resistance Symbol, $R_{D(dc)}$. The static dc resistance of an FET's drain element; $R_{D(dc)} = V_D/I_D$.

dc drain voltage Symbol, $V_{D(dc)}$. The static dc voltage at the drain element of a field-effect transistor.

dc dump In digital computer operation, removing dc power from a computer, which would eradicate material stored in a volatile memory.

dc emitter current Symbol, $I_{E(dc)}$. The static direct current in the emitter element of a bipolar transistor.

dc emitter resistance Symbol, $R_{E(dc)}$. The static dc resistance of a bipolar transistor's emitter element; $R_{E(dc)} = V_E/I_E$.

dc emitter voltage Symbol, $V_{E(dc)}$. The static dc voltage at the emitter element of a bipolar transistor.

dc equipment Apparatus designed expressly for operation from a dc power supply. Compare AC EQUIPMENT and AC/DC.

dc erase head In a magnetic recorder, a head supplied with a dc current for the purpose of removing data.

dc error voltage In a television receiver, the dc output of the phase detector, which is used to control the frequency of the horizontal oscillator.

dc gate current Symbol, $I_{G(dc)}$. The very small static direct current in the gate element of a field-effect transistor.

dc gate resistance Symbol, $R_{G(dc)}$. The very high, static dc resistance of an FET's gate element; $R_{G(dc)} = V_G/I_G$.

dc gate voltage Symbol, $V_{G(dc)}$. The static dc voltage at the gate element of a field-effect transistor.

dc generator **1.** A rotating machine (dynamo) for producing direct current. Also see DYNAMO-ELECTRIC MACHINERY. **2.** Generically, a device that produces direct current: batteries, photocells, thermocouples, etc.

dc generator amplifier A special type of generator that provides power amplification. The input signal energizes the field winding of a constant-speed machine; because the output voltage is proportional to field flux and armature speed, a high output voltage is obtained. Also see AMPLI-DYNE.

dc grid bias Steady dc control-grid voltage used to set the operating point of an electron tube.

dc grid current Symbol, $I_{G(dc)}$. The static direct current in the control-grid element of an electron tube.

dc grid resistance Symbol, $R_{G(dc)}$. The static dc resistance in the control-grid element of an electron tube; $R_{G(dc)} = V_G/I_G$.

dc grid voltage Symbol, $V_{G(dc)}$. The static dc voltage at the control grid of an electron tube.

dc inserter In a television transmitter, a stage that adds the dc pedestal (blanking) level to the video signal.

dc inverter An electrical, electronic, or mechanical device that converts dc to ac. Also called INVERTER.

dcl Abbreviation of *dynamic load characteristic.*

dc leakage The unintended flow of direct current.

dc leakage current **1.** The direct current that normally passes through a correctly polarized electrolytic capacitor operated at its rated dc working voltage. **2.** The zero-signal reverse current in a semiconductor pn junction.

DCM Abbreviation of DIGITAL CAPACITANCE METER.

D/CMOS Combination of DMOS and CMOS on a monolithic chip.

dc motor A motor that operates from direct current only.

dc noise Noise heard during the playback of magnetic tape that was recorded while direct current was in the record head.

dc noise margin In a digital or switching circuit, the difference $V_o - V_i$, where V_o is the output-voltage level of a driver gate and V_i is the input threshold voltage of a driven gate.

dc operating point For a bipolar transistor, field-effect transistor, or vacuum tube, the static, zero-signal dc voltage and current levels.

dc overcurrent relay A relay or relay circuit actuated by dc coil current rising above a specified level. Compare DC UNDERCURRENT RELAY.

dc overvoltage relay A relay or relay circuit actuated as a result of the dc coil voltage rising above a specified level. Compare DC UNDERVOLTAGE RELAY.

dc patch bay A patch bay in which the dc circuits of a system are terminated.

dc picture transmission In television, transmission of the dc component of the video signal; this component corresponds to the average illumination of the scene.

dc plate current Symbol, $I_{P(dc)}$. The static direct current in the plate element of an electron tube.

dc plate resistance Symbol, $R_{P(dc)}$. The static dc resistance of the internal plate-cathode path of an electron tube; $R_{P(dc)} = V_P/I_P$.

dc plate voltage Symbol, $V_{P(dc)}$. The static dc voltage at the plate electrode of an electron tube.

dc positioning Alignment of the spot on the screen of an oscilloscope tube, by means of adjustable dc voltages applied to the horizontal and vertical deflecting plates.

dc power Symbol, P_{dc}. Unit, watt. The power in a dc circuit; $P_{dc} = EI$, where E is in volts and I is in amperes. Compare AC POWER. Also see POWER.

dc power supply A power unit that supplies direct current only. Examples: battery, transformer/rectifier/filter circuit, dc generator, and photovoltaic cell. Compare AC POWER SUPPLY.

dc relay A relay having a simple coil and core system for closure by direct current, which can be rectified ac.

dc resistance Resistance offered to direct current, as opposed to in-phase ac resistance.

dc resistivity The resistivity of a sample of material measured using a pure dc voltage under specified conditions (physical dimensions, temperature, etc.).

dc restoration The reinsertion of the dc component into a signal from which the component has been extracted through a capacitor or transformer.

dc restorer A circuit that reinserts the average dc component of a signal after the component has been lost because the signal passed through a capacitor or transformer.

DCS Abbreviation of DORSAL COLUMN STIMULATOR.

dc shift A shift in the DC OPERATING POINT.

dc short A coaxial fitting providing a dc path between the center and outer conductors, while permitting radio-frequency (RF) current to flow easily through the coaxial section. Compare DC BLOCK.

dc signaling A signaling procedure that uses direct current as the medium (e.g., simple wire telegraphy or telephony).

dc source 1. DC GENERATOR. 2. A live circuit point from which one or more direct currents can be taken.

dc source current Symbol, $I_{S(dc)}$. The static direct current in the source element of a field-effect transistor.

dc source resistance Symbol, $R_{S(dc)}$. The static dc resistance of an FET's source element.

dc source voltage Symbol, $V_{S(dc)}$. The static dc voltage at the source element of a field-effect transistor.

DCTL Abbreviation of DIRECT-COUPLED TRANSISTOR LOGIC.

dc-to-dc inverter See DC INVERTER.

dc transducer 1. A transducer that depends on direct current for its operation (i.e., it has a dc power supply whose output is modulated by the sensed phenomenon). 2. A transducer that converts a direct current into some other form of energy, such as heat, pressure, or sound.

dc transformer A dc-to-dc converter providing voltage step-up. The applied dc is usually first converted to ac, which is then stepped up by a transformer. The higher-voltage ac is then rectified to produce a high dc output voltage.

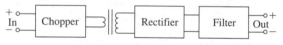

dc transformer

dc transmission 1. Sending dc power from a generating point to a point of use. 2. In television transmission, the retention of the dc component in the video signal.

dc tuning voltage The capacitance-varying dc voltage applied to a varactor in an inductance-capacitance (LC) tuned circuit.

dcu Abbreviation of decimal counting unit.

dc undercurrent relay A relay or relay circuit that is actuated as a result of the dc coil current dropping below a specified level. Compare DC OVERCURRENT RELAY.

dc undervoltage relay A relay or relay circuit that is actuated as a result of the dc voltage dropping below a specified level. Compare DC OVERVOLTAGE RELAY.

dcv Abbreviation of DC VOLTS or DC VOLTAGE.

dc voltage Abbreviation, dcv. A voltage that does not change in polarity, an example being the voltage delivered by a battery or dc generator. Also see VOLTAGE.

dc working voltage Abbreviation, dcwv. The rated dc voltage at which a component can be operated continuously with safety and reliability.

dc working volts   Abbreviation, dcwv. The actual value, expressed in volts, of a DC WORKING VOLTAGE.

dcwv   Abbreviation of DC WORKING VOLTAGE.

dD   Symbol for *differential of electric displacement.*

DDA   Abbreviation of *digital differential analyzer.*

DDD   Abbreviation of DIRECT DISTANCE DIALING (telephone).

D display   See D SCOPE.

DE   Abbreviation of *decision element.*

dE   Symbol for *differential of voltage.*

deac   In frequency-modulation (FM) receivers, a device used for deemphasis. The name is short for *deaccentuator.*

deactuating pressure   For an electrical contact, the pressure at which contact is made or broken as the pressure reaches the level of activation.

dead   **1.** Unelectrified. **2.** Lacking electromagnetic signals or fields. **3.** Electrically or mechanically inoperative.

dead band   **1.** A radio-frequency band on which no signals are heard. **2.** A range of values for which an applied control quantity (e.g., current or voltage) has no effect on the response of a circuit.

deadbeat   The state wherein a moving body (such as the pointer of a meter or the voice coil of a loudspeaker) comes to rest without overswing or oscillation.

deadbeat galvanometer   See DEADBEAT INSTRUMENT.

deadbeat instrument   A meter or recorder that is highly damped to ensure that overswing or oscillation does not occur.

deadbeat meter   See DEADBEAT INSTRUMENT.

dead break   An unreliable contact of a relay, caused by insufficient pressure.

dead circuit   A circuit that is electrically disabled.

dead end   The unused end of a tapped coil (i.e., the turns between the end of the coil and the last turn used).

dead-end tower   A supporting tower for an antenna or transmission line that can withstand stresses caused by loading or pulling.

dead file   A computer file that is not in use, but is being kept in a record.

dead front panel   A metal panel that, for safety and desensitization, is completely insulated from voltage-bearing components mounted on it; it is often grounded.

dead interval   See DEAD TIME.

dead line   A deenergized line or conductor.

dead period   See DEAD TIME.

dead room   An anechoic room in which acoustic tests and studies are made.

dead short   A short circuit with extremely low (virtually no) resistance from dc into the radio-frequency spectrum.

dead space   See DEAD BAND.

dead spot   **1.** An area in which radio waves from a particular station are not received. **2.** On a vacuum-tube cathode (directly or indirectly heated), a spot from which no electrons are emitted.

dead stretch   The tendency of insulating materials to permanently retain their approximate dimensions after having been stretched.

dead time   **1.** DOWN TIME. **2.** An interval during which there is no response to an actuating signal. **3.** In a computer system, an interval between related events that is allocated to prevent interference between the events.

dead volume   In a pressure transducer, the zero-stimulus volume of the pressure port cavity.

dead zone   See ZONE OF SILENCE.

debatable time   Computer time that cannot be placed in any other category.

debounced switch   A switch in sensitive computer or control systems that has circuitry for eliminating the electrical effects of bounce (see BOUNCE, 1).

de Broglie waves   Electromagnetic waves that are believed to be associated with moving particles (such as electrons, protons, and neutrons).

debug   **1.** To eliminate errors in, and maximize the efficiency of, a computer program or group of programs. **2.** To optimize the design and construction of electronic equipment.

debugging   A process by which engineers eliminate the flaws in a circuit, machine, or computer program.

debugging aid routine   A computer program used to test other programs.

debugging period   The time interval following completion of a software design, a hardware interconnection, or the manufacture of a piece of electronic equipment, during which errors and imperfections are sought and corrected.

debunching   In a velocity-modulated tube, such as a Klystron, a beamspreading space-charge effect that destroys electron bunching.

Debye length   The maximum distance between an electron and a positive ion over which the electron is influenced by the field of the ion.

Debye shielding distance   See DEBYE LENGTH.

deca-   A prefix that indicates multiplication by 10.

decade   **1.** A frequency band whose upper limit is 10 times the lower limit. Example: 20 Hz to 200 Hz. **2.** A set of 10 switched or selectable components in which the total value is 10 times that of individual values. Example: a *decade capacitor.* Also called DECADE BOX. **3.** A group, sometimes a unit of access, of 10 computer storage locations.

decade amplifier   An amplifier or preamplifier whose gain can be adjusted in increments of 10 ($\times1$, $\times10$, $\times100$, etc.).

decade box   A group of components that provides values in 10 equal steps selected by a switch or jacks. For compactness, the components and the associated hardware are enclosed in a box or can. See, for example, DECADE CAPACITOR.

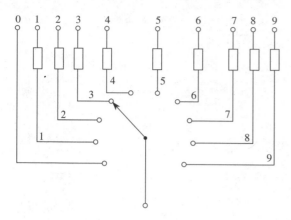

decade box

decade capacitor A composite capacitor whose value is variable in 10 equal steps. For example, the values might be set at 100 picofarads (pF), 200 pF, 300 pF, etc., up to 1000 pF. Compare DECADE INDUCTOR and DECADE RESISTOR.

decade counter A counter (see COUNTER, **1, 2**) in which the numeric display is divided into sections, each having a value 10 times that of the next and displaying a digit from zero to nine.

decade inductor An inductor whose value is variable in 10 equal steps. Compare DECADE CAPACITOR and DECADE RESISTOR.

decade resistor A resistor whose value is variable in 10 equal increments. Compare DECADE CAPACITOR and DECADE INDUCTOR.

decade scaler A scale-of-10 electronic counter (i.e., a circuit delivering one output pulse for each group of 10 input pulses).

decametric waves Waves in the 10- to 100-meter band (30 to 3 MHz).

decay **1.** The decrease in the value of a quantity, e.g., current decay in a resistance-capacitance circuit. **2.** The gradual, natural loss of radioactivity by a substance.

decay characteristics **1.** The decay of a parameter; usually an exponential function. **2.** The persistence time in a storage oscilloscope.

decay curve A curve, usually logarithmic, representing the function of quantity versus time for a signal decrement, the decrement of radioactivity, or other natural process.

decay rate A quantitative expression for the rapidity with which a quantity decreases. Generally listed in decibels per second (dB/s) or decibels per millisecond (dB/ms).

decay time The time required for pulse amplitude to fall from 90% to 10% of the peak value. Also called FALL TIME.

Decca A 70- to 130-kHz CW radio navigation system (British).

decelerated electron A high-speed electron that is abruptly decelerated upon striking a target, causing X-rays to be emitted.

decelerating electrode A charged electrode that slows the electrons in an electron beam.

deceleration Acceleration that results in a decrease in speed.

deceleration time **1.** The time taken by magnetic tape to stop moving after the last recording or playback has finished. **2.** The time taken by a mechanical data storage medium, such as a hard disk, to come to rest after completion of a read or write operation, or on powering-down.

decentralized data processing Data processing in which the computing equipment is distributed among managerial subgroups.

deception A method of producing misleading echoes in enemy radar.

deception device A radar device, or radar-associated device, for deception.

deci- Abbreviation, d. A prefix meaning one-tenth (10^{-1}). Examples: DECIBEL, DECIMETER.

decibel Abbreviation, dB. A practical unit of relative gain. In terms of power, the relative gain in decibels is equal to:

$$\text{Gain (dB)} = 10 \log_{10}(P_{out}/P_{in}),$$

where P_{out} is the output power and P_{in} is the input power. For voltage, if the input and output impedances are the same, the gain in decibels is given by:

$$\text{Gain (dB)} = 20 \log_{10}(V_{out}/V_{in}),$$

where V_{out} is the output voltage and V_{in} is the input voltage. For current, if the input and output impedances are the same, the gain in decibels is given by:

$$\text{Gain (dB)} = 20 \log_{10}(I_{out}/I_{in}),$$

where I_{out} is the output current and I_{in} is the input current. Losses are indicated by negative dB gain values.

decibels above reference acoustic power Abbreviation, dBrap. The ratio of a given acoustic power level to a lower reference acoustic power level, specified in decibels.

decibels above reference noise Abbreviation, dBrn. The ratio of the noise level at a selected point in a circuit to a lower reference noise level, in decibels.

decibels referred to 1 millivolt Abbreviation, dBmV. The relative voltage level of a signal when compared with a 1-mV signal measured at the same terminals.

decibels referred to 1 milliwatt Abbreviation, dBm. The ratio, in decibels, of an applied power level to the power level of 1 mW.

decibels referred to 1 volt Abbreviation, dBV. The ratio, in decibels, of a given voltage to 1 V, expressed in decibels.

decibels referred to 1 watt Abbreviation, dBW. The ratio of a given power level to the power level of 1 W, expressed in decibels.

decider See DECISION ELEMENT.

decigram A unit of mass equal to 0.1 gram.

deciliter A unit of volume equal to 0.1 liter, or 10^{-4} cubic meter.

decilog A unit equal to 0.1 times the common logarithm of a ratio.

decimal 1. Pertaining to the base-10 number system (see DECIMAL NUMBER SYSTEM). 2. A base-10 numerical fraction, represented by figures to the right of the radix point (decimal point), and arranged serially according to negative powers of 10. Examples: $0.12 = 1.2 \times 10^{-1}$, $0.00135 = 1.35 \times 10^{-3}$.

decimal attenuator An attenuator circuit whose resistances are chosen for attenuation in decimal steps. Thus, one section provides attenuation in steps of 0.1 times the applied voltage, another in steps of 0.01 times the applied voltage, another in steps of 0.001 times the applied voltage, etc.

decimal code A method of defining numbers, in which each place has a value of ten times that immediately to the right.

decimal-coded digit 1. A numeral from 0 to 9. 2. A numeral in the DECIMAL NUMBER SYSTEM. 3. A binary representation of a decimal value from 0 to 9.

decimal digit A numeral from 0 to 9.

decimal equivalent The decimal number equal to a given fraction (e.g., the decimal equivalent of $^{21}/_{64}$ is 0.3281).

decimal fraction See DECIMAL, 2.

decimal notation See DECIMAL NUMBER SYSTEM.

decimal number system The familiar base-10 or radix-10 number system, in which the digits 0 through 9 represent values according to their position, relative to the decimal point (also called the *radix point*). Positions to the left of the point represent successive positive powers of 10, and those to the right represent successive negative powers of 10.

decimal point The radix point in a decimal number. It serves to separate the integral part from the fractional part of the number.

decimeter waves See MICROWAVES.

decimetric waves Electromagnetic waves having lengths ranging from 0.1 meter to 1 meter (3000 MHz to 300 MHz). Also known as *ultrahigh frequency (UHF)*.

decineper A natural-logarithmic unit equal to 0.1 *neper*.

decipher See DECODING, 3.

decision 1. A choice based on the evaluation and comparison of data, and the identification of a specified objective. 2. In digital computer operations, the automatic selection of the next step in a sequence, on the basis of data being compared by a relational test.

decision box A block on a computer flowchart indicating the point at which a decision (see DECISION, 2) must be made as to which of several branches the program will take.

decision elements See LOGIC CIRCUITS.

decision instruction A computer program instruction to compare the values of operands and take an appropriate action, as per the BASIC instruction "IF A = B THEN GO TO (line number)."

decision procedure In decision theory, a series of calculations made to optimize the speed or efficiency of a process, or to minimize risk, failure, cost, etc.

decision theory A statistical discipline concerned with identifying and evaluating choices and alternatives, and determining the best sequence of steps to take in reaching an objective.

decision tree In decision theory, a diagram showing alternative choices, so called from its resemblance to a tree with branches.

decision value A value that defines the boundary between two intervals in the encoding process.

deck 1. See TAPE DECK. 2. A pack of punched cards in a computer file.

declarative macroinstruction As part of an assembly language, instructions to the compiler to do something or record a condition without affecting the object program.

declarative statement A computer source program instruction specifying the size, format, and kind of data elements and variables in a program for a compiler.

declination 1. The angle representing the deviation of magnetic north from true north; it is the angle subtended by a freely turning magnetic needle and the meridian. Compare INCLINATION. 2. Celestial latitude.

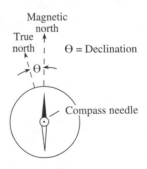

declination, 1

declinometer An instrument for measuring declination.

decode 1. To unscramble a coded message. 2. In digital computer operations, to deliver a specific output from character-coded inputs.

3. In a multiplex system, the separation of the subcarrier from the main carrier.

decoder A circuit or device for performing DECODING.

decoder/demultiplexer A circuit that places an input signal on a selected output line.

decoder/driver An integrated circuit containing a decoder and driver.

decoding **1.** In computer and data-processing operations, DIGITAL-TO-ANALOG CONVERSION. **2.** The conversion to English of a message received in a code. **3.** Translating a message from a secret code (i.e., deciphering a message). **4.** The automatic conversion of a signal into the appropriate switching action (as the enabling of a transmitter or receiver by a tone in a selective calling system).

decoding circuit A circuit intended for the purpose of translating a code into ordinary language.

decollator An offline computer device for separating the parts of output continuous stationery sets. Also see CONTINUOUS STATIONERY.

decommutation The extraction of a signal component from the composite signal, resulting from commutation.

decommutator A circuit or device for performing decommutation, including demodulators, demultiplexers, and signal separators.

decoupler A device that isolates two circuits so that a minimal amount of coupling exists between them.

decoupling The elimination or effective minimization of coupling effects, as in decoupling amplifier stages to prevent interaction through a common power-supply lead.

decoupling capacitor **1.** A capacitor that provides a low-impedance path to ground to prevent undesired stray coupling among the circuits in a system. **2.** The capacitive member of a resistance-capacitance (RC) decoupling filter.

decoupling filter A resistance-capacitance (RC) filter, usually inserted into a common dc line in a multistage amplifier to prevent interstage feedback coupling through the common impedance of the line.

decoupling network One or more decoupling filters.

decoupling resistor The resistive member of a resistance-capacitance (RC) decoupling filter.

decoy In radar, an object that provides misleading reflections. Also see CHAFF.

decreasing function A function whose curve has a negative slope at all points in the domain.

decrement **1.** Also called *logarithmic decrement*. The rate at which a damped wave dies down. The decrement value is the natural (base-e) logarithm of the ratio of two successive peaks of the same polarity. **2.** A quantity used to lessen the value of a variable. **3.** To lower the value (of a register, for example) by a single increment.

decremeter An instrument for measuring the decrement of a radio wave.

decremeter capacitor A variable capacitor for use in a decremeter. The rotor plates are shaped so that equal angular rotations correspond to the same decrement at all settings. Thus, the percentage of capacitance change for a given angle of rotation is constant throughout the capacitance range.

dedicated Assigned exclusively to a certain purpose [e.g., a dedicated facsimile (fax) line].

deductive logic A form of symbolic logic used to demonstrate that a certain conclusion will always follow, given a certain set of circumstances. The logic of digital circuits is deductive. Compare INDUCTIVE LOGIC.

dee In a cyclotron, one of the D-shaped chambers in and between which particles accelerate in a spiral path to high velocity.

dee line In a cyclotron, a support for the dee, with which it forms a resonant circuit.

deemphasis In frequency modulation, the introduction of a low-pass characteristic (response falls as modulating frequency increases) to complement the rising response of preemphasis. Also called *postemphasis* or *postequalization*. Compare PREEMPHASIS.

deemphasis amplifier An amplifier used to remove the high-frequency preemphasis applied to signals prior to broadcasting, multiplexing, tape recording, or telemetering. Also see DEEMPHASIS and PREEMPHASIS.

deemphasis circuit A low-pass filter that provides deemphasis in an FM receiver.

deemphasis network See DEEMPHASIS CIRCUIT.

deenergize To take a circuit or device out of operation (i.e., to remove its power or signal excitation).

deep cycle Pertaining to a rechargeable cell or battery that can operate until it is almost completely discharged. It generally has a high ampere-hour capacity.

deep-diffused junction A pn junction made by diffusing the impurity material deep in the semiconductor wafer. Compare SHALLOW-DIFFUSED JUNCTION.

deep discharge The nearly complete discharge of a cell or battery; usually done prior to recharging.

deep-space net A radar system intended for constant monitoring of spacecraft.

defeating **1.** The disabling or circumvention of an alarm or security system, leaving the protected property vulnerable to intrusion. **2.** The dangerous, and potentially lethal, disabling of a safety device in an electrical or electronic system.

defect **1.** Absence of an electron (hence, presence of a hole) in the lattice of a semiconductor crystal. **2.** An abnormality of design, construction, or performance of an electronic circuit or device. **3.** In a computer system, a hardware or software fault that could be the eventual cause of a failure. **4.** A flaw in a crystalline substance.

defect conduction In a semiconductor material, conduction via holes.

deferred addressing Indirect addressing in which a preset counter makes several references to find a desired address.

deferred entry An entry into a computer subroutine, delayed because of a delay in the exit from a control program.

deferred exit An exit from a computer subroutine, delayed because of a particular command.

defibrillation Use of a CARDIAC STIMULATOR to halt fibrillation of the heart, as caused by electric shock.

defibrillator See CARDIAC STIMULATOR.

definite-purpose component A component designed for a specific use, rather than for a wide range of possible applications (e.g., a video detector diode, as opposed to a general-purpose diode). Compare GENERAL-PURPOSE COMPONENT.

definition **1.** Clarity of a video image (i.e., one having good contrast and faithful tones). **2.** Good intelligibility of reproduced sounds.

deflecting coil One of a set of external coils carrying sawtooth currents, which provide electromagnetic deflection of the cathode-ray beam in picture tubes, camera tubes, radar display tubes, sonar display tubes, and some oscilloscopes. Also called *deflection coil.*

deflecting electrode An electrode, such as a deflecting plate, used to alter the direction an electron beam. Also called *deflection electrode.*

deflecting plate In a cathode-ray tube, a plate that attracts or repels the electron beam, causing the spot to move horizontally or vertically on the screen. Also called *deflection plate.*

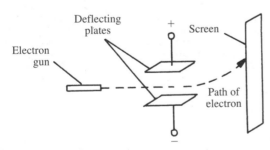

deflecting plate

deflecting torque The torque required to move the pointer of a meter, or the pen or mirror of a recorder.

deflection **1.** In a cathode-ray tube, movement of the electron beam by electric or magnetic fields. **2.** Movement of the pointer of a meter or the pen or mirror of a recorder by an applied current or voltage.

deflection factor Symbol, G. The reciprocal of DEFLECTION SENSITIVITY.

deflection plane In a cathode-ray tube, the plane perpendicular to the axis of the tube. This plane contains the electromagnetic and/or electrostatic lines of flux that result in deflection of the electron beam.

deflection coil See DEFLECTING COIL.

deflection electrode See DEFLECTING ELECTRODE.

deflection plate See DEFLECTING PLATE.

deflection polarity In a cathode-ray tube, the polarity of the voltage applied to a particular deflecting plate to move the electron beam in a particular direction.

deflection sensitivity Symbol, S. A quantitative measure of the extent to which the input voltage will displace the electron beam on the screen of an electrostatic cathode-ray tube. Expressed in volts per centimeter (V/cm) or volts per inch (V/in).

deflection voltage The potential difference between the deflection plates of an electrostatic cathode-ray tube. It is used to control the direction of the electron beam striking the phosphor screen.

deflection yoke An assembly of deflection coils in picture and camera tubes, and in some magnetically deflected oscilloscope tubes. The usual combination is two series-connected horizontal deflection coils and two series-connected vertical deflection coils.

deflector **1.** A beam-forming plate in a beam-power tube. **2.** A deflection plate in a cathode-ray tube. **3.** A deflection coil or yoke in a picture tube, camera tube, or magnetic-deflection oscilloscope tube. **4.** A mechanical attachment for improving the angle of radiation of a loudspeaker by spreading the higher-frequency waves.

defocusing Blurring of the image on the screen of a cathode-ray tube, caused by spreading of the electron beam.

deformation potential The voltage generated when a crystal lattice is subjected to pressure. An example is the voltage produced by a crystal microphone when acoustic waves strike the crystal.

defruiting The elimination of non-synchronized echoes in a radar system.

deg Abbreviation of DEGREE.

degassing During the evacuation of a vacuum tube or similar device, the removal of gas, including that which has bonded to the glass and metal parts.

degauss See DEMAGNETIZE.

degausser **1.** A circuit that performs DEGAUSSING. **2.** A device for bulk erasing magnetic tape; also called a *bulk tape eraser.*

degaussing **1.** The demagnetization of an object; in particular, the removal of all residual magnetism. **2.** The erasure of data from a magnetic or magneto-optical data-storage medium.

degaussing circuit   In a color television receiver, a circuit including a thermistor, voltage-dependent resistor, and coil for automatically demagnetizing the picture tube when the receiver is switched on.

degaussing coil   A coil carrying an alternating current; the resulting magnetic field demagnetizes objects that have become accidentally magnetized.

degeneracy   In microwave practice, the appearance of a single resonant frequency for two or more modes in a resonator.

degenerate modes   In microwave operations, a set of modes with the same resonant frequency or propagation constant.

degenerate parametric amplifier   An inverting parametric amplifier, in which the two signals are of the same frequency, which is half the pump frequency.

degenerate semiconductor   A semiconductor that behaves like a metal over a wide range of temperatures.

degeneration   In an amplifier, the technique of feeding a portion of the output back to the input out of phase with the input signal, to improve fidelity at the expense of gain. Also called *negative feedback* or *inverse feedback*. Compare REGENERATION.

degenerative resistor   An unbypassed emitter resistor in a common-emitter bipolar-transistor circuit, or an unbypassed source resistor in a common-source field-effect transistor circuit. Signal current flowing through the resistor produces negative feedback current (degeneration), which reduces the gain of the stage, but increases the linearity of the transfer characteristic.

degradation   **1.** Gradual deterioration in the condition or performance of a circuit or device. **2.** In a computer system, compromised performance caused by component failure.

degradation failure   Failure occurring at the terminal point of degradation.

degraded operation   See DEGRADATION.

degreaser   See ULTRASONIC CLEANING TANK.

degree   **1.** A unit of circular angular measurement equal to 1/360 of the circumference of a circle. Also called GEOMETRIC DEGREE. **2.** A unit of temperature measurement. See DEGREE ABSOLUTE, DEGREE CELSIUS, DEGREE CENTIGRADE, DEGREE FAHRENHEIT, and DEGREE REAUMUR.

degree absolute   Symbol, K. The unit of temperature on the absolute scale. Also see ABSOLUTE SCALE.

degree Celsius   Symbol, °C. The unit of temperature on the CELSIUS SCALE.

degree centigrade   Symbol, °C. The unit of temperature on the *centigrade scale* (now called CELSIUS SCALE).

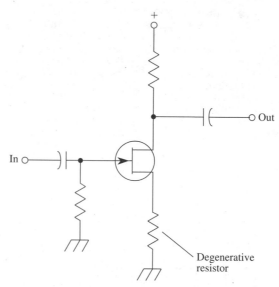

degenerative resistor

degree Fahrenheit   Symbol, °F. The unit of temperature on the FAHRENHEIT SCALE.

degree of current rectification   For a rectifier, the ratio of the average direct output current to the root-mean-square (rms) alternating input current.

degree of voltage rectification   For a rectifier, the ratio of the average direct-current (dc) output voltage to the root-mean-square (rms) alternating-current (ac) input voltage.

degree Reaumur   Symbol, °R. The unit of temperature on the REAUMUR SCALE.

degrees of freedom   **1.** The ways in which a point can move or a system can change. In three-dimensional space, a rigid body has six degrees of freedom: motion in three linear directions, and rotation around three linear axes extending through its center. **2.** The ways in which a robot arm can move, including linear motion and rotational motion.

degrees of rotation   A measure of the extent to which a robot joint, or a set of robot joints, can be turned. Some reference axis is always used; angles are specified in degrees, relative to that axis.

degrees-to-radians conversion   The conversion of angles in degrees to angles in radians. To change degrees to radians, multiply degrees by 0.01745. Compare RADIANS-TO-DEGREES CONVERSION.

deion circuit breaker   A circuit breaker in which the arc occurring when the contacts open is quickly extinguished by an external magnetic device.

deionization   The conversion of an ionized substance, such as a gas, to a neutral (non-ionized) state. The process changes the ions into uncharged atoms.

deionization potential The voltage at which an ionized substance becomes deionized; for example, the voltage at which a glow discharge is extinguished when the gas ions become neutral atoms at that voltage. Also called *extinction potential.*

deionization time The time required for an ionized gas to become neutral after the removal of the ionizing voltage.

deionization voltage See DEIONIZATION POTENTIAL.

deionize To restore to an electrically neutral condition (i.e., to convert ions to neutral atoms, as in the deionization of the gas when the discharge in a glow tube is extinguished).

deka- A prefix meaning ten(s) (e.g., DEKAMETER).

dekahexadecimal number system See HEXADECIMAL NUMBER SYSTEM.

delamination The splitting apart, in layers, of an insulating material, such as mica or bonded plastic film.

delay 1. The interval between the instant at which a signal or force is applied or removed and the instant at which a circuit or device subsequently responds in a specified manner. 2. The time required for a signal to traverse a given medium, such as air, mercury, or quartz.

delay action Response occurring some time after a stimulus has been applied or removed (e.g., the retarded opening of a delayed-dropout relay).

delay circuit 1. A circuit, such as a resistance-capacitance (RC) or resistance-inductance (RL) combination, that introduces a time delay. 2. See DELAY LINE.

delay coincidence circuit A coincidence circuit (see AND CIRCUIT) triggered by two pulses, one of which lags behind the other.

delay counter In a digital computer, a device that halts a program run long enough for an operation to be completed.

delay distortion 1. Distortion resulting from variations in the phase delay of a circuit or device at different points in its frequency range. 2. In a facsimile (fax) signal, variations in the delay of different frequency components of the signal.

delayed AGC See DELAYED AUTOMATIC GAIN CONTROL.

delayed automatic gain control An automatic gain control circuit that operates only when the signal amplitude exceeds a predetermined threshold level, thus providing maximum amplification of weaker signals.

delayed automatic volume control See DELAYED AUTOMATIC GAIN CONTROL.

delayed break In relay or switch operation, contacts separating some time after the switch has been thrown or the relay deenergized. Compare DELAYED MAKE.

delayed close See DELAYED MAKE.

delayed closure See DELAYED MAKE.

delayed contacts Contacts that open or close at a predetermined instant after their activating signal is applied or removed.

delayed drop-in See DELAYED MAKE.

delayed dropout See DELAYED BREAK.

delayed loop In security applications, a circuit or system that registers an alarm some time after intrusion is first detected. The delay can usually be selected or preadjusted.

delayed make In relay or switch operation, contacts closing some time after the switch has been thrown or the relay has been energized. Compare DELAYED BREAK.

delayed open See DELAYED BREAK.

delayed PPI Plan-position indicating radar having a delayed time base.

delayed pull-in See DELAYED MAKE.

delayed repeater A repeater that receives and stores information, and retransmits the information later, in response to a switching or interrogation signal.

delayed repeater satellite An active communications satellite that acts as a delayed repeater (i.e., it receives and records information at one time and retransmits it at a later time).

delayed sweep 1. In an oscilloscope or radar, a sweep that starts at a selected instant after the signal under observation has started. 2. The (usually calibrated) circuit for producing a sweep, as defined in (1).

delayed updating Updating a computer record or record set so that the record fields are left unchanged until all other changes attendant to the pertinent event are processed.

delay equalizer A network that corrects DELAY DISTORTION.

delay-frequency distortion Distortion caused by variation of envelope delay within a frequency band.

delay line A device (not always a line) that introduces a time lag in a signal. The lag is the time required for the signal to pass through the device, minus the time necessary for the signal to traverse the same distance through a wire, cable, optical fiber, or free space.

delay-line memory In a digital computer, a memory that uses a delay line, associated input- and output-coupling devices, and an external regenerative-feedback path. Information is kept stored by causing it to recirculate in the line by regeneration.

delay-line register In a digital computer, a register that operates in the manner of a DELAY-LINE MEMORY and has a register length (capacity) of an integral number of words.

delay-line storage See DELAY-LINE MEMORY and DELAY-LINE REGISTER.

delay multivibrator See MONOSTABLE MULTIVIBRATOR.

delay-power product   Unit, watt-second. The figure of merit for an integrated circuit (IC) gate. Increasing gate power reduces propagation delay. Also called PROPAGATION DELAY-POWER PRODUCT.

delay relay   A relay that opens or closes at the end of a predetermined time interval.

delay switch   A switch having delayed make, delayed break, or both.

delay time   1. The interval between the instant a voltage or current is applied and the instant a circuit or device operates. 2. In an output pulse, the interval between the instant an ideal pulse is applied to the input of a system and the instant the output pulse reaches 10% of its maximum amplitude. 3. The time elapsed between the presentation of a pulse to the input of a delay line and the appearance of the pulse at the output.

delay timer   1. A timer that starts or stops an operation after a prescribed length of time. 2. A delay relay or switch.

delay unit   In a radar system, a circuit for delaying pulses.

delete   1. To erase or blank out a signal. 2. The elimination from a computer file of a record or record group. 3. To remove a computer program from memory or storage.

deletion record   In the master file of a digital computer, a new record that causes existing ones to be deleted.

delimiter   In digital computer operations, a character limiting a sequence of characters of which it is not itself a member.

Dellinger effect   The sudden disappearance of a radio signal as a result of an abrupt increase in atmospheric ionization caused by a solar eruption.

deliquescent material   A material that absorbs enough moisture from the air to get wet. For example; calcium chloride, a deliquescent material, is often used to keep electronic equipment dry. Compare HYGROSCOPIC MATERIAL.

delta circuit   A three-phase electrical circuit with no common ground.

delta connection   A triangular connection of coils or load devices in a three-phase system, so called from its resemblance to the Greek letter delta. Compare WYE-CONNECTION.

delta-matched antenna   See WYE-MATCHED IMPEDANCE ANTENNA.

delta-matched impedance antenna   See WYE-MATCHED IMPEDANCE ANTENNA.

delta matching transformer   In a WYE-MATCHED IMPEDANCE ANTENNA, the fanned-out (roughly delta-shaped) portion of the two-wire feeder at its point of connection to the radiator. It matches the impedance of the feeder to that of the radiator.

delta modulation   The conversion of an analog signal into a digital pulse train that can be decoded to yield the original analog signal.

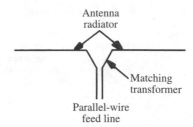

delta-matching transformer

delta network   See DELTA CONNECTION.

delta pulse-code modulation   In wire or radio communications, the conversion of an audio signal into a digital pulse train.

delta quantity   An increment (i.e., the difference between two values of a variable).

delta rays   The emission of secondary electrons as a result of radioactivity.

delta-sigma modulation   A method of analog-to-digital conversion. The output is a pulse density function of the input. The input can be obtained by low-pass filtering of the output.

delta tune   Also called *receiver incremental tuning (RIT)*. In high-frequency (HF) communications transceivers, a control that allows the receiver frequency to be adjusted up to several kilohertz higher or lower than the transmitter frequency.

delta waves   Brain waves having a frequency less than 9 Hz. Also see ELECTROENCEPHALOGRAPH and ELECTROENCEPHALOGRAM.

Deluc's pile   See DRY PILE.

dem   Abbreviation of DEMODULATOR.

demagnetization curve   The portion of a magnetic hysteresis curve, showing reduction of demagnetization.

demagnetization effect   The phenomenon in which uncompensated magnetic poles at the surface cause a reduction of the magnetic field inside a sample of a material.

demagnetize   To remove magnetism from an object, either temporarily or permanently.

demagnetizer   See DEGAUSSER.

demagnetizing current   The half-cycle of an alternating current (or polarity of a direct current) flowing through a coil wound on a permanent magnet (as in a headphone, permanent-magnet loudspeaker, or polarized relay), that reduces the magnetic field.

demagnetizing force   1. A magnetic force whose direction reduces the residual induction of a magnetized material. 2. An effect that reduces the magnetism of a permanent magnet, such as high temperature or a physical blow.

demand factor   In the use of electric power, the ratio of the consumer's maximum demand to the actual power consumed.

demand processing Descriptive of a system that processes data as it is available, without storing it.

demarcation strip An interface between a terminal unit and a carrier line.

Dember effect The appearance of a voltage between regions in a semiconductor when one of the regions is illuminated.

demodulation The process of retrieving the information (modulation) from a modulated carrier. In receivers and certain test instruments, this process is called DETECTION.

demodulator 1. A circuit that recovers the information from a modulated analog or digital signal. In radio communications, such a device is usually called a DETECTOR. 2. In computer communications, a device that performs ANALOG-TO-DIGITAL CONVERSION of incoming online signals.

demand read (write) Inputting or outputting data blocks to or from a central processor, as needed for processing.

demodulator probe A diode probe that removes the modulation envelope from an applied amplitude-modulated signal, and presents the envelope to a voltmeter or oscilloscope.

demonstrator A device used to show and teach the way in which a component, circuit, or system operates.

DeMorgan's theorem A rule of sequential or digital logic. It states that the negation of (A AND B), for any two statements A AND B, is equivalent to NOT A OR NOT B. Also, the negation of (A OR B) is equivalent, logically, to NOT A AND NOT B.

demultiplexer A circuit or device that separates the components of a multiplexed signal transmitted over a channel.

demultiplexing circuit See DEMULTIPLEXER.

denary band A band in which the highest frequency is 10 times the lowest frequency.

dendrite 1. The branching (tree-like) structure formed by some materials, such as semiconductors, as they crystallize. 2. The branching portion of a nerve cell; hence, the corresponding circuit element in the electronic model of such a cell.

dendritic growth 1. Dendrite (see DENDRITE, 1). 2. The process of growing long, flat semiconductor crystals.

dendron See DENDRITE, 2.

dens Abbreviation of DENSITY.

dense binary code A binary representation system, in which any possible combination of characters is assigned some correspondent.

densitometer An instrument for measuring the density of a body.

density 1. Mass per unit volume of a material. 2. Concentration of charge carriers or of lines of flux. 3. The number of items per unit volume, area, distance, or time.

density modulation Modulation of the density, with respect to time, of electrons in an electron beam.

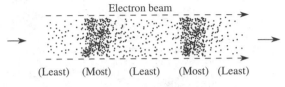

Electron beam

(Least) (Most) (Least) (Most) (Least)

density modulation

density of electrons The concentration of electrons (i.e., the number per unit volume, area, distance, or time).

density packing A figure indicating the quantity of bits per inch or per centimeter, stored on a magnetic tape.

dependent equations Equations that are alike and have an infinite number of solutions. Compare INDEPENDENT EQUATIONS and INCONSISTENT EQUATIONS.

dependent linearity Linearity (especially in its deviation from an ideal slope) as a dependent variable.

dependent variable A changing quantity whose value at any instant is governed by the value at that instant of another changing quantity (the independent variable). Compare INDEPENDENT VARIABLE.

depletion-enhancement-mode MOSFET A metal-oxide-semiconductor field-effect transistor (MOSFET) designed for zero gate-bias voltage. An ac gate signal voltage drives the MOSFET alternately into the depletion mode (negative signal half-cycle) and enhancement mode (positive signal half-cycle). Compare DEPLETION-TYPE MOSFET and ENHANCEMENT-TYPE MOSFET.

depletion field-effect transistor A field-effect transistor whose operation is based on the control of depletion layer width.

depletion layer See BARRIER, 1.

depletion-layer capacitance See JUNCTION CAPACITANCE.

depletion-layer rectification Rectification provided by a semiconductor junction.

depletion-layer transistor A transistor whose action depends on modulation of current carriers in a space-charge region (depletion layer).

depletion mode Operation characteristic of the DEPLETION-TYPE MOSFET.

depletion region See BARRIER, 1.

depletion-type MOSFET A metal-oxide-semiconductor field-effect transistor (MOSFET) in which the channel directly under the gate electrode is narrowed by a negative gate voltage (in an n-channel device) or by a positive gate voltage (in a p-channel device).

depolarization   **1.** In a primary cell, the removal of the agents that have caused polarization. **2.** The addition of a polarization-inhibiting substance to the electrolyte of a primary cell.

depolarizer   A substance that retards polarization in an electrochemical cell. An example is the manganese dioxide used in dry cells.

depolarizing agent   See DEPOLARIZER.

deposition   The application of a layer of one substance (usually a metal) to the surface of another (the substrate), as in evaporation, sputtering, electroplating, silk-screening, etc.

depth finder   See ACOUSTIC DEPTH FINDER.

depth indicator   **1.** A sounding instrument for determining the depth of a body of water. **2.** On an ACOUSTIC DEPTH FINDER, the meter that indicates the depth of water.

depth of cut   On a phonograph disk, the depth of the recorded groove.

depth of discharge   Abbreviation, DOD. In a rechargeable cell or battery, a measure of the extent to which discharging has occurred. It is generally specified as a percentage. For example, if the DOD of a 10-ampere-hour (10-AH) battery is 80 percent, then 8 AH have been used up, and 2 AH remain before recharging will be necessary.

depth of heating   In dielectric heating, the depth of heat penetration in the sample when both electrodes are applied to one of its faces.

depth of modulation   The degree to which a carrier wave is modulated.

depth of penetration   The extent to which a skin-effect current penetrates the surface of a conductor.

depth sounder   See ACOUSTIC DEPTH FINDER.

de-Q   **1.** To reduce the Q of a component or tuned circuit. **2.** To inhibit laser action during an interval when an ion population excess is pumped up.

derating   To reduce an operating parameter (e.g., current, voltage, power) as another factor (such as temperature) increases, to ensure efficient, reliable, and safe operation.

derating curve   A graph that shows the extent to which a quantity (such as allowable power dissipation) must be reduced as another quantity (such as temperature) increases.

derating factor   The amount by which a current, power, or voltage must be decreased to ensure safe and efficient operation of a circuit or device in a given environment (temperature, altitude, humidity, etc.). Also see DERATING and DERATING CURVE.

derivative   **1.** A mathematical expression indicating the rate at which a function changes, with respect to the independent variable. See DERIVATIVE FUNCTION. **2.** The slope of a line tangent to a curve at a given point. **3.** The output signal of a DIFFERENTIATOR, relative to the input signal.

derivative action   In a control system, an action producing a corrective signal proportional to

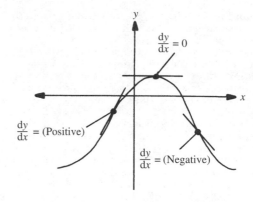

derivative

the rate of change (derivative) of the controlled variable.

derivative control   A method of automatic control, actuated according to the number of errors per second.

derivative function   For a mathematical function $f(x)$, the function $f'(x) = df(x)/dx$, over the domain of f. For any specific point x_0 in the domain of f, the value of $f'(x_0)$ is equal to the slope of a line tangent to f at the point $(x_0, f(x_0))$.

derived center channel   The sum or difference of the left and right channels in a stereophonic system.

Dershem electrometer   A variation of the *quadrant electrometer.* In the Dershem instrument, the needle (to which a small mirror is attached) rotates within slots cut in the quadrant plates and, therefore, can never accidentally touch the plates.

description   A data element that is part of a record and is used to identify it.

desensitization   **1.** The process of making a circuit or device less responsive to small values of a quantity. **2.** Also called *desensing.* In a communications receiver, an unwanted, often intermittent reduction in front-end gain, caused by an extremely strong local signal.

desensitize   **1.** To reduce the sensitivity of a receiver. **2.** To reduce the gain of an amplifier. **3.** To reduce the small-quantity response of an instrument.

desiccant   A compound, such as cobalt chloride, used for the purpose of keeping enclosed items dry.

design   **1.** A unique, planned arrangement of electronic components in a circuit, in accordance with good engineering practice, to achieve a desired end result. **2.** A unique layout of components or controls, in accordance with good engineering practice, esthetics, and (often) ergonomics. **3.** Invention. **4.** Plan. **5.** To produce a design, as defined in **1**, **2**, **3**, or **4**.

designation   Within a computer record, coded information identifying the record so that it can be handled accordingly.

design-center rating   A specified parameter that, if not exceeded, should provide acceptable average performance for the greatest number of the components so rated.

design compatibility   The degree to which a transmitter and receiver are designed for the rejection of unwanted electromagnetic noise.

design engineer   An engineer who is skilled in the creation of new designs and in the comparative analysis of designs.

design-maximum rating   See MAXIMUM RATING.

design-proof test   A performance test made on a newly completed circuit or device to determine the suitability of the design.

Desk-Fax   A facsimile transceiver that can be placed on a desktop, used for wire or radio transmission and reception of still images.

desk microphone   A microphone equipped with a stand that sits on a table or desktop. It allows the operator to use both hands for equipment adjustment, taking notes, etc.

desktop computer   A personal computer designed for nonportable use, usually equipped with a built-in hard disk, one or more diskette drives, a CD-ROM drive, and a fax/modem. It generally uses an external cathode-ray-tube display, printer, and keyboard. The power supply is intended for use with 117-volt utility circuits.

desolder   To unsolder joints, usually with a special tool that protects delicate parts and removes melted solder by suction.

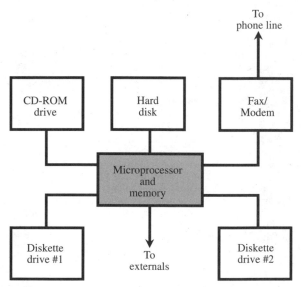

**desktop computer
(main unit only)**

destaticization   A chemical process used to minimize the retention of electrostatic charges by certain substances.

destination   1. The point in a system to which a signal of any sort is directed. 2. In communications, a receiving station.

destination file   A computer file that receives data output during a specific program run.

destination register   In a digital computer, a register into which data is entered.

Destriau effect   Light emission resulting from the action of an alternating electric field on phosphors embedded in a dielectric.

destructive addition   A computer logic operation in which the sum of two operands appears in the memory location occupied by one of the operands.

destructive breakdown   A breakdown in which the effects are irreversible (e.g., permanent damage to a dielectric by excessive applied voltage).

destructive interference   Interference resulting from the addition of two waves that have the same frequency, but opposite phase.

destructive read   In a computer or calculator, the condition in which reading the answer erases the data (as from a location) used in the calculation.

destructive test   A test that unavoidably destroys the test sample. Compare NONDESTRUCTIVE TEST.

DETAB   A COBOL-based computer programming language permitting the programmer to present problems as decision tables.

detail constant   Pertaining to a video signal, the ratio V_H/V_L, where V_H is the amplitude of high-frequency components, and V_L is the amplitude of the low-frequency reference component.

detected error   In a computer system, an error that is identified, but remains uncorrected until final output is available.

detection   1. See DEMODULATION. 2. The sensing of a change in the operating parameters of a circuit or system.

detection range   In security applications, the radius within which transducers or sensors can be expected to reliably operate. This radius varies, depending on the environment, the sensitivity of the receiving circuits and transducers, and the strength of the transmitted signal (if any).

detectophone   A device for eavesdropping on a conversation. The device can use a tape recorder or a tiny radio transmitter.

detector   1. In radio communications, a device or circuit that extracts the information from a modulated carrier. Also sometimes called a *demodulator*. 2. A device that senses a signal or condition and indicates its presence.

detector balanced bias   In a radar system, bias obtained from a controlling circuit and used to reduce or eliminate clutter.

detector bias   Steady dc voltage applied to a detector to set its operating point.

detector blocking   In a regenerative receiver, a phenomenon in which a strong signal tends to pull the detector oscillator into phase with itself, thereby causing the detector to oscillate at the signal frequency.

detector circuit   A demodulator circuit (i.e., one used to recover the intelligence from a modulated carrier).

detector probe   See DEMODULATOR PROBE.

detector pull-in   See DETECTOR BLOCKING.

detector stage   In a receiver or instrument, the separate stage that contains the detector circuit. Some systems, such as a superheterodyne receiver, have more than one detector. Also see FIRST DETECTOR and SECOND DETECTOR.

detent   A mechanical stop used on a rotary switch to hold the switch pole securely in each selected position.

detune   1. To adjust a circuit to some frequency other than its resonant frequency. 2. To set the frequency of a receiver or transmitter to some point other than the frequency normally used. 3. To stagger-tune a receiver intermediate-frequency system.

detuning   Tuning to a point above or below the frequency to which a device or system is normally (or initially) adjusted (usually the resonant frequency of the device).

detuning stub   A device used for the purpose of coupling a feed line to an antenna, while choking off currents induced on the feed line as a result of the near-field radiation of the antenna.

deupdating   Producing an earlier form of a computer file by substituting older records for current ones.

deuterium   Symbol, D, d, H^2, or ^2H. Also called *heavy hydrogen*. The hydrogen isotope having a nucleus consisting of one proton and one neutron.

deuterium oxide   Symbol, D_2O. Also called *heavy water*. This compound has wide use in nuclear reactors.

deuteron   The nucleus of a deuterium atom.

deuton   See DEUTERON.

deutron   See DEUTERON.

deviation   1. In a frequency-modulated (FM) radio signal, the instantaneous amount of carrier frequency shift away from the unmodulated frequency. It is usually expressed in kilohertz; directly proportional to the amplitude of the modulating signal, up to a certain maximum that depends on the bandwidth allowed. 2. The maximum instantaneous carrier frequency shift in a FM signal. 3. The extent or amount by which a quantity drifts from its proper value.

deviation distortion   In a frequency-modulation (FM) receiver, distortion resulting chiefly from discriminator nonlinearity and restricted bandwidth.

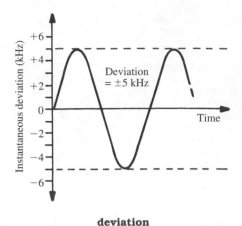

deviation

deviation ratio   In a frequency-modulated (FM) signal, the ratio between the highest modulating frequency and the maximum carrier deviation.

deviation sensitivity   For a frequency-modulation (FM) receiver, the smallest deviation that will produce a specified audio output power. Expressed in kilohertz, or as a percentage of rated deviation of the receiver, measured with the receiver set for maximum gain.

device   1. A simple or complex discrete electronic component. 2. A subsystem used as a unit, and regarded as a single component.

device complexity   The number of components in an integrated circuit.

device independence   A characteristic of a computer, that allows operation independent of the types of input/output devices used.

dew point   For a gas containing water vapor (typically air), the highest temperature at which the vapor condenses as the gas is cooled. The dew point depends on the amount of vapor in the gas.

dew-point recorder   An instrument for determining and recording the temperature at which water vapor in the air condenses to a liquid.

DF   Abbreviation of DIRECTION FINDER.

DF antenna   An antenna that is mechanically rotatable or has an electrically rotatable response pattern for use with a direction finder.

DF antenna system   Two or more DF antennas arranged for maximum directivity and maneuverability, together with associated feeders and couplers.

D flip-flop   A delayed flip-flop. The state of the input determines the state of the output during the following pulse, rather than during the current pulse.

dg   Abbreviation of *decigram*.

dia   Abbreviation of *diameter*.

diac   A two-terminal, bilateral, three-layer semiconductor device that exhibits negative resistance. When the applied voltage exceeds a critical value, the device conducts.

diagnosis **1.** Determination of the cause and location of a hardware malfunction. **2.** In computer operations, determination of the cause of a system operation error.

diagnostic routine **1.** An efficient sequence of diagnostic tests for rapid, foolproof troubleshooting of electronic hardware. **2.** A computer software package intended for debugging programs, or for finding the cause of a hardware or operating-system malfunction. Also called *diagnostic*, *diagnostic program*, or *diagnostic utility*.

diagnostic test **1.** A test made primarily to ascertain the cause of dysfunction in electronic equipment. Compare PERFORMANCE TEST. **2.** To apply a diagnostic routine to hardware faults, or to implement one to prevent such a fault.

diagnotor In digital computer operations, a troubleshooting routine combining both diagnosis and editing.

diagram A (usually line) drawing depicting a circuit, assembly, or organization. See, for example, BLOCK DIAGRAM and CIRCUIT DIAGRAM.

dial **1.** A graduated scale, arranged horizontally, vertically, in a circle, or over an arc. Used to show the distance through which a variable component (such as a potentiometer, variable capacitor, or switch) has been adjusted. A pointer can move over the scale, or the scale can be moved past a stationary pointer. **2.** The graduated face of a meter. **3.** In a telephone system, to press the keys or actuate the tones that establish contact with another subscriber.

dial cable A flexible cable or belt conveying motion on the shaft of an adjustable component (such as a potentiometer or variable capacitor) to a dial.

dial-calibrated attenuator A variable attenuator with a dial reading directly in decibels.

dial-calibrated capacitor A variable capacitor with a dial reading directly in picofarads.

dial-calibrated inductor A variable inductor with a dial reading directly in microhenrys.

dial-calibrated potentiometer A potentiometer with a dial reading directly in output volts, percentage of input voltage, number of turns (when resistance is a linear function), or other quantity.

dial-calibrated resistor A variable resistor with a dial reading directly in ohms, kilohms, or megohms.

dial-calibrated rheostat See DIAL-CALIBRATED RESISTOR.

dial cord A form of dial cable. Cord usually designates a fabric string, whereas a cable is a flexible, braided wire.

dial knob The knob used to turn a dial under a pointer, or to turn a pointer over a dial scale.

dial lamp See DIAL LIGHT.

dial light A small lamp sometimes used to illuminate a dial. Can also serve as a pilot light.

dial lock A small mechanism used to lock a dial at a particular setting to prevent further turning.

dialer See AUTOMATIC DIALING UNIT.

dialing key In a telephone system, a dial that uses keys, rather than a rotary dial.

dial jack In a telephone system, a set of jacks that facilitates interconnections between dial cords and external lines.

dial light A lamp or light-emitting diode placed in the dial mechanism of a radio receiver, transmitter, or transceiver. Allows the dial to be read in dim light or in darkness.

dialog equalizer In sound transmission and recording, a high-pass filter that reduces low-frequency response during dialog and extreme closeups.

dial pulse An interruption of the direct current in a telephone system when the dial contacts of the calling telephone open. The number of such interruptions corresponds to the digit dialed.

dial scale The graduated portion of a dial.

dial system **1.** See DIAL TELEPHONE SYSTEM. **2.** The arrangement of dials and knobs that facilitates adjustment of electronic equipment.

dial telephone A telephone set in which a numbered rotatable disk is used to produce the switch interruptions that cause generation of the transmitted multidigit telephone numbers.

dial telephone system The complete automatic circuit, including central-office facilities, for dial telephone operation.

dial tone In a telephone system, a constant hum or whine heard before dialing, indicating that the system is operational.

dial-up In a telephone system, the calling of one subscriber by another, using a dial system.

diam Abbreviation of *diameter*.

diamagnetic Pertaining to a material having magnetic permeability less than unity.

diamagnetism The state of having magnetic permeability less than unity. A material with this property reduces the flux density of a magnetic field, relative to the flux density in air or in free space.

diamond antenna Also called *rhombic antenna*. A nonresonant wideband directional antenna whose horizontal wire elements are arranged in the shape of a diamond (rhombus). The arrangement is fed at one corner, the opposite corner being terminated with a noninductive resistor.

diamond lattice The orderly internal arrangement of atoms in a redundant pattern in crystalline materials, such as germanium or silicon.

diamond stylus A phonograph "needle" having as its point a small, ground diamond.

diapason **1.** Either of the two principal stops (open and closed) of an electronic organ that cover the entire range of the instrument. When

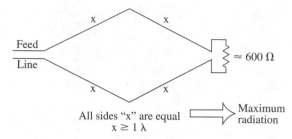

All sides "x" are equal
$x \geq 1 \lambda$

Maximum
radiation

diamond antenna

one is used, a note played is automatically sounded in several octaves. **2.** Tuning fork.

diaphony See DISSONANCE.

diaphragm A usually thin metal or dielectric disk used as the vibrating member in headphones, loudspeakers, and microphones, and as the pressure-sensitive element in some sensors and barometers.

diaphragm gauge A sensitive gas pressure gauge using a thin metal diaphragm stretched flat. Increments of pressure move the diaphragm, relative to a nearby electrode, varying the capacitance between the two.

diathermic Pertaining to a substance that efficiently transfers heat or infrared energy.

diathermotherapy The use of diathermy in the treatment of various physiological disorders.

diathermy **1.** In medicine and physical therapy, the production of heat in subcutaneous (below the skin) tissues by means of high-frequency radio waves. **2.** A radio-frequency (RF) power oscillator and associated equipment used to produce heat in subcutaneous tissues.

diathermy interference Radio-frequency interference (RFI) resulting from the operation of unshielded and/or unfiltered diathermy equipment.

diathermy machine See DIATHERMY, **2**.

diatomic Having two atoms (e.g., a DIATOMIC MOLECULE).

diatomic molecule A molecule (such as that of oxygen) composed of two atoms. Compare MONATOMIC MOLECULE.

dibble A mathematical function in which a number (usually an integer) is doubled, and then one is added to the result. Thus, dibble $n = 2n + 1$.

dibit A combination of two binary digits (bits). The four possible dibits are 00, 01, 10, and 11.

dice Plural of DIE, **1**, **3**.

dichotomizing search Also called *binary search.* In digital computer operations, locating an item in a table of items that are arranged by key values in serial order. The required key is compared with a key halfway through the table; according to this relational test, half of the table is accepted and again divided for comparison, etc. until the keys match and the item is found.

dichotomy Characterized by the usually repetitive branching into two sets, groups, or factions.

dichroism Also called *dichromatism.* **1.** The property of a crystal showing different colors, depending on which axis corresponds to the line of sight. **2.** The property of a solid taking on different colors as the thickness of the transmitting layer changes. **3.** The property of a liquid changing color, according to solution concentration.

dichromate cell An electrolytic cell consisting of electrodes of carbon and zinc. The zinc electrode is immersed in a diluted solution of sulfuric acid, and the carbon electrode in a solution of potassium dichromate.

dicing The cutting of a semiconductor melt, crystal wafer, or other material into dice (see DIE).

dictionary A table of specifications for the size and format of computer file operands, and data names for field and file types.

die **1.** A small wafer of useful electrical material, such as a semiconductor or a precision resistor chip. **2.** A casting designed to mold molten metal into a specific configuration until the metal hardens. **3.** Any small object of roughly cubical proportions. **4.** To lose power or energy completely, usually unintentionally. **5.** In a computer program, to produce unpredicted and useless results following an initial run.

die bonding The bonding of dice or chips to a substrate.

die casting Making a casting by forcing molten metal (such as an aluminum alloy, lead, tin, or zinc) under high pressure into a die or mold.

dielectric A material that is a nonconductor of electricity; especially, a substance that facilitates the storage of energy in the form of an electric field. Such materials are commonly used in capacitors and transmission lines.

dielectric absorption The ability of certain dielectric materials to retain some of their electric charge—even after being momentarily short-circuited. Capacitors with this property must be shorted out continuously for a certain length of time before the dielectric has completely discharged.

dielectric amplifier A voltage amplifier circuit in which the active component is a capacitor having a nonlinear dielectric. A signal voltage applied to the capacitor varies the capacitance, thus varying the current. The modulated current flows through a load resistor, developing an output-signal voltage higher than the input-signal voltage.

dielectric antenna An antenna in which some or all of the radiating element is made of a dielectric material, such as polystyrene. Primarily used at microwave frequencies.

dielectric breakdown Sudden, destructive conduction through a dielectric when the applied voltage exceeds a critical value.

dielectric breakdown voltage   The voltage at which DIELECTRIC BREAKDOWN occurs in an insulating material. Varies, depending on the particular dielectric substance.

dielectric capacity   See DIELECTRIC CONSTANT.

dielectric constant   Symbol, *k*. For a dielectric material, the ratio of the capacitance of a two-plate capacitor using the dielectric material, to the capacitance of the equivalent capacitor with dry air as a dielectric. Also called *inductivity* and *specific inductive capacity.*

dielectric current   **1.** Current flowing over the surface of a dielectric material in response to a varying electric field. **2.** Current flowing through a dielectric as a result of its finite insulation resistance.

dielectric dissipation   For a dielectric material in which an electric field exists, the ratio of the lost (dissipated) electrical energy to the recoverable electrical energy.

dielectric dissipation factor   The cotangent of the dielectric phase angle, also equal to the reciprocal of the *Q* factor.

dielectric fatigue   In some dielectric materials subjected to a constant voltage, the deterioration of dielectric properties with time.

dielectric guide   A waveguide made from a solid dielectric, such as polystyrene.

dielectric heater   A high-frequency power generator used for DIELECTRIC HEATING.

dielectric heating   The heating and forming of a dielectric material, such as a plastic, by temporarily making the material the dielectric of a two-plate capacitor. This capacitor is connected to the output of a high-power radio-frequency (RF) generator. Losses in the dielectric cause its heating. Compare INDUCTION HEATING.

dielectric hysteresis   See DIELECTRIC ABSORPTION.

dielectric isolation   In a monolithic integrated circuit (IC), the isolation of circuit elements from each other by a dielectric film, as opposed to isolation by reverse-biased pn junctions.

dielectric lens   A molded piece of dielectric material used to focus microwaves. Its operation is analogous to that of an optical lens.

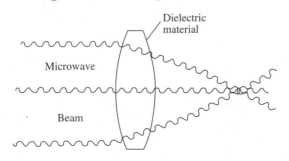

dielectric lens

dielectric loss   For a dielectric material subjected to a changing electric field, the rate of transformation of electric energy into heat.

dielectric loss angle   Ninety degrees minus the DIELECTRIC PHASE ANGLE.

dielectric loss factor   For a dielectric material, the product of the dielectric constant and the tangent of the dielectric loss angle.

dielectric loss index   See DIELECTRIC LOSS FACTOR.

dielectric matching plate   A dielectric plate used in some waveguides for impedance matching.

dielectric mirror   A reflector containing a number of layers of dielectric material. Its action depends on electromagnetic energy being partially reflected from the interfaces between materials having unequal indexes of refraction.

dielectric phase angle   For a dielectric material, the angular phase difference between a sinusoidal voltage applied to the material and the component of the resultant current having the same period as that of the voltage.

dielectric phase difference   See DIELECTRIC LOSS ANGLE.

dielectric polarization   The effect characterized by the slight displacement of the positive charge in each atom of a dielectric material, with respect to the negative charge, under the influence of an electric field.

dielectric power factor   The cosine of the dielectric phase angle, or the sine of the dielectric loss angle.

dielectric puncture voltage   See DIELECTRIC BREAKDOWN VOLTAGE.

dielectric rating   The breakdown voltage, and sometimes the power factor, of the dielectric material used in a device, such as a relay, motor, or switch.

dielectric ratings   Electrical characteristics of a dielectric material: breakdown voltage, power factor, dielectric constant, etc.

dielectric resistance   See INSULATION RESISTANCE.

dielectric rigidity   See DIELECTRIC STRENGTH.

dielectric-rod antenna   A unidirectional antenna that uses a dielectric substance to obtain power gain.

dielectric soak   See DIELECTRIC ABSORPTION.

dielectric strain   The distorted internal state of a dielectric, caused by the influence of an electric field. Also called DIELECTRIC STRESS.

dielectric strength   The highest voltage a dielectric can withstand before DIELECTRIC BREAKDOWN occurs. Usually expressed in volts or kilovolts per mil of material thickness.

dielectric stress   The distortion of electron orbits in the atoms of a dielectric material subjected to an electric field.

dielectric susceptibility   For a polarized dielectric, the ratio of polarization to electric intensity.

dielectric tests Laboratory experiments performed to determine the dielectric characteristics of a substance—especially the dielectric constant and the dielectric breakdown voltage.

dielectric waveguide See DIELECTRIC GUIDE.

dielectric wedge A wedge-shaped dielectric slug placed inside a waveguide for impedance matching.

dielectric wire A small dielectric waveguide that acts as a wire to carry signals between points in a circuit.

Dietzhold network A four-terminal, shunt m-derived circuit used in some wideband amplifiers.

Dietzhold peaking In some wideband amplifiers, frequency compensation obtained with a shunt m-derived network (see DIETZHOLD NETWORK).

difference amplifier See DIFFERENTIAL AMPLIFIER.

difference channel In a stereophonic amplifier, an audio channel that handles the difference between signals in the right channel and those in the left channel.

difference detector A detector whose output is the difference between two simultaneous input signals.

difference frequency A signal frequency produced by mixing or heterodyning of signals at two other frequencies. If the lower input signal frequency is f_1 and the higher input signal frequency is f_2, then the difference frequency f_d is equal to $f_2 - f_1$.

difference of potential The absolute value of the algebraic difference of voltages at two points of different electrical potential. Thus, the difference of potential between a +5-V point and a –5-V point is +5 – (–5) V = 10 V. Also see POTENTIAL DIFFERENCE.

difference quantity See INCREMENT.

difference signal **1.** The resultant signal obtained by subtracting, at every instant for at least one full cycle, the amplitudes of two signals. **2.** The difference of the left- and right-channel outputs in a stereo system.

differential **1.** A device, consisting of a gear system, that adds or subtracts angular motions and delivers the result. **2.** A gear system in which the motion of a shaft is transferred to two other shafts aligned with each other and perpendicular to the first shaft. **3.** One of two coils arranged to produce opposite polarities at a point in a circuit. **4.** Pertaining to a difference between two signals or quantities.

differential amplifier A circuit, usually an operational amplifier, that amplifies the voltage difference between two input signals. The instantaneous output voltage is equal to some constant multiple of the difference between the instantaneous input voltages.

differential analyzer An analog computer that solves differential equations using integrators.

differential angle For a mercury switch, the angle between operation and release positions.

differential capacitor A dual variable capacitor with two identical stator sections, and a single rotor section that turns into one stator section and out of the other. The capacitance of one section decreases while that of the other increases.

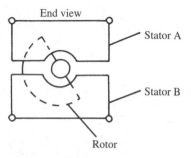

differential capacitor

differential coil See DIFFERENTIAL, **3**.

differential comparator A linear integrated circuit (IC) that delivers an output proportional to the difference between two input signals.

differential compound dc generator A compound-wound dc generator in which the magnetomotive force of the series field opposes that of the shunt (main) field.

differential compound dc motor A compound-wound dc motor in which the magnetomotive force of the series field coil opposes that of the shunt (main) field coil.

differential cooling Reducing temperature at different points on a surface at different rates.

differential delay The difference $d_{max} - d_{min}$ across a frequency band, where d_{max} is the maximum frequency delay and d_{min} is the minimum frequency delay.

differential discriminator A device that passes pulses, whose amplitudes are between two predetermined values above or below zero.

differential distortion In an automatic-gain-control circuit, distortion from effects that cause shunting of the diode load resistor.

differential flutter Fluctuations in the speed of a magnetic tape that are nonuniform in different parts of the tape.

differential gain In a differential amplifier, the average gain of the two sections of the amplifier. Compare DIFFERENTIAL UNBALANCE.

differential gain control A circuit or device for setting the gain of a radio receiver in terms of an anticipated change in signal strength, to reduce the receiver output signal differential.

differential galvanometer A galvanometer in which currents in two similar coils neutralize each other; thus, there is zero deflection when the currents are equal.

differential gap The smallest range of values that a controlled variable must take to change a three-position controller's output from on to off, or vice versa.

differential heating Increase of temperature at different points on a surface at different rates.

differential impedance See DIFFERENTIAL-INPUT IMPEDANCE.

differential induction coil An induction coil having two differentially wound primary coils.

differential input In a differential amplifier, the circuit between input terminals 1 and 2, as opposed to the circuit between input 1 or input 2 and ground.

differential-input amplifier A differential amplifier whose output is proportional to the difference between two input signals—each applied between an input terminal and common ground.

differential-input capacitance In a differential amplifier, the capacitance between the input terminals.

differential-input impedance In a differential amplifier, the impedance between the input terminals.

differential-input measurement For a differential amplifier, a floating measurement made between the input terminals.

differential-input rating In an operational amplifier, the greatest difference signal that can be placed between the inputs while allowing proper operation.

differential-input resistance In a differential amplifier, the resistance between the input terminals.

differential-input voltage In a differential amplifier, the signal voltage presented to the floating input terminals.

differential-input voltage range In a differential amplifier, the range of signal voltages that can be applied between the differential input terminals without overdriving the amplifier.

differential input-voltage rating The maximum differential-input voltage that can be applied safely to a differential amplifier.

differential instrument A galvanometer or other meter in which deflection results from the differential effect of currents flowing in opposite directions through two identical coils. Also see DIFFERENTIAL GALVANOMETER.

differential keying A system of break-in keying, in which the oscillator stage of a transmitter containing a keyed amplifier is disabled when the key is open to prevent interference with the receiver at the keying station, and is enabled when the key is closed.

differential-mode gain In an operational amplifier, the ratio, in decibels, between the output voltage and the differential input voltage.

differential-mode input In an operational amplifier in differential mode, the difference between the two input signal voltages.

differential-mode signal In a balanced three-terminal circuit, such as the input of a differential amplifier, a signal applied between the floating (ungrounded) input terminals.

differential multiplexer An analog multiplexer that selects both the high and low portion of the input signal.

differential nonlinearity Incremental error from an ideal analog output difference when the input is changed by a certain value. Generally expressed as a fraction of full-scale output.

differential permeability The derivative of normal induction, with respect to magnetizing force.

differential phase In a television system tested with a low-level, high-frequency sine-wave signal (f_1) superimposed on a low-frequency, sine-wave signal (f_2), the difference in phase shift of f_1 throughout the system for two specified levels of f_2.

differential phase-shift keying Keying of a carrier by varying the carrier phase.

differential pressure The difference in pressure between two points.

differential-pressure transducer A transducer that delivers an output proportional to the difference between two sensed actuating pressures.

differential protective relay A differential relay that operates to protect equipment or personnel when the difference between the two actuating quantities reaches a prescribed level.

differential receiver A synchro differential that receives the electrical output of two synchro transmitters. The receiver can subtract one input voltage from the other.

differential relay A relay actuated by the difference between two currents or voltages.

differential selsyn A selsyn in which the position assumed by the rotor is proportional to the sum of rotor and stator field values.

differential stage See DIFFERENTIAL AMPLIFIER.

differential synchro See DIFFERENTIAL RECEIVER and DIFFERENTIAL TRANSMITTER.

differential transducer A dual-input, single-output sensor, such as a pressure transducer, that is actuated by two sensed quantities and delivers an output proportional to their difference.

differential transformer A variable inductance transformer having a (usually cylindrical) core that is moved in and out to provide adjustable coupling between the interwound primary and secondary windings. This permits adjustment of the amplitude and phase of the transformer output voltage, with respect to the input voltage.

differential transmitter A synchro differential connected to a synchro transmitter. In a synchro receiver supplied by this combination, the change in rotor position is the algebraic difference between the transmitter-rotor position and the differential-rotor position.

differential unbalance   For a differential amplifier, the average difference in gain between the two amplifier sections. Compare DIFFERENTIAL GAIN.

differential voltage   1. The voltage difference between the input signals to a differential device. **2.** The breakdown voltage minus the operating voltage for a lamp.

differential voltage gain   1. The ratio, in decibels, between the differential output and differential input voltages of an amplifier. **2.** The instantaneous ratio, in decibels, between the rate of change of the output signal voltage and the rate of change of the input signal voltage in an amplifier.

differential-wound field   In a motor or generator, a field winding having series and shunt coils whose fields are opposing.

differentiate   1. To produce an output signal, the instantaneous amplitude of which is proportional to the instantaneous rate of change of the input amplitude. **2.** To determine the derivative of a mathematical function.

differentiating circuit   See DIFFERENTIATING NETWORK.

differentiating network   A four-terminal resistance-capacitance (RC) network whose output voltage is the derivative of the input voltage, with respect to time. Compare INTEGRATING NETWORK.

differentiation   1. The processing of an input signal to create an output signal whose voltage waveform represents the derivative, with respect to time, of the input voltage waveform. **2.** The process of computing a mathematical derivative.

differentiator   1. See DIFFERENTIATING NETWORK. **2.** An operational amplifier whose output waveform is the mathematical derivative of the input waveform.

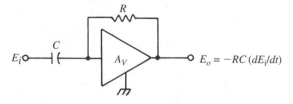

$$E_o = -RC\,(dE_i/dt)$$

differentiator, 2

diffracted wave   A wave or ray of energy undergoing DIFFRACTION.

diffraction   1. Interference of one part of an energy beam with another part when the beam is deflected along two or more paths having different lengths. When this happens with visible light, dark and light bands or colored bands appear. This effect is responsible for the rainbow-like appearance of light reflected from the surface of a compact disc. **2.** The bending of electromagnetic waves around an object. This effect explains why radio signals can propagate around large obstructions, such as buildings and hills. The effect becomes more pronounced as the wavelength increases (the frequency decreases). **3.** The bending of acoustic waves around an object. This effect explains why sound propagates around large obstructions, such as buildings. The effect becomes more pronounced as the wavelength increases (the frequency decreases).

diffraction grating   A transparent plate containing thousands of parallel lines or grooves spaced extremely close together. Light passing through the slits between the lines produces a rainbow spectrum as a result of DIFFRACTION.

diffraction spectrum   1. The spectrum produced in visible light by a diffraction grating. **2.** The distribution of energy at various frequencies, produced by diffraction of electromagnetic waves. **3.** The distribution of energy at various frequencies, produced by diffraction of acoustic waves.

diffractometer   An instrument for measuring the diffraction of radiation, such as light or X-rays.

diffuse   1. To produce or cause DIFFUSION. **2.** Energy that is diffused.

diffused-alloy transistor   See DRIFT-FIELD TRANSISTOR.

diffused-base transistor   A bipolar transistor in which the base region has been diffused into the semiconductor wafer. Also see DIFFUSED JUNCTION.

diffused device   A semiconductor device in which the junction is produced by diffusion (see DIFFUSION, **1**). Examples: DIFFUSED-BASE TRANSISTOR, DIFFUSED DIODE, DIFFUSED-JUNCTION RECTIFIER, and DIFFUSED-MESA TRANSISTOR.

diffused diode   A semiconductor diode having a diffused junction.

diffused-emitter-and-base transistor   A transistor in which n and p materials both have been diffused into the semiconductor wafer to provide emitter and base junctions. Also see DIFFUSION, **1** and DIFFUSED TRANSISTOR.

diffused junction   In a semiconductor device, a pn junction formed by diffusing a gas into a semiconductor at a high temperature that is below the melting point of the semiconductor. Typically, a gas containing an n-type impurity is diffused into p-type semiconductor material. Compare ALLOY JUNCTION.

diffused-junction rectifier   A semiconductor rectifier using a diffused junction.

diffused-junction transistor   See DIFFUSED-BASE TRANSISTOR, DIFFUSED-MESA TRANSISTOR, and DIFFUSED TRANSISTOR.

diffused-layer resistor   In an integrated circuit, a resistor produced by diffusing a suitable material into the substrate.

diffused-mesa transistor   A transistor whose base is a n-type layer diffused into a p-type wafer (the remaining p-type material serving as the collector); its emitter is a small p-type area diffused into or alloyed with the n-layer. Unwanted diffused portions are etched away, leaving the transistor in a mesa shape.

diffused planar transistor   A diffused transistor in which emitter, base, and collector electrodes are exposed at the face of the wafer, which has an oxide layer to forestall leakage between surface electrodes.

diffused resistor   See DIFFUSED-LAYER RESISTOR.

diffused sound   **1.** Sound distributed so that its energy flux is the same at all points. **2.** Sound whose source is difficult to locate or seems to shift, as that heard from out-of-phase stereo channels.

diffused transistor   A transistor in which one or both electrodes are created by diffusion. See DIFFUSED JUNCTION.

diffused-junction transistor   See DIFFUSED-BASE TRANSISTOR, DIFFUSED-MESA TRANSISTOR, and DIFFUSED TRANSISTOR.

diffusion   **1.** In the fabrication of semiconductor devices, the slow, controlled introduction of a material into the semiconductor, for example, the high-temperature diffusion of a n-type impurity (from a gas containing it) into a p-type wafer to form a diode. **2.** The random velocity and movement of current carriers in a semiconductor, resulting from a high-density gradient. **3.** The characteristic spreading of light reflected from a rough surface or transmitted through a translucent material. **4.** The spreading-out of sound waves, for example when reflected from acoustic baffles. **5.** The migration of atoms from one substance to another, as in the spreading of one gas throughout another.

diffusion bonding   A method of joining different substances by diffusing atoms of one into the other. This technique is employed in the manufacture of certain semiconductor diodes, transistors, and other devices.

diffusion capacitance   The current-dependent capacitance of a forward-biased semiconductor junction.

diffusion current   Current resulting from the diffusion of carriers within a substance (see DIFFUSION, **2**).

diffusion length   In a semiconductor junction, the distance a current carrier travels to the junction during carrier life.

diffusion process   **1.** The technique of processing semiconductor devices by diffusion (see DIFFUSION, **1**). **2.** Producing a high vacuum by means of diffusion (see DIFFUSION PUMP).

diffusion pump   A pump for fast, efficient creation of a high vacuum in electron tubes and similar devices. In one form, the pump, in conjunction with a force pump, uses mercury vapor as the pumped medium. Gas molecules evacuated from the device diffuse into a chamber, where condensing mercury vapor traps and carries them off.

diffusion theory   The notion that, in a homogeneous medium, current density is directly proportional to the gradient of particle flux density.

diffusion transistor   A transistor whose operation is based principally on the diffusion of current carriers (see DIFFUSION, **2**).

diffusor   In acoustics, a device or structure deliberately installed to spread sound waves throughout a region.

dig-in angle   A stylus angle of 90 degrees, relative to the surface of a phonograph disc. Compare DRAG ANGLE.

DIGIRALT   Acronym for *digital radar altimetry*. A system that utilizes digital techniques to enhance the accuracy of an altimeter using radar.

digit   A single symbol in a numbering system (e.g., 0 through 9 in the decimal system, or 0 or 1 in the binary system), whose value depends on its position in a group and on the radix of the particular system used.

digital   **1.** Pertaining to components, circuits, or systems that use signals having an integral number of discrete levels or values, rather than signals, whose levels or values vary over a continuous range. **2.** Pertaining to a numeric readout or display. **3.** See BINARY, **1**.

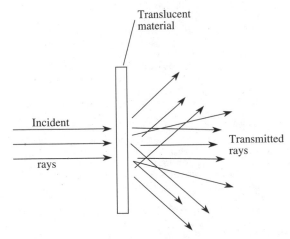

diffusion, 3

digital annunciator   An annunciator that gives an alphanumeric digital display of information, as well as sounding an alarm.

digital audio tape   Abbreviation, DAT. A magnetic tape intended for recording digitally encoded audio data. Used in some high-fidelity applications, and also for computer data storage.

digital barometer   An electronic barometer providing a digital readout.

digital capacitance meter   Abbreviation DCM. A meter with a digital readout for measuring capacitance values.

digital circuit   A circuit affording a dual-state switching operation (i.e., on or off, high or low, etc.). Also called *binary circuit*.

digital communications   Radio or wire communications using a dual-state mechanism (on/off, positive/negative, or modulated/unmodulated) to represent information.

digital comparator   A comparator that presents two digital values, one for each of the quantities being compared.

digital computer   A high-speed, electronic machine for performing mathematical operations, file management, machine control, or other "intelligent" functions, and whose basic internal operations (data storage, comparing, and computation) are based on semiconductor devices assuming one of two states (on or off, high or low). Compare ANALOG COMPUTER.

digital data   Information represented and processed in the form of combinations of digits (0 and 1, in the binary system).

digital-data cable   A cable designed to conduct high-speed digital pulses with minimal distortion and loss.

digital data-handling system   A system that accepts, sorts, modifies, classifies, or records digital data, displaying the final result or passing the data to a computer.

digital delay circuit   A device that stores digitized audio data, and releases it after a specified delay.

digital device   **1.** A digital integrated circuit (IC). **2.** Any circuit or system that operates by digital means.

digital differential analyzer   Abbreviation, DDA. A digital computer that can perform integration using specialized circuitry.

digital display   A presentation of information (such as the answer to a problem) in the form of actual digits, as opposed to one in the form of, for example, a meter deflection. See, for example, DIGITAL-TYPE METER.

digital divider   In a computer, a device that can divide (i.e., provide a quotient and remainder using dividend and divisor signals).

digital electrometer   An electrometer that has a digital current or voltage indicator.

digital electronics   The branch of electronics concerned with components, circuits, and systems that use signals having an integral number of discrete levels or values, as opposed to signals whose levels or values vary over a continuous range. Compare ANALOG ELECTRONICS.

digital frequency meter   A direct-reading frequency meter using high-speed electronic switching circuits and a digital readout. Such instruments read frequency from less than 1 Hz to many gigahertz.

digital HIC   A hybrid integrated circuit (HIC) designed for digital applications. Also see DIGITAL INTEGRATED CIRCUIT.

digital IC   See DIGITAL INTEGRATED CIRCUIT.

digital incremental plotter   A device that can draw, according to signals received from a computer, graphs depicting solutions to problems.

digital information   See DIGITAL DATA.

digital information display   See DIGITAL DISPLAY.

digital integrated circuit   An integrated circuit (IC) intended for binary operations, such as switching, gating, etc. Compare LINEAR INTEGRATED CIRCUIT.

digital integrator   A device that can perform integration, in which increments in input variables, and an output variable, are represented by digital signals.

digital logic   A form of Boolean algebra, consisting of negation, conjunction, and disjunction, in which the binary digit 1 has the value "true" and 0 the value "false" (in positive logic) or vice-versa (in negative logic). Digital logic is the basis by which all digital devices function.

digital-logic module   **1.** A circuit that performs digital operations. **2.** A logic gate.

digital multimeter   Abbreviation, DMM. A voltohm-milliammeter producing a digital readout of measured values.

digital multiplex   **1.** The combination of several or many digital signals into a single digital signal. **2.** Also called *digital demultiplex*. The reverse process from that defined in 1, in which the original signals are obtained from the combination signal. **3.** Communication using the techniques defined in 1 and 2.

digital multiplex equipment   Equipment that accomplishes digital multiplexing or the reverse process, digital demultiplexing.

digital multiplier   In a digital computer, a device that produces a product signal from multiplier and multiplicand signals.

digital output   An output signal of digital pulses representing a number equal or proportional to the value of a corresponding input signal.

digital panel meter   A numeric-readout meter whose relatively small size allows mounting on a panel.

digital phase shifter   A phase shifter actuated by a digital control signal.

digital photometer   An electronic photometer providing a digital readout of illumination values.

digital power meter An electronic wattmeter providing a digital readout of measured power.

digital readout An indicating device that displays a sequence of numerals that represent a measured value.

digital recording A system for tape-recording high-fidelity sound. The audio is converted from analog to binary digital form, and the binary digits (bits) are recorded on magnetic tape.

digital representation The use of digital signals to represent information as characters or numbers.

digital rotary transducer A device that delivers a digital output signal proportional to the rotation of a shaft.

digital signal A signal having an integral number of discrete levels or values, as opposed to a signal whose levels or values vary over a continuous range.

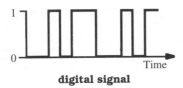

digital signal

digital signal processing Abbreviation, DSP. A method of signal enhancement that operates by eliminating confusion between digital states. This improves dynamic range and frequency response, reduces the number of errors, and virtually eliminates noise. It is used extensively in digital communication and recording, often in conjunction with analog-to-digital (A/D) and digital-to-analog (D/A) conversion to enhance the quality of analog signals and recordings.

digital sound Sound recording and reproduction accomplished with digital, rather than analog, signals. Advantages include wideband frequency response, superior dynamic range, and relative immunity to noise.

digital speech communications A system of voice communications, in which the analog voice signal is encoded into digital pulses at the transmitter, and decoded at the receiver.

digital subtractor In a computer, a device that produces an output signal whose value is equal to the difference of the values of two input signals.

digital switching Routing operations carried out on digital signals to establish communications links between specified system users.

digital television 1. A television system in which the picture information is encoded into digital form at the transmitter, and decoded at the receiver. 2. A form of television picture transmission that functions according to picture motion, rather than absolute brightness.

digital temperature indicator See DIGITAL THERMOMETER.

digital thermometer An electronic thermometer that provides a digital readout of temperature.

digital-to-analog conversion The conversion of a digital quantity into an analog representation, such as shown by a performance curve. Compare ANALOG-TO-DIGITAL CONVERSION.

digital-to-analog converter A circuit or device that performs DIGITAL-TO-ANALOG CONVERSION.

digital transmission 1. A method of signal transmission in which the modulation occurs in defined increments, rather than over a continuous range. 2. A message that is sent in digital form.

digital-type meter An indicating instrument in which a row of numeral indicators displays a value. Compare ANALOG-TYPE METER.

digital voltmeter Abbreviation, DVM. An electronic voltmeter having a direct numerical readout, rather than an analog display.

digital wattmeter See DIGITAL POWER METER.

digital compression In digital computer operation, the process of representing data with an economy of characters to reduce file size.

digit current In digital computer operations, the current associated with writing or reading a digit into or out of a memory cell.

digit delay element A logic element (gate) whose output signal lags the input signal by one digit period.

digit filter A device for detecting designations. See DESIGNATION.

digitize 1. To express the results of an analog measurement in digital units. 2. To convert an analog signal into corresponding digital pulses.

digitizer See ANALOG-TO-DIGITAL CONVERTER.

digit period In a digital circuit or system, the time interval between the start of one digital pulse and the start of the next pulse.

digit place See DIGIT POSITION.

digit plane In a matrix-type computer memory, the plane within a three-dimensional array of memory storage elements representing a DIGIT POSITION.

digit position The ordinal position of a digit in a numeral, the first position being occupied by the least-significant digit (e.g., 7 is in the third position in the numeral 756).

digit pulse A pulse that energizes magnetic core memory elements representing a digit position in several words.

digitron A display in which all of the characters lie in a single, flat plane.

digit time The duration of a digit signal in a series of signals.

digit time slot In digital communications, the interval of time assigned to one bit or one digit.

digit-transfer bus In a digital computer, a main line (of conductors) that transfers information among various registers; it does not handle control signals.

diheptal CRT base   The 14-pin base of a cathode-ray tube. Also see BIDECAL, DUODECAL, and MAGNAL.

DIIC   Abbreviation for *dielectric-isolated integrated circuit*. Several separate integrated-circuit wafers are contained in a single package, and kept electrically insulated by layers of dielectric.

dilatometer   An instrument used to measure expansion.

dimension   **1.** Any measurable quantity, such as distance, time, temperature, humidity, etc. **2.** An axis in the three-dimensional Cartesian coordinate system. **3.** An independent variable in a function of one or more variables.

dimensional analysis   A mathematical procedure whereby an equation involving quantities with different units is verified as being *dimensionally correct*. The original variables are replaced with fundamental quantities, such as resistance (R), current (I), length or displacement (d), and time (t), applicable to electrical systems. The equation is dimensionally correct if it can be shown that the left and right sides of the equation are identical.

dimensional ratio   In magnetism, the ratio of the longest diameter of an elongated ellipsoid of revolution to the shortest.

dimensional stability   Nonvariance or little variance in the shape and size of a medium (such as film) during the processing of that material.

dimensionless quantity   A quantity that is merely a real number. Example: logarithm, exponent, numerical ratio, etc. In contrast are physical quantities: 3 volts, 5000 hertz, 10 amperes, etc.

diminished radix complement   See COMPLEMENT.

dimmer   An electronic device used for controlling the brightness of incandescent lamps. Using amplified control, the device enables high-wattage lamp loads to be smoothly adjusted via a small rheostat or potentiometer. A photoelectric-type dimmer automatically controls lamps in accordance with the amount of daylight.

dimmer curve   The function of a light-dimmer voltage output as a function of setting on a linear scale.

DIN   Abbreviation for *Deutsche Industrie Normenausschuss*. A German association that sets standards for the manufacture and performance of electrical and electronic equipment, as well as other devices.

D indicator   In radar operations, an indicator combining type B and C indicators (see B DISPLAY and C DISPLAY).

Dingley induction-type landing system   An aircraft landing system that provides lateral and vertical guidance; instead of radio, it uses the magnetic field surrounding two horizontal cables laid on or under either side of the runway.

diode   A two-element device containing an anode and a cathode, and providing unidirectional conduction. The many types are used in such devices as rectifiers, detectors, peak clippers, mixers, modulators, amplifiers, oscillators, and test instruments.

diode action   **1.** The characteristic behavior of a diode (i.e., rectification and unidirectional conduction). **2.** Two-electrode rectification or unidirectional conductivity in any device other than a diode (e.g., asymmetrical conductivity between the collector and base of a transistor).

diode amplifier   **1.** A parametric amplifier employing a varactor. **2.** An amplifier utilizing hole-storage effects in a semiconductor diode. **3.** A negative-resistance amplifier using a tunnel diode.

diode array   A combination of several diodes in a single housing.

diode assembly   See DIODE ARRAY.

diode bias   A steady direct-current (dc) voltage applied to a diode to establish its operating point.

diode capacitance   The capacitance existing at the p-n junction of a semiconductor diode when the junction is reverse-biased. The capacitance generally varies, depending on the reverse-bias voltage.

diode capacitor   **1.** A capacitor normally operated with a diode. **2.** A voltage-variable capacitor utilizing the junction capacitance of a semiconductor diode (e.g., a varactor).

diode-capacitor memory cell   A high-value capacitor in series with a high-back-resistance semiconductor diode. A data pulse forward-biases the diode and charges the capacitor, which remains charged, thus holding the data bit, because of the long time constant of the high capacitance and the high back resistance of the diode.

diode characteristic   The current-versus-voltage curve for a diode.

diode checker   An instrument for testing semiconductor diodes. There are two forms: A static checker, which measures forward and reverse current; and a dynamic checker (see DYNAMIC DIODE TESTER), which displays the entire diode response curve on an oscilloscope screen.

diode chopper   A chopper using an alternately biased diode as the switching element.

diode clipper   A clipper using one or more diodes. A single biased diode will limit the positive or negative peak of an applied alternating-current (ac) voltage, depending on diode polarity and bias. Two biased diodes with opposing polarity will clip both peaks. Also see LIMITER.

diode converter   See DIODE MIXER.

diode current   The forward or reverse current flowing through a diode.

diode current meter   A direct-current (dc) milliammeter or microammeter with a semiconduc-

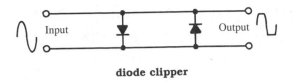

diode clipper

tor-diode rectifier that allows the measurement of alternating current (ac).

diode curve changer A diode or network of diodes used to make a linear current-voltage curve acquire some nonlinear shape.

diode demodulator See DEMODULATOR PROBE and DIODE DETECTOR.

diode detector A detector circuit in which a diode demodulates a signal. The diode, a simple device, provides linear response at high signal amplitudes, but affords no amplification.

diode feedback rectifier **1.** In a rectified-carrier, negative-feedback system for an amplitude-modulated (AM) transmitter, the diode that rectifies the modulated carrier and provides the audio envelope for use as negative-feedback voltage. This voltage is applied to the speech amplifier/modulator channel to reduce distortion, noise, and hum, at the same time providing automatic modulation control. **2.** The diode that rectifies a part of the signal at the output of an audio amplifier and provides a proportional direct-current (dc) voltage for use as bias in an automatic-gain-control (AGC) circuit.

diode field-strength meter A simple meter for measuring the intensity of a radio-frequency (RF) electromagnetic field. It consists of a short whip antenna, an inductance-capacitance (LC) tuned circuit, a diode detector, and a direct-current (dc) microammeter. The deflection of the meter is roughly proportional to the RF signal voltage.

diode gate A passive switching circuit of biased diodes. Also see AND CIRCUIT and OR CIRCUIT.

diode impedance The vector sum (resultant) of the resistive and reactive components of a diode. In a semiconductor diode, the inductive component of reactance is almost entirely the inductance of leads and electrodes, whereas the capacitive component of reactance is the shunting capacitance between leads and electrodes, plus the voltage-variable capacitance of the pn junction. The resistive component is almost entirely the voltage-variable resistance of the pn junction.

diode isolation A means of insulating an integrated-circuit chip from its substrate. The chip is surrounded by a pn junction that is reverse-biased. This prevents conduction between the chip and the substrate.

diode lamp See LASER DIODE.

diode laser See LASER DIODE.

diode light source See LASER DIODE.

diode limiter See DIODE CLIPPER.

diode load **1.** The current drawn from a diode acting as a rectifier or demodulator. **2.** The output (load) resistor into which a diode operates.

diode load resistance The required value for a diode load resistor.

diode load resistor A resistor usually connected to the output of a diode rectifier or diode detector.

diode logic Digital circuitry, such as AND and OR circuits, using diodes as the principal components.

diode matrix In some digital devices, a grid of wires, the intersections of some being interconnected through diodes, whose polarities determine circuit operation. A series of AND circuits is provided by this arrangement, which acts as a high-speed rotary switch when it is supplied with input pulses.

diode mixer A frequency converter that operates via the nonlinearity of semiconductor diodes.

diode noise limiter A noise limiter circuit having one or more biased diodes.

diode oscillator An oscillator based on the negative resistance or breakdown characteristics of certain diodes, such as high-reverse-biased germanium diodes, tunnel diodes, Gunn diodes, and four-layer diodes. It is generally used at microwave frequencies.

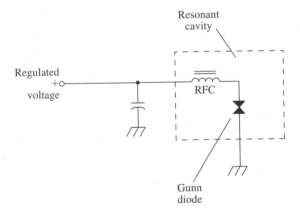

diode oscillator, 1

diode pack A device containing more than one diode. An example is the full-wave bridge-rectifier integrated circuit.

diode peak detector A diode detector whose load resistance is high at modulation frequencies; the voltage across the resistance is proportional to the peak amplitude of the modulated signal.

diode peak voltmeter A diode-type alternating-current (ac) voltmeter, in which the deflection of the direct-current (dc) milliammeter or microammeter is proportional to the peak value of the applied ac voltage.

diode probe   A test probe containing a diode used as either a rectifier or demodulator.

diode recovery time   The interval during which relatively high current continues to flow after the voltage across a semiconductor junction has been abruptly switched from forward to reverse. Recovery time is attributable to DIODE STORAGE.

diode rectification   Conversion of alternating current (ac) to pulsating direct current (dc) by diode action.

diode rectifier   **1.** A diode device that converts alternating current (ac) to pulsating direct current (dc) in a power supply. **2.** A small-signal diode device that converts ac to dc in the automatic-gain-control (AGC) circuit of a superheterodyne receiver. Also called *AGC rectifier*.

diode resistor   **1.** A resistor usually operated with a diode. **2.** A voltage-variable resistor utilizing the (usually forward) resistance of a semiconductor diode.

diode storage   The charge carriers (electrons and holes) remaining within a pn junction for a short time after forward bias has been either removed or switched to reverse polarity.

diode storage time   See DIODE RECOVERY TIME.

diode switch   See DIODE GATE.

diode sync separator   A diode used in a television receiver circuit to separate and deliver the sync pulses from the composite video signal.

diode temperature stabilization   **1.** Keeping the temperature of a diode at a constant level. **2.** Using the temperature-resistance characteristic of a forward-biased semiconductor diode to stabilize a circuit (such as a transistor amplifier stage) (i.e., to prevent variations caused by temperature changes).

diode tester   See DIODE CHECKER.

diode transistor   **1.** See UNIJUNCTION TRANSISTOR. **2.** A semiconductor diode whose operation simulates that of a transistor by means of pulsed operation that alternately makes the single junction an emitter or collector. **3.** A transistor connected to operate solely as a diode.

diode-transistor logic   Abbreviation, DTL. Logic circuitry in which a diode is the logic element and a transistor acts as an inverting amplifier.

diode-type meter   A rectifier-type alternating-current (ac) meter consisting of a semiconductor diode(s) and a direct-current (dc) milliammeter or microammeter. The diode rectifies the ac input, the resulting dc deflecting the meter.

diode varactor   A conventional semiconductor diode or rectifier used as a makeshift varactor (voltage-variable capacitor).

diode variable resistor   See DIODE VARISTOR.

diode varistor   A conventional diode used as a makeshift varistor (voltage-variable resistor).

diode voltage reference   See ZENER VOLTAGE REFERENCE.

diode voltage regulator   See ZENER VOLTAGE REGULATOR.

DIP   Abbreviation of DUAL IN-LINE PACKAGE.

dip   **1.** A distinct decrease in the value of a varying quantity, followed by an increase [e.g., the sudden drop, followed by a rise, in collector current when a bipolar-transistor radio-frequency (RF) power amplifier is tuned through resonance]. **2.** Also called *magnetic inclination*. The slanting of a compass needle, resulting from the orientation of the geomagnetic lines of flux, with respect to the earth's surface. It varies, depending on magnetic latitude.

dip adapter   An external accessory that allows a radio-frequency (RF) signal generator to be used as a DIP METER.

dip coating   **1.** Applying a protective coat of insulating material to a conductor or component by dipping it into the liquid material, then draining and drying it. Compare SPRAY COATING. **2.** The coat applied in this way.

dip encapsulation   Embedding a component or circuit in a protective block of insulating material (such as a plastic) while the material is in a liquid state, and then allowing the material to harden in ambient air or in an oven.

dip impregnation   Saturating a component or material (such as absorbent film) with a substance (such as oil or wax) by dipping or vacuum forcing.

diplexer   A coupler that permits two or more transmitters to operate simultaneously into a single antenna.

diplex operation   **1.** Simultaneous transmission or reception of two signals using a single antenna. **2.** Simultaneous transmission or reception of two signals on a single carrier.

diplex reception   The reception of signals while transmitting with the same antenna.

diplex transmission   The transmission of signals while receiving with the same antenna.

dip meter   A tunable radio-frequency (RF) instrument that, by means of a sharp dip of an indicating meter, indicates resonance with an external circuit under test. Specific names are derived from the active component used: *grid-dip meter*, *gate-dip meter*, etc.

dip needle   See INCLINOMETER.

dipolar   Also, *bipolar*. Possessing two poles (usually electric or magnetic).

dipolarization   See DEPOLARIZATION.

dipole   **1.** A molecule having an electronic moment (i.e., one in which the center of the negative charges is not also the center of the positive charges). **2.** DIPOLE ANTENNA.

dipole antenna   A fundamental form of antenna from which many others are derived. It consists of a center-fed single wire a half-wave-

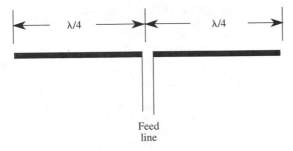

Feed
line

dipole antenna

length long (at the operating frequency) that is suitably corrected for end effects.

dipole disk feed   A method of coupling radio-frequency energy to a disk-shaped antenna. The energy is applied to a dipole located adjacent to the disk.

dipole feed   A method of coupling radio-frequency energy to an antenna by means of a half-wave dipole. The dipole is directly fed by the transmission line, and the dipole radiates energy to the rest of the system.

dip oscillator   The oscillator that provides the signal for a DIP METER.

dipotassium tartrate   Abbreviation, DKT. An organic piezoelectric material.

dipped component   A discrete electronic component that has been given a protective coating by dipping into a suitable material (such as oil, varnish, or wax) and draining off the surplus.

dipper   Collective term for resonance-type instruments, such as a DIP METER or DIP ADAPTER.

dipper interrupter   A cyclic switching device in which a contact pin is part of a revolving wheel partially immersed in mercury.

dipping   1. The application of a protective coating or impregnant to a component by immersing it in a suitable material. Also see DIP COATING, DIP ENCAPSULATION, and DIP IMPREGNATION. **2.** In a resonant (tuned) amplifier circuit, the adjustment of the resonant circuit for minimum current through the amplifying device.

dipping needle   See INCLINOMETER.

dip soldering   1. Soldering leads or terminals by dipping them into molten solder and then removing excess solder. **2.** Tinning printed-circuit patterns by dipping the boards into molten solder or placing them in contact with the surface of a solder bath. **3.** Soldering leads in printed circuits by the methods defined in (2).

DIP switch   A switch (or group of miniature switches) mounted in a dual-inline package (DIP) for easy insertion into an integrated-circuit socket or printed-circuit board.

direct-access storage device   A computer memory in which data access time is unaffected by the data location. Also called *random-access memory device*.

direct-acting recorder   See GRAPHIC RECORDER.

direct-acting recording instrument   See GRAPHIC RECORDER.

direct address   The actual address of a computer storage location (i.e., the one designated by machine code 0. Also called *absolute address* or *real address*.

direct capacitance   The capacitance between two points in a circuit, as opposed to the capacitance between either point and other objects (including ground).

direct allocation   In digital computer operations, to specify the necessary memory locations and peripherals for a particular program when it is written.

direct coding   Computer programming in machine language.

direct control   Control of one machine by another, for example, the control of a computerized mobile robot by a central computer system.

direct-conversion receiver   A heterodyne receiver in which the incoming radio-frequency (RF) signal is amplified, then mixed with the RF output of a tunable local oscillator, producing an audio-frequency (AF) beat note. The AF is amplified; audio filtering can be added. Although the direct-conversion receiver somewhat resembles the superheterodyne type, it has no intermediate-frequency (IF) chain, and does not normally provide single-signal reception. Also see ZERO-BEAT RECEPTION.

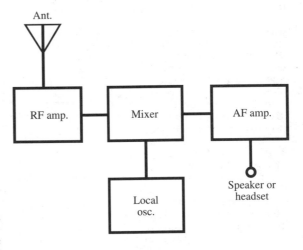

direct-conversion receiver

direct-coupled amplifier   An amplifier in which the output circuit of one stage is wired directly to the input circuit of the following stage (i.e., there is no intervening capacitor or transformer). Such an amplifier can handle alternating-current (ac) or direct-current (dc) signals, and has wide frequency response.

direct-coupled transistor logic Abbreviation, DCTL. In digital computer and switching circuits, a logic system using only direct-coupled transistor stages.

direct coupling Direct connection of one circuit point to another for signal transmission (i.e., without intermediate capacitors or transformers). Because coupling devices aren't used, direct coupling provides transmission of direct current (dc), as well as alternating current (ac).

direct current **1.** Abbreviation, dc. A current that always flows in the same direction (i.e., the polarity never reverses). The current might be constant, as from a battery or a regulated power supply; it might be pulsating, as from an unfiltered rectifier. **2.** Pertaining to current that always flows in the same direction. **3.** Descriptive of a voltage, resistance, or other parameter under conditions in which there is a usually constant current that always flows in the same direction.

direct-current amplifier An amplifier for boosting direct-current (dc) signals, as opposed to dc voltage signals.

direct-current bar See DC BAR.

direct-current beta See DC BETA.

direct-current block See DC BLOCK.

direct-current bus See DC BUS.

direct-current circuit breaker See DC CIRCUIT BREAKER.

direct-current component See DC COMPONENT.

direct-current converter See DC CONVERTER.

direct-current coupling See DC COUPLING.

direct-current dump See DC DUMP.

direct-current equipment See DC EQUIPMENT.

direct-current erase head See DC ERASE HEAD.

direct-current generator See DC GENERATOR.

direct-current inverter See DC INVERTER.

direct-current leakage See DC LEAKAGE.

direct-current motor See DC MOTOR.

direct-current noise See DC NOISE.

direct-current power See DC POWER.

direct-current relay See DC RELAY.

direct-current resistance See DC RESISTANCE.

direct-current shift See DC SHIFT.

direct-current short See DC SHORT.

direct-current signaling See DC SIGNALING.

direct-current source See DC SOURCE.

direct-current transducer See DC TRANSDUCER.

direct-current transformer See DC TRANSFORMER.

direct-current transmission See DC TRANSMISSION.

direct digital control In a digital computer, multiplexing or time sharing among a number of controlled loops.

direct display unit A cathode-ray-tube (CRT) peripheral that displays data recalled from memory.

direct-distance dialing A form of telephone service that allows dialing of long-distance numbers without involving a human operator.

direct drive **1.** Pertaining to electromechanical accessories for electronic equipment. **2.** The transmission of power directly from a source (such as a motor) to a driven device without intermediate gears, belts, or clutches.

direct-drive robot A robot that uses the minimum possible number of gears and other drive systems.

direct-drive torque motor In a positioning or speed-control system, a servoactuator connected directly to the driven load.

direct-drive tuning A tuning or adjusting mechanism in which the shaft of the variable component (such as a potentiometer or variable capacitor) is turned directly by a knob (i.e., without gearing, dial cable, or similar linkage).

directed number A number having direction as well as magnitude; a vector quantity.

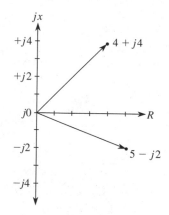

directed number

direct electromotive force A direct-current (dc) voltage that does not fluctuate or pulsate.

direct emf See DIRECT ELECTROMOTIVE FORCE.

direct ground **1.** A ground connection made by the shortest practicable route. Compare INDIRECT GROUND. **2.** An earth ground.

direct induced current A transient current induced in the same direction as the induction current when it is interrupted.

directing antenna See DIRECTIONAL ANTENNA.

direct-input circuit A circuit, especially an amplifier, whose input is wired directly to the input electrode of the active device (i.e., without a coupling capacitor or transformer).

direct-insert subroutine In digital computer operations, a subroutine directly inserted into a larger instruction sequence. It must be rewritten at every point it is needed.

direct instruction A computer program instruction that indicates the location of an operand in memory.

directional 1. Depending on direction or orientation. 2. Having a concentration in an identifiable direction. 3. Pertaining to a transducer in which radiation, or sensitivity, is concentrated in certain directions at the expense of radiation or sensitivity in other directions.

directional antenna An antenna that transmits and receives signals more effectively in some directions than in others. Also called *beam*, *beam antenna*, and *directive antenna*.

directional array 1. A directional antenna having a set of elements assembled in such a way that their combined action shapes the radiation into a unidirectional pattern. 2. A group of antennas spaced and phased to produce unidirectional radiation and reception patterns.

directional beam 1. An antenna whose radiation or reception pattern strongly favors a specific direction. 2. The radiation or reception pattern of such an antenna.

directional characteristic The precise directional properties of an antenna or transducer.

directional CQ In amateur radio, a transmission that invites replies only from stations in a certain direction or in a particular city, state, or country.

directional coupler A microwave device that couples an external system to waves traveling through the coupler in one direction.

directional diode A high-back-resistance semiconductor diode inserted into a direct-current (dc) signal circuit or control circuit. Permits unidirectional current flow.

directional filter In carrier-current transmission, a filter that halves the frequency band, one half being for transmission in one direction, and the other half being for transmission in the opposite direction.

directional gain Symbol, k_S. The ratio of the power that would be radiated by a loudspeaker if the free-space axial sound pressure were constant over a sphere, to the actual radiated power. Usually expressed in decibels.

directional homing A scheme for locating the source of a radio signal. An effort is made to keep the bearing of the target or guiding station constant. Therefore, the search path is as direct (as nearly a straight line) as practicable.

directional horn See DIRECTIVE HORN.

directional hydrophone A hydrophone whose response pattern strongly favors one direction.

directional lobe In the spatial response pattern of a device, such as an antenna or loudspeaker, a portion showing emphasized response in a given direction.

directional microphone A microphone that strongly favors sound emanating from in front of it.

directional pattern See DIRECTIVITY PATTERN.

directional phase shifter A phase-shifting circuit in which the characteristics are different in one direction, as compared with the other direction.

directional power relay A relay that is actuated when the monitored power reaches a prescribed level in a given direction.

directional relay See POLARIZED RELAY.

directional response For any form of transducer, a radiation or sensitivity pattern that is concentrated in certain directions.

directional separation filter See DIRECTIONAL FILTER.

directional transducer A device that senses or emits some effect to an extent that depends on the direction from which the effect comes. Directional effects are often, but not always, accompanied by gain in the favored direction(s). Examples: *directional microphone*, *directional speaker*, and *directional antenna*.

directional variation of radio waves Changes in the field strength of radio waves, depending on the direction. There are various causes, including antenna directivity, ground characteristics, ionospheric factors, weather conditions, and the presence of obstructing objects.

direction angle In radar operations, the angle between the center of the antenna baseline and a line going to the target.

direction finder A receiver specially adapted to show the direction from which a signal is received, thus revealing the direction of the receiver with respect to the transmitting station, and vice versa. In its simplest form, it is a receiver with a loop antenna that is rotatable over a map or compass card. For increased accuracy, checks are made with signals from two transmitting stations; the exact location of the receiver is pinpointed by triangulation.

direction finding The taking of bearings by means of a direction finder.

direction of lay In a multiconductor cable, the lateral direction of winding of the topmost conductors as they recede from the observer; called *left-hand lay* or *right-hand lay*. If the cable is viewed from either end, left-hand lay is equivalent to conductors that rotate clockwise as they recede from the viewer; right-hand lay is equivalent to conductors that rotate counterclockwise as they recede from the viewer.

direction of polarization The direction of the electrostatic field in a linearly polarized wave.

direction of propagation The direction in which energy moves from a transmitter, or between equivalent points in a sector of space under consideration.

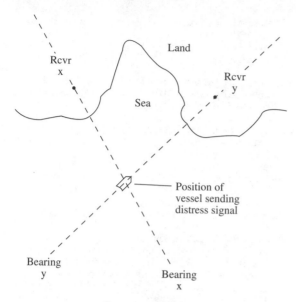

direction finding

direction rectifier   In a control system, a rectifier whose direct-current (dc) output voltage has a magnitude and polarity dependent on the magnitude and phase of an alternating-current (ac) selsyn error voltage.

direction resolution   **1.** The smallest difference in azimuth that a direction-finding device can detect. **2.** The smallest angular separation between two targets that allows a radar set to show two separate echoes rather than a single echo.

directive   In a computer source program, a statement directing the compiler in translating the program into machine language without being translated itself. Also called *control statement.*

directive antenna   An antenna designed for best propagation or reception in one (often steerable) horizontal direction. Also called *beam antenna* and *directional antenna.*

directive gain   For a directional antenna, a rating equal to $12.566(Pr/Pt)$, where Pr is the radiated power per steradian in a given direction and Pt is the total radiated power.

directive horn   A microwave antenna having the shape of a (usually rectangular) horn.

directivity   **1.** In an antenna, a directional response. **2.** The degree to which the radiation or sensitivity of a transducer is concentrated in certain directions. **3.** The angle between the half-power points of a directive antenna in the azimuth plane. **4.** In an antenna system, the ratio, in decibels, between the power in the favored direction and the power in the exact

opposite direction; also called front-to-back ratio. **5.** The forward power gain of an antenna, with respect to a dipole in free space. **6.** The forward power gain of an antenna, with respect to an isotropic radiator in free space.

directivity diagram   A graph of the radiation/response pattern of a beam antenna or other directional device, usually in a horizontal or vertical plane. Also see DIRECTIVITY PATTERN.

directivity factor   **1.** A measure of the directivity of an antenna or transducer. **2.** In acoustics, the ratio, in decibels, between the gain in the maximum direction and the gain in the minimum direction, for a transducer, such as a speaker or microphone.

directivity index   **1.** For an acoustic-emitting transducer, the ratio, in decibels, of E_1 to E_2, where E_1 is the average intensity over an entire sphere surrounding the transducer, and E_2 is the intensity on the acoustic axis. **2.** For an acoustic pickup transducer, the ratio, in decibels, of E_1 to E_2, where E_1 is the average response over an entire sphere surrounding the transducer, and E_2 is the response on the acoustic axis.

directivity of antenna   For a beam antenna, the ratio E_{max}/E_{avg}, where E_{max} is the maximum field intensity at a selected distance from the antenna and E_{avg} is the average field intensity at the same distance.

directivity of directional coupler   The ratio, in decibels, of P_1 to P_2, where P_1 is the power at the forward wave-sampling terminals (measured with a forward wave in the transmission line) and P_2 is the power at the terminals when the wave is reversed in direction.

directivity pattern   The calculated or measured radiation or response pattern (transmission or reception) of an antenna, microphone, loudspeaker, or similar device, with particular attention to the directional features of the pattern.

directivity signal   A spurious output signal resulting from finite directivity in a coupler.

direct light   Light rays traveling directly from a source to a receptor or target without reflection.

directly grounded   Connected to earth or to the lowest-potential point in a circuit, without any intervening resistance or reactance.

directly heated cathode   A vacuum-tube filament. It is so called because, when heated, it becomes the cathode of the tube (i.e., the emitter of electrons).

directly heated thermistor   A thermistor whose temperature changes with the surrounding temperature, and also as a result of power dissipation in the device itself. Compare INDIRECTLY HEATED THERMISTOR.

directly heated thermocouple   A meter thermocouple heated directly by signal currents passing through it. Compare INDIRECTLY HEATED THERMOCOUPLE.

direct measurement Immediate measurement of a quantity, rather than determining the value of the quantity through adjustments of a measuring device (e.g., measuring capacitance with a capacitance meter, rather than with a bridge). Compare INDIRECT MEASUREMENT.

direct memory access Abbreviation, DMA. The transfer of data from a computer memory to some other location, without the intervention of the central processing unit (CPU).

direct numerical control In a computer or data system, the capability for distributing information among numerically controlled machines whenever desired.

director In a multielement directional antenna, an element that is usually mounted in front of the radiator element, and that is phased and spaced to direct the radiation forward. The director functions in conjunction with the reflector element, which is usually mounted behind the radiator.

directory See DICTIONARY.

direct pickup The broadcasting, especially in television, of events at the same time as they occur (e.g., without recording/reproduction).

direct piezoelectricity The production of a piezoelectric voltage by mechanically stressing a suitable crystal.

direct playback In audio or video recording, the reproduction of a recording without additional processing (e.g., the playing of an original recorded tape, rather than a tape that has been mass produced).

direct-point repeater A relay-operated telegraph repeater. The received signals actuate the relay, which switches the second line.

direct-radiator loudspeaker A loudspeaker whose cone or diaphragm is directly coupled to the air.

direct ray An electromagnetic ray (wave) that reaches a receiver without reflection or refraction, and without encountering obstructions.

direct recording **1.** A record produced by a graphic recorder. **2.** The technique of producing such a record.

direct-recording instrument A device, such as a graphic recorder, that directly produces a permanent record (such as an inked trace) of the variations of a quantity.

direct resistance coupling A form of coupling in which the output of the first amplifying device is connected through a resistor directly to the input of the second device. The resistance value can vary; sometimes the connection is a short circuit.

directrix A fixed line to which a curve is referred (e.g., the axis of a parabola).

direct scanning In television, the sequential viewing of parts of a scene by the camera—even though the entire scene is continuously illuminated.

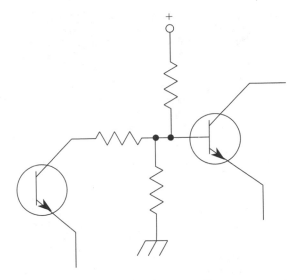

direct resistance coupling

direct serial file organization A technique of organizing files stored in a direct access device, in which a record can be chosen by number and amended where it is without altering other members of the file.

direct sound wave A sound wave arriving directly from its source—especially a wave within an enclosure that is not affected by reflection.

direct substitution **1.** An exact component replacement. **2.** Installing an exact component replacement.

direct synthesizer A device for producing random, rapidly changing frequencies for security purposes. A reference oscillator provides a comparison frequency; the output frequency is a rational-number multiple of this reference frequency.

direct voltage See DC VOLTAGE.

direct wave A wave that travels from a transmitter to a receiver without being reflected by the ionosphere or the ground. Compare SKYWAVE.

direct Wiedemann effect Twisting force (torque) in a wire carrying current in a longitudinal magnetic field. Occurs because of interaction between the longitudinal field and the circular magnetic field around the wire.

direct-wire circuit A communications or control line of wires connecting a transmitter (or control point) and a receiver (or controlled point) without an intermediary, such as a switchboard.

direct-writing recorder See GRAPHIC RECORDER.

direct-writing telegraph **1.** See PRINTING TELEGRAPH. **2.** See TELAUTOGRAPH.

dis-   A prefix meaning "deprived of." For the formation of electronic terms, the prefix must be distinguished from *un-*, meaning "not." For example, a *discharged* body is one that was charged, but has been emptied of its charge. An *uncharged* body is one that ordinarily or presently is not charged.

disable   **1.** To deliberately render a circuit, device, or system inoperative. **2.** In digital computer operations, to defeat a software or hardware function.

disc   See DISK.

disc engraving   **1.** Recording sound by cutting a groove in a record disc. **2.** The groove resulting from such a process.

discharge   The emptying or draining of electricity from a source, such as a battery or capacitor. The term also denotes a sudden, heavy flow of current, as in DISRUPTIVE DISCHARGE. Compare CHARGE.

discharge current   **1.** Current flowing out of a capacitor. **2.** Current flowing out of a cell—especially a storage cell. Compare CHARGING CURRENT.

discharge key   See DISCHARGE SWITCH.

discharge lamp   A gas-filled tube or globe in which light is produced by ionization of the gas between electrodes. Familiar examples are the neon bulb and fluorescent tube.

discharge phenomena   The effects associated with electrical discharges in gases, such as luminous glow.

discharge potential   See IONIZATION POTENTIAL.

discharger   **1.** A short-circuiting tool for discharging capacitors. **2.** A spark gap or other device for automatically discharging an overcharged capacitor.

discharge rate   **1.** The current that can be supplied by an electrochemical cell or battery reliably during its discharging cycle. Usually expressed in milliamperes or amperes. **2.** An expression of the speed with which a battery is being discharged at a specific point in time. It is usually specified in amperes or milliamperes.

discharge switch   A switch for connecting a charged capacitor to a resistor or other load, through which the capacitor discharges. In some circuits, when the switch is in its resting position, it connects the capacitor to the charging source.

discharge voltage   See IONIZATION POTENTIAL.

discharging   **1.** The conversion of chemical energy to electrical energy by an electrochemical cell or battery. **2.** The release of stored electrical energy from a capacitor, or from a network containing capacitors.

discharging tongs   See DISCHARGER, **1.**

discone antenna   An antenna consisting of a horizontal metal or wire-mesh disk above a metal or wire-mesh cone. The antenna has an omnidirectional radiation pattern in the horizontal plane, and provides a good match to a coaxial transmission line over a frequency range of several octaves. Commonly used at very-high frequencies (VHF) and ultra-high frequencies (UHF).

disconnect   **1.** To separate leads or connections, thereby interrupting a circuit. **2.** A type of connector whose halves can be pulled apart to open a cable or other circuit quickly. **3.** To open a switch or relay.

disconnector   See DISCONNECT, **2** and DISCONNECT SWITCH.

disconnect signal   A signal sent over a telephone line, ending the connection.

disconnect switch   A switch whose main function is to open a circuit quickly (either manually or automatically) in the event of an overload.

discontinuity   **1.** A break in a conductor. **2.** A point at which the impedance in a transmission line abruptly changes.

discontinuous wave trains   See DAMPED WAVES.

discrete   **1.** Complete and self-contained, as opposed to a part of something else. **2.** Composed of individual, separate members.

discrete capacitor   Capacitance that is entirely self-contained, rather than being electrically distributed. Also called LUMPED CAPACITOR. Compare DISTRIBUTED CAPACITANCE.

discrete circuit   A circuit comprised of discrete components, such as resistors, capacitors, diodes, and transistors, not fabricated into an integrated circuit.

discrete component   A self-contained device that offers one particular electrical property in lumped form (i.e., concentrated at one place in a circuit, rather than being distributed). A discrete component is built especially to have a specific electrical property, and exists independently, not in combination with other components. Examples: disk capacitor, toroidal inductor, and carbon-composition resistor. Compare DISTRIBUTED COMPONENT.

discrete device   Any component or device that operates as a self-contained unit.

discrete element   A discrete device that forms part of a larger system.

discrete inductor   An inductive component that is entirely self-contained, rather than being electrically spread out. Also called *lumped inductor*. Compare DISTRIBUTED INDUCTANCE.

discrete information source   A source of data containing a finite number of individual elements, rather than a continuously variable parameter.

discrete part   See DISCRETE COMPONENT.

discrete resistor   A resistive component that is entirely self-contained, rather than being electrically spread out. Also called *lumped resistor*. Compare DISTRIBUTED RESISTANCE.

discrete sampling   Sampling of individual bits or characters, one or more at a time.

discrete thin-film component   A discrete component produced by the thin-film process (e.g., thin-film capacitor, thin-film potentiometer, etc.).

discretionary wiring A method of interconnecting the components and circuits on a semiconductor wafer for optimum performance. This requires a separate analysis and wiring pattern for every chip.

discrimination 1. Sharp distinction between electrical quantities of different value. **2.** The detection of a frequency-modulated (FM) signal (i.e., the delivery of an audio signal corresponding to the frequency or phase variations in the FM carrier).

discriminator A second detector for frequency-modulated (FM) signals, in which two diodes are operated from the center-tapped secondary of a special intermediate-frequency (IF) transformer. The circuit is balanced for zero output when the instantaneous received signal frequency is at the unmodulated carrier frequency; the circuit delivers output when the instantaneous received signal frequency swings above or below the unmodulated carrier frequency. Also see FOSTER-SEELEY DISCRIMINATOR and TRAVIS DISCRIMINATOR.

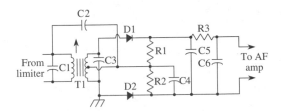

discriminator

discriminator transformer The special input transformer in a DISCRIMINATOR.

discriminator tuner A device that tunes a discriminator to a selected subcarrier.

discriminator tuning device See DISCRIMINATOR TUNER.

dish See DISH ANTENNA.

dish antenna A transmitting and/or receiving antenna consisting of a driven element and a large reflector. The reflector has the shape of a shallow, circular section of a paraboloid or sphere. The feed point is at the focus of the reflector. This antenna, noted for its high directivity and gain, is used mainly at ultra-high and microwave frequencies for communications and satellite television. Large antennas of this type are used in some radio telescopes.

dish-type construction A type of panel-and-chassis construction in which the chassis is fastened vertically to the back of the panel.

disintegration 1. The destructive breakdown of a material. **2.** The stripping of a vacuum-tube cathode of its emissive coating (see DISINTEGRATION VOLTAGE). **3.** The decay of a radioactive material.

disintegration voltage The anode voltage at which the cathode of a gas tube begins to be stripped of its electron-emitting material. For safety and reasonable tube life, the anode working voltage must be between the ionization and disintegration values.

disintegrator An ultrasonic device for reducing crystals or particles to fine suspensions.

disjunction The logical inclusive-OR operation.

disk 1. A flat, circular plate (e.g., *rectifier disk*). **2.** See DISKETTE. **3.** See HARD DISK. **4.** See COMPACT DISC. **5.** See CD-ROM. **6.** A phonograph record or the equivalent unrecorded blank.

disk capacitor A fixed (usually two-plate) capacitor consisting of a disk of dielectric material on whose faces are deposited metal-film plates.

disk capacitor

disk coil See DISK WINDING.

disk dynamo A rudimentary direct-current (dc) generator, in which a copper disk rotates between the poles of a permanent magnet. The outer edge of the disk becomes positively charged; the center of the disk becomes negatively charged.

diskette A magnetic recording disk used for microcomputer data storage. Housed in a square, flat case. In personal computing, there are two sizes: 5.25 inches square and 3.5 inches square. The 5.25-inch version is flexible and is sometimes called a *floppy disk.*

disk files An information-storage system in which data are recorded on rotating magnetic disks.

disk generator 1. See DISK DYNAMO. **2.** A disk-type electrostatic generator.

disk memory A common misnomer for DISK STORAGE.

Disk Operating System Abbreviation, DOS. Any of several command-driven operating systems commonly used in IBM-compatible personal computers.

disk pack In disk files, a set of disks that can be handled as a single unit.

disk recorder A device for recording (and usually also playing back) sound or other signals on record disks.

disk recording 1. Recording sound or other signals on disks. **2.** A disk resulting from such a recording. See DISK.

disk rectifier   A semiconductor rectifier (such as copper-oxide, selenium, magnesium-copper-sulfide, or germanium type) in which the active material is deposited on a metal disk.

disk resistor   A resistor consisting of a resistive material deposited on a metal disk; or a disk of resistive material. In the latter, electrodes are plated on the faces of the disk, one or more of which are held between clips or screws for connections.

disk storage   In digital computer systems, an on-line or offline data storage scheme, in which information is recorded on the magnetic coating of a rotating disk or set of disks. See DISKETTE, and HARD DISK.

disk system   A sound-motion-picture system using audio disks synchronized with the film.

disk thermistor   A thermistor having the general shape of a disk.

disk-type storage   See DISK STORAGE.

disk varistor   A varistor having the general shape of a disk.

disk winding   An armature or coil winding that is flat, rather than cylindrical. Also called *disk coil*, *pancake coil*, and *spiral coil*.

dislocation   A crystal region in which the arrangement of atoms does not have the perfect lattice structure of the crystal.

dispersion   **1.** The property of a material that causes energy at different wavelengths to pass through it at different speeds. **2.** The separation of a wave into its various component frequencies (as when white light is broken up into the color spectrum by a prism). **3.** The scattering of a microwave beam when it strikes an obstruction. **4.** The scattering of sound or ultrasound as it emanates from an acoustic transducer. **5.** A suspension of finely divided particles within another substance.

dispersive medium   A medium that disperses a wave passing through it.

displacement   **1.** A change in the position of a point, particle, figure, or body. **2.** The vector representing a change in the position of a point, particle, figure, or body. **3.** Movement of a member through a specified distance.

displacement current   **1.** An alternating current proportional to the rate of change of an electric field, and existing in addition to usual conduction current. **2.** The current flowing into a capacitor immediately after application of a voltage. This current continues to flow, although continually diminishing in value, until the capacitor becomes fully charged.

displacement of porches   In a television signal, the amplitude difference between the front porch and back porch of a horizontal sync pulse.

displacement of vectors   Vector rotation through a specified number of angular degrees or radians.

displacement transducer   A transducer in which movement (displacement) of a rod, armature, core, reed, or other object converts mechanical energy into proportionate electrical energy.

display   **1.** Visually observable presentation of information, such as data entered into a computer, an answer to a problem solved by a computer, the value of a measured quantity, or a graph of a function. **2.** The screen in a computer system or terminal that visually portrays text and graphical data. In laptop, notebook, and portable computers, this is usually a *liquid-crystal display (LCD)*; in desktop computers and terminals, it is usually a *cathode-ray tube (CRT)*. **3.** To portray information in a visual manner (e.g., as text, numerals, symbols, or graphic images).

display blanking   See DISPLAY INHIBIT.

display console   In a computer system, a peripheral that is used to access and display data being processed or stored; often, it is a unit with a cathode-ray tube (CRT), keyboard, and light pen.

display control   An interface device between a central processor and several visual display units (terminals).

display dimming   See DISPLAY INHIBIT.

display inhibit   In a digital meter, the blanking or dimming of the display when the instrument is not being used. It is used to conserve battery energy.

display loss   The ratio P_1/P_2, where P_1 is the minimum input-signal power that can be detected by an ideal output device at the output of a receiver, and P_2 is the minimum input-signal power value seen by an operator using an output device with the same receiver. Also called *visibility factor*.

display mode   **1.** A particular method of presenting a display. For example, a character display on a video unit might consist of bright characters on a dark background, or dark characters on a light background. **2.** An operating mode for a particular device, in which a display is used.

display module   A self-contained unit with circuitry and readouts for indicating a numerical count.

display primaries   Also called *primary colors*. In a color television receiver, the colors red, green, and blue. When mixed correctly, these three colors can produce any visible hue.

display-storage tube   A special cathode-ray tube in which patterns and other information can be stored for later viewing. The tube has two electron guns: a writing gun and a reading (viewing) gun.

display unit   A device that presents information for visual reading. Included are analog and digital meters, cathode-ray tubes, data printers, graphic recorders, etc. Also see DISPLAY CONSOLE.

display visibility   The ease with which a display can be read by an operator.

display window   **1.** In a panoramic display, the width of the presented frequency band in hertz. **2.** The panel opening through which the indication of a display unit appears.

displayed part   That portion of a number displayed in the readout of a calculator or computer. There might be digits that are not displayed, but which the machine might take into consideration when making calculations. For example, in a 10-digit calculator display, the number 245.789378214895 would be displayed as 245.7893782. Depending on the calculator design, the machine might truncate (disregard) the undisplayed digits (14895), or take the undisplayed digits into account when making calculations.

disposable component   A circuit component or machine part that is so inexpensive that it is more cost-effective to discard it than to repair it when it fails.

disruptive discharge   Sudden, heavy current flow through a dielectric material when it fails completely under electric stress.

dissector   A transducer that samples an illuminated image point by point.

dissector tube   A camera tube using a flat photocathode, upon which the image is focused by the lens system. Electromagnetic deflection from external coils provides scanning. Electrons pass sequentially from the image cathode to a scanning tube at the opposite end of the camera tube. Also called *Farnsworth dissector tube* and *orthiconoscope.*

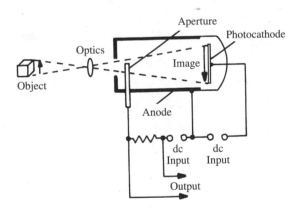

dissector tube

dissipation   **1.** The consumption of power, often without contributing to a useful end, and usually accompanied by the generation of heat. **2.** In an amplifier, the difference between the collector, drain, or plate input power and the usable output power.

dissipation constant   For a thermistor, the ratio of the change in power dissipation to a corresponding change in body temperature.

dissipation factor   **1.** For a dielectric material, the tangent of the dielectric loss angle. Also called *loss tangent.* **2.** Symbol, D. For an impedance (such as a capacitor), the ratio of resistance to reactance; $D = R/X$. It is the reciprocal of the *figure of merit (Q).*

dissipation line   A resistive section of transmission line, used for dissipating power at a certain impedance. Two parallel lengths of resistance wire are terminated by a large, noninductive resistor that has a value equal to the characteristic impedance of the line.

dissipator   **1.** A device used primarily to consume power (i.e., a power sink). **2.** A device for removing heat generated by a device's operation (e.g., a heatsink attached to a power transistor).

dissociation   The condition that characterizes electrolytes (certain acids, bases, or salts in water solution) in which the molecules of the material break up into positive and negative ions.

dissonance   The unpleasant effect (especially in music) produced by nonharmonious combinations of sounds.

dissymmetrical network   A network having unequal input and output image impedances.

dissymmetrical transducer   A transducer having unequal input and output image impedances.

distance-double law   A theoretical rule for determining the rate at which sound intensity decreases as distance increases. Under ideal conditions, when the distance from a sound source is doubled, the sound pressure is reduced to one-fourth of its original level, a reduction of 6 decibels. This is analogous to the *inverse-square law* for visible light and other radiant energy.

distance mark   On a radar screen, a mark indicating the distance from the radar set to the target.

distance measurement   Also called *ranging.* A method or system that allows a robot to navigate in its environment. It also allows a central computer to track the locations of robots under its control. Can use radar, sonar, visible light, or infrared.

distance-measuring equipment   In radionavigation, a system that measures the distance of the interrogator to a transponder beacon in terms of the transmission time to and from the beacon.

distance protection   The use of a protective device within a specified electrical distance along a circuit.

distance relay   In circuit protection, a relay that operates to remove power when a fault occurs within a predetermined distance along the circuit.

distance resolution   **1.** The smallest difference in radial distance between two objects that a distance-measurement or range-finding device can detect. **2.** In radar operations, the minimum distance over which targets can be separated.

distant control   See REMOTE CONTROL.

distorted-drive multiplier   A frequency multiplier whose excitation signal is a peaked wave that has been predistorted to decrease the angle of flow in the device, thus increasing its efficiency.

distorted nonsinusoidal wave   A nonsinusoidal wave whose ideal shape (square, rectangular, sawtooth, etc.) has been altered.

distorted sine wave   A wave that is approximately of sinusoidal shape (i.e., it is not an exact plot of a sine wave because of the presence of harmonics).

distortion   **1.** Deformation of a signal waveform. **2.** The additional deformation of a signal exhibiting a less-than-ideal waveshape when it passes through a circuit. Some distortion originates within the signal generator itself; other forms result from circuits and devices transmitting the signal. **3.** Any degradation in the quality of a high-fidelity audio signal. **4.** See TOTAL HARMONIC DISTORTION.

distortionless   **1.** Having no distortion. **2.** Having a propagation velocity that does not depend on frequency.

distortion meter   An instrument for measuring harmonic distortion. It consists of a highly selective band-rejection filter (notch filter) that removes the fundamental frequency of the signal under test, and a sensitive voltmeter that can be switched between the filter input and the filter output. The distortion percentage is determined from the ratio between filter-output and filter-input voltages.

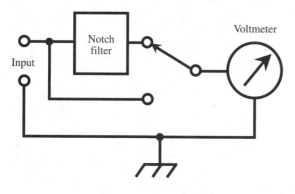

distortion meter

distortion tolerance   The maximum amount of distortion that can be present in a signal without making it useless. This varies over wide limits. The maximum harmonic distortion that might be acceptable in a high-fidelity sound system could be less than 0.1% total, whereas in some applications of ac power, 10% would be acceptable.

distress frequency   A radio frequency on which an emergency signal is transmitted. Ships at sea and aircraft over the sea use 500 kHz (by international agreement). In Citizen Band communications, channel 9 has been set aside for emergency use.

distress signal   A signal indicating that trouble exists at the transmitting station and imploring aid from the recipient. The international radiotelegraph distress signal is the three-letter combination *SOS*; the international radiotelephone distress signal is the word *mayday*, the phonetic equivalent of the French *m'aidez* (help me).

distributed   Existing over a measurable interval, area, or volume; not concentrated in a single place or places.

distributed amplifier   A wideband, untuned amplifier whose active devices are spaced (distributed) along parallel, artificial delay lines consisting of coils that act in combination with the input and output capacitances of the active devices. Adding active devices to the lineup increases the gain. Commonly used as preamplifiers for television receivers.

distributed capacitance   Symbol, C_d. Capacitance that is dispersed throughout a component or system, rather than being lumped in one place. An example is the distributed capacitance of a coil.

distributed component   An electrical property that is spread throughout a circuit or device, rather than being concentrated at one point, as in a discrete component. For example, DISTRIBUTED CAPACITANCE and DISTRUBUTED INDUCTANCE are spread along the length of a transmission line. Another example is the DISTRIBUTED RESISTANCE of a wire coil. Distributed components are often unintended, but they can be useful. Compare DISCRETE COMPONENT and LUMPED COMPONENT.

distributed constant   See DISTRIBUTED COMPONENT.

distributed-constant delay line   A delay line whose capacitance and inductance are distributed throughout the line. Compare LUMPED-CONSTANT DELAY LINE.

distributed inductance   Symbol, L_d. Inductance that is dispersed throughout a system or component, rather than being lumped in one place, such as in a coil (e.g., the inductance of an antenna or capacitor).

distributed network   **1.** A network in which electrical properties (such as resistance, inductance, and capacitance) are distributed over a measurable interval, area, or volume. **2.** A network whose characteristics do not depend on frequency within a given range.

distributed-parameter network   A network composed of distributed components, rather than lumped components.

distributed pole In a motor or generator, a pole having a DISTRIBUTED WINDING.

distributed resistance Symbol, R_d. Resistance that is dispersed throughout a component or circuit, rather than being lumped in one place, such as in a resistor. An example is the high-frequency resistance of an antenna system.

distributed-shell transformer A transformer having two complete closed cores that are perpendicular to each other.

distributed winding In a motor or generator, a winding that is placed in several slots (rather than in one slot) under a pole piece.

distributing amplifier An amplifier having a single input and two or more outputs that are isolated from each other; it distributes signals to various points.

distributing cable 1. In cable television, the cable connecting the receiver to the transmission cable. 2. In power service, the cable running between a feeder and a consumer's house.

distribution 1. The selective delivery of a quantity (e.g., *power distribution*). 2. In statistical analysis, the number of times particular values of a variable appear. Also called *frequency distribution*.

distribution amplifier A low-output-impedance power amplifier that distributes a radio, television, or audio signal to a number of receivers or speakers.

distribution cable See DISTRIBUTING CABLE.

distribution center 1. The central point from which a signal is routed to various points of use. 2. In electric power operations, the point at which generation, conversion, and control equipment is operated to route power to points of use.

distribution factor For a polyphase alternator, the factor by which the total voltage V_T can be determined in terms of the coil voltage V_C and the number of coils n: $V_T = nV_C$. Distribution factor $k_d = (\sin(sd/2))/(s \times \sin(d/2))$, where s is the number of slots per phase per pole, and d is the angle between adjacent slots.

distribution function In statistical analysis, the function $F(x)$ expressing the probability that F takes on a value equal to or less than x.

distribution switchboard 1. A switchboard through which signals can be routed to or among various points. 2. A switchboard for routing electric power to points of use.

distribution transformer A step-down transformer used to supply low-voltage alternating-current (ac) utility power to one or more consumers from a high-voltage line.

distributor 1. See COMMUTATOR. 2. A switching device consisting of a rotating blade and a number of contacts arranged in a circle. Accomplishes sequential switching of a voltage to a number of points in a circuit. A common example is the distributor in the ignition system of an automotive engine.

disturbance An undesired variation in, or interference with, an electrical or physical quantity.

disturbed-one output In digital computers, the one output of a magnetic cell that has received only a partial write pulse train because it was last written into. Compare UNDISTURBED-ONE OUTPUT.

disturbed-zero output In digital computers, the zero output of a magnetic cell that has received only a partial write pulse train since it was last read from. Compare UNDISTURBED-ZERO OUTPUT.

dither 1. Vibrate; quiver. 2. The condition of vibration or quivering (e.g., the dither of a meter pointer). 3. To blend pixels in a digitized image to obtain various shades and colors.

divergence 1. The tendency of a collimated beam of energy to spread out. 2. The extent to which a collimated beam of energy spreads out, generally measured in seconds of arc, minutes of arc, angular degrees, or angular radians.

divergence loss Loss of transmitted sound energy, resulting from spreading.

diverging lens A lens having a virtual focus for parallel rays; generally a *concave lens*.

diversity 1. The property of consisting of two or more independent components or media. 2. See DIVERSITY RECEPTION. 3. See DIVERSITY TRANSMISSION.

diversity factor 1. A measure of the degree to which a system exhibits unity among its constituents. 2. The sum of the requirements of each constituent of a system, divided by the total requirement of the system.

diversity gain 1. Signal gain achieved by using two or more receiving antennas. 2. Signal gain achieved by using two or more transmitting antennas.

diversity reception Also called *dual-diversity reception*. A method of minimizing the effects of fading in ionospheric communication at high frequencies (HF). Accomplished using two receivers whose antennas are 5 to 10 wavelengths apart. Each receiver, tuned to the same signal, feeds a common audio amplifier. The timing of the fading is different at the two antennas because of phasing effects. The composite signal, therefore, fades less than either of the component signals. Some diversity systems use three or more antennas and receivers to reduce the effects of fading even further; this is sometimes called *multiple-diversity reception*.

diversity transmission Also called *dual-diversity transmission* or *multiple-diversity transmission*. A scheme similar to DIVERSITY RECEPTION, except applied at the transmitting end of a communication circuit. The signals from two or more transmitters, at identical frequencies, are fed to antennas spaced several wavelengths apart.

diverter-pole generator A well-regulated direct-current (dc) generator, whose shunt winding is

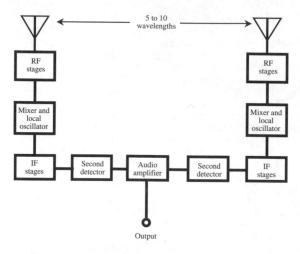

diversity reception

on the main field pole, the series winding being on a diverter pole whose flux opposes that of the main pole.

divide-by-seven circuit   A three-stage binary circuit having feedback from stage three to stage one. Stage three is switched on by the fourth input pulse; at that time, the feedback pulse switches on stage one, simulating one input pulse and reducing the usual counting capacity from eight to seven.

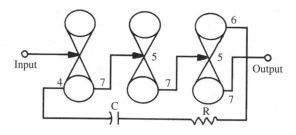

divide-by-seven circuit

divide-by-two circuit   A circuit that delivers one output pulse for each two successive input pulses (i.e., a *flip-flop*).

divided-carrier modulation   Modulation obtained by adding two identical frequency carriers that are 90 degrees out of phase.

divided circuit   A *parallel circuit.*

divided equipment   A system of modular electronic components interconnected with cables. A simple example is a radio receiver having an external power supply and external loudspeaker.

divider   **1.** See VOLTAGE DIVIDER. **2.** See FREQUENCY DIVIDER. **3.** See PULSE-COUNT DI-

VIDER. **4.** A computing circuit or device for performing mathematical division.

divider probe   A test probe that divides an applied signal voltage by some factor (such as 2, 5, or 10) to place it within the range of the instrument with which the probe is used.

dividing network   See CROSSOVER NETWORK.

division   **1.** Separating a quantity into a number of equal parts, as indicated by the divisor. **2.** Voltage division (see VOLTAGE DIVIDER). **3.** Frequency division (see FREQUENCY DIVIDER). **4.** Pulse-count division (see PULSE-COUNT DIVIDER).

division of vectors   **1.** The quotient of two rectangular vectors determined by the principle of rationalization in algebra (i.e., by multiplying the numerator and denominator of the indicated division by the conjugate of the denominator, simplifying, and performing the division). **2.** To find the quotient of two polar vectors: the quotient of their moduli and the difference of their arguments.

dj   Abbreviation of *diffused junction.*

DKT   Abbreviation of *dipotassium tartrate.*

D layer   A layer of the ionosphere that is below the E layer; its altitude is approximately 60 kilometers.

dm   Abbreviation of *decimeter.*

DMA   Abbreviation of DIRECT MEMORY ACCESS and *direct memory addressing.*

DME   Abbreviation of DISTANCE-MEASURING EQUIPMENT.

DMM   Abbreviation of DIGITAL MULTIMETER.

DMOS   Abbreviation for *double-diffused metal-oxide semiconductor*, a type of field-effect transistor that exhibits extremely low capacitance and low source-drain resistance when conducting.

DNL   See DIFFERENTIAL NONLINEARITY.

DNS   Abbreviation of *Doppler navigation system.*

doctor   To use unconventional (sometimes substandard) methods in fixing a circuit or device or in correcting a bad design.

document   **1.** In digital computer operations, especially in file maintenance, a form that provides information pertinent to a transaction. Also see TRANSACTION. **2.** To perform documentation (see DOCUMENTATION, **2**). **3.** A computer text file.

documentation   **1.** Paperwork explaining the scope of programs and how they can be optimized. **2.** Annotating a computer program at critical points during its writing (e.g., so that the purpose of various segments are understood). A measure of good programming, documentation becomes especially valuable for program modification or debugging.

document reader   An electronic device that reads printed cards, usually for data entry into a computer.

dog   **1.** A malfunctioning circuit or device. **2.** The cause of a circuit or device malfunction.

doghouse An enclosure for antenna loading inductors and other resonating components, placed at the base of a vertical broadcasting tower.

dog whistle See ULTRASONIC WHISTLE.

Doherty amplifier A highly efficient linear radio-frequency (RF) amplifier in which a *carrier tube* and a *peak tube* operate jointly, both receiving amplitude-modulated RF excitation. During unmodulated intervals, the carrier tube supplies carrier power to the load, while the peak tube, biased to cutoff, idles. On positive modulation peaks, the peak tube supplies output power that combines with that of the carrier tube, the increase in power corresponding to the condition of full modulation of the carrier. On negative modulation peaks, the peak tube does not supply power, and the output of the carrier tube is reduced to zero.

Dolby An electronic method of improving the audio reproduction quality of magnetic-tape systems. The gain is increased for low-level sounds during the recording process. During playback, the gain of the low-level sounds is reduced back to its original level.

Dolby A A Dolby system with four frequency ranges, operated independently. It is used mostly by recording professionals.

Dolby B A modified form of Dolby A, with only one band of noise-reducing circuitry. It is used primarily by hobbyists.

Dolezalek electrometer See QUADRANT ELECTROMETER.

dolly 1. A low, wheeled frame or platform for transporting electronic equipment. 2. A tool with which one end of a rivet is held while the head is hammered out of the other end.

DOM Abbreviation of DIGITAL OHMMETER.

domain 1. A region of unidirectional magnetization in a magnetic material. 2. A region of unidirectional polarization in a ferroelectric material. 3. A region in which a variable is confined.

domestic electronics Also called *consumer electronics*. The branch of electronics concerned with appliances, automatic controls, protective devices, entertainment systems, communications devices, and other equipment for the home.

domestic induction heater A household cooking utensil heated by currents induced in it. A primary coil (connected to the power line) is imbedded in the utensil, which acts as a short-circuited secondary coil.

dome tweeter A speaker designed for high-frequency (treble), high-fidelity audio, and often functional at frequencies considerably above the limit of the human hearing. Characterized by a convex diaphragm. Usually part of an assembly including a woofer and midrange speaker.

dominant In statistical analysis, the nature of any quantity that imposes its effects even in the presence of other quantities.

dominant mode In a waveguide, the propagation mode exhibiting the lowest cutoff frequency.

dominant wave In a waveguide, the wave having the lowest cutoff frequency.

dominant wavelength For visible light of a given hue, the wavelength at which the emitted energy is the greatest.

donor An electron-rich impurity added to a semiconductor to make it into an n-type material. So called because it donates its excess electrons. Compare ACCEPTOR.

donor atom An atom having an excess electron. When a substance having such atoms is added to an intrinsic semiconductor, the extra electron is donated, making the semiconductor into an n-type material.

donor impurity A substance whose atoms have excess electrons, and that donates electrons to the atomic structure of the semiconductor crystal to which it is added. Donor elements make semiconductors into n-type materials. Also see DONOR ATOM. Compare ACCEPTOR IMPURITY.

do-nothing instruction A computer program instruction that causes no action to be taken. Can be used to provide space for future program updating, or to fill out a block of instructions, as needed by a compiler. Also called *dummy instruction*.

don't-care state In a logic function or gate, an input digit whose state (high or low) does not affect the output.

donut capacitor A flat, ring-shaped capacitor.

donut coil See TOROIDAL COIL.

donut crystal A relatively large, zero-temperature-coefficient piezoelectric quartz crystal cut in the form of a torus with the y-axis passing through the center of rotation.

donut magnet See RING MAGNET.

donut pattern The three-dimensional radio-frequency (RF) radiation/response pattern of a free-space straight antenna element measuring ½ wavelength, neglecting the effects of ground and nearby objects.

doohickey A usually unnamed device—especially one used to achieve some significant modification of circuit performance.

doorknob capacitor A high-voltage fixed capacitor, so called from its round package, which somewhat resembles a doorknob.

doorknob tube A special UHF vacuum tube, so called from its characteristic shape. The unique design provides short electron-transit time and low interelectrode capacitance. Largely replaced in recent years by semiconductor devices.

dopant An impurity added in controlled amounts to a semiconductor to make it an n-type or p-type material. Also see ACCEPTOR and DONOR.

dope To add impurities to a semiconductor material. Doping allows the manufacture of n-type or p-type semiconductors with varying degrees of conductivity. In general, the greater the extent of doping, the higher the conductivity.

doped junction   In a semiconductor device, a junction produced by adding a dopant to the semiconductor melt.

doping   Adding a dopant to a semiconductor to alter the way it conducts current.

doping agent   See DOPANT.

doping compensation   Opposite doping (i.e., adding a donor impurity to p-type semiconductor material or adding an acceptor impurity to n-type semiconductor material).

doping gas   A gas diffused into a semiconductor material to dope it. For example, phosphorus pentoxide gas can be used to create an n-type region in a p-type silicon chip.

doping level   The relative concentration of impurity added to a semiconductor material to obtain a certain resistivity and polarity. The greater the doping level, the lower the resistivity.

Doppler broadening   In a spectrum, the spreading out or blurring of a spectral line caused by DOPPLER EFFECT, in turn resulting from motion of molecules, atoms, or other particles in the medium.

Doppler cabinet   A loudspeaker enclosure with which a vibrato effect is achieved by rotating or reciprocating either the loudspeaker or a baffle board; the length of the sound path is altered cyclically.

Doppler effect   A change in the frequency of a wave that occurs when the source and observer are in relative motion. The frequency of the wave increases (the wavelength shortens) as the source and observer approach each other; the frequency decreases (the wavelength becomes greater) as the source and observer recede from each other. This effect is often observed with sound waves, as when the pitch of an automobile horn seems to rise as the car approaches and to fall as the car passes. The effect is also observable in electromagnetic radiation at all wavelengths. It affects satellite communication and space communication.

Doppler enclosure   See DOPPLER CABINET.

Doppler radar   A radar that uses the change in carrier frequency of the signal returned by a moving target (approaching or receding) to measure its velocity. Used by law enforcement officers to determine the speed of moving vehicles. Also used by meteorologists to evaluate air circulation patterns in thunderstorms, and to determine wind speeds in hurricanes and tornadoes.

Doppler ranging   See DORAN.

Doppler shift   The extent to which the frequency or wavelength of a signal changes because of DOPPLER EFFECT. Can be measured in Hertz (for frequency) or in meters (for wavelength). In astronomy, the shift is also measured as displacement of absorption or emission lines in an infrared, visible, or ultraviolet spectrum.

Doppler's principle   See DOPPLER EFFECT.

doran   A continuous-wave trajectory-measuring system utilizing Doppler shift (see DOPPLER EFFECT). The name is a contraction of *doppler ranging*.

dorsal column stimulator   Abbreviation, DCS. A machine that generates radio-frequency energy that is applied to human tissues for the temporary relief of pain.

dosage meter   See DOSIMETER.

dose   The total quantity of radiation received upon exposure to nuclear radiation or X-rays.

dosimeter   An instrument for measuring the amount of exposure to nuclear radiation or X-rays.

dot   1. The shorter of the two characters (dot and dash) of the telegraph code. The dot, a short sound, mark, or perforation, is one-third the length (duration) of a dash. Compare DASH. 2. One of the small spots of red, green, or blue phosphor on the screen of a color-television picture tube or cathode-ray-tube (CRT) computer display. 3. A small spot of material alloyed with a semiconductor to form an alloy junction. 4. The junction of two lines on a schematic diagram, representing a wired connection; also called *solder dot*.

dot AND   Externally connected circuits or functions whose combined outputs result in an AND function. Compare DOT OR.

dot-and-dash telegraphy   Telegraphy (wire or radio) by means of dot and dash characters.

dot cycle   One period of an alternation between two signaling conditions, each of which is of unit duration (e.g., a unit mark followed by a unit space).

dot encapsulation   A method of packaging cylindrical components by pressing them into the holes of perforated disks; interconnections are made, to complete a circuit, on each face of the disks.

dot generator   A special radio-frequency (RF) signal generator used to produce a pattern of red, green, and blue dots on the screen of a color television receiver.

dot matrix   A rectangular array of spaces, some of which are filled in to form alphanumeric and punctuation characters.

dot-matrix display   A display that shows characters in dot-matrix form.

dot-matrix printer   A computer output peripheral that prints characters and images on paper as a fine grid of dots. A print head, containing several pins, presses the ribbon against the paper as it moves laterally across each line. Can be used to print text and/or graphics.

dot movement pattern   The movement of the red, green, and blue dots on the screen of a color television picture tube as the red, green, and blue magnets and the lateral magnet are adjusted for convergence of the dots at the cen-

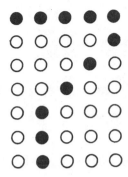

dot matrix

ter. The blue dots move horizontally or vertically; the red and green dots, diagonally.

dot OR Externally connected circuits or functions whose combined outputs result in an OR function. Compare DOT AND.

dot pattern In color television testing with a dot generator, dots of color (a red group, green group, and blue group) produced on the screen. With overall beam convergence, the three groups blend to produce white.

dot-sequential system The color television system in which the image is reproduced by means of primary-color dots (red, green, blue) sequentially activated on the screen of the picture tube. Compare FIELD-SEQUENTIAL SYSTEM and LINE-SEQUENTIAL SYSTEM.

double-amplitude-modulation multiplier A modulating system in which a carrier is amplitude-modulated first by one signal and then by a second signal. The resulting signal is fed to a detector, the output of which contains the product of the two modulating signals.

double-anode diode A semiconductor diode having two anodes and a common cathode.

double armature An armature (such as that of a dynamotor or a two-voltage generator) that has two separate windings on a single core, and has two separate commutators.

double-balanced mixer See BALANCED MIXER.

double-balanced modulator See BALANCED MODULATOR.

double-base diode See UNIJUNCTION TRANSISTOR.

double-base junction transistor A junction transistor having the usual emitter, base, and collector electrodes, plus two base connections, one on either side of the base region. The additional base connection acts as a fourth electrode to which a control voltage is applied. Also called *tetrode transistor*.

double-beam CRT See DUAL-BEAM OSCILLOSCOPE.

double-beam oscilloscope See DUAL-BEAM OSCILLOSCOPE.

double-bounce calibration In radar operations, a calibration technique for determining zero-beat error. Round-trip echoes are observed, the correct range being the difference between the two echoes.

double-bounce signal A signal that is received after having been reflected twice.

double-break contacts The member of a set of contacts that is normally closed on two others. Compare DOUBLE-MAKE CONTACTS.

double-break switch A switch that opens a previously closed circuit at two points simultaneously on closing. Compare DOUBLE-MAKE SWITCH.

double bridge See KELVIN DOUBLE BRIDGE.

double buffering In the input/output operation of a computer peripheral, the use of two memory areas for temporary storage.

double-button microphone A carbon microphone having two buttons mounted on each side of the center of a stretched diaphragm, and connected in push-pull. Also see BUTTON MICROPHONE.

double-channel duplex Two-way communication over two independent channels. One station transmits on one channel, and the other station transmits on the other channel. The result is conversation-mode communications, in which one operator can interrupt the other at any time; both receivers are always operational.

double-channel simplex A system of communication in which two channels are used. One station transmits on one channel, and the other station transmits on the other channel. Interruption is not possible because whenever either operator transmits, the station receiver is muted.

double-checkerboard pattern In a magnetic core memory, the maximum noise that appears when half of the half-selected cores are in the one state and the others are in the zero state. Also called *worst-case noise pattern*.

double circuit tuning A circuit whose output and input are tuned separately. Such tuning provides increased selectivity when the input and output are resonant at the same frequency, and decreased selectivity when they are tuned to different frequencies. Also see DOUBLE-TUNED AMPLIFIER.

double clocking A phenomenon that occurs in some digital circuits when the input pulse is nonuniform, and appears as two pulses to the device. The device is thus actuated at twice the desired frequency.

double-coil direction finder A radio direction finder (RDF) using an antenna that consists of two identical, perpendicular coils. The directivity of the antenna is the resultant of the directivity of the individual coils.

double conversion 1. Two complete frequency conversions in a superheterodyne system. For

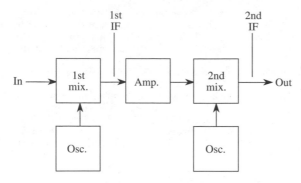

double conversion

example, the incoming signal might be converted to a 9-MHz first intermediate frequency (first IF); at a later stage, this signal might be converted to a 455-kHz second IF. The high first IF widely separates the signal from the image; the low second IF allows superior selectivity to be achieved at a reasonable cost. Also called *dual conversion.* **2.** Pertaining to a superheterodyne receiver with two intermediate frequencies.

double-conversion receiver   Also called *double-conversion superheterodyne.* A superheterodyne receiver using DOUBLE CONVERSION to achieve optimum selectivity and image rejection.

double-current generator   **1.** A dynamo-type generator supplying both alternating current (ac) and direct current (dc) from one armature winding. **2.** A rotary converter operating on dc and delivering ac.

double-diamond antenna   A broadband antenna consisting of two rhomboid plates, one attached to each side of the feeder.

double-diffused epitaxial mesa transistor   A transistor in which a thin mesa crystal is overlaid on another mesa crystal. Also called *epitaxial-growth mesa transistor.*

double-diffused transistor   See DIFFUSED-EMITTER-AND-BASE TRANSISTOR.

double diode   See DUODIODE.

double-diode limiter   A limiter in which two diodes are connected back to back in parallel, to limit both peaks of an alternating-current (ac) signal.

double-doped transistor   See GROWN-JUNCTION TRANSISTOR.

double edit   In audio tape recording, to make two changes in a given span of the tape. For example, a producer might dislike the wording of a certain sentence, and re-record the sentence. Then, changing his or her mind, the producer might record the original sentence back over the re-recorded sentence. These changes increase the risk of audible irregularities appearing in the final recording.

double emitter follower   See COMPOUND CONNECTION.

double-ended amplifier   See PUSH-PULL AMPLIFIER and DOUBLE-ENDED CIRCUIT.

double-ended circuit   A symmetrical circuit (i.e., one having identical halves, each operating on a half-cycle of the input signal). Example: a push-pull amplifier.

double-extended Zepp antenna   A horizontal, collinear, center-fed antenna, in which each section measures 0.65 wavelength. This antenna gives increased gain over that of the Zepp and double Zepp (see DOUBLE ZEPP ANTENNA).

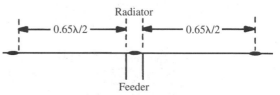

double-extended Zepp antenna

double-hump resonance curve   A resonant response that is flattened by double tuning; it exhibits two resonance peaks. Also see DOUBLE-TUNED AMPLIFIER.

double-hump wave   See DOUBLE-PULSE WAVE.

double image   Two overlapping television pictures, one usually fainter than the other. Caused by the signal arriving over two different paths (one possibly attributable to reflection of the wave) and, hence, at different instants in time. The fainter image is called a GHOST.

double insulation   The use of two layers of insulation on a conductor, made of different materials.

double ionization   Ionization resulting from an electron colliding with an ion. In a gas, for example, a neutral atom might collide with an electron, which can knock an electron out of the atom. The atom then becomes a positive ion; it might in turn be bombarded by an electron, releasing still another electron.

double-junction photosensitive semiconductor   See PHOTOTRANSISTOR.

double layer   See HELMHOLTZ DOUBLE LAYER.

double local oscillator   A mixer system in which a local oscillator generates two accurate radio-frequency (RF) signals separated by a few hundred hertz. The difference frequency is used as a reference in some applications.

double-make contacts   A set of normally open contacts of which one closes against two others simultaneously. Compare DOUBLE-BREAK CONTACTS.

double-make switch   A switch that closes a previously open circuit at two points simultaneously. Compare DOUBLE-BREAK SWITCH.

double moding   In microwave operations, the abrupt changing of frequency at irregular intervals.

double modulation   Using a modulated carrier to modulate another carrier of a different frequency.

double-play tape   A thin magnetic recording tape that has approximately twice the playing time of the usual tape. Although the playing time is longer, double-play tape is more subject to jamming and stretching than standard-thickness recording tape.

double-pole   Having two poles or switchable circuits (e.g., a double-pole switch).

double-pole, double-throw switch or relay   Abbreviation, DPDT. A switch or relay having two contacts that can be closed simultaneously in one of two directions, to close or open two circuits.

double precision   The use of two computer words to represent a single number to gain precision.

double-pole, single-throw switch or relay   Abbreviation, DPST. A switch or relay having two contacts that can be closed in only one direction, to simultaneously close or open two circuits.

double precision hardware   Within a computer, arithmetic units permitting the use of double-precision operands, sometimes also accommodating floating-point arithmetic.

double-precision number   In digital computer operations, a number represented by two words for greater precision.

double pulse reading   Pertaining to a magnetic core in a computer memory, recording bits as two states held simultaneously by one core having two areas that can be magnetized with alternate polarities. For example, positive-negative could represent zero, and negative-positive could represent one.

double-pulse wave   An alternating-current (ac) wave having two successive positive peaks followed by two successive negative peaks within each cycle. The output voltage of a varistor bridge has such a waveshape for an ac input.

double-pulsing station   A loran station that transmits at two pulse rates upon receiving two pairs of pulses.

double pumping   A method of obtaining increased peak output power from a laser by pumping it for a comparatively long interval and then immediately pumping it for a short interval.

doubler   **1.** A circuit or device for multiplying a frequency by two (see FREQUENCY DOUBLER). **2.** A circuit or device for multiplying a voltage by two (see VOLTAGE DOUBLER).

double probe   A test probe that multiplies an applied signal voltage by two, so it can be handled more effectively by the instrument with which the probe is used.

double punching   In perforating a punched card, putting two holes in one column; it is an error if it occurs in a field of a card that is part of a record.

double rail   A form of logic system in which two lines are used, with three possible states. The output can be high, low, or undecided.

double response   **1.** Two-point response, as that associated with tuning a receiver to a signal and then to its image. **2.** See DOUBLE-HUMP RESONANCE CURVE.

double screen   A cathode-ray tube having a two-layer screen on which there is an additional, long-persistence coating of a different color.

double shield   Two independent electromagnetic shields for a circuit enclosure or cable. The shielding structures are concentric, and can be connected together at a single point (the common point).

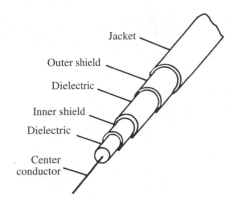

double shield

double sideband   Abbreviation, DSB. In a modulated signal, the presence of both sidebands.

double-sideband suppressed carrier   Abbreviation, DSSC. A transmission technique in which both sideband products of modulation are transmitted and the carrier is suppressed. Compare LOWER SIDEBAND, SUPPRESSED CARRIER, UPPER SIDEBAND, and SUPPRESSED CARRIER.

double-sideband system   A modulation or demodulation system utilizing both sidebands, with or without the carrier.

double-sideband transmitter   A modulated transmitter using a double-sideband system.

double signal   In reception, the property of having a signal on either side of the carrier frequency, as in a direct-conversion receiver. The two signals represent the sum and difference of the local oscillator signal and the actual received signal. Because the two signals convey identical information, the phenomenon is wasteful of received spectrum, and degrading to receiver selectivity and sensitivity.

double-signal receiver   A receiver, such as a direct-conversion type, in which the signals occur in replicated form on either side of the local oscillator signal. Compare SINGLE SIGNAL.

double-spot tuning   In a superheterodyne receiver, tuning in the same signal at two different places on the dial, a condition caused by image response.

double squirrel-cage induction motor   A polyphase induction motor having a double squirrel-cage rotor. The rotor slots contain two bars, an upper bar having low reactance (being near the air gap) and high resistance, and a lower bar having high reactance and low resistance. This motor has low starting current, high starting torque, and a full-load slip of less than 5%.

double-stream amplifier   A traveling-wave tube in which microwave amplification results from the interaction of two electron beams of different average velocity.

double-stub tuner   Two stubs (see STUB) connected in parallel with a transmission line and usually spaced 0.375 wavelength (135 electrical degrees) apart; it is used as an impedance matcher.

double superheterodyne   See DOUBLE-CONVERSION SUPERHETERODYNE.

double superheterodyne reception   See DOUBLE-CONVERSION SUPERHETERODYNE.

double-surface transistor   See COAXIAL TRANSISTOR.

doublet   1. A polarized atom (electric dipole). For example, an atom under electric stress in the dielectric of a capacitor behaves, as if it has a positive charge on one side and a negative charge on the other. 2. A system of two equal and opposite magnetic poles situated close together (magnetic dipole). 3. The waveform of the output voltage delivered by a linear-response delay line that is excited by a current step function (see UNIT FUNCTION). 4. See DOUBLET ANTENNA.

doublet antenna   Also called *dipole antenna*. A center-fed antenna consisting of a single, usually straight conductor measuring 0.5 wavelength.

double-throw   Operating in opposite directions as selected (e.g., a double-throw relay or switch).

double-throw circuit breaker   A circuit breaker that closes in both its pull-in and dropout positions.

double-throw switch or relay   A switch or relay having two ganged poles.

double-trace recorder   See DOUBLE-TRACK RECORDER, 2.

double tracing   Displaying two signals simultaneously on the screen of an oscilloscope through the use of an electronic switch.

double-track recorder   1. A tape recorder whose head is positioned so that separate recordings can be made as two tracks on the tape. 2. A graphic recorder that produces two separate parallel tracings.

doublet trigger   A two-pulse, constant-spaced trigger signal used for coding.

double-tuned amplifier   An amplifier whose input and output circuits are both tuned.

double-tuned circuit   A circuit, such as an amplifier or filter, using separate input and output tuning. Also see DOUBLE CIRCUIT TUNING and DOUBLE-TUNED AMPLIFIER.

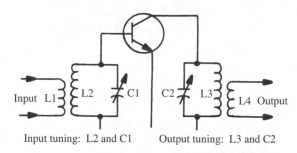

Input L1   L2   C1   C2   L3   L4 Output

Input tuning: L2 and C1   Output tuning: L3 and C2

double-tuned circuit

double-tuned detector   A form of frequency-modulation (FM) discriminator with two resonant circuits. One is tuned slightly higher than the channel center frequency, and the other is tuned an equal amount below the center.

double-vee antenna   A broadband, modified dipole antenna resembling two vees in line. Also see VEE ANTENNA.

double-winding generator   A dynamo-type generator having separate armature windings for supplying two voltages, either of which can be direct (dc voltage) or alternating (ac voltage).

double-wye rectifier   A heavy-load circuit using six rectifier diodes, each conducting for 120 degrees of the cycle. An interphase winding is used. The circuit is equivalent to two three-phase, half-wave rectifiers connected in parallel.

double-Y rectifier   See DOUBLE-WYE RECTIFIER.

double Zepp antenna   A usually horizontal, straight, center-fed, full-wavelength antenna. Also called *two half waves in phase*. Its name was derived because it is, in fact, two Zepp antennas forming a collinear array.

doubling   1. Producing the second harmonic of a signal. 2. In communication, unintentional simultaneous transmission by both operators, resulting in missed information. 3. In a speaker, distortion resulting in large amounts of second-harmonic output.

doubly balanced modulator   See BALANCED MODULATOR.

doughnut capacitor   See DONUT CAPACITOR.

doughnut coil   See TOROIDAL COIL.

doughnut crystal   See DONUT CRYSTAL.

doughnut magnet   See RING MAGNET.

down convert   In superheterodyne conversion, to heterodyne a signal to an intermediate frequency lower than the signal frequency. Compare UP CONVERT.

down lead   See LEAD-IN.

downlink   The signal sent down from an active communications satellite to the earth, usually on a different frequency than the signal sent up. See UPLINK.

downlink beamwidth   The angle subtended between the half-power points of the downlink signal from an active communications satellite.

downlink frequency   The frequency of the downlink signal from an active communications satellite. Usually, the downlink signals occupy a certain band of frequencies, anywhere from several kilohertz to several megahertz wide.

downlink power   **1.** The output power of the downlink transmitter in an active communications satellite. **2.** The effective radiated power (ERP) of the downlink signal from an active communications satellite.

down time   A period of time during which electronic equipment is completely inoperative (for any reason).

downturn   A usually sudden dip in a performance curve. Compare UPTURN.

downward modulation   Modulation in which the average carrier component decreases during modulation. Example: amplitude modulation of a transmitter in which the antenna current decreases during modulation. Compare UPWARD MODULATION.

DP   Abbreviation of DATA PROCESSING.

DPDT   Abbreviation of *double-pole, double-throw* (switch or relay).

DPM   **1.** Abbreviation of *digital power meter.* **2.** Abbreviation of DIGITAL PANEL METER. **3.** Abbreviation of *disintegrations per minute.*

DPS   Abbreviaton of *disintegrations per second.*

DPST   Abbreviation of *double-pole, single-throw* (switch or relay).

dr   Abbreviation of *dram.*

drag   **1.** A retarding force, caused by friction, acting on a moving body in contact with another moving or stationary body or medium. **2.** A retarding force introduced by an applied magnetic or electric field.

drag angle   In disk recording, an angle of less than 90° between the stylus and the disk. The acute angle causes the stylus to drag instead of digging in.

drag cup   A cup of nonmagnetic metal (usually copper or aluminum) that, when rotated in a magnetic field, acquires a voltage proportional to the speed of rotation. The device is often used as a brake.

drag-cup motor   A servomotor whose shaft has a copper or aluminum drag cup that rotates in the field of a two-phase stator. Eddy currents

set up in the cup by the field winding produce torque; braking action, direction control, and speed control are obtainable by means of associated electronics.

drag magnet   In a motor-type meter, a braking magnet (i.e., one used to reduce speed through eddy-current effects). Also called *retarding magnet.*

drain   **1.** The current or power drawn from a signal or power source. **2.** A load that absorbs current or power. **3.** The electrode in a field-effect transistor (FET) from which the output is usually taken; equivalent to the collector of a bipolar transistor.

drainage equipment   Devices and systems for protecting circuits against transients generated by circuit breakers and similar safety devices.

drain-coupled multivibrator   An oscillator that uses two field-effect transistors (FETs) in the circuit equivalent of a collector-coupled bipolar-transistor multivibrator. The drain of one stage is capacitance-coupled to the gate of the other stage.

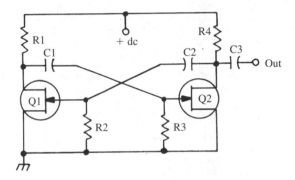

drain-coupled multivibrator

D-region   A low region of the ionosphere beneath the E-region, whose ionization varies with the inclination of the sun. The greatest ionization is at midday; the layer disappears at night.

dress   The (usually experimental) arrangement of leads for optimum circuit operation (minimum capacitance, best suppression of oscillation, minimum pickup, etc.).

dressed contact   A contact having a permanently attached locking spring member.

drift   **1.** Within a conductor or semiconductor, the controlled, directed movement of charge carriers resulting from an applied electric field. **2.** A usually gradual and undesirable change in a quantity, such as current, as a result of a disturbing factor, such as temperature or age.

drift current   In a semiconductor, the current resulting from a flow of charge carriers in the presence of an electric field. The charge carriers are electrons in n-type material and holes in p-type material.

drift field   The inherent internal electric field of a DRIFT-FIELD TRANSISTOR.

drift-field transistor   An alloy-junction, bipolar, radio-frequency (RF) transistor for which the impurity concentration is graded from high on the emitter side of the base wafer to low on the collector side. This creates an internal drift field that accelerates current carriers and raises the upper frequency limit of the transistor.

drift-matched components   Active or passive components that have been closely matched in terms of the drift of one or more parameters, with respect to time, temperature, etc.

drift mobility   For current carriers in a semiconductor, the average drift velocity per unit electric field.

drift space   **1.** In a vacuum tube, a space that is nearly free of alternating-current (ac) fields from the outside, and in which the repositioning of electrons is governed by the space-charge forces and the velocity distribution of the electrons. **2.** In a Klystron, the space between buncher and catcher cavities in which there is no field.

drift speed   The average velocity of charge carriers moving through a medium.

drift transistor   See DRIFT-FIELD TRANSISTOR.

drift velocity   The net velocity of a charged particle (electron, hole, or ion) in the direction of the field applied to the conducting medium.

drift voltage   The usually gradual change in voltage resulting from such causes as internal heating. Also called voltage drift.

drip loop   In a transmission line for an antenna or power service, a loop near the point of entry to the building for the purpose of allowing condensation or rain water to drip off.

drip-proof motor   A motor with ventilating apertures arranged so that moisture and particles cannot enter the machine.

drip-tight enclosure   A housing designed to prevent entry of rain, snow, and dust; it also prevents accidental contact with the enclosed apparatus or machinery.

drive   **1.** To excite (i.e., to supply with input-signal current, power, or voltage) (see DRIVING CURRENT, DRIVING POWER, and DRIVING VOLTAGE). **2.** Input-signal excitation (see DRIVING CURRENT, DRIVING POWER, and DRIVING VOLTAGE). **3.** A device that moves a recording medium (e.g., *tape drive* and *diskette drive*). **4.** The transmission of mechanical energy from one place to another (e.g., *motor drive*).

drive array   A set of two or more hard-disk drives in a computer system. They function together to minimize the possibility of data loss. Such a system can also increase the amount of fast-access data storage.

drive belt   A continuous belt used to transmit mechanical energy from a driving pulley to a driven pulley.

drive circuit   **1.** A circuit used to provide the excitation to a motor. **2.** An amplifier that supplies drive to a more powerful amplifier.

drive control   In a television receiver, the potentiometer used to adjust the ratio of horizontal pulse amplitude to the level of the linear portion of the sawtooth scanning-current wave.

driven element   In a multielement antenna, an element to which electromagnetic energy is fed directly, as opposed to a PARASITIC ELEMENT, which is excited by a nearby radiator element.

driven-element directive antenna   A multielement directional antenna whose elements are driven from the feed line (i.e., no element is parasitic). Compare PARASITIC-ELEMENT DIRECTIVE ANTENNA.

driven multivibrator   A multivibrator whose operation or frequency is controlled by an external synchronizing or triggering voltage. Compare FREE-RUNNING MULTIVIBRATOR.

driven single sweep   A single oscilloscope sweep that is initiated by the signal under observation.

drive pattern   A pattern of interference in a facsimile system that is caused by improper synchronization of the recording spot.

driven sweep   An oscilloscope sweep that is initiated by the signal under observation.

drive pin   A pin used to prevent a record from slipping on the rotating turntable of a recorder or reproducer. It is similar to, and located near, the center pin of the turntable.

drive pulse   In digital computer operations, a pulse that magnetizes a cell in a memory bank.

driver   **1.** A device that supplies a useful amount of signal energy to another device to ensure its proper operation (e.g., a current driver for a magnetic-core memory, an oscillator driving a loudspeaker). **2.** A power amplifier stage that supplies signal power to a higher-powered amplifier stage. **3.** In a digital computer, a stage that increases the output current or power of another stage (e.g., a clock driver). **4.** The cone and magnet of a dynamic speaker.

driver element   In a multielement directive antenna, the element excited directly by the feeder, the other elements (directors and reflectors) being parasitic.

driver impedance   **1.** The output impedance of a driver stage. **2.** The impedance "seen" from the driven stage of an amplifier, through the driver transformer, to the driver stage. It is the vector sum of driver reactance and resistance.

driver inductance   In an amplifier's driver transformer, the inductance, as "seen" looking through the transformer from the driven stage into the driver stage.

driver resistance   In an amplifier's driver transformer, the resistance "seen" looking through the transformer from the driven stage into the driver stage.

driver stage An amplifier stage whose chief purpose is to supply excitation (input-signal current, power, or voltage) to the next stage. Also see DRIVER.

driver transformer The transformer that couples a driver stage to a driven stage. Example: the interstage transformer inserted between the collector of a single-ended driver transistor and the two bases of a push-pull power-output stage in an audio amplifier.

driving current In a power amplifier, the input signal current required to produce a given amount of output power.

driving-point admittance The reciprocal of DRIVING-POINT IMPEDANCE.

driving-point impedance The input impedance of a network.

driving power In a power amplifier, the input signal power required to produce a given amount of output power.

drive wire The wire forming the coil around the toroidal cell in a magnetic core memory; supplies pulses that magnetize the cell.

driving-range potential In cathodic protection, the difference of potential between the anode and (protected) cathode.

driving signal 1. Drive (see DRIVE, **2**). **2.** In television, time-scanning signals (line-frequency pulses and field-frequency pulses) at the pickup location.

driving spring In a stepping relay, the spring that moves the wiper blades.

driving voltage In a power amplifier, the input signal voltage required to produce a given amount of output power.

DRO Abbreviation of DIGITAL READOUT.

drone A pilotless radio-controlled aircraft without a human pilot.

drone cone An undriven loudspeaker cone that is mounted in a bass-reflex enclosure with other speakers. Also called PASSIVE RADIATOR.

droop 1. A dip in the graph of a function. **2.** In a pulse train, the decrease in mean amplitude (in percent of maximum amplitude) at a given instant after attainment of maximum amplitude.

drooping radials In a ground-plane antenna, radials that slope downward to provide a transmission-line impedance match. The slope angle depends on the characteristic impedance of the

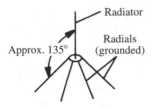

drooping radials

line; typically, the angle is between 45 degrees and 70 degrees, relative to horizontal.

drop 1. In wire communications, the line connecting a telephone cable to a subscriber's building. **2.** See VOLTAGE DROP.

drop bar A device that automatically grounds or short-circuits a capacitor when the door of a protective enclosure is opened.

drop cable See DISTRIBUTING CABLE, **1**.

drop channel In a communications system utilizing several channels, a channel that is not used.

drop-in The unintentional creation of bits when a magnetic storage device is being read from or written into. Compare DROP-OUT, **4**.

drop indicator In a signaling system, such as an annunciator, a hinged flap that drops into view when the signaling device is actuated.

drop-out 1. The opening of a relay or circuit breaker. **2.** In digital computer operations, variation in signal level of the reproduced tape-recorded data. Such variation can result in errors in data reproduction. **3.** In the production of monolithic circuits, a special image placed at a desired point on the photomask. **4.** Digit loss during a read or write operation involving a magnetic storage device.

dropout current See DROPOUT VALUE.

dropout power See DROPOUT VALUE.

dropout value The level of current, power, or voltage at which a device, such as a circuit breaker or relay, is released.

dropout voltage See DROPOUT VALUE.

dropping resistor A series resistor providing a voltage reduction equal to the voltage drop across itself. For example, a 1000-ohm resistor in series with a 45-V battery, and carrying a current of 10 mA, will provide a voltage reduction equal to 10 V ($IR = 0.01 \times 1000 = 10$ V), thus dropping the 45 V to 35 V.

drop relay In a telephone system, a relay that is activated by the ringing signal. The relay is used to switch on a buzzer, light, or other device.

drop repeater A repeater intended for a termination of a communications circuit in a telephone system.

dropsonde A parachute-supported radiosonde dropped from a high-flying aircraft.

drop-tracks The tracks of radioactive particles made visible by moisture in an ionization chamber.

drop wire A wire that runs from a building to a pole (for line extension) or to a cable terminal (for cable extension).

drum 1. A rotating cylinder coated with a magnetic material on which digital information can be recorded in the form of tiny magnetized spots. These spots are read as the drum rotates under pickup heads, or erased when the stored information is no longer needed. **2.** In some graphic recorders, facsimile receivers, etc., a rotating cylinder carrying the recording sheet.

drum capacitor See CONCENTRIC CAPACITOR.

drum controller The device that regulates the recording process on a drum memory.

drum mark On a track of a magnetic drum, a character that signifies the end of a character group.

drum memory In digital computers, a memory based on a magnetic drum (see DRUM, **1**). They have been largely replaced in recent years by electronic random-access memory, in the form of integrated circuits (ICs) and/or PCMCIA standard adapter cards.

drum parity The degree of accuracy in a drum recording/reproducing system.

drum programmer A device for sequencing operations. Its heart is a rotating drum, around whose surface contacts or points can be placed to actuate or terminate operations at selected times.

drum receiver A facsimile receiver using recording paper or photographic film wound around a revolving drum.

drum recorder A graphic recorder in which the record sheet is wound around a rotating drum.

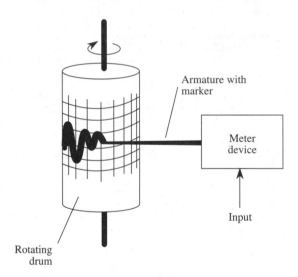

Armature with marker

Meter device

Input

Rotating drum

drum recorder

drum resistor A resistor consisting of a hollow cylinder of resistive material. Such a resistor can be cooled by circulating air or liquid through the cylinder.

drum speed The speed, usually measured in revolutions per minute (rpm), of the rotating drum in a graphic recorder, facsimile transmitter, or facsimile receiver.

drum storage The storage of data as magnetic impulses on a cylindrical, or drum-shaped, medium. Largely supplanted in recent years by magnetic disks, optical disks, and magnetic tapes.

drum switch A sequential switch whose contacts are pins or teeth placed at points around the outside of a revolving drum.

drum transmitter A facsimile transmitter in which the sheet bearing the material to be transmitted is wound around a revolving drum.

drum-type controller A motor-driven drum switch arranged to time various operations through sequential switching.

drum varistor A varistor that is a hollow cylinder of nonlinear resistance material. This varistor can be cooled by circulating air or liquid through it.

drum winding In a motor or generator, an armature whose conductors are on the outer face of the core, the two branches of a turn lying under adjacent poles of opposite polarity.

drunkometer An instrument for testing the extent of alcoholic intoxication. It electronically measures blood alcohol content through analysis of the subject's breath.

dry In an electric cell, a term used to describe an electrolyte that is semiliquid or solid.

dry battery A battery of dry cells.

dry cell **1.** A Leclanche primary cell in which the positive electrode is carbon, the negative electrode is zinc, and the electrolyte is a gel of ammonium chloride and additives. Also see CELL and PRIMARY CELL. **2.** A cell whose electrolyte is a gel or paste.

dry circuit A circuit in which the maximum voltage is 50 mV and the maximum current 200 mA.

dry-contact rectifier See DRY-DISK RECTIFIER.

dry contacts Contacts that neither make nor break a circuit.

dry-disk rectifier A solid-state rectifier, such as a copper-oxide, magnesium-copper-sulfide, or selenium type, that consists of a metal disk coated with a semiconductor material. The name was originally used to distinguish this rectifier from the *wet electrolytic rectifier*.

dry electrolytic capacitor An electrolytic capacitor whose electrolyte is a paste or solid. Compare WET ELECTROLYTIC CAPACITOR.

dry flashover voltage The breakdown voltage between electrodes in dry air when all insulation is clean and dry.

dry pile A voltaic pile containing numerous disks silvered or tinned on one face and covered with manganese dioxide on the other.

dry reed A metal contact, generally used as a relay or switch, that moves toward or away from another fixed contact under the influence of a magnetic field.

dry-reed relay See DRY-REED SWITCH.

dry-reed switch A switch consisting of two thin, metallic strips (reeds) hermetically sealed in a glass tube. The tube is surrounded by a coil of wire. When a current flows in the coil, a magnetic field affects the reeds. In the *normally open dry-reed switch*, the magnetic field causes the reeds to come together and close the circuit. In the *normally closed dry-reed switch*, the magnetic field causes the reeds to separate, opening the circuit. Compare MERCURY-WETTED REED RELAY.

dry run 1. The preliminary operation of equipment for testing and appraisal. Such a procedure precedes putting the equipment into regular service. 2. A step-by-step, paper-and-pencil "run" of a computer program before it is machine-implemented.

dry shelf life The life of a battery cell stored without its electrolyte.

dry-transfer process A method of transferring printed-circuit patterns and panel labels from sheets by rubbing them onto the substrate or panel.

dry-type forced-air-cooled transformer A DRY-TYPE TRANSFORMER that is cooled by convection of air circulated by a blower or fan. This increases the amount of power that the transformer can safely handle.

dry-type self-cooled transformer A DRY-TYPE TRANSFORMER that is cooled by natural air circulation (convection), without the use of a blower or fan.

dry-type transformer A transformer that, rather than being immersed in oil, is cooled entirely by the circulation of air.

DSB Abbreviation of DOUBLE SIDEBAND.

DSBSC Abbreviation of DOUBLE-SIDEBAND SUPPRESSED CARRIER. Also abbreviated DSSC.

dsc Abbreviation of *double silk covered* (wire).

D scope A radar whose display resembles that of a C scope, the difference being that blip height gives an approximation of the distance.

D service A Federal Aviation Agency service providing radio broadcasts of weather data, notices to aircraft personnel, and other advisory messages.

dsp Abbreviation of *double silver plated*.

DSR Abbreviation of DYNAMIC SPATIAL RECONSTRUCTOR.

DSS Abbreviation of *direct station selection* (telephone).

DSSC Abbreviation of DOUBLE-SIDEBAND SUPPRESSED CARRIER. Also abbreviated DSBSC.

DT Abbreviation of DATA TRANSMISSION.

DTA Abbreviation of *differential thermoanalysis*.

DT-cut crystal A piezoelectric plate cut from a quartz crystal at an angle of rotation about the z-axis of –53 degrees. It has a zero temperature coefficient of frequency at approximately 30 degrees Celsius. Also see CRYSTAL AXES and CRYSTAL CUTS.

DTL Abbreviation of DIODE-TRANSISTOR LOGIC.

DTn Abbreviation of DOUBLE TINNED.

DTS 1. Abbreviation of DATA-TRANSMISSION SYSTEM. 2. Abbreviation of *digital telemetry system*.

DU Abbreviation of DUTY CYCLE.

dual 1. Pertaining to a combination of two components such as diodes, transistors, etc., in a single housing. The components are often carefully matched. Compare QUAD. 2. Pertaining to a device or circuit that behaves in a manner analogous to that of another operating with component and parameter counterparts. Thus, a current amplifier can be the dual of a voltage amplifier; a series-resonant circuit, the dual of a parallel-resonant circuit; or a field-effect transistor, the dual of a bipolar transistor.

dual-beam CRT A cathode-ray tube having two separate electron guns, for use in a dual-beam oscilloscope.

dual-beam oscilloscope Also called *dual-trace oscilloscope*. An oscilloscope having two electron guns and deflection systems; it can display two phenomena on the screen simultaneously for comparison.

dual capacitor 1. Two fixed capacitors combined in a single housing, sometimes sharing a common capacitor plate. 2. A two-section, ganged variable capacitor.

dual-channel amplifier An amplifier having two separate, independent channels (e.g., a stereo high-fidelity audio amplifier).

dual-cone speaker A speaker designed for a wide range of audio frequencies. One cone responds to the bass (low) and midrange audio frequencies, and a smaller cone responds to the treble (high) audio frequencies.

dual diode A discrete component consisting of two diodes in one package.

dual-diversity receiver A receiver or receiver system for DIVERSITY RECEPTION.

dual-diversity reception See DIVERSITY RECEPTION.

dual-emitter transistor A low-level silicon pnp chopper transistor of the planar passivated epitaxial type; it has two emitter electrodes.

dual-frequency calibrator A secondary frequency standard providing two fundamental test frequencies (e.g., 100 kHz and 1 MHz).

dual-frequency induction heater An induction heater whose work coils carry energy of two different frequencies. The coils heat the work either simultaneously or successively.

dual gate 1. A digital integrated circuit (IC) consisting of two logic gate units. 2. Pertaining to a field-effect transistor (FET) with two gates or gate electrode connections.

dual-gate FET A field-effect transistor with two gate (input) electrodes.

dual-gate MOSFET A metal-oxide-semiconductor field-effect transistor (MOSFET) with two gate (input) electrodes.

dual-inline package Abbreviation, DIP. A flat, molded integrated-circuit (IC) package having terminal pins along both long edges.

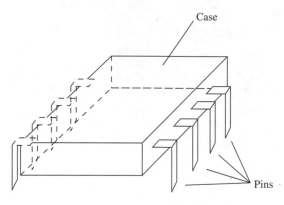

dual-inline package

duality   **1.** The condition of being dual (see DUAL). This can be an aid in the design of certain circuits requiring complementary parameters, e.g., current-operated circuit analogs of voltage-operated circuits. **2.** See DUALITY OF NATURE.

duality of nature   **1.** Any of various situations in which a phenomenon exhibits two distinct and different natures. A commonly cited example is the dual model of light. In some instances, visible light behaves like a barrage of particles, but in other environments it appears to be a wave effect. Another example is the dual model of electrostatic energy, behaving as point charges in some scenarios and as force fields in other situations. **2.** The tendency of a set of principles to be duplicated in sense by predictable analogies, as between inductance and capacitance, electrostatics and magnetics, etc.

dual local oscillator   See DOUBLE LOCAL OSCILLATOR.

dual meter   A meter having two meter movements and scales in a single case; the arrangement permits simultaneous monitoring of two quantities.

dual modulation   The modulation of a single carrier or subcarrier by two different types of modulation—each carrying different information.

dual network   A network that is the dual of another network having complementary parameters. For example, a common-emitter, current-sensitive, bipolar-transistor circuit is the dual of a common-source, voltage-sensitive, field-effect-transistor (FET) circuit. Also see DUALITY.

dual operation   In digital logic, the operation resulting from inverting all of the digits. Every 1 is replaced with a 0, and vice-versa.

dual-output power supply   A power supply with two outputs. Often, one output is positive and the other is negative. In some cases, one output consists of alternating current (ac) and the other consists of direct current (dc).

dual pickup   In disk reproduction, a pickup having two styli, one for large-groove records and one for fine-groove records.

dual potentiometer   A ganged assembly of two potentiometers. The resistance values might or might not be the same.

dual preset counter   A preset counter that will set alternately to two different numbers.

dual rail   See DOUBLE RAIL.

dual resistor   See DUAL POTENTIOMETER and DUAL RHEOSTAT.

dual rheostat   A ganged assembly of two rheostats. The resistance values might or might not be the same.

dual stereo amplifier   **1.** A two-channel audio amplifier for stereophonic audio applications. **2.** A two-channel linear integrated circuit (IC) for stereophonic audio applications.

dual-system loudspeaker   See TWO-WAY SPEAKER.

dual trace   In a cathode-ray oscilloscope, the use of two separate electron beams, which can show two different signals simultaneously on a single screen.

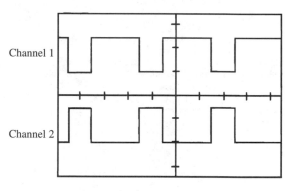

dual trace

dual-trace recorder   See DOUBLE-TRACK RECORDER, **2.**

dual-track recorder   See DOUBLE-TRACK RECORDER.

dual recording   In digital computer operations, updating two sets of master files simultaneously.

dual use   The use of a communications system for two modes of data transfer at the same time.

Duant electrometer   See BINANT ELECTROMETER.

duct   **1.** A narrow propagation path, sometimes traveled by microwaves, created by unusual atmospheric conditions. **2.** A pipe or channel for cables and wires.

dubbing   The adding of sound to a recorded magnetic tape, record disk, or film (e.g., replacing the sound track of a film in one language with that of another language).

duct **1.** A narrow propagation path, sometimes traveled by microwaves, created by unusual atmospheric conditions. **2.** A pipe or channel for cables and wires. **3.** An opening, vent, or other airway used for various purposes, such as cooling and acoustic wave transmission.

ducted port An opening in a speaker cabinet that has an airway (duct) extending several inches into the cabinet. It improves the quality of sound from a speaker system by equalizing the air pressure inside and outside the cabinet. Also provides resonant audio effects at frequencies that depend on the dimensions of the duct.

duct effect The creation of a duct (see DUCT, **1**) along which radio waves at some frequencies travel when temperature inversions are present in the atmosphere.

ductilimeter An instrument used for measuring the ductility of metals.

ducting The confinement of a radio wave to a duct (see DUCT, **1**) between two layers of the atmosphere or between an atmospheric layer and the earth.

Duddell arc A carbon copper arc circuit that produces audible continuous waves. Consists of a series inductance-capacitance (LC) circuit shunting an electric arc.

Duerdoth's multiple feedback system In an amplifier, feedback through several paths to improve response over that afforded by single-path feedback. In a simple application of multiple feedback, a single external loop is augmented with unbypassed emitter resistors in the amplifier stages.

Duerdoth's stability margin A feedback-amplifier stability margin equal to a 6-dB increase in gain at low and high frequencies over beta values between 0.3 and somewhat less than 2. For higher beta values, Duerdoth adopts an angular margin (for example, 15°); below $\beta = 0.3$, no danger of instability is present.

dummy **1.** A nonoperative model of a piece of equipment, usually assembled with dummy components (see DUMMY COMPONENT, **1**) for the purpose of developing a layout. **2.** DUMMY ANTENNA, DUMMY COMPONENT, or DUMMY LOAD. **3.** Part of a computer program that, rather than being useful for the problem at hand, only serves to satisfy some other format or logic requirement.

dummy antenna **1.** A nonradiating device that serves as a load for a transmitter (i.e., it takes the place of the regular antenna during tests and adjustments of the transmitter). **2.** A device containing a network of discrete inductive, capacitive, and resistive elements, inserted between a radio-frequency signal generator and receiver to simulate a standard antenna.

dummy component **1.** A nonoperative component used in developing a layout or package. **2.** A nonoperative component fraudulently included in a piece of equipment (e.g., an unwired transistor in a receiver circuit, a common occurrence during the early days of the transistor, when a 10-transistor radio brought more money than an 8-transistor radio, without regard to the circuit itself).

dummy instruction In a computer, a command that serves no operational purpose, other than to fill a format requirement.

dummy load **1.** A load device, usually consisting of resistance without reactance, used to terminate a power generator or power amplifier during adjustments and tests. The load resistance is equal to the output impedance of the generator or amplifier. **2.** See DUMMY ANTENNA.

dummy resistor A power-type resistor used as a dummy load.

dump **1.** In digital-computer operations, to transfer, completely or partially, the contents of memory into a peripheral. **2.** To switch off all power to a computer, deliberately or accidentally, thereby losing what is in the volatile memory.

dump and restart During a halt in a computer program run, to backtrack to the last dump point and use the data there to resume the run. Also see DUMP POINT.

dump check In digital-computer operations, the checking of all digits being transferred (see DUMP, **1**) to prevent errors when they are retransferred.

dumping To transfer the output at various stages in a computer program run to an external storage medium, so it will be available (in case of a failure) for the program's resumption from a point other than at the beginning.

dump point In writing a computer program, a point at which instructions are given to transfer data processed thus far to a storage medium that would be unaffected by a software or hardware failure. Also see DUMP AND RESTART and DUMPING.

dumping resistor **1.** See BLEEDER. **2.** A resistor having the minimum resistance permissible in a given situation. Used to discharge a capacitor, it acts to provide an alternative path to a potentially destructive short circuit.

duo Any pair of matched components, usually in a single package.

duodecal CRT base The 12-pin base of a cathode-ray tube. Also see BIDECAL, DIHEPTAL, and MAGNAL.

duodecal socket A 12-pin tube socket. Also see DUODECAL CRT BASE.

duodecimal **1.** Having 12 possibilities, states, choices, etc. **2.** Pertaining to the DUODECIMAL NUMBER SYSTEM. **3.** A number or numeral in the DUODECIMAL NUMBER SYSTEM.

duodecimal number system   A system of numbering in which the radix, also called the base or modulus, is 12. The system uses the digits 0 through 9, plus two other characters (usually A and B) to represent 10 and 11. Thus, counting proceeds as 0, 1, 2,. . ., 9, A, B, 10, 11, 12,. . ., 19, 1A, 1B, 20, 21, 22, etc. At one time, some people seriously proposed that this system replace the DECIMAL NUMBER SYSTEM for general use.

duodiode   See DUAL DIODE.

duolateral coil   A multilayer, lattice-wound coil (see UNIVERSAL WINDING) in which the turns in successive layers are staggered slightly. Also called *honeycomb coil.*

duopole   A two-pole all-pass device.

duplex   **1.** A mode of communication in which two channels are used so that either operator in a conversation can interrupt the other at any time. **2.** The transmission of two messages over a single circuit, at the same time.

duplex artificial line   In wire telephony, a balancing network that simulates the impedance of the actual line and the remote terminal equipment; it prevents an outgoing transmission from interfering with the local receiver.

duplex cable   A cable consisting of a twisted pair of insulated stranded-wire conductors.

duplex channel   A channel used for wire or radio DUPLEX OPERATION.

duplex communication   See DUPLEX OPERATION.

duplex diode   See DUAL DIODE.

duplexer   In radar operations, a device operated by the transmitted pulse to automatically switch the antenna from the receiver to the transmitter.

duplexing assembly   In a radar system, a device that automatically makes the receiver unresponsive to the outgoing transmitted signal while allowing incoming signals to reach the receiver easily. Also see TRANSMIT-RECEIVE SWITCH.

duplex computer system   An installation of two computer systems, one standing by to take over in case the other fails.

duplex operation   The simultaneous operation of a transmitter and receiver at a single location. This becomes possible (without mutual interference) through the use of two sufficiently separated carrier frequencies.

duplex system   A system composed of two identical equipment sets—either of which will perform the intended function while the other stands by.

duplication check   In digital-computer operations, the checking of an operation by doing it twice, using different methods in each case, to ensure the accuracy of results.

duplication house   A professional person or company who makes high-quality copies of tape recordings (either audio or video). Charges vary, depending on the type and length of the recording.

duplicate   To transfer data from one storage location to another. Compare DUMP, **1.**

dural   See DURALUMIN.

duralumin   An alloy of aluminum, copper, magnesium, manganese, and silicon. It offers strength with minimal weight.

duration control   A potentiometer or variable capacitor for adjusting the duration of a pulse.

duration time   The period during which a pulse is sustained (i.e., the interval between turn-on and turn-off time).

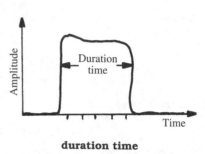

duration time

during cycle   The interval during which a timer is in operation.

durometer   An instrument for measuring the hardness of a material.

dust collector   See DUST PRECIPITATOR.

dust core   A magnetic core for radio-frequency coils consisting of very minute particles of iron or an alloy, such as Permalloy.

dust cover   A removable, usually plastic cover for electronic and computer equipment, to protect hardware during periods of nonuse.

dust-ignition-proof motor   A motor whose housing completely prevents the entry of dust, virtually eliminating the danger of fine dust sparking inside the machine.

dust precipitator   An electrostatic device for removing dust, lint, and other particles from the air. It consists essentially of a pair of screens or wires through which the air passes; a potential of several thousand volts is maintained between them. The particles acquire a charge, then stick to the oppositely charged screen.

Dutch metal   A copper-zinc alloy.

duty cycle   **1.** The proportion or percentage of time during which a device, circuit, or system is operating or handling power. For example, when a radiotelegraph transmitter is keyed on and off to send Morse code, the duty cycle is approximately 50 percent; with frequency-shift keying, the duty cycle is 100 percent. **2.** The conditions under which an electrochemical cell or battery is used. In particular, the proportion or percentage of time during which current is drawn from the cell or battery for the purpose of operating an electrical or electronic circuit, device, or system.

duty cyclometer   A direct-reading instrument for measuring duty cycle.

duty factor   **1.** The ratio P_{avg}/P_{pk}, where P_{avg} is the average power in a system and P_{pk} is the peak power. **2.** The product of the duration and the repetition rate of regularly recurring pulses comprising a carrier.

duty ratio   See DUTY FACTOR, 1.

DVM   Abbreviation of DIGITAL VOLTMETER.

DVOM   Abbreviation of DIGITAL VOLT-OHM-MILLIAMMETER.

dwell meter   An instrument that shows the period (or angle) during which contacts remain closed.

dwell switching   Switching action in which the contacts are held closed (or a circuit kept on) for specified periods, as opposed to MOMENTARY SWITCHING.

dwell tachometer   A combination dwell meter/tachometer for automobile engine testing and adjustment. The dwell meter allows observation and adjustment of the ignition point cam angle; the tachometer shows the motor speed in revolutions per minute (rpm).

DX   **1.** Radiotelegraph abbreviation meaning *long distance* or *foreign country.* **2.** A communication or broadcast station located far away and/or in a foreign country. **3.** Abbreviation of DUPLEX.

DXer   An amateur radio operator who prefers to communicate with stations far away and/or in foreign countries.

Dy   Symbol for DYSPROSIUM.

dyadic operation   A binary operation (i.e., one using two operands).

dyn   Abbreviation of DYNE.

dyna-   A prefix (combined form) meaning *power* (e.g., dynamometer and dynatron).

dynamic acceleration   Acceleration whose magnitude and direction are constantly changing.

dynamic allocation   In multiprogramming, a system in which a monitor program assigns peripherals and areas of memory to a program.

dynamic analogy   A mathematical similarity between or among various phenomena involving the motion of particles.

dynamic base current   See AC BASE CURRENT.

dynamic base resistance   See AC BASE RESISTANCE.

dynamic base voltage   See AC BASE VOLTAGE.

dynamic behavior   **1.** The behavior of a component, device, or system when signals are applied, as opposed to *static behavior* under no-signal conditions. **2.** The behavior of a device or system involving the motion of particles over a period of time.

dynamic braking   A technique for stopping a motor quickly using a resistor (the dynamic braking resistance) connected across the spinning armature. The resistor dissipates the energy generated by the motor, producing a damping action that results in braking.

dynamic characteristic   The performance characteristic of a device or circuit under alternating-current (ac) operating conditions, as opposed to the *static characteristic,* when only direct current (dc) flows.

dynamic check   **1.** A test made under actual operating conditions of a device or circuit. **2.** A test made with an alternating-current (ac) applied signal, rather than with direct-current (dc) quantities.

dynamic collector current   See AC COLLECTOR CURRENT.

dynamic collector resistance   See AC COLLECTOR RESISTANCE.

dynamic collector voltage   See AC COLLECTOR VOLTAGE.

dynamic contact resistance   In relay or switch contacts, variation in the electrical resistance of the closed contacts because of variations in contact pressure.

dynamic convergence   In a color picture tube, the meeting of the three beams at the aperture mask during scanning.

dynamic curve   A characteristic curve that accounts for the presence of resistance in series with the device to which the curve applies.

dynamic debugging   Any debugging operation performed on a computer system during a normal-speed program run.

dynamic decay   Decay resulting from such factors as ion charging in a storage tube.

dynamic demonstrator   A teaching aid consisting of a board displaying an electronic circuit, behind which is mounted the actual circuit. Various circuit components (especially adjustable ones) are mounted on the front of the board, in clear view at places where their circuit symbols appear. Pin jacks at important test points in the circuit allow connection of a meter, signal generator, and oscilloscope leads for testing or demonstrating the circuit.

dynamic deviation   The difference between ideal output and actual output of a circuit or device operating with a reference input that changes at a constant rate and is free of transients.

dynamic diode tester   An instrument that displays the response curve (or family of curves) of a diode on a calibrated oscilloscope screen. The horizontal axis of the screen indicates voltage, the vertical axis shows current, and zeros for both quantities are at center screen. Also see DYNAMIC RECTIFIER TESTER.

dynamic drain current   See AC DRAIN CURRENT.

dynamic drain resistance   See AC DRAIN RESISTANCE.

dynamic drain voltage   See AC DRAIN VOLTAGE.

dynamic dump   A dump that occurs during a program run. See DUMPING.

dynamic electric field   An electric field whose intensity is constantly changing, either periodically or in a complex way.

dynamic emitter current   See AC EMITTER CURRENT.

dynamic emitter resistance   See AC EMITTER RESISTANCE.

dynamic emitter voltage   See AC EMITTER VOL-TAGE.

dynamic equilibrium   **1.** The state of balance between constantly varying quantities. **2.** The tendency of two current-carrying circuits to maintain at a maximum the magnetic flux linking them.

dynamic error   In a periodic signal delivered by a transducer, an error resulting from the restricted dynamic response of the device.

dynamic flip-flop   A flip-flop (bistable multivibrator) that is kept on by recirculating an alternating-current (ac) signal. The device can be switched on or off by a single pulse. Compare STATIC FLIP-FLOP.

dynamic focus   Compensation for defocusing, caused by the electron beam sweeping in an arc across a flat color picture-tube screen; the method uses an alternating-current (ac) focusing-electrode voltage.

dynamic gate voltage   See AC GATE VOLTAGE.

dynamic impedance   The impedance of a device (such as a transistor or diode) when it is operating with an applied alternating-current (ac) signal, as opposed to its *static resistance* with only direct current (dc) applied.

dynamic limiter   A limiter, such as is used in frequency-modulation (FM) receivers, that maintains the output-signal level, despite appreciable excursions of input-signal amplitude.

dynamic loudspeaker   See DYNAMIC SPEAKER.

dynamic magnetic field   A magnetic field whose intensity is constantly changing, either periodically or in a complex way.

dynamic memory   A usually random-access data storage method in which the memory cells must be electrically refreshed periodically to avoid the loss of held data.

dynamic microphone   A microphone in which a small coil attached to a vibrating diaphragm or cone moves in a uniform magnetic field to generate the output signal.

dynamic mutual conductance   See DYNAMIC TRANSCONDUCTANCE.

dynamic noise suppressor   A noise limiter consisting of an audio filter whose bandwidth is directly proportional to signal strength (i.e., it is varied automatically by signal amplitude).

dynamic operating line   A curve displaying the control function of a device. For example, the collector-current-versus-base-current curve of a bipolar transistor is drawn between the limits of saturation and cutoff.

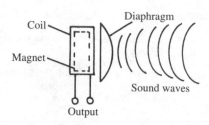

dynamic microphone

dynamic output impedance   The output impedance of a power supply, as "seen" by the load.

dynamic pickup   A phonograph pickup whose stylus causes a small coil to vibrate in the field of a permanent magnet. Works on the same principle as the DYNAMIC MICROPHONE.

dynamic printout   A printout that occurs as a single function, actuated by one command, and completing itself in one operation.

dynamic problem checking   A method of checking the solution obtained by an analog computer, to see that it makes sense (is not absurd).

dynamic programming   A method of problem solving in which continual checks are made to ensure accuracy or conformance to a certain set of rules.

dynamic range   **1.** In high-fidelity audio, the ratio of the loudest sound to the faintest sound that can be reproduced without significant distortion or noise. It is usually expressed in decibels. **2.** In a communications receiver, a measure of the ability to receive both weak and strong signals without excessive noise, distortion, desensitization or other undesirable effects. It is expressed in various ways, typically in decibels. **3.** The ratio between the loudest and faintest sounds, or between the strongest and weakest signals, encountered in a given environment or situation. It is usually expressed in decibels.

dynamic rectifier tester   An instrument that displays the response curve of a rectifier on a calibrated oscilloscope screen. During the test, the rectifier receives an alternating-current (ac) voltage with a low positive peak and high negative peak, both corresponding to the rated forward and reverse voltages (respectively) of the rectifier. The horizontal axis of the screen indicates voltage, the vertical axis indicates current, and zeros for both quantities are at center screen.

dynamic regulation   In an automatically regulated system, such as a voltage-regulated power supply, the transient response of the system. Dynamic regulation is determined from maximum overshoot and recovery time when the load or line value is suddenly changed.

dynamic regulator A circuit or device providing dynamic regulation.

dynamic reproducer **1.** See DYNAMIC MICROPHONE. **2.** See DYNAMIC PICKUP. **3.** See DYNAMIC SPEAKER.

dynamic resistance See DYNAMIC IMPEDANCE.

dynamic run See DYNAMIC CHECK, **1.** See also DYNAMIC DEBUGGING.

dynamics The study of bodies, charges, fields, forces, or pulses in motion. Compare STATICS.

dynamic sequential control In digital computer operation, the computer's changing the sequence of instructions during a run.

dynamic source current See AC SOURCE CURRENT.

dynamic source resistance See AC SOURCE RESISTANCE.

dynamic source voltage See AC SOURCE VOLTAGE.

dynamic spatial reconstructor Abbreviation, DSR. An advanced x-ray machine, developed at the Mayo Clinic, that displays organs in three-dimensional views in motion, and allows them to be electronically dissected without actually operating on the patient.

dynamic speaker A loudspeaker in which a small coil (voice coil), attached to a diaphragm or cone and carrying an audio-frequency signal current, moves back and forth in a permanent magnetic field and, accordingly, causes the diaphragm or cone to vibrate (emit sound). Compare MAGNETIC SPEAKER.

dynamic stability A measure of the ability of a robot to maintain its balance while in motion.

dynamic stop As caused by a computer program instruction, a loop indicating the presence of an error.

dynamic storage See DYNAMIC MEMORY.

dynamic subroutine A form of computer subroutine that allows the derivation of other subroutines in various forms.

dynamic test See DYNAMIC CHECK.

dynamic transconductance Transconductance determined from alternating-current (ac) signal parameters, rather than from direct-current (dc) parameters.

dynamic transducer A coil-and-magnet device that converts mechanical vibration into electric currents, or vice-versa. Common examples include most microphones, headphones, and loudspeakers.

dynamic transfer characteristic An input-output characteristic determined, with respect to the load of a transfer device. Also see DYNAMIC CHARACTERISTIC.

dynamic transistor tester **1.** An instrument for checking the alternating-current (ac) gain of a transistor, rather than its direct-current (dc) beta. **2.** An instrument for determining the condition of a transistor from its performance in a simple oscillator circuit. **3.** An instrument that displays a transistor response curve, or a family of such curves, on a calibrated oscilloscope screen. Also see DYNAMIC DIODE TESTER and DYNAMIC RECTIFIER TESTER.

dynamo A mechanical generator of electricity; typically a rotating machine.

dynamoelectric machinery Rotating electric machinery. Examples: amplidynes, generators, dynamotors, rotary converters.

dynamometer **1.** See ELECTRODYNAMOMETER. **2.** A device for mechanically measuring the output power of a motor.

dynamometer ammeter See ELECTRODYNAMOMETER.

dynamometer voltmeter See ELECTRODYNAMOMETER.

dynamophone A dynamometer (see DYNAMOMETER, **2**) that uses two telephone circuits to measure the twist of a shaft.

dynamostatic machine A machine driven by alternating-current (ac) or direct-current (dc) power for the generation of static electricity.

dynamotor A (usually small) self-contained motor-generator. The motor and generator portions are enclosed in a common housing, giving the machine the appearance of a simple motor.

dynaquad A pnpn four-layer semiconductor device with three terminals, similar to the silicon-controlled rectifier or thyristor.

dynatron A form of vacuum tube that displays a negative-resistance characteristic, resulting in oscillation at ultra-high and microwave frequencies.

dynatron frequency meter A heterodyne-type frequency meter using a dynatron oscillator.

dyne Abbreviation, d. A unit of force. One dyne (10^{-5} newton) is the force that will give a mass of 1 gram an acceleration of 1 centimeter per second per second. Compare NEWTON.

dyne-centimeter See ERG.

dyne-five In the Giorgi mks system, a unit of force equal to 1 newton.

dyne per square centimeter Abbreviation, d/cm^2. A unit of pressure equal to 0.1 pascal (9.869×10^{-7} atmosphere).

dyne-seven A unit of force equal to 10^7 dynes.

dynistor A semiconductor diode that continues to conduct after the forward voltage is reduced below the normal threshold point. To stop the conduction, a reverse voltage must be applied, or voltage must be entirely removed from the device. It is used in switching applications.

dynode In a photomultiplier tube, any of several slanting electrodes that receives a beam of electrons generated by the light-sensitive cathode and reflects it, along with secondary electrons. This amplifies the beam; the process is repeated several times. Thus, the emission from the cathode is greatly amplified when it reaches the plate.

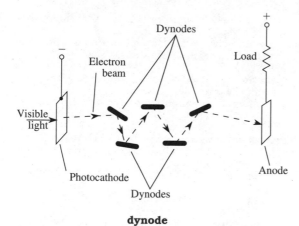

dynode

dysprosium Symbol, Dy. An element of the rare-earth group. Atomic number, 66. Atomic weight, 162.50. Dysprosium is a highly magnetic substance.

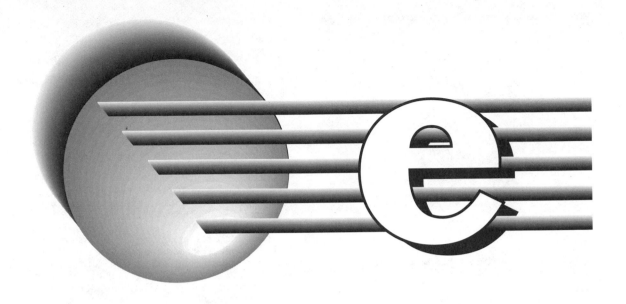

E **1.** Symbol for VOLTAGE. **2.** Symbol for ELEC-
TRIC FIELD STRENGTH. **3.** Abbreviation of
EMITTER. **4.** Symbol for prefix EXA. **5.** Symbol
for ENERGY.

e **1.** Symbol for VOLTAGE. **2.** Abbreviation of
EMITTER. **3.** Symbol for ELECTRON CHARGE.
4. Symbol for the natural logarithm base (approximately equal to 2.71828). **5.** Symbol for
ECCENTRICITY. **6.** Abbreviation of ERG.

EAM Abbreviation of *electronic accounting machine.*

E and M terminals The output and input leads
in some signaling systems. Also called *E and M
leads.*

early early sound Sound propagated through
solids and/or liquids that reaches a pickup device (such as a microphone) before the sound
propagated through the air. In general, sound
waves travel faster as the medium becomes
more dense.

early-failure period The period immediately after
manufacture of a device, during which the failure rate (caused by defects in equipment or
workmanship) is high.

early-warning radar Abbreviation, EWR. A radar
system that produces immediate warning when
enemy aircraft enter the monitored area.

earphone **1.** *Headphone* (usually a single unit).
2. Telephone receiver. **3.** A miniature acoustic
transducer that is small enough to be inserted
into the ear.

earpiece See EARPHONE, 3.

earth **1.** The ground. **2.** An electrical connection
to the earth (see GROUND CONNECTION, 2). **3.**
In space communications, the planet Earth.

earth connection See GROUND CONNECTION, **2.**

earth currents **1.** Electric currents induced in
the earth by current flowing through underground or underwater cables. **2.** Electric currents flowing through the earth between ground
connections of electrical equipment.

earth ground **1.** A common connection to an
electrode buried in the earth so that good conductivity is maintained between the common
circuit point and the earth itself. **2.** A rod driven
into the surface of the earth for use as a common circuit connection.

earth inductor A magnetometer consisting of a
coil that is rotated in the earth's magnetic field.
It delivers an alternating-current (ac) voltage
proportional to the field strength. Also called
generating magnetometer.

earth-moon-earth See MOONBOUNCE.

earth resonance A resonant effect at extremely
low frequencies, caused by reflection of currents
within the earth. Resonant currents have been
tested as a means of communicating with submarines worldwide.

earth's magnetic field Also called *geomagnetic
field.* The natural magnetic field whose lines of
flux extend from north to south. The earth's
magnetic poles, also called the *geomagnetic
poles,* do not exactly coincide with the geographic poles. The field somewhat resembles
that of a bar magnet.

Eastern Standard Time Abbreviation, EST. Local mean time at the 75th meridian west of
Greenwich.

east-west effect The phenomenon in which the
number of cosmic rays approaching earth near

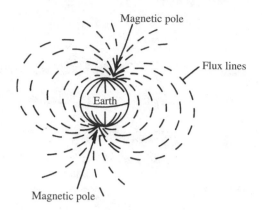

earth's magnetic field

the equator from the west is greater than that from the east by 10 percent.

E_{avg} Symbol for AVERAGE VOLTAGE.

E_b Symbol for BATTERY VOLTAGE.

E bend In a waveguide, a smooth change in the direction of the axis, which remains parallel to the direction of polarization.

EBI Abbreviation of EQUIVALENT BACKGROUND INPUT.

ebiconductivity Conductivity resulting from electron bombardment.

ebonite Hard rubber used as an insulant. Dielectric constant: 2.8. Dielectric strength: 30 to 110 kV/mm.

EBR Abbreviation of ELECTRON-BEAM RECORDING.

EBS Abbreviation of ELECTRON-BOMBARDED SEMICONDUCTOR.

EBS amplifier An amplifying device using an electron-bombarded semiconductor. The electron beam is modulated by the input signal, and the modulated resistance of the semiconductor target modulates a relatively heavy current to provide an amplified output. Current gains on the order of 2000 are possible.

ec Abbreviation of ENAMEL-COVERED (in reference to wire).

eccentric circle See ECCENTRIC GROOVE.

eccentric groove On a phonograph record, an off-center groove in which the stylus rides at the end of the recording, where it causes the tone arm to trip the record-changing mechanism.

eccentricity **1.** The condition of being off center, intentionally or not. It is often a consideration in the behavior of dials, potentiometers, and servomechanisms. **2.** On a phonograph record, the condition in which the spiral recording groove and the center hole of the disk are not concentric. **3.** A quantitative expression for the extent to which an ellipse is elongated.

ECCM Abbreviation of ELECTRONIC COUNTER-COUNTERMEASURES.

ECDC Abbreviation of *electrochemical diffused collector.*

ECG Abbreviation of electrocardiogram. (Also, EKG.)

ECG telemetry Use of a radio telemetering system to monitor the heart function of a person from a distance.

echelon **1.** A level of calibration accuracy, the highest echelon being the national standard for the particular measurement involved. **2.** A level of maintenance in which lower ordinal numbers refer to less-critical tasks, and higher ordinal numbers refer to tasks requiring progressively higher skills and technological expertise.

echelon grating A diffraction grating with extremely high resolution. Generally useful only over a small range of wavelengths.

echo **1.** A signal that is reflected back to the point of origin. **2.** A reflected or delayed signal component that arrives at a given point behind the main component. **3.** A radar blip, indicating an object or thundershower. **4.** Reflection of the signal on a telephone line, caused by improper impedance matching, or by overload of the system by too many subscribers attempting to use the system at the same time. **5.** In audio systems, a circuit that causes sounds to repeat one or more times, at intervals ranging from a fraction of a second to several seconds. **6.** The effect produced by a circuit, as defined in 5.

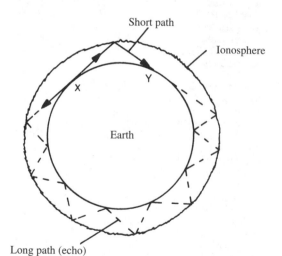

echo

echo area The area of a target that will return a radar signal as an echo.

echo attenuation In a bidirectional wire-communication circuit equipped with repeaters or multiplexers, the attenuation of echo currents set up by conventional operation.

echo box   A resonant-cavity device used to test a radar set. Part of the transmitted energy enters the box, which retransmits it to the receiver. The signal reaching the receiver is a slowly decaying transient whose intensity eventually falls below the level that can be displayed on the screen; the time required to reach this level indicates radar performance.

echo chamber   A reverberation chamber, electronic recording device, or room for acoustic tests or for simulating sonic delays.

echo check   In data communication, a means of checking the accuracy of received data by sending it back to the transmitting station for comparison with the original data.

echo depth sounder   See ACOUSTIC DEPTH SOUNDER.

echo eliminator   **1.** A device that quiets a navigational instrument after receipt of a pulse, to prevent reception of a subsequent, delayed pulse. **2.** In a two-way telephone circuit, a voice-operated device that suppresses echo currents caused by conversation currents going in the opposite direction.

echoencephalograph   An ultrasonic medical instrument that allows viewing of internal organs. Used for diagnostic purposes in certain situations, instead of the X-ray machine.

echogram   In acoustics, a graph of the sound decrement in an enclosure. Time is plotted on the horizontal axis; signal amplitude is plotted on the vertical axis. An intense pulse is transmitted from a speaker; a microphone picks up the echoes and sends them to a pen recorder or microprocessor.

echo intensifier   A device used at a radar target to boost the intensity of reflected energy.

echo interference   Radio interference resulting from a reflected signal arriving slightly later than the direct signal.

echo matching   In an echo-splitting radar system, the trial-and-error orientation of the antenna to find the direction from which the pulse indications are identical.

echo ranging   An ultrasonic method of determining the bearing and distance of an underwater object.

echo send   In an audio mixer, an output for delivering signals to external systems, such as an echo box (see ECHO, **5**). It can also provide an auxiliary output for a second set of speakers, a tape recorder, etc.

echo sounder   See ACOUSTIC DEPTH SOUNDER.

echo splitting   Separating a radar echo into two parts so that a double indication appears on the radar screen.

echo suppression   In a telephone circuit, a device that chokes off reflected waves, thereby minimizing audible echo.

echo suppressor   See ECHO ELIMINATOR.

echo talk   Echo in a telephone system that results in distracting interference.

echo wave   A reflected wave, such as a radio wave reflected alternately between earth's surface and the ionosphere.

ECL   Abbreviation of EMITTER-COUPLED LOGIC.

eclipse effect   A decrease in the critical frequency of the E and F1 layers of the ionosphere during a solar eclipse.

ecliptic orbit   Any orbit that lies in the same plane as the orbit of the earth around the sun (the *ecliptic plane*). The ecliptic plane is slanted about 23.5° from the plane of the earth's equator.

ECM   Abbreviation of ELECTRONIC COUNTERMEASURES.

ECO   Abbreviation of ELECTRON-COUPLED OSCILLATOR.

econometer   An instrument for continuously monitoring the amount of carbon dioxide in (factory) flue gases.

E core   A transformer or transducer core having the shape of an E. Coils can be wound on one, two, or all three of the crosspieces.

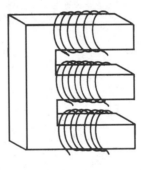

E core

ECPD   Abbreviation of *Engineer's Council for Professional Development.*

ECTL   Abbreviation of *emitter-coupled transistor logic.*

EDD   Abbreviation of ENVELOPE-DELAY DISTORTION.

eddy current   A circulating current induced in a conducting material by a varying magnetic field, often parasitic in nature. Such a current can, for example, flow in the iron core of a transformer.

eddy-current device   A brake, coupling, clutch, drag cup, drive unit, or similar device whose operation is based on the generation of torque, pull, or opposition by the action of eddy currents.

eddy-current heating   Heating caused by eddy-current loss in a material.

eddy-current loss   Power loss resulting from eddy currents induced in nearby structures by an electromagnetic field. Eddy currents in the core of a transformer give rise to such loss.

edge connector   A terminal block with a number of contacts, attached to the edge of a printed-circuit board for easy plugging into a foundation circuit.

edge control   In the manufacture of paper, a robotic system for maintaining the width of a sheet by sensing the edges and correcting the machine accordingly. Transducers that sense the passing edges deliver output signals proportional to variations from standard width.

edge detection   The ability of a machine vision system to locate and follow boundaries. Used extensively in mobile robots.

edge effect   The extension of electric lines of flux between the outer edges of capacitor plates. This portion of the interplate field contributes a small amount of capacitance. Because the lines of flux are not confined to the space between plates, they can cause capacitive coupling with external bodies.

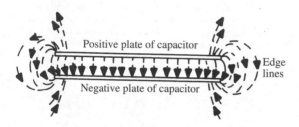

edge effect

edge-punched card   In digital computer operations, a punched card whose edge is perforated in a narrow column, the center being used for written annotation.

edgewise meter   A meter having a curved horizontal scale; this arrangement allows mounting the instrument edgewise in a panel.

edgewise-wound coil   A coil made of a flat metal strip cut in the shape of a coil spring. The design allows the use of clips to vary the inductance, but this advantage is often offset by the coil's high distributed capacitance.

edging   In a color television picture, extraneous color of a different hue than the objects around whose edges it appears.

Edison base   A threaded base on light bulbs, cone-type heaters, and some pilot lamps.

Edison battery   A group of Edison cells connected in series, parallel, or both, and contained in a single package with two electrodes.

Edison cell   A secondary (storage) cell in which the active positive plate material consists of nickel hydroxide held in steel tubes assembled into a steel grid; the active negative plate material is powdered iron oxide mixed with cadmium; the electrolyte is potassium hydroxide. The open-circuit voltage of the cell is typically 1.2 V at full charge.

Edison distribution system   A three-wire, 110- to 250-volt direct-current (dc) power-distribution system.

Edison effect   Thermionic emission of negatively charged particles (electrons) from a hot filament sealed in an evacuated bulb; they are attracted by a cold, positively charged metal plate in the bulb.

E display   A radar display in which the horizontal coordinate indicates distance, and the vertical coordinate indicates elevation.

edit   **1.** In tape recording, the modifying of the recorded material by deleting (cutting out or erasing), adding (splicing or overrecording), or changing the sequence of the material by physically or magnetically altering the tape. **2.** In digital computer operations, to make data ready for processing.

edit decision list   In the editing of a digital audio/video presentation, a record of every change (cut and paste). The list is automatically made by the computer and stored on disk for later reference if needed.

editing   **1.** Alteration of a magnetic-tape recording by means of splicing. **2.** Alteration of data stored in memory, either by adding information, removing information, changing information, or (usually) a combination of these operations.

EDL   Abbreviation of EDIT DECISION LIST.

EDM   Abbreviation of ELECTRICAL-DISCHARGE MACHINING.

EDP   Abbreviation of *electronic data processing.*

EDPC   Abbreviation of ELECTRONIC DATA-PROCESSING CENTER.

EDPM   Abbreviation of ELECTRONIC DATA-PROCESSING MACHINE.

EDPS   Abbreviation of ELECTRONIC DATA-PROCESSING SYSTEM.

EDT   **1.** Abbreviation of *ethylene diamine tartrate* (a synthetic piezoelectric material). **2.** Abbreviation of *Eastern Daylight Time.*

EDU   Abbreviation of *electronic display unit.*

educational robot   A robot that can be programmed for the purpose of teaching its users something. Popular as an educational toy for children.

EDVAC   Acronym for *Electronic Discrete Variable Automatic Computer*, a development of the University of Pennsylvania.

EE   Abbreviation of ELECTRICAL ENGINEER or ELECTRONICS ENGINEER.

E$_{eff}$ Symbol for EFFECTIVE VOLTAGE.

EEG   Abbreviation of ELECTROENCEPHALOGRAM.

EEPROM   Abbreviation of ELECTRICALLY ERASABLE PROGRAMMABLE READ-ONLY MEMORY. See PROM and ROM.

EES   Abbreviation of EARLY EARLY SOUND.

effective acoustic center   The apparent point of propagation of spherically divergent sound waves radiated by an acoustic generator.

effective actuation time   The total actuation time of a relay (i.e., the sum of the initial actuation time and subsequent intervals of contact chatter).

effective address The address a computer uses in implementing an instruction (i.e., one not necessarily coinciding with the address given in the instruction).

effective ampere An effective current of 1 ampere. Also see EFFECTIVE CURRENT.

effective antenna length See ELECTRICAL LENGTH.

effective antenna resistance The radiation resistance of an antenna, as measured at the input point.

effective bandwidth The bandwidth of an ideal bandpass filter, which, at a reference frequency, has the same transfer ratio as an actual bandpass filter under consideration; it also has the same current and voltage characteristics.

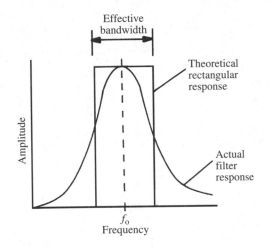

effective bandwidth

effective capacitance The actual capacitance between two points in a circuit resulting from the combination of inherent, lumped, and stray capacitances.

effective conductivity Conductivity measured between the parallel faces of a unit cube of a material.

effective confusion area In a radar system, an area in which interference makes it impossible to see whether a target is present.

effective current Symbol, I_{eff}. The root-mean-square (rms) value of alternating current (see EFFECTIVE VALUE). For a sinusoidal current, $I_{eff} = 0.707 I_{max}$, where I_{max} is the maximum value of the current. Also called *rms current*.

effective cutoff See EFFECTIVE CUTOFF FREQUENCY.

effective cutoff frequency For a filter or similar device operated between specified impedances, the frequency at which insertion loss is higher than the loss at a specified reference frequency in the passband.

effective field intensity The root-mean-square (rms) value of the field-strength voltage, averaged for all points at a horizontal distance of one mile from a transmitting antenna.

effective height The height of an antenna in terms of its performance as a transmitter or receiver of electromagnetic energy.

effective input capacitance The actual operative capacitance present at the input terminals of a circuit or device, caused by the shunt capacitance of the terminals themselves and the net capacitance of the circuit connected to the terminals.

effective internal resistance In an electrochemical cell or battery, a resistance that originates within the electrolyte and electrodes. This resistance is low when the current drain is low; it rises as the current drain increases. It limits the maximum current that the cell or battery can deliver.

effective isolation The condition of components or circuits being so well isolated or shielded that no significant direct coupling, capacitive coupling, or inductive coupling exists between them.

effective instruction The machine-language version of an instruction given in a computer program, as produced by resident software.

effectively bonded The condition afforded by an extremely low-resistance union between two conducting surfaces that are solidly fastened together.

effectively grounded The condition of being connected to earth or to the low-potential end of a circuit by means of an extremely low-resistance connection.

effective parallel capacitance Inherent capacitance that manifests itself in parallel with two circuit points in combination with any lumped capacitance.

effective parallel resistance **1.** The leakage resistance that manifests itself in parallel with a dielectric (e.g., the leakage resistance of a capacitor). **2.** Parallel-resistance effects caused by stray shunt-resistance components.

effective percentage of modulation For a complex waveform, an expression of the equivalent percentage of modulation by a pure sine wave. Given a certain proportion of power in the sidebands with modulation by a complex signal, the effective percentage of modulation is that percentage which, when the modulating signal is sinusoidal, results in the same proportion of power in the sidebands.

effective phase angle In alternating-current (ac) circuits, the phase angle, with respect to waveforms for current and voltage. When both waveforms are sinusoidal, the effective phase angle is the actual phase angle. But when harmonics are present in current or voltage, the angles differ, the difference being greater in capacitive circuits than in inductive circuits.

effective radiated power Symbol, P_{er}; abbreviation, ERP. The radio-frequency (RF) power delivered by an antenna in terms of antenna gain; $P_{er} = P_i A_p$, where P_{er} is the effective radiated power (watts), P_i is the antenna input power (watts), and A_p is the power gain of the antenna.

effective resistance 1. In a coupled circuit, the sum of the actual resistance of the circuit and the reflected resistance of the load. 2. See EFFECTIVE ANTENNA RESISTANCE.

effective series inductance Inherent (distributed) inductance acting in series with other components in a circuit. The inherent inductance of the wire in a wirewound resistor, for example, manifests itself in series with the resistance of the device.

effective series resistance Inherent (distributed) resistance acting in series with other components in a circuit. Thus, the inherent resistance of the wire in a coil appears in series with the inductance of the coil. Likewise, a capacitor has an effective series resistance because of the resistance of the leads, plates, and connections.

effective shunt capacitance See EFFECTIVE PARALLEL CAPACITANCE.

effective shunt resistance See EFFECTIVE PARALLEL RESISTANCE.

effective sound pressure The root-mean-square (rms) value of instantaneous sound pressure at one point in a sound cycle.

effective speed of transmission In telegraphy (wire or radio) and in electronic data transmission, the transmission speed (characters per minute, bits per second, etc.) that can be reliably maintained for a given period.

effective thermal resistance The effective temperature rise (in degrees per watt of dissipation) of a semiconductor junction above an external reference temperature that is at equilibrium.

effective time For a computer, the time during which useful work is performed.

effective transmission speed See EFFECTIVE SPEED OF TRANSMISSION.

effective value The root-mean-square (rms) value of an alternating-current (ac) quantity. The effective value an alternating current produces in a pure resistance has the same heating effect as the equivalent direct current. See also ROOT MEAN SQUARE.

effective volt An effective potential of one root-mean-square (rms) volt. Also see EFFECTIVE VOLTAGE.

effective voltage Symbol, E_{eff}. The root-mean-square value of alternating-current (ac) voltage (see EFFECTIVE VALUE). For a sinusoidal voltage, $E_{eff} = 0.707 E_{max}$, where E_{max} is the maximum value of the voltage. Also called *rms voltage*.

effective wavelength Wavelength in terms of measured frequency and effective propagation velocity.

effects processor In audio systems, a circuit that produces various sound effects via digital signal processing.

efficiency 1. The ratio of useful power or energy output to total power or energy input to a device or system. 2. The proportion of applied audio-frequency (AF) power that a loudspeaker converts into acoustic energy. 3. See ELECTRICAL EFFICIENCY.

efficiency modulation A system of amplitude modulation in which the efficiency of a radio-frequency (RF) power amplifier is varied at an audio-frequency (AF) rate.

efficiency of rectification For a rectifier, the ratio of the direct-current (dc) output voltage to the peak value of alternating-current (ac) input voltage. For percent efficiency, the ratio is multiplied by 100.

efflorescence The giving up of water by a substance upon exposure to air. Some materials used in electronics exhibit this property. Common efflorescent compounds are hydrated ferrous carbonate, ferrous sulfate, and sodium carbonate.

efflorescent material A material exhibiting efflorescence. Compare DELIQUESCENT MATERIAL.

E field 1. An electric field. 2. the electric-field component of an electromagnetic wave.

EFL Abbreviation of *emitter-follower logic*.

E_g Symbol for GENERATOR VOLTAGE.

EHD Abbreviation of *electrohydrodynamic(s)*.

EHF Abbreviation of EXTREMELY HIGH FREQUENCY.

EHP Abbreviation of *effective horsepower*.

E-H tee A waveguide junction in which E- and H-plane tee junctions intersect the main waveguide at the same point. Also see WAVEGUIDE TEE.

E-H tuner An impedance-transforming E-H tee with two arms that are terminated in tunable plungers for critical adjustments. See WAVEGUIDE PLUNGER.

EHV Abbreviation of *extra-high voltage*.

E_i Symbol for INPUT VOLTAGE.

EIA Abbreviation of *Electronics Industries Association*.

eight-level code A code, such as the *American Standard Code for Information Interchange (ASCII)*, in which each character is represented by eight bits.

E indicator A radar elevation display, in which the horizontal scale shows range and the vertical scale shows elevation.

Einstein equation The equation depicting the interconversion of mass and energy; $E = mc^2$, where E is energy (ergs), m is mass (grams), and c is the speed of light in a vacuum (centimeters per second).

einsteinium Symbol, Es. A radioactive element produced artificially. Atomic number, 99. Atomic weight, 252.

Einstein/Dehaas effect The tendency for an iron or steel cylinder to become magnetized as it rotates.

Einstein shift The decrease in frequency and loss of energy experienced by quanta acted upon by gravitation.

Einthoven string galvanometer A simple galvanometer in which a silvered glass filament carrying current is mounted in a magnetic field set up by either a permanent magnet or an electromagnet. The current causes the filament to be deflected through a distance proportional to current strength, the deflection being observed through a microscope.

EIT Abbreviation of *engineer-in-training*.

either-or operation The logical inclusive-OR operation.

EJC Abbreviation of *Engineers' Joint Council*.

eka-aluminum See GALLIUM.

eka-silicon See GERMANIUM.

EKG Abbreviation of ELECTROCARDIOGRAM. (Also, ECG.)

EKG telemetry See ECG TELEMETRY.

EL Abbreviation of ELECTROLUMINESCENCE.

elapsed time **1.** In data-processing and computer operations, what appears to be the duration of a process, compared with actual processing time, as measured by internal clocks, for example. **2.** The accumulated time, usually expressed in hours, minutes, and seconds, that an operation takes or a machine runs.

elapsed-time meter An instrument that indicates the time an electronic device or system has been in operation. Most such meters are based on electric clockwork that runs only while the system is in operation, holding the count during shutdown periods. Also see ELECTROLYTIC ELAPSED-TIME METER.

elastance Unit, daraf. The opposition of a capacitor to being charged. It is the reciprocal of capacitance.

elastic collision A collision between two charged particles in which neither loses energy—even though they are deflected from their normal paths.

elasticity **1.** The ability of a body to return to its original shape after being deformed. See YOUNG'S MODULUS. **2.** See ELASTIVITY.

elastic limit The maximum stress that can be tolerated by a material without being permanently deformed.

elastic wave A wave in an elastic medium, such as air or water; thus, a wave that is mechanically produced.

elastivity **1.** Specific elastance (i.e., the elastance in darafs per cubic unit of a dielectric). **2.** The ratio of electric stress to displacement.

elastomer A compressible, conducting substance used in pressure sensing. In one arrangement, an array of electrodes is connected to each side of a pad of the material. When pressure appears at some point, the material compresses, lowering the resistance in the pressure zone. A microprocessor determines the location and extent of the pressure.

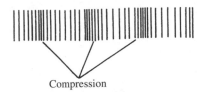

Compression

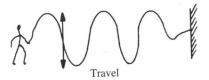

Travel

elastic waves

E layer A layer in the ionosphere that is 50 to 90 miles above the surface of the earth, and is noted for returning radio waves at high and very-high frequencies.

elbow bend A 90-degree bend in a waveguide.

ELD Abbreviation of *edge-lighted display*.

electra A radio-navigational system in which equal-intensity signal zones (usually 24) are provided.

electralloy A nonmagnetic alloy used in the manufacture of radio hardware, such as chassis.

electre See ELECTRUM.

electrepeter A device used to change the direction of an electric current.

electret A device whose heart is a dielectric disk or slab that is permanently polarized electrically, and so possesses a permanent electric field. The electrical equivalent of the permanent magnet. Certain waxes, ceramics, and plastics acquire permanent polarization after they have been heated, then cooled slowly in an intense electric field.

electret microphone Also called *electret capacitor microphone*. A microphone in which sound waves cause an electret to vibrate and generate audio-frequency (AF) output current. An internal power supply (such as a battery) supplies the necessary voltage.

electric **1.** Pertaining to electricity and its various manifestations. **2.** See ELECTROSTATIC.

electric absorption See DIELECTRIC ABSORPTION.

electric accounting machine A self-contained data-processing machine that is neither a computer nor a computer peripheral.

electrical-acoustical transducer A transducer, such as a headphone, sonic applicator, or buzzer, that converts electrical energy into sound energy. Compare ACOUSTICAL-ELECTRICAL TRANSDUCER.

electrical angle The angle assumed at any instant by the rotating vector representing an alternating current or voltage. A complete cycle is divided into 360 electrical degrees. Thus, for an

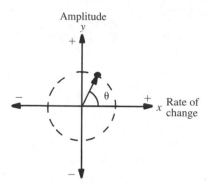

electrical angle

alternating-current (ac) sine wave, the angle is 0 degrees for zero and positive-going, 90 degrees for positive maximum, 180 degrees for zero and negative-going, and 270 degrees for negative maximum.

electrical attraction   The attraction between two oppositely charged bodies or particles. Compare ELECTRICAL REPULSION.

electrical axis   In a quartz crystal, the axis through opposite corners of the hexagonal cross section. The various electrical axes are x, x', and x'' (or x-x, x'-x', and x''-x''). The electrical axis is perpendicular to the mechanical axis, which runs through the crystal's length. Also see CRYSTAL AXES and X-AXIS, **2**.

electrical bail   An action in which a special switch changes contact position and locks itself in that position after a station has been actuated, at the same time releasing a previously actuated station.

electrical bandspread   In a tuned circuit, bandspread obtained by changing values of inductance or capacitance, rather than by mechanical gearing.

electrical bias   A current maintained in a relay coil (sometimes an auxiliary coil) to keep the relay partially closed, thus sensitizing it. Compare MECHANICAL BIAS.

electrical boresight   In radar operations, the tracking axis, as determined by an electrical test, such as one involving a sharp null or sharp peak response.

electrical center   The point at which an adjustable component (variable resistor, variable inductor, etc.) has exactly half its total value. This point does not always coincide with the physical center.

electrical conductance   See CONDUCTANCE.

electrical conduction   The flow of charge carriers through a material. The degree of conduction is indicated by the material's value of conductance.

electrical conductivity   See CONDUCTIVITY.

electrical coupling   The coupling of two or more circuits or elements by means of electric-field effects.

electrical degree   **1.** In a periodic waveform, the length of time corresponding to $\frac{1}{360}$ of the time for completion of one cycle. **2.** In space, that distance representing $\frac{1}{360}$ of the wavelength in the medium through which electromagnetic energy travels.

electrical discharge   The flow of current out of a voltage reservoir, such as a battery or capacitor.

electrical discharge in gases   The phenomenon of electric conduction (current) by a gas, caused by sudden breakdown as a result of gas ionization. The discharge is often accompanied by light, as in the red glow of a neon bulb.

electrical-discharge machining   A method of machining metals in which the metal is vaporized by an arc formed between an electrode and the metal workpiece (anode). In this way, metal is removed in tiny bits from the surface of the workpiece.

electrical distance   Distance in terms of the time required for an electromagnetic wave to travel between two points in a particular medium.

electrical drainage   The diversion of electric currents away from underground pipes to prevent corrosion by electrolysis.

electrical efficiency   The ratio of the output of an electrical or electronic device to the total input. It can be expressed as a decimal or percentage. For example, for a bipolar transistor amplifier, the percent efficiency is equal to $100(P_{out}/P_{in})$, where P_{in} is the collector input in volt-amperes, and P_{out} is the output power in watts.

electrical elasticity   See CAPACITANCE.

electrical element   See ELEMENT, **2**.

electrical energy   Energy in the form of electricity (see ELECTRICITY, **1**). The term is often used in place of ELECTRICITY.

electrical engineer   Abbreviation, EE. A trained professional skilled in applying physics and mathematics to electricity, and in the theory and application of basic engineering and related subjects. Of particular interest to the EE are the generation and distribution of electrical energy and the design and application of electromechanical devices. Compare ELECTRONICS ENGINEER.

electrical erosion   In electrical contacts, the loss of metal as a result of the evaporation or transfer of metal during switching.

electrical filter   A bandpass, band-rejection, high-pass, or low-pass filter that operates by electrical means. Examples: Butterworth filter and Chebyshev filter.

electrical forming   See ELECTROFORM, **1**.

electrical gearing   In an electromechanical system, such as a servo, the condition in which an output shaft is electrically rotated at a speed different from that of an input shaft.

electrical glass   High-temperature insulating materials made from glass fibers.

electrical inertia   See INDUCTANCE.

electrical initiation **1.** Starting an action (electrical or nonelectrical) by means of an electrical signal. **2.** Using an enabling pulse.

electrical instrument A device for measuring an electrical quantity (such as voltage, current, or power).

electrical interlock Also called an *interlock switch* or *door-interlock switch.* A door- or lid-operated switch connected in series with the power switch of a piece of equipment. The interlock causes power to be removed from internal circuits whenever the door is opened, the lid lifted, or the case removed. This minimizes the chance for electric shock to occur to service personnel.

electrical length The length, in wavelengths, of an antenna or transmission line. The electrical length usually differs from the actual length because of ground-capacitance effects, end effects, and the speed of electromagnetic waves in conductors and/or dielectrics.

electrical load A device connected to a source of electricity (generator, amplifier, network, etc.) for a useful purpose (heat, work, etc.).

electrically connected Connected via direct path, such as through a wire, resistance, inductance, or capacitance.

electrically erasable PROM A programmable read-only memory (PROM) that can be erased by an electrical signal, rather than by exposure to ultraviolet light. Also see PROM and ROM.

electrically variable capacitor See VOLTAGE-VARIABLE CAPACITOR.

electrically variable inductor An inductor whose value varies inversely with the amount of direct current that is caused to flow through it or through an auxiliary winding on the same core.

electrically variable resistor See VOLTAGE-DEPENDENT RESISTOR.

electrical nature of matter The general behavior of matter as a complex interplay of waves and particles. Also see ELECTRON THEORY OF MATTER, WAVE MECHANICS, and WAVE THEORY OF MATTER.

electrical network A circuit containing two or more components (including generators and loads), usually arranged in some pattern.

electrical noise Extraneous currents and/or voltages that interfere with desired electrical quantities. Compare ACOUSTIC NOISE.

electrical polarity The distinct difference observable in electrification, designated positive (or plus) and negative (or minus). Negative electrification is generally characterized by a surplus of electrons; positive electrification is characterized by a deficiency of electrons.

electrical quantity **1.** See COULOMB and QUANTITY, **3. 2.** An electrical unit (e.g., AMPERE, OHM, VOLT, and WATT).

electrical repulsion The mutual repulsion of bodies or particles having similar electric charges. Two positively charged objects will repel each other, as will two negatively charged objects.

electrical reset An electromechanical device for resetting a relay that ordinarily remains in the position resulting from actuation.

electrical resistance The in-phase current-retarding effect that all conductors exhibit to some extent. Also see RESISTANCE.

electrical resistivity See RESISTIVITY.

electrical resolver A synchro whose rotor has two perpendicular windings in addition to another winding.

electrical scan A method of changing the orientation of the major lobe of an antenna. The antenna is kept physically stationary, but the phase/amplitude relationships of the signals applied to different driven elements are varied.

electrical sheet Sheet iron or steel used for motor laminations.

electrical system **1.** The overall configuration of electrical elements for a set of apparatus. **2.** The wiring system that supplies power to a set of devices. **3.** One of several methods of quantizing electrical properties, such as METER-KILOGRAM-SECOND (mks), CENTIMETER-GRAM-SECOND (cgs) electromagnetic, cgs electrostatic, and the INTERNATIONAL SYSTEM OF UNITS (SI).

electrical taste See GALVANIC TASTE.

electrical technology The theory and practical application of electricity. Taught as a subengineering major, usually in two-year colleges that award the degree of Associate in Arts (AA) or Associate in Science (AS).

electrical time constant For a torque motor, the ratio of armature inductance to effective armature resistance. Compare MECHANICAL TIME CONSTANT.

electrical transcription **1.** A phonograph record made electrically, as opposed to one made mechanically. **2.** A radio program in which such a record is played. **3.** Any direct mechanical or electrical recording of an audio signal.

electrical transducer **1.** A transducer that converts a nonelectrical phenomenon into a proportional current, voltage, or frequency. **2.** A transducer that converts electricity in one form to electricity in another [e.g., a transducer actuated by direct-current (dc) voltage, delivering an alternating-current (ac) output, whose frequency is proportional to the dc input voltage].

electrical twinning A defect in which two quartz crystals intergrow in such a way that the electrical sense of their axes becomes reversed. Compare OPTICAL TWINNING.

electrical unit A standard for measuring an electrical quantity (e.g., ampere, ohm, volt, watt, siemens, etc.).

electrical wavelength The distance over which an electromagnetic wave propagates in the time required for completion of one cycle. In free space, the electrical wavelength in meters is

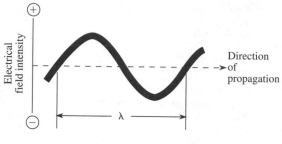

electrical wavelength

equal to 300 divided by the frequency in mega-hertz. In other media, the wavelength might be shorter, depending on the velocity factor.

electrical zero 1. A zero-output or minimum-output point resulting from the adjustment of a bridge or other zero-set circuit. **2.** In a meter whose pointer is mechanically set to some point above or below the zero on the scale, the zero setting obtained when the meter is deflected to scale zero by a current or voltage. **3.** For a synchro, the position at which the amplitudes and time phase of the outputs are defined.

electric and magnetic double refraction See KERR ELECTRO-OPTICAL EFFECT and KERR MAGNETO-OPTICAL EFFECT.

electric arc A sustained luminous discharge in the space between two electrodes. Compare ELECTRIC SPARK.

electric aura See ELECTRIC WIND.

electric balance See BRIDGE, **1** and **2**.

electric bell See BELL.

electric brazing A method of brazing in which electric current generates the required heat.

electric breakdown 1. The usually sudden ionization of a gas by an electric field and the accompanying heavy current flow through the gas. **2.** The (destructive) puncture of a dielectric by the strain produced by high voltage. Also see DIELECTRIC STRENGTH. **3.** The usually non-destructive, abrupt increase in semiconductor junction current at a high reverse voltage. See, for example, AVALANCHE BREAKDOWN.

electric breakdown voltage 1. The voltage at which avalanche effect occurs. **2.** Dielectric strength.

electric breeze See ELECTRIC WIND.

electric buzzer See BUZZER. Compare ELECTRONIC BUZZER.

electric calculator An electrically driven machine for performing mathematical operations. Its electromechanical nature distinguishes it from the electronic calculator, which features no moving parts, other than keys. Also see CALCULATOR.

electric catfish A fish native to tropical and northern Africa, capable of delivering a strong electric shock.

electric cell See CELL, **1**.

electric chair An electrode-bearing chair used in some states for administering the death penalty via high-voltage electricity. See ELECTROCUTION.

electric charge Potential energy as the electrification of a body or component. For a capacitance of C farads charged to a potential of E volts, the charge Q, in coulombs, is equal to the product CE. Also see ENERGY STORED IN CAPACITOR.

electric chronograph An instrument for accurately recording time intervals.

electric chronometer A precision electric or electronic timepiece. Also see ELECTRIC CLOCK and ELECTRONIC CLOCK.

electric circuit A network of interconnected components and devices, often including a source of electric power. Current flowing through a circuit is acted on by components, which produce specific desired effects.

electric clock A clock driven by electric current. Electric clocks fall into two categories: those driven by synchronous alternating-current (ac) motors, and those driven by stepping mechanisms that usually operate from direct current (dc).

electric column See VOLTAIC PILE.

electric conduction The flow of current carriers through a conductor.

electric constant Also called *permittivity of vacuum*. The fixed electrical permittivity of free space, the value of which is 8.8542×10^{-12} farad per meter.

electric contact See CONTACT, **1**, **2**.

electric controller An adjustable device for modifying the operating voltage or power of a component or system. Compare ELECTRONIC CONTROLLER.

electric cooling 1. Cooling via PELTIER EFFECT. **2.** See ELECTROSTATIC COOLING. **3.** Forced-air cooling (of equipment) by electric blowers or fans.

electric current The phenomenon wherein charge carriers move in a directed manner through a material or vacuum. In most electrical conductors, current results from movement of electrons. In a semiconductor material, electric current can result from the movement of holes, as well as electrons; the proportion of holes to electrons depends on the nature of the semiconductor. In a gas or electrolyte, current consists of a flow of ions. In certain situations, electric currents can result from the movement of positrons, protons, anti-protons, alpha particles, and various atomic nuclei.

electric current density See CURRENT DENSITY.

electric delay line See DELAY LINE.

electric density See ELECTRIC SPACE DENSITY and ELECTRIC SURFACE DENSITY.

electric dipole A pair of equal charges having opposite polarity and separated by a fixed distance.

electric discharge See ELECTRICAL DISCHARGE.

electric-discharge lamp See DISCHARGE LAMP.

electric disintegration See ELECTRIC DISPERSION.

electric dispersion In a colloidal suspension, dispersion accomplished by passing an electric current through the material.

electric displacement The movement of a body or particle in response to an electric current or field.

electric double refraction See KERR ELECTRO-OPTICAL EFFECT.

electric dust precipitator See DUST PRECIPITATOR.

electric eel An eel (fish) capable of delivering a disabling shock on contact.

electric elasticity See ELASTIVITY, **1**, **2**.

electric endosmosis See ELECTRO-OSMOSIS.

electric eye A sensing device that uses a radiant energy beam to detect objects. It generally uses a laser diode as the beam source, and a photoelectric cell, phototransistor, or photovoltaic cell as the beam detector. The output is used to control some external machine or system.

electric fence A wire fence through which an electric current is passed. Anyone touching the fence will receive a shock. It is used in some prisons, and also by cattle ranchers to keep people or animals contained.

electric fidelity The frequency response of a circuit or device.

electric field The space surrounding an electric charge or charged body, in which electric energy acts (electric lines of flux fill the space).

electric field intensity See ELECTROSTATIC FIELD INTENSITY.

electric field strength **1.** Symbol, E. In an electromagnetic wave, the amplitude of the electric component of the field, expressed in volts per meter. **2.** Dielectric strength.

electric-field vector See ELECTRIC-FIELD STRENGTH, **1**.

electric filter See ELECTRIC WAVE FILTER.

electric fish Fish capable of generating intense electric shocks (e.g., *electric catfish* and *electric eel*).

electric flux See ELECTROSTATIC FLUX.

electric flux density Symbol, D. In an electric field, the number of lines of flux per unit area, usually expressed in coulombs per square meter.

electric flux lines The direction of the electric field in the vicinity of a charged object. The field is denoted by means of "lines of flux" or "lines of force," with each line representing a designated electric field intensity. The closer together the lines, the more intense the field in a given region.

electric focusing See ELECTROSTATIC FOCUSING.

electric force The force exerted by an electrically charged particle or an electric field.

electric forces The forces exerted by electric charges or electric fields. Also see UNIT ELECTROSTATIC CHARGE.

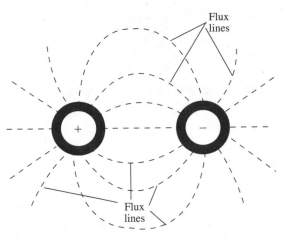

electric flux lines

electric furnace An electrically heated chamber (sometimes heated by an electric arc) used in ore reduction, carbide manufacture, and other high-temperature processes.

electric generator A device for producing electricity. Thus, many different devices, such as batteries, dynamos, oscillators, solar cells, and thermocouples, are classed as generators.

electric glow The light (usually pale blue) that occasionally accompanies an electric discharge in air.

electric guitar A guitar whose acoustic vibrations are converted by a transducer to an electrical signal for amplification.

electric hygrometer An instrument for measuring humidity in terms of the moisture-sensitive resistance of a sensor. A relatively simple direct-current (dc) circuit is used. Compare ELECTRONIC HYGROMETER.

electric hysteresis See ELECTROSTATIC HYSTERESIS.

electrician A professional person who installs and services electrical equipment and wiring.

electric image For solving certain problems involving electricity, an array of electrical points forming an image of certain other electrical points.

electricity **1.** Phenomena resulting from the existence of stationary or moving electric charge carriers, such as electrons, holes, and ions. **2.** A branch of physics concerned with phenomena resulting from the existence of stationary or moving charge carriers. **3.** Electrical energy or power. **4.** The voltage existing at utility outlets. In the North America, this is nominally an alternating-current (ac) voltage of 117 or 234 V at 60 Hz.

electric lamp An electric-powered device used primarily as a source of light. Common types are arc, incandescent, and fluorescent.

electric light   **1.** Visible light produced by means of electricity. **2.** Electric lamp.

electric lines of flux   Lines of flux associated with an electric charge and constituting the charge's electric field.

electric machine   A mechanical device for generating static electricity. See, for example, ELECTROSTATIC GENERATOR, VAN DE GRAAFF GENERATOR, and WIMSHURST MACHINE.

electric meter   **1.** An instrument such as an ammeter, voltmeter, or wattmeter, used to indicate an electrical quantity (usually directly). **2.** See KILOWATT-HOUR METER.

electric mirror   See ELECTRON MIRROR.

electric moment   In an electric field of unit intensity, the maximum torque exerted on an electric dipole.

electric motor   A machine that converts electrical energy into mechanical work. The familiar form is a machine in which an armature rotates between the poles of a field magnet, mechanical energy being produced at the armature's revolving shaft.

electric needle   A needle electrode carrying high-frequency current; it is used in surgery to cut tissue and sear it immediately to prevent bleeding.

electric network   See ELECTRICAL NETWORK.

electric organ   See ELECTRONIC ORGAN.

electric oscillations   The alternate flow of electric charges in opposite directions, occurring at a defined frequency or frequencies.

electric osmosis   See ELECTRO-OSMOSIS.

electric piano   See ELECTRONIC PIANO.

electric polarization   **1.** The orientation of flux lines in an electric field. **2.** The orientation of the electric field component in an electromagnetic field.

electric potential   See ELECTROSTATIC POTENTIAL.

electric power   Symbol, P. Unit, watt. The rate at which electrical energy is used. Power is energy per unit time; in the context of electricity, it is expressed as the product of current and voltage. In terms of heat losses, it is often expressed as I^2R (current in amperes squared, multiplied by resistance in ohms).

electric precipitator   See DUST PRECIPITATOR.

electric probe   A pin or rod inserted into an electrostatic field to sample it, or into an electromagnetic field to sample its electric component. See, for example, WAVEGUIDE PROBE. Compare MAGNETIC PROBE.

electric radiation   **1.** The radiation of energy by means of electric waves. **2.** The energy so radiated.

electric recording   Inkless recording on paper by direct use of an electric current. The two principal types are: (1) A current-carrying stylus burns away (in a fine line) the metallic coating of the recording paper, exposing the dark underlying layer. (2) A stylus delivers current that produces a line by means of electrolysis in a special paper (see ELECTROLYTIC RECORDER). Compare ELECTROSTATIC PRINTER.

electric reset   See ELECTRICAL RESET.

electric residue   A residual electric charge, such as might remain on a capacitor after it has been incompletely discharged.

electric rings   Colored rings formed on a plate by the electrolytic deposition of substances, such as copper and some peroxides.

electric screen   See ELECTROSTATIC SCREEN.

electric shield   See ELECTROSTATIC SCREEN.

electric shock   A physiological reaction caused by the passage of electric current through living tissue. When slight, it is characterized by tingling sensations and involuntary contractions of the muscles; a severe shock can cause paralysis, unconsciousness, heart fibrillation, and/or burns. If heart fibrillation occurs or if burns are severe, death can result.

electric spark   A momentary, luminous discharge of electricity in the space between two electrodes. Compare ARC, **1**.

electric steel   Steel that has been processed in an electric furnace.

electric strain   See DIELECTRIC STRAIN.

electric strain gauge   A device for detecting the strain that a certain stress produces in a body. Typically, such a gauge consists of one or more fine insulated wires cemented to the surface under test. As the surface becomes strained, the wire stretches, undergoing a change in electrical resistance that is proportional to the change in strain.

electric strength   See DIELECTRIC STRENGTH.

electric stress   See DIELECTRIC STRESS.

electric stroboscope   See ELECTRONIC STROBOSCOPE.

electric surface density   The ratio of the electric charge on a surface to the area of the surface. Compare ELECTRIC VOLUME DENSITY.

electric tachometer   See ELECTRONIC TACHOMETER.

electric telemeter   A device that sends metered data over a wire transmission line to a remote point for monitoring.

electric thermometer   See ELECTRONIC THERMOMETER.

electric transcription   See ELECTRICAL TRANSCRIPTION.

electric transducer   A transducer that responds to non-electric energy, then delivers a proportional electric current or voltage to another circuit.

electric tuning   A means of adjusting the frequency of a receiver, transmitter, transceiver, or oscillator, without the use of mechanical devices. An example is the use of a varactor diode, whose capacitance varies with voltage.

electric utilities   The power companies that supply electric current for industrial and consumer use.

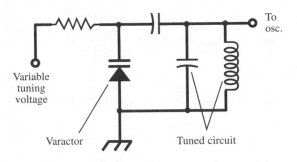

Variable tuning voltage

Varactor

Tuned circuit

To osc.

electric tuning

electric vane   A small demonstration device consisting of a rotor having several spokes terminating in points. The rotor is mounted on a pivot bearing and, when it is connected to a source of high voltage, spins from the force of electricity escaping from the points into the surrounding air.

electric vector   In an electromagnetic field, the vector representing the electric component. It is perpendicular to the magnetic vector.

electric volume density   The ratio of the electric charge in a space to the volume of the space. Compare ELECTRIC SURFACE DENSITY.

electric watch   A small timepiece driven by a tiny, self-contained electrochemical cell that drives an electrical escapement or other stepping mechanism. Compare ELECTRONIC WATCH.

electric wave   See ELECTROMAGNETIC WAVES.

electric-wave filter   A circuit or device for separating signals of one frequency from those of other frequencies.

electric whirl   See ELECTRIC VANE.

electric wind   1. Air currents set up by electrons escaping from the sharp point of a high-voltage electrode. 2. The outward-rushing plasma (solar wind) ejected by the sun and traveling through space.

electrification   1. Generating an electric charge in a body, as in charging a glass rod by rubbing it with a silk cloth. 2. Providing electric service (e.g., RURAL ELECTRIFICATION). 3. The conversion of a system from purely mechanical to electrical or electromechanical.

electroacoustic   Pertaining to devices and systems that exhibit both electrical and acoustic effects. For example, speakers and microphones are electroacoustic devices.

electroacoustic device   A device that transfers energy by converting it from electrical to acoustic form or vice-versa.

electroacoustic transducer   A transducer that converts sound vibrations into electrical pulsations or, conversely, one that converts electricity into sound.

electroanalysis   Chemical analysis performed by electrolytic methods.

electroanesthesia   Anesthesia produced by an electric current going through some part of the body.

electroballistics   A branch of physics concerned with the electrical or electronic measurement of the velocities and trajectories of projectiles.

electrobath   A solution in which ELECTROPHORESIS or ELECTROPLATING is done.

electrobiology   Biology concerned with electrical phenomena in living organisms.

electrobioscopy   The examination of a body for viability by inducing muscular contractions with an electrical impulse.

electrocapillarity   The production of capillary effects by means of electricity. See, for example, CAPILLARY ELECTROMETER.

electrocardiogram   Abbreviation, ECG or EKG. A record made by an electrocardiograph of the changes in potential caused by the heartbeat; used as a diagnostic aid.

electrocardiograph   An instrument that records changes in electrical potential caused by the heartbeat.

electrocardiophonograph   A medical instrument that detects and records the impulses of the heart.

electrocatalysis   Catalytic action produced by electricity (see CATALYSIS).

electrocautery   1. In medicine, a cauterizing instrument consisting essentially of a platinum wire (at the tip of an insulated probe) that is heated by an electric current. Also see ELECTRIC NEEDLE. 2. Cauterizing with an electrocautery.

electrochemical deterioration   An electrochemical reaction that results in the permanent or temporary failure of a device.

electrochemical diffused-collector transistor   A high-current pnp transistor in which metal has replaced the etched-away mass of p material, providing a built-in heatsink.

electrochemical equivalent   In electrolysis or electroplating, a constant (Z) for the metal in plates. For a given metal, Z is the mass (in grams) of the metal deposited by 1 coulomb of electricity.

electrochemical junction transistor   See SURFACE-BARRIER TRANSISTOR.

electrochemical measurements   1. Measurements made on chemical substances with electrical instruments to determine such factors as conductivity, pH, dielectric strength, dielectric constant, etc. 2. Measurements of electrical or electronic phenomena in terms of electrochemical response (e.g., current drain in terms of weight of plated metal, or voltage in terms of gas breakdown).

electrochemical polarization   The disabling of a primary cell caused by gas products deposited around or on one of the electrodes.

electrochemical recording See ELECTRIC RECORDING.

electrochemical reduction Extracting a metal from a compound by means of electrolysis.

electrochemical series See ELECTROMOTIVE SERIES.

electrochemical switch A static, ionic alternating-current (ac) switch consisting of an anode, cathode, and a control electrode, all immersed in an electrolyte. A positive control-electrode voltage switches the device on, initiating ion current from anode to cathode through the liquid.

electrochemical transducer A transducer that converts chemical changes into electrical quantities, or vice versa. Examples: soil-acidity probe and electrolytic elapsed-time meter.

electrochemistry The branch of chemistry, overlapping with physics, concerned with chemical action arising from the effect of electricity on substances, and electrical effects produced by chemical action.

electrochromic display A display that operates by means of electric fields, which control the light-transmission and light-reflection characteristics in different regions of the material.

electrochronometer A precision electric or electronic clock. Also see ELECTRIC CLOCK and ELECTRONIC CLOCK.

electrocoagulation Use of a high-frequency alternating current to solidify tissue, as in arresting bleeding.

electrocorticogram See ELECTROENCEPHALOGRAM.

electroculture Acceleration or modification of plant growth through the application of electricity to plants, seeds, or soil.

electrocution **1.** Death resulting from electric shock. **2.** An electric shock inflicted for the purpose of causing death (e.g., in an ELECTRIC CHAIR).

electrode A body, point, or terminal in a device or circuit that delivers electricity, or to which electricity is applied. A positive electrode is usually an ANODE; a negative electrode is usually a CATHODE.

electrode admittance The admittance encountered by current flowing through an electrode; the property is entirely that of the electrode and is the reciprocal of ELECTRODE IMPEDANCE. Consists of a real-number component (ELECTRODE CONDUCTANCE) and an imaginary-number component that is 90 degrees out of phase (ELECTRODE SUSCEPTANCE).

electrode capacitance The capacitance between an electrode and a reference body, such as ground or another electrode.

electrode characteristic The mathematical function or graph of electrode current versus electrode voltage.

electrode conductance The conductance encountered by current flowing through an electrode; the property is entirely that of the electrode and is the reciprocal of ELECTRODE RESISTANCE.

electrode current Current entering or leaving an electrode.

electrode dark current See DARK CURRENT.

electrode dissipation The power lost in the form of heat in an electrode.

electrode drop Voltage drop resulting from ELECTRODE RESISTANCE.

electrode efficiency In an electrolytic cell, the ratio of the yield of metal deposited to the maximum possible theoretical yield. This value ranges between 0 and 1 (0 percent and 100 percent).

electrode impedance The impedance encountered by alternating current flowing through an electrode; the property is entirely that of the electrode and is the reciprocal of ELECTRODE ADMITTANCE. Consists of a real-number component (ELECTRODE RESISTANCE) and an imaginary-number component that is 90 degrees out of phase (ELECTRODE REACTANCE).

electrodeless discharge Discharge in a gas tube that is not directly connected to a power source. A familiar example is the glow of a neon lamp held in a strong radio-frequency (RF) electromagnetic field.

electrodeposit **1.** To deposit a substance by electrical action. Also see ELECTROPHORESIS and ELECTROPLATING. **2.** A deposit that is formed on an electrode by electrophoresis or electroplating.

electrodeposition The electrical application of a layer of one material (such as a metal) on the surface of another (the substrate) (e.g., electroplating, evaporation, and sputtering).

electrode potential See ELECTRODE VOLTAGE.

electrode reactance The imaginary-number component of ELECTRODE IMPEDANCE.

electrode resistance The resistance encountered by current flowing through an electrode; the property is entirely that of the electrode and is the reciprocal of ELECTRODE CONDUCTANCE.

electrodermography A method of monitoring the functions of the human body by measuring the resistance between two electrodes placed on the surface of the skin.

electrode susceptance The imaginary-number component of ELECTRODE ADMITTANCE.

electrode voltage The voltage between an electrode and a reference point, such as ground or another electrode.

electrodiagnosis **1.** The diagnosis of a disease or disorder through the use of electromedical instruments. **2.** Troubleshooting the electrical portion of electromechanical equipment.

electrodialysis See ELECTRO-OSMOSIS.

electrodissolution Dissolving a constituent substance of an immersed electrode by means of electrolysis.

electrodynamic Pertaining to electricity in motion (i.e., current flow and its accompanying electric and magnetic fields).

electrodynamic braking Stopping a tape-deck motor quickly by applying a braking voltage. In this method, direct braking current flows through the shaded-pole alternating-current (ac) reel motor.

electrodynamic instrument See ELECTRODYNAMOMETER.

electrodynamic loudspeaker See DYNAMIC SPEAKER.

electrodynamics The branch of physics concerned with moving electric charge carriers, such as electrons, holes, and ions. Also concerned with the interaction of electrical and mechanical phenomena. Important in the design and manufacture of devices, such as motors and generators.

electrodynamic speaker See DYNAMIC SPEAKER.

electrodynamism See ELECTRODYNAMICS.

electrodynamometer An indicating meter whose movable coil rotates between two stationary coils. All three coils are connected in series, and the magnetic fields of the two stationary coils are additive. This meter produces a positive indication for alternating current (ac), as well as for direct current (dc). Can be adapted for use as an ammeter, voltmeter, or wattmeter.

electroencephalogram Abbreviation, EEG. A record made by an ELECTROENCEPHALOGRAPH, showing changes in electric potential resulting from bioelectric action in the brain. The record is used as a diagnostic aid.

electroencephalograph An instrument that produces a record of voltage changes resulting from the brain's bioelectricity.

electroencephaloscope A type of oscilloscope used to pick up, amplify, and display changes in potential caused by the brain's bioelectric action.

electroextraction Extracting a substance from a mixture (e.g., a metal from an ore) by an electrical process, such as electrolysis.

electroform 1. To precondition a material or device (e.g., a semiconductor junction) by passing a current through it for a specified period. 2. To form articles by electrodepositing material on a mold or core.

electrogalvanized Electroplated with zinc.

electrogastrogram A recording of the electrical impulses and other functions of the stomach, for medical diagnostic purposes.

electrograph 1. A picture transmitting or receiving device (see FACSIMILE RECEIVER and FACSIMILE TRANSMITTER). 2. A device used for the electrolytic etching or transfer of designs.

electrographic recording A method of producing a visible pattern or record, using electrodes to create discharge through an insulating material.

electrographite Synthetic graphite prepared by heating carbon in an electric furnace.

electrojet A region of high current concentration in the sky near bright auroral displays or along the magnetic equator.

electrokinetic energy The energy of electric charge carriers in motion; a form of kinetic energy. The current in a wire (a flow of electrons) is a common manifestation of this form of energy. Compare ELECTROSTATIC ENERGY.

electrokinetics A branch of electricity concerned with (1) the behavior of moving charged particles (such as ions and molecules) and bodies in motion, and (2) the generation of static charges by moving liquids or solids in contact with each other.

electroless process Plating a metal from a solution of one of its salts without using electricity.

electroluminescence The ability of certain phosphors to emit light continuously when an alternating-current (ac) voltage is applied to them.

electroluminescent cell A device for generating light by electroluminescence. It consists of a luminescent-phosphor layer and two transparent metal films. An alternating-current (ac) voltage applied between the films causes the phosphor to glow through the transparent metal.

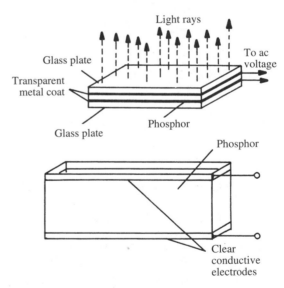

electroluminescent cell

electroluminescent lamp A lamp using one or more electroluminescent panels.

electroluminescent panel A panel that forms a complete electroluminescent cell. It delivers low-intensity visible light when an alternating-current (ac) voltage is applied to it. Available in various sizes and shapes.

electrolysis 1. The action whereby a current passing through a conductive solution (electrolyte) produces a chemical change in the solution and the electrodes. **2.** An electrical method of destroying hair roots.

electrolyte A substance that ionizes in solution. Electrolytes conduct electricity; in batteries, they are instrumental in producing electricity by chemical action.

electrolytic 1. Containing an electrolyte substance. **2.** See ELECTROLYTIC CAPACITOR.

electrolytic capacitor A capacitor (commonly called an *electrolytic*) in which one "plate" is an electrolyte (a liquid, such as boric acid, or a paste); the other plate is an aluminum can containing liquid electrolyte, or an aluminum foil against which paste electrolyte presses. A thin oxide film electroformed on the foil or the can serves as the dielectric. Because it is very thin, the oxide film results in a high value of capacitance in a small physical volume. Also see DRY ELECTROLYTIC CAPACITOR and WET ELECTROLYTIC CAPACITOR.

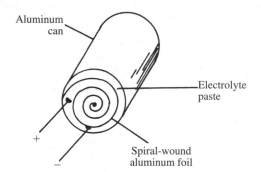

Aluminum can

Electrolyte paste

+

−

Spiral-wound aluminum foil

electrolytic capacitor

electrolytic cell An electrochemical device containing an electrolyte and at least two electrodes. Included in this category are voltaic cells, electrolytic capacitors, and electrolytic resistors.

electrolytic conduction Electric current flowing through an electrolyte, an action characterized by (1) positive electrolyte ions migrating to the negative electrode, where they acquire electrons; (2) negative ions migrating to the positive electrode, where they lose electrons; and (3) current flow in the external circuit, which consists of conventional electron flow (current in the electrolyte is a movement of ions).

electrolytic conductivity Conductance of an electrolyte. It is the conductance of a cube of the electrolyte, measuring one centimeter along each edge, at a specified temperature.

electrolytic corrosion Corrosion caused by an applied voltage, or that is accelerated by the voltage. Compare GALVANIC CORROSION.

electrolytic current meter See VOLTAMMETER.

electrolytic dissociation See DISSOCIATION.

electrolytic elapsed-time meter An instrument that indicates the time that equipment has been in operation in terms of the amount of metal electroplated on the cathode of an electrolytic cell by energy consumed during the period.

electrolytic gas A gas produced by electrolysis. Examples are hydrogen (H) and oxygen (O), generated in a ratio of two to one, by the electrolysis of water (H_2O).

electrolytic iron Very pure iron obtained by electrolytic refining.

electrolytic polarization In electrolysis, the tendency for the products to recombine. In an electrolytic cell, this effect interferes with the performance of the cell, reducing the voltage.

electrolytic potential The difference of potential that appears between a metal electrode in an electrolyte and the electrolyte immediately surrounding it. Also see ELECTROMOTIVE SERIES.

electrolytic recorder A data recorder that uses a paper impregnated with a chemical that turns dark when an electric current passes through the paper from the point of a stylus.

electrolytic rectifier A rectifier consisting of an aluminum electrode and a lead or carbon electrode in a solution of borax or sodium bicarbonate, or in a solution of ammonium citrate, ammonium phosphate, and potassium citrate. Also called *chemical rectifier.*

electrolytic refining Extracting or purifying metals by electrolysis.

electrolytic resistor An emergency resistor made by immersing two wire leads in an electrolyte; the weaker the solution, the higher the resistance.

electrolytic switch See ELECTROCHEMICAL SWITCH.

electrolyze To subject something to electrolytic action.

electrolyzer A cell used in the production of various materials by electrolysis. See, for example, ELECTROCHEMICAL REDUCTION and ELECTROLYTIC REFINING.

electromagnet 1. A coil of insulated wire wound around an iron or steel cylinder, intended for use as a magnet. When current flows through the coil, a magnetic field develops, in effect rendering the cylinder a strong bar magnet. **2.** Any device that exhibits magnetism only while an electric current flows through it.

electromagnetic Exhibiting both electric and magnetic properties (e.g., an *electromagnetic wave*).

electromagnetic attraction 1. The attraction of iron or steel to an electromagnet. **2.** The attraction of an electromagnetic pole to the opposite pole of another electromagnet. A unit pole attracts another unit pole 1 centimeter away with a force of 1 dyne or 10^{-5} newton. Compare ELECTROMAGNETIC REPULSION.

electromagnetic communication   1. Any form of communication using a combination of electric and magnetic phenomena. Examples include wire telegraphy, wire telephony, radiotelegraphy, radiotelephony, facsimile, and television. **2.** Electronic communication via electromagnetic fields (i.e., radio communication).

electromagnetic compatibility   1. The ability of a set of electronic devices to work together without being adversely affected by each other's electromagnetic fields. **2.** In radio communication, the relative immunity of a device or devices to the effects of electromagnetic fields.

electromagnetic complex   A system that produces electromagnetic radiation.

electromagnetic component   1. The magnetic component of an electromagnetic wave, which is perpendicular to the electrostatic component, and can be thought of as the wave's current component. **2.** A device operated by electromagnetism, such as a coil-type relay or a current-operated field magnet.

electromagnetic constant   1. Symbol, c. The propagation speed of electromagnetic waves in a vacuum, approximately equal to 299,792 kilometers per second or 186,282 miles per second. Also called SPEED OF LIGHT and VELOCITY OF LIGHT. **2.** The propagation speed of electromagnetic waves in a particular medium. Equal to vc, where v is the VELOCITY FACTOR of the medium, and c is the speed of electromagnetic waves in a vacuum (299,792 kilometers per second or 186,282 miles per second).

electromagnetic   coupling   See   INDUCTIVE COUPLING.

electromagnetic crack detector   An instrument that uses electromagnetic fields to find cracks in iron or steel.

electromagnetic CRT   A cathode-ray tube using electromagnetic deflection.

electromagnetic cylinder   See SOLENOID.

electromagnetic deflection   In a television picture tube and some oscilloscopes, deflection of the electron beam by the magnetic fields of external horizontal- and vertical-deflection coils. Compare ELECTROSTATIC DEFLECTION.

electromagnetic deflection coil   See DEFLECTION COILS.

electromagnetic delay line   See DELAY LINE.

electromagnetic energy   Energy in the form of electric and magnetic fields. A radio wave traveling through space, for example, has electric and magnetic components, between which energy oscillates.

electromagnetic energy conversion   The conversion of electrical energy into mechanical work and vice versa, through the intermediary of an electromagnetic field.

electromagnetic   environment   A   region   in which electric and magnetic fields are present.

electromagnetic field   A combination of alternating electric and magnetic fields. The electric

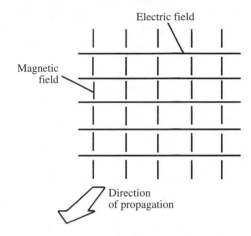

electromagnetic field

lines of flux are perpendicular to the magnetic lines of flux at every point in space. The field propagates in a direction perpendicular to both the electric and magnetic lines of flux. The frequency of oscillation can range from a fraction of one Hz to many quadrillions of Hz. In order from longest wavelength (lowest frequency) to shortest wavelength (highest frequency), effects of this type include radio waves, infrared, visible light, ultraviolet, X rays, and gamma rays.

electromagnetic flux   The magnetic field surrounding a coil or conductor carrying an electric current.

electromagnetic focusing   In a television picture tube, electron-beam focusing obtained by varying the direct current flowing through an external focusing coil.

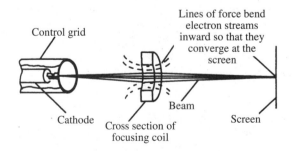

electromagnetic focusing

electromagnetic force   The force that causes a conductor to be displaced from its position in a magnetic field when it conducts current.

electromagnetic frequency spectrum   The frequency range of electromagnetic fields including radio waves, infrared, visible light, ultraviolet,

Wavelength
(meters)

10^{-16}
10^{-14}
10^{-12} — Gamma rays
10^{-10} — X rays
10^{-8} — Ultraviolet rays
10^{-6} — Infrared
10^{-4} — Microwaves
10^{-2} — FM broadcast short waves
1 — AM broadcast
10^2
10^4
10^6 — 60 Hz alternating current
10^8

electromagnetic frequency spectrum

X rays, and gamma rays. Ranges from a fraction of one Hz to many quadrillions of Hz.

electromagnetic horn radiator A horn used to radiate microwave energy. Also see HORN ANTENNA.

electromagnetic induction Inducing a voltage in a circuit or conductor by causing alternating current to flow in another nearby circuit or conductor. Compare ELECTROSTATIC INDUCTION.

electromagnetic inertia The tendency for the current in a circuit to lag the voltage at high frequencies.

electromagnetic interference Disturbances of equipment operation caused by electromagnetic fields from outside sources.

electromagnetic lens A coil or coil system whose magnetic field causes an electron beam passing through it to converge or diverge as a light beam does in passing through an optical lens. Compare ELECTROSTATIC LENS. Also see ELECTROMAGNETIC FOCUSING.

electromagnetic mass The mass that a moving electric charge is thought to possess.

electromagnetic microphone A microphone in which sound energy is converted into proportionate electrical energy by electromagnetism. Common examples are the *dynamic microphone* and *velocity microphone*.

electromagnetic mirror A reflector of electromagnetic waves (e.g., antenna elements, ionospheric layers, buildings, and hills).

electromagnetic momentum The momentum of a moving electric charge, comparable to that of matter in motion. Electromagnetic momentum is the product of electromagnetic mass and charge velocity.

electromagnetic oscillograph **1.** An electromechanical data recorder for tracing the waveform or variations of a signal. **2.** See ELECTROMECHANICAL OSCILLOSCOPE.

electromagnetic oscilloscope **1.** An oscilloscope using electromagnetic deflection. **2.** See ELECTROMECHANICAL OSCILLOSCOPE.

electromagnetic pump A device used for moving conducting or semiconducting fluids. When a current is passed through the fluid, a force is exerted on the molecules of the fluid because of the magnetic field set up by the current.

electromagnetic pulse Abbreviation, EMP. **1.** A broadband electromagnetic field emitted in a short, intense burst from a lightning stroke or nuclear explosion. This field can disrupt the operation of, and (in some cases) cause damage to, electrical and electronic apparatus. **2.** In electromagnetic induction, the displacement of an electron in a conductor by the magnetic field.

electromagnetic radiation The propagation of electromagnetic fields through space; it normally occurs at approximately 299,792 kilometers per second or 186,282 miles per second.

electromagnetic reaction The reaction between magnetic fields. Also see ELECTROMAGNETIC ATTRACTION and ELECTROMAGNETIC REPULSION.

electromagnetic reconnaissance In military applications, the use of electromagnetic apparatus to detect potential enemy activity in a certain geographic region.

electromagnetic relay See ELECTROMECHANICAL RELAY.

electromagnetic repulsion The repulsion of a pole of an electromagnet by the pole of another electromagnet (north pole opposing north pole, south opposing south). Compare ELECTROMAGNETIC ATTRACTION.

electromagnetics A branch of physics concerned with the theory and application of electromagnetism.

electromagnetic screen See ELECTROMAGNETIC SHIELD.

electromagnetic shield **1.** A partition, can, or box made of magnetic material (iron, steel, or special alloy) enclosing a magnetic component. The magnetic flux generated by the component is confined by the shield, thus preventing interference with external components. Likewise, external magnetic fields are prevented from reaching the component. **2.** A grounded partition, metal sheet, wire braid, or other barrier that prevents electromagnetic fields from passing through. Commonly used in electronic equipment to prevent ELECTROMAGNETIC INTERFERENCE. Also used in COAXIAL CABLE to confine electromagnetic fields to the transmission line.

electromagnetic shielding The use of an ELECTROMAGNETIC SHIELD to prevent undesired interaction among electrical and electronic devices and systems.

electromagnetic spectrum See ELECTROMAGNETIC FREQUENCY SPECTRUM and ELECTROMAGNETIC WAVELENGTH SPECTRUM.

electromagnetic switch **1.** A switch actuated by magnetism produced by control current flowing through a coil wound on an iron core. **2.** See ELECTROMECHANICAL RELAY.

electromagnetic theory of light The theory that light consists of electromagnetic waves that are similar to radio waves, but of shorter wavelength.

electromagnetic tube A cathode-ray tube using electromagnetic deflection (e.g., a television picture tube).

electromagnetic unit Abbreviation, emu. A unit of measure in the electromagnetic system of CENTIMETER-GRAM-SECOND (cgs) units.

electromagnetic vibrator See INTERRUPTER.

electromagnetic wavelength spectrum The wavelength range of electromagnetic fields, including radio waves, infrared, visible light, ultraviolet, X rays, and gamma rays. It ranges from many kilometers to a tiny fraction of one millimeter.

electromagnetic waves Waves produced in a conductor or in space by the acceleration or oscillation of electric charge carriers. Such waves have an electric and a magnetic component acting at right angles to each other. The waves propagate at right angles to both the electric and magnetic flux lines.

electromagnetism **1.** Magnetism resulting from the movement of electric charge carriers (e.g., the magnetic field surrounding a coil of wire carrying an electric current). **2.** See ELECTROMAGNETICS.

electromagnetizer A magnetizer using continuous direct current (dc) as the magnetic-field source.

electromechanical Descriptive of any device that converts energy from electrical to mechanical form or vice-versa. Examples are the motor and the generator.

electromechanical amplifier An amplifier that converts an electrical input signal into mechanical motion (vibratory or rotary), which it then converts back into an electrical output signal of higher current, voltage, or power.

electromechanical chopper A vibrator-type interrupter used primarily to chop direct current, converting it into a square-wave signal, whose amplitude is proportional to current strength. Also see CHOPPER.

electromechanical counter A device that indicates the number of pulses that have been applied to it. Typically, it has a series of dials—each capable of displaying the numerals 0 to 9 in sequence, one for each decade in the count. The dials are geared together, the train being operated by the stepping action of an electromagnetic escapement. Compare ELECTRONIC COUNTER.

electromechanical energy The energy stored by an inductor or capacitor in an electromechanical device.

electromechanical filter See ULTRASONIC FILTER, **1.**

electromechanical flip-flop See BISTABLE RELAY.

electromechanical frequency meter A usually direct-reading instrument for measuring frequency in the lower and middle portions of the audio spectrum. It works via the mechanical motion resulting from the applied signal. The two varieties are the movable-iron type and the reed type.

electromechanical modulator See CHOPPER.

electromechanical oscillator An oscillator consisting of an electromechanical amplifier provided with regenerative feedback.

electromechanical oscilloscope A galvanometer-type instrument for displaying a varying or alternating current or voltage. The signal is applied to a meter movement having a movable coil, which swings or vibrates in response to the signal. A tiny mirror cemented to the coil reflects a beam of light to a rotating mirror that sweeps the beam across a translucent screen on which the image is produced.

electromechanical recorder An instrument in which a pen or stylus is moved on a sheet of paper by the varying signal current or voltage being recorded.

electromechanical rectifier A rectifier in which a moving part, such as a vibrating reed or rotating commutator-slip-ring unit, is driven by alternating current (ac) to close the circuit during positive or negative ac half-cycles, thus rectifying the ac. Compare ELECTROLYTIC RECTIFIER and ELECTRONIC RECTIFIER.

electromechanical relay An electromagnetic switch consisting of a multiturn coil wound on an iron core near an armature with a movable end contact. When control current flows through the coil, it becomes magnetized and attracts the armature, closing the movable contact against a stationary one.

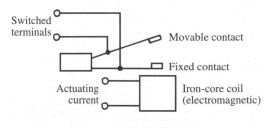

electromechanical relay

electromechanical timer A device for automatically timing a process or an observed event. Most such timers are based on an accurate clock (electric or spring driven) that opens or closes contacts at predetermined instants. Compare ELECTRONIC TIMER.

electromechanical transducer A transducer that translates mechanical signals directly into electrical ones or vice-versa, without the intermediary of active devices, such as transistors or integrated circuits.

electromechanical valve A usually poppet-type valve for gases or liquids. The valve is operated by electromagnetic action and is often aided by an electronic (servo) circuit.

electromechanics The theory and application of electromechanical devices.

electromedical engineering The branch of electronics engineering concerned with the theory, design, and application of electronic equipment for medical diagnosis or treatment.

electromedical equipment Electrical or electronic equipment used in medical diagnosis or treatment.

electromerism Ionization in gases.

electrometallurgy The branch of metallurgy concerned with the use of electricity (especially in electrolysis) to separate or purify metals or to furnish heat for metallurgical processes.

electrometer A specially designed, highly sensitive electronic voltmeter used to measure extremely low voltages and, indirectly, extremely low currents. It is sometimes used as a galvanometer.

electrometer amplifier A stable low-noise amplifier for increasing the sensitivity of an electrometer.

electrometry The science of electrical measurements.

electromigration The movement of atoms in a substance from one place to another, because of interaction between electrons and ions in the presence of electric currents. This effect can cause the eventual deterioration of certain semiconductor devices.

electromotion Motion produced by electric charges or electrons.

electromotive force Abbreviation, emf. Electrical pressure, the potential that causes charge carriers to move through a substance or circuit. See VOLTAGE.

electromotive series A list of metals arranged according to the potential between the surface of the metals and an electrolyte into which they are immersed. Some metals acquire a positive potential (with respect to hydrogen, for which the potential is zero) and others, a negative potential.

electromotor A generator or motor, depending upon the context in which the term is used.

electromyogram The record produced by an ELECTROMYOGRAPH.

electromyograph An instrument for detecting, measuring, and analyzing the weak electrical currents generated by muscular activity.

electromyography The monitoring and analysis of the electrical activity of human muscles.

electron The subatomic particle that carries the unit negative charge of electricity. The electron has a mass of 9.109×10^{-31} kilogram and carries a charge of 1.602×10^{-19} coulomb.

electron acceleration See ELECTRON MOTION, **2**.

electronarcosis Loss of consciousness caused by passing a weak current through the brain. Useful in treating certain mental disorders, the process is somewhat similar to ELECTROSHOCK.

electron attachment The bonding of an electron to a neutral atom to form a negative ion. Also see ANION and ION.

electron avalanche See AVALANCHE and ELECTRON MULTIPLICATION.

electron band **1.** An emission line in the spectrum of an element or compound, caused by the movement of electrons from higher to lower energy levels within the atoms. **2.** An absorption line in the spectrum of an element or compound, caused by the movement of electrons from lower to higher energy levels within the atoms.

electron beam See ELECTRON STREAM, **1**.

electron-beam bender Any element that causes intentional deflection of the electron stream in a cathode-ray tube.

electron-beam focusing Reducing the size of the spot produced by the electron beam in a cathode-ray tube or television picture tube. This is accomplished by adjusting the direct-current (dc) bias voltage on a focusing electrode.

electron-beam generator **1.** See ELECTRON GUN. **2.** A tube, such as a Klystron, in which velocity modulation of the electron beam generates extremely high radio frequencies.

electron-beam instrument An instrument, such as an oscilloscope, based on a cathode-ray tube.

electron-beam machining Welding or shaping materials by controlled electron beams.

electron-beam magnetometer A magnetometer in which the magnetic field under measurement deflects the electron beam in a cathode-ray tube over a distance that is proportional to field intensity.

electron-beam recording In digital computer operations, a technique whereby the output of a computer is recorded on microfilm by an electron beam.

electron-beam scanning tube A tube in which an electron beam strikes a sensitized screen to produce a spot of light, which is deflected electrically or magnetically across a screen. Examples are oscilloscope tubes, storage tubes, and television picture tubes.

electron-beam tube Electron tubes (such as beam-power tubes, klystrons, oscilloscope tubes, and television picture tubes), in which an electron beam is generated and controlled.

electron-beam welding A method of welding in which an electron beam is focused on the workpiece to heat it.

electron-bombarded semiconductor A semiconductor wafer, plate, or junction that is acted on by an electron beam; it alters the resistance of the semiconductor to control the current in an external circuit.

electron-bombarded semiconductor amplifier See EBS AMPLIFIER.

electron bunching See BUNCHING.

electron charge See ELEMENTARY CHARGE.

electron cloud A mass of free electrons.

electron diffraction Diffraction that occurs when a beam of electrons passes through a crystal material. Fast-moving electrons have wavelike properties; the wavelength depends on the speed of the particles. This effect can also occur with beams of other particles, such as neutrons, protons, or alpha particles.

electron drift 1. The movement of an electron from atom to atom in a conductor, as caused by the influence of an applied voltage. **2.** In a semiconductor, directed electron movement. Also see DRIFT, **1.**

electronegative Having negative electrification or polarity (see ELECTRICAL POLARITY). Compare ELECTROPOSITIVE.

electron emission The emission of electrons into surrounding space by a material. Depending on the material, this effect can be initiated by application of heat, light, torsion, electron impact, a high-voltage field, and other actions.

electron flow See ELECTRON DRIFT.

electron g-factor A physical constant that expresses the ratio of electron magnetic moment to the Bohr magneton, and equal to approximately 1.00116. Also called *free-electron g-factor*.

electron-gas binding forces See METALLIC BINDING FORCES.

electron-gas bonding See BONDING, **1** and METALLIC BINDING FORCES.

electron gun A composite electrode for generating an electron beam (see ELECTRON STREAM, 1) in a vacuum. In a cathode-ray tube, the gun comprises a heated cathode, control electrode, accelerating electrodes, and a focusing electrode.

electron-hole pair In a semiconductor, an electron and a related hole. Each electron in the conduction band has a counterpart in the valence band, a vacancy (hole) left by the electron's moving to the conduction band.

electronic 1. Descriptive of any component, device, or system that functions, according to the principles of ELECTRONICS. **2.** Pertaining to electrons.

electronic adder A circuit (such as an operational amplifier) for performing arithmetic addition. In such a circuit, the output-signal amplitude is the sum of the input-signal amplitudes. Also see ADDER and ANALOG ADDER.

electronic aid An electronic device or circuit that contributes to the operation of a nonelectronic device or system; a pH meter, for example, is an electronic aid to chemistry.

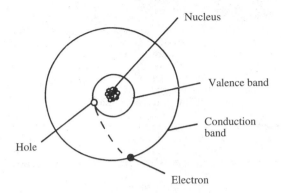

electron-hole pair

electronics aide See ELECTRONICS TECHNICIAN.

electronic attenuator An attenuator in which the variable resistor is the output section of an active device, such as a transistor. Varying the direct-current (dc) bias of the input section varies the resistance of the output section.

electronic autopilot A servo system for detecting and automatically correcting an aircraft's flight path.

electronic balance An electronic scale, which uses a sensitive current-measuring device in conjunction with a movable tension device.

electronic brain 1. A high-end computer. **2.** A robot controller. **3.** A system that possesses or uses artificial intelligence (AI).

electronic breadboard 1. A thin, usually nonmetallic board or card having prepunched holes for the quick assembly of electronic circuits for test and evaluation. **2.** Any circuit prototype that is manually wired during the experimental phase of product development.

electronic bug 1. A semiautomatic telegraph key that produces dots via an oscillating mechanical arm. The operator produces dashes manually. **2.** A telegraph keying device that automatically generates dots and dashes. Also see ELECTRONIC KEY, **1. 3.** An undetermined source of problems or improper operation in an electronic circuit.

electronic buzzer 1. A mechanical buzzer driven by a direct-current (dc) amplifier. **2.** An oscillator circuit that produces a sound similar to that of a mechanical buzzer.

electronic calculating punch A machine that punches on a card the result of calculations it has performed on data it has read from another punched card.

electronic calculator A fully electronic machine for performing mathematical calculations. The simplest machines perform basic arithmetic; more sophisticated ones can do operations with trigonometric, logarithmic, hyperbolic, and other scientific functions. Basic machines are available in department stores for about five dollars. It is usually powered via a small cell or battery, or by a small photovoltaic panel.

electronic camouflage The use of electronics by a target craft to minimize or prevent the reflection of radar echoes.

electronic carillon An electronic system that produces sounds resembling those of a bell carillon.

electronic chime See ELECTRONIC CARILLON.

electronic circuit An electric circuit containing active electronic components, such as transistors and integrated circuits, as opposed to a circuit containing only passive electrical components (such as resistors, switches, heating elements, etc.).

electronic clock **1.** An electric clock whose motor is driven by a constant-frequency oscillator (crystal or tuning fork type), followed by multivibrators and amplifiers. **2.** Any electronic timing circuit that produces pulses at predetermined intervals for the purpose of regulating the operation of other circuits, subsystems, or assemblies.

electronic commutator See COMMUTATOR, **2.**

electronic conduction A flow of electric current resulting from the movement of electrons among atoms in a conductor.

electronic control **1.** The science of automatically controlling machines and devices by means of electronic circuits. **2.** A circuit or device that provides automatic electronic control.

electronic controller A controller (see CONTROLLER, **2**) having no moving parts. For automatic operation, such a device often contains a circuit that senses control signals, compares them with a signal standard, and automatically adjusts the output control power accordingly.

electronic counter A fully electronic circuit that indicates the number of pulses that have been applied to it (see COUNTER, **1**). Unlike the electromechanical counter, the electronic counter has no moving parts and is therefore capable of extremely high-speed, noiseless operation.

electronic counter-countermeasures Abbreviation, ECCM. Military procedures for interfering with a foe's electronic countermeasures.

electronic countermeasures Abbreviation, ECM. Interference with enemy radio and radar emissions by electronic means. Also see JAMMING.

electronic coupling Coupling via electronic effects or devices.

electronic crowbar A switch that prevents destructive currents from flowing through the components of a circuit.

electronic current meter A current meter that uses an amplifier ahead of an analog or digital indicator to provide increased sensitivity.

electronic data processing Abbreviation, EDP. See DATA PROCESSING and ELECTRONIC INFORMATION PROCESSING.

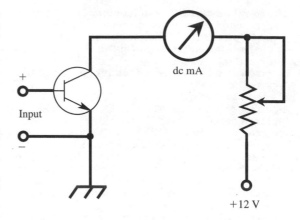

electronic current meter

electronic data-processing center Abbreviation, EDPC. An installation of electronic equipment and accessories for processing and storing data, usually in digital form. Also see DATA PROCESSING and ELECTRONIC INFORMATION PROCESSING.

electronic data-processing machine Abbreviation, EDPM. A device, such as an electronic computer, used in the automatic processing of data, usually in digital form.

electronic data-processing system **1.** A unique arrangement of machines for processing data. **2.** The sequence of steps in, and the underlying rationale for, the processing of data by automated equipment.

electronic deception See DECEPTION and DECEPTION DEVICE.

electronic differential analyzer See ANALOG DIFFERENTIATOR, DIGITAL DIFFERENTIAL ANALYZER, and DIFFERENTIAL ANALYZER.

electronic differentiator A circuit that performs mathematical differentiation. Also see DIFFERENTIATOR, **2.**

electronic divider **1.** An electronic device for performing arithmetic division. In a digital computer, such a divider can be a sequence of flip-flops, each of which produces a single output for every two input pulses. In an analog computer, the output signal amplitude is equal to the quotient of two input-signal amplitudes. **2.** See FREQUENCY DIVIDER. **3.** A voltage divider using active components, rather than resistors.

electronic dust precipitator See DUST PRECIPITATOR.

electronic efficiency A quantitative expression for the effectiveness of an electron beam as a medium of power transmission. The electronic efficiency, in percent, is equal to $100P_{out}/P_{in}$, where P_{out} is the (output) power delivered by the beam, and P_{in} is the (input) power supplied to the beam.

electronic equivalent of gravity In equations for the acceleration, velocity, and distance traveled for an electron, the factor equal to eF/m, where e is the electron charge, F is the potential gradient of field, and m is the electron mass. Also see ELECTRON MOTION, **2**.

electronic flash **1.** A device containing a circuit that uses an electronic flash tube as a light source for photography or other purposes. Also called *photoflash*. **2.** A bright momentary light burst produced by the equipment described in **1**, above.

electronic flash tube A tube used to produce brilliant bursts of light in photoflash units, stroboscopes, and laser exciters. A flash tube usually contains xenon gas, which is fired by a high-voltage pulse.

electronic frequency meter **1.** An instrument that gives direct readings of frequency in hertz, kilohertz, or megahertz on an analog scale or as a digital readout. **2.** Any device that indicates the operating frequency of another device, directly or indirectly, when used for such purpose.

electronic frequency synthesizer An instrument that supplies a number of selectable frequencies derived from one or more internally generated fixed frequencies.

electronic gas A collection of free electrons whose behavior resembles that of a gas.

electronic gate **1.** A logic gate that operates by electronic means. **2.** A security system, consisting of a mechanical gate controlled electronically. Similar to an electronic garage door.

electronic guitar See ELECTRIC GUITAR.

electronic heating The production of heat in an object via high-frequency energy. The two principal methods are *dielectric heating* and *induction heating*.

electronic hygrometer An electrical device for measuring relative humidity, whose sensitivity and stability have been increased by the addition of active amplifying devices.

electronician See ELECTRONICS TECHNICIAN.

electronic induction See ELECTROSTATIC INDUCTION.

Electronic Industries Association Abbreviation, EIA. An American association of electronic manufacturers and engineers. It sets standards, disseminates information, provides industry-government liaison, and maintains public relations for the industry.

electronic information processing The use of electronic equipment (especially digital computers and attendant devices) to perform mathematical operations on data entered into the system in the form of electrical signals. Also see DATA PROCESSING.

electronic instrument An instrument whose circuit uses active devices for increased sensitivity over that of the electrical counterpart, and for minimum loading of a device under test. Compare ELECTRICAL INSTRUMENT.

electronic integrator A active device (such as an operational amplifier) for performing mathematical integration. Also see INTEGRATOR, **2**.

electronic intelligence **1.** Information exchanged by electronic means. Examples: radio messages, radar information, and computer data. **2.** The faculties of reasoning and decision making, as apparently simulated by a high-level computer.

electronic interference The malfunctioning of a device because of nearby currents, voltages, or electromagnetic fields.

electronic inverter An electronic device for converting direct current (dc) to alternating current (ac). Typically, an inverter is a transistorized square-wave oscillator inductively coupled to ac output terminals. The dc to be inverted energizes the transistors, which perform the switching function at the rate determined by the components of the circuit. Also see INVERTER, **1**.

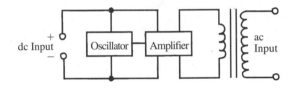

electronic inverter

electronic jamming The deliberate transmission of electromagnetic energy for the purpose of interfering with the operation of a device or devices.

electronic key **1.** For telegraphy (radio or wire), an electronic circuit that generates a continuous string of accurately spaced and timed Morse code dots or dashes, depending on its lever's position (right or left). **2.** For telegraphy (radio or wire), a keyboard that produces perfectly timed Morse code output that corresponds to the operator's typed input. **3.** An electronic device for opening an electronic lock.

electronic keyer See ELECTRONIC KEY, **1**.

electronic lock A lock that will open only after application of a special coded sequence of signals.

electronic mail Also called *e-mail*. A communications system that allows people to leave digital text messages for each other. It is popular among users of personal computers. Operates through the telephone lines using terminal emulation software and a modem. It can also be used via amateur radio packet communications.

electronic microammeter See FET CURRENT METER and TRANSISTOR CURRENT METER.

electronic microvoltmeter See MICROVOLTMETER.

electronic milliammeter See FET CURRENT METER and TRANSISTOR CURRENT METER.

electronic millivoltmeter A millivoltmeter that uses an amplifier ahead of an analog or digital indicator to provide high input impedance and increased sensitivity.

electronic multimeter   A *voltohm-milliammeter* that uses active amplifying devices. Also see ELECTRONIC INSTRUMENT.

electronic multiplier   A device, such as a Hall generator, whose output is equal (or proportional) to the product of two inputs (i.e., it can perform arithmetic multiplication).

electronic music   **1.** Music produced by a combination of electronic oscillator, amplifier, and loudspeaker. A number of successful instruments have been developed. See, for example, ELECTRONIC CARILLON, ELECTRONIC ORGAN, ELECTRONIC PIANO, and THEREMIN. **2.** The electronically amplified sounds of conventional musical instruments.

electronic organ   A musical instrument with a keyboard similar to that of a conventional organ, in which tones produced by oscillators or electrically driven reeds are processed and amplified for delivery to a system of loudspeakers.

electronic packaging   See ENCAPSULATION.

electronic part   A lowest replaceable unit, or component, in an electronic circuit.

electronic phase meter   An electronic instrument for measuring phase difference. Direct readings, in degrees of lead or lag, are visible on an analog scale or as a digital readout.

electronic photoflash   A transistorized light-intensity meter. Also see ELECTRONIC INSTRUMENT.

electronic piano   A musical instrument having the keyboard of a conventional piano and provided with electronic amplification.

electronic power supply   A power supply using transistors or integrated circuits for stabilization and output control.

electronic precipitator   See DUST PRECIPITATOR.

electronic product   Any commercially manufactured electronic device, intended for purchase by the public, by industry, or by government.

electronic profilometer   An electronic instrument for measuring surface roughness.

electronic ratchet   A stair-step circuit or other arrangement functioning in the manner of an equivalent electromechanical stepping switch. Also see COMMUTATOR.

electronic reconnaissance   In military applications, the use of electronic systems to locate enemy installations (such as radio stations, guided-missile sites, and radar bases).

electronic rectifier   A rectifier that uses active devices to change alternating current (ac) to direct current (dc).

electronic regulator   A voltage regulator that uses active electronic circuits, as opposed to a reactor-type or electromechanical device. See, for example, VOLTAGE REGULATOR.

electronic relay   **1.** A switching circuit that uses one or more transistors, and performs the relay

function without moving parts. **2.** An electronic component designed to switch when gating signals are applied (e.g., triac, diac, or silicon-controlled rectifier).

electronic resistor   **1.** The effective internal collector-emitter resistance of a common-emitter bipolar-transistor stage. **2.** The effective internal drain-source resistance of a field-effect transistor (FET) stage.

electronics   The branch of physics concerned with the behavior and application of electric charge carriers in components, devices and systems that accomplish amplification, oscillation, signal processing, and/or switching.

electronics engineer   A trained professional skilled in the physics and mathematics of electronics, and in the theory and application of basic engineering and related subjects. Compare ELECTRICAL ENGINEER.

electronics service person   An electronics technician skilled in repairing and maintaining electronic equipment. Also called *electronics service technician.*

electronic shutter   See KERR CELL.

electronics technician   A professional skilled in building, testing, repairing, or maintaining electronic equipment.

electronics technology   The theory and practical application of electronics. Taught as a subengineering major, usually in two-year junior colleges or technical institutes, awarding the degree of associate in arts (AA) or associate in science (AS).

electronic stethoscope   A stethoscope employing a miniature microphone, amplifier, and earphones. The amplifier gain is continuously controllable, and its bandwidth often selectable for emphasizing particular heart sounds and other body noises.

electronic stimulator   A device for applying controlled electrical pulses to the body to stimulate muscles or nerves during diagnosis or therapy.

electronic stroboscope   A stroboscope that uses a rate-calibrated oscillator, rather than a mechanical contactor to generate pulses that strobe the lamp.

electronic subtracter   An electronic circuit for performing arithmetic subtraction.

electronic surge   A sudden, large increase in the current in a conductor. Can be caused by an electromagnetic pulse; can also occur when utility power is restored following a blackout.

electronic switch   **1.** A nonmechanical device, such as a flip-flop or gate, whose characteristic on-off operation can be used to make and break an electric circuit. Compare CONTACT SWITCH. **2.** A device using electronic gating and sequencing circuits to present several signals alternately to the single input of an oscilloscope, allowing simultaneous viewing of the signals.

electronic tachometer   An instrument for measuring angular velocity, usually in revolutions per minute (rpm). Ideally, the response is independent of sensor voltage amplitude, showing only the number of pulses per unit time reaching the meter circuit.

electronic thermal conductivity The thermal-conductivity component, resulting from the transfer of heat by electrons and holes.

electronic thermometer An instrument for measuring temperature as a result of variations in a temperature-sensitive component, such as a resistor, thermocouple, or thermistor.

electronic timer An electronic circuit or device for automatically timing a process or observed event. Most are based on the time constant of a stable resistance-capacitance (RC) circuit. Compare ELECTROMECHANICAL TIMER.

electronic tube See ELECTRON TUBE.

electronic tuning Variation of the resonant frequency of a device or circuit by changing the bias voltage or current of a controlling electronic component.

electronic voltmeter A voltmeter that uses electronic amplification ahead of the indicating meter to provide high input impedance and increased sensitivity. Also see FET VOLTMETER and TRANSISTOR VOLTMETER.

electronic voltohmmeter A voltohmmeter that uses electronic amplification ahead of the indicating meter to provide high input impedance and increased sensitivity.

electronic typewriter A typewriter with a microcomputer that provides features, such as buffering, automatic repeat, erase memory, and paragraph/page memory.

electronic warfare The use of electronic systems for military purposes, including interfering with an enemy's use of similar systems.

electronic watch **1.** A watch whose movement is a tiny, high-frequency, alternating-current (ac) motor driven by a stable oscillator. **2.** Any miniature timepiece incorporating solid-state circuitry, but especially one using a digital readout.

electronic wattmeter A wattmeter in which an amplifier is used for increased sensitivity.

electronic waveform synthesizer A signal generator that delivers an alternating or pulsating signal whose waveform can be tailored by means of adjustable circuit components.

electron lens A device that focuses an electron beam in a manner similar to the focusing of light rays by a glass lens. Also see ELECTROSTATIC LENS, ELECTROMAGNETIC LENS, and WAVE-GUIDE LENS.

electron magnetic moment The energy per unit flux density available in an electron. Approximately equal to 9.2848×10^{-24} joule per tesla.

electron mass See MASS OF ELECTRON AT REST.

electron microscope A microscope in which the source of illumination is an electron beam focused by electromagnetic lenses. It allows much

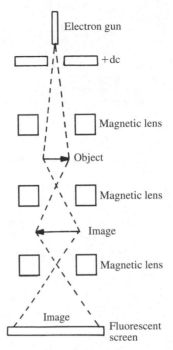

electron microscope

greater magnification than is possible with optical microscopes.

electron mirror A reflector of electrons—especially a dynode element in a photomultiplier tube or electron-multiplier tube.

electron motion **1.** The movement of electrons in a conductor, semiconductor, or space, as the result of electric or magnetic attraction or repulsion. **2.** The movement of an electron as a charged mass. In an electric field, this movement simulates that of a free-falling body in a gravitational field.

electron multiplication **1.** In a gas discharge, the production of additional electrons as a result of collisions between electrons, atoms, and molecules. **2.** The increased production of electrons in a semiconductor when avalanche occurs.

electron-multiplier tube **1.** A vacuum tube utilizing a sequence of secondary emissions for increased current amplification. Electrons from the cathode strike a positively biased dynode with a force that dislodges secondary electrons, which, upon joining those first emitted, are reflected to a second positive dynode that contributes more secondary electrons, reflecting the total to a third positive dynode, etc. The last dynode in the chain reflects the enhanced beam to an anode collector that passes the high current to an external circuit. **2.** See PHOTOMULTIPLIER TUBE.

electronography   Printing by means of the electrostatic transfer of ink from a printing plate across a gap to an impression cylinder.

electron optics   See ELECTRO-OPTICS.

electron orbits   See ELECTRON SHELLS.

electron oscillator   A device in which oscillation is obtained by causing electrons to move in an oscillatory path, to travel in bunches, etc. Examples: klystron, magnetron, and traveling-wave tube.

electron pair   Two electrons from adjacent atoms, which sometimes share the same orbits, but always produce a bond between two adjacent atoms.

electron-pair bond   The bond between an electron pair.

electron physics   The physics of electronics, usually from a highly theoretical viewpoint.

electron-proton magnetic moment ratio   A physical constant whose value is approximately equal to 658.211, derived from the division of the magnetic moment of the electron by that of the proton.

electron recoil   The recoil of an electron from a photon it has collided with.

electron rest mass   See MASS OF ELECTRON AT REST.

electron scanning   Deflection of an electron beam. See, for example, ELECTROSTATIC DEFLECTION and ELECTROMAGNETIC DEFLECTION.

electron shells   The spheres, concentric with the nucleus of an atom, that represent the median distances from the nucleus around which electrons migrate.

electron spin   The rotation of an electron (i.e., around its axis). This motion is independent of the electron's movement around the nucleus of an atom.

electron stream   **1.** The beam of electrons generated by the electron gun in a cathode-ray tube. **2.** The electrons moving between the cathode and plate in an electron tube.

electron-stream instrument   See ELECTRON-BEAM INSTRUMENT.

electron-stream meter   An oscilloscope (or cathode-ray tube alone) used as a device for making measurements.

electron-stream transmission efficiency   The ratio of the current through a positive electrode to the current impinging on it. In a tube, for example, some electrons are absorbed by the plate, and others are reflected.

electron telescope   A telescope using a combination of a glass lens, photocathode, and electrostatic focusing. Light from the object is focused on the photocathode by the lens, the electrons emitted being focused electrostatically on a phosphorescent viewing screen.

electron transit time   The time required for an electron to travel a given distance. For a vacuum tube, the upper frequency limit of operation is governed by the time required for an electron to reach the plate after leaving the cathode. Transit time is usually stated in fractions of a microsecond.

electron tube   An evacuated or gas-filled chamber in which electrons are emitted (usually by a hot cathode) and controlled (usually by a voltage applied to a grid electrode).

electron unit   See ELEMENTARY CHARGE.

electron velocity   The velocity acquired by an electron that moves between two points having a given potential difference. Also see ELECTRON MOTION, **2.**

electronvolt   Abbreviation, eV. The energy acquired by a unit charge moving through a potential difference of one volt; it is equal to approximately 1.6022×10^{-19} joule.

electron-wave tube   A tube, such as a klystron or traveling-wave tube, in which electrons traveling at different velocities interact with each other, modulating the electron stream.

electro-oculogram   A recording of the voltage that is found between the anterior and posterior parts of the eyeball.

electro-optical transistor   A phototransistor or pair of phototransistors in a single package. Used in electronic circuits to sense changes in light levels.

electro-optical valve   See KERR CELL.

electro-optic radar   A form of radar that makes use of visual apparatus for locating a target.

electro-optics   The branch of electronics dealing with related electrical and optical phenomena: photoelectricity, light generation, laser technology, light amplification, etc. It is also concerned with electronic phenomena that are analogous to optical phenomena, such as electronic focusing, reflection, refraction, diffraction, etc. Also called *electron optics* and *optoelectronics.*

electro-osmosis   Causing liquids to flow by applying an electric field across the walls of a porous plug. The force exerted by the field on ions in the liquid causes it to flow.

electropad   The skin-contacting electrode of an electrocardiograph.

electropathy   See ELECTROTHERAPY.

electrophilic   Pertaining to the tendency to seek electrons.

electrophobia   An irrational fear of electricity, a psychological condition sometimes exhibited by victims of serious electric shock.

electrophonic effect   Sound heard by a person when an alternating current is passed through some part of the body.

electrophoresis   The movement of dielectric particles through a liquid in which they are suspended, produced by the electric field between electrodes immersed in the suspension.

electrophoresis equipment   **1.** Any device intended for the purpose of depositing a dielectric material onto a metal by means of electrophoresis. **2.** Any equipment in which electrophoresis occurs.

electrophoresis scanner   A device that senses the movement of charged particles caused by electrophoresis effects.

electrophoretic deposition   A type of deposition in which a low-voltage direct current passing through a colloidal suspension of dielectric polymer particles deposits them as a coating on a metallic body (the anode in the process). It can provide a better coating than one obtained with spray painting or dipping.

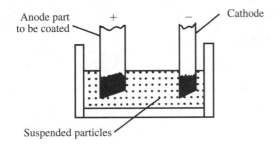

electrophoretic deposition

electrophorus   A simple device used to demonstrate electrostatic generation and induction. It consists of a smooth metal plate at the end of an insulating handle and an accompanying cake of resin or hard rubber. The cake is rubbed with cat's fur, making it negatively charged. The metal plate is touched to the charged cake; by induction, it acquires a bound positive charge on the face that touched the cake and a free negative charge on the opposite face. When the plate is lifted and its top face touched momentarily with the finger or grounded, the negative charge leaks off, often with a sharp spark, but the positive charge remains.

electrophotographic process   See XEROGRAPHY.

electrophotography   The production of photographs by means of electricity. See XEROGRAPHY.

electrophotometer   A light-intensity meter using a photoelectric sensor and a meter, but usually not incorporating an amplifier. Compare ELECTRONIC PHOTOMETER.

electrophrenic respiration   A system of inducing respiration in which one or both of the phrenic nerves (i.e., of the diaphragm) are stimulated electrically to produce contractions of the diaphragm muscles.

electrophysiology   **1.** The study of electrical processes in the human body. **2.** The study of how electrical impulses affect, and are produced by, body organs.

electroplaques   In electric fish, small voltage-generating cells that are connected in series-parallel networks.

electroplate   **1.** To cause one metallic substance to adhere to the surface of another through the effects of electrolysis. **2.** A metal plating deposited via electrolysis.

electroplating   Depositing one metal on the surface of another by electrolytic action.

electropolar   Having electrical polarity (either positive or negative).

electropolishing   An electrolytic method of smoothing a rough metal surface. The workpiece to be polished becomes the anode of an electrolytic cell in which electrolytic action dissolves tiny surface irregularities.

electropositive   Having positive electrification or polarity. Compare ELECTRONEGATIVE.

electropotential series   See ELECTROMOTIVE SERIES.

electropsychrometer   An electronic instrument for humidity measurements.

electroreduction   In electrolysis, reduction of the cathode electrode.

electrorefining   The refining of metals by means of electrolysis.

electroretinograph   An instrument used to measure the electrical response of the human retina to light.

electroretinography   The process of detecting and measuring electrical impulses from the retina.

electroscope   An instrument for detecting electric charges and fields. The common type uses a pair of gold-leaf strips hung from the end of a metal rod in a glass tube or jar. When the exposed end of the rod is brought near a charged object, the leaves repel each other and spread apart.

electrosection   The use of an arc-generating device for making surgical incisions.

electrosensitive recording   See ELECTRIC RECORDING.

electroshock   **1.** The system of creating a controlled electric shock in the brain as a treatment for certain mental disorders. **2.** The electric shock used in the therapy described in **1.**

electrospinograph   An instrument that senses and records electrical impulses from the spinal cord.

electrostatic   Pertaining to stationary electric charges and fields, and their application.

electrostatic actuator   A device for measuring the sensitivity of a microphone. Electrostatic charges produce forces on the diaphragm of the microphone, and the resulting output is recorded.

electrostatic amplifier   See DIELECTRIC AMPLIFIER.

electrostatic charge   See ELECTRIC CHARGE.

electrostatic component   The electric component of an electromagnetic wave. It is perpendicular to the magnetic component and can be thought of as the wave's voltage component.

electrostatic constant See ELECTRIC CONSTANT.

electrostatic convergence See ELECTROSTATIC FOCUSING.

electrostatic cooling Accelerated cooling of a body through the application of an intense electrostatic field. The body must be in a free convection state, a corona discharge must be present, and the field must not be uniform.

electrostatic copier A document-copying apparatus that uses electrostatic effects to reproduce printed material.

electrostatic coupling See CAPACITANCE COUPLING.

electrostatic deflection In a cathode-ray tube, deflection of the electron beam by the electrostatic fields between pairs of internal horizontal and vertical deflecting plates. It is primarily used in laboratory oscilloscopes. Compare ELECTROMAGNETIC DEFLECTION.

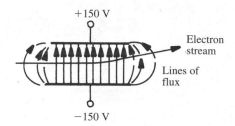

electrostatic deflection

electrostatic electrometer See KELVIN ABSOLUTE ELECTROMETER.

electrostatic electrophotography See XEROGRAPHY.

electrostatic energy The potential energy contained in an electrostatic field (e.g., the energy in a charged capacitor). Compare ELECTROKINETIC ENERGY.

electrostatic field A stationary electric field.

electrostatic field intensity An expression of the strength of an electrostatic field. Usually expressed in volts per meter, millivolts per meter, or microvolts per meter.

electrostatic flux The flux existing around an electric charge or a charged body.

electrostatic focusing In a cathode-ray tube, electron-beam focusing achieved by varying the dc bias voltage on a focusing electrode. Compare ELECTROMAGNETIC FOCUSING.

electrostatic galvanometer A galvanometer operating on the principle of the electrostatic voltmeter.

electrostatic generator A device for producing high-voltage electric charges; e.g., a *Van de Graaff generator.*

electrostatic headphone A device similar to an electrostatic speaker, but held against the head for private listening. Incoming audio signals cause attraction and repulsion among charged plates, resulting in acoustic vibration.

electrostatic hysteresis The tendency of some dielectrics (especially ferroelectric materials) to saturate and retain a portion of their polarization when an alternating electric field to which they are exposed reverses polarity. This causes the charge to lag behind the charging force.

electrostatic induction The charge acquired by a body inserted into an electric field. Compare ELECTROMAGNETIC INDUCTION.

electrostatic instrument See ELECTROSTATIC VOLTMETER.

electrostatic lens An assembly of deflecting plates or cylinders, whose electric field causes an electron beam to converge or diverge in much the same way as a visible light beam passing through an optical lens. Compare ELECTROMAGNETIC LENS.

electrostatic loudspeaker See ELECTROSTATIC SPEAKER.

electrostatic memory A memory unit in which an information bit is stored as an electric charge.

electrostatic memory tube A cathode-ray tube in which information bits are stored in capacitive cells swept by the scanning electron beam.

electrostatic microphone See CAPACITOR MICROPHONE.

electrostatic phase shifter See PHASE-SHIFTING CAPACITOR.

electrostatic potential In an electric field, the potential energy represented by the voltage between the two elements creating the field, or between any two points within the field.

electrostatic precipitator See DUST PRECIPITATOR.

electrostatic printer A computer output peripheral in which the printing medium, a fine dust, is fused by heat onto paper that has been charged according to the data being represented.

electrostatic process 1. Any process that uses electrostatic action. 2. A method of photography in which visual images are converted to electrostatic images.

electrostatic recording A method of recording that employs a signal-controlled electric field.

electrostatic relay A high-input-impedance relay consisting of two polarity-controlled contacts; opposite charges on the contacts close the relay, and like charges open it.

electrostatics The branch of electricity concerned with electrical charges at rest. Compare ELECTRODYNAMICS and ELECTROKINETICS.

electrostatic screen A shield against electric flux consisting of a number of straight, narrowly separated rods or wires joined at only one end. The shield has little effect on magnetic flux. Also called *Faraday shield.*

electrostatic **separator** A device for separating fine particles from a mixture by exposing the mixture to an intense electrostatic field.

electrostatic **series** A list of materials arranged in this sequence: any one of them becomes positively electrified when rubbed with another lower in the list, or negatively electrified when rubbed with another higher in the list. Compare ELECTROMOTIVE SERIES.

electrostatic **shield** Any metallic enclosure designed to confine an electric field.

electrostatic **speaker** A loudspeaker whose vibrating diaphragm is one of two plates in a large air-dielectric capacitor, the other being a closely situated metal plate (or plug). An audio voltage applied to the plates causes them to vibrate. Also called *capacitive loudspeaker* and *capacitor loudspeaker.*

electrostatic **sprayer** An equipment for spray painting in which fine droplets of paint are attracted by an electrostatic field to the surface to be coated.

electrostatic **storage** See ELECTROSTATIC MEMORY.

electrostatic **stress** **1.** Stress in the vicinity of a charged body or particle. **2.** See DIELECTRIC STRESS.

electrostatic **transducer** See CAPACITANCE TRANSDUCER.

electrostatic **tube of flux** The space between electric lines of flux going through adjacent points on the boundary of a given area in an electric field.

electrostatic **tweeter** A small electrostatic speaker for reproducing high-frequency sounds. Compare WOOFER.

electrostatic **unit** Abbreviation, esu. A unit of measure in the electrostatic system of cgs units. Also see CENTIMETER-GRAM-SECOND. Compare ELECTROMAGNETIC UNIT.

electrostatic **vector** See ELECTRIC VECTOR.

electrostatic **voltmeter** An indicating meter whose movement consists of a stationary metal

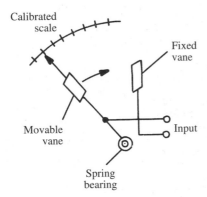

electrostatic voltmeter

plate near a rotating metal plate. A voltage applied to the plates charges them, and the attraction between them causes the movable member to rotate against the torque of a returning spring over an arc proportional to the voltage.

electrostatography See XEROGRAPHY.

electrosteel See ELECTRIC STEEL.

electrostenolysis The deposition of certain metals from a solution in capillary tubes when an electric current passes through the solution.

electrostimulation Electrical excitation of nerves for the relief of pain.

electrostriction In certain materials, the physical contraction that occurs when a voltage is applied. Compare MAGNETOSTRICTION.

electrostrictive **ceramic** A ceramic exhibiting ELECTROSTRICTION when voltage is applied.

electrostrictive **relay** A relay in which the movable contact is carried by a bar of electrostrictive material, such as barium titanate. A control voltage deforms the material, causing the contacts to close.

electrosurgery Surgery, sometimes bloodless, achieved with diathermy-like equipment. See DIATHERMY, **2.**

electrosynthesis Chemical synthesis produced by means of electric currents or fields.

electrotape Also called *electronic tape measure.* Any device that measures distance by electronic means, such as radar or sonar.

electrotechnology See ELECTRICAL TECHNOLOGY and ELECTRONICS TECHNOLOGY.

electrotellurograph An instrument for measuring ground currents.

electrotherapeutics See ELECTROTHERAPY.

electrotherapy The treatment of disorders or diseases by electrically induced heat—especially by DIATHERMY.

electrothermal **1.** Pertaining to electrically generated heat. **2.** Pertaining to a combination of electricity and heat.

electrothermal **device** A device whose operation depends on the heat generated by an electric current (e.g., a bolometer, hot-wire ammeter, thermocouple, or varistor).

electrothermal **expansion element** A thermostatic element, such as a bimetallic strip, whose expansion is used in heat-sensitive switches.

electrothermal **instrument** A hot-wire or thermocouple-type meter.

electrothermal **recorder** See ELECTRIC RECORDING, **1** and THERMAL RECORDER.

electrothermic See ELECTROTHERMAL.

electrothermics The study and application of the heating effects of electricity in conductors and junctions.

electrotitration In chemistry, the completion of titration, as indicated by an electrical measurement, such as of the resistance of the solution being titrated.

electrotonic Pertaining to ELECTROTONUS.

electrotonus Modification of a nerve's sensitivity by passing a constant current through it.

electro-ultrafiltration In physical chemistry, filtering a colloidal suspension by electro-osmosis.

electrovalence **1.** The number of charges acquired by an atom gaining electrons. **2.** The number of charges forfeited by an atom losing electrons. **3.** Valence resulting from electron transfer between atoms and the resulting creation of ions.

electrovalency See ELECTROVALENCE.

electrovalent bond See IONIC BOND.

electrowin To recover (win) a metal from a solution of its salts by means of electrolysis.

electrum A natural alloy of gold and silver.

element **1.** See ELECTRODE. **2.** A circuit component intended for a specific purpose. **3.** A specific part of an antenna array (e.g., *driven element* or *parasitic element*). **4.** A fundamental, unique substance whose atoms are of only one kind (examples: aluminum, carbon, silicon, and sulfur). There are more than 100 elements, some man-made. Elements combine to form compounds. **5.** A circuit, such as an AND gate, that can be taken as a unit because it performs a special function. **6.** In digital computer operations, a subunit of a category that cannot be further categorized [e.g., a *bit* (word element) or a *record* (file element)].

elemental area In a facsimile or television picture, a scanning line segment as long as the line's width.

elemental charge See ELEMENTARY CHARGE.

elemental semiconductor A semiconductor containing one undoped chemical element.

elementary charge Symbol, *e.* Also called *unit electric charge.* The electric charge of a single electron or proton. This charge is approximately equal to 1.6022×10^{-19} coulomb.

elementary particle **1.** A minute charged or uncharged particle within the atom (i.e., electron, proton, neutron, quark, etc.). **2.** In theory, a subatomic particle that cannot be broken down into smaller particles.

element error rate In communications or data transfer, the ratio n_i/n_t, where n_i is the number of elements received incorrectly and n_t is the number of elements transmitted.

element spacing **1.** The spacing between radiator, director, and reflector elements in a directional antenna. **2.** The spacing between the internal electrodes of a vacuum tube.

elevation Angular position (in degrees) of a point above the horizontal.

elevation-position indicator A type of radar display simultaneously indicating the elevation of, and the line-of-sight distance to, the target.

elevator control **1.** An electronic system for automatically stopping an elevator and opening the doors. Various safety functions are included, an example being the reopening of a closing door when a passenger steps into the car. **2.** In an aircraft, the mechanical, electronic, or electromechanical devices or circuits involved in actuation of the elevators.

eliminator **1.** A device or circuit acting as a surrogate for an inconvenient or undesirable component (e.g., battery eliminator). **2.** A device for removing or minimizing an undesirable signal or quantity (e.g., harmonic eliminator); interference eliminator.

ell A coaxial fitting that is a right-angle line section with a coaxial connector at each end. It takes its name from its L shape.

ellipse A geometric figure having the Cartesian-plane formula $(x - x_0)^2/a^2 + (y - y_0)^2/b^2 = 1$, where a and b are constants, and x_o and y_o represent the center point.

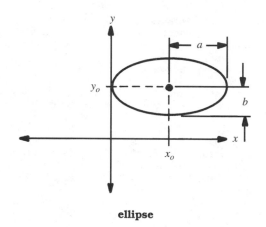

ellipse

elliptical filter See ELLIPTIC FILTER.

elliptical function See ELLIPTIC FUNCTION.

elliptical load line For any amplifier with an output transformer, a load line in the shape of an ellipse, obtained when the load connected to the output element is reactive, rather than purely resistive.

elliptically polarized wave An electromagnetic wave in which the rotation of the electric-intensity vector at one point describes an ellipse.

elliptical orbit A satellite orbit that is not a perfect circle. In theory, all satellites deviate slightly from perfectly circular orbits. Sometimes a satellite is deliberately put into an orbit that is greatly elongated. The closer the satellite is to the earth, the faster it moves.

elliptical polarization Polarization characterized by elliptical rotation of the wave vector at a given point.

elliptical stylus In a phonograph (turntable) system, a stylus with a characteristic ellipsoidal shape.

elliptic filter A band-pass, band-stop, high-pass, or low-pass inductance-capacitance (LC) filter, designed according to an ELLIPTIC FUNCTION. Characterized by a steep attentuation-versus-frequency cutoff response with ripple in both the passband and the stopband.

elliptic function A function, similar to the Chebyshev and Butterworth functions, used in the design of certain selective filters. The elliptic function results in a better filter magnitude response than the Chebyshev or Butterworth functions in some applications. See ELLIPTIC FILTER.

elongation A form of modulation distortion resulting from multipath propagation. Some of the paths result in greater propagation delay than other paths; this causes the modulation envelope to spread out. The higher the modulating frequency, the greater the effect.

ELSE A word used in a BASIC computer program that provides an instruction based on a relational test and, in this respect, is related to IF-THEN, ON-GOTO, etc. It specifies the operation to be done if the conditions given in the same program line don't occur.

ELSIE Abbreviation of *electronic letter-sorting and indicator equipment.*

EM 1. Abbreviation of EFFICIENCY MODULATION. **2.** Abbreviation of ELECTROMAGNETIC(S). **3.** Abbreviation of *electromagnetic iron.* **4.** Abbreviation of ELECTROMAGNETIZER. **5.** Abbreviation of ELECTRON MICROSCOPE. **6.** Abbreviation of EXPOSURE METER. **7.** Abbreviation of *electromotive.*

E_m 1. Symbol for MAXIMUM VOLTAGE. **2.** Symbol for MAXIMUM JUNCTION FIELD.

emanation 1. Emission of electrons. **2.** Emission of radioactive particles or ionizing radiation. **3.** Emission of electromagnetic energy.

E_{max} Symbol for MAXIMUM VOLTAGE.

embedded path A means of guiding a mobile robot along a specific route. One common scheme uses a buried, current-carrying wire that produces a magnetic field. The robot can sense and follow this field. Colored paints and tapes can also be used in conjunction with machine vision systems. Compare EDGE DETECTION.

embedded training The inclusion of training/tutorial programs in computerized equipment that assist users in the operation of the equipment.

embedding See ENCAPSULATION.

embossed-foil printed circuit A printed circuit made by pressing the pattern from metal foil into the insulating substrate and then removing the surplus foil.

embossed-groove recording 1. A phonograph record into which grooves are embossed, rather than scribed. **2.** Recording sound by embossing grooves on record disks.

embossing stylus The rounded-tip stylus used to make an embossed-groove recording.

EMC Abbreviation of ELECTROMAGNETIC COMPATIBILITY.

EME Abbreviation of *earth-moon-earth.* See MOONBOUNCE.

e/m_e The ratio of the elementary electron charge to its mass: 1.7588×10^{11} coulombs per kilogram. Also see CHARGE-MASS RATIO.

Emergency Broadcast System In the United States, a general plan for dissemanating information via broadcast stations in the event of a national emergency.

emergency channel A communication channel allocated for emergency service.

emergency communication Radio or other electronic transmission and reception of urgent messages (e.g., distress signals, storm warnings, etc.).

emergency equipment 1. Apparatus kept in standby status for immediate operation when regularly used equipment fails. **2.** Equipment, especially vehicular, for use in emergency situations. Examples are ambulances, fire-fighting trucks and equipment, etc.

emergency power supply An alternating-current (ac) or direct-current (dc) power unit kept in standby status for immediate use when the regular power supply fails.

emergency service A communications service devoted exclusively to emergency communication.

EMF, emf Abbreviation of ELECTROMOTIVE FORCE.

emf standard See STANDARD CELL.

EMG 1. Abbreviation of ELECTROMYOGRAM. **2.** Abbreviation of ELECTROMYOGRAPH.

EMI Abbreviation of ELECTROMAGNETIC INTERFERENCE.

E microscope See ELECTRON MICROSCOPE.

emission 1. The ejection of particles, especially electrons, from a material. **2.** Waves radiated from any source (as from a transmitting antenna or from an amplifier stage). **3.** The emanation of radiant, electromagnetic, acoustical, electrical, or magnetic energy.

emission code A system of abbreviating the various types of radio emission. See EMISSION MODE.

emission frequency 1. In communications, the carrier frequency of the transmitted signal as it is radiated from the antenna or fed into a transmission line. **2.** The actual frequency or frequency range of a signal as it is transmitted or radiated. This might be the carrier frequency. **3.** The frequency of energy in an emission band or bands in a spectrum.

emission lines In a spectrum, radiation intensity peaks that appear as bright lines in a visible display. In a radio-frequency spectrum, the emission lines occur as sharp peaks in radiated energy at specific wavelengths.

emission mode Any of various official classifications of radio communication emission types.

Emissions are designated according to the modulation method used (e.g., continuous waves, amplitude modulation, single-sideband with suppressed carrier, frequency modulation, pulse modulation, etc.).

emission power **1.** The rate at which energy is radiated from an object. **2.** In radio communication, the transmitter output power.

emission spectrum The radiation spectrum of a substance that emits energy (e.g., the light spectrum of an incandescent metal).

emission types See EMISSION MODE.

emission velocity The initial velocity of an electron as it leaves an emitting surface.

emission wavelength **1.** In communications, the carrier wavelength of the transmitted signal as it is radiated from the antenna or fed into a transmission line. **2.** The actual wavelength or wavelength range of a signal as it is transmitted or radiated. This might or might not be the carrier wavelength. **3.** The wavelength of energy in an emission band or bands in a spectrum.

emissive power The rate at which a surface emits energy of all wavelengths in all directions, per unit area of radiating surface, regardless of temperature.

emissivity For a radiating source, the ratio W_1/W_2, where W_1 is the energy emitted by the source at a particular temperature, and W_2 is the energy emitted by a blackbody (i.e., a theoretically perfect radiator) at the same temperature.

emittance For an energy-radiating source, the radiated power per unit area of radiating surface.

emitted electron An electron that has left an atom of a material and has escaped into surrounding space or entered a neighboring material.

emitter **1.** A body that discharges particles or waves (see EMISSION). **2.** In a semiconductor device, the area, region, or element from which current carriers are injected into the device. In a transistor symbol, the emitter is that electrode shown with an arrowhead.

emitter-base junction In a bipolar transistor, the boundary between base and emitter regions.

emitter bias Emitter current or voltage maintained to set the operating point of a bipolar transistor.

emitter bulk resistance The portion of the resistance of the semiconductor material in a transistor that affects emitter resistance.

emitter-coupled logic A bipolar form of digital logic, abbreviated ECL.

emitter-coupled multivibrator A two-transistor multivibrator circuit in which the emitters share a common resistor.

emitter-coupled phase inverter A transistor phase inverter in which the out-of-phase component is taken from the collector and the in-phase component from the emitter resistor (of the same transistor). Another transistor is often used to amplify the in-phase component so that both outputs are equal in magnitude.

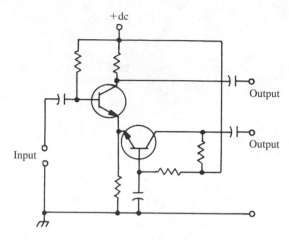

emitter-coupled phase inverter

emitter current Symbol, I_E. The current in the emitter electrode of a bipolar transistor.

emitter degeneration In a transistor amplifier, current degeneration obtained by use of an unbypassed emitter resistor. The arrangement results in virtually distortion-free amplification at a sacrifice in voltage gain.

emitter follower A transistor circuit in which the input signal is applied to the base, and the output signal is taken from the emitter resistor. Gain is always less than unity; output impedance is low.

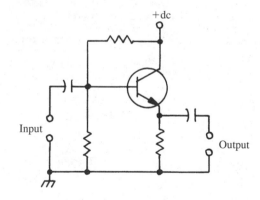

emitter follower

emitter-input circuit See COMMON-BASE CIRCUIT.

emitter junction See EMITTER-BASE JUNCTION.

emitter resistance Symbol, R_E. **1.** The resistance of the emitter electrode in a bipolar transistor. **2.** External resistance connected to a transistor's emitter terminal.

emitter stabilization In a common-emitter transistor stage, an emitter resistor that stabilizes the circuit against temperature variations.

emitter-to-base junction See EMITTER-BASE JUNCTION.

emitter voltage Symbol, V_E. The voltage at the emitter electrode of a bipolar transistor.

EMP, emp 1. Abbreviation of ELECTROMAGNETIC PULSE. **2.** Abbreviation of *electromagnetic power.*

emphasis Modification of the amplitude-versus-frequency output or response of an audio circuit, for the purpose of optimizing signal intelligibility.

emphasizer An audio-frequency device with a specially tailored response, intended to maximize intelligibility of a voice.

Empire cloth Varnished cambric used as an insulating sheet or tape.

empirical Observable; derived from experimentation.

empirical curve A curve plotted from data acquired from observations, tests, and calculations, rather than from mathematical laws or other theory.

empirical design The design of electronic circuits by cut-and-try methods and, to some extent, through intuition arising from experience (i.e., practical as opposed to theoretical design).

empirical probability Probability estimated from experience and observations. This method is often used in quality-control and reliability procedures.

empty medium A computer storage medium, such as a magnetic tape or disk, that is ready to accept data (i.e., rather than being completely blank, it contains the signals necessary for processing the to-be-added data).

EMU, emu Abbreviation of ELECTROMAGNETIC UNIT(S).

emulator In computer engineering, a sophisticated device that substitutes for a similar device or stage in the computer, and thereby provides a basis for experimenting and troubleshooting without disturbing the equivalent part of the computer.

E$_n$ Symbol for *voltage remaining at null.*

enable To initiate the operation of a circuit or device by applying a pulse or trigger signal.

enable pulse 1. A pulse that initiates the operation of a circuit or device. **2.** A binary pulse that augments a write pulse to make a magnetic core change state.

enabling gate A digital device that regulates the length of a pulse for specialized use.

enameled wire Wire that is insulated by a thin coat of baked enamel. Commonly used in coil winding because the thin enamel allows for a maximum number of turns in a given volume for a given wire gauge.

encapsulant A material, such as potting resin, used to embed (encapsulate) a component, circuit, or device.

encapsulated circuit A component, circuit, or device embedded in plastic or wax (see ENCAPSULATION).

encapsulated component An electronic part that is embedded in plastic or wax (see ENCAPSULATION).

encapsulating material See ENCAPSULANT.

encapsulation The embedding of a circuit or component in a solid mass of plastic or wax. The mold or container remains as part of the assembly after the plastic or wax has solidified. Protects against the environment, and/or against the effects of physical vibration. Compare POTTING.

encephalogram See ELECTROENCEPHALOGRAM.

encephalograph See ELECTROENCEPHALOGRAPH.

enciphered facsimile Facsimile communications that have been rearranged or scrambled at the transmitting location so that it cannot be intercepted by a third party. A deciphering device is needed at the receiver end of the circuit.

enclosure 1. A cabinet, case, or other housing for electronic equipment, such as a receiver, transmitter, or test instrument. **2.** A specially designed housing for a loudspeaker.

encode 1. To convert signals or data into a desired (usually digital) form. Also called CODE. **2.** To equip a transmitter with a tone-producing device (encoder). **3.** To develop and apply an encoding system to a group of transceivers or transmitters of a communications network.

encoder 1. An analog-to-digital or digital-to-analog converter. **2.** An electromechanical device for translating the angular position of a rotating shaft into a corresponding series of digital pulses. Also see SHAFT-ANGLE ENCODER. **3.** A device for encoding data (see ENCODE). **4.** A machine with a keyboard for printing characters that can be read by optical character recognition (OCR) equipment. **5.** A tone generator used as a receiver enabler in the transmitters of a communications network.

encoding 1. The translation, either by a machine or by a human operator, of a spoken or written language into digital code. **2.** Any function performed by an ENCODER.

end-around carry In a computer, a carry produced in the most significant position, causing a carry into the least-significant position.

end-around shift In digital-computer operations, the transfer of characters from one end of a register to the other end. Also called LOGICAL SHIFT.

end bell 1. The part of a motor housing that supports the bearing and protects internal rotating parts. **2.** A clamping part fastened to the back of a plug or receptacle. **3.** Either of the two frames of a transformer that contains the mounting lugs.

end bracket See END BELL, 2.

end cell A cell intended for series operation in conjunction with a storage battery. As the voltage of the battery drops, the end cell can be added into the circuit.

end effect   **1.** In a tapped coil, losses because of induced currents flowing in the inductance and distributed capacitance of the unused end of the coil. **2.** EDGE EFFECT in a capacitor. **3.** An effective capacitance at the ends of an antenna, resulting from air discharge. This lowers the resonant frequency slightly below that predicted by theory. The effect is exaggerated by the proximity of objects, such as trees and buildings, or when an antenna is placed close to the earth.

end effector   The device or tool connected to the end of a robot arm (e.g., a gripper, screwdriver, drill, or soldering iron).

end-fed antenna   An antenna whose lead-in or feeders are attached to an end of the radiator.

end feed   A method of feeding electromagnetic fields to an antenna by connecting the transmission line to the end. Ordinarily, the antenna must be a multiple of 0.5 wavelength long for end feed to be effective.

end-fire antenna   An antenna that exhibits maximum radiation or best reception off its ends. Also see END-FIRE ARRAY.

end-fire array   A beam antenna of multiple elements providing end-fire directivity. Compare BROADSIDE ARRAY.

end-fire directivity   In a directive antenna, beaming a signal along the plane of the antenna (i.e., off its ends).

end instrument   A device capable of converting intelligence into electrical signals or vice-versa, and that needs to be connected to only one terminal of a loop.

end item   A final, completed product or component.

endless loop   Also called *infinite loop*. A computer programming bug that causes the machine to go in an indefinite, and often useless, logical circle. For example, suppose that at line 180, the computer encounters the command GOTO 250, meaning "Go to line 250," but line 250 gives the command GOTO 180. Once the computer gets to line 180, it enters a loop in which nothing is accomplished, and from which the only escape is intervention by the operator (e.g., terminating the program).

end mark   In digital-computer operations, a signal or code indicating the close of an information unit.

endodyne reception   See ZERO-BEAT RECEPTION.

end-of-charge voltage   For a rechargeable cell or battery, the voltage at full charge (i.e., just after disconnection of the charging apparatus and before use).

end-of-data mark   A code or character signaling that all the data in a computer storage medium has been read or used.

end-of-discharge voltage   For a rechargeable cell or battery, the voltage at the termination of a discharging cycle, immediately before the unit is taken out of use and the charging apparatus is connected.

end-of-field mark   In computer operations, a "flag" code that signals when the end of a field has been reached.

end-of-file mark   In computer operations, a code instruction that signals when the last record in a file has been read.

end-of-line unit   The last device or circuit in a chain.

end-of-message character   A character or code signaling the end of a message.

end-of-run   The end of a computer program or program run, as indicated by the program.

end-of-tape mark   A physical marker at the end of a magnetic tape (e.g., something that can be sensed by methods other than that used to read the tape).

end-of-tape routine   A computer program that handles the processing needed after the last record on a reel of magnetic tape has been reached.

end-on armature   A relay armature that moves in the direction of the core's axis.

end-on directional antenna   See END-FIRE ANTENNA and END-FIRE ARRAY.

endoradiograph   An X-ray picture, derived or enhanced by the introduction of substances into the body.

endoradiosonde   A tiny pill-enclosed transducer and radio transmitter for sensing physiological conditions in the stomach and intestines; it transmits corresponding signals to instruments outside.

endothermic reaction   A chemical reaction producing cold (i.e., one in which kinetic energy is lost). Compare EXOTHERMIC REACTION.

end-plate magnetron   A magnetron whose oscillation intensity is increased by a positive

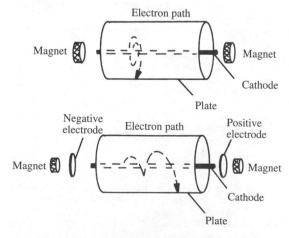

end-plate magnetron

and a negative end plate, the electric field between them causes the electrons to move axially while spinning.

end point   1. For a precision potentiometer, the shaft position between the last and first positions of measurement. **2.** The point at which the useful life of a device can be considered spent. **3.** The point at which a time interval or operational sequence ends. **4.** The end-point voltage of a primary or Edison storage cell. **5.** For a lead-acid storage cell, the specific-gravity value of the electrolyte at which the cell is considered in need of recharging (nominally 1.150 to 1.175).

end-point control   A form of quality control in which the end item is checked for defects.

end-point sensitivity   A means of expressing the sensitivity of a meter or other indicating device: the ratio, in decibels, between the input signal required to produce a full-scale or maximum reading and the smallest detectable input signal.

end-point voltage   The voltage of a battery or cell terminal when the device is no longer useful.

end resistance   In a rheostat or potentiometer, the resistance between the wiper and the end terminal when the wiper is set to the end point of the device.

end-resistance offset   In a potentiometer, the resistance between the wiper and an end terminal when they are in contact.

end-scale deflection   See END-SCALE VALUE.

end-scale value   For an indicating meter, the electrical quantity indicated at the last graduation on the scale.

end section   Either the input or output section of a multisection filter.

end setting   1. The fully clockwise or fully counterclockwise setting of a rotatable control. **2.** The minimum or maximum setting of a control.

end shield   In a magnetron, a shield that confines the space charge to the interaction space.

end spaces   The cavities at either end of the anode block in a multicavity magnetron tube; they terminate all the anode-block cavity resonators.

end use   The intended application of a circuit or device.

energize   To apply operating power and input signals to a circuit or device.

energized   The condition of a circuit or device that is powered or excited.

energy   Symbol, W. Common units: joule, watt-hour, and kilowatt-hour. **1.** The capacity for doing work. Some common forms of energy are electrical, mechanical, and chemical. Also see CONSERVATION OF ENERGY, KINETIC ENERGY, and POTENTIAL ENERGY. **2.** The work performed by electric power. The unit used by utility companies is the kilowatt-hour (kWh), equal to the product Pt, where P is power in kilowatts and t is the period (hours) during which the power is used.

energy-band diagram   A diagram depicting the various energy levels within the atom of a conductor, semiconductor, or insulator.

energy barrier   The natural potential gradient across a semiconductor junction. In the absence of an applied voltage, the gradient, not measurable from the outside, prevents total interaction between the n- and p-type materials.

energy cell   1. A usually small primary or secondary cell—especially the kind used in hearing aids and electronic watches. **2.** A capacitive-type direct-current (dc) source (see ENERGY-STORAGE DEVICE, **2**).

energy consumption   1. The conversion of energy from one form to another by a component, circuit, system, or machine, in the process of performing some useful task. **2.** The amount of energy involved in the process defined in **1**.

energy conversion   The transformation of energy from one form to another. See also CONSERVATION OF ENERGY and ENERGY TRANSFORMATION.

energy-conversion device   A component, circuit, system, or machine that changes energy from one form to another. See also CONSERVATION OF ENERGY.

energy density   1. For an energy-producing cell, such as an electrochemical cell, the ratio of available energy to cell mass. It is expressed in joules per gram or in watt-hours per kilogram. **2.** For an energy-producing cell, the ratio of available energy to cell volume. Expressed in joules per cubic centimeter or in watt-hours per cubic centimeter.

energy gap   In the energy-level diagram for a semiconductor or insulator, the region between valence and conduction bands representing the minimum energy required to make the electron pass from the valence to the conduction band (i.e., to become a current carrier). Also called *forbidden energy band.*

energy level   A constant-energy state, such as one of the energy levels of an electron in an atom.

energy-level diagram   1. A diagram showing the energy levels (in electronvolts) of electrons in the various shells of an atom. **2.** A diagram showing variations in power that correspond to variations in current in a channel.

energy loss   In any system, the energy that is unavoidably lost (i.e., it is not converted into useful work). Also see ENTROPY and POWER LOSS.

energy of a charge   The energy level of an electrostatic charge. It is $QV/2$ ergs, where Q is the quantity of electricity in coulombs, and V is the potential in volts.

energy product   An expression of the effectiveness of a permanent magnet. The magnetic flux density is multiplied by the magnetic field strength to obtain the energy product, specified in gauss-oersteds.

energy redistribution A mathematical process for determining the effective duration of an irregular pulse. The instantaneous power output of the irregular pulse is integrated from the start to the end of the pulse. Then, a rectangular pulse is constructed having the same peak power and the same total energy content (area under the power curve). The length of this rectangular pulse is considered to be the effective duration of the irregular pulse.

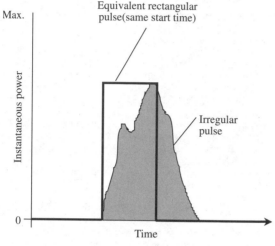

energy redistribution

energy state The condition of an electron, as expressed by its position and velocity, with respect to the position and velocity of other electrons.

energy-storage capacitor A usually high-value capacitor used primarily to store the charge used to fire a lamp (as in a photoflash unit), create a spark discharge (as in electronic ignition), or perform some similar function.

energy-storage device **1.** See CAPACITOR. **2.** A small, electrochemical component offering very high capacitance (e.g., several farads) and low leakage current (less than 1 pA). It has a number of applications, including long-interval timing, power-supply filtering, and energy-cell service. Its active ingredients are compressed powders.

energy stored in capacitor The electrical energy in the field between the plates of a charged capacitor. In this instance, energy $W = CE^2/2$, where W is the energy in joules, C is the capacitance in farads, and E is the voltage in volts.

energy stored in inductor The magnetic energy in the field surrounding an inductor carrying current. In this instance, energy $W = LI^2/2$, where W is the energy in joules, L is the inductance in henrys, and I is the current in amperes.

energy transformation The conversion of one form of energy into another, as with a transducer.

engine analyzer An instrument for checking the performance of an automobile engine. In addition to measuring voltage and resistance throughout a car's electrical system, the instrument measures engine speed, cam dwell angle, and other factors.

engineer **1.** A person who designs machines, circuits, and other devices. **2.** A person who develops methods of utilizing machines, circuits, or other devices more efficiently, or for new applications. **3.** To design or implement an apparatus.

engineering The science of applying scientific laws to technical problems and designing practical devices. Also see ELECTRICAL ENGINEER and ELECTRONICS ENGINEER.

enhanced-carrier demodulation A method of reducing distortion in the demodulation of amplitude-modulated (AM) signals. A properly phased and synchronized local carrier is added to the signal in the demodulator.

enhancement mode Operation characteristic of an ENHANCEMENT-TYPE MOSFET.

enhancement-type MOSFET A metal-oxide semiconductor field-effect transistor (MOSFET) in which the channel directly under the gate electrode is widened (enhanced) by a negative gate voltage in the n-channel unit or by a positive gate voltage in the p-channel unit. Compare DEPLETION-TYPE MOSFET.

ENIAC An electronic computer developed at the University of Pennsylvania. The name is an acronym for *Electronic Numerical Integrator And Calculator.*

ENIC Abbreviation of *voltage negative-impedance converter.*

enrichment In a mixture of different isotopes of a given element, the increase in the relative concentration of one particular isotope.

ensemble **1.** A collection of devices that functions together as a complete unit. **2.** In music recording, the ability of all the musicians to hear each other during the session. **3.** A set of random mathematical functions, all starting at the same point.

ENSI Abbreviation of EQUIVALENT-NOISE-SIDEBAND INPUT.

entladungsstrahlen Ultraviolet radiation emitted by electric arcs. At atmospheric pressure, the wavelength is approximately 40 to 90 nanometers, depending on the arc length. The term is derived from the German word for *discharge rays.*

entrainment Providing a path for gases to escape from an electrochemical cell or battery.

entrance delay In security applications, a delay that allows authorized people time to leave the protected area after activating the alarm system, or to deactivate the system after entering the protected area. The delay is approximately 30 to 45 seconds.

entropy **1.** In all closed physical systems, the measure of energy wasted. According to the second law of thermodynamics, for example, supplied heat can never be converted entirely into work. **2.** In communications, the amount of information in a message, defined as the base-10 logarithm of the number of equivalent messages that can exist. **3.** A natural process in which the energy in the universe tends to become more uniformly distributed with the passage of time.

entropy coding A form of digital encoding that minimizes redundancy, thereby increasing the amount of data in a given amount of memory or storage space.

entry **1.** A unit of computer input or output information. **2.** A data item in a table or list. **3.** A computer source program statement. **4.** In a computer program, the address of the first instruction.

entry condition A condition that must be specified before a computer program is run (e.g., establishing operand values).

entry-level system **1.** The least-sophisticated computer that will perform the things that a user requires. **2.** A simple electronic or computer system (e.g., an amateur radio transciever or personal computer, intended for ease of operation, and from which the user expects to upgrade to a more powerful system at a later date).

entry point In a computer program, the first instruction to be implemented, or a point during the run when data can be entered.

envelope **1.** On a graph, the imaginary line joining successive signal peaks. In the graph for an amplitude-modulated signal, the line reproduces the modulating wave. **2.** The enclosure of a transistor or integrated circuit. **3.** The glass shell of a vacuum tube.

envelope delay In a tuned amplifier, time delay introduced in the envelope of a modulated signal by varying the phase of the envelope· with the modulating frequency. This delay varies directly with the amount by which the sidebands shift, with respect to the carrier frequency.

enveloped file A computer file with labels permitting it to be handled by a computer of a type different from that used to make the file.

environmental conditions See ENVIRONMENTAL FACTORS.

environmental factors Aspects of the space immediately surrounding and sometimes influencing electronic equipment. Examples: altitude, dust, light, moisture, noise, pressure, shock, temperature, and vibration.

environmentally sealed Sealed against the effects of adverse environmental factors.

environmental test chamber See CLIMATE CHAMBER.

E$_o$ **1.** Symbol for OUTPUT VOLTAGE. **2.** Symbol for *zero reference voltage*.

EOF Abbreviation of *end of file*.

EOL Abbreviation of *end of line*.

EOLM Abbreviation of *electro-optical light modulator*.

EOR Abbreviation of END OF (program) RUN.

EOS Abbreviation of *electro-optical system(s)*.

EOT Abbreviation of *end of tape*.

EOTS Abbreviation of *electro-optical tracking system*.

E$_P$ **1.** Symbol for PLATE VOLTAGE. **2.** Symbol for PEAK VOLTAGE.

EP Abbreviation for EXTENDED PLAY.

ephemeris time Time measured with respect to the orbit of the earth around the sun. Initiated in the year 1900 AD.

epipolar navigation A scheme for position sensing and navigation that uses an artificially intelligent vision system. Allows calculation of position and velocity, based on changes in the visualized direction, size, and shape of an object whose actual location, size, and shape are precisely known. It is used in some mobile robots.

episcotister A mechanical light beam modulator. The device consists of a series of rotating disks having transparent and opaque sections that alternately interrupt and pass the light beam at an audio-frequency rate.

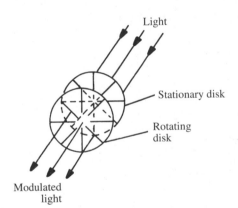

episcotister

epitaxial Pertaining to, or having the property of, EPITAXY.

epitaxial deposition The tendency of certain materials to grow on a semiconductor substrate under certain conditions.

epitaxial device A semiconductor device built by means of EPITAXIAL GROWTH.

epitaxial film A film of single-crystal semiconductor material deposited onto a single-crystal semiconductor substrate.

epitaxial growth Growing monocrystalline silicon on a silicon wafer by precipitating silicon from a gas in which the wafer is placed. Epitaxy is secured between the precipitate and the wafer.

epitaxial layer A semiconductor layer exhibiting epitaxy. Also see EPITAXIAL GROWTH.

epitaxial mesa transistor See DOUBLE-DIF-FUSED EPITAXIAL MESA TRANSISTOR.

epitaxial planar transistor A planar transistor having an epitaxially grown collector on a low-resistivity substrate, and a diffused base and emitter.

epitaxial process See EPITAXIAL GROWTH PROCESS.

epitaxial transistor A transistor in which an epitaxial layer (into which a base region later is diffused and an emitter region alloyed) is grown on the face of a semiconductor wafer, which serves as the collector. Also see DOUBLE-DIFFUSED EPITAXIAL MESA TRANSISTOR.

epitaxy The condition in which atoms in a thin film of single-crystal semiconductor material grown on the surface of the same kind of wafer continue their characteristic alignment. Also see EPITAXIAL GROWTH.

E plane The plane of an antenna containing the electric field.

E plane bend See E BEND.

E-plane tee junction A waveguide junction whose structure changes in the plane of the electric field.

epoxy resin A synthetic resin used to encapsulate electronic equipment, or as a cement. Epoxy resins are based on ethylene oxide or its derivatives.

EPROM Abbreviation of *erasable programmable read-only memory.*

EPU **1.** Abbreviation of *electronic power unit.* **2.** Abbreviation of *emergency power unit.*

Eq **1.** Abbreviation of *equation.* **2.** Abbreviation of EQUALIZER or EQUALIZATION.

equal alternations Positive and negative half-cycles of a wave that have identical shape and amplitude.

equal-energy source A light source that has a constant emission rate (energy per unit wavelength).

equal-energy white The color of light emitted by a source radiating equally the wavelengths of the visible-light spectrum.

equal heterodyne In a beat-frequency system, the condition in which the outputs of the two heterodyning oscillators are identical.

equality circuit A logic circuit that, when two numbers are put into it, outputs logic 1 if the numbers are equal, and logic 0 if the numbers are not equal.

equalization **1.** The use of an EQUALIZER to make the frequency response of a line, amplifier, or other device uniform over a given frequency range. **2.** The use of an EQUALIZER to modify the frequency response of a line, amplifier, or other device.

equalizer A circuit or device, such as a compensated attenuator, that allows the user to tailor the frequency response of a line, amplifier, or

other device. Sometimes used in sophisticated high-fidelity stereo amplifier systems, to obtain a desired bass/midrange/treble frequency output.

equalizer circuit breaker A form of circuit breaker that trips in the event of unbalance in an electrical system.

equalizing current A current that flows in the circuit of two compound generators connected in parallel.

equalizing network A circuit used to equalize a line.

equalizing pulses In a television signal waveform, several pulses (preceding and following the vertical sync pulse and having a repetition rate of twice the power-line frequency) that start the vertical retrace at the correct instant for good interlace.

equal-loudness curves See AUDIBILITY CURVES.

equal vectors Vectors having the same magnitude and the same direction. They do not necessarily originate at the same point. Compare IDENTICAL VECTORS.

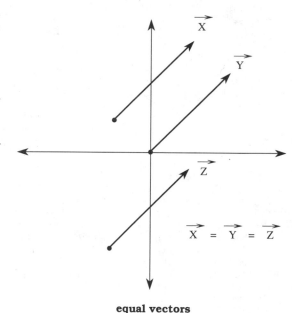

equal vectors

equation solver A (usually analog) computer for solving linear simultaneous equations or for determining the roots of polynomials.

equatorial orbit A satellite orbit that lies in the plane of the earth's equator.

equiphase surface Any surface in a wave, over which the field vectors at a particular instant have either 0° or 180° phase difference.

equiphase zone The space region in which two radionavigation signals show no phase difference.

equipment **1.** Collectively, apparatus or components designated for a specific purpose (e.g., *radio equipment*). **2.** A functional electronic unit, such as a test instrument, receiver, or memory unit.

equipment chain A system consisting of series-connected circuits or devices.

equipment ground An electrical ground connection intended to reduce the chances of electric shock. An equipment ground does not necessarily constitute a good radio-frequency ground; it serves only to eliminate potential differences among the individual units in a system.

equipment life The period during which electronic equipment functions according to specifications; it is terminated at an END POINT.

equipment test A usually preliminary, qualifying test of electronic equipment.

equipotential Having a potential difference of zero; being at the same voltage level.

equipotential line Between two charged plates, the locus (an imaginary line) of points having the same potential, with respect to the plates.

equipotential surface A surface on which all points have the same electrical potential.

equisignal Pertaining to signals having equal intensity.

equisignal localizer See TONE LOCALIZER.

equisignal radio-range beacon For aircraft guidance, a radio-range beacon that transmits two distinct signals that are received by aircraft with equal intensity only in certain directions.

equisignal surface The "surface" around a transmitting antenna formed by points of equal field intensity.

equisignal zone The region in which two radionavigation signals have identical amplitude.

equivalence The condition existing when one network can be substituted for another without disturbing currents, impedances, and voltages at the terminals.

equivalent absorbing power See EQUIVALENT STOPPING POWER.

equivalent absorption Unit, sabin. The rate at which a surface absorbs sound energy.

equivalent binary digits For a given decimal number or specific character, the corresponding binary digits (bits).

equivalent bit rate The number of binary digits (bits) that can be sent in a given unit of time, such as one second, in a digital communications system.

equivalent capacitance The value of a single lumped capacitance, that would cause the same action as the capacitance distributed throughout a circuit.

equivalent circuit A circuit that has the same overall current, impedance, phase, and voltage relationships as a more-complicated counterpart that it usually replaces for analysis.

equivalent component density For a circuit in which discrete components are not used or are not evident, the volume of that circuit divided by the number of discrete components that would be required if the circuit used them.

equivalent conductivity The conductivity of a solution that contains 1 gram equivalent of the solute in the space between electrodes 1 centimeter apart.

equivalent dark-input current For a photoelectric device, the illumination required for an output current equal to the DARK CURRENT of the device.

equivalent decrement The value of decrement in a damped wave that would result in the same amount of interference at a receiver as the interference caused by the sidebands of an amplitude-modulated signal.

equivalent delay line A comparatively simple network, such as a resistance-capacitance (RC) circuit, that will provide the attenuation and phase characteristics of an ideal delay line.

equivalent delta In a three-phase system, a delta-connected circuit that is equivalent to a given wye-connected circuit, from the standpoint of impedance and phase. Also see DELTA CONNECTION and WYE CONNECTION. Compare EQUIVALENT WYE and WYE-EQUIVALENT CIRCUIT.

equivalent differential input capacitance For a differential amplifier, the equivalent input capacitance (see EQUIVALENT CAPACITANCE) at one input (inverting or noninverting) when the opposite input is grounded.

equivalent differential input impedance For a differential amplifier, the equivalent input impedance at one input (inverting or noninverting) when the other input is grounded.

equivalent differential input resistance For a differential amplifier, the equivalent input resistance at one input (inverting or noninverting) when the other input is grounded.

equivalent equations Two equations for an unknown that have the same root.

equivalent four-wire system A two-wire line over which full-duplex operation is obtained by use of frequency division.

equivalent height See VIRTUAL HEIGHT.

equivalent impedance **1.** The value of a single lumped impedance that would cause the same action as the impedance distributed throughout a circuit. **2.** An impedance that draws current of the same strength and phase as that drawn by an impedance it replaces.

equivalent inductance The value of a single lumped inductance that would cause the same action as the inductance distributed throughout a circuit.

equivalent input offset current For a differential amplifier, the difference between currents flowing into the inverting and noninverting inputs when the output voltage is zero.

equivalent input offset voltage For a differential amplifier, the input voltage required to reduce the output voltage to zero.

equivalent input wideband noise voltage   For a differential amplifier, the ratio V_o/G_v, where V_o is the root-mean-square (rms) output-noise voltage, and G_v is the direct-current (dc) voltage gain.

equivalent length of antenna   1. The electrical length of an antenna, as measured in degrees or wavelengths. **2.** The free-space length of an antenna. **3.** The length d (in feet) of a quarter-wave resonant antenna at a specific frequency f (in megahertz), given by the formula $d = 234/f$. **4.** The length d (in feet) of a half-wave resonant antenna at a specific frequency f (in megahertz), given by the formula $d = 468/f$.

equivalent length of electric dipole   The distance, measured in a straight line, separating the points that represent the charge centers of an electric dipole.

equivalent length of feed line   The electrical length of a feed line as measured in degrees or wavelengths. Generally, this is equal to $1/v$ times the line length in free-space wavelengths, where v is the VELOCITY FACTOR of the line, expressed as a fraction between 0 and 1.

equivalent length of magnet   The distance separating the poles of a magnet. In a bar magnet, these poles are not exactly at the ends. The actual equivalent length is about 83% of the length of the bar magnet.

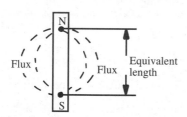

equivalent length of magnet

equivalent loudness   The actual intensity, in decibels, of a given sound whose apparent loudness changes with frequency.

equivalent network   A network that can replace a more-complex network for analysis purposes.

equivalent noise input   The value of modulated luminous flux that, when applied to a photoelectric device, produces a root-mean-square (rms) output current equal to the device's rms noise current.

equivalent-noise-sideband input   Abbreviation, **ENSI.** A specification for receiver noise characteristics. Numerically, $ENSI = 0.3E_s(P_n/P_s)^{1/2}$, where E_s is the voltage of an unmodulated radiofrequency (RF) carrier applied to the receiver, P_n is the resulting noise-output power of the receiver (measured with an rms meter), and P_s is the noise-output power measured with the RF signal 30% amplitude modulated at 400 Hz with a 400-Hz bandpass filter inserted between the receiver output terminals and the meter.

equivalent noise temperature   For a component having resistance, the temperature (degrees absolute) at which a theoretically perfect resistor having the resistance of the component would generate the same noise the component generates at room temperature.

equivalent optics   The analogy between certain optical lenses and prisms and the electrostatic deflection of an electron beam. Thus, when the upper deflecting plate in an electrostatic deflection system is made negative and the lower plate is positive, the beam is deflected downward, like horizontal light rays bent by a prism. When both plates are made equally negative, the beam converges to a point, as light rays do when they pass through a double convex lens. When both plates are made equally positive, the beam spreads out, as do light rays passing through a double concave lens.

equivalent permeability   The permeability of a component made of certain materials, compared with that of a component having the same reluctance, shape, and size, but made of different materials.

equivalent reactance   The value of a single lumped reactance that would cause the same action as the reactance distributed throughout a circuit.

equivalent resistance   The value of a single lumped resistance that would cause the same action as the resistance distributed throughout a circuit.

equivalent series and parallel circuits   Series and parallel circuits in which current, voltage, phase, and frequency relationships are identical. Any series circuit can be transformed into an equivalent parallel circuit.

equivalent series resistance   The equivalent resistance acting in series with circuit components.

equivalent sine wave   A sine wave of the same frequency and effective voltage as a given wave.

equivalent stopping power   For a material in the path of radioactive particles, the thickness of the material that produces the same energy loss as that produced by one centimeter of air.

equivalent time   The effective duration of some phenomenon, such as a pulse.

equivalent volt   See ELECTRONVOLT.

equivalent wye   In a three-phase system, a wye-connected circuit that is equivalent to a given delta-connected circuit from a standpoint of impedance and phase. Also see DELTA CONNECTION, EQUIVALENT DELTA, WYE CONNECTION, and WYE-EQUIVALENT CIRCUIT.

equivalent Y   See EQUIVALENT WYE.

equivocation   A condition in which the meaning of data depends on certain parameters.

ER   Abbreviation of ECHO RANGING.

Er   Symbol for ERBIUM.

E$_r$ Symbol for voltage drop across a resistance.

erasable storage   In computer operations, any storage medium holding information that can be erased.

erasable PROM   A programmable read-only memory (PROM) from which the data can be removed, usually by exposure to ultraviolet light. Also see PROM.

erase   To obliterate or remove a signal, especially a recorded one, as in the erasure of recorded material from a magnetic tape or the data from a computer disk.

erase button   A pushbutton that actuates the circuit supplying a signal that erases stored material (as the display on a storage oscilloscope).

erase current   In an electromagnetic erase head, the current flowing through the coil of the head. In most instances, it is a high-frequency current (usually the regular bias current), but it can be as low as 60 Hz, as long as the speaker does not respond to what remains of it on the tape after erasure.

erase head   In a tape recorder, a head used to erase recorded material from tape. It can contain a permanent magnet (see ERASE MAGNET) or an electromagnet whose coil carries erase current.

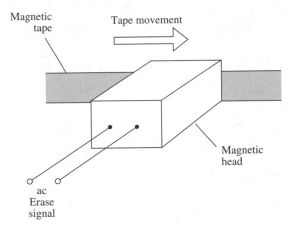

erase head

erase magnet   In a tape recorder, a magnet used to erase recorded material from tape. Because the strength of the magnet is greater than that of the magnetized areas on the tape, erasure is complete (the tape left demagnetized).

erase oscillator   In a tape recorder, a high-frequency (typically 30 to 80 kHz) oscillator that supplies erase current.

eraser   See BULK ERASER.

erase signal   A signal that causes recorded material to be erased (see ERASE and ERASE CURRENT).

erasing speed   The rate at which successive storage elements are erased, as in a charge-storage tube.

erasure   **1.** In tape-recording and digital-computer operations, the process of erasing a recorded signal (see ERASE). **2.** An erasure accomplished by the process described in 1, above.

erbium   Symbol, Er. A metallic element of the rare-earth group. Atomic number, 68. Atomic weight, 167.26.

E region   See E LAYER.

e register   In a computer, a register used in double-precision calculations.

E$_r$-E$_y$ signal   In color television, the resultant signal that is the difference between the original full-red and E_y signals.

ERG   Abbreviation of ELECTRORETINOGRAPHY.

erg   Abbreviation, e. A unit of work. It is the work done by a force of one dyne (10^{-5} newton) acting through a distance of one centimeter.

ergograph   An instrument used to measure and record work done by muscles.

ergometer   An instrument for measuring energy consumed or work accomplished.

ergon   See ERG.

E$_{rms}$ Symbol for ROOT-MEAN-SQUARE VOLTAGE.

ERP   Abbreviation of EFFECTIVE RADIATED POWER.

error   **1.** In calculations and measurements, the difference between a true value and an observed or calculated value. **2.** In electronic circuits, especially those of automatic control systems, the difference between a required (or reference signal) level and the actual signal level. **3.** In communications, a discrepancy between the transmitted data and the received data.

error accumulation   The adding-up of maximum possible error when measurements are repeatedly made. Generally, the maximum plus-or-minus error per measurement is multiplied by the number of measurements.

error amplifier   An amplifier for boosting error current or voltage.

error-checking code   An error-correcting or error-detecting code.

error-correcting code   An error-detecting code that, in addition to the function indicated by its name, indicates the correct code.

error-correcting telegraph   A digital communications system in which an improbable or incorrect character is not accepted. In the event that such a character is received, the receiver instructs the transmitter to send that character again.

error correction   **1.** The restoration of mutilated, corrupted, or missing data in a digital system, especially in magnetic data storage media, such as tapes and disks. **2.** In digital communications, any scheme in which the receiver (destination) automatically eliminates (to the greatest possible extent) errors in data from a transmitter (source). For example, the destination can instruct the source to repeat questionable characters or words.

error-correction routine In computer operations, a series of programmed instructions to detect and correct errors in files. A common example is a spell-checking program for word-processed document files.

error current An error signal that is a feedback current for automatically correcting a system.

error curve A bell-shaped curve that describes the distribution of errors in measurement around a true value.

error-detecting code In computer operations, a character-coding system that ensures that an impossible combination (forbidden characters) will be generated by an error (for error detection).

error-detecting routine A computer program that detects errors by checking the validity of data.

error detection and feedback In computer operations, a system in which an error (sensed by an error-detecting code) automatically generates a request to repeat the suspect signal.

error detector A sensor that responds to an error signal by delivering a signal proportional to the error.

error diagnostics As performed by a compiler, detecting and indicating the presence of errors in source language statements.

error interrupt A computer program halt caused by a software or hardware error and accompanied by a display of what has happened.

error list As produced by a compiler, a list of source language statement faults.

error message During a computer program run, a statement (displayed on a peripheral) of what is in error.

error of measurement The positive or negative difference between the value of an actual measurement and the true (or most probable) value.

error range For a data item, the range of values over which it will cause an error.

error rate In data transmission, the ratio of errors transmitted to the data transmitted.

error-rate damping Damping that involves adding to an error signal another signal that is proportional in rate of change.

error ratio 1. In a received message, the number of incorrect characters divided by the total number of characters. Can be represented as a fraction between 0 and 1 or as a percentage by multiplying the fraction by 100. 2. A measure of distortion for digital signal communications. The number of inaccurately received bits divided by the total number of received bits.

error routine A computer program segment that is input when an error is detected so that an appropriate action is taken (correct the error, repeat the process, etc.).

error-sensing circuit A circuit that samples the output current or voltage of a power supply, amplifier, or control system, compares this output with a standard value, and delivers a feedback (correction) signal whose amplitude is proportional to the difference (error).

error signal In a servo system, an output signal whose value is proportional to the difference between the actual operating quantity of the system and a standard reference quantity. The signal is fed back to the input of the system for automatic correction.

error tape In data processing, a record tape designed and used for storing errors for subsequent study.

error voltage An error signal that is a feedback voltage for automatically correcting a system.

Es Symbol for EINSTEINIUM.

Esaki diode See TUNNEL DIODE.

E scope See E DISPLAY.

escape character In computer operations, a character indicating that the next character belongs in a new group.

escapement A (usually oscillating) mechanical or electromechanical device that stores energy (often in a spiral spring) on one swing, and returns that energy on the next swing. Such a mechanism advances a shaft progressively in a clock or watch, and in some control equipment.

escape velocity 1. The minimum velocity (about 25,000 miles per hour or seven miles per second) required for a space vehicle to completely escape the gravitational field of the earth. 2. The minimum velocity required for a space vehicle to completely escape the gravitational field of a planet or star. 3. The minimum velocity required for an electron to escape the electrical influence of an atomic nucleus.

escutcheon A usually decorative plate that frames an opening or covers a panel in a piece of equipment (e.g., the escutcheon of a radio tuning dial).

ESD Abbreviation of ENERGY-STORAGE DEVICE.

ESG Abbreviation of *electronic sweep generator*.

Esnault-Pelterie formula A formula for approximately calculating the inductance of a single-layer solenoidal coil:

$$L = 0.1008(a^2n^2)/(s + 0.92a)$$

where L is the coil inductance in microhenrys, a is the radius of the coil in inches, s is the length of the coil in inches, and n is the number of turns in the winding. The formula is accurate to 0.1 percent for all values of $2a/s$ between 0.2 and 1.5.

ESS Abbreviation of *electronic switching system*.

EST Abbreviation of EASTERN STANDARD TIME.

esu Abbreviation of ELECTROSTATIC UNIT(S).

ET Abbreviation of EPHEMERIS TIME.

ETC Abbreviation of *electronic temperature control*.

etchant   Any substance such as cupric chloride, ferrous chloride, or hydrochloric acid, used in etching.

etched circuit   A circuit produced by etching the metallic coating of a substrate to provide the required pattern of conductors and terminals to which discrete components are soldered.

etched circuit

etch factor   The ratio of the depth to the width of an etched track in an etched circuit.

etching   **1.** Chemically eating away a metal to form a desired pattern, such as an etched circuit. **2.** Thinning a quartz-crystal plate by slowly eroding one or both of its faces with hydrofluoric acid to fine-tune the resonant frequency.

ET-cut crystal   A piezoelectric plate cut from a quartz crystal at an angle of +66°, with respect to the z-axis. Also see CRYSTAL AXES and CRYSTAL CUTS.

ether   **1.** Also called *luminiferous ether*. A nonviscous fluid once thought to fill space, convey waves (radio, light, etc.), and sustain fields. **2.** A volatile liquid occasionally used in electronics as a solvent [e.g., ethyl oxide $(C_2H_5)_2O$].

ether drift   The postulated motion between a material body and the ether (see ETHER, **1**). The concept was checked by Michelson and Morley, who failed to find that the earth moves relative to the ether. This eventually led to scientific rejection of the so-called *ether theory* of the propagation of light.

ethical slave   A machine, especially a smart robot, that is treated in the manner of a slave, based on the notion that a machine cannot have "feelings." Some researchers fear that the use of ethical slaves could lead to technological nightmares. For example, robots might be used as soldiers in a marauding offensive army; the commanders could rationalize that there is nothing immoral about the war because there is no loss of life on their side.

E transformer   A differential transformer whose primary is wound on the center leg of an E core, the secondaries being wound on the outer legs.

Ettinghausen effect   A phenomenon somewhat like the HALL EFFECT. It occurs when a metal strip, carrying current longitudinally, is placed into a magnetic field perpendicular to the plane of the strip: corresponding points on opposite edges of the strip exhibit different temperatures.

Eu   Symbol for EUROPIUM.

eudiometer   **1.** An instrument for measuring the amount of oxygen in the air. **2.** An instrument for analyzing gases.

eureka   **1.** See CONSTANTAN. **2.** The ground transponder beacon in the British rebecca-eureka radar navigational system (see REBECCA-EUREKA SYSTEM).

europium   Symbol, Eu. An element of the rare-earth group. Atomic number, 63. Atomic weight, 151.96.

eutectic   **1.** A form of reaction in which mixed liquids solidify when cooled. **2.** The solid substance resulting from a reaction as defined in **1**.

eutectic alloy   A metallic alloy with a specific melting point, made via eutectic process.

eutectic bond   A connection between two dissimilar metals, facilitated by a third metal alloyed, via eutectic process, to the adjoining faces.

eV   Symbol for ELECTRONVOLT.

evacuation   The removal of air or other gases from a tube or chamber, specifically, the envelope of a vacuum tube that houses the internal elements.

evaporation   **1.** A technique for electrically depositing a film of a selected metal on a metallic or nonmetallic surface. A filament of the metal to be deposited is heated by an electric current in a vacuum chamber, which makes filament particles travel to the (nearby) object to be coated, where they condense as a film. In an alternate method, a piece of the metal to be deposited is laid on or wrapped around a filament of some other metal. **2.** Electron emission by a hot cathode.

evaporation theory   The theory that electrons will acquire sufficient escape velocity to leave a material when the energy acquired by (or imparted to) the electron exceeds the work function of the material. Also see WORK FUNCTION.

E vector   The vector that represents the electric component of an electromagnetic wave.

even-even nucleus   An atomic nucleus containing an even number of protons and an even number of neutrons. An example is the alpha particle, or helium nucleus, which contains two protons and two neutrons.

even harmonic   In a complex waveform, an even-numbered multiple of the fundamental frequency. Compare ODD HARMONIC.

even line   In a television picture, an even-numbered member of the 262.5 horizontal lines scanned by the spot in developing the even-line field. Compare ODD LINE.

even-line field   On a television screen, the complete field obtained when the spot has traced all the even-numbered lines. Compare ODD-LINE FIELD.

even-line field

even parity check   A check to verify the presence of an even number of ones or zeros in a group of bits.

event   An occurrence that affects the state of a computer file.

event counter   Any device that measures the number of specified events taking place within a certain interval of time.

evolution   Extracting a root of a number (e.g., square root, cube root, etc.).

E wave   In microwave operations, the transverse magnetic (TM) wave. Also see WAVEGUIDE MODES.

EWR   Abbreviation of EARLY-WARNING RADAR.

EWS   Abbreviation of *early-warning system.*

E_x   **1.** Symbol for voltage drop across a reactance. **2.** Symbol for EXCITATION ENERGY.

exa-   Symbol, E. A prefix meaning 10^{18} (International System of Units).

exalted-carrier reception   In radio reception, overcoming the effects of selective fading by maintaining the carrier at a high amplitude. This is accomplished before demodulation by removing the carrier from an amplitude-modulated or phase-modulated signal, amplifying it, and reinserting it at a higher amplitude with the sidebands.

exc   **1.** Abbreviation of EXCITER. **2.** Abbreviation of EXCITATION.

except gate   A logic gate that delivers an output pulse when an input pulse is present at one or more of a set of input terminals, and absent from one or more of another set of input terminals. Also called *exclusive-OR element.*

excess charge   The amount of overcharge for a storage battery.

excess conduction   In a semiconductor, current conduction by excess electrons.

excess electron   **1.** An electron that, when introduced into an atom, results in a negative ion. **2.**

An electron resulting from the addition of a donor impurity to a semiconductor substance.

excess meter   A meter that integrates the amount of power in excess of some predetermined level.

excess minority carriers   The number of minority carriers in excess of the normal equilibrium number in a semiconductor material.

excess modified index of refraction   Symbol, M. For waves transmitted through a refracting medium, a modified index of refraction greater than unity.

excess noise   Electrical noise caused by current in a semiconductor material.

excess sound pressure   Unit, dyne/cm². In a medium conducting sound waves, the quantity P_t - P_s, where P_t is total instantaneous pressure at a given point in the medium, and P_s is static pressure in the absence of the sound waves.

excess-three code   A computer code derived from binary notation by adding binary three (i.e., 0011) to each four-bit group. Thus, decimal seven is 1010 in the code (it is 0111 in binary). Unlike the binary representation for zero, the excess-three representation (0011) contains two ones, a feature that distinguishes actual zero from a machine fault.

exchange   **1.** To reverse the contents of two memory banks. For example, if the memory banks are called A and B, an exchange is the placing of the contents of memory A into memory B, and the placing of the contents of memory B into memory A. The original contents are removed. **2.** A two-way sequence of data transmissions. **3.** A designated location in a telephone circuit.

exchange line   A telephone line.

exciplex   In a laser, a method of adjusting the color by means of chemical reactions in organic dyes.

excitant   The electrolyte in a voltaic cell.

excitation   **1.** Supplying input-signal driving current, driving power, or driving voltage. **2.** Input-signal driving current, driving power, or driving voltage.

excitation anode   In a mercury-pool tube, an auxiliary anode whose operation maintains the cathode spot when no output current is being drawn from the tube.

excitation current   **1.** Input-electrode current in an excited transistor amplifier. **2.** Grid current in an excited vacuum-tube amplifier. **3.** Current flowing in the circuit of the excitation anode of a mercury-pool tube. **4.** Current flowing in the exciter circuit of an alternator. **5.** Shunt-field current in a motor.

excitation energy   **1.** Symbol, E_x. In artificial transmutation, the energy of a nucleus when protons of less than maximum energy have been emitted from the atom. **2.** Electrical energy required by a transducer.

excitation purity   In color television, complete saturation of a hue (i.e., there is no contamination by other colors, and the saturated hue is distributed uniformly).

excitation voltage **1.** The signal voltage that achieves, or is required for, excitation (see EXCITATION, **1**). **2.** The value of driving voltage.

excitator An electrical discharger.

excited atom An atom in which one or more electrons have been pushed out of their normal orbits into higher ones by energy applied from the outside.

excited-field speaker A dynamic speaker in which the magnetic field is provided, not by a permanent magnet, but by direct current flowing through a large coil of wire wound around the speaker core. The coil usually acts as a filter choke in the power supply of the attendant amplifier or receiver.

excited state In artificial transmutation, the state of the nucleus when protons of less-than-maximum energy have been emitted from the atom. The energy of the protons, in this instance, is greater than the ground state.

exciter **1.** An amplifier or oscillator (or a system of such units) that supplies the input (driving) signal to the output amplifier in a radio transmitter or similar device. **2.** A small direct-current (dc) generator that supplies direct current to the field winding of an alternating-current (ac) generator. **3.** See INDUCTION COIL.

exciter lamp **1.** A concentrated-filament, high-intensity incandescent lamp used in sound-on-film recording and reproduction and in some types of electromechanical television. **2.** In a facsimile transmitter, the lamp illuminating what is being scanned.

exciter relay In an electromechanical generator, the relay that activates the direct-current (dc) field excitation during machine startup.

exciter response **1.** A change in the exciter voltage of a motor when the field-circuit resistance changes. **2.** A change in the operating conditions of a radio frequency exciter, as a result of a change in the impedance at the input of the final amplifier.

exciter unit See EXCITER.

exciting current **1.** The output current produced by the exciter of a generator (see EXCITER, **2**). **2.** The field current of a dynamo-type generator. **3.** Primary current in an unloaded transformer.

exciting power **1.** The output power produced by an exciter. **2.** The input-signal power required for full output from a power amplifier. Also called DRIVING POWER.

exciting voltage **1.** Input-signal voltage. **2.** The input-signal-voltage amplitude required for full rated output from a power amplifier. Also called DRIVING VOLTAGE. **3.** The output voltage produced by an exciter.

exciton In a semiconductor or dielectric, a bound electron-hole pair.

excitron A mercury-pool rectifier whose arc is initiated mechanically (e.g., by means of a magnetic plunger in the tube).

exclusion principle The rule that only one particle of a particular kind can occupy a given quantum state at one time.

exclusive-NOR A logic function where the output is 1 if both inputs are 1 or both are 0 (same). The output is 0 if one input is 0 and the other is 1 (different). Compare EXCLUSIVE OR.

exclusive-OR A logic function in which the output is 1 when the two inputs are different, and is 0 when the two inputs are the same.

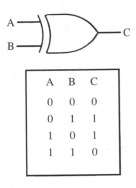

A	B	C
0	0	0
0	1	1
1	0	1
1	1	0

exclusive-OR

excursion **1.** A change in the value of a quantity in a given direction. **2.** In an oscillatory system, a body's moving away from the point of equilibrium or mean position.

execution A computer's performance of the operations required by an instruction.

execution time The length of time required for a computer to complete a designated operation.

executive routine In computer operations, a program that controls and processes other routines. Also called *monitor program*. Compare MONITOR SYSTEM.

exhaust analyzer An instrument for examining the exhaust fumes of an internal combustion engine, to measure the presence of noxious materials and to evaluate air-to-fuel ratio and combustion efficiency.

exhaustion See EVACUATION.

exit **1.** In computer operations, the last instruction in a program or program segment, often taking a subroutine back to the main program. **2.** To leave a computer application, routine or subroutine.

exoskeleton A robot that resembles a suit of armor, and that greatly magnifies the force of physical movements. A human operator occupies the interior. Thus, for example, the operator might use the machine to throw a football

2500 yards, or to run 50 miles an hour, or to smash through walls. Primarily a tool of science fiction writers, this machine is within the scope of current robotic technology.

exosphere   The extreme outer layer of the earth's atmosphere.

exothermic   Pertaining to a chemical or electro-chemical reaction in which heat is given off. Compare ENDOTHERMIC.

exothermic reaction   In a chemical reaction, the production of positive reaction energy (i.e., kinetic energy is gained). Compare ENDOTHER-MIC REACTION.

exp 1. Symbol for EXPONENTIAL. **2.** Abbreviation of EXPERIMENT(AL).

expand 1. In communications, to increase the bandwidth of a signal, restoring it to normal bandwidth after it has been compressed. **2.** In communications, to increase the dynamic range of a signal. **3.** In computer operations, to restore a file to full or normal size after it has been compressed. **4.** To widen the scale of a meter. **5.** To widen (or magnify a portion of) the trace of an oscilloscope beam. Compare COMPRESS.

expandable   Capable of being built up into larger circuits or systems.

expandable gate   In digital logic, a gate that can be provided with an unlimited number of input lines by electrical interconnection with other gates.

expanded memory   In personal computer systems, memory beyond the basic 640 kilobytes (640 kb), up to one megabyte (1 MB). This memory resides in integrated circuits (ICs) in the computer, and is normally volatile (i.e., it is not retained when power is removed). Compare EX-TENDED MEMORY.

expanded-scale meter   A meter having a scale designed to display a narrow range of values. Such a meter used for monitoring the 117-V power line might have a scale reading 100 to 140 V, instead of a conventional scale beginning at zero.

expanded sweep 1. In an oscilloscope, speeding up the deflection of the beam during a selected portion of the trace. **2.** The circuit for the action described in **1**.

expander   A circuit for increasing the dynamic range over which a signal or quantity can vary. A typical example is the volume expander, a device that greatly increases the amplitude of strong signals while weakening, or having no effect on, signals of low amplitude.

expansion 1. In communications, the process of increasing the bandwidth of a signal, restoring it to normal bandwidth after it has been compressed. **2.** In communications, a process in which stronger components are amplified more than weak ones, restoring a signal to its normal dynamic range after it has been compressed. **3.** In computer operations, the restoration of a file to full or normal size after it has been com-

pressed. **4.** The widening of a meter scale. **5.** The widening or magnification of an oscilloscope trace. Compare COMPRESS.

expansion chamber   A cloud chamber for viewing the paths of radioactive particles. It consists of a closed glass cylinder containing humid air and a piston. An electrostatic field is applied through the cylinder, the piston is pulled quickly, and the volume of the chamber expands. The temperature inside falls below the dew point, a cloud is formed, and droplets of water condense on ions, making their paths visible for observation or photography through the cylinder walls.

expansion ratio   In communications, the inverse of COMPRESSION RATIO.

expansion time   For an expansion chamber, the interval during which expansion occurs. The interval is kept short to ensure that the temperature will drop low enough for vapor condensation, and to minimize the possibility of continuing gas motion distorting the track of a particle.

expectation   In probability theory, the middle value (average or mean) of a random variable.

expendable   A component or system that, for economy, is best discarded instead of repaired when it fails. Also called DISPOSABLE COMPONENT.

experiment   One or a series of carefully planned tests carried out under controlled conditions to obtain data or to check performance.

experimental chassis   See ELECTRONIC CHASSIS.

experimental model   A prototype of an electronic circuit or device, produced solely for operational tests or as a model against which theory and design can be checked.

experimental service   A special, nonamateur radio service intended for on-the-air testing of new methods and equipment.

experimental station   A station specially licensed to operate on specific frequencies in the experimental service.

expert system   Also called *rule-based system*. A form of artificial intelligence (AI) that allows a computer or smart robot to act as a highly talented specialist in a specific field. An example is the use of a computer to help a physician diagnose a complex disease. A smart robot might be used as a surgical assistant.

exploring coil   A pickup coil for sensing a signal or magnetic field. Sometimes called a *sniffer*.

exploring electrode 1. A sampling electrode sealed in a discharge tube for measuring ionization at the point of insertion. **2.** Broadly, a test probe.

explosion-proof device   A device that is housed and operated so that its sparking, heating, or production of radiant energy will not cause materials in the environment to explode.

exponent   A number written as a superscript indicating the power to which another number (called the *base*) is to be raised. For example, 2^2

is the square (second power) of 2; x^3 is the cube (third power) of x.

exponential   **1.** A base (such as the natural number e) modified by an exponent. **2.** Related to a change in value as determined by an exponent. Thus, using increments for x in the equation $y = e^x$ produces an exponential curve.

exponential curve   A curve based on powers of a number (such as for $y = e^x$). Also see EXPONENTIAL, EXPONENTIAL DECREASE, and EXPONENTIAL INCREASE.

exponential damping   Damping action described by an exponential curve.

exponential decay   See EXPONENTIAL DECREASE.

exponential decrease   The continuous reduction in the value of a quantity, according to the equation $y = e^{-x}$, which depicts the natural decay curve.

exponential function   A function, such as $f(x) = e^x$, that varies exponentially. See, for example, EXPONENTIAL DECAY, EXPONENTIAL GROWTH, and EXPONENTIAL SERIES.

exponential horn   A horn of circular or rectangular cross section, whose cross-sectional area S at any point x feet along its axis is given by the formula $S = S_0 e^{mx}$, where S_0 is the cross-sectional area at the throat, e is the natural logarithm base (approximately 2.71828), and m is the horn flaring constant.

exponential increase   The continuous increase of a quantity, according to the equation $y = e^x$, which depicts the natural growth curve.

exponential line   A transmission line whose characteristic impedance varies exponentially with its electrical length.

exponential quantity   A quantity involving an exponential (e.g., $3e^x$).

exponential series   A mathematical series based on exponential expressions. Example: $e^x = 1 + x + (x^2/2!) + (x^3/3!) + (x^4/4!) + \dots$

exponential sweep   In cathode-ray-tube (CRT) devices, such as oscilloscopes, a beam sweep that starts fast and slows exponentially.

exponential transmission line   See EXPONENTIAL LINE.

exponential waveform   Any waveform in which the rate of change in the amplitude is directly or inversely proportional to the instantaneous amplitude. The absolute value of the derivative of such a waveform is equal to the absolute value of the instantaneous amplitude, multiplied by a constant that depends on the amplitude units.

exposure   **1.** The total amount of radiation received in a given area, or by a given sample, or by a person, over a specified length of time. **2.** The extent to which a photographic film has been darkened or otherwise modified by visible light, infrared, ultraviolet, or X rays.

exposure meter   **1.** A usually simple instrument for measuring light intensity—especially for photographic purposes. A common form con-

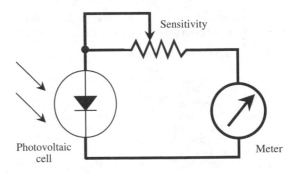

exposure meter

sists of a self-generating photocell connected to a direct-current microammeter. **2.** A device that indicates the amount of ionizing radiation that has been received over a given period of time.

expression control   A volume control in an electronic organ.

extended double Zepp antenna   See DOUBLE-EXTENDED ZEPP ANTENNA.

extended memory   In personal computer systems, memory beyond the first megabyte (1 MB). There is no limit in theory to the extent of this memory, although it is limited by current technology. Used in high-level programs—especially those involving graphical applications, artificial intelligence, or intensive calculations. Resides in integrated circuits (ICs) in the computer, and is normally volatile (i.e., it is not retained when power is removed). Compare EXPANDED MEMORY.

extended octaves   Audio-frequency tones above or below the normal range of an electronic musical instrument. Special circuits must be added to make the extended octaves available.

extended play   Pertaining to a recorded phonograph disc that provides a longer playing time than conventional discs of the same size and recording speed.

extender   A substance added to an encapsulant to make it go further.

extensimeter   See EXTENSOMETER.

extension cable   A flexible, low-capacitance (usually concentric) cable for connecting part of one circuit to part of another. Extension cables are available with a variety of end connectors.

extension cord   A flexible power cord having a male plug on one end and female receptacle on the other.

extension loudspeaker   An auxiliary loudspeaker serving areas in which the main speakers can't be adequately heard.

extensometer   An instrument used to measure small amounts of expansion, contraction, or deformation.

exterior label   On a diskette or tape cartridge used for computer data storage, a written identification on the housing or cartridge, as opposed to the label, which is recorded on the diskette or tape itself.

external armature In a dynamo-type machine, an armature that rotates around the outside of the field magnets, as opposed to the usual (inside) arrangement.

external capacitor A high-value capacitor connected externally to an oscillator or sweep generator to lower its frequency.

external circuit A circuit or subcircuit connected and external to a main equipment.

external controls 1. Control devices that are connected to, but operated away from, a main circuit. **2.** Manual or screwdriver-adjusted controls that are mounted on the panel of an equipment, as opposed to those mounted in the case or behind the panel.

external critical damping resistance The value of external resistance that must be connected to a galvanometer or other meter to produce critical damping.

external damping device A resistor or short-circuiting bar connected temporarily between the terminals of a meter to keep its movement immobile during transportation.

external feedback Negative or positive feedback through a separate path outside of and around the main circuit. Example: negative feedback through a resistance-capacitance (RC) path between the output terminals and the input terminals of an amplifier.

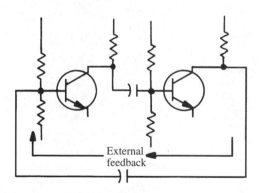

external feedback

external impedance Load impedance (i.e., an impedance connected to the output terminals of a generator or amplifier).

external load See EXTERNAL IMPEDANCE.

external loudspeaker See EXTERNAL SPEAKER.

externally caused chatter In a relay, contact chatter caused by mechanical vibration outside of the relay.

externally caused failure Failure of a circuit or component resulting from unfavorable environmental factors.

external memory In computer operations, a memory unit outside of the computer mainframe.

external power supply A power supply unit situated apart from the powered equipment. Such separation is helpful in eliminating the disturbing effects of heat, hum, and vibration associated with internal power units.

external Q For a microwave tube, the quantity $1/(1/Q_1 + 1/Q_2)$, where Q_1 is the loaded Q and Q_2 is the unloaded Q.

external S-meter A signal-strength meter connected to a receiver, but not installed in its panel.

external speaker A loudspeaker that doesn't share an enclosure with an amplifier, receiver, or other device that drives it. Such isolation is helpful in eliminating the undesirable effects of vibration and acoustic feedback.

external storage In computer operations, storage media (such as magnetic diskettes or tapes) that are outside of the computer.

extinction potential See DEIONIZATION POTENTIAL.

extinction voltage See DEIONIZATION POTENTIAL.

Extra-class license An amateur-radio license that conveys all available amateur operating privileges in the United States. The highest class of amateur license.

extract 1. To remove a signal or quantity from some product containing it, or from its source. Examples: extracting a fifth harmonic from a complex signal, extracting the direct-current (dc) component from a signal containing both alternating current (ac) and dc. **2.** To derive a factor (e.g., to extract a root). **3.** To separate certain classes of information from an aggregate of information.

extract instruction In computer operations, the instruction to generate a new word by the serial arrangement of designated segments of specified words.

extractor 1. A circuit or device for removing a signal (or a signal component) from another circuit or device. A demodulator probe, for example, extracts the modulation from a modulated signal. **2.** A device for removing used active devices from a circuit board. Such extractors can also employ heat to desolder, as well as remove the devices.

extraneous component A usually undesired inherent effect that results from the physical nature of a component or device. Examples: distributed capacitance of a coil, internal inductance of a capacitor.

extraneous emission Undesired emission from a transmitter (e.g., excessive harmonics).

extraneous response The unintended response of a circuit or device (e.g., image response in a superheterodyne communications receiver).

extraneous root In the solution of an equation derived from another equation, one or more roots that satisfy the derived equation but not the original one.

extraneous signal A superfluous and potentially interference-causing signal.

extranuclear Outside the nucleus of an atom.

extraordinary ray Of the two rays resulting from the double refraction of electromagnetic waves, the one that does not follow the usual laws of refraction. Also see X WAVE.

extraordinary wave See X WAVE.

extrapolar 1. Outside of electrical or magnetic poles. **2.** Not between electrical or magnetic poles.

extrapolation Estimation of values beyond the range of available data. An example is the extension of a curve beyond its final plotted point to determine a value for a variable. There is always some margin for error, which increases as the process is extended further and further beyond the range of actual data values. Commonly done by computers (e.g., prediction of the probable path of a hurricane 12, 24, 36, and 48 hours in advance).

extrared See INFRARED.

extraviolet See ULTRAVIOLET.

extreme 1. The lowest or highest value of a quantity. **2.** The lowest or highest point of the dependent variable in the range of a function. **3.** An unusual value for a parameter (e.g., temperature extreme and pressure extreme).

extremely high frequency Abbreviation, EHF. A frequency near the upper limit of the radio-frequency spectrum—especially one in the 30- to 300-GHz band.

extremely low frequency 1. Abbreviation, ELF. Pertaining to a signal or current within the audio-frequency (AF) range, but not used for audio applications. **2.** Electromagnetic emissions from a cathode-ray tube (CRT), resulting from the currents in the deflecting coils and/or electron beam. **3.** The 60-Hz electromagnetic field generated by utility power lines and wiring.

extrinsic base-resistance/collector-capacitance product Units: seconds, milliseconds, and mi-

croseconds. For a bipolar transistor, the product $R_B C_C$, where R_B is the base resistance and C_C is the collector capacitance. This product is a time constant that determines the high-frequency operating limit of the transistor.

extrinsic conductance For a material, the conductance resulting from impurities or such external factors as environmental conditions.

extrinsic properties For a semiconductor material, properties resulting from doping (e.g., altered resistivity or majority/minority carrier differentiation). Also see EXTRINSIC SEMICONDUCTOR.

extrinsic semiconductor A semiconductor material, such as germanium or silicon, to which a controlled amount of a suitable impurity material has been added to give the semiconductor a desired resistivity and polarity. Compare INTRINSIC SEMICONDUCTOR.

extrinsic transconductance Symbol, g_m. For a bipolar transistor, the first derivative of collector current, with respect to base-emitter voltage. It is the ratio of a small change in collector current (dI_C) to the small change in base-emitter voltage (dV_{BE}) that produced it, collector voltage being constant; $g_m = dI_C/dV_{BE}$.

extrusion The process of forming a material such as metal or plastic, by forcing it through dies. Many pieces of electronic hardware are mass produced in this manner. Examples are insulating rods and tubes, metal cans, and metal tubing.

eye-in-hand system In robotics, a scheme that uses a vision system, servo, and microprocessor to precisely manipulate an END EFFECTOR, such as a robot gripper ("hand"). A camera (the "eye") is contained in the end effector itself, and is designed to work at close range (i.e., approximately one meter down to a fraction of a millimeter).

eyelet connection A connection made by fastening conductors together with an eyelet or by soldering leads or pigtails to an eyelet.

eyepiece A small lens system for viewing an oscilloscope screen through a camera setup.

E_Z Symbol for *voltage drop across an impedance*.

E zone A portion of the earth including most of the eastern hemisphere. When propagation forecasts are made, this region is one of three longitude zones specified.

F **1.** Symbol for FORCE. **2.** Symbol for FLUO-RINE. **3.** Abbreviation of FAHRENHEIT. **4.** Abbreviation of FARAD. **5.** Abbreviation of FERMI. **6.** Symbol for FOCAL LENGTH. **7.** Symbol for FUSE. **8.** Symbol for FARADAY CONSTANT.

f **1.** Abbreviation of FEMTO. **2.** Symbol for FREQUENCY. **3.** Symbol for FUNCTION.

F_0 Symbol for DAMPING FACTOR.

F1 layer The lower part of the ionosphere's F REGION. Also called *F1 region.*

F2 layer The upper part of the ionosphere's F REGION. Also called *F2 region.*

fA Abbreviation of FEMTOAMPERE.

fabrication tolerance The amount of variation that can be tolerated in the manufacture of components.

Fabry-Perot interferometer A resonant cavity, often used with lasers, that has mirrors at each end; the interferometer produces the optical equivalent of standing waves.

face **1.** A flat crystal surface whose orientation can be expressed as its position relative to other faces. **2.** The viewer's side of a screen. **3.** The scale part of a meter.

face material In a tape recorder, the plastic used to coat the face of a head.

face-parallel cut See Y-CUT CRYSTAL.

face-perpendicular cut See X-CUT CRYSTAL.

face side The side of pressure-sensitive insulating tape that is coated with adhesive.

facom A radionavigation system that operates by means of phase comparison at low frequencies. Effective over long distances and under poor conditions.

facsimile Also called *fax.* The transmission and reception, through the medium of radio or by wire, of permanent pictures, writing, and other graphic material.

facsimile receiver The complete device or system that selects, amplifies, and demodulates a picture signal received up from the air, wires, or cable, and uses the elements of this signal to reproduce the picture. Also see FACSIMILE.

facsimile recorder The machine that puts a transmitted facsimile image on paper.

facsimile transmitter The complete device or system that generates signals depicting graphic material (pictures, writing, printing, etc.) and sends them to a distant point via cable, wire lines, or radio for subsequent reproduction. Also see FACSIMILE.

factor **1.** A data element that is an operand in an arithmetic operation. **2.** To find the two or more numbers whose product is the number being factored. **3.** One of two or more numbers whose product is the number being factored.

factorial Symbol, !. For an integer n, the product of all positive integers up to and including n. Thus, $5! = 1 \times 2 \times 3 \times 4 \times 5 = 120$. The term $n!$ is read "n factorial."

factor of merit See FIGURE OF MERIT.

factor of safety See SAFETY FACTOR.

fade in To gradually increase an audio or video signal—especially for recording.

fade out **1.** To gradually decrease an audio or video signal—especially for recording. **2.** The complete disappearance of a radio communications signal. See FADING.

fader **1.** In sound amplification systems, an attenuator circuit that enables the operator to fade out one signal and fade in another. Ordinarily, a fader does not provide mixing action. **2.**

In an automotive high-fidelity sound system, a control that adjusts the volume of the front speaker set and rear speaker set. Usually, this is a single knob; increasing the front volume decreases the rear volume, and vice-versa.

fading 1. Repeated increases and decreases of radio communications signal amplitude at the reception point. Fading of a radio wave results from multiple propagation paths from transmitter to receiver, causing the received waves to arrive in constantly varying phase relationships. **2.** In a cell or battery power supply, a gradual loss of power-delivering capability that occurs during the discharge cycle.

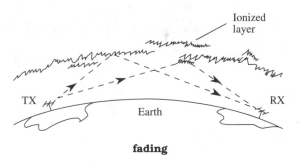

fading

factory automation The use of robotic devices, to the greatest extent possible, as laborers in manufacturing plants.

Fahnestock clip A flat, sheet-metal spring clip for holding a wire (usually in a temporary breadboard setup).

Fahrenheit scale A temperature scale on which the freezing point of water is 32 degrees, and the boiling point of water is 212 degrees. Compare ABSOLUTE SCALE and CELSIUS SCALE.

failsafe Pertaining to devices or circuits that, upon failure, cause no damage or serious malfunction.

failsoft In a computer, a system in which operation is maintained—even in the event of partial failure. Efficiency is reduced but the computer does not completely shut down.

failure The condition wherein a circuit, system, or device is not operating correctly.

failure analysis 1. The process of determining the failure rate for a component, system, or device. **2.** The process of determining the cause of a failure.

failure mode The particular way in which a failure of equipment or a method occurs.

failure unit A unit of machine or device failure: one failure per billion (10^9) hours of operation.

fall-in The time when synchronous speed is attained in a synchronous motor.

falling characteristic A NEGATIVE RESISTANCE characteristic.

fall time 1. Decay time. **2.** The time required for the amplitude of a pulse to decrease from 90 percent to 10 percent of its peak amplitude. Compare RISE TIME.

false add A logic add (i.e., addition without carries).

false alarm 1. Improper operation of an electronic security system, resulting in actuation of the device when no breach of security has occurred. **2.** In radar, the presence of a false echo that causes the attendant circuits or personnel to act as though an enemy target is present.

false error A condition in which a computer system erroneously signals the existence of an error.

false precision See MISLEADING PRECISION.

false retrieval The incorrect specification of criteria for information to be selected for retrieval so that an unwanted item of data is selected. Also called *false drop.*

family Any group of components, circuits, ratings, or characteristics, classed together because of some common or analogous feature or application. Examples: IC family, family of curves, and family of equations.

family of curves A group of curves plotted on the same axes, that depict the performance of a circuit or device at several levels of a third parameter (e.g., curves showing transistor collector current vs. collector voltage for several levels of base current).

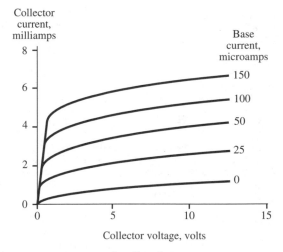

family of curves

fan antenna See DOUBLE-V ANTENNA.

fan-in 1. A number of inputs entering a common input terminal. **2.** In digital computer operations, the number of inputs that can be accommodated by a logic circuit. Compare FAN-OUT.

fan-in circuit A circuit having a number of input lines entering a common input point. Also see FAN-IN, **1**.

fan-out **1.** One common output terminal feeding a number of output lines. **2.** In digital computer operations, the number of outputs that can be fed by a logic circuit. Compare FAN-IN.

fan-out circuit A circuit in which a number of output lines leave a common output terminal. Also see FANOUT, **1.**

fantasy robot A robot as portrayed in science fiction or fantasy. Such robots are usually, but not always, *androids* (that is, they have humanoid form). Some fictional robot characteristics are later realized. Science fiction can even give roboticists ideas for future designs.

Fanuc A factory complex located at the foot of Mount Fuji in Japan. Known for its innovation, discipline, and quality control, the factory is almost entirely automated; that is, most of the labor is done by robots. Many engineers regard this factory as a model for automated complexes.

farad (Michael Faraday, 1791–1867) Abbreviation, F. The basic unit of capacitance. A capacitor has a capacitance of 1 F when a charge of 1 volt per second across the capacitor produces a current of 1 ampere through it.

faraday An electrical quantity approximately equal to 9.65×10^4 coulombs; it is the quantity of electricity required in electrolysis to free 1 gram atomic weight of a univalent element. The equivalent, and preferred, unit is the COULOMB. Also called *Faraday constant.*

Faraday cage See ELECTROSTATIC SCREEN.

Faraday constant See FARADAY.

Faraday cylinder A cylindrical metal shield placed around electrical equipment or circuits to prevent electromagnetic fields from affecting the equipment or circuits.

Faraday rotation A change in the polarization of an electromagnetic wave as it travels through certain substances.

Faraday effect See MAGNETO-OPTICAL ROTATION.

Faraday's disk dynamo See DISK DYNAMO.

Faraday shield See ELECTROSTATIC SCREEN.

Faraday's law The voltage induced in a conductor moving in a magnetic field is proportional to the rate at which the conductor cuts the magnetic lines of flux.

Faraday's laws of electrolysis **1.** In electrolysis, the mass of a substance liberated from solution is proportional to the strength and duration of the current. **2.** For different substances liberated by the same current in a certain time, the masses are proportional to the electrochemical equivalents of the substances. Also see ELECTROCHEMICAL EQUIVALENT; ELECTROLYSIS, **1**; and ELECTROLYTE.

faradic current The lopsided alternating current produced by an induction coil.

faradmeter An alternate term for MICROFARAD METER.

far field **1.** The region beyond the near field of an antenna (see NEAR FIELD, **1**). **2.** The region beyond the near field of a loudspeaker (see NEAR FIELD, **2**).

far infrared Also called far IR. The lower-frequency portion of the infrared (IR) spectrum.

farming robot A robot that performs labor in an agricultural setting. Examples: fruit-picking robot, field-watering robot, cow-milking robot. Such machines are usually overseen by a central computer, via which the farmer can monitor and control the robots' actions.

far zone See FAR FIELD, **1**, **2**.

fast access storage In a computer memory, the section from which information can be most quickly accessed, depending on the relative speed of other system devices.

fast-break, fast-make relay A relay that opens and closes rapidly.

fast-break, slow-make relay A relay that opens rapidly and closes slowly.

fast charge The rapid charging of a rechargeable cell or battery, particularly of a nickel-cadmium (NICAD) or nickel-metal-hydride (NiMH) device.

fast diode See COMPUTER DIODE.

fast drift The rapid change of a quantity or setting, usually in one direction. Compare SLOW DRIFT.

fast-food robot A robot that prepares and/or serves items in a fast-food establishment. Robots have not yet gained wide acceptance in this setting, mainly because of technical difficulties and prohibitive cost. Another problem is that some customers are put off or intimidated by robots.

fast-forward Abbreviation, FF or FFWD. In a tape recorder, a mechanism for running the tape through the machine rapidly.

fast groove The informationless groove between tracks on a disk recording.

fast-make/fast-break relay A relay that closes and opens rapidly.

fast-make, slow-break relay A relay that closes rapidly and opens slowly.

fast-forward playback In a videotape recorder, the playing back of the tape at faster than real-life speed. It allows the viewer to move quickly ahead in a program, and also to watch the images so as to know when to resume normal replay.

fast-reverse playback In a videotape recorder, the playing back of the tape rapidly backwards. It allows the viewer to move quickly back in a program, and also to watch the images so as to know when to resume normal replay.

fast time constant **1.** The property of responding quickly to changes in input parameters. **2.** In radar, a method of defeating attempts at jamming by modification of the receiving circuitry.

fathometer See ACOUSTIC DEPTH FINDER.

fathom **1.** To measure the depth of a body of water, as in the use of sonar for this purpose. **2.** A unit of length (distance) equal to six feet.

fatigue **1.** The degradation of the performance of circuits or materials with time. **2.** The tendency of bodies and materials to weaken, deform, or fracture under repeated strain.

fault **1.** A defective point or region in a circuit or device. **2.** A failure in a circuit or device.

fault current **1.** A momentary current surge. **2.** A leakage current.

fault finder A troubleshooting instrument or device (e.g., a multimeter).

fault resilience **1.** A design scheme for an electronic or computer device or system so that if a component or circuit fails, the system will continue to operate, although perhaps at reduced efficiency. The operator is notified of the problem so that it can be repaired with minimal downtime. **2.** In a computer system, the property of being as nearly sabotage-proof as possible.

fault tolerance Total redundancy in an electronic or computer system so that if a component or circuit fails, the system will continue to function at full efficiency. Every component has a backup that automatically takes over in case of failure. The operator is notified of the problem, so the defective part or circuit can be replaced while its backup keeps the circuit working continuously at 100-percent capacity.

Faure plate A storage battery plate consisting of a lead grid containing a chemical electrolytic paste.

fax Abbreviation of FACSIMILE.

fc Abbreviation of FOOT-CANDLE.

f$_c$ Abbreviation of CARRIER FREQUENCY.

FCC See FEDERAL COMMUNICATIONS COMMISSION.

f$_{co}$ Abbreviation of CUTOFF FREQUENCY.

F connector A type of antenna feedline connection especially common on television receivers and videocassette recorders.

F display See F SCAN.

FDM Abbreviation of *frequency-division multiplex*.

FE Abbreviation of FERROELECTRIC. See FERROELECTRICITY.

Fe Symbol for IRON.

feasibility study The procedures for evaluating the potential gains in applying a computer system to a job or to an organization's process, or in modifying or replacing an existing system.

FEB Abbreviation of FUNCTIONAL ELECTRONIC BLOCK.

Federal Communications Commission Abbreviation, FCC. Established in 1934, the U.S. Government agency that regulates electronic communications. The FCC succeeded the Federal Radio Commission (FRC), which was established in 1927; the FRC succeeded the Radio Division of the Bureau of Navigation in the Department of Commerce, whose jurisdiction over radio began in 1912.

feed **1.** To supply power or a signal to a circuit or device. **2.** The method of supplying such a signal or power. See, for example, PARALLEL FEED and SERIES FEED. **3.** To cause data to be entered into a computer for processing.

feedback **1.** The transmission of current or voltage from the output of a circuit or device back to the input, where it interacts with the input signal to modify operation of the device. Feedback is positive when it is in phase with the input, and is negative when it is out of phase. **2.** To input the result at one point in a series of operations to another point; the method allows a system to monitor its actions and make necessary corrections.

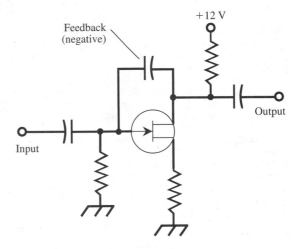

feedback, 1.

feedback amplifier **1.** An amplifier whose performance (especially frequency response) is modified by means of positive, negative or both positive and negative feedback. **2.** An amplifier placed in the feedback path of another circuit to increase the amplitude of feedback.

feedback attenuation **1.** In an operational-amplifier circuit, the attenuation in the voltage from output to input. **2.** In an audio-frequency or radio-frequency amplifier circuit, the reduction of feedback by electronic means.

feedback bridge A bridge circuit in the feedback channel of an amplifier or oscillator.

feedback capacitance **1.** A capacitance through which feedback current is coupled from the output to the input of a circuit or system. **2.** The interelectrode capacitance of a vacuum tube.

feedback control **1.** The variable component (potentiometer or variable capacitor) used to adjust the level of feedback current or voltage. **2.** The control of circuit performance by means of feedback.

feedback cutter A device used for the purpose of cutting grooves in phonograph disks. Feedback is used to provide a flat frequency response.

feedback factor For a feedback amplifier, the quantity $1 - bA$, where A is the open-loop gain of the amplifier and b is the FEEDBACK RATIO.

feedback input current   In a feedback network, the current drawn by the feedback input. This current affects the design parameters of a network.

feedback loop   The part of a circuit that provides controlled feedback in an operational-amplifier circuit.

feedback oscillator   A circuit in which oscillation is obtained by feeding a portion of the output of an active amplifying device back to the input circuit by inductive coupling. Also called *tickler oscillator*.

feedback path   A path over which feedback, either positive or negative, can occur in a circuit. The feedback can be intentionally produced, or it can be undesirable.

feedback percentage   Symbol, n. In a feedback circuit, the percentage of output voltage that is fed back; $n = 100V_f/V_o$, where V_f is the feedback voltage and V_o is the open-loop output voltage. Compare FEEDBACK RATIO.

feedback ratio   For a feedback system, the ratio V_f/V_o, where V_f is the voltage that is fed back and V_o is the open-loop output voltage of the system.

feedback rectifier   See DIODE FEEDBACK RECTIFIER.

feedback regulator   In a controlled-feedback circuit, the device that determines the amount of feedback.

feedback resistance   **1.** The internal base resistance of a point-contact transistor. **2.** The resistance in a feedback loop.

feedback transfer function   The transfer function of a feedback loop exclusively.

feedback winding   A special winding on a magnetic amplifier or saturable reactor, for the introduction of feedback currents.

feeder   **1.** A conductor or set of conductors that carries electric power from one point to another. **2.** The transmission line connecting a transmitter to an antenna.

feeder cable   **1.** A communication cable running in a primary route from a central station (or in a secondary route from a main feeder cable) as a means of making connections to distribution cables. **2.** In a cable television system, the cable carrying transmission from the head end to the trunk amplifier. Also called TRUNK CABLE.

feeder loss   Loss of energy resulting from resistance in, or radiation from, feeder lines.

feeding   In character recognition, a system in which documents go into the transport of a character reader at a steady, specified rate.

feed pitch   The distance between feed holes.

feed reel   The tape supply reel of a tape recorder.

feedthrough   **1.** The usually undesirable transmission of a signal through a circuit without being processed by the circuit, because of unavoidable capacitive coupling, for example. **2.** Contraction of FEEDTHROUGH COMPONENT.

feedthrough capacitor   A capacitor whose design is like that of a feedthrough terminal; it is mounted in a hole in a chassis. The center screw or wire is the "high" terminal of the capacitor, to which connections can be made above or below the chassis. The body of the device is the "low" terminal of the capacitor; it is soldered to the chassis or secured with a nut.

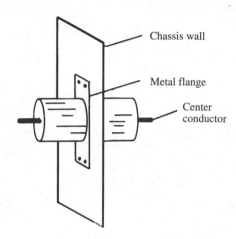

feedthrough capacitor

feedthrough component   A passive device permanently installed in a panel or plate (e.g., a FEEDTHROUGH CAPACITOR or FEEDTHROUGH INSULATOR).

feedthrough insulator   An insulator mounted tightly in a hole in a wall or chassis, and provided with a center hole for a lead.

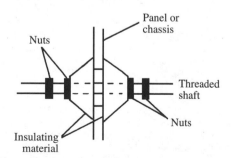

feedthrough insulator

feedthrough terminal   A terminal mounted tightly in a hole in a chassis or wall; it consists of a screw going through a feedthrough insulator. Connections can be made to either end of the screw.

FE-EL Abbreviation of *ferroelectric-electroluminescent*.

feeler 1. A wire or blade contact (e.g., a finger that senses holes in a punched card). **2.** The wire portion of a point-contact diode.

Felici mutual-inductance balance An inductive null circuit for determining mutual inductance (M_x) in terms of a standard mutual inductance (M_s). The secondary coils of two mutual-inductance circuits are connected in phase opposition. The standard mutual inductor, which is variable, is adjusted for null. At null, $M_x = M_s$.

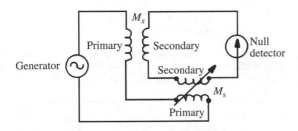

Felici mutual-inductance balance

female plug A plug whose contacts are separated by a recess into which the prongs of a mating male plug are inserted. Compare HERMAPHRODITE PLUG and MALE PLUG.

femto- Abbreviation, f. A prefix meaning quadrillionth (10^{-15}).

femtoampere Abbreviation, fA. A unit of extremely low current; 1 fA equals 10^{-15} A.

femtofarad Abbreviation, fF. A unit of extremely low capacitance; 1 fF equals 10^{-15} F.

femtovolt Abbreviation, fV. A unit of extremely low voltage; 1 fV equals 10^{-15} V.

fence A system or string of early warning radar stations.

Fermat's principle The principle that the path of a ray of radiant energy between two points in any medium is the shortest distance between those points in that medium. This path is also the path of least propagation time. This might not necessarily be a straight line. On a flat plane, the path of least time between any two points is always a straight line, assuming constant velocity of propagation. However, on a sphere, the path of least time between two points is represented by a great circle.

fermi Abbreviation, F. An extremely small unit of length and wavelength, equal to one quadrillionth (10^{-15}) of a meter.

Fermi-Dirac distribution function The probability that an electron will be in a certain quantum state under conditions of thermal equilbrium. This is determined as the probability that the electron will be in a given energy band at a particular instant of time.

fermium Symbol, Fm. A radioactive metallic element that is artificially produced. Atomic number, 100. Atomic weight, 257.

ferpic Acronym for *ferroelectric ceramic picture* device. An image-storing device containing a photoconductive film, transparent electrodes, and a ferroelectric ceramic, in layers.

ferreed A form of magnetic switching device, similar to a reed relay, that maintains its position indefinitely without the need for a continuous current.

ferret A vehicle or craft equipped for determining the locations of enemy radar transmitters.

ferri- A prefix used to denote magnetic properties.

ferric oxide Formula, Fe_2O_3. A red oxide of iron used to coat magnetic recording tape.

ferristor A high-frequency magnetic amplifier using a ferroresonant circuit.

ferrite A high-resistance magnetic material consisting principally of ferric oxide and one or more other metals. After being powdered and sintered, ferrites exhibit low eddy-current loss at high frequencies and make ideal core material for inductors and switching elements. Also used in television deflection yokes and in miniature antennas. Also see FERROSPINELS.

ferrite antenna See FERRITE-ROD ANTENNA.

ferrite bead 1. A magnetic storage device in the form of a bead of ferrite powder fused onto the signal conductors of a memory matrix. **2.** A tiny ring of ferrite that can be slipped over a wire or cable to choke off radio-frequency (RF) currents.

ferrite bead

ferrite core A coil or switching-element core made from a ferrite; specifically, in a core memory, a small magnetic toroid that can retain its polarity when charged by a pulse.

ferrite core memory A magnetic memory in which ferrite cores are interconnected by a network of input and output wires.

ferrite isolator A microwave device that permits energy to pass with negligible loss in one direction through a waveguide or coaxial line, while absorbing energy passing in the opposite direction.

ferrite limiter A device used in the antenna circuit or front end of a receiver, to prevent overload while maintaining a linear response. Used mostly at ultra-high and microwave frequencies.

ferrite loopstick See FERRITE-ROD ANTENNA.

ferrite memory A static memory using ferrite cores. See CORE MEMORY.

ferrite-rod antenna A small receiving antenna consisting of a coil of wire wound on a ferrite rod a few inches long. Exhibits a sharp null along the axis of the coil. Can be tuned with a variable capacitor, usually connected in parallel, for narrow-band frequency response. Used mainly at low and medium frequencies.

ferrite switch A device that regulates the flow of power through a waveguide. The electric-field vector is rotated, resulting in a high degree of attenuation when actuated, but little or no attenuation when not activated.

ferroelectric 1. Producing ferroelectricity. 2. A ferroelectric material.

ferroelectric amplifier See DIELECTRIC AMPLIFIER.

ferroelectric capacitor A capacitor in which a ferroelectric material is the dielectric.

ferroelectric cell See FERROELECTRIC CAPACITOR.

ferroelectric crystal A crystal of ferroelectric material.

ferroelectric flip-flop A flip-flop based on the hysteresis of a ferroelectric capacitor. Compare FERRORESONANT FLIP-FLOP.

ferroelectricity Electric polarization in certain crystalline materials. The effect is analogous to the magnetization of a ferromagnetic material by a magnetic field.

ferroelectric-luminescent Pertaining to a ferroelectric cell that emits light.

ferroelectric material A nonlinear dielectric material capable of producing ferroelectricity. Examples: barium titanate, barium strontium titanate, potassium dihydrogen phosphate, guanadine aluminum sulfate hexahydrate (GASH), Rochelle salt, and triglycene sulfate.

ferromagnetic 1. Pertaining to a substance that conducts a magnetic field with relative ease. 2. Pertaining to a material in which a magnetic-field change causes a voltage, which in turn results in a measurable current flow.

ferromagnetic material A substance that concentrates magnetic lines of flux relative to their concentration in free space. Iron, powdered iron, and ferrite are common examples.

ferromagnetic resonance The point at which the permeability of a magnetic material peaks at a microwave frequency.

ferromagnetic spinels Highly permeable and resistive ceramic-like materials. The low eddy-current losses and high permeability of these materials suit them for use as cores in radio-frequency (RF) transformers and inductors. Also see FERRITE.

ferromagnetic tape Magnetic tape used for winding closed transformer cores.

ferrometer An instrument for testing hysteresis and permeability in steel and iron.

Ferron detector See IRON-PYRITES DETECTOR.

ferroresonant circuit An inductance-capacitance (LC) circuit in which the coil is a saturable reactor. Because of coil nonlinearity, the circuit is resonant at only one value of alternating-current (ac) voltage, and exhibits both negative resistance and bistable operation.

ferroresonant counter A digital counter using ferroresonant flip-flops, rather than semiconductor devices.

ferroresonant flip-flop A flip-flop using one or two ferroresonant circuits instead of semiconductor devices. See BISTABLE MULTIVIBRATOR. Compare FERROELECTRIC FLIP-FLOP.

ferroresonant shift register A shift register using ferroresonant circuits instead of semiconductor devices.

ferrosoferric oxide See MAGNETITE.

ferrospinels See FERROMAGNETIC SPINELS.

ferrous Pertaining to a substance that contains iron and is magnetizable.

Ferroxcube A nonmetallic ferromagnetic material having high permeability and resistivity, and a Curie point near room temperature. These characteristics make the material suitable for the cores of radio-frequency (RF) inductors and transformers, and for high-frequency magnetic shields.

Fessenden oscillator In underwater communications, a transmitter of acoustic waves.

FET Abbreviation of FIELD-EFFECT TRANSISTOR.

fetch An operation in a computer run in which the location of the next instruction is taken from memory and changed if necessary; it then goes to the control register.

FET current meter An ammeter, milliammeter, or microammeter having a self-contained amplifier that uses field-effect transistors. Also see ELECTRONIC CURRENT METER.

FET op-amp 1. An operational amplifier composed of field-effect transistors and associated components. 2. An operational amplifier having a field-effect transistor in its input stage.

FET voltmeter A voltmeter using a field-effect transistor amplifier for high-impedance input. Also see ELECTRONIC VOLTMETER.

FET VOM A volt-ohm-milliammeter (VOM) using a field-effect transistor amplifier for increased sensitivity and high input impedance.

FF Abbreviation of FLIP-FLOP.

fF Abbreviation of FEMTOFARAD.

FFI Abbreviation of FUEL-FLOW INDICATOR.

fhp Abbreviation of FRACTIONAL HORSEPOWER.

fiber 1. A tough, vulcanized insulating material. Dielectric constant, 2.5 to 5. Dielectric strength, 2 kV/mm. 2. A thin thread of a material. 3. Also called *optical fiber*. A light-conductive transparent filament; see FIBEROPTICS, 1.

fiber electrometer An instrument for measuring small quantities of electricity. It consists of a thin thread, such as one of plasticized quartz, hanging freely between two knife-edged metal pieces that are charged by the electricity being measured. The charge draws the fiber away from its position of rest. The movement can be observed with a microscope. A special form of this instrument, using two fibers, is the *bifilar electrometer.*

fiber needle A soft phonograph needle made from a fiber. It produces less disk wear than other styli, but is short-lived.

fiber metallurgy A process in which metallic fibers or filaments are grown.

fiberoptic bundle A cable of optical fibers. See FIBEROPTICS, **1.**

fiberoptic coupling Also called *optical coupling.* A method of coupling in which a light-conducting fiber is placed between a light (signal) source and a photoreceptor. Also see FIBEROPTICS, **1, 2.**

fiberoptics 1. Also called *optical fibers.* Extruded materials, such as certain plastic filaments, that provide paths for light. **2.** The science of developing and using communications systems that use optical fibers to transfer data.

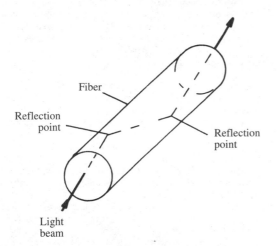

Fiber

Reflection point

Reflection point

Light beam

fiberoptics

fiberoptic scrambler A fiberscope in which a center section of fibers in the core is deliberately disoriented before the bundle is encapsulated; when cut, one half can decode the image encoded by the other half. See FIBERSCOPE.

fiberscope A flexible bundle of optical fibers having a lens at each end; it is used to view areas that are otherwise inaccessible to view.

fiber stylus See FIBER NEEDLE.

fibre Alternate (Brit.) spelling of FIBER.

fibrillation Dangerous, irregular beating of the heart that often follows electric shock. Also see CARDIAC STIMULATOR and DEFIBRILLATION.

fidelity The degree to which a circuit or device transmits a signal without distorting it. Pertains especially to acoustic devices and stereo audio equipment.

field 1. A volume of space in which a force is operative. See, for example, ELECTRIC FIELD and MAGNETIC FIELD. **2.** Half of a video image, consisting either of all the even-numbered lines, or all the odd-numbered lines. **3.** A computer record subdivision containing an information unit (e.g., a bank account record might have deposits as a field).

field circuit breaker A circuit breaker designed to control the field excitation of a motor or other device.

field coil 1. The winding on the field pole of a motor or generator. **2.** The winding on the pole of an electrodynamic speaker. **3.** The main coil of a relay. **4.** The fixed coil in an electrodynamometer.

Field Day In amateur radio, an annual contest sponsored by the American Radio Relay League (ARRL) to simulate emergency communication conditions. It occurs during the last full weekend in June.

field direction The direction in which an electric field or magnetic field exerts its force.

field effect The phenomenon in which the flow of current carriers in a solid substance is controlled by an external electric field. A useful application is the FIELD-EFFECT TRANSISTOR (FET).

field-effect tetrode Also called *dual-gate FET.* A field-effect transistor (FET) in which the gate electrode is split into two parts, each connected to a separate external lead. The reverse bias between the channel and either gate lead affects the conductivity through the device.

field-effect transistor Abbreviation, FET. A monolithic semiconductor amplifying device in which a high-impedance GATE electrode controls the flow of current carriers through a thin bar of silicon (rarely, germanium) called the CHANNEL. Ohmic connections made to the ends of the channel constitute SOURCE and DRAIN electrodes. Also see JUNCTION FIELD-EFFECT TRANSISTOR, METAL-OXIDE SEMICONDUCTOR FIELD-EFFECT TRANSISTOR, and CHANNEL JUNCTION FIELD-EFFECT TRANSISTOR.

field-effect varistor A nonlinear dual-terminal semiconductor device capable of maintaining a value of current for a range of voltages.

field-emission microscope An instrument for examining the atomic structure of high-melting-point metals; it magnifies more than 2 million times. The metal to be examined is made into a needle that is subjected to 5 to 30 kV; electrons emitted by the tip of the needle form an image on a fluorescent screen.

field forcing A method of controlling a motor by changing the magnetic field in the windings.

field frequency In television, the product of frame frequency and fields per frame (in the United States, 60 per second).

field intensity   **1.** The strength of an electric or magnetic field. **2.** The strength of an electromagnetic field, usually expressed in microvolts per meter or millivolts per meter.

field-intensity meter   See FIELD-STRENGTH METER.

field ionization   The tendency for atoms to be ionized in a gas by a high-intensity electric field. The ionization occurs mostly near the poles of the electric field.

field-ion microscope   A high-resolution field-emission microscope that uses helium ions instead of electrons. The ions are repelled by the tip of the metal needle under observation, forming an image on a fluorescent screen. Also see FIELD-EMISSION MICROSCOPE.

field length   Record field size in applicable units, usually bytes, characters, or words.

field magnet   **1.** The permanent magnet in a dynamic speaker. **2.** A similar magnet in an earphone, generator, microphone, motor, phono pickup, transducer, etc.

field pickup   **1.** A probe or sensor for insertion into an electric or magnetic field. **2.** An on-location radio or television program (i.e., one coming from outside the studio). Also called remote or NEMO.

field resistor   A resistive component consisting of an insulated form with a thin layer of conductive material.

field rheostat   The rheostat whose setting determines the amount of current flow through the field coil of a motor or generator.

field scan   A form of television scanning in which the lines are scanned alternately.

field-sequential system   A color-television system in which the image is reproduced by means of primary color fields (red, green, and blue) flashed sequentially on the screen of the picture tube. Compare DOT-SEQUENTIAL SYSTEM and LINE-SEQUENTIAL SYSTEM.

field strength   See FIELD INTENSITY.

field-strength meter   An instrument for measuring the radio-frequency (RF) voltage of a signal reaching a chosen location. The instrument consists essentially of a radio detector equipped with a portable antenna and an output meter.

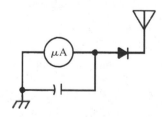

field-strength meter

field telephone   A rugged, portable telephone system for outdoor use.

field test   A test of equipment under actual operating conditions (i.e., outside the laboratory or factory).

field winding   See FIELD COIL, **1, 2**.

fig.   Abbreviation of *figure* (usually in reference to an illustration).

figure-8 pattern   **1.** A bidirectional antenna pattern whose cross section, in a specified plane, resembles the numeral 8. **2.** A Lissajous figure resembling the numeral 8.

figure of merit   **1.** For a capacitor, inductor, or tuned circuit, the ratio of reactance to resistance. Also called *Q factor* or *Q*. **2.** For a magnetic amplifier, the ratio of power amplification to control time constant. **3.** For a transistor, the *gain-bandwidth factor.*

fil   Abbreviation of FILAMENT.

filament   In a vacuum tube or incandescent lamp, the thin wire heated by electric current; it emits electrons, light, and heat. The filament is the cathode in a filament-type tube, but serves only to heat indirectly the cathode sleeve in an indirectly heated tube.

filament battery   See A BATTERY.

filament choke   A radio-frequency (RF) choke operated in the filament lead of an electron tube. Such chokes are necessary in filament-type tubes in RF power amplifiers.

filament circuit   The circuit carrying filament current.

filament coil   See FILAMENT WINDING.

filament current   Symbol, I_F. The current flowing through the filament of a vacuum tube.

filament emission   Electrons emitted directly by the filament in an electron tube (thermionic emission) or the amount of such emission.

filament hum   A hum signal caused by voltage induced in a circuit by the alternating-current (ac)-operated filaments (heaters) of tubes or by the filament wiring.

filament lag   The time delay in the heating and cooling of an ac tube or lamp filament as filament-current changes polarity.

filament power supply   A source of power, usually alternating-current, for heating the filament of a vacuum tube or tubes.

filament resistance   **1.** The resistance of the filament in an electron tube or incandescent lamp. **2.** The resistance of an external dropping resistor in the filament circuit of a tube or lamp.

filament transformer   A step-down transformer that supplies power exclusively to the filament (heater) of an electron tube.

filament-type bolometer   A BOLOMETER in which the sensitive element is a wire filament. Examples: barretter, incandescent lamp, and wire fuse.

filament voltage   Symbol, V_F. The voltage across the filament of an electron tube.

filament winding   In a power transformer, the coil that supplies heating power to the filament of a vacuum tube. Also called FILAMENT COIL.

file An organized collection of records related by a common format, data source, or application.

file conversion Converting data files from one form to another, often for the purpose of making them compatible with other computers.

file gap An area of a data medium that signifies the end of a file; it can also mark the start of another file.

file identification A code that identifies a file.

file label File identification in which the first record in the file is a set of characters unique to the file; it conveys such information about (for example, a tape file as a description of content, generation number, reel number, date of writing, etc.). Also called HEADER LABEL.

file layout How the contents of a file are organized; usually defined by the system or specified by a program.

file maintenance To delete, add, or correct records in a file. Unlike updating, which is done to reflect changes in events recorded in the file, maintenance ensures that the contents of the file are accurate records of the necessary data.

file management A method of storing and recalling data from computer storage media, such as magnetic disks.

filename In a computer file label, the alphanumeric character set that identifies and describes the file. It generally consists of one to eight characters, often including an extension of one to three characters. In some computer operating systems, filenames can be much longer (e.g., up to 32 characters). See FILENAME EXTENSION.

filename extension A group of one, two, or three characters following the main body of a FILENAME, and separated from it by a period (.). It generally denotes the application or purpose of the file. The extension .BAK, for example, denotes a backup file; .TXT denotes a text file; .BMP denotes a bit-mapped graphics file.

file organization The way words, bits, or records are physically arranged in the storage medium for a file, possibly including the method of access (serial, alphabetical, random, etc.).

file-oriented programming Computer programming that uses a general file and record-control program to simplify I/O coding.

file-oriented system A system having file storage as its basis.

file print A hard copy (printout) of the contents of a file.

file processing The operations associated with making and using files.

file protection Preventing the possibility of writing over data files before they are made available for use. It is usually done by having a program check file labels.

file reconstitution Restoring a partially or completely damaged file by updating a previous generation of the file using a file of interim transactions.

file recovery Following the interruption of file processing because of system failure, the procedure for reestablishing the file's condition as necessary for the resumption of processing without losing accuracy.

file section Part of a file in certain consecutive locations on a storage medium.

file security Protective and security measures (e.g., the issuance of clearances, status markers, etc.) as they relate to computer files.

file set A collection of interrelated files stored consecutively in a magnetic disk volume (package).

fill The percentage of lines in a cable that are actually in use at a given time.

filler A nonessential data part used, for example, to bring a record to a standard size.

film See THIN-FILM MEMORY.

film capacitor A capacitor in which the electrodes are plated or deposited on the faces of a thin film of plastic or other dielectric material.

film chain A system designed for the transmission of movies over a television system. This requires synchronization of the movie frame rate with the television scanning rate.

film frame A single picture on a strip of motion picture film.

film-frame blanking interval The interval during which a film frame is blanked out as motion-picture film moves through a camera, projector, or pickup. The blanking action allows a frame to move into position without blurring the image as seen by viewers.

film integrated circuit A monolithic circuit whose elements are films formed on an insulating substrate.

film pickup A photocell, photodiode, or phototransistor circuit used to pick up recordings from the sound track of motion-picture film.

film reader A device for converting data on film into digital form for a computer.

film recorder An apparatus that records data as a sound pattern on film. Compare FILM REPRODUCER.

film reproducer An apparatus that plays back data recorded on photographic film. Compare FILM RECORDER.

film resistor A resistor whose resistance material is a thin film deposited on a substrate.

film scanning The conversion of a movie into a form suitable for transmission by television.

film speed 1. The speed at which motion-picture film moves intermittently through a camera, projector, or pickup, measured in feet or frames per second. 2. A measure of film's light sensitivity, given as an ASA (American Standards Association) or DIN (European) number; in either system, the higher the number, the greater the light sensitivity.

filter 1. A circuit or device that passes alternating currents at some frequencies while attenuating or blocking currents at other frequencies. Examples: BANDPASS FILTER, BAND-REJECTION

FILTER, HIGH-PASS FILTER, and LOW-PASS FILTER. **2.** An inductance-capacitance (LC) or resistance-capacitance (RC) circuit for removing the ripple from the output of a power-supply rectifier. **3.** A transparent disk with special optical properties placed in front of a camera lens for a special photographic effect. **4.** A character patterned to control the elimination or selection of characters in another pattern. **5.** A device or program that separates information, according to certain specifications or characteristics. **6.** A machine word that specifies the elements to be treated in another machine word; also called MASK.

filter attenuation   In a selective filter, the power, current, or voltage loss, in decibels, that occurs within the passband.

filter attenuation band   In a selective filter, the frequency band(s) outside the passband; that is, the frequency range over which signals are significantly attenuated.

filter bank   In audio applications, a set of bandpass filters, each of which covers a specific portion of the audio-frequency (AF) spectrum. There is some (minimal) overlap between the passbands of the filters, so an AF signal of a specific frequency will always pass through at least one of the filters, but will never pass through more than two of the filters.

filter capacitor   A capacitor that provides capacitive reactance in a wave filter or power-supply filter while also blocking direct current.

filter center   A place where information is modified for transmission to aircraft pilots. Such information can include weather data, course changes, or other instructions.

filter choke   An inductor that provides inductive reactance in a wave filter or power-supply filter while affording relatively easy conduction of direct current.

filter crystal   A piezoelectric crystal used in a CRYSTAL RESONATOR.

filter cutoff   The frequency or frequencies at which the transmission figure of a filter is below its maximum value by a prescribed amount, usually 3 dB, representing the half-power point(s).

filter discrimination   The amount of fluctuation in the insertion loss of a bandpass, band-rejection, high-pass, or low-pass selective filter. The fluctuation is measured at various points in the filter passband.

filter inductor   See FILTER CHOKE.

filter passband   The frequency range over which a selective filter passes signals with minimum attenuation.

filter reactor   See FILTER CHOKE.

filter slot   In a waveguide, a slot that acts as a choke to suppress undesirable modes.

filter stopband   See FILTER ATTENUATION BAND.

filter transmission band   See FILTER PASSBAND.

fin   **1.** A metal disk or plate attached to a component for the purpose of radiating heat. **2.** A projection in an irregular heatsink.

final amplifier   The last amplifier in a cascade of amplifier stages, as in a transmitter or instrument circuit. It often includes an impedance-matching circuit for optimum coupling to the load. Also called OUTPUT AMPLIFIER.

final result   A result displayed at the end of a data processing operation. Compare INTERMEDIATE RESULT.

finder   The switch or group of relays that selects the path for a call going through a telephone switching system. Also called LINE FINDER.

fine adjustment   Adjustment of a quantity in small increments or as a smooth, continuous variation. Compare COARSE ADJUSTMENT.

fine-chrominance primary   See I SIGNAL.

fine frequency control   A variable component, such as a potentiometer or variable capacitor, that permits a signal or response frequency to be varied over a small increment; it is often used in conjunction with a coarse frequency control.

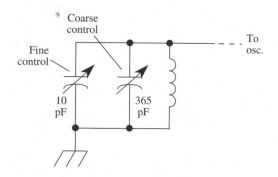

fine frequency control

fine-groove record   See MICROGROOVE RECORD.

fine index   In computer operations, a secondary, supplemental index used with a main, or gross, index when the latter does not adequately detail the differences between the items being indexed.

fine-motion planning   The scheme used by a robotic end effector ("hand") to get in exactly the correct position. It uses machine vision, tactile sensors, pressure sensors, or high-precision displacement transducers.

finger   See FEELER, **1.**

finger plethysmograph   A device that senses and records the resistance through the human finger during various parts of the heart cycle.

finger rules   See FLEMING'S LEFT-HAND RULE, FLEMING'S RIGHT-HAND RULE, and RIGHT-HAND RULE FOR WIRE.

finish lead   The lead attached to the last turn of a coil. Also called *outside lead.* Compare START LEAD.

finished blank   The end product in the crystal manufacturing process, often including electrodes.

finishing The careful handwork and testing involved in bringing a crystal blank to a condition that is acceptable as finished, according to specifications.

finishing rate The rate of charging a battery, as the battery approaches a full charge. Generally, the finishing rate is less than the normal charging rate.

finite Pertaining to that which has defined limits.

finite sample space In statistics, a sample space having definite limits.

finite series A mathematical series having a limited number of terms. Example: $1 + 0.1 + 0.01 + 0.001$, a finite series containing four terms and whose sum is equal to 1.111.

finned surface The irregular surface of a heatsink. The ratio of surface area to volume is greater than with a flat surface; this increases the cooling effectiveness of the heatsink.

fins Metal vanes radiating from components that dissipate large amounts of power as heat.

FIR Abbreviation of FAR INFRARED.

fire A transition from non-conduction to conduction in an ionizing switching device.

fire control The aiming and firing of guns automatically via radar and associated electronic systems.

firefighter robot A robotic device or system intended to protect lives and property from fire. Such a robot can be simple, such as an automatic sprinkler system actuated via heat sensors and/or smoke detectors. More-sophisticated systems might use autonomous or remotely controlled androids that perform the same functions as human firefighters.

Fire Underwriter's regulations See NATIONAL ELECTRIC CODE.

firing The pulse that initiates conduction in an ionization switching device.

firing angle **1.** For a magnetic amplifier, the angular distance through which the input-voltage vector rotates before the core is driven into saturation. **2.** For a silicon-controlled rectifier (SCR), the point, as an angle (in degrees or radians), along the control voltage half-cycle at which the SCR fires.

firing circuit Any circuit, such as a phase shifter, that permits adjustment of the firing angle of a silicon-controlled rectifier (SCR) or similar device, or which delivers the required pulse or other signal to initiate firing.

firmware **1.** Programs (software) in nonvolatile computer memory [e.g., in a read-only memory (ROM), that can only be changed by replacement with an alternate unit]. **2.** Unalterable internal interconnections that determine what a computing device or system can do. Also called MICROPROGRAM.

first detector In a superheterodyne circuit, the signal frequency detector. Compare SECOND DETECTOR.

first filter capacitor The input capacitor in a capacitor-input power-supply filter.

first Fresnel region A portion of a directional transmitted electromagnetic ray, shaped generally like a paraboloid with the apex at the transmitter and the axis in the direction of transmission. Any point in the first Fresnel zone is in such a position that the sum of the lengths of the paths from the point to the receiver, and the point to the transmitter, is no greater than 0.5 wavelength more than the distance from the transmitter to receiver.

first harmonic The fundamental frequency in a complex waveform from which multiples are generated.

first-in/first-out Acronym, FIFO. A read-write memory commonly used as a buffer to smooth out the flow of data bits in a digital system. The output bits are in the same order (sequence) as the input bits. If a data bit x goes into the FIFO before data bit y, then x will always emerge from the FIFO before y. Compare PUSHDOWN STACK.

first-in/last-out See PUSHDOWN STACK.

first law of thermodynamics Quantities of heat can be converted into mechanical work, and vice versa. Also see MECHANICAL EQUIVALENT OF HEAT.

first level address See ABSOLUTE ADDRESS.

first selector The selector that responds to the first-digit dial pulses when a telephone number is called.

fishbone antenna An untuned, wideband directional antenna of the general end-fire type. Consists of a number of collector antennas, each capacitively coupled to the resistor-terminated transmission line in collinear pairs. It is so called from its resemblance to the skeleton of a fish.

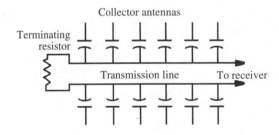

fishbone antenna

fishpaper A chemically treated, vulcanized-fiber paper used for electrical insulation.

fish pole A microphone boom that can be held in the hand.

fist In radiotelegraphy and wire telegraphy, an operator's manual sending style.

fitting A device intended to mechanically fasten a wire or cable in place.

five-element code A five-impulse telegraph code that describes a character (e.g., Baudot, which also includes start and stop elements).

five-layer device A semiconductor device containing four pn junctions. Examples: diac and triac.

five-level code A teletype code that utilizes five binary elements to define a character.

fix **1.** In direction finding, the point at which two lines of direction intersect. **2.** In electronics maintenance, to repair successfully. **3.** To subject an in-process circuit board to a solution or other medium to stop a photographic action permanently. Also, the solution in which such photosensitive materials can be immersed to halt development.

fixed bias Bias voltage or current supplied from a fixed external source (such as a battery or power supply) independent of the operation of the biased device. Compare AUTOMATIC BIAS.

fixed block length Blocks of data having a fixed number of words or characters, as required because of hardware limitations or a program instruction. Compare VARIABLE BLOCK LENGTH.

fixed capacitor A nonadjustable capacitor (i.e., one having a single unalterable value).

fixed component Any component (e.g., a capacitor, inductor, or resistor that has one unalterable value).

fixed contact The stationary contact in a relay or switch. Compare MOVABLE CONTACT.

fixed-crystal detector A simple crystal detector in which the point of the contact wire is permanently placed in contact with a sensitive spot on the surface of the crystal.

fixed field Fields in records organized so that those containing similar information in each record are the same length and in the same relative position in the record. Compare VARIABLE FIELD.

fixed form coding The coding of source languages so that each part of the instruction is in a fixed field.

fixed-frequency amplifier An amplifier that is pretuned to operate on one frequency, or in a relatively narrow band of frequencies.

fixed-frequency oscillator An oscillator that is preset to operate on one frequency. Such an oscillator can be self-excited or controlled (crystal, fork, magnetostriction, etc.).

fixed-frequency receiver A receiver that is pretuned to receive signals of one frequency.

fixed-frequency transmitter A transmitter that is pretuned to radiate signals of one frequency. Such a transmitter can contain a self-excited or crystal-controlled oscillator.

fixed inductor A nonadjustable inductor (i.e., one having an unalterable value of inductance).

fixed-length record A record in which word or character size is constant. Compare VARIABLE LENGTH RECORD.

fixed logic Applicable to computers or peripherals whose logic can only be altered internally by changing connections.

fixed memory A nonvolatile readout computer memory that can only be altered mechanically.

fixed placement file A file that has been allocated a fixed location in storage.

fixed-point system A notation system in which a single set of digits represents a number, and the radix point (in the decimal system, the decimal point) can only be placed in one position for the value being expressed. Also see FLOATING-POINT CALCULATION.

fixed resistor A nonadjustable resistor (i.e., one having an unalterable value of resistance).

fixed-sequence robot A robot that performs one task or set of tasks, making exactly the same movements every time. The sequence is programmed in the robot controller via firmware. Many assembly robots and toy robots are of this type. Compare FLEXIBLE AUTOMATION.

fixed station A radio station operating from a stationary point; one that is not mobile.

fixed-step potentiometer A potentiometer whose output is varied in one or more discrete steps by fixed-resistor sections. Also see POTENTIOMETER.

fixed word length Applicable to the organization of information in storage in which each computer word stored has a fixed number of characters or bits.

fixture A piece of hardware used in equipment set-ups (e.g., microwave couplers, joints, sections, etc.).

fL Abbreviation of FOOT-LAMBERT.

flag **1.** A piece of information added to a data item that gives information about the data item. **2.** A bit added to a character or word to delineate a field boundary. **3.** An indication that an operation is complete and need not be done by the program. **4.** An indicator identifying the members of mixed sets. **5.** A character that signals the presence of some condition (e.g., an *error flag* indicates that a data item caused an error).

flag event A program condition that causes a flag to be set.

flag line An input pulse to a microprocessor that depends on specific external instructions. Indicates a certain condition or change of state.

flagpole antenna **1.** Any of several vertical UHF or VHF antennas consisting of a radiator mounted atop a coaxial pipe or cable (see, for example, COAXIAL ANTENNA). It takes its name from its resemblance to a flagpole. **2.** A vertical antenna formed by shunt-feeding a pole already in existence, such as a flagpole. This can be done to conceal the antenna.

flag terminal A form of terminal that does not require soldering for electrical contact. A protruding "flag" is crimped around the conductor.

flame alarm A (usually photoelectric or thermoelectric) device or circuit for detecting a flame and actuating an alarm.

flame control A (usually photoelectric or thermoelectric) device or circuit for sensing and automatically controlling the height of a flame, such as a gas pilot.

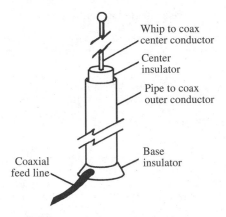

flagpole antenna, 1

flame-failure control A FLAME CONTROL that automatically cuts off the fuel if the flame goes out.

flame microphone A microphone in which two electrodes in a flame undergo a change in electrical resistance when the flame is influenced by sound waves, thus modulating current passing between the electrodes.

flange 1. A flat, protruding edge used for fastening a connector or plug to the chassis of a piece of equipment. 2. In a waveguide, a coupling used for connection to another section of waveguide, or to a horn or other external device.

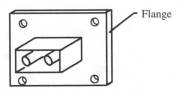

flange

flange focus The focal length of a lens, based on the distance from the mounting flange to the focal plane.

flanging In sound systems, a means of obtaining special effects using a COMB FILTER. Creates an "extraterrestrial," digitized sound. Commonly used by rock music bands.

flanking Modification of the response of a selective filter, resulting from the parallel connection of two or more similar filters.

flap See DROP INDICATOR.

flap attenuator A waveguide attenuator consisting of a sheet of resistance material inserted transversely into the waveguide through a slot.

flare 1. The hyperbolic cross section of a horn antenna or loudspeaker. 2. A transient or station-

ary bright area with (usually) a central pip on the screen of an otherwise blank oscilloscope or television picture tube.

flare angle The gradual change in a waveguide's diameter over its length.

flare factor The angle at which the faces of a horn speaker are curved or turned outward.

flaring constant Symbol, m. A number expressing the degree of flare (see FLARE, 1) in a horn antenna or loudspeaker. The value of m is equal to $0.6931/d$, where d is the distance along the axis required for the cross-sectional area A of the horn to double. If d is given in feet (ft), for example, then A is in units of square feet (ft^2) and m is in units of reciprocal feet (1/ft). If d is in centimeters (cm), then A is in units of square centimeters (cm^2) and m is in units of reciprocal centimeters (1/cm).

flash 1. A photographic camera flash. 2. To vaporize a metal (such as magnesium) in an electron tube being evacuated, to absorb gases. 3. Flashover.

flash arc In a vacuum tube, a sudden high-current arc between cathode and plate at high plate voltages; it can short-circuit the plate power supply.

flashback voltage The maximum inverse voltage that causes the gas in a tube to ionize.

flash delay A device that automatically postpones the operation of a FLASHTUBE until a predetermined instant, such as the moment when a moving object arrives at a particular point before a camera.

flasher An electrical or electronic device or circuit that flashes a light or a series of lights sequentially.

flasher LED A light-emitting diode (LED) that, when connected to a low-voltage direct-current (dc) source, emits light that flashes at a basic rate of a few pulses per second.

flashlamp 1. See FLASHTUBE. 2. A small portable light operated from self-contained cells; a flashlight or lantern.

flashlight See FLASHLAMP, 2.

flashover The sudden discharge of electrical energy between electrodes or conductors, often accompanied by light; it is usually the result of excessive voltage.

flashover voltage 1. The peak voltage at which FLASHOVER occurs. 2. The voltage at which disruptive discharge occurs between electrodes and across the surface of an insulating material.

flash plating Electroplating in which a thin layer is deposited quickly.

flash test Insulation testing by applying a higher-than-normal voltage for a short time.

flashtube A straight or coiled glass tube filled with gas and provided with electrodes. When a high voltage is applied to the electrodes, the tube emits a brilliant flash of light.

flat cable Also called *ribbon cable*. A cable whose flexible conductors are molded side by side in a flexible, flat ribbon of plastic (such as polyethylene).

flat-compounded generator A compound-wound generator whose windings are proportioned so that the full-load and no-load voltages are identical.

flat fading Fading of a radio signal that occurs independently of frequency; all frequency components of the signal fade to the same extent at the same time.

flat file A computer file containing unfolded documents.

flat frequency response Relatively equal response to all fixed-point frequencies within a given spectrum, exhibited by an amplifier or other circuit that must transmit a band of frequencies.

flat line A transmission line in which there are no standing waves, or for which the standing-wave ratio is very low.

flat pack An integrated circuit package consisting of a square or rectangular flat housing, with pins projecting straight outward from the edges.

flat response A response characteristic in which the dependent variable is substantially constant over a specified range of values of the independent variable. For example, in amplifier operation, an output signal whose component fundamental frequencies and their harmonics are in the same proportion as those of the input signal being amplified.

flat-ribbon line A transmission line (feeder) consisting of two flexible conductors molded in a flexible, flat ribbon of plastic, such as polyethylene. Also called *twinlead*.

flattening The leveling-off or blunting of a normally peaked or curved response, often caused by signal saturation within a circuit. Sine-wave clipping is an example.

flat top **1.** The horizontal radiating portion of an antenna. **2.** See FLAT-TOP ANTENNA. **3.** Of an amplifier, to distort by clipping of the positive half-cycles.

flat-top antenna An antenna having a horizontal wire or wires at the top to lower the resonant frequency and increase the bandwidth.

flat-top beam A bidirectional, end-fire antenna consisting of two close-spaced dipoles center-fed out of phase. Also see KRAUS ANTENNA.

flat-topping The positive-peak clipping of a modulation envelope that occurs when an amplifier

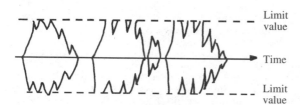

flat-topping

is overdriven or when a signal is overmodulated. This is in contrast to deliberate clipping. Flat-topping results in "splatter" and is, therefore, an undesirable characteristic in an amplitude-modulated signal.

flat-top response The ability to uniformly transmit frequencies in a given band.

flat transmission line **1.** A transmission line that is free of standing waves. Also see MATCHED TRANSMISSION LINE. **2.** See FLAT-RIBBON LINE.

flaw An irregularity in a substance that can result in problems, such as mechanical failure or poor equipment performance.

flaw detector An instrument that uses ultrasonic waves to detect internal flaws in metal. The waves are reflected by flaws.

F layer See F REGION.

fLb Abbreviation of FOOT-LAMBERT.

Fleming/Kennelly law Under conditions at or near magnetic saturation in a ferromagnetic substance, the reluctivity is directly proportional to the intensity of the magnetic field.

Fleming's generator rule See FLEMING'S RIGHT-HAND RULE.

Fleming's left-hand rule A simple way of indicating certain relationships in the behavior of electric generators and motors. If the thumb, index finger, and middle finger of the left hand are positioned so that they are at right angles to each other, the thumb will point in the direction of force or motion when the index finger is pointed in the direction of flux; the middle finger points in the direction of current flow. Compare FLEMING'S RIGHT-HAND RULE.

Fleming's motor rule See FLEMING'S LEFT-HAND RULE.

Fleming's right-hand rule A simple way of indicating certain relationships in the behavior of electric generators and motors. If the thumb, index finger, and middle finger of the right hand are positioned so that they are at right angles to each other, the middle finger points in the direction of an induced voltage, the thumb in the direction of the motion of a conductor, and the index finger in the direction of the magnetic field. Compare FLEMING'S LEFT-HAND RULE.

Fletcher-Munson curves A set of curves depicting the uneven frequency response of human hearing. Also called AUDIBILITY CURVES.

flexible automation The ability of a robot or system to do various different tasks. Changing from one task to another is simply a matter of changing software. Compare FIXED-SEQUENCE ROBOT.

flexible collodion A viscous solution of pyroxylin (cellulose nitrates) used sometimes as a binder for coils.

flexible contact A contact made from flat, metal spring stock; it is usually bent or curved. Also called *spring contact*.

flexible coupling   A device for joining two shafts and conveying rotary motion from one to the other; it is elastic, so the shafts need not be exactly aligned with each other.

flexible flat cable   See FLAT CABLE.

flexible manufacturing system   A roboticized manufacturing plant that can turn out a variety of different products. One or more central computers oversee the operation of the facility. Such factories are commonly used in the production of electronic devices (such as printed circuits, calculators, and portable radios).

flexible resistor   An insulated, wirewound resistor that can be bent, coiled, or knotted.

flexible shaft   A control shaft that can be bent somewhat while still allowing easy adjustment.

flex life   A measure of how much bending a conductor or other flexible object can take without breaking.

flexode   A diode that is flexible in that its junction can be changed (i.e., reversed without reversing its leads, its resistance being variable from the forward- to backward-resistance value).

flicker   1. A tendency for a video image to appear, disappear, and reappear, or to increase and decrease in intensity frequently. 2. The effect created by such action (as in a flickering light).

flicker frequency   The number of times the screen illumination flashes on and off in the projection of a motion picture. It is 48 per second (twice the frame rate) in conventional movie projectors; for each frame, the screen is blanked once when the frame is pulled into position and once again during projection of the frame.

flight control   Electronic monitoring and control of an aircraft in flight.

flight path   The course planned for an aircraft's flight.

flight-path computer   A computer that controls the course of an aircraft in flight, from takeoff to landing.

flight-path deviation   The departure of an aircraft in flight from the course in the flight plan. Also see FLIGHT PATH.

flight-path-deviation meter   An instrument that provides a visual indication of the departure of an aircraft in flight from the course in the flight plan.

flight telerobotic servicer   A remotely controlled robot used to maintain and repair space vehicles and satellites. The machine can be controlled by a computer program or by a human operator. The most-sophisticated machines can use TELEOPERATION and/or TELEPRESENCE so that a human can perform dangerous work without being placed at personal risk.

flight test   1. To test airborne electronic equipment in actual flight. 2. Any test made as in 1.

Flinders bar   In a magnetic compass, a metal bar that corrects for the vertical component (inclination) of the earth's magnetic field. The bar must be designed differently in different geographic locations, because the inclination varies from place to place. Inclination is greatest near the geomagnetic poles, and is zero at the geomagnetic equator.

flint glass   A hard, bright, lead glass. Dielectric constant, 7 to 9.9. Dielectric strength, 30 to 150 kV/mm. Also see GLASS.

flip chip   A monolithic semiconductor device (such as a diode, transistor, or integrated circuit), in which bead-like terminals are provided on one face of the chip for bonding.

flip-chip bonding   A scheme for making connections between a semiconductor chip and a header, in which leads are not run between chip and header. Instead, bead-like projections are electrodeposited as terminals around one face of the chip, which is then registered with the header terminals and bonded to them.

flip-flop   1. See BISTABLE MULTIVIBRATOR. 2. A two-position relay that locks in alternate positions upon receiving successive actuating pulses.

flip-flop key   In a video display, a key that, when pressed, allows viewing of one half of the screen and then the other.

flip-flop memory   A bistable computer memory that stores bits of data as flip-flop states.

flip-flop relay   See BISTABLE RELAY.

float charging   The constant charging of a storage battery, keeping the battery at or near the fully charged state at all times.

floated battery   A storage battery connected in parallel with a generator, which supplies the load; the battery, always completely charged, helps during high-current demands.

floating   1. To float a storage battery; see FLOAT. 2. An ungrounded device or circuit that is not connected to a source of voltage. 3. Not loaded or driven. 4. Not fixed in position. 5. A dedicated ground connection that remains isolated from the common circuit ground.

floating address   See RELATIVE ADDRESS.

floating charge   See TRICKLE CHARGE.

floating control   1. A potentiometer, such as a gain control, installed with its shaft insulated from ground and, accordingly, subject to body-capacitance effects. 2. A type of automatic control in which the rate of final control element movement depends on the amount that the controlled variable deviates from a prescribed value.

floating ground   See FLOATING, 5.

floating input   An ungrounded input circuit.

floating-input measurement   See DIFFERENTIAL-INPUT MEASUREMENT.

floating instrument   An instrument whose signal terminals are above ground.

floating I/O port   An input/output (I/O) terminal that is not loaded or being driven.

floating junction   A junction (in a semiconductor device, for example), that has no net current flowing through it.

floating neutral A circuit with a variable common voltage reference.

floating paraphase inverter A dual-transistor adaptation of the paraphase inverter. The second stage receives its input signal from a tap on the load resistor of the first stage and provides the additional phase shift that is required.

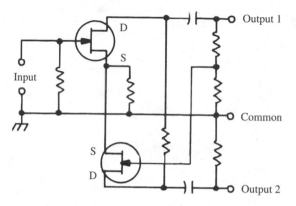

floating paraphase inverter

floating-point calculation An electronic calculation using a floating point number [i.e., a number whose value is represented by two sets of digits, a fixed-point part (see FIXED-POINT SYSTEM) and a radix (base number) with an exponent]. Important in the operation of microprocessors, especially in computer systems.

floating-point number A number expressed in the floating-point system.

floating-point package Computer-vendor software that enables that computer to perform floating-point calculations.

floating-point system A system of notation in which a number n is represented by two sets of numbers: a fixed-point part (see FIXED-POINT SYSTEM) a, the radix (base number) r, and an exponent b as follows: $n = a \times r^b$. For example, in the floating-point system, 623 can be written 6.23×10^2. Floating-point numbers can be stored economically (in terms of memory) and in magnitudes that might otherwise be beyond the capacity of the computer to operate upon with relatively consistent accuracy. Compare FIXED-POINT SYSTEM.

floating probe A test electrode (wire or plate) inserted in a discharge tube at a desired point to sample the potential gradient, but which acquires a misleading negative charge, with respect to the gas cloud, because electrons (traveling faster than the positive ions) tend to accumulate on the probe.

floating zero A control system in which the reference point is easily moved.

floating zone In a semiconductor ingot undergoing purification, a molten zone in which impurities float. The material in the zone is melted by the radio-frequency (RF) field of an external heating coil, which is passed along the ingot to move the molten zone to one end, picking up impurities along the way and concentrating them at the end that is later sawed off.

float switch A switch operated by a float, such as in a sump pump.

flocking 1. Particulate felt used on phonograph turntables to protect disks from being scratched. 2. To coat with flocking.

flood gun In a storage (image-holding) oscilloscope, the electron gun that sprays the storage target with low-velocity electrons and makes the image visible on the viewing screen. The gun is mounted next to one pair of deflection plates. Compare WRITING GUN.

floor stand A support for a microphone, consisting of a heavy base that rests on the floor, and an adjustable, vertical boom that allows the microphone to be set at various heights.

floppy disk A flexible magnetic disk used in recording, as in computer and data system storage. It usually refers to a 5.25-inch diskette.

flow 1. The movement of current carriers under the influence of an electric field. 2. See ANGLE OF CONDUCTION. 3. A series of interrelated events in a time sequence.

flow angle See ANGLE OF CONDUCTION.

flowchart 1. A diagram depicting the logic steps in a digital-computer program. 2. A diagram showing the flow of material through a sequence of processes.

flow direction The method of delineating antecedent and successor events on a flowchart; usually arrows and flowlines connecting the events in the way a page is read (top to bottom, left to right).

flowed-wax disk A form of recording disk, in which wax is melted onto a plastic or metal base. The grooves are cut in the wax layer.

flowline A line showing flow direction on a flowchart.

flowmeter An instrument for measuring liquid flow rate.

flow relay A relay that is actuated by a predetermined rate of fluid flow.

fluctuating current See COMPOSITE CURRENT.

fluctuating voltage See COMPOSITE VOLTAGE.

fluid absorption See LIQUID ABSORPTION.

fluid analogy The comparison of electric current flow to the movement of a simple fluid. Also see WATER ANALOGY.

fluid capacitor See WATER CAPACITOR.

fluid computer A digital computer that uses fluid logic elements (i.e., one that contains no electronic circuits or moving parts).

fluid damping Use of a viscous fluid to damp a mechanical member's movement.

fluid-flow alarm   An electronic circuit that actuates an alarm when fluid flowing through pipes or other channels changes from a predetermined rate.

fluid-flow control   A servo system that automatically maintains or adjusts liquid flow through pipes or other channels.

fluid-flow gauge   See FLUID-FLOW METER.

fluid-flow indicator   See FLUID-FLOW METER.

fluid-flow meter   An instrument that indicates fluid flow rate through pipes or other channels.

fluid-flow switch   In a fluid-cooled system, a switch that actuates an alarm when the fluid slows or stops.

fluidics   **1.** A form of digital logic in which circuits operate by means of fluid flow. **2.** A branch of physics concerned with the behavior of fluids; more commonly called *fluid dynamics.*

fluid-level control   A servo system that automatically maintains the level of a fluid in a tank.

fluid-level gauge   An electronic system that provides direct readings of the level of a fluid in a tank.

fluid-level indicator   See FLUID-LEVEL GAUGE.

fluid logic   Logic operations carried out by varying the flow and pressure of a gas or liquid in a circuit of channels. Also see FLUID COMPUTER.

fluid ounce (U.S.)   Abbreviation, fl. oz. A unit of volume equal to 2.957×10^{-5} cubic meters, or 0.02957 liter. A quart is 32 ounces; a gallon is 128 ounces.

fluid-pressure alarm   An electronic circuit that actuates an alarm when fluid pressure rises or falls beyond set limits.

fluid-pressure control   A servo system that automatically maintains or adjusts fluid pressure in pipes or other channels.

fluid-pressure gauge   See FLUID-PRESSURE METER.

fluid-pressure indicator   See FLUID-PRESSURE METER.

fluid-pressure meter   An instrument that indicates the pressure of a fluid in a pipe or other channel.

fluid valve   See ELECTROMECHANICAL VALVE.

fluorescence   The property of some materials to glow when excited by a stimulus, such as ultraviolet, X rays, or an electron beam. Compare PHOSPHORESCENCE.

fluorescent lamp   See FLUORESCENT TUBE.

fluorescent materials   Materials that glow when irradiated, but cease to glow when the source of excitation is removed. An example is the phosphor coating on the screen of a cathode-ray tube (CRT).

fluorescent screen   A transparent or translucent plate (such as the end of a cathode-ray tube or fluoroscope) coated with phosphors that glow when struck by an electron beam, or by high-energy electromagnetic radiation, such as ultraviolet or X rays.

fluorescent tube   A mercury-vapor glow lamp distinguished by having a glass tube whose inner wall is coated with a phosphor that emits light when excited by the ultraviolet glow discharge in the vapor.

fluorescent X rays   X rays reradiated by the atoms of a material that has absorbed X radiation. During initial exposure, energy absorbed from the radiation raises the energy level of electrons in the atoms; when the electrons return to their normal energy levels, they reradiate some of the absorbed energy.

fluorine   Symbol, F. A gaseous element of the halogen family. Atomic number, 9. Atomic weight, 18.998.

fluoroscope   A device used for viewing the internal structures of objects. A screen coated with material that fluoresces when exposed to X rays is mounted in one end of a light-tight viewing hood. When an object is placed between the screen and an X-ray tube, an image is produced on the screen. In medical applications, this device has been supplanted by methods that do not use ionizing radiation; *nuclear magnetic resonance imaging (NMRI)* is one example.

fluoroscopy   The art of using a fluoroscope in the inspection of materials and parts or in medical examinations.

flush   A form of mounting in which there is little or no protrusion from the panel surface.

flutter   **1.** In a high-frequency superheterodyne receiver, a rapid fluctuation in signal strength, caused by tuning and detuning of the oscillator stage. This usually results from poor direct-current (dc) power-supply regulation. **2.** Repetitive, rapid fluctuations in the output of a sound reproducer. Also see WOW. **3.** An echo effect sometimes observed in rooms or auditoriums of poor acoustic design.

flutter bridge   A bridge-type instrument for measuring flutter in constant-speed machines, such as sound recording and reproducing devices.

flutter rate   The frequency of flutter, in cycles per second (Hertz).

flux   **1.** Theoretical lines of force that extend in all directions from an electric charge (electric flux) or from a magnetic pole (magnetic flux). **2.** A material that makes metals more amenable to being joined by soldering. **3.** The number of photons that pass through a surface for a given time.

flux density   Symbol, B. Unit, tesla. The degree of concentration of magnetic lines of force. One tesla represents a flux density of one volt-second per square meter $(V{\cdot}s/m^2)$.

fluxgate   A device that controls the azimuth bearing of a directional system by means of interaction with the geomagnetic field.

fluxgate magnetometer   A magnetic compass for robot guidance. Uses coils to sense changes in artificially generated reference fields. Output from the sensors is sent to a computer that calculates the robot's position, based on the orientation and intensity of the lines of flux in the reference fields.

flux graph A device that graphically records the intensity of a magnetic field around a permanent magnet or electromagnet, or around an inductor carrying a current.

flux leakage See MAGNETIC LEAKAGE.

flux lines The theoretical lines of force in an electric or magnetic field.

flux linkage The passage of lines of force set up by one component through another component, so as to enclose most of the penetrated component's volume.

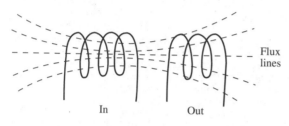

flux linkage

fluxmeter An instrument for measuring magnetic flux density. Also called *gaussmeter*.

flux refraction The tendency for magnetic lines of flux to change direction at the boundary between substances having different permeability. Flux refraction resembles refraction of electromagnetic radiation in or at a boundary between substances having different indices of refraction.

flyback **1.** The abrupt drop or reversal of a current or voltage that was previously increasing (e.g., the rapid fall of a sawtooth wave). Also see KICKBACK. **2.** The duration of the drop of a current or voltage that was previously increasing, for a sawtooth or similar wave. **3.** In an oscilloscope or picture tube, the rapid return of the beam to its starting position.

flyback checker An apparatus that senses the presence of short or open circuits in motors, transformers, and generators, by measuring the amount of flyback (kickback).

flyback power supply See KICKBACK POWER SUPPLY.

flyback time The time taken for the electron beam in an oscilloscope tube, picture tube, or camera tube to return to its starting point after it has reached the point of maximum deflection.

flyback transformer In a television receiver circuit, the horizontal output transformer. The unit supplies horizontal scanning voltage and kickback voltage, which is rectified to produce the high-voltage direct-current (dc) anode potential.

Also see FLYBACK and KICKBACK POWER SUPPLY.

flying eyeball An undersea exploration robot consisting of a television camera, illumination lamps, and thrusters (such as jets or propellers). A cable, which also serves as a tether, sends data to a human operator, and allows the operator to control the movements of the robot. In some cases, the tether/cable can be replaced by an infrared or visible-light laser data link.

flying-spot tube A tube, such as a camera tube, in which a rapidly deflected spot of light scans an image on a transparent screen; the spot is projected through the picture to a photomultiplier.

fly's-eye lens A lens consisting of hundreds of much smaller lenses. Used in microelectronic circuit fabrication to produce many images of the same circuit.

flywheel effect **1.** In an inductance-capacitance (LC) tank circuit, the completion of a partial input wave cycle at the resonant frequency, resulting from the storage and release of energy. This provides a nearly perfect sine-wave output for class-AB, class-B, and class-C radio-frequency (RF) power amplifiers. **2.** In an LC tank circuit, the action in which energy continues to oscillate between the capacitor and inductor after an input signal has been removed. The oscillation stops when the tank-circuit finally loses the energy absorbed. The lower the inherent resistance of the circuit, the longer the decrement (decay time).

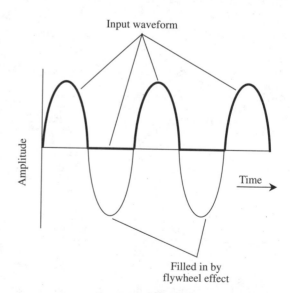

flywheel effect, 1.

flywheel synchronization A form of television scanning synchronization used when the received signal is very weak. The synchronization signals from the transmitter are sensed by the receiver, which then produces its own local pulses based on the rate of received pulses.

flywheel tuning A tuning dial mechanism in which the control shaft has a flywheel for the smoother tuning action afforded by the added momentum.

Fm Symbol for FERMIUM.

FM Abbreviation of FREQUENCY MODULATION.

f$_m$ Abbreviation of MODULATION FREQUENCY.

FM-AM Pertaining to equipment that will operate with either amplitude-modulated or frequency-modulated signals.

FM-AM multiplier A method of frequency multiplication using both amplitude and frequency modulation of a carrier wave.

FM broadcast band The 88- to 108-MHz frequency band, within which channels spaced 200 kHz apart occupy positions from 88.1 to 107.9 MHz.

FM detector See DISCRIMINATOR, RATIO DETECTOR, and SLOPE DETECTOR.

FM-FM Frequency modulation by one or more FM subcarriers.

FM limiter In a frequency-modulation circuit, a stage which holds the amplitude of the FM signal to a constant value. The limiter can be active (e.g., an amplifier-limiter transistor) or passive (e.g., a diode clipper).

FM multiplex See MULTIPLEX ADAPTER.

FM noise Unintentional modulation of a frequency-modulated transmitter, resulting from noise in the audio-input stages.

FM-PM A system of modulation in which a carrier is phase modulated by frequency-modulated subcarriers.

FM radar A radar system in which the signal is frequency modulated; the distance to the target is measured in terms of the beat note between transmitted and reflected waves.

FM repeater A two-way radio system composed of a simultaneously operating receiver and transmitter, the latter of which retransmits (usually on a different frequency) all signals picked up by the receiver. The system is usually tower- or hilltop-mounted, and is used to extend the range of two-way units in a communications network.

FM stereo The use of multiplex methods to transmit and receive stereophonic programs in an FM channel. Also see MULTIPLEX ADAPTER.

FM tuner A compact radio receiver that handles frequency-modulated (FM) signals, and delivers its low-amplitude audio output to a high-fidelity system. Compare AM TUNER and AM-FM TUNER.

focal length Symbol, F. The distance from the center of a lens or dish antenna to the principal focus. Also see PRINCIPAL FOCUS.

focus 1. The point at which rays converge. Also see PRINCIPAL FOCUS. 2. To bring rays to a point of convergence.

focus coil See FOCUSING COIL.

focus control In an oscilloscope or television circuit, the potentiometer that controls the voltage on the focusing electrode of the cathode-ray tube and, accordingly, the sharpness of the image.

focus grid 1. The focusing electrode in an electrostatic cathode-ray tube. 2. The focusing electrode in an oscilloscope tube.

focusing Bringing a ray of particles or energy to a common point. This can be done using lenses, deflecting coils, deflecting plates, or reflecting devices. Focusing can be done with acoustic waves, electromagnetic waves, and theoretically with any kind of disturbance propagated through any medium.

focusing anode See FOCUSING ELECTRODE.

focusing coil An external coil used to focus an electron beam in a cathode-ray tube. Also see ELECTROMAGNETIC FOCUSING.

focusing electrode The internal electrode (grid or ring) used to focus the electron beam in a cathode-ray tube. Also called focus electrode. Also see ELECTROSTATIC FOCUSING and FOCUS GRID, 1, 2.

focusing magnet A permanent magnet assembly for focusing the electron beam in a cathode-ray tube.

foil 1. The thin conductive strips on a printed-circuit board. 2. Also known as *tape*. Thin metal supplied in strips, intended for use in certain security systems. It can be installed in closed loops at potential points of entry.

foil capacitor A capacitor whose plates are sheets or strips of metal foil separated by a dielectric film.

foil coil See FOIL-WOUND COIL.

foil conductor A conductor that is a strip of metal foil, rather than wire. Also see FOIL PATTERN.

foil electroscope See LEAF ELECTROSCOPE.

foil pattern The pattern of thin metal circuit paths that constitute the "wiring" of a printed circuit. Also see ETCHED CIRCUIT and PRINTED CIRCUIT.

foil-wound coil A coil wound with metal foil (usually aluminum or copper) instead of wire. Such coils substantially reduce the weight of large transformers and filter chokes.

foldback 1. See FOLDBACK CURRENT LIMITING. 2. In audio recording, the routing of sound (via an audio mixer) to some other destination in addition to the recording medium. Example: playing an electronic organ while singing, recording the arrangement on tape, and also listening to it (organ and voice) in a headset.

foldback current limiting In a power supply, a method of automatically reducing the output current to a safe level when the load current exceeds the maximum recommended value. This action protects both the power supply and the powered equipment.

folded dipole A doublet antenna consisting of two straight, parallel, half-wave conductors

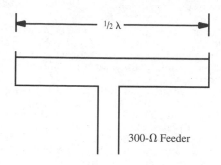

folded dipole

joined at their ends, one being center fed. Exhibits a pure resistive impedance of about 300 ohms at its fundamental frequency.

folded horn   A loudspeaker having a horn whose flare is divided into several zigzagging chambers; that is, the horn is, in effect, folded to squeeze a required length into a small cabinet.

folded-horn enclosure   See   LABYRINTH SPEAKER.

folded pattern   An oscilloscope image having an elongated time axis obtained by successive horizontal sweeps—each placed slightly lower on the screen than the preceding one. The folded-pattern technique provides a time axis several times longer than the screen width.

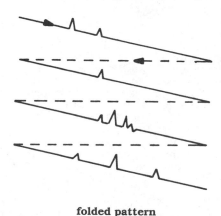

folded pattern

folding frequency   In a system where sampling is made at uniform frequency increments, the frequency corresponding to half the sampling rate in hertz.

foldover   Distortion characterized by the horizontal or vertical overlapping of a television picture.

follower   A single-stage, active circuit characterized by zero phase reversal, and voltage gain less than unity. The *emitter follower* is also called a *common-collector circuit*; the *source fol-*

lower is also known as a *common-drain circuit*. Characterized by moderate to high input impedance, and low output impedance over a wide band of frequencies.

follower drive   In a servo system, the drive that mechanically follows the master drive.

following blacks   In a television picture, the effect in which a moving white object has a black border following it.

following whites   In a TV picture, the effect in which a moving dark object has a white border following it.

follow-up motor   See SERVOMOTOR.

font   The physical shape and size of the letters and numbers in an alphanumeric system.

font reticle   In optical character recognition, an overlay reference pattern of lines used to check the size and configuration of an input character, the size of punctuation marks, and spacing between lines and characters.

food-service robot   Any robot that is used for the purpose of packaging, preparing, and/or serving food.

foot   Abbreviation, ft. A unit of linear measure in the English system equal to 0.3048 meter.

foot-candle   Abbreviation, fc. A unit of illuminance; 1 fc is the amount of direct light emitted by 1 candela (see CANDLEPOWER) that falls on 1 square foot of a surface on which every point is 1 foot away from the source. In the International System of Units, the unit is *lux* (lumens per square meter). Compare METER-CANDLE.

foot-candle meter   A light meter whose scale reads directly in foot-candles.

foot-lambert   Abbreviation, fL. A unit of luminance; the average brightness of a surface that emits or reflects 1 lumen per square foot. The Standard International (S.I.) unit is the *candela per square meter* (cd/m^2); 1 fL = 3.426 cd/m^2.

foot-pound   Abbreviation, ft-lb. In the English system, a unit of energy equal to 1 pound displaced through 1 foot in the direction of the exerting force. The Standard International (S.I.) unit is the *joule* (j); 1 ft-lb = 1.356 j.

foot-pound-second system   See FPS SYSTEM OF UNITS.

foot switch   A switch operated by the foot, generally used for the purpose of turning a playback or recording system on and off. Often used for taking dictation.

forbidden band   See ENERGY GAP.

forbidden character code   An error-finding code using forbidden characters: combinations of prohibited bits. Also called *forbidden combination*.

forbidden energy band   See ENERGY GAP.

force   1.   Symbol, F. Units: newton, dyne, poundal. The agency or influence that accomplishes work. **2.** An operator interjection made during a program run that causes the computer to execute a branch instruction; it is usually necessary when a condition responsible for halting a program must be bypassed.

forced coding   Programming that minimizes the time required to retrieve information from storage. Also called *minimum latency programming* or *minimum access programming*.

forced oscillations   Oscillations in a circuit, such as in an inductance-capacitance (LC) tank, that result from continuously applied alternating-current (ac) excitation. Compare FREE OSCILLATIONS.

foreground job   A relatively high-priority, short-running program that is carried out by interrupting a low priority, long-running program. Compare BACKGROUND JOB.

force pump   In a multistage vacuum system, the first pump that reduces the pressure considerably below atmospheric pressure. Also see DIFFUSION PUMP and VACUUM PUMP.

force summing device   A transducer element that is physically moved by a force being transduced.

foreshortened addressing   In control computers, the mixing of available storage by using simplified addressing instructions.

fork oscillator   An audio-frequency oscillator controlled by a tuning fork. The dimensions of the fork determine its vibration frequency and, accordingly, the frequency of the oscillator.

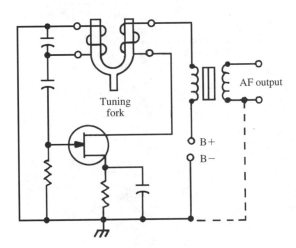

fork oscillator

form   1. The core or frame upon which an inductor is wound. 2. A vessel, such as a mold, used in the shaping stage of a manufacturing process.

formaldehyde   Formula, HCHO. A colorless, pungent gas that is a constituent of many well-known plastic insulating materials (see PHENOLFORMALDEHYDE PLASTICS).

formant   1. The audio-frequency range in which the sound of a spoken syllable is concentrated. 2. Any general group of audio frequencies.

formant filter   In an electronic organ, an audio filter that changes the waveshape of a tone so that the tone will have the desired characteristics.

format   1. The form in which data is presented (e.g., the arrangement of characters, fields, words, totals, etc.). 2. To prepare a computer disk or tape so that it will accept data.

form factor   1. The SHAPE FACTOR for a filter or tuned circuit. 2. For a half-cycle of an alternating-current (ac) quantity, the ratio of the root-mean-square (rms) value to the average value.

form feed   1. A mechanical system that positions paper being supplied to a line printer. 2. The FF character that initiates advancement of printout paper in a printer. 3. The advancement of printout paper in a printer.

form feed character   In a control loop, a character (symbol, FF) used on printing devices for controlling form feed.

forming   See ELECTROFORM, 1.

form stop   An automatic device that stops a printer when the paper runs out.

FORTH   A high-level computer programming language used in certain robots, automated factories, medical electronic devices, and electronic games. It was originally developed in the 1970s to facilitate computer control of equipment in astronomical observatories.

FORTRAN   A high-level computer programming language developed in the 1950s, and still used in some scientific and mathematical applications. It is not especially useful for the control of electronic or mechanical devices.

fortuitous conductor   A medium that creates an unwanted electrical path.

fortuitous distortion   Waveform distortion that results from causes other than characteristic effects or bias effects.

forward AGC   Automatic gain control provided by special transistors whose transconductance decreases with increasing emitter current, and vice versa. Compare REVERSE AGC.

forward-backward counter   A counter that runs forward to perform addition and backward to perform subtraction.

forward bias   Forward voltage or current in a transistor or semiconductor diode.

forward-blocking state   For a silicon-controlled rectifier, the off state, during which the forward bias is so much less than the forward breakover voltage that only small off-state current flows.

forward breakover voltage   1. For a semiconductor pn junction, the smallest forward voltage at which appreciable conduction occurs. This is about 0.3 V for germanium and 0.6 V for silicon. 2. For a silicon-controlled rectifier, the forward voltage value at which the device abruptly switches on.

forward characteristic   The current-voltage response of a semiconductor junction that is biased in the forward (high-conduction) direction. Compare REVERSE CHARACTERISTIC.

forward compatibility standards   Standards developed to make programs for one computer system usable for additional or replacement equipment.

forward conduction   The increased current conduction through a pn junction that is forward biased. Compare REVERSE CONDUCTION.

forward current   Symbol, I_f. The increase in current flow through a pn junction that is forward biased. Compare REVERSE CURRENT.

forward current-transfer ratio   The current gain of a bipolar transistor (alpha for the common-base connection and beta for the common-emitter connection).

forward power   1. In a transmission line, the power leaving the generating source, as measured by a directional wattmeter at that location. **2.** The power arriving at the load at the terminating end of a transmission line.

forward propagation by ionospheric scatter   See FORWARD SCATTER.

forward propagation by tropospheric scatter   Abbreviation, FPTS. A method of transmitting part of a radio signal beyond the horizon using the scattering effect of the troposphere. Also see FORWARD SCATTER and TROPOSPHERE.

forward resistance   Symbol, R_f. The resistance of a forward-biased pn junction. Also see FORWARD BIAS. Compare REVERSE RESISTANCE.

forward-reverse ratio   See FRONT-TO-BACK RATIO.

forward scatter   Also called *forward propagation by ionospheric scatter*. The scattering of a radio wave in the normal direction of propagation to points beyond the skip zone. The phenomenon occurs because of waves returned from regions in the ionosphere. Compare BACK SCATTER.

forward transconductance   Symbol, g_{fs}. For a common-source-connected FET, the ratio of a drain-current differential to the differential of gate-to-source voltage that produces it; $g_{fs} = 1000(dI_D/dV_{GS})$, where g_{fs} is in microsiemens, I_D is the drain current in milliamperes, and V_{GS} is the gate-to-source voltage in volts.

forward voltage   Symbol, E_f or V_f. Voltage whose polarity causes maximum current to flow through a pn junction. Compare REVERSE VOLTAGE.

forward voltage drop   The voltage across a semiconductor junction that is biased in the forward (high-conduction) direction. Compare REVERSE VOLTAGE DROP.

FOSDIC   Acronym for *film optical scanning devices for input to computer.*

Foster-Seeley discriminator   A discriminator circuit in which the diodes are operated from a single-tuned, center-tapped secondary of the input transformer. The center tap is also capacitively coupled to the top of the transformer's primary coil. Compare TRAVIS DISCRIMINATOR.

Foucault currents   See EDDY CURRENTS.

four-address instruction   A computer instruction in which the address is comprised of four addresses: two for operands, one for the result

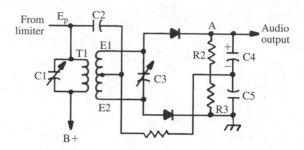

Foster-Seeley discriminator

of the operation, and one for the upcoming instruction.

four-channel sound system   Also called *quadraphonic sound system*. A high-fidelity, stereophonic sound reproduction system, in which there are four channels, rather than the usual two. The channels are generally designated left front, left rear, right front, and right rear. The four-channel system is an enhancement of two-channel stereo.

four-dimensional continuum   1. In relativistic theory, the space-time continuum. There are three spatial dimensions and one time dimension. A point in the continuum can be uniquely defined by three space coordinates and one time coordinate. **2.** Any continuum that requires four and only four coordinates to uniquely determine the position of a point.

Fourier analysis   Use of the FOURIER SERIES to evaluate the components of a complex wave, or to define a complex wave in terms of its components.

Fourier series   An infinite mathematical series that shows any periodic function to be a combination of sine terms and cosine terms. Any complex wave (e.g., a square wave) consists of fundamental and harmonic sine-wave components. In simplified form, the series is:

$$f(x) = A_0/2 + A_1 \cos x + B_1 \sin x + A_2 \cos 2x + B_2 \sin 2x + A_3 \cos 3x + B_3 \sin 3x + \ldots$$

In general, the more terms to which the series is calculated, the better the approximation of a complex waveform.

four-layer diode   A dual-terminal npnp device that is usable as a bistable switch, sawtooth or pulse generator, memory device, etc.

four-layer transistor   A transistor in which the wafer or block has four processed regions; however, the device might have only three terminals. Some examples are the silicon-controlled rectifier, silicon-controlled switch, and thyristor.

four-level laser   A laser identical to the three-level laser, except for the addition of one excited state.

four-phase system   A two-phase system in which the center taps of the coils are interconnected. Also called QUARTER-PHASE SYSTEM.

four-terminal network A network having two input terminals and two output terminals. One input terminal can be internally connected to one output terminal (as when a common ground is present), but this is not mandatory.

four-space 1. A mathematical space in which four coordinates (w,x,y,z) are necessary to uniquely define a point. **2.** Three-dimensional space with the addition of time as a fourth dimension; coordinates are, for example, (x,y,z) for space and t for time.

four-space coordinates 1. A system of coordinates for uniquely determining points in four-space. Such a system can be Euclidean or non-Euclidean, as with space of any number of dimensions. **2.** The set of numbers that defines a particular point uniquely in four-space; for example, $P = (3,-15,0,-7)$.

four-sphere The set of all points equidistant from a given point P in four-space. Formula is $w^2 + x^2 + y^2 + z^2 = r^2$, where r is the radius and the coordinates are (w,x,y,z) in the Euclidean, Cartesian system.

four-track recording A tape recording in which four channels are recorded in two adjacent tracks on the tape. Usually, tracks number 1 and 3 are in the forward direction, and tracks number 2 and 4 are in the reverse direction.

four-track tape A magnetic tape with four parallel sound paths.

four-wire wye system A three-phase system in which three wires supply the respective phases, a fourth being the neutral conductor.

F_p Symbol for POWER-LOSS FACTOR.

fp Abbreviation of FREEZING POINT.

FPC Abbreviation of *Federal Power Commission.*

FPI Abbreviation of FUEL-PRESSURE INDICATOR.

FPIS Abbreviation of *forward propagation by ionospheric scatter.* See FORWARD SCATTER.

fpm Abbreviation of *feet per minute.*

fps 1. Abbreviation of *feet per second.* **2.** Abbreviation of *frames per second.* **3.** Abbreviation of *foot-pound-second (fps)*, a chiefly British system of units.

fps system of units The British system of units of measurement that uses the foot for length, the pound for mass, and the second for time. Compare CENTIMETER-GRAM-SECOND and INTERNATIONAL SYSTEM OF UNITS.

FPTS Abbreviation of FORWARD PROPAGATION BY TROPOSPHERIC SCATTER.

Fr Symbol for FRANCIUM.

fr Abbreviation of FRANKLINE.

fractional exponent An exponent indicating that a number is to be raised to a fractional power (e.g., $10^{4/3}$). The numerator of the exponent indicates the power to which the base number must be raised; the denominator of the exponent indicates the root that must be taken of the result. Thus, na/b is equal to the bth root of na.

fractional gain Amplification less than unity. A notable example is the transfer function of a source follower or emitter follower.

fractional horsepower Any power rating lower than one horsepower (1 hp). Also see HORSEPOWER.

fractional uncertainty See RELATIVE UNCERTAINTY.

frame 1. A single, complete video image, scanned in $\frac{1}{30}$ second in conventional television receivers. **2.** A single motion-picture (film) image. **3.** In packet communications, a fundamental unit of data. The three types are called *information (I) frame, supervisory (S) frame*, and *unnumbered (U) frame.* **4.** One of a recurring cycle of pulses. **5.** In pulse-code modulation (PCM), a cyclic word group including a sync signal. **6.** A complete commutator cycle. **7.** A digital representation of a set of objects, useful in robotics and artificial intelligence (AI).

frame alignment The condition in which the receiver, or receiving apparatus, is in correct alignment with the signal to be received. In television, for example, this results in true rendition of the picture. Incorrect frame alignment (misalignment) might result in the picture being split with the top and bottom interposed. For other types of signals, misalignment would result in garbled reception.

frame-alignment signal In television, a transmitted signal that is used to ensure that frame alignment occurs in the receiver. It is a form of synchronizing pulse.

frame-alignment time slot In a transmitted television frame, an interval of time that is used for the purpose of transmitting a frame-alignment signal. There might or might not be other signal information transmitted during this time interval.

frame frequency The number of frames of a motion-picture film that come into position per unit of time in a camera, projector, or pickup.

frame of reference Geometric relationships used to describe the location of a body in space.

frame rate See FRAME FREQUENCY.

frame-repetition rate See FRAME FREQUENCY.

frame roll Momentary vertical roll in a television picture.

frame synchronizing signal 1. In pulse amplitude modulation (PAM), a coded pulse indicating initiation of a commutation frame. **2.** In pulse-code modulation (PCM), a signal used to identify an information frame.

framing 1. Synchronization of the vertical component of a video signal so that the top and bottom of the transmitted and received pictures line up. **2.** The process of lining up the top and bottom of a movie picture. **3.** Alignment of the characters in a digital alphanumeric transmission.

francium Symbol, Fr. A radioactive metal element of the alkali-metal group. Produced artificially through radioactive disintegration. Atomic number, 87. Atomic weight, 223.

Frankenstein scenario A theme often depicted in science fiction, in which intelligent machines seize power from their human creators. With the rapid advance of technology, especially in robotics and artificial intelligence (AI), some people, including a few educated researchers, believe this scenario is within the realm of possibility. Most scientists think it is highly improbable.

Franklin antenna   A vertical collinear array that produces omnidirectional gain because of phasing among the individual components.

frankline   (Benjamin Franklin, 1706–1790) Abbreviation, fr. A name that has been suggested for the unit of electric charge; 1 fr is the charge that exerts a force of 1 dyne on an equal charge at a distance of 1 centimeter in a vacuum.

Franklin oscillator   A dual-terminal, audio/radio-frequency (AF/RF) oscillator circuit. Consists of a two-stage, resistance-capacitance (RC) coupled amplifier, with a tuned inductance-capacitance (LC) tank in the input gate circuit, and with capacitive feedback from the second drain to the tank.

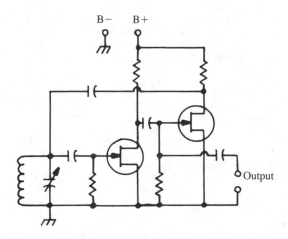

Franklin oscillator

Fraunhofer region   The area surrounding a radiating antenna, throughout which the energy appears to come from a single point located near the actual antenna.

free air resonance   For a speaker, the resonant frequency or frequencies exhibited when the device is not mounted in a cabinet.

free carrier   A free electron or, in a semiconductor material, the equivalent hole. Also see ELECTRON and HOLE.

free charge   The portion of a charge on a conductor that, being unaffected by a neighboring charge, will escape to ground when the conductor is grounded. Compare BOUND CHARGE.

free electron   **1.** An electron situated in one of the outer orbits of an atom, held loosely by the nucleus. Because free electrons can easily escape

the attraction of atomic nuclei, they will drift among atoms if the material is subjected to an electric potential. The result is electric current. Also see ELECTRON and BOUND ELECTRON. **2.** An electron that is not associated with any atomic nucleus.

free field   Data organized in a storage medium in such a way that a data item or field can be anywhere in the medium. Compare FIXED FIELD.

free impedance   For a transducer, the input impedance produced by a perfectly short-circuited load.

free magnetic pole   A magnetic pole that is so well isolated from its opposing pole that it experiences little or no influence from the latter.

free magnetism   A theoretical medium or fluid to which magnetic effects are conventionally given. The sum of free magnetism in any given object is always zero. Within any small part of the field, the free magnetism is thought of as flux lines. This theoretical medium can be any nonmagnetic material.

free net   In radio communications, a network in which stations are free to communicate with other stations in the net without constant supervision by the net control station. Such communication is carried out on a frequency slightly above or below that of the net's formal operation.

free oscillations   Oscillations in a circuit, such as an inductance-capacitance (LC) tank, that continue after excitation has been removed. Also see FLYWHEEL EFFECT. Compare FORCED OSCILLATIONS.

free path   In a gas tube, the path taken by an electron as it collides with atoms. Also see MEAN FREE PATH.

free-power supply   **1.** A simple tuned radio-frequency (RF) detector diode, used to rectify a radio signal and supply small amounts of direct current for the operation of low-powered transistor circuits. **2.** See SOLAR BATTERY.

free reel   The supply reel of a magnetic-tape recorder.

free-running frequency   The frequency at which a synchronized generator, such as a multivibrator or self-excited oscillator, will operate when the synchronizing voltage is removed.

free-running multivibrator   See ASTABLE MULTIVIBRATOR and UNCONTROLLED MULTIVIBRATOR.

free space   Empty space; a theoretical ideal.

free-space loss   Radio transmission loss disregarding variable factors (a theoretical condition).

free-space pattern   The ideal directivity pattern of an antenna that is situated many wavelengths above ground. In use, this pattern is modified by reflections from ground.

free speed   The angular velocity of an unloaded motor.

free-standing display   In a computer system, a remote display unit for prompting peripheral operators.

freezing point   Abbreviation, fp. The temperature at which a liquid starts becoming a solid at normal pressure. Compare MELTING POINT.

F region   Also called *F layer*. A region of the ionosphere with an altitude at night of approximately 175 miles. In daytime, the region splits into the lower *F1 region* and the higher *F2 region*. This layer is primarily responsible for long-distance propagation of radio waves at high frequencies (3 MHz to 30 MHz). At times it returns waves at frequencies as high as about 70 MHz.

Fremodyne detector   A frequency-modulation (FM) detector that is essentially a conventional amplitude-modulation (AM) circuit detuned to one side of resonance (slope-tuned) to demodulate a frequency-modulated signal. Also see SLOPE DETECTOR.

French phone   See CRADLEPHONE.

freqmeter   Contraction of FREQUENCY METER.

frequency   Symbol, f. The rate at which a phenomenon is repeated. The basic unit of frequency is the *Hertz (Hz)*, which represents one complete cycle per second. Common units encountered in electronics are the *kilohertz (kHz)*, *megahertz (MHz)*, and *gigahertz (GHz)*, where 1 kHz = 10^3 Hz, 1 MHz = 10^6 Hz, and 1 GHz = 10^9 Hz. Occasionally, the *terahertz (THz)* is used; 1 THz = 10^{12} Hz.

frequency-agile radar   A radar system in which the transmitter frequency is shifted in a predetermined pattern for the purpose of avoiding detection. A frequency-agile radar system, with a complex frequency control program, is very difficult to jam.

frequency allocation   **1.** The assignment of frequencies to radio and allied services by the licensing authority (in the United States, the Federal Communications Commission). **2.** A specific assignment of a frequency or a band of frequencies. Also see RADIO SPECTRUM.

frequency band   A given range of frequencies, usually specified for some application (e.g., the band allocated for standard radio broadcast service). Also see BAND.

frequency bias   An intentional change in the frequency of a transmitted signal.

frequency bridge   **1.** Any alternating-current bridge, such as the *Wien bridge* or *resonance bridge*, that can be nulled at only one frequency for a given set of bridge-arm values. **2.** Any alternating-current bridge that is used to measure unknown frequencies.

frequency calibrator   A device, such as a crystal oscillator, that provides a signal of precise frequency with which other signals can be compared. Also see SECONDARY FREQUENCY STANDARD.

frequency changer   **1.** A superheterodyne converter (see CONVERTER). **2.** A motor-generator in which the output voltage has the same value as the input voltage, but is of a different frequency. **3.** See FREQUENCY-MULTIPLYING TRANSFORMER. **4.** See FREQUENCY MULTIPLIER.

frequency-change signaling   See FREQUENCY-SHIFT KEYING.

frequency channel   A relatively narrow segment of a frequency band allocated to a station in a particular service. The bandwidth of the channel depends on the type of modulation used, the type of data to be transmitted, and the speed or fidelity of the data to be transmitted.

frequency comparator   A device, such as an oscilloscope or zero-beat indicator, used to check one frequency against another. Also see FREQUENCY COMPARISON.

frequency comparison   The observation of a current or voltage of one frequency for similarities in that of another frequency. Comparisons (as in frequency matching) can be made by audio means, by visual means, or both. Common instruments used are oscilloscopes, beat-note detectors, and beat-note meters.

frequency-compensated attenuator   An attenuator, such as one in an electronic voltmeter or wideband oscilloscope, that has been modified by the addition of capacitors or inductors to achieve reasonably flat response over a wide range of frequencies.

frequency compensation   The modification of a circuit, such as an amplifier or attenuator, by the addition of capacitors or inductors to tailor its response at specified frequencies.

frequency control   **1.** An adjustable component (potentiometer, variable capacitor, or variable inductor) with which the frequency or frequency response of a circuit is adjusted. **2.** A device, such as a quartz crystal or tuning fork, that automatically sets the frequency of an oscillator.

frequency conversion   The process of changing a signal from one frequency to another, usually without altering the signal bandwidth. In some cases, a signal is turned "upside down" by this process [e.g., an upper-sideband (USB) signal might be changed to a lower-sideband (LSB) signal]. Generally accomplished by means of a MIXER.

frequency converter   **1.** An active or passive device for changing the frequency of a signal. **2.** The mixer in a superheterodyne circuit.

frequency correction   Manual or automatic resetting of a deviated frequency to its original value.

frequency counter   An instrument that counts signal cycles or pulses over a standard time base (a frequency measurement). Often used to accurately measure the frequencies of radio or television signals; in this application, it is a precision FREQUENCY METER.

frequency cutoff   See CUTOFF FREQUENCY.

frequency detector   See FREMODYNE DETECTOR.

frequency deviation   **1.** The degree to which a frequency changes from a prescribed value.

Thus, if the frequency of a 1000-Hz oscillator drifts between 990 and 1010 Hz, the deviation is ±10 Hz. **2.** In a frequency-modulated (FM) signal, the amount of instantaneous frequency shift above and below the unmodulated carrier frequency.

frequency-deviation meter In frequency-modulation (FM) communications operations, a meter that gives a direct reading of frequency deviation resulting from a modulating signal. It uses either a tuned circuit or a frequency comparator.

frequency difference 1. In a superheterodyne circuit, the difference between the signal frequency and the oscillator frequency. **2.** In any beat-frequency operation, the quantity $f_2 - f_1$, where f_2 is the higher frequency and f_1 is the lower frequency. Compare FREQUENCY SUM.

frequency discriminator See DISCRIMINATOR.

frequency distortion A form of distortion in which the amplification of some frequencies is different from that of others.

frequency distribution See DISTRIBUTION, **2.**

frequency diversity The transmission and reception of signals at two or more frequencies for the purpose of reducing the effects of fading. It is generally used in long-distance, high-frequency circuits.

frequency divider A circuit or device whose output frequency is a fraction of the input frequency. Compare FREQUENCY MULTIPLIER.

frequency-dividing network See CROSSOVER NETWORK.

frequency-division multiplex A form of multiple-signal parallel transmission in which a single carrier is modulated by two or more signals simultaneously.

frequency doubler A circuit that multiplies an input frequency by two. If a doubler's input circuit is tuned to frequency f, then its output circuit is generally tuned to $2f$. Frequency doubling is performed by various nonlinear devices, including transistors, varactors, and biased diodes.

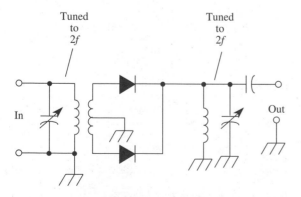

frequency doubler

frequency drift An undesired, usually gradual, change in the frequency of a signal from its intended frequency or channel; expressed in hertz or kilohertz.

frequency function See PROBABILITY DENSITY FUNCTION.

frequency indicator 1. A device that indicates when a phase or frequency is common to two alternating currents. **2.** The display or dial that shows the operating frequency of a radio receiver or transmitter. **3.** See FREQUENCY METER.

frequency keying See FREQUENCY-SHIFT KEYING.

frequency meter An instrument for measuring the frequency of an alternating current. The several different types are used in different applications. Also see AUDIO FREQUENCY METER, FREQUENCY COUNTER, POWER-FREQUENCY METER, and WAVEMETER.

frequency-modulated radar See FM RADAR.

frequency modulation Abbreviation, FM. A method of conveying data via an alternating-current (ac) carrier. The frequency of the carrier is varied at the frequency of the modulating voltage, the instantaneous amount of carrier frequency variation being proportional to the instantaneous amplitude of the modulating signal. Compare AMPLITUDE MODULATION.

frequency modulation deviation 1. In frequency modulation (FM), the largest difference between the instantaneous signal frequency and the unmodulated carrier frequency. **2.** The maximum bandwidth of an FM signal at its audio modulation amplitude peak.

frequency modulator 1. A circuit or device that modulates the frequency of an oscillator. **2.** The modulator section of an FM transmitter.

frequency monitor A device used (often continuously) to check the frequency of a signal (e.g., a frequency-deviation meter used in radio broadcast stations or a frequency meter used in electric-generating stations).

frequency multiplier A circuit or device whose output frequency is a multiple of the input frequency. See, for example, FREQUENCY DOUBLER.

frequency-multiplying amplifier See MULTIPLIER AMPLIFIER.

frequency-multiplying transformer A magnetic amplifier that generates harmonics of the supply frequency. The effect results from the nonlinearity of the transformer core material.

frequency offset 1. The difference between an actual frequency and the desired frequency. **2.** In a communications transceiver, the difference between the receiver frequency and the transmitter frequency. In some modes, such as single-sideband (SSB), the offset is normally zero. In other modes, notably continuous-wave (CW) Morse code, the offset is normally several hundred Hz. **3.** See FREQUENCY SPLIT, **1.**

frequency overlap **1.** A common band of frequencies between two adjacent channels in a communications system. **2.** A common frequency region between two assigned bands. **3.** A condition in which parts of the sidebands of two signals occupy the same range of frequencies.

frequency pulling A change in the frequency of a circuit, especially of a self-excited oscillator, resulting from the detuning effects of an external circuit, device, or condition (such as body capacitance or a change in the temperature).

frequency pushing An effect in which a current change in a source oscillator causes a shift in source frequency.

frequency quadrupler See QUADRUPLER, **2**.

frequency quintupler See QUINTUPLER, **2**.

frequency range **1.** A communication system's frequency transmission limits, beyond which the power output is attenuated below a specified amount. **2.** The frequency band or bands within which a radio transmitter, receiver, or transceiver is designed to operate.

frequency ratio counter See FREQUENCY RATIO METER.

frequency ratio meter A meter that indicates the ratio between two frequencies, and is useful in the quick identification of harmonics.

frequency record A phonograph test disk containing recordings of various frequencies at specified amplitudes.

frequency rejection The elimination, usually by a filter, of a single frequency (or narrow band of frequencies) from a mixture of frequencies. Compare FREQUENCY TRANSMISSION.

frequency relay A frequency-sensitive relay (see SELECTIVE RELAY, **1**).

frequency response A performance characteristic that describes the operation of a device or circuit over a specified range of signal frequencies (e.g., the gain-versus-frequency characteristic of an amplifier).

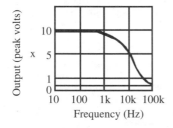

frequency response

frequency-response recorder A graphic recorder that automatically plots a frequency-response curve for a device under test.

frequency run A test, or test sequence, that determines the loss characteristics of a circuit as a function of the operating frequency.

frequency scanning **1.** A controlled fluctuation of the transmitter frequency in a frequency-agile radar or communications system. **2.** In a programmable, digital communications receiver or transceiver, a form of simultaneous digital monitoring of two or more channels. **3.** The frequency-response change in a spectrum analyzer.

frequency scaler See SCALER.

frequency-selection sensor A sensor that passes or rejects phenomena at certain frequencies while ignoring those at other frequencies.

frequency-selective relay See SELECTIVE RELAY, **1**.

frequency-sensitive bridge A bridge, such as the *Wien bridge* or *resonance bridge*, that can be balanced at only one frequency for a given set of bridge-arm values.

frequency separator In a television receiver, the circuit that separates horizontal- and vertical-scanning sync pulses.

frequency-shift keying Abbreviation, FSK. In wire or radio digital communications, the keying of a transmitter, or the actuation of a modem, by shifting the frequency of a carrier over a range of a few hundred hertz. One frequency is called *mark* and the other is called *space*. Various sets of standard mark/space FSK combinations are used in different communications services. When FSK is done with tones in the audio-frequency (AF) range, the scheme is called AUDIO-FREQUENCY-SHIFT KEYING (AFSK).

frequency-shift radar See DOPPLER RADAR.

frequency span The difference $f_2 - f_1$, where f_1 is the lowest frequency in a given range of frequencies and f_2 is the highest frequency. Compare FREQUENCY SPREAD.

frequency spectrum All electromagnetic radiation, from longest to shortest wavelengths, within a set of specified limits.

frequency split **1.** The difference between the receiver frequency and the transmitter frequency in a communications repeater. **2.** See FREQUENCY OFFSET, **2**.

frequency spotting The setting-up of signals at reference frequencies (usually harmonics of a standard-frequency oscillator), and their use in identifying unknown frequencies. Also see FREQUENCY CALIBRATOR.

frequency spread The ratio f_2/f_1, where f_1 is the lowest frequency in a given range of frequencies and f_2 is the highest frequency. Compare FREQUENCY SPAN.

frequency stability The degree to which a frequency remains constant during variations in temperature, current, voltage, and similar factors. It is specified in Hertz (Hz), kilohertz (kHz), or megahertz (MHz), or in parts per million per unit of the variable parameter.

frequency standard A signal source of a precise frequency, against which other signal sources can be calibrated. See specifically PRIMARY

FREQUENCY STANDARD and SECONDARY FREQUENCY STANDARD.

frequency sum   In a beat-frequency system, the quantity $f_1 + f_2$, where f_1 is the lower frequency and f_2 is the higher frequency. Compare FREQUENCY DIFFERENCE, **2**.

frequency swing   See FREQUENCY DEVIATION, **1, 2**.

frequency synthesizer   A generator of signals at a precise frequency or set of frequencies, generally adjustable in discrete frequency steps. It is used for test or communications purposes. The signals are derived from a single-frequency source, usually a crystal oscillator. Also see SIGNAL SYNTHESIZER.

frequency tolerance   The acceptable amount by which a frequency can vary from its intended value. The tolerance can be specified as a percentage of the stated frequency, a certain number of parts per million, or a certain number of hertz (Hz), kilohertz (kHz), or megahertz (MHz). Example: 3.675000 MHz ±10 Hz.

frequency-to-voltage converter   A device or circuit that delivers an output voltage that is proportional to the input frequency.

frequency translation   **1.** The conversion of a given frequency band from one part of the electromagnetic spectrum to another, without changing the actual separation of channels or the overall width of the band. **2.** See FREQUENCY CONVERSION.

frequency transmission   The passage of a frequency or band of frequencies from a mixture of frequencies through a filter or other circuit. Compare FREQUENCY REJECTION.

frequency tripler   See TRIPLER, **2**.

frequency-variation method   A method of determining the figure of merit (Q) of a tuned circuit by varying the frequency of the applied test voltage from resonance (f_r) to a high point (f_2) and a low point (f_1). At the high and low points, the circuit voltage is 0.707 times the voltage at resonance. The figure of merit then is calculated from the formula $Q = f_r/(f_2 - f_1)$.

frequency-voltage converter   See FREQUENCY-TO-VOLTAGE CONVERTER.

frequency-wavelength conversion   See WAVELENGTH-PERIOD-FREQUENCY RELATIONSHIPS.

fresnel   (A.J. Fresnel, 1788–1827) A unit of frequency equal to 10^{12} Hz. Also called *terahertz* and abbreviated THz.

fresnel lens   A usually square plastic sheet with progressively thicker concentric areas; its effect is similar to that of an automotive headlight lens.

Fresnel number   A measure of the relative effects of diffraction in an optical lens. The Fresnel number is equal to the radius of the lens divided by the product of the light wavelength and the lens focal length, all measured in the same units.

Fresnel region   For a radio-frequency transmitting antenna, the zone between the antenna and the FRAUNHOFER REGION. The size of the Fresnel region depends on the wavelength of the radiated energy.

friction   The resistance to mechanical motion when one material is rubbed against another. Friction was one of the earliest sources of human-made electricity (see FRICTIONAL ELECTRICITY and ELECTRIC MACHINE). Electrical resistance, opposing the flow of current, is analogous to friction.

frictional electricity   Static electricity generated by rubbing one material against another.

frictional electric machine   See ELECTRIC MACHINE.

frictional error   The change in parameters of a phonograph pickup, resulting from friction with the disk surface.

frictional loss   A decrease or impairment in the efficiency with which energy is converted into useful work, caused by friction between moving parts.

fringe area   The region in which a signal falls to the minimum field strength necessary for satisfactory communication.

fringe howl   In a regenerative detector, a howling sound that occurs when the transistor first begins to oscillate, obscuring the signal. The term is used because the circuit is operated at the fringe of oscillation.

fringing   See EDGE EFFECT.

Fritch   Trade name (American Telephone & Telegraph Co.) for *frequency-selective switch*.

fritting   A condition in which electrical contact corrosion creates a small hole, through which molten contact material passes to form a conductive bridge.

front contact   The movable contact of a relay.

front end   **1.** The first radio-frequency (RF) amplifier stage in a radio or television receiver. **2.** The converter portion of a superheterodyne communications receiver (i.e., the RF amplifier, first detector, and local oscillator). Compare REAR END.

front layer photocell   See RECTIFIER PHOTOCELL.

front porch   In a television horizontal sync pulse, the interval between the end of the sync pulse and the fall of the blanking pedestal. Compare BACK PORCH.

front projection   In big-screen video, a scheme in which the images from a set of bright cathode-ray tubes (CRTs) are projected onto a reflective screen, in a manner similar to the way the film is projected in a movie theater.

front-surface mirror   Also called *first-surface mirror*. A mirror that has its reflective material on the front, instead of on the back.

front-to-back ratio   **1.** For a semiconductor junction, the ratio of forward (positive) current to reverse (negative) current for the same value of voltage. Also called *forward-reverse ratio.* **2.** In a unidirectional antenna, the ratio of signal strength in the favored direction to signal strength 180 degrees opposite the favored direction. It is usually expressed in decibels (dB).

frost alarm   A device or circuit that responds to the presence of frost and actuates an alarm. Such alarms are sensitive to temperature, moisture, or both.

FRUGAL   Acronym for *FORTRAN rules used as a general applications language.*

FRUSA   Acronym for *flexible rolled-up solar array,* such as the type used in spacecraft and communications satellites.

F scan   In radar operations, a display in which a central blip represents the target at which the antenna is pointed; horizontal and vertical displacement of the blip indicate corresponding horizontal and vertical aiming errors.

FSK   Abbreviation of FREQUENCY-SHIFT KEYING.

FSM   Abbreviation of FIELD-STRENGTH METER.

FS meter   See FIELD-STRENGTH METER.

FSR   Abbreviation of *feedback shift register.*

ft   Abbreviation of *foot* or *feet.*

FT-cut crystal   A piezoelectric plate cut from a quartz crystal at an angle of +57°, with respect to the z-axis. Also see CRYSTAL AXES and CRYSTAL CUTS.

ft-Lb   Abbreviation of FOOT-LAMBERT.

ft-lb   Abbreviation of FOOT-POUND.

Fuchs antenna   A simple antenna consisting of a single-wire radiator without feeder or transmission line, connected directly to the transmitter. It is usually an odd multiple of 0.25 wavelength long. When a good radio-frequency (RF) ground is used, this antenna can be effective at high frequencies, although part of its radiated field is often inside the transmitter building.

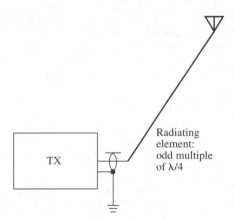

Radiating element: odd multiple of λ/4

TX

Fuchs antenna

fuel alarm   A sensing circuit that actuates an alarm when the fuel in a tank or reservoir falls to a prescribed level.

fuel cell   A generator that produces electricity directly from a reaction between fuel substances, such as hydrogen and oxygen.

fuel-flow alarm   An electronic circuit that actuates an alarm when fuel flow changes from a prescribed value.

fuel-flow control   A servo system that automatically maintains or corrects the flow rate of a fuel.

fuel-flow gauge   See FUEL-FLOW METER.

fuel-flow indicator   See FUEL-FLOW METER.

fuel-flow meter   An instrument for measuring fuel flow rate.

fuel-flow switch   A switch that is actuated by fuel flowing in pipes or other channels.

fuel gauge   An instrument consisting of a transducer that senses the level of liquid fuel in a tank and delivers a proportional output current or voltage, and an electric meter whose needle is deflected in proportion to the current or voltage and, therefore, to the fuel level. Alternatively, the meter can be a direct-readout digital device, showing the number of gallons remaining in the tank, and/or the extent to which the tank is full (fraction or percentage).

fuel meter   See FUEL GAUGE.

fuel-pressure indicator   An instrument for measuring fuel pressure in pipes or other channels.

fuel-pressure meter   See FUEL-PRESSURE INDICATOR.

full adder   In a digital computer, an adder circuit that can handle the carry signal, as well as the binary elements that are to be added. Also see ADDER and CARRY. Compare HALF ADDER.

full bridge   A bridge-rectifier circuit in which each of the four arms contains a diode. By comparison, the three-quarter bridge contains a resistor in one arm; the half bridge, resistors in two arms; and the quarter bridge, resistors in three arms.

full-duplex system   In data communications, a system that transmits data in both directions simultaneously and continuously. Compare HALF-DUPLEX SYSTEM.

full-focus yoke   See COSINE YOKE.

fullhouse   A multichannel radio-control model plane system that allows the use of a realistic complement of working control surfaces.

full-load current   The output current from a source when the load is maximum (that is, the load resistance is minimum).

full-load power   The power drawn from a source when the load is maximum (that is, the load resistance is minimum).

full-load voltage   The output voltage of a source when full power is drawn [i.e., when the load is maximum (that is, the load resistance is minimum)].

full-load wattage   See FULL-LOAD POWER.

full-power frequency response   The highest frequency at which a signal can fluctuate at full voltage (peak-to-peak) without causing distortion of more than a certain specified amount.

full-range speaker See MONORANGE SPEAKER.

full scale 1. The operating range of an instrument. **2.** In an analog meter, the quantity indicated by maximum deflection of the needle (usually at the extreme right-hand end of the calibrated scale). **3.** Transducer output as a function of highest allowable input stimulus.

full-scale current Symbol, I_{FS}. In a digital-to-analog converter, the maximum current that can occur at the output.

full-scale error For an electrical indicating instrument, the rated full-scale input signal minus the actual input signal that causes a full-scale deflection. Thus, the predictable error in an instrument, expressed as a percentage of the full-scale reading.

full-scale frequency Generally expressed in Hertz (Hz) or kilohertz (kHz). The maximum frequency at which a voltage-to-frequency converter can operate while remaining within its specifications.

full-scale sensitivity The current, voltage, or power required to deflect a meter mechanism to full scale.

full-scale symmetry Expressed in microamperes (mA). The mathematical difference between the full-scale current outputs in a complementary-output digital-to-analog converter.

full track A recording track covering the full width of a magnetic tape.

full-track head A tape-recorder head having a gap that covers the full width of the tape.

full-track recording Usually applicable to quarter-inch or narrower magnetic recording tape, a one-track recording made by a head that magnetizes essentially the entire width of the tape.

full-wave bridge rectifier See BRIDGE RECTIFIER.

full-wave, center-tap rectifier A circuit in which the center-tapped secondary winding of a transformer operates two rectifier diodes, each on an alternate half-cycle of secondary voltage. The frequency of the ripple in the direct-current (dc) output is equal to twice the alternating-current (ac) input frequency. Compare BRIDGE RECTIFIER.

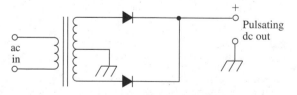

full-wave, center-tap rectifier

full-wave detector A detector circuit using two diodes in a full-wave, center-tap rectifier configuration.

full-wave doubler See FULL-WAVE VOLTAGE DOUBLER.

full-wave loop antenna A loop antenna with a circumference of one wavelength, fed at a break. The loop can be circular, square, triangular, or occasionally some odd shape. The most efficient configuration is the circular loop. Maximum radiation occurs perpendicular to the plane of the loop.

full-wave rectifier A rectifier that delivers a half-cycle of pulsating direct-current (dc) output voltage for each half-cycle of applied alternating-current (ac) voltage. The successive output half-cycles have the same polarity. See, specifically, BRIDGE RECTIFIER and FULL-WAVE, CENTER-TAP RECTIFIER. Compare HALF-WAVE RECTIFIER.

full-wave vibrator 1. In a vibrator-type power supply, an interrupter that closes contacts on both ends of its swing, thus causing direct current (dc) to flow through the transformer in alternate directions. **2.** A vibrator-type rectifier that closes in both directions.

full-wave voltage doubler A voltage-doubler circuit whose direct-current (dc) output has a ripple of twice the alternating-current (ac) supply frequency. Compare HALF-WAVE VOLTAGE DOUBLER.

function 1. A mapping between two sets of quantities or points A and B, such that: (1) For each y in B, there exists at least one corresponding x in A; and (2) For each x in A, there exists exactly one y in B. In this case y is said to be a function of x; this can be written as $y = f(x)$. The set A is called the *domain* of f; the set B is called the *range* of f. **2.** A mathematical expression, using symbols, relating variables (e.g., the expression $x - y = z$ is a function of variables x, y, and z). **3.** The behavior and application for which a device or system is designed. **4.** Part of a computer instruction specifying the operation to be done.

functional blocks Combinations of substances or components that perform specific tasks in an electronic circuit. An example is a tuned circuit, containing inductive reactance, capacitive reactance, and resistance.

functional character See CONTROL CHARACTER.

functional design Design specifications encompassing a description of how system elements will interrelate, and what their logic design will be.

functional diagram FUNCTIONAL DESIGN represented in graphic form; that is, as an illustration or set of illustrations.

functional electronic block Abbreviation, FEB. A complete integrated circuit. See INTEGRATED CIRCUIT.

functional end (FE) point In a system operating from a battery power supply, the lowest voltage at which the equipment will properly operate. As a battery discharges, the voltage decreases;

when the voltage drops to the FE point, the battery must be replaced or recharged.

functional test A performance test of a device or circuit, to see that it behaves as intended in the environment in which it is to be used.

function generator **1.** A signal generator whose output is any of several selectable waveforms (e.g., sine, square, triangular, step-pulse) and frequencies (or repetition rates). **2.** An analog computer circuit that produces a variable based on a mathematical function and one or more input variables.

function hole See CONTROL HOLE.

function key **1.** In digital communications, a keyboard key used to control the form in which a message will be received. **2.** On a computer keyboard, any of 12 keys (usually designated F1 through F12) that activates special functions. The precise action of a given key depends on the program being run.

function polling A polling technique in which a disabled device signals its condition and specifies the remedy.

function switch In a multifunction instrument, such as a voltohm-milliammeter, the switch that permits selection of the various functions.

function table **1.** A table of mathematical function values. **2.** Hardware or software that translates one representation of information into another. **3.** A routine that allows a computer to use the values of independent variables to determine the value of a dependent variable.

fundamental Contraction of FUNDAMENTAL FREQUENCY.

fundamental component The FUNDAMENTAL FREQUENCY of a complex wave.

fundamental frequency **1.** The lowest frequency in a complex wave containing harmonic energy. **2.** In a radio or television transmitter, the intended frequency of operation. **3.** In acoustics and audio applications, the predominant pitch of a musical tone.

fundamental group A set of trunk lines in a telephone system, through which zone centers are interconnected.

fundamental mode See DOMINANT MODE.

fundamental suppression Removal of the fundamental frequency from a complex wave, leaving only the harmonics, as in the operation of a null network adjusted to the fundamental frequency.

fundamental units Base units of an absolute system of units. Example: the meter (m), the kilogram (kg), and the second (s) in the mks system.

fundamental wavelength The wavelength that corresponds to the FUNDAMENTAL FREQUENCY of a wave or signal.

fuse A safety device consisting of a wire of low-melting-point metal. When current passing through the wire exceeds a prescribed (safe) level, the resulting heat melts the wire and opens the circuit, protecting equipment from damage. See PROXIMITY FUSE.

fuse box A set of electrical fuses, usually enclosed in a metal box.

fused junction In a semiconductor, a junction produced by alloying metals to the semiconductor material.

fused junction See ALLOY JUNCTION.

fuse resistor See FUSIBLE RESISTOR.

fuse wire The low-melting-point wire used in fuses. See FUSE.

fusible resistor A low-value resistor that also serves as a fuse in certain appliances, such as television receivers.

fusing current The specified current level at which a wire of a given diameter and material composition will melt.

fusion **1.** In acoustics, pertaining to delayed or reflected waves that arrive within approximately ⅕ of a second of the direct wave. So called because the human ear/brain "fuses" (blends) sounds together when they are separated by less than about ⅕ second. If the delay is longer, the ear/brain usually perceives an echo instead. **2.** In a nuclear reaction, the uniting of two atomic nuclei, accompanied by the release of energy.

future labels In a computer system, program instruction labels that refer to locations not designated as absolute addresses by a compiler or assembler.

futurist A person who tries to anticipate or predict, based on current technology and trends, what will be accomplished in a given field in the next several years or decades.

fuzz A form of deliberate distortion in the waveform produced by an electric guitar.

fuzzbox A circuit that distorts the waveform produced by an electric guitar, for the purpose of creating various musical sound effects.

fuzz buster Slang for a specialized mobile radio receiver, used by drivers of vehicles to signal the presence of law-enforcement radar equipment.

fV Abbreviation of *femtovolt*.

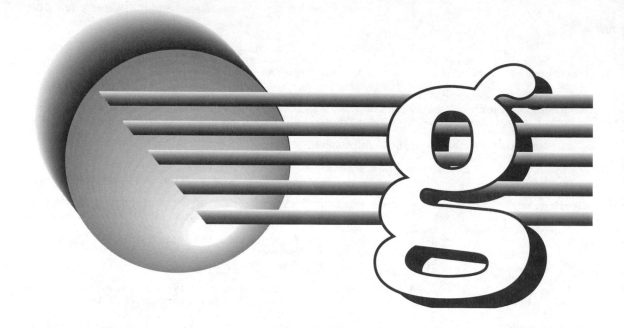

G **1.** Symbol for CONDUCTANCE. **2.** Abbreviation of GIGA-. **3.** Symbol for DEFLECTION FACTOR. **4.** Symbol for PERVEANCE. **5.** Symbol for GRAVITATIONAL CONSTANT. **6.** Symbol for GENERATOR. **7.** Symbol for GATE. **8.** Abbreviation for GAUSS.

g **1.** Symbol for CONDUCTANCE. **2.** Abbreviation of GRAM. **3.** Subscript for GATE. **4.** Subscript for GENERATOR. **5.** Symbol for GRAVITY.

GA Radiotelegraph abbreviation of "Go ahead."

G/A Abbreviation of *ground-to-air*.

Ga Symbol for GALLIUM.

GaAs **1.** Formula for *gallium arsenide*. **2.** Pertaining to semiconductor devices based on gallium arsenide.

GA coil A special form of coil, wound with extra space among the turns to reduce the distributed capacitance.

gadget **1.** A device or component. **2.** A superfluous or makeshift device.

gadolinium Symbol, Gd. A metallic element of the rare-earth group. Atomic number, 64. Atomic weight, 157.25.

gage See GAUGE.

gain The extent to which a component, circuit, device, or system increases current, voltage, or power. Applicable especially to active devices, such as transistors and integrated circuits (ICs), and to amplifiers and filters that use them. Also used to express the directional properties of some antenna systems. Usually specified in decibels (dB). See AMPLIFICATION, CURRENT AMPLIFICATION, DECIBEL, VOLTAGE AMPLIFICATION, and POWER AMPLIFICATION.

gain-bandwidth product Symbol, f_T. The product of an amplifier's gain and bandwidth.

gain control **1.** To adjust the gain of an amplifier. **2.** A potentiometer used to adjust amplifier gain.

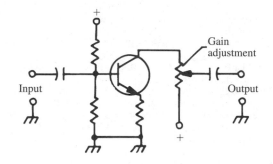

gain control

gain function A function between two currents or voltages in a circuit with gain.

gain-level linearity The quantitative measure of the extent to which the gain of a device depends on the signal level. The level is found by comparing the output to the input level over a range of input signal levels.

gain reduction The drop in gain of an amplifier at high- and low-frequency extremes.

gain sensitivity control See DIFFERENTIAL GAIN CONTROL.

gain stability The degree to which the gain of a system remains constant during changes in related factors, such as temperature, supply power, and loading.

gain temperature coefficient The extent to which the full-scale current varies over a certain temperature range, expressed in parts per million per degree Celsius (ppm/°C).

galactic noise Radio noise propagated from the plane of our galaxy, and especially from the center, located in the direction of the constellation Sagittarius. It is of significance in space communications and radio astronomy.

galena Formula, PbS. Natural lead sulfide, which in nature takes the form of bluish-gray, cubical crystals.

gallium Symbol, Ga. Atomic number, 31. Atomic weight, 69.72. One of the constituents of the semiconductor compound GALLIUM ARSENIDE.

gallium arsenide Formula, GaAs. A compound of gallium and arsenic, used as a semiconductor material. It is noted for its low-noise characteristics.

gallium-arsenide diode A diode in which the semiconductor material is processed gallium arsenide.

gallium-arsenide varactor A low-noise, microwave varactor in which the semiconductor material is gallium arsenide.

gallium-phosphide diode A light-emitting diode in which the semiconductor material is processed gallium phosphide.

galloping ghost A form of radio-control system in which the elevation and rudder can be moved to the desired extent.

Galton whistle A device for producing high-frequency acoustic waves (ultrasound), similar to a common dog whistle.

galvanic cell Generic term for any electrochemical primary voltaic cell.

galvanic corrosion Corrosion that occurs on one of two dissimilar metals when they are immersed in an electrolyte. Caused by battery action between them. Compare ELECTROLYTIC CORROSION.

galvanic couple See VOLTAIC COUPLE.

galvanic current A very small direct current such as that produced by dissimilar metals in acid or by nervous reaction in living tissue.

galvanic pile See VOLTAIC PILE.

galvanic series A list of metals and alloys arranged in order of the most to least likely to oxidize in a given environment.

galvanic skin response Abbreviation, GSR. The variations in electrical resistance of the (usually human) skin. This phenomenon is a useful indicator in physiology, psychology, and criminology.

galvanic taste A sharp, metallic taste experienced when a small electric current is passed through the tip of the tongue.

galvanism (After Luigi Galvani, 1737–1798) The production of an electric current by chemical action, as in a battery.

galvanize To coat steel with zinc to forestall corrosion.

galvanometer A sensitive, bi-directional current meter. Used in various electrical tests—especially as a null indicator in bridge operation. Also see MICROAMMETER.

galvanometer constant The number by which a galvanometer reading must be multiplied in order to obtain the current in microamperes, milliamperes, or amperes.

galvanometer recorder A graphic recorder in which a mirror in a movable-coil galvanometer reflects a beam of light to a passing strip of photographic film.

galvanometer shunt A resistor placed in parallel with a galvanometer to decrease its sensitivity. Also see SHUNT RESISTOR.

galvanometry The use of galvanometers to determine the intensity and direction of electric currents.

galvanoplastics The science of ELECTROPHORESIS and ELECTROPLATING.

galvanoscope An instrument for detecting and showing the direction of very weak electric currents.

galvanotherapy The use of electric currents to produce heat in the body of a human or animal.

gamma ferric oxide A form of coating used in formulation of magnetic recording tape.

gamma match A linear transformer for matching an unbalanced (usually coaxial) feed line to a balanced (usually half-wave) antenna. The outer conductor of the cable is connected to the center of the radiator, and an extension of the center conductor runs for a short distance parallel to the radiator, making a right-angle bend before connecting to the radiator.

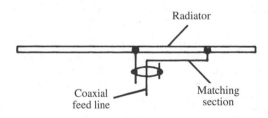

gamma match

gamma rays High-energy, ionizing radiation emitted by radioactive substances; similar to X rays, but of a shorter wavelength.

gamma section See GAMMA MATCH.

gang To mechanically couple components (pots, switches, etc.) for operation by a single knob.

gang capacitor A variable capacitor consisting of sections mounted on the same shaft for simultaneous variation. It is usually specified by the number of sections (e.g., four-gang capacitor). Compare GANGED CAPACITORS.

ganged capacitors Separate variable capacitors mechanically connected together (e.g., by belt or gear drive) for simultaneous variation. Compare GANG CAPACITOR.

ganged potentiometers Separate potentiometers mechanically connected together (e.g., by belt or gear drive) for simultaneous variation. Compare GANG POTENTIOMETER.

ganged rheostats See GANGED POTENTIOMETERS.

ganged switches Separate switches mechanically connected together for simultaneous operation. Compare MULTISWITCH.

ganged tuning Simultaneous tuning of separate circuits by means of ganged capacitors or ganged potentiometers.

gang potentiometer A potentiometer consisting of sections mounted on the same shaft for simultaneous variation. Usually specified according to the number of sections (e.g., *dual potentiometer*).

gang printer In digital computer and data processing operations, an electromechanical printer capable of printing an entire line at one time.

gang punch **1.** To punch identical or nonvarying information into the cards of a group. **2.** A machine for this operation.

gang rheostat See GANG POTENTIOMETER.

gang switch See MULTISWITCH.

Gantt chart A chart of activity versus time used in industry as an aid in making decisions regarding the allocation of resources for specific activities [e.g., as applied to PERT (project evaluation and review techniques)].

gap **1.** A space between electrodes or magnetic poles. **2.** A device consisting essentially of separated electrodes (e.g., *spark gap*). **3.** A relatively narrow space cut in iron cores to provide a break in a magnetic circuit. Also see SLOT, **1. 4.** The opening between the opposite poles of a tape recorder or playback head.

gap arrester A lightning arrester consisting of a number of metal cylinders separated by air gaps.

gap coding A system in which silent periods are inserted, according to a specific timing code, into a transmission.

gap depth In a magnetic recording head, the depth of the gap (taken perpendicular to the face). Compare GAP WIDTH.

gap digit A digit that contributes no intelligence to the word in which it appears (e.g., a *parity bit*).

gap energy The energy represented by the forbidden gap in electron energy levels (e.g., between the M-valence band and the N-conduction band in a material).

gap filling Modification of an antenna for the purpose of eliminating nulls in the directional pattern.

gap insulation See SLOT INSULATION, **1, 2**.

gap loss In a reproducing head, the loss that occurs because of the GAP DEPTH.

gap-type protector A spark gap used to protect equipment from high-voltage transients.

gap voltmeter See NEEDLE GAP and SPHERE GAP.

gap width In a magnetic recording head, the width of the gap (taken parallel with the face). Compare GAP DEPTH.

garbage **1.** In digital computer operations, a colloquialism for useless or incorrect data. **2.** Colloquialism for unreadable signals or severe intermodulation in a radio communications circuit. **3.** Colloquialism for an unsound theory.

garble **1.** Garbled matter. **2.** Also called *scramble*. To purposely render communications or data unintelligible to everyone, except the intended recipient(s). See SCRAMBLER CIRCUIT.

garbled matter Confused communications or data, usually resulting from distortion in a circuit or system. Also called GARBLE.

garbler See SCRAMBLER CIRCUIT.

garnet maser A maser that uses natural or synthetic garnet as the stimulated material. Also see YTTRIUM-IRON-GARNET.

gas One of the states of matter, characterized by molecules that are widely separated and are in continual, relatively rapid motion. Because it is a fluid, a gas will readily conform to a container of any shape. Gases can readily be compressed and liquefied. Compare LIQUID, PLASMA, and SOLID.

gas amplification In a radiation-counting device, the ratio, in decibels, of the charge collected to the charge produced in the gas.

gas breakdown The ionization of a gas by means of high voltage. The intensity of the electric field prevents recombination of ions. Collisions among atoms cause further ionization. Thus, the gas becomes a good conductor of current.

gas cell A cell whose operation depends on gas absorption by the electrodes.

gas cleanup Loss of pressure in a gas-filled tube, eventually leading to failure. Caused by gas ions forming compounds with metal parts or with the glass envelope.

gas detector A device for sensing presence of various gases in the air—especially toxic or explosive gases (such as chlorine, hydrogen, or methane).

gaseous conduction The conduction of an electric current through an ionized gas.

gaseous phototube A PHOTOTUBE containing a small amount of a gas suitable for ionic conduction.

gaseous voltage regulator A gas-filled diode across which the voltage drop is substantially constant during the gas discharge and which accordingly delivers a constant output voltage.

gas-filled cable A sealed cable filled with an inert gas that serves as a low-loss dielectric and moisture barrier.

gas-filled counter tube A radiation counter tube containing a gas that ionizes when irradiated. See GEIGER-MUELLER TUBE.

gas-filled lamp **1.** An incandescent lamp filled with a gas, such as nitrogen, for improved performance. **2.** Discharge lamp.

gas-filled tube An enclosure filled with gas that is subjected to an electric potential, intended to produce specific effects, such as light emission or voltage regulation.

gas-flow alarm An electronic circuit that actuates an alarm when the flow of gas through a pipe changes from a predetermined rate.

gas-flow control A servo system for automatically maintaining or adjusting the flow of gas through pipes.

gas-flow gauge See GAS-FLOW METER.

gas-flow indicator See GAS-FLOW METER.

gas-flow meter An instrument that indicates the rate of gas flow through a pipe, in terms of volume per unit time (e.g., cubic feet per minute).

gas-flow switch In a gas-circulating system, a switch that actuates an alarm when the gas flow rate changes.

gas focusing In a cathode-ray tube, a technique by which a gas is used for the purpose of focusing an electron beam. The ionization of the gas causes the electron beam to be made more narrow.

GASH Acronym for *guanidine aluminum sulfate hexahydrate*, an organic crystalline material used as the dielectric in certain ferroelectric capacitors and ferroelectric memory elements.

gas laser A LASER that uses a gas or mixture of gases (instead of a solid rod) as the stimulated medium. Some of the gases used are argon, carbon dioxide, helium, krypton, and neon.

gas maser A MASER in which the stimulated material is a gas, such as ammonia.

gas multiplication See GAS AMPLIFICATION.

gas noise Electrical noise resulting from the undirected motion of gas molecules in a gas-filled tube.

gas-pressure alarm An electronic circuit that actuates an alarm when gas pressure rises or falls.

gas-pressure control A servo system for automatically maintaining or adjusting gas pressure in pipes or other channels.

gas-pressure gauge See GAS-PRESSURE METER.

gas-pressure indicator See GAS-PRESSURE METER.

gas-pressure meter An instrument that indicates gas pressure in a pipe or container, but provides no means for automatically correcting the pressure.

gas ratio For a gas-filled tube, the ratio I_i/E_i, where I_i is the ion current and E_i is the ionization potential.

gas sensor Any element, such as the filament in a hot-filament gas detector, that responds to the presence of a gas in the environment and activates the detector or alarm circuit.

gassing **1.** The generation of gas by a storage battery, especially while it is being charged. **2.** The generation of gas during electrolysis.

gas sniffer See GAS DETECTOR.

gaston A device intended for the purpose of modulating an aircraft signal, making the signal difficult to jam. The signal is randomly modulated by noise from the device.

gas tube See GAS-FILLED TUBE.

gas-tube lightning arrester A lightning arrester, consisting of a special gas diode. The tube has virtually infinite resistance at low voltages, but provides a low-resistance path to ground when the high voltage of a lightning stroke ionizes the gas.

gas-tube oscillator A relaxation oscillator using a two-element gas tube, such as a neon lamp, as the breakdown device.

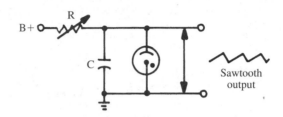

gas-tube oscillator

gas valve See ELECTROMECHANICAL VALVE.

gas X-ray tube An X-ray tube in which the positive ions of a gas bombard the cathode, which emits electrons.

gate **1.** A device or circuit that has no output until it is triggered into operation by one or more enabling signals, or until an input signal exceeds a predetermined threshold amplitude. **2.** The input (control) electrode of a field-effect transistor or thyristor device (e.g., silicon-controlled rectifier). **3.** A signal that triggers the passage of other signals through a circuit.

gate array Basic gates arranged in a pattern on a chip; the gates can be interconnected during manufacture to form a unit that performs whatever function is needed.

gate circuit **1.** An electronic switching circuit (see GATE, 1). **2.** The circuit associated with the gate electrode of a field-effect transistor.

gate-controlled switch A device similar to a silicon-controlled rectifier or thyristor. A negative current, applied to the gate, switches the device off.

gate current Symbol, I_G. Current flowing in the gate (control) circuit of a semiconductor device. The current is finite in thyristors, but is almost zero in some types of field-effect transistors.

gated amplifier An amplifier whose input is effectively switched on and off by gating signals.

gated buffer A low-voltage, high-current driver, used for differentiation in a multivibrator circuit.

gated flip-flop A flip-flop in which it is impossible for both outputs to be low simultaneously.

gate-dip meter A dip meter using a field-effect-transistor oscillator with the indicating microammeter in the gate circuit.

gate-dip oscillator   See GATE-DIP METER.

gated multivibrator   A rectangular-wave generator that produces a gate voltage when triggered.

gate-drain voltage   Symbol, V_{GD}. In a field-effect transistor, the maximum voltage permitted between the gate and drain electrodes.

gated sweep   **1.** In radar, a sweep whose initiation and duration are closely controlled to eliminate echoes in the image. **2.** A circuit providing the action described in **1**.

gate electrode   See GATE, **2**.

gate impedance   **1.** The impedance of the gate electrode of a field-effect transistor with respect to the other electrode, which serves as the return. **2.** The impedance of the gate winding of a magnetic amplifier.

gate leakage current   See GATE REVERSE CURRENT.

gate nontrigger voltage   Symbol, V_{Gnt}. For a thyristor, the direct-current (dc) voltage applied between the gate and the cathode, above which the device fails to maintain its rated blocking voltage.

gate power dissipation   Symbol, P_G. In a silicon controlled rectifier, the power consumed by the gate-cathode path.

gate-protected MOSFET   A metal-oxide-semiconductor field-effect transistor in which the gate electrode is protected from accidental burnout via built-in Zener diodes, connected back-to-back.

gate pulse   **1.** A pulse applied to the gate electrode to actuate a gate-controlled semiconductor device. **2.** An actuating pulse in a gate circuit.

gate recovery time   Symbol, t_{Gr}. For a silicon-controlled rectifier, an extension of the reverse recovery time: the interval following application of the reverse voltage required before the forward blocking voltage can be reapplied and then blocked by the device.

gate reverse current   Symbol, I_{GSS}. In a field-effect transistor, reverse current in the gate-source circuit. Also called *gate leakage current.*

gate signal   **1.** The input or control signal applied to the gate electrode of a semiconductor device. **2.** An actuating signal in a gate circuit.

gate-source breakdown voltage   Symbol, BV_{GSS}. The voltage at which the gate junction of a junction field-effect transistor (JFET) enters avalanche.

gate-source pinchoff voltage   Symbol, V_P. In a field-effect transistor, the gate-source voltage at which the conduction channel just closes.

gate-source voltage   Symbol, V_{GS}. In a field-effect transistor, the direct-current (dc) voltage between the gate and source electrodes.

gate terminal   **1.** The terminal connected to the gate semiconductor in a field-effect transistor. **2.** The terminal, or terminals, connected to the input or inputs of a digital-logic network.

gate trigger current   In a gate-controlled semiconductor switch, the current flowing in the gate circuit when the device is being switched on by a gate trigger voltage.

gate trigger voltage   In a gate-controlled semiconductor switch, the trigger voltage required to actuate the device.

gate turn-off current   In a gate-controlled semiconductor switch, the low value of gate current that flows when the device is being switched off. Turn-off current varies with collector (anode) current.

gate turn-off voltage   In a gate-controlled semiconductor switch, the low value of gate voltage that causes the device to switch off.

gate voltage   **1.** The voltage applied to the gate electrode of a field-effect transistor. See GATE-SOURCE VOLTAGE. **2.** The instantaneous gate-cathode voltage in a silicon-controlled rectifier. **3.** The voltage across the gate winding of a magnetic amplifier.

gate winding   In a magnetic amplifier, a winding that produces gating action.

gating   **1.** The process of using one signal to switch another (or part of another) on or off for a desired interval. **2.** Selecting a part of a wave for observation or for control purposes.

gauge   **1.** Any device, such as a METER, used for the purpose of measuring the magnitude of a quantity. **2.** Wire data and measurements (see WIRE GAUGE, **1**, **2**, **3**). **3.** Sheet metal thickness (e.g., 10 gauge).

gauss   (Karl F. Gauss, 1777–1855) Unit of magnetic flux density, equivalent to one line of flux per square centimeter. The SI (preferred) unit of magnetic flux density is the TESLA (webers per square meter); 1 gauss equals 10^{-4} teslas (symbol, T). Also see FLUX DENSITY.

Gaussian curve   See BELL-SHAPED CURVE.

Gaussian distribution   In statistics, the symmetrical distribution described by a bell-shaped curve. Also called NORMAL DISTRIBUTION.

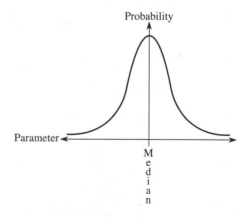

Gaussian distribution

Gaussian function   A mathematical function used in the design of lowpass filters. The Gaussian response is characterized by low band-edge selectivity, high transition bandwidth, negligible step response overshoot, and low step-response delay time.

Gaussian noise Electrical noise whose amplitude-versus-frequency characteristic is described by the GAUSSIAN DISTRIBUTION.

Gaussian waveform A waveform that results in minimal side lobes in a pulse-compression system.

gaussmeter See FLUXMETER.

Gauss' theorem Across any closed surface within an electric field, the total flux is approximately equal to 12.566 times the enclosed quantity of electric charge.

gauze resistor See WOVEN RESISTOR.

GAVRS Abbreviation of *gyrocompass attitude vertical reference system.*

GCA Abbreviation of GROUND-CONTROLLED APPROACH.

GCI Abbreviation of GROUND-CONTROLLED INTERCEPTION.

GCM Abbreviation of *gyrocompass module.* See GYROCOMPASS.

GCT Abbreviation of GREENWICH CIVIL TIME.

Gd Symbol for GADOLINIUM.

G display See G SCAN.

GDO **1.** Abbreviation of GRID-DIP OSCILLATOR. **2.** Abbreviation of GATE-DIP OSCILLATOR.

Ge Symbol for GERMANIUM.

gear **1.** Collectively, electronic equipment. **2.** A toothed wheel commonly used in mechanical devices.

gearmotor An electric motor with a gear train for speed changing.

gear-wheel pattern A pattern produced on an oscilloscope by intensity-modulating a circular trace. A signal of unknown frequency f_x is applied to the intensity-modulation (z-axis) input. The signal produces corrugations in the trace. If there are n corrugations around the trace, and if the trace itself completes f_s revolutions per second, then the unknown frequency f_x, in Hz, is equal to nf_s. Compare SPOT-WHEEL PATTERN.

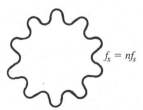

$$f_x = nf_s$$

gear-wheel pattern

Geiger counter A radioactivity rate-counting instrument based on the GEIGER-MUELLER TUBE. Pulses from the tube drive a transistor,

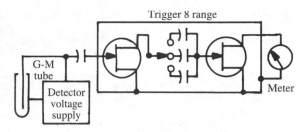

Geiger counter

which, in turn, drives a meter or digital counter to indicate the count.

Geiger-Mueller counter See GEIGER COUNTER.

Geiger-Mueller region For a GEIGER-MUELLER TUBE, the range of voltages within which the output pulse amplitude is constant, regardless of ionizing radiation intensity.

Geiger-Mueller threshold The lowest voltage in the Geiger-Mueller region.

Geiger-Mueller tube A gas-filled radiation detector/counter tube consisting of a straight wire as an anode, surrounded by a cylindrical cathode. The tube is biased by high voltage. Radiation penetrating the tube ionizes the gas; each ionizing event causes an output pulse.

Geiger point counter See POINT COUNTER.

Geiger region See GEIGER-MUELLER REGION.

Geiger threshold See GEIGER-MUELLER THRESHOLD.

Geissler tube A simple gas-filled glow-discharge tube with metal electrodes sealed in each end. When a sufficiently high voltage is applied between the electrodes, the highly rarefied gas ionizes and glows with the color associated with the particular gas used.

gel A substance equivalent to colloidal solution in the solid phase (e.g., silica gel).

gel battery A rechargeable electrochemical BATTERY designed for use with portable electronic and computer equipment. Noted for its ability to deliver high current for short periods, when necessary, and also to deliver moderate current continuously throughout its discharge cycle.

gen Abbreviation of GENERATOR.

genemotor Contraction of *generator/motor*, a (usually battery-driven) dynamotor that has separate motor and generator windings on the same armature core.

general class license An amateur-radio license that conveys some privileges in the high-frequency bands, and all operating privileges in the very-high-frequency region and above. An examination of moderate difficulty is required.

general-purpose bridge See UNIVERSAL BRIDGE.

general-purpose component A component designed or used for a wide range of applications. For example, a general-purpose germanium diode is useful as a detector, mixer, limiter, clipper, meter rectifier, automatic-gain-control (AGC) rectifier, and curve changer.

general-purpose computer A computer that can be used in a number of applications for which it was not specifically designed.

general-purpose diode A small-signal semiconductor diode that is useful for a variety of applications, such as detection, light-duty rectification, limiting, logic switching, etc.

general-purpose function generator A nonspecialized function generator that is capable of generating a variety of different waveforms.

general-purpose program A program for the solution of a class of problems or for a specific problem, according to certain parametric values. Also called *general routine*.

general-purpose relay Any relay that can be used in various situations, such as for switching alternating or direct currents.

general-purpose tester An instrument, such as a voltohm-milliammeter, that offers several test capabilities.

general-purpose transistor A transistor that can be used in several applications, such as audio amplification, detection, and oscillation.

general service code See CONTINENTAL CODE.

generate **1.** To produce a signal or carrier wave. **2.** To convert some non-electrical form of energy (usually mechanical) into electrical energy. **3.** To develop subroutines from parameters applied to skeletal coding. **4.** To use a program generator to produce a specialized version of a general-purpose program.

generated address An address developed by program instructions for later use by that program.

generated noise **1.** Electrical noise caused by battery action (i.e., between dissimilar metals) in a component, such as in a potentiometer. **2.** Electrical noise caused by small output variations of generating devices (rotating machines, vibrators, etc.). Also called *generator noise*.

generating magnetometer See EARTH INDUCTOR.

generating station An electric power station.

generating voltmeter An instrument based on a rapidly spinning variable capacitor. A direct-current (dc) voltage applied to the capacitor is converted into an alternating current (ac) by the varying capacitance; the ac is proportional to the voltage.

generation **1.** The production of a signal or carrier wave. **2.** The conversion of some non-electrical form of energy (usually mechanical) into electrical energy. **3.** The number of recording steps between a master recording and a copy. **4.** A copy of data in any form (e.g., tape recording, disk file, and photocopy).

generation number A number that identifies the age of a file; it is included in the file label on the disk or tape containing the file.

generator **1.** Symbol, G. Any signal source. **2.** A rotating machine for producing electricity. **3.** An electronic device for converting direct current into alternating current of a specific frequency and waveshape. **4.** In computer operation, a routine (akin to a compiler) that will produce a program to perform a specific version of some general operation by implementing skeletal coding, according to specific parameters (e.g., *sort generator*).

generator efficiency The ratio of consumed power to delivered power in a generator. It is usually expressed as a percentage.

generator noise Electrical noise caused by a rotating generator. Also see GENERATED NOISE, **2.**

generator-type microphone A microphone that produces an output voltage without the need for a supply voltage. Examples: ceramic, crystal, dynamic, electret, and velocity types.

generator-type transducer A transducer that converts mechanical motion into an electrical signal of a proportional voltage. In such a transducer, an armature or conductor moves in a magnetic field.

generic A form of software collection. Several specialized software packages can be derived from the generic collection, for use in different systems.

geodesic **1.** On a surface, the shortest path between two points. **2.** The shortest path between two geographical locations, measured over the surface of the earth. Also called *geodetic* and *great circle*.

geodesy The branch of applied mathematics concerned with the precise dimensions of the earth.

geodetic system The application of a computer to seismographic studies for the purpose of reducing drilling and mining costs.

geomagnetic field See EARTH'S MAGNETIC FIELD.

geomagnetism The earth's magnetism. Also see EARTH'S MAGNETIC FIELD.

geometric capacitance The ratio of the free charge of a capacitor to the voltage across its terminals.

geometric mean The nth root of the product of n quantities.

geometric progression A mathematical sequence in which each term after the first is obtained by multiplying the preceding one by a constant quantity (e.g., 1, 2, 4, 8, 16, 32, 64,...). Also called *geometric sequence*.

geometric symmetry In a bandpass or band-rejection filter, a condition in which the response is identical on either side of the center frequency. Also called *mirror-image symmetry*.

george box In an intermediate-frequency amplifier, a device used to reject jamming signals. Any jamming signal with an amplitude lower than a certain minimum is rejected.

geostationary orbit An orbit in which a satellite revolves around the earth exactly once a day, so it remains over the same place on the earth all the time. The altitude must be 22,300 miles,

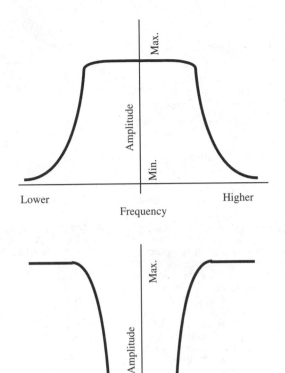

geometric symmetry

and the orbit must lie in the plane of the earth's equator.

geostationary satellite A satellite in GEOSTATIONARY ORBIT. It is always in the same spot in the sky from any given observing point. A geostationary satellite provides coverage over about 40 percent of the earth, and is commonly used for communications and weather-observation purposes.

germanium Symbol, Ge. A metalloidal element. Atomic number, 32. Atomic weight, 72.59. Used in semiconductor diodes, photocells, rectifiers, and transistors.

germanium diode A diode in which the semiconductor material is specially processed germanium.

germanium dioxide Formula, GeO_2. A gray or white powder obtainable from various sources; it is reduced in an atmosphere of hydrogen or helium to yield germanium, a semiconductor material.

germanium junction diode A germanium diode that contains a pn junction.

germanium photocell A photoconductive cell consisting of a reverse-biased germanium point-contact diode or germanium junction diode.

germanium point contact The contact between a pointed metal wire and a germanium wafer, as in a point-contact diode or point-contact transistor.

germanium rectifier A power rectifier that contains a germanium pn junction.

germanium transistor A transistor in which germanium is the semiconductor material. Such a transistor has lower internal resistance and greater temperature drift than a silicon transistor.

German silver A copper-nickel-zinc alloy used in some resistance wires. Also called NICKEL SILVER.

GEV Abbreviation of *ground effect vehicle.*

GeV Abbreviation of GIGAELECTRONVOLT.

gfi Abbreviation of GROUND-FAULT INTERRUPTER.

g-force See GRAVITY, **2.**

g_{FS} Symbol for FORWARD TRANSCONDUCTANCE.

G/G Abbreviation of GROUND-TO-GROUND.

ghost In television reception, a slightly displaced image appearing on the screen simultaneously with its twin (the false member of a double image).

ghost signal Any signal (such as an undesired reflection) that produces a ghost.

GHz Abbreviation of GIGAHERTZ.

G_i Symbol for INPUT CONDUCTANCE.

Gibson girl A portable radio transmitter, powered by an integral crank-operated generator, introduced during World War II for pilots forced down at sea.

giga- Abbreviation, G. **1.** A prefix meaning billion (10^9). **2.** In digital data applications, a prefix meaning 2^{30}.

gigabit A unit of digital data, equal to 2^{30} bits or 1024 megabits. Also see BIT and MEGABIT.

gigabyte A unit of digital data, equal to 2^{30} bytes or 1024 megabytes. Also see BYTE and MEGABYTE.

gigacycle See GIGAHERTZ.

gigaelectronvolt Abbreviation, GeV. A large unit of voltage; 1 GeV equals 10^9 eV. Also see BEV, ELECTRONVOLT, MEV, and MILLION ELECTRON VOLTS.

gigahertz Abbreviation, GHz. A unit of ultra-high frequency; 1 GHz equals 1,000,000,000 Hz = 10^9 Hz.

gigaohm A unit of extremely high resistance, reactance, or impedance, equal to 1,000,000,000 ohms = 10^9 ohms.

GIGO Abbreviation of *garbage in = garbage out,* an expression signifying that incorrect or improper input to a computer will produce meaningless output.

gilbert (William Gilbert, 1540–1603) A unit of magnetomotive force, equal to 1.26 times the number of ampere-turns. The SI (preferred) unit of magnetomotive force is the ampere (symbol, A); 1 gilbert = 0.796 A.

gilbert per centimeter   See OERSTED.

gimbal   A suspension device whose orientation can be changed without affecting the attitude of the body being suspended.

gimmick   **1.** Colloquialism for any unnamed device. Also see GADGET. **2.** Colloquialism for any tricky manipulation or design. **3.** A low-value capacitor made by twisting two short pieces of insulated wire together.

gimp   Colloquialism for the tinsel and cloth conductor used in some earphone cords.

Giorgi system   The *meter-kilogram-second (mks)* system of units.

GJD   Abbreviation of GERMANIUM JUNCTION DIODE.

glass   A hard, brittle, amorphous, and usually transparent substance that is largely silicon dioxide. Glass has a multitude of uses in electronics, and there are several kinds, each having different electrical properties. The dielectric constant ranges from about 4 to 10; the dielectric strength ranges from about 20 to 300 kilovolts per millimeter.

glass arm   A stiffness of the wrist or forearm, somewhat resembling writer's cramp, sometimes experienced by radiotelegraph operators or wire telegraph operators after prolonged use of a hand key.

glass bulb   The glass enclosure of electron tubes and incandescent lamps.

glass capacitor   A capacitor that uses thin glass as the dielectric, and usually has plates consisting of metal electroplated or electrodeposited on opposite faces of the glass. Also see MOLDED GLASS CAPACITOR.

glass diode   A semiconductor diode molded in glass.

glass electrode   A probe used with a pH meter; it consists of a thin-walled glass tube containing potassium chloride and mercurous chloride. Also see CALOMEL ELECTRODE.

glass envelope   See GLASS BULB.

glassivation   A procedure for encapsulating semiconductor devices in glass or other dielectric material.

glass-metal seal   See GLASS-TO-METAL SEAL.

glass plate capacitor   See GLASS CAPACITOR.

glass shell   See GLASS BULB.

glass-to-metal seal   A bond between glass and metal in electronic devices, such as vacuum tubes, feedthrough terminals, and glass capacitors.

glass tube   A vacuum tube whose elements are housed in an evacuated glass envelope.

glide path   The guidance beam used by aircraft making instrument landings.

glide-path transmitter   A radio-frequency transmitter that produces a guidance beam for aircraft landing purposes. The aircraft follows the beam toward the runway.

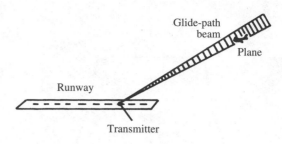

glide-path transmitter

glide slope   See GLIDE PATH.

G line   A microwave conductor consisting of a round wire coated with a dielectric.

glitch   **1.** In a television image, a narrow, horizontal interference bar that moves vertically. **2.** A very short and unwanted high-amplitude transient that recurs irregularly in an electronic system.

glitter   **1.** In radar, an echo or set of echoes that fluctuates rapidly in intensity because of motion in the target. **2.** A system in which moving devices are used to confuse enemy radar systems.

gloss factor   For a reflecting surface, the ratio of reflected light in a selected direction to reflected light in all directions.

glossmeter   An instrument for determining GLOSS FACTOR.

glow discharge   The luminous electrical discharge resulting from the passage of current through ionized gas in a partially evacuated tube. The color of the glow is characteristic of the particular gas used.

glow-discharge microphone   A device that produces audio-frequency currents from the action of sound waves in a glow-discharge tube.

glow-discharge tube   A partially evacuated tube that contains two or more electrodes. The rarefied gas in the tube glows when a sufficient voltage is applied to the electrodes. See DISCHARGE LAMP, FLUORESCENT TUBE, and NEON BULB.

glow lamp   See DISCHARGE LAMP.

glow modulator tube   A gas tube whose luminous output can be modulated by an audio input signal.

glow potential   The voltage at which glow discharge just begins in a gas-filled tube.

glow switch   In fluorescent light circuits, an electron tube containing two bimetal strips that make mutual contact when heated by the glow discharge.

glow tube   See DISCHARGE LAMP, FLUORESCENT TUBE, GLOW MODULATOR TUBE, NEON BULB, and STROBOTRON.

glow voltage   See BREAKDOWN VOLTAGE, **2.**

glucinium   See BERYLLIUM.

gluon   A subatomic particle that is believed to bind quarks together (coined by Prof. Murray Gell-Mann of California Institute of Technology).

GM   Abbreviation of *Geiger-Mueller* (see, for example, GEIGER-MUELLER TUBE).

gm   Abbreviation of *gram*. Also abbreviated g.

g_m   Symbol for TRANSCONDUCTANCE.

g-m   Abbreviation of GRAM-METER.

gm-cal   Abbreviation of GRAM-CALORIE.

gm-cm   Abbreviation of GRAM-CENTIMETER.

G-M counter   See GEIGER COUNTER.

GMT   Abbreviation of GREENWICH MEAN TIME.

G/M tube   See GEIGER-MUELLER TUBE.

gnd   Abbreviation of GROUND.

g_o   Symbol for OUTPUT CONDUCTANCE.

gold   Symbol, Au. A precious metallic element. Atomic number, 79. Atomic weight, 196.967. Electrical contacts that must have low radio-frequency resistance, and that must be relatively immune to corrosion, are often plated with gold.

gold-bonded diode   A germanium point-contact diode having a fine gold wire whose point is bonded to the germanium wafer. Its principal features are high forward current and almost constant, low reverse current.

gold doping   The diffusion of gold into the base and collector regions of a diffused-mesa transistor; it shortens carrier storage time.

golden ratio   A set of proportions used in the design of some speaker cabinets. The width (W) is ⅝ of the height (H); the depth (D) is ⅝ of the width. These correspond to a ratio $H : W : D =$ 1.000 : 0.625 : 0.391. These proportions are thought by some acoustics engineers to result in the best possible sound quality.

gold-leaf electroscope   See ELECTROSCOPE.

Goldschmidt alternator   An early dynamo for generating radio-frequency power. The high-frequency energy was not generated directly by the machine, but by resonant circuits and frequency-multiplying interaction between components.

Golf   Standard phonetic alphabet code word for the letter G.

goniometer   **1.** Generically, any radio direction finder. **2.** An inductive coupler having a secondary coil rotated by a dial calibrated to read azimuth. The coupler, when used with a suitable antenna system, comprises a direction finder. **3.** A device for electrically varying the directional pattern of an antenna.

go-no test   A test that indicates only acceptance or rejection of a device. No diagnosis is made.

GOTO   In computers and programmable calculators, an instruction that, followed by a suitable label, directs the program to that label.

goto circuit   In a digital-logic circuit, a device that senses the direction of electric current.

goto pair   A pair of diodes connected in reverse series used in digital-logic circuits.

governor   **1.** A device that prevents a motor or engine from running faster than a certain speed. **2.** Any device that limits a circuit parameter.

g parameters   Conductance parameters obtained for the equivalent-pi model of a transistor: g_{BE}, g_{GC}, g_{CE}, and g_m.

gpc   Abbreviation of GERMANIUM POINT CONTACT.

GPI   Abbreviation of GROUND-POSITION INDICATOR.

gr   Abbreviation of *grain(s)*.

graceful degradation   A computer programming technique used to prevent debilitating breakdown by operating the system—even though several subsystems have malfunctioned; also known as *crippled mode*.

grad   A unit of angular measurement equal to 0.9 degree.

graded-base transistor   See DIFFUSED-BASE TRANSISTOR.

graded filter   A power-supply filter that supplies direct-current output at various points in the filter sequence. Thus, the points in the powered equipment that can tolerate the least ripple are connected to the filter output, and those that can tolerate appreciable ripple are connected to the filter input; fairly critical points are connected to an intermediate position in the filter, such as at the junction of two chokes.

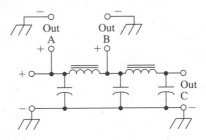

graded filter

graded-junction transistor   A grown-junction transistor in which the temperature of the melt and the rate at which the crystal is pulled from it are closely controlled as the n and p layers are formed.

gradient   The rate at which a variable quantity increases or decreases. See, for example, VOLTAGE GRADIENT.

gradient microphone   A microphone whose output varies with sound pressure. Also see PRESSURE MICROPHONE.

Graetz bridge   A full bridge rectifier (i.e., one having a diode in each arm).

grain boundary   In a polycrystalline solid, a boundary between single crystalline regions.

gram   **1.** Abbreviation, g. A unit of mass and weight, equal to 0.001 kilogram or 0.0353 ounce. **2.** A suffix meaning something drawn (written), or recorded, as in *radiogram* or *electrocardiogram*.

gram atom   See GRAM ATOMIC WEIGHT.

gram atomic weight   Also called *gram-equivalent*. The quantity of an element with a mass in grams that is equal to the atomic weight of the element. For example, copper has an atomic weight of 63.546; therefore, one gram atomic weight of copper has a mass of 63.546 grams.

gram-calorie Abbreviation, gm-cal. The amount of heat required to raise the temperature of one gram of water by one degree Celsius.

gram-centimeter Abbreviation, gm-cm. The work done by a force of one gram exerted over a distance of one centimeter. Also see JOULE.

gram-equivalent See GRAM ATOMIC WEIGHT.

grammar **1.** The sequence of words and/or abbreviations in a communication or part of a communication. **2.** The sequence of codes and/or commands in a high-level computer programming language.

gramme armature See GRAMME RING.

Gramme ring A type of armature for a motor or generator, consisting of an iron ring onto which is wound a coil of wire, each turn being connected to a commutator bar.

gram-meter Abbreviation, g-m. A unit of work equal to a force of one gram exerted over a distance of one meter. Compare JOULE.

gram-molecular weight See MOL.

gram molecule See MOL.

gramophone Archaic term for *phonograph*.

grandfather cycle A backup scheme in a magnetic reproduction system. The original records are retained for a period of time so that new copies of high precision can be made in case of loss.

grandfather file An original copy of a file on a magnetic disk or tape, retained as a source for reconstruction as needed. Usually, three generations of a file (grandfather, father, and son) are kept, each identified by a generation number. Sometimes the terms *grandparent*, *parent*, and *child* are used instead. See GENERATION NUMBER.

grand synthesizer A hypothetical child with a mind perfectly attuned to artificial intelligence (AI), who grows up to revolutionize the whole industry; a "grand master of AI."

granular carbon Carbon in the form of fine granules, used in the button of a carbon microphone.

granularity **1.** In a digital device, the smallest increment that can be differentiated. **2.** The limit of detail in a reproduction system.

granule One of many narrow frequency subbands, the combination of which composes a complete signal. Each subband carries its own specific data.

graph **1.** A presentation of data, particularly a depiction of the manner in which one variable or set of variables changes, with respect to another. Can be in the form of discrete points, curves, bars, columns, pie-shaped slices, etc. **2.** A curve or set of curves in a coordinate system.

graphical analysis The solution of problems through the use of graphic devices, such as vector diagrams, load lines, Nyquist plots, topological flow diagrams, etc.

graphical harmonic analysis See SCHEDULE METHOD.

graphical user interface Acronym, GUI (pronounced "gooey"). An operating system or software that makes it easy for lay people to use a computer. Commands are given by making choices from among items displayed on the screen. Popular versions use symbols, called *icons*, along with a pointing device, such as a *mouse* or *trackball*.

graphic documentation Records of data in the form of graphs, charts, tables, diagrams, etc.

graphic equalizer A device for tailoring the amplitude-versus-frequency response of a high-fidelity audio system. Consists of a splitter, several audio filters, and a mixer. The gain of each filter is adjustable via a slide potentiometer. The potentiometers are arranged on the front panel in such a way that their relative positions show the approximate shape of the response curve.

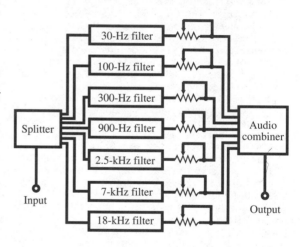

graphic equalizer

graphic instrument See GRAPHIC RECORDER.

graphic-level recorder An instrument that makes a permanent recording of signal amplitude as a function of some independent variable (such as time, frequency, or direction).

graphic panel In process control, a panel of illuminated lights or dials that display the status of a process.

graphic recorder An instrument in which a signal-driven pen or stylus makes a permanent record of a quantity on graph paper. The paper passes at a controlled speed beneath the pen.

graphics **1.** Diagrams, charts, photos, tables, or similar, often symbolic, artwork used to convey information. **2.** The video display in a computer system. **3.** Computer software designed specifically to create and edit illustrations.

graphic solution   **1.** A method of depicting the solution(s) to a problem or equation by means of graphs. **2.** The process of solving problems or equations with the aid of graphs.

graphic terminal   A display or plotter that provides visual output of a computer run.

graphite   A soft form of carbon used in resistors, attenuators, contacts, brushes, vacuum-tube plates, cathode-ray tube coatings, etc.

graphite-line resistor   An emergency, makeshift resistor consisting of a pencil line drawn on a piece of paper. The heavier the line for a given width and length, the lower its resistance.

graphophone   Archaic term for *phonograph.*

grasping planning   A scheme that a robot arm and gripper use to get hold of a particular object. It can use a vision system, a bar-code reader, tactile sensing, and/or proximity sensing. The robot controller (computer) must be programmed to recognize the input from these devices, and to seek out the object.

grass   The background noise (noise floor) on the display of a spectrum analyzer; it also appears on certain types of radar displays.

grasshopper fuse   A special type of spring-operated fuse. When it burns out, it actuates an alarm that alerts personnel of a possible circuit or system malfunction.

graticule   Calibrated gridwork, as on the face of an oscilloscope or spectrum-analyzer screen.

grating   A set of parallel, closely spaced, equidistant conductors or bars. When an electromagnetic field that has a wavelength comparable to the conductor spacing passes through the plane containing the conductors, diffraction occurs, producing an interference pattern. An adaptation of this device, called a DIFFRACTION GRATING, is used to separate visible light into its constituent spectral colors.

grating reflector   A metal antenna reflector consisting of numerous parallel, straight, closely spaced conductors. When the conductor spacing is much smaller than the wavelength, the set behaves like a solid sheet of metal.

Gratz rectifier   A form of full-wave rectifier circuit in a three-phase, alternating-current system.

gravitational constant   Symbol, g. The acceleration produced by the attraction of a unit mass at unit distance; $g = 6.673 \times 10^{-11}$ N•m^2/kg^2.

gravitational wave   See GRAVITY WAVE.

gravity   **1.** The universal force of attraction between material bodies—especially that force evidenced by the earth's drawing of bodies toward its center, causing them to have weight. **2.** Abbreviation, g. The rate at which a free-falling mass accelerates in a vacuum at the earth's surface; equal to 9.802 meters per second per second (m/s^2). **3.** The rate at which a free-falling mass accelerates in a vacuum in the vicinity, or at the surface, of an astronomical object, such as a planet or star.

gravity cell   An electrochemical cell in which the positive electrode is made of copper and the negative electrode is made of zinc. The copper electrode is placed at the bottom of a jar, and the zinc electrode is placed at the top. The jar is half filled with copper sulfate solution, and then filled with zinc sulfate solution. The solutions remain separate because copper sulfate has a higher specific gravity than zinc sulfate.

gravity wave   A disturbance in a gravitational field, such as might be caused by a collapsing star. These waves might emanate from black holes or rapidly spinning neutron stars.

gray body   A radiating body exhibiting constant spectral emissivity at all wavelengths. That is, the emitted energy is the same at all wavelengths and all frequencies.

Gray code   A computer code in which the expressions representing sequential numbers differ in only one bit.

gray scale   A reference scale for use in black-and-white television and video display images, consisting of several defined levels of brightness with neutral color.

**Gray scale:
hypothetical 16-shade binary codes.**

Code	Relative shade	Percent brightness
0000	Black	0.00
0001		6.67
0010	Very dark gray	13.33
0011		20.00
0100	Dark gray	26.67
0101		33.33
0110	Medium-dark gray	40.00
0111		46.67
1000	Medium gray	53.33
1001		60.00
1010	Medium-light gray	66.67
1011		73.33
1100	Light gray	80.00
1101		86.67
1110	Off-white	93.33
1111	White	100.00

gray tin   A form of tin that exhibits some properties of a semiconductor at temperatures below 18 degrees Celsius.

greatest lower bound   The largest value of a parameter that can be obtained without changing some characteristic of a circuit, program, or system.

Greek alphabet   The 24-letter alphabet of the Greek language. Virtually all of letters are used as symbols in electronics and related sciences.

Green Book   A specialized format for *compact-disk read-only memory (CD-ROM)* computer data storage media, developed by Sony and Philips. Requires the use of a *Compact Disk-Interactive*

(CD-I) player for data retrieval. See also CD-ROM, ORANGE BOOK, RED BOOK, and YELLOW BOOK.

green gun   The electron gun in a color cathode-ray tube whose correctly adjusted beam strikes only the green phosphors on the screen.

green video voltage   In a three-gun color cathode-ray-tube circuit, the green-signal voltage, which actuates the green gun.

Greenwich Civil Time   Abbreviation, GCT. Mean time counted from mean midnight at Greenwich, England, the location of zero meridian.

Greenwich Mean Time   Abbreviation, GMT. Mean solar time at zero degrees longitude, also called the *Greenwich meridian* because it passes through Greenwich, England. In recent years, GMT has been supplanted by COORDINATED UNIVERSAL TIME (UTC) as the basis of standard time throughout the world.

grid   **1.** The prime control electrode in a vacuum tube. Usually, it is a coil or mesh, but it can have other forms. Also called *control grid.* **2.** Any electrode in a vacuum tube placed between the cathode and the anode (plate) (e.g., *screen grid* and *suppressor grid*). **3.** Two sets of straight, uniformly spaced, parallel conducting wires or rods, one set perpendicular to the other. The conductors are electrically connected at all crossing points. Used as an electrostatic or electromagnetic shield, or as a reflector of electromagnetic waves. **4.** Two sets of uniformly spaced parallel lines, one set perpendicular to the other, used as a system of coordinates or as a basis for physical measurements.

grid capacitor   **1.** A capacitor in series with the grid of a vacuum tube, used for blocking purposes. **2.** A bypass capacitor in a grounded-grid tube type amplifier. **3.** The capacitor in the grid tank circuit of a tube type oscillator or amplifier.

grid-cathode capacitance   Symbol, C_{GK}. The internal capacitance between the control grid and cathode of an electron tube. Also called INPUT CAPACITANCE.

grid characteristic   The grid-current-versus-grid-voltage performance curve for a vacuum tube.

grid circuit   The external circuit associated with the control grid of a vacuum tube.

grid current   Symbol, I_G. Current flowing between the control grid and cathode in a vacuum tube.

grid cylinder   The metal cylinder that acts as a control grid in a cathode-ray tube.

grid-dip meter   **1.** A dip meter that contains a vacuum-tube oscillator; the indicating microammeter is in the grid circuit. **2.** Loosely, any frequency-sensitive wavemeter that indicates resonance by a marked dip in input (base, grid, and gate) current.

grid-dip oscillator   See GRID-DIP METER.

grid dissipation   **1.** The amount of power given up as heat in the grid circuit of a vacuum-tube amplifier. **2.** The maximum amount of power that a tube can safely dissipate as heat in the grid.

grid drive   See GRID EXCITATION.

grid-driving power   The signal power required by the control grid of a power tube.

grid emission   Electron or ion emission by the control grid of a vacuum tube.

grid excitation   Signal voltage or power applied to the control grid in a vacuum-tube amplifier circuit.

grid impedance   Symbol, Z_G. The internal impedance of the grid-cathode path in a vacuum tube.

grid input impedance   The impedance of the grid input section of a vacuum-tube circuit. It is a complex combination of grid impedance and the impedance of input-circuit components.

gridistor   A special form of field-effect transistor with several channels.

grid-limiter resistor   A resistor connected in series with the grid of a tube to limit grid current during the positive half-cycle of grid-signal voltage.

grid limiting   The cutting off of plate current in a vacuum tube, with consequent limiting action, by means of a high, negative grid voltage developed by overdriving the grid.

grid loading effect   The tendency of the internal grid-cathode path of a vacuum tube to load a tuned circuit—especially when the grid draws current.

grid locking   A vacuum-tube fault in which the grid potential has become permanently positive because of excessive grid electron emission.

grid mesh   The mechanical structure of a grid (e.g., gauze or a metal screen).

grid neutralization   See GRID-NEUTRALIZED AMPLIFIER.

grid-neutralized amplifier   A neutralized radio-frequency power amplifier in which the neutralizing capacitor is connected from the plate of the tube to the free end of a center-tapped grid-tank coil.

grid north   In the grid system of navigation, the direction most nearly corresponding to geographic north.

grid-plate capacitance   See PLATE-GRID CAPACITANCE.

grid pool tube   A gas-discharge tube in which the cathode is a pool of mercury.

grid power loss   Driving-power loss in the grid-input circuit of a power amplifier.

grid resistor   A high-value resistor connected between the control grid and ground in a vacuum-tube amplifier circuit.

grid return   The circuit path through which the control grid of a vacuum tube is returned to ground or to the negative grid bias supply.

grid-separation circuit   A vacuum-tube circuit in which the control grid is grounded. See COMMON-GRID CIRCUIT.

grid swing   The peak-to-peak variation of a grid excitation signal.

grid tank A resonant inductance-capacitance circuit operating in the control-grid circuit of a vacuum tube. Compare PLATE TANK.

grid tank capacitance The capacitance required to tune a GRID TANK to resonance.

grid tank inductance The inductance of the coil in a GRID TANK.

grid tank voltage The alternating-current (ac) voltage developed across the grid tank of a vacuum-tube circuit.

grid tuning Tuning of a vacuum-tube circuit by varying the capacitance, inductance, or both in the GRID TANK.

grid voltage 1. Symbol, V_G. The direct-current (dc) bias voltage applied to the control grid of a vacuum tube. 2. Symbol, $V_{G(ac)}$. The voltage of the radio-frequency (RF) or audio-frequency (AF) signal in the grid circuit.

grille A covering for an acoustic speaker, used primarily to protect the speaker cone, but also for esthetic appeal.

grille cloth A durable fabric often used for speaker grilles in high-fidelity sound systems. It transmits sound at all audio frequencies, but protects the speaker(s) and provides an attractive physical appearance.

gripper See ROBOT GRIPPER.

grommet An elastic washer inserted through a hole in a chassis to prevent accidental grounding of a conductor or to reduce wear on a cord or cable exiting the chassis.

groove 1. See KEYWAY. 2. The fine, spiral line cut into a phonograph disc when it is manufactured.

groove angle On a phonograph disk, the angle between the walls of the unmodulated groove.

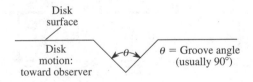

groove angle

groove speed In a phonograph recording or reproducing system, the speed of the cutter or needle, with respect to the disc. The speed is greatest near the outer edge of the disk, and least near the center.

gross content The overall amount of data contained in a message. It can be expressed in bits, bytes, words, or other units.

gross index One of a pair of indexes, used to give a reference in the *fine index*, a supplement; both indexes are used to locate computer records in storage.

gross-motion planning The method(s) that a robot uses to navigate in a general area without running into objects, knocking things over, falling down stairs, or losing its balance. It is often performed using a COMPUTER MAP of the work environment.

ground 1. The earth in relation to electricity and magnetism. 2. An electrical connection to the earth. 3. The return point in a circuit. 4. A short-circuit to the earth or to a circuit return point. 5. A short-circuit to the metal chassis, case, or panel of a piece of equipment.

ground absorption The absorption (and resulting loss) of radio-frequency electromagnetic energy by the earth.

ground bus A conductor connected to an earth ground, and to which devices in a system are individually connected. The common ground points (e.g., chassis) of the individual devices are not directly connected to each other, so *ground loops* are avoided. This scheme minimizes the probability of ELECTROMAGNETIC INTERFERENCE to or from the system. Compare GROUND LOOP.

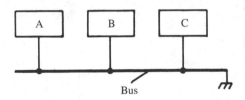

ground bus

ground clamp A device that provides a mechanical and electrical bond between a conductor and a ground rod or pipe. It is generally capable of passing a large amount of current.

ground clutter 1. In a surface-based radar system, echoes from nearby buildings, hills, and other objects, producing blips or blobs near the center of the screen. 2. In radar operations, an interference pattern on the screen, caused by accidental grounding in the system.

ground conductivity The ease with which the earth will carry electrical current. Saltwater has the best conductivity; dark, moist soil and fresh water (because of the mineral content) rate from fair to good. Sandy soil has the poorest ground conductivity.

ground conduit A pipe housing one or more ground leads.

ground connection 1. A low-resistance connection to the earth. 2. The common point, such as a chassis, to which zero-potential terminals of circuit components are connected.

ground constants The conductivity and dielectric constant of the earth for a particular kind of terrain and soil at a given location. Affects the behavior of radio antenna systems and electrical utility systems. Usually, high conductivity (low resistance) and low dielectric constant are desirable characteristics.

ground-controlled approach Abbreviation, GCA. In air navigation, a ground radar system that provides information for radio-directed aircraft approaches.

ground-controlled interception Abbreviation, GCI. A ground radar system by which an aircraft can be directed to intercept enemy aircraft.

ground current **1.** A direct electric current flowing into the earth from an electrical or electronic device, or into a device from the earth. **2.** An alternating current flowing between the earth and a device. **3.** An electric current flowing through the earth between two points. **4.** A current flowing in the normal ground (low-potential) line of a circuit.

ground detector A device that indicates whether or not a given circuit point is at direct-current ground.

grounded antenna See MARCONI ANTENNA.

grounded-base circuit See COMMON-BASE CIRCUIT.

grounded-cathode circuit See COMMON-CATHODE CIRCUIT.

grounded-collector circuit See COMMON-COLLECTOR CIRCUIT.

grounded-drain circuit See COMMON-DRAIN CIRCUIT.

grounded-emitter circuit See COMMON-EMITTER CIRCUIT.

grounded-gate circuit See COMMON-GATE CIRCUIT.

grounded-grid circuit See COMMON-GRID CIRCUIT.

grounded outlet An outlet with a receptacle having a ground contact that can be connected to equipment-grounding conductors.

grounded-source circuit See COMMON-SOURCE CIRCUIT.

grounded system A set of electrical conductors or a transmission line in which one conductor is deliberately grounded.

ground effect **1.** Modification or distortion of the ideal free-space directivity pattern of an antenna by reflections from, and absorption by, the earth. **2.** Effects of the earth on radio-wave propagation (e.g., the production of a *reflected wave* and a *surface wave*, neither of which can exist if the earth is not part of the signal path). **3.** Effects on antenna behavior, such as modification of the impedance and resonant frequency, caused by the proximity of the earth.

ground efficiency In an antenna system, the quality of the ground circuit. For some antenna systems, such as a balanced dipole at great height, this is not a consideration. Ideal ground efficiency (100%) results in zero ground loss.

ground environment **1.** See GROUND CONSTANTS. **2.** The ground characteristics in the vicinity of an unbalanced antenna working against ground. **3.** In aviation, the set of ground-based installations.

ground fault **1.** Loss of a ground connection. **2.** A short-circuit to ground.

ground-fault interrupter Abbreviation, GFI. A fast-acting electronic circuit breaker that opens the power-line circuit breaker to prevent electric shock or equipment damage when the path of current flow is through the earth.

grounding electrode A device, such as a ground plate or ground rod, that facilitates low-resistance connections to the earth.

grounding plate A metal plate connected to the earth, on which a person stands to discharge static electricity from the body.

grounding rod See GROUND ROD.

ground insulation Electrical insulation used between adjacent energized and grounded parts, such as transformer windings and metal cores.

ground level See GROUND STATE.

ground loop A closed current path resulting from improper grounding of the components in a system. A loop is formed when two devices are connected to each other, and also to separate earth grounds or to a single earth ground via conductors of appreciable length. The loops can act as antennas, increasing the likelihood of ELECTROMAGNETIC INTERFERENCE to or from the system. The use of a single GROUND BUS is preferred.

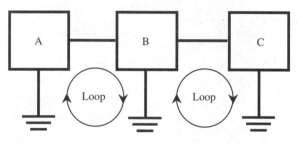

ground loop

ground mat A grid or network of conductors, connected to earth ground, for the purpose of improving the earth conductivity.

ground noise **1.** Electrical noise that results from a faulty ground connection. **2.** Background noise. **3.** In wire circuits, such as a telephone system, electrical noise that results from fluctuations in ground current.

ground plane **1.** A metal plate or a system of horizontal rods or wires mounted high on a mast, at the base of a vertical antenna, to provide a radio-frequency ground at a point several wavelengths above the surface of the earth. Also see

GROUND-PLANE ANTENNA. **2.** In noise and interference tests, a sheet metal structure used to simulate the skin of an aircraft or missile. **3.** On a circuit board, a thin metallic sheet, usually bound to the underside, that serves as a common ground and RF shield.

ground-plane antenna   An elevated vertical radiator at whose base is mounted a GROUND PLANE consisting of a metal disk or cone, or a system of radial wires or rods. The radius of the ground plane is ¼ wavelength. The antenna is fed with coaxial cable or hard line. The feed-line shield is connected to the ground plane, and the center conductor is connected to the vertical radiator.

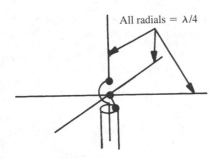

All radials = $\lambda/4$

ground-plane antenna

ground plate   A metal plate buried in the earth to provide a low-resistance ground connection.

ground-position indicator   Abbreviation, GPI. A computer system that gives a continuous indication of an aircraft's position in terms of heading, elapsed time, and speed, with respect to the surface. This provides a more useful indication of the aircraft position than an *air-speed indicator* because it is not affected by high-altitude winds.

ground potential   See ZERO POTENTIAL, **3.**

ground protection   The use of a GROUND-FAULT INTERRUPTER.

ground-reflected wave   A radio wave component that results from ground reflection.

ground reflection   The reflection of a radio wave by the earth.

ground resistance   The direct-current resistance of a connection to the earth, or the resistance between two points through the earth. The magnitude of the resistance depends on several factors: composition of the soil, amount of moisture, soil electrolytic action, and the area of contact with the earth.

ground return   **1.** The point or path used to return a circuit to ground for completion. **2.** In radar, echoes returned from the earth's surface (including reflections from objects on it).

ground-return circuit   A circuit, such as a single-wire telephone line, in which earth ground forms one leg of the circuit. Compare METALLIC CIRCUIT.

ground rod   A strong metal rod driven deep into the earth as a point of ground connection.

ground speed   The speed of an aircraft or missile, relative to the surface of the earth.

ground state   The least-energy level of all possible states in a system.

ground support equipment   Electronic surface-based apparatus upon which the functioning of a weapons system is dependent.

ground switch   A switch for grounding an outside antenna during idle periods. Also called *lightning switch*. Ideally, antennas should be disconnected from equipment, as well as grounded, when not in use.

ground-to-air communication   Radio or radar transmission from a land station to an aircraft in flight.

ground-to-ground   **1.** Pertaining to communications between land-based stations. **2.** Pertaining to missiles intended for use between points on the surface of the earth.

ground-to-ground communication   Communications between land-based stations.

ground wave   **1.** A radio wave that travels along the surface of the earth. Consists of a *line-of-sight wave*, a *reflected wave*, and/or a *surface wave*. **2.** A shock wave transmitted by the earth.

ground wire   A conductor between an equipment and a ground connection, either for circuit completion or for safety.

group   **1.** A series of computer storage locations containing a specific record or records. **2.** The data in these locations. **3.** A record set having a common key value in a sorted file.

group busy   In a telephone system, an audio signal indicating that all of the lines in a group are in use.

group code   In digital communications, an error-detecting code used to verify a character group transferred between terminals.

group delay   In a modulated signal, a delay in the transmission of data.

grouped-frequency operation   In a two-wire communications system, the grouping of directional signals into certain frequency bands.

grouped records   A set of data records in which the key of one record identifies the entire set.

grouping   **1.** The arrangement of data into blocks or sets. **2.** On a phonograph disc, the insertion of gaps in the arrangement of grooves. **3.** Any periodic irregularity in the spacing of a data transmission. **4.** The bunching of grooves on a disc recording. **5.** In a facsimile system, occasional spacing errors between recorded lines. **6.** A mass of data arranged into groups, according to common characteristics.

group mark   **1.** In telegraphy, an indicator that signals the end of a data unit. **2.** A character indicating the end of a character group; usually, it is a logical record that is addressed and processed as a unit.

group velocity   The velocity at which a group of waves or a pulse is propagated.

Grove cell   A closed-circuit primary cell in which the positive electrode, platinum, is immersed in nitric acid; the negative electrode, zinc, is immersed in sulfuric acid. The nitric acid is held in a porous cup, surrounded by a larger jar of sulfuric acid.

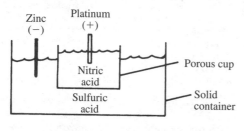

Grove cell

growler   **1.** An electromechanical troubleshooting device that indicates the location of short circuits and grounds (especially in electric motors) by emitting a growling or rumbling sound. **2.** Any tester that provides an audible signal, which indicates electrical continuity.

grown-diffused transistor   A transistor that is made by first growing the emitter and collector regions as a crystal, into which the base region is later diffused while the crystal is being pulled.

grown diode   A semiconductor diode created by growing a layer of p-type material into n-type material (or vice-versa) as the single-crystal material is being pulled from the melt.

grown junction   A pn junction produced by adding impurities in various amounts to a crystal while it is being pulled from molten semiconductor material.

grown-junction diode   See GROWN DIODE.

grown-junction photocell   A grown-junction diode used as a photoconductive cell.

grown-junction transistor   A transistor made by adding n-type and p-type impurities successively to a crystal in its molten state, then slicing the resulting npn formations from the finished crystal.

G-scan   A rectangular radar display consisting of a laterally centered blip that "grows wings" as a target approaches. Horizontal and vertical displacement of the blip indicate horizontal and vertical aiming errors.

G scope   See G SCAN.

GSR   Abbreviation of GALVANIC SKIN RESPONSE.

G-string antenna   In microwave operations, a communications path provided by a dielectric-coated wire that behaves like an extremely low-

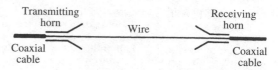

G-string antenna

loss coaxial line with its outer conductor removed to infinity. A horn at each end matches the line to the transmitter and receiver. The term comes from the first initial of Dr. George Groubau, inventor of the device, and the stringy appearance of the wire.

GTO   Abbreviation of GOTO.

guard band   A narrow unoccupied band of frequencies at the upper and lower limits of an assigned channel; its purpose is to prevent adjacent-channel interference by ensuring adequate separation between channels.

guard circle   On a phonograph disk, an inner groove that prevents collision of the pickup with the spindle at the center of the disc.

guard circuit   An auxiliary circuit added to an alternating-current bridge to compensate for the effects of stray capacitance in the bridge arms. One of its several forms is the WAGNER GROUND.

guarded input   An input-terminal arrangement in which one terminal, maintained at the proper potential, shields the entire input-terminal combination.

guarding   A method of short-circuiting a leakage current to ground. On a printed-circuit board, guarding is usually accomplished by the use of a large conducting foil surface near critical components.

guard relay   A relay that ensures that only one linefinder will be connected to a line circuit when other line relays are in operation.

guard ring   A metal ring (or other configuration) surrounding, but separate from, a charged body or terminal, for the purpose of evenly distributing the electric charge over the latter's surface.

guard shield   A shield that encloses the input circuit of an amplifier or instrument.

guard terminal   In a GUARDED INPUT, the terminal that shields the combination.

guard wire   A grounded wire that is intended to catch and ground a broken high-voltage line.

Gudden-Pohl effect   The tendency of an ultraviolet irradiated phosphor to glow momentarily when subjected to an electric field.

GUI   Acronym for GRAPHICAL USER INTERFACE. Can be spelled out or pronounced "gooey."

guidance   Electronic control of the path or course of a robot, missile, or other vehicle.

guidance system   The complete electromechanical system for control of a robot, missile, or other vehicle. It consists of hardware and software. The hardware includes beacons, sensors, drive systems, rockets, etc. The software interprets data from, and transmits commands to, the hardware. The nature of the hardware and software depend on the application.

guidance tape In a guided missile, a magnetic tape containing computer instructions for steering the missile in a designated course.

guide See WAVEGUIDE.

guide connector See WAVEGUIDE CONNECTOR.

guided missile A missile whose progress to a target is controlled electronically by signals from a control station or by sensing equipment aboard the missile.

guided propagation A form of radio-wave propagation in which air masses of different temperatures or humidity levels cause refraction and/or reflection of electromagnetic waves, guiding signals over long distances with very little attenuation. Commonly observed at very-high and ultra-high frequencies.

guide elbow See WAVEGUIDE ELBOW.

guide flange See WAVEGUIDE FLANGE.

guide gasket See WAVEGUIDE GASKET.

guide junction See WAVEGUIDE JUNCTION.

guide load See WAVEGUIDE LOAD.

guide slot See KEYWAY.

guide wavelength See WAVEGUIDE WAVELENGTH.

Guillemin effect The tendency for a strip of ferromagnetic material to become straight in a strong magnetic field. This is a form of MAGNETOSTRICTION.

Guillemin line In radar operations, a special pulse-forming network for controlling modulation pulse duration.

guillotine capacitor A variable capacitor in which a sliding (instead of rotary) plate moves between two stator plates. Its name results from its resemblance to the infamous beheading apparatus.

gulp Several bytes of digital information.

gun See ELECTRON GUN.

Gunn diode A semiconductor diode that exhibits NEGATIVE RESISTANCE and GUNN EFFECT. It is useful as an oscillator and amplifier at microwave radio frequencies.

Gunn effect The appearance of radio-frequency (RF) current oscillations in a direct-current-biased slab of n-type gallium arsenide in an electric field of sufficient strength.

Gunn-effect circuit Any circuit exploiting the Gunn effect, especially a GUNN OSCILLATOR.

Gunn oscillator A discrete semiconductor microwave oscillator using a GUNN DIODE.

gutta percha A hard, rubberlike, organic insulating material. Dielectric constant, 3.3 to 4.9. Dielectric strength, 203 to 508 kV/in.

guyed tower In radio communications or in microwave links, a structure that is supported by one or more sets of guy wires to add strength and to prevent collapse.

guying The support of a radio communications or microwave-link tower by the use of one or more sets of guy wires.

guy insulator Also called *egg insulator*. An insulator designed to electrically break a guy wire while maintaining its ability to support a structure. Such an insulator has two slots with holes placed at right angles, in such a position that the wire will not separate even if the insulator breaks. The stress exerted on the insulator is compression, and the insulating material is stronger under this type of stress than under tension (pulling).

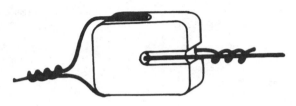

guy insulator

guy wire A bracing wire for antenna masts or towers.

gyrator An active (usually cascaded-transistor) device exhibiting nonreciprocal phase shift. It provides, among other functions, the simulation of inductance using capacitors.

gyro Contraction of GYROSCOPE.

gyro- A prefix meaning "pertaining to gyroscopes," "containing a gyroscope," or "behaving like a gyroscope."

gyrocompass A type of compass in which a spinning gyroscope, acted upon by the earth's rotation, causes the device to point to true north. Compare MAGNETIC COMPASS.

gyrofrequency The natural frequency of rotation of charged particles around the earth's magnetic lines of flux.

gyromagnetic Pertaining to the magnetic properties of rotating electric charges (e.g., the effect of electrons spinning inside an atom).

gyromagnetic effect The tendency of a rotating body to become magnetized because of the magnetic field of the earth.

gyropilot See AUTOPILOT.

gyroscope A device that consists of a spinning wheel mounted in a gimbal. The shaft of the wheel will point in one direction, despite the movement of the earth beneath it.

gyrostat See GYROSCOPE.

G-Y signal In a color-television circuit, the signal representing primary green (G) minus luminance (Y). A primary green signal is obtained when the G-Y signal is combined with the luminance (Y) signal. Compare B-Y SIGNAL and R-Y SIGNAL.

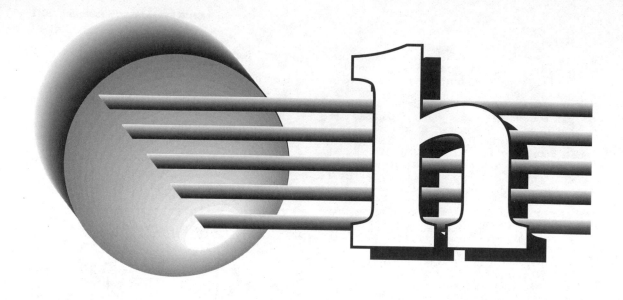

H **1.** Symbol for *magnetic field strength.* **2.** Symbol for MAGNETIZING FORCE. **3.** Symbol for HYDROGEN. **4.** Symbol for UNIT FUNCTION. **5.** Abbreviation of HORIZONTAL. (Also, hor and horiz.) **6.** Symbol for HENRY. **7.** Symbol for HARMONIC.

h **1.** Abbreviation of prefix HECTO-. **2.** Symbol for the PLANCK CONSTANT. **3.** Abbreviation of HOUR.

Haas effect See FUSION, **1.**

hack In computer networking, to access, and sometimes to change, sensitive data without authorization.

hacker A person knowledgeable in computer networking who uses his or her expertise to access, and sometimes to alter, sensitive data. This is illegal and can sometimes be destructive. For example, a hacker might change people's credit information, create criminal records for people who have committed no crimes, etc.

HACKER program A computer program developed by Gerry Sussman as an early experiment with artificial intelligence (AI), to see how the machine would deal with complex decision-making problems.

hadron A subatomic particle consisting of quarks.

hafnium Symbol, Hf. A metallic element. Atomic number, 72. Atomic weight, 178.49. Readily emits electrons.

hailer **1.** A marine microphone-amplifier-speaker system for calling to other boats or persons ashore. **2.** A comparable system for land vehicles, such as police cars. Also see MEGAPHONE, **1.**

hair See HAIRLINE.

hair hygrometer A device for measuring relative humidity, in which a stretched hair is the moisture-sensitive element.

hairline A fine line used as an index or a graticule marker in a precision instrument.

hairpin coil A quarter-turn coil, so called from its resemblance to a hairpin.

hairpin coupling coil A hairpin coil used as a low-impedance primary or secondary coil for input or output coupling.

hairpin match A form of impedance-matching network used at the feed point of a half-wave dipole antenna. A short length of open-wire transmission line, short-circuited at the far end, is connected in parallel with the antenna at the feed point.

hairpin pickup A short, doubled length of wire that acts as a pickup coil at very-high and ultrahigh frequencies.

hairspring A fine, usually spiral spring—especially the one in a movable-coil meter or the one connected to the balance wheel of a watch or clock.

hair-trigger Pertaining to extreme sensitivity of response, such as the tendency of a switching device to change state when excited by a weak pulse.

hair wire **1.** An extremely thin wire filament in a lamp or bolometer. **2.** Very small gauge wire (e.g., #44).

hal Abbreviation of HALOGEN.

half-add The sum of two binary digits, in which the carry operation is omitted. Thus $0 + 0 = 0$, $0 + 1 = 1$, $1 + 0 = 1$, and $1 + 1 = 0$.

half-adder In digital systems, an adder circuit that can handle the two binary bits that are to be added, but that cannot accommodate a carry signal. Compare FULL ADDER.

half-bridge A bridge rectifier that has diodes in two arms and resistors in the other two.

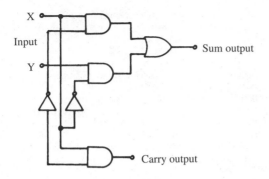

half-adder

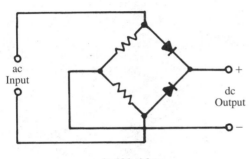

half-bridge

half-cell A voltaic cell consisting of a single electrode immersed in an electrolyte and having a definite difference of potential; it is, in effect, half of a primary cell. Also see HELMHOLTZ DOUBLE LAYER.

half-cycle Half of a complete alternation (i.e., 180 degrees of phase).

half-cycle magnetizer A magnetizer using half-cycles of rectified alternating current as the magnetic-field source.

half-duplex channel A communications channel in a HALF-DUPLEX SYSTEM.

half-duplex system In data communications, a system that transmits data in both directions, but not simultaneously. Compare FULL-DUPLEX SYSTEM.

half-lattice crystal filter A band-pass crystal-filter circuit using two piezoelectric crystals in a four-arm bridge. Also see CRYSTAL RESONATOR.

half-nut In a facsimile receiver, a device that guides the lead screw.

half-power point In a response curve or directional pattern, such as for a selective filter or a unidirectional antenna, the points on each side of maximum at which the power is 3 dB below the peak value.

half-power width In a directional antenna system, an expression of beamwidth. It is usually listed as the horizontal-plane angle, in degrees, between the half-power points in the main lobe of the directive pattern.

half-step **1.** In audio engineering, the frequency interval between two sounds, whose ratio is 1.06:1. **2.** The difference in pitch between the notes produced by two adjacent keys on a piano.

half tap A bridging circuit or device that can shunt another circuit with the least electrical disturbance.

half-track recorder A magnetic tape recorder that applies signals to both halves of a tape with a head that covers only half the tape's width in each of two directions. Also called *dual-track recorder.*

half-track tape Magnetic tape recorded by a HALF-TRACK RECORDER.

half-wave Half of a complete wave (i.e., a complete rise and fall in one direction). Its graphic representation is similar in appearance to that for a half-cycle.

half-wave antenna An antenna whose radiator measures an electrical half wavelength from end to end. Such a radiator is about 5 percent less than a free-space half-wavelength long, because of capacitive effects and the velocity factor of the conductor.

half-wave chopper A chopper that closes a circuit during only half the switching signal cycle.

half-wave dipole A center-fed antenna whose radiator measures 0.5 electrical wavelength from end to end. Also see DIPOLE ANTENNA.

half-wave doubler See HALF-WAVE VOLTAGE DOUBLER.

half-wave feeder See HALF-WAVE TRANSMISSION LINE.

half-wave loop antenna A loop antenna having a circumference of 0.5 wavelength with a break opposite the feed point. It is, in effect, a HALF-WAVE DIPOLE bent into a circle or square (although any symmetrical configuration can be used). The circle is the most efficient configuration.

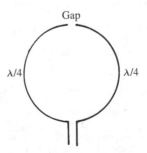

half-wave loop antenna

half-wave radiator See HALF-WAVE ANTENNA.

half-wave rectification The conversion of alternating current (ac) to direct current (dc) during half of each ac cycle. Also see HALF-WAVE RECTIFIER.

half-wave rectifier A rectifier that delivers a half-cycle of direct-current (dc) output for every other half-cycle of applied alternating-current (ac) voltage. Because the successive dc half-cycles are 180 degrees apart, they have the same polarity. Compare FULL-WAVE RECTIFIER.

half-wave transmission line A transmission line measuring 0.5 electrical wavelength at the transmission frequency. The physical length is somewhat less than a free-space half wavelength because of the VELOCITY FACTOR of the line.

half-wave vibrator A vibrator (see INTERRUPTER) whose reed operates against only one stationary contact. Compare FULL-WAVE VIBRATOR.

half-wave voltage doubler A voltage-doubler circuit whose direct-current (dc) output has a ripple frequency equal to that of the alternating-current (ac) supply. Although its output is harder to filter than that of a full-wave doubler, this circuit has the advantage of a common ground. Compare FULL-WAVE VOLTAGE DOUBLER.

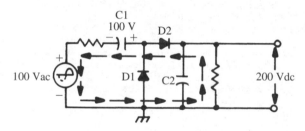

half-wave voltage doubler

voltage is positive in some metals (such as zinc) and negative in others (such as gold). Also see ETTINGHAUSEN EFFECT, NERNST EFFECT, and RIGHT-LEDUC EFFECT.

Hall-effect modulator A device that uses the HALL EFFECT to modulate a signal, or to mix two signals.

Hall-effect multiplier A device based upon the Hall generator and used in analog mathematical operations, such as multiplication and the extraction of roots.

Hall field The transverse electric field of a conductor carrying current in a magnetic field.

Hall generator A semiconductor device exhibiting the HALL EFFECT. It is a thin wafer or film of indium antimonide or indium arsenide with leads on opposite edges.

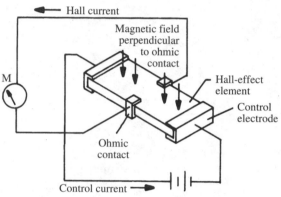

Hall generator

halide A compound of a HALOGEN. Examples: sodium iodide, used as a scintillating crystal; ammonium chloride, used as the electrolyte in a dry cell.

halide crystal A halogen-compound crystal, such as mercuric iodide and sodium iodide, useful in detecting radioactivity.

Hall coefficient For a current-carrying conductor, the constant relationship between the Hall (transverse electric) field and the magnetic flux density.

Hall constant For a current-carrying conductor, the constant of proportionality k given by the equation $k = e/(im)$, where e is the transverse electric field (Hall field), i is the current density, and m is the magnetic field strength.

Hall effect A phenomenon observed in thin strips of metal and in some semiconductors. When a strip carrying current longitudinally is placed in a magnetic field that is perpendicular to the strip's plane, a voltage appears between opposite edges of the strip that, although feeble, will force a current through an external circuit. The

Hall mobility For a conductor or semiconductor, the product of conductivity and the HALL CONSTANT.

Hall network A resistance-capacitance null circuit whose general configuration is two cascaded high-pass tee-sections bridged by a high resistance. The circuit can be tuned with one potentiometer.

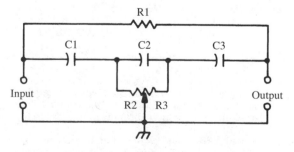

Hall network

Hallwacks effect   The phenomenon (observed by Hallwacks in 1888) in which ultraviolet light falling on a polished zinc plate causes a negatively charged electroscope to which it is connected to discharge.

hallucination   In complex computers and artificially intelligent systems, the generation or appearance of data for no apparent reason.

halo   See AFTERGLOW and PERSISTENCE.

halo antenna   A horizontally polarized antenna, consisting of a circular half-wave dipole whose ends are capacitance loaded. Commonly used at very high frequencies (VHF).

halogen   Abbreviation, hal. A group of five very active nonmetallic elements whose similar chemical properties put them in group VIIA of the periodic table; they are *astatine*, *bromine*, *chlorine*, *fluorine*, and *iodine*.

Halowax   A chlorinated naphthalene wax used as an impregnant for paper capacitors. Dielectric constant, 3.4 to 5.5. Resistivity, 10^{13} to 10^{14} ohm-cm.

halt   A stop during the execution of a computer program run, often resulting from a HALT INSTRUCTION.

halt instruction   An instruction in a computer program that causes a break in the program's execution, as by BASIC's STOP command, for example.

ham   Colloquialism for AMATEUR RADIO operator.

ham radio   See AMATEUR RADIO.

Hamilton's principle   Also called the *principle of least action*. Motion tends to occur in such a way that the integral of the product of kinetic energy and elapsed time is minimal.

hammer   **1.** The striking member in a WHEEL PRINTER. **2.** The clapper in an electric bell or gong.

hammer-and-wheel   See WHEEL PRINTER.

Hamming code   An error-correction code used in some digital communications circuits.

hand capacitance   Also called *body capacitance*. Capacitive coupling effects between a circuit and the human body (e.g., as evidenced between an operator's hand and a device having extremely high impedance and poor grounding and/or shielding).

hand generator   An electric generator operated by turning a hand crank.

Handie-Talkie   Abbreviation, HT. Tradename for a portable transceiver small enough to be held in the hand during operation.

hand key   Also called *brass pounder*. An old-fashioned, hand-operated telegraph key, operated by manual downward pressure.

hand-operated device   A device manipulated directly and manually by the operator's hand(s). Also called *manual device*.

hand receiver   **1.** A single earphone that must be held against the ear. **2.** A telephone receiver.

hand rules   See FLEMING'S LEFT-HAND RULE, FLEMING'S RIGHT-HAND RULE, and RIGHT-HAND RULE FOR WIRE.

handset   See CRADLEPHONE.

handshaking   **1.** A controlled, periodic exchange of synchronizing pulses between a digital transmitter and receiver. **2.** In a digital communications system, a method of error correction. The receiver detects nonstandard or improbable character sequences, and instructs the transmitter to repeat them for double-checking.

hand-type pointer   In an electric meter, a spearlike pointer (resembling the hand of a clock), as opposed to a knife-edged pointer.

hand-wired   Pertaining to electronic equipment wired by hand, rather than being assembled on printed-circuit boards. This form of construction is rarely seen nowadays, except in some radio-frequency power amplifiers.

hang AGC   An automatic-gain-control (AGC) circuit whose action is sustained for a brief interval after an actuating signal has passed, an advantage in some applications. Also called *fast-attack/slow-release AGC*.

hangover   In sound operations, the blurring or smearing of low-frequency (bass) notes by a poorly damped or poorly mounted loudspeaker.

hangup   **1.** In phonograph operation, the state in which the same material is played repetitiously (i.e., the stylus does not move toward the spindle). **2.** In digital-computer operations, an unexpected break during a program run as a result of software or hardware failure. Sometimes called UNEXPECTED HALT.

H antenna   See LAZY-H ANTENNA.

hard copy   **1.** In digital computer operations, a readable document (printout) of material being translated to a form understood by a computer. **2.** Generally, written or typed documents, as opposed to data on other media, such as diskettes, tapes, CD-ROM, etc.

hard disk   An electromechanical data storage medium commonly used in personal computers. Consists of several rigid disks, called *platters*, coated with ferromagnetic material.

hard-drawn wire   High-tensile-strength unannealed wire.

hard dump   See HARDWARE DUMP.

hard magnetic material   High-retentivity magnetic material. Also see RETENTIVITY.

hardness   **1.** The property that causes a material to resist penetration, deformation, scratches, etc. **2.** The penetrative ability of ultraviolet rays, X rays, or other ionizing radiation. Generally, the radiation hardness increases as the wavelength decreases, and as the photon or particle energy increases.

hardness tester   A device for measuring the hardness of a solid in terms of the force required to penetrate its surface. Also see HARDNESS, 1.

hard radiation   In general, any radiation with high penetrating power. Usually, this term is used in reference to short-wavelength (high-energy) ultraviolet rays or X rays.

hard solder   Solder that melts at a comparatively high temperature. Compare SOFT SOLDER.

hard vacuum A nearly perfect vacuum, that is, a medium essentially devoid of atomic or sub-atomic particles.

hardware **1.** Collectively, electronic circuit components and associated fittings and attachments. **2.** In a computer system, the electronic and electromechanical components (e.g., integrated circuits, keyboards, and disk drives) associated with operation. Compare SOFTWARE.

hardware availability ratio A figure depicting the availability of a computer system to do productive work; as a percentage, it is given by the formula:

$$A = 100(ta - td)/ta,$$

where A is the availability ratio, ta is the operational time, and td is the downtime over a specified time period.

hardware check A check on data being transferred within a computer, as done by hardware (e.g., a parity check).

hardware cloth A finely woven wire screen sometimes used in place of a metal plate for an antenna element, an antenna reflector, or a shielded enclosure. Especially useful when free-air circulation is required.

hardware dump During a computer program run, data sent to a storage device for later evaluation; it occurs at the time of a failure. Also called AUTOMATIC HARDWARE DUMP.

hardware engineer A person who designs and perfects the actual electronic circuitry in a system. The hardware engineer is not involved with the programming of the system.

hardware recovery A computer system's ability (through software or hardware) to recover from a failure (i.e., to proceed from the point of failure).

hardware serviceability ratio See HARDWARE AVAILABILITY RATIO.

hardwire **1.** To construct a circuit for direct-current conductivity. **2.** A circuit exhibiting direct-current conductivity over a complete, closed path.

hard-wire telemetry See WIRE-LINK TELEMETRY.

hard wiring **1.** In computer systems, functions or programs built directly into the machine hardware. In order to alter such functions or programs, the system wiring and/or components must be physically changed. **2.** A system interconnected entirely by wires and cables, and using no free-space links, such as radio or infrared.

hard X rays High-frequency (shortwave) X rays. Such radiation has high penetrating power. Compare SOFT X RAYS.

harmonic **1.** Symbol, H. In a complex sound or signal wave, a component whose frequency is a multiple of the FUNDAMENTAL FREQUENCY by a whole-number factor of 2 or more. **2.** Pertaining to whole-number multiples of the FUNDAMENTAL FREQUENCY of a sound or signal, as defined in **1**.

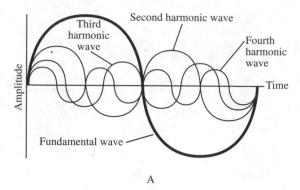

A

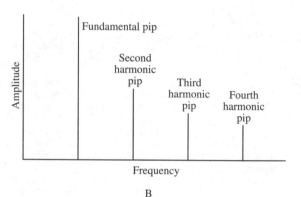

B

harmonic: waves (A)
and spectrum-analyzer display (B)

harmonic accentuation Increasing the amplitude of harmonic components in a complex wave using filters, amplifiers, or special modes of operation.

harmonic accentuator A circuit or device, such as a harmonic amplifier or bandpass filter, for emphasizing signal harmonics.

harmonically related bands In communications, frequency bands arranged so that the frequencies in one band are harmonics of the frequencies in another band. An example of bands that are precisely related in this way are 4.1 to 4.3 MHz and 8.2 to 8.6 MHz. Various amateur radio bands are harmonically related to some extent, such as 40 meters (7.0 to 7.3 MHz) and 20 meters (14.0 to 14.35 MHz).

harmonic amplifier An amplifier, such as one used with a frequency standard, used to increase the amplitude of weak harmonics. Also see HARMONIC ACCENTUATION.

harmonic analysis **1.** The evaluation of the harmonic content of a complex wave. See, for example, HARMONIC WAVE ANALYZER; SCHEDULE METHOD, **2**; SPECTRUM ANALYZER; and WAVE ANALYZER. **2.** See FOURIER ANALYSIS.

harmonic analyzer See HARMONIC WAVE ANALYZER, SPECTRUM ANALYZER, and WAVE ANALYZER.

harmonic antenna An antenna operated· at a harmonic of the lowest frequency at which it is resonant. For example, a half-wave dipole cut for 7.0 MHz, but used for transmitting and receiving at 21.0 MHz, is functioning at the third harmonic.

harmonic attenuation Reduction of the amplitude of harmonic components in a complex wave using filters, tuned amplifiers, or special modes of operation.

harmonic attenuator A circuit, device, or method of operation (such as a filter, tuned amplifier, special biasing, or special bypassing) for reducing the amplitude of harmonics.

harmonic component See HARMONIC.

harmonic composition See HARMONIC DISTRIBUTION.

harmonic content The amount of harmonic energy present in a complex wave. Also see HARMONIC-DISTORTION PERCENTAGE and HARMONIC RATIO.

harmonic-cut crystal Also called *overtone crystal*. A quartz crystal that, when operated in the proper circuit, oscillates at a harmonic of the (fundamental) frequency dictated by its thickness.

harmonic detector A detector tuned to respond to a harmonic of a signal.

harmonic distortion 1. The generation of harmonics by the circuit or device by which the signal is processed. 2. The deformation of the original signal that results from the action described in 1. 3. The disproportionate reproduction of a signal's harmonic components.

harmonic distortion meter See DISTORTION METER.

harmonic-distortion percentage In a signal containing harmonics, the harmonic energy as a percentage of the total signal energy (fundamental plus all harmonics). Also called *total harmonic distortion (THD)*.

harmonic distribution For a given signal, the various frequencies and amplitudes of its harmonics, specified within a certain range of frequencies.

harmonic elimination The complete removal of one or more harmonics from a complex wave using a filter or special mode of operation.

harmonic eliminator A circuit or device, such as a band-suppression filter, for removing harmonics.

harmonic filter 1. A bandpass filter for transmitting one or more harmonics of a complex input wave. 2. A band-suppression filter for removing one or more harmonics of a complex input wave.

harmonic frequency 1. In a complex wave, the frequency of a component that is a multiple of the FUNDAMENTAL FREQUENCY by a whole-number factor of two or more. 2. A frequency that is a whole-number (two or more) multiple of another frequency to which it is referred. Compare NONHARMONIC FREQUENCY.

harmonic generator 1. An oscillator operated so that it generates strong harmonics of the fundamental frequency. 2. See FREQUENCY MULTIPLIER. 3. See HARMONIC AMPLIFIER.

harmonic intensification See HARMONIC ACCENTUATION.

harmonic intensifier See HARMONIC ACCENTUATOR.

harmonic interference Interference resulting from the harmonics of radio or test signals.

harmonic motion Periodic motion typified by a swinging pendulum and illustrated by the plot of a sine wave.

harmonic oscillator A crystal oscillator whose output frequency is a harmonic of the crystal frequency.

harmonic percentage See HARMONIC-DISTORTION PERCENTAGE.

harmonic producer 1. An oscillator that uses a tuning fork to establish the fundamental frequency. The output can be an odd or even harmonic of this frequency. 2. See FREQUENCY MULTIPLIER. 3. A nonlinear circuit used in a calibrator to generate markers at integral multiples of the fundamental frequency.

harmonic ratio 1. In a complex wave, the ratio of harmonic energy to total signal energy (fundamental plus all harmonics). 2. In a complex wave, the ratio of harmonic energy to fundamental-frequency energy.

harmonic reducer See HARMONIC ATTENUATOR.

harmonic reduction See HARMONIC ATTENUATION.

harmonic resonance Resonance of an antenna or a circuit at a whole multiple of the applied signal frequency.

harmonic ringing In wire telephony, the use of alternating-current signal harmonics for selective ringing.

harmonic series of tones A set of audio-frequency tones in which the frequencies can be specified by f, $2f$, $3f$, $4f$, and so on.

harmonic suppression See HARMONIC ELIMINATION.

harmonic suppressor See HARMONIC ELIMINATOR.

harmonic tolerance The harmonic content permissible in a given system.

harmonic totalizer An instrument for measuring *total harmonic distortion*. See, for example, DISTORTION METER.

harmonizer A circuit that changes the frequency of an audio signal, or produces an output at several audio frequencies from an input having only one audio frequency. Used in sound recording for special effects.

harness A tied bundle of wires or cables for wiring electronic equipment.

harp antenna   A vertical antenna consisting of a number of wires that fan out from point to point along a horizontal supporting wire.

hartley   A unit of digital information equivalent to 3.32 bits. Used in certain computer applications.

Hartley oscillator   A self-excited oscillator circuit in which the two sections of a tapped tank coil supply the main coil and feedback coil required for a feedback system. The emitter or source is connected to the tap.

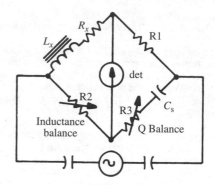

Hay bridge

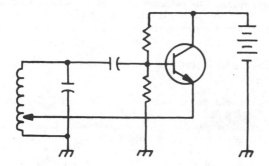

Hartley oscillator

hash   **1.** Electrical noise, especially wideband noise with a characteristic hissing sound in a radio receiver. **2.** Undesirable or purposefully meaningless information, as used in a hash total (checksum).

hash filter   A radio-frequency filter for eliminating HASH noise in a radio receiver.

hat   **1.** Also called *capacitance hat*. A small disk or set of wires attached to the end(s) of an antenna radiator, lowering the resonant frequency and increasing the usable bandwidth. **2.** A procedure for randomizing data.

hash total   See CHECKSUM.

hatchdot pattern   A television test pattern consisting of a crosshatch pattern with dots around its outer edges and one dot at its center.

hatted code   A form of code in which randomization is used to maximize the difficulty of breaking the code.

Hay bridge   An alternating-current bridge for measuring the inductance and Q of an inductor in terms of resistance, frequency, and a standard capacitance.

haywire   Loose, disorderly, or apparently careless wiring.

haz   Abbreviation of HAZARD.

hazard   Abbreviation, haz. A dangerous or potentially dangerous circuit, device, material, method, situation, or system (e.g., *electric-shock hazard*).

H beacon   A form of homing beacon with an omnidirectional radiation pattern and a radio-frequency output of between 50 W and 2 kW.

H bend   See H-PLANE BEND.

HCD   Abbreviation of *hard-copy device*.

HCM   Abbreviation of HALF-CYCLE MAGNETIZER.

HDB-3 code   Abbreviation of HIGH-DENSITY BIPOLAR-3 CODE.

HDF   Abbreviation of HIGH-FREQUENCY DIRECTION FINDER.

HDTV   Abbreviation of HIGH-DEFINITION TELEVISION.

H-display   See H-SCAN.

He   Symbol for HELIUM.

head   **1.** The top or operating portion of a device (e.g., microphone head or dynamic-speaker head). **2.** In magnetic recording and reproduction, the magnetic device (transducer) that delivers or picks up recorded impulses. **3.** In a hard disk or diskette drive, a transducer that delivers and picks up recorded data.

head alignment   **1.** Positioning the cone of a dynamic speaker so that the voice coil moves freely (i.e., without rubbing against the core). **2.** Positioning a magnetic-recorder head so that a proper relationship to the moving tape is maintained.

head amplifier   A self-contained amplifier or preamplifier in the head of a microphone or sound-on-film pickup.

head degausser   A device used for the purpose of demagnetizing the head of a tape recorder. Unwanted magnetization can build up because of direct-current components in the driving signal.

head demagnetizer   See HEAD DEGAUSSER.

head end   In a television network or system, the location from which signals are sent to subscribers.

header   **1.** A (usually glass) disk or wafer through which one or more leads pass and to which they are fully sealed. Can be used as the terminal base of an enclosed plug-in unit, such as a miniature coil, filter, or similar components. Also see GLASS-TO-METAL SEAL. **2.** A data set placed before other sets as a means of identifying them and, possibly, including control data pertinent to the sets so identified.

header capacitance   Capacitance between or among the leads in a header (see HEADER, **1**).

header label A header recorded on a magnetic tape file (see HEADER, **2**).

head gap **1.** In computer disk or tape drives, the distance between the head and the magnetic medium. **2.** In audio operations, the spacing between tape-unit head electrodes; also called *gap width.*

heading The direction taken by a vehicle with reference to some point (such as a radio beacon, true north, or magnetic north).

headlight In radar operations, a small rotating antenna.

headphone A small acoustic transducer worn against the ear for listening to music without disturbing others, or for monitoring live or recorded material without being disturbed by noise in the environment. Also see RECEIVER, **2.**

headphone amplifier An audio-frequency amplifier designed and operated primarily to supply a signal to headphones.

headphone receiver A portable radio receiver, usually for AM and/or FM broadcast, consisting of a pair of headphones or a headset with the radio built into it.

head room **1.** In a high-fidelity sound system, the extent, measured in decibels, to which an amplifier can be operated beyond the zero point on its volume-unit (VU) meter without causing objectionable distortion on sound peaks. **2.** In tape recording, the region between the maximum recording level specified by the manufacturer of the equipment, and the amplitude at which tape overload occurs. It is specified in decibels.

headset An assembly consisting of one or two earphones, a headband, and a flexible cord. Also see HEADPHONE and RECEIVER, **2.**

head stack In magnetic recording, an assembly of two or more heads for multitrack service. Also see HEAD, **2.**

head station See BASE STATION.

head-to-tape contact In magnetic-tape recording or playback, physical contact between the tape and the head.

hearing aid A miniature audio-frequency device that amplifies sound for people with impaired hearing. It consists of a microphone, a high-gain amplifier, and an earphone or bone-conduction transducer.

hearing-aid battery A physically small battery designed for use with hearing aids. Such a battery is usually of the lithium type, or some other type that has long life under conditions of low current drain.

hearing loss A measure of hearing impairment. Generally expressed as the ratio, in decibels, of an individual's threshold of hearing to the normal threshold of hearing. Also see AUDIOLOGIST, AUDIOMETER, and AUDIOMETRIST.

heart fibrillation A condition in which the heart muscle twitches at random, rather than pumping blood normally. This can be caused by an electric shock through the heart of 100 mA to 300 mA. If normal heart function is not restored, death will follow.

heart pattern See CARDIOID PATTERN.

heart telemetry See ECG TELEMETRY.

heat A form of energy transferred by conduction, convection, or radiation between two bodies having different temperatures. The amount of heat is expressed in degrees, British thermal units, calories, joules, or kelvins.

heat aging **1.** The degeneration of a substance, aggravated by high temperatures. **2.** A test that indicates the immunity of a substance to degeneration because of high temperatures.

heat coil A device that disconnects a circuit when the temperature reaches a certain minimum level.

heat detector A sensor of heat. See, for example, BOLOMETER, INFRARED DETECTOR, MICRORADIOMETER, RADIOMETER, THERMISTOR, THERMOCOUPLE, and THERMOPILE.

heated-pen recorder See THERMAL RECORDER.

heated-stylus recorder See THERMAL RECORDER.

heated-wire flowmeter See HOT-WIRE FLOWMETER.

heated-wire sensor A hot wire used to discriminate between substances, according to how they affect its heating. See, for example, GAS DETECTOR (also usable as a vacuum gauge), HOT-WIRE ANEMOMETER, and HOT-WIRE MICROPHONE.

heat engine A machine that converts heat energy into mechanical energy.

heater **1.** The filament of an indirectly heated vacuum tube. **2.** The filament in an indirectly heated thermistor.

heater-voltage coefficient The amount of frequency change per volt of fluctuation in the filament voltage of a Klystron.

heat exchanger A device or system that removes heat from a hot body and transfers it to another body or to the surrounding air.

heat-eye tube An infrared-sensitive device used for the purpose of locating objects in visible darkness. The tube consists of a cathode-ray device that is sensitive to infrared radiation.

heat gradient The temperature difference between two points on a body, divided by the distance between the two points.

heating depth See DEPTH OF HEATING.

heating effect The production of heat (power loss) by electric current flowing in a conductor.

heating element **1.** See HEATER. **2.** The resistance element (such as a strip or coil) that generates heat in an electric-heating device.

heat loss **1.** Heat emitted by conduction, convection, or radiation from a body at a relatively high temperature. **2.** Power loss as a result of the heating effect of an electric current.

heat of fusion   The amount of heat required to melt a unit mass of a solid that has reached its melting point.

heat of radioactivity   Heat generated during the process of radioactive disintegration.

heat of reaction   In a chemical or electrochemical reaction, the heat (in calories) absorbed or released.

heat of vaporization   The amount of heat required to convert 1 gram of a liquid to a vapor without raising its temperature.

heat radiator   See HEATSINK.

heat rays   See INFRARED RAYS.

heat remover   **1.** See HEATSINK. **2.** A forced-air or forced-liquid cooling system.

heat-resistant glass   See PYREX.

heat-sensitive resistor   See THERMISTOR.

heat-sensitive switch   A make-and-break device, such as a thermostat, that is actuated by a change in temperature.

heat-shrink tubing   An insulated flexible sleeving made from a plastic that shrinks permanently for a tight fit when heated; it is commonly used at the joint between a cable and connector.

heatsink   A heat exchanger in the form of a heavy, metallic mounting base or a set of radiating fins. It conducts heat away from such devices as power transistors, heavy-duty resistors, or power tubes, and dissipates the heat into the surrounding environment via convection and radiation.

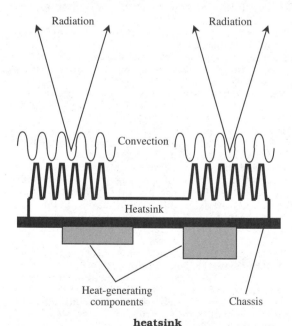

heatsink

heatsink resistance   The opposition offered by a heatsink to the flow of heat.

heat therapy   **1.** The use of radio-frequency heating for therapeutic purposes. Also see DIATHERMY. **2.** The use of infrared rays for therapeutic purposes.

heat transfer   The movement of heat from one point to another by absorption, conduction, convection, or radiation.

heatronic   Pertaining to the heating of a dielectric material subjected to a high voltage.

heat unit   **1.** See BRITISH THERMAL UNIT. **2.** See CALORIE. **3.** See KELVIN.

heat waves   See INFRARED RAYS.

heat writer   See THERMAL RECORDER.

Heaviside-Campbell bridge   A form of mutual-inductance bridge. Mutual inductance is determined without regard to the operating frequency.

Heaviside layer   See KENNELLY-HEAVISIDE LAYER.

heavy hydrogen   An isotope of hydrogen. The term is applied to *deuterium*, whose nucleus consists of one proton and one neutron, and also to *tritium*, whose nucleus consists of one proton and two neutrons.

heavy metal   A metal having a specific gravity of 5.0 or higher. Examples: iron (7.85 to 7.88), lead (11.3), nickel (8.6 to 8.9), mercury (13.6), platinum (21.4).

heavy water   Formula, D_2O. Water in which deuterium (HEAVY HYDROGEN), rather than ordinary hydrogen has combined with oxygen.

hecto-   Abbreviation, h. A prefix meaning hundred(s), (i.e., 10^2).

hectometric wave   An electromagnetic field whose wavelength is on the order of hundreds of meters (i.e., at least 100 meters, but less than 1000 meters). The frequency ranges from 300 kHz to 3 MHz.

hectowatt   Abbreviation, hW. A unit of power equal to 100 watts. Seldom used; power in this range is usually expressed in terms of the WATT or the KILOWATT.

heelpiece   A part of an electronic relay that provides mechanical support for the armature.

Hefner candle   A unit of luminous intensity equal to 0.9 candela; the standard (German) is the HEFNER LAMP.

Hefner lamp   A standard light source whose luminous intensity is 0.9 candela. It burns amyl acetate (banana oil) and its flame has been the standard of the HEFNER CANDLE, a unit of luminous intensity devised in Germany. Also see CANDLE POWER and LUMINOUS INTENSITY.

height control   In a television receiver circuit, the potentiometer or rheostat that controls the vertical dimension of the picture by varying the amplitude of vertical scanning pulses.

height finder   An altitude-measuring radar system.

height-position indicator   Abbreviation, HPI. A radar displaying the height of a target, its angular elevation, and the slant range.

Heil oscillator   An oscillator based on a special tube consisting of a heated cathode, first anode,

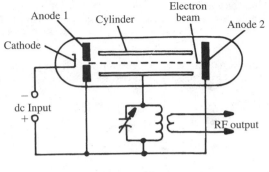

Heil oscillator

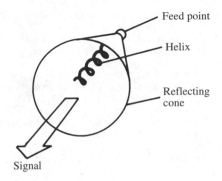

helicone

metal cylinder, and second anode. Electrons emitted by the cathode pass through a hole in the first anode and become a beam, which passes through the cylinder and strikes the second anode (collector). Electron bunching in the cylinder causes energy to be transferred to a tank circuit between the cylinder and anodes.

Heisenberg uncertainty principle See UNCERTAINTY PRINCIPLE.

hekto- See HECTO-.

heliacal cycle See SUNSPOT CYCLE.

helical antenna A spring-shaped antenna mounted perpendicular to a flat metal-plate reflector, an arrangement that produces circularly polarized waves in a narrow beam. It is used primarily at ultra-high and microwave radio frequencies.

helical-beam antenna See HELICAL ANTENNA.

helical line The helix in a backward-wave oscillator or traveling-wave tube.

helical potentiometer A potentiometer whose resistance element is a wire wound into a coil of several turns. The slider moves over the wire (or the larger coil) from one end to the other as the slider or coil is turned through several complete revolutions. Also called MULTITURN POTENTIOMETER.

helical scanning Radar scanning by an antenna that moves vertically as it moves horizontally, producing a spiral motion to the radiated beam.

helical sweep See SPIRAL SWEEP, **1**, **2**.

helical transmission line See HELICAL LINE.

helicone An antenna used at ultra-high and microwave frequencies, consisting of a helical radiator within a cone-shaped reflector.

helionics The science of converting solar heat into electrical energy. The term is an acronym from *helio-* (pertaining to the sun) and *electronics*.

heliostat **1.** A servo-controlled motor-driven device that drives a mirror to keep sunlight trained upon a specific target. **2.** By extension, any similar device to keep a solar cell pointed to the sun.

helitron A form of oscillator used at ultra-high and microwave frequencies. The output frequency is variable over a wide range.

helium Symbol, He. A gaseous element. Atomic number, **2**. Atomic weight, 4.0026.

helium group The six inert gases in group 0 of the periodic table: *argon, helium, krypton, neon, xenon,* and *radon.*

helium-neon laser A laser in which the lasing substance is a mixture of helium and neon. Produces a characteristic brilliant red visible output. Also see HELIUM and NEON.

helix **1.** A single-layer coil. **2.** That which is coil-shaped (i.e., spiral in configuration). **3.** See HELICAL ANTENNA. **4.** See HELICAL LINE.

helix line See HELICAL LINE.

helix recorder An information recorder using a spiral method of scanning. The recording medium is usually drum-shaped.

Helmholtz coil A device consisting of two crossed-field primary windings in which an inductively coupled secondary winding rotates. The primary windings carry currents that differ in phase by 90 degrees. Rotating the secondary coil provides 360 degrees of continuously variable phase shift.

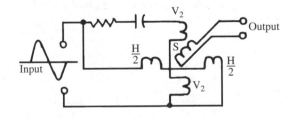

Helmholtz coil

Helmholtz double layer An intermolecular layer between a metal and an electrolyte in which it is immersed. It is formed when the adhesive force between the metal and electrolyte decreases the surface tension of the metal, causing positive ions to migrate from the metal into the liquid. The metal, charged negatively, and the electrolyte, charged positively, form a capacitor whose dielectric is the Helmholtz layer.

Helmholtz resonator   An acoustic (sound) chamber whose geometry, in combination with the size of a small opening, results in resonance at a specific frequency.

HEM   Abbreviation of *hybrid electromagnetic* (see, for example, HYBRID ELECTROMAGNETIC WAVE).

hemimorphic   Pertaining to an object with ends that have unlike faces.

He-Ne laser   See HELIUM-NEON LASER.

henry   Symbol, H. The standard unit of inductance. It is the inductance exhibited by a closed circuit in which one volt is produced by a current changing uniformly at one ampere per second. This is a large unit of inductance; more common units are the MILLIHENRY and the MICROHENRY.

hermaphroditic plug   A plug that has the prongs of a male plug and the recessed contacts of a female plug. Compare FEMALE PLUG and MALE PLUG.

hermetically sealed   Constructed in manufacture so as to be permanently closed against the entry of air or other gases, dust, and moisture.

hermetic seal   A permanent, air-tight seal that effectively prevents corrosion from elements in the outside environment.

herringbone pattern   A pattern of interference in a television picture, so named because of its resemblance to the skeleton of a fish.

Herschel-Quincke tube   An acoustic device that demonstrates sound interference. The device has two hollow cylinders, one of which can be adjusted in length. At the far end of the apparatus, the cylinders are joined together. The resultant amplitude depends on the difference in length between the cylinders. Sound wavelengths can be measured using this apparatus.

hertz   Abbreviation, Hz. The standard unit of frequency (of periodic phenomena, such as alternating or pulsating currents); 1 Hz = 1 cycle per second. One Hz is an extremely small unit of frequency; more common units are the KILOHERTZ, the MEGAHERTZ, and the GIGAHERTZ.

Hertz antenna   An ungrounded halfwave antenna fed by a transmission line attached to one end or to the center of the radiator. See, for example, CENTER-FED ANTENNA and END-FED ANTENNA. Compare MARCONI ANTENNA.

Hertz effect   Ionization of a gas, produced by intense ultraviolet radiation.

Hertzian antenna   See HERTZ ANTENNA.

Hertzian oscillator   See HERTZ OSCILLATOR.

Hertzian radiation   Radiation of electromagnetic (radio) waves.

Hertzian waves   Electromagnetic waves in the radio spectrum, with wavelengths longer than those of infrared, visible light, ultraviolet, X rays, or gamma rays.

Hertz oscillator   A damped-wave generator of oscillations, used by Hertz in his demonstration of radio waves in 1888 (verifying the earlier prediction by James Clerk Maxwell). The oscillator contains a spark gap supplied by an induction coil, attendant coils, capacitors (in the prototype, Leyden jars), and two large metal plates.

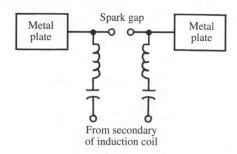

Hertz oscillator

Hertz vector   A single vector that specifies the electromagnetic field (electric and magnetic components) of a radio wave.

hesitation   As distinct from a halt, a brief break in a computer program run during which internal operations are occurring, such as data transfer to a peripheral.

heterochromatic   Consisting of different frequencies, wavelengths, or colors. Compare MONOCHROMATIC.

heterodyne   **1.** To beat one alternating-current signal against another to produce one or more beat-frequency signals. Also see BEAT FREQUENCY and BEAT NOTE. **2.** The whistle produced when two signals very close in frequency are mixed in a radio receiver. **3.** To combine radio signals in a mixer, the purpose of which is to produce a sum or difference signal for further processing.

heterodyne detection   **1.** Signal detection by beating the incoming signal against one produced by a local oscillator. In this way, an unmodulated signal is made audible (the beat note is an audio frequency). **2.** Signal detection by a superheterodyne circuit.

heterodyne detector   **1.** A detector that makes a radio-frequency (RF) signal audible by beating it against the RF signal of a local oscillator, the product being an audio-frequency (AF) beat note. **2.** The FIRST DETECTOR or SECOND DETECTOR in a SUPERHETERODYNE CIRCUIT. **3.** A combination linear detector and local RF oscillator used to detect and measure the frequency of test signals. Also see HETERODYNE FREQUENCY METER.

heterodyne eliminator   See WHISTLE FILTER.

heterodyne filter   See WHISTLE FILTER.

heterodyne frequency The frequency of the signal obtained by beating one signal against another.

heterodyne frequency meter A tunable radio-frequency meter that zero-beats a signal of an unknown frequency (or one of its harmonics) against an internally generated signal of a standard frequency (or one of its harmonics).

heterodyne method See HETERODYNE, 1.

heterodyne oscillator A signal generator whose output is the beat product of outputs from two internal oscillators. The output frequency can be either the sum or the difference of the oscillator frequencies, as selected by output filtering or tuning. See BEAT-FREQUENCY OSCILLATOR.

heterodyne reception Radio reception (especially in telegraphy) by means of the beat-note process. Also see HETERODYNE DETECTION, 1 and HETERODYNE DETECTOR, 1.

heterodyne repeater A REPEATER in which the received signals are converted to another frequency before transmission.

heterodyne-type frequency meter See HETERODYNE FREQUENCY METER.

heterodyne wave analyzer A type of audio-frequency (AF) wave analyzer. The input signal is heterodyned in a balanced modulator with the signal from an internal tunable oscillator. One of the resulting sidebands is passed through a sharp bandpass filter, whose output actuates an alternating-current (ac) voltmeter. The internal oscillator is tuned slowly so that different components of the balanced-modulator output sideband pass successively through the filter. The amplitude-versus-frequency function of the input signal is determined by noting the meter readings as the internal oscillator is tuned.

heterodyne wavemeter See HETERODYNE FREQUENCY METER.

heterodyne whistle See HETERODYNE, 2.

heterogeneous Pertaining to a group of objects or devices that have differing characteristics.

heterogeneous radiation Any broadband form of radiation. In particular, broadbanded radio waves, infrared radiation, visible light, ultraviolet, X rays, or gamma rays.

heterolysis The HYDROLYSIS of a compound into two oppositely charged ions.

heteropolar generator An electric generator in which the active conductors move through magnetic fields, first in one direction, then in the other direction. This is done by means of rotation in a nonuniform magnetic field. Most generators in common use are of this kind.

heuristic knowledge In artificial intelligence (AI), a form of machine knowledge in which a computer learns from its mistakes. As a complex program is repeatedly run over a period of time, the number of errors per run approaches zero.

heuristic program In artificial intelligence (AI), a program with which the computer solves a problem by trial and error, often learning in the process so that mistakes will not be repeated on subsequent runs.

Heusler's alloys Ferromagnetic alloys that contain one or more non-magnetic metals (such as aluminum, copper, or manganese).

hexadecimal number system An alphanumeric, base-16 system of number notation used in some computers. The system uses the usual digits plus the letters A through F to represent the numbers 10 through 15 (each place can only hold one symbol).

hex inverter A collection of six digital inverters, or NOT gates, contained within one package, usually an integrated circuit.

Hf Symbol for HAFNIUM.

HF Abbreviation of HIGH FREQUENCY.

Hg Symbol for MERCURY.

HH beacon In radionavigation, a nondirectional homing beacon.

hi 1. Contraction of HIGH. 2. Radiotelegraph symbol for a laugh, often verbalized by radio amateurs.

HIC Abbreviation of HYBRID INTEGRATED CIRCUIT.

HIDM Abbreviation of HIGH-INFORMATION DELTA MODULATION.

hi-fi 1. Contraction of HIGH-FIDELITY. 2. In video recording, the addition of sound having high fidelity.

high 1. Pertaining to a circuit point or condition at some potential above ground. 2. The logical digit 1. 3. The condition of having relatively large magnitude (e.g., HIGH FREQUENCY and HIGH VOLTAGE). 4. Pertaining to the upper portion of a range, as in HIGH BAND or HIGH FREQUENCY. 5. Characterized by greater-than-normal response or performance, as in HIGH Q or HIGH FIDELITY.

high band 1. The higher or highest frequency band used in communications, testing, or processing, when several bands are available. 2. The very-high-frequency (VHF) television channels 7 through 13. 3. The communications frequency range from about 144 MHz to about 170 MHz.

high boost In sound recording and reproduction, the emphasis of high frequencies in an operating spectrum. Also called HIGH-FREQUENCY COMPENSATION.

high-C circuit A tuned circuit having high capacitance and low inductance at a given frequency. Such a circuit is characterized by high selectivity and low voltage. Compare HIGH-L CIRCUIT. Also see LC RATIO.

high contrast In an image, a limited range of gray values between black and white, or a similar condition in a color image (overbright whites, little shadow detail). Also see CONTRAST.

high definition In facsimile or television, a condition of minute detail so that the original scene is faithfully reproduced.

high-definition television Abbreviation, HDTV. A digital television broadcast scheme in which images have greater detail (more scanned lines and more pixels) than the images in conventional television. The audio quality is also improved.

high-density bipolar-3 code A communications or digital code in which two logic highs (ones) can occur in sequence, without the need for an intervening logic low (zero) to separate them.

high-efficiency linear amplifier A LINEAR AMPLIFIER with higher operating efficiency than is obtainable with conventional class-B linear amplifiers. Efficiencies on the order of 60% at 100% modulation are possible.

high-energy materials See HARD MAGNETIC MATERIALS.

high-energy particle **1.** A SUBATOMIC PARTICLE that has been given high velocity by a particle accelerator. **2.** High-speed subatomic particles emitted by the sun during a solar flare, or arriving from outer space.

high-energy physics The discipline dealing with the characteristics, properties, and applications of HIGH-ENERGY PARTICLES.

higher-order language See HIGH-LEVEL LANGUAGE.

high fidelity Abbreviation, hi-fi. Pertaining to an audio-frequency system that is very faithful to the signal it is processing (i.e., one characterized by extremely low distortion and wide frequency response).

high frequency Abbreviation, HF. Pertaining to frequencies in the 3- to 30-MHz band (wavelengths from 10 to 100 meters). Also see RADIO SPECTRUM.

high-frequency alternator A dynamo for generating radio-frequency energy.

high-frequency bias In a tape recorder, a high-frequency sinusoidal signal superimposed on the signal being recorded, for improving linearity and dynamic range.

high-frequency compensation See HIGH BOOST.

high-frequency converter See SHORTWAVE CONVERTER.

high-frequency crystal See HARMONIC CRYSTAL.

high-frequency direction finder Abbreviation, HDF. A direction finder operated at high radio frequencies (i.e., between about 3 MHz and 30 MHz).

high-frequency heating Electronic heating of materials by high-frequency energy. See, for example, DIELECTRIC HEATING and INDUCTION HEATING.

high-frequency resistance See RADIO-FREQUENCY RESISTANCE.

high-frequency speaker See TWEETER.

high-frequency trimmer **1.** In older high-frequency communications receivers, a low-value variable capacitor operated in parallel with a usually front-panel tuning capacitor to set the high-frequency end of the tuning range. See, for example, OSCILLATOR TRIMMER. **2.** A small variable capacitor used in conjunction with a larger tuning capacitor, the function of which is to permit precision tuning of the larger device.

high-impedance-state output current Pertaining to tests that ensure that an integrated circuit will not overload a bus line.

high-impedance voltmeter A voltmeter having an input impedance of at least several megohms.

high-information delta modulation A companded form of delta modulation, operating at comparatively low sample rate.

high-L circuit A tuned circuit having high inductance and low capacitance at a given frequency. Such a circuit is characterized by low selectivity and high voltage. Compare HIGH-C CIRCUIT. Also see LC RATIO.

high-level audio signal An audio-frequency signal that has been preamplified (e.g., the output of a compact-disc player). Compare LOW-LEVEL AUDIO SIGNAL.

high-level input current **1.** Pertaining to the testing of intertransistor leakage in an integrated circuit (IC) having multiple emitter inputs. **2.** The current into an IC input at minimum high-level voltage.

high-level language Also called *higher-order language*. A computer programming language in which the operator is easily able to communicate with the machine. It generally serves as an interface between a human programmer and the MACHINE LANGUAGE. Examples are BASIC, C, C++, COBOL, and FORTRAN.

high-level modulation In an amplitude-modulated transmitter, introduction of the audio at the final stage of radio-frequency amplification, permitting 100% modulation of the full-power signal.

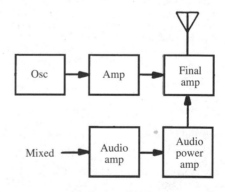

high-level modulation

high-level output current **1.** Pertaining to the testing of drive capability and fanout of an integrated circuit (IC). **2.** The current flowing from an IC output when in the high state.

high-level recovery Hardware recovery using data not involved in the failure, such as that on a magnetic storage medium. Also see HARDWARE RECOVERY.

highlight 1. A bright area in a television picture. **2.** In computer data processing, the defining or setting-off of a block of data (such as text), with the intention of relocating, editing, or deleting it.

high-noise-immunity logic Abbreviation, HNIL. A form of bipolar digital logic designed for minimal sensitivity to noise. Also known as *high-threshold logic (HTL)*.

high order Descriptive of the relationship between bits or digits in a word or number. Of two digits, the one holding the higher place value is the high-order digit (e.g., 2 is the high-order digit in 25).

high-pass filter A selective filter that transmits (with little attenuation) frequencies above a critical (cutoff) frequency and blocks frequencies below the cutoff value. Such filters can be inductance-capacitance (LC) circuits, resistance-capacitance (RC) circuits, or a combination of these.

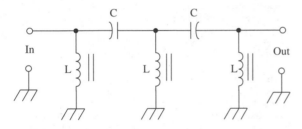

high-pass filter

high-pass-filter method A method of measuring the total harmonic distortion (THD) percentage using a high-pass filter to separate the harmonics from the fundamental. The output voltage V_o of the filter is compared with the input voltage V_i; then THD $= 100 V_o / V_i$.

high-performance Pertaining to apparatus designed for continuous operation with maximum reliability.

high-performance navigation system Acronym HIPERNAS. An electromechanical guidance system that is purely inertial and self-compensating.

high-potential test A high-voltage test of insulation, in which the applied voltage is continuously increased until the breakdown point of the dielectric is reached.

high-power rectifier A rectifier designed for high-voltage, high-current operation.

high Q For a component or circuit, a high value for the ratio X/R (reactance to resistance). This is a relative term because a particular numerical value of Q, considered high in one situation, might be regarded as low under other circumstances. Also see FIGURE OF MERIT.

high-resistance joint In the wiring of electronic equipment, a joint or connection between conductors that is poorly made, thereby introducing a high resistance between the parts.

high-resistance voltmeter A voltmeter having an input resistance of at least several megohms.

high-speed carry In computer operation, a carry into a column causing a carry out, circumventing the usual intermediate adding circuit.

high-speed diode See COMPUTER DIODE.

high-speed flip-flop A flip-flop having short switch-on and switch-off time.

high-speed oscilloscope An oscilloscope with excellent high-frequency and unit-function response. It can reproduce high-speed pulses faithfully.

high-speed relay A relay with a short make or short break interval.

high-speed transistor See SWITCHING TRANSISTOR.

high tension Pertaining to utility power-transmission lines on which there are very high voltages, typically 100 kilovolts (100 kV) or more.

high-tension line A power-transmission line carrying a very high voltage. It is generally used for the transfer of electric power over long distances.

high-threshold logic See HIGH-NOISE-IMMUNITY LOGIC.

high voltage 1. A voltage considerably higher than those ordinarily encountered in a particular application. The term is comparative; a few hundred volts might be considered high in one situation, but low in another. **2.** In a cathode-ray tube, the voltage that accelerates the beam electrons. **3.** In a television receiver, the picture-tube anode voltage. **4.** In a vacuum-tube power amplifier, the plate supply voltage.

high-voltage probe A very-high-resistance probe for measuring high voltages with a low-range voltmeter.

highway A path over which multiple signals are propagated using time-division multiplexing.

HILAC Acronym for *heavy-ion linear accelerator*.

hill-and-dale recording See VERTICAL RECORDING.

hinged-iron instrument An alternating-current meter whose input transformer core is hinged in two parts. By means of a thumb trigger, the core can be opened, then closed around the current-carrying conductor that induces magnetism in the core; a secondary coil delivers current to the meter. Also called *clamp ammeter* or *clamp voltmeter*.

HIPERNAS Acronym for HIGH-PERFORMANCE NAVIGATION SYSTEM.

hipernick A high-permeability alloy of iron and nickel.

hipot Contraction of *high potential*. See HIGH-POTENTIAL TEST.

hiss 1. A high-pitched sound rich in sibilants (*s*, *sh*, and *z* sounds) produced by random high-frequency fluctuations in current. **2.** The characteristic, high-pitched background noise (as in 1) accompanying super-regeneration. **3.** Internally generated noise in a communications receiver, amplified by the audio-frequency stages and appearing at the speaker or headphones.

hiss filter See HASH FILTER.

hit 1. The occurrence of a lightning stroke at a specific point on the ground. Also called *direct hit.* **2.** The coincidence of two pulses.

H lines Magnetic lines of flux.

HLL Abbreviation of HIGH-LEVEL LANGUAGE.

H network A network of five impedances: two connected in series between the upper input and output terminals, two between the lower input and output terminals, and one shunted between the junctions of the series-connected impedances. Also called *H pad*, *balanced tee network*, and *balanced tee pad*.

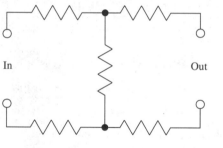

H network

Ho Symbol for HOLMIUM.

hobby robot A robot intended for amusement and, sometimes, for education. Such robots often take humanoid form. Some are programmable, and can give demonstrations, play musical instruments, and do other complex routines.

hockey-stick lead On a capacitor, resistor, or other component, a pigtail lead that is given a single crimp for easy insertion into a printed-circuit board.

hodoscope An instrument consisting essentially of closely spaced ion counters, for studying the path of an ionizing particle.

Hoffmann electrometer See BINANT ELECTROMETER.

hog horn A form of horn antenna used in microwave applications. It is generally used in the feed system of a dish antenna. The horn opening points in the direction of the feed waveguide.

hold 1. To retain data in a storage device after the data has been duplicated in another location or device. **2.** A momentary halt of an operation or process. **3.** In a television receiver, a control that stabilizes the vertical or horizontal synchronization.

hold circuit 1. See HOLDING CIRCUIT. **2.** In a television receiver, the circuit associated with the hold control(s). Also see HORIZONTAL-HOLD CONTROL and VERTICAL-HOLD CONTROL.

hold control See HORIZONTAL-HOLD CONTROL and VERTICAL-HOLD CONTROL.

hold current Symbol, I_h. The minimum current that will keep a normally open relay closed or a normally closed relay open.

hold electrode In a mercury switch, the electrode that is in permanent contact with the mercury.

holding beam In an electrostatic cathode-ray storage tube, the electron beam that generates replacement charges for those that were stored on the dielectric surface and then lost.

holding circuit In an electromechanical relay, a separate circuit that, when energized, keeps the relay actuated.

holding coil In an electromechanical relay, the extra coil that is associated with the holding circuit.

holding current 1. Current in the holding coil of a relay. **2.** In a gas tube, the minimum current required to maintain ionization.

holding gun In an electrostatic cathode-ray storage tube, the electron gun that generates the holding beam.

hold mode A condition in which the output state of a digital-logic circuit remains unchanged while the input signals are removed.

hold-off voltage The highest voltage that can be applied to a flashtube without causing it to fire.

holdover The flow of current through the ionized path created by an electric arc.

hold time 1. The time permitted for a weld to harden in resistance welding. **2.** In digital communications, the time for which a signal is maintained at a certain input after changing state at another specified input.

hole 1. In a semiconductor atom, the vacancy resulting from the loss of an electron. When an electron is lost, so is its negative charge, leaving an equivalent net positive charge. This charge, like that of an electron, can move as a current carrier. **2.** The punched-out portion of a chassis or panel, through which wires can be passed or components mounted.

hole conduction In a semiconductor material, electrical conduction as a result of HOLE CURRENT.

hole current In a semiconductor material, the electrical current resulting from the movement of positive charge carriers (holes). Also see HOLE.

hole density The degree of concentration of holes in a semiconductor. Also see HOLE.

hole-electron pair In a semiconductor, a hole and a related electron. Each electron in the conduction band has a counterpart in the valence band, a vacancy (HOLE) left by the movement of the electron to the conduction band.

hole injection The creation of mobile holes in a semiconductor by applying an electric charge. Also see HOLE.

hole injector **1.** The emitter electrode of a bipolar pnp transistor. **2.** The metal whisker of a point-contact diode having an n-type wafer. **3.** The p-layer of a forward-biased junction diode.

hole mobility The ease with which a hole moves within a semiconductor. Also see CARRIER MOBILITY.

hole storage See CARRIER STORAGE.

hole storage factor In a bipolar transistor biased to saturation, the amount of storage charge caused by excess base current.

hole trap In a semiconductor, an impurity that can cancel holes by releasing electrons to fill them.

hollow coil A coreless inductor.

hollow conductor Tubing used as a low-loss conductor at radio frequencies.

hollow core A core that is not solid throughout—especially one that has a central mounting hole.

holmium Symbol, Ho. A metallic element of the rare-earth group. Atomic number, 67. Atomic weight, 164.93. Forms highly magnetic compounds.

holocamera A camera for making holograms. Also see HOLOGRAM, 1 and HOLOGRAPHY.

hologram **1.** A wavefront recording made on photographic film by the process of HOLOGRAPHY. By changing the frequency of the light transmitted, various magnifications of the image can be obtained. Produces a true three-dimensional image. **2.** A visible, three-dimensional display projected in the air or underwater by means of lasers. They are often used at outdoor music concerts and other events.

holography A method of producing a wavefront recording of an object illuminated by laser light. The result, an interference pattern, appears meaningless when viewed in ordinary diffuse light. But when a point source of illumination is used, especially a laser, an image appears that is convincingly three-dimensional.

homeostasis The condition of being in static equilibrium.

home station See BASE STATION.

homing **1.** Guidance by means of an electronic beacon. The vehicle maintains a course toward the beacon. **2.** Guidance by means of some form of emission from a target object. The emission can be acoustic or electromagnetic energy.

homing antenna A direction-finding antenna—especially one on a mobile vehicle.

homing beacon A station radiating a beam for use in direction finding by mobile vehicles.

homing device A receiving device mounted on a mobile vehicle, and that continuously indicates the direction of a selected transmitting station that is the vehicle's destination.

homing relay A stepping relay that returns to its starting position after each switching sequence. Also see STEPPING SWITCH.

homing station See HOMING BEACON.

homodyne reception See ZERO-BEAT RECEPTION.

homogeneous **1.** Uniform in structure; similar at all points or locations. **2.** Consisting of many identical elements.

homogous field A field whose lines of flux in one plane pass through a single point.

homolysis The decomposition of a compound into a pair of neutral atoms or radicals.

homomorphism A one-to-one correspondence between the elements of two sets.

homopolar Pertaining to the union of atoms of the same polarity; nonionic.

homopolar generator A direct-current (dc) generator whose poles have the same polarity, with respect to the armature. Thus, no commutator is necessary.

homopolar magnet A magnet whose pole pieces are concentric.

homunculus In artificial intelligence (AI), a computer or robot that exhibits characteristics of a living being; especially, an ANDROID.

honeycomb coil A multilayer coil having a UNIVERSAL WINDING.

honeycomb winding See UNIVERSAL WINDING.

honker Also called *midrange speaker*. A loudspeaker that favors the middle audio frequencies. Compare TWEETER and WOOFER.

hood A light shield for a cathode-ray tube; it allows the screen to be viewed with a minimum of interference from room light.

Hooke's law Strain is proportional to the stress that produces it, as long as the ELASTIC LIMIT is not exceeded.

hook switch A switch that closes a circuit when a headset or handset is lifted from the resting position. The common telephone receiver uses such a switch.

hook transistor A four-layer pnpn semiconductor device, in which the outer p and n layers serve as emitter and collector, the inner n layer being the base. This places a p layer between the base and collector, resulting in a transistor that provides high alpha as a result of carrier multiplication by the additional junction in the collector layer.

hookup See SCHEMATIC DIAGRAM.

hookup wire Flexible, insulated wire used in the wiring of some electrical and electronic devices.

hoop antenna See CAGE ANTENNA.

hoot stop During a computer program run, a loop made evident by a sound signal.

hop In long-distance radio communications, the transmission of a wave and its subsequent return to the earth from the ionosphere; it is of importance mainly at low, medium, and high frequencies.

hor   Abbreviation of HORIZONTAL. (Also, *H* and *horiz.*)

horiz   Occasional abbreviation of HORIZONTAL. The usual form is *hor*; another alternate is *H*.

horizon   **1.** For a specific location, the circle on the celestial sphere midway between the zenith (the point directly overhead) and the nadir (the point directly underfoot). **2.** Also called *visual horizon.* The set of points, as viewed from a particular location, where the sky and the earth appear to meet (i.e., the last visible part of the earth's surface from a given observation point). **3.** Also called *radio horizon.* The set of points, from a particular location at a given radio frequency, representing the maximum communications range via the ground wave under normal conditions. Also see ARTIFICIAL HORIZON.

horizontal   **1.** Pertaining to objects or effects in a plane perpendicular to a line connecting the zenith (the point directly overhead) and the nadir (the point directly underfoot). **2.** Pertaining to that which is parallel to an assumed flat surface. **3.** Pertaining to width deflection on a cathode-ray tube.

horizontal AFC   In a television receiver circuit, *automatic frequency control (AFC)* of the horizontal sweep. It keeps the receiver's horizontal scanning in step with that of the camera at the transmitting station.

horizontal amplification   Gain provided by the horizontal channel of a device, such as an oscilloscope, cathode-ray electrocardiograph, or television receiver. Compare VERTICAL AMPLIFICATION.

horizontal amplifier   A circuit or device that provides HORIZONTAL AMPLIFICATION. Compare VERTICAL AMPLIFIER.

horizontal angle of radiation   For an antenna, the direction of maximum radiation in the horizontal plane (see HORIZONTAL, **1**), provided as an azimuth angle measured clockwise from geographic north.

horizontal angle of deviation   In a communications circuit, the angular difference, in degrees, between the compass direction from which a received signal arrives, and the great-circle path connecting the receiving station with the transmitting station.

horizontal axis   The axis that is parallel to an assumed horizontal surface (of the earth, for example) or the one so represented in a diagram. Also see X-AXIS.

horizontal beamwidth   In a directional antenna system, the angle, measured in the horizontal plane, between the half-power points in the major lobe.

horizontal blanking   See HORIZONTAL RETRACE BLANKING.

horizontal-blanking pulse   In a television signal, the rectangular pedestal-shaped pulse that oc-

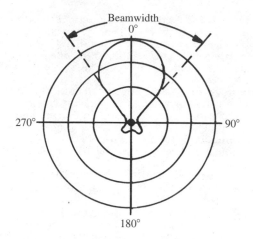

horizontal beamwidth

curs between the active horizontal lines to achieve horizontal retrace blanking. Compare VERTICAL-BLANKING PULSE.

horizontal centering control   See CENTERING CONTROL.

horizontal channel   The system of amplifiers, controls, and terminations that constitute the path of the horizontal signal in an equipment, such as an oscilloscope or graphic recorder. Compare VERTICAL CHANNEL.

horizontal-convergence control   In a color television receiver, the variable component for adjusting the horizontal dynamic convergence voltage.

horizontal coordinates   See CARTESIAN COORDINATES.

horizontal deflection   In a cathode-ray tube, the lateral movement of the electron beam on the screen. Compare VERTICAL DEFLECTION.

horizontal deflection coils   The pair of coils that produces the magnetic field to horizontally deflect the electron beam in an electromagnetic cathode-ray tube. Also see DEFLECTION COIL.

horizontal-deflection electrodes   See HORIZONTAL DEFLECTION COILS and HORIZONTAL DEFLECTION PLATES.

horizontal deflection plates   In an electrostatic cathode-ray tube (typical of laboratory oscilloscopes and some early television picture tubes), a pair of plates that produces an electric field to horizontally deflect the electron beam. Compare VERTICAL DEFLECTION PLATES.

horizontal directivity   The radiation or reception pattern of a directional antenna in the horizontal plane.

horizontal-drive control   See DRIVE CONTROL.

horizontal dynamic convergence   During the scanning of a horizontal line in a color picture tube, convergence of the electron beams at the aperture mask. Compare VERTICAL DYNAMIC CONVERGENCE.

horizontal field strength The field strength of signals passing through an antenna in a horizontal plane. Compare VERTICAL FIELD STRENGTH.

horizontal-field-strength diagram A plot of horizontal field strength, usually in polar form. Compare VERTICAL-FIELD-STRENGTH DIAGRAM.

horizontal flowcharting Flowcharting the movement of documents or files, rather than the data bits themselves, through a digital system.

horizontal frequency In television circuits, the horizontal scanning frequency [i.e., the frequency at which the horizontal lines are traced (generally 15.750 kHz)].

horizontal frequency response The gain-vs.-frequency characteristic of the horizontal channel of an oscilloscope or graphic recorder. Compare VERTICAL FREQUENCY RESPONSE.

horizontal gain At a specified frequency, the overall amplification of the horizontal channel of an oscilloscope or graphic recorder. Compare VERTICAL GAIN.

horizontal-gain control A control, such as a potentiometer, for adjusting horizontal gain. Compare VERTICAL-GAIN CONTROL.

horizontal-hold control In a television receiver, the control for adjusting the horizontal oscillator frequency to prevent horizontal tearing of the picture. Compare VERTICAL-HOLD CONTROL.

horizontal hum bars Dark, horizontal interferential bars in a television picture, caused by HUM interference.

horizontal linearity The precision of gain and deflection in the horizontal channel of an oscilloscope, graphic recorder, or television receiver. A linear picture is a faithful (undistorted) reproduction of the original image. Compare VERTICAL LINEARITY.

horizontal-linearity control In an oscilloscope or television receiver, the control with which horizontal linearity is adjusted. Compare VERTICAL-LINEARITY CONTROL.

horizontal line frequency See HORIZONTAL FREQUENCY.

horizontal lock See HORIZONTAL-HOLD CONTROL.

horizontally polarized wave An electromagnetic wave whose electric lines of flux are parallel to the plane of the horizon. Compare VERTICALLY POLARIZED WAVE.

horizontal multivibrator In a television receiver, a 15.750-kHz multivibrator that generates the horizontal sweep signal.

horizontal oscillator In a TV receiver, the oscillator (usually a multivibrator) that generates the horizontal sweep signal. Compare VERTICAL OSCILLATOR.

horizontal output stage In a television receiver, an output amplifier following the horizontal oscillator. Compare VERTICAL OUTPUT STAGE.

horizontal output transformer In a television receiver, the output transformer in the horizontal-oscillator-output amplifier section. Also called FLYBACK TRANSFORMER.

horizontal polarization Pertaining to an electromagnetic wave whose electric lines of flux are horizontal. In general, when the radiating element of an antenna is horizontal, the electric lines of flux in the transmitted waves are horizontal, and the antenna is most sensitive to incoming signals whose electric lines of flux are horizontal. Compare VERTICAL POLARIZATION.

horizontal positioning control See CENTERING CONTROL.

horizontal quantity The quantity measured along the X-axis of a graph represented by the horizontal deflection of an oscilloscope beam. Compare VERTICAL QUANTITY.

horizontal recording See LATERAL RECORDING.

horizontal repetition rate See HORIZONTAL FREQUENCY.

horizontal resolution In a television picture, the number of picture elements (*pixels*) that can be discerned in a horizontal scanning line. Compare VERTICAL RESOLUTION.

horizontal retrace In a cathode-ray device, such as an oscilloscope or television receiver, the rapid return of the electron beam to its starting point after completing a horizontal sweep of the screen. Compare VERTICAL RETRACE.

horizontal retrace blanking In oscilloscopes and television receivers, the automatic cutoff of the electron beam during a horizontal retrace period, preventing an extraneous line on the screen during the period. Compare VERTICAL RETRACE BLANKING.

horizontal scanning 1. The lateral sweeping of the electron beam in a cathode-ray tube. 2. The sampling of x-axis values in a repetitive or nonrepetitive sweep of that axis.

horizontal scanning frequency See HORIZONTAL FREQUENCY.

horizontal sensitivity The signal voltage required at the input of a horizontal channel for full horizontal deflection. Also see HORIZONTAL GAIN. Compare VERTICAL SENSITIVITY.

horizontal signal A signal serving as a horizontal quantity. Compare VERTICAL SIGNAL.

horizontal sweep 1. In a cathode-ray tube, the horizontal movement of the spot on the screen; in particular, the movement from left to right, during which a line of the image is formed on the screen. 2. The circuit that produces horizontal sweep.

horizontal sweep frequency The frequency at which horizontal sweep occurs; in a television receiver, it is generally 15.750 kHz. Also called *horizontal sweep rate*. Compare VERTICAL SWEEP FREQUENCY.

horizontal sweep rate See HORIZONTAL SWEEP FREQUENCY.

horizontal-sync discriminator In a television receiver, a circuit that compares horizontal sync-pulse phase with the phase of the signal from the horizontal sweep oscillator.

horizontal synchronization In a television receiver, synchronization of the horizontal component of scanning with that of the transmitting camera. Also see HORIZONTAL SYNC PULSE. Compare VERTICAL SYNCHRONIZATION.

horizontal sync pulse In a video signal, the pulse that synchronizes the horizontal scanning component in a television receiver with that of the camera; it also triggers horizontal retrace and blanking. Also see BACK PORCH. Compare VERTICAL SYNC PULSE.

horizontal wave See HORIZONTALLY POLARIZED WAVE.

horizontal-width control See WIDTH CONTROL, **1**, **2**.

horn A radiating device that is essentially a cylindrical or rectangular pipe, whose surface flares from a narrow entry to a wide exit. See, for example, HORN ANTENNA, HORN SPEAKER, and MEGAPHONE.

horn antenna An antenna that resembles a round, square, or elliptical horn. The feed point is at the apex, where the cross-sectional area is the smallest. The maximum radiation occurs in the direction opposite of the HORN MOUTH.

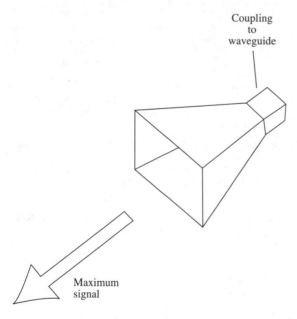

Coupling to waveguide

Maximum signal

horn antenna

horn cutoff frequency The lowest frequency at which an exponential horn will function properly.

horn loading In a sound-transmission system, a form of propagation that makes use of a horn-shaped speaker.

horn mouth The wider (radiating) end of a horn antenna or speaker. Compare HORN THROAT.

horn radiator See HORN ANTENNA.

horn speaker A loudspeaker using a horn in conjunction with an acoustic transducer. It generally produces sound of low fidelity, and is intended for use in marginal environments, such as outdoor public-address (PA) systems.

horn throat The narrower (input) end of a horn antenna or speaker. Compare HORN MOUTH.

horsepower Abbreviation, hp. A unit of power equal to 746 watts. It is generally used to express mechanical power delivered by engines and electric motors.

horsepower-hour Abbreviation, hp-hr. A unit of energy or work represented by the equivalent of one horsepower delivered for a period of one hour; equal to 746 watt-hours.

horseshoe coil See HAIRPIN COIL and HAIRPIN COUPLING COIL.

horseshoe magnet A (usually permanent) magnet having the shape of a horseshoe or a U and a rectangular cross section.

host A programmable computer that gathers and stores the information from all of the data-entry terminals in a system.

HOT **1.** Abbreviation of HORIZONTAL OUTPUT TRANSFORMER. **2.** Abbreviation of HORIZONTAL OUTPUT TUBE.

hot **1.** Pertaining to an object from which heat energy is transferred to the environment by radiation, convection, and/or conduction. **2.** Charged to an electrical potential, either positive or negative, with respect to common ground. **3.** Pertaining to a conductor that carries a high radio-frequency (RF) current or voltage.

hot carrier In a semiconductor, a charge carrier (electron or hole) whose energy is higher than that of majority carriers normally encountered in the same material.

hot-carrier diode A semiconductor diode having a metal base that receives HOT CARRIERS from a semiconductor layer. The unit has a fast switching speed because there are virtually no minority carriers—either injected or stored.

Hotel Phonetic alphabet code word for the letter H.

hot-filament gas detector A gas detector in which the sensor is a heated filament acting as one arm of a Wheatstone bridge circuit. The bridge, previously balanced, becomes unbalanced when gas impinges upon the filament and changes its resistance.

hot junction The heated junction in a two-junction thermocouple circuit. Compare COLD JUNCTION.

hot line **1.** An energized wire, transmission line, or busbar. **2.** A private communications channel (wire or radio) kept in constant readiness for instant use between persons of high authority.

hot-pen recorder See THERMAL RECORDER.

hot plate A metal device, usually heated by means of electricity, used for the purpose of conducting certain experiments.

hot resistance The resistance of a component during its operation (i.e., after it has been heated by ambient temperature or internal power dissipation). Compare COLD RESISTANCE.

hot spark A brilliant flash seen when a capacitor discharges through a spark gap in a vacuum.

hot spot 1. In a circuit or component, an area whose temperature is ordinarily higher than that of the surrounding area. 2. A local current or voltage maximum on an antenna or transmission line. 3. In communications operations, a geographic location in which reception is markedly better than in other nearby places or from which the transmitted signal appears to be stronger.

hot-strip ammeter A current meter similar to the hot-wire meter, except that it has a heated metallic strip instead of a heated wire.

hot-stylus recorder See THERMAL RECORDER.

hot-tip writing The use of a heated-tip stylus in graphic recording. Also see THERMAL RECORDER.

hot-wire ammeter See HOT-WIRE METER.

hot-wire anemometer An electrical anemometer whose indication is based on the cooling effect of the wind on a heated filament.

hot-wire flowmeter An instrument for determining the rate of flow of a gas in a pipe or other channel. The circuit is similar to that of the gas detector and hot-wire anemometer.

hot-wire gasmeter See GAS DETECTOR.

hot-wire instrument See HOT-WIRE METER.

hot-wire meter A meter in which current heats a wire, stretching it so that it moves a pointer across a scale over a distance proportional to the magnitude of the current.

hot-wire microphone A microphone in which sound waves vary the temperature of a heated wire and, accordingly, its electrical resistance.

hot-wire relay A time-delay relay in which actuating current heats a wire, causing it to expand, eventually opening or closing the contacts. Also see DELAY RELAY.

hot-wire sensor See HEATED-WIRE SENSOR.

hot-wire transducer See HOT-WIRE MICROPHONE.

hour Abbreviation, h; (sometimes, hr). A unit of time measure equal to 60 minutes or 3600 seconds. Compare MINUTE, 1 and SECOND, 1. Also see TIME.

housekeeping In digital-computer operations, the part of a program that attends to chores (e.g., setting variables to zero), rather than being involved in making computations for a solution.

howl A discordant sound produced in headphones or a loudspeaker, usually as a result of acoustic or electrical feedback.

howler 1. An audio-frequency alarm device. 2. A sound-emitting test device (see GROWLER, 1, 2).

howl repeater A form of electric feedback in which a hum or howl occurs because of oscillation. The term is used to describe an oscillating conduction in a wire-communications-system repeater.

hp Abbreviation of HORSEPOWER.

h-p Abbreviation of HIGH PRESSURE.

H pad See H NETWORK.

h parameters Parameters of the four-terminal network equivalent of a transistor. They are *hybrid parameters* (thus, *h*) because of their appearance in mesh and nodal equations. The basic *h* parameters are h_{11}, input resistance with output short-circuited; h_{12}, reverse voltage ratio with input open-circuited; h_{21}, forward current gain with output short-circuited; and h_{22}, output conductance with input open-circuited.

h particle A positive hydrogen ion or proton obtained by bombarding a hydrogen atom with alpha particles or high-velocity positive ions.

HPF Abbreviation of *highest probable frequency.*

hp-hr Abbreviation of HORSEPOWER-HOUR.

HPI Abbreviation of HEIGHT-POSITION INDICATOR.

H plane The plane of the magnetic field of an antenna, or the magnetic component of an electromagnetic field. Compare E PLANE.

H-plane bend In a waveguide, a smooth change in the direction of the axis perpendicular to the direction of polarization.

H-plane tee junction A waveguide tee junction, whose structure changes in the magnetic-field plane. Also see WAVEGUIDE JUNCTION and WAVEGUIDE TEE.

hr Abbreviation of HOUR. (Also, h.)

H scan A radar display in which the target is represented by two close blips, approximating a line, whose shape is proportional to the sine of the target's angle of elevation.

H scope See H SCAN.

HSM Abbreviation of *high-speed memory.*

HTL Abbreviation of HIGH-THRESHOLD LOGIC.

hub The hole in the center of a magnetic tape reel.

hue The quality of having a particular visible color; an attribute that depends on the wavelength(s) of light emitted or reflected. Thus, electromagnetic energy at a wavelength of 700 nanometers (nm) has a red hue; energy at a wavelength of 400 nm has a violet hue. Compare SATURATION, 2.

hue control Also called *tint control.* In a color television receiver, a control that allows adjustment of the color wavelength, but does not affect the saturation (intensity).

hum 1. Alternating current having a frequency of 60 Hz. 2. Residual ripple in the output of a power supply, having a frequency of 60 Hz or 120 Hz, depending on the type of rectifier circuit used. 3. An electromagnetic field of long wavelength, usually originating from utility lines and having a primary frequency of 60 Hz. 4. The effects of low-frequency electromagnetic fields or currents, such as moving horizontal bars on a television screen. 5. An acoustic disturbance of long wavelength (low pitch).

human engineering 1. Also called *user-friendliness.* The extent to which an electronic or electromechanical device or system is easy to operate. **2.** The branch of engineering devoted to interfacing human beings with the machines and instruments they operate. Both a science and an art, the discipline is concerned with the safest and most efficient design, arrangement, and operation of equipment.

human interface The interface between a sophisticated electronic device and a human operator.

human-made interference Also called *artificial interference.* Electromagnetic interference to radio and television receiving systems or to data terminals, originating from artificial sources (such as radio transmitters, certain electrical appliances, and internal-combustion engines). Of the numerous different forms, some affect only a narrow band of frequencies or set of frequencies, and others affect a wide band of frequencies.

humanoid robot A robot that bears structural resemblance to a human being (e.g., has arms, a head, and perhaps legs). In its most advanced form, such a robot is an ANDROID.

hum-balance potentiometer A potentiometer connected across an alternating-current power supply, with its slider grounded. At a certain setting, hum interference is nulled.

hum bars See HORIZONTAL HUM BARS.

hum bucking The reduction of hum interference by introducing an alternating-current voltage of the same frequency and amplitude as the hum, but opposite in phase.

hum-bucking coil An auxiliary coil used in conjunction with the field and voice coils of an electrodynamic speaker. Reduces hum interference via HUM BUCKING.

hum field The magnetic field surrounding a conductor carrying hum-frequency alternating current.

humidity The amount of moisture in the air. Also see ABSOLUTE HUMIDITY and RELATIVE HUMIDITY.

humidity meter See ELECTRIC HYGROMETER and ELECTRONIC HYGROMETER.

humidity sensor A pickup whose resistance or capacitance varies proportionally with ambient humidity.

hum interference Electrical interference resulting from HUM in any of its various electrical forms (see HUM, **1–4**).

hum loop A ground loop that results in undesired hum in the output of an amplifier.

hummer A nonelectronic audio oscillator similar to the fork oscillator, but using a thick, metal reed, instead of a tuning fork. A carbon microphone button attached to the reed provides the feedback path necessary for sustained oscillation.

hum modulation Undesirable modulation of a radio signal or audio amplifier output signal by HUM interference.

hump 1. Either the positive or the negative half-cycle of a sine wave; that is, either the portion

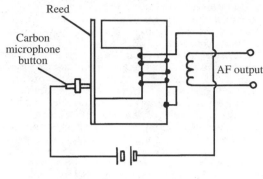

hummer

from 0 degrees to 180 degrees, or the portion from 180 degrees to 360 degrees. **2.** A curve whose graph is a multiple of the sine function, and whose domain is restricted to a half-cycle (0 to 180 degrees or 180 to 360 degrees). See, for example, DOUBLE-HUMP RESONANCE CURVE and DOUBLE-HUMP WAVE.

hunting An undesirable condition in which an electrical or electromechanical system oscillates back and forth, relative to some mean mode of operation ("hunts" for the mode), sometimes eventually settling down at the mode. It can occur in a servo system because of overcompensation, lack of hysteresis, or both.

Huygens' principle The observation that an advancing wave is the resultant of secondary waves that arise from points in the medium that have already been passed.

HV Abbreviation of HIGH VOLTAGE.

H vector A vector representing the magnetic field of an electromagnetic wave. Compare E VECTOR.

hW Abbreviation of HECTOWATT.

H-wave mode In a waveguide, a mode of transmission in which the electric lines of flux are at right angles to the direction of the waveguide. Also called *transverse-electric (TE) mode.*

hy Occasional abbreviation of HENRY. The SI abbreviation and symbol, H, is preferred.

hybrid Descriptive of a device that is an offspring of other devices or a product of dissimilar technologies (but using elements of each). See, for example, HYBRID JUNCTION and HYBRID COIL.

hybrid active circuit An active circuit (such as an amplifier, oscillator, or switch) using a combination of two dissimilar active devices (e.g., transistors and vacuum tubes).

hybrid coil A special type of bridging transformer used in wire telephony to prevent self-oscillation in a repeater amplifier that operates in both directions.

hybrid computer A computer system incorporating more than one major computer technology. Examples: analog/digital and digital/neural-network.

hybrid electromagnetic wave Abbreviation, HEM wave. An electromagnetic wave whose electric-field and magnetic-field vectors are both in the direction of propagation.

hybrid IC See HYBRID INTEGRATED CIRCUIT.

hybrid integrated circuit Abbreviation, HIC. An integrated circuit embodying both integrated and microminiature discrete components (i.e., one combining both monolithic and thin-film construction).

hybrid junction 1. See MAGIC TEE. 2. A four-terminal device, such as a resistor circuit, special transformer, or waveguide assembly, in which a signal applied to one pair of terminals divides and appears at only the two adjacent terminals.

hybrid microcircuit A microcircuit containing diffused or thin-film elements interconnected with separate chip elements.

hybrid parameters See H PARAMETERS.

hybrid ring A hybrid waveguide junction (see HYBRID JUNCTION, **2**) consisting essentially of a reentrant line with four side arms. Used as an equal power divider.

hybrid-tee See HYBRID JUNCTION, **1**.

hybrid thin-film circuit A microcircuit in which semiconductor devices and discrete components are attached to passive components and conductors that have been electrodeposited on a substrate.

hybrid transformer See HYBRID COIL.

hydroacoustic Pertaining to the sound of fluids, especially water, under pressure.

hydroacoustic transducer A transducer that converts energy from the high-pressure flow of a fluid into acoustic energy.

hydrodynamic pressure The pressure of a fluid in motion. Compare HYDROSTATIC PRESSURE.

hydroelectric Pertaining to the production of electricity by water power, as by a generator turned by water turbines.

hydroelectric machine A device for generating electricity from high-pressure steam escaping from a series of jets.

hydroelectric power See WATER POWER.

hydrogen Symbol, H. A gaseous element. Atomic number, **1**. Atomic weight, 1.00794. Used in making semiconductor materials, it is the lightest and most abundant element in the universe. Compare DEUTERIUM and TRITIUM.

hydrogen atmosphere The nonoxidizing atmosphere in which semiconductor materials are melted and processed, and in which semiconductor crystals are grown. Occasionally, helium is used instead of hydrogen.

hydrogen atom A single atom of the element hydrogen, consisting of one electron and one proton.

hydrogen-ion concentration See pH.

hydrogen lamp A glow-discharge lamp that produces light by means of the ionization of rarefied hydrogen gas. Visible light is emitted at discrete wavelengths.

hydrokinetic Pertaining to fluids in motion or the forces behind such motion.

hydrolysis The process whereby chemical substances become ionized in water solution, producing electrolytes.

hydromagnetics See MAGNETOHYDRODYNAMICS.

hydromagnetic wave In a fluid, a wave in which the energy is propagated via magnetic and dynamic modes.

hydrometer An instrument for measuring the specific gravity of liquids.

hydrophone An underwater sound-to-electricity transducer (microphone).

hydropower See WATER POWER.

hydrostatic pressure The pressure of a fluid at rest. Compare HYDRODYNAMIC PRESSURE.

hygristor A resistor, the resistance of which depends on humidity. A common application is in the measurement of relative atmospheric humidity.

hygrogram A graphic rendition of atmospheric humidity versus time, made by a HYGROGRAPH.

hygrograph A device that produces a graphic recording of atmospheric humidity as a function of time. Consists essentially of a HYGROMETER connected to a permanent data-storage device, such as a computer or pen recorder.

hygrometer An instrument for measuring humidity. Also see ELECTRIC HYGROMETER, ELECTRONIC HYGROMETER, and HAIR HYGROMETER.

hygroscopic material A material that absorbs moisture from the air, but not enough to get wet (e.g., lime and silk). Compare DELIQUESCENT MATERIAL.

hygrostat A humidity-sensitive relay or switching circuit.

hygrothermograph A graphic recorder indicating humidity and temperature on the same chart, both as functions of time.

hyperacoustical zone In the upper atmosphere, a region in which the distance between air molecules is comparable to the wavelengths of audible sound. As the altitude increases within this zone, the upper-frequency limit of effective sound propagation decreases. At altitudes above this zone, no audible sound can be propagated.

hyperbola A conic-section curve satisfying the equation:

$$(x - x_0)^2 / a^2 - (y - y_0)^2 / b^2 = 1$$

where x and y are the independent and dependent variables, x_0 and y_0 are the coordinates of the center, a is half the length of the major axis, and b is half the length of the minor axis.

hyperbolic angle An angle subtended by a sector of a hyperbola in a manner analogous to that in which a circular angle is subtended by an arc of a circle.

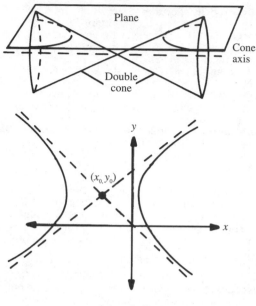

hyperbola

hyperbolic-cosine horn   See CATENOIDAL HORN.

hyperbolic error   **1.** In an interferometer, a miscalculation in the direction of arrival of a signal. The signal from one antenna in the system can be assumed to be in phase with the signal from another antenna, when actually the two components differ by an integral number of whole wavelengths. **2.** The angular error, in degrees, minutes, or seconds of arc, resulting from a miscalculation of phase in an interferometer.

hyperbolic face contour   See HYPERBOLIC GRIND.

hyperbolic functions   The nonperiodic functions of a hyperbolic angle. Hyperbolic functions are related to the hyperbola in the same manner that common trigonometric functions are related to the circle. Hyperbolic functions are useful in calculations involving traveling waves on transmission lines, attenuator design, and wave-filter design.

hyperbolic grind   The shape (approximately hyperbolic) to which the face of a magnetic recording head is ground. It provides optimum contact with the tape and ensures good high-frequency response.

hyperbolic horn   A horn antenna whose cross-sectional area is a hyperbolic function of the distance along the axis.

hyperbolic logarithm   See NAPIERIAN LOGARITHM.

hyperbolic navigation   A radionavigation system in which the operator of an aircraft or boat determines position by comparison of two received signals. The two transmitters radiate signals from known positions and with known timing characteristics. The time delay from each transmitter is determined, resulting in two hyperbolic curves on a map. The point of intersection of the curves is the location of the aircraft or ship.

hyperbolic radian   A unit of measure derived from a hyperbolic angle. A hyperbolic radian is the hyperbolic angle that encloses an area of 0.5 when the distance along the x-axis to the hyperbola is unity. Also see HYPERBOLIC ANGLE. Compare CIRCULAR RADIAN.

hyperbolic trigonometry   The branch of mathematics dealing with the theory and application of hyperbolic angles and their functions.

hypercardioid microphone   A unidirectional microphone with exceptional sensitivity in front, and minimal responsiveness from the sides and rear.

hypercardioid pattern   A directional CARDIOID PATTERN with accentuated responsiveness or emission in the favored direction (front), and greatly suppressed responsiveness or emission in other directions (sides and rear).

hyperfocal distance   The shortest distance to which a lens can be focused without degrading definition at infinity.

hyperfrequency waves   See MICROWAVES.

hypernik   See HIPERNICK.

hyperon   Any one of various particles having a mass greater than that of a neutron or proton.

hyperpolarization   The production of an increased voltage across a biological membrane.

hypersonic   Pertaining to speeds of at least five times that of sound. In air at normal atmospheric pressure, such speeds are more than approximately 1700 meters, or 5600 feet, per second.

hypersonic speed   Any speed greater than five times the speed of sound in a given medium.

hypersyn motor   A high-efficiency, high-power-factor synchronous motor combining the advantages of the *direct-current-excited synchronous motor* (stiffness), the *hysteresis motor* (synchronizing torque), and the *induction motor* (high starting torque).

hypervelocity   Velocity in excess of 3 kilometers per second.

hypotenuse   The side of a right triangle opposite to the right angle.

hypothesis   An idea, concept, or system that seems true or workable, but must be subjected to logical analysis and/or practical testing to prove its validity.

hypsometer   An altimeter in which a thermistor (connected to a battery and current meter) is immersed in a boiling liquid. Because the liquid's boiling point is proportional to altitude, it affects the resistance of the thermistor and, hence, the deflection of the meter.

hysteresigram   The hysteresis-curve record produced by a HYSTERESIGRAPH.

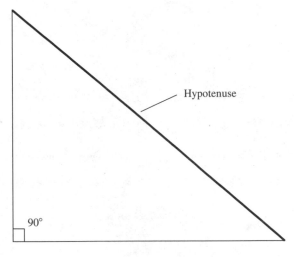

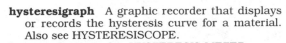

Hypotenuse

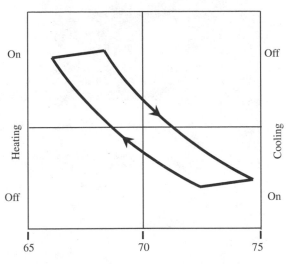

Temperature, Fahrenheit

hysteresis curve

hysteresigraph   A graphic recorder that displays or records the hysteresis curve for a material. Also see HYSTERESISCOPE.

hysteresimeter   See HYSTERESIS METER.

hysteresis   **1.** The tendency of a magnetic material to saturate and retain some of its magnetism after the alternating magnetic field to which it is subjected reverses polarity, thus causing magnetization to lag behind the magnetizing force. **2.** A similar electrostatic action in a ferroelectric dielectric material. **3.** In a servo system, the condition in which a variable quantity lags the effect or stimulus that causes it to change. The plot for this is a double-line HYSTERESIS CURVE.

hysteresis brake   A brake whose retarding action comes from hysteresis in a permanent-magnet motor.

hysteresis clutch   A magnetic clutch whose output torque (for synchronous drive or continuous slip) comes from hysteresis in a permanent-magnet motor.

hysteresis coefficient   In a sample of iron whose volume is one cubic centimeter, the energy in ergs dissipated during one cycle of magnetization. Also called *coefficient of hysteresis.*

hysteresiscope   An oscilloscope that is specially designed to display the hysteresis curve of a material. Compare HYSTERESIGRAPH.

hysteresis curve   A response curve depicting hysteresis in a magnetic material, a dielectric, or a servo system. A graph of the extent to which a variable quantity lags the effect or stimulus that causes it to change (e.g., a curve showing the effect of response delay in a thermostatically controlled heating/cooling system).

hysteresis cycle   A complete hysteresis curve.

hysteresis distortion   Signal distortion in iron-core components, such as coupling transformers, resulting from hysteresis in the iron.

hysteresis error   In a meter, a difference in indications for increasing and decreasing current, an effect caused by hysteresis in iron meter parts.

hysteresis heater   An induction heater in which heating results from hysteresis loss in the load.

hysteresis loop   See HYSTERESIS CURVE.

hysteresis loss   Power loss caused by hysteresis in a magnetic material exposed to an alternating magnetic field, or in a dielectric material exposed to an alternating electric field. It is characterized by the generation of heat.

hysteresis meter   An instrument that determines the hysteresis loss in a ferromagnetic material in terms of the torque produced when the material is rotated in a magnetic field, or vice versa.

hysteresis motor   A synchronous motor that does not require direct-current excitation, and does not have salient poles. It is started by means of hysteresis losses that the rotating magnetic field causes in the secondary.

hysteretic constant   For a ferromagnetic material, hysteresis loss in ergs per cubic centimeter of material per cycle of magnetization.

hysteretic loss   See HYSTERESIS LOSS.

hystoroscope   A device used to determine the magnetic characteristics of a material.

Hz   Abbreviation of HERTZ.

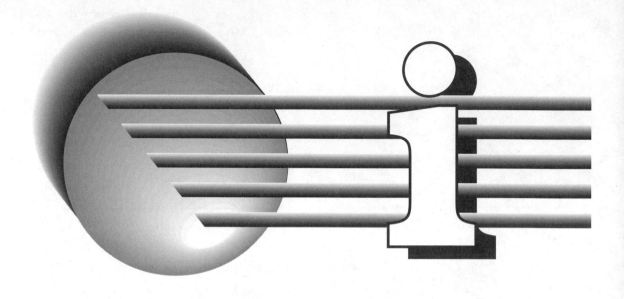

I **1.** Symbol for CURRENT. **2.** Symbol for INTRINSIC SEMICONDUCTOR. **3.** Symbol for LUMINOUS INTENSITY. **4.** Symbol for IODINE.

i **1.** Symbol for the unit imaginary number, the square root of -1. (Also, j.) **2.** Subscript for INSTANTANEOUS VALUE. **3.** Symbol for INTRINSIC SEMICONDUCTOR. **4.** Symbol for ANGLE OF INCIDENCE. **5.** Symbol for INSTANTANEOUS CURRENT. (Also, I_t.) **6.** Symbol for a unit vector parallel to the x-axis. **7.** Symbol for INCIDENT RAY.

I_{ac} Symbol for the ac component of a COMPOSITE CURRENT.

I_{AF} Symbol for AUDIO-FREQUENCY CURRENT.

IAGC   Abbreviation of INSTANTANEOUS AUTOMATIC GAIN CONTROL.

IAVC   Abbreviation of INSTANTANEOUS AUTOMATIC VOLUME CONTROL.

I_B **1.** Symbol for *plate power-supply current.* **2.** Occasional symbol for *plate current* (usually, I_P).

IBM   Abbreviation for *International Business Machines* Corporation.

IC   **1.** Abbreviation of INTEGRATED CIRCUIT. **2.** Abbreviation of INTERNAL CONNECTION.

I_C **1.** Symbol for transistor COLLECTOR CURRENT. **2.** Occasional symbol for *grid current* (usually, I_G).

ICAD   Abbreviation of *integrated control and display.*

ICAS   Abbreviation of INTERMITTENT COMMERCIAL AND AMATEUR SERVICE.

I_{CBO} Symbol for the static reverse collector (leakage) current in a common-base connected transistor with an open-circuited emitter.

ICBS   Abbreviation of *interconnected business system.*

I_{CEO} Symbol for the static reverse collector (leakage) current in a common-emitter-connected transistor with an open-circuited base.

ice loading   **1.** In an antenna, power-line system, or other structure, the additional stress caused by accumulation of ice. **2.** The weight or thickness of ice a structure can safely withstand.

ice-removal circuit   A high-voltage, low-frequency power supply used to heat certain antennas to melt ice that accumulates on them.

ICET   Abbreviation of *Institute for the Certification of Engineering Technicians* (National Society of Professional Engineers).

ICME   Abbreviation of *International Conference on Medical Electronics.*

I_{co} Symbol for the collector cutoff current (static leakage current) of a bipolar transistor (see CUTOFF CURRENT).

icon   In a graphical computer interface, a symbol that aids the user in recognizing a selection that can be made.

iconoscope   A camera tube in which an electron beam scans a photomosaic on which the image is focused. The light-sensitive droplets of the mosaic form tiny capacitors with the insulated, metallic backplate of the mosaic, each capacitor becoming charged by the light of the picture. As the electron beam scans the mosaic, each capacitor discharges as the beam strikes it, delivering an output pulse proportional to the light intensity at that spot in the picture.

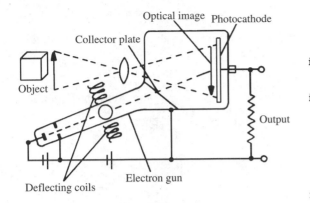

iconoscope

IC tester An instrument for checking the operation of an integrated circuit.

ICW Abbreviation of INTERRUPTED CONTINUOUS WAVE.

ID Abbreviation of INSIDE DIAMETER.

IDA Abbreviation of *integrodifferential analyzer*.

I_{dc} Symbol for the dc component of a COMPOSITE CURRENT.

ideal Pertaining to a circuit, device, material, or manner of operation that is assumed to conform to the theoretical best-case example; it is not usually realized in real life. Thus, an ideal reactance has no inherent resistance.

ideal capacitor A capacitor having zero dielectric loss and a constant value of capacitance at all alternating-current frequencies.

ideal component A theoretical component that is assumed to be 100-percent efficient and to have no extraneous properties. Compare PRACTICAL COMPONENT.

ideal crystal A piezoelectric crystal that acts as a theoretically perfect tuned circuit, that is, an ideal capacitor and inductor.

ideal inductor An inductor having zero loss and a constant value of inductance at all alternating-current frequencies.

I demodulator In a color-television receiver circuit, a demodulator that receives the chrominance and 3.58-MHz oscillator signals and delivers a video output corresponding to color in the picture.

identical vectors Equal vectors that have the same initial point or point of application.

identification 1. In radar operations, the (often automatic) determination of the target's identity. See, for example, IDENTIFICATION, FRIEND OR FOE. **2.** In digital computer operations, a symbol or set of symbols within a label identifying a unit of data or its location.

identification beacon 1. A beacon used for the determination of a particular geographic location.

2. An automatically transmitted station-identification signal or code, usually superimposed on the regular transmission in the form of a subcarrier or subaudible signal.

identification division The division (one of four) in a COBOL program that describes and identifies the program being compiled.

identification, friend or foe Abbreviation, IFF. A technique in which a radar station transmits an interrogating signal and the station questioned replies automatically with a suitable pulse or other signal if it is aboard a friendly aircraft or vessel. If it is aboard an enemy vehicle, the station gives no reply or sends an unsatisfactory one.

identifier A data file identification label in an input/output device, or a label that identifies a specific storage location.

identity element A logic element that, upon receipt of two input signals, provides an output that is logic 1 (high) only if the input signals are both logic 1 (high) or logic 0 (low).

idiochromatic Possessing the photoelectric properties of a true crystal.

I display See I SCAN.

idle channel noise A measurement of wideband noise. The total energy at an output of an integrated circuit or other communications stage with that output grounded (idle).

idle character A digital character that conveys no information, but helps maintain synchronization between the transmitter and receiver. Sometimes called a *blank*.

idler wheel In a phonograph or magnetic tape recorder, an auxiliary, rubber-coated wheel that transfers rotary motion from the motor pulley to the platter or the rim of the capstan flywheel.

idle time The period during which data processing equipment, although operable, is not in use.

idling Standby equipment operation, as when vacuum-tube filaments in a radio-frequency power amplifier are kept hot—even when the amplifier is not actually being used to transmit a signal.

idling current The current flowing in a device during a standby period, as opposed to operating current. Also called STANDBY CURRENT.

idling frequency In a parametric amplifier, the difference between the signal frequency and pump frequency.

idling power See STANDBY POWER.

idling voltage The voltage required by or measured in a device that is in standby mode.

$I_{D(off)}$ Symbol for drain cutoff current in a field-effect transistor.

IDOT Abbreviation of *instrumentation online transcriber*.

IDP 1. Abbreviation of INDUSTRIAL DATA PROCESSING. **2.** Abbreviation of INTEGRATED DATA PROCESSING. **3.** Abbreviation of INTERMODULATION-DISTORTION PERCENTAGE.

I$_{DSS}$ Symbol for DRAIN CURRENT AT ZERO GATE VOLTAGE in a field-effect transistor.

I$_E$ Symbol for EMITTER CURRENT.

IEC Abbreviation of *integrated electronic component*.

IEE Abbreviation of *Institution of Electrical Engineers* (British).

IEEE Abbreviation of *Institute of Electrical and Electronics Engineers*.

IES Abbreviation of *Illuminating Engineering Society*.

IF Abbreviation of INTERMEDIATE FREQUENCY.

IF amplifier See INTERMEDIATE-FREQUENCY AMPLIFIER.

I$_{FB}$ In an integrated circuit, current limit feedback or feedback current.

IF channel See INTERMEDIATE-FREQUENCY CHANNEL.

IF converter The converter (first detector-oscillator) section of a superheterodyne radio receiver.

IFF Abbreviation of IDENTIFICATION, FRIEND OR FOE.

IF gain **1.** The amplification provided by the intermediate-frequency (IF) channel of a superheterodyne receiver, usually specified in decibels. **2.** A control that allows adjustment of the amplification in the IF channel of a superheterodyne radio receiver.

IF interference See INTERMEDIATE-FREQUENCY INTERFERENCE.

IFIPS Abbreviation of *International Federation of Information Processing Societies*.

IF selectivity See INTERMEDIATE-FREQUENCY SELECTIVITY.

IF strip A (sometimes removable) circuit section containing a complete intermediate-frequency channel.

IF/THEN/ELSE In computer systems and artificial intelligence, a two-way choice that is made during the execution of a program. For example, in finding the absolute value of a number, the logic proceeds as follows: "IF $x < 0$, THEN multiply x by -1; otherwise (ELSE) leave it alone."

IF transformer See INTERMEDIATE-FREQUENCY TRANSFORMER.

I$_G$ Symbol for GATE CURRENT.

I$_G$ Symbol for GRID CURRENT.

IGFET Abbreviation of INSULATED-GATE FIELD-EFFECT TRANSISTOR.

ignition coil A small open-core transformer having a high step-up turns ratio for converting 6- or 12-volt battery potential to the high voltage needed in an automotive ignition system.

ignition interference Electrical noise generated by the ignition system of an internal combustion engine.

ignition potential **1.** The minimum voltage needed to cause electrical discharge in an internal combustion engine. **2.** See BREAKDOWN VOLTAGE, **1**, **2**.

ignition reserve The extra voltage provided by the starter, as compared with the voltage actu-

ally needed for ignition of an internal-combustion engine.

ignition system An electrical or electronic system that supplies the high voltage in an automotive engine. See, for example, CAPACITOR-DISCHARGE IGNITION SYSTEM.

ignition voltage See IGNITION POTENTIAL.

ignitron A form of rectifier tube that contains ionized mercury. It is used with some extremely high-voltage power supplies.

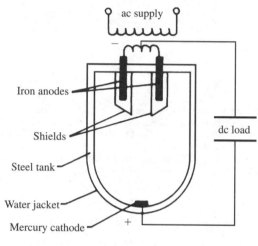

ignitron

ignore character **1.** A character used as a signal to inhibit an action. **2.** A digital character that is ignored by the system.

I$_{GSS}$ Symbol for GATE REVERSE CURRENT in a field-effect transistor.

IGY Abbreviation for INTERNATIONAL GEOPHYSICAL YEAR.

I$_H$ **1.** Symbol for HOLD CURRENT. **2.** Symbol for HOLDING CURRENT.

IHF Abbreviation of INHIBIT FLIP-FLOP.

IHFM Abbreviation for *Institute of High Fidelity Manufacturers*.

ihp Abbreviation of INDICATED HORSEPOWER.

ihp-hr Abbreviation of INDICATED HORSEPOWER-HOURS.

I$_i$ **1.** Symbol for INPUT CURRENT. **2.** Symbol for INSTANTANEOUS CURRENT (also, i).

I$_K$ Symbol for CATHODE CURRENT.

I$_L$ Symbol for current in an inductor.

I^{2}L Abbreviation of INTEGRATED INJECTION LOGIC. (Also IIL.)

illegal character **1.** A character or bit group that is, according to some standard, invalid. **2.** A bit group that represents a symbol in a character set.

illuminance The amount of luminous flux received per unit surface area, measured in lux (lumens per square meter).

illuminant-C In color television, the reference white that closely resembles average daylight.

illuminated pushbutton See LIGHTED PUSHBUTTON.

illuminated switch See LIGHTED SWITCH.

illumination **1.** Visible light. **2.** The condition of being irradiated by visible light. **3.** The intensity of visible light irradiating an object or region.

illumination control A photoelectric circuit that automatically regulates electric lights, according to the amount of daylight.

illuminometer A device for measuring ILLUMINANCE.

ILS Abbreviation of INSTRUMENT LANDING SYSTEM.

IM Abbreviation of INTERMODULATION.

I$_m$ **1.** Abbreviation of *maximum current*. (Also, I$_{max}$). **2.** Abbreviation of *meter current*.

image **1.** In a superheterodyne circuit, a spurious response whose frequency differs from that of the desired signal by twice the intermediate frequency. **2.** A picture on the screen of a television receiver or computer display. **3.** A pattern on the screen of an oscilloscope tube. **4.** A picture on the mosaic of a television camera tube. **5.** A duplicate of a computer storage area that is in another part of storage or on another medium.

image admittance The reciprocal of IMAGE IMPEDANCE.

image antenna An imaginary "mirror" antenna below the effective radio-frequency (RF) ground surface, at a depth equal to the height of the true radiating antenna above effective RF ground.

image attenuation constant The real-number part of the IMAGE TRANSFER CONSTANT. Also see IMAGE PHASE CONSTANT.

image compression Any of various methods by which the number of bytes in a digital image can be reduced, without significant degradation of image quality. The two most common methods are *JPEG (Joint Photographic Experts Group) image compression* and *fractal image compression*. Other schemes include *MPEG (Moving Picture Experts Group) image compression* and *Indeo*, developed by Intel Corporation. Fractal image compression can provide a compression factor of as much as 100:1 without significant degradation of image quality.

image converter **1.** A device that changes an invisible image into a visible image. Examples include the *snooperscope*, an infrared-to-visible converter, and photographic apparatus for infrared, ultraviolet, and X-ray wavelengths. **2.** A tube that operates as an image converter.

image dissector See DISSECTOR TUBE.

image effect The effect of reflection of electromagnetic waves from the ground. An IMAGE ANTENNA appears to radiate from a point beneath the effective RF ground plane. The depth of the image antenna below the effective RF ground plane is equal to the height of the actual antenna above the effective RF ground plane.

image frequency The frequency of the image response in a superheterodyne radio receiver. See IMAGE, 1.

image impedance The property of a network in which the load impedance is "seen," looking into the output terminals with the generator connected to the opposite end, and the generator impedance is "seen," looking into the input terminals with a load connected to the opposite end.

image intensification An increase of the brightness of the display on a cathode-ray tube.

image intensifier A device that increases the brightness of the spot produced when a beam of electrons or X rays hits a fluorescent screen.

image interference A type of interference that can occur in superheterodyne circuits. It occurs when there is a sufficiently strong signal on the IMAGE FREQUENCY.

image orthicon See ORTHICON.

image phase constant The imaginary-number part of the IMAGE TRANSFER CONSTANT. Also see IMAGE ATTENUATION CONSTANT.

image potential The potential energy of a charged particle at a given distance from a metal surface. The metal surface acts in a way similar to a mirror; a reflected image of the object, having equal charge but opposite polarity, is formed on the other side of the surface.

image ratio See SIGNAL-TO-IMAGE RATIO.

image rejection In a superheterodyne radio receiver, the suppression or elimination of IMAGE INTERFERENCE by means of a selective circuit, such as a radio-frequency preamplifier.

image response In a superheterodyne receiver, an undesired response to signals removed from the desired frequency by twice the intermediate frequency.

image transfer constant A number depicting the transfer of power by an impedance network. It has the same value, regardless of the direction of transmission through the network. Also see IMAGE ATTENUATION CONSTANT and IMAGE PHASE CONSTANT.

imaginary axis In a vector diagram of complex impedance, the axis of the imaginary-number component (jX).

imaginary number A real-number multiple of the positive square root of -1. Engineers depict the positive square root of -1 by the lowercase letter j; mathematicians use the lowercase letter i. Engineers write imaginary numbers in the form jX, and mathematicians write Xi, where X is a real number.

imaginary-number component The imaginary-number part of a COMPLEX NUMBER.

I$_{max}$ Abbreviation of *maximum current*.

IM distortion meter INTERMODULATION METER.

IM distortion percentage See INTERMODULATION-DISTORTION PERCENTAGE.

I$_{min}$ Abbreviation of *minimum current*.

imitation The transmission of false signals for purposes of deception. For example, during wartime, the signals from an enemy station might be recorded and retransmitted.

immediate access 1. The ability of a computer to store and retrieve data in a minimal amount of time. 2. Computer storage that can be accessed in a minimal amount of time.

immediate address An instruction address that is used as data by that instruction.

IM meter See INTERMODULATION METER.

immitance Impedance or admittance; a contraction of IMPEDANCE and ADMITTANCE. Example: a *negative-immitance circuit*.

immortal knowledge Knowledge that can be kept indefinitely in the form of detailed computer data files. Some scientists and sociologists believe that this will eventually have a profound effect on the way that future generations view history.

impact excitation See SHOCK EXCITATION.

impact strength 1. The ability of a component or material to withstand mechanical shock loading. 2. The work required to fracture the material under shock loading.

IMPATT diode Acronym for *impact avalanche transit time* diode. A microwave semiconductor (silicon or gallium arsenide) diode exhibiting negative resistance resulting from the combined effects of charge-carrier transit time and impact avalanche breakdown. It is used as an oscillator or amplifier.

IMPATT oscillator A microwave oscillator that uses an IMPATT DIODE.

impedance Symbol, Z. Unit, ohm. The total opposition offered by a circuit or device to the flow of alternating current. It is the vector sum of RESISTANCE and REACTANCE. This is a COMPLEX NUMBER whose real-number component is resistance R, and whose imaginary-number component is reactance jX; mathematically, $Z = R + jX$.

impedance angle The angle between the resistance and impedance vectors in an IMPEDANCE TRIANGLE.

impedance arm The network branch that contains one or more impedances, as opposed to an arm that contains only resistance or (predominantly, reactance). Also called *impedance leg*.

impedance branch See IMPEDANCE ARM.

impedance bridge 1. An alternating-current (ac) bridge (commonly operated at 1 kHz) used to measure resistance, inductance, capacitance, and resistive components associated with inductors and capacitors, from which impedance can be calculated. 2. Sometimes, an ac half-bridge circuit in which an unknown impedance is compared with a known resistance. 3. A radio-frequency bridge circuit whose balancing element reads impedance directly in ohms.

impedance bump A discontinuity in the characteristic impedance of a radio-frequency transmission line. It is often caused by the use of improper splicing techniques.

impedance coil See CHOKE COIL.

impedance converter See IMPEDANCE TRANSFORMER.

impedance-coupled amplifier An amplifier using capacitor/coil combinations for interstage and output load coupling.

impedance drop In an alternating-current circuit, the complex sum of the resistance drop and reactance drop.

impedance ground A ground connection in which the impedance at the operating frequency is determined by a network of resistors, capacitors, and/or inductors.

impedance leg See IMPEDANCE ARM.

impedance magnetometer A device that is used for measuring small local variations in the intensity of the earth's magnetic field. A small change in the intensity of the magnetic field will cause a change in impedance of a nickel-iron wire having high permeability.

impedance match The condition (for maximum power transfer) when the transmitting impedance equals the receiving impedance, or when a suitable transformer is inserted between different impedances for matching purposes. Also see IMPEDANCE MATCHING.

impedance matching 1. The adjustment or modification of two impedances so that they are identical, that is, the two resistive components are equal, and the two reactive components are equal. 2. The insertion of a suitable transformer or network between circuits having different impedances, for the purpose of optimizing power transfer.

impedance-matching network A network of discrete components, often adjustable, that is used to match a circuit having a certain impedance to a circuit having a different impedance. An example is the inductive-capacitive (LC) coupler, also called a *transmatch*, commonly used to match a radio transmitter to an antenna system.

impedance-matching transformer See IMPEDANCE TRANSFORMER.

impedance meter See Z METER.

impedance plethysmograph An electronic device used to measure changes in the chemical content of body cells.

impedance poles See POLES OF IMPEDANCE.

impedance ratio The quotient of two impedances that are related in some situation, such as impedance match or impedance mismatch. The impedance ratio of a transformer is equal to the square of the turns ratio.

impedance transformer 1. A transformer for converting an impedance to a different value. The turns ratio is equal to the square root of the impedance ratio. 2. An emitter follower or source follower circuit, used primarily to match a high impedance to a lower impedance. 3. A short-circuited transmission-line section used to match or convert impedances at radio frequencies.

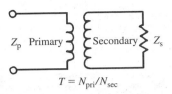

$$T = N_{\text{pri}}/N_{\text{sec}}$$

impedance transformer

impedance triangle   A triangular vector diagram in which the impedance vector is the hypotenuse, and the reactance and resistance vectors are the perpendicular sides.

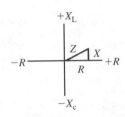

impedance triangle

impedance vector   In a vector diagram, the resultant (vector) representing the combined reactance and resistance vectors. Also see IMPEDANCE TRIANGLE.

impedance zeros   See ZEROS OF IMPEDANCE.

imperative macroinstruction   A MACROINSTRUCTION used to create object (machine language) program instructions.

imperative statement   A source language program instruction that is converted into object program (machine language) instructions.

imperfection   A fault in the lattice of a crystal. Also see CRYSTAL LATTICE.

implementation   **1.** Putting a system into operation and evaluating its performance. **2.** Doing all that is necessary to install a device or system.

implosion   The inward collapse of an evacuated chamber, such as the envelope of a cathode-ray tube. It is the opposite of explosion, an outward bursting.

impregnant   A substance for the IMPREGNATION of electronic components. Examples: waxes, oils, liquid plastics, and varnish.

impregnation   The process of filling the spaces within a material or structure with an insulating compound. Various electronic components, such as capacitors, inductors, transformers, transistors, and diodes, are impregnated for protection and stability.

impressed voltage   The voltage applied or presented to a circuit or device.

impulse   **1.** A signal of extremely short duration (e.g., a noise burst). **2.** A brief, unidirectional surge in voltage (usually) or current.

impulse excitation   Driving a tank circuit with a single pulse, then allowing it to oscillate at its own frequency until another driving pulse arrives.

impulse frequency   In a digital telephone, the number of pulse periods per second, corresponding to a dialed digit, generated by the pulse springs.

impulse generator   See MARX GENERATOR.

impulse noise   Electrical noise from short-duration pulses, such as those produced by an automotive ignition system.

impulse ratio   The ratio V_p/V_s, where V_p is the breakdown (or flashover or sparkover) voltage caused by an impulse, and V_s is the corresponding voltage at the crest of the power-frequency cycle.

impulse relay   A relay that is able to close or open completely when driven by a short pulse.

impulse speed   The switching rate of a telephone dialing device as it transmits pulses.

impulse timer   A synchronous-motor-driven timer whose cams can control many circuits; it can advance by a number of specified increments, as controlled by an integral stepping mechanism.

impulse transmission   A method of transmission in which defined impulses are used to denote changes in signal content or format.

impurity   A substance added to an intrinsic semiconductor to alter its electrical properties.

impurity atom   In a processed semiconductor material, an atom of an IMPURITY material that produces either n- or p-type properties to the intrinsic semiconductor.

impurity density   In the manufacturing process of a semiconductor material, the amount of impurity added to the original semiconductor.

impurity ion   In a crystal, an ion in a space between atoms, or one taking the place of an atom.

impurity level   **1.** The energy existing in a semiconductor material as a result of doping (the addition of an impurity). **2.** See IMPURITY DENSITY.

impurity material   See IMPURITY.

In   Symbol for INDIUM.

I_n   Symbol for the nth value of current in a series of values.

in   **1.** Abbreviation of INPUT. **2.** Abbreviation of INCH.

inaccuracy   **1.** The state or condition of instrument error. **2.** The difference between the actual value of a parameter and the value indicated by an instrument. **3.** The percentage of instrument error.

inactive leg   Within a transducer, an electrical component whose characteristic remains unchanged when the stimulus (quantity being transduced) is applied; specifically, a Wheatstone bridge element in a transducer.

inactive lines   In a conventional television picture, blanked lines that do not contribute to the visible part of the image. Approximately half of these lines are at the top of the screen; the other half are at the bottom.

inactive time   The period during which a radioactivity counter is insensitive to ionizing agents.

incandescence   The state of glowing from intense heat, as when a metal becomes white hot from an electric current flowing through it.

incandescent lamp   A filament-type lamp. The filament becomes so hot when an electric current passes through it that it glows brilliantly.

inch   Abbreviation, in. A unit of linear measure in the English system; 1 in. = 2.54 centimeters = 0.0254 meter.

inching   See JOGGING.

inch-pound   Abbreviation, in-lb. A unit of work equal to a force of 1 pound exerted over a distance of 1 inch. Compare FOOT-POUND.

incident   **1.** A failure in a computer system requiring the intervention of an operator in removing or revising the job involved. **2.** Pertaining to a ray or rays of energy striking a surface or boundary, or encountering a device (such as an antenna or photovoltaic cell).

incidental AM   Undesired amplitude modulation in a frequency-modulated signal. Compare INCIDENTAL FM.

incident field intensity   The field strength of an electromagnetic field as it arrives at a receiving antenna.

incidental FM   Undesired frequency modulation in an amplitude-modulated signal. Compare INCIDENTAL AM.

incidental time   Computer time devoted to other than program runs or program development.

incident light   The light that strikes or enters an altering device or medium. See INCIDENT RAY.

incident power   In a transmission line, the power that reaches the end of the line. Compare REFLECTED POWER.

incident ray   The ray that strikes the surface of a reflecting, refracting, or absorbing body. Compare REFLECTED RAY and REFRACTED RAY.

incident wave   **1.** A wave propagated to the ionosphere. Compare REFLECTED WAVE and REFRACTED WAVE. Also see IONOSPHERE and IONOSPHERIC PROPAGATION. **2.** A wave that encounters a change (in density, for example) in a propagation medium or the transition point between media.

in-circuit tester   An instrument that permits the checking of components (especially transistors) without removing them from the circuit in which they are wired.

inclination   The angle between the horizon and the lines of flux of the earth's magnetic field. Varies with geographic location, being 90 degrees at the geomagnetic poles, and zero at the geomagnetic equator. Compare DECLINATION.

inclinometer   An instrument for measuring INCLINATION. One form consists of a magnetic needle mounted so that it can swing inside a vertically mounted circular scale.

inclusive-OR   Also called OR operation. A logical operation between two operands, the result of which depends on rules for combining bits in each position within the operands: an output of 1 results if one or both of the bits have a value of 1; zero only if both are zero. Compare EXCLUSIVE-OR.

incoherent light   Electromagnetic radiation in the visible spectrum in which the waves are not aligned (not in phase) and can be of more than one wavelength.

incoherent radiation   Electromagnetic radiation in which the waves are not aligned (not in phase) and can be of more than one frequency or wavelength.

incoming inspection   The examination of equipment and materials as they enter a factory or laboratory, for the purpose of identifying damaged or faulty units.

incoming line   A line that enters a device, facility, or stage. Compare OUTGOING LINE.

Incompleteness Theorem   A mathematical theorem of significance in artificial intelligence. For any consistent set of axioms (postulates), there are always more true statements than provable statements.

incomplete program   Also called *incomplete routine*. A computer program of generalized steps that must be augmented with specific requirements to be implemented for a given operation.

inconsistency   Contradictory computer statements, as detected by the program.

inconsistent equations   A set of equations that have no common solution.

Increductor   A specialized radio-frequency magnetic amplifier or saturable reactor.

increment   **1.** The difference between two successive values of a variable. **2.** A small change in a quantity, such as mass, distance, or time. **3.** A quantity to be added to another quantity. **4.** The difference in value between adjacent hash marks on a meter scale.

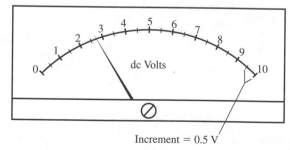

Increment = 0.5 V

increment, 4

incremental computer   A computer that operates on changes in variables. Example: differential analyzer.

incremental digital recorder   A magnetic tape recorder that moves the tape across the record head in increments.

incremental display A device that converts digital data into a form for display (characters; graphs).

incremental inductance The inductance exhibited by an inductor, such as an iron-core choke, carrying a direct current.

incremental permeability The permeability exhibited by a material when an alternating-current magnetizing force is superimposed upon a direct current.

incremental plotter A device that, by direction of a computer program, provides the results of a program run in the form of curves or points on a curve, along with annotational characters.

incremental representation For incremental computers, a method of representing variables in terms of changes in the variables.

incremental sensitivity The smallest change in a quantity under measurement that can be detected by the instrument used.

ind **1.** Abbreviation of *indicator*. **2.** Abbreviation of INDUCTANCE (More commonly, *L*). **3.** Abbreviation of INDUCTOR (More commonly, *L*).

indefinite integral See INTEGRAL, 1.

Indeo Also called *Digital Video Interactive (DVI)*. A method of IMAGE COMPRESSION developed by Intel Corporation.

independent equations A set of equations having one common solution.

independent events In probability and statistics, the case where the occurrence of one event has no effect on the occurrence of another.

independent failure A circuit failure whose direct cause is not related to malfunctions elsewhere in the system.

independent mode In tracking supplies, an optional method of operation in which the separate units are adjustable independently of each other. Compare TRACKING MODE.

independent variable A changing quantity whose value at any instant is not governed by the value of any other quantity. Compare DEPENDENT VARIABLE.

index **1.** A reference line, hair, or point (e.g., a *file index*). **2.** In mathematics, an exponent. **3.** A ratio of one quantity to another, as *index of refraction*. **4.** In a computer memory, a table of references in a key sequence; it can be addressed to find the addresses of other data items. **5.** A number that is used to select a specific item within an array of items in memory.

index counter Also called *tape counter*. In a magnetic tape recorder, a (usually electromechanical) counting device that the operator can refer to in order to find material on the tape.

indexed address During or preceding the execution of a computer program instruction, an address that is modified by the content of an index register.

indexing **1.** An information retrieval technique used with files on a direct-access storage medium or on tables in memory. **2.** To modify an instruction using an index word.

index of modulation In frequency modulation, the ratio of carrier frequency deviation to modulating frequency.

index of refraction Symbol, *n*. The ratio v_1/v_2, where v_1 is the speed of energy propagation in the first medium through which the energy passes, and v_2 is the speed in the second medium.

index register Abbreviation, XR. In digital computer operations, a register holding a modifier that allows data to be directly addressed (each program refers to an index register when addressing storage locations). Also called MODIFIER REGISTER.

index word A word (bit group) containing a modifier that will be added to a basic instruction when it is executed during a program run.

India mica High-grade mica mined in India. Its excellent dielectric properties make it useful for capacitor stacks, high-*Q* radio-frequency circuits, and other critical applications.

indicated horsepower Abbreviation, ihp. Horsepower calculated from data or ratings, as opposed to measured horsepower.

indicated horsepower-hours Abbreviation, ihp-hr. Horsepower-hours based on calculation of indicated horsepower.

indicating fuse A fuse that provides some signal (such as a protruding pin) to show that it has blown.

indicating instrument An instrument, such as a meter, that provides direct readings of a measured quantity, as opposed to an instrument, such as a bridge, that must be manipulated and whose operation must often be followed by calculations.

indicating lamp A lamp that is marked or coded so that when it is on or off it conveys information.

indicator **1.** Meter (see METER, 1). **2.** See MONITOR. **3.** See ANNUNCIATOR. **4.** In a computer, a device that can be set by a specific condition (e.g., by a negative result or error indicator).

indicator probe A test probe having a built-in meter.

indicial response Symbol, I(T). The sum of the transient and steady-state responses to a unit function.

indirect addressing In computer programming, a technique in which the address in an instruction refers to a different location containing another address, that can specify yet another address or an operand. Also called *multilevel addressing*.

indirect coupling Collectively, capacitive and inductive coupling, as opposed to direct coupling.

indirect ground An unintentional ground connection (e.g., accidental grounding of part of a circuit) or one obtained through a roundabout path. Compare DIRECT GROUND.

indirect light Light that has been reflected from one or more surfaces. Compare DIRECT LIGHT.

indirectly controlled Influenced by a directly controlled parameter, but not itself directly controlled.

indirectly grounded Connected to earth or to the lowest-potential point in a system inadvertently or through a roundabout path (e.g., by means of an indirect ground). Compare DIRECTLY GROUNDED.

indirectly heated cathode An electron-tube cathode consisting of a cylindrical or rectangular sleeve coated with a substance that is a rich emitter of electrons; it is heated by a filament inside the cylinder.

indirectly heated thermistor A thermistor whose temperature is changed by a built-in heater (filament) operated by the control current.

indirectly heated thermocouple A meter thermocouple heated by a small heater (filament) through which the signal current passes.

indirect material A semiconductor substance in which electrons move from the conduction band to the valence band in discrete jumps or steps.

indirect measurement The measurement of a quantity by comparing it with a similar quantity, using an instrument that requires adjustment or manipulation (rather than a simple meter). For example, resistance can be measured with a bridge, instead of an ohmmeter. Compare DIRECT MEASUREMENT.

indirect piezoelectricity In a piezoelectric crystal, the application of a voltage for the purpose of producing a strain on the crystal. A piezoelectric buzzer operates on this principle.

indirect scanning A method of video scanning, in which a fast-moving spot of light scans the film or an object and is passed through the film (or reflected by the object) to a photocell.

indirect wave **1.** In communications, a wave that arrives at a receiver after having traveled via refraction, reflection, or both. **2.** A radio wave propagated via the ionosphere. **3.** A wave reflected from some object, such as the moon or a meteor trail. **4.** A wave received from a satellite, originating from a distant earth station.

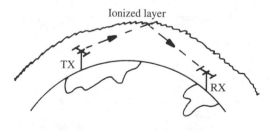

Ionized layer

TX

RX

indirect wave

indium Symbol, In. A metallic element. Atomic number, 49. Atomic weight, 114.82. Used as a dopant in semiconductor processing.

indoor antenna An antenna erected and operated in a building, but kept away from other objects as much as possible.

indoor radiation Electromagnetic radiation from the part of an antenna feeder or lead-in that is inside the transmitter building.

indoor transformer A power service transformer that, for protection against the elements, is installed inside the building it serves.

induced Brought about by the influence of a magnetic or electric field.

induced charge An electric charge produced in a body by the electric field surrounding another charge.

induced current An alternating current established in one circuit by the alternating magnetic field of another circuit. Also see INDUCTION.

induced EMF See INDUCED VOLTAGE.

induced failure A form of component failure that occurs because of operation beyond the normal specifications.

induced voltage An alternating voltage set up across one circuit (especially a coil) by the alternating magnetic field of another circuit. Also see INDUCTION.

inductance Symbol, L. Unit, henry. In a conductor, device, or circuit, the inertial property (caused by an induced reverse voltage) that opposes the flow of current when a voltage is applied; it opposes a change in current that has been established. Also see HENRY, INDUCTION, and MUTUAL INDUCTANCE.

inductance bridge An alternating-current bridge for measuring inductance in terms of a standard inductance or a standard capacitance. See, for example, HAY BRIDGE, MAXWELL BRIDGE, and OWEN BRIDGE.

inductance-capacitance Abbreviation, LC. **1.** A combination of inductance and capacitance in a circuit, such as a filter, a parallel-resonant circuit, or a series-resonant circuit. **2.** Pertaining to a device for measuring inductance and capacitance (e.g., LC bridge and LC meter).

inductance-capacitance bridge An alternating-current bridge for measuring inductance and capacitance only.

inductance-capacitance filter A filter composed of inductors and capacitors. Also called LC filter.

inductance-capacitance meter A direct-reading meter for measuring inductance and capacitance.

inductance-capacitance-resistance Abbreviation, LCR. **1.** A combination of inductance, capacitance, and resistance in a circuit, such as a basic tuned circuit. The resistive component represents loss in the inductor and capacitor. **2.** Pertaining to a device for measuring inductance, capacitance, and resistance (e.g., LCR bridge and LCR meter).

inductance-capacitance-resistance bridge See IMPEDANCE BRIDGE.

inductance coil See INDUCTOR.

inductance filter A filter using only an inductor, usually a coil of wire.

inductance-resistance time constant The time constant t (see ELECTRICAL TIME CONSTANT) of a circuit containing, ideally, only inductance and resistance. Mathematically, $t = LR$, where t is in seconds, L is the inductance in henrys, and R is the resistance in ohms. Also called *LR time constant*.

inductance standard A highly accurate, stable inductor used in precision measurements. Also see PRIMARY STANDARD and SECONDARY STANDARD.

induction 1. The ability of an alternating, pulsating, or otherwise changing current flowing in one circuit to set up a current in a nearby circuit. The circuits need not be physically connected, but need only be linked by magnetic lines of flux. Also see SELF-INDUCTION. 2. The phenomenon whereby a body becomes electrically charged by the field surrounding a nearby charged body. Also see ELECTRIC CHARGE.

induction coil A special high-voltage step-up transformer having an open core and a vibrator-interrupter in series with the primary winding, which carries direct current from a battery. The current is broken up into short pulses by the interrupter, and a high alternating-current voltage is generated in the secondary winding.

induction compass A compass whose indications depend on current induced in a coil revolving in the earth's magnetic field. Compare GYROCOMPASS and MAGNETIC COMPASS.

induction factor The ratio of total current to nonproductive current in an alternating-current circuit.

induction field The portion of an electromagnetic field that returns to a radiator, such as a coil, as opposed to the RADIATION FIELD.

induction frequency converter A mechanical device used for converting a signal at a fixed frequency to a signal at another fixed frequency.

induction furnace A furnace in which high-frequency magnetic fields induce currents in metal ores, causing the ore to become hot enough to melt.

induction heater A high-power, radio-frequency generator designed especially for induction heating.

induction heating The heating of metallic work samples by placing them in (but insulated from) a WORK COIL carrying current from a high-power radio-frequency generator. The workpiece is heated by radio-frequency currents induced in it as a result of the intense alternating magnetic field within the coil. Compare DIELECTRIC HEATING.

induction loss Loss of energy from a current-carrying conductor because of inductive coupling to a nearby conductor.

induction modulator See ELECTROMECHANICAL MODULATOR.

induction motor An electric motor in which the stator's rotating magnetic field makes the rotor revolve.

induction speaker An acoustic loudspeaker in which an audio-frequency current is passed through a diaphragm or coil located in a constant magnetic field. This results in movement of the diaphragm or coil.

induction transducer See INDUCTIVE TRANSDUCER.

induction-type landing system See DINGLEY INDUCTION-TYPE LANDING SYSTEM.

induction welding Welding in which the heating current flowing in the workpieces is induced by an electromagnetic field.

inductive capacitor A wound capacitor in which the inductance of the roll is controlled and specified. Such a capacitor is useful in compact filters and in single-frequency by-passing, where the reactive components are supplied by the capacitor. Compare NONINDUCTIVE CAPACITOR.

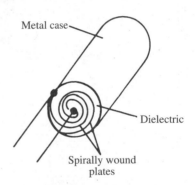

Metal case

Dielectric

Spirally wound plates

inductive capacitor

inductive circuit 1. A circuit in which inductance predominates. 2. A (theoretical) circuit containing inductance only.

inductive coupling The transfer of energy between two inductors (or inductive devices) by a linking electromagnetic field. Also see COEFFICIENT OF COUPLING, COUPLING, INDUCTION, and MUTUAL INDUCTANCE.

inductive feedback See MAGNETIC FEEDBACK.

inductive heater See INDUCTION HEATER.

inductive heating See INDUCTION HEATING.

inductive kick See BACK VOLTAGE and KICK-BACK.

inductive load A load device that approaches a pure inductive reactance (e.g., loudspeaker and electric motor).

inductive logic A form of reasoning that demonstrates that a certain conclusion is highly probable, given a certain set of circumstances. This is of interest to researchers in artificial intelligence (AI). Compare DEDUCTIVE LOGIC.

inductive microphone   A microphone in which sound waves vibrate a conductor or coil in a strong magnetic field, producing a corresponding alternating-current output by the resulting induction. Example: *dynamic microphone*.

induction neutralization   Neutralization of a vacuum-tube radio-frequency power amplifier, via negative feedback from the output to the input through coupling coils.

inductive reactance   Symbol, X_L. Unit, ohm. The reactance exhibited by an ideal inductor, considered as a positive imaginary-number quantity; $X_L = j6.28fL$, where X_L is in ohms, f is the frequency in Hertz, L is the inductance in henrys, and j is the unit imaginary number (the square root of -1). Alternatively, f can be specified in megahertz, and L in microhenries. In a pure inductive reactance, current lags 90 degrees behind voltage. Also see INDUCTANCE, INDUCTION, INDUCTOR, and REACTANCE.

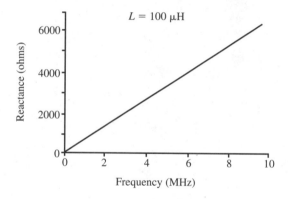

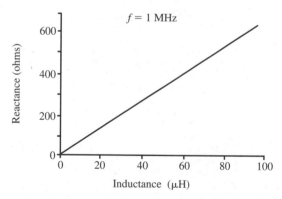

inductive reactance

inductive switching   Switching operations in a circuit containing an inductor. Switching time is influenced by the INDUCTANCE-RESISTANCE TIME CONSTANT of the inductor; overall operation is affected by the back voltage generated by the inductor.

inductive transducer   A transducer in which the sensed phenomenon causes a change in inductance (or reluctance), which, in turn, causes a proportional change in output current, voltage, frequency, or bridge balance. Compare CAPACITIVE TRANSDUCER, CRYSTAL TRANSDUCER, MAGNETIC TRANSDUCER, and RESISTIVE TRANSDUCER.

inductive trimmer   See TRIMMER INDUCTOR.

inductive tuning   Also called *permeability tuning*. In a radio receiver, transmitter or transceiver, the adjustment of frequency by changing the inductance of a coil having a movable core.

inductivity   See DIELECTRIC CONSTANT.

inductometer   An instrument for measuring inductance in terms of the resonant frequency of an INDUCTANCE-CAPACITANCE (*LC*) circuit, in which L is the unknown inductance and C is calibration capacitance.

inductor   A coil of wire wound according to various designs, with or without a core of ferromagnetic material, to concentrate the magnetic flux resulting from current flowing in the wire. The coiling of the wire and/or the addition of a ferromagnetic core increases the self-inductance compared with that of a straight wire having the same length. Also see INDUCTANCE; INDUCTION, **1**; and SELF-INDUCTANCE, **1**.

inductor alternator   See ALTERNATOR.

inductor amplifier   See MAGNETIC AMPLIFIER.

inductor decade   See DECADE INDUCTOR.

inductor microphone   See INDUCTIVE MICROPHONE.

inductors in parallel   See PARALLEL INDUCTORS.

inductors in parallel-series   See PARALLEL-SERIES INDUCTORS.

inductors in series   See SERIES INDUCTORS.

inductors in series-parallel   See SERIES-PARALLEL INDUCTORS.

inductor substitution box   An enclosed assortment of common-value inductors that can be switched, one at a time, to a pair of terminals. In troubleshooting and circuit development, any of several useful fixed inductances can be thus obtained.

industrial data processing   Abbreviation, IDP. The application of digital computers and associated equipment to industrial problems, through the classification, sorting, storing, and manipulation of information.

industrial electronics   The branch of electronics concerned with manufacturing processes and their control, and with the operation and safeguarding of factories.

industrial instrumentation   **1.** Supplementing an industrial process with electrical and electronic measuring instruments. **2.** The instruments used for the purpose defined in **1**.

industrial television   Abbreviation, ITV. A usually closed-circuit television (CCTV) system, used as an adjunct to a manufacturing process, or as a means of communication or surveillance within an industrial plant.

industrial robot A robotic device used in industrial applications (e.g., mining, construction, manufacturing, or laboratory work).

industrial tube An (often heavy-duty) highly reliable vacuum tube designed expressly for industrial service, such as high-power radio or television broadcasting.

ineffective time The period during which an otherwise operational computer is not being used effectively because of delays or idle time.

inelastic collision A collision between charged particles in which one gains energy and the other loses energy.

inert gas A gas that does not readily react with other elements. Inert gases include *argon*, *helium*, *krypton*, *neon*, and *xenon*. Such gases are often used in hermetically sealed devices to retard corrosion.

inertance See ACOUSTIC INDUCTANCE.

inertia The tendency of a body at rest to remain at rest unless acted on by an outside force. Also, the tendency for a body in motion to maintain that motion unless acted on by an outside force. Compare MOMENTUM.

inertia in electric circuit The condition in a circuit containing inductance, in which a current change lags behind a voltage change (analogous to mechanical inertia; see INERTIA).

inertial guidance A system that automatically guides missiles and satellites in a desired trajectory without the need for continuous control by signals from a station.

inertia relay A time-delay relay whose operation is slowed by the addition of weights or other attachments.

inertia switch A switch that can sense a disturbance of its inertia.

inference engine A circuit that gives instructions to a computer or robot, by applying programmed rules to commands issued by a human operator. Comprises the functional portion of an EXPERT SYSTEM.

infinite Pertaining to a quantity or region that has no defined limits.

infinite baffle A loudspeaker baffle having no openings for the passage of sound from the front to the back of the speaker cone.

infinite-impedance detector A detector that offers the very high input impedance of a gate-source circuit and the large-signal capabilities of a diode detector. Audio-frequency output is taken across the source resistor, which is bypassed for radio-frequency signals. There is no drain resistor. Drain current increases with the input signal from a very low value at zero signal level.

infinite line See INFINITE TRANSMISSION LINE.

infinite regress A reasoning pattern (either human or machine-based) that is fallacious because it defines or explains something in terms of itself.

infinite sample space In statistics, a sample space having no definite limits.

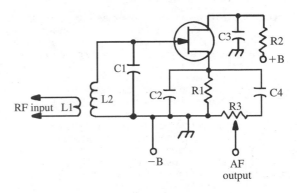

infinite-impedance detector

infinite series A mathematical series in which the number of terms is limitless. For example, $\frac{1}{9}$ = 0.1 + 0.06 + 0.006 + 0.0006 + ...

infinitesimal **1.** A quantity, such as a differential, that approaches zero as the limit. **2.** Pertaining to a quantity whose magnitude is extremely small or negligible. **3.** Pertaining to an extremely small change in a quantity or measured value.

infinite transmission line A theoretical transmission line with normal characteristics, but extending away from the signal generator or receiver for a limitless distance.

infinity Symbol, ∞. A quantity that is unlimited in duration or dimension. A quantity that increases without limit is sometimes said to "approach infinity."

infix notation A system of logical operation notation wherein operands are separated by operators, thus, A & B, where the ampersand means AND. Compare PREFIX NOTATION.

Infobahn See INFORMATION SUPERHIGHWAY.

infobond On a printed circuit board, a form of wiring on the side opposite the components. The wiring is used in place of the foil normally on such a circuit board.

information **1.** Collectively, data or communications, excluding the symbols or signals used to describe, present, or store them. **2.** The result of data processing (i.e., that which is derived from the compilation, analysis, and distillation of data).

information bits In an encoded signal, data characters or digits that can be treated to give information (excluding control characters).

information center A storage bank designed for use by many different subscribers, via computer.

information channel A channel through which data and associated signals are transmitted and received.

information feedback system In message transmission, a control system in which intelligence received at a terminal is returned to the sending unit for automatic verification.

information gate A device or circuit that opens and closes an information channel.

"information processor" species Anything that uses data to derive conclusions, to produce other data, or to take specific actions, and whose functioning can be explained entirely on the basis of data-processing operations. This includes computers and smart robots. Many (but not all) scientists believe that animals are also included; some believe that human beings qualify as well.

information retrieval In digital computer and data-processing operations, the categorizing and storage of information and the automatic recall of specific file items. Also see ACCESS TIME.

information separator An indicator that separates items of information or fields in a (usually variable-length) record.

information storage In digital computer and data processing operations, holding information in memory pending retrieval.

information superhighway 1. General expression for a worldwide network consisting of computers (personal, educational, industrial, and government) interconnected by telephone lines. **2.** See INTERNET. **3.** A massive, evolving, somewhat controversial data communication network linking computers, television, and telephone systems. It uses high-speed, high-volume data links. Communication technologies include fiberoptics, radio-frequency repeaters, microwaves, geostationary satellites, and low-earth-orbit (LEO) satellite systems.

information word A character group representing stored information and managed, as a unit, by hardware or software.

infra- Prefix meaning *below* or *lower than* (e.g., INFRARED).

infrablack region In a composite video signal, the blacker-than-black region (see BLACKER THAN BLACK).

infradyne receiver A superheterodyne receiver in which the intermediate frequency is the sum of the signal and oscillator frequencies, rather than their (usual) difference.

infrared Pertaining to electromagnetic energy in a band whose wavelength is longer than that of visible light, but shorter than that of microwave energy.

infrared communication Communication by keying or modulating infrared rays.

infrared counter-countermeasure A military tactic in which action is taken against an enemy infrared countermeasure.

infrared countermeasure A military tactic using countermeasure methods to cripple enemy infrared equipment.

infrared detector A device that senses the presence of infrared energy. Some such detectors are bolometers, radiometers, radiomicrometers, and photocells.

infrared-emitting diode Abbreviation, IRED. A semiconductor diode, such as the gallium-arsenide type, that emits infrared rays when a current passes through the p-n junction in the forward direction.

infrared guidance A navigation and reconnaissance system using infrared rays.

infrared homing The method whereby a guided missile uses infrared rays to guide it to its target.

infrared light See INFRARED RAYS.

infrared motion detector See MOTION DETECTOR and INFRARED.

infrared photography Photography in which the scene is illuminated with infrared light or emits infrared rays, and the film is infrared sensitive.

infrared radiation See INFRARED RAYS.

infrared rays Radiation at frequencies in the INFRARED region. Also (somewhat mistakenly) called *heat rays.*

infrared remote control 1. The use of an infrared link, usually over short line-of-sight distances, for the purpose of controlling the operation of electronic equipment. A common example is the local remote control of a television receiver or high-fidelity system. **2.** A small box, containing buttons, a transmitter and an infrared-emitting diode (IRED), used for local remote control of devices, such as television receivers and high-fidelity sound systems.

infrared spectrum The region of the electromagnetic spectrum in which INFRARED radiation is found. This band lies between the microwave radio spectrum and the visible-light spectrum.

infrared therapy The use of infrared rays by physicians and other practitioners to treat certain disorders.

infrared waves Electromagnetic waves whose lengths are greater than those of visible light waves, but less than those of microwaves.

infrared window Any portion of the infrared spectrum in which energy is easily transmitted through the lower atmosphere of the earth.

infrasonic Pertaining to acoustic disturbances whose frequencies are below the range of human hearing (less than about 20 Hz).

infrasonic intrusion detector A system that detects the presence of extremely low-frequency acoustic disturbances, and sends a signal to an alarm. Such INFRASONIC waves can be caused by various actions such as walking on a wooden floor, opening or closing a door, etc.

infrasonics The branch of physics dealing with INFRASONIC phenomena.

infrasound Acoustic disturbances in the air, whose frequencies are lower than about 20 Hz, and whose wavelengths are longer than about 55 feet (17 meters).

inharmonic distortion Distortion in which the frequencies of extraneous components are not harmonically related to the fundamental frequency. It is sometimes experienced when a tone-burst signal is applied to a loudspeaker.

inherent component A (usually extraneous) property possessed by a device because of its internal peculiarities. Thus, an inductor has

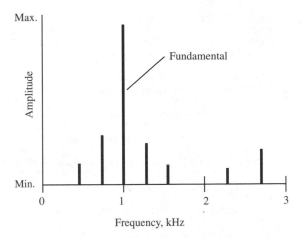

inharmonic distortion

inherent capacitance; a capacitor has inherent inductance.

inherited error In an extended calculation, an error carried through from one of the earlier steps.

inhibit **1.** In digital computer and logic operations, to prevent an action or block the input of data by means of a pulse. **2.** To delay an action or process.

inhibit gate A pulse-actuated gate circuit that acts as an INHIBITOR.

inhibitor **1.** A device or circuit that produces a pulse or signal that prevents an action, or that blocks data input. **2.** An additive, such as an organic liquid, that delays the hardening of a mixture, such as an encapsulating compound.

inhibit pulse In a computer, a drive pulse that prevents other pulses from changing the direction of magnetization in the cells of a magnetic core memory.

inhibit signal In digital computer and logic operations, the signal that causes an INHIBIT action.

initial drain **1.** The current supplied by a battery or cell at its rated voltage. **2.** The current delivered by a rechargeable battery or cell when it is put to use immediately after receiving a full charge.

initial failure The first failure occurring in the operation of a circuit or device.

initial instructions A resident computer routine used to aid program loading. Also called *initial order.*

initial ionizing event In the operation of a radioactivity counter, the first event that starts the chain of similar events constituting the count.

initialization A computer program instruction that sets the value of a variable to zero.

initial permeability Permeability in the low magnetization region of a material.

initial time delay Abbreviation, ITD. In acoustics, the elapsed time between the instant the

direct sound wave is first heard, and the instant the first echoes (reflected sound waves) arrive.

initiate See TRIGGER.

injection **1.** Introducing a signal into a circuit or device. **2.** Introducing charge carriers (electrons or holes) into a semiconductor.

injector **1.** An element or electrode for INJECTION. **2.** A device or circuit that injects a signal into another device or circuit.

injector electrode See INJECTOR, 1.

ink bleed In the printing of matter for optical character recognition, ink flow around the characters, often making them unrecognizable to the reader.

inkjet galvanometer A galvanometer whose movement controls the pressure of a jet of ink for making a recording on a paper chart. Also see LIQUID-JET OSCILLOGRAPH.

inkjet printer A printer commonly used with personal computers, in which images are created by jets of ink sprayed directly onto the paper. Noted for low operating noise level, high image resolution, and excellent color-reproduction capability.

ink-mist recorder A graphic recorder in which the line is traced by a mist of ink.

ink recorder A graphic recorder using a pen-and-ink stylus.

ink squeeze-out In the printing of matter for optical character recognition, the squeezing of ink from a character's center.

ink-vapor recorder See INK-MIST RECORDER.

in-lb Abbreviation of INCH-POUND.

inlead The part of an electrode that passes through the external shell or case of a component.

inline procedure The main portion of a COBOL computer program, responsible for the primary operations.

inline processing The action peculiar to a system that processes data almost immediately upon receipt (i.e., one that need not be capable of storing a lot of unprocessed data).

inline readout In digital computer operations, a readout device that displays digits side-by-side horizontally.

inline subroutine A subroutine that must be written each time it is needed, as compared with one that can be accessed by a program branch.

inline tuning Tuning of all the stages of a channel, such as an intermediate-frequency amplifier, to the same frequency.

inner conductor The inner wire or rod of a coaxial cable or coaxial tank. It generally carries the signal, and is isolated from the surrounding environment by the grounded OUTER CONDUCTOR.

inorganic Consisting of materials other than carbon compounds; therefore, it is not related to living things.

inorganic electrolyte Any electrolyte that is completely inorganic: containing no compounds of carbon.

in phase The condition in which alternating or pulsating waves or wave phenomena are in step

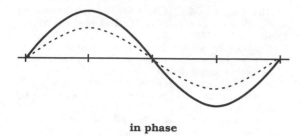

in phase

with each other at all points. Compare OUT-OF-PHASE.

in-phase carrier   See I-PHASE CARRIER.

in-phase current   Resistive current in an ac circuit (i.e., current in phase with voltage). Compare QUADRATURE CURRENT.

in-phase feedback   Feedback in phase with a main signal. Also called POSITIVE FEEDBACK and REGENERATION.

in-phase voltage   A voltage that is in phase with another (reference) voltage.

in-plant system   An automatic data communications system within a specific building or complex.

input   **1.** Energy or information delivered or transferred to a circuit or device. **2.** The terminals of a device or circuit to which energy or information is applied. **3.** To deliver or transfer energy or information to a circuit or device (as to input data from a computer peripheral to memory).

input admittance   Symbol, Y_i. The internal admittance of a circuit or device, as "seen" from the input terminals; the reciprocal of input impedance. Compare OUTPUT ADMITTANCE.

input area   In a computer memory, an area set aside for data input from a source other than a program.

input bias current   The input bias required by an operational amplifier.

input capacitance   Symbol, C_i. **1.** The internal capacitance of a circuit or device, as "seen" from the input terminals. Compare OUTPUT CAPACITANCE. **2.** The grid-cathode capacitance of a vacuum tube.

input capacitor   **1.** In a capacitance-coupled circuit, the input coupling capacitor. Compare OUTPUT CAPACITOR. **2.** The first capacitor in a capacitor-input filter (i.e., that capacitor electrically nearest the rectifier output electrode).

input choke   The first choke in a choke-input filter (i.e., that choke electrically nearest the rectifier output electrode, when no preceding capacitor is used).

input circuit   The circuit or subcircuit constituting the input section of a network or device. Compare OUTPUT CIRCUIT.

input clamp current   The current from an input when the input is in a state below ground potential. A test for the input clamp diode.

input conductance   Symbol, G_i. The internal conductance of a circuit or device, as "seen" from the input terminals; it is the reciprocal of INPUT RESISTANCE. Compare OUTPUT CONDUCTANCE.

input coupling capacitor   See INPUT CAPACITOR, **1**.

input coupling transformer   See INPUT TRANSFORMER.

input current   Symbol, I_i. **1.** The current delivered to a circuit or device. **2.** Current flowing in the input leg or electrode of a circuit or device.

input device   **1.** A device, such as an input transformer, that couples energy or information to a circuit or device. Compare OUTPUT DEVICE. **2.** A device through which another device receives data.

input equipment   Collectively, input devices used with a computer.

input error voltage   In an operational amplifier, the error voltage at the input terminals when a feedback loop operates around the amplifier.

input extender   A diode network that provides increased fan-in for a logic circuit. Also see FAN-IN, **1**.

input gap   In a velocity-modulated tube, the gap in which the electron stream is initially modulated.

input guarding   A method of eliminating stray coupling among inputs in an integrated circuit. A shield is provided at the input; it is driven to follow along with the input voltage. This ensures low loss and minimum errors resulting from unwanted coupling.

input impedance   Symbol, Z_i. The internal impedance of a circuit or device, as "seen" from the input terminals. Compare OUTPUT IMPEDANCE.

input limited   The processing time limitation imposed by an input unit on the speed of a program run.

input noise current   At the input of an integrated circuit, the root-mean-square (rms) or peak-to-peak (pk-pk) noise current existing within a specified range of frequencies.

input noise current density   The noise current, usually expressed as a root-mean-square (rms) value, in a band 1 Hz wide around a given frequency.

input noise voltage   At the input of an integrated circuit, the root-mean-square (rms) or peak-to-peak (pk-pk) noise voltage existing within a specified range of frequencies.

input noise voltage density   The noise voltage, usually expressed as a root-mean-square (rms) value, in a band 1 Hz wide around a given frequency.

input offset current   In an operational amplifier, the difference between the currents going to the input terminals when the output is zero.

input offset voltage   In an operational amplifier, the potential that has to be applied between the input terminals for a zero output voltage.

input/output   Abbreviation, I/O. **1.** Data transmitted to, or received from, a computer. **2.** A terminal through which data is transmitted to, or received from, a device.

input/output bound A condition affecting a system in which the time consumed by input and output operations is greater than that required for other processes.

input/output buffer A computer memory area specifically reserved for the receipt of data coming from or going to a peripheral.

input/output control The part of a computer system that coordinates activity between a central processor and peripherals.

input/output equipment **1.** In digital computer operations, devices for entering information into the computer or for reading information from it. Examples: keyboard, mouse, display, and optical scanner. **2.** In robotics and artificial intelligence, a data link between a controller and one or more robots, and/or between or among two or more controllers.

input/output isolation Arrangement or operation of a circuit or device so that there is no direct path between input and output terminals around the circuit or device. Also see ISOLATION.

input/output module See INPUT/OUTPUT EQUIPMENT.

input/output routine A routine for simplifying the programming of standard input/output equipment operations.

input/output switching The allocation of more than one channel to peripherals for communications with a central processor.

input/output voltage differential At a given load current, the potential difference that is necessary for an integrated circuit to operate according to its output voltage specifications.

input power Symbol, P_i. **1.** The power presented to the input terminals of a circuit or device. Also called POWER INPUT. Compare OUTPUT POWER. **2.** The operating power of a circuit or device (i.e., the power-supply requirement).

input protection In an integrated circuit, a means of preventing damage to the device from excessive voltage at the input, such as transient spikes or the result of malfunctioning of some other circuit.

input record **1.** A computer record of immediate interest that is ready for processing. **2.** During a computer program run, a record read into memory from an input record.

input recorder A device that makes a permanent record of the signals or data input to a circuit or system.

input register In a computer, a register that receives data from a peripheral relatively slowly and then passes it on to a central processor at a faster speed as a sequence of informational units. Also see REGISTER.

input resistance Symbol, R_i. The internal resistance of a circuit or device, as "seen" from the input terminals. Compare OUTPUT RESISTANCE.

input resonator In a velocity/modulated tube, the resonator in which electron bunching occurs.

input routine A computer program section that manages data transferal between an external storage medium and a memory input area.

input section **1.** See INPUT ROUTINE. **2.** See INPUT AREA.

input sensitivity **1.** The level of input-signal amplitude that will result in a certain signal-to-noise ratio at the output of a device. The specified signal-to-noise ratio is usually 10 or 20 dB. **2.** The level of input signal in a frequency-modulated device, required to produce a specified amount of noise quieting. The specified level of noise quieting is usually 20 dB. Alternatively, 12-dB SINAD (ratio of signal to the level of noise and distortion) can be specified. **3.** The minimum level of input voltage required to actuate a logic gate.

input signal The signal (current, voltage, and power) presented to the input terminals of a circuit or device for processing.

input tank In a double-tuned stage of a transmitter or power generator, the tank circuit in which the input signal is resonated. This is generally the base or gate circuit. Compare OUTPUT TANK.

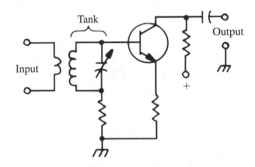

input tank

input terminals Terminals (usually a pair) associated with the input section of a circuit or device. Compare OUTPUT TERMINALS.

input transformer The transformer that delivers signal voltage or power to the input circuit of a network or device. Compare OUTPUT TRANSFORMER.

input uncertainty The combination of all parameters that result in adverse behavior in an operational amplifier.

input unit In a digital computer, the device or circuit that receives information from peripherals.

input voltage **1.** Symbol, E_i or V_i. The voltage presented to a circuit or device. Compare OUTPUT VOLTAGE, 1. **2.** The voltage across the input leg or electrode of a circuit or device. Compare OUTPUT VOLTAGE, 2.

input-voltage drift For an integrated circuit (IC), the time- and temperature-dependent change in output voltage divided by the IC's open-loop voltage gain.

input-voltage offset   For a differential amplifier, the input signal voltage at the differential input that results in zero output voltage.

input-voltage range   The range, in volts, over which the input voltage can fluctuate in an integrated circuit so that the common-mode rejection ratio (CMRR) specifications are not exceeded.

input winding   The signal winding of a magnetic amplifier.

inquiry   A programmed request for information from storage in a computer.

inquiry display terminal   A video display/keyboard terminal used to make an inquiry to a computer system, and display the response.

inquiry station   A terminal from which an inquiry can be sent to a central computer.

inrush   The initial surge of current that occurs when voltage is first applied to the primary winding of a transformer with no load connected.

inscribe   To convert data to a form on a document that is readable by a character-recognition device, as through the use of magnetic ink, for example.

insect robot   A member of a fleet of robots, all of which are under the control of a single computer. The term arises because the system functions like an anthill or beehive, in which the individual machines are "stupid," but the system as a whole is "smart." Such robots often have six legs, like insects. Compare AUTONOMOUS ROBOT.

insert   A (usually metallic) bushing that can be molded into a plastic part (or pressed into it after molding is completed) to provide a bearing sleeve or threaded hole.

insert core   A ferromagnetic core whose position can be adjusted to vary the inductance of the coil surrounding it.

insert edit   **1.** In magnetic tape recording, a section of tape on which new audio is recorded over existing audio. **2.** The process of recording new audio over existing audio in a defined interval on a magnetic tape.

insertion gain   In a circuit or system, the gain resulting from the amplifier inserted into the system; it is usually expressed in decibels. Compare INSERTION LOSS.

insertion loss   Loss of energy or gain by placing certain devices or subcircuits (filters, impedance matchers, etc.) in a circuit. It is usually expressed in decibels. Also see INSERTION RESISTANCE.

insertion phase shift   The difference in phase produced by a circuit installed in an electrical transmission line.

insertion resistance   The resistance of a component or instrument that is introduced into a circuit. Thus, the internal resistance of a microammeter becomes an insertion resistance in the circuit in which the meter is connected for current measurement.

inside antenna   See INDOOR ANTENNA.

inside diameter   Abbreviation, ID. The innermost diameter of a body or figure having two concentric diameters. Compare OUTSIDE DIAMETER.

inside lead   See START LEAD.

inside radiation   See INDOOR RADIATION.

inside spider   A voice-coil centering device within a loudspeaker.

inst   **1.** Abbreviation of INSTRUMENT or INSTRUMENTATION. **2.** Abbreviation of INSTANT.

instability   Inconsistency in the operation of a circuit or device, in the parameters of a device, or in an electrical quantity. It can be attributed to a number of causes, including temperature, loading, age, humidity, negative resistance, and radioactivity.

installation tape number   An identification number given to a reel of magnetic tape by the processing facility.

instant   Abbreviation, inst. The point in time at which an event occurs, or at which a quantity reaches a particular value.

instantaneous   Occurring at a specified moment, or instant, of time.

instantaneous amplitude   The amplitude, specified in amperes, volts, or watts, of a signal, specified at a particular moment in time.

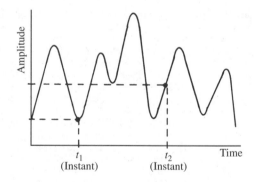

instantaneous amplitude

instantaneous automatic gain control   Abbreviation, IAGC. An automatic gain control whose operation almost immediately follows a change in signal amplitude.

instantaneous automatic volume control   Abbreviation, IAVC. An instantaneous automatic gain control system for the immediate control of volume in receivers and audio-frequency amplifiers.

instantaneous companding   A form of companding that operates according to the instantaneous amplitude of the input signal.

instantaneous contacts   Timer contacts that open or close almost immediately upon application of the control signal.

instantaneous current   Symbol, i or I_t. The value of an alternating or fluctuating current at a particular instant in the cycle.

instantaneous disc   A phonograph disc that can be played back immediately after being recorded.

instantaneous frequency   The frequency of a signal at a particular moment in time. The instantaneous frequency changes in frequency-modulated or phase-modulated signals.

instantaneous power   **1.** In a single-sideband, suppressed-carrier signal, the power at a specified instant in time. It varies between zero and the peak envelope power (PEP). **2.** The output power of an audio amplifier at a specified instant in time.

instantaneous power output   The rate of power delivery to a load at a given instant.

instantaneous relay   A relay, such as a fully electronic type (having no moving parts), that shows virtually no delay in its operation.

instantaneous sample   A measurement obtained by INSTANTANEOUS SAMPLING.

instantaneous sampling   The measurement of wave or signal amplitude at a specific moment in time. See, for example, INSTANTANEOUS CURRENT and INSTANTANEOUS VOLTAGE.

instantaneous speech power   In the output of an audio amplifier, the instantaneous value of power in a speech wave, as opposed to that in a sine wave. Also see INSTANTANEOUS VALUE and SPEECH POWER, **1**.

instantaneous value   The magnitude of a fluctuating value at a selected instant in time. See, for example, INSTANTANEOUS CURRENT, INSTANTANEOUS POWER, INSTANTANEOUS SPEECH POWER, and INSTANTANEOUS VOLTAGE. Compare AVERAGE VALUE, and EFFECTIVE VALUE.

instantaneous voltage   Symbol, e or E_t. The value of an alternating or fluctuating voltage at a particular instant in the cycle.

instant loop   In electronic security applications, a circuit that actuates an alarm without delay when an intrusion is detected.

instruction   In digital computer operations, a set of bits defining an operation. Consists of an operation code specifying the operation to be performed, one or more operands or their addresses, and one or more modifiers or their addresses (to modify the operand or its address).

instruction address   In a computer memory, the address of a location containing an instruction.

instruction address register   Also called *program counter*. A register that holds instruction addresses so that the retrieval of the instructions from memory can be controlled during a program run.

instruction code   Also called INSTRUCTION SET. The symbols and characters that compose the syntax of a computer programming language.

instruction format   In a computer's basic machine code, the part that specifies how characters or digits are used to represent the codes within the machine's instruction set.

instruction modification   In a computer instruction, a change in the instruction code that makes the computer do a different operation when the routine containing the code is encountered again.

instruction register   A register in a computer containing the address of the current instruction. Also called CONTROL REGISTER (abbreviation, CR).

instruction set   **1.** The range of commands that form a programming language. **2.** See INSTRUCTION CODE.

instruction storage   A memory circuit that stores computer instructions or programs.

instruction time   The time required for a control unit to analyze and implement a computer program instruction.

instruction word   In digital computer programming, a word containing the instruction code (type of operation to be performed) and the address part (location of the associated data in storage).

instrument   A device for measuring electrical quantities or the performance of electronic equipment. A *meter* provides a direct indication; other devices, such as a *bridge*, must be adjusted, the measured quantities being determined from one or more adjustments (sometimes augmented with calculations).

instrumental error   See INSTRUMENT ERROR.

instrument amplifier   Also called INSTRUMENTATION AMPLIFIER. A high-gain, wideband amplifier that increases the sensitivity of an instrument (such as an oscilloscope, meter, or graphic recorder).

instrument-approach system   See INSTRUMENT LANDING SYSTEM.

instrumentation   Planning and providing instruments and instrument systems for the collection and, sometimes, storage and analysis of data.

instrumentation amplifier   **1.** A form of integrated-circuit voltage amplifier designed for high linearity, high input impedance, and high common-mode rejection. It is intended for use with electronic instruments. **2.** See INSTRUMENT AMPLIFIER.

instrument chopper   A refined chopper for converting a direct-current (dc) signal to alternating current (ac) for an ac instrument, such as a voltmeter or recorder.

instrument error   Discrepancy in measured quantities resulting from inaccuracy of the instrument used, insertion resistance, environmental factors, operator error, etc.

instrument flight   Also called *blind flight*. Aircraft flight guided by navigational instruments and signals alone. Required when visibility is extremely poor.

instrument fuse   A fast-acting, low-current fuse used to protect a sensitive instrument, such as a galvanometer, milliammeter, and/or microammeter.

instrument lamp A light or lamp that illuminates the face of an instrument to facilitate viewing in the dark.

instrument landing Also called *blind landing*. Aircraft landing guided entirely by instruments. Required when visibility is poor and when landing is imperative at a given location at a given time.

instrument landing station The radio or radar station in a blind-landing system (see INSTRUMENT LANDING SYSTEM).

instrument landing system Abbreviation, ILS. The complete instrument and signal system (on the ground or in aircraft) required for an INSTRUMENT LANDING.

instrument multiplier See MULTIPLIER PROBE, **1**.

instrument preamplifier An external, sensitive amplifier for an instrument that has an internal input amplifier. Also see INSTRUMENT AMPLIFIER.

instrument relay See METER RELAY.

instrument resistance See METER RESISTANCE.

instrument shunt A resistance connected in parallel with a current-measuring instrument, used to increase the range of currents that can be measured.

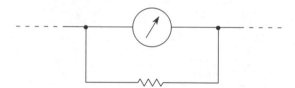

instrument shunt

instrument transformer A transformer used to change the range of an alternating-current meter. For ammeters, it is called a *current transformer*; for voltmeters, it is called a *potential transformer*.

insulant A nonconducting material, used to prevent the flow of electric current between or among points. See INSULATOR, **1**.

insulated Isolated from conductors by an INSULANT.

insulated-gate field-effect transistor Abbreviation, IGFET. See METAL-OXIDE SILICON FET.

insulated resistor A resistor around which is molded a nonconducting material, such as vitreous enamel or a plastic.

insulating tape Electrical insulation in the form of a thin, usually adhesive, strip of fabric, paper, or plastic.

insulation **1.** A coating of dielectric material that prevents a short circuit between a conductor and the surrounding environment. **2.** The application of a dielectric coating to an electrical conductor.

3. Electrical separation between or among different components, circuits, or systems.

insulation breakdown Current leakage through, and rupture of, an insulating material because of high-voltage stress.

insulation ratings Collectively, the dielectric constant, dielectric strength, power factor, and resistivity of an insulating material. Sometimes included are such physical properties as rupture strength, melting point, etc.

insulation resistance The very high resistance exhibited by a good insulating material. It is expressed in megohms (or higher units of resistance) for a sample of material of stated volume or area.

insulation system Collectively, the materials needed to insulate a given electronic device.

insulator **1.** A material that, ideally, conducts no electricity; it can, therefore, be used for isolation and protection of energized circuits and components (also see DIELECTRIC). Actually, no insulator is perfectly nonconductive (see, for example, INSULATION RESISTANCE). **2.** A molded piece of solid insulating material, used to electrically isolate conductors—especially in antenna systems and power transmission lines. **3.** Any body made from an insulating material.

insulator arcover A sudden arc, or flow of current, over the surface of an insulator, because of excessive voltage.

integer A positive or negative whole number, as opposed to a fraction or mixed number.

integral **1.** Also called *indefinite integral* and *antiderivative*. For given mathematical function f, function g, whose derivative is equal to f. **2.** Also called *definite integral*. The area under a curve of a function, between two vertical lines defined by two specific points in the domain of the function. **3.** The part of a number to the left of the radix point. **4.** Pertaining to integers (positive or negative whole numbers) or quantities that can be represented by integers.

integral action In automatic control operations, a control action delivering a corrective signal proportional to the time that the controlled quantity has differed from a desired value.

integral contact In a relay or switch, a contact that carries current to be switched.

integral-horsepower motor A motor rated at one horsepower.

integral multiple A whole multiple of a number. Thus, a harmonic is an integral multiple of fundamental frequency f: $2f$, $3f$, $4f$, etc.

integral number See INTEGER.

integrate **1.** To perform the function of mathematical or electrical INTEGRATION. **2.** To construct a circuit on a piece of semiconductor material.

integrated Constructed on a single piece of material, such as a semiconductor wafer.

integrated amplifier An audio-frequency (AF) amplifier having a preamplifier, intermediate amplifier, and output amplifier on a single chassis.

integrated capacitor In an integrated circuit, a fixed capacitor in which one plate is a layer of material diffused into the substrate, the dielectric is a thin-oxide film grown on top of the first layer, and the other plate is a metal layer deposited on top of the oxide film.

integrated circuit Abbreviation, IC. A circuit whose components and connecting "wires" are made by processing distinct areas of a chip of semiconductor material, such as silicon. Classified according to construction (e.g., *monolithic IC, thin-film IC, hybrid IC*).

integrated data processing Abbreviation, IDP. The detailed electronic classification, sorting, storage, and mathematical processing of data within a coordinated system of equipment, usually at one location.

integrated electronics The branch of electronics that is concerned with the design and fabrication of integrated circuits.

integrated resistor See DIFFUSED-LAYER RESISTOR.

Integrated Services Digital Network Abbreviation, ISDN. A scheme via which the signal-carrying ability of metallic wires is optimized. Involves the digitization of data, including text, images, and voices/music.

integrating circuit See INTEGRATING NETWORK.

integrating galvanometer A device for measuring the change in electric flux produced in a coil in an electric field. Even very slow changes can be measured.

integrating meter An instrument whose indication is a summation (usually) of an electrical quantity that is time-dependent (e.g., *ampere-hour meter* and *watt-hour meter*).

integrating motor An electric motor that follows the integral of the input signal. The angle of rotation of the motor shaft is equal to the integral of the input waveform.

integrating network A four-terminal network whose output voltage is proportional to the time integral of the input voltage. It can be a passive resistance-capacitance (RC) circuit or it can use

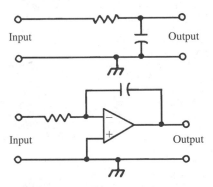

integrating networks

an operational amplifier. Compare DIFFERENTIATING NETWORK.

integrating photometer A photometer whose reading is the average candlepower at all angles in one plane.

integration 1. The process of determining a mathematical function when its derivative is given. 2. The processing of a signal by an INTEGRATOR circuit. 3. Collectively, the processes by which an INTEGRATED CIRCUIT is manufactured.

integrator 1. See INTEGRATING NETWORK. 2. A device having an output variable whose value is proportional to the integral of one variable, with respect to another, or is proportional to the integral of an input variable, with respect to elapsed time.

intelligence 1. Meaningful data that modulates a carrier [e.g., the voice or music in a frequency-modulated (FM) radio signal, or the image in a television signal]. 2. Also called *machine intelligence.* The quality of a system or device, especially a computer, that allows it to "learn" (i.e., to better its capability by repeatedly operating on a given problem).

intelligence bandwidth 1. The bandwidth necessary to convey a specified amount of data within a certain period of time. 2. The total bandwidth of one complete signal channel in a communications or broadcast system.

intelligence signal 1. A signal that conveys data or information. 2. The modulating waveform in a communications or broadcast transmission.

intelligent terminal A computer terminal (e.g., an input/output video display/keyboard unit) that through its circuitry (i.e., by use of a microprocessor) has some data-processing ability.

intelligibility tests Tests that measure the coherence of electronically reproduced speech.

intensification of image See IMAGE INTENSIFICATION.

intensifying ring In some electrostatic cathode-ray tubes, an internal metal ring serving as an extra anode to accelerate the beam and, thus, brighten the image.

intensity The degree or extent of a phenomenon (such as amplitude, brightness, loudness, power, force, etc.).

intensity control In an oscilloscope circuit, the potentiometer that adjusts the direct-current voltage on the control electrode of the cathode-ray tube and, accordingly, the brightness of the image. Also called BRIGHTNESS CONTROL and BRILLIANCE CONTROL.

intensity level 1. A measure of sound magnitude, expressed in decibels, with respect to a value of one microwatt per square centimeter (10^{-6} W/cm^2) at sea level in the atmosphere. 2. The setting of the brightness control in a cathode-ray-tube device.

intensity modulation 1. Modulation of electron-beam intensity in a cathode-ray tube. Also called *z-axis modulation*. **2.** Sometimes, the video-signal modulation in a television image.

intensity-modulation amplifier The z-axis amplifier in an oscilloscope. Also see INTENSITY MODULATION.

interaction The (sometimes mutual) influence of one circuit or device on the behavior of another, as in induction.

interactive display A computer display device with which its operator can supply data to the computer in response to what is displayed. Example: *touch screen*.

interactive graphics A computer graphics system using a cathode-ray tube to draw or modify three-dimensional representations.

interactive program A computer program in which the machine and its operator engage in two-way communication. Most personal computing software is of this type, in contrast to programs that carry out all their functions without operator intervention (other than initialization).

interactive television Television provided to consumers, in which viewers can transmit data, as well as receive it. For example, a survey might be conducted in which viewers are polled and send in their responses. Another example: products might be ordered while viewing an advertisement.

interactive mode See CONVERSATIONAL MODE.

interbase resistance The internal resistance between the bases of a unijunction transistor.

interblock A part of a computer program or a hardware device that will prevent interference between parts of a computer system.

interblock space **1.** On a magnetic tape, the space between recordings, caused by starting and stopping the tape. **2.** On magnetic tape used as a computer storage medium, the interval between recorded blocks.

intercarrier receiver A television (TV) receiver circuit in which video, sound, and sync components of the composite TV signal are amplified together in the radio-frequency (RF), intermediate-frequency (IF), and video IF stages; then they are separated in the video detector and video amplifier stages. Compare SPLIT-SOUND RECEIVER.

intercept receiver In military service, a search receiver tuned over a wide band of frequencies to locate and evaluate enemy signals.

interchangeability The ability of one component to substitute directly for another component of the same kind. Example: capacitor interchangeability, transistor interchangeability. Also see REPLACEMENT.

intercharacter space The three-unit interval between letter symbols in telegraphy. Compare INTERWORD SPACE.

intercom A comparatively simple two-way telephone or low-power radio system for use on the premises of a home or business.

intercommunicator See INTERCOM.

interconnection **1.** A mutual connection of separate circuits. **2.** The interconnection of two or more separate power-generating systems.

interdigital contacts A pair of contacts with "fingers" that are plated, printed, or deposited on the surface of a resistor material or semiconductor substrate. The fingers of each contact are interconnected at one end, the fingers of one contact being interleaved with those of the other.

interdigital tube A magnetron having a cathode surrounded by anode segments that are alternately interconnected at opposite ends in the manner of INTERDIGITAL CONTACTS.

interelectrode capacitance Capacitance between or among electrodes—especially between the plate and control grid of a vacuum tube.

interelement capacitance Internal pn-junction capacitance in a semiconductor device, such as a diode or transistor.

interface **1.** The circuitry that interconnects and provides compatibility between a central processor and peripherals in a computer system. **2.** Collectively, the hardware and software that allows a computer to interact with its operator. **3.** To provide an efficient pathway for data between two devices or systems. **4.** The meeting of surfaces or regions in a material. **5.** The surface of a body that mates with another body similar or identical to it.

interface resistance See CATHODE INTERFACE.

interface routine A computer program routine that links one system to another.

interfacial connection A connection that runs through a printed-circuit board and joins circuit joints on opposite faces of the board.

interference **1.** In communications, degradation of reception caused by noise or undesired signals. **2.** The interaction of acoustic or electromagnetic waves from more than one source, especially when they are of the same frequency, producing a characteristic INTERFERENCE PATTERN of high-amplitude and low-amplitude regions.

interference attenuator A device or mode of operation that reduces the amplitude of interference.

interference eliminator A filter, wavetrap, or similar device that removes interfering signals or noise. Also see INTERFERENCE.

interference filter See INTERFERENCE ELIMINATOR.

interference pattern A regular pattern of high-amplitude and low-amplitude regions, lobes, or bands, produced when waves of identical frequency from two or more sources combine in varying phase. Such patterns can be observed with sound, radio waves, infrared, visible light, ultraviolet, X rays, and gamma rays. The phenomenon is of interest in acoustic engineering, the design of radio antenna systems, and in physics (particularly optics).

interference stub A length of twin-lead feeder cut to appropriate length, connected to the antenna-input terminals of a television receiver, and short-circuited at the opposite end. A stub of the correct length resonates at the frequency of an interfering signal and, acting as a wavetrap, keeps it out of the receiver. Also see STUB.

interference trap   A wavetrap that suppresses interfering signals at the rejection frequency of the trap.

interferometer   **1.** A radio telescope having two antennas spaced at a distance of many wavelengths, providing much greater resolution than a single antenna. Pioneered by M. Ryle of England and J.L. Pawsey of Australia. **2.** Any device that displays an INTERFERENCE PATTERN for testing or experimental purposes.

interfix   A method used in information-retrieval systems that eliminates ambiguity in the responses to inquiries by describing the relationship between keywords in a record.

Interframe   A method of digital IMAGE COMPRESSION developed by *MPEG (Moving Picture Experts Group)*. It operates by eliminating redundant data from between image frames. Compare INTRAFRAME.

interharmonic beats   Beat notes produced by various combinations of the harmonics of a signal.

interim storage   See TEMPORARY STORAGE.

interior label   On a magnetic tape used as a computer-storage medium, a label recorded at the beginning of the tape. Compare EXTERIOR LABEL.

interior protection   **1.** In electronic security applications, a set of sensors contained entirely within the region to be protected. **2.** The installation and operation of a security system whose sensors are all within the region to be protected.

interlace   A form of data storage in which portions of the data are stored in alternate locations in the tape or disk.

interlaced field   A video image field produced by INTERLACED SCANNING.

interlaced scanning   In the display of a video image, the alternate presentation of the even- and odd-line fields. This process increases the obtainable image resolution for a given refresh rate, but can result in "jerkiness" of the image when rapid motion is portrayed.

interlace factor   A number expressing the extent to which two fields are interlaced. Also see INTERLACED SCANNING.

interleaving   In multiprogramming, the inclusion in a program of segments of another program so that both can be effectively executed simultaneously.

interlock switch   See ELECTRICAL INTERLOCK.

intermediate amplifier   See BUFFER.

intermediate frequency   Abbreviation, IF. In a superheterodyne circuit, the frequency of the signal that results from beating the incoming signal with the signal produced by the local oscillator.

intermediate-frequency amplifier   In a superheterodyne circuit, the fixed-frequency ampli-

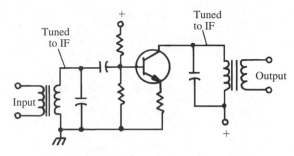

intermediate-frequency amplifier

fier that boosts the intermediate-frequency signal. Also see INTERMEDIATE FREQUENCY.

intermediate-frequency channel   Usually, the intermediate-frequency amplifier in a superheterodyne circuit, but sometimes including the second detector, automatic gain control (AGC), and oscillator stages.

intermediate-frequency converter   See IF CONVERTER.

intermediate-frequency interference   Interference from signals at the intermediate frequency of a receiver or instrument.

intermediate-frequency selectivity   The selectivity of an intermediate-frequency (IF) channel alone, usually determined by the characteristics of the bandpass filter(s) in the IF channel.

intermediate-frequency transformer   A coupling transformer designed for use in an intermediate-frequency amplifier.

intermediate-puck drive   In a tape recorder, a speed-reducing drive system in which an intermediate wheel conveys motion from the motor shaft to the rim of the flywheel.

intermediate puck wheel   See IDLER WHEEL.

intermediate repeater   In wire telephony, a repeater inserted into a line or trunk at some point other than the end.

intermediate result   Obtained during a program run or the execution of a subroutine, a result that is used again as an operand in deriving the final result.

intermediate section   Any of the internal sections of a multisection filter. Thus, the middle section of a three-section filter.

intermediate storage   In a computer system, a storage medium for temporarily holding totals or working figures. Also called WORK AREA.

intermediate subcarrier   A modulated or unmodulated subcarrier that modulates either a carrier or another intermediate subcarrier.

intermittent   **1.** Pertaining to a circuit fault, such as an open or short circuit, that occurs some of the time, but not all the time. **2.** See INTERMITTENT CONDITION. **3.** Pertaining to a phenomenon that is observed some of the time, but not all the time; sporadic. **4.** Pertaining to a

DUTY CYCLE greater than zero, but less than 100 percent; usually between 25 and 50 percent.

intermittent commercial and amateur service Abbreviation, ICAS. Operation of equipment, such as radio transmitters, for short, irregular periods, as in amateur (hobbyist) activity or infrequent commercial service. ICAS ratings are higher than continuous commercial service (CCS) ratings. Compare CONTINUOUS COMMERCIAL SERVICE.

intermittent condition A defect in a circuit or device that causes erratic and unreliable operation. The cause of such a problem is often difficult to determine.

intermittent dc See INTERMITTENT DIRECT CURRENT.

intermittent direct current A regularly pulsed unidirectional current. Also called PULSATING DIRECT CURRENT.

intermittent duty A DUTY CYCLE of less than 100 percent, but greater than zero. Generally, an operating duty cycle of 25 to 50 percent.

intermittent-duty rating The dissipation or power rating of a component, circuit, or system, under conditions of intermittent use, usually a 25-percent to 50-percent DUTY CYCLE.

intermittent operation Operation characterized by often long nonoperating intervals. Intermittent operation is often random, whereas on-off operation tends to be regular.

intermittent signal An interrupted signal resulting from the intermittent operation of a circuit or device.

intermodulation Abbreviation, IM. **1.** The (usually undesired) modulation of one signal by another, caused by nonlinear processing of the signals. **2.** The heterodyning of components in the sidebands produced by an amplitude-modulated (AM) or single-sideband (SSB) transmitter.

intermodulation distortion Abbreviation, IMD. **1.** Distortion products in the output of an amplitude-modulated (AM) or single-sideband (SSB) transmitter, caused by heterodyning of components in the sidebands. **2.** Distortion products in the output of an audio amplifier, caused by heterodyning of the fundamental components. **3.** The extent to which distortion as defined in 1 occurs. See INTERMODULATION-DISTORTION PERCENTAGE.

intermodulation-distortion meter See INTERMODULATION METER.

intermodulation-distortion percentage Abbreviation, IDP. The degree to which a low-frequency test signal modulates a higher-frequency test signal when both are applied simultaneously (in a prescribed amplitude ratio) to a device under test; $IDP = 100(b - a)/a$, where a is the peak-to-peak amplitude of the unmodulated high-frequency wave and b is the peak-to-peak amplitude of the modulated high-frequency wave.

intermodulation meter An instrument for measuring percentage of intermodulation distortion (IMD). The instrument combines a dual-frequency signal generator, filter circuits, and percent-of-modulation meter. Also see INTERMODULATION-DISTORTION PERCENTAGE.

intermodulation noise Electrical noise produced in one channel by signals in another; it is caused by INTERMODULATION.

internal absorptance The ratio of flux absorbed in a substance to the flux leaving at the entry surface of the substance. It does not include energy reflected at the entry surface.

internal amplification In a radioactivity counter tube, current enhancement resulting from cumulative ionization initiated by an ionizing particle.

internal arithmetic In a digital computer, arithmetic operations performed in the computer, as opposed to those performed by peripherals.

internal impedance The impedance in a device, as opposed to that added from the outside. Compare INTERNAL RESISTANCE.

internal input impedance The impedance in a circuit or device, as "seen" from the input terminals. Compare INTERNAL OUTPUT IMPEDANCE.

internal input resistance The resistance in a circuit or device, as "seen" from the input terminals. Compare INTERNAL OUTPUT RESISTANCE.

internal noise Electrical noise generated within a circuit, as opposed to that picked up from outside. Such noise comes from transistors, diodes, integrated circuits, resistors, and any other component through which current flows.

internal output impedance The impedance in a circuit or device, as "seen" from the output terminals. Compare INTERNAL INPUT IMPEDANCE.

internal output resistance The resistance in a circuit or device, as "seen" from the output terminals. Compare INTERNAL INPUT RESISTANCE.

internal resistance **1.** The resistance of a device, as opposed to added resistance. See, for example, METER RESISTANCE. **2.** In a cell or battery, the equivalent resistance, resulting from imperfect conductivity of the electrolyte and electrodes, which limits the maximum deliverable current.

internal thermal shutdown In an integrated circuit, the junction temperature at which thermal shutdown occurs. It is generally indicated in degrees Celsius (°C).

internal transmittance The ratio of flux reaching the exit surface of a material to the flux leaving the entry surface. Reflection is not taken into account. The sum of internal transmittance and INTERNAL ABSORPTANCE is always equal to 1.

international broadcast station A shortwave broadcast station transmitting programs for international reception between 6 and 26.6 MHz.

international callsign The call letters of a station, assigned within a country, according to the method of arrangement (identifying letters, or letters and numerals) prescribed by the International Telecommunication Union.

international candle See CANDLE.

international coulomb   A unit of electrical quantity, equal to 0.99985 absolute coulomb.

international farad   A unit of capacitance, equal to 0.99952 absolute farad.

international henry   A unit of inductance, equal to 1.00018 absolute henry.

international joule   A unit of energy, equal to 1.00018 absolute joule.

International Morse Code   See CONTINENTAL CODE.

international ohm   A unit of electrical resistance, equal to 1.000495 absolute ohm. The other international units are derived from this value.

International Radio Consultative Committee   Abbreviation, CCIR (*Comite Consultatif International Radiodiffusion*). An international organization reporting to the International Telecommunication Union, and studying technical operations and tariffs of radio and television.

International Steam Table calorie   A unit of heat energy equal to 4.1868 joules.

International System of Units   Abbreviation, SI (*Systeme International d'Unites*). The system of units of measurement established in 1960 under the Treaty of the Meter. The base units are as follows.

–METER (m), length: 1,650,763.73 times the wavelength of the light emitted in a vacuum of krypton 86

–KILOGRAM (kg), mass: the mass of the protype kilogram kept at Sevres, France

–SECOND (s), time: the duration of 9,192,631,770 periods of the radiation that corresponds to the transition between the two hyperfine levels of the ground state of cesium 133

–KELVIN (K), thermodynamic temperature: $\frac{1}{273.16}$ the thermodynamic temperature of the triple point of water

–AMPERE (A), electric current: the current that, flowing through two infinitely long parallel wires in a vacuum and separated by 1 meter, produces a force of 2×10^{-7} newton per meter of length between the wires

–CANDELA (cd), luminous intensity: the luminous intensity of $\frac{1}{600,000}$ square meter of perfectly radiating surface at the temperature of freezing platinum

International Telecommunication Union   Abbreviation, ITU. An international, nongovernmental organization devoted to standardizing worldwide communications practices and procedures.

International Telegraph and Telephone Consultative Committee   See CCITT.

International Telegraph Consultative Committee   See CCIT.

international units   A system of electrical units, based on the resistance through a specified quantity and configuration of the element mercury. The INTERNATIONAL OHM forms the basis for the international system of units.

international volt   A unit of electrical potential, equal to 1.00033 absolute volt.

international watt   A unit of power, equal to 1.00018 absolute watt.

Internet   A worldwide, interconnected system of computer networks. Originated in the late 1960s as *ARPAnet* (Advanced Research Projects Agency network). Still used extensively by educators and scientists, but gaining popularity among personal-computer users. Sometimes called the INFORMATION SUPERHIGHWAY.

interphone   An intercom aboard a mobile vehicle.

interpolation   Finding a value that falls between two values listed in a table, indicated by a dial, plotted on a graph, derived by estimate, or given by intermediate calculation. For example, if a linear variable capacitor has a value of 100 pF when its dial is set to 10, and 140 pF when the dial is set to 20, then the capacitance when the dial reads 15 (midway between 10 and 20) can be assumed to be 120 pF (midway between 100 pF and 140 pF). When functions are not linear, interpolation is usually not exact.

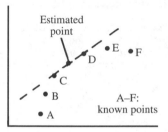

interpolation

interpolation meter   See INTERPOLATION-TYPE INSTRUMENT.

interpolation oscillator   A frequency-measuring signal generator with a built-in crystal oscillator, whose harmonics provide calibration points on the tuning dial. The dial provides a continuous indication of generator frequencies between crystal-harmonic points. Also see INTERPOLATION-TYPE INSTRUMENT.

interpolation-type instrument   An instrument, such as a meter or signal generator, that is used to transfer an accurate quantity point from a standard to another instrument and to provide a range of values between such points. A secondary standard is sometimes used as an interpolation-type instrument (see, for example, INTERPOLATION OSCILLATOR).

interpole motor   A direct-current motor with small auxiliary poles (*interpoles*) between its main field poles. The interpoles reduce sparking at the commutator.

interpreter   A computer program that can convert instructions given in a high-level language (BASIC, for example) into the machine language that a computer uses; if it is not resident in the computer's nonvolatile memory, it must be loaded each time the machine is activated.

interrecord gap   See INTERBLOCK SPACE.

interrupt   A break in a computer program, as when a background job is interrupted so that a foreground job can be run. Also see BACKGROUND JOB and FOREGROUND JOB.

interrupted commercial and amateur service   See INTERMITTENT COMMERCIAL AND AMATEUR SERVICE.

interrupted continuous wave   Abbreviation, ICW. A continuous wave that is interrupted at regular intervals, as in the chopping of a wave at a regular rate. Compare CONTINUOUS WAVE (CW) and MODULATED CONTINUOUS WAVE (MCW).

interrupted dc   A direct current or voltage that is periodically started and stopped by switching or chopping.

interrupter contacts   Auxiliary contacts operated directly by the armature of a stepping switch.

interruption frequency   See QUENCHING FREQUENCY.

interruption-frequency oscillator   See QUENCH OSCILLATOR.

interrupt signal   The signal that causes a break (INTERRUPT) in a computer program.

intersatellite communication   **1.** Communication between or among satellites. **2.** Communication between two earth-based stations, using two or more satellites. **3.** Communication between an earth-based station and a satellite-based station, using at least one intermediate relaying satellite.

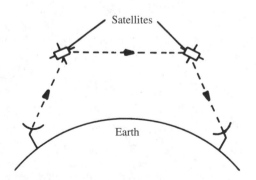

Satellites

Earth

intersatellite communication

intersecting storage ring   A device for producing great amounts of energy. It is similar to a vacuum tube. High-speed subatomic particles are fed to a ring-shaped evacuated structure in opposite directions. The two particle beams collide at various points, yielding high energy.

intersection   The logical AND operation.

interstage capacitor   A coupling capacitor used between two circuit stages.

interstage coupling   The transfer of a signal between two circuit stages, such as those of an amplifier. Common forms of interstage coupling include *direct coupling*, *capacitive coupling*, *transformer coupling*, *diode coupling*, and *optoisolator coupling*.

interstage diode   A semiconductor coupling diode used between two circuit stages.

interstage transformer   A coupling transformer used between two circuit stages. It provides direct-current isolation, and also can match purely resistive impedances.

intersymbol interference   In a digital communications signal, a condition in which a given symbol overlaps with one or more other symbols (either immediately preceding it or immediately following it), upsetting the ability of the receiver to decipher signals in certain time intervals. The phenomenon is sometimes a problem in time-division multiplexing—especially at data speeds near the maximum for the system.

intersystem   A power-generating network of interconnected separate systems.

intersystem communications   Communications between computer systems, either through direct linking of central processors, or by mutual use of peripherals and input/output channels.

intertie   See INTERCONNECTION, 2.

interval   **1.** The amount of separation between successive points, events, or quantities. **2.** The continuous range of values between two defined points. **3.** A specific period of time, with defined beginning and ending points.

intervalometer   A timing device for operating equipment over a precisely defined time interval.

interval timer   A device that provides power to an equipment for a precise interval upon application of a simple initiating signal or action. See also INTERVALOMETER.

interword space   The seven-unit interval between words or code groups in telegraphy. Compare INTERCHARACTER SPACE.

intoxication tester   See DRUNKOMETER.

intracoding   The coding of data using only data that it contains.

Intrafax   Western Union's private facsimile system.

Intraframe   A method of digital IMAGE COMPRESSION developed by *MPEG (Moving Picture Experts Group)* and *JPEG (Joint Photographic Experts Group)*. It operates by eliminating redundant data within image frames. Compare INTERFRAME.

intrinsic-barrier diode   See PIN DIODE.

intrinsic-barrier transistor   A bipolar transistor with a layer of intrinsic semiconductor between one of its pn junctions.

intrinsic concentration   The number of minority carriers exceeding the normal equilibrium number in a semiconductor.

intrinsic conduction The flow of electron/hole pairs in an intrinsic semiconductor subjected to an electric field.

intrinsic flux A quantity equal to the product of the intrinsic flux density and the cross-sectional area in a magnet.

intrinsic flux density The increased flux density of a magnet in its actual environment, as compared with the flux density resulting from the same magnetizing force in a perfect vacuum.

intrinsic mobility Electron mobility in an intrinsic semiconductor. Also see CARRIER MOBILITY and MOBILITY.

intrinsic Q The value of the Q, also known as the FIGURE OF MERIT, for an unloaded circuit. This value is generally higher than the value when a load is connected to the circuit.

intrinsic semiconductor A semiconductor whose characteristics are identical to those of a pure crystal of the material. In this condition, the semiconductor is nearly an insulator. Example: highly purified germanium or silicon before n- or p-type impurities have been added. Compare EXTRINSIC SEMICONDUCTOR.

intrusion alarm A set of electronic sensors and associated circuitry composing a system that detects and warns of the presence of unauthorized personnel within a specific region.

intrusion sensor A sensitive pickup (such as a photocell, ultrasonic detector, or capacitive transducer) that responds to a nearby body by delivering an actuating signal to an intrusion alarm.

INV Abbreviation of INVERTER.

inv Abbreviation of INVERSE.

Invar A nickel-steel alloy (36% nickel) having a low temperature coefficient of linear expansion (1 ppm/°C). Invar is used in electronic equipment where mechanical distortion resulting from temperature changes must be negligible, and in magnetostrictive circuits (see MAGNETOSTRICTION).

inverse 1. Opposite in nature (e.g., an INVERSE CHARACTERISTIC). 2. Of opposite sign (e.g., a negative current or voltage). 3. An operation of opposite kind; thus, subtraction is the inverse of addition, and division is the inverse of multiplication.

inverse beta The beta of a transistor operated with the emitter and collector interchanged.

inverse bias See REVERSE BIAS.

inverse characteristics The characteristics of a bipolar transistor when operated with the emitter and collector reversed.

inverse conduction See REVERSE CONDUCTION.

inverse cube law A principle relating the intensity of an effect to the reciprocal of the cube of the distance from the source. The magnetic field around a solenoidal coil of wire obeys this principle.

inverse current See REVERSE CURRENT.

inverse-distance law The inverse-square law applied to the propagation of radio waves, assuming that the waves do not encounter obstacles.

inverse feedback See DEGENERATION.

inverse fourth-power law A rule of propagation for certain complex forms of energy: $I = k/d^4$, where I is the intensity of the field, d is the distance from the source, and k is a constant.

inverse impedances Impedances (Z_1 and Z_2) that are the reciprocal of another impedance (Z_3), satisfying the relationship $Z_1 Z_2 = (Z_3)^2$. Also called RECIPROCAL IMPEDANCES.

inverse leakage The flow of a small static reverse current in semiconductor devices.

inverse-parallel circuit See BACK-TO-BACK CIRCUIT and BACK-TO-BACK CONNECTION.

inverse peak voltage See PEAK INVERSE VOLTAGE.

inverse piezoelectric effect Mechanical movement in a piezoelectric material, caused by application of voltage.

inverse resistance See REVERSE RESISTANCE.

inverse resonance See PARALLEL RESONANCE.

inverse-square law The energy or power intensity of a phenomenon is inversely proportional to the square of the distance from the source. This is often applied to quantitative reasoning about radiant energy, electromagnetic energy, and acoustic energy. Thus, if the distance doubles, the energy or power drops to ¼ its previous value.

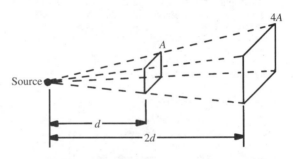

inverse-square law

inverse trigonometric function An angle expressed in terms of a given trigonometric function, followed by the exponent -1 or preceded by "arc" (sin^{-1} is the equivalent of *arcsin*).

inverse voltage 1. The negative voltage at the anode of a rectifier during the negative half-cycle of alternating-current (ac) input. 2. The voltage across a power-supply filter capacitor during the negative half-cycle of ac input. 3. Semiconductor-junction reverse voltage.

inverse Wiedeman effect See DIRECT WIEDEMAN EFFECT.

inversion 1. A reversal of the normal vertical temperature gradient of the atmosphere, often resulting in long-distance tropospheric radio-wave propagation. 2. Speech scrambling (see SCRAMBLER CIRCUIT). 3. Phase inversion (see PHASE INVERTER). 4. Changing direct current into alternating current, often increasing the voltage (see INVERTER, 1).

inverted amplifier   A push-pull, grounded-gate, field-effect-transistor (FET) amplifier.

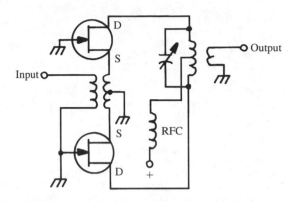

inverted amplifier

inverted-L antenna   An antenna having a horizontal radiator and a vertical feeder or lead-in attached to one end of the radiator. The entire arrangement resembles an upside-down L. The overall length is generally ¼ to ½ wavelength.

inverted speech   See SCRAMBLED SPEECH.

inverter   1. Also called *power inverter*. A device that converts direct current (dc) into alternating current (ac), often of a much higher voltage (e.g., 12 Vdc into 117 Vac). 2. A logic circuit that pro-

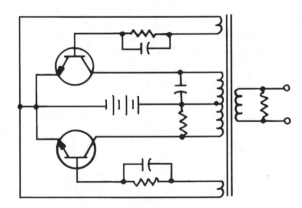

inverter, 1

Input o——▷o—— o **Output**

In	Out
0	1
1	0

inverter, 2

vides an output pulse that is a negation of the input pulse. Also called a COMPLEMENTER or a NOT CIRCUIT. 3. See PHASE INVERTER.

inverting adder   An analog adder circuit that is provided with an amplifier for a 180° phase shift.

inverting amplifier   An amplifier providing a 180° phase shift between input and output.

inverting connection   Connection to the inverting input terminals of a differential amplifier or operational amplifier. Also see INVERTING INPUT. Compare NONINVERTING INPUT.

inverting input   In a differential amplifier or operational amplifier, the input circuit that produces a phase reversal between the input and output. Compare NONINVERTING INPUT.

invisible failure   In a computer system, a hardware or software failure whose effect on the system is unnoticeable in a given application. A failure that is invisible in one application might be vividly apparent in some other application.

invister   A unipolar semiconductor material, capable of operation at very high frequencies.

involution   Raising a number to a power: squaring, cubing, etc. Compare EVOLUTION.

inward-outward dialing   Also called *direct dialing.* In a telephone system, a method of dialing in which calls can be made to and from branch exchanges, without operator assistance.

I/O   Abbreviation of *input/output* (see INPUT/ OUTPUT EQUIPMENT).

I_o Symbol for OUTPUT CURRENT.

iodine   Symbol, I. A nonmetallic element of the halogen family. Atomic number, 53. Atomic weight, 126.905. Also see HALOGEN.

ion   A charged atom [i.e., one that has gained one or more electrons (a negative ion, or *anion*) or lost one or more electrons (a positive ion, or *cation*)].

ion burn   A spot burned on the screen of a cathode-ray tube by negative ions from the cathode striking a single point on the faceplate with high intensity for long periods.

ion concentration   1. The number of ions, expressed as a percentage or as a number per unit volume, in a substance. 2. Ionization density in the atmosphere.

ion exchange resins   Granular resins that contain acid or base groups, and that trade ions with salts in solutions. The resins play a part in the purification of water for various industrial processes.

ionic binding forces   In a crystal, the binding forces that occur when valence electrons of one atom are joined to those of a neighboring atom whose outer shell they fill.

ionic bond   In a solid, a bond between atoms, formed as a result of the attraction between oppositely charged atoms (ions).

ionic conduction   Conduction, as in a gas or electrolyte, by ion migration (positive to the cathode, negative to the anode).

ionic crystal   A crystal whose lattice is held together by the electric forces between ions. Also see IONIC BINDING FORCES and IONIC BOND.

ionic current   Current caused by ion movement in a gas or liquid. Also see ION, IONIZATION, and IONIC CONDUCTION.

ionic semiconductor   A semiconductor in which the carrier is an ion, as opposed to an electron or hole.

ionic switch   See ELECTROCHEMICAL SWITCH.

ionization   **1.** The loss or gain of one or more electrons by an atom. Also see ANION, CATION, and ION. **2.** The formation or existence of significant numbers of ions in a gas, liquid, or solid (e.g., ionization of the upper atmosphere).

ionization arc   The electrical discharge resulting from the ionization of a material because of high voltage.

ionization chamber   An enclosure containing a gas and a pair of electrodes between which a high voltage is applied. Radiation, such as X rays or radioactive particles, passing through the walls of the chamber ionize the gas, creating an ionization current that is proportional to the intensity of the radiation.

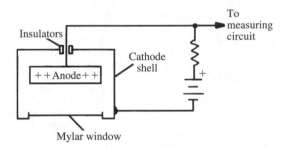

ionization chamber

ionization current   **1.** Current in an ionized gas (such as air). **2.** Current flowing in an electrolyte. **3.** Current in an ionization chamber, Geiger-Mueller tube, or similar gaseous device. **4.** In a gas tube, current flowing after the ignition potential has been reached. **5.** Negative grid current resulting from gassiness in a vacuum tube.

ionization density   The extent to which ionization exists in an ionized layer of the atmosphere. The higher the ionization density, the greater the effect on radio waves—especially at frequencies below about 150 MHz.

ionization gauge   A form of vacuum tube that can be used to measure the hardness of a vacuum. It consists of a cathode, an anode (plate), and a positively charged grid. Plate current flows as a result of ionization of the atoms within the tube. The more nearly perfect the vacuum, the lower the plate current.

ionization potential   The voltage at which a substance (especially a gas) ionizes. Also called (for a gas) *ignition potential* (see BREAKDOWN VOLTAGE).

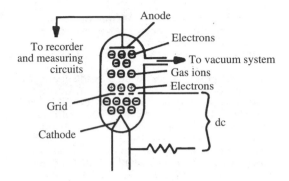

ionization gauge

ionization pressure   In an ionized gas, the pressure increase resulting from the ionization, as compared with the same volume and mass of gas when not ionized.

ionization resistance   See CORONA RESISTANCE.

ionization smoke detector   A device that senses the presence of smoke or other particles as a result of changes in the IONIZATION CURRENT through the air. When the ionization current suddenly changes, a signal is sent to an alarm circuit.

ionization time   The interval, usually measured in microseconds or milliseconds, between the instant that an ionizing potential is applied to a gas, and the instant at which the gas begins to ionize. Compare DEIONIZATION TIME.

ionization trail   The ionized path of a meteor as it passes through the upper atmosphere.

ionize   To cause the electrons in a substance, particularly a gas, to move freely from atom to atom.

ionized gas   A gas whose atoms, under the influence of a strong electric field or IONIZING RADIATION, have become positive or negative ions.

ionized layer   See KENNELLY-HEAVISIDE LAYER.

ionized liquid   See ELECTROLYTE.

ionizing radiation   **1.** Any high-energy electromagnetic radiation that causes ionization in a gas through which the field passes. Examples: ultraviolet, X rays, and gamma rays. **2.** High-speed atomic nuclei (e.g., protons or alpha particles).

ion migration   The movement of ions through a solid, liquid, or gas because of the influence of an electric field.

ionosphere   **1.** Collectively, the several regions (layers) in the upper atmosphere that are ionized by radiation from the sun. These ionized layers are responsible for the absorption, reflection, and refraction of radio waves—especially at frequencies below about 150 MHz. Also see KENNELLY-HEAVISIDE LAYER. **2.** Any of the individual IONOSPHERIC LAYERS.

ionospheric disturbance   See IONOSPHERIC STORM.

ionospheric forecasting   Predicting ionospheric conditions. Radio propagation data is derived from such predictions.

ionospheric layers   The respective layers of the ionosphere: *D layer* (at an altitude of about 30 mi or 50 km), *E layer* (at an altitude of about 50 mi or 80 km), the *F1 layer* (at an altitude of about 125 mi or 200 km), and the *F2 layer* (at an altitude of about 180 mi or 300 km). The F1 layer is generally present only in the daytime.

ionospheric propagation   Propagation of radio waves by means of reflection or refraction by the ionosphere. Also see HOP; INCIDENT WAVE; IONOSPHERE; MULTIHOP PROPAGATION; REFLECTED WAVE, **1**; REFRACTED WAVE; and SKYWAVE.

ionospheric storm   Turbulence in the ionosphere, usually accompanied by a magnetic storm and caused by high-speed particles emitted from an eruption on the sun.

ion sensor   A device whose operation is based on the detection of ions and the delivery of a proportionate voltage. Examples are the *Geiger counter*, *halogen gas leak detector*, *mass spectrometer*, and *vacuum gauge.*

ion spot   See ION BURN.

ion trap   See BENT-GUN CRT.

ion-trap magnet   An external (usually double) magnet used with a television picture tube to deflect the ion beam away from the screen. This prevents ION BURN.

I/O port   That part of a computer providing, via a connector, a point through which data can enter from, or exit to, peripheral equipment.

I_P **1.** Abbreviation of PLATE CURRENT. **2.** Abbreviation of PEAK CURRENT.

I-phase carrier   In color television, a carrier separated by 57 degrees from the color subcarrier.

I-picture   A video image that is coded using only data that it contains.

ipm   Abbreviation of INCHES PER MINUTE.

ips   Abbreviation of INCHES PER SECOND.

IR   **1.** The product of current and resistance (see, for example, IR DROP). **2.** Abbreviation of INSULATION RESISTANCE. **3.** Abbreviation of INFRARED.

Ir   Symbol for IRIDIUM.

I_r Symbol for CURRENT in a resistor.

IRAC   Abbreviation for *Interdepartment Radio Advisory Committee* (a federal government group in the United States).

IR diode   See INFRARED DIODE.

IR drop   The voltage drop (E) across a resistance (R) when there is a current (I) through the resistor; according to Ohm's law, $E = IR$.

IRE   Abbreviation for *Institute of Radio Engineers*, the predecessor of the IEEE (*Institute of Electrical and Electronics Engineers*).

IRED   Abbreviation for INFRARED-EMITTING DIODE.

I_{RF} Symbol for RADIO-FREQUENCY CURRENT.

iridescence   A sparkling, colorful appearance in a material, resulting from refraction, internal reflection, and interference in light waves passing through the substance. It is especially noticeable in quartz and certain gems.

iridium   Symbol, Ir. A metallic element of the platinum group. Atomic number, 77. Atomic weight, 192.22.

iron   Symbol, Fe. A ferromagnetic, metallic element. Atomic number, 26. Atomic weight, 55.847. Iron (and its special form, steel) is widely used in magnetic circuits.

iron/constantan thermocouple   A thermocouple consisting of a junction between wires or strips of IRON and CONSTANTAN.

iron core   A transformer or choke core made from iron or steel. The core is usually laminated to reduce eddy-current loss.

iron-core coil   An inductor having an iron or steel core, usually laminated to reduce eddy-current loss.

iron-core IF transformer   An intermediate-frequency transformer having a core of powdered iron, a form of iron that has the advantage of high permeability while greatly minimizing eddy currents.

iron-core transformer   A transformer whose coils are wound on a core of laminated iron or steel.

iron loss   Power lost in the iron cores of transformers, inductors, and electrical machinery as a result of eddy currents and hysteresis.

iron magnet   A permanent magnet consisting of magnetized iron or a mixture of iron and nickel.

iron oxide   A compound of iron and oxygen, whose most familiar form is common rust. The several variants have characteristics that depend on the number of iron and oxygen atoms in the iron-oxide molecule. See, for example, MAGNETITE and RED OXIDE OF IRON.

iron pyrites   Formula, FeS_2. Natural iron sulfide that occurs as bright yellow crystals in its natural state.

iron-vane meter   An alternating-current meter whose movable element, a soft iron vane, carries the pointer and pivots near a similar, stationary vane. The vanes are mounted in a multiturn coil

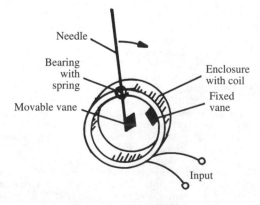

iron-vane meter

of wire. The current flows through the coil, the resulting magnetic field magnetizing the vanes. Because the magnetic poles of the vanes are identical, they repel each other; the movable vane is deflected (against the torque of returning springs) over an arc proportional to the current, carrying the pointer over the scale.

irradiance   The amount of radiant flux impinging on a unit surface area; it is generally specified in watts per square meter (W/m^2).

irradiation   **1.** Exposure of a device to radioactivity or X rays. **2.** The total radiant power density that is incident upon a receiving surface.

irrational number   A number that cannot be expressed as the quotient of two integers. Its decimal expansion is nonterminating and nonrepeating.

irregularity   **1.** The condition of being nonuniform, or rapidly fluctuating, rather than constant. **2.** A departure from normal operating conditions. **3.** Nonuniformity in a surface. **4.** Nonuniform distribution of matter. **5.** Nonuniform distribution of data.

IR viewer   A device that allows observation of images at infrared wavelengths. See SNIPERSCOPE and SNOOPERSCOPE.

I_s **1.** Symbol for source current in a field-effect transistor. **2.** Symbol for *screen current* in a vacuum tube.

ISDN   Abbreviation for INTEGRATED SERVICES DIGITAL NETWORK.

ISCAN   Abbreviation of *inertialess steerable communications antenna.*

I-scan   A radar display in which the target is shown as a complete circle, whose radius is proportional to the distance to the target.

I-signal   With the Z-signal, one of the two signals that modulates the chrominance subcarrier in color television. The I-signal results from mixing a B-Y signal (with -0.27 polarity) and an R-Y signal (with +0.74 polarity).

Isinglass   Thinly laminated mica.

ISO   Abbreviation for *International Standards Organization.*

ISO 9660   A standard format for producing CD-ROM (COMPACT DISK READ-ONLY MEMORY) mass storage media for use with computers. It is a part of the YELLOW BOOK scheme.

isobar   **1.** An atom whose nucleus has the same weight as that of another atom but differs in atomic number. **2.** On a weather map, a line connecting points of equal pressure. Also see BAR, **1.**

isochromal phenomena   **1.** Effects occurring at regular time intervals. **2.** Effects of equal duration.

isochromatic   Also *orthochromatic.* **1.** The quality of having or producing natural visible-light hues. **2.** Color sensitivity excluding a response to red.

isochronal   See ISOCHRONE.

isochrone   On a map, a line connecting points of constant time difference in radio-signal reception. It is useful in radiolocation and radionavigation.

isochronous   Having identical resonant frequencies or wavelengths.

isoclinic line   See ACLINIC LINE.

isodose   Pertaining to points receiving identical dosage of radiation.

isodynamic line   On a map of the geomagnetic field (the earth's magnetic field), a line connecting points of equal flux density.

isoelectric   Having a potential difference of zero.

isoelectronic   Having the same number of electrons.

isogonal   **1.** See ISOGONIC LINE. **2.** Having uniform magnetic declination at all points.

isogonic line   On a map of the geomagnetic field (the earth's magnetic field), a line connecting points of equal magnetic declination.

isolantite   An insulating ceramic. Dielectric constant, 6.1.

isolated   **1.** Electrically insulated. **2.** Separated in such a way that interaction does not take place.

isolated input   **1.** An ungrounded input. **2.** An input circuit with a blocking capacitor to prevent the passage of direct current.

isolated location   In a computer, a storage location that is hardware-protected from being addressed by a user's program.

isolating amplifier   See BUFFER, **1.**

isolating capacitor   A series capacitor inserted in a circuit to pass an alternating-current signal while blocking direct current. Also called a BLOCKING CAPACITOR.

isolating diode   A diode used (because of its unidirectional conduction) to pass signals in one direction, but block them in the other direction.

isolating resistor   A high-value resistor connected in series with the input circuit of a voltmeter or oscilloscope to protect the instrument from stray pickup. In most voltmeters, this resistor is built into the probe.

isolating transformer   A power transformer, usually having a 1:1 turns ratio, for isolating equipment from direct connection to the power line.

isolation   The arrangement or operation of a circuit so that signals in one portion are not transferred to (nor affect) another portion.

isolation amplifier   See ISOLATING AMPLIFIER.

isolation capacitor   See ISOLATING CAPACITOR.

isolation diode   **1.** In an integrated circuit, a reverse-biased diode that is formed in the substrate to prevent cross-coupling and grounds. **2.** See ISOLATING DIODE.

isolation resistor   See ISOLATING RESISTOR.

isolation transformer   See ISOLATING TRANSFORMER.

isolator   See OPTOELECTRONIC COUPLER.

isolith   A form of monolithic integrated circuit, in which the semiconductor is removed in certain places for the purpose of isolating different parts of the circuit.

isomagnetic   Having equal magnetic intensity.

isomer   A material that has the same atomic number or chemical formula as some other substance, but, because of a difference in the

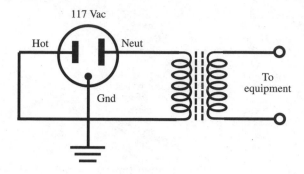

117 Vac

Hot   Neut

Gnd

To equipment

isolating transformer

atomic structure, is an entirely different substance. An example is carbon; it can be either
graphite (by far the more common form) or *diamond.*

isophote   On a graph of visible-light intensity, a
curve joining points of equal brightness.

isoplanar   An integrated-circuit configuration in
which insulating barriers or metal oxides are
fabricated among the bipolar elements.

isothermal process   A physical or chemical process in which there is no temperature change as
other factors vary. Compare ENDOTHERMIC
REACTION and EXOTHERMIC REACTION.

isotope   An atom having the same number of protons as another atom, thereby composing the
same chemical element, but having a different
number of neutrons. Thus, *deuterium* is an isotope of *hydrogen.* Some isotopes are radioactive
[e.g., *carbon 14* (an isotope of the more-common
carbon 12)]. The two extra neutrons in carbon
14 make it less stable than carbon 12.

isotropic antenna   See UNIPOLE, **2.**
isotropic radiator   See UNIPOLE, **2.**
I_{sup} Symbol for *suppressor current.*
I(t)   Symbol for INDICIAL RESPONSE.
ITD   Abbreviation for INITIAL TIME DELAY.
item   **1.** Component. **2.** Any one of a number of
similar or identical components, circuits, or
systems.
iteration   Repeating a series of arithmetic operations to arrive at a solution to a problem. Computers are commonly programmed to do this
thousands, millions, or billions of times. Such a
program must include a statement of acceptable
accuracy so that it knows when to leave the iteration loop.
iterative impedance   In a network consisting of
identical, cascaded sections, the input impedance of a section to which the output impedance
of the preceding section is made equal.
iterative routine   A program or subroutine that
provides a solution to a problem by iteration.
iterative transfer constant   Symbol, *P*. A property of ITERATIVE IMPEDANCE networks. If I_i is
the network input current and I_o is the network
output current, then $P = \log_e(I_o/I_i)$.
ITU   Abbreviation for *International Telecommunication Union.*
ITV   **1.** Abbreviation of INDUSTRIAL TELEVISION.
2. Abbreviation for INTERACTIVE TELEVISION.
I-type semiconductor   See INTRINSIC SEMI-
CONDUCTOR.
I_X Symbol for *current in a reactance.*
I_Y Symbol for *current in an admittance.*
I_Z Symbol for *current in an impedance.*
-ize   A suffix used, with some liberty, to form
verbs from nouns. In electronics, this commonly
refers to procedures or processes (e.g., to AN-
ODIZE, ELECTROCIZE, PLASTICIZE, or TRAN-
SISTORIZE).

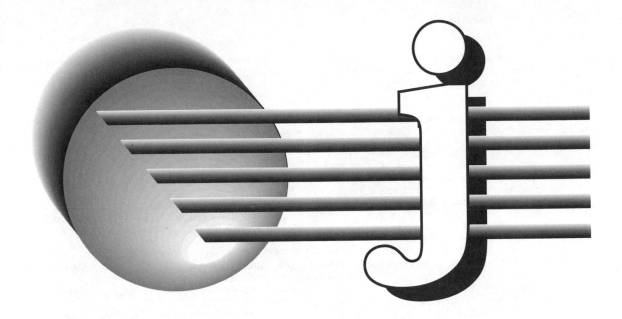

J **1.** Abbreviation for JOULE. **2.** Symbol for JACK or CONNECTOR. **3.** Symbol for EMISSIVE POWER.

j (*j* **operator**) The square root of −1; an imaginary number (usually denoted *i* in mathematics). Assigned to reactance values depicted on the vertical axis of the resistance-reactance (RX) plane in impedance vector diagrams, and whose currents are 90 degrees out of phase with the current in the resistive part of an alternating-current circuit.

jack A receptacle for a plug. A plug (a male connector) is inserted into a jack (a female connector) to complete a circuit or removed from it to break a circuit.

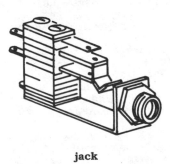

jack

jack box A (usually metallic) box or can used to hold, shield, or protect a jack or group of jacks.

jacket **1.** The outer covering on a cable, as opposed to the insulation or dielectric separating the individual conductors within the cable. **2.** An insulat-

ing outer case or wrapper on a component, such as a capacitor. **3.** A shield can or shield box. **4.** A heat-radiating or water-conducting enclosure used in cooling a power vacuum tube.

jack panel A (usually metallic) panel in which a number of jacks are mounted, usually in some order or sequence as denoted by labels.

jack panel

jackscrew In a two-piece connector, a screw for mating or separating the halves of the connector.

Jacob's law A principle concerning the behavior of motors. An electric motor develops maximum power when $E_i = 2E_{bk}$, where E_i is the applied voltage and E_{bk} is the back voltage.

JAES Abbreviation for *Journal of the Audio Engineering Society.*

jaff Colloquial term for radar jamming that combines electronic and chaff techniques.

jag Distortion caused by temporary loss of synchronization between the scanner and recorder in a facsimile system.

jam input **1.** A means of setting a logic line to the desired condition by directly applying the desired high or low voltage. **2.** A voltage applied to a logic line to force it high or low.

jammer **1.** A radio transmitter or station used for the purpose of JAMMING communications between or among other stations. **2.** A radio operator who engages in the practice of deliberately JAMMING communications between or among other stations.

jamming   The deliberate use of countermeasures, such as malicious transmission of interfering signals, to obstruct communications.

jamming effectiveness   The extent to which JAMMING is able to disrupt a service. It can be expressed quantitatively as the ratio of jamming signal voltage to jammed signal voltage. It can also be determined according to the percentage of data that is effectively obliterated.

JAN   Abbreviation of JOINT ARMY-NAVY.

janet   A system for point-to-point communication via meteor-trail forward scatter. It is generally used at very high frequencies (VHF).

Jansky noise   Wideband, high-frequency electromagnetic noise generated by objects in interstellar and intergalactic space.

J antenna   An end-fed half-wave antenna having a quarter-wave, parallel-wire matching section. The entire antenna, when oriented vertically, resembles the letter J.

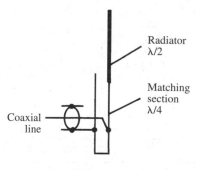

J antenna

Janus antenna array   (from *Janus*, an ancient Roman god.) A Doppler-navigation antenna array radiating forward and backward beams.

jar   **1.** (From *Leyden jar*) An obsolete unit of capacitance equal to 1/900 microfarad. **2.** The container for the elements of a storage cell.

JASA   Abbreviation for *Journal of the Acoustical Society of America.*

J-carrier system   In carrier-current (wired/wireless) telephony, a broadband system that provides 12 telephone channels at frequencies up to 140 kHz.

JCET   Abbreviation of *Joint Council on Educational Television.*

JCL   Abbreviation of *job control language.*

J-display   A radar display having a circular time base. The transmitted pulse and reflected (target) pulse are spaced around the circumference; distances can be measured circumferentially between them.

JEDEC   Acronym for *Joint Electron Device Engineering Council.*

jerk   The rate of change of acceleration; the third derivative of displacement.

JETEC   Acronym for *Joint Electron Tube Engineering Council.*

jewel bearing   A low-friction bearing used in electric meters and other sensitive devices. It takes its name from a jewel pivot (such as a sapphire) in the groove of which rides the pointed end of a rotating shaft. Also called *jeweled bearing* or *jewel.*

jezebel   A passive sonobuoy used in military applications. It detects enemy submarine noises, and transmits them by radio to a monitoring station.

JFET   Abbreviation of *junction field-effect transistor.*

JHG   Abbreviation of JOULE HEAT GRADIENT.

jig   A device constructed especially for the purpose of holding an equipment or circuit board during its repair.

jitter   A (usually small and rapid) fluctuation in a phenomenon, such as a quantity or wave, because of noise, mechanical vibration, interfering signals, or similar internal or external disturbances. It is used especially in reference to cathode-ray-tube (CRT) displays.

J/K   Abbreviation for *joule(s) per Kelvin,* the SI unit of entropy; also the unit for the Boltzmann constant.

J-K flip-flop   A transistor-resistor flip-flop stage producing an output signal even when both inputs are in the logic 1 state (high). It is so called because its input terminals are labeled J and K.

J/(kg·K)   Abbreviation for *joule(s) per kilogram Kelvin,* the SI unit of specific heat capacity.

job   A unit of computer work, usually consisting of several program runs.

job control language   An operating system language used to describe the control requirements for jobs within the system.

job control program   A program that uses control language statements and implements them as instructions controlling a job in an operating system.

job control, stacked   See SEQUENTIAL-STACKED JOB CONTROL.

job flow control   To control the order of jobs being processed by a computer to make the most efficient use of peripherals and central processor time—either manually or by an operating system.

job library   A series of related sets of data that will be loaded for a given job.

job-oriented terminal   A terminal that produces data in computer-ready form.

job statement   A control statement identifying the beginning of a series of job control statements for a job.

job step   The execution of a computer program according to a job control statement; several job steps can be specified by a job.

job stream In a processing system, a group of consecutively run jobs.

jogging Rapid, repetitive switching of power to a motor to advance its shaft by small amounts. Also called *inching*.

Johnson counter See RING COUNTER.

Johnson curve A spectral curve (important in appraising solar cell performance) for air mass zero (i.e., for conditions beyond the earth's atmosphere).

Johnson-Lark-Horowitz effect The resistivity gained by a metal or degenerate semiconductor (one in which conduction is nearly equal to that of a simple metal) because of electron scattering by impurity atoms.

Johnson noise See THERMAL NOISE.

Johnson-Q feed system See Q-ANTENNA.

join Also called *disjunction*. The logical inclusive-OR operation.

joined actuator A form of multiple circuit breaker in which the opening of one circuit results in the opening of all circuits.

joint See JUNCTION, 1.

joint circuit A communications circuit shared by two or more services.

joint communications Communication facilities being used by more than one service of the same country.

joint denial The logical NOR (NOT-OR) operation.

joint-force sensor A feedback servo device that prevents a robot joint from exerting excessive force. It works by detecting the mechanical resistance the robot arm encounters. If the resistance becomes too great, the joint force is reduced or removed.

jolt **1.** Colloquialism for KILOVOLT. **2.** Colloquialism for ELECTRIC SHOCK. **3.** Colloquialism for TRANSIENT. **4.** Colloquialism for a lightning discharge.

Joly transformer A frequency-tripling transformer whose frequency-multiplying action depends on the nonlinearity of the magnetic induction curve of the core material.

Jones plug A special form of polarized receptacle having numerous contacts.

Jones plug

j **operator** See *J*.

Josephson effect The phenomenon, predicted by Brian Josephson, wherein a current flows across the gap between the tips of two super-conductors brought close together; a high-frequency wave is generated.

Joshi effect The phenomenon whereby current in a gas changes as the result of irradiation by light.

joule Abbreviation, J. The SI unit of work. One joule is the work performed when the point of application of one newton is moved one meter in the direction of the applied force. Also see NEWTON.

Joule calorimeter A heat-measuring device that operates electrically.

Joule constant See MECHANICAL EQUIVALENT OF HEAT.

Joule effect **1.** The heat resulting from current flowing through a resistance. **2.** See MAGNETOSTRICTION.

joule heat See JOULE EFFECT, 1.

joule heat gradient The rate of change in the temperature of a resistive object through which a current flows.

joule meter An integrating wattmeter producing readings in joules.

Joule's law The rate at which heat is produced by current flowing in a constant-resistance circuit is proportional to the square of the current.

journal A file of messages within an operating system, providing information for restarts and historical analysis of system functioning.

joystick A two- or three-dimensional potentiometer with a movable lever, allowing control of a parameter, according to the position of the lever in the up/down and left/right directions. It is often used in computer games for the purpose of manipulating images on a screen. In some such devices, the lever can be rotated clockwise or counterclockwise to obtain additional functions.

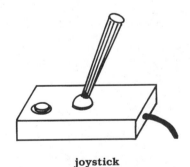

joystick

JPEG Abbreviation of *Joint Photographic Experts Group*.

JPEG image compression An image-compression scheme that eliminates redundancies, greatly reducing the necessary digital storage space. The process is fast enough to allow animated graphics at moderate speed.

JPL Abbreviation of *Jet Propulsion Laboratory*.

J-pole antenna See J ANTENNA.

J rule During transitions of orbital electrons from higher to lower energy states (accompanied by the emission of photons), changes in the inner quantum number can only be by a factor of 0 or +1, or –1.

J scan See J DISPLAY.

J scope A radar device that produces a J DISPLAY.

JSR Abbreviation of *jump to subroutine*.

JTAC Abbreviation of *Joint Technical Advisory Committee*.

judder In facsimile transmission, distortion caused by movements of the transmission or reception equipment.

juice Colloquialism for electric voltage or current.

jukebox An automatic phonograph (usually found in public places) that contains a large assortment of records.

Juliet Phonetic representation for the letter J, used in voice communications.

jump **1.** To purposely provide a short circuit around some component or circuit. **2.** Also called *branch*. In digital computer operations, a programming instruction specifying the memory location of the next instruction and directing the computer to it.

jump, conditional See CONDITIONAL BRANCH.

jump, unconditional See UNCONDITIONAL BRANCH INSTRUCTION.

jumper A short piece of wire (usually flexible, insulated, and equipped with clips) for jumping a component or circuit. See JUMP, **1.**

jumper

jump instruction See BRANCH INSTRUCTION.

junction **1.** A joint (connection) between two conductors. **2.** The region of contact between semiconductor materials of opposite type (e.g., *pn junction*). **3.** A waveguide fitting used to attach a branch waveguide to a main waveguide at an angle.

junction barrier See DEPLETION REGION.

junction battery A nuclear battery in which a silicon pn junction is irradiated by strontium 90.

junction box A (usually metal) protective box or can into which several conductors are brought together and connected.

junction capacitance In a semiconductor pn junction, the internal capacitance across the junction; it is of special interest when the junction is reverse-biased. Also called *barrier capacitance*.

junction capacitor See VOLTAGE-VARIABLE CAPACITOR.

junction diode A semiconductor diode created by joining an n-type region and p-type region as a wafer of semiconductor material, such as germanium or silicon.

junction field-effect transistor Abbreviation, JFET. A field-effect transistor in which the gate electrode consists of a pn junction.

junction filter A combination of separate low- and high-pass filters having a common input, but separate outputs. The filter is used to separate two frequency bands and transmit them to different circuits.

junction laser See LASER DIODE.

junction light source See LIGHT-EMITTING DIODE.

junction loss **1.** The loss that occurs in a telephone circuit at connecting points. **2.** Loss in a semiconductor pn junction. **3.** Loss occurring at an electrical connection because of poor bonding.

junction photocell A photoconductive or photovoltaic cell that is essentially a light-sensitive JUNCTION DIODE.

junction point **1.** A point at which two or more conductors, components, or circuits join in an electrical connection. **2.** The point in a computer routine at which one of several choices is made.

junction rectifier A semiconductor rectifier that is, in effect, a heavy-duty junction diode, or the equivalent of several heavy-duty junction diodes in combination.

junction station A microwave relay station joining one or more microwave radio legs to the main route or through route.

junction transistor A transistor in which the emitter and collector consists of junctions (see JUNCTION, **2**) between p and n semiconductor regions. Compare POINT-CONTACT TRANSISTOR.

junctor In a crossbar system, a circuit that bridges frames of a switching unit and terminates in a switching device on each frame.

Jungian-world theory The theory that societies keep repeating the same mistakes, generation after generation. Of interest to some researchers in artificial intelligence. It has been suggested that supercomputers might help find solutions to recurring social problems.

justification **1.** The alignment of text along the left margin, the right margin, or both margins. **2.** A method of altering the speed of a digital signal so that it can be received by equipment designed for a different data speed. The rate of speed is lower after this process is applied. Also called *pulse stuffing*.

justify **1.** To adjust the printing of words for aligned left and/or right margins. **2.** In computer operations, to shift an item in a register so that the most- or least-significant digit is at the corresponding end of the register.

just-operate value The current or voltage level at which a relay or similar device just closes. Also called *just-close value*.

just-release value The current or voltage level at which a relay or similar device just opens. Also called *just-open value*.

just scale A musical scale of three consecutive triads, the highest note of each being the lowest note of the next. Each triad has the ratio 4:5:6 or 10:12:15.

jute Tar-saturated fiber, such as hemp, used as a protective covering for cable.

jute-protected cable A cable whose outer covering is a wrapping of JUTE or similar material.

juxtaposed elements Components placed or mounted side by side.

juxtaposed images Images (e.g., those on the screen of a dual-beam cathode-ray tube) that are close to each other for simultaneous viewing, but do not overlap at any point.

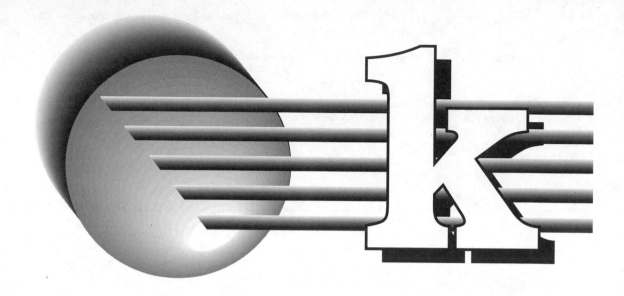

K **1.** General symbol for CONSTANT. **2.** Symbol for POTASSIUM. **3.** Symbol for KELVIN. **4.** Radiotelegraph symbol for *go ahead* or *over.* **5.** Symbol for CATHODE. **6.** Symbol for KILOBYTE. **7.** Abbreviation of KILOHM (k is preferred). **8.** Abbreviation of KILO-.

k **1.** Abbreviation of KILO-. **2.** Symbol for the BOLTZMANN CONSTANT. **3.** General symbol for a mathematical constant. **4.** Symbol for DIELECTRIC CONSTANT. **5.** Abbreviation for KILOHM.

kA Abbreviation of KILOAMPERE.

Karnaugh map A logic chart showing switching-function relationships and used in computer logic analysis to determine quickly the simplest form of logic circuit for a given function. The Karnaugh map is sometimes regarded as a tabular form of the Venn diagram.

Kansas City standard A frequency-shift modulation standard for a computer/tape-recorder interface. Also called *byte standard.*

KB **1.** Abbreviation of KEYBOARD. **2.** Abbreviation of KILOBYTE.

K band The 18- to 27-GHz band of frequencies, pertaining to their use in radar applications.

kcal Abbreviation of KILOCALORIE.

K carrier system A four-wire carrier-current telephone system using frequencies up to 60 kHz and providing 12 channels.

kCi Abbreviation of KILOCURIE.

kcs Abbreviation of *kilocharacter per second* (1000 characters per second).

K display See K SCAN.

KDP Abbreviation of POTASSIUM DIHYDROGEN PHOSPHATE, a ferrolelectric material.

keeper A small iron bar placed across the poles of a permanent magnet to forestall demagnetization.

K electron In certain atoms, one of the electrons whose orbit is nearest the nucleus.

Kel-f Abbreviation of *polymonochlorotrifluorethylene,* a high-temperature insulating material.

Kellie bond **1.** The junction of two mated electrically conductive surfaces that are held together by an adhesive that exhibits negligible resistance thermally and electrically when set. **2.** To make a thermally conductive joint, as from a heatsink to a chassis or component.

kelvin (Lord Kelvin, 1824–1907) Symbol, K. The SI unit of thermodynamic temperature; 1 K = 1/273.16, the thermodynamic temperature of the triple point of water.

Kelvin absolute electrometer An electrostatic voltmeter consisting of a movable metal plate (or plates) and a stationary metal plate (or plates)

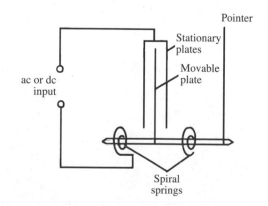

Kelvin absolute electrometer

between which voltage is applied. The movable plate(s) is displaced over a distance that is proportional to the potential, against the torque of a return spring.

Kelvin balance An apparatus for measuring current in terms of magnetic pull. A coil is attached to each end of the beam of a balance, and coils ride directly above two stationary coils. Current flows through all coils, making one pair attractive and the other repellent, thus unbalancing the beam. Balance is restored by sliding a weight whose position along a graduated scale indicates the current strength.

Kelvin contacts Electrical contacts designed to eliminate the effect of lead resistance on the accuracy of measurement. Two leads run to each test point, one lead carrying the test signal and the other leading directly to the measuring instrument.

Kelvin double bridge A special bridge for measuring very low resistance (0.1 ohm or less). The arrangement of the bridge reduces the effects of contact resistance that causes significant error when such low resistances are connected to conventional resistance bridges.

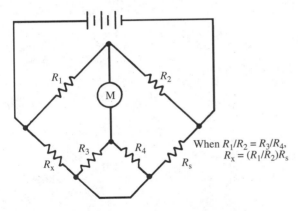

When $R_1/R_2 = R_3/R_4$,
$R_x = (R_1/R_2)R_s$

Kelvin double bridge

Kelvin replenisher A static generator consisting of two pairs of concentric, rotating semicircular conductors connected to brushes. The machine can be regarded as a rotating electric doubler.

Kelvin scale See ABSOLUTE SCALE.

Kelvin temperature scale See ABSOLUTE SCALE.

Kelvin voltmeter An electrostatic voltmeter in which an assembly of figure-8-shaped metal plates rotates between the plates of a stationary assembly when a voltage is applied between the assemblies. The length of the arc of rotation is proportional to the electrostatic attraction and, thus, to the applied voltage.

Kendall effect Distortion in a facsimile record caused by unwanted modulation produced by a carrier signal.

Kennelly-Heaviside layer (A.E. Kennelly, 1861–1939; Oliver Heaviside, 1850–1925) An early name for ionized regions in the upper atmosphere. These regions reflect and refract radio waves at certain frequencies. There are several layers at various altitudes. Also see IONOSPHERE and IONOSPHERIC LAYERS.

keraunograph A meteorological instrument for detecting distant electrical storms. In its simplest form, it consists of a galvanometer connected in series with an antenna and ground.

keraunophone A radio-receiving KERAUNOGRAPH.

kernel Inside an electrical conductor, a line along which the magnetic field strength is zero. Generally, this line is near the center of the conductor.

Kerr cell A nitrobenzene-filled cell that makes use of the KERR ELECTRO-OPTICAL EFFECT. It can function as an electric light shutter or control.

Kerr electro-optical effect The tendency of certain dielectric materials to become double-refracting in an electric field.

Kerr magneto-optical effect The tendency of glass and some other solids and liquids to become double-refracting in a magnetic field.

Kerst induction accelerator See BETATRON.

keV Abbreviation of KILOELECTRONVOLT.

Kew magnetometer A special magnetometer used to measure the intensity of the earth's magnetic field, and also the magnetic declination at a given point on the earth's surface. The device is designed for very high accuracy, using magnifying lenses.

key 1. A specialized hand-operated switch, used to make and break a circuit repetitively to form the dot and dash signals of telegraphy. In recent years, this device has been largely replaced by electronic keyers. **2.** A projection or pin that guides the insertion of a plug-in component into a holder or socket. **3.** A digit or digits used to locate or identify a computer record (but not necessarily part of the record).

keyboard An array of lettered or numbered, low-torque push buttons, used to enter information into a computer, telegraph, teletypewriter, or automatic control system.

keyboard computer A digital computer in which the input device is an electrical keyboard of the typewriter or calculator type.

keyboard entry The operation of a keyboard to enter information into a computer for processing.

keyboard keyer A device for automatically sending Morse code using a typewriter-like keyboard, rather than a paddle or straight key. Each key on the keyboard, when pressed, produces the complete character and a space following it. Most keyboard keyers have buffers to allow typing well ahead of the code being sent, with insertion of all the correct spaces. The speed range is usually from about 5 words per minute (wpm) to 60 or 70 wpm, although some keyboard keyers are programmed for speeds over 100 wpm.

keyboard lockout   A keyboard interlock in a data transmission circuit that prevents data from being transmitted while the transmitter of another station on the same circuit is operating.

keyboard send-receive unit   A teletypewriter lacking an automatic input device.

key cabinet   In a telephone system, a facility that shows a subscriber which lines are busy and which lines are open.

key chirp   A chirping sound in a received signal, resulting from slight frequency shift when a radiotelegraph transmitter is keyed. It does not occur with a well-designed transmitter.

key-click filter   An inductance-capacitance (LC) or resistance-capacitance (RC) filter for smoothing a keying wave to eliminate KEY CLICKS. It functions by optimizing the rise and decay times of the keyed waveform.

key clicks   Excessive bandwidth of a radiotelegraph signal that can result when a keyed signal has rise and decay times that are too rapid. Produces characteristic clicking or popping sounds, with resulting interference, in receivers tuned to frequencies near that of the transmitted signal. A KEY-CLICK FILTER can eliminate this.

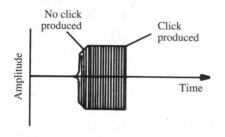

key clicks

keyed AGC   A controlled automatic gain control (AGC) system in a television receiver circuit. The AGC acts when the horizontal sync pulse appears; it is inactive between pulses. This prevents unwanted actuation of the AGC by noise transients and picture-signal elements.

keyed clamp   A clamping circuit that uses a control signal to determine the clamping time.

keyed interval   In a transmission system that is keyed periodically, an interval beginning with a change in state and having a duration of the shortest time between changes in state.

keyed rainbow generator   For testing of color-television receivers, a signal generator that produces a rainbow color pattern on the screen (i.e., a set of 10 vertical color bars representing the spectrum, with blank bars in between). The pattern results from gating the 3.56-MHz oscillator in the receiver at a frequency of 189 kHz.

keyer   An automatic device for keying a radiotelegraph transmitter or wire telegraph circuit. The keyer can operate from perforated tape, an embossed disk, magnetic tape, or other similar recording.

keyer adaptor   A modulated-signal detector that produces a direct-current signal having an amplitude sympathetic with the modulation; it provides the keying signal for a frequency-shift exciter in radio facsimile transmission.

keying   1. The modulation of a carrier by switching it on and off. It is commonly used in radiotelegraphy. 2. The modulation of a carrier by switching its frequency between two defined values. It is also called FREQUENCY-SHIFT KEYING (FSK) and it is used in data transmission. 3. The modulation of a carrier with an audio tone that is switched on and off. The carrier can be modulated via amplitude modulation (AM), frequency modulation (FM), pulse modulation, or any other form that will convey the audio tone. It is occasionally used in radiotelegraphy at very-high frequencies (VHF) and above. Also called *audio keying.* 4. The modulation of a carrier with an audio tone whose frequency is switched between two defined values. The carrier can be modulated via amplitude modulation (AM), frequency modulation (FM), pulse modulation, or any other form that will convey the audio tone. It is commonly used in data transmission at VHF and above. Also called AUDIO FREQUENCY-SHIFT KEYING (AFSK).

keying chirp   A rapid change in the frequency of a continuous-wave signal, occurring at the beginning of each code element. In the receiver, the resulting sound is a chirp.

keying error rate   In data transmission, the ratio of incorrectly keyed signals to the total number of signals keyed.

keying filter   See KEY-CLICK FILTER.

keying frequency   1. In audio-keyed radiotelegraphy, the audio frequency (tone) of the dot and dash signals (as opposed to the carrier frequency). 2. In radiotelegraphy, the transmission speed (see KEYING SPEED). 3. The number of times per second that a black-line signal occurs while an object is scanned in a facsimile system.

keying monitor   A simple detector used by an operator to listen to the keying of a radiotelegraph transmitter.

keying speed   The speed (in words per minute) of a telegraph or radio-telegraph transmission.

keying transients   1. Transients arising from the keying of a radiotelegraph transmitter or wire telegraph circuit. 2. Transients that arise from the repetitive making and breaking of any circuit.

keyless ringing   In a telephone system, ringing that begins as soon as the calling plug is put in the appropriate jack on the jack panel.

key pulse   In telephone operations, a signaling system in which the desired numbers are entered by pressing corresponding pushbuttons or keys.

key punch A keyboard-operated machine for recording information by perforating a tape or cards.

keyshelf A shelf that supports manually operated telephone switchboard keys.

key station The master (control) station in a communications or control network.

keystoning A form of video image distortion in which the top of the picture is wider than the bottom, or vice versa. Thus, the image area is shaped like a trapezoid, rather than a rectangle.

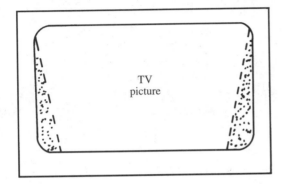

keystoning

key switch 1. A lockable switch that is operated by inserting and turning a key in it. 2. A switch having a long handle that transmits motion to the mechanism through a cam. 3. See KEY, 1. 4. The separate short-circuiting switch sometimes mounted on the base of a telegraph key (see KEY, 1). 5. A switch that actuates the keys of an electronic organ.

key-to-disk unit A keyboard-to-magnetic-disk data-processing unit.

keyway A groove or slot into which a mating key slides to position a plug-in component (see KEY, 2).

keyword In information retrieval systems, the significant word in the title describing a document (e.g., in the title "A Primer on French Cuisine," the word *cuisine* would be the keyword, the others having no singular significance).

kg Abbreviation of KILOGRAM.

kgC Abbreviation of KILOGRAM-CALORIE.

kgm Abbreviation of KILOGRAM-METER.

kg/m³ Symbol for KILOGRAMS PER CUBIC METER, the SI unit of density.

K-H layer See KENNELLY-HEAVISIDE LAYER.

kHz Abbreviation of KILOHERTZ.

kick 1. To place into sudden operation, as by the quick, forcible closure of a switch or the rapid application of an enabling pulse. 2. See TRIGGER. 3. Colloquialism for an abrupt, momentary electric shock.

kickback 1. The counter EMF that appears across an inductor when current is interrupted. 2. See FLYBACK.

kickback power supply A high-voltage power supply using the flyback principle. See FLYBACK.

kidney joint A waveguide coupling used in radar. The joint is flexible, or can consist of an air gap, to allow rotation of the antenna.

Kikuchi lines A characteristic spectral pattern produced by the electrons scattered when an electron beam strikes a crystal.

killer 1. A pulse or other signal used to disable a circuit temporarily (e.g., a blanking pulse). 2. In personal computing, an application of such importance that it alone serves as the motivation for someone to purchase or upgrade a system. Common examples are word processing and on-line communications.

killer circuit 1. A circuit that disables some function of a system, such as the audio in a television receiver. 2. The blanking circuit in a radar receiver. 3. A circuit that prevents responses to side-lobe signals in a repeater or transponder.

Kilo Pronunciation, *KEY-low*. Phonetic alphabet code word for the letter K.

kilo- Abbreviation, K or k. 1. A prefix meaning thousand(s). 2. In digital data applications, a prefix meaning 2^{10} (1024).

kiloampere Abbreviation, kA. A unit of current equal to 1000 amperes.

kilobit A unit of digital data equal to 2^{10} (1024) bits. Also see BIT.

kilobyte Abbreviation, K or KB. A unit of digital data equal to 2^{10} (1024) bytes. Also see BYTE.

kilocalorie Abbreviation, kcal. A large unit of heat; 1 kcal equals 1000 calories. See CALORIE.

kilocurie Abbreviation, kCi. A large unit of radioactivity equal to 3.71×10^{13} disintegrations per second; 1 kCi equals 1000 curies. Also see CURIE, MEGACURIE, MICROCURIE, and MILLICURIE.

kilocycle See KILOHERTZ.

kiloelectronvolt Abbreviation, keV. A large unit of electrical energy equal to 1000 electronvolts. See ELECTRONVOLT.

kilogauss A large unit of magnetic flux density; 1 kilogauss equals 1000 gauss or 0.1 tesla.

kilogram Abbreviation, kg. The SI base unit of mass; it is equal to 1000 grams.

kilogram-calorie The heat required to raise 1 kilogram of water 1°C.

kilogram-meter Abbreviation, kgm. A unit of mechanical energy (work); 1 kgm is the energy required to raise a mass of 1 kilogram vertically by a distance of 1 meter (equal to 7.2334 foot-pounds). Also see JOULE.

kilohertz Abbreviation, kHz. A unit of frequency; 1 kHz equals 1000 Hz.

kilohm Symbol, kΩ. A unit of high resistance, reactance, or impedance; 1 kΩ equals 1000 ohms.

kilojoule Abbreviation, kJ. A unit of energy or work; 1 kJ equals 1000 joules. See JOULE.

kilolumen Abbreviation, klm. A unit of luminous flux equal to 1000 lumens. See LUMEN.

kilomega- See GIGA-.

kilomegahertz See GIGAHERTZ.

kilometer Abbreviation, km. A large metric unit of linear measure; 1 km equals 1000 meters (3280.8 feet).

kilo-oersted Abbreviation, kOe. A unit of magnetic field strength; 1 kOe equals 1000 oersteds. See OERSTED.

kiloroentgen Abbreviation, kr. A large unit of radioactive radiation; 1 kr equals 1000 roentgens. See ROENTGEN.

kilorutherford Abbreviation, krd. A large unit of radioactivity equal to 10^9 disintegrations per second.

kilovar A compound term coined from *kilo-* and *VAR* (the abbreviation of *volt-amperes reactive*). It is equal to a reactive power of 1000 watts.

kilovar-hour A large unit of reactive electrical energy, equivalent to 1000 reactive watts manifested for a period of one hour.

kilovolt Abbreviation, kV. A unit of high voltage; 1 kV equals 1000 V.

kilovolt-ampere Abbreviation, kVA. A unit of high power that gives the TRUE POWER in a direct-current circuit and the APPARENT POWER in an alternating-current circuit; 1 kVA equals 1000 W. Also see DC POWER.

kilovolt-ampere reactive See KILOVAR.

kilovoltmeter A voltmeter designed to measure thousands of volts (kilovolts).

kilowatt Abbreviation, kW. A unit of high power; 1 kW equals 1000 watts. Also see WATT.

kilowatt-hour Abbreviation, kWh. A common unit of electrical energy; 1 kWh equals 1000 watt hours, or the equivalent of 1000 watts dissipated for a period of one hour. Also see ENERGY, KILOWATT-HOUR, POWER, WATT-HOUR, and WATT-SECOND.

kilowatt-hour meter A motorized meter for recording (electrical) power consumption in kilowatt-hours. Also see KILOWATT-HOUR.

kinematograph A motion picture camera. Also called CINEMATOGRAPH and KINETOGRAPH.

kine **1.** See KINESCOPE, **1.** **2.** See KINESCOPE RECORDING.

kinescope **1.** The picture tube in a television receiver. **2.** See KINESCOPE RECORDING.

kinescope recorder A film or tape apparatus for recording television pictures.

kinescope recording A motion-picture or videotape made from the screen (or taken from the circuit) of a television picture tube.

kinetic energy The energy associated with particles, bodies, or electric charge carriers in motion.

kinetograph See KINEMATOGRAPH.

kinetoscope A motion-picture projector.

kiosk A computer and peripherals set up for the purpose of multimedia use by the general pub-

lic. It generally uses a touch screen for inputting data and must be ruggedly constructed to tolerate rough treatment.

Kirchhoff's first law The sum of the currents flowing out of a point in a direct-current circuit equals the sum of the currents flowing into that point.

Kirchhoff's laws (Gustav Robert Kirchhoff, 1824–1887) Two laws of electric circuits that account for the behavior of certain networks. See KIRCHHOFF'S FIRST LAW and KIRCHHOFF'S SECOND LAW.

First law: $I_1 + I_2 + I_3 = I_4 + I_5$

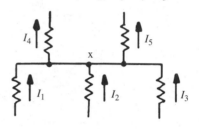

Second law: $V_1 + V_2 + V_3 + V_4 = V_5$

Kirchhoff's laws

Kirchhoff's second law The algebraic sum of all the voltage drops around a direct-current circuit (including supply voltages) is always equal to zero.

kit A selection of components, associated equipment, supplies (such as wire and hardware), and instructions for constructing a piece of electronic equipment.

kite-supported antenna A longwire antenna that uses a kite as a support for the far (nonstation) end. A tether is used to reduce the chance that the kite will fly away with wire attached. It was used by Marconi in early experiments with radio. Radio amateurs and shortwave listeners sometimes use this scheme at low and medium frequencies. It is a dangerous antenna because of electrostatic buildup, a tendency to attract lightning, the possibility of its breaking loose, and the risk that it might contact utility lines.

kJ Abbreviation of KILOJOULE.

k-line programming A method by which an artificially intelligent robot can learn as it does a job, so it will have an easier time doing the same job in the future. The robot controller actually learns from the robot's mistakes.

Klipsch horn A loudspeaker that includes a folded low-frequency horn housed in a corner enclosure.

klm Abbreviation of KILOLUMEN.

kludge **1.** A crude, useless, or grossly inefficient machine or process. **2.** A hastily contrived prototype of a circuit or device, put together for the purpose of testing a concept, but not intended as a representative of a production unit.

klydonograph A device that photographically records the voltage gradient in the presence of an electric field.

klystron A microwave tube whose operation is based on the velocity modulation of an electron beam by buncher and cavity reentrant cavities.

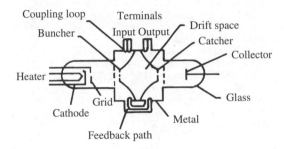

klystron

klystron amplifier A microwave amplifier using a klystron.

klystron harmonic generator A frequency-multiplying power amplifier using a klystron. It is used at microwave radio frequencies.

klystron oscillator A klystron operated as a self-excited microwave oscillator.

klystron repeater A microwave amplifier in which a klystron inserted in a waveguide boosts the amplitude of an incoming signal.

km Abbreviation of KILOMETER.

knee **1.** A sharp bend in a response curve for a device, usually indicating the onset of conduction, saturation, cutoff, pinchoff, or limiting action. It applies especially to semiconductor diodes and transistors. **2.** The characteristics of a device when it is operated at a point in the vicinity of a sharp bend in its response curve.

knee noise Electrical noise generated by rapidly repeating current fluctuations at the knee in a Zener diode.

knife-edge diffraction The lessening of atmospheric signal attenuation when the signal passes over a sharp obstacle and is diffracted.

knife switch A switch composed of one or more flat blades roughly resembling knife blades, which are slid firmly between the jaws of pinching contacts to close a circuit.

knob **1.** A (usually round and insulated) finger dial for adjusting a variable electronic component, such as a potentiometer, variable capacitor, or rotary switch. **2.** A solid round insulator usually having a low diameter to height ratio. **3.** A small ball- or rod-shaped electrode or protuberance.

knocker A fire-control radar subassembly of synchronizing and triggering circuits.

knockout An area in a metal box or chassis that is easily removed by tapping or knocking to provide an opening.

knot A unit of speed, corresponding to 1 nautical mile per hour. A speed of 1 knot is about 1.15 statute miles per hour; a speed of 1 statute mile per hour is about 0.868 knots. It is used by mariners for specifying speeds at sea, and also occasionally by meteorologists in specifying wind speeds.

knowledge The data in a computer and in mass-storage media, accumulated over time and capable of being put to practical use.

kOe Abbreviation of KILO-OERSTED.

Kolster decremeter An absorption wavemeter with a movable scale; it permits measurement of the decrement of a radio wave.

Kooman antenna A unidirectional antenna consisting of stacked, full-wave, center-fed driven elements, and a reflecting screen.

Korner Killer Trade name for an acoustically absorbent object that reduces sound echoes that can occur in enclosed rooms. The name results because the device works best when placed in a corner (where two walls meet).

Kovar An alloy of cobalt, iron, and nickel. It is used mostly in glass-to-metal seals because it has characteristics of both kinds of material.

Kozanowski oscillator A positive-grid vacuum-tube UHF oscillator circuit using two tubes having cylindrical elements, and a pair of parallel-wire tanks.

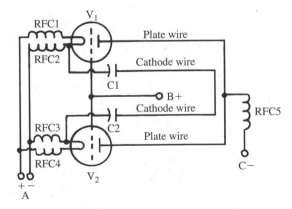

Kozanowski oscillator

Kr Symbol for KRYPTON.

kr Abbreviation of KILOROENTGEN.

K radiation   X rays emitted from an atom when an electron becomes a K electron.

kraft paper   Strong brown paper used for insulation and as the dielectric of paper capacitors.

Kramer system   A system of three-phase motor control providing constant horsepower, and having a direct-current (dc) motor coupled to the shaft of a wound-rotor three-phase induction motor. The dc supply for the motor also supplies a rotary converter. The speed-control rheostat is connected in series with the field of the motor and the dc power supply.

Kraus antenna   A bidirectional, flat-top beam antenna consisting of a pair of closely spaced dipoles. Several such sections can be connected in series by crisscrossing the wires at voltage loops.

krd   Abbreviation of KILORUTHERFORD.

Kryptol   A mixture of clay, graphite, and silicon carbide. It is used in electric heater elements because of its low resistance and high melting point.

krypton   Symbol, Kr. An inert, gaseous element. Atomic number, 36. Atomic weight, 83.80. Krypton is present in trace amounts in the earth's atmosphere.

K scan   In radar operations, a modified A-scan used in aiming antennas in which two pips are displayed; their relative amplitudes indicate the antenna-aiming error.

K series   A series of spectral lines for the shortest wavelengths of radiation from the innermost electron shell of a radiating atom.

KSR   Abbreviation of *keyboard send-receive* unit.

Ku band   A band of microwave frequencies between approximately 12 and 18 GHz.

Kundt's law   The index of refraction of a medium does not change continuously with wavelength in the absorption bands.

Kundt tube   A device used to measure the speed of sound in gases under various conditions. Suspended particles in the gas form standing waves that can be easily seen. Knowing the frequency of the disturbance and the distance between nodes of the standing waves, the speed can be determined. The pressure and density of the gas, as well as temperature and humidity, affect the speed.

kV   Abbreviation of KILOVOLT.

kVA   Abbreviation of KILOVOLT-AMPERE.

kVAR   Abbreviation of REACTIVE KILOVOLT-AMPERE.

kVARh   Abbreviation of KILOVAR-HOUR.

kW   Abbreviation of KILOWATT.

kWh   Abbreviation of KILOWATT-HOUR.

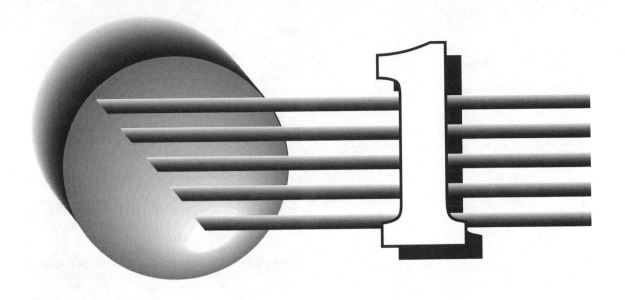

L **1.** Symbol for INDUCTANCE. **2.** Symbol for MEAN LIFE. **3.** Abbreviation of LOW. **4.** Resembling the capital letter L in physical shape. **5.** Symbol for LAPLACE TRANSFORM.

l **1.** Symbol for LENGTH. **2.** Abbreviation of LITER. **3.** Subscript for LOW. **4.** Abbreviation of LUMEN; also abbreviated *lm* (preferred) and *lum.*

La Symbol for LANTHANUM.

label **1.** A symbolic group of characters that identifies an area of memory, an item of data, a file, or a record. **2.** A name assigned to a source program instruction step to identify the step as a coding entry point, or to make the step usable as a reference point for entry to the routine or subroutine in which it appears.

label group A collection of labels, usually of the same type, held in an operating system.

label identifier Within a label, a character set used to name the kind of item labeled.

label record A record identifying a file recorded on a magnetic storage medium (e.g., magnetic tape).

label set A collection of labels having a common label identifier.

labile oscillator A frequency-controlled local oscillator.

laboratory conditions The environmental, mechanical, and electrical parameters characteristic of controlled conditions. Actual operating conditions can be much different.

laboratory-grade instrument An instrument having the high accuracy and stability that suit it to precision measurements in a laboratory. Also called PRECISION INSTRUMENT. Compare SERVICE-TYPE INSTRUMENT.

laboratory power supply A regulated direct-current source whose adjustable output is less than 10 kV at no more than 500 W.

laboratory standard See PRIMARY STANDARD and SECONDARY STANDARD.

labyrinth speaker A loudspeaker whose enclosure (a wooden cubicle) includes a folded pipe or acoustic transmission line (behind the speaker); the inner walls are lined with a sound-absorbent material. When the pipe, which is open-ended, is half as long as the wavelength of the frequency being reproduced, the sound emerging from the open end is in phase with that radiated by the front of the speaker and, therefore, reinforces it.

laced wiring Circuit wiring in which wires or cables run parallel in bundles that are tied together with LACING CORD.

lacing cord Strong, sometimes waxed cord used to tie together wires running parallel in a bundle. Also see LACED WIRING.

lacquer disk See CELLULOSE-NITRATE DISK.

lacquer-film capacitor A fixed capacitor with a plastic film dielectric; the film is applied as liquid lacquer to the metal foil.

lacquer master A master recording made on a CELLULOSE-NITRATE DISK.

lacquer original See LACQUER MASTER.

ladar Abbreviation of LASER DOPPLER RADAR. Also abbreviated *lopplar.*

ladder attenuator See LADDER-TYPE ATTENUATOR.

ladder filter A form of delay line or filter. It generally consists of series and parallel impedances, either in a balanced or unbalanced form.

ladder line   See AIR-INSULATED LINE.

ladder network   A network consisting of several L sections in cascade. See L SECTION, **1, 2, 3**.

ladder-type attenuator   An attenuator consisting of a ladder network equipped with a switching circuit for selecting the output at various sections.

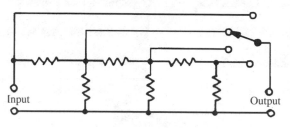

ladder-type attenuator

LAFOT   Coded weather broadcasts aired every six hours by the U.S. Weather Bureau through marine radiotelephone broadcasting stations for the Great Lakes region.

lag   In computations relating the phase of alternating-current signals, the extent to which one quantity follows another in time (e.g., the current lags the voltage by 90 degrees in a pure inductive reactance). Compare LEAD.

lagged-demand meter   A meter with a built-in time delay.

lagging current   Current that follows voltage (in time). Also see LAG.

lagging load   A load in which current lags behind voltage (i.e., an inductive load). Compare LEADING LOAD.

lag network   A phase-shifting circuit containing series-resistance and shunt-capacitance arms. It produces a lagging phase shift. Compare LEAD NETWORK.

lambda wave   An electromagnetic disturbance that travels along the surface of an object. An example is the surface wave characteristic of low-frequency propagation.

lambert   Symbol, L. The centimeter-gram-second (cgs) unit of luminance, equal to the brightness of an ideal diffusing surface that radiates or reflects light at 1 lumen per square centimeter. The SI (preferred) unit of luminance is the candela per square meter (cd/m^2); 1 lambert equals 10^4 cd/m^2. Also see CANDELA.

Lambert's law of illumination   The illumination of a surface by a point light source is inversely proportional to the square of the distance between the surface and the source. If the surface is not perpendicular to the rays, the illumination is proportional to the cosine of the angle of incidence.

laminated armature   An armature for a motor or generator, made of stacked laminations.

laminated contact   A switch contact consisting of a number of laminations—each contacting a conducting counterpart.

laminated core   A core for a transformer, choke, relay, or similar device, made of stacked laminations.

laminated disk   A layered recording disk.

laminated pole   A pole within a motor, generator, relay, electromagnet, or similar device, made of stacked laminations.

lamination   **1.** A relatively thin sheet of metal cut to a required shape to be stacked with other similar sheets to form a laminated core or pole. **2.** A relatively thin sheet of plastic that is bonded together and heat-formed with other similar sheets to produce a sheet or piece of desired thickness and strength.

lamp   A device for converting electrical energy into visible light. The term includes a number of devices (e.g., arc lamp, fluorescent tube, incandescent lamp, mercury-vapor lamp, and neon bulb).

lamp-bank resistor   A makeshift heavy-duty resistor consisting of several incandescent lamps arranged so that they can be switched in various series, parallel, and series-parallel combinations to vary the resistance provided by the filaments.

lampblack   Carbon obtained from soot deposited by a smoky flame. The substance is used as the basic material for some resistors.

lamp cord   A two-wire insulated cord, used with low-wattage alternating-current appliances at 117 volts. The wire is usually stranded copper equivalent to American Wire Gauge (AWG) #16.

lamp dimmer   See DIMMER.

lamp driver   A usually single-stage circuit for amplifying a small pulse to drive an indicator lamp.

lamp extractor   A special tool used to insert or extract miniature lamps for electronic equipment.

lamp jack   A receptacle with a spring release that holds a small incandescent bulb. The bulb is removed and replaced by pushing and twisting.

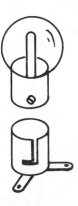

lamp jack

lamp-type expander   A volume expander in which the tungsten filament in an incandescent lamp serves as the nonlinear resistor.

lamp-type readout   For counters, calculators, and digital meters, a readout device in which each digit is indicated by a lamp.

LAN   Abbreviation of LOCAL AREA NETWORK.

land   **1.** The flat, reflective surface between pits on a compact disc (CD). Compare PIT, **1**. **2.** The thin vinyl wall between grooves on a phonograph record. **3.** A bonding point in a microcircuit. **4.** Pertaining to earthbound communications stations.

Land camera   See POLAROID CAMERA.

landing beacon   The aircraft landing-beam transmitter. Also see LANDING BEAM.

landing beam   A highly directional airport radio signal beamed upward to guide aircraft landing during conditions of poor visibility.

landline   A telephone or telegraph circuit completed with wires.

landmark beacon   Any beacon that is not an airway or airport beacon.

land mobile service   Two-way radio service between a base station and mobile land vehicles, or among mobile land vehicles.

land mobile station   A radio station aboard a mobile, earthbound vehicle.

land return   Ground reflection of radar signals back to the transmitter.

land station   A fixed ground station.

Langevin ion   An electrically charged particle, such as a grain of dust or droplet of water, resulting from the accumulation of ions.

Langmuir dark space   In a luminous gas discharge, the dark region around a negatively charged probe inserted into the positive column. Compare CROOKES' DARK SPACE.

Langmuir's law   See CHILD'S LAW.

language   In digital-computer operations, any one of the detailed systems for representing data, instructions, and procedures through the use of symbols and symbol sequences. See MACHINE LANGUAGE, ASSEMBLY LANGUAGE, COBOL, FORTRAN, and BASIC.

language laboratory   An electronic contribution to the teaching and learning of languages. It consists of recordings in a language being studied and all the equipment associated with recording, playback, and monitoring. Students listen to the speech of experts in the language record, listen to, and later erase their own utterances in the language.

language translation   **1.** The conversion of statements in one computer language to equivalent statements in another. **2.** The conversion of one written natural language into another (e.g., French to Russian) by means of a computer program.

language translator   **1.** An assembly program, compiler, or other routine used for translation between computer languages. **2.** A high-level program that allows a computer to translate one written natural language into another (e.g., Chinese to Italian).

L antenna   See INVERTED-L ANTENNA.

lanthanum   Symbol, La. An elemental metal of the rare-earth group. Atomic number, 57. Atomic weight, 138.906.

lanyard   A wire or cable used to quickly pull apart the halves of a quick-disconnect connector.

lap   A device used for grinding piezoelectric crystals for resonance at a desired frequency.

lap dissolve   The simultaneous fading out of one televised scene while another is fading in so that one is apparently dissolving into the next. It is also applicable to motion pictures.

lapel microphone   A small microphone that is clipped to a lapel of a user's jacket or coat.

lap joint   An overlapping splice of two conductors.

Laplace transform   Symbol, *L*. An operator that reduces the work of solving certain differential equations by permitting them to be handled by simpler algebraic methods.

lapping   Fine-tuning quartz crystal plates by moving them over a flat plate coated with a liquid abrasive.

laptop computer   See NOTEBOOK COMPUTER.

lap winding   In a motor or generator armature, a winding in which the opposite ends of each coil are connected to the adjoining segments of the commutator.

lap wrap   **1.** A form of asbestos cloth wire insulation. **2.** A method of wrapping with electrical tape, in which there is considerable overlap among the turns of the tape.

large calorie   See KILOGRAM-CALORIE.

large-scale integration   Abbreviation, LSI. The inclusion of more than 100 transistors, performing various individual, but interrelated circuit functions, on a single integrated-circuit chip.

large signal   A relatively high-amplitude signal that traverses so large a part of the operating characteristic of a device that nonlinear portions of the characteristic are usually encountered. Compare SMALL SIGNAL.

large-signal analysis   The rigorous study of circuits and devices that process large signals.

large-signal component   **1.** A coefficient or parameter such as amplification, transconductance, or dynamic resistance, measured under conditions of large-signal operation. Also see LARGE SIGNAL and LARGE-SIGNAL EQUIVALENT CIRCUIT. **2.** A device designed for operation at high signal levels.

large-signal equivalent circuit   For a given transistor circuit, the equivalent circuit at high signal levels (i.e., at amplitudes approaching saturation and cutoff levels). Also see EQUIVALENT CIRCUIT.

large-signal operation   The use of a circuit or device at signal levels sufficiently high so that nonlinear portions of the characteristic are usually encountered. Compare SMALL-SIGNAL OPERATION.

large-signal transistor   See POWER TRANSISTOR.

large-signal voltage gain   In an integrated-circuit amplifier, the voltage gain under open-loop conditions, determined as the difference in the output voltage divided by the difference in the input voltage. It is usually specified in volts per millivolt or volts per microvolt.

Larmor orbit   The path followed by a charged particle in a constant magnetic field. Because of interaction between the external field and the field generated by the particle, the charged particle travels in a circular path.

laryngaphone   See THROAT MICROPHONE.

LASCR   Abbreviation of LIGHT-ACTIVATED SILICON-CONTROLLED RECTIFIER.

LASCS   Abbreviation of LIGHT-ACTIVATED SILICON-CONTROLLED SWITCH.

lase   To emit coherent electromagnetic energy in the visible-light spectrum. See LASER.

laser   Acronym for *light amplification by stimulated emission of radiation.* A device that produces coherent radiation in the visible-light range, that is, between 750 and 390 nanometers (one nanometer is 10^{-9} meter). Some devices that produce coherent radiation in the infrared, ultraviolet, or X-ray parts of the spectrum are also referred to as lasers. Lasers can be either continuous or pulsed, and are characterized by coherent, monochromatic emissions. The peak intensity ranges from a few microwatts to many megawatts.

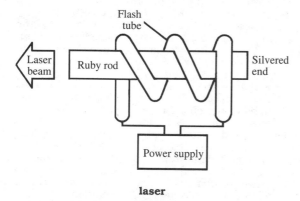

laser

laser beam   The radiation from a laser—especially if the divergence is very low, that is, the rays are almost perfectly parallel, resulting in minimal divergence.

laser-beam communication   A form of coherent infrared or optical communication in which a laser beam is the link between transmitting and receiving stations. Also see LASER, LASER DIODE, and LIGHT-BEAM COMMUNICATION.

laser capacitor   An energy-storage capacitor used to discharge-fire the exciter lamp of a laser. Also see LASER.

laser cavity   An optical-resonant cavity that results in the emission of coherent light.

laser cutting   A method of using a laser for severing materials.

laser diode   A special form of semiconductor light-emitting diode (LED), usually of the gallium-arsenide type, that emits coherent light when a voltage is applied to its terminals. Also see LASER.

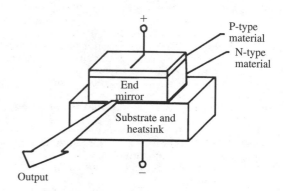

laser diode

laser disk   A method of reproducing sound in which a laser is used to recover the sound from a compact disk.

laser Doppler radar   Acronyms, *ladar* or *lopplar.* A form of Doppler radar using the light beam of a laser instead of radio waves.

laser eye surgery   A method of repairing the retina of the eye without cutting the eyeball, using laser beams to push loose retina tissue back into place.

laser gun   A colloquial term for a weapon that makes use of a laser as a device of destruction.

laser optical videodisc system   A system in which a low-powered laser reads audio and video information from a videodisc and delivers it to a television receiver.

laser ranger   A radar-like device using intense light (instead of microwaves).

laser show   A three-dimensional, midair display having motion, made by using lasers in various combinations.

laser surgery   The application of a laser in medicine for the purpose of assisting in, or actually performing, operations on human subjects.

laser welding   Welding (especially of tiny pieces) with the heat produced by a laser beam.

lasing   The emission of coherent electromagnetic energy in the visible-light spectrum. See LASER.

lat Abbreviation of LATITUDE.

latch **1.** A feedback loop in a symmetrical digital circuit, such as a flip-flop, used to maintain a given state. **2.** A simple logic-circuit storage element that consists of two gates as a unit. **3.** To maintain a closed (energized) state in a pair of relay contacts after initial energization from a single electrical pulse. See LATCHING RELAY.

latching current In a thyristor, the minimum value of anode current (slightly higher than the holding current) that will sustain conduction immediately after switch-on.

latching relay An electromechanical or fully electronic relay that locks into whichever mode it is energized for (on or off).

latch-on relay See LOCKING RELAY.

latchup In a transistor switching circuit, the abnormal condition in which the collector voltage remains at its switched-on level after the transistor is switched to cutoff from saturation.

latch voltage The input voltage at which a flip-flop changes states.

late contacts Relay contacts that are operated following the movement of other contacts during the relay's operation.

latency **1.** The time taken by a digital computer to deliver information from its memory. **2.** In a serial storage system, the access time less the word time.

latent image **1.** In a storage tube, a stored image that is not yet visible. **2.** An image stored in the mosaic of an iconoscope. **3.** The image that will appear when photographic film or paper is developed.

lateral chromatic aberration An aberration affecting the sharpness of off-axis color television images.

lateral compliance In phonograph reproduction, the ease with which the stylus can move laterally as it follows the groove. Also see COMPLIANCE and LATERAL RECORDING.

lateral-correction magnet In a color picture tube, a magnet operated with a set of pole pieces attached to the focus element of the blue gun; it controls horizontal positioning of the blue beam for convergence.

lateral magnet See LATERAL-CORRECTION MAGNET.

lateral recording A disc recording in which the groove undulates from side to side. Compare VERTICAL RECORDING.

latitude Abbreviation, lat. Angular distance measured around the earth's circumference to the north and south from the equator. Compare LONGITUDE.

latitude effect The tendency of the earth's magnetic field to decrease the number of charged subatomic particles that reach the surface of the earth near the equator, as compared with the number reaching the surface at other latitudes.

Latour alternator See BETHENOD ALTERNATOR.

lattice **1.** The orderly internal pattern (matrix) of atoms in a crystal. Also see CRYSTAL LATTICE. **2.** A symmetrical arrangement of components in a network (such as an attenuator, a filter, or a bridge circuit).

lattice filter A lattice network having reactance in its arms that makes it a selective circuit.

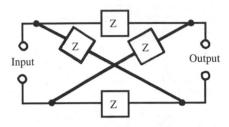

latttice filter

lattice network See LATTICE, **2.**

lattice section See LATTICE, **2.**

lattice structure See LATTICE, **1.**

lattice winding See UNIVERSAL WINDING.

laue diagram A pattern of spots on a photographic plate produced by the scattering of high energy radiation as it falls on a thin crystal. This pattern is used to determine the nature of the crystal material.

launching The energy transference from a cable into a waveguide.

lavalier microphone A small microphone that can be hung from the user's neck on a cord or chain.

law **1.** A general, verifiable statement that describes the behavior of entities or the relationships between phenomena or concepts. The product of inductive reasoning that follows many observations and controlled experiments (e.g., *first law of thermodynamics*, *inverse-square law*, *Kirchhoff's laws*, and *Ohm's law*. **2.** The nature of the change of a dependent variable, particularly as depicted by a response curve (e.g., *square law*).

LAWEB Civilian weather bulletins issued every six hours from ship and shore positions along the Great Lakes during the sailing season.

lawn mower **1.** A facsimile term for a helix recording mechanism. **2.** A radar receiver preamplifier.

law of a curve See LAW, **2.**

law of averages In probability and statistics, a principle stating that for a large sampling of events, the numerical probability value will be more closely approached than when the sampling is small. Compare LAW OF LARGE NUMBERS.

law of charges Different electric charges attract each other, and similar charges repel each other.

law of electric charges See LAW OF CHARGES.

law of electromagnetic induction See LENZ'S LAW.

law of electrostatic attraction See COULOMB'S LAWS.

law of electrostatic repulsion See COULOMB'S LAWS.

law of first wavefront In acoustics, a rule stating that the perceived direction from which a sound arrives is determined by the first wavefront that reaches the listener's ears.

law of induction See FARADAY'S LAW.

law of inverse squares See INVERSE-SQUARE LAW.

law of large numbers In probability and statistics, a principle stating that with a large sample, the sample average will approximate the population average. It is often erroneously called LAW OF AVERAGES.

law of magnetism Different magnetic poles attract each other, and similar magnetic poles repel each other.

law of natural decay See EXPONENTIAL DECREASE.

law of natural growth See EXPONENTIAL INCREASE.

law of normal distribution Gauss' law of the frequency distribution of a repetitive function, describing the probability of deviations from the mean.

law of octals Chemical activity occurs between two atoms lacking eight valence electrons, and continues until the requirement of eight electrons is satisfied for all but the first orbit, where only two electrons are required. Of interest in the study of semiconductors.

law of radiation See QUANTUM THEORY.

law of reflection For a ray of energy striking a smooth reflective surface, the angle of reflection is equal to the angle of incidence, with respect to a plane tangent to the surface at the point of incidence.

Lawrence accelerator See CYCLOTRON.

lawrencium Symbol, Lr (occasionally Lw). A short-lived radioactive element produced artificially from californium. Atomic number, 103. Atomic weight, about 260.

lay See DIRECTION OF LAY.

layer **1.** A complete coil winding consisting of turns laid side by side (not on top of each other). **2.** In a semiconductor device, a region having unique electrical properties (e.g., n $layer$). **3.** A region of the ionosphere. See IONOSPHERIC LAYERS. **4.** The tape on a reel or in a cassette, encompassing one complete turn (rotation). **5.** In general, a single stratum of a stratified medium.

layer-to-layer transfer In a roll of magnetic tape, unwanted transfer of data between adjacent turns on the reel. If severe, this transfer can cause drop-in or drop-out in a computer. In audio applications, it can sometimes be heard as a delayed echo or a faint sound occurring just prior to the actual recorded sound.

layer winding A coil winding in which the turns are arranged in two or more concentric layers.

layerwound coil An inductor wound in layers, one on top of the other. Also see LAYER, **1**. Compare SINGLE-LAYER COIL.

layout The arrangement of components on a chassis, printed circuit board, or panel.

lazy-H antenna An antenna consisting of two vertically stacked collinear elements, producing both horizontal and vertical directivity.

Lb Abbreviation of LAMBERT; also, L (preferred).

lb Abbreviation of POUND.

L band A radio-frequency band extending from 390 MHz to 1.55 GHz. For subdivisions of this band, see L_C BAND, L_F BAND, L_K BAND, L_L BAND, L_P BAND, L_S BAND, L_T BAND, L_X BAND, L_Y BAND, and L_Z BAND.

LC **1.** Abbreviation of LIQUID CRYSTAL; also abbreviated lix. **2.** Abbreviation of INDUCTANCE-CAPACITANCE. **3.** Symbol for LC CONSTANT.

L carrier In a telephone system, a carrier having a frequency between approximately 68 kHz and 10 MHz. It can be used in wire-transmission or radio links.

L_C band A section of the L BAND extending from 465 MHz to 510 MHz.

LC bridge See INDUCTANCE-CAPACITANCE BRIDGE.

LC constant Abbreviation, LC. The product of the inductance and capacitance required for resonance at a given frequency.

LCD Abbreviation of LIQUID-CRYSTAL DISPLAY.

LC filter See INDUCTANCE-CAPACITANCE FILTER.

L circuit See L NETWORK.

LC meter See INDUCTANCE-CAPACITANCE METER.

LCR See INDUCTANCE-CAPACITANCE-RESISTANCE.

LC ratio In a tuned circuit, the ratio of inductance to capacitance.

LCR bridge See IMPEDANCE BRIDGE, **1**.

L_d Symbol for DISTRIBUTED INDUCTANCE.

LDF See LOW-FREQUENCY DIRECTION FINDER.

L display Also called L $scan$. A radar display in which the target appears as two horizontal traces, one extending from a vertical timebase to the right, the other to the left.

lead Pronunciation, $leed$. **1.** A conductor (usually a wire) leading to or emerging from a terminal or electrode. **2.** In computations relating phase, the extent to which one quantity precedes another (e.g., current leads voltage by 90 degrees in a pure capacitance). Compare LAG.

lead Pronunciation, led. Symbol, Pb. A heavy metallic element. Atomic number, 82. Atomic weight, 207.2. It can be used as a shield against atomic radiation, and has various applications in electronics (e.g., as electrodes in batteries and as a component of solder). See LEAD-ACID BATTERY, FUSE, and SOLDER.

lead-acid battery A storage battery in which the cells contain lead plates immersed in an electrolyte (sulfuric acid). The positive plate contains lead peroxide, and the negative plate, spongy lead.

lead-acid cell One cell of a LEAD-ACID BATTERY.

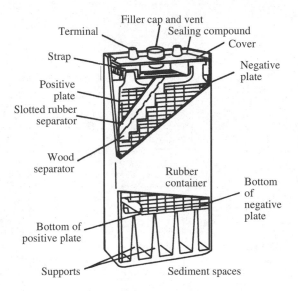

lead-acid cell

lead cell 1. A lead-acid cell. 2. A lead-sulfide photocell; see LEAD SULFIDE, 1.

lead dress See DRESS.

leader 1. The blank section at the beginning of a magnetic tape. It is usually made of plastic. 2. A record, preceding a group of records, that identifies the group and provides other data pertinent to the group. 3. In a lightning stroke, the initial movement of electrons or positive ions, creating the ionized path that allows discharge.

lead frame The metal frame holding the leads of a circuit package (DIP) in place before encapsulation.

lead-in The wire connecting an antenna to a receiver or transmitter.

leading current Current that precedes voltage in time. Also see LEAD.

leading edge The rising edge of a pulse; compare TRAILING EDGE.

leading ghost A twin television image to the left of the original on the screen.

leading load A load in which current leads voltage (i.e., a capacitive load).

lead-in groove Around the outer edge of a phonograph record, a blank spiral groove that leads the stylus into the first groove of the recording. Compare LEAD-OUT GROOVE.

leading whites In a television picture, an abnormal condition in which the leading (left) edge of a black object has a white border.

leading-zero suppression In a digital meter, the blanking out of all zeros to the left of the decimal point.

lead-in spiral See LEAD-IN GROOVE.

lead-in tube A tube of insulating material, such as plastic or ceramic, used to conduct an antenna lead-in through a wall.

lead-in wire 1. A single wire, used as a feed line for a shortwave receiving antenna. 2. The feed line for a television receiving antenna. 3. A feed line for a transmitting antenna.

lead network A phase-shift circuit containing series capacitance and shunt resistance; it produces a leading phase shift. Compare LAG NETWORK.

lead-out groove Around the inner edge of a phonograph record, a blank spiral groove leading into the eccentric or locked groove.

lead-over groove On a phonograph record containing several recorded tracks, a blank groove that conducts the stylus from the end of one recording to the beginning of the next.

lead screw 1. A threaded rod that guides the cutter across the surface of a disc during its recording. 2. In facsimile transmission, a threaded shaft that moves the drum or scanning mechanism lengthwise.

lead sulfate Formula, $PbSO_4$. An insulating compound formed in a LEAD-ACID CELL by the chemical action between the lead in the plates and the sulfuric-acid electrolyte. If the sulfate is not broken down during charging of the cell, it will eventually ruin the cell.

lead sulfide Formula, PbS. A compound of lead and sulfur used as the light-sensitive material in some photoconductive cells.

lead zirconate titanate A synthetic piezoelectric material.

leaf electroscope An electroscope using a pair of gold leaves or a single gold leaf and a solid strip of metal.

leak 1. The loss of energy through a stray path not intended for conduction. 2. A point from which energy is lost through a stray path not intended for conduction.

leakage 1. The small current that flows through an electrical insulator. 2. The electromagnetic field that is radiated or received by a feed line that should theoretically have 100-percent shielding.

leakage current The zero-signal current flowing across a reverse-biased semiconductor junction.

leakage flux Collectively, magnetic lines of flux around a transformer that do not link the primary and secondary coils.

leakage inductance Self-inductance caused by LEAKAGE FLUX. Leakage inductance is effectively in series with the primary or secondary winding of a transformer.

leakage resistance   **1.** In an imperfect insulator, the ohmic resistance, calculated by dividing the voltage across the insulator by the current flowing through the insulator. **2.** The quotient of voltage and current in a reverse-biased semiconductor junction.

leakage radiation   Radiation from parts of a system, as compared with that from the true radiator.

leakage reactance   Inductive reactance caused by leakage inductance in the primary or secondary circuit of a transformer.

leakance   The conductance of an insulating material, measured in siemens. It is equal to the reciprocal of the leakage resistance in ohms.

leaky   **1.** Descriptive of a capacitor in which the dielectric material is not a perfect insulator. **2.** Descriptive of imperfect shielding in a coaxial transmission line. **3.** Descriptive of a waveguide with imperfect shielding.

leaky dielectric   See LEAKY INSULATOR.

leaky insulator   An insulator that conducts significant current at a specified (test) voltage.

leaky waveguide   A waveguide that has imperfect shielding, allowing some electromagnetic field to escape.

leapfrogging   In radar, a phasing process that eliminates false echoes resulting from the signals of other radar sets.

leapfrog test   A test performed on different locations by a computer program in memory; it moves to another memory area to continue tests on other locations.

learning   The ability of an artificially intelligent machine to improve or expand its knowledge with time. This can occur as a result of accumulation of information; it can also occur in systems that track their errors to avoid repeating them.

leased line   A communications circuit reserved exclusively for a specific user.

least-significant bit   Abbreviation, LSB. The digit with the lowest place value in a binary number.

least-significant character   Abbreviation, LSC. In positional notation, the extreme right-hand character in a group of significant characters. See POSITIONAL NOTATION.

least-significant digit   Abbreviation, LSD. The digit in a number that is at the extreme right (i.e., the one having the lowest place value).

least upper bound   The smallest value of a parameter that can be obtained without changing some characteristic of a circuit, program or system.

Lecher frame   A sturdy assemblage of LECHER WIRES.

Lecher lines   See LECHER WIRES.

Lecher oscillator   A self-excited radio-frequency oscillator using Lecher wires in place of an inductance-capacitance (LC) tank circuit. Also see LINE-TYPE OSCILLATOR.

Lecher wires   A circuit segment consisting of two parallel wires or rods joined by a coupling loop

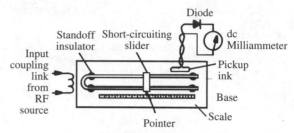

Lecher frame

on one end, the other end being open. A short-circuiting bar is moved along the wires to vary the effective length of the circuit. Radio-frequency energy is inductively coupled into the system through the loop, and the bar is slid along to various response points, as indicated by a meter or lamp coupled to the wires. The frequency can be determined by measuring the distance between adjacent response points. It is used at very-high frequencies (VHF), ultra-high frequencies (UHF), and microwave frequencies. Also called *Lecher frame* and *Lecher lines*.

Leclanche cell   See DRY CELL, **1**.

LED   See LIGHT-EMITTING DIODE.

LED phototransistor isolator   An optoelectronic isolator in which the light source is a light-emitting diode and the light-sensitive component is a phototransistor.

LEDE   Abbreviation for LIVE END/DEAD END.

LEF   See LIGHT-EMITTING FILM.

left-hand lay   See DIRECTION OF LAY.

left-hand motor rule   See FLEMING'S LEFT-HAND RULE.

left-hand polarized wave   See COUNTERCLOCK-WISE-POLARIZED WAVE.

left-hand taper   Potentiometer or rheostat taper in which most of the resistance is in the counterclockwise half of rotation as viewed from the front. Compare RIGHT-HAND TAPER.

left justified   An item of data that occupies consecutive locations in storage, starting at the left-hand end of its area; empty locations might appear consecutively at the right-hand end if the item needs fewer positions than have been provided.

left shift   A shift operation in which the digits of a word are displaced to the left; the effect is multiplication in an arithmetic shift.

leg   **1.** Any one of the distinct branches of a circuit or network; also called ARM or BRANCH. **2.** In a computer program, a path in a routine or subroutine.

L electron   In certain atoms, an electron whose orbit is outside of, and nearest to, the orbit of the K electrons.

Lenard rays   See CATHODE RAYS.

length   **1.** The number of bits or characters in a record, word, or other data unit. **2.** The end-to-end dimension of a device, circuit, line, etc. **3.** The start-to-finish duration of a time interval.

length to fault   In cable or line measurements from the home station, the distance (i.e., the cable or line length) to the point at which a fault, such as a short circuit or ground, is located.

lens   **1.** A usually circular piece of transparent material with one or both surfaces curved in cross section, used (through its refractive properties) to focus or spread rays that pass through it. Lenses for visible light must be transparent, but those for other radiation, such as radio waves, need not transmit light. Also see ANTENNA LENS. **2.** In a cathode-ray tube, one or more high-voltage electrodes for focusing an electron beam to a fine point on the screen.

lens antenna   See ANTENNA LENS.

lens disk   A NIPKOW DISK having a lens in each hole.

lens speed   The light-transmitting ability of a lens, given as an f-stop number: the lens' focal length divided by its diameter.

lens turret   A multiple-lens mount on a camera that can be rotated for quick lens interchange.

Lepel discharger   See QUENCHED SPARK GAP.

letter-identification word   See PHONETIC ALPHABET CODE WORD.

letters patent   See PATENT.

letters shift   In a text communications terminal, a control character that causes all of the following characters to occur in the lower case. This can be an automatic or a manual control character.

let-through current   The current conducted by a circuit breaker during a short-circuit.

level   **1.** The amplitude at which a device is functioning or at which a phenomenon occurs (e.g., collector-current level, or received signal level). **2.** The minimum amplitude at which a phenomenon occurs; also called *threshold amplitude*. **3.** A functional plateau or echelon.

level clipper   See CLIPPER.

level compensator   **1.** An automatic gain control (AGC) that effectively reduces amplitude variations in a received signal. **2.** An automatic gain control in telegraph receiving equipment.

level control   **1.** The adjustment of amplitude or threshold. **2.** A potentiometer or other variable component for adjusting the amplitude or threshold of a quantity.

level indicator   See VOLUME INDICATOR.

level translator   Any circuit or device that alters the voltage levels of input signals. An example is a converter that changes positive-logic signals to negative-logic signals.

level-triggered flip-flop   A flip-flop that responds to voltage level, rather than to the frequency of an input signal.

lever switch   **1.** A switch designed for rapid making and breaking of a circuit. **2.** A radiotelegraph key.

Lewis antenna   A form of antenna used at ultrahigh and microwave frequencies. It resembles a horn antenna.

Leyden bottle   See LEYDEN JAR.

Leyden jar   [Leyden, Holland (also Leiden), site of the invention in 1745 by Peiter van Musschenbroek, 1692–1761.] The first practical capacitor. In modern form, it is a glass jar covered inside and out with metal foil and has a rod topped by a metal ball that touches the inner foil. It is still used occasionally in classrooms for demonstrating static electricity. The Leyden jar was co-invented by van Musschenbroek and invented independently by E. G. von Kleist of Pomerania, among others.

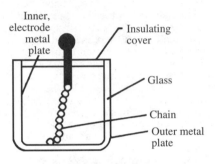

Leyden jar

Leyden phial   See LEYDEN JAR.

Leyden vial   See LEYDEN JAR.

LF   Abbreviation of LOW FREQUENCY.

L_F band   A section of the L BAND extending from 1.35 to 1.45 GHz.

L fitting   See ELL.

LHD   Abbreviation of LOAD/HAUL/DUMP.

Li   Symbol for LITHIUM.

librarian program   A computer program controlling a LIBRARY.

library   In digital-computer and data-processing operations, the permanent storage of data or instructions. Also called *permanent mass storage*.

licrystal   An acronym from *liquid* and *crystal*. See LIQUID CRYSTAL.

lidar   See LIGHT DETECTION AND RANGING.

lie detector   See POLYGRAPH.

life   **1.** The duration of useful service (or of operation before failure) of electronic equipment. **2.** For a non-rechargeable cell or battery, the length of time it will last in a given application before it must be discarded and replaced. **3.** In robotics and artificial intelligence (AI), a general term that refers to qualitative similarities between machines and animate creatures, including human beings.

life test   An assessment of the life of electronic equipment—either by means of full-time test runs or accelerated time tests.

lifetime See CARRIER LIFETIME.

lifter A device in a magnetic tape recorder that removes the tape from the recording and playback heads under fast-forward and rewind conditions.

light Visible electromagnetic radiation occurring in the wavelength band of about 750 nanometers (red light) to 390 nanometers (violet light). Included sometimes in the category of light are infrared and ultraviolet rays.

light-activated silicon-controlled rectifier Abbreviation, LASCR. A silicon-controlled rectifier that functions both as a photosensor and a heavy-duty bistable electronic switch, allowing high currents to be switched by means of a light beam.

light-activated silicon-controlled switch Abbreviation, LASCS. A pnpn device that acts simultaneously as photocell and electronic switch.

light adaption **1.** The process whereby the eye adjusts itself to an increase or decrease in illumination. **2.** Similar action in photoelectric devices. **3.** The length of time required for the eye to adjust itself to an increase or decrease in illumination.

light amplifier A solid-state amplifier using an input electroluminescent cell and an output photocell, or some similar pair of components. The device is essentially an optoelectronic coupler with gain.

light-beam communication A system of communication in which a beam of light between transmitting and receiving stations is modulated or interrupted to convey intelligence. A laser is commonly used because it has minimal beam divergence, allowing maximum communication range.

light-beam meter An electric meter using a LIGHT-BEAM POINTER.

light-beam pointer A slender beam of light that replaces the pointer in a moving-coil meter. The light comes from a small incandescent lamp and is reflected by a mirror attached to the coil; when the coil moves, a spot of light moves over the scale of the meter.

light-beam receiver The receiver in a LIGHT-BEAM COMMUNICATION system.

light-beam recorder A graphic recorder using a light-beam pointer. In this device, a small spot of light traces a pattern on moving photographic film, which is subsequently developed to produce a permanent record.

light-beam transmitter The transmitter in a LIGHT-BEAM COMMUNICATION system.

light cable A cable, consisting of numerous thin optical fibers, through which light can be transmitted for communication or control purposes. See, for example, LIGHT-WAVE TELEPHONY.

light chopper A device that modulates a light beam by interrupting it repetitively.

light detection and ranging Acronym, lidar. A navigation and surveillance system in which

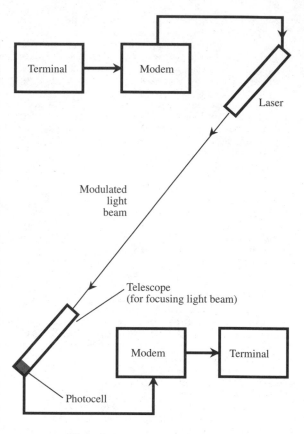

light-beam communication

laser light scans in a manner similar to that of RADAR.

light dimmer See DIMMER.

lighted pushbutton See LIGHTED SWITCH.

lighted switch A pushbutton switch containing a pilot light that glows to show when the switch is on. Also called *illuminated switch*.

light-emitting diode Abbreviation, LED. A semiconductor device that emits visible light when forward biased. Also see LASER DIODE.

light-emitting film A thin phosphor film that becomes luminescent when a high-frequency voltage is applied across its surface. Also see ELECTROLUMINESCENCE and ELECTROLUMINESCENT CELL.

light flasher An electronic circuit or simple automatic flasher switch for flashing a lamp at regular intervals.

light flicker See LOAD FLICKER.

light flux See LUMINOUS FLUX.

light hood See HOOD.

light-induced electricity See PHOTOELECTRICITY.

light load A load that is a fraction of the usual value for a given application. That is, its resistance or impedance is several times higher than normal.

light meter An electronic instrument for measuring the intensity of light. It generally consists of a photodiode, a battery, and a direct-current microammeter connected in series. A direct-current amplifier can be used to increase the sensitivity.

light microsecond A unit of electrical distance; the distance that light, or any electromagnetic disturbance, travels in free space in 1 microsecond. Approximately equal to 300 meters.

light modulation Variation of the instantaneous brightness of a visible light beam in synchronization with the instantaneous amplitude of a modulating signal. Also see LIGHT MODULATOR.

light modulator A device with which a beam of light can be modulated by an electrical signal.

light negative Pertaining to negative photoconductivity, the decrease in conductivity of a photosensitive material under illumination. Compare LIGHT POSITIVE.

lightning The discharge that occurs between positive and negative poles in the atmosphere. Common in and near areas where heavy rainfall is occurring. It also can occur in snow storms, in sand storms, and over erupting volcanoes. Generally, the negative pole is in a cloud and the positive pole is at the surface of the earth, resulting in a flow of electrons from cloud to ground. Some lightning occurs as a flow of electrons from ground to cloud, or between two clouds. Such discharges sometimes attain current levels of more than 1,000,000 amperes.

lightning arrester A device that bypasses high-voltage pulses from most nearby lightning discharges to the earth, helping to protect electronic equipment connected to an outdoor antenna or power line. Is not a total guarantee of protection, however.

lightning conductor 1. A system for protecting buildings from lightning strikes. A common system includes a lightning rod, heavy conductor, and ground rod. The ground rod is placed at least six feet from the base of a building and is at least eight feet long. 2. The conductor between the lightning rod and ground rod in a system, as defined in 1.

lightning detector See KERAUNOGRAPH and KERAUNOPHONE.

lightning rod A protective device mounted on the outside of structures, consisting of a pointed, grounded metal rod that will conduct a lightning discharge to earth.

lightning strike A direct hit of an object by a lightning stroke. It usually causes extensive damage to electrical and electronic equipment through which the discharge passes.

lightning stroke The discharge that occurs with lightning. The peak current is typically several

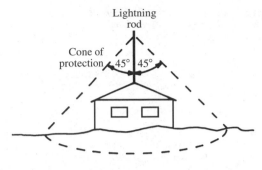

lightning rod

tens of thousands of amperes, but in some cases can exceed 1,000,000 amperes. A stroke can consist of one discharge or several individual discharges in rapid succession.

lightning switch See GROUND SWITCH.

light-operated relay See PHOTOELECTRIC RELAY.

light-operated switch A PHOTOELECTRIC RELAY, or a switch operated by such a relay.

light pen A probe containing a tiny photosensor in its tip. The tip of the light pen is touched to the screen of a cathode-ray tube to sense the beam when it passes the spot of contact. It is used as an input device in some computers and terminals.

light pipe 1. An OPTICAL FIBER. 2. A cable consisting of numerous optical fibers in a bundle. See FIBEROPTICS, 1.

light positive Pertaining to positive photoconductivity, when the conductivity of a photosensitive material increases under illumination. Compare LIGHT NEGATIVE.

light quantum See PHOTON.

light ray A thin beam of light. Theoretically, a ray emerges from a point source (i.e., it has no width).

light receiver See LIGHT-BEAM RECEIVER.

light relay A photoelectric device that operates a relay, according to fluctuations in the intensity of a light beam.

light-sensitive cathode Also called *photocathode*. A cathode that emits electrons when exposed to light.

light-sensitive diode A semiconductor diode usable as a photoconductive cell. Such diodes are available as both junction and point-contact types.

light-sensitive material A photoconductive or photoemissive substance.

light-sensitive resistor See PHOTOCONDUCTIVE CELL.

light sensor 1. A light-sensitive device, such as a photocell, photodiode, phototransistor, or phototube. 2. A light-sensitive substance, such as cesium, selenium, silicon, cadmium selenide, or lead sulfide.

light source Any generator of light. Under some conditions, the source is regarded as a point.

light spectrum See ELECTROMAGNETIC THEORY OF LIGHT.

light-spot scanner Also called *flying-spot scanner*. A television camera using (as a source of illumination) a spot of light that scans what is to be televised.

light transmitter See LIGHT-BEAM TRANSMITTER.

light valve **1.** An electromechanical device for varying the intensity of light passing through its adjustable aperture. **2.** See KERR CELL.

light-wave telephony Telephone communication by means of modulated-light transmission, usually through an OPTICAL FIBER.

light-year Abbreviation, lt-yr. Pertaining to astronomy, a unit of distance equal to the distance traveled by light in one year in a vacuum: $9.460\ 55 \times 10^{15}$ meters (5.878×10^{12} miles).

likelihood In probability and statistics, the chance that an event will occur or that an outcome will be realized. Also see PROBABILITY, **1**, **2**.

lim Abbreviation of LIMIT.

Lima Pronunciation, *LEE-ma*. Phonetic alphabet word for the letter L.

limen A unit that has been proposed as the minimum audible change in frequency that can be detected by at least half of a group of listeners.

limit **1.** The lowest or highest frequency in a band. **2.** In mathematics, a fixed value that a variable approaches. **3.** The upper and lower extremes in any performance range or value range.

limit bridge A bridge used to check a component (e.g., resistance, capacitance, or inductance) in terms of the tolerance limits, rather than the nominal (named) value, of that component. Also see BRIDGE, **2**.

limited integrator A circuit that integrates two input signals until the corresponding output signal exceeds a certain limit.

limited stability A characteristic of a circuit or system, allowing proper operation only if the input signal and applied voltages are within certain maximum and minimum limits.

limiter A device or circuit whose output-signal amplitude remains at some predetermined level, despite wide variations in input-signal amplitude.

limiting The restriction of the maximum peak amplitude of a signal to a designated level.

limiting amplifier An amplifier that automatically holds the output-signal level to a prescribed value.

limiting current In electrolysis, the highest current that conducts under certain conditions of ion concentration. This current depends on the electrolyte material, the concentration of the electrolyte in solution, the electrode substance, and the size of the electrolytic cell.

limiting error The anticipated maximum value of the absolute error in a computation.

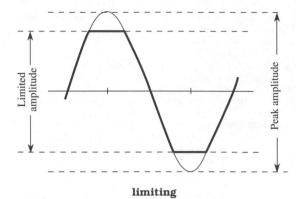

limiting

limiting resistor See CURRENT-LIMITING RESISTOR.

limiting resolution As a measure of video image resolution, the maximum number of lines for picture height that can be discriminated on a test chart.

limit switch A switch that is actuated when a monitored quantity (e.g., current, voltage, or illumination) reaches the limit of its range.

line **1.** A wire, cable, or waveguide, along which electrical or electromagnetic energy travels from one defined place to another. **2.** One lengthwise path in which a force, such as electricity or magnetism, is evidenced. Such a *line of flux* has theoretically zero width.

line advance **1.** The physical separation between the centers of adjacent scanning lines in a television system. **2.** Line feed in a text data transmission system.

line amplifier An amplifier in a telephone line or similar channel, or one feeding such a line from the input end.

linear **1.** In a straight line. **2.** In the manner of a straight line. Thus, linear response is indicated when one quantity varies directly with another; the graph of this response is a straight line (i.e., one of constant slope). **3.** The characteristic of a signal that is a replica of another (e.g., an amplifier output signal of the same waveform as that of the input signal).

linear absorption coefficient A number expressing the extent to which the intensity of an X-ray beam is reduced per centimeter of the material through which it passes.

linear accelerator A device in which subatomic particles are accelerated in a straight line through a long tube. This action is in contrast with that occurring in a circular accelerator, such as a CYCLOTRON.

linear algebra A branch of mathematics that deals with the solving of linear equations or sets of linear equations.

linear amplifier **1.** An amplifier for which a linear relationship exists between input and output parameters (e.g., a high-fidelity audio amplifier). **2.** A class-AB radio-frequency power amplifier that does not distort the envelope of an amplitude-modulated (AM) or single-sideband (SSB) signal. It is commonly used by amateur radio operators.

linear array   A directional antenna having equally spaced, in-line elements.

linear circuit   **1.** A circuit whose output is a faithful reproduction of the input. See LINEAR AMPLIFIER, **1** and LINEAR DETECTOR. **2.** A circuit whose performance is linear. See LINEAR RESPONSE, **1.**

linear decrement   In a damped wave, a constant decrease in amplitude with time, as opposed to a decrease that is a logarithmic or otherwise nonlinear function of time. Compare DECREMENT.

linear detector   A detector whose output/input relationship is linear. Also see LINEAR, **2, 3**; LINEAR CIRCUIT, **1**; and LINEAR RESPONSE, **1, 2, 3.**

linear differential transformer   A device that converts the physical position of an object into an output voltage or current. The voltage or current is directly proportional to the displacement.

linear distortion   Amplitude distortion in which the output and input signal envelopes are disproportionate (in the absence of spurious frequencies).

linear equation   See FIRST-DEGREE EQUATION.

linear function   **1.** In Cartesian two-space, a function of the form $y = mx + b$, where the coordinates are (x,y), the slope is m (any real number) and b is the point on the y axis at which the graph crosses the axis. **2.** Any function in any number of dimensions whose graph appears as a straight line in the Cartesian system of coordinates.

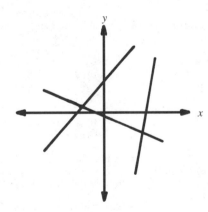

linear function

linear IC   See LINEAR INTEGRATED CIRCUIT.

linear integrated circuit   An integrated circuit designed for analog operations (such as signal amplification, oscillation, nondigital regulation, analog instrumentation, and similar applications). Compare DIGITAL INTEGRATED CIRCUIT.

linearity   **1.** The degree to which performance or response approaches the condition of being linear, expressed in percent or parts per million. Also see LINEAR AMPLIFIER, **1**; LINEAR CIRCUIT, **1, 2**; LINEAR OSCILLATOR, **1**; LINEAR RESPONSE, **1, 2, 3**; and LINEAR TAPER. **2.** In a cathode-ray-tube image, absence of compression or stretching of any portion of the image; that is, an undistorted reproduction.

linearity control   In a cathode-ray-tube display, the potentiometer used to correct image linearity. See LINEARITY, **2.**

linearity error   **1.** The difference between a theoretically linear function and the actual function, as observed under experimental conditions. **2.** The degree of nonlinearity in an amplifier that is supposed to be linear.

linear modulation   **1.** Modulation in which the instantaneous amplitude of the input signal is directly proportional to the instantaneous amplitude of the output signal. **2.** Modulation in which the instantaneous amplitude of the input signal is inversely proportional to the instantaneous amplitude of the output signal. **3.** Modulation in which the instantaneous amplitude of the input signal is directly proportional to the frequency or phase deviation of the output signal.

linear motor   A motor in which the stator and rotor are parallel and straight.

linear oscillator   **1.** An oscillator whose alternating-current output amplitude varies linearly with its direct-current input. **2.** A line-type oscillator.

linear programming   A method of determining the optimum value for a certain set of linear equations. Generally, this is done by finding the point on a plane in space closest to some point not on the plane.

linear quantizing   A method of quantizing in which all of the intervals are of equal size or duration. An example is a linear analog-to-digital converter circuit.

linear reflex detector   See INFINITE-IMPEDANCE DETECTOR.

linear response   **1.** A response in which the value of the dependent variable is equal or directly proportional to the value of the independent variable. Thus, the graph of the response function is a straight line over the range of normal operating values. Compare LOGARITHMIC RESPONSE, **1** and SQUARE-LAW RESPONSE. **2.** A type of response in which a quantity (such as current) varies directly with another quantity (such as voltage). Compare LOGARITHMIC RESPONSE, **2**. **3.** Low-distortion response. Also see HIGH FIDELITY.

linear scale   A scale in which all of the divisions represent the same differential and are equally

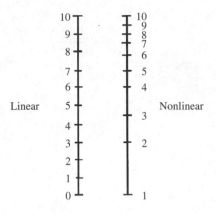

linear scale

spaced. On a linear scale, a given difference always has the same physical length, no matter where on the scale it appears. For example, the interval between 3 and 4 on a linear scale is the same as any interval between x and $x + 1$, where x is any real value on the scale.

linear sweep   In a television or oscilloscope circuit, the scanning of the electron beam across the screen at a constant speed. Also see LINEAR, **1**; LINEAR RESPONSE, **1**; and LINEARITY, **2**.

linear taper   In a potentiometer or rheostat, resistance variation that is directly proportional to shaft rotation. Thus, half the total resistance corresponds to movement of the shaft over half the arc of full rotation. Compare LOG TAPER. Also see TAPER.

linear time base   For an oscilloscope, the base provided by sweeping the electron beam horizontally at a uniform rate. Also see LINEAR SWEEP.

linear track   On a video tape, the track that contains audio information that accompanies the video data. It was so named because it is a single, straight track, in contrast to the video tracks, which are angled.

linear tracking   In a turntable system, a design scheme in which the lateral movement of the stylus, as the disc is played, occurs in a straight line, rather than in an arc.

linear transformer   A radio-frequency transformer consisting of a section of transmission line.

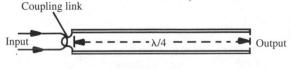

linear transformer

linear variable differential transformer   Abbreviation, LVDT. A differential transformer ex-

hibiting linear response. Also see LINEAR RESPONSE, **1**, **2**.

line balance   The degree of electrical similarity between transmission line conductors, or between a conductor and ground.

line-balance converter   A device used to isolate the outer conductor at the end of a coaxial line from ground.

line characteristic distortion   Fluctuations in the duration of received signal impulses in text data communications, caused by changing current transitions in the wire circuit.

line circuit   The telephone system relay equipment associated with stations connected to a switchboard.

line code   A code between the digits in processing equipment and the pulses representing the digits in a line transmission.

line conditioning   In data communications, the modification of private or leased lines by adding compensating reactances to reduce amplitude variations or phase delays over a band of frequencies.

line contact stylus   A needle used to reproduce stereo high-fidelity sound from vinyl discs. It has a characteristic oblate ellipsoidal shape.

line coordinate   A symbol identifying a specific row of cells in a matrix; a specific cell can be located with an additional column coordinate.

line cord   A flexible two- or three-wire insulated cable connecting equipment to the power line by means of a plug that mates to a standard electrical outlet.

line current   **1.** Current flowing from a power line into equipment. **2.** Current flowing in a transmission line. **3.** Current flowing into a parallel-resonant circuit.

line diffuser   A circuit that creates minor vertical oscillations of the spot on a television screen, making the individual scanning lines less noticeable.

line driver   An integrated circuit capable of transmitting logic signals through long lines.

line drop   The voltage drop along a line supplying power to a device.

line equalizer   See EQUALIZER.

line fault   A discontinuity in a transmission line, resulting in signal loss at the receiving end of a circuit.

line feed   In a text data transmission system, the movement of the paper, platen, or cursor to allow for printing or displaying an additional line of text.

line filter   A circuit of one or more inductors and capacitors inserted between an alternating-current-powered device and the power line. It is used to attenuate noise signals.

linefinder   A switching device that finds one of a group of calling telephone lines and connects it to a trunk, connector, or selector.

line frequency   **1.** The frequency of power-line voltage in the United States, 60 Hz. **2.** The rate at

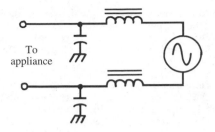

line filter

which the horizontal lines are traced in a video image. Also see HORIZONTAL FREQUENCY.

line group 1. A group of signals sent by wire transmission. **2.** The frequency spectrum occupied by a group of signals sent by wireless transmission.

line leakage Resistance between insulators of two wires in a telephone line loop.

line loss The sum of energy losses in a transmission line.

lineman A technician who works mainly with telephone or telegraph lines.

line matching transformer A device that provides an impedance match in an audio circuit, and also can adapt balanced to unbalanced audio transmission lines (or vice-versa).

line noise 1. Electrical noise (as received by a radio) arising from fluctuations of current or voltage in a power line. **2.** Noise in a data transmission line.

line of flux 1. A line (usually curved) depicting the points of equal-intensity field strength in the vicinity of an electric charge or a charged body. Also see FLUX. **2.** A line depicting the points of equal-intensity field strength in the vicinity of a magnetic pole or a magnetized body. Also see FLUX.

line-of-sight communication Radio communications between points located so that a straight line between them does not pass through the earth, or through any major obstructions. Also see LINE-OF-SIGHT DISTANCE.

line-of-sight distance The maximum distance over which an ultra-high-frequency (UHF) or microwave signal can be directly transmitted along the surface of the earth. It is slightly more than the maximum optical line-of-sight distance.

line oscillator See LINE-TYPE OSCILLATOR.

line plug The plug terminating a line cord. Also see MALE PLUG.

line printer A machine that prints the results of a computer run, line by line.

line radio See WIRED RADIO.

line regulation Automatic stabilization of power-line voltage.

line-sequential system The color television system in which the image is reproduced by means of primary color lines (red, green, and blue) sequentially beamed across the screen of the pic-

ture tube. Compare DOT-SEQUENTIAL SYSTEM and FIELD-SEQUENTIAL SYSTEM.

lines of cleavage See CLEAVAGE.

lines oscillator See LINE-TYPE OSCILLATOR.

line supervision In electronic security systems, a method of monitoring circuit characteristics to detect possible tampering.

line switch 1. The main power-line switch to a system. **2.** Within a piece of electronic equipment, the switch that opens and closes the circuit to the incoming power line.

line-type amplifier A radio-frequency amplifier in which the tuned circuits are transmission lines consisting of parallel wires, rods, or tubing, or of coaxial cable sections.

line-type oscillator A radio-frequency oscillator in which the tuned circuits are transmission lines consisting of parallel wires, rods, or tubing, or of coaxial cable sections.

line unit In a wire data transmission system, the terminal unit, or device that converts the text signals into electrical impulses and vice-versa.

line voltage 1. The voltage between the conductors in a power line. **2.** The voltage between the conductors of a transmission line.

line-voltage drop See LINE DROP.

line-voltage monitor See POWER-LINE MONITOR.

linguistics The study of languages, including structure, symbology, and phonetics.

link 1. The small coupling coil used in link coupling. **2.** A communication path between two radio facilities for the purpose of extending the range of one, as between a remote pickup point and a broadcast transmitter. **3.** A data connection between two different computers. **4.** The act or process of creating a signal path or data connection, as defined in **1**, **2**, or **3**. **5.** In a digital computer, a branch instruction, or an address in such an instruction, used to leave a subroutine to return to some point in the main program.

linkage Coupling between separated conductors or devices through the medium of electric or magnetic lines of flux.

link circuit A closed-loop coupling circuit having two coils of a few turns of wire; each coil is placed near one of the circuits to be coupled.

link coupling Low-impedance coupling via a small (usually one-turn) input or output coil fed by a twisted pair or a coaxial line.

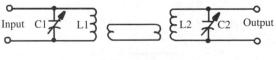

link coupling

linked subroutine A subroutine, entered by a branch instruction from a main routine, that executes a branch instruction returning control to the main routine.

link fuse A fuse consisting of an exposed length of fuse wire.

link neutralization Neutralization achieved by out-of-phase current fed back via link coupling from the output to the input of an amplifier. Also called INDUCTIVE NEUTRALIZATION.

lin-log receiver A radar receiver whose amplitude response is linear for small signals, but logarithmic for large ones.

lip microphone A small microphone operated close to or in contact with the lips.

liquid A state of matter characterized by a level of molecular motion intermediate between that of gases and solids; liquids have the ability (like gases) to take the shape of a container and are only slightly compressible. Compare GAS, PLASMA, and SOLID. Also see STATE OF MATTER.

liquid absorption For a solid material, such as dielectric, the ratio of the weight of liquid absorbed by the material to the weight of the material.

liquid capacitor See WATER CAPACITOR.

liquid cell See ELECTROLYTIC CELL.

liquid conductor See ELECTROLYTE.

liquid cooling Use of circulating water, oil, or other fluid to remove heat from components or equipment, such as microprocessors or power amplifiers.

liquid crystal A liquid exhibiting some of the characteristics of a crystal. Also see NEMATIC CRYSTAL and SMECTIC CRYSTAL.

liquid-crystal display Abbreviation, LCD. For counters, calculators, digital meters, digital clocks, and certain computer displays, a device in which each digit or pixel is formed by strips or squares of liquid-crystal material. Also see NEMATIC CRYSTAL and SMECTIC CRYSTAL.

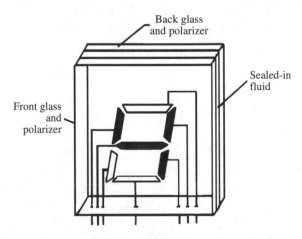

liquid-crystal display

liquid-filled transformer A transformer filled with a protective liquid insulator, such as oil.

liquid-flow alarm An electronic circuit that actuates an alarm when the flow of a liquid through pipes or other channels changes from a desired rate.

liquid-flow control A servo system that automatically maintains or corrects the rate of liquid flow through pipes or other channels.

liquid-flow gauge See LIQUID-FLOW METER.

liquid-flow indicator See LIQUID-FLOW METER.

liquid-flow meter An instrument that indicates the rate at which a liquid moves through pipes or other channels.

liquid-flow switch In a liquid-cooled system, a switch that actuates an alarm when the liquid slows or stops.

liquid-jet oscillograph A graphic recorder using an ink-jet galvanometer to trace the pattern on a paper chart.

liquid laser A laser in which the active material is a liquid.

liquid-level alarm An electronic device that actuates visual or audio signal devices when the surface of a liquid inside a tank rises or falls to a predetermined level.

liquid-level control A servo system that automatically maintains the liquid in a tank at a predetermined level.

liquid-level gauge An electronic system that provides direct readings of the level of a liquid in a tank.

liquid-level indicator See LIQUID-LEVEL GAUGE.

liquid-level meter See LIQUID-LEVEL GAUGE.

liquid load See WATER LOAD.

liquid-pressure alarm An electronic circuit that actuates an alarm when the pressure of a liquid changes.

liquid-pressure control A servo system that automatically maintains or corrects liquid pressure in pipes or other channels.

liquid-pressure gauge See LIQUID-PRESSURE METER.

liquid-pressure indicator See LIQUID-PRESSURE METER.

liquid-pressure meter An instrument that provides direct readings of liquid pressure in a pipe or other channel.

liquid-pressure switch A switch that actuates an external circuit or device when the pressure of a liquid changes.

liquid rheostat See WATER RHEOSTAT.

liquid valve See ELECTROMECHANICAL VALVE.

liser An oscillator that produces an extremely pure microwave carrier signal.

LISP A digital-computer language written in the form of lists. A program can be directly interpreted as data, and vice-versa. The entire language is derived from a few basic functions. Programs are easy to debug. It is used in artificial intelligence (AI) research. Also see LANGUAGE.

Lissajous figure Any one of several curves resulting from the combination of two harmonically related sine waves. These figures are familiar in electronics; they are obtained when signals are applied simultaneously to both axes of an oscilloscope. It is also called *Lissajous pattern.*

list **1.** To print serially the records in a file or in memory. **2.** To print (instruct a computer to display) every item of input data in a program. **3.** A one-dimensional array of numbers.

listener fatigue Physiological symptoms, such as headaches, caused by prolonged listening to certain sounds (e.g., a pure sine wave or poorly reproduced music).

listening angle In stereo sound reproduction, the angle between the speakers, with respect to the listener. This angle can vary from zero to 180 degrees. Larger angles result in increased apparent channel separation.

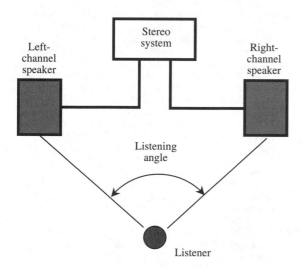

listening angle

listening test The subjective evaluation of audio equipment by listeners.

liter Abbreviation, l. A metric unit of volume equal to 1.0567 U.S. liquid quarts or 0.908 U.S. dry quart. A liter is the volume of 1 kilogram of water at 4⁻C and under a pressure of 1 pascal.

literal operands It is usually applicable to source language instructions, operands that specify the value of a constant, rather than an address of a location in which the constant is stored.

lithium Symbol, Li. An element of the alkalimetal group, and the lightest elemental metal. Atomic number, 3. Atomic weight, 6.941.

lithium battery See LITHIUM CELL.

lithium cell A vented, steel-jacketed PRIMARY CELL in which the anode element is LITHIUM. The electrolyte is an organic substance without water. Nominal voltage is 2.8 V. The lithium cell has long shelf life.

Litzendraht wire See LITZ WIRE.

Litz wire A woven wire having a number of copper strands, each separately enameled to insulate it from the others. The wire is woven so that inner strands come to the surface at regular intervals. It is noted for its low losses at radio frequencies.

live **1.** Electrically activated (i.e., sustaining voltage or current). **2.** Being broadcast as it occurs. **3.** Acoustically reflective, as in a LIVE ROOM (contrasted with one that is acoustically absorbent).

live end **1.** In a recording or broadcasting studio, the part of the room in which the acoustic concentration is greatest. **2.** In a utility circuit, the wire or terminal that carries 117 volts alternating current (the ungrounded end).

live end/dead end Pertaining to a room that is acoustically reflective (live) at one end, and acoustically absorbent (dead) at the other end.

live room A room with little or no acoustically absorbent material in its ceiling, walls, and floor, with the result that echoes and reverberation are pronounced. Compare DEAD ROOM.

lix Abbreviation of LIQUID CRYSTAL.

L_K band A section of the L BAND that extends from 1.150 to 1.350 GHz.

L_L band A section of the L BAND that extends from 510 to 725 MHz.

LLL Abbreviation of LOW-LEVEL LOGIC.

lm Preferred abbreviation of LUMEN.

lm/ft² Abbreviation of *lumens per square foot.* Also see LUMEN.

lm-hr Abbreviation of LUMEN-HOUR.

lm/m² Abbreviation of *lumens per square meter.* Also see LUMEN and LUX.

lm/W Abbreviation of *lumens per watt,* a unit of luminosity. Also see LUMEN.

ln Representation of the natural (base-*e*) logarithm function (see NAPIERIAN LOGARITHM). Also written *loge.*

L network An impedance-matching circuit, filter, or attenuator whose schematic representation resembles an inverted letter L.

LO Abbreviation of LOCAL OSCILLATOR.

lo Abbreviation of *low,* usually as a prefix or subscript. Also abbreviated L.

load **1.** Also called *electrical load.* A device or circuit that is operated by the electrical power output of another device or circuit. Examples: speaker, light bulb, power amplifier, antenna system. **2.** Also called *mechanical load.* The mechanical power output demanded of a machine—especially a motor. **3.** To fill an internal computer storage with information from an external storage [e.g., from a magnetic disk to a computer's random access memory (RAM)]. **4.** To add inductors and/or capacitors to an antenna system to alter the characteristics of the system—especially the resonant frequency. **5.** To adjust the output circuit of a radio-frequency power amplifier for optimum energy transfer to the antenna system.

load-and-go Automatic coding in which a user's (source) program is translated automatically into machine language and stored.

load capacitance **1.** The capacitance present in an electrical load (see LOAD, 1). **2.** A capacitance used as an electrical load.

load capacity **1.** In pulse-code modulation, the level at which a sine-wave signal has peaks coinciding with the plus/minus virtual decision values of the encoder. **2.** The maximum number of signals that a medium or line can carry without serious degradation of reception.

load circuit **1.** The circuit that forms the load, or power-consuming portion, of a system. **2.** A circuit that facilitates transfer of power to a load.

load coil See WORK COIL.

load current The current flowing in a load. See LOAD.

load division A method of connecting two or more power sources to a single load, for optimum power transfer.

loaded antenna An antenna incorporating a LOADING COIL and/or LOADING DISK to increase its electrical (effective) length. See LOADING COIL and LOADING DISK.

loaded line A transmission line in which inductors or capacitors are inserted at appropriate points to alter the characteristics of the line.

load end The end of a transmission line to which a radiator or receiver is connected.

load flicker Fluctuations in the brightness of lamps, caused by intermittent loading of the power line by other devices.

load/haul/dump Abbreviation, LHD. A remote-controlled or computer-controlled robot used in mining and construction work. Under the direction of a human operator or a computer, it loads, hauls, and dumps materials (hence its name). It can use various navigation methods, including beacons, computer maps, position sensors, and vision systems.

load impedance Symbol, Z_L. The impedance presented by a load connected to a generator or other source.

loading **1.** The matching of source impedance to load impedance, usually by means of the introduction of an inductance or capacitance into the load itself. **2.** Any form of impedance matching. **3.** The addition of inductance and/or capacitance to an antenna system to alter the characteristics of the system—especially the resonant frequency. **4.** The modification of the acoustic impedance of a loudspeaker.

loading coil An inductor inserted in a circuit to increase its total inductance or to provide some special effect, such as canceling capacitive reactance. See LOADED ANTENNA and PUPIN COIL.

loading disk Also called *capacitance hat.* A metal disk mounted atop a vertical antenna to increase its effective length and thereby lower its resonant frequency. It also increases the bandwidth of the system.

loading factor The ratio of source impedance to load impedance before the introduction of loading circuits.

loading inductance **1.** The inductance present in a load. **2.** An inductance used as a load.

loading routine Also called *loading program.* A routine permanently in memory; it allows a program to be loaded into memory from an external storage medium.

load life The longevity of a device in terms of the number of hours it can withstand its full power rating.

load line In a group of voltage-current (*EI*) curves, a line connecting points of equal resistance (*E/I*) that are equal to a particular value of load resistance (impedance).

load power The power dissipated in a load.

load regulation Automatic stabilization of load resistance (impedance) at a constant value.

load resistance **1.** The resistance present in a load. **2.** A resistance used as load.

load stabilizer A device for holding load current or load voltage to a constant value.

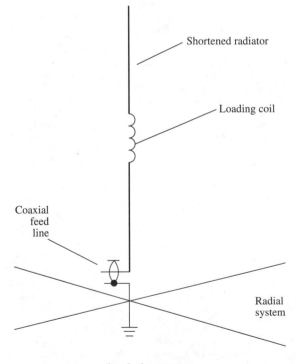

Shortened radiator

Loading coil

Coaxial feed line

Radial system

loaded antenna

loadstone   Alternate spelling of LODESTONE.

load termination   The load connected to the output of a circuit or device as the terminal element in a circuit or system.

load voltage   The voltage developed across a load.

load-voltage stabilization   Automatic regulation of load voltage.

load wattage   See LOAD POWER.

lobe   In the directivity pattern of a transducer, a figure, such as a circle or ellipse enclosing an area of intensified response. Applicable especially to antennas.

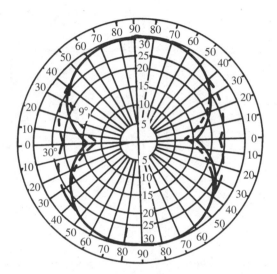

lobe (pattern of horizontal half-wave antenna)

lobing   **1.** In a transmitting or receiving antenna, the effect of ground reflection, resulting in phase reinforcement (lobes) at some elevation angles and phase opposition (nulls) at other angles. **2.** The pattern of secondary maxima in the radiation response of a directional antenna.

local action   Electrolysis between separate areas of a single electrode immersed in an electrolyte. The action is caused by impurities at different spots in the electrode metal, causing one spot to act as an anode and the other as a cathode, thereby creating a small battery cell.

local alarm   In security applications, a visible and/or audible alarm that can be seen and/or heard easily throughout the protected zone.

local area network   Abbreviation, LAN. A group of computers and/or terminals that are linked together within a relatively small geographic area, such as a college campus. Interconnections are usually made via cable. There are several different configurations, called *topologies*.

local battery   In wire telephony, a battery installed on the subscriber's premises.

local broadcast station   A standard broadcast station licensed in the local service. See LOCAL CHANNEL and LOCAL STATION.

local channel   A channel in the standard amplitude-modulation (AM) broadcast band, intended to serve only the area near the station. Transmitter power and operating time are restricted to prevent long-distance propagation.

local control   The control of a radio transmitter from the site (in contrast to remote control).

local feature focus   In robotic systems, the use of only a small portion of the available image data to perform a function. The robot computer recognizes and acts on the data it needs, disregarding the rest.

local feedback   Feedback within a circuit stage.

localizer   A radionavigation transmitter whose signal guides aircraft to the centerline of a runway.

local oscillator   Abbreviation, LO. An oscillator, such as a beat-frequency type, included in a piece of equipment, as contrasted to the oscillator in a distant transmitter.

local program   A program that originates at the same single broadcast station from which it is transmitted.

local reception   The reception of signals from local stations. Compare LONG-DISTANCE COMMUNICATIONS.

local side   The group of circuits and components associated with a communications terminal at a given location.

local station   A station situated within the same general area as the receiver, as opposed to a distant station.

local system library   A computer program library containing standard software associated with a specific system.

local transmission   The sending of signals to receivers in the same general locality as the transmitter, as opposed to long-distance transmission.

local trunk   In a telephone system, the interconnecting line between local and long-distance lines.

location   In digital computer operation, a memory position (often a register) specified by an address and usually described in terms of the basic storage unit a particular system uses (e.g., a character is a location in a character-oriented machine).

location counter   A register in the control section of a computer containing the address of the instruction being executed.

locked groove   A continuous blank groove around the inside of a phonograph record. When the disc is done playing, this groove keeps the stylus from running into the label or sliding across the disc.

locked oscillator   **1.** A fixed-frequency oscillator, such as a crystal-controlled oscillator. **2.** See BRADLEY DETECTOR.

lock-in   A state of synchronism, as when a self-excited oscillator is synchronized (locked-in) with a standard-frequency generator.

lock-in amplifier   A detector that makes use of a balanced amplifier. The output is the difference between the collector or drain currents of the two devices.

locking circuit   See HOLDING CIRCUIT.

locking relay   See LATCHING RELAY.

lock-in relay   See LATCHING RELAY.

lock-out   **1.** To prevent a hardware unit or routine from being activated (e.g., when there would be a conflict between operations using the same areas of memory). **2.** A safeguard against an attempt to refer to a routine in use.

lock-up relay   An electromagnetic relay that can be locked in the actuated state nonmechanically (i.e., by means of an electromagnet or permanent magnet).

locus   The set of all points located by stated conditions (e.g., the locus of secondary points that are all equidistant from a primary point is a sphere).

lodestone   A natural magnet; a form of the mineral magnetite. Also spelled *loadstone*.

log   **1.** Abbreviation of LOGARITHM. **2.** A continuous record of communications kept by a station, or a record of the operation of an equipment.

log₁₀ $\log_{10}$ Abbreviation of *common logarithm* (base-10 logarithm). Also called *Briggsian logarithm*.

logarithm   Abbreviation, log. The power y to which a fixed number a, called the *base*, must be raised to equal a given number x. Suppose $x = a^y$, where a, x, and y are real numbers. Then, $\log_a x = y$. The most common logarithmic bases are 10 and the transcendental number e, approximately equal to 2.71828. See COMMON LOGARITHM and NAPIERIAN LOGARITHM.

logarithmic amplifier   An amplifier whose output-signal amplitude is proportional to the logarithm of the input-signal amplitude.

logarithmic curve   A graphical representation of a logarithmic function, having the form $y = k \log_a x$, where k is a nonzero real-number constant, and a is a positive real number (the logarithmic base).

logarithmic decrement   See DECREMENT.

logarithmic graph   Also called *log-log graph*. A graph in which the x and y axes are both incremented logarithmically. Compare SEMILOGARITHMIC GRAPH.

logarithmic horn   A horn whose diameter varies directly, according to the logarithm of the displacement along the axis. See HORN.

logarithmic mean   See GEOMETRIC MEAN.

logarithmic meter   A current meter or voltmeter whose deflection is proportional to the logarithm of the quantity under measurement. The increments on the scale of such an instrument are closer together in the upper portion.

logarithmic rate of decay   See EXPONENTIAL DECREASE.

logarithmic rate of growth   See EXPONENTIAL INCREASE.

logarithmic response   **1.** Response in which the value of a dependent variable is at every point proportional to the logarithm of the independent variable. **2.** A type of response in which a quantity (such as current) varies directly with the logarithm of another quantity (such as voltage).

logarithmic scale   A graduated scale in which the coordinates are positioned, according to the logarithm of the actual distance from the origin.

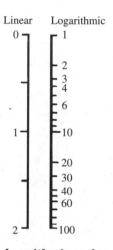

logarithmic scale

logarithmic voltmeter   See LOGARITHMIC METER.

logₑ $\log_e$ Abbreviation of *logarithm to the base e* (the NAPIERIAN LOGARITHM). Also written *ln*.

logic   **1.** In digital circuits, the mathematics dealing with the truth or falsity of statements (represented by variables) and their combinations. Also see SYMBOLIC LOGIC. Generally, "truth" is represented by the binary digit 1, and "falsity" is represented by the binary digit 0. **2.** Collectively, the switching circuits and associated hardware for implementing digital functions (see 1), such as AND, NAND, NOR, OR, etc.

logical decision   During a computer program run, a choice between alternatives based on specified conditions. For example, one alternative path in a routine might be selected because an intermediate result was negative.

logical diagram   A schematic diagram showing the interconnection between gates of a logic circuit.

logical equivalence   The condition in which two logical statements have identical truth value for all possible combinations of truth value of their constituents.

logical file   A data set composing one or several logical records.

logical implication   For logical statements x and y, the condition that y is true whenever x is true: If x, then y.

logical operation   **1.** An operation using logical operators: AND, NOR, OR, and NAND. **2.** A processing operation in which arithmetic is not involved (e.g., a shift).

logical operator   A word or symbol representing a logic function operating on one or more operands. Examples: NOT, OR, AND, NOR, and NAND.

logical shift   A shift operation in which digits in a word are moved to the left or right in circular fashion; digits displaced at one end of the word are returned at the other. Also called CYCLIC SHIFT.

logic array   In logic circuits, a redundant arrangement of identical components in a single package.

logic circuit   In digital systems, a gating or switching circuit that performs such logical operations as AND, NAND, NOR, OR, and XOR. It can use diodes, transistors, charge-coupled devices, tunnel diodes, thyristors, ferroelectric elements, magnetic-core elements, or a combination of these. It usually consists of diodes and transistors fabricated onto an integrated-circuit (IC) chip.

logic circuits (or gates)

logic comparison   An operation in which two operands are compared for equal value.

logic connectives   Words connecting operands in a logic statement; the truth or falsity of the statements can be determined from their content and the connectives' meanings.

logic diagram   **1.** A graphic representation of a logic function (e.g., AND, NAND, NOR, OR, and XOR). **2.** The design of a device or system represented by graphic symbols for logic elements and their relationships.

logic diode   See COMPUTER DIODE.

logic flowchart   The logical steps in a program or subroutine represented by a set of symbols.

logic function   An expression for an operation involving one or a combination of logic operators.

logic gate   See LOGIC CIRCUIT.

logic input current   In an integrated circuit, the input current to the logic gate at a certain voltage value.

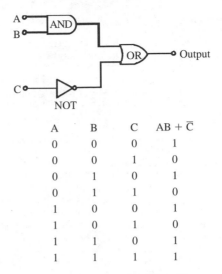

A	B	C	$AB + \overline{C}$
0	0	0	1
0	0	1	0
0	1	0	1
0	1	1	0
1	0	0	1
1	0	1	0
1	1	0	1
1	1	1	1

logic diagram and truth table

logic input levels   The range of voltages over which the logic trip level occurs, from low to high or high to low. It is usually expressed in volts for the low state and the high state; for example, low is −1 to +2 volts, high is +4 to +6 volts.

logic instruction   A command to execute a logical function.

logic level   **1.** One of the two logic states 0 or 1 (on or off, high or low). **2.** Of the two logic states, that which represents the "true" condition. **3.** The voltage amplitude of digital signals in a logic system.

logic probe   A test probe with a built-in amplifier and (usually) indicating LEDs; its tip is touched to various test nodes in a digital logic circuit to trace logic levels and pulses.

logic relay   See BISTABLE RELAY.

logic swing   In a logic circuit, the difference between the voltage corresponding to the high state and the voltage corresponding to the low state.

logic symbol   **1.** A symbol used to represent a logic element in a circuit diagram. **2.** A symbol used to represent a logic connective.

log-log graph   See LOGARITHMIC GRAPH.

LOGO   A high-level computer programming language used for robot control and as an education aid. It is especially useful for teaching children how to operate computers and computerized robots. Statements are simple enough so that elementary-school children can learn to write short programs.

log-periodic antenna   Also called *log-periodic dipole array (LPDA)*. A broad-spectrum, multiband directional antenna in which the lengths and spacing of the radiator and elements increase logarithmically from one end of the antenna to the other.

log polar navigation A computerized navigation system in which polar-coordinate data is converted into rectangular-coordinate data. In the transformation process, the logarithm of the radius (range) is taken. This results in improved image resolution at close range, although it sacrifices resolution at greater ranges.

log taper In a potentiometer or rheostat, resistance variations that correspond to the logarithm of shaft rotation, or vice versa. Compare LINEAR TAPER. Also see TAPER.

long Abbreviation of LONGITUDE.

long-distance communication 1. Radio communication between stations separated by distances too great for ground-wave propagation to be effective. **2.** In telephone service, communications that require the dialing of an area code in addition to the local exchange number.

long-distance loop A direct telephone line connecting a subscriber's station to a long distance switchboard.

long-distance reception Reception of radio signals from stations beyond the range of ground-wave propagation. See also LONG-DISTANCE COMMUNICATION, 1.

long-distance transmission Transmission of radio signals to points beyond the range of ground-wave propagation. See also LONG-DISTANCE COMMUNICATION, 1.

longitude Abbreviation, long. Angular displacement, measured in degrees around the earth's circumference, to the east and west of the prime meridian that passes through Greenwich, England. Compare LATITUDE. Also see MERIDIAN.

longitude effect The variation (caused by the earth's rotation and magnetic field) of the strength of cosmic rays arriving at different longitudes on the surface of the earth.

longitudinal current Current flowing in the same direction in the parallel wires of a pair (the return circuit is via ground).

longitudinal parity Parity associated with bits recorded on one track of a magnetic storage medium to indicate whether the number of bits is even or odd.

longitudinal redundancy A computer condition, generally affecting magnetic tape records, in which the bits in each track of a record do not meet the required parity, as determined by a LONGITUDINAL REDUNDANCY CHECK.

longitudinal redundancy check A parity check performed on a block of characters or bits (for example, on a track of a magnetic disk). A parity character is generated and transmitted as the last character of the block; thus, each longitudinal block has either even or odd parity.

longitudinal wave A wave in which the movement of particles in a medium is parallel with the direction of propagation.

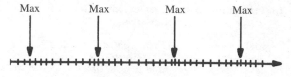

longitudinal wave

long line 1. A single-wire antenna whose length is greater than the length of the wave fed to it for propagation. Also see LONG-WIRE ANTENNA. **2.** In wire telegraphy, an electrical line that has great physical length. **3.** In electronics theory, a transmission line of indeterminate length, but whose characteristics remain stable and predictable to infinity.

long-persistence screen A cathode-ray-tube screen on which the image remains for a time after the electron beam has passed.

long-play Abbreviation, LP. Descriptive of phonograph discs designed to play at 33.3 revolutions per minute (rpm). Also see MICROGROOVE RECORD.

long-play record See MICROGROOVE RECORD.

long-range navigation See LORAN.

long-range radar Radar that can detect targets at distances of 200 miles or more.

long skip Ionospheric radio-wave propagation, usually via the F layer, between or among stations separated by large geographic distances. The wave angles of departure (from transmitting stations) and arrival (at receiving stations) are very small relative to the horizon. Compare SHORT SKIP.

long-term drift Gradual change in the value of a quantity, such as voltage or frequency, observed over a long period, in contrast to that noted for a brief interval. Compare SHORT-TERM DRIFT.

long-term input offset voltage stability Expressed in microvolts per month. The extent to which the input offset voltage in an integrated circuit stays stable over long periods of time.

long-term stability Stability reckoned over a period of weeks, months or years, as contrasted to that noted for brief intervals of time (minutes or hours).

long throw A speaker design term that describes a woofer moving through long excursions; the objective is to provide good low-frequency response with low distortion.

long waves Low-frequency radio waves, particularly those in the frequency range of 30 kHz to 300 kHz (10 km to 1 km).

long-wire antenna An antenna whose radiating element(s) measure at least one wavelength, but more typically several wavelengths. The several variants are generally used at radio frequencies between about 500 kHz and 30 MHz.

lookup A computer programming technique in which a data item identified by a key is selected from an array.

loop **1.** An electrical circuit consisting of elements connected in series. **2.** In a standing-wave system, a maximum-response point (e.g., *current loop* and *voltage loop*). Compare NODE, **2. 3.** See LOOP ANTENNA. **4.** A signal path (e.g., *feedback loop*). **5.** A one- or two-turn coil for low-impedance coupling. Also see LINK, 1. **6.** In a computer program run, the repetitious execution of a series of instructions that terminates when some specified condition is satisfied by a relational test, at which point the next instruction in the main program is obeyed.

loop antenna **1.** A small portable receiving antenna in the form of a wire coil. **2.** A half-wave conductor bent into a circle or square. The conductor is broken at the point opposite the feed point. It can be used for transmitting and receiving. **3.** A full-wavelength, continuous conductor bent into a circle or square. It can be used for transmitting and receiving.

loop checking A method of checking the accuracy of data transmitted over a data link by returning signals received at one terminal to the transmitting terminal for comparison with the original data.

looped amplification See FEEDBACK FACTOR.

looping plug A double phone-plug unit for simultaneously plugging into two phone jacks. Completes (loops) the circuit between the two jacks.

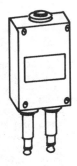

looping plug

loop-input signal A signal introduced into a feedback control loop.

loop pulsing The regular, intermittent breaking of the direct-current path at the transmitting end of a transmission line; also called DIAL PULSING.

loop resistance The resistance of the electrical path around a complete loop (see LOOP, 1).

loop response time In a security system, the length of time between the first sensing of an abnormal condition (e.g., an intrusion) and the recognition of that condition by the controller.

loopstick antenna See FERRITE-ROD ANTENNA.

loop test A means of locating a discontinuity in a circuit by creating a closed loop, including the suspected fault point.

loose coupling Coupling that transfers only small amounts of energy, as when a primary and secondary coil are spaced so far apart that the coefficient of coupling is small. Compare CLOSE COUPLING.

loosely coupled twin In computer operations, a system in which two processors, each having its own operating system, are used with switches so that they can use common peripherals. Also see SWITCH.

lopplar Acronym for *laser Doppler radar*. Also abbreviated as ladar.

lorac A radio-navigation system that operates by means of phase comparison. Similar to LORAN. Trade name of Seismograph Service Corporation.

loran A long-range radionavigation system in which two pairs of ground stations transmit pulsed signals that are used by aircraft and ships to determine their positions. The name is an acronym for *long-range navigation*.

loran C A radionavigation system that operates at a frequency of 100 kHz. It operates on the hyperbolic principle.

loran D A radionavigation system similar to loran C. It is used by aircraft, operates independent of ground stations, and prevents unwanted enemy detection of aircraft position.

Lorentz force For a charge Q moving with velocity v in a magnetic field B and an electric field E, the force $F = Q(E + (v \times B))$.

loss Energy that is dissipated without doing useful work in a circuit or system. See POWER LOSS.

loss angle For an insulating material, 90 degrees minus the PHASE ANGLE.

loss index For an insulating material, the product of the POWER FACTOR and the DIELECTRIC CONSTANT.

lossless data compression A process in which the number of bits in a data file is reduced by eliminating redundancies, without sacrificing any of the precision or detail in the file. Compression of text and programs must usually be lossless. Image compression need not generally be lossless. Compare LOSSY DATA COMPRESSION.

lossless line A perfect transmission line (i.e., one having no resistance loss, no dielectric loss, and no radiation loss). It is not realizable in practice, but useful in some theoretical calculations.

loss tangent See DISSIPATION FACTOR, 1.

lossy data compression A process in which the number of bits in a data file (especially a digital image) is reduced by eliminating redundancies, with some sacrifice of precision or detail. In image compression, some loss can usually be tolerated, allowing larger compression ratios than would be possible if zero loss were mandatory.

Lossy compression is not generally acceptable for text files and programs. Compare LOSSLESS DATA COMPRESSION.

lossy line   A line or cable having comparatively high or excessive attenuation per unit length.

loudness   The amplitude of sound, especially in audio reproduction equipment, such as a high-fidelity stereo amplifier. Also called VOLUME.

loudness control   See COMPENSATED VOLUME CONTROL.

loudness curves   See AUDIBILITY CURVES.

loudness switch/button   In a high-fidelity audio amplifier, a switch or button that can be actuated when music is played at low loudness. Increases the volume of the bass relative to the midrange and treble.

loudspeaker   A transducer that converts electrical impulses into sound waves of sufficient volume to be heard easily by a number of listeners situated at some distance from the device. Also called *speaker*.

loudspeaker damping   See DAMPED LOUD-SPEAKER.

loudspeaker dividing network   See CROSSOVER NETWORK.

low   **1.** The logical digit 0. **2.** Of relatively small magnitude (e.g., LOW VOLTAGE and LOW-FREQUENCY). **3.** In a rechargeable cell or battery, the condition of being near the end of the discharge cycle.

low band   **1.** The low or lowest frequency band used in communications, testing, or processing in a given situation. **2.** Television channels 2 to 6 (54 to 88 MHz). **3.** In two-way radio operations, those radio channels between 30 MHz and about 70 MHz.

low battery   **1.** The condition of a battery needing replacement or recharging. **2.** An indicating device that shows when a battery needs to be replaced or recharged.

low-battery bias current   The current into a designated pin of an integrated circuit required for proper operation of the LOW-BATTERY INDICATOR.

low-battery indicator   A device, such as a light-emitting diode (LED) and associated circuitry, that gives a visible indication of the condition of LOW BATTERY.

low-capacitance probe   A test probe in which capacitance has been minimized to reduce loading and detuning of the circuit under test.

low-energy criterion   See VON HIPPEL BREAK-DOWN THEORY.

lower sideband   Abbreviation, LSB. In an amplitude-modulated wave, the lower band of frequencies equal to the difference between the carrier frequency and the modulating frequency. Compare UPPER SIDEBAND.

lower sideband suppressed carrier   Abbreviation, LSSC. A single-sideband transmission technique in which the lower sideband is transmitted, but the upper sideband and carrier are suppressed. Compare DOUBLE SIDEBAND SUPPRESSED CARRIER and UPPER SIDEBAND SUPPRESSED CARRIER.

lowest usable frequency   Abbreviation, LUF. The lowest frequency that can be used successfully at a given time for communication via the ionosphere. Compare MAXIMUM USABLE FREQUENCY.

low filter   A highpass filter that removes low-frequency audio noise from the modulating waveform of a broadcast station. The result is a lower level of transmitted hum and rumble.

low-frequency   Abbreviation, LF. **1.** Pertaining to radio frequencies in the band from 30 kHz to 300 kHz (wavelengths from 10 kilometers to 1 kilometer). Also see RADIO SPECTRUM. **2.** Pertaining to audio frequencies below 500 Hz.

low-frequency compensation   **1.** In video-amplifier design, special measures, such as use of high coupling and bypass capacitances, to boost low-frequency gain. **2.** Use of special circuits to increase the low-frequency response of an audio amplifier. Also see BASS BOOST, **1**, **2**.

low-frequency direction finder   Abbreviation, LDF. A direction finder operated in or below the standard amplitude-modulation (AM) broadcast band, that is, below 1.605 MHz.

low-frequency padder   See OSCILLATOR PADDER.

low-frequency parasitics   Parasitic oscillations of a frequency lower than that being processed by the amplifier or generated by the oscillator in which they occur.

low-level   **1.** A logic term for the more negative of the two (binary) logic levels. **2.** Having an amplitude that is below that normally available in comparable circuits or systems. **3.** In computer operations, pertaining to programming languages (such as assembly language or machine language) that control the machine, but do not directly interface with the operator.

low-level audio signal   In audio operations, a signal that has not been amplified by any means (e.g., the output of a dynamic microphone). Compare HIGH-LEVEL AUDIO SIGNAL.

low-level contact   A switch or relay contact intended for use with low values of current and voltage.

low-level input current   **1.** A test used to check an input pull-up resistor in an integrated circuit to ensure that the fan-in is as specified. **2.** The current flowing from an input when the highest low-level output voltage specified is applied to the input of the device.

low-level language   A computer programming language in which each instruction has only one equivalent machine code. Examples are *machine language* and *assembly language*. Compare HIGH-LEVEL LANGUAGE.

low-level logic   Abbreviation, LLL. In digital-computer operations, any logic system that operates at low voltage or current levels.

low-level modulation Modulation of a radio or television transmitter at a stage preceding the final radio-frequency (RF) power amplifier.

low-level output current **1.** A test to ascertain that the fan-out and current-sinking capability of an integrated circuit are as specified. **2.** The current flowing into an output with input conditions that cause the output to be at logic low.

low-level signal **1.** A signal with small amplitude. **2.** A signal with peak-to-peak voltage so low that it does not drive an amplifier circuit out of the linear range of operation.

low-loss material A material, particularly a dielectric, having low electrical loss at a given frequency. Also see LOSS.

low-noise Pertaining to circuits, especially weak-signal communications receiving amplifiers and converters, designed to generate the smallest possible amount of internal noise.

low-noise down converter In a satellite television receiving system, a circuit that converts the signals from the dish antenna to frequencies that correspond to the channels on a conventional television set.

low order The lesser-value place(s) of characters or digits in the hierarchy of a group (number or word). For example, 5 and 6 are low-order digits in the number 123,456.

low-order position The extreme right-hand (least significant) position in a number or word.

low-pass filter A selective filter that transmits (with little attenuation) frequencies below a critical (cutoff) frequency and blocks frequencies above the cutoff value. Such filters can be inductance-capacitance (LC) circuits, resistance-capacitance (RC) circuits, or a combination of these.

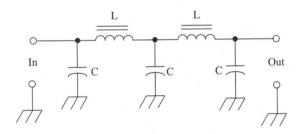

low-pass filter

low power Abbreviation, LP. Power considerably lower than that ordinarily encountered in a particular application. The term is arbitrary; several hundred watts might be regarded as low power in one situation, whereas a fraction of a watt would be implied in another.

low-print recording tape Magnetic tape that is less susceptible to print-through than conventional tape.

low Q For a component or circuit, a low quotient for the ratio of reactance to resistance (X/R). This is a relative term because a particular Q value considered low in one situation might be high in other circumstances. Also see FIGURE OF MERIT, **1**.

low tension See LOW VOLTAGE.

low voltage **1.** A voltage considerably lower than that ordinarily encountered in a particular application. The term is arbitrary; several hundred volts might be regarded as low in one situation, and a fraction of a volt would be implied in another. **2.** In a television receiver, the supply voltage applied to all points other than the high-voltage circuit or the picture tube.

low-voltage rectifier In a television receiver, the rectifier that supplies power for the low-voltage stages. See LOW VOLTAGE, **2**.

LP **1.** Abbreviation of LOW POWER. **2.** Abbreviation of LONG PLAY. **3.** Abbreviation of *low pressure*.

L pad An attenuator consisting of one series arm and one shunt arm, arranged in such a way that the schematic representation of the circuit resembles an inverted capital letter L. It is noted for its constant input resistance or impedance as the amount of attenuation is varied.

LPB Abbreviation of LIGHTED PUSHBUTTON.

L_P band A section of the L BAND extending from 390 to 465 MHz.

lpm Abbreviation of *lines per minute*: the output speed of a line printer.

lpW Abbreviation of *lumens per watt*; lm/W is preferred.

Lr Symbol for LAWRENCIUM.

L + R, L − R The sum and difference of the left (L) and right (R) channel signals in a stereo high-fidelity sound system. The L + R signal is the in-phase combination of the two channels; the L − R signal is the out-of-phase combination.

L regulator See L-TYPE VOLTAGE REGULATOR.

LRR Abbreviation of LONG-RANGE RADAR.

LR time constant See INDUCTANCE-RESISTANCE TIME CONSTANT.

LSA diode Abbreviation for *limited-space-charge-accumulation diode*. A solid-state diode that acts as a microwave oscillator.

LSB **1.** Abbreviation of LOWER SIDEBAND. **2.** Abbreviation of LEAST-SIGNIFICANT BIT.

L_S band A section of the L band that extends from 900 to 950 MHz.

LSC Abbreviation of LEAST-SIGNIFICANT CHARACTER.

LSD Abbreviation of LEAST-SIGNIFICANT DIGIT.

L section **1.** A filter section whose schematic representation has the general shape of an inverted capital letter L. **2.** An attenuator circuit whose schematic representation has the general shape of an inverted capital letter L. **3.** A network section consisting of a series (input) impedance arm and a shunt (output) impedance arm. See L PAD. **4.** A right-angle bend in coaxial cable (see ELL).

LSI   See LARGE-SCALE INTEGRATION.

LSSC   Abbreviation of LOWER SIDEBAND SUPPRESSED CARRIER.

L$_T$ band   A section of the L BAND extending from 780 to 900 MHz.

LTROM   Abbreviation of LINEAR-TRANSFORMER READ-ONLY MEMORY.

L-type antenna   See INVERTED-L ANTENNA.

L-type voltage regulator   A simple voltage regulator containing a series current-limiting resistor and shunt regulator (zener diode, VR tube, voltage-dependent resistor, etc.). The schematic representation resembles an inverted capital letter L.

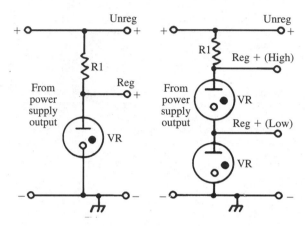

L-type voltage regulator

lt-yr   Abbreviation of LIGHT-YEAR.

Lu   Symbol for LUTETIUM.

Lucalox   General Electric's translucent ceramic; its chief constituent is polycrystalline alumina. The material has many applications in electro-optics.

Lucite   Trade name for METHYL METHACRYLATE RESIN.

Luddites   During the Industrial Revolution, people who sabotaged automated factory equipment because they believed the machines would put them out of work. The word comes from the name of Ned Ludd, their supposed leader. The term is sometimes applied nowadays to people who fear computers, robots, and other technological innovations because of real or imagined threats to personal job security.

LUF   Abbreviation of LOWEST USABLE FREQUENCY.

lug   **1.** A contact attached to the end of a wire lead to facilitate connection to a binding post. **2.** A contact attached to a terminal strip, to which wire leads are soldered.

lum   Abbreviation of LUMEN. The preferred (SI) form is lm.

lumen   Abbreviation, lm, and sometimes l or lum. The SI unit of luminous flux; it is equal to the light that is emitted in one steradian (the unit solid angle) by a uniform point source of one candela. Also see CANDLE POWER, ILLUMINANCE, LUMINOUS INTENSITY, SOLID ANGLE, and STERADIAN.

lumen-hour   Abbreviation, lm-hr. The amount of light that a source having a luminous flux of one LUMEN delivers in a time period of one hour.

luminaire   A complete and self-contained lighting system, for television-studio use or photographic use. The kit includes all of the needed parts and accessories.

luminance   The amount of light emitted or scattered by a surface. This property is expressed in *candelas per square meter (cd/m²)*.

luminance channel   In a color television circuit, the channel that processes the Y SIGNAL.

luminance signal   See Y SIGNAL.

luminescence   The production of visible light, but not heat, by a material stimulated by radiation or electron bombardment. See ELECTROLUMINESCENT CELL and LUMINESCENT SCREEN.

luminescent cell   See ELECTROLUMINESCENT CELL.

luminescent screen   A cathode-ray tube whose screen is coated with a material that glows under the influence of ionizing radiation, X rays, or electron beams.

luminiferous ether   See ETHER, 1.

luminosity   The luminous efficiency of radiant energy, as given by the ratio of luminous flux to radiant flux (lumens per watt) for a specific wavelength.

luminosity factor   Abbreviated K, and expressed in lumens per watt. The luminous intensity divided by the actual radiant intensity at a given wavelength of visible light.

luminous energy   The energy in visible electromagnetic radiation.

luminous flux   The rate of transfer or flow of luminous energy.

luminous intensity   Luminous flux through a unit solid angle, expressed in candelas. Also see CANDELA.

lumistor   An amplifier or coupling device in which the input signal varies the brilliance of a

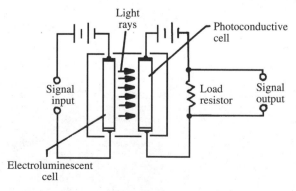

lumistor

lamp, electroluminescent cell, or light-emitting diode, and a photocell (or other light-sensitive device) picks up the fluctuating light and uses it to modulate an output current. In a compact lumistor, the light-emitting and light-sensing components are separate layers in a wafer or block of material. Compare LIGHT AMPLIFIER.

lumped Pertaining to a property that is concentrated at or around a single point, rather than being distributed through a circuit (e.g., *lumped capacitance* and *lumped inductance*).

lumped capacitor See DISCRETE CAPACITOR.

lumped component A discrete component (i.e., one that is self-contained). Compare DISTRIBUTED COMPONENT.

lumped constant The total value of any single electrical property in an electrical or electronic component.

lumped-constant delay line A delay line having discrete capacitance and inductance components. Compare DISTRIBUTED-CONSTANT DELAY LINE.

lumped impedance A reactance and/or resistance manifested in a definite location. Examples are ordinary components, such as capacitors, inductors, and resistors.

lumped inductor See DISCRETE INDUCTOR.

lumped parameter Any circuit parameter that can be considered as a discrete parameter—even if it is not made up of a single component.

lumped resistor See DISCRETE RESISTOR.

lutetium Symbol, Lu. A metallic element of the rare-earth group. Atomic number, 71. Atomic weight, 174.967.

lux The unit of illuminance, equivalent to one LUMEN per square meter.

Luxemberg effect The generation of interference by cross-modulation of two or more signals whose paths intersect in the same region of the ionosphere.

luxmeter A device for measuring visible illuminance.

LV Abbreviation of LOW VOLTAGE.

LVDT Abbreviation of LINEAR VARIABLE DIFFERENTIAL TRANSFORMER.

Lw Symbol for LAWRENCIUM; more commonly *Lr*.

lx Abbreviation of LUX.

L_X band A section of the L BAND that extends from 950 MHz to 1.15 GHz.

L_Y band A section of the L BAND that extends from 725 to 780 MHz.

L_Z band A section of the L BAND that extends from 1.450 to 1.550 GHz.

LZT Abbreviation of LEAD ZIRCONATE-TITANATE, a ceramic used in electronics.

M 1. Abbreviation of prefix MEGA-. **2.** Symbol for MUTUAL INDUCTANCE. **3.** Symbol for MODIFIED INDEX OF REFRACTION.

m 1. Abbreviation of prefix MILLI-. **2.** Symbol for MASS. **3.** Abbreviation of METER. **4.** Abbreviation of MILE. (Also, mi.) **5.** Symbol for MODULATION COEFFICIENT.

m^2 Abbreviation of *square meter*, the SI unit of area.

m^3 Abbreviation of *cubic meter*, the SI unit of volume.

MA 1. Abbreviation of MAGNETIC AMPLIFIER. (Also, *magamp.*) **2.** Abbreviation of MEGAMPERE.

mA Abbreviation of MILLIAMPERE.

Mache unit A unit of radioactivity equivalent to 13.47 disintegrations per second (3.64×10^{-10} curie) per liter. It represents the concentration of radon gas per liter (when all radiation is absorbed) that will result in a saturation current of 10^{-3} esu (not to be confused with MACH NUMBER).

machine address See ABSOLUTE ADDRESS.

machine code See MACHINE LANGUAGE.

machine cycle In a machine whose operation is periodic, a complete sequence constituting a period of operation.

machine error In a computer or data-processing system, an error attributable to a hardware failure, rather than to a software fault.

machine instruction A computer program instruction written in MACHINE LANGUAGE.

machine knowledge General term for data stored in an artificially intelligent computer system, and the ability of the computer to use that data in meaningful ways.

machine language Computer program instructions and data represented in binary form. In the hierarchy of programming languages, it is the lowest; the computer works directly with it. All high-level languages are translated to machine language by an assembler, compiler, interpreter, or monitor system.

machine learning In artificial intelligence, a computer's ability to learn through repeated calculations for particular problems.

machine logic 1. The way that a computer's functional parts are interrelated. **2.** The facility whereby a computer solves problems.

machine operation The performance by a computer of a built-in function (e.g., subtraction).

machine operator A person participating in implementing and overseeing the processing of computer programs.

machine word In computer operations, the address of a memory location composed of the full number of bits normally handled by each register of the machine.

machining In industrial robotics, the mechanical modification of parts during assembly. Examples: drilling, welding, sanding, polishing, and painting.

Mach number For a medium such as air, the ratio of the speed of a body in motion to the speed of sound in the medium. (Not to be confused with MACHE UNIT.)

macro 1. A control shortcut, in which a function requiring the actuation of several switches is abbreviated, via a microcomputer, so that it can be executed by actuating only one or two switches. **2.** Abbreviation of MACROINSTRUCTION.

macro- Prefix denoting extremely large. Compare MICRO-.

macro assembly program An assembly program whose source statements are translated to several machine-language instructions.

macroinstruction A source program instruction that becomes several machine-language instructions when operated on by a compiler.

macroknowledge In artificial intelligence, knowledge in the large sense (i.e., knowledge about information). Example: a set of definitions in an expert system. Compare MICROKNOWLEDGE.

macroprogram A computer program consisting of macroinstructions.

macrosonics The theory and applications of high-amplitude sound waves.

madistor A component that produces changes in current by means of magnetic-field effects. It is used as an oscillator or amplifier.

MADT Abbreviation of MICROALLOY DIFFUSED TRANSISTOR.

MAG Abbreviation of MAXIMUM AVAILABLE GAIN.

magamp Acronym for MAGNETIC AMPLIFIER.

magazine A tape or film cartridge.

magenta One of the primary pigments used in color printers. It has a pinkish-red hue.

magnal CRT base An 11-pin base typical of many cathode-ray tubes.

magnesium Symbol, Mg. A metallic element. Atomic number, 12. Atomic weight, 24.305.

magnesium fluoride phosphor A substance used as a phosphor coating on the screen of a very-long-persistence cathode-ray tube. The fluorescence and phosphorescence are orange.

magnesium silicate phosphor A substance used as a phosphor coating on the screen of a cathode-ray tube. The fluorescence is orange-red.

magnesium tungstate phosphor A substance used as a phosphor coating on the screen of a cathode-ray tube. The fluorescence is very light blue.

magnet A device or body of material that has the ability to attract to itself pieces of iron and other magnetic metals, and the ability to attract or repel other magnets. Also see ELECTROMAGNET, PERMANENT MAGNET, and TEMPORARY MAGNET.

magnet armature See KEEPER.

magnet battery A group of several magnets placed together in parallel (i.e., with similar poles touching or resting nearby) to act as a single magnet.

magnet charger A device that produces an intense magnetic field for restoring weakened magnets or for making new magnets.

magnetic 1. Pertaining to MAGNETISM. 2. Possessing MAGNETISM. 3. Capable of being magnetized. 2. See MAGNETIC MATERIAL.

magnetic air-gap A space between two magnetic poles, either the same (in which case the force is repulsive) or opposite (in which case the force is attractive).

magnetic amplifier An iron-core device that uses the principle of the saturable reactor to obtain amplification. In its simplest form, it consists of input and output coils wound on a core of square-loop magnetic metal. The input coil consists of two identical windings connected in series-opposition so that currents in the output winding cannot induce voltage in the input winding. The output coil is connected in series with a load and an alternating-current (ac) supply. A small ac signal applied to the input winding causes a large change in the impedance of the output winding and, therefore, a large change in the voltage across the load.

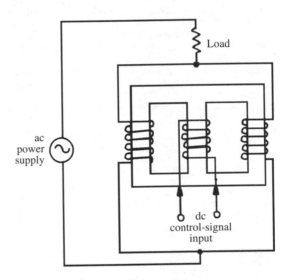

magnetic amplifier

magnetic analysis See MASS SPECTROMETER.

magnetic attraction 1. The force that causes a magnetic pole to draw to itself an opposite magnetic pole. Thus, a north pole attracts a south pole, and a south pole attracts a north pole. Compare MAGNETIC REPULSION. 2. The force that causes a magnetic pole to draw to itself a piece of magnetic material, such as iron or steel.

magnetic axis A straight line joining the poles of a magnet.

magnetic bearing The azimuth, or compass direction, measured with respect to magnetic north (the direction of the north geomagnetic pole). It is usually expressed in degrees and can be read directly from a compass.

magnetic azimuth An azimuth bearing relative to magnetic north (the direction of the north geomagnetic pole).

magnetic balance   An instrument for measuring the force, either attractive or repulsive, between two objects that are magnetized, or between a magnet and a magnetic substance. The device can also be used for measuring the intensity of a magnetic field, either from a permanent magnet, an electromagnet, or from the earth.

magnetic bias   A steady magnetic force applied to another magnetic field to set the latter's quiescent point (e.g., sensitizing a relay by using a permanent magnet to lower the relay draw-in point).

magnetic blowout   **1.** The extinction of an electric arc by a strong magnetic field. **2.** The apparatus for accomplishing the action described in **1**.

magnetic bottle   A container envisioned for atomic fusion reactions, and that would consist of a magnetic field. Conventional containers cannot withstand the extremely high temperatures involved in atomic fusion.

magnetic braking   See ELECTROMAGNETIC BRAKING.

magnetic bridge   An instrument comparable to the WHEATSTONE BRIDGE, used to measure magnetic permeability.

magnetic bubble memory   See BUBBLE MEMORY.

magnetic capacity   The maximum magnetization a given material can receive.

magnetic card   A computer storage medium in the form of a card that can be selectively magnetized or imprinted with magnetic ink to represent data.

magnetic cartridge   A variable-reluctance phonograph pickup. As the stylus moves in the groove, the vibrations are translated into electric currents by a magnet and coil.

magnetic centering   Centering the beam in a television picture tube by means of an electromagnetic focusing coil, a permanent magnet, or both.

magnetic character   A letter, numeral, or other symbol written or printed in (visible) magnetic ink for its automatic sensing or reading in computing and signaling operations.

magnetic circuit   The closed path determined by a line of magnetic flux or by a set of lines of flux.

magnetic clutch   A clutch in which the magnetism of one rotating member causes a second member to lock in and rotate. There need not be physical contact between the two.

magnetic coil   The winding in an electromagnet or similar device.

magnetic compass   A direction-indicating device using a horizontally suspended magnetic needle as the indicator. The needle tends to point in the direction of the north geomagnetic pole. Compare GYROCOMPASS.

magnetic component   See ELECTROMAGNETIC COMPONENT.

magnetic conductivity   See PERMEABILITY.

magnetic constant   The absolute permeability of free space. It is approximately 1.26×10^{-6} H/m.

magnetic controller   A controller that uses electromagnets for some of its functions.

magnetic core   The iron core of an electromagnet, choke, transformer, relay, or similar device.

magnetic coupling   See INDUCTIVE COUPLING.

magnetic course   In navigation, a course referenced to geomagnetic north, rather than geographic north.

magnetic crack detector   See ELECTROMAGNETIC CRACK DETECTOR.

magnetic creeping   A gradual increase in the magnetization of a material under the influence of a steady magnetizing force.

magnetic cycle   **1.** For a material in an alternating magnetic field, the change in magnetic flux as a function of time. **2.** The change in the magnetic-field polarity of the earth. This polarity reverses every few thousand years.

magnetic damping   The production of a damping effect or drag in a machine or meter by means of magnetic action on a moving member, in accordance with LENZ'S LAW.

magnetic declination   See DECLINATION.

magnetic deflection   See ELECTROMAGNETIC DEFLECTION.

magnetic density   The concentration of magnetic flux in a region, expressed as the number of lines per unit area of cross section.

magnetic dip   At a particular location on the earth's surface, the angle between the terrestrial magnetic field and a horizontal line.

magnetic dipole   **1.** A molecule or particle with a north and south magnetic pole. **2.** Any pair of adjacent north and south magnetic poles.

magnetic direction finder   Abbreviation, MDF. A type of compass operated by an electric signal delivered by a gyrostabilized magnetic-compass movement.

magnetic disk   A rotating disk coated with a layer of magnetic material for the recording, storage and retrieval of information. They are available in various sizes, configurations, and storage capacities. Commonly used with personal computers. Also see DISKETTE and HARD DISK.

magnetic doublet   See DOUBLET, **2**.

magnetic drive   A device in which mechanical movement is conveyed from one moving part to another by means of a magnetic clutch.

magnetic drum   See DRUM.

magnetic effect of electric current   The presence of a magnetic field around a conductor carrying electric current.

magnetic equator   Also called *geomagnetic equator*. An imaginary circle around the earth, along which a magnetic needle shows no dip. It is near, but slightly displaced from, the geographic equator, and is midway between the geomagnetic poles.

magnetic feedback   Feedback by means of inductive coupling between the output and input circuits of a system. It can be positive or negative.

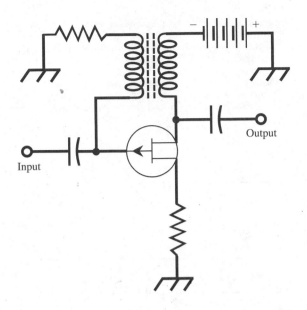

magnetic feedback

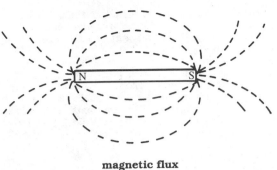

magnetic flux

magnetic field   The space around a magnetic pole or magnetized body in which magnetic energy acts.

magnetic field intensity   See MAGNETIC INTENSITY.

magnetic field strength   See MAGNETIC INTENSITY.

magnetic-field viewer   A device for visually examining a magnetic field. It consists of a clear plastic watchcase filled with iron-oxide particles in liquid suspension. When it is placed within a magnetic field, the particles align themselves in the direction of the magnetic lines of flux.

magnetic-film memory   A magnetic memory in which memory cells consist of a thin film (thick film in some instances) of a magnetic material deposited on a substrate. Information is written into and read out of the cell through coils. Also called *thin-film memory*.

magnetic flip-flop   A bistable multivibrator using magnetic amplifiers or square-loop cores in place of transistors.

magnetic flux   The intensity of a magnetic field through a given area. The unit of magnetic flux is the weber, and the symbol is F. It can loosely be expressed as the number of lines passing through a region of a certain area or of a unit area, such as one square meter. See FLUX.

magnetic flux density   See FLUX DENSITY.

magnetic flux linkage   The passage of magnetic lines of flux through separate materials or circuits, thereby coupling them magnetically.

magnetic focusing   See ELECTROMAGNETIC FOCUSING.

magnetic force   The force exerted by a magnet on a body of magnetic material, or on another magnet, within its field.

magnetic friction   1. See HYSTERESIS, 1. 2. The resistance experienced by a magnetic material moving in a magnetic field.

magnetic gap   A space separating the materials in a magnetic circuit. This break is either an air space or one filled with a comparatively thin piece of nonmagnetic material (e.g., the gap in a choke-coil core).

magnetic head   See MAGNETIC PICKUP HEAD and MAGNETIC RECORDING HEAD.

magnetic hysteresis   See HYSTERESIS, 1.

magnetic inclination   See MAGNETIC DIP.

magnetic induction   1. The magnetization of a magnetic material, such as iron or steel, when it is placed in a magnetic field. 2. The induction of an alternating voltage in a conductor by a nearby alternating magnetic field. Also see ELECTROMAGNETIC INDUCTION.

magnetic ink   Writing or printing ink that is a suspension of finely divided particles of magnetic material. Also see MAGNETIC CHARACTER.

magnetic instability   1. The tendency of a magnetic recording medium to deteriorate with time. 2. Any fluctuation in the intensity of a magnetic field.

magnetic intensity   The free-space strength of a magnetic field at a particular point. Specifically, the force (in dynes) that the magnetic field would exert on a unit magnetic pole placed at that point.

magnetic iron oxide   See MAGNETITE.

magnetic leakage   The usually undesired extension of magnetic flux beyond the confines of a magnetic body, such as the core of a choke.

magnetic lens   See ELECTROMAGNETIC LENS.

magnetic line of flux   See LINE OF FLUX, 2.

magnetic load   An electromagnetic device operating on the output of an electrical source. Such devices include actuators, alarms, electromagnets, magnetic tapes and disks, relays, and loudspeakers.

magnetic loudspeaker   See MAGNETIC SPEAKER, 1, 2.

magnetic material   **1.** A material, such as magnetite, that exhibits natural magnetism. **2.** A material, such as iron or steel, that is capable of being magnetized.

magnetic media   Any medium that stores data as tiny magnetic fields; in particular, MAGNETIC DISK or MAGNETIC TAPE.

magnetic memory   **1.** See RETENTIVITY. **2.** A digital memory circuit using magnetic fields to store data bits. Example: BUBBLE MEMORY.

magnetic meridian   The circle of the celestial sphere that passes through the zenith and earth's magnetic poles.

magnetic mine   A naval mine detonated by a magnetic switch that is closed by the proximity of the steel hull of a ship.

magnetic modulator   A core-type device that is somewhat similar to a magnetic amplifier used for amplitude modulation. Modulating current passes through the control winding, and the carrier current through the output winding.

magnetic moment   Unit, joule per tesla. For a magnet, the product of pole strength and the distance between poles.

magnetic needle   The pivoted magnetic pointer in a magnetic compass.

magnetic north   See NORTH MAGNETIC POLE.

magnetic oxide   Iron oxide used as the sensitive coating of magnetic recording tape.

magnetic pickup   **1.** A phonograph pickup of the variable-reluctance type (see VARIABLE-RELUCTANCE PICKUP). **2.** A magnetic transducer (such as a phono cartridge, tape recording head, or similar input element).

magnetic-pickup head   In a tape recorder, the transducer that receives up magnetic impulses from the passing tape and converts them into alternating currents. These currents are amplified to obtain the original sound. Compare MAGNETIC RECORDING HEAD.

magnetic-plate wire   Wire in which a magnetic metal has been plated on top of a nonmagnetic metal.

magnetic poles   **1.** The points in a MAGNET at which the magnetic lines of flux converge. **2.** The points on the earth at which the geomagnetic lines of flux converge. See NORTH MAGNETIC POLE and SOUTH MAGNETIC POLE.

magnetic   pressure   See   MAGNETOMOTIVE FORCE.

magnetic printing   **1.** Also called *magnetic print-through*. In a recording material, such as magnetic tape, the transfer of information from one part of the material to another part (or from one medium to another) by the magnetic field of the recorded material. This phenomenon, which is also called PRINT-THROUGH, sometimes occurs in recording tape on a reel. **2.** Conventional lithography, letterpress, or other reproduction process in which MAGNETIC INK is used.

magnetic print-through   See MAGNETIC PRINTING, **1.**

magnetic probe   A loop or coil inserted in an electromagnetic field to sample the magnetic component. See, for example, WAVEGUIDE PROBE. Compare ELECTRIC PROBE.

magnetic recording   **1.** The recording of sounds or data by varying the magnetization of a medium, such as a magnetic disk or tape. **2.** A magnetic medium on which data has been recorded.

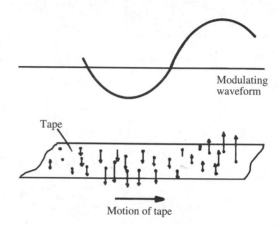

Modulating waveform

Tape

Motion of tape

magnetic recording

magnetic recording head   In a tape recorder, the transducer that receives current impulses (analogs of the original sound vibrations) from an amplifier and converts them into magnetic impulses that magnetize spaces on the passing tape. Compare MAGNETIC PICKUP HEAD.

magnetic recording medium   **1.** A magnetic cylinder, disk, drum, tape, or wire used in the recording of sound or data. **2.** The sensitive material with which any of these is coated.

magnetic relay   A relay having a permanent magnet in whose field a coil, bar, or reed moves to open or close a pair of contacts.

magnetic   remanence   See   RESIDUAL   MAGNETISM.

magnetic repulsion   The force that causes a magnetic pole to push away a similar magnetic pole, although they are not in mutual contact. Thus, two north poles repel each other, and so do two south poles. Compare MAGNETIC ATTRACTION.

magnetic-resonance accelerator   See CYCLOTRON.

magnetics   **1.** Collectively, magnetic components and equipment. **2.** Collectively, magnetic materials. **3.** A branch of physics dealing with magnets and magnetism.

magnetic saturation   The condition in which a magnetic material passes all of the magnetic lines of flux that its permeability allows. Increasing the intensity of the magnetizing force will produce no increase in magnetization.

magnetic scan See ELECTROMAGNETIC DEFLECTION.

magnetic screen See ELECTROMAGNETIC SHIELD.

magnetic shield See ELECTROMAGNETIC SHIELD and MAGNETIC SHIELDING.

magnetic shielding 1. Enclosing a magnetic field to confine its flux, thus preventing interaction with outside bodies. 2. Devices (such as boxes, cans, or shells of iron, steel, or a magnetic alloy) used for the purpose described in 1.

magnetic shift register A shift register using magnetic flip-flops.

magnetic shunt A device that allows the useful magnetic flux of an instrument's magnet to be controlled. The device consists of a piece of magnetic material near the magnet in an electrical measuring instrument.

magnetic south See MAGNETIC SOUTH POLE.

magnetic speaker 1. A loudspeaker that is essentially an enlarged earphone with a horn that conveys and intensifies the sound from the vibrating diaphragm. 2. A loudspeaker in which the vibration of a diaphragm or reed in the field of a permanent magnet is conveyed by a pin to a paper or composition cone. Compare DYNAMIC SPEAKER.

magnetic storage 1. A data bank or memory that stores information in the form of magnetic fields. 2. The data on a magnetic tape or disk.

magnetic storm A disturbance in the earth's magnetic field that typically follows a solar flare. Often causes interference to radio communications at low, medium and high frequencies.

magnetic strip A strip of powdered iron or ferrite on the back of an identification card, bank cash card, or credit card, that carries a code to identify the account number and verify that the secret entry code (if any) is correct, or that the credit is good.

magnetic susceptibility See SUSCEPTIBILITY.

magnetic switch 1. In security systems, a switch kept open by the presence of a magnet attached to a door, window, or other movable object. When the object is moved, the magnet moves away from the switch, closing the switch and actuating an alarm. 2. A REED SWITCH operated by a magnetic field.

magnetic tape Plastic tape coated with a film of magnetic material; it can be magnetized along its length to record sounds, video signals, and computer information.

magnetic-tape core A strip of magnetic metal wound spirally to create a toroid (donut) shape. Such construction is sometimes used in choke or transformer cores. Also see TOROID.

magnetic tape deck See TAPE DECK.

magnetic tape drive See TAPE TRANSPORT.

magnetic tape head See MAGNETIC PICKUP HEAD and MAGNETIC RECORDING HEAD.

magnetic tape library In a computer installation, the place where magnetic tape files are kept, or magnetic tape files and the records needed to utilize them.

magnetic tape parity As a safeguard against losing information bits during the transfer of information between magnetic tape and a memory device, a technique in which an extra bit is generated and added to characters under certain conditions, to make the output uniform temporarily. Lack of uniformity in output then serves as an error indicator. The original quantity is recovered by dropping the extra bit following a parity check.

magnetic tape reader A tape deck for playing back data on magnetic tape.

magnetic tape recorder A recorder-reproducer using magnetic tape.

magnetic test coil See SEARCH COIL.

magnetic thick film A film of magnetic material at least 10^{-6} meter in thickness, deposited on a substrate. Compare MAGNETIC THIN FILM.

magnetic thin film A film of magnetic material, less than 10^{-6} meter in thickness, deposited on a substrate. Compare MAGNETIC THICK FILM.

magnetic transducer A transducer that uses a coil, magnet, or both, to convert displacement into variable magnetic fields or electric currents. Common varieties are the inductance type, transformer type, and generator type. Compare CAPACITIVE TRANSDUCER, CRYSTAL TRANSDUCER, and INDUCTIVE TRANSDUCER.

magnetic tuning In a microwave oscillator, a means of tuning in which a ferrite rod in the cavity resonator is made to have adjustable magnetization so that the resonant frequency of the cavity varies and the frequency of the oscillator is thus adjustable. It is also used at ultra-high frequencies (UHF) and occasionally at very-high frequencies (VHF).

magnetic-vane meter See IRON-VANE METER.

magnetic vector In an electromagnetic field, the vector representing the magnetic component. It is perpendicular to the electric vector.

magnetic viscosity A property of certain materials, described in terms of the time required to magnetize a given substance to a specified level.

magnetic whirl One of the circular magnetic lines of flux around a straight conductor that carries electric current.

magnetic wire The thin wire used in wire recording and playback. See WIRE RECORDER.

magnetism The property of having or causing a magnetic field. It occurs when magnetic dipoles are aligned and when electric charge carriers are in motion.

magnetite A natural magnetic oxide of iron. Also called LODESTONE.

magnetization curve A curve depicting the magnetization of a material versus the applied magnetizing force. See, for example, HYSTERESIS CURVE.

magnetizer A device for magnetizing magnetic materials, as in the making of permanent mag-

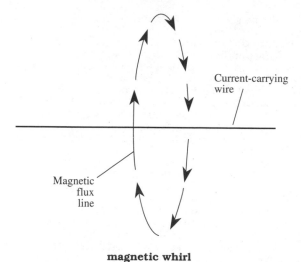

Current-carrying wire

Magnetic flux line

magnetic whirl

nets. Also see MAGNET CHARGER. Compare DEMAGNETIZER.

magnetizing current   **1.** A current that sets up a magnetic field of useful intensity. **2.** The half-cycle of an alternating current or the polarity of a direct current flowing through a coil wound on a permanent magnet (as in a headphone, permanent-magnet loudspeaker, or polarized relay) that increases magnetic field strength. Compare DEMAGNETIZING CURRENT. **3.** The field current of a dynamo.

magnetizing force   **1.** Magnetomotive force (in gilberts) divided by spatial distance (in meters). **2.** The intensity of a magnetic field that causes a material to become magnetized.

magnet keeper   See KEEPER.

magnet meter   See MAGNET TESTER.

magnet motor   See PERMANENT-MAGNET MOTOR.

magneto   See PERMANENT-MAGNET GENERATOR.

magnetocardiogram   Abbreviation, MCG. A record, made by a MAGNETOCARDIOGRAPH, of the pulsating magnetic field of the heart. It is used as a diagnostic aid.

magnetocardiograph   An instrument that produces a record of the pulsating magnetic field generated around the torso by natural ion currents in the heart.

magnetoelectric generator   See MAGNETO-GENERATOR.

magnetofluid mechanics   See MAGNETOHYDRODYNAMICS.

magnetofluidynamics   See MAGNETOHYDRODYNAMICS.

magnetogasdynamics   See MAGNETOHYDRODYNAMICS.

magnetoionic duct   A propagation path for radio waves between two points that have the same

geomagnetic longitude on the surface of the earth. The radio waves tend to travel with the geomagnetic lines of flux at some frequencies under certain conditions.

magnetoionics   The study of the effects of the geomagnetic field on the propagation of radio waves.

magnetogenerator   See PERMANENT-MAGNET GENERATOR.

magnetograph   An instrument for automatically recording a magnetic field.

magnetohydrodynamic generator   A device using magnetohydrodynamic principles to generate electric power directly from gases. In the generator, a hot gas is passed through an intense magnetic field; a pair of collector plates picks up electrons from the ionized gas.

magnetohydrodynamic gyroscope   A gyroscope whose spin is obtained by a rotating magnetic field circulating a conducting fluid, such as mercury, around a closed loop. Also see MAGNETOHYDRODYNAMICS.

magnetohydrodynamic power generator   See MAGNETOHYDRODYNAMIC GENERATOR.

magnetohydrodynamics   Abbreviation, MHD. The theory and application of phenomena produced by electrically conductive fluids and gases in electric and magnetic fields.

magnetometer   An instrument for measuring the strength and direction of magnetic fields.

magnetomotive force   Abbreviation, mmf. Unit, ampere. The phenomenon that is sometimes descriptively called *magnetic pressure*. It is analogous to electromotive force (and to water pressure) and is the agent that produces a magnetic field.

magneton   See BOHR MAGNETON.

magneto-optical rotation   The tendency of a magnetic field to rotate the plane of polarization of light passing through a substance. Also see KERR MAGNETO-OPTICAL EFFECT.

magneto-optical technology   A computer data-storage technology that uses lasers to guide the read/write head in a magnetic disk drive. This greatly increases the amount of data that can be effectively stored on, and retrieved from, a magnetic disk.

magneto-optical valve   See KERR MAGNETO-OPTICAL EFFECT.

magnetopause   The high-altitude limit of the MAGNETOSPHERE.

magnetoplasmadynamics   See MAGNETOHYDRODYNAMICS.

magnetoresistance   The phenomenon whereby the resistance of a material, such as a semiconductor, changes when it is exposed to a magnetic field. Also see MAGNETORESISTOR.

magnetoresistor   A material (such as bismuth wire, indium antimonide, or indium arsenide) whose resistance varies with the strength of a magnetic field in which it is placed.

magnetosphere   In the upper atmosphere, a region extending thousands of kilometers from

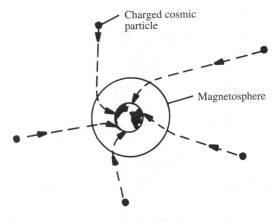

magnetosphere

the earth, in which charged particles are trapped by the earth's magnetic field.

magnetostatic field   A stationary magnetic field, such as that produced by a permanent magnet.

magnetostriction   The expansion or contraction of a bar or rod of magnetic material (such as Invar, Monel metal, Nichrome, nickel, or Stoic metal) in proportion to the strength of an applied magnetic field. Magnetostrictive vibration in such a rod is comparable to piezoelectric vibration in a quartz crystal.

magnetostriction filter   See ULTRASONIC FILTER, **1**.

magnetostriction oscillator   An oscillator whose frequency is controlled by a magnetostrictive rod (see MAGNETOSTRICTION). The dimensions of the rod and the type of metal it contains determine its vibration frequency and, accordingly, the operating frequency of the oscillator.

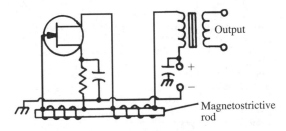

magnetostriction oscillator

magnetostrictive delay line   A delay line in which the signal is propagated through a magnetostrictive rod. Also see MAGNETOSTRICTION.

magnetostrictive microphone   A microphone in which sound vibrations produce changes in a magnetostrictive element, which, in turn, are converted into output-voltage changes. Also see MAGNETOSTRICTION.

magnetostrictive transducer   A transducer in which some phenomenon, such as vibration or pressure, produces changes in a magnetostriction element, which in turn are converted into output-voltage changes. Also see MAGNETOSTRICTION.

magnet protector   See KEEPER.

magnetrode   The trademark of a radio-frequency device for externally producing hyperthermia (elevated temperature) inside the body, as in heating a cancerous tumor for therapeutic purposes.

magnetron   A microwave vacuum tube consisting of a diode (with a cylindrical anode) through which the field of a powerful external permanent magnet passes. The magnetic field causes electrons leaving the cathode to travel in spiral paths between the electrodes. This action gives the tube a negative-resistance characteristic, resulting in oscillation when the tube is connected in an appropriate circuit. Some magnetrons have a built-in resonant cavity.

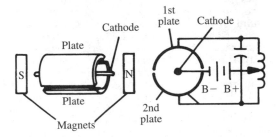

magnetron

magnet steel   A high-retentivity alloy of chromium, cobalt, manganese, steel, and tungsten, used in the manufacture of permanent magnets.

magnet tester   An instrument used to measure the flux of a magnet. Also see FLUXMETER.

magnet wire   Insulated wire (usually solid copper) of 14 to 40 gauge, so called because of its original major use in winding the coils of electromagnets.

magnitude   **1.** General expression for degree, size, or extent. **2.** Signal strength (amplitude). **3.** For a number or vector quantity, the absolute value or length. **4.** A measure of the relative or absolute brightness of celestial objects.

mAh   Abbreviation of *milliampere-hour*.

main   British expression for the alternating-current (ac) utility power available in a house or building.

main bang   **1.** In a radar display, the pip or pulse resulting from the actual transmitted signal. This pulse is blanked out. **2.** In a spectrum analyzer, the pip corresponding to a frequency of zero, and caused by the local oscillator.

mainframe   **1.** The chassis containing the central processor and arithmetic and logic circuits for a large computer. **2.** The general term for a large, powerful computer.

main memory The principal (immediate process) memory unit in a digital computer or data-processing system.

main path In a computer program, the sequence of instruction execution disregarding the execution of subroutines.

main program The part of a computer program other than a subroutine.

main routine See MAIN PROGRAM.

mains **1.** In a power-distribution center, the lines that supply the entire system. An example is the set of lines leading into a house. **2.** The utility wires and associated outlets in a house or building.

maintenance The process of keeping a system, circuit, or component in operating condition, with minimal down time.

maintenance routine A computer program used by computer service personnel for diagnosis during a regular service interval.

major beats The principal beats produced in a beat-note system; they are usually the sum and/or difference of two fundamental frequencies. Compare MINOR BEATS.

major face In a hexagonal quartz crystal, one of the three larger faces. Compare MINOR FACE.

majority carrier The predominant charge carrier in processed semiconductor material. Electrons are the majority carriers in n-type material; holes are the majority carriers in p-type material. Compare MINORITY CARRIER.

majority logic A logic gate in which the output is high whenever the majority of its inputs is high, regardless of which inputs are high. Thus, in a five-input gate of this type, the output is high when any three or more of the inputs are high.

major lobe The principal lobe in an antenna directivity pattern. Also see LOBE. Compare MINOR LOBE.

major loop The principal path for the circulation of information or control signals in an electronic system (e.g., *major feedback loop*). Compare MINOR LOOP.

make **1.** The closing of a pair or set of contacts. **2.** To close a pair or set of contacts.

make-before-break contacts A pair of contacts in which the movable arm closes with the next contact before breaking with the previous one. Compare BREAK-BEFORE-MAKE CONTACTS.

make time The time required for a relay to latch completely, or for a switch (either mechanical or electronic) to close completely. Compare BREAK TIME.

male plug A plug having one or more protruding contacts in the form of pins, blades, or prongs. Compare FEMALE PLUG and HERMAPHRODITIC PLUG.

Malter effect The tendency for a layer of semiconductor having a high secondary emission ratio to become positively charged when bombarded

male plug

by electrons. This occurs when a thin insulator separates the semiconductor from a metal plate. The insulator must be very thin (on the order of 10^{-7} meters). This results in a potential difference of up to about 100 volts.

manganese Symbol, Mn. A metallic element. Atomic number, 25. Atomic weight, 54.938.

manganese-dioxide depolarizer In a dry cell, manganese dioxide mixed with powdered carbon, the mixture being a depolarizing agent. Also see DEPOLARIZER.

manganin A low-temperature-coefficient alloy used in making wire for precision resistors. A typical composition is: copper (84 percent), manganese (12 percent), and nickel (4 percent).

manipulator A robot arm and end effector, as used in mechanical processes.

man-made interference See HUMAN-MADE INTERFERENCE.

man-made static See HUMAN-MADE INTERFERENCE.

manometer An instrument for measuring gas or vapor pressure—especially at low levels.

manpack A portable radio transceiver that can be used while walking.

mantissa **1.** The portion of a logarithm to the right of the decimal point. Thus, in 3.952502 ($\log_{10}$ 8964), the mantissa is 0.952502. **2.** The fixed point part of a number in scientific notation; thus, in 4×10^3, the mantissa is 4.

manual **1.** Actuated or operated directly by mechanical means, rather than automatically. **2.** A book, or a set of online information files, detailing the operation and maintenance procedures for a device or system.

manual input Use of a keyboard, mouse, trackball, or other electromechanical input device to enter data into a computer program or system.

manual operation In data processing, an operation in which automatic machines are not involved.

manual telegraphy Telegraphy that consists signals transmitted by a hand-operated key and recorded by hand (pen, pencil, or typewriter).

manual tuning Tuning performed entirely by adjusting variable circuit components by hand.

manual word generator A device by which an operator can originate information words for input into computer memory.

manufacturing automation protocol In a factory using computer-controlled robots, the set of standards for data communication between the robots and the controller and/or between individual robots. It keeps the factory operating smoothly.

MAR   Abbreviation of MEMORY-ADDRESS REGISTER.

Marconi antenna   A quarter-wave radio transmitting or receiving antenna operated against an earth ground.

Marconi effect   The undesired tendency of an entire receiving antenna system, including lead-in or feeders, to act as a MARCONI ANTENNA.

margin   **1.** A gap or space between two objects, such as adjacent plates of a capacitor. **2.** Clearance. **3.** The maximum error that can be tolerated without risk of improper or abnormal operation. **4.** In a teletypewriter, the range of adjustments in which the error frequency is acceptable.

marginal relay   A relay having a small difference between its on and off currents or voltages.

marginal test   As performed on equipment in a computer installation, a test to either determine the cause of an intermittent malfunction, or verify an equipment's operating tolerances.

marine broadcast station   A coastal station that broadcasts information of interest to shipping: time, weather, ocean currents, etc.

marine radio   Radio communications between seagoing vessels or between vessels and shore stations.

marine radiobeacon station   A land-based radionavigation station whose transmitted signals are used for taking bearings.

mariner's compass   See MAGNETIC COMPASS.

mark   **1.** In telegraphy, the dot or dash portion of a character, as opposed to the dead space between such portions. **2.** The intelligence part of a similar signal (such as sound, light, etc.). **3.** The high (logic 1) state represented by a binary bit, as opposed to the low (logic 0) state. **4.** A character identifying the end of a data set. Also called MARKER (see MARKER, **2**).

marker   **1.** A pip that indicates a particular frequency on a response curve displayed on an oscilloscope screen. **2.** A character that identifies the end of a data set. Also called MARK (see MARK, **4**).

marker beacons   Individual coded-signal transmitters placed along a radio range and indicating features of the course marked by them.

marker frequency   **1.** A known frequency that can be used to identify a spot-frequency harmonic of a frequency-standard signal. **2.** A known accurate signal used to identify the limit of a radio band. **3.** The frequency at some point on a response curve as identified by a marker pip (see MARKER).

marker generator   An oscillator that supplies a marker pip (see MARKER).

mark hold   In telegraphy, an unmodulated signal meaning information is not being sent.

mark reading   The reading by an optical scanning device of marks made in specific areas of a docu-

ment; the process also includes the marks' conversion to digital signals for input to a computer.

mark scanning   See MARK READING.

mark sensing   A process similar to MARK READING, except that the marks are sensed electrically.

marker trap   A wave trap that supplies a dip-type marker pip when used in conjunction with a radio-frequency test oscillator (see MARKER).

market scanner   Also called *bar-code reader.* A device that scans a black-bar binary label printed on a carton or other package (or magazine), and indicates the price of the merchandise on the readout of the checkout register.

mark-to-space ratio   In radiotelegraphy, the ratio of the duration (mark) of a dot to the interval (space) between successive dots.

Marx generator   An impulse-type high-voltage direct-current generator circuit in which several capacitors are charged in parallel through a high-resistance network. When the capacitor voltage reaches a critical high value, discharge occurs in series through spark gaps, producing a high-voltage pulse for each discharge.

Marx generator

maser   A low-noise microwave amplifying device in which a microwave input signal causes high-energy-state molecules of ammonia or ruby to fall to the low-energy state and, as a result, to emit large amounts of energy as an output signal. The name is an acronym for *microwave amplification by stimulated emission of radiation.*

mask   **1.** A kind of stencil through which plating, electrodeposition, or diffusion can be done. **2.** The viewing screen, or GRATICULE, of an oscilloscope. **3.** To obliterate a signal with a stronger one. **4.** A bit or character pattern used to change or extract bit positions in another pattern.

masking   **1.** The use of a MASK of any type. **2.** The tendency of one effect or phenomenon to obscure another. It applies especially in audio systems, where certain sounds impair the ability of a listener to hear other sounds that occur at the same time. **3.** The extent to which one effect or phenomenon obscures another.

Masonite   Masonite Corporation's tough fiberboard used for panels and bases of some electronic equipment.

mass   The quantity of matter in a body. Like weight, mass is expressed in kilograms in the metric (SI) system and in pounds in the English system. For a given piece of material, mass can be determined by dividing the weight by the acceleration of gravity.

mass data   Data in excess of the maximum amount that can be stored in the main (internal) storage unit of a digital computer (i.e., that which can only be accommodated by external media such as magnetic disks or tapes).

mass-energy equation   Energy (E) is the product of a given mass (m) and the square of the speed of light (c^2): $E = mc^2$. It is also called the *Einstein equation.*

mass number   1. Symbol, A. A number representing the total of neutrons and protons in the nucleus of an atom. The approximate mass of an atom is equal to $A \times m_p$, where m_p is the total proton (rest) mass. 2. The number indicating the sum of nuclear protons and neutrons in an atom. It is usually written following the symbol for the atom: thus, U238 is uranium having 238 nucleons. An isotope of an element will have a different mass number than that of the normal atom.

mass of electron at rest   Symbol, m_e. The amount of matter in an electron; $m_e = 9.1093897 \times 10^{-31}$ kg.

mass of neutron at rest   Symbol, m_n. The mass of a neutron in the nucleus of an atom; $m_n = 1.6749286 \times 10^{-27}$ kg.

mass of proton at rest   Symbol, m_p. The mass of a proton in the nucleus of an atom; $m_p = 1.6726231 \times 10^{-27}$ kg.

mass resistivity   1. The resistance of a wire one meter long having a mass of one gram. It varies, depending on the composition of the wire. 2. The resistance of a wire one mile long having a weight of one pound. It varies, depending on the composition of the wire.

mass spectograph   An instrument used to analyze chemical compounds and mixtures in terms of their distinctive mass spectra, exhibited by ionized samples of the materials in a magnetic field.

mass spectrometer   Abbreviation, MS. An instrument that permits rapid analysis of chemical compounds via the MASS SPECTRUM.

mass spectrum   An electron spectrum that can be used to identify a chemical element. Different elements have nuclei with different charge-to-mass ratios. This results in each element having a unique mass spectrum.

mass storage   In a computer system, a magnetic or optical storage medium capable of holding large amounts of data. Examples: magnetic diskette, magneto-optical diskette, external hard disk, compact-disk read-only memory (CD-ROM), and magnetic tape.

mass unit   See ATOMIC MASS UNIT.

master   1. The primary or main element or device in a system. 2. A primary data medium or recording from which copies are made. 3. A primary reference standard. See the following several definitions.

master clock   1. In a digital computer, the primary generator of timing pulses. 2. A standard time clock that drives other (slave) clocks, or to which clocks of lesser accuracy can be referred.

master console   In a computer system, an equipment with panel instruments and controls, which permits operations to be governed, monitored, and controlled by a human operator.

master control   1. The main control circuit in a system. 2. A point from which signals or programs are distributed in a communications or broadcast system.

master data   Also called *archives.* In a computer record, data elements that remain unaltered for a long time, and from which copies are made.

master file   A computer file of data used routinely and remaining unchanged for a long time.

master gain control   The principal gain control in an audio amplifier or mixer [i.e., the one used to adjust the gain (volume) of the entire system].

master instruction tape   Magnetic tape on which various related computer programs are recorded.

master library tape   See MASTER PROGRAM FILE.

master oscillator   Abbreviation, MO. The main oscillator in an electronic system (e.g., the oscillator stage in an oscillator-amplifier type of radio transmitter). This oscillator can be either self-excited or crystal-controlled.

master oscillator-power amplifier   Abbreviation, MOPA. A type of transmitter or signal generator in which a frequency-determining oscillator drives a power amplifier, which in turn delivers an output signal. Because the oscillator is isolated from the output load, this arrangement has greater stability than one in which the oscillator alone supplies power to the load.

master pattern   The etching pattern used for manufacture of a batch of identical printed-circuit boards.

master program file   A reel of magnetic tape on which is recorded the programs regularly used in a data-processing installation. It is also called *master library tape.*

master record   In a data-processing system, the current record (usually stored on a disk or tape) that will be used for the next computer run.

master relay   A relay that operates other (slave) relays. Compare SLAVE RELAY.

master station   See KEY STATION.

master switch   A switch that can actuate or de-actuate an entire installation or system.

master tape   1. In sound recording and reproduction, a magnetic tape that contains material from which other tapes and discs can be made. 2. In automation, a magnetic tape on which is recorded the basic signal sequence for controlling a process and other recorders. 3. In data processing, a magnetic tape that must not be erased.

master volume control   See MASTER GAIN CONTROL.

masurium See TECHNETIUM.

MAT Abbreviation of MICROALLOY TRANSISTOR.

match **1.** To mate devices, signals, impedances, etc. for optimum compatibility in terms of signal transfer, equipment interfacing, and other optimizing qualities. **2.** The condition of being compatibly mated, physically or electrically.

matched components Circuit components (capacitors, coils, diodes, resistors, transistors, etc.) that are carefully selected for similar or particularly compatible operating characteristics.

matched filter **1.** A filter with input and output impedances matched to the input line and output load, respectively. **2.** A filter designed for separating a signal with a particular waveform from other signals and noise.

matched impedance A usually non-reactive impedance that has the same value as that of another impedance with which it is operated. Maximum power is transferred between impedances that are matched.

matched load A purely resistive load, the impedance of which is the same as the characteristic impedance of the feed line. This results in optimum power transfer from the line to the load.

matched pair A pair of matched components offered in a single package.

matched transmission line A transmission line terminated in a purely resistive impedance whose value is identical to the characteristic impedance of the line. Such a line transfers all of its energy to its load without reflection; no standing waves are on the line.

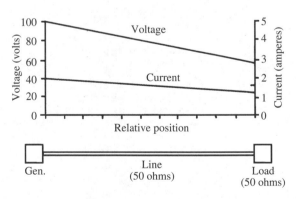

matched transmission line

matching pad An inductance-capacitance (LC) network for matching the impedance of a load to the output impedance of a signal generator.

matching stub See STUB.

matching transformer An audio-frequency (AF) or radio-frequency (RF) transformer used to match one purely resistive impedance to another.

matchtone A transistorized, single-frequency audio oscillator that can be used to monitor transmitted radiotelegraph signals. The carrier wave from the transmitter is rectified by a small semiconductor diode, whose direct-current output powers the oscillator.

Mateucci effect The generation of a potential difference in a helically wound, ferromagnetic wire when its magnetization fluctuates.

mathematical check A test of the validity of the result of an arithmetic process (by using alternate methods, for example).

mathematical logic **1.** A branch of mathematics that involves the theoretical behavior of various systems of reasoning. **2.** See BOOLEAN ALGEBRA. **3.** See DIGITAL LOGIC.

mathematical model See MODEL, 2.

mathematical subroutine Within a computer program, a subroutine serving as an arithmetic function (i.e., one for performing an operation not integral to the monitor program).

matrix **1.** A high-speed switching or memory array used in counters and computers. **2.** Generally, any two-dimensional array of objects. **3.** A device for solving linear simultaneous equations, consisting of a rectangular array of coefficients.

matrix printer See WIRE PRINTER.

mat switch A form of PRESSURE SENSOR used in some security systems. When weight appears on the mat, switches close, actuating an alarm.

matter The building material of the universe that occupies space and has mass that can be measured. See, for illustration, ATOMIC THEORY and STATES OF MATTER.

matter waves See DE BROGLIE WAVES.

max Abbreviation of MAXIMUM.

maxima Points along a curve at which a function reaches a local maximum value. Also see MAXIMA AND MINIMA.

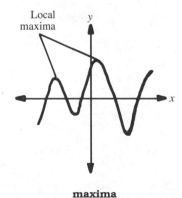

maxima

maxima and minima **1.** The loops and nodes of current or voltage on an antenna or transmission line. **2.** The lobes and nulls in a directivity pattern. **3.** The bright and dark bands in a visible-light interference pattern. **4.** In radar reflections, regions of localized maximum and minimum intensity. **5.** The study and solution of maximum, minimum, and inflection points on the curve of a function.

maximal flatness   For an amplifier or network, the condition in which peaks are not present in the normal passband response.

maximum   Abbreviation, max. The highest value in a range or set. Also see MAXIMA AND MINIMA and PEAK.

maximum available gain   Abbreviation, MAG. The amplification provided by a circuit or device whose input and output impedances are correctly matched to source and load.

maximum current   **1.** Symbol, I_m or I_{max}. The highest value reached by an alternating-current half-cycle or by a pulse current. Also called PEAK CURRENT. **2.** The highest value of current in a series of current values.

maximum power   **1.** Symbol, P_m or P_{max}. The highest value of power that an equipment can be called upon to supply. **2.** The highest value of power in a series of measurements or calculations.

maximum-power discharge current   For a cell or battery, the current at which the greatest amount of power is delivered.

maximum power output   See MAXIMUM POWER, **1.**

maximum power transfer   The condition in which the largest amount of power is delivered by a source to a load.

maximum power transfer theorem   Maximum power is transferred from a generator to a load when the impedance of the load equals the internal impedance of the generator. Compare COMPENSATION THEOREM, NORTON'S THEOREM, RECIPROCITY THEOREM, SUPERPOSITION THEOREM, and THEVENIN'S THEOREM.

maximum rating   **1.** The highest value of a quantity (e.g., current, voltage, or power) that can safely be used with a given device. **2.** The highest value of a quantity afforded by a given device (e.g., *maximum capacitance* of a variable capacitor).

maximum record level   **1.** In a magnetic tape, magnetic disk, or phonograph disc, the highest amplitude of input signal that can be recorded with an acceptable amount of distortion. **2.** The recording-head current or power that results in third-harmonic distortion of three percent.

maximum signal level   **1.** In an amplitude-modulated signal, the peak power. **2.** In an amplitude-modulated facsimile or television system, the amplitude that results in a black or white picture (depending on whether the highest amplitude produces black or white).

maximum undistorted power output   Abbreviation, MUPO. The highest power that an active amplifying device will deliver before significant distortion occurs.

maximum usable frequency   Abbreviation, MUF. The highest frequency that can be used successfully at a given time, between two specific geographic locations, for communication via the ionosphere.

maximum voltage   **1.** Abbreviation, E_m, E_{max}, V_m, or V_{max}. The peak value reached by an alternating-current voltage half-cycle, or by a voltage pulse. **2.** The highest value of voltage in a series of voltage measurements or calculations.

maximum wattage   See MAXIMUM POWER.

maxterm form   In mathematical calculations, the factored form of a function, expressed as a product of sums. For example, the maxterm form of $f(x) = x^2 + 5x + 6$ is $f(x) = (x + 2)(x + 3)$.

maxwell   Symbol, Mx. The cgs unit of magnetic flux, equivalent to one line of flux or 10^{-8} weber.

Maxwell bridge   A four-arm alternating-current bridge for measuring inductance against a standard capacitance.

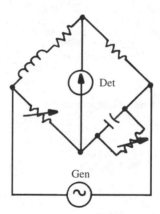

Maxwell bridge

Maxwell's equations   A set of four equations developed by James Clerk Maxwell in 1864 and 1873, describing vector quantities pertaining to points in space subjected to varying electric and magnetic forces. Through his classic presentation, Maxwell predicted the existence of electromagnetic waves, whose later discovery made radio possible.

Maxwell's law   Also called *Maxwell's rule.* Every part of an electric circuit is acted upon by a force tending to move it in the direction that results in the maximum magnetic flux being enclosed.

maxwell-turn   A unit of magnetic coupling (linkage) equal to 1 maxwell per turn of wire in a coil linked by magnetic flux. Also see MAXWELL.

mayday   In radiotelephony, a word spoken as an international distress signal equivalent to SOS in radiotelegraphy. The word is the phonetic equivalent of the French *m'aidez* (help me).

MB   Abbreviation of MIDBAND.

Mb   Abbreviation of MEGABAR.

MBB   Abbreviation of MAKE BEFORE BREAK.

MBM   Abbreviation of *magnetic bubble memory.*

MBO   Abbreviation of MONOSTABLE BLOCKING OSCILLATOR.

MBS   Abbreviation of *magnetron beam switching.*

mc   **1.** Symbol for MILLICURIE (mCi is preferred). **2.** Symbol for METER-CANDLE.

Mc   **1.** Symbol for MEGACURIE (MCi is preferred). **2.** Obsolete abbreviation of *megacycle(s)*, a term superseded by MEGAHERTZ.

MCG   Abbreviation of MAGNETOCARDIOGRAM.

McLeod gauge   An instrument for measuring gas under low pressure. A measured volume of the gas under test is first compressed (to a lower known volume) to a pressure more easily measured via a mercury manometer and the application of Boyle's law.

MCM   Abbreviation of MONTE CARLO METHOD.

McProud test   A simple test for checking the tracking efficiency of a phonograph pickup and arm for microgroove discs.

Mc/s   Obsolete abbreviation of *megacycle(s) per second*, a term superseded by MEGAHERTZ.

MCS   **1.** Abbreviation of *Master of Computer Science.* **2.** Abbreviation of *missile control system.*

MCW   Abbreviation of MODULATED CONTINUOUS WAVE.

Md   Symbol for MENDELEVIUM.

MDAS   Abbreviation of *medical data acquisition system.*

m-derived filter   A filter whose inductance (L) and capacitance (C) values are derived by multiplying those of a constant-k filter by a factor m between zero and 1. This factor is a function of the ratio f_i/f_c, where f_i is the frequency of infinite attenuation, and f_c is the cutoff frequency. This type of filter exhibits sharper response than the equivalent constant-k filter.

MDI   Abbreviation of MAGNETIC DIRECTION INDICATOR.

M-display   See M-SCAN.

MDS   Abbreviation of MINIMUM DISCERNIBLE SIGNAL.

m_e   Symbol for MASS OF ELECTRON AT REST.

Meacham oscillator   A highly stable radio-frequency oscillator consisting of an amplifier pro-

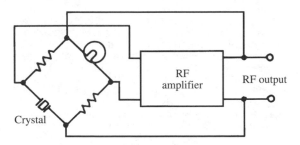

Meacham oscillator

vided with a feedback circuit containing a four-arm bridge, one arm of which is a quartz crystal, and another, a tungsten-filament lamp acting as a nonlinear resistor. Also called *bridge-stabilized oscillator.*

mean   **1.** A general term meaning *average.* **2.** See ARITHMETIC MEAN. **3.** See GEOMETRIC MEAN.

mean charge   **1.** In an object that is nonuniformly charged, the average charge per unit distance, area, or volume. **2.** In a capacitor carrying a fluctuating current, the average amount of charge held by the plates.

mean free path   **1.** In acoustics, the average distance that sound waves travel before striking a barrier or reflecting surface. **2.** The average distance that sound waves travel between reflections (echoes) in a chamber. **3.** In a gas tube, the average of all the free paths of electrons at a specified temperature.

mean life   **1.** Symbol, L. The average life of a radioactive substance [i.e., the time taken for $1/e$ (e = base of natural logarithms) of the substance to disintegrate]. **2.** The time required for excess carriers injected into a semiconductor to recombine with carriers of opposite sign. Also called *average life.*

mean proportional   See GEOMETRIC MEAN.

mean time before failure   Abbreviation, MTBF. The average length of time that a component or system will perform before the first failure occurs. It is generally specified in hours.

mean time between failures   Abbreviation, MTBF. The average length of time that a component or system will perform before failure occurs—either initially or after repair or replacement. It is generally specified in hours.

measured   A quantity that is presented to an instrument for measurement.

measured service   Any service in which charges are assessed per unit-time usage block. Online computer services are a common example. In some cases, other factors, such as distance, affect the cost per unit time; most long-distance telephone services fall into this category.

measurand   Any quantity that is measured with an instrument.

measurement   **1.** The process by which the magnitude, extent, or duration of a parameter is found. **2.** The value of a parameter, as obtained, according to **1.**

measurement error   The difference between the measured value of a quantity and its true value. Also see NEGATIVE ERROR OF MEASUREMENT and POSITIVE ERROR OF MEASUREMENT.

measurement range   In a measuring device, the range within which the error is smaller than a specified value.

mechanical analogs   Familiar mechanical devices, systems, or effects with which certain electrical counterparts can be compared for ease in teaching or understanding (e.g., inductance compared with mass, capacitance with elasticity, voltage with pressure, and current with velocity).

mechanical axis In a quartz crystal, the axis perpendicular to the faces of the hexagon. Also see Y-AXIS, **2**.

mechanical bandspread Bandspread tuning obtained by reduction-ratio gearing of the tuning mechanism. Compare ELECTRICAL BAND-SPREAD.

mechanical bias **1.** A steady pull applied by a spring to the armature of a relay to sensitize it by decreasing the distance that the armature must move to close the contacts. **2.** Bending of a relay frame to position the armature closer to the magnet for the purpose defined in **1**.

mechanical damping Damping action obtained entirely by mechanical devices (such as weights, dashpots, etc.).

mechanical equivalent of heat The amount of mechanical work required to produce a unit quantity of heat. For example, 4.183 joules can be converted into 1 calorie of heat.

mechanical equivalent of light The expression of luminous energy in equivalent power units. In practical measurements, this is taken as the total power output of a lamp minus the power absorbed by a transparent jacket used to remove the infrared and ultraviolet rays.

mechanical filter See ULTRASONIC FILTER, **1**.

mechanical joint A union of electrical conductors consisting exclusively of a junction or splice made without brazing, soldering, or welding.

mechanical load An electromechanical device that uses the output of an electrical source. Such devices include actuators, brakes, clutches, meters, motors, and relays.

mechanical rectifier A vibrator or commutator used to change an alternating current into a direct current by selecting and passing only positive or negative half-cycles. Also see ELECTROMECHANICAL RECTIFIER.

mechanical scanner **1.** A mechanical device for scanning an object or scene and breaking it into horizontal lines that are converted to signals. **2.** A device that scans the reproducer lamp in a mechanical television receiver. See, for example, NIPKOW DISK.

mechanical switch A switch actuated by moving or sliding a lever, pressing a button, or otherwise applying mechanical pressure.

mechanical time constant For a torque motor, the ratio of moment of inertia to damping factor. Compare ELECTRICAL TIME CONSTANT.

mechanical wave filter See ULTRASONIC FILTER, **1**.

mechanics The branch of physics concerned with forces and motion and the laws of gases and liquids. It is subdivided into *kinematics* and *kinetics*.

mechatronics Combination of the words *mechanics* and *electronics*, referring to the use of electromechanical devices (especially robots) in manufacturing. The term was originally coined in Japan.

median **1.** The middle value in a sequence of numbers. For example, in the series: 1, 2, 3, 4, 5, 6, 7, the median is 4. Compare ARITHMETIC MEAN and GEOMETRIC MEAN. **2.** In a statistical distribution, the value s in the domain so that the area under the curve for all values less than s is equal to the area under the curve for all values greater than s.

medical electronics See ELECTROMEDICAL ENGINEERING.

medical robot **1.** A robot used in a doctor's office, or in a hospital to assist doctors and nurses. There are various applications, some of which have provoked controversy (e.g., *robotic surgical assistant*). It generally performs simple, noncritical tasks. It has been suggested as a means of entertaining hospital patients—especially children. **2.** See BIOMECHANISM.

medium In a computer system, that storage device onto or into which data is recorded for input into memory (e.g., magnetic disk, magnetic tape, optical disk, etc.).

medium-frequency Abbreviation, MF. Pertaining to frequencies in the range 300 kHz to 3 MHz, representing wavelengths from 1000 meters to 100 meters.

medium of propagation The substance (or vacuum) through which electromagnetic energy is transmitted (e.g., outer space, the atmosphere, or a dielectric material).

medium-scale integration A method of manufacturing integrated circuits, in which there are at least 10, but less than 100, individual gates on each chip. Abbreviated MSI.

medium-scan television A television (TV) communications medium in which the scanning rate is slowed down compared to regular (fast-scan) TV, but is faster than the commonly used slow-scan TV. It provides some conception of motion, although not as realistic as fast-scan TV.

medium tension Medium voltage. A relative term, but generally referring to common alternating-current utility voltage (e.g., 117 volts or 234 volts).

medium wave Abbreviation, MW. Pertaining to wavelengths corresponding to medium frequencies (see MEDIUM-FREQUENCY) (i.e., those in the 100- to 1000-meter range).

meg **1.** Colloquialism for MEGOHM(s). **2.** Colloquialism for MEGABYTE(s).

mega- Abbreviation, M. **1.** A prefix meaning *million(s)*, (i.e., 10^6 or 1,000,000). **2.** In digital data applications, a prefix meaning 2^{20} or 1,048,576.

megabar Abbreviation, Mb. A cgs unit of high pressure. 1 Mb = 10^6 bars = 10^{11} pascals. Also see BAR, **1**.

megabit A unit of digital data equal to 2^{20} (1,048,576) bits. Also see BIT.

megabyte Abbreviation, M or MB. A unit of digital data equal to 2^{20} (1,048,576) bytes. Also see BYTE.

megacurie Abbreviation, MCi. A large unit of radioactivity equal to 3.71×10^6 disintegrations per second; 1 MCi = 10^6 curies. Also see CURIE.

megacycle See MEGAHERTZ.

megaelectronvolt Abbreviation, MeV. A large unit of electrical energy; 1 MeV = 10^6 eV. Also see ELECTRONVOLT.

megahertz Abbreviation, MHz. A unit of frequency; 1 MHz = 10^6 Hz = 1,000,000 Hz.

megampere Abbreviation, MA. A unit of high current; 1 MA = 10^6 A = 1,000,000 A.

megaphone **1.** A hand-held microphone/amplifier/loudspeaker used to amplify the voice of a person who must be heard over an appreciable area. **2.** A simple horn for amplifying the voice.

megarutherford Abbreviation, Mrd. A large unit of radioactivity equal to 1 trillion (10^{12}) disintegrations per second; 1 Mrd = 10^6 rd = 1,000,000 rd. Also see RUTHERFORD.

megavolt Abbreviation, MV. A unit of extremely high voltage; 1 MV = 10^6 V = 1,000,000 V.

megavolt-ampere Abbreviation, MVA. A unit of extremely high reactive power; 1 MVA = 10^6 VA = 1,000,000 VA. Also see VOLT-AMPERE.

megawatt Abbreviation, MW. A unit of high power; 1 MW = 10^6 W = 1,000,000 W. Also see WATT.

megawatt-hour Abbreviation, MWh. A large unit of electrical energy or of work; 1 MWh = 10^6 Wh = 1,000,000 Wh = 3.6×10^9 joules. Also see WATT-HOUR.

megger An instrument containing an internal high-voltage direct-current power supply, used for measuring high values of resistance. Compare MEGOHMMETER.

meg-mike **1.** Colloquialism for MEGOHM-MICROFARAD(s). **2.** Colloquialism for MEGOHM-FARAD(s).

megohm Symbol, M. A unit of high resistance, reactance, or impedance; 1 M = 10^6 ohms = 1,000,000 ohms.

megohm-farads For a large capacitor, the product of leakage resistance (megohms) and capacitance (farads). Also see MEGOHM-MICROFARADS.

megohmmeter A special ohmmeter for measuring resistances in the megohm range.

megohm-microfarads For a capacitor, the product of leakage resistance (megohms) and capacitance (microfarads). The figure is an expression for the relative insulation resistance of a capacitor.

Meissner circuit An oscillator tuned by means of LECHER WIRES (parallel-conductor resonant circuits). It is used primarily at ultra-high frequencies (UHF).

Meissner effect In a superconductive material, the abrupt loss of magnetism when the temperature of the material is reduced to a value below that required for superconductivity.

Meissner oscillator See MEISSNER CIRCUIT.

mel An expression of apparent or perceived sound pitch. A tone of 1 kHz, at a level of 40 dB, with respect to the threshold of hearing, represents 1 mel. The perceived pitch depends, to some extent, on the intensity of the sound, as well as on the actual frequency.

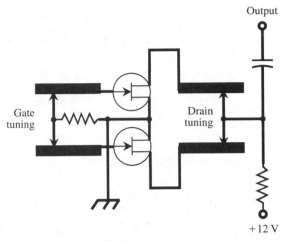

Meissner circuit

M electron In certain atoms, one of the electrons whose orbits are outside of and nearest to those of the L electrons.

meltback process The technique of remelting a doped semiconductor material and allowing it to refreeze to form a grown junction.

meltback transistor A grown-junction transistor produced by the MELTBACK PROCESS.

melting point Abbreviation, mp. The temperature at which a solid starts becoming liquid at a pressure of one atmosphere. Compare FREEZING POINT and MIXTURE MELTING POINT.

memory **1.** The section of a digital computer that records and holds data until it is necessary. In personal computers, the term generally refers to RANDOM-ACCESS MEMORY and READ-ONLY MEMORY, contained in integrated circuits (ICs). Compare STORAGE. **2.** See MEMORY DRAIN.

memory address register In computer storage, a register in which is stored the address of operands in other locations.

memory area A portion of computer memory reserved for a specific type of data. Also called *area*.

memory capacity As a function of the number of memory locations available, the number of bytes that can be stored. It is usually specified in kilobytes, megabytes, or gigabytes. Also see GIGABYTE, KILOBYTE, and MEGABYTE.

memory cycle **1.** The period of execution of a sequence of operations. **2.** The complete operational cycle for inputting data to memory or retrieving it.

memory dialing In a telephone set, a feature that allows rapid dialing of stored digits. The simplest version is the "redial" feature, in which the most recently dialed number is rapidly dialed at the touch of a button. Some sets can store several different numbers, usually including area codes, and sometimes country codes as well.

memory drain Also called *memory* and *memory effect*. In a nickel-cadmium (NICAD) cell or battery, a loss of effective energy capacity when subjected to repeated partial discharge. It can be prevented by always using the cell or battery until it is almost totally discharged before recharging.

memory dump In computer operations, to either print out what is stored in some of or all of the memory locations or transfer the data from a bank of memory cells to some external storage medium.

memory effect See MEMORY DRAIN.

memory guard In a computer, hardware or software that keeps certain memory locations from being addressed by a program being run.

memory location In a computer memory, a place where an information unit (word or character) can be stored; the stored information can be retrieved by appropriate addressing instructions.

memory organization packets In artificial intelligence (AI) and expert systems, a method of arranging computer memory into general rules or statements. The statements are used by software to derive models, forecasts, diagnoses, etc.

memory power Computer memory efficiency in terms of data processing (cycle) speed.

memory protection A hardware device in a multiple programming computer that prevents programs from being altered by other operating programs in the installation.

memory register In a digital computer, a register used in all instruction and data transfers between the memory and other sections of the machine.

memory unit See MEMORY.

mendelevium Symbol, Md. A radioactive element produced artificially. Atomic number, 101. Atomic weight, 258 (approx.).

menu In computer operations, a list of commands for using various functions of the system.

MEP Abbreviation of *mean effective pressure.*

mercuric iodide Formula, HgI_2. A compound whose crystals are useful at room temperature as detectors in high-resolution gamma-ray spectroscopy.

mercury Symbol, Hg. A metallic element. Atomic number, 80. Atomic weight, 200.59. The only metal that is liquid at room temperature. It is used extensively in switches, certain high-voltage rectifiers, high-vacuum pumps, and thermometers.

mercury arc The arc discharge occurring in mercury vapor between solid or liquid (mercury) electrodes. The discharge emits ultraviolet radiation.

mercury-arc rectifier A heavy-duty rectifier tube utilizing ionized mercury vapor. The two general types are MERCURY-VAPOR RECTIFIER and MERCURY-POOL RECTIFIER.

mercury battery A series or parallel combination of mercury cells. Also see MERCURY CELL.

mercury cadmium telluride Formula HgCdTe. An alloy used as a semiconductor in certain transistors, integrated circuits, and infrared detectors.

mercury cell A primary cell housed in a steel container and having a mercuric-oxide cathode, amalgated-zinc anode, and potassium hydroxide and zinc-oxide electrolyte. The output voltage remains reasonably constant throughout the life of the cell.

mercury delay line A delay line in which delay is obtained by propagating the signal through a pipe of mercury.

mercury diffusion pump A vacuum diffusion pump using mercury vapor.

mercury displacement relay A form of switching relay in which the electrical contact is made by moving mercury.

mercury-jet switch A multipoint switch using a jet of mercury instead of the conventional wiper arm, for high-speed operation and reduced wear.

mercury memory A recirculating memory using a mercury delay line. Also see DELAY LINE and DELAY-LINE MEMORY.

mercury-pool cathode In certain industrial electron tubes, such as the ignitron, a cathode electrode consisting of a pool of mercury.

mercury-pool rectifier A type of mercury-arc rectifier whose cathode is a pool of mercury. In one type, the arc is initiated by tilting the tube momentarily to bring the mercury into contact with a third electrode, thus causing a starting current to flow through the pool. In another type, the *ignitron*, a starter electrode is in continual contact with the mercury.

mercury pump See MERCURY DIFFUSION PUMP.

mercury rectifier See MERCURY-POOL RECTIFIER and MERCURY-VAPOR RECTIFIER.

mercury relay A relay in which at least one of the contacts is mercury.

mercury storage See MERCURY MEMORY.

mercury switch A switch consisting essentially of two or more stiff wire electrodes and a drop of mercury hermetically sealed in a glass tube. Tilting the tube causes the mercury to flow toward one end, where it immerses the electrodes, providing a conductive path between them.

mercury-vapor lamp A glow lamp emitting blue-green light that causes ionization of mercury vapor by an electric current.

mercury-vapor rectifier A tube-type high-voltage diode rectifier containing a small amount of mercury that vaporizes and ionizes during tube operation.

mercury-vapor tube 1. See MERCURY-VAPOR LAMP. 2. See MERCURY-VAPOR RECTIFIER.

mercury-wetted reed relay A reed relay in which the reeds are wetted with mercury in a pool by capillary action. The film of mercury forms a tiny bridge when the reeds open; when this bridge separates, a clean, high-speed break occurs without contact bounce. Compare DRY-REED SWITCH.

merge 1. In computer operations, to make a single set or file from two or more record sets. 2. In word processing, to create a corrected master recording from two input media: the original master recording and the recording that contains the corrections.

meridian 1. A great circle passing through earth's geographic poles and a given point on the surface of the earth. **2.** A line of longitude on a map or globe. Also see TIME ZONE, ZERO MERIDIAN, and ZONE TIME.

mesa A flat-topped, protruding region in a semiconductor wafer. The mesa is produced by etching the surrounding part of the material. Some bipolar transistors are manufactured in this way.

mesa diffusion A method of manufacturing bipolar transistors. The different semiconductor materials are first diffused together. Then part of the resulting wafer is etched away, resulting in a mesa shape.

mesa transistor A diffused planar transistor in which the silicon area around the base has been etched away to reduce collector-to-base capacitance; the base-emitter region remains elevated like a high plateau (mesa).

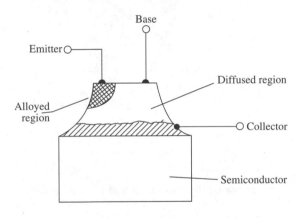

mesa transistor

MESFET A form of field-effect transistor combining depletion-mode and enhancement-mode properties. A Schottky barrier forms the gate electrode.

mesh 1. A combination of the elements that form a closed path in a network. **2.** The closed figure (such as the delta or star) obtained by connecting polyphase windings together. **3.** A grid, screen, or similar structure in a vacuum tube.

mesh equations Equations describing fully the current and voltage relations in a network of meshes (see MESH, **1**).

Mesny circuit A push-pull ultra-high-frequency (UHF) oscillator whose gate or base tank is a pair of parallel wires short-circuited by a slider; the drain or collector tank is a similar pair of wires. The frequency is varied by moving the sliders along the wires.

mesochronous A condition for signals in which significant instants pass at identical average speeds, such as bits per second.

meson An unstable nuclear particle first observed in cosmic rays. A meson can be electrically positive, negative, or neutral. Its mass lies between that of the electron and proton.

mesotron See MESON.

message 1. In communications, a body of information sent from a source (transmitter) to a destination (receiver). **2.** Data entered into a transaction-processing system.

message exchange In a digital communications channel, a hardware unit that carries out certain switching functions that would otherwise have to be done by a computer.

message switching system A data communications system having a central computer that receives messages from remote terminals, stores them, and transfers them to other terminals as needed.

metadyne See DC GENERATOR AMPLIFIER.

metal An elemental material that exhibits several familiar properties (such as luster, ductility, malleability, good electrical and heat conductivity, relatively high density, and the ability to emit electrons). Common examples are aluminum, copper, gold, lead, and silver. Compare METALLOID and NONMETAL.

metal-base transistor A bipolar transistor in which the base is a metal film, and the emitter and collector are films of n-type semiconductor material.

metal-ceramic construction The building of certain electronic components by bonding ceramic parts to metal parts. Also see CERMET.

metal-film resistor A fixed or variable resistor in which the resistance element is a film of a metal alloy deposited on a substrate such as a plastic or ceramic.

metal finder See METAL LOCATOR.

metallic binding forces In a crystal, the binding electrostatic force between cations and electrons. Also called *electron-gas binding forces.*

metallic bonding See BONDING, **1** and METALLIC BINDING FORCES.

metallic circuit A circuit, such as a two-wire telephone line, in which earth ground is not a part of the circuit. Compare GROUND-RETURN CIRCUIT.

metallic crystal A crystal substance in which positive ions and free electrons exist; it is, therefore, a good electrical conductor.

metallic insulator A short-circuited quarter-wave section of transmission line that acts as an insulator at the quarter-wavelength frequency.

metallicize To make a circuit fully metallic, as when two wires are used instead of one wire and a ground connection. (Not to be confused with METALLIZE.)

metallic rectifier   A dry rectifier using a metal disk or plate coated with a material (such as selenium, an oxide, or a sulfide).

metallic tape   Recording tape made from metal, rather than from plastic. Noted for its excellent audio-reproduction characteristics.

metallize   To treat, coat, or plate with a metal. (Not to be confused with METALLICIZE.)

metallized capacitor   A capacitor in which each face of a dielectric film is metallized to form conductive plates.

metallized-paper capacitor   A paper-dielectric capacitor whose plates are metal areas electrodeposited on each side of a paper film.

metallized-polycarbonate capacitor   A fixed capacitor in which the dielectric is a polycarbonate plastic film, and the plates are metal areas electrodeposited on each face of the film.

metallized resistor   See METAL-FILM RESISTOR.

metal locator   An electronic device for locating metal deposits, pipes, or wires underground, in walls, or under floors. It operates via the disturbance that these objects cause to a radio-frequency or magnetic field.

metalloid   An element that has some of the properties of a metal. Examples of metalloidal elements widely used in electronics are antimony, arsenic, germanium, silicon, and tin.

metal master   See ORIGINAL MASTER.

metal negative   See ORIGINAL MASTER.

metal-oxide resistor   A resistor in which the resistance material is a film of tin oxide deposited on a substrate.

metal-oxide semiconductor field-effect transistor   Abbreviation, MOSFET. A field-effect transistor in which the gate electrode is not a pn junction (as in the junction field-effect transistor), but a thin metal film insulated from the semiconductor channel by a thin oxide film. Gate-control action is entirely electrostatic. Also called *insulated-gate field-effect transistor*. Also see DEPLETION-TYPE MOSFET, DEPLETION-ENHANCEMENT-TYPE MOSFET, and ENHANCEMENT-TYPE MOSFET.

metal-oxide varistor   A VOLTAGE-DEPENDENT RESISTOR in which the resistance material is a metallic oxide, such as zinc oxide.

metal-plate rectifier   See METALLIC RECTIFIER.

metal tube   A vacuum tube housed in a metal envelope for self-shielding and mechanical ruggedness.

metamer   A visible-light beam that is identical in color (hue), but different in concentration (saturation), with respect to a reference color.

meteor-burst signals   Momentary signals, or increases in signal strength, resulting from reflection of electromagnetic energy from meteor ionization trails. See METEOR SCATTER, 1.

meteor ionization trail   A cloud of ions left in the upper atmosphere as a meteor passes. This cloud tends to reflect radio signals at certain frequencies for a short period of time. During a meteor shower, there could be a sufficient number of such trails to allow continuous over-the-horizon communication when other over-the-horizon modes are unusable.

meteorograph   An instrument for the simultaneous measurement of various meteorological phenomena such as temperature, humidity, etc.

meteorology   The science of the atmosphere, especially the study of weather and climate. (Not to be confused with METROLOGY.)

meteor scatter   **1.** The reflection of electromagnetic waves, especially at very-high frequencies (VHF), by the ionization trails left by meteors in the upper atmosphere. **2.** Communications by means of radio waves reflected by meteor ionization trails.

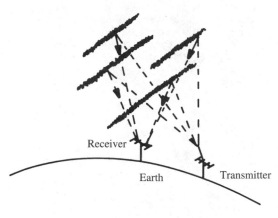

meteor scatter

meteor-trail reflections   Momentary reflection of signals by the ionized trails of meteors passing through a signal path.

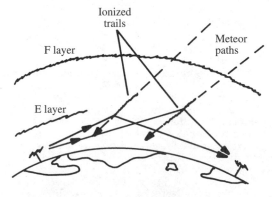

meteor-trail reflections

meter   1. An instrument for measuring and indicating the value of a particular quantity. See, for example, CURRENT METER and VOLTMETER. **2.** Abbreviation, m. A unit of linear measure and of electrical wavelength, equivalent to 1.65076373×10^6 wavelengths (in a vacuum) of the radiation corresponding to the transition between the two levels of the krypton-86 atom, and approximately equal to 39.37 inches. **3.** To supply in specific increments or by a governed amount.

meter alignment   See VISUAL ALIGNMENT.

meter-ampere   A unit of transmitted radio signal intensity. Determined by multiplying the antenna current (in amperes) by the height (in meters) of the antenna above ground.

meter-candle   Abbreviation, mc. A metric unit of illuminance, equivalent to the illumination on a surface 1 meter from a light source of 1 candle power. Compare FOOT-CANDLE and LUX.

meter equivalent   The number of meters equal to a given English measure of length (e.g., the meter equivalent of 3 feet is approximately 0.9144).

meter-kilogram-second   Abbreviation, mks. The system of units in which the meter is the standard unit of length, the kilogram is the standard unit of mass, and the second is the standard unit of time. Compare CENTIMETER-GRAM-SECOND and INTERNATIONAL SYSTEM OF UNITS.

meter multiplier   See MULTIPLIER RESISTOR.

meter protector   A nonlinear resistor, such as a varistor or semiconductor diode, used to prevent overswing in an electric meter by limiting the current flowing through it.

meter rating   The maximum reading on a meter, at or below which the accuracy is within a specified limit, but above which the error might exceed that limit.

meter rectifier   A light-duty semiconductor diode or bridge circuit, used to change alternating current (ac) to direct current (dc) for deflection of a D'Arsonval-type dc milliammeter or microammeter.

meter relay   A sensitive relay that is essentially a moving-coil meter, whose pointer closes against a stationary contact mounted at some point along the scale.

meter resistance   Symbol, R_m. The internal resistance of an electric meter. In a simple D'Arsonval meter, it is the resistance of the movable coil. In more-complicated meter circuits, it is the resistance of the parallel combination of the coil and METER SHUNT.

meter scale factor   See SCALE FACTOR, **1.**

meter sensitivity   See VOLTMETER SENSITIVITY.

meter shunt   A resistor connected in parallel with an ammeter, milliammeter, or microammeter to increase the range of currents that the device can measure.

meter torque   See DEFLECTING TORQUE.

meter-type relay   See METER RELAY.

methyl methacrylate resin   Also known by the trade name *Lucite*. A plastic insulating material. Dielectric constant, 2.8 to 3.3. Dielectric strength, 20 kV/mm.

metre   Abbreviation, m. Alternate spelling of *meter* when used to specify displacement or wavelength. See METER, **2.**

metric system   The decimal system of weights and measures based on the meter, kilogram, and second. Also see CENTIMETER-GRAM-SECOND, METER-KILOGRAM-SECOND, and INTERNATIONAL SYSTEM OF UNITS.

metric ton   Abbreviation, MT. A metric unit of weight equal to 1000 kilograms or 1.1023 English tons.

metric waves   British designation for electromagnetic energy having wavelengths ranging from 10 meters down to 1 meter, corresponding to frequencies from 30 MHz up to 300 MHz.

metrology   The science of weights and measures, including electrical standards and electronic instruments and measurements. (Not to be confused with METEOROLOGY.)

metronome   A mechanical or electronic device that produces audible beats (ticks). It is commonly used in setting the tempo for music, and for audibly timing certain processes.

MeV   Abbreviation of MEGAELECTRONVOLT(s).

MEW   Abbreviation of MICROWAVE EARLY WARNING.

mF   Abbreviation of MILLIFARAD.

MF   1. Abbreviation of MEDIUM FREQUENCY. **2.** Abbreviation of MIDFREQUENCY.

MFD   Abbreviation of MAGNETOFLUID DYNAMICS (see MAGNETOHYDRODYNAMICS).

MFSK   Abbreviation of MULTIPLE FREQUENCY-SHIFT KEYING.

Mg   Symbol for MAGNESIUM.

mg   Abbreviation of MILLIGRAM.

MGD   Abbreviation of MAGNETOGASDYNAMICS (see MAGNETOHYDRODYNAMICS).

MHD   Abbreviation of MAGNETOHYDRODYNAMICS.

MHD generator   See MAGNETOHYDRODYNAMIC GENERATOR.

MHD   gyroscope   See   MAGNETOHYDRODYNAMIC GYROSCOPE.

MHD power generation   See MAGNETOHYDRODYNAMIC GENERATOR.

mho   Obsolete term for the standard unit of electrical conductance. See SIEMENS.

mhp   Abbreviation of MILLIHORSEPOWER.

MHz   Abbreviation of MEGAHERTZ.

mi   Abbreviation of MILE. (Also, m.)

MIC   Abbreviation of MICROWAVE INTEGRATED CIRCUIT.

mic   Abbreviation of MICROPHONE.

mica   A dielectric mineral of complex silicate composition, easily separated into numerous thin, transparent sheets. It is widely used as a capacitor dielectric and high-temperature electrical insulator. Dielectric constant, 2.5 to 7. Dielectric strength, 50 to 220 kV/mm. Also see MUSCOVITE.

mica capacitor A capacitor using a thin film of mica as the dielectric. Such a capacitor exhibits high Q and good stability. Also see MICA and SILVERED-MICA CAPACITOR.

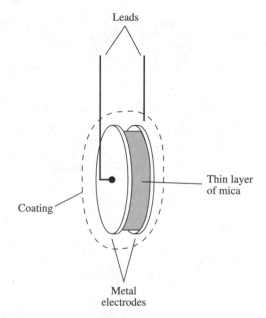

mica capacitor

Leads

Thin layer of mica

Coating

Metal electrodes

MICR Abbreviation of MAGNETIC INK CHARACTER RECOGNITION.

micro- **1.** A prefix meaning MILLIONTH(S) (i.e., 10^{-6}). **2.** A prefix meaning extremely small (as in microstructure). Compare MACRO-.

microalloy diffused transistor Abbreviation, MADT. A MICROALLOY TRANSISTOR having a uniform base region that is diffused into the wafer before the emitter and collector electrodes are produced by alloying.

microalloy transistor Abbreviation, MAT. A transistor having tiny emitter and collector electrodes that are formed by alloying a thin film of impurity material with a collector pit and emitter pit facing each other on opposite surfaces of the semiconductor wafer. Also see SURFACE-BARRIER TRANSISTOR.

microammeter A usually direct-reading instrument used to measure current in the microampere range. Also see CURRENT METER.

microampere A small unit of current, equal to 10^{-6} (0.000001) A.

microbalance A sensitive electronic weighing device. One type uses one or more servo amplifiers for the balancing operation.

microbar A cgs unit of low pressure, equal to 10^{-6} b or 0.1 pascal. Also see BAR, **1** and MILLIBAR.

microbarograph A barograph that is sensitive to small changes in pressure.

microbeam An energy beam (ray) having extremely small cross section.

microcircuit An extremely small circuit fabricated upon and within a substrate, such as a semiconductor chip. Also see INTEGRATED CIRCUIT.

microcode **1.** See MICROINSTRUCTION. **2.** A code for MICROPROGRAMMING.

microcomponent A tiny component in an electronic circuit. Examples are the resistors, capacitors, diodes, and transistors fabricated onto an integrated-circuit chip.

microcomputer **1.** Any small computer whose central processing unit (CPU) is contained on a single small circuit board or within a single integrated circuit. **2.** A self-contained computer designed around a MICROPROCESSOR.

microcrystal A crystal that is invisible to the naked eye.

microcurie A small unit of radioactivity equal to 3.71×10^4 disintegrations per second or 10^{-6} curie. Also see CURIE.

microelectrode **1.** An electrode used in MICROELECTROLYSIS. **2.** A tiny electrode, especially one of those used in integrated circuits and in certain biological applications.

microelectrolysis Electrolysis of tiny amounts of material. Also see ELECTROLYSIS, **1**.

microelectronic circuit **1.** A tiny electronic circuit other than an INTEGRATED CIRCUIT (i.e., one assembled in a small space with small discrete or integrated components). **2.** See MICROCIRCUIT.

microelectronic device See MICROELECTRONIC CIRCUIT.

microelectronics The branch of electronics dealing with extremely small components and circuits fabricated on substrates. Also see INTEGRATED CIRCUIT.

microelectrophoresis Electrophoresis of single particles.

microelectroscope A very sensitive electroscope used to detect minute quantities of electricity.

microelement A tiny component (capacitor, resistor, coil, semiconductor device, or transformer) mounted on a wafer and used in a MICROCIRCUIT.

microelement wafer A microwafer on which a microelement is mounted or deposited.

microfarad Abbreviation, μF. A unit of capacitance equal to 10^{-6} (0.000001) F.

microfarad meter **1.** A dynamometer-type meter that indicates the value of a capacitor directly in microfarads. Such instruments operate from an alternating-current power line. **2.** A direct-reading capacitance meter.

microfiche A method of storing printed information on small film cards. The pages are reduced and arranged in order from left to right and top to bottom. The card is inserted into a projecting machine to allow retrieval of the information. The photographic method is similar to that used in MICROFILM.

microfilm   A method of storing printed or photographic information. The pages are reduced and arranged sequentially on a strip of film, usually 35-mm size. The film is inserted into a projecting device for retrieval of the information.

microgalvanometer   A highly sensitive GALVANOMETER.

microgauss   A magnetic unit equal to 10^{-6} (0.000001) gauss.

microgram   A metric unit of weight or mass equal to 10^{-6} (0.000001) gram.

microgroove record   A phonograph disc with a very fine groove (200 to 300 per inch), designed for playback at 33⅓ revolutions per minute (rpm).

microhenry   Symbol, µH. A unit of inductance, equal to 10^{-6} (0.000001) H.

microhm   Symbol, µΩ. A unit of low resistance, reactance, or impedance, equivalent to 10^{-6} (0.000001) ohm.

microhm-centimeter   A unit of low resistivity, equal to 10^{-6} (0.000001) ohm-cm. See OHM-CENTIMETER and RESISTIVITY.

microhmmeter   An instrument for measuring ultra-low resistance. Such an instrument must have a special provision for canceling the effects of contact and lead resistance.

microinch   A unit of linear measure equal to 10^{-6} (0.000001) inch.

microinstruction   A machine-code instruction that controls the operation of a computer directly (i.e., it is a "wired-in" instruction, or one set by DIP switches, independent of programs loaded into the machine).

microknowledge   In artificial intelligence (AI), detailed machine knowledge. It includes logic rules, computer programs, and data in memory. Compare MACROKNOWLEDGE.

microliter   A unit of volume, equal to 10^{-6} (0.000001) liter.

microlock   A special form of phase-locked-loop system, used especially with radar to improve the signal-to-noise ratio.

micromanipulator   A machine that permits handling tiny parts in very small areas. An example of its use is in placing connections close together in microcircuits.

micrometer   **1.** An instrument for measuring very small thicknesses, diameters, etc. **2.** Also called *micron.* The SI unit of length, equal to 10^{-6} (0.000001) meter, or 10^{-3} (0.001) millimeter.

micromho   See MICROSIEMENS.

micromicro-   See PICO-.

micromicrofarad   See PICOFARAD.

micromicrohenry   See PICOHENRY.

micromicron   A unit of linear measure equal to 10^{-12} meter, or 10^{-6} (0.000001) micrometer.

micromillimeter   See NANOMETER.

microminiature   Pertaining to an extremely small body, component, or circuit; the last adjective in the sequence of those describing size: *standard, small, midget, miniature, subminiature,* and *microminiature.*

micromodule   A small, encapsulated circuit, consisting of smaller components. The components can be discrete, can consist of integrated circuits, or can be a combination of both. The module is easily removed and replaced by means of a plug-in socket.

micron   See MICROMETER.

microphone   A transducer that converts sound waves, especially speech and music, into electrical voltage analogs.

microphone amplifier   A high-gain, low-noise audio preamplifier used to boost the output of a microphone.

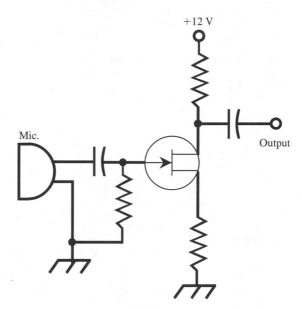

microphone amplifier

microphone boom   A device used to hang a microphone, with the base out of the way. It is often used in radio broadcasting.

microphone hummer   See HUMMER.

microphone input   In an audio amplifier, a jack or other receptacle provided for connection to an external microphone. It can also be used with other low-level audio apparatus. The jack is connected to a MICROPHONE AMPLIFIER that provides high gain with minimum internal noise.

microphone oscillator   See HUMMER.

microphonics   Ringing (electrical noises) set up by the vibration of a component having loose or movable elements. For example, ringing noises are generated in some circuit boards when they receive a physical blow.

microphonograph A recorder of very low-intensity sound.

microphonoscope An electronic stethoscope, using amplification to enhance the response.

microphotograph An extremely small photograph, often of a pattern or mask used in producing transistors and integrated circuits. Not to be confused with *photomicrograph*, a photograph taken through a microscope.

microphotometer A sensitive instrument for measuring small-area light intensity.

microphysics The branch of physics concerned with atoms, molecules, and subatomic particles.

micropower Extremely small amounts of power—especially the very low direct-current supply power required by some transistors.

microprocessor A usually single-chip computer element that contains the control unit, central processing circuitry, and arithmetic and logic functions; it is suitable for use as the central processing unit (CPU) of a microcomputer or a dedicated automatic control system.

microprogram 1. In computer operations, a routine of microinstructions that provides a computer a specific function, independent of those established by programs being run or by the monitor program. Also see MICROINSTRUCTION. 2. In the direction of a computer, use of a routine that is stored specifically in the memory, instead of elsewhere.

microprogramming In the direction of a computer, the use of a routine that is stored specifically in the memory, instead of elsewhere.

micropulsation Also called *micropulse.* A pulse of extremely short duration.

microradiometer A sensitive detector of heat and infrared radiation, consisting essentially of a thermopile carried by the moving coil of a galvanometer.

microrutherford A unit of radioactivity equal to one disintegration per second or 10^{-6} (0.000001) rutherford. Also see RUTHERFORD.

microsecond A unit of time measure equal to 10^{-6} (0.000001) second.

microsiemens A unit of conductance equal to 10^{-6} (0.000001) siemens.

microspectrophotometer An extremely sensitive spectrophotometer for examining light from tiny areas.

microstrip A microwave component that is, in effect, a single-wire transmission line operating above ground.

microsyn A device that translates rotational position into an electrical signal. Similar to a SELSYN. It is used for such purposes as rotator-direction reading.

microsystems electronics The technology of electronic systems using tiny electronic components. Also see INTEGRATED CIRCUIT, MICROELEC-TRONIC CIRCUIT, MICROELEMENT, MICRO-ELEMENT WAFER, and MICROWAFER.

microvolt A unit of low voltage, equal to 10^{-6} (0.000001) volt.

microvolter An accurate, external attenuator (usually for an audio signal generator) providing stepped and continuously variable output in microvolts and millivolts.

microvoltmeter A usually direct-reading instrument used to measure voltages in the microvolt range. An input amplifier boosts the test voltage sufficiently to deflect the indicating meter.

microvolts per meter A unit of radio-frequency (RF) field strength. It refers to the RF voltage (in microvolts) between an antenna and ground, divided by the height of the antenna (in meters) above ground. Compare MILLI-VOLTS PER METER.

microvolts per meter per mile A means of expressing absolute radio-frequency (RF) field strength. Generally, the numerical value is based on the field strength, in MICROVOLTS PER METER, at a distance of 1 statute mile (5280 feet) from the source.

microwafer A wafer of insulating material, such as a ceramic, on which one or more microelements are mounted and terminals deposited or plated.

microwatt A unit of low power, especially electrical power, equal to 10^{-6} (0.000001) watt.

microwattage See MICROPOWER.

microwattmeter An instrument for measuring power in the microwatt range. Such an instrument obtains its sensitivity from a built-in input amplifier.

microwave See MICROWAVES.

microwave security system A circuit using microwave radio-frequency energy to detect intruders. When an object moves within the field, the intensity of the field changes at one or more pickup sensors, triggering an alarm.

microwave acoustics See ACOUSTOELECTRON-ICS and ACOUSTIC DELAY LINE.

microwave dish A dish antenna for use at microwave frequencies.

microwave early warning Abbreviation, MEW. A high-power early warning radar system that affords large traffic-handling capacity and long range.

microwave filter A bandpass filter built into a waveguide for use at microwave frequencies.

microwave frequencies The general expression for radio frequencies above the ultra-high range, that is, 3 GHz or more, but below the frequencies of infrared energy. This corresponds to radio wavelengths of 10 centimeters or less.

microwave integrated circuit Abbreviation, MIC. An integrated circuit designed for use at microwave frequencies.

microwave lens See WAVEGUIDE LENS.

microwave mirror A reflector of microwaves.

microwave oven A device consisting essentially of a radio-frequency heater using a magnetron oscillator. It produces microwave energy that causes heating of certain substances via excitation of the molecules.

microwave plumbing Collectively, the waveguides, tees, elbows, and similar fixtures and connections used in microwave setups.

microwave radio relay The use of microwaves to relay radio, television, and control signals from point to point.

microwave refractometer An instrument using microwaves (around 10 GHz) to measure the refractive index of the atmosphere.

microwave region See MICROWAVE FREQUENCIES and MICROWAVES.

microwave relay See MICROWAVE RADIO RELAY.

microwave relay system A series of microwave transmitter-receiver stations for relaying communications in several line-of-sight hops.

microwaves Radio-frequency electromagnetic energy at wavelengths shorter than about 10 centimeters, but longer than the wavelengths of infrared energy. See also MICROWAVE FREQUENCIES.

microwave spectrum See MICROWAVE FREQUENCIES and MICROWAVES.

microwave transistor A transistor whose semiconductor properties and special fabrication enable it to operate at microwave frequencies.

microwave tube A KLYSTRON, MAGNETRON, or similar tube, used to generate or amplify microwave radio-frequency signals.

midband Abbreviation, MB. The region whose limits are immediately above and below a MIDFREQUENCY; the limits are usually specified for a particular case.

midband frequency See MIDFREQUENCY.

midfrequency The center frequency in a specified band of frequencies.

midget Of reduced size (smaller than *small* and larger than *miniature*).

MIDI Acronym for MUSICAL INSTRUMENT DIGITAL INTERFACE.

midpoint voltage The voltage at the terminals of a cell or battery when it has been discharged halfway (i.e., when the amount of energy used up is equal to the amount of energy remaining).

midrange Pertaining to audio frequencies in the middle of the human hearing range, where the ear is the most sensitive. These frequencies lie between the BASS and TREBLE.

midrange horn A MIDRANGE SPEAKER equipped with a flared horn to give the device a unidirectional sound-emission pattern. It is used primarily in high-power systems and by popular music bands or high-end audio enthusiasts.

midrange speaker A loudspeaker operating most efficiently at frequencies in the middle of the audio spectrum. Such a speaker is intermediate in performance between a WOOFER and a TWEETER.

midsection The center section of a multisection filter having an odd number of sections; thus, the second section of a three-section filter.

migration See ION MIGRATION.

mike 1. See MICROPHONE. 2. See MICROFARAD. 3. See MICROMETER.

MIL Abbreviation of *military*.

mil 1. A small unit of linear measure; 1 mil = 10^{-3} (0.001) inch = 0.0254 mm. 2. Thousand, as in *n* parts per mil.

mile Abbreviation, m or mi. A large unit of linear measure, 1 mi = 1.609 km = 5280 feet.

military robot A robot designed and used for the purpose of executing some task in warfare. The two general types are: human-operated and computer-controlled. An example of a human-operated military robot is an aircraft that is flown by remote control by a ground-based pilot. The same robot, or a whole fleet of them, might be flown by a computer using sophisticated EXPERT SYSTEMS.

mill A telegraph operator's typewriter.

Miller oscillator A crystal oscillator circuit in which the crystal is connected between the control electrode and ground. The tuned tank is connected in the output circuit. The internal capacitance of the active device provides feedback coupling. Sometimes called *conventional crystal oscillator.*

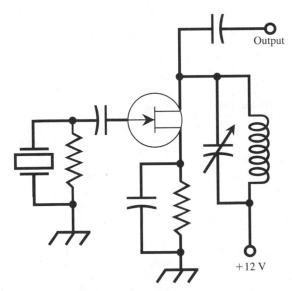

Miller oscillator

milli- Abbreviation, m. A prefix meaning thousandth(s): 10^{-3} (0.001).

milliammeter A usually direct-reading instrument for measuring current in the milliampere range. Also see CURRENT METER.

milliampere Abbreviation, mA. A unit of current equal to 10^{-3} (0.001) ampere.

milliampere-hour Abbreviation, mAh. A unit of low current drain or charging rate, equal to 10^{-3} (0.001) ampere-hour. Also see AMPERE-HOUR and BATTERY CAPACITY.

millibar Abbreviation, mb. A unit of low pressure equal to 10^{-3} (0.001) bar or = 100 pascals.

millicurie Abbreviation, mCi. A small unit of radioactivity equal to 3.71×10^7 disintegrations per second, or 10^{-3} (0.001) curie. Also see CURIE.

millifarad Abbreviation, mF. A seldom-used unit of capacitance, equal to 10^{-3} (0.001) farad or 1000 microfarads.

milligram Abbreviation, mg. A metric unit of weight equal to 10^{-3} (0.001) gram.

millihenry Abbreviation, mH. A unit of inductance, equal to 10^{-3} (0.001) henry.

millihorsepower Abbreviation, mhp. A unit of power equal to 10^{-3} (0.001) horsepower or 0.746 watt. Also see HORSEPOWER.

millilambert Abbreviation, mL. A small unit of brightness equal to 10^{-3} (0.001) lambert.

milliliter Abbreviation, ml. A metric unit of volume equal to 10^{-3} (0.001) liter.

millimaxwell Abbreviation, mMx. A small unit of magnetic flux equal to 10^{-3} (0.001) maxwell or 10^{-11} weber.

millimeter Abbreviation, mm. A metric unit of linear measure equal to 10^{-3} (0.001) meter or 0.03937 inch.

millimeter equivalent The number of millimeters equal to a given English measure fraction (e.g., the millimeter equivalent of $\frac{5}{16}$ inch is 7.937).

millimeter waves Wavelengths between 0.6 and 10 mm (frequencies from 30 to 500 GHz).

millimicro- See NANO-.

millimicrofarad See NANOFARAD.

millimicrohenry See NANOHENRY.

millimicron Abbreviation, mm. A unit of wavelength equal to 10^{-3} micron or one nanometer (10^{-9} meter).

millimilliampere See MICROAMPERE.

millimole Abbreviation, mmol. A unit in chemistry equal to 10^{-3} (0.001) mole.

milliohm A small unit of resistance, reactance, or impedance, equal to 10^{-3} (0.001) ohm.

milliohmmeter An ohmmeter for measuring resistances in the milliohm range.

million electronvolt(s) See MEGAELECTRON-VOLT.

milliphot A unit of illumination equal to 10^{-3} (0.001) phot.

millipuffer See PUFFER.

milliradian Abbreviation, mrad. A unit of angular measure equal to 10^{-3} (0.001) radian.

milliroentgen Abbreviation, mr. A small unit of radioactive dosage; 1 mr = 10^{-3} (0.001) roentgen = 2.57976×10^{-7} Ci/kg.

millirutherford Abbreviation, mrd. A small unit of radioactivity equal to 1000 disintegrations per second; 1 mrd = 10^{-3} (0.001) rutherford.

millisecond Abbreviation, ms or msec. A small unit of time equal to 10^{-3} (0.001) second.

millitorr Abbreviation, mT. An obsolete unit of low pressure equal to 10^{-3} (0.001) torr, or 0.133322 pascal. Also see TORRICELLI.

millivolt Abbreviation, mV. A unit of voltage equal to 10^{-3} (0.001) volt.

millivoltmeter A usually direct-reading instrument for measuring low electric potential. Its sensitivity is provided by a high-gain amplifier operated ahead of the indicating meter.

millivolt potentiometer Abbreviation, MVP. A potentiometer-type null instrument for accurately measuring small direct-current voltages, such as those delivered by a thermocouple. Also see POTENTIOMETRIC VOLTMETER.

millivolts per meter Abbreviation, mV/m. A unit of radio-frequency (RF) field strength. It refers to the RF voltage (in millivolts) developed between an antenna and ground, divided by the height (in meters) of the antenna above ground. Compare MICROVOLTS PER METER.

milliwatt Abbreviation, mW. A unit of power equal to 10^{-3} (0.001) watt.

milliwattmeter An instrument for measuring power in milliwatts. Such instruments usually obtain their sensitivity from a built-in preamplifier.

Mills cross A radio-telescope antenna, consisting of two collinear or phased arrays with a common intersecting lobe. The result is high resolution.

min **1.** Abbreviation of MINIMUM. **2.** Abbreviation of MINUTE.

mineral An element or compound that occurs naturally in the earth's crust. Most minerals are crystalline and many of these have found use in electronics. Some have been produced artificially.

mineral oil A natural liquid insulant derived from petroleum. Dielectric constant, 2.7 to 8.0. Power factor, 0.08 to 0.2 percent at 1 kHz.

mineral-oil capacitor An oil capacitor whose paper dielectric has been impregnated with mineral oil, which is also the filler.

miniature Very small (smaller than midget and larger than subminiature).

miniature cell An electrochemical cell of very small size (e.g., a *button cell* of the kind used in cameras and watches).

miniaturization The technology of minimizing the physical size of a circuit or system, while maintaining its ability to accomplish a given task.

minicalculator A pocket-size electronic calculator.

minicomputer General term for a computer that is more sophisticated than a MICROCOMPUTER, but less powerful than a MAINFRAME.

mini connector A jack or plug having two or three conductors, and measuring $\frac{1}{8}$ (0.125) inch in diameter. It is commonly used with audio equipment.

minifloppy A smaller than standard flexible magnetic disk (floppy).

minima Points along a curve at which a function reaches a local minimum value. Also see MAXIMA AND MINIMA.

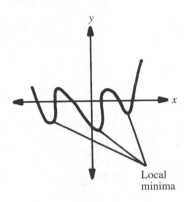

minima

minimum Abbreviation, min. The smallest value in a range or set. Also see MAXIMA AND MINIMA.

minimum detectable signal A signal whose intensity is just higher than the threshold of detection.

minimum discernible signal Abbreviation, MDS. The lowest input-signal amplitude that will produce a discernible output signal in a radio receiver.

miniscope A very-small-sized, lightweight oscilloscope.

minitrack A system used to track an earth satellite, using signals transmitted to the satellite by a line of ground radio stations.

minometer A radioactivity-measuring instrument composed of an ionization chamber and a string galvanometer.

minor beats Secondary or extraneous beats produced in a beat-note system, caused by various sum and difference frequency byproducts of the heterodyne process. Compare MAJOR BEATS.

minor bend A bend in a rectangular waveguide, made without twisting.

minor cycle See WORD TIME.

minor face In a hexagonal quartz crystal, one of the three smaller faces. Compare MAJOR FACE.

minority carrier The type of charge carrier present in relatively small numbers in a processed semiconductor material. Electrons are minority carriers in p-type material; holes are minority carriers in n-type material. Compare MAJORITY CARRIER.

minor lobe One of the lobes of lesser intensity in an antenna directivity pattern. Also see LOBE. Compare MAJOR LOBE.

minor loop A subordinate path for the circulation of information or control signals in an electronic system (e.g., *minor feedback loop*). Compare MAJOR LOOP.

minute **1.** Abbreviation, min. A unit of measure of time equal to 60 seconds or 1/60 hour. **2.** Also called *minute of arc*. Symbol ('). A unit of arc measure equal to 1/60 angular degree or 60 seconds. **3.** General term meaning "extremely small."

MIR Abbreviation of *memory-information register*.

mirror **1.** A device consisting chiefly of a highly polished or silvered surface that reflects a large part of the radiation (such as light) striking it. **2.** Radar-interference material (see CHAFF). **3.** To reflect, as by a mirror.

mirror galvanometer A galvanometer in which a mirror is moved by the coil. The mirror either reflects a spot of light along an external scale, or it reflects the scale, which is then read through a small telescope.

mirror-galvanometer oscillograph See ELECTROMECHANICAL OSCILLOSCOPE.

mirror image **1.** An image or curve that is exactly reversed relative to a straight line or flat plane, compared to a reference image or curve. Compare BILATERAL SYMMETRY. **2.** For a quarter-wave Marconi antenna, the extra quarter-wave element supplied by the earth. **3.** For an antenna at a distance d above a ground plane, an effective antenna at an equal distance d below the ground plane.

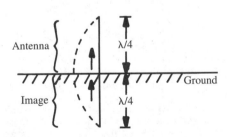

mirror image, 2

mirror-reflection echo A false radar echo or set of echoes, caused by reflection of the radar beam from a plane surface prior to its encountering the target or targets. The beam can also be reflected from one target to another.

mirror-type meter A meter whose movable coil carries a small mirror (rather than a pointer) that reflects a beam of light to produce a spot on a translucent scale.

misaligned head In a tape recorder, a record or a pickup head that is incorrectly oriented, with respect to the passing tape.

misfire Failure of a gas tube or mercury-arc tube to ignite at the correct instant.

misleading precision In electronic calculations and data recording, greater precision than the instruments or conditions justify. Also see SIGNIFICANT FIGURES.

mismatch The condition resulting from joining two circuits, or connecting a line to a circuit, in which the impedances are substantially different.

mismatched impedances Impedances that are unequal, and thus do not satisfy the conditions for maximum power transfer.

mismatch factor For a load not perfectly matched to a driving circuit, the ratio of current flowing in the load to the current that would flow in the load if its impedance were perfectly matched to the output impedance of the driving circuit.

mismatch loss For a load that is mismatched to a source, the ratio P_1/P_2, where P_1 is the power a matched load would absorb from the source, and P_2 is the power actually absorbed by the mismatched load.

mistor A variable-resistance device, used to detect the presence of a magnetic field and to measure magnetic-field strength.

MIT Abbreviation of MASTER INSTRUCTION TAPE.

mix **1.** To produce a beat signal (either the sum or the difference frequency) from two input signals. **2.** The proportion of powdered iron and other inert substances in a ferromagnetic transformer core. Different mixes result in different operating characteristics.

mixdown A method of combining recorded sound from two or more audio tracks, and recording the result onto an audio tape or disc. It is used to create special audio effects.

mixed-base notation A number system in which the base (radix) alternates between two digit positions. Also called *mixed radix notation*.

mixed calculation A mathematical calculation or expression in which more than one operation is used.

mixed modulation Modulation of several kinds coexisting in a system. Thus, a small amount of undesired frequency modulation might accompany amplitude modulation, or vice versa.

mixed number A number having integral (whole) and fractional parts (e.g., 3.14159).

mixer **1.** A device, such as a transistor or semiconductor diode, used to mix two input signals and deliver an output equal to their difference and/or sum (see MIXING). **2.** See AUDIO MIXER. **3.** Any device that combines two or more signals, yielding one output signal whose nature is determined by the characteristics of the circuit.

mixer noise Electrical noise that occurs in a MIXER.

mixing Combining several signals so that some desired mixture of the original signals is obtained. Compare MODULATION.

mixture **1.** A combination of two or more signals that retain their characteristics—even when they interact to produce beat-frequency products. **2.**

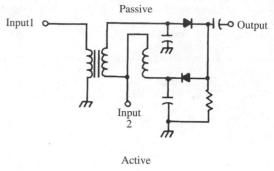

Passive

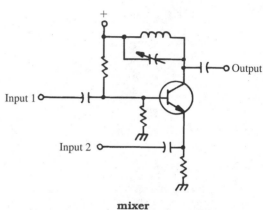

Active

mixer

A diffusion of one substance throughout another, without a solution or a chemical reaction resulting.

mixture melting point Abbreviation, mmp. The temperature at which a mixture of solid substances starts turning into a liquid at 1 atmosphere of pressure. This melting point depends upon the melting points of the substances and their relative concentration in the mixture. Also see MELTING POINT and MIXTURE.

mks Abbreviation of METER-KILOGRAM-SECOND.

mL Abbreviation of MILLILAMBERT.

ml Abbreviation of MILLILITER.

mm Abbreviation of MILLIMETER.

mmf Abbreviation of MAGNETOMOTIVE FORCE.

mmol Abbreviation of MILLIMOLE.

mmp Abbreviation of MIXTURE MELTING POINT.

mmv Abbreviation of MONOSTABLE MULTIVIBRATOR.

Mn Symbol for MANGANESE.

m_n Symbol for MASS OF NEUTRON AT REST.

mnemonic **1.** Pertaining to MEMORY or to memory systems. **2.** A memory code or device.

mnemonic code In computer operations, a programming code, such as assembly language, that, although easily remembered by the programmer, requires subsequent conversion to machine language.

mntr Abbreviation of MONITOR. (Also, mon.)

MO Abbreviation of MASTER OSCILLATOR.

Mo Symbol for MOLYBDENUM.

mobile communications 1. Radio communications between or among stations on board moving or stationary land, waterborne, or airborne vehicles. **2.** Radio communications between at least one fixed station and one or more moving or stationary land, waterborne, or airborne stations.

mobile radio service See MOBILE COMMUNICATIONS.

mobile receiver A radio, television, or other receiver aboard a moving or stationary land, waterborne, or airborne vehicle.

mobile-relay station A fixed station that receives a signal from a MOBILE STATION and retransmits it to one or more other mobile stations.

mobile station A station installed and operated aboard a moving or stationary vehicle. The vehicle might be on land, under water, or in the air. Compare PORTABLE STATION.

mobile transmitter A radio, television, or other transmitter aboard a moving or stationary vehicle. The vehicle might be on land, under water, or in the air.

mobility See CARRIER MOBILITY.

mockup See DUMMY, 1.

mod 1. Abbreviation of MODULATOR. **2.** Abbreviation of MODULUS. **3.** Abbreviation of MODIFICATION.

mode 1. One of the ways a given resonant system can oscillate. **2.** One of the ways that electromagnetic energy can be propagated through a device or system. See MODES OF PROPAGATION. **3.** The method via which intelligence is conveyed in a communications or broadcast signal. See EMISSION MODE. **4.** Resonance of sound waves within an acoustic chamber.

mode coupling The exchange or interaction of energy between identical modes (see MODE, **1, 2**).

mode filter A waveguide filter that separates waves of different propagation mode, but of the same frequency (see MODES OF PROPAGATION).

model 1. A working or mockup version of a circuit, system, or device, illustrative of the final version. **2.** A mathematical representation of a process, device, circuit, or system. Example: the Rutherford model of the atom.

modeling The creation of an object in three-dimensional computer graphics.

modem See MODULATOR-DEMODULATOR.

mode purity In a modulated radio-frequency signal, the condition in which no undesirable types of modulation exist. For example, a frequency-modulated signal in which there is zero amplitude modulation.

moderator A substance, such as graphite or heavy water, used to slow neutrons in an atomic reactor. Also see ACCELERATOR, **1** and REACTOR, **2**.

modes of propagation The configurations in which microwave energy can be transmitted through a WAVEGUIDE.

modes of resonance In a microwave cavity, the configurations in which resonant oscillation can exist, depending on the way the cavity is excited.

modification 1. Changing the configuration of a circuit, device, or system, usually to a minor extent, to tailor its characteristics for a specific purpose. **2.** Changing some aspect of a signal for a specific purpose (e.g., reducing the emission bandwidth to allow more signals to fit within a given band of frequencies). **3.** In computer operations, changing program addresses and instructions by performing logic and arithmetic on them, as if they were data. Also see PROGRAM MODIFICATION.

modified alternate mark inversion A signal that is similar to alternate mark inversion (AMI), but contains certain differences that are specified by a rigorous set of standards for the particular signal.

modifier A data item used to change a computer program instruction so that it can be used to implement different successive operations. Also see PROGRAM MODIFICATION.

modifier register See INDEX REGISTER.

modify To perform a MODIFICATION to a circuit, device, system, signal, program address, etc.

moding A fault characterized by oscillation of a MAGNETRON in undesirable modes.

modular technique See BUILDING-BLOCK TECHNIQUE.

modulated amplifier A usually high-frequency amplifier whose output is varied in some way for the purpose of conveying intelligence. Compare

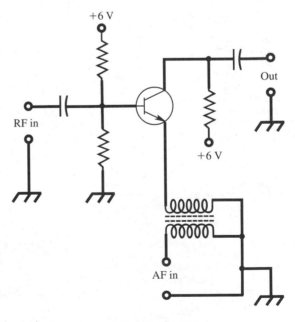

modulated amplifier

MODULATED OSCILLATOR. In the amplitude modulation of an amplifier, there is little or no disturbance of the carrier frequency. Also see MODULATION.

modulated beam   **1.** An electron beam (as in a cathode-ray tube), whose intensity is varied by a desired signal. **2.** A light beam whose intensity is varied for communications or control purposes.

modulated carrier   A carrier wave whose amplitude, frequency, or phase is varied to convey intelligence.

modulated continuous wave   Abbreviation, mcw. A high-frequency carrier wave modulated by a continuous, lower-frequency wave, as in MCW telegraphy.

modulated CW   See MODULATED CONTINUOUS WAVE.

modulated electron beam   See MODULATED BEAM, **1**.

modulated light beam   See MODULATED BEAM, **2**.

modulated oscillator   A usually high-frequency oscillator whose output is varied in some way to convey intelligence. Compare MODULATED AMPLIFIER. Also see MODULATION.

modulated-ring pattern   See GEAR-WHEEL PATTERN and SPOT-WHEEL PATTERN.

modulated stage   A transmitter, amplifier, or oscillator in which the signal information is impressed on the carrier.

modulated wave   See MODULATED CARRIER.

modulatee   A stage or circuit upon which modulation is impressed (e.g., a MODULATED AMPLIFIER or a MODULATED OSCILLATOR).

modulating electrode   **1.** In an oscilloscope, an electrode (usually the intensity electrode) to which a signal can be applied to intensity-modulate the electron beam. **2.** In a cathode-ray tube, the electrode to which the video signal is applied.

modulating signal   Intelligence that modulates a carrier (e.g., binary data in radioteletype, or music in broadcasting).

modulation   Combining two signals with the result that some aspect of one signal (the carrier) is varied by and in sympathy with the other (the modulating signal). Usually, the carrier has a frequency considerably higher than that of the modulating signal.

modulation bars   A form of television interference in which an amplitude-modulated signal causes horizontal bars, alternating light and dark, to appear on the picture screen. The higher the modulating frequency, the closer together the bars appear. In severe cases, the bars completely obliterate the picture.

modulation capability   The maximum percentage of modulation a transmitter will permit before nonlinearity occurs. Also see MODULATION LINEARITY.

modulation characteristic   For an amplitude-modulated wave, the ratio of the instantaneous

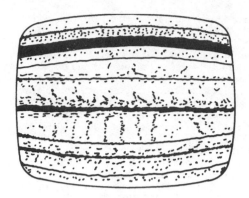

modulation bars

amplitude of the modulated signal to the instantaneous modulating voltage.

modulation code   In a modulated transmitter, a system of modulation in which certain signal variations or pulses represent particular characters. Examples are ASCII, BAUDOT CODE, and MORSE CODE.

modulation coefficient   Symbol, m. A figure expressing the depth (extent) to which a signal is amplitude-modulated. For a signal in which the upward modulation is equal to the downward modulation, $m = (E_m - E_c)/E_c$, where E_c is the peak-to-peak voltage of the unmodulated signal, and E_m is the peak-to-peak voltage of the modulated signal. For full (100%) modulation, $m = 1$.

modulation depth   See DEPTH OF MODULATION.

modulation distortion   **1.** In a modulated signal, envelope distortion introduced by the modulation process or by the receiver circuit. **2.** External cross modulation (see CROSS MODULATION, **1**).

modulation envelope   See ENVELOPE, **1**.

modulation-envelope distortion   Undesirable distortion in the ENVELOPE of the modulating intelligence in an amplitude-modulated or single-sideband signal at the output of a radio transmitter.

modulation factor   See MODULATION COEFFICIENT.

modulation frequency   Abbreviation, f_m. The frequency of a modulating signal.

modulation linearity   In a modulated signal, the degree to which the instantaneous signal amplitude or frequency follows the instantaneous amplitude of the modulating signal.

modulation meter   See PERCENTAGE-MODULATION METER.

modulation monitor   **1.** A linear detector with a pickup coil (or antenna) and headphones for listening to an amplitude-modulated signal. **2.** See PERCENTAGE-MODULATION METER. **3.** A device that displays the modulation characteristics of a signal (e.g., the envelope for amplitude modulation and single sideband or the frequency-vs.-time function for frequency modulation).

modulation noise   See NOISE BEHIND THE SIGNAL.

modulation percentage   A measure of the extent to which a signal is amplitude modulated. It is expressed as the MODULATION COEFFICIENT multiplied by 100.

modulation ratio   For a modulated signal, the quotient M_r/M_i, where M_r is the percentage of radiated-signal modulation, and M_i is the percentage of current modulation.

modulator   A device or circuit for modulating a carrier.

modulator cell   See KERR CELL.

modulator crystal   A transparent piezoelectric crystal to which a signal voltage can be applied to modulate a beam of polarized light passing through it.

modulator-demodulator   Also called *modem*. **1.** A device that converts binary data to audio-frequency-shift-keyed (AFSK) analog signals, and vice-versa. It is commonly used to interface computers and terminals with telephone lines and radio transceivers. **2.** A circuit or device, such as a biased diode or diode bridge, that can perform either modulation or demodulation.

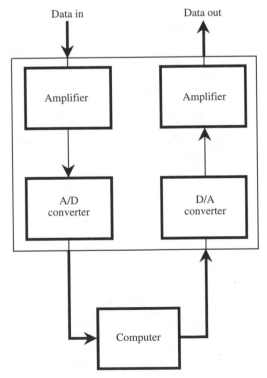

modulator-demodulator

modulator driver   An amplifier stage that delivers excitation current, voltage, or power to a modulator stage.

module   An assembly containing a complete self-contained circuit (or subcircuit), often miniaturized and made for plug-in operation.

modulometer   Any instrument, such as a percentage-modulation meter, used to measure the degree of modulation of a signal. Often, it can also measure other signal characteristics (e.g., carrier shift, extraneous amplitude modulation, and extraneous frequency modulation).

modulo n check   In computer operations, a technique for verifying the validity of a number used as an operand. The number being so checked is divided by another number to provide a remainder (check digit) that goes with the number. After the number is, for example, transmitted through some part of a computer system, it is again divided by the original divisor, and if the remainder is the check digit, the data has retained its integrity.

modulus   **1.** Absolute magnitude. Also see ABSOLUTE VALUE and IMPEDANCE. **2.** Abbreviation, mod. In computer operations, a whole number that indicates the number of states a counter sequences through in each cycle. **3.** Abbreviation, mod. A number (constant or coefficient) expressing the degree to which some property is possessed by a material or body (e.g., *modulus of elasticity*, *shear modulus*, and *bulk modulus*). **4.** A constant by which a logarithm to one base must be multiplied to obtain a logarithm of the same number to another base.

modulus of elasticity   The stress-to-strain ratio in a material under elastic deformation.

moire   In a television or facsimile picture, an effect produced by the convergence of straight lines. When the lines are nearly parallel to the scanning lines, the converging lines appear irregular.

moisture meter   See ELECTRIC HYGROMETER and ELECTRONIC HYGROMETER.

mol   Abbreviation of MOLE.

molar conductance   See MOLECULAR CONDUCTANCE.

molar polarization   Any molecule in an electric field undergoes a small displacement of the positive and negative electrical centers. This results in an electric dipole.

molar solution   A solution, such as an electrolyte, containing 1 mol of solute per liter of solvent. Compare NORMAL SOLUTION.

mold   **1.** To form matter into a desired shape, as by pouring liquefied material into a container or liquefying the material in the container, then allowing the liquid material to solidify. In *hot molding*, the material is melted in the container and then cooled to hardness; in *cold molding*, the material is shaped without heat and it solidifies with time. **2.** The hollow container used to shape a material, as in **1**.

molded capacitor   A capacitor that is molded into a protective body of insulating material. Also see MOLD, **1**, **2** and MOLDED COMPONENT.

molded ceramic capacitor   A ceramic-dielectric capacitor enclosed in a molded housing. Also see MOLD, **1**, **2**; MOLDED CAPACITOR; and MOLDED COMPONENT.

molded coil   See MOLDED INDUCTOR.

molded component   A part (such as a capacitor, coil, or resistor) that is completely enclosed in a protective material (such as a plastic) that is molded around it. Also see MOLD, **1**, **2**.

molded electrolytic capacitor   A solid-dielectric electrolytic capacitor enclosed in a molded housing. Also see MOLD, **1**, **2**; MOLDED CAPACITOR; MOLDED COMPONENT; and SOLID-ELECTROLYTIC CAPACITOR.

molded glass capacitor   A glassplate-dielectric capacitor enclosed in a molded glass housing. Also see GLASS CAPACITOR; MOLD, **1**, **2**; MOLDED CAPACITOR; and MOLDED COMPONENT.

molded inductor   An inductor that is molded into a protective housing of insulating material. Also see MOLD, **1**, **2** and MOLDED COMPONENT.

molded mica capacitor   A mica-dielectric capacitor enclosed in a molded housing. Also see MICA CAPACITOR; MOLD, **1**, **2**; MOLDED CAPACITOR; and MOLDED COMPONENT.

molded mud   A molding compound that has inferior electrical characteristics. Also see MOLD, **1**, **2** and MOLDED COMPONENT.

molded paper capacitor   A paper-dielectric capacitor enclosed in a molded housing. Also see MOLD, **1**, **2**; MOLDED CAPACITOR; MOLDED COMPONENT; and PAPER CAPACITOR.

molded porcelain capacitor   A capacitor enclosed in a body of molded porcelain. Also see MOLD, **1**, **2**; MOLDED CAPACITOR; MOLDED COMPONENT; and PORCELAIN.

molded resistor   A resistor that is molded in a protective housing of insulating material. Also see MOLD, **1**, **2** and MOLDED COMPONENT.

molded transistor   A transistor that is encapsulated in a protective molding compound, such as epoxy resin. Also see MOLD, **1**, **2** and MOLDED COMPONENT.

mole   Abbreviation, mol. **1.** The amount of substance in a system containing as many specified entities (atoms, molecules, ions, subatomic particles, or groups of such particles) as there are atoms in 12 grams of carbon 12. **2.** It is also called the *Avogadro constant*. A unit of quantity in chemistry, equal to approximately 6.022×10^{23}.

molectronics   See MOLECULAR ELECTRONICS.

molecular circuit   See MONOLITHIC INTEGRATED CIRCUIT.

molecular conductance   For a solution, such as an electrolyte, the product of specific conductivity and the volume (in liters) of a solution that contains 1 gram molecule of the solute. Also see SOLUTE; SOLUTION, **1**; and SOLVENT, **1**, **2**.

molecular conductivity   See MOLECULAR CONDUCTANCE.

molecular electronics   The technique of processing a single block of material so that separate areas perform the functions of different electronic components. The entire block constitutes a circuit (e.g., a MONOLITHIC INTEGRATED CIRCUIT).

molecular magnets   According to the molecular theory of magnetism, the elemental magnets formed by individual molecules.

molecular theory of magnetism   Each molecule in a piece of magnetic metal is itself a magnet (possessing a north and a south pole). These tiny magnets are thought to be normally oriented at random, but when the material is magnetized by an external force, they align themselves with each other.

molecular weight   Abbreviation, mol wt. In a molecule of a substance, the sum of the atomic weights of the constituent atoms.

molecule   The basic particle of a compound; each molecule usually contains two or more atoms. For example, the formula $AgNO_3$ represents silver nitrate, each molecule of which contains one atom of silver (Ag), one atom of nitrogen (N), and three atoms of oxygen (O).

moletronics   See MOLECULAR ELECTRONICS.

mol wt   Abbreviation of MOLECULAR WEIGHT.

molybdenum   Symbol, Mo. A metallic element. Atomic number, 42. Atomic weight, 95.94. It is used in the grids and plates of certain vacuum tubes.

moment   The tendency to produce motion around a point, as by torque, or the product of a quantity and the distance to a point. The moment of force is expressed as the product Fd, where F is force and d is distance.

momentary-contact switch   A switch that maintains contact only while it is held down. Such a device is usually a *pushbutton switch*, although it might be a *toggle switch*, a *slide switch*, or a *lever switch*.

momentary switching   Switching of short duration, often characterized by a quick make and break immediately following activation of the switch. Compare DWELL SWITCHING.

moment of inertia   For a torque motor, the inertia of the armature around the axis of rotation. Also see MOMENT.

mon   **1.** Abbreviation of MONITOR. **2.** Abbreviation of MONAURAL.

monatomic   **1.** Pertaining to a molecule with only one atom. **2.** Pertaining to a molecule with only one replaceable atom or radical.

monatomic molecule   A molecule having a single atom (e.g., argon, helium, and neon). Compare DIATOMIC MOLECULE.

monaural   **1.** Pertaining to an audio system having one channel. **2.** Pertaining to hearing with one ear, as opposed to BINAURAL.

monaural recorder A single-track recorder, as opposed to a stereophonic recorder.

Monel metal An alloy of nickel (67%), copper (28%), iron, manganese, and other metals (5%). Its resistivity is approximately 42 microhm-centimeters at 20°C.

monimatch An amateur version of the reflected-power meter and SWR meter.

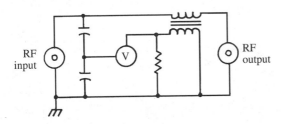

RF input   V   RF output

monimatch

moniscope A special cathode-ray tube that produces a stationary picture for testing television equipment. Its name is a contraction of monitor and scope.

monitor 1. A device that allows the sampling of a signal or quantity. Examples: *line-voltage monitor*, *television monitor*, and *modulation monitor*. **2.** A cathode-ray-tube (CRT) computer display.

monitor head A separate playback head included in some tape recorders for listening to the tape as it is being recorded.

monitoring The act, process, or technique of observing an action while it is in progress or checking a quantity while it is varying. Examples: *carrier monitoring*, *modulation monitoring*, and *line-voltage monitoring*.

monitoring amplifier An auxiliary amplifier used in monitoring an audio-frequency system.

monitoring antenna A usually small pickup antenna used with a signal monitor or monitoring receiver.

monitoring key In a telephone system, a device used to listen to a two-way conversation.

monitoring receiver A radio or television receiver used specifically to monitor a transmission directly.

monitoring station In a security system, a central control location from which personnel can observe the input from sensors, cameras, and other devices at remote locations throughout the secured area.

monitor system A computer program usually stored in the read-only memory (ROM) supplied by the hardware vendor. It controls the implementation of programs written by the user, and the operation of peripherals associated with program runs and inputting or outputting data to or from memory. Also called *executive program*.

monkey chatter The characteristic sound of a single-sideband (SSB) signal when the receiver is mistuned, or when the receiver is set for the wrong sideband.

monk's cloth A coarse drapery fabric sometimes used to soundproof the walls and ceiling of a radio studio or recording booth.

mono See MONAURAL.

mono- Prefix meaning *single*.

monobrid circuit An integrated circuit in which either several monolithic IC chips are interconnected to form a larger, single-package circuit, or monolithic IC chips are interwired with thin-film components into a single-package circuit. The name is a contraction of *monolithic hybrid*.

monochromatic 1. Being of one color (hue) in nature. **2.** Being of a single wavelength in nature (pertaining to radiation of any kind). **3.** Pertaining to black-and-white television.

monochromaticity Consisting of one color of visible light. The brightness can vary from black to maximum.

monochromatic power density At a given temperature, the energy radiated per square centimeter of blackbody surface per second per unit wavelength range. Also see BLACKBODY and BLACKBODY RADIATION.

monochromatic sensitivity Sensitivity to light of one color only.

monochrome television Black-and-white television.

monoclinic crystal A crystal having three axes of unequal length; two of them intersect obliquely and are perpendicular to the third [e.g., the type of crystal found in one form of sulfur (monoclinic sulfur)].

monocrystalline material See SINGLE-CRYSTAL MATERIAL.

monode A one-element device, such as a filament-type lamp, thermistor, voltage-dependent resistor, barretter, etc.

monogroove stereo A method of making a stereophonic phonograph disc in which both channels are recorded as a single groove.

monolayer A thin film having a thickness of one molecule.

monolithic integrated circuit An integrated circuit (IC) formed in a single block or wafer of semiconductor material. The name is derived from the Greek monolithos ("one stone"). Compare HYBRID INTEGRATED CIRCUIT and THIN-FILM INTEGRATED CIRCUIT.

monometallic Containing or using only one metal.

monomolecular film See MONOLAYER.

monophonic recorder See SINGLETRACK RECORDER.

monophonic system A single-channel sound system. Compare STEREO SYSTEM.

monopole antenna See QUARTER-WAVE MONOPOLE.

monopulse In radar and electronic-navigation operations, using one pulse to determine azimuth and elevation simultaneously.

monorange speaker A loudspeaker that reproduces most of the full audio range. Also called *extended range speaker.* Compare TWEETER and WOOFER.

monostable   Having one stable state.

monostable blocking oscillator   Abbreviation, MBO. A blocking oscillator that behaves somewhat like a one-shot multivibrator. The oscillator delivers a single output pulse each time it receives an input (trigger) pulse.

monostable multivibrator   A multivibrator that delivers one output pulse for each input (trigger) pulse. Also called *one-shot circuit* and *single-shot multivibrator.* Compare ASTABLE MULTIVIBRATOR and BISTABLE MULTIVIBRATOR.

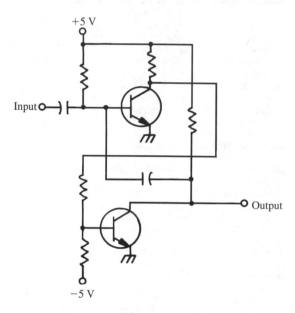

monostable multivibrator

monostatic reflectivity   The property whereby, for certain reflectors (such as a tricorner reflector), all incident rays are reflected in exactly the opposite direction from which they arrive.

monotone   A sound or series of sounds having a single, constant pitch (frequency).

monotonicity   In a digital-to-analog converter, a condition where the output either remains the same or increases for any single increase in the input code.

monovalent   See UNIVALENT.

Monte Carlo method   **1.** The use of statistical sampling in the approximate solution of an engineering problem. **2.** In computer operations, the construction of mathematical models from randomly selected components taken from representative statistical populations.

Moog synthesizer   An electronic device that can be made to simulate virtually any sound, including that of musical instruments and the

human voice, through the use of several audio oscillators, whose output can be controlled to produce tones of various harmonic content, duration, attack, and decay periods.

moonbounce   Also called *earth-moon-earth (EME).* Radio communication, usually at very-high frequencies (VHF) or ultra-high frequencies (UHF), in which the moon is used as a passive reflector. This is a popular mode among some amateur radio operators.

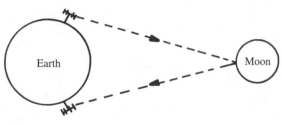

moon bounce

MOPA   Abbreviation of MASTER OSCILLATOR/POWER AMPLIFIER.

morphological electronics   See MOLECULAR ELECTRONICS.

Morse   **1.** See MORSE CODE. **2.** Telegraphy (wire or radio). **3.** To signal by means of the Morse code.

Morse code   Either of two similar binary codes used in radio and wire telegraphy. It uses short pulses (dots or dits) and long pulses (dashes or dahs) to represent letters of the alphabet, numerals, and punctuation marks. It usually refers to the CONTINENTAL CODE, but occasionally it refers to the AMERICAN MORSE CODE.

MOS   Abbreviation of *metal-oxide-semiconductor.*

mosaic   **1.** See PHOTOMOSAIC. **2.** The pattern of tiny photoelectric particles in a television camera tube that convert the image into electric charges.

mosaic crystal   A form of imperfect crystal. The defects have certain properties, one of which is to cause additional energy levels in semiconductor materials manufactured from such crystals.

MOS capacitor   A capacitor using metal-oxide-semiconductor (MOS) technology. It is used in MOS integrated circuits. A silicon substrate forms one electrode (generally p-type material). An oxide layer forms the dielectric. An electrode forms the other plate of the capacitor. The capacitance might be variable by changing the applied voltage at the metal gate electrode.

MOSFET   Abbreviation of METAL-OXIDE-SEMICONDUCTOR FIELD-EFFECT TRANSISTOR.

MOSROM   Abbreviation of *metal-oxide-semiconductor read-only memory* (see READ-ONLY MEMORY).

MOST Abbreviation of *metal-oxide-semiconductor transistor.*

most significant character Abbreviation, MSC. In positional number representation, the leftmost character in a significant group, such as a word.

most significant digit Abbreviation, MSD. In a number, the leftmost digit that is not zero (zero being insignificant in this context).

mother **1.** A term or prefix referring to a component that supports (or appears to support) other similar components (e.g., MOTHERBOARD). **2.** A term referring to the source from which samples or components are derived (e.g., MOTHER CRYSTAL). **3.** A mold that has been electroformed from a master phonograph disc.

motherboard In a computer or data-processing device, the circuit board on which most of the main circuitry is mounted.

mother crystal A natural quartz crystal from which is produced the piezoelectric plates and other components used in electronics.

motion detector A device for sensing the movement or stopping of a body, such as a rotating shaft. Various sensors are used in different detectors: magnetic, photoelectric, capacitive, etc.

motion frequency The natural frequency (especially that of oscillation) of a servo.

Motion Picture Experts Group Abbreviation, MPEG. A data-compression standard used for animated digital video. It is useful in computer videoconferencing and telecommuting, and for the development of multimedia presentations.

motion-picture pickup In television operations, a camera (and the technique for using it) for picking up scenes directly from motion-picture film.

motion sensor In security systems, a set of devices that produces an output signal whenever anything moves within a certain area. Such equipment might use infrared, ultrasound, microwaves, capacitive effects, thermal sensors, air-current detectors, sound detectors, video cameras, or a combination of these.

motor **1.** A machine for converting electrical energy into mechanical energy. **2.** The driving mechanism of a loudspeaker.

motorboard The basic mechanism of a tape recorder, embodying motor, flywheel, capstan, rollers, etc., assembled on a board or panel.

motorboating A repetitive, low-frequency popping or puffing noise sometimes observed in malfunctioning audio circuits. It was so named because of its resemblance to the sound of a motorboat.

motorboating filter In an audio amplifier circuit, a simple filter installed to prevent MOTORBOATING caused by unwanted positive feedback. Also see DECOUPLING FILTER.

motor capacitor See MOTOR-RUN CAPACITOR and MOTOR-START CAPACITOR.

motor constant The ability, expressed numerically, of a torque motor to convert electric input power into torque.

motor converter An electromechanical device for converting alternating current to direct current.

motor-driven relay An electromechanical relay whose contacts are opened and closed by a rotating motor.

motor effect Magnetic force between adjacent current-carrying conductors.

motor-generator A combination of motor and generator in a single machine assembly. A common arrangement is a low-voltage motor turning a high-voltage generator. The machine shafts can be coupled, or the motor can turn the generator through a belt, chain, or gear train.

motor meter A meter in which the movable element is essentially a continuously rotating motor. See, for example, KILOWATT-HOUR METER.

motor-run capacitor A power-factor-boosting capacitor connected (together with its auxiliary winding) in parallel with the main winding in an induction motor. Also see CAPACITOR MOTOR.

motor-speed control A method of controlling the speed of a motor by varying the magnitude and/or phase of its current. Electronic devices usually use diode, diac, or triac circuits.

motor-start capacitor A capacitor that, with an auxiliary winding, is switched into a motor circuit during the starting period, and is automatically disconnected (with the winding) after the motor reaches normal running speed. Also see CAPACITOR MOTOR.

motor starter See STARTING BOX.

mould See MOLD.

mount **1.** A mechanical device with which a component is attached to a circuit board or chassis. **2.** The attachment of a circuit board to a chassis. **3.** The hardware with which an antenna is attached to a mast. **4.** The hardware with which a microphone is attached to a boom or other support. **5.** In general, any attaching hardware.

Mountain standard time Abbreviation, MST. Local mean time at the 105th meridian west of Greenwich. Also see GREENWICH MEAN TIME, STANDARD TIME, TIME ZONE, and COORDINATED UNIVERSAL TIME.

mounting flange The portion of a speaker frame, usually made of metal, that is equipped with holes for attachment to a cabinet or panel.

mouse A pointing device commonly used with personal computers. It is about the size of a candy bar. The computer operator moves the display pointer or cursor by sliding the mouse on a flat surface. Functions and commands are executed by pressing a button (clicking) on the device.

mouth The radiating end of a horn (antenna, loudspeaker, etc.).

MOV Abbreviation of METAL-OXIDE VARISTOR.

movable-coil meter See D'ARSONVAL METER.

movable-coil modulator See ELECTROMECHANICAL MODULATOR.

movable contact The traveling contact in a relay or switch. Compare FIXED CONTACT.

movable-iron meter　See IRON-VANE METER.

movies on demand　In television, a system that makes it possible for subscribers to choose the programs they want to see, and also to choose the viewing times for the programs.

moving-coil galvanometer　A galvanometer whose movable element is a coil of fine wire suspended or pivoted between the poles of a magnet.

moving-coil microphone　See DYNAMIC MICROPHONE.

moving-coil motor　The driving mechanism of a moving-coil DYNAMIC SPEAKER.

moving-coil pickup　See DYNAMIC PICKUP.

moving-coil speaker　See DYNAMIC SPEAKER.

moving-conductor microphone　See VELOCITY MICROPHONE.

moving-diaphragm meter　A headphone used as a sensitive indicator in alternating-current bridge measurements.

moving element　In an electromechanical device, the portion that moves physically under variable operating conditions.

moving-film camera　An oscilloscope camera in which the film is drawn past the lens continuously at a constant speed, rather than being advanced frame by frame, as in a motion-picture camera.

moving-iron meter　See IRON-VANE METER.

moving-vane meter　See IRON-VANE METER.

mp　Abbreviation of MELTING POINT.

m$_p$　Symbol for MASS OF PROTON AT REST.

MPEG　Abbreviation for MOTION PICTURE EXPERTS GROUP.

MPG　Abbreviation of *microwave pulse generator*.

mph　Abbreviation of *miles per hour*. Also, mi/h.

MPO　Abbreviation of *maximum power output*.

mps　1. Abbreviation of *meters per second*. Also, m/s. 2. Abbreviation of *miles per second*. Also, mi/s.

MPT　Abbreviation of MAXIMUM POWER TRANSFER.

MPX　Abbreviation of MULTIPLEX.

MR　Abbreviation of MEMORY REGISTER.

mrad　Abbreviation of MILLIRADIAN.

MRIA　Abbreviation of *Magnetic Recording Industry Association*.

mrm　Abbreviation of *milliroentgens per minute*.

MS　Abbreviation of MASS SPECTROMETER.

m^2/s　Abbreviation of *meters squared per second*. The unit of kinematic viscosity.

M scan　In radar operations, a modified A-scan display in which a pedestal signal is moved along the base line to a point where it coincides with the base line of the reflected signal to determine the distance to the target.

msec　Abbreviation of MILLISECOND. Also, ms.

msg　Abbreviation of MESSAGE.

MSI　Abbreviation of MEDIUM SCALE INTEGRATION.

MST　Abbreviation of MOUNTAIN STANDARD TIME.

MT　Abbreviation of METRIC TON.

MTR　Abbreviation of MAGNETIC TAPE RECORDER.

mtr　Alternate abbreviation of METER.

MTS　Abbreviation for MULTICHANNEL TELEVISION SOUND.

M-type backward-wave oscillator　A broadband, voltage-tuned oscillator in which the electrons interact with a backward traveling radio-frequency wave. Compare O-TYPE BACKWARD-WAVE OSCILLATOR.

mu　Symbol, μ. 1. Abbreviation of the prefix MICRO-. 2. Expression for AMPLIFICATION FACTOR. 3. Expression for PERMEABILITY. 4. Expression for MICRON. 5. Expression for ELECTRIC MOMENT. 6. Expression for INDUCTIVITY. 7. Expression for MAGNETIC MOMENT. 8. Expression for MOLECULAR CONDUCTIVITY.

μ　1. Symbol for MU.

μ**A**　Abbreviation of MICROAMPERE.

μ_B　Symbol for BOHR MAGNETON.

μ**b**　Abbreviation of MICROBAR.

μ**Ci**　Abbreviation of MICROCURIE.

μ_e　Symbol for ELECTRON MAGNETIC MOMENT.

μ**F**　Abbreviation of MICROFARAD.

μ**g**　Abbreviation of MICROGRAM.

μ**H**　Abbreviation of MICROHENRY.

μ**in**　Abbreviation of MICROINCH.

μ**l**　Abbreviation of MICROLITER.

μ**mm**　Abbreviation of *micromillimeter* (see NANOMETER).

μ_n　Symbol for NUCLEAR MAGNETON.

μ_o　Symbol for FREE-SPACE PERMEABILITY CONSTANT.

μ_p　Symbol for PROTON MAGNETIC MOMENT.

μ**P**　Abbreviation of MICROPROCESSOR.

μ**rd**　Abbreviation of MICRORUTHERFORD.

μ**S**　Abbreviation of MICROSIEMENS.

μ**s**　Abbreviation of MICROSECOND. (Also, μsec.)

μ**V**　Abbreviation of MICROVOLT.

μ**V/m**　Abbreviation of MICROVOLTS PER METER.

μ**W**　Abbreviation of MICROWATT.

MUF　Abbreviation of MAXIMUM USABLE FREQUENCY.

mu factor　See MU, 2.

mu law　In communications, a companding standard generally used in the United States and Canada.

Muller tube　A tube that conducts by means of ionization of an internal gas. It is used for radiation detection.

multiaddress　In a computer, a multiple memory location.

multiband amplifier　A radio-frequency power amplifier capable of operation on more than one frequency band. The bands are often (but not always) harmonically related. Compare WIDEBAND AMPLIFIER.

multiband antenna　A single antenna, such as one used in amateur radio and television reception, operated in several frequency bands or channels. The bands are often (but not always) harmonically related.

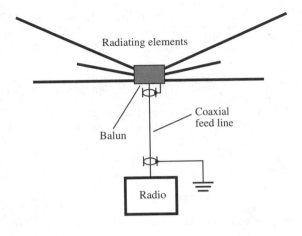

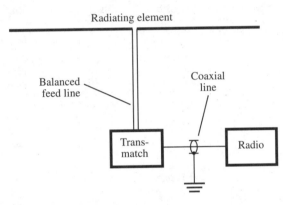

multiband antenna

multiband device   A device (such as a tuner, receiver, transmitter, or test instrument) that operates in several selectable frequency bands.

multiband oscilloscope   See WIDEBAND OSCILLOSCOPE.

multiband receiver   A communications receiver capable of operation on more than one frequency band. Such a receiver might, but does not necessarily, provide continuous coverage over a wide range of frequencies. Compare WIDEBAND RECEIVER.

multicasting   The use of two frequency-modulation (FM) broadcast stations, or one FM station and one television station, to broadcast separately the two channels of a stereo program. The program is picked up simultaneously with two receivers.

multicavity magnetron   A magnetron whose anode block has two or more cavities.

multicellular horn   A loudspeaker in front of which are placed rectangular cells through which the sound passes.

multichannel   Pertaining to a radio-communication system that operates on more than one channel at the same time. The individual channels might contain identical information, or they might contain different signals.

multichannel analyzer   A test instrument, such as a spectrum analyzer, that splits an input into several channels for testing.

multichannel television sound   Abbreviation, MTS. In television broadcasting, audio transmitted on more than one channel to provide stereo sound to subscribers.

multichip circuit   A MICROCIRCUIT composed of interconnected active and passive chip-type components.

multichip integrated circuit   An INTEGRATED CIRCUIT composed of circuit elements on separate, interconnected chips.

multicontact switch   A switch having more than two contacting positions.

multicoupler   An impedance-matching device used to couple several receivers to a single antenna.

multielement antenna   A directive antenna having more than one element. Such antennas include phased arrays and parasitic arrays. Common examples are the LOG-PERIODIC ANTENNA, the QUAD ANTENNA, and the YAGI ANTENNA.

multiemitter transistor   **1.** A bipolar transistor having more than one emitter. **2.** A bipolar power transistor having several emitters connected in parallel in the transistor structure.

multiframe   A set of frames in a signal that are adjacent to each other in time (consecutive) and positioned according to an alignment signal.

multigun CRT   A cathode-ray tube (CRT) having more than one electron gun.

multihop propagation   Propagation of a radio wave by several successive reflections between the ionosphere and the surface of the earth.

multilayer circuit   A circuit consisting of several sections printed or deposited on separate layers, which are subsequently stacked in a sandwich-like manner.

multilayer coil   A coil in which the turns of wire are wound in several complete layers, one on top of the other. Compare SINGLE-LAYER COIL.

multimedia   In personal computing, the use of video and sound effects together. It is useful especially in education, but also as a form of entertainment. Data is typically recorded on CD-ROM (compact-disk read-only memory).

multimedia computer   A personal computer designed especially for multimedia use. It includes a sound board, speakers, a microphone, and a CD-ROM (compact-disk read-only memory) drive. It often has a large-screen, high-resolution monitor (17 inches or greater diagonal measure).

multimeter   A meter that allows measurement of different quantities (e.g., current, voltage, and resistance); the functions are usually made available through a selector switch.

multimode operation **1.** In radio communication, the use of two or more transmitters simultaneously, operating in different modes [e.g., one using single-sideband (SSB) and another using frequency modulation (FM)]. **2.** The transmission of visible light or infrared energy through an optical fiber in more than one mode at the same time. **3.** The operation of any device in more than one of its modes simultaneously.

multipactor A microwave switching tube capable of operating at high power levels. Characterized by high operating speed.

multipath cancellation A phenomenon sometimes observed in radio-wave propagation. Separate signal components arrive at the receiver in equal amplitude, but opposite phase. Also see MULTIPATH FADING and MULTIPATH RECEPTION.

multipath delay In MULTIPATH RECEPTION, the lag between signal components arriving over different paths.

multipath effect At a receiver, the difference in arrival time of multipath signals. Also see MULTIPATH DELAY.

multipath fading In radio communication, variations in the received signal that result from phasing various components of the transmitted signal that are propagated over different paths. At low, medium, and high frequencies, this effect is usually the result of ionospheric fluctuation. At very-high and ultra-high frequencies, it could occur as a result of changes in the state of the intervening atmosphere or, occasionally, reflection from objects, such as aircraft.

multipath reception Reception of a signal over more than one path. This often results in fading (see MULTIPATH FADING) and other undesirable effects, such as ghosting in television reception.

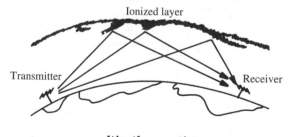

Ionized layer

Transmitter

Receiver

multipath reception

multipath transmission **1.** Transmission of a signal over two or more paths. Also see MULTIPATH RECEPTION. **2.** See MULTIHOP PROPAGATION.

multiphase system See POLYPHASE SYSTEM.

multiple access system A timesharing data processing system that can be used by a number of people at remote locations, usually through peripherals other than conventional terminals (e.g., cash registers linked to a computer system for inventory control).

multiple-address code In computer operations, an instruction code that requires the user to specify the address of more than one operand per instruction.

multiple address instruction A computer program instruction specifying the address of more than one operand.

multiple break **1.** Interruption of a circuit at several points. **2.** Contact bounce.

multiple-chip circuit See HYBRID INTEGRATED CIRCUIT.

multiple connector In a flowchart, a symbol showing the merging of several flowlines.

multiple ionization Successive ionization, as when an ion repeatedly collides with electrons. Also see DOUBLE IONIZATION.

multiple-length number In computer operations, a number occupying more than one register.

multiple-loop feedback system A feedback system using more than one feedback loop. An example is a tunable audio amplifier (see PARALLEL-TEE AMPLIFIER) in which a negative-feedback path provides tuning, while a positive-feedback path sharpens selectivity.

multiple modulation See COMPOUND MODULATION.

multiple precision arithmetic An arithmetic process using several words (bit groups) for an operand to ensure accuracy.

multiple programming **1.** Computer operation in which several programs in memory share peripherals and processor time. **2.** Programming a computer so that several logic or arithmetic operations can be carried out at the same time.

multiple-purpose meter See MULTIMETER.

multiple-purpose tester A multimeter sometimes combined with some other instrument, such as a test oscillator.

multiple reel file In a data-processing system, a magnetic tape data file of more than one reel.

multiple speakers A group of more than two loudspeakers, usually operated from a single amplifier system.

multiple-stacked broadside array A stacked array in which a number of collinear elements are stacked above and below each other. Also see BROADSIDE ARRAY and COLLINEAR ANTENNA.

multiple station Descriptive of a communications network in which more than one terminal is used.

multiple-unit steerable antenna A shortwave antenna system intended to prevent or minimize the effects of fading in received signals. It consists principally of a number of rhombic antennas feeding the receiver. The system utilizes the various waves arriving at different angles. An electric steering system causes the antennas to be selected automatically in the best combination and with their outputs in the proper phase. Also see DIVERSITY RECEPTION.

multiple winding   See DRUM WINDING.

multiplex   Pertaining to a communications or broadcasting system in which *multiplexing* is used. See MULTIPLEXING, **1**, **2**, **3**.

multiplex adapter   A special circuit (or auxiliary unit) used in frequency-modulated radio receivers for stereophonic reception from a station transmitting a multiplex broadcast. Also see MULTIPLEXING, **1** and MULTIPLEX STEREO.

multiplex code   The transmission of multiple signals over a single medium, using a code (such as Morse, Baudot, or ASCII). See MULTIPLEXING, **2**, **3**.

multiplex data terminal   A computer terminal acting as a modem by virtue of its accepting and transferring signals between its input/output devices and a data channel.

multiplexer   A device that allows two or more signals to be transmitted simultaneously on a single carrier wave, communications channel, or data channel. See MULTIPLEXING, **2**, **3**.

multiplexing   **1.** A process in which a comparatively low-frequency carrier is modulated, then mixed with a signal that has a higher frequency. Also see SUBCARRIER and SUBSIDIARY COMMUNICATION AUTHORIZATION. **2.** The simultaneous transmission of numerous relatively low-frequency signals on a single carrier having a higher frequency. Also called *frequency-division multiplexing*. **3.** The transmission of numerous signals on a single channel by breaking each signal into timed fragments (intervals) and transmitting the fragments in a rotating sequence. Also called *time-division multiplexing*. **4.**

In certain digital light-emitting-diode (LED) displays, the lighting of various parts of the display in a rapidly rotating sequence.

multiplex stereo   The use of *multiplexing* to broadcast both channels of a stereophonic program on a single carrier wave. See MULTIPLEXING, **1**, **2**.

multiplex telegraphy   **1.** A system of wire telegraphy in which two or more messages are sent simultaneously in one or both directions. **2.** A system of radiotelegraphy in which two or more messages can be sent simultaneously on the same carrier wave.

multiplex telephony   **1.** A system of wire telephony in which two or more messages can be sent simultaneously in one or both directions over the same line. **2.** A system of radiotelephony in which two or more messages can be sent simultaneously on the same carrier wave.

multiplication   **1.** The arithmetic process whereby a certain factor is added to itself the number of times indicated by another factor (the multiplier). **2.** A method of increasing a quantity, magnitude, or rate by some desired factor. See, for example, FREQUENCY MULTIPLIER and VOLTAGE MULTIPLIER.

multiplier   **1.** See FREQUENCY MULTIPLIER. **2.** See VOLTAGE MULTIPLIER. **3.** A circuit or device for performing arithmetic multiplication. **4.** See VOLTMETER MULTIPLIER.

multiplier amplifier   A frequency-multiplying amplifier (such as a doubler, tripler, or quadrupler), whose output circuit is tuned to an integral multiple of the input frequency. Compare STRAIGHT-THROUGH AMPLIFIER.

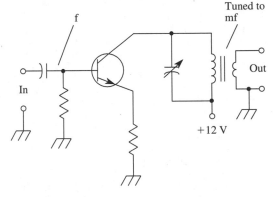

multiplier amplifier

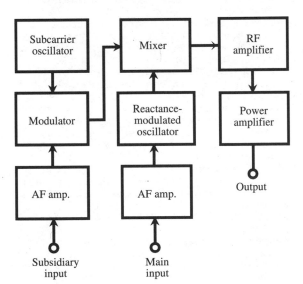

multiplexing, 1.

multiplier phototube   See PHOTOMULTIPLIER TUBE.

multiplier prefix   A prefix that, when affixed to the name of a quantity (e.g., Hertz and byte) indicates the amount, usually a power of 10 or a power of 2, by which that quantity is to be multiplied. Also called *prefix* and *prefix multiplier*. See PREFIXES table in Appendix B. Also see, for example, GIGA-, KILO-, MEGA-, MICRO-, MILLI-, NANO-, and PICO-.

multiplier probe **1.** A resistor-type test probe for a voltmeter, which increases the range of the meter and, therefore, acts as a voltmeter multiplier. **2.** A voltage-multiplier type of test probe for a voltmeter, which multiplies the test voltage before it is applied to the instrument (e.g., voltage-doubler probe).

multiplier register In a computer, a register that retains a number during a multiplication operation.

multiplier resistor A resistor connected in series with a current meter (usually a milliammeter or microammeter) to make it a voltmeter. Also called VOLTMETER MULTIPLER.

multiplier tube See PHOTOMULTIPLIER TUBE.

multipoint circuit A transmission circuit or system, in which information can be entered or retrieved at two or more locations.

multipoint distribution service In radio broadcasting, the transmission of programs via microwave links from a central facility to various local stations.

multipolar Pertaining to the presence of more than two magnetic poles.

multipolar machine A motor or generator having a number of poles in its armature and field.

multiposition relay A relay having more than two positions of closure. See, for example, SELECTOR RELAY.

multiposition switch A switch having more than two contacting positions. See, for example, SELECTOR SWITCH and STEPPING SWITCH.

multiprocessing **1.** In a computer system, the running of more than one program at once. **2.** The use of more than one microprocessor simultaneously in a single computer. Also called *parallel processing*. **3.** See TIME SHARING.

multiprogramming Also called *multitasking*. In a computer system, a technique that allows two or more programs to be executed at the same time.

multipurpose meter An electric meter that performs several functions, usually available through a function selector. Examples: VOLTAMMETER, VOLT-OHMMETER, and VOLT-OHM-MILLIAMMETER.

multirange instrument An instrument provided with several separate ranges, usually selectable by range switching (e.g., five-range voltmeter, two-scale ammeter, and four-band oscillator).

multisection filter A filter having two or more selective sections connected in cascade.

multisegment magnetron See MULTICAVITY MAGNETRON.

multiskip propagation See MULTIHOP PROPAGATION.

multistage device A device having several stages operating in cascade or otherwise coordinated with each other (e.g., a five-stage amplifier).

multistage feedback Feedback (positive or negative) between several stages in a system, as opposed to feedback between the output and input of a single stage.

multistage oscillation Oscillation resulting from positive feedback between or among two or more stages of an amplifier chain, as opposed to oscillation occurring between the output and input of a single amplifier stage.

multistage X-ray tube An X-ray tube providing electron acceleration by means of successive ring-shaped anodes—each biased to a higher voltage than the preceding one.

multiswitch A switch having a number of poles and contacts.

multitester An instrument, such as a multimeter or a combined signal generator and oscilloscope, that performs a number of different test functions.

multitrack recording **1.** A recording on two or more tracks (e.g., *multitrack disk* and *multitrack tape*). **2.** Making a recording on a tape or disc with two or more tracks.

multiturn potentiometer A potentiometer whose shaft must be rotated through several complete revolutions to cover the full resistance range.

multivalent Having a valence greater than 2. Compare UNIVALENT.

multivibrator A circuit usually containing two transistors in a resistance-capacitance (RC) coupled amplifier, whose output is capacitance-coupled to the input. The two stages switch each other alternately in and out of conduction at a frequency determined by the R and C values. Also see ASTABLE MULTIVIBRATOR, BISTABLE MULTIVIBRATOR, and MONOSTABLE MULTIVIBRATOR.

multiwire antenna An antenna having more than one wire in the radiating section. In early flat-top antennas, such wires were usually connected together at one end.

multiwire doublet antenna A doublet antenna having more than one wire in its radiator. A common form is the *folded dipole*, in effect two closely spaced dipole radiators connected together at both ends, one being center-fed.

Mumetal A high-permeability alloy of iron and nickel, valued especially for use as a magnetic shield for cathode-ray tubes.

Munsell color system A system for specifying colors in terms of hue, saturation, and brilliance, according to charts. Also see COLOR MATCHING.

Muntz metal See YELLOW METAL.

MUPO Abbreviation of MAXIMUM UNDISTORTED POWER OUTPUT.

Murray-loop bridge A specialized form of Wheatstone bridge in which two of the resistance arms are supplied by a two-wire line (such as a telephone line). By means of resistance measurements made with the bridge, the distance from an office or station to a ground fault on the line can be determined.

MUSA   Abbreviation of *multiple-unit steerable antenna.*

muscovite   Formula, $KH_2Al_2(SiO_4)_3$. A high-grade variety of mica having low dielectric loss.

Musical Instrument Digital Interface   Acronym, MIDI. A computer language used in electronic music. It "tells" the computer when to play a note, how long to play it, and how loud to play it. It also sets the tempo of the music, based on how long a quarter-note lasts. It controls the operation of a music synthesizer, and allows two or more synthesizers to communicate.

musical quality   See TIMBRE.

musical scale   A series of tones between a given tone and its second harmonic, scaled in intervals of ⅙ octave. The most common example can be found on a piano. Variations exist (e.g., *13-note scale, six-note scale,* and *five-note scale*).

music chip   An integrated circuit for producing various musical effects (such as tones, percussion, etc.).

music power   For a power amplifier, the short-term output power obtained in the reproduction of music waveforms, in contrast to root-mean-square (rms) or effective power output.

music synthesizer   A set of oscillators, usually operated with a computer, used to create or playing electronic music. Also see MOOG SYNTHESIZER and MUSIC INSTRUMENT DIGITAL INTERFACE.

music under   Pertaining to low-volume, continuous, background music, often added to presentations, radio and television advertisements, educational programs, etc.

muting   **1.** Disabling a receiver or amplifier under no-signal or weak-signal conditions. **2.** Softening or muffling a sound.

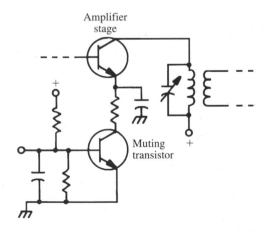

Amplifier
stage

Muting
transistor

muting

muting circuit   **1.** An interference-preventing device that automatically shuts off a radio receiver during the operation of a transmitter, and vice

versa. **2.** A squelch circuit. **3.** In a stereo receiver, an electronic element that cuts off all audio when no signal is present or when the receiver is being tuned between carriers.

muting switch   A switch or relay that cuts off a receiver during periods of transmission, or when reception is not desired. Generally, a cut-off voltage is applied to one of the intermediate-frequency stages to accomplish muting. In some cases, the audio-frequency circuit is disabled.

mutual antenna coupling   Electromagnetic coupling between or among antennas when they are placed too close together. Usually, it is an undesirable phenomenon.

mutual capacitance   Inherent capacitance between two conductors.

mutual-capacitance attenuator   An attenuator that, in its simplest form, is essentially a shielded, two-plate variable capacitor.

mutual conductance   See TRANSCONDUCTANCE.

mutual impedance   An impedance shared by two or more branches of a circuit.

mutual inductance   Symbol, *M.* Unit, henry. The property shared by neighboring inductors or inductive devices that enables induction to occur. A mutual inductance of 1 henry is present when a current change of 1 ampere per second in one inductor induces 1 volt across another inductor. Also see INDUCTANCE.

mutual-inductance attenuator   An attenuator consisting essentially of two coupled coils (input and output), whose spacing can be gradually changed.

mutual-inductance bridge   See CAREY-FOSTER MUTUAL-INDUCTANCE BRIDGE.

mutual induction   The action whereby the magnetic field produced by alternating current in one conductor produces a voltage in another isolated conductor.

mutual interference   **1.** See ADJACENT-CHANNEL INTERFERENCE. **2.** Any kind of interference between or among radio-frequency communications circuits.

mutually exclusive events   Two or more events (or data points) so that the occurrence of one prevents the occurrence of the other(s). That is, two events cannot take place simultaneously.

MV   **1.** Abbreviation of MEGAVOLT. **2.** Abbreviation of MULTIVIBRATOR.

mV   Abbreviation of MILLIVOLT.

MV   Abbreviation of MEDIUM VOLTAGE.

MVA   Abbreviation of MEGAVOLT-AMPERE.

mV/m   Abbreviation of millivolts per meter.

mVP   Abbreviation of MILLIVOLT POTENTIOMETER.

MW   Symbol for MEGAWATT.

mW   Symbol for MILLIWATT.

mw   Abbreviation of MEDIUM WAVE.

MWH   Abbreviation of MEGAWATT-HOUR.

mW RTL   Abbreviation of *milliwatt resistor-transistor logic* or *low-power resistor-transistor logic.*

Mx   Abbreviation of MAXWELL.

Mycalex   Trade name for an insulating material consisting of mica bonded with glass. Dielectric constant, 6 to 8. Resistivity, 10^{13} ohm-cm.

Mylar   A DuPont registered trademark. A tough, plastic insulating material commonly used as a magnetic tape base. Dielectric constant, 2.8 to 3.7. Dielectric strength, 7000 V/mil.

Mylar capacitor   A capacitor in which the dielectric film is Mylar.

Mylar tape   Magnetic recording tape using a Mylar film as the substrate.

mym   Abbreviation of MYRIAMETER.

myoelectricity   1. Bioelectric pulses of 10- to 1000-mV amplitude produced by muscular activity and detectable by electrodes attached to the skin. Also see ELECTROMYOGRAM, ELECTROMYOGRAPH, and ELECTROMYOGRAPHY. **2.** The study of phenomena, as defined in **1**.

myogram   See ELECTROMYOGRAM.

myograph   See ELECTROMYOGRAPH.

myography   See ELECTROMYOGRAPHY.

myriameter   Abbreviation, mym. A metric unit of linear measure equal to 10 kilometers (10^4 meters).

myriametric waves   British designation for electromagnetic energy having wavelengths from 100 kilometers down to 10 kilometers, corresponding to frequencies from 3 kHz up to 30 kHz.

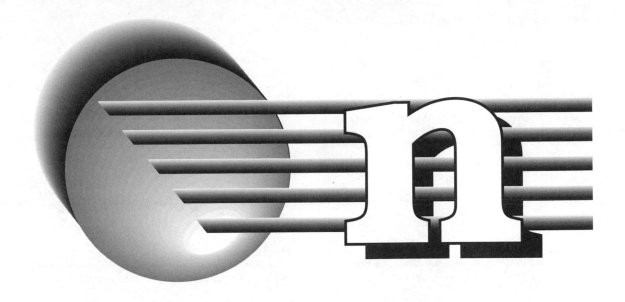

N **1.** Symbol for NUMBER. **2.** Symbol for NITRO-GEN. **3.** Abbreviation for NEWTON. **4.** Abbreviation of NUMBER (also, No.). **5.** Symbol for the set of natural (counting) numbers (0, 1, 2, 3, ...).

n **1.** Abbreviation of prefix NANO-. **2.** Symbol for NUMBER. **3.** Symbol for a term (e.g., a multiplier) having an assigned value. **4.** Symbol for part of an expression or operator (as in $2n$, $n - 1$, n^2, etc.). **5.** Symbol for INDEX OF REFRACTION. **6.** Symbol for amount of substance (unit, mole).

NA **1.** Abbreviation of *not available* (as on a specifications sheet). **2.** Abbreviation of *not applicable*.

N_A Symbol for AVOGADRO'S CONSTANT.

Na Symbol for SODIUM.

nA Abbreviation of NANOAMPERE.

NAB Abbreviation of NATIONAL ASSOCIATION OF BROADCASTERS.

NAB curve In audio-frequency operations, the standard magnetic tape playback equalization curve developed by the National Association of Broadcasters (NAB).

NAE Abbreviation of *National Academy of Engineering*.

NAND circuit Also called *NOT-AND circuit*. A binary digital circuit whose output is high (logic 1) if any of the input signals are low (logic 0); the output is low only when all the inputs are high. The performance of the NAND circuit is the inverse of that of the AND circuit.

NAND gate A gate that performs the function of a NAND circuit.

nano- Abbreviation, n. A prefix meaning billionth(s) (i.e., 10^{-9}).

nanoampere Abbreviation, nA. A unit of current; 1 nA equals 10^{-9} ampere.

nanofarad Abbreviation, nF. A unit of capacitance; 1 nF equals 10^{-9} farad.

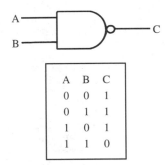

NAND circuit

A	B	C
0	0	1
0	1	1
1	0	1
1	1	0

nanohenry Abbreviation, nH. A unit of low inductance; 1 nH equals 10^{-9} henry.

nanometer Abbreviation, nm. A unit of short wavelength or displacement; 1 nm equals 10^{-9} meter.

nanosecond Abbreviation, ns. A time interval of 10^{-9} second.

nanotechnology The design and construction of superminiature electronic and electromechanical devices. For example, microscopic, computer-controlled robots might someday be used as programmable antibodies to fight infectious diseases, or to build integrated circuits, atom by atom.

nanovolt Abbreviation, nV. A unit of low voltage; 1 nV equals 10^{-9} volt.

nanovoltmeter A sensitive voltmeter for measuring potential in the nanovolt range.

nanowatt Abbreviation, nW. A unit of low power; 1 nW equals 10^{-9} watt.

nanowattmeter A meter for measuring power in the nanowatt range.

NAP Abbreviation of *nuclear auxiliary power.*

napier See NEPER.

Napierian base Symbol, *e.* An irrational number, equal to approximately 2.718282, and used as the NAPIERIAN LOGARITHM base.

Napierian logarithm Abbreviation, ln or log$_e$. A logarithm to the base *e* (see NAPIERIAN BASE). Also called NATURAL LOGARITHM. Compare COMMON LOGARITHM.

NAPU Abbreviation of *nuclear auxiliary power unit.*

narrative A computer program statement that, rather then being an instruction, merely describes the purpose of what follows (usually the steps in a routine or a block of instructions) as a debugging or program modification aid. In a program written in BASIC, such a statement is preceded by the abbreviation REM, for remark. Also called COMMENT.

narrowband **1.** A frequency band in which the difference between upper and lower limits is small, compared with bandwidths typical of the service specified. **2.** Pertaining to a radio-frequency emission whose bandwidth is limited or restricted. **3.** Pertaining to a circuit or device that operates over a comparatively small range of frequencies.

narrowband amplifier An amplifier whose passband is restricted to a fraction of the frequency spread common to the amplifier's application.

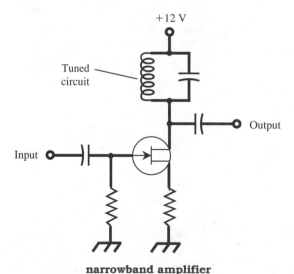

narrowband amplifier

narrowband FM See NARROWBAND FREQUENCY MODULATION.

narrowband frequency modulation Abbreviation, NBFM or NFM. Frequency modulation in which the maximum instantaneous frequency deviation is no greater than the highest modulating frequency.

narrowband interference Signal interference whose bandwidth is narrow, compared with that of the circuit affected.

narrowband voice modulation Abbreviation, NBVM. A scheme via which an analog voice signal is compressed into a band of frequencies narrower than that normally required for effective communication.

narrow bandwidth Pertaining to a radio-frequency emission whose bandwidth is comparatively narrow (e.g., a small fraction of the available spectrum space in the frequency band being used).

narrow-sector recorder A directional radio receiver for locating sources of atmospheric noise.

NARTB Abbreviation of *National Association of Radio and Television Broadcasters.*

NAS Abbreviation of *National Academy of Sciences.*

National Association of Broadcasters Abbreviation, NAB. A countrywide organization of radio and television broadcasters.

National Bureau of Standards Abbreviation, NBS. An agency in the U.S. that maintains values for physical constants in the Standard International (SI) System of Units. It also maintains radio broadcast stations that transmit standard time and frequency signals.

National Electrical Manufacturers Association Abbreviation, NEMA. A countrywide organization of manufacturers of electrical and electronic equipment and supplies.

National Electric Code Abbreviation, NEC. Safety regulations and procedures issued by the National Fire Protection Association for the installation of electrical wiring and equipment in the United States. Although the code is advisory from the Association's standpoint, it is enforced to various degrees by local authorities.

National Television Standards Committee Abbreviation, NTSC. A U.S. organization of television companies and other interested organizations. It developed the original black-and-white and color television standards that were approved by the Federal Communications Commission.

natural-decay curve See EXPONENTIAL DECREASE.

natural antenna frequency The fundamental resonant frequency of an electromagnetic antenna.

natural disintegration **1.** The decay of a radioactive substance as a result of the continuous emission of particles and rays. **2.** Also called *half life.* The time required for half of a quantity of a radioactive substance to decay into a different isotope or element.

natural electricity **1.** Atmospheric electricity. **2.** The electricity in living organisms, that is, BIOELECTRICITY.

natural frequency See NATURAL RESONANT FREQUENCY.

natural-growth curve See EXPONENTIAL INCREASE.

natural interference Interference from atmospheric and celestial sources, as opposed to human-made interference.

natural language A spoken or written human language (such as French or Japanese), as opposed to a computer language (such as machine language, C++, or LISP). Translation between natural language and machine language is important in optical character recognition, speech recognition, and speech synthesis.

natural logarithm See NAPIERIAN LOGARITHM.

natural magnet A material, such as magnetite (lodestone), found in nature and exhibiting permanent magnetism.

natural magnetism Magnetism found in some natural materials (see NATURAL MAGNET) and in the earth itself.

natural number **1.** Any nonnegative whole number, that is, a member of the set $N = (0, 1, 2, 3, ...)$. **2.** See NAPIERIAN BASE.

natural period The time required for one complete wave cycle to occur in a device at its NATURAL RESONANT FREQUENCY.

natural radiation Noise in the form of radiation emitted by natural radioactive substances, cosmic rays, etc. Also called BACKGROUND RADIATION.

natural resonance Resonance resulting from the unique physical constants of a body, circuit, or system. Also see NATURAL RESONANT FREQUENCY.

natural resonant frequency **1.** The frequency at which a circuit or device responds with maximum amplitude to applied signals. **2.** The frequency at which a circuit or device generates maximum energy. **3.** The frequency at which an object vibrates at maximum amplitude.

natural wavelength The wavelength corresponding to the NATURAL RESONANT FREQUENCY of a circuit, device, or object.

nautical mile A nautical unit of linear measure equal to 1.852 kilometers (1.1508 statute miles).

nav **1.** Abbreviation of *navigation*. **2.** Abbreviation of *navigational*.

Navaglobe A radionavigation system used at very-low or low frequencies over long distances.

NAVAIDS Abbreviation of NAVIGATIONAL AIDS.

navar A radar system in which a ground radar scans the immediate vicinity of an airport, observes the flight activity, and transmits such observations to aircraft in flight. The name is a contraction of the term *navigation and ranging*.

navigation aid An electronic device or system, such as radar or radio direction finding, that assists in the navigation of vehicles on land, at sea, or in the air.

navigation beacon A beam that provides aircraft and ships with navigational aid.

NAWAS Abbreviation of *National Attack Warning System*.

Nb Symbol for NIOBIUM.

nb Abbreviation of NARROWBAND.

NBFM Abbreviation of NARROWBAND FREQUENCY MODULATION. Also abbreviated NFM.

NBS Abbreviation for NATIONAL BUREAU OF STANDARDS.

NBTDR Abbreviation of *narrowband time-domain reflectometry*.

nbw Abbreviation of NOISE BANDWIDTH.

NC **1.** Abbreviation of NORMALLY CLOSED. **2.** On drawings, abbreviation of *no connection*. **3.** Abbreviation of NUMERICAL CONTROL.

N/C Abbreviation of NUMERICAL CONTROL.

nc Abbreviation of *no connection*.

n-channel junction field-effect transistor Abbreviation, NFET. A junction field-effect transistor in which the gate junction is formed on a bar or die of n-type semiconductor material.

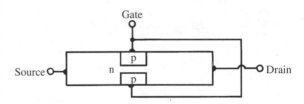

n-channel junction field-effect transistor

n-channel MOSFET A metal-oxide-semiconductor (MOS) field-effect transistor in which the channel is n-type material.

NCMT Abbreviation of NUMERICALLY CONTROLLED MACHINE TOOL.

NCS Abbreviation of *net control station(s)*.

N curve A negative-resistance voltage-current curve having a shape roughly resembling an uppercase letter N. Compare S CURVE.

Nd Symbol for NEODYMIUM.

N display A radar display in which the target is represented by a pair of vertical blips, whose amplitude indicates target direction and whose position along the horizontal base line (as determined by lining up a pedestal signal with the blips) is read from the pedestal-adjustment calibration.

n-doped zinc-oxide ceramic A nonlinear-resistance material used in the manufacture of some voltage-dependent resistors.

NDR Abbreviation of NONDESTRUCTIVE READ.

NDT Abbreviation of NONDESTRUCTIVE TEST.

Ne Symbol for NEON.

near-end crosstalk Crosstalk originating at, or near, the telephone subscriber line in which the interference is noticed.

near field **1.** The radiation field within a radius of 1 wavelength from a transmitting antenna.

2. The sound field near a loudspeaker or other reproducer.

near infrared   Pertaining to electromagnetic radiation of 3 to 30 micrometers in wavelength.

near ultraviolet   That part of the ultraviolet spectrum nearest the visible light wavelengths. These are the least-penetrating ultraviolet rays. They are also called *soft ultraviolet.*

near video on demand   In television, a local service in which various programs/videos are broadcast at specified times.

near zone   See NEAR FIELD, **1**.

NEB   Abbreviation of *noise equivalent bandwidth.*

NEC   Abbreviation of NATIONAL ELECTRIC CODE.

necessary bandwidth   The minimum bandwidth needed (with a given emission) to transmit information at a required rate and of a required quality. In general, as data speed increases (as measured in bits per second, baud, or words per minute), the minimum required bandwidth increases. For slow-speed Morse code signals, it can be as small as a few Hertz; for fast-scan television, it is several megahertz.

neck   The straight portion of a cathode-ray-tube (CRT) envelope (i.e., the part between the base and the flared portion).

NEDA   Abbreviation of *National Electronic Distributors' Association.*

needle   **1.** The stylus of a phonograph cartridge. **2.** The pointer of an indicating meter. **3.** One of the electrodes in a voltage-measuring spark gap (see NEEDLE GAP). **4.** The slender, pointed metal tip of a test probe.

needle chatter   See NEEDLE TALK.

needle drag   In disc recording and reproduction, friction between the needle (stylus) and disc. Also called *stylus drag.*

needle electrode   See NEEDLE, **3**, **4**.

needle gap   A spark gap composed of two needles having an adjustable air gap between their points. An unknown high voltage is measured in terms of the gap width necessary for sparking.

needle memory   A computer memory in which the dual-state elements are thin magnetic needles.

needle pointer   The pointer of a meter or compass.

needle pressure   See VERTICAL STYLUS FORCE.

needle probe   See NEEDLE-TIP PROBE.

needle scratch   In disc recording and reproduction, noise resulting from vibration of the needle (stylus) because of an irregular groove surface. Also called *surface noise.*

needle talk   Direct radiation of sound by the stylus of a phonograph pickup. Also called *needle chatter.*

needle telegraph   A telegraph in which the Morse code characters are converted into magnetic needle deflections.

needle test point   See NEEDLE, **4**.

needle-tip probe   A test probe that terminates in a sharp point. Also see NEEDLE, **4**.

needle voltmeter   See NEEDLE GAP.

neg   Abbreviation of NEGATIVE.

negate   **1.** To insert the NOT operation in front of a digital expression. **2.** To change logic 1 to logic 0 (high to low) or vice-versa.

negation   The logical NOT operation (see NOT) in digital systems. Also see NAND CIRCUIT, NOR CIRCUIT, NOR GATE, NOT CIRCUIT, and NOT-OR CIRCUIT.

negation element   In a computer system, a device that can give the reverse of a condition, event, or signal.

negative   **1.** Possessing NEGATIVE ELECTRIFICATION. **2.** In voice communications, a word often used for "no," especially when interference is present or signals are weak. **3.** Pertaining to a real number less than zero. **4.** An image whose shadings are opposite to those in the scene.

negative acceleration   A decrease in speed or velocity; also called *deceleration.*

negative acknowledgment character   In a handshaking or forward-error-correction (FEC) system, a response by the receiving station that indicates a missed bit or bits.

negative angle   **1.** An angle in the third or fourth quadrant in a system of rectangular coordinates. **2.** An angle measured clockwise from the positive x-axis in a rectangular coordinate system. Compare POSITIVE ANGLE.

negative bias   A steady, negative direct-current voltage or current applied continuously to an electrode of a device, such as a transistor to establish the operating point. Compare POSITIVE BIAS.

negative bus   See NEGATIVE CONDUCTOR.

negative charge   An electric charge consisting of a quantity of NEGATIVE ELECTRIFICATION. Also see CHARGE, **1**; ELECTRIC CHARGE; and UNIT ELECTROSTATIC CHARGE. Compare POSITIVE CHARGE.

negative conductor   The conductor or wire connected to the negative terminal of a current, power, or voltage source. Compare POSITIVE CONDUCTOR.

negative electricity   See NEGATIVE CHARGE and NEGATIVE ELECTRIFICATION.

negative electrification   Electrification characterized by an excess of electrons. For example, when a glass rod is rubbed with a silk cloth, the cloth becomes negatively charged because electrons are transferred from the glass to the cloth. Similarly, when a neutral atom acquires an extra electron, the atom becomes negatively charged because it has an excess of electrons. Compare POSITIVE ELECTRIFICATION.

negative electrode   **1.** An electrode connected to the negative terminal of a current, power, or voltage source. **2.** The negative output terminal of a current, power, or voltage source, such as a battery or generator.

negative error of measurement   An error of measurement in which the difference between a measured value and the true or most probable value is negative. Compare POSITIVE ERROR OF MEASUREMENT.

negative exponent In mathematical notation, an exponent indicating that a number is to be raised to a negative power. Raising a number x to a negative power $-n$ means taking the reciprocal of the number raised to the power n. That is, $x^{-n} = 1/x^n$; for example, $10^{-2} = 1/10^2 = 1/100 = 0.01$.

negative feedback Feedback that is out of phase with the input signal. Also called INVERSE FEEDBACK, DEGENERATION, and DEGENERATIVE FEEDBACK. Compare POSITIVE FEEDBACK.

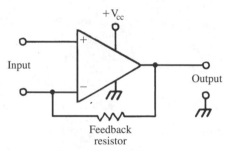

negative feedback

negative-feedback amplifier An amplifier in which negative feedback is used to improve performance or modify response.

negative function A trigonometric function having the negative sign. In a rectangular coordinate system, the sine function is negative in the third and fourth quadrants, the cosine in the second and third, and the tangent in the second and fourth. Compare POSITIVE FUNCTION.

negative gain A misnomer for FRACTIONAL GAIN, arising because fractional gain can be expressed in negative decibels.

negative ghost In a television picture, a ghost with negative (see NEGATIVE, **4**) shading.

negative ground In a direct-current power system, the connection of the negative pole to common ground.

negative image **1.** A picture in which the blacks, whites, and shades in between are the reverse of those in the scene (see NEGATIVE, **4**). **2.** An abnormal image that has the reverse shading described in **1**.

negative impedance An impedance that displays the same behavior as that of NEGATIVE RESISTANCE.

negative ion An atom with an excess of electrons and, consequently, a net negative charge. Also called ANION. Compare POSITIVE ION.

negative-ion generator A device for generating negative ions and circulating them into the surrounding air. This is believed by some people to be beneficial to health.

negative lead See NEGATIVE CONDUCTOR.

negative-lead filtering Power-supply filtering in which the choke coils and capacitors are in the negative direct-current lead, rather than in the positive lead (the usual position). One advantage of this arrangement is the lower insulation requirement of the choke.

negative light modulation In television image transmission, the condition in which transmitted power is increased by a decrease in the initial intensity of light. Compare POSITIVE LIGHT MODULATION.

negative line See NEGATIVE CONDUCTOR.

negative logic **1.** Binary logic in which a high negative state represents logic 1, and a low negative state represents logic 0. **2.** Binary logic in which a low positive state represents logic 1, and a high positive state represents logic 0. Compare POSITIVE LOGIC.

negative measurement error See NEGATIVE ERROR OF MEASUREMENT.

negative modulation Amplitude-modulated television transmission in which the transmitted power decreases as image brightness increases. Compare POSITIVE MODULATION.

negative modulation factor For an amplitude-modulated wave having unequal positive and negative modulation peaks, a ratio expressing the maximum negative deviation from the average for the envelope. Compare POSITIVE MODULATION FACTOR.

negative number A real number less than zero (i.e., one to which the minus sign is assigned).

negative peak The maximum negative instantaneous current or voltage in an alternating-current waveform.

negative-peak voltmeter An electronic meter for measuring the NEGATIVE PEAK voltage of an alternating-current waveform.

negative phase-sequence relay A relay that responds to the negative phase sequence in a polyphase circuit. Compare POSITIVE PHASE-SEQUENCE RELAY.

negative picture modulation See NEGATIVE MODULATION.

negative picture phase In a television signal, the picture-signal voltage swing from zero to negative, in response to an increase in brightness. Compare POSITIVE PICTURE PHASE.

negative plate The negative member of a battery cell; electron flow is from the plate through the external circuit.

negative pole See NEGATIVE ELECTRODE, **1**, **2**.

negative positive zero Abbreviation, NP0. Pertaining to temperature-compensating capacitors having a temperature coefficient of capacitance that changes sign within a specified temperature range.

negative potential **1.** The potential measured at a negative electrode, with respect to the positive electrode or to ground. **2.** Potential less than that of the earth as a reference.

negative resistance 1. A decrease in voltage across a device as the current through it increases, and an increase in voltage as the current decreases. **2.** A decrease in current through a device as the voltage across it increases, and an increase in current as the voltage decreases. This is opposite to the behavior of an ohmic (positive) resistance. Also see N-CURVE, NEGATIVE-RESISTANCE REGION, NEGATIVE RESISTOR, and S CURVE.

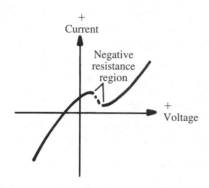

negative resistance

negative-resistance amplifier A simple circuit in which a negative-resistance device, such as a TUNNEL DIODE, cancels the positive resistance of the circuit, causing amplification or oscillation.

negative-resistance device See NEGATIVE RESISTOR.

negative-resistance diode 1. See TUNNEL DIODE. **2.** A reverse-biased germanium diode (and occasionally a silicon diode) that exhibits NEGATIVE RESISTANCE. **3.** A special diode tube that, when operated at ultrahigh frequencies, exhibits negative resistance because of transit-time effects.

negative-resistance magnetron A split-anode magnetron operated at a combination of anode voltage and magnetic field strength corresponding to cutoff; it exhibits negative resistance to voltage applied symmetrically between the anode halves. The frequency of oscillation is determined by an external tank circuit.

negative-resistance oscillator An oscillator that consists of a negative-resistance device connected across a tuned circuit. The arrangement oscillates because the negative resistance cancels the positive resistance (losses) of the tuned circuit. See, for example, NEGATIVE-RESISTANCE MAGNETRON and TUNNEL-DIODE OSCILLATOR.

negative-resistance region In certain devices, a portion of the voltage-versus-current curve hav-

ing negative slope (i.e., the current decreases as the voltage increases, or vice versa). Also see N CURVE, NEGATIVE RESISTANCE, and S CURVE.

negative-resistance repeater A repeater that produces gain by means of NEGATIVE RESISTANCE effects.

negative resistor Any device exhibiting NEGATIVE RESISTANCE.

negative space charge The cloud of electrons (negative particles) in the region surrounding an emitter, such as the hot cathode of a vacuum tube.

negative temperature coefficient Abbreviation, NTC. A number expressing the amount by which a quantity (such as the rating of a component) decreases when the temperature is raised. The coefficient is stated as a percentage, or as a certain number of parts per million (ppm) per degree temperature rise. Compare POSITIVE TEMPERATURE COEFFICIENT and ZERO TEMPERATURE COEFFICIENT.

negative terminal See NEGATIVE ELECTRODE, 2.

negative torque In an electric motor, a torque that acts against the operating torque.

negative transmission In a television or facsimile system, the condition in which brighter light corresponds to lower transmitted power, and dimmer light corresponds to higher transmitted power.

negative valence The valence of a negative ion. Also see VALENCE.

negator A logical NOT element [i.e., one that outputs the complement of an input bit (1 for 0 and vice-versa)].

negatron The term that specifically differentiates the familiar ELECTRON from a POSITRON (positive electron).

NEI Abbreviation of *noise equivalent input.*

neighborhood node A local site at which a fiberoptic television (video) signal is converted to a cable signal.

NEL Abbreviation of *National Electronics Laboratory.*

NELA Abbreviation of *National Electric Light Association.*

N electron In certain atoms, an electron whose orbit is outside of, and nearest to, those of the M electrons.

NEMA Abbreviation of *National Electrical Manufacturers' Association.*

nematic crystal A normally transparent liquid crystal that becomes opaque when an electric field is applied to it, and becomes transparent again when the field is removed. The crystal material is cut in the form of a letter or numeral and provided with a reflecting backplate for display readouts in calculators, watches, and various electronic devices.

nematic-crystal display A device in which an electrically controlled film of nematic-crystal material is used to transmit and interrupt light from a lamp or from a reflecting mirror, in this way displaying characters in whose shape the film has been formed.

nematic liquid In a liquid-crystal display (LCD), a normally clear liquid that becomes opaque in the presence of an electric field.

nemo A radio or television program that is picked up from a location outside the studio. Also called *field pickup* or *remote*.

neodymium Symbol, Nd. A metallic element of the rare-earth group. Atomic number, 60. Atomic weight, 144.24.

neodymium-YAG laser A laser that uses neodymium and yttrium-aluminum-garnet (YAG) crystal. It is used in medical applications, such as surgery and various other jobs where high precision is required. Generally, it is a low-to-medium-power laser.

neomatachograph An instrument used in psychology to measure complex reaction time. Compare NEOMATACHOMETER.

neomatachometer An instrument used in psychology to measure simple reaction time. Compare NEOMATACHOGRAPH.

neon Symbol, Ne. An inert-gas element. Atomic number, 10. Atomic weight, 20.179. Neon, present in trace amounts in the earth's atmosphere, is used in some glow tubes, readout devices, and indicator lamps.

neon bulb A (usually small) neon-filled gas diode. It has a characteristic pink glow and is ignited by a firing voltage for the particular unit. Also called *neon glow lamp* and *neon tube*.

neon-bulb flip-flop A flip-flop circuit (bistable multivibrator) using two neon bulbs as the bistable components.

neon-bulb gate A gate circuit containing a neon bulb biased below the firing point. A trigger voltage added to the bias voltage raises the applied voltage and fires the bulb, producing an output pulse.

neon-bulb logic Logic circuits composed of neon-bulb gates.

neon-bulb memory See NEON-BULB STORAGE.

neon-bulb multivibrator A multivibrator using two neon bulbs as the switching components.

neon-bulb oscillator A simple relaxation oscillator consisting essentially of a neon bulb, capacitor, resistor, and direct-current supply. The frequency of the sawtooth-wave output depends principally on the capacitance and resistance values. The maximum operating frequency is limited to about 5 kHz by the deionization time of the gas.

neon-bulb overmodulation indicator The application of a neon-bulb overvoltage indicator as a monitor for amplitude-modulated radio-frequency signals. The bulb flashes each time the modulation percentage exceeds a predetermined value. Also called *neon-bulb modulation alarm*.

neon-bulb overvoltage indicator A relatively simple circuit in which a neon bulb flashes each

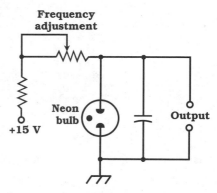

neon-bulb oscillaor

time a voltage monitored by the circuit exceeds a predetermined value. The flash shows that the portion of the voltage presented to the bulb has exceeded the firing potential.

neon-bulb peak indicator See NEON-BULB OVERVOLTAGE INDICATOR.

neon-bulb ring counter A ring counter composed of neon-bulb flip-flops. The maximum counting speed is limited by the deionization time of the neon bulbs to approximately 300 events per second.

neon-bulb sawtooth generator A relatively simple relaxation oscillator using a neon bulb, capacitor, and resistor. The output is a sawtooth wave, whose frequency is determined principally by the capacitance and resistance values.

neon-bulb scale-of-two circuit A scale-of-two circuit (frequency halver) using neon bulbs as the bistable elements.

neon-bulb storage A storage (memory) device composed of neon bulbs. A fired bulb (representing a bit of stored information) remains fired until turned off by an erase signal.

neon-bulb stroboscope A stroboscope in which a neon bulb supplies the light flashes. The circuit is essentially that of the neon-bulb oscillator, the flash rate being continuously variable by an adjustable frequency control.

neon-bulb voltage regulator A simple circuit utilizing the constant voltage drop across a fired neon bulb as a regulated voltage. The usual circuit configuration is a neon bulb and current-limiting resistor in series with a power supply.

neon-bulb volume indicator A neon-bulb overvoltage indicator used in some tape recorders to show when the volume exceeds a predetermined level—especially when the volume is high enough to cause an unacceptable amount of distortion.

neon glow lamp See NEON BULB.

neon lamp See NEON BULB.

neon pilot lamp A neon bulb used as a pilot lamp operated from the power-line circuit of an electronic equipment. Also called *neon pilot light*.

neon tube See NEON BULB.

NEP Abbreviation of NOISE EQUIVALENT POWER.

NEPD Abbreviation of *noise equivalent power density.*

neper Abbreviation, Np. A Napierian-logarithmic unit expressing a ratio of power levels; $Np = \log_e (P_1/P_2)^{1/2}$, where P_1 and P_2 are the power values being compared and e is the Napierian logarithm base, equal to approximately 2.71828. The neper is related to the decibel (dB), a similar unit based on common logarithms, in the following manner: 1 Np = 8.686 dB; 1 dB = 0.1151 Np.

neptunium Symbol, Np. A radioactive metallic element produced artificially. Atomic number, 93. Atomic weight, 237.05.

Nernst effect The appearance of a voltage between the opposite edges of a metal strip that is conducting heat longitudinally when the strip is placed in a magnetic field perpendicular to the plane of the strip.

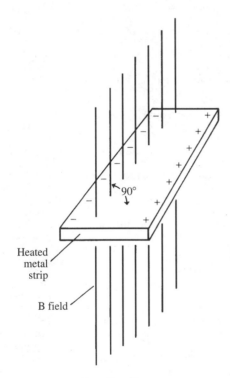

Heated metal strip

B field

Nernst effect

Nernst-Ettinghausen effect In a piezoelectric crystal, the tendency for a temperature gradient to exist as a result of applied electromagnetic fields.

Nernst lamp An incandescent lamp in which the filament material is a mixture of magnesia and certain rare oxides (such as yttria). A surrounding current-carrying coil heats the filament, low-ering its resistance and causing it to glow, after which it continues to operate on a low current.

nerve center The most essential part of a control system or communication network.

nerve current In an animal organism, the small electrical current that flows along nerve fibers.

nervous breakdown The upset of a function in a digital computer (which becomes disabled as a result).

NESC Abbreviation of *National Electrical Safety Code.*

nested loops See NESTING.

nesting In digital computers and data processing, the inclusion of one or more loops or subroutines inside a larger loop or subroutine. Nested loops, for example, can be used to assign values to double-subscripted variables.

NET Abbreviation of *noise equivalent temperature.*

net 1. An effective, useful, or resultant quantity (e.g., NET CAPACITANCE). 2. Colloquialism for *communications network.* See NETWORK, 2.

net authentification A password or other special identification used in a radio network.

net capacitance The resultant capacitance in a circuit in which capacitances act in combination with each other.

net component The total value of two or more passive components of the same sort. See, for example, NET CAPACITANCE, NET CURRENT, NET IMPEDANCE, NET INDUCTANCE, NET POWER, NET REACTANCE, NET RESISTANCE, and NET VOLTAGE.

net current The current flowing in a circuit in which currents aid or oppose each other.

net gain For an amplifier, the amount of gain remaining after all losses in the device have been subtracted.

net impedance The impedance of a circuit in which impedances act in combination with each other.

net inductance The inductance of a circuit in which inductances act in combination with each other.

net loss For an amplifier or other system, the algebraic sum of gains and losses between two points in the system.

net power The resultant power observed when power signals aid or oppose each other in a single circuit or system.

net radiometer A device for measuring the difference in intensity between radiation entering the earth's surface and radiation leaving it. This is generally visible light or infrared radiation from the sun.

net reactance Symbol, X_t. The combined inductive reactance (X_L) and capacitive reactance (X_C) in a circuit or device.

net resistance The resistance of a circuit in which resistances act in combination with each other.

net voltage The resultant voltage at a point where voltages aid or oppose each other.

network **1.** A circuit arrangement of electronic components, sometimes redundant in its design [e.g., resistance-capacitance (RC) network]. **2.** A group of interconnected computers, communications stations, or other facilities, often organized for simultaneous operation and data transfer. **3.** To conduct research or gather information using a group of interconnected computers, communications stations, or other facilities.

network analog A circuit or circuits representing variables and used to express and solve a mathematical relationship between the variables.

network analysis The rigorous examination of a network to determine its properties and performance. Compare NETWORK SYNTHESIS.

network analyzer An analog or digital circuit for simulating and analyzing a network (see NETWORK, **1**) by means of measurements and calculations from the model so obtained.

network assurance The construction and operation of a network in such a manner that failures can be quickly and easily located and corrected.

network calculator An analog or digital device for determining the component values and performance of a given network (see NETWORK, **1**).

network constant The value of a passive component (capacitance, inductance, resistance, etc.) used in a network (see NETWORK, **1**).

network filter A transducer that passes or rejects signals, depending on their frequency.

network interface unit Abbreviation, NIU. A device, provided to each subscriber, that connects telephones, television sets, and personal computers to an electrical or fiberoptic cable. Envisioned as an integral component of the multimedia INFORMATION SUPERHIGHWAY.

network provisioning The control of a network by means of computer software, rather than via manual rearrangement of system devices.

network relay **1.** A relay that provides protection of the circuits in a network (see NETWORK, **1**); a circuit breaker. **2.** In a communications network (see NETWORK, **2**), the reception and retransmission of a message by a human operator.

network synthesis The design and fabrication of a network (see NETWORK, **1**) by rigorous engineering methods to achieve a prescribed performance.

network theorems See COMPENSATION THEOREM, MAXIMUM POWER TRANSFER THEOREM, NORTON'S THEOREM, RECIPROCITY THEOREM, SUPERPOSITION THEOREM, and THEVENIN'S THEOREM.

network topology The analysis of networks (see NETWORK, **1**) with signal-flow diagrams. Components of the diagram represent signal paths, open loops, closed loops, and node points.

network transfer function A function describing the overall processing of energy by a network (see NETWORK, **1**); it is equal to V_o/V_i, where V_i is the input voltage and V_o is the output voltage of the network.

Neuman's law A property of mutual inductances. For a given orientation and environment for two inductors, the value of the mutual inductance does not change, regardless of the magnitude, frequency, or phase of the currents in the coils. That is, mutual inductance is subject only to the physical environment surrounding the coils.

neuristor A two-terminal semiconductor device that simulates the behavior of a neuron (nerve cell) and allows machines to duplicate some of the neurological phenomena observed in the human body.

neuroelectricity Low-voltage electricity in the nervous system of a human being or animal.

neuron A nerve cell in a living organism.

neurosurgery assistance robot An electromechanical device, controlled by a human operator and assisted by computers, that helps to perform simple neurosurgical operations requiring extreme precision and steadiness. One procedure for which a robot has been used is the drilling of holes in the skull prior to brain surgery.

neutral **1.** Having no electric charge; thus, an atom is normally neutral because its internal positive charges neutralize its internal negative charges. **2.** Devoid of voltage (e.g., a neutral line). **3.** Pertaining to a chemical, especially a solution, that is neither acidic nor alkaline.

neutral bus See NEUTRAL WIRE.

neutral circuit **1.** A deenergized circuit (i.e., a "dead" one). **2.** In a teletypewriter system, a circuit in which current flows in one direction.

neutral conductor See NEUTRAL WIRE.

neutral ground A ground connection to a neutral wire or to the neutral point of a circuit.

neutralization The process of balancing out positive feedback in an amplifier to prevent self-oscillation. Also see NEUTRALIZING CAPACITOR and NEUTRALIZING COIL.

neutralization indicator A neon bulb or radio-frequency meter used during neutralization of an amplifier. When the amplifier is properly neutralized, the bulb or meter will show zero signal with no input to the amplifier, indicating that the circuit is not oscillating.

neutralize To eliminate positive feedback in a radio-frequency amplifier.

neutralized amplifier An amplifier in which neutralization has been performed to prevent self-oscillation.

neutralizing capacitor In a capacitively neutralized circuit, a small capacitor that serves as a coupler of signal energy from the output back to the input in reverse phase, to cancel self-oscillation of the circuit.

neutralizing circuit Any component or set of components that is used to neutralize a radio-frequency amplifier.

neutralizing coil In an inductively neutralized circuit, a small coupling coil that picks up signal energy from the output and applies it in reverse phase to the input, to cancel circuit self-oscillation.

neutralizing tool   A nonconducting screwdriver-like device for adjusting a neutralizing capacitor or coil. It is usually made of fiber or plastic.

neutralizing voltage   The feedback voltage that cancels self-oscillation in the process of neutralization.

neutralizing wand   See NEUTRALIZING TOOL.

neutral line   See NEUTRAL WIRE.

neutral relay   See UNPOLARIZED RELAY.

neutral wire   In a polyphase power-transmission system, the line (wire) that does not carry current until the system is unbalanced.

neutrodon   See NEUTRODYNE.

neutrodyne   A radio-frequency amplifier that is neutralized by feeding energy through a small capacitor from a tap on the secondary coil of the collector or drain output transformer back to the base or gate.

neutron   An uncharged atomic particle having a mass approximately equal to that of the proton. The neutron is present in the nucleus of every atom, except that of hydrogen.

neutron age   16.7% of the mean square displacement of a neutron as it moves through a specified energy range.

neutron rest mass   See MASS OF NEUTRON AT REST.

new candle   See CANDELA.

newton   (Sir Isaac Newton.) Symbol N. The SI unit of force. A force of 1 newton imparts an acceleration of 1 meter per second per second to a mass of 1 kilogram. The newton is equal to 10^5 dynes.

Newton's laws of motion   Three natural laws discovered in 1686 by Sir Isaac Newton. First law: A body at rest or in motion tends to remain in that state, unless it is acted upon by some force. Second law: A body tends to accelerate or decelerate when it is acted upon by a force, the acceleration or deceleration being directly proportional to the force and inversely proportional to the mass of the body. Third law: For every action or acting force, there is an equal and opposite reaction or reacting force.

nexus   An interconnection point in a system.

NF   Abbreviation of NOISE FIGURE.

nF   Abbreviation of NANOFARAD.

NFET   Abbreviation of N-CHANNEL JUNCTION FIELD-EFFECT TRANSISTOR.

NFM   Abbreviation of NARROWBAND FREQUENCY MODULATION. Also abbreviated NBFM.

NFM reception   Reception of a signal having NARROWBAND FREQUENCY MODULATION. Standard discriminators and ratio detectors can be used. Slope detection can be achieved with an amplitude-modulation (AM) receiver by tuning slightly to one side of the center frequency of the FM signal.

NFM transmission   Transmission of a signal via NARROWBAND FREQUENCY MODULATION. A simple method consists of frequency modulat-

ing the master oscillator of the transmitter at the modulation frequency. Phase modulation can also be used.

NFPA   Abbreviation of *National Fire Protection Association* (see NATIONAL ELECTRIC CODE).

NFQ   Abbreviation of *night frequency*.

NG   **1.** Abbreviation of NEGATIVE GLOW. **2.** Abbreviation of *no good*, used for marking inoperative or malfunctioning components.

nH   Abbreviation of NANOHENRY.

nhp   Abbreviation of NOMINAL HORSEPOWER.

Ni   Symbol for NICKEL.

nibble   In computer operations, a four-bit word.

NICAD   Acronym for NICKEL-CADMIUM BATTERY or NICKEL-CADMIUM CELL.

Ni-Cd   Abbreviation for NICKEL-CADMIUM BATTERY or NICKEL-CADMIUM CELL.

Nichrome   A nickel-chromium alloy used in the form of a wire or strip for resistors and heater elements.

nickel   Symbol, Ni. A metallic element. Atomic number, 28. Atomic weight, 58.69. Nickel is familiar as an alloying metal in some resistance wires and as the material used in some electron-tube elements.

nickel-cadmium battery   **1.** A battery of nickel-cadmium cells (see NICKEL-CADMIUM CELL). **2.** Loosely, a nickel-cadmium cell.

nickel-cadmium cell   A small, rechargeable, electrochemical cell. The anode is cadmium, the cathode is nickel hydroxide, and the electrolyte is potassium hydroxide.

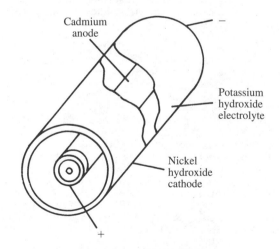

Cadmium anode

Potassium hydroxide electrolyte

Nickel hydroxide cathode

nickel-cadmium cell

nickel-iron battery   See EDISON BATTERY.

nickel-oxide diode   A diode fabricated from nickel-oxide semiconductor material.

nickel silver   An alloy of copper, nickel, and zinc, sometimes used for making resistance wire. Also called GERMAN SILVER.

Nicol prism   An optical component for producing or analyzing plane-polarized light. It consists of two prisms of Iceland spar cemented together. Light entering the device strikes the interface, where the ordinary ray is totally reflected and the extraordinary ray passes through, both rays being plane-polarized perpendicular to each other.

NIDA   Abbreviation of *numerically integrating differential analyzer.*

NIF   Abbreviation of NOISE IMPROVEMENT FACTOR.

night effect   A phenomenon sometimes observed at frequencies below approximately 500 kHz. Direction-finding signals received between sunset and the following sunrise appear to come from a transmitter that moves slowly back and forth.

night-effect errors   In radio direction-finding, inaccurate or uncertain readings resulting from the NIGHT EFFECT.

night range   The distance over which signals from a given transmitter are consistently received after sunset.

ni junction   In a semiconductor device, the junction between an n-type layer and an intrinsic layer.

nil   **1.** Colloquialism for *negligible.* **2.** British expression for *zero.* Also, *nought.* **3.** Colloquialism for *nothing.*

niobium   Symbol, Nb. A metallic element chemically resembling tantalum. Atomic number, 41. Atomic weight, 92.91.

NIPO   Abbreviation of *negative input/positive output.*

NIR   Abbreviation of NEAR INFRARED.

nit   In digital-computer operations, a unit of data equal to 1.44 bits.

nitrocellulose   See CELLULOSE NITRATE.

nitrogen   Symbol, N. A gaseous element. Atomic number, 7. Atomic weight, 14.007. Nitrogen is the most-abundant component (about 78%) of the Earth's atmosphere.

NIU   Abbreviation of NETWORK INTERFACE UNIT.

Nixonite   A trade name for cellulose acetate, a plastic.

Nixonoid   A trade name for cellulose nitrate, a plastic.

NJCC   Abbreviation of *National Joint Computer Conference.*

n layer   A semiconductor layer doped to provide current carriers that are predominantly electrons. Compare P LAYER.

n-level logic   **1.** A multilevel form of logic, with *n* different possible states. **2.** In a computer, the connection of up to *n* logic gates.

NLR   **1.** Abbreviation of *nonlinear resistance.* **2.** Abbreviation of NONLINEAR RESISTOR.

NLS   Abbreviation of NO-LOAD SPEED.

N/m²   Abbreviation of *newtons per meter squared* (pascals).

Nm²/kg   Newton meters squared per kilogram, the SI unit of the *gravitational constant.*

NMAA   Abbreviation of *National Machine Accountants Association.*

NMOS   A metal-oxide semiconductor device made on a p-type substrate whose active carriers, electrons, migrate between n-type source and drain contacts.

NMR   **1.** Abbreviation of NUCLEAR MAGNETIC RESONANCE. **2.** Abbreviation of NORMAL-MODE REJECTION.

n-n junction   In a semiconductor device, especially an integrated circuit, the junction between two n-type regions having somewhat different properties (sometimes designated n_1 and n_2).

NO   Abbreviation of NORMALLY OPEN.

No   Symbol for NOBELIUM.

No.   Abbreviation of NUMBER.

no-address instruction   In digital computer operations, an instruction requiring no reference to storage or memory for its execution.

nobelium   Symbol, No. A radioactive element produced artificially. Atomic number, 102. Atomic weight, approximately 259 (varies with isotope).

Nobili's rings   See ELECTRIC RINGS.

noble   Chemically inert or inactive. For example, *noble metals* oxidize less rapidly than *base metals.*

noble gas   An inert rare gas (such as argon, helium, krypton, neon, or xenon). It is used in electronic glow devices.

noble metal   A comparatively nonreactive metal (such as gold, silver, or platinum).

noctovision   A television transmission system using infrared rays instead of visible light to scan the object. This makes it possible to televise images in complete visual darkness (hence, the prefix *nocto-*, meaning "night").

no-charge machine fault time   Unproductive computer time resulting from errors or a malfunction.

nodal point   See NODE.

node   **1.** The terminal point at which two or more branches of a circuit meet, or a point that is common to two circuits. **2.** In a standing-wave system, a zero point or minimum point (e.g., *current node*). Compare LOOP, **1**. **3.** A database management system expression defining the location of information about a record, user, field, etc.

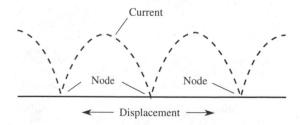

node, 2

nodules **1.** Oxide particles that protrude above the surface of magnetic tape. **2.** In a planar pattern describing radiation or pickup characteristics (as for antennas, microphones, loudspeakers), a small peak aligned in a direction other than that of the main lobe.

no-field release In the starting box for a shunt motor, the electromagnet that normally holds the arm in full-running position; it is connected in series with the field winding. When the field current is lost, the arm is released, disconnecting the armature for safety. Compare NO-VOLTAGE RELEASE.

noise **1.** A random-frequency current or voltage signal extending over a considerable frequency spectrum and having no useful purpose, unless it is intentionally generated for test purposes. **2.** Dissonant, interferential sound; unlike harmonious sound, it is disagreeable. **3.** In audio operations, unwanted hiss and/or hum. **4.** Extra bits or bytes that must be removed from digital data before it can be useful.

noise abatement The elimination or reduction of noise intensity—especially a measure in a program concerned with noise pollution in the environment.

noise analysis The measurement of the amplitude and spectral distribution of noise and the determination of its character.

noise analyzer An instrument for evaluating the nature of noise in a communications system. See, for example, NOISE METER. Noise analyzers are sometimes adapted for vibration analysis.

noise-balancing system A bridge circuit inserted between a receiver and antenna for balancing out interferential signals resulting from nearby power-line leaks or similar causes.

noise bandwidth Abbreviation, NBW. A figure obtained by dividing the area under the power-output-vs.-frequency curve of a device by the power amplitude at the noise frequency of interest.

noise behind the signal Noise caused by, but exclusive of, a signal.

noise blanker A device that cuts off one of the intermediate-frequency stages of a radio receiver during a noise pulse. The noise blanker is effective against high-amplitude impulses of short duration.

noise-canceling microphone A microphone that discriminates against background sounds. It is usually directional and relatively insensitive, requiring the user to talk directly into it at close range.

noise clipper A biased-diode circuit used as an automatic noise limiter. The device cuts off all signals above a predetermined amplitude on the theory that noise peaks are high-level transients in an otherwise uniform signal. Noise is reduced at the sacrifice of system reproduction fidelity.

noise criteria An expression for the level of ambient acoustic noise.

noise current Noise-generated current.

noise-current generator A noise generator that supplies a useful current. Compare NOISE-VOLTAGE GENERATOR.

noise digit A digit (usually zero) generated during normalization of a floating-point number. See NORMALIZE.

noise diode A reverse-biased semiconductor diode that produces a standard noise voltage.

noise elimination The nearly complete removal of noise effects from a system. Noise can never be eliminated altogether because the movement of electrons and atoms generates some electrical and thermal noise. However, in some digital systems, the effects of noise can be almost totally overcome. Compare NOISE SUPPRESSION.

noise equivalent power Abbreviation, NEP. The power that produces an rms signal-to-noise ratio of 1 in a detector.

noise factor For a circuit, especially a communications receiver or weak-signal amplifier, the ratio R_1/R_2, where R_1 is the signal-to-noise power ratio of an ideal circuit, and R_2 is the signal-to-noise ratio of the circuit under test. Compare NOISE FIGURE.

noise figure The NOISE FACTOR of a circuit, expressed in decibels. If N is the noise factor expressed as a ratio, then noise figure N_{dB} can be determined by $N_{dB} = 10 \log_{10} N$.

noise filter A filter designed to suppress noise that would otherwise enter an electronic circuit (e.g., a power-line noise filter).

noise floor **1.** In a receiver, the level of noise in microvolts that determines the weakest signal that can be heard or accurately received. **2.** In a spectrum analyzer, the level of noise that determines the weakest signal that will be visibly displayed.

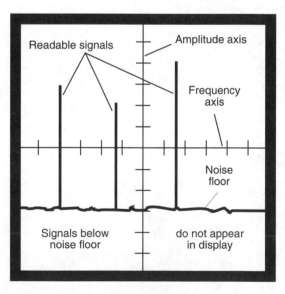

noise floor, 2.

noise generator A device for generating precise amounts of noise voltage for test purposes.

noise grade 1. The relative level of radio-frequency background noise, over all electromagnetic frequencies, in a particular geographic location. The noise grade is generally lowest near the poles and highest near the equator. 2. The mathematical function of relative electromagnetic noise intensity versus latitude and longitude.

noise immunity The degree to which a circuit or device is insensitive to extraneous energy—especially noise signals.

noise-improvement factor Abbreviation, NIF. For a radio receiver, the ratio SN_i/SN_o, where SN_i is the input signal-to-noise ratio and SN_o is the output signal-to-noise ratio.

noise killer 1. See AUTOMATIC NOISE LIMITER. 2. See NOISE FILTER. 3. See NOISE BLANKER.

noiseless alignment See VISUAL ALIGNMENT.

noise level 1. The amplitude of ambient electrical noise generated outside an electronic system of interest. 2. The amplitude of electrical noise generated in an electronic system of interest. 3. The intensity of ambient acoustic noise.

noise limiter See AUTOMATIC NOISE LIMITER.

noise margin In a binary logic circuit, the difference between operating and threshold voltages.

noise-measuring set See NOISE METER.

noise meter An instrument for measuring acoustic noise level. It consists essentially of a sensitive, multirange voltmeter provided with a microphone, amplifier, and attenuators. The meter scale reads noise level directly in decibels.

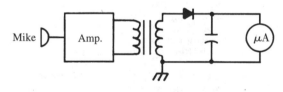

noise meter

noise power The power component of a noise signal.

noise power ratio The ratio of noise power at the output of a circuit (such as a receiver) to the noise power at the input.

noise pulse A random short-duration noise burst whose amplitude exceeds the average peak noise level.

noise quieting In a radio receiver, the reduction (in decibels) of background noise, with respect to a signal of interest.

noise ratio See NOISE POWER RATIO.

noise-reducing antenna A receiving antenna having a balanced transmission line and usually some form of noise-balancing system for reducing electrical noise picked up by the antenna.

noise reduction See NOISE SUPPRESSION.

noise residue The residual output (see NULL VOLTAGE, 1) of a balanced bridge, caused entirely by noise.

noise silencer A noise-limiting circuit that removes noise-pulse transients with little or no effect on the signal from which the noise is removed. Compare NOISE CLIPPER.

noise source See NOISE GENERATOR.

noise spike See NOISE PULSE.

noise suppression 1. In communications, the reduction of noise amplitude to a level that is noncompetitive with desired signals. 2. In audio recording and reproduction, reduction of unwanted noise (e.g., hiss) to the greatest extent possible without degrading the fidelity of the desired audio. Compare NOISE ELIMINATION.

noise suppressor A device for eliminating electrical noise or reducing its amplitude. See, for example, AUTOMATIC NOISE LIMITER and NOISE BLANKER.

noise temperature At a given frequency, the temperature of a passive system that has the same noise power per unit bandwidth as that observed at the terminals of a device under test.

noise voltage The voltage component of an electrical noise signal.

noise-voltage generator A signal generator that supplies an alternating-current waveform containing random-frequency pulses of relatively uniform distribution over a given frequency spectrum. Compare NOISE-CURRENT GENERATOR.

noisy mode During normalization of a floating-point number, the generation of digits, excluding zero, as part of the fixed-point part (see NORMALIZE).

NOL 1. Abbreviation of *National Ordnance Laboratory*. 2. Abbreviation of *Naval Ordnance Laboratory*.

no-load current 1. Output-electrode current (e.g., drain, plate, or collector current) when a device is not delivering output to an external load. 2. Current flowing in the primary winding of an unloaded transformer.

no-load losses Losses in an unloaded transformer (see NO-LOAD CURRENT, 2).

no-load speed The rotational speed of an unloaded motor.

no-load voltage The open-circuit output voltage of a power supply, amplifier, generator, or network.

nominal 1. Named, rated, or specified. The nominal value of a speaker, for example, might be 8 ohms, even though the actual impedance value depends on the frequency of the applied signal. 2. Approximate, and specified as a typical example only, for the purpose of identifying the operating or value range. For example, an automotive circuit might have a nominal rating of 12 volts—even though it can be operated at 10 volts to 14.6 volts.

nominal band In a facsimile signal, the waveband extending between zero and the maximum frequency of modulation.

nominal bandwidth 1. For a filter, the difference $f_{c2} - f_{c1}$, where f_{c1} is the nominal lower cutoff frequency and f_{c2} is the nominal upper cutoff frequency. **2.** For an allocated communication channel, the total bandwidth, including upper and lower guard frequencies. **3.** The intended and specified bandwidth of a given channel, regardless of the bandwidth of the signal on that frequency at any given time.

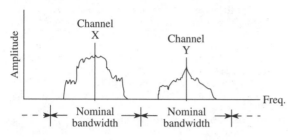

nominal bandwidth, 2

nominal capacitance The rated ("label") value of a capacitor. Also see NOMINAL VALUE.

nominal current The rated ("nameplate") value of required current or of current output. Also see NOMINAL VALUE.

nominal horsepower The rated ("nameplate") horsepower of a machine, such as a motor. Also see NOMINAL VALUE.

nominal impedance The rated impedance of a circuit or device. Also see NOMINAL VALUE.

nominal inductance The rated ("label") value of a coil's inductance. Also see NOMINAL VALUE.

nominal line pitch In a television raster, the average center-to-center separation between adjacent lines.

nominal line width 1. For a television raster, the factor $1/n$, where n is the number of lines per unit width for the direction in which the lines progress. **2.** In facsimile, the average center-to-center separation of scanning or recording lines.

nominal power factor The rated ("nameplate") value of power factor of a device. Also see NOMINAL VALUE.

nominal power rating The rated ("nameplate") value of power output, power drain, or power dissipation. Also see NOMINAL VALUE.

nominal Q The rated ("nameplate") value of Q of a capacitor, inductor, transformer winding, or tank circuit. Also see NOMINAL VALUE.

nominal rating See NOMINAL, **1**, **2**.

nominal resistance The rated ("label") value of a resistor or similar device. Also see NOMINAL VALUE.

nominal speed The highest speed of a data-processing unit or system, disregarding slowdowns because of factors other than computational operations.

nominal value A named, specified, rated, or labeled value, given without reference to tolerance. This can differ significantly from the actual value. For example, the nominal value of a capacitor might be 100 pF; but if the tolerance is ±10 percent, the actual capacitance might be any value between 90 pF and 110 pF.

nominal voltage 1. The rated ("nameplate") value of required voltage or of voltage output. Also see NOMINAL VALUE. **2.** In a cell or battery, the MIDPOINT VOLTAGE.

nomogram See ALIGNMENT CHART.

nomograph See ALIGNMENT CHART.

nomography The geometric representation of a mathematical function or relation by means of alignment charts.

nonaccountable time The period during which a computer system is unavailable to the user (because of a power outage, for example).

nonarithmetic shift See LOGICAL SHIFT.

nonblinking meter A digital meter that does not alternate, or oscillate, between two different values when the measured parameter is between two discrete values. Instead, the display is rounded off to the nearest value, and the display remains at that value continuously.

nonblocking system In a telephone communications network, a system that ensures a circuit will be completed when necessary. That is, at no time is it impossible for a connection to be made. Under conditions of extremely heavy usage, the quality of communications might be degraded, but the connection will not be cut off.

nonbridging contact In a switch or relay, a movable contact that leaves one stationary contact before contacting another.

nonchargeable battery A primary battery (i.e., one that cannot ordinarily be recharged). An example is a battery of common zinc-carbon or alkaline cells.

noncoherent Pertaining to electromagnetic radiation in which the wave disturbances are not all precisely aligned in frequency and phase.

nonconductor See DIELECTRIC.

noncontact temperature measurement The use of infrared or optical electronic equipment to measure the temperature of bodies without touching them.

noncorrosive flux A solder flux that does not corrode the metals to which solder is applied.

noncrystalline Pertaining to materials that possess none of the characteristics of crystals. Compare CRYSTALLINE MATERIAL.

nondestructive read In digital computer and counter operation, the process of reading data without erasing it as a result. The name is also applied to the readout device.

nondestructive test Abbreviation, NDT. A test that does little or no irreversible harm to the test sample. Compare DESTRUCTIVE TEST.

nondeviated absorption Absorption that slows waves by a negligible amount; also, normal sky-wave absorption.

nondirectional antenna An antenna that displays equally intense radiation or equally sensitive reception in all directions within a specified plane. An example is a vertical dipole antenna, which is nondirectional in the horizontal plane.

nondirectional microphone A microphone that responds equally well to sound from any direction; an omnidirectional microphone.

nondissipative load A purely reactive load. In such a load, the only power consumed is that which is dissipated in the inherent resistance (losses) of the load.

nondissipative stub A stub that exhibits only slight losses; it consumes no power, except that dissipated in small, inherent losses. Also see STUB.

nonelectrical Not electrical in nature. The term is commonly used to designate the mechanical parts of electromechanical systems, such as robots and servomechanisms.

nonelectrolyte A substance that does not ionize in water solution. Compare ELECTROLYTE.

nonelectronic meter A meter that uses no electronic devices (such as transistors, liquid crystals, light-emitting diodes, or integrated circuits). Also called *conventional meter.*

nonequivalence operation See EXCLUSIVE-OR OPERATION.

nonerasable storage In digital-computer and data-processing operations, storage media that cannot be erased under ordinary circumstances. A common example is CD-ROM (compact-disk read-only memory).

nonferrous metal A metal or alloy that does not contain iron, and is not related to iron in the sense that it is not attracted to magnets.

nonflammable Pertaining to a material that is resistant to burning.

nonharmonic frequency A frequency that has no integral numerical relationship to another frequency of interest. Compare HARMONIC FREQUENCY.

nonharmonic oscillations Parasitic oscillations that do not occur at the fundamental frequency nor at any harmonic frequency of an oscillator or amplifier in which they appear.

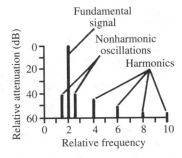

nonharmonic oscillations

nonillion The number 10^{30}, so called because when written out, the number contains nine groups of three zeros (following the first 1000).

noninductive capacitor A wound capacitor in which the edges of one of the spiral windings are connected together to minimize the inductance of the roll. Compare INDUCTIVE CAPACITOR.

noninductive resistor A wirewound resistor constructed so that the magnetic field of the coil is self-canceling. Therefore, the inductance is practically eliminated.

noninterlaced scanning In the display of a video image, the presentation of all the raster lines in a single scan. It is commonly used in cathode-ray-tube (CRT) computer monitors. This process minimizes "jerkiness" in rapidly moving images.

noninverting connection Connection to the noninverting input of a differential or operational amplifier. Also see NONINVERTING INPUT. Compare INVERTING CONNECTION.

noninverting input In a differential or operational amplifier, the input that provides an output signal in phase with the input. Compare INVERTING INPUT.

nonionic **1.** Possessing none of the properties of ions. **2.** Electrically neutral.

nonionizing radiation Electromagnetic radiation that does not cause ionization of gases under a given set of conditions. Examples: radio signals, television signals, and visible light.

nonlinear **1.** Pertaining to components, circuits, or devices in which the instantaneous output signal amplitude is not directly proportional to the instantaneous input signal amplitude. The graph of instantaneous output versus instantaneous input is a curve, not a straight line. Example: CLASS-C AMPLIFIER. **2.** Pertaining to components, circuits, or devices in which a specified value is not directly proportional to some other specified value. Example: NONLINEAR CAPACITOR.

nonlinear bridge See VOLTAGE-SENSITIVE BRIDGE.

nonlinear capacitor A capacitor whose value varies nonlinearly with applied voltage. Also see VOLTAGE-VARIABLE CAPACITOR, 1, 2.

nonlinear coil See SATURABLE REACTOR.

nonlinear dielectric A material (such as processed barium-strontium titanate) whose dielectric constant varies with applied voltage.

nonlinear distortion Distortion caused by nonlinear response of an amplifier or component. This causes different parts of the signal to be amplified or transmitted by different amounts; therefore, the amplitude variations in the output signal differ from those in the input signal.

nonlinear inductor See SATURABLE REACTOR.

nonlinearity **1.** The condition of being NONLINEAR. In an amplifier, this means that the output signal is not a faithful reproduction of the input signal, and distortion occurs. **2.** A measure of the extent to which a circuit is nonlinear. Expressed as a percentage of peak-to-peak full-scale output, the maximum extent to which the output differs from a perfect reproduction of the input.

nonlinearity error   An error in received signals resulting from nonlinearity in one or more of the stages in the communications circuit.

nonlinear mixing   The mixing of signals as a result of the nonlinear response of a device (such as a semiconductor diode operated in its square-law region) through which they are passed simultaneously. Also see MIXER and MIXING.

nonlinear network   A circuit that produces distortion in an input waveform; the output and input waves are not related by a linear function.

nonlinear quantizing   A method of signal quantizing in which the intervals are not all the same size or duration.

nonlinear resistor   A resistor whose value varies with applied voltage. Also see VOLTAGE-DEPENDENT RESISTOR.

nonlinear response   Any response for which the corresponding plot is not a straight line; doubling the independent variable, for example, does not double the dependent variable.

nonloaded *Q*   See UNLOADED *Q*.

nonmagnetic   **1.** Possessing no magnetism. **2.** Incapable of being magnetized.

nonmathematical   Pertaining to materials and methods that rely upon physical description and qualitative procedures instead of mathematical development, prediction, and quantitative procedures.

nonmetal   An elemental material devoid of the properties exhibited by metals (e.g., luster, good ductility, electrical conductivity, heat conductivity, and malleability). Examples: carbon, phosphorus, sulfur. Compare METAL and METALLOID.

nonmetallic conduction   Collectively, ionic conduction in liquids and gases, conduction in dielectrics by small leakage currents, and thermionic conduction in a vacuum.

nonmicrophonic   Without microphonic properties, e.g., a nonmicrophonic integrated circuit does not produce electrical ringing when physically struck.

nonnumeric character   A character that is not a numeral, i.e., a symbol or letter.

nonohmic response   **1.** Nonlinear resistance or reactance. Compare OHMIC RESPONSE. **2.** See NEGATIVE RESISTANCE.

nonoscillating detector   A detector devoid of positive feedback action and, therefore, unable to generate a signal on its own. Compare OSCILLATING DETECTOR.

nonplanar   **1.** Existing in three spatial dimensions. **2.** Pertaining to a circuit that cannot be fabricated on a two-dimensional board without the use of jumper wires.

nonpolar   **1.** Having no pole(s). **2.** Pertaining to atoms that share electrons to complete their outer shells. **3.** Not polarized nor requiring po-

larization. Example: a 100-pF disk ceramic capacitor is nonpolar because it can be used in circuits without consideration of voltage polarity.

nonpolar crystal   A crystal in which lattice points are identical.

nonpolarized electrolytic capacitor   An electrolytic capacitor that has no definite negative and positive terminals and, consequently, can be used in alternating-current circuits, as well as in direct-current circuits. See also NONPOLAR, **3.**

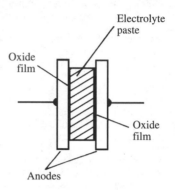

Electrolyte paste

Oxide film

Oxide film

Anodes

nonpolarized electrolytic capacitor

nonpolarized reactor   A saturable reactor in which the lines of flux produced in the three-leg core by the coils on the two outer legs oppose each other in the center leg. When direct current (dc) is passed through the coil on the center leg to saturate the core, operation remains the same for either dc polarity. Compare POLARIZED REACTOR.

nonpolarized relay   See UNPOLARIZED RELAY.

nonprint code   In telegraphy, a code used to start teleprinter functions excluding printing.

nonreactive circuit   A circuit containing pure resistance only.

nonrechargeable battery   See NONCHARGEABLE BATTERY.

nonrecurrent   Pertaining to phenomena that do not repeat periodically. Thus, a single sweep in an oscilloscope is nonrecurrent.

nonrecurrent sweep   See NONREPETITIVE SWEEP.

nonregenerative detector   A detector having no regenerative feedback. Such a detector is stable, but relatively insensitive. Compare REGENERATIVE DETECTOR.

nonregenerative receiver   A radio receiver in which no local signal whatever is generated.

nonrepetitive phenomena   See NONRECURRENT.

nonrepetitive sweep   In an oscilloscope, a single horizontal sweep of the electron beam, initiated either by the operator or by the signal under observation. Also called SINGLE SWEEP. Compare RECURRENT SWEEP.

nonreset timer   A timer that must be reset manually.

nonresident routine   A computer routine not permanently stored in memory. Compare RESIDENT ROUTINE.

nonresonant   **1.** Pertaining to a resonant circuit or device operated at some frequency other than one of its resonant frequencies. Thus, reactance is present at the operating frequency. See RESONANCE. **2.** Pertaining to a circuit or device that exhibits pure resistance (without reactance) over a wide range of frequencies.

nonresonant lines   Transmission lines so dimensioned and operated that they do not resonate at the operating frequency.

nonresonant load   An alternating-current load that is either purely resistive or is detuned from the fundamental and harmonic frequencies of the source from which it is operated.

nonreturn to zero   In the magnetic recording of digital data, the system in which the current flowing in the write-head coil is sustained (i.e., does not return to zero) after the write pulse.

nonsalient pole   A nonprojecting (often flush) pole. Compare SALIENT POLE.

nonsaturated color   **1.** Visible light that consists of energy at more than one wavelength. **2.** A color that contains some white, in addition to the pure color.

nonsaturated logic   A logic circuit in which transistors are prevented from saturating. This results in higher operating speed than SATURATED LOGIC using the same transistors.

nonshorting switch   A multiple-throw switch that disconnects one circuit before completing another; that is, no two poles are ever connected simultaneously.

nonsinusoidal waveform   A waveform whose curve cannot be represented by the equation $y = c \sin a(x + b)$, where a, b, and c are constants, y is the dependent variable (usually instantaneous amplitude or frequency), and x is the independent variable (usually time), for any real-number values of a, b, and c. Examples: BACK-TO-BACK SAWTOOTH, SAWTOOTH, and SQUARE WAVE. The COSINE WAVE is sinusoidal, being a SINE WAVE shifted in phase by 90 degrees.

nonsymmetrical wave   See ASYMMETRIC WAVE.

nonsynchronous   Unrelated in cyclic quality to other such qualities in the system.

nonsynchronous network   A communications network in which the clocks are not all synchronized.

nonsynchronous vibrator   A power-supply vibrator that is essentially a single-pole, double-throw switch providing no mechanical rectification. A separate rectifier must be used. Compare VIBRATOR-TYPE RECTIFIER. Also see VIBRATOR-TYPE POWER SUPPLY.

nontechnical   Pertaining to circuits, devices, systems, or phenomena described in lay terms, using concise graphics and little or no mathematics. An example is the simplified explanation of the operation of a spread-spectrum radio transmitter.

nontonal components   See NOISE, **3.**

nontrigger voltage   For a thyristor, the maximum gate-to-cathode voltage that can be applied without triggering the device. The amplitude of interferential signals, including noise, must be below this level to prevent accidental triggering.

nonuniform field   An electric or magnetic field whose intensity is not the same at all points.

nonvolatile memory   A computer storage medium whose contents remain unaltered when the power is switched off (i.e., they are available when power is switched on again). Example: READ-ONLY MEMORY.

nonvolatile storage   A computer storage medium in which the data does not require a source of power to be retained. Examples: MAGNETIC DISK, MAGNETIC TAPE, and COMPACT-DISK READ-ONLY MEMORY.

no-op instruction   An instruction that commands a computer to perform no operation, other than to proceed to the following instruction.

NOR circuit   Also called NOT-OR CIRCUIT. In computer and control operations, a circuit that delivers a zero output signal, except when two or more input signals are zero. The NOR circuit function is the inverse of that of the OR circuit.

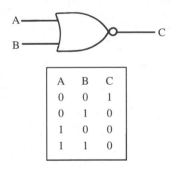

A	B	C
0	0	1
0	1	0
1	0	0
1	1	0

NOR circuit

NOR gate   A gate that performs the functions of a NOR circuit.

norm   The average or ambient condition.

normal   **1.** Pertaining to the most commonly observed set of conditions or parameters. **2.** Standard. **3.** Perpendicular; oriented at right angles. **4.** Pertaining to a NORMAL DISTRIBUTION. **5.** Pertaining to a NORMAL SOLUTION. **6.** Pertaining to an atom at its lowest energy state. See NORMAL STATE OF ATOM.

normal curve   See BELL-SHAPED CURVE.

normal distribution   In a statistical evaluation, a probability distribution represented by the so-called bell-shaped curve. The maximum probability occurs at the 50-percent value.

normal-distribution curve See BELL-SHAPED CURVE.

normal electrode A standard electrode used in electrode-potential measurements.

normal fault An unintended path between the hot terminal of a load and ground.

normal fault plus grounded neutral fault A combination of NORMAL FAULT and GROUNDED NEUTRAL FAULT.

normal glow discharge In a glow-discharge tube, the discharge region between the Townsend discharge and the abnormal glow in which current increases sharply, but a constant voltage drop is maintained across the tube.

normal impedance A transducer's input impedance when the load impedance is zero.

normal induction curve A saturation curve for a magnetic material. Also see BOX-SHAPED LOOP and SATURABLE REACTOR.

normalize In computer programming, to use floating-point numbers to modify the fixed-point part of a number so that it is within a desired range.

normalized admittance The quantity $1/Z_n$, where Z_n is NORMALIZED IMPEDANCE.

normalized frequency The unitless number represented by the ratio f/f_r, where f_r is a reference frequency and f is a frequency of interest. Response plots are sometimes conveniently drawn on the basis of normalized frequency, the reference (or resonant) frequency being indicated as **1**, twice the reference frequency as **2**, etc.

normalized impedance A value of impedance divided by the characteristic impedance of a waveguide.

normally closed Abbreviation, NC. Pertaining to a switch or relay whose contacts are closed when the device is at rest. Compare NORMALLY OPEN.

normally open Abbreviation, NO. Pertaining to a switch or relay whose contacts are open when the device is at rest. Compare NORMALLY CLOSED.

normal mode Pertaining to a device or system operated in its usual or most common manner.

normal mode A state of acoustic resonance in an enclosure, such as a speaker cabinet or a room.

normal-mode rejection Abbreviation, NMR. In a digital direct-current voltmeter, the level of noise on the applied voltage that will be rejected by the instrument. Compare COMMON-MODE REJECTION.

normal position In a switch or relay, the state of the contacts when the device is at rest.

normal solution A solution, such as an electrolyte, in which the amount of dissolved material is chemically equivalent to 1 gram-atomic weight of hydrogen per liter of the solution. Compare MOLAR SOLUTION.

normal state of atom The condition in which an atom is at its lowest energy level. For the hydrogen atom, for example, the state in which the electron is in the lowest-energy orbit.

normal-through A feature in an audio PATCH BAY or PATCH PANEL that connects two sockets by default. The top socket and the one immediately below it are connected, even when a patch cord is not plugged into either of them.

northern lights See AURORA.

north magnetic pole The north pole of the equivalent bar magnet constituted by the EARTH'S MAGNETIC FIELD. The north magnetic pole lies close to the geographic north pole. Compare SOUTH MAGNETIC POLE.

north pole **1.** See NORTH MAGNETIC POLE. **2.** The earth's geographic north pole. **3.** See NORTH-SEEKING POLE.

north-seeking pole Symbol, N. The so-called north pole of a magnet. When the magnet is suspended horizontally, this pole points in the direction of the earth's north magnetic pole. Compare SOUTH-SEEKING POLE.

Norton's equivalent An equivalent circuit based on NORTON'S THEOREM, replacing a Thevenin equivalent for a current-actuated device, such as a bipolar transistor. Also see THEVENIN'S THEOREM.

Norton's theorem With reference to a particular set of terminals, any network containing any number of generators and any number of constant impedances can be simplified to one constant-current generator and one impedance. The equivalent circuit will deliver to a given load the same current that would flow if the output terminals of the original circuit where short-circuited. Compare COMPENSATION THEOREM, MAXIMUM POWER TRANSFER THEOREM, RECIPROCITY THEOREM, SUPERPOSITION THEOREM, and THEVENIN'S THEOREM.

NOT In binary logic, an operation that changes high to low and vice-versa. Also see NAND CIRCUIT, NOR CIRCUIT, NOR GATE, NOT CIRCUIT, and NOT-OR CIRCUIT.

NOT-AND circuit See NAND CIRCUIT.

notation The way that numbers, quantities, or formulas are represented (e.g., *binary notation*, *Polish notation*, and *scientific notation*).

notch A dip in frequency response, typical of a band-suppression (band-elimination) filter or other frequency-rejection circuit. Compare PEAK, 3.

notch amplifier An amplifier containing a notch filter or other arrangement that permits it to reject one frequency or a given band of frequencies while passing all higher and lower frequencies.

notch antenna An antenna with a slot in the radiating surface, for the purpose of obtaining a directional response.

notcher See NOTCH FILTER.

notcher-peaker A circuit or device that can be set to perform either as a NOTCH FILTER or PEAK FILTER.

notch filter A frequency-rejection circuit, such as a band-suppression filter, for producing a notch.

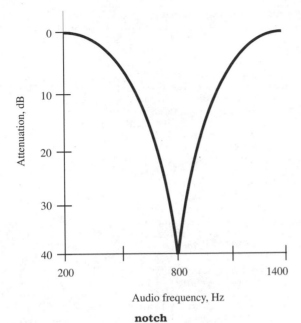

notch

notch gate   In radar, a gate that determines the minimum and maximum range.

notch sweep   An oscilloscope sweep that expands only a small portion (notch) of the pattern on the screen, leaving the portions on either side of the notch untouched. Thus, the first dozen or so cycles might appear at the normal sweep speed, the next two cycles expanded, and the remaining two or three at normal sweep speed.

NOT circuit   A logic circuit that provides an output pulse when there is no input pulse, and vice-versa. Also called COMPLEMENTER, NEGATOR, and INVERTER.

note   See BEAT NOTE.

notebook computer   A portable personal computer, also called a *laptop computer*. It is about the size of a typical three-ring notebook, and generally contains a DISKETTE DRIVE, a HARD DISK, a MODEM, and attachments for peripherals, such as printers. It uses rechargeable batteries and can be operated for approximately two to six hours between battery charges.

NOT gate   A digital circuit that inverts a logical condition—either from high (logic 1) to low (logic 0) or vice-versa. Also called an *inverter*.

NOT-OR circuit   A logical OR CIRCUIT combined with a NOT CIRCUIT.

novelty calculator   See SPECIAL-PURPOSE CALCULATOR.

November   Phonetic alphabet code word for the letter N.

novice   **1.** A beginner class of amateur radio license. **2.** Any beginner or inexperienced practitioner.

no-voltage release   In the starting box for a shunt motor, the electromagnet that normally holds the arm in full-running position. It is connected directly across the power line to disconnect the motor in the event of power failure. When the arm is released, it falls to its off position, thereby preventing burnout that would result if the motor were left connected to the line in the full-running position when power resumed. Compare NO-FIELD RELEASE.

noys scale   A scale of apparent acoustic noise, based on a linear function instead of the more common logarithmic function.

Np   **1.** Symbol for NEPTUNIUM. **2.** Abbreviation of NEPER.

N_p Symbol for number of primary turns in a transformer.

n-phase system   A polyphase system having n phases.

npin transistor   A junction transistor having an intrinsic layer between a p-type base and an n-type collector. The emitter is a second n-type layer on the other side of the base.

N plant   See NUCLEAR POWER PLANT.

n-plus-one address instruction   A computer program instruction containing two addresses, one of which specifies the location of an upcoming instruction to be executed.

NPM   Symbol for *counts per minute*.

npnp device   A semiconductor switching device having three junctions. Examples: FOUR-LAYER DIODE, and SILICON-CONTROLLED RECTIFIER. Also called *pnpn device*.

npn transistor   A bipolar transistor in which the emitter and collector layers are n-type semiconductor material, and the base layer is p-type semiconductor material. Compare PNP TRANSISTOR.

NPO   Abbreviation of NEGATIVE POSITIVE ZERO.

NPO capacitor   A fixed capacitor exhibiting temperature-compensating ability over a wide temperature range, in which the coefficient has negative, positive, and zero values.

NPS   Symbol for *counts per second*.

N radiation   X rays emitted as a result of an electron becoming an N electron.

NRD   Abbreviation of NEGATIVE-RESISTANCE DIODE.

N region   See N LAYER.

NRZ   Abbreviation of NONRETURN TO ZERO.

N_s Symbol for number of secondary turns in a transformer.

ns   Abbreviation of NANOSECOND.

N scan   See N DISPLAY.

N scope   Colloquialism for a radar set using an N DISPLAY.

nsec   Alternate abbreviation of NANOSECOND.

Ns/m²   Newton-seconds per meter squared, the unit of dynamic viscosity.

n-space   A coordinate system in n variables. It is generally of mathematical interest. The coordinates are written $(x_1, x_2, x_3,...,x_n)$ and are called *ordered n-tuples*.

NSPE   Abbreviation of *National Society of Professional Engineers.*

NTC   Abbreviation of NEGATIVE TEMPERATURE COEFFICIENT.

nth harmonic   An unspecified harmonic, having a frequency of n times the fundamental frequency, where n is some positive integer. Also see HARMONIC and HARMONIC FREQUENCY.

nth term   An unspecified term in a mathematical sequence or series.

NTP   Abbreviation of NORMAL TEMPERATURE AND PRESSURE.

NTSC   Abbreviation of *National Television Standards Committee.*

NTSC color signal   The color-television signal specified by the National Television Systems Committee. In the signal, the phase of a 3.58-MHz signal varies with the instantaneous hue of the transmitted color, and the amplitude varies with the instantaneous saturation of the color.

NTSC triangle   On a chromaticity diagram, a triangle whose sides encompass the range of colors obtainable from the additive primaries.

NTSC-type generator   A special radio-frequency signal generator for color-television tests. It provides separate, individually selected color bars that are fully saturated. The signals are strictly in accordance with NTSC standards.

n-type conduction   In a semiconductor, current flow consisting of electron movement. Compare P-TYPE CONDUCTION.

n-type material   Semiconductor material that has been doped with a donor-type impurity and, consequently, conducts a current via electrons. Germanium, for example, when doped with arsenic, becomes n-type. Compare P-TYPE MATERIAL.

n-type semiconductor   See N-TYPE MATERIAL.

nuclear battery   See ATOMIC BATTERY.

nuclear bombardment   In nucleonics, the bombarding of the nucleus of an atom with subatomic particles, usually neutrons.

nuclear charge   The net positive charge of the nucleus of an atom.

nuclear clock   A chronometer based on the rate of disintegration of a radioactive material.

nuclear energy   Energy resulting from the splitting of the nucleus of an atom or from the fusion of nuclei. Also see ATOMIC ENERGY, ATOMIC POWER, NUCLEAR FISSION, NUCLEAR FUSION, NUCLEAR REACTOR, and NUCLEUS.

nuclear fission   A nuclear reaction resulting from the bombardment of nuclei in the atoms of certain radioactive materials. The bombardment with neutrons creates two new nuclei (by splitting) and several new neutrons that split several other nuclei, producing still more nuclei and neutrons, etc. The result is a *chain reaction* that can lead to a violent explosion if not checked. Compare NUCLEAR FUSION.

nuclear force   A strong attraction that holds together pairs of nucleons in an atomic nucleus. This prevents an electric charge of protons from driving the nucleus apart. Nuclear force acts only over very minute distances. At greater distances, electrostatic repulsion is stronger.

nuclear fusion   A nuclear reaction resulting from the violent collision of the nuclei of the atoms of a hydrogen isotope (such as deuterium) at extremely high temperature. The process produces more energy than does NUCLEAR FISSION, and leaves no hazardous radioactive waste.

nuclear magnetic resonance   An atomic phenomenon in which a particle, such as a proton, in a steady magnetic field "flips over" when an alternating magnetic field is applied perpendicular to the steady field.

nuclear magnetic resonance imaging   Abbreviation, NMRI. The use of NUCLEAR MAGNETIC RESONANCE effects to produce a picture of internal body organs. Using computers, three-dimensional renditions can be generated. It is useful in medicine as a diagnostic aid.

nuclear medicine   A branch of medicine involving the use of radioactive isotopes in diagnosing and treating disease. A radioactive isotope is put inside the body and it tends to accumulate in certain areas. Abnormal concentration of radioisotopes might indicate abnormal body activity in a certain area.

nuclear pile   See NUCLEAR REACTOR.

nuclear power plant   A power-generating plant using a NUCLEAR REACTOR.

nuclear reaction   1. A reaction in which a heavy atomic nucleus is split into two or more lighter nuclei, with an accompanying release of radiant energy. Also called NUCLEAR FISSION. 2. A reaction in which two or more light nuclei combine to form a heavier nucleus, accompanied by the release of radiant energy. Also called NUCLEAR FUSION.

nuclear reactor   1. A device in which nuclear fission can be initiated and controlled. At the center of the reactor is a core of nuclear fuel, such as a fissionable isotope of uranium. The core is surrounded by a graphite moderator jacket that is, in turn, surrounded by a coolant jacket; the whole is surrounded by a thick concrete shield. Neutron-absorbing rods are inserted through various walls to different depths in the fuel to control the reaction. Also called *atomic pile.* 2. A controlled nuclear fusion device, not yet perfected, but under development. It would provide all the benefits of an atomic pile (fission reactor), but would be more efficient and would not produce hazardous radioactive waste.

nuclear recoil   An observable vibration of an atomic nucleus when it disintegrates.

nuclear resonance   The condition wherein a nucleus absorbs a gamma ray emitted by an identical nucleus.

nuclear service robot   A remotely controlled (teleoperated) robot used for general work in environments where the level of radioactivity is too high for humans (e.g., the maintenance of a nuclear reactor). It could also be used, if necessary, for such tasks as disarming nuclear warheads and cleaning up after a nuclear accident.

nucleon   A proton or neutron in the nucleus of an atom.

nucleonics   The branch of physics concerned with nucleons and nuclear phenomena. The name is an acronym for *nuclear electronics.*

nucleon number   See MASS NUMBER.

nucleus   The center or core of an atom. Contains neutrons, protons, and other particles. The net electric charge of the nucleus is positive, and is equal to the sum of the negative charges of the orbital electrons of the atom.

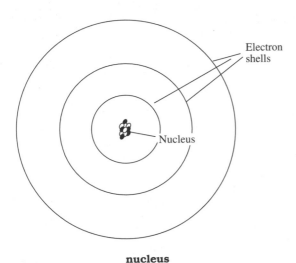

Electron shells

Nucleus

nucleus

null   **1.** The condition of zero output current or voltage resulting from adjusting or balancing a circuit, such as a bridge. **2.** A local minimum in an interference pattern or directivity pattern.

null balance   In potentiometric-measuring circuits for comparing one voltage to another, the balance condition in which no current flows through the galvanometer.

null current   In potentiometric-measuring circuits for comparing one voltage to another, the galvanometer current remaining at null when the null point is not fully zero.

null detection   Direction finding by means of an antenna with a bidirectional or unidirectional null response.

null detector   See BRIDGE DETECTOR.

null frequency   The frequency at which a frequency-sensitive circuit, such as a Wien bridge or twin-tee network, can be balanced.

null meter   See BRIDGE DETECTOR.

null method   See ZERO METHOD.

null point   In a balanced circuit, such as a bridge or potentiometer, the point of zero output voltage (or current) or minimum output voltage (or current).

null potentiometer   **1.** The variable resistor that constitutes one arm of a four-arm bridge and is used to balance the bridge. **2.** A potentiometric circuit using the null method to compare one voltage with another. Also see POTENTIOMETER, **2.**

null setting   **1.** The setting of a bridge circuit or other null device that balances the circuit. **2.** The electrical zero setting of an electronic voltmeter.

null voltage   **1.** In a conventional bridge, the output voltage remaining when the bridge is set for its best null. **2.** For a voltage-sensitive bridge, the input voltage that will produce zero output voltage.

number   The mathematical representation of a quantity. It is generally used in electronics to denote coefficients, magnitudes, component values, frequencies, etc.

number cruncher   A computer with great computational power, but one not necessarily able to process large amounts of data (such as payroll information).

number system   A systematic sequence of numbers based on a radix and a logical arrangement. See, for example, BINARY NUMBER SYSTEM and DECIMAL NUMBER SYSTEM.

numeral   A member of a digit set in a number system.

numerical analysis   A mathematical approach to solving problems numerically, including finding the limits of error in the results.

numerical code   A code having a character set restricted to digits.

numerical control   A method of programming computer-controlled mechanical devices, used in some early robots. An automated system in which number sequences fed to a digital computer cause it to control machines or processes in a manufacturing operation.

nV   Abbreviation of NANOVOLT.

nW   Abbreviation of NANOWATT.

nybble   A piece of digital information that is larger than a bit and smaller than a byte. Compare GULP.

Nylon   The trade name for a synthetic fiber-forming polyamide, useful for electrical insulation.

Nyquist criterion of stability   With reference to a NYQUIST DIAGRAM for a feedback amplifier, the amplifier is stable if the polar plot of loop amplification for all frequencies from zero to infinity is

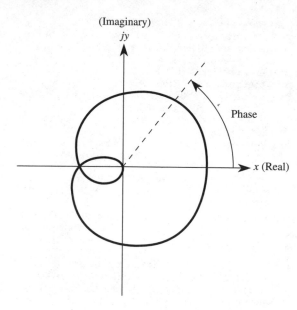

(Imaginary)
jy

Phase

x (Real)

Nyquist diagram

a closed curve that neither passes through nor encloses the point $1 + j0$.

Nyquist diagram   A graph of the performance of a reactive feedback system (such as a degenerative amplifier) that depicts the variation of amplitude and phase of the feedback factor with frequency. The plot is polar and accounts for the real and imaginary components.

Nyquist noise rule   The power dissipated in a resistor because of thermal noise at a given frequency. The derivative of frequency, with respect to power, is equal to the absolute temperature times the Boltzmann constant.

N zone   See N LAYER.

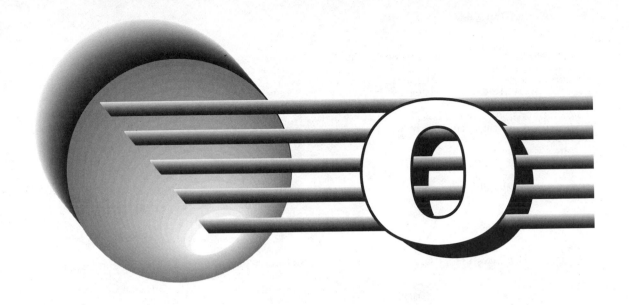

O **1.** Symbol for OXYGEN. **2.** Abbreviation of OUTPUT.

o **1.** Symbol for OUTPUT. (Also, OUT; both are used as subscripts.) **2.** Symbol for ORIGIN.

O_2 Symbol for OXYGEN.

O_3 Symbol for OZONE.

OAT Abbreviation of OPERATING AMBIENT TEMPERATURE.

object code **1.** In a computer system, the machine-language output of the compiler, directed to the computer. **2.** In a computer, the high-level output of the compiler, directed to the operator. **3.** The assembly language, directed to the compiler for translation between machine language and high-level language and vice versa.

object language The computer language that a compiler derives from a high-level (source) language (such as C++, LISP, etc.); it is usually machine language, but it can be an intermediate code that requires further conversion.

object-oriented graphics Also called *vector graphics*. In computer graphics, the use of equations to represent curves in a coordinate plane to define shapes, rather than defining the shapes pixel-by-pixel.

object-oriented language A computer program that uses on-screen objects, called icons, to represent commands. A movable device, such as a mouse or trackball, is used to move an arrow or other pointer to the icon; then a button is pressed to carry out the function indicated by the icon.

object-oriented programming Abbreviation, OOP. A computer programming language that builds sophisticated programs from basic programs called modules.

object program A machine or high-level language version of a user's computer program, as produced by a compiler.

object recognition In robotic systems, any method used to identify specific objects, according to characteristics, such as shape, texture, weight, etc. Common schemes use bar-code labels and machine vision. More-complex methods make use of pattern-recognition programs.

oblique-incidence transmission Transmission of radio signals via ionospheric reflection.

oblique mode In acoustics, a resonance within a room that involves all four walls, the floor, and the ceiling.

oboe A system of radar navigation in which a pair of ground stations measures the distance to an airborne transponder beacon and then transmits the information to the aircraft.

obsolescence-free Pertaining to a design or process that is not likely to become obsolete in the near future. Compare OBSOLESCENCE-PRONE.

obsolescence-prone Pertaining to a design or process subject to being soon outdated. Compare OBSOLESCENCE-FREE.

OBWO Abbreviation of O-TYPE BACKWARD-WAVE OSCILLATOR.

o/c Abbreviation of OPEN CIRCUIT.

occluded gas Gas that has been absorbed or adsorbed by solid material, such as glass or metals, and that must be eliminated during the evacuation of an electronic device, such as a vacuum tube. Also see OUTGASSING.

occultation **1.** The passage of the moon or other planetary body in front of a more distant celestial object, resulting in the cutting off of electromagnetic radiation from that object. **2.** The eclipsing of one object by another.

occupied band A frequency band used by at least one transmitting station regularly.

occupied bandwidth For a given emission, the continuous band of frequencies (f_2 - f_1) for which the mean (average) radiated power above f_2 and below f_1 is 0.5 percent of the total mean radiated power.

occupied orbit In an atom, an orbit in which an electron is present.

Ocean Phonetic alphabet code word for the letter O.

OCR Abbreviation of OPTICAL CHARACTER RECOGNITION.

oct Abbreviation of OCTAL.

octal Abbreviation, oct. Based on the number eight. See, for example, OCTAL NUMBER SYSTEM.

octal digit One of the figures in the group 0 through 7 used in the OCTAL NUMBER SYSTEM.

octal notation See OCTAL NUMBER SYSTEM.

octal number system The base-eight system of number notation. It uses digits 0 through 7. Compare BINARY NUMBER SYSTEM and DECIMAL NUMBER SYSTEM. The octal system is often used as shorthand for otherwise-cumbersome binary numbers. The binary number is separated into groups of three digits from right to left; each such group is then converted into its decimal equivalent, with the result being the octal form of the binary number [e.g., binary 111 001 011 = octal 713 (111 = decimal 7; 001 = decimal 1; and 011 = decimal 3)].

Decimal	Octal
0	0
1	1
2	2
3	3
4	4
5	5
6	6
7	7
8	10
9	11
10	12
11	13
12	14
13	15
14	16
15	17
16	20

octal number system

octal-to-decimal conversion Conversion of numbers in the octal number system to numbers in the more-familiar decimal number system. This is done by expressing the octal number serially in powers of eight. Thus, octal 12 = (1×8^1) + (2×8^0) = 8 + 2 = decimal 10.

octant One-eighth of a circle; therefore, 45 degrees, or 0.5 quadrant.

octave **1.** The range of frequencies between a given frequency (f) and twice that frequency ($2f$). **2.** The range of frequencies between a given frequency (f) and half that frequency ($f/2$).

octave band A band of frequencies one octave wide (see OCTAVE).

octave-band noise analyzer A noise analyzer having bandpass-filter channels whose center frequencies are one octave apart.

octave-band pressure level Sound pressure level within an OCTAVE BAND.

octave pressure level See OCTAVE-BAND PRESSURE LEVEL.

OCTL Abbreviation of OPEN-CIRCUITED TRANSMISSION LINE.

octonary signal An eight-level signaling code.

octonary system See OCTAL NUMBER SYSTEM.

OD Abbreviation of OUTSIDE DIAMETER.

odd-even check A method of checking the integrity of data transferred in a computer system, in which each word carries an extra digit to show whether the sum of ones in the word is odd or even.

odd harmonic In a complex waveform, a harmonic that is an odd-numbered multiple of the fundamental frequency (e.g., third harmonic, fifth harmonic, etc.). Compare EVEN HARMONIC.

odd-harmonic intensification In a complex waveform, emphasis of the amplitude of odd harmonics, with respect to that of even harmonics, a property of some multivibrators and non-sinusoidal waves.

odd line In a conventional television picture, one of the 262.5 odd-numbered horizontal lines scanned by the electron beam in developing the odd-line field. Compare EVEN LINE.

odd-line field On a conventional television screen, the complete field obtained when the electron beam has traced all the odd-numbered lines. Compare EVEN-LINE FIELD.

odd-line interlace See ODD-LINE FIELD.

odd parity check A computer check for an odd number of ones or zeros in digital data.

Odex Trade name for a series of autonomous robots developed by Odetics, Inc. They use legs for locomotion. Noted for their ability to maneuver in places that most robots cannot reach.

odograph An electromechanical or electronic plotter that traces the path of a vehicle on a map, or on the image of a map as portrayed on a display screen.

odometer An electromechanical device that indicates the speed of, and distance covered by, a moving vehicle or robot. Some such devices give a constant position indication, via mathematical integration of the measured velocity (speed and direction), relative to time. It can function in one, two, or three dimensions.

odometry A method of speed, velocity, and/or position sensing. It is commonly used in mobile vehicles and mobile robots. The most-sophisticated systems give a constant indication of position on the basis of a starting point (origin) and mathematical integration of the velocity (speed and direction), with respect to time. It can function in one, two, or three dimensions.

Oe   Symbol for OERSTED.

oersted   Symbol, Oe. The cgs unit of magnetic field intensity; 1 Oe = 79.58 A/m. Formerly the unit of reluctance.

off-air alarm   A device that gives a visible or audible indication when the carrier of a transmitter is lost. In its most rudimentary form, the device consists of a radio-frequency relay that actuates a bell, buzzer, horn, or lamp.

off-center display   A radar display whose center point does not correspond to the location of the antenna.

off-center-fed antenna   An antenna in which a feeder is attached to one side of the center point of the radiator. See, for example, WINDOM ANTENNA.

off-center feed   The connection of a feed line to an antenna radiator at some point other than the physical center of the radiator.

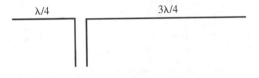

off-center feed

off delay   The interval during which a circuit remains on after the control signal has been switched off. Compare ON DELAY.

off-ground   **1.** An above- or below-ground operating voltage. **2.** The ground return for a voltage, as defined in **1**, not common with the system ground.

offhook   In a telephone system, the condition in which the receiver is removed from its receptacle, or in which the line is otherwise engaged (e.g., a fax machine or modem is in use).

off isolation   A measure of the extent to which an open switch isolates the output from the input, specified as the output voltage divided by the input voltage. For percentage, multiply this quantity by 100. The ideal value is zero (or zero percent).

off-limit   In a stepping relay, a condition in which the armature has gone past the limit of its travel.

offline   **1.** In a computer installation, equipment that is not controlled by the central processor. **2.** In computers and data processing, operations that are not under the direct real-time control of a central processor. **3.** A computer memory facility or device not connected to a central processor. **4.** In personal computing, the

use of a computer by itself (i.e., not connected in a network). Compare ONLINE.

offline editing   In video production, a process in which copies are made of the original recording; these copies are edited in a trial-and-error scheme to develop the final presentation. Compare ONLINE EDITING.

offloading   The use of computers and/or robots to perform repetitive, mundane tasks, leaving people free to do more interesting things. Example: a personal robot that mows the lawn.

off-on operation   See ON-OFF OPERATION.

off period   **1.** The interval during which an on-off circuit or device is off. **2.** The time during which an equipment is shut down.

offset   An imbalance between the halves of a normally symmetrical circuit, such as that of a differential amplifier. Also see OFFSET CURRENT and OFFSET VOLTAGE.

offset adjustment range   The change in offset voltage, in millivolts or in microvolts, that can be affected by means of the external offset adjustment circuit(s).

offset current   For an operational amplifier, the input current when the offset voltage is zero.

offset voltage   For an operational amplifier, the particular value of direct-current bias voltage required at the input to produce zero output voltage.

off state   **1.** The condition of an on-off circuit or device, such as a flip-flop, that is off. Compare ON STATE, **1**. **2.** The condition in which a circuit or device is shut down. Compare ON STATE, **2**.

off-state voltage   The voltage drop across a semiconductor device, such as a diode, rectifier, or thyristor, when the device is in its normal off (nonconducting) state. Compare ON-STATE VOLTAGE.

off-target jamming   In radio or radar jamming, the use of a remote jamming transmitter that will not betray the location of the base station.

off time   The period during which no useful work is being performed, as of equipment when it is not functioning because of a circuit breakdown.

OGL   Abbreviation of OUTGOING LINE.

OGO   Abbreviation of *orbiting geophysical observatory.*

ohm   Symbol, Ω. The basic unit of resistance, reactance, or impedance. A resistance of 1 ohm passes a current of 1 ampere in response to an applied emf of 1 volt.

ohmage   Electrical resistance or resistivity expressed in ohms.

ohm-centimeter   A unit of volume resistivity (see RESISTIVITY): the resistance of a centimeter cube of the material under measurement. Also see MICROHM-CENTIMETER.

ohmic component   A resistive or reactive circuit or device exhibiting an OHMIC RESPONSE.

ohmic contact   A usually very-low-resistance connection between two materials that provides bilateral linear conduction. It exhibits none of the properties of a rectifying junction or a nonlinear resistance.

ohmic heating   1. Heating caused by current passing through a resistive material (i.e., I^{2R} losses in the material). **2.** In an electric field, heat generated by charged particles when they collide with other particles.

ohmic loss   Loss resulting from the direct-current resistance in a circuit or transmission line.

ohmic region   The portion of the response curve of a negative-resistance device that exhibits positive (ohmic) resistance. The E-I curve of a tunnel diode, for example, has two such positive-slope regions with a negative-slope (negative-resistance) region between them.

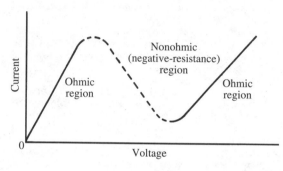

ohmic region

ohmic resistance   A resistance exhibiting OHMIC RESPONSE.

ohmic response   Response that follows OHM'S LAW: $I = E/R$. In strictly ohmic devices, neither resistance nor reactance changes with current or voltage. Compare NONOHMIC RESPONSE.

ohmic value   Electrical resistance expressed in ohms, or in multiples or fractions of ohms (kilohms, megohms, milliohms, etc.)

ohmmeter   An instrument for the direct measurement of electrical resistance. It usually consists of a milliammeter or microammeter, a battery, and several switchable resistors having very close tolerances. The scale is calibrated in ohms; the switch selects multiplier factors (e.g., ×100, ×10,000, ×1,000,000). The scale is usually reversed (i.e., 0 is at the extreme right and "infinity" is at the extreme left).

ohmmeter zero   1. The condition of proper adjustment of an ohmmeter, indicating zero resistance for a direct short circuit. **2.** The potentiometer, or other control, used for adjusting an ohmmeter to obtain a reading of zero with a short circuit.

ohm-mile   A rating meaning 1 mile of wire having a resistance of 1 ohm.

ohms adjust   The rheostat or potentiometer used to set the pointer of an ohmmeter before it is used to take resistance readings.

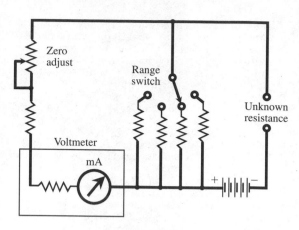

ohmmeter

Ohm's law   The statement of the relationship among current, voltage, and resistance. In a direct-current circuit, current varies directly with voltage and inversely with resistance: $I = E/R$, where I is the current in amperes, E is the voltage in volts, and R is the resistance in ohms. For alternating current, Ohm's law states that $I = E/X = E/Z$, where X is reactance and Z is impedance.

ohms per square   The resistance (in ohms) between two parallel edges of a square of thin-film resistance material.

ohms-per-volt   A specification that indicates the sensitivity and impedance of a voltmeter. In general, the higher the rating, the better. When measuring voltage in high-impedance circuits, the rating should be as high as possible. Field-effect-transistor (FET) voltmeters and vacuum-tube voltmeters have the highest ratings.

oil-burner control   An electronic system for starting and stopping the operation of an oil burner to prevent puffback and to interrupt the supply when the flame becomes erratic.

oil calorimeter   A calorimeter used to measure power in terms of the rise in temperature of oil heated by the electrical energy of interest.

oil capacitor   A capacitor impregnated or filled with oil, such as high-grade castor or mineral oil. Also see OIL DIELECTRIC.

oil circuit breaker   A circuit breaker filled with a high-grade insulating oil for cooling and arc elimination.

oil-cooled transformer   A heavy-duty transformer, through which oil is circulated for heat removal and arc prevention.

oil dielectric   A highly refined oil used as an electrical insulating material (e.g., between the plates of a capacitor). Familiar examples are *castor oil*, *mineral oil*, and the synthetic oil *chlorinated diphenyl*.

oil diffusion pump   See OIL PUMP.

oiled paper Insulating paper impregnated with oil for waterproofing and to increase its dielectric strength.

oil-filled cable A cable whose insulation is impregnated with oil that can be maintained at a constant pressure.

oil-filled capacitor See OIL CAPACITOR.

oil-filled circuit breaker See OIL CIRCUIT BREAKER.

oil-filled transformer A transformer whose case is filled with an insulating oil.

oil fuse cutout A fuse cutout that is filled with an insulating oil. Compare OPEN-FUSE CUTOUT.

oil-immersed transformer See OIL-FILLED TRANSFORMER.

oil-impregnated capacitor See OIL CAPACITOR.

oil pump A vacuum diffusion pump using oil instead of mercury. Also see DIFFUSION PUMP.

oil switch A switch enveloped by insulating oil.

OLRT Abbreviation of *online real time* (operation).

OM Amateur radio jargon for OLD MAN: chief (male) operator, or husband of female operator.

omega A phase-dependent radionavigation system using single-frequency, time-shared, ICW transmissions from two or more locations.

omnibearing A navigational bearing obtained by means of OMNIRANGE.

omnibearing converter An electromechanical device in which an OMNIRANGE signal and vehicle heading information are combined, the output being a signal that is fed to a meter.

omnibearing indicator Abbreviation, OBI. An omnibearing converter with a dial and pointer.

omnibearing line In an OMNIRANGE system, one of the imaginary lines extending from the geographic center of the omnirange.

omnibearing selector A device that can be set manually to a selected omnibearing.

omniconstant calculator A calculator that adds or multiplies numbers in succession in such a manner as to arithmetically or geometrically increase the exponent as a single button is repeatedly pressed.

omnidirectional 1. Pertaining to a device that responds equally well to acoustic or electromagnetic energy from any direction in three dimensions. 2. Pertaining to a device that radiates acoustic or electromagnetic energy equally well in any direction in three dimensions. 3. Also, NONDIRECTIONAL. Pertaining to an antenna that intercepts or radiates equally well in any azimuth (horizontal) direction.

omnidirectional antenna See NONDIRECTIONAL ANTENNA.

omnidirectional hydrophone A hydrophone that picks up underwater sounds coming from any direction.

omnidirectional microphone A microphone that picks up sounds coming from any direction.

omnidirectional radio range See OMNIRANGE.

omnidirectional range See OMNIRANGE.

omnidirectional range station Abbreviation, ORS. A radionavigation station for OMNIRANGE service.

omnigraph A Morse-code generator that operates via marked or perforated paper tape.

omnirange A radionavigation system in which each station in a chain broadcasts a beam in all directions. It usually operates at very-high frequencies (VHF) or ultra-high frequencies (UHF). Pilots of aircraft home on a particular station by tuning it in and noting its bearings.

OMR Abbreviation for OPTICAL MARK RECOGNITION.

on air See ON THE AIR.

on-call channel An assigned radio channel of which exclusive, full time use is not demanded.

on-course curvature In navigation, the rate at which the course of a vehicle deviates with reference to the distance along the true course.

on-course signal A single-tone-modulated signal indicating to an aircraft pilot following a radio beam that the flight is substantially on course.

on current See ON-STATE CURRENT.

on delay An interval during which a circuit remains off after an actuating signal has been supplied. Compare OFF DELAY.

on-demand system A system, especially in computer and data-processing operations, that delivers information or service immediately upon request.

ondograph An electromechanical device that graphically draws alternating-current waveforms on paper.

ondoscope A radio-frequency (RF) energy detector that consists of a neon bulb attached to the end of an insulating rod. When a bulb is held in an intense RF field, the field energy ionizes the gas in the bulb, causing it to glow without direct connection to the RF circuit.

one-address code In computer programming, a code in which the address in an instruction refers to only one memory location.

one condition See ONE STATE.

one-digit adder See HALF ADDER.

one-element rotary antenna A directional antenna consisting of a radiator only (no directors or reflectors) that can be rotated. A straight, rigid, half-wave rotatable dipole is the most common configuration.

one-for-one compiler A compiler that generates one machine language instruction from one source language instruction.

one-input terminal In a flip-flop, the input terminal that must be energized to switch the circuit to its logic 1 output.

one-level address See ABSOLUTE ADDRESS.

one-level subroutine In a computer program, a subroutine in which no reference is made to other subroutines.

one-lunger Colloquialism for a radio transmitter consisting entirely of a one-transistor oscillator.

one output   See ONE STATE.

one-output signal   The signal that results from reading a computer memory unit that is in the logic 1 state.

one-output terminal   In a flip-flop, the output terminal that is energized when the circuit is in its logic 1 state.

one-plus-one address   A method of computer programming in which instructions contain two addresses and an operation, the addresses referring to the location of the next instruction and the location of the data to be used.

ones complement   Binary notation in the *radix-minus-one-complement form.*

one shot   See MONOSTABLE MULTIVIBRATOR.

one-shot circuit   See MONOSTABLE MULTIVIBRATOR.

one-shot multivibrator   See MONOSTABLE MULTIVIBRATOR.

one-sided wave   A waveform consisting of only negative or positive half-cycles. Example: a rectified alternating-current signal.

one state   Also, *logic 1 state*. The high, on, or true logic state of a bistable device, such as a flip-flop. Compare ZERO STATE. In binary notation, the one state is represented by the digit 1.

one-third-octave band   A frequency band that is ⅓ octave wide; that is, the difference between the upper-frequency limit (f_2) and the lower-frequency limit (f_1) is one-third of an octave. Also see OCTAVE BAND.

one-to-one assembler   An assembler computer program that produces a machine language instruction as a result of translating a source-language statement.

one-to-one correspondence   A mapping between two sets A and B so that every element in set A has exactly one correspondent in B, and every element in B has exactly one correspondent in A.

O network   A four-impedance network containing two series (upper and lower) arms and two shunt (input and output) arms.

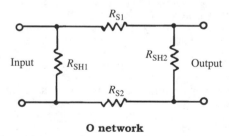

O network

one-way communication   **1.** The transmission of a message to one or more stations that receive only. Compare TWO-WAY COMMUNICATION. **2.** See BROADCASTING.

one-way conduction   See UNILATERAL CONDUCTIVITY.

one-way radio   See ONE-WAY COMMUNICATION.

one-way repeater   In wire telephony, a device that amplifies and retransmits a signal in the direction the signal was traveling when it arrived at the repeater. Compare TWO-WAY REPEATER.

one-way valve   A diode or rectifier (British variation).

on interval   See ON TIME.

online   **1.** Descriptive of equipment under the control of a central processor. **2.** Pertaining to operations being controlled by a central processor. **3.** Relating to a computer storage device independent of a central processor. **4.** In personal computing, the use of a computer in a network (e.g., with a modem for operation on the Internet). Compare OFFLINE.

online data reduction   Processing data as it enters a computer system.

online editing   In video production, the final phase of editing. The original recording (not copies) is used to prepare the presentation, based on the trials that were performed using the copies. Compare OFFLINE EDITING.

online service   A computer network accessible via telephone lines, television cable systems, and/or radio. It is generally available to owners of personal computers. It provides such services as electronic mail, special-interest forums, news, weather, sports, shopping, and general information.

on-off keying   Keying, as in radiotelegraphy and wire telegraphy, by switching a signal source on and off to form dots and dashes or a binary code, rather than alternately changing the amplitude or frequency of the signal.

on-off operation   A switching operation, especially that performed by nonmechanical (fully electronic) circuits.

on-off ratio   **1.** For a circuit or device, the ratio of off time to on time. **2.** For a pulse, the ratio of pulse duration to the dead space between pulses.

on-off switch   **1.** In electronic equipment, the switch by which the equipment can be started or stopped. It can be, but is not necessarily, the power-line or B-plus switch. **2.** An electronic circuit or stage that is designed to operate as a conventional switching element when triggered by an appropriate signal.

on period   See ON TIME.

ONR   Abbreviation of *Office of Naval Research*.

on resistance   See ON-STATE RESISTANCE.

on state   **1.** For a switch or switching device (such as a flip-flop), the condition of the device when it conducts current or delivers an output voltage. Compare OFF STATE, **1**. **2.** The condition of a circuit or device that is activated for operation. Compare OFF STATE, **2**.

on-state current   The current flowing through a semiconductor device (such as a diode, rectifier, or thyristor) when it is conducting. Also see ON-STATE VOLTAGE.

on-state resistance The resistance of a voltage-dependent resistor that is conducting current.

on-state voltage The voltage drop across a semiconductor device (such as a diode, rectifier, or thyristor) when the device is conducting current. Also see ON-STATE CURRENT.

on the air 1. The state of a radio station that is transmitting. 2. In broadcasting, the condition in which the transmitter is operational and the sound and/or video from the studio is being disseminated.

on time The length of time a switch or switching device (such as a flip-flop) remains on.

on voltage See ON-STATE VOLTAGE.

OOP Abbreviation of OBJECT-ORIENTED PROGRAMMING.

op 1. Abbreviation of OPERATE. 2. Abbreviation of *operator* (see OPERATOR, 1). 3. Abbreviation of OPERATION. 4. Abbreviation of *operational*.

opacimeter 1. An instrument for measuring the extent to which a material blocks light. 2. An instrument, such as a field-strength meter, used to measure the effectiveness of an electrical shielding material in blocking radio waves, X rays, or other radiation.

opacity The condition of being opaque. This applies to all forms of radiation. For example, a material can be opaque to light rays, but be transparent to radio waves, or it can be transparent to gamma rays while being opaque to alpha particles.

op amp Abbreviation of OPERATIONAL AMPLIFIER.

op code Abbreviation of OPERATION CODE.

open-air line See OPEN-WIRE LINE.

open-back cabinet A loudspeaker enclosure in which the space behind the speaker is open to the room.

open capacitance The value of a variable capacitor whose rotor plates have been rotated completely out of mesh with the stator plates. Compare CLOSED CAPACITANCE.

open-center display A radar display in which a ring around the center indicates zero range.

open-chassis construction A method of assembling electronic equipment by mounting components and wiring them on an unenclosed chassis, often without a front panel. Similar to breadboard construction.

open circuit 1. A discontinuous circuit (i.e., one that is broken at one or more points and, consequently, cannot conduct current nor present a voltage at its extremities). Compare CLOSED CIRCUIT. 2. Pertaining to no-load conditions, for example, the open-circuit voltage of a battery. 3. For a bipolar transistor, the operating characteristics under independent input and output conditions.

open circuit breaker A circuit breaker whose contacts are open.

open-circuit current Current flowing in the primary winding of an unloaded transformer.

open-circuited line See OPEN-CIRCUITED TRANSMISSION LINE.

open-circuited transmission line Abbreviation, OCTL. An unterminated transmission line in which the conductors at the far end are not connected together.

open-circuit impedance For a transmission line or a four-terminal network, the input or driving-point impedance when the output end of the line or network is open-circuited.

open-circuit jack A telephone jack that introduces a break in a circuit until a plug connected to a closed external circuit is inserted.

open-circuit plug See OPEN PLUG.

open-circuit resistance For a four-terminal network, the input or driving-point resistance when the output end of the network is unterminated.

open-circuit signaling A system of signaling in which no current flows until the signal circuit is in active operation. In a simple telegraph circuit, for example, current flows only when the key is pressed (to form a dot or dash).

open-circuit alarm system A security system in which all the actuating sensors are normally open and connected in parallel. When one of the sensors is actuated, it closes, causing a short circuit that triggers the alarm.

open-circuit voltage See NO-LOAD VOLTAGE.

open-collector configuration In an integrated circuit, an output scheme utilizing no internal pull-up resistor. Wired-OR outputs can thus have opposite states without risk of damage to the device.

open component An open-circuit component (e.g., an open diode, coil, resistor, etc.).

open core A magnetic core having a cylindrical shape. A disadvantage of this core configuration, in some applications, is that much of the magnetic flux extends outside the core. Compare CLOSED CORE.

open-core choke A choke coil wound on an open core. Also called OPEN-CORE INDUCTOR. Compare CLOSED-CORE CHOKE.

open-core transformer A transformer wound on an open core. Compare CLOSED-CORE TRANSFORMER.

open-delta connection See VEE-CONNECTION OF TRANSFORMERS.

open-ended Pertaining to a circuit or device that can be built upon without modifying its original configuration.

open-end stub A stub that is neither short-circuited nor terminated at its far end.

open-end stub tuning Adjustment of an OPEN-END STUB, by pruning its length, for optimum operation at a given frequency.

open-entry contact In a connector, an unprotected, opening contact of the female type.

open feeder See OPEN-WIRE LINE.

open-frame machine See OPEN GENERATOR and OPEN MOTOR.

open-fuse cutout   A type of enclosed-fuse cutout having an exposed fuse holder and support. Compare OIL FUSE CUTOUT.

open generator   An unsealed generator (i.e., one that has openings in its housing for air circulation).

open line   **1.** See OPEN-WIRE LINE. **2.** See OPEN-CIRCUITED TRANSMISSION LINE.

open loop   **1.** In a control system, a feedthrough path having no feedback and that is not self-regulating. **2.** In an operational amplifier, the configuration in which there is no feedback, and in which the device operates at maximum gain. **3.** A loop within a program from which the computer automatically exits after a specific number of iterations.

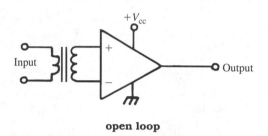

open loop

open-loop bandwidth   The bandwidth of an open-loop device, such as an amplifier, without feedback. Also see OPEN LOOP.

open-loop control system   A control system having no feedback and that is not self-regulating. An example is a fluid-level gauge that indicates the height of fluid in a tank, but that cannot correct the level automatically. Compare CLOSED-LOOP CONTROL SYSTEM.

open-loop differential voltage gain   For a differential amplifier, the overall voltage gain (when either input is used) when the amplifier has no feedback.

open-loop gain   The overall gain (ratio of output to input) of an open-loop device, such as an amplifier without feedback. Also see OPEN LOOP.

open-loop input impedance   The input impedance of an open-loop device, such as an amplifier without feedback. Also see OPEN LOOP.

open-loop output impedance   The output impedance of an open-loop device, such as an amplifier without feedback. Also see OPEN LOOP.

open-loop output resistance   The output resistance of an open-loop device, such as an amplifier without feedback. Also see OPEN LOOP and OPEN-LOOP IMPEDANCE.

open-loop system   **1.** A circuit in which the input and output currents are independent. **2.** A robot that does not use a servo system. It depends entirely on alignment and precision for positioning accuracy. **3.** An electromechanical device that does not use corrective feedback.

open-loop voltage gain   The overall voltage gain of an open-loop amplifier (i.e., one having no feedback). Also see OPEN LOOP.

open magnetic circuit   A magnetic circuit in which a complete path is not provided for magnetic flux. See, for example, OPEN CORE. Compare CLOSED MAGNETIC CIRCUIT.

open motor   An unsealed motor (i.e., one that has openings in its housing for air circulation).

open-phase protection   Use of an automatic device, such as an open-phase relay, to interrupt the power to a polyphase system when one or more phases are open-circulated.

open-phase relay   In a polyphase system, a protective relay that opens when one or more phases are open-circuited. Also see OPEN-PHASE PROTECTION.

open plug   A phone plug to which no external connections are made; it is used to hold the blades of a jack as if they were plugged in.

open-reel   A tape-recording system in which the tape, during record or playback condition, is wound into a take-up reel that is physically separate from the tape reel. Also called *reel-to-reel arrangement.*

open relay   **1.** A relay in its open-contact state. **2.** A relay having an open-circuited coil. **3.** An unenclosed relay.

open routine   In computer operations, a routine that can be inserted directly into a larger routine and requires no link to the main program.

open subroutine   In computer operations, a subroutine that can be inserted into a larger instructional sequence and must be recopied whenever it is required. Also called *direct-insert subroutine.*

Open Systems Interconnection Reference Model   Abbreviation, OSI-RM. A standard set of protocols for computer network communication. It consists of seven levels, also called layers: *physical layer, link layer, network layer, transport layer, session layer, presentation layer,* and *application layer.* It is used extensively in packet communications and amateur packet radio.

open temperature pickup   A temperature transducer that must be placed directly in contact with the monitored medium.

open volume   Pertaining to the maximum-gain operation of a sound-reproducing system (i.e., operation at full volume).

open wire   **1.** An unterminated wire. **2.** A wire supported above the surface of the earth and often ungrounded. **3.** See OPEN-WIRE LINE.

open-wire feeder   See OPEN-WIRE LINE.

open-wire line   A transmission line or feeder usually consisting of two straight, parallel wires held apart by bars of low-loss insulating material at regular intervals along the line.

open-wire loop   A branch line connected to a main open-wire line.

open-wire transmission line   See OPEN-WIRE LINE.

open-wire wavemeter See LECHER WIRES.

operand In computer operations, a quantity that enters into or results from an operation.

operate **1.** To manipulate according to an established procedure (e.g., to operate an instrument). **2.** To perform according to specifications, in the sense that an electronic circuit functions.

operate current A signal current or trigger current required to actuate a device. Compare OPERATE VOLTAGE.

operate delay See OPERATE TIME, **1**.

operate interval See OPERATE TIME, **2**.

operate time **1.** The interval starting after the application of an operate current or voltage to a device, and ending when the device operates. **2.** The period during which an electronic equipment is in operation. Also see OPERATING TIME, **1**.

operate voltage The signal voltage or trigger voltage required to actuate a device. Compare OPERATE CURRENT.

operating ambient temperature Abbreviation, OAT. The maximum or recommended temperature in the space immediately surrounding an equipment in operation.

operating angle In an amplifier circuit, the excitation-signal cycle, in degrees, during which drain, collector, or plate current flows. Class-A amplifiers operate for 360 degrees of the input signal cycle; class-AB amplifiers operate for more than 180 degrees, but less than 360 degrees of the input signal cycle; class-B amplifiers operate for 180 degrees of the input signal cycle; class-C amplifiers operate for less than 180 degrees of the input signal cycle.

operating bias In a circuit containing transistors, diodes, or vacuum tubes, the value(s) of direct-current bias required for normal operation.

operating code The code used by the operator in a computer or data-processing system.

operating conditions The environment in which a circuit or system functions in normal use.

operating current The current required by a device during its operation. Compare IDLING CURRENT.

operating cycle The sequence of events in the operation of a device. For example, the repetitive operation of a neon-bulb relaxation oscillator is a sequence of three events: (1) slow charge of capacitor, (2) firing of bulb, and (3) abrupt discharge of capacitor.

operating frequency **1.** The fundamental frequency at which a circuit or device is operated. **2.** The frequency of the current, voltage, or power delivered by a generator.

operating frequency range **1.** The range of operating frequencies, expressed as a minimum and maximum, for a communications receiver, transmitter, or transceiver. **2.** For an integrated-circuit oscillator, the minimum and maximum frequency, and all frequencies in between, at which the device is guaranteed to operate.

operating life The maximum period (from seconds to years) over which a device will operate before failure (from which it usually cannot recover). Compare SHELF LIFE.

operating line A line drawn across a family of curves depicting the performance of a device. It intersects each curve at a single point and graphically displays the performance of the device for a given condition. Thus, an operating line on a family of output curves for a transistor might depict operation with a given load resistor.

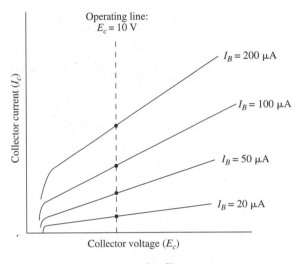

Operating line: $E_c = 10$ V

$I_B = 200$ μA

$I_B = 100$ μA

$I_B = 50$ μA

$I_B = 20$ μA

Collector current (I_c)

Collector voltage (E_c)

operating line

operating overload The extent and/or duration of overload to which an equipment can be exposed during customary operation, and still continue to properly function.

operating point On the response curve for a device, the point indicating the quiescent level of operation (such as determined by a fixed bias voltage or current). An alternating-current signal applied at this point oscillates above and below the point as a mean.

operating-point shift A movement of an operating point due to faulty operation of a circuit or device, or to a value change in some critical component.

operating position **1.** The control point in a system, [i.e., the place where an operator (see OPERATOR, **1**) normally functions]. **2.** The actual or recommended physical orientation of a device during its operation (e.g., a vertical operating position for a power vacuum tube).

operating power **1.** The power actually used by a device during its operation. **2.** The antenna power of a radio station.

operating ratio For a given period, the ratio t_o/t, where t_o is the time during which an equipment is operating correctly, and *t* is the duration of the period.

operating station   In a computer installation, one or more consoles for the control of a data-processing system by an operator.

operating system   Abbreviation, OS. In a computer, a set of programs that oversee the functioning of the hardware and application software. It works with the basic input/output system (BIOS).

operating temperature   The actual or recommended temperature of a device during its operation.

operating-temperature range   For a given device, the spread between maximum and minimum values of operating temperature.

operating time   **1.** The interval during which an equipment is in operation. **2.** The period corresponding to OPERATING ANGLE.

operating-time characteristic   For a coil-type relay, the relationship between operating time and operating power.

operating voltage   The voltage required by a device, or measured at the device, during its operation. Compare IDLING VOLTAGE.

operation   **1.** The working of a circuit or device (i.e., its performance). **2.** A process usually involving a sequence of steps (e.g., a mathematical operation).

operational amplifier   Abbreviation, op amp. An extremely stable (usually direct-coupled) linear amplifier originally intended for performing mathematical operations; see, for example, DIFFERENTIATOR, **2** and INTEGRATOR, **2**. This amplifier, especially the integrated-circuit variety, has a wide range of applications.

operational differential amplifier   An OPERATIONAL AMPLIFIER preceded by a DIFFERENTIAL AMPLIFIER.

operational readiness   In statistical analysis, the probability that a system will, at a certain time, be correctly operating or ready to operate.

operational reliability   Reliability determined empirically from a study of the actual operation of a device or system under controlled conditions. Also called ACHIEVED RELIABILITY.

operational transconductance amplifier   Abbreviation, OTA. An integrated-circuit amplifier that differs from the conventional operational amplifier in that its output current is proportional to its input-signal voltage.

operation code   In computer operations, the part of an instruction that specifies an operation.

operation decoder   In a digital computer, the circuit that reads an OPERATION CODE and directs other circuitry in the execution of the code.

operation envelope   See WORK ENVELOPE.

operation number   In computer programming, a number that indicates the position in the program of a particular operation or subroutine.

operation part   In a computer program, the part of an instruction containing the OPERATION CODE.

operation register   In a digital computer, the register that stores the operation code of an instruction.

operations research   A branch of computer engineering, devoted to the solution and/or optimization of functions of many variables.

operation time   The interval between the instant of application of all voltages to a circuit, and the instant when the current reaches a specified percentage of its final steady value.

operator   **1.** A person who performs an operation (see OPERATE, **1**). **2.** In mathematics, a symbol indicating an operation (e.g., j, $+$, $-$, $\times$, etc.).

operator j   See J OPERATOR.

opposition   **1.** The state of two quantities that are 180 degrees out of phase with each other. **2.** A state in which two effects or quantities operate against each other in some manner (e.g., physically, mathematically, electrically, etc.).

opt   Abbreviation of OPTICAL.

Optacon   An electronic aid for the blind. It has a camera that scans printed matter and a device that forms corresponding raised letters that can be read, as would Braille, with the fingertips. The name is a contraction of *optical to tactile converter.*

optical   **1.** Generating or sensing visible light. **2.** Visible electromagnetic radiation in the range of approximately 390 to 750 nanometers wavelength.

optical ammeter   A type of OPTICAL PYROMETER that measures the current flowing through the filament of an incandescent lamp.

optical axis   The z-axis of a quartz crystal (see Z-AXIS, **4**).

optical character reader   A device that uses OPTICAL CHARACTER RECOGNITION to discern printed characters.

optical character recognition   Abbreviation, OCR. In computer and data-processing operations, the reading of alphabetical, numerical, and other characters from hard copy (usually printed matter) by photoelectric methods. It converts the characters into digital data that can be stored in computer memory, on disks and tapes, and transmitted via digital communications networks. It can also allow a computer or robot to read signs, maps, etc.

optical communications   One-way or two-way communications via modulated visible light. It can be conducted through optical fibers, the atmosphere, water, or any other transparent medium.

optical coupler   A coupling device consisting essentially of a light source (actuated by an input

optical coupler

signal) mounted in an opaque housing with a light-sensitive device (that delivers the output signal). In its simplest form, the arrangement consists of a light-emitting diode (LED) and a photodiode.

optical detector An integrated-circuit (IC) that provides light-to-voltage conversion. Its direct-current output voltage is proportional to the intensity of light impinging on its sensor.

optical encoder An electronic device that measures the extent to which a mechanical shaft has rotated. It can also measure the rate of rotation (angular speed). It consists of a light-emitting diode (LED), a photodetector, and a disk with alternate light and dark bands (chopping wheel). It is commonly used in digital controls and jointed robot arms.

optical fiber A glass or plastic medium through which light is propagated for optical-communications purposes. The refractive characteristics of the fiber keep the visible light inside.

optical lever A device for amplifying the effect of a small rotation. The rotating member carries a small mirror that reflects a light beam over a curved scale, the distance through which the light spot travels on the scale being proportional to the distance between the scale and the rotating mirror. In this way, the deflection on the scale is several times the length of the arc described by the mirror, the rotation being thus amplified.

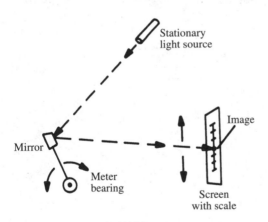

optical lever

optical link See OPTICAL COUPLER.

optical mark recognition A method of data transfer that involves the use of optical techniques.

optical maser See LASER.

optical mode The vibration mode that produces an oscillating dipole in a crystal lattice.

optical pattern A Christmas-tree-like pattern produced by parallel rays of light striking a phono disk. Also see DIFFRACTION.

optical playback See OPTICAL SOUND REPRODUCER.

optical pyrometer A pyrometer for measuring the temperature of a hot body in terms of the intensity and color of light it emits.

optical sound recorder A photoelectric machine for recording sound on photographic film. Also see OPTICAL SOUND RECORDING.

optical sound recording A system for recording sound on photographic film, as in sound motion pictures. The sound is picked up by a microphone and amplified to vary the intensity of a light source. The film passing this modulated beam becomes exposed to a variable-width or variable-density track corresponding to the modulation (see VARIABLE-DENSITY SOUND RECORD and VARIABLE-WIDTH SOUND RECORD). When developed film is played back, its sound track modulates a light beam in the reproducer by actuating a photocell or phototube to produce the audio signal, which is then amplified.

optical sound reproducer A photoelectric machine for reproducing sound on film. A light beam in the device is modulated by the passing sound track, and it, in turn, modulates photocell or phototube current, which is amplified to drive a loudspeaker. Also see OPTICAL SOUND RECORDING.

optical system Collectively, the functional arrangement of lenses, mirrors, prisms, and related devices in optoelectronic apparatus.

optical tachometer An optoelectronic instrument for measuring (by means of reflected-light variations) the speed of a body, such as a rotating shaft, without electrical or mechanical attachments to the latter.

optical thermometer See OPTICAL PYROMETER.

optical twinning A kind of defect in which two types of quartz occur in the same crystal. Compare ELECTRICAL TWINNING.

optical type font A special type (printing) style designed for use with OPTICAL CHARACTER RECOGNITION equipment.

optical wand A pencil-like optical probe, used to read bar codes from a printed page and translate the codes into information that is then loaded into a computer or calculator.

optic axis See OPTICAL AXIS.

optic flow See EPIPOLAR NAVIGATION.

optics 1. The science of light, its measurement, application, and control. 2. A system of lenses, prisms, filters, or mirrors used in electronics to direct, control, or otherwise modify light rays.

optimization The adjustment or manipulation of the elements of a process or system for the best operation or end result.

optimize 1. To manipulate a set of variables or parameters for the best possible performance of a circuit or system. 2. To maximize the value of a multivariable function.

optimum angle of radiation For a given altitude of the ionosphere, the angle, with respect to the horizon, at which a radio signal should be transmitted from a specific geographic location to provide optimum reception at some other specific location. This angle varies, depending on the altitude of the ionospheric layer from which signals are returned, the distance between the transmitting and receiving stations, and the number of hops taken by the signal between the earth and the ionosphere.

optimum bunching In a velocity-modulated tube, such as a klystron, the bunching associated with maximum output.

optimum collector load The ideal load impedance (see OPTIMUM LOAD) for a particular transistor operated in a specified manner.

optimum coupling The degree of coupling between two circuits tuned to the same frequency that results in maximum energy transfer. Also called CRITICAL COUPLING.

optimum current The value of current that produces the most-effective performance of a circuit or device.

optimum frequency See OPTIMUM WORKING FREQUENCY.

optimum load The value of load impedance that produces maximum transfer of power from a generator or amplifier.

optimum plate load The ideal load impedance (see OPTIMUM LOAD) for a particular electron tube operated in a specified manner.

optimum *Q* The most effective figure of merit for a capacitor, inductor, or tuned circuit at a specified frequency.

optimum reliability The value of reliability that ensures minimum project cost.

optimum voltage The value of voltage that results in the most effective performance of a circuit or device.

optimum working frequency In radio transmission involving reflection from the ionosphere, the frequency of use that results in the most reliable communication between two points.

optoelectronic coupler An assembly consisting of an LED and a phototransistor. An input signal causes the diode to glow, and the light activates the transistor, which in turn delivers an output signal of higher amplitude than that of the input signal.

optoisolator See OPTICAL COUPLER and OPTO-ELECTRONIC COUPLER.

optoelectronics A branch of electronics that involves the use of visible light for communications or data-transfer purposes.

optoelectronic transistor A transistor having an electroluminescent emitter, transparent base, and photoelectric collector.

optophone A photoelectric device for converting light into sounds of proportionate pitch to enable blind persons to "see" by ear.

Orange Book Trade name (Sony and Philips) for a specialized format for *compact-disc recordable (CD-R)* computer data storage media. It allows recording of data onto, as well as retrieval of data from, an optical compact disc. See also GREEN BOOK, RED BOOK, and YELLOW BOOK.

orange peel On a phonograph disc, a mottled surface that produces high background noise; so called from its resemblance to an orange peel.

orbit 1. Also called *shell*. The median path of an electron around the nucleus of an atom. 2. The circular or elliptical path of an artificial satellite (e.g., a communications satellite) around the earth. 3. The elliptical path of the moon around the earth. 4. The elliptical path of the earth or another planet around the sun. 5. Any closed, usually circular or elliptical path, that an object follows around another object.

orbital-beam multiplier tube An electron-multiplying UHF oscillator or amplifier tube in which a positively charged electrode focuses electrons in a circular path.

orbital electron An electron in orbit around the nucleus of an atom.

orbital period The length of time required by a satellite to go around a celestial body, usually the earth. It can vary from about 90 minutes for very low orbits to months or even years for orbits beyond that of the moon. The moon's period is about a month.

OR circuit Also called *inclusive-OR circuit*. In digital systems and other switching circuits, a logic gate whose output is high (logic 1) when any of the input signals is high. The output is low (logic 0) only when all of the inputs are low. Compare AND CIRCUIT.

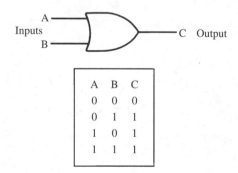

A	B	C
0	0	0
0	1	1
1	0	1
1	1	1

2-input OR circuit

order 1. An instruction to a digital computer. 2. Sequence.

OR element See OR CIRCUIT.

ordered pair A set of two variables or numbers that can be mapped one-to-one onto a set of points in a plane. The most familiar example is (x,y), used to depict the Cartesian (rectangular) coordinate system on which characteristic curves and other functions are plotted.

order of interference The position of an interference fringe that depends on whether the interference arises from one, two, three, or more wavelength differences. Generally, the first fringe results from a difference of one wavelength, the second fringe from a difference of two wavelengths, etc. The center fringe indicates that the two signals are exactly in phase; that is, the difference is zero wavelengths.

order of logic 1. A mathematical expression for the complexity of a system of logic. 2. The relative speed with which logical information is processed in a system.

order tone A warning signal to receiving operators in the form of a tone transmitted over a trunk preceding the transmission of an order.

ordinary ray As a result of the double refraction of electromagnetic waves, the member of a pair of rays that follows the usual laws of refraction. Also see O WAVE. Compare EXTRAORDINARY RAY.

ordinary wave See O WAVE.

ordinate In the rectangular coordinate system, a point located on the vertical axis.

organ 1. A computer subsystem. 2. An electronic device used for the purpose of generating music.

organic decay See EXPONENTIAL DECREASE.

organic electricity Electricity in the living tissues of animals and plants.

organic growth See EXPONENTIAL INCREASE.

organic semiconductor A semiconductor material consisting of, or combined with, some compound of carbon.

OR gate See OR CIRCUIT.

orientation 1. The direction or position of an object in space, expressed in terms of coordinate values. 2. In a teleprinter, the calibration or alignment that determines the speed of response to a received character.

orientation of quartz plates See CRYSTAL AXES and CRYSTAL CUTS.

orifice An opening or window, such as that in a loudspeaker enclosure or waveguide, through which energy is transmitted.

origin 1. The starting point in a coordinate system. 2. Relative to address modification in computer operations, an address to which a modifier is added to derive a variable operand address.

original lacquer In disc-recording operations, an original recording made on a lacquer-surfaced disc that is subsequently used to make a master.

original master In disk recording, the master disc produced from a wax or lacquer disc (see ORIGINAL LACQUER) by means of electroforming.

origin distortion The change in the shape of a wave as it swings through zero (polarity).

OR operation See OR CIRCUIT.

ORS Abbreviation of OMNIDIRECTIONAL RANGE STATION.

orthicon A television camera tube somewhat similar to the iconoscope, but which provides internal amplification of light and, accordingly, can be used in dimmer places than the iconoscope. Light amplification is provided by an arrangement similar to that of a photomultiplier tube.

orthiconoscope See ORTHICON.

orthoacoustic recording 1. A system of disc recording in which the inherent differences between high-frequency recording and low-frequency recording are compensated to provide reproduction that more closely resembles the actual sound. 2. A disc made by the method defined in 1.

orthogonal axes Perpendicular axes [e.g., those in a Cartesian (rectangular) coordinate system].

Os Symbol for OSMIUM.

OS Abbreviation of OPERATING SYSTEM.

osc Abbreviation of OSCILLATOR.

OSCAR Abbreviation for *Orbiting Satellite Carrying Amateur Radio*. A satellite with a transponder that has an uplink in one amateur band and a downlink in another amateur band.

osciducer See OSCILLATING TRANSDUCER.

oscillate 1. To fluctuate in amplitude in a uniform manner. 2. To vary above and below a specified value at a constant rate.

oscillating arc A small arc, especially one produced by slow-opening relay contacts, that generates high-frequency oscillations.

oscillating circuit A closed circuit containing inductance, capacitance, and inherent resistance, in which energy passes back and forth between inductor and capacitor at a frequency determined by the inductance (L) and capacitance (C) values.

oscillating crystal 1. A piezoelectric plate maintained in a state of oscillation in a circuit. See, for example, CRYSTAL OSCILLATOR and QUARTZ CRYSTAL. 2. An oscillating semiconductor diode (see NEGATIVE-RESISTANCE DIODE, 1, 2).

oscillating current See OSCILLATORY CURRENT.

oscillating detector A detector provided with positive feedback; therefore, it is capable of generating a signal of its own. Compare NON-OSCILLATING DETECTOR.

oscillating diode 1. A semiconductor diode biased into its negative-resistance region so that it oscillates in a suitable circuit. 2. An oscillating tunnel diode. 3. Any of several microwave diodes, such as the IMPATT diode, which will oscillate in a suitable system. 4. See MAGNETRON. Also see DIODE OSCILLATOR.

oscillating field An alternating electric or magnetic field.

oscillating rod A rod of magnetostrictive metal maintained in a state of oscillation in a circuit. See, for example, MAGNETOSTRICTION and MAGNETOSTRICTION OSCILLATOR.

oscillating transducer A transducer in which an input quantity varies a frequency proportionately from its center value.

oscillating wire   A wire of magnetostrictive metal maintained in a state of oscillation in a circuit. See, for example, MAGNETOSTRICTION and MAGNETOSTRICTION OSCILLATOR.

oscillation   The periodic change of a body or quantity in amplitude or position (e.g., oscillation of a pendulum, voltage, or crystal plate).

oscillation constant   For an oscillating inductance-capacitance (LC) circuit, the expression $(LC)^{1/2}$, where L is the inductance in henrys and C is the capacitance in farads. The reciprocal of the OSCILLATION NUMBER.

oscillation control   A manual or automatic device for adjusting the frequency or amplitude of the signal generated by an oscillator.

oscillation efficiency   The ratio, as a percentage, of the alternating-current (signal) power output of an oscillator (P_{out}) to the corresponding direct-current power input (P_{in}). *Efficiency* = $100 P_{out}/P_{in}$.

oscillation number   For an oscillating circuit, the number of complete oscillation cycles that occur in 6.28 (2 pi) seconds.

oscillation test   **1.** A test of an oscillator to determine if a signal is being generated. **2.** A test for transistors wherein the transistor is used as an oscillator to give a rough indication of its condition in terms of oscillation amplitude.

oscillation transformer   A tank coil of a radio transformer—especially one that includes an output coupling coil.

oscillator   A device that produces an alternating or pulsating current or voltage electronically. The term is sometimes used to describe any alternating-current-producing device other than an electromechanical generator.

oscillator circuit   The specific manner in which the components of an OSCILLATOR are interconnected. The three general types are: positive-feedback, negative-resistance, and relaxation.

oscillator coil   A tapped coil that provides the input and output windings required for an oscillator circuit. Such coils are used in signal generators, oscillators, and superheterodyne receivers.

oscillator-doubler   A circuit consisting of an oscillator and a frequency doubler (e.g., a crystal oscillator whose output frequency is twice the crystal frequency).

oscillator drift   A usually gradual change in frequency of an oscillator caused by such factors as warmup time, voltage variations, capacitance change, inductance change, or change in transistor characteristics.

oscillator frequency   The fundamental frequency at which an oscillator operates. It can be determined by a tuned circuit, crystal, cavity, section of waveguide or transmission line, or by a resistance-capacitance circuit.

oscillator harmonic interference   In a superheterodyne receiver, interference that is the beat product of local oscillator harmonics and received signals.

oscillator interference   Radio-frequency interference caused by signals from the high-frequency oscillator of a receiver.

oscillator keying   Keying by making and breaking the signal output, direct-current (dc) power, or dc bias of the oscillator stage of a radiotelegraph transmitter.

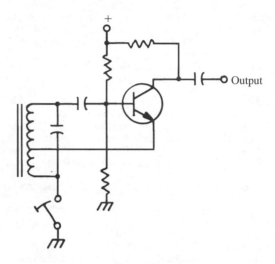

oscillator keying

oscillator-mixer   **1.** A combination stage in which a transistor functions as a local oscillator and mixer in a receiver or test instrument. **2.** A device designed specifically to function as a local oscillator and mixer.

oscillator-mixer-detector   **1.** In a superheterodyne receiver, a stage in which the functions of high-frequency oscillator, mixer, and first detector are performed by a single transistor. **2.** A device designed specifically to function as a local oscillator, mixer, and detector.

oscillator-multiplier   A single circuit that serves simultaneously as an oscillator and frequency multiplier. See, for example, OSCILLATOR-DOUBLER.

oscillator padder   In a superheterodyne receiver, a small, limited-range variable capacitor connected in series with the oscillator coil for tracking oscillator tuning at the low end of a band. Compare OSCILLATOR TRIMMER.

oscillator power supply   **1.** The direct-current or alternating-current power supply for an oscillator. **2.** See OSCILLATOR-TYPE POWER SUPPLY.

oscillator radiation   The emission of radio-frequency energy by the oscillator stage of a superheterodyne receiver. Also see OSCILLATOR INTERFERENCE.

oscillator-radiation voltage   The radio-frequency voltage at the antenna terminals of a superheterodyne receiver that results from signal emission by the oscillator stage.

oscillator stabilization 1. The automatic compensation of an oscillator circuit for the frequency drift resulting from changes in temperature, current, voltage, or component parameters. **2.** The automatic stabilization of the operating point of an oscillator circuit against variations resulting from changes in temperature, supply current or voltage, or component parameters.

oscillator synchronization The locking of an oscillator in step with another signal source, such as a frequency-standard generator.

oscillator tracking In a superheterodyne receiver, the constant separation of the oscillator frequency from the signal frequency by an amount equal to the intermediate frequency at all settings of the tuning control.

oscillator transmitter A radio transmitter consisting only of a radio-frequency oscillator and its power supply. The oscillator can be modulated in various ways [e.g., on-off keying, frequency-shift keying, voice amplitude modulation (AM), voice frequency modulation (FM)].

oscillator trimmer In a superheterodyne receiver, a small, limited-range capacitor connected in parallel with the oscillator coil for tracking oscillator tuning at the high end of a band. Compare OSCILLATOR PADDER.

oscillator tuning The separate, often ganged, tuning of the oscillator stage in a circuit.

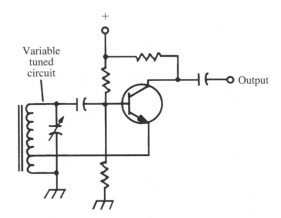

oscillator tuning

oscillator-type power supply A high-voltage, direct-current (dc) power supply in which a radio-frequency (RF) oscillator generates a low-voltage alternating current (ac). This ac voltage is stepped up by an RF transformer, and is finally rectified to obtain high-voltage dc.

oscillator-type transmitter See OSCILLATOR TRANSMITTER.

oscillator wavelength The fundamental wavelength at which an oscillator operates. It is usually expressed in meters, centimeters, or millimeters. It can be determined by a tuned circuit, crystal, cavity, section of waveguide or transmission line, or by a resistance-capacitance circuit.

oscillatory current A current that alternates periodically, particularly the current in an inductance-capacitance (LC) tank circuit that results from the oscillation of energy back and forth between the inductor and capacitor.

oscillatory discharge An electrical discharge, such as that of a capacitor, that sets up an OSCILLATORY CURRENT.

oscillatory surge A current or voltage surge that includes both positive and negative excursions.

oscillatory transient See OSCILLATORY SURGE.

oscillistor A device consisting essentially of a bar of semiconductor material positioned in a magnetic field; it will produce oscillations under certain conditions.

oscillogram 1. The image produced on the screen of an oscilloscope. **2.** A permanent, usually photographic, record made from the screen of an oscilloscope.

oscillograph 1. An instrument that makes a permanent record (photograph or pen recording) of a rapidly varying electrical quantity. Also called *recorder* (see RECORDER, **2**). Compare OSCILLOSCOPE. **2.** An obsolete term for OSCILLOSCOPE.

oscillograph recorder A direct-writing recorder (see RECORDER, **2**).

oscillography The use of a graphic oscillation recorder (OSCILLOGRAPH).

oscillometer A device used for determining the peak amplitude of an oscillation.

oscilloscope An instrument that presents for visual inspection the pattern representing variations in an electrical quantity. Also see CATHODE-RAY OSCILLOSCOPE. Compare OSCILLOGRAPH.

oscilloscope camera A special high-speed, short-focus camera with fixtures for attachment to an oscilloscope to record images from the screen. Standard and instant-film types are available.

oscilloscope differential amplifier An amplifier that processes the difference between two signals, for the purpose of displaying on an oscilloscope or oscillograph.

oscilloscope tube A cathode-ray tube for use in an oscilloscope. It contains an electron gun, accelerating electrode, horizontal and vertical deflecting plates, and a fluorescent screen.

Os-Ir Symbol for OSMIRIDIUM.

OSI-RM Abbreviation of OPEN SYSTEMS INTERCONNECTION REFERENCE MODEL.

OSL Abbreviation of *orbiting space laboratory*.

osmiridium Symbol, Os-Ir. A natural alloy of osmium and iridium.

osmium Symbol, Os. A metallic element of the platinum group. Atomic number, 76. Atomic weight, 190.2.

osmotic pressure The force that causes the positive ions to pass out of a solution toward a metal body immersed in an electrolyte. Also see HELMHOLTZ DOUBLE LAYER.

OSO Abbreviation of *orbiting solar observatory.*

osteophone A bone-conduction hearing aid.

OTA Abbreviation of OPERATIONAL TRANSCONDUCTANCE AMPLIFIER.

OTL Abbreviation of OUTPUT-TRANSFORMER-LESS.

O-type backward-wave oscillator Abbreviation, OBWO. A backward-wave oscillator using harmonics having opposing phases.

ounce Abbreviation, oz. A unit of weight equal to ¹⁄₁₆ pound or 28.35 grams.

ounce-inch Abbreviation, oz-in. A unit of torque equal to the product of a force of 1 ounce and a moment arm of 1 inch. Compare POUND-FOOT.

outage **1.** Loss of power to a system. **2.** Loss of a received signal.

outboard components **1.** Discrete components (capacitors, coils, resistors, or transformers) connected externally to an integrated circuit. **2.** Discrete components connected externally to any existing electronic device.

outcome In statistical analysis, the result of an experiment or test. An outcome can be numerical or nonnumerical.

outdoor antenna An antenna erected outside, usually high above the surface of the earth clear of obstacles. It generally provides superior performance compared with an INDOOR ANTENNA. Also reduces the probability of radio-frequency interference (RFI) when used for transmitting.

outdoor booster A signal preamplifier mounted on an outdoor television receiving antenna for improved reception.

outdoor transformer A weatherproof distribution transformer installed outside the building it services.

outer conductor The outer metal cylinder or jacket of a coaxial cable or coaxial tank. Compare INNER CONDUCTOR.

outgassing **1.** In the evacuation of electronic devices, such as vacuum tubes, the removal of occluded gases from glass, ceramic, and metal by means of slow baking and by flashing an internal metal getter (such as one of magnesium). **2.** The production of gases in certain electrochemical cells and batteries during the final stage of charging.

outgoing line A power or signal line that leaves a device, facility, or stage. Compare INCOMING LINE.

outlet A female receptacle that delivers a signal or operating power to equipment plugged into it.

outline flowchart In computer operations, a preliminary flowchart showing how a program will be divided into routines and segments, input and output functions, program entry points, etc.

out-of-line coding Instructions for a computer program routine stored in an area of memory other than that in which the routine's program is stored.

out of phase Pertaining to the condition in which the alternations or pulsations of two or more separate waves or wave phenomena, having identical frequencies, are out of step with each other. Compare IN PHASE.

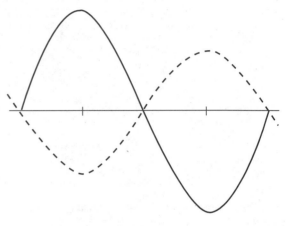

out of phase

out-of-phase current Reactive current in an alternating-current circuit (i.e., current that is out of phase with voltage. Also see QUADRATURE CURRENT).

out-of-phase voltage Voltage across a reactance; so called because it is out of phase with the current.

outphaser A device that converts a sawtooth wave to a square wave. It is used in electronic organs and synthesizers.

outphasing modulation A system of modulation in which the sideband frequencies are shifted 90 degrees from the phase position in an amplitude-modulated wave. The resulting constant-envelope wave is then amplified with high efficiency and low distortion by a class-C stage; then the signal is reconverted to an amplitude-modulated one by phase shifting the carrier, with respect to the sidebands.

out-plant system A data-processing system in which a central computer receives data from remote terminals.

output **1.** Energy or information delivered by a circuit, device, or system. Compare INPUT, **1. 2.** The terminals at which energy or information is taken from a circuit, device, or system. Compare INPUT, **2.**

output admittance   Symbol, Y_o. The internal admittance of a circuit or device, as "seen" at the output terminals; the reciprocal of OUTPUT IMPEDANCE. Compare INPUT ADMITTANCE.

output amplifier   **1.** The last stage in a multistage amplifier. **2.** A separate amplifier that boosts the current, voltage, or power delivered by another amplifier.

output area   In a computer system, the portion of storage holding information for delivery to an output device. Also called *output block*.

output axis   For a gyroscope that has received an input signal, the axis around which the spinning wheel precesses.

output block   See OUTPUT AREA.

output buffer   **1.** A circuit that follows an oscillator and reduces the effects of variable load impedance on the oscillator frequency or signal amplitude. **2.** An amplifier, usually with a voltage gain of 6 dB, that follows a video multiplexer. The amplifier drives a coaxial transmission line.

output bus driver   In a computer, a device that amplifies output signals sufficiently to provide signals to other devices without undue loading of the supply line (bus).

output capability   The maximum power or voltage output that a circuit can deliver without distortion or other improper operating conditions.

output capacitance   Symbol, C_o. The internal capacitance of a circuit or device, as seen at the output terminals. Compare INPUT CAPACITANCE.

output capacitive loading   For an operational amplifier at unity gain, the maximum capacitance that can be connected to the output of the amplifier before phase shift increases to the point of oscillation.

output capacitor   **1.** In a capacitance-coupled circuit, the output coupling capacitor. Compare INPUT CAPACITOR. **2.** The last capacitor in a power-supply filter circuit.

output capacity   The maximum output capability of a device or system expressed in appropriate units, such as current, voltage, power, torque, horsepower, etc.

output choke   The last choke (inductor) in a power-supply filter circuit.

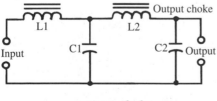

output choke

output circuit   The circuit or subcircuit that constitutes the output portion of a network or device.

Also see OUTPUT and OUTPUT TERMINALS. Compare INPUT CIRCUIT.

output-circuit distortion   Distortion in the output portion of a circuit or device (such as a transistor or transformer), usually caused by an overload or nonlinear response.

output conductance   Symbol, G_o. The internal conductance of a circuit or device, as "seen" at the output terminals. It is the reciprocal of OUTPUT RESISTANCE. Compare INPUT CONDUCTANCE.

output control   **1.** The gain control of an amplifier. **2.** The level control of a variable power supply.

output coupling capacitor   See OUTPUT CAPACITOR.

output coupling transformer   See OUTPUT TRANSFORMER.

output current   **1.** Symbol, I_o. The current delivered by a source, such as a battery, generator, or amplifier. Compare INPUT CURRENT, **1.** **2.** Symbol, I_o. Current flowing in the output leg or electrode of a circuit or device. Compare INPUT CURRENT, **2.**

output device   **1.** A load device, such as a resistor, loudspeaker, lamp, relay, motor, etc., that utilizes the output energy delivered by a generator, amplifier, or network. **2.** A device, such as an output transformer, that serves to transfer energy or information from a circuit or device. Compare INPUT DEVICE. **3.** In computer operations, a device that presents the results of computer operation in a comprehensible form. Examples: printer, monitor, disk drive, tape drive, modem, etc.

output efficiency   The efficiency of a device, such as a generator or amplifier, in delivering an output signal. For an amplifier, the efficiency ($Eff_\%$) is given as a percentage by the formula $Eff_\% = 100 P_o/P_i$, where P_i is the direct-current power input, and P_o is the alternating-current (signal) power output.

output equipment   See OUTPUT DEVICE, **3.**

output filter   The direct-current filter of a power supply operating from alternating current. Also see CAPACITOR-INPUT FILTER and CHOKE-INPUT FILTER.

output gap   A device via which current or power is intercepted from an electron beam in a beam-power tube.

output impedance   Symbol, Z_o. The impedance "looking" into the output terminals of an amplifier, generator, or network. Compare INPUT IMPEDANCE.

output indicator   A device, such as an analog meter, digital meter, or bar-graph meter, that provides a visual indication of the output-signal amplitude of an equipment.

output leakage current   In an open-collector integrated circuit, the current from collector to emitter with the output in the "off" condition and a certain specified voltage applied to the device. It can be expressed in milliamperes or microamperes.

output limiting A process for automatically maintaining the amplitude of the signal delivered by a generator or amplifier. See, for example, AUTOMATIC GAIN CONTROL, AUTOMATIC MODULATION CONTROL, VOLUME COMPRESSION, and VOLUME LIMITER.

output load See OUTPUT DEVICE, **1**.

output load current **1.** The current through the output load of an amplifier. Generally, this current is expressed in root-mean-square (rms) form. **2.** The highest rms current that an amplifier can deliver to a load of a specified impedance.

output meter A meter that gives a quantitative or qualitative indication of the output of an amplifier or generator. See, for example, OUTPUT-POWER METER.

output offset In an integrated circuit, the voltage at the output when the inputs are grounded.

output port The output terminal of a logic device.

output power Symbol, P_o. The power deliverable by an amplifier, generator, or circuit. Also called *power output*. Compare INPUT POWER.

output-power meter A type of direct-reading wattmeter for measuring the power output of an amplifier or generator.

output regulator A circuit or device that automatically maintains the output of a power supply or signal source at a constant amplitude.

output resistance Symbol, R_o. The internal resistance of a circuit or device, as "seen" at the output terminals. Compare INPUT RESISTANCE.

output routine In computer operations, a routine (program segment) that performs the work involved in moving data to an output device, often including intermediate transferals and modifying the data as necessary.

output section See OUTPUT AREA.

output sink current In an integrated circuit, for a specified set of conditions at the input and output, current into the output as measured in milliamperes or microamperes.

output source current In an integrated circuit, for a specified set of conditions at the input and output, the current out of the output, as measured in milliamperes or microamperes.

output stage The last stage of an amplifier. Delivers the signal to the load.

output terminals Terminals (usually a pair) associated with the output of a circuit or device (see OUTPUT, **1**, **2**). Compare INPUT TERMINALS.

output tank In a transmitter or power generator, a parallel-tuned combination of inductance and capacitance in the collector, drain, or plate circuit, that is generally tuned to resonance at the operating frequency. IT optimizes efficiency and couples the signal to the load. Compare INPUT TANK.

output transformer The output-coupling transformer that delivers signal voltage or power from

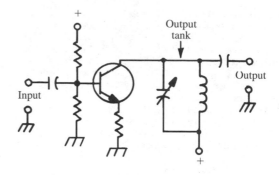

output tank

an amplifier, generator, or network to a load or to another circuit. Compare INPUT TRANSFORMER.

output-transformerless Abbreviation, OTL. Pertaining to an oscillator, amplifier, or generator that requires no output coupling transformer.

output transistor A transistor in the final stage of an amplifier or generator; usually, it is a power transistor.

output tube A vacuum tube in the final stage of an amplifier or generator; usually, it is a power tube.

output unit See OUTPUT DEVICE.

output voltage **1.** Symbol, E_o or V_o. The voltage delivered by a source, such as a battery, generator, or amplifier. Compare INPUT VOLTAGE, **2**. **2.** Symbol, E_o or V_o. The voltage across the output leg or electrode of a circuit or device. Compare INPUT VOLTAGE, **2**.

output voltage compliance In an integrated circuit, the voltage range over which the output can be made to swing, while keeping the operation of the circuit within a certain maximum allowable nonlinearity limit. It is measured in volts or millivolts.

output voltage noise In an integrated circuit, the output noise over a given range of frequencies, as measured in peak-to-peak millivolts or microvolts. It can also be measured as the root-mean-square (rms) value.

output voltage swing In an integrated circuit with a specified load, the output-voltage change measured as a difference between maximum and minimum in volts or millivolts.

output voltage tracking For an integrated-circuit dual regulator, the difference between the absolute values of the output voltages of a dual regulator. It can be expressed as a specific voltage or as a percentage of the specified output voltage of the device.

output winding The secondary coil of an output transformer.

outside antenna See OUTDOOR ANTENNA.

outside booster See OUTDOOR BOOSTER.

outside diameter Abbreviation, OD. The outermost diameter of a body or figure having two concentric diameters (e.g., tubing or conduit). Compare INSIDE DIAMETER.

outside lead See FINISH LEAD.

outside transformer **1.** See OUTDOOR TRANSFORMER. **2.** A transformer mounted outside of an equipment in whose circuit it is included. External mounting can eliminate hum in the equipment circuit, and can help to prevent overheating.

oven **1.** Also called *crystal oven*. A chamber providing a closely controlled operating temperature for an electronic component, such as a quartz crystal. **2.** An enclosure in which electronic equipment can be tested at selected, precise high temperatures. Compare COLD CHAMBER.

overall feedback Positive or negative feedback around an entire system (such as a public-address system), as opposed to feedback confined to one stage or a few stages within the system.

overall gain The total gain of an entire system (such as a multistage amplifier), as opposed to that of one or several stages.

overall loudness The apparent intensity of an acoustic disturbance, generally measured with respect to the threshold of hearing, and expressed in decibels, relative to the threshold level.

overbiased unit A component, such as a transistor or vacuum tube, whose bias current or voltage is higher than the correct value for a given mode of operation. Compare UNDERBIASED UNIT.

overbunching In a velocity-modulated tube, such as a Klystron, the condition in which the buncher voltage exceeds the value required for optimum bunching.

overcharging In a secondary cell or battery, the application of charging current longer than necessary to obtain full charge. This can sometimes cause problems, such as cell heating.

overcompounded generator A dynamo-type generator having a compound field winding in which the series-field winding increases the field intensity beyond the point needed to maintain the output voltage. Compare UNDERCOMPOUNDED GENERATOR.

overcompounding A characteristic of electromechanical motors, resulting in increased running speed with decreasing load resistance.

overcoupled transformer A transformer having greater than critical coupling between its primary and secondary windings. In tuned circuits, such as intermediate-frequency (IF) transformers, this produces a double-peak response.

overcoupling Extremely close coupling (see CLOSE COUPLING).

overcurrent A current greater than the specified, nominal, or desired level. Compare UNDERCURRENT.

overcurrent circuit breaker A circuit breaker that opens when current exceeds a predetermined value.

overcurrent protection The use of a circuit breaker, relay, or other device to protect a circuit or system from damage resulting from an excessive flow of current.

overcurrent relay A protective relay that opens a circuit when current exceeds a predetermined value. Compare UNDERCURRENT RELAY.

overcutting In disc recording, the condition in which an excessively high amplitude signal causes the stylus to cut through the wall between adjacent grooves. Compare UNDERCUTTING.

overdamping Damping greater than the critical value (see DAMPING ACTION, **2**). Compare UNDERDAMPING.

overdesign Also called *overengineering*. **1.** To use an unnecessarily high safety factor in the design of equipment. **2.** To design equipment for performance superior to that which is required in the intended application. **3.** A design that results from operations defined in **1** and **2**.

overdrive **1.** To deliver a signal having excessive amplitude to the input of a power amplifier. **2.** The undesirable operating conditions resulting from the delivery of a signal having excessive amplitude to the input of a power amplifier. **3.** The addition of a special-purpose integrated circuit to a personal computer to increase processing power and/or speed.

overdriven amplifier See OVERDRIVEN UNIT.

overdriven unit An amplifier, oscillator, or transducer whose driving signal (current, voltage, power, or other quantity) is higher than that which the device can properly or efficiently handle for correct or intended operational performance.

overdub In audio recording, a method of combining two or more signals onto a single tape track. For example, a live voice can be recorded on a tape containing pre-recorded music.

overexcited Receiving higher than normal excitation, as in radio-frequency amplifiers or alternating-current generators.

overflow **1.** In computer or calculator operation, the condition in which an arithmetic operation yields a result exceeding the capacity of the location or display for a result. **2.** The carry digit that results from the condition described in (1).

overflow indicator **1.** In a digital calculator, a display that indicates that a numerical value is too large or too small to be shown with the available number of decimal places. **2.** In data processing, a display that indicates the presence of too many bits or characters for the available storage capacity.

overflow position In a digital computer, an auxiliary register position for developing the overflow digit (see OVERFLOW, **1**, **2**).

overflow record In data processing, a record that will not fit the storage area allotted for it, and that must be kept where it can be retrieved, according to some reference stored in its place.

overflow storage In a calculator or computer, extra storage space, allowing a small amount of overflow without loss of accuracy.

overhanging turns The turns in the unused portion(s) of a tapped coil.

overhead line A power or transmission line suspended above the ground between poles or towers.

over-horizon radar A form of radar used at high frequencies, in which pulses are transmitted and received. The signals are returned to earth via the ionosphere, both in the forward and reflected directions, making it possible to detect such things as missile launchings from thousands of miles away.

over-horizon transmission See FORWARD SCATTER.

overinsulation Use of excessive insulation for a particular application. Compare UNDERINSULATION.

over insulation The insulation (usually a strip of tape) laid over a wire brought up from the center of a coil. Compare UNDER INSULATION.

overlap **1.** The time during which two successive operations are performed simultaneously. **2.** In a facsimile or television system, a condition in which the scanning line is wider than the center-to-center separation between adjacent scanning lines.

overlap radar A long-range radar situated in one sector and covering part of another sector.

overlay **1.** A sheet of transparent or translucent material laid over a schematic diagram for the purpose of tracing connections that have been made in wiring an equipment from the diagram. **2.** In computer operations, a method whereby the same internal storage locations are used for different parts of a program during a program run. It is used when the total storage requirements for instructions exceed the available main storage capacity.

overlay transistor A double-diffused epitaxial transistor having separate emitters connected together by means of diffusion and metallizing to increase the edge-to-area ratio of the emitters. This design raises the current-handling ability of the transistor. Also see DIFFUSED TRANSISTOR and EPITAXIAL TRANSISTOR.

overload **1.** Current or power drain in excess of the rated output of a circuit or device. **2.** An excessive driving signal.

overload circuit breaker See CIRCUIT BREAKER.

overloaded amplifier A power amplifier delivering excessive output power. Compare UNDERLOADED AMPLIFIER, **2.**

overloaded oscillator An oscillator from which excessive power is drawn, causing instability, frequency shift, lowered output voltage, and overheating.

overload indication Any attention-catching method, such as an audible or visual alarm, for warning that a prescribed signal or power level has been exceeded.

overload level The amount of overload that can safely be applied to an equipment (see OVERLOAD, **1**).

overload protection The use of circuit breakers, relays, automatic limiters, and similar devices to protect equipment from overload damage by reducing current or voltage, disconnecting the power supply, or both.

overload recovery time Following an overdrive at the input of an integrated-circuit device, the time required for the output to resume its normal characteristics.

overload relay A relay actuated when circuit current exceeds a predetermined value. Compare UNDERLOAD RELAY.

overload time The maximum length of time that an equipment can safely be subjected to an overload level of current.

overmodulation Modulation in excess of a prescribed level—especially amplitude modulation greater than 100%. Compare COMPLETE MODULATION and UNDERMODULATION.

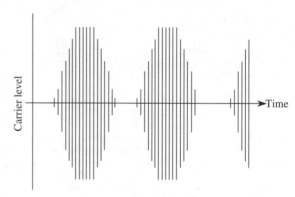

overmodulation

overmodulation alarm See OVERMODULATION INDICATOR.

overmodulation indicator A device, such as a neon bulb, incandescent lamp, light-emitting diode, analog meter, or digital meter, adapted to give an alarm when the modulation percentage of a signal exceeds a predetermined value.

overpotential See OVERVOLTAGE.

overpower relay A relay actuated by a rise in power above a predetermined level. Compare UNDERPOWER RELAY.

overpressure For a pressure transducer, pressure in excess of the maximum rating of the device.

override **1.** To intentionally circumvent an automatic control system. **2.** To bridge a functional stage of a system.

overscanning   The deflection of the beam of a cathode-ray tube beyond the edges of the screen.

overshoot   **1.** The momentary increase of a quantity beyond its normal maximum value (e.g., the spike sometimes seen on a square wave because of the overswing of a rising voltage). **2.** Momentary overtravel of the pointer of an analog meter.

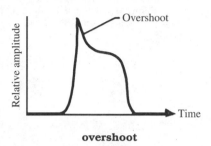

overshoot

overswing   See OVERSHOOT, 2.

overtemperature protection   The use of an automatic device, such as a thermal relay or thermostat, to disconnect a device from the power supply when the device's temperature becomes excessive.

overthrow   See OVERSHOOT, 2.

overtone   See HARMONIC.

overtone crystal   A piezoelectric quartz crystal that oscillates at odd multiples of the frequency for which it was cut. This allows crystal operation at frequencies otherwise obtainable only from a fundamental-frequency crystal ground so thin as to be prohibitively fragile.

overtone oscillator   A crystal oscillator using an OVERTONE CRYSTAL.

overtravel   See OVERSHOOT, 2.

overvoltage   A voltage higher than a specified or rated value. Compare UNDERVOLTAGE.

overvoltage circuit breaker   A circuit breaker that opens when voltage exceeds a predetermined value.

overvoltage protection   The use of a special circuit or device to protect equipment from excessive voltage. When voltage increases beyond the overvoltage limit, the protective circuit causes shutdown.

overvoltage relay   A relay actuated when voltage rises above a predetermined value. Compare UNDERVOLTAGE RELAY.

overwrite   In computer operations, to record new data over existing data (e.g., to update the files on a magnetic disk or tape).

Ovshinsky effect   In thin-film solid-state devices, the tendency for switches to have the same characteristics for currents in either direction.

O wave   One (the ordinary) of the pair of components into which an ionospheric radio wave is divided by Earth's magnetic field. Compare X WAVE.

Owen bridge   A wide-range four-arm bridge that measures inductance in terms of a standard capacitance and bridge-arm resistances.

own coding   Additional program steps added to vendor-supplied software so that it can be modified to fit special needs.

ox   Abbreviation of OXYGEN.

oxidation   **1.** The combination of a substance with oxygen. Generally a slow process, such as the corrosion of iron or aluminum in the atmosphere. The process is accelerated by the presence of moisture and/or high temperatures. **2.** The loss of electrons from a cell or battery during discharge.

oxidation-reduction potential   The potential at which oxidation occurs at the anode of an electrolytic cell, and at which reduction occurs at the cathode.

oxide-coated cathode   See OXIDE-COATED EMITTER.

oxide-coated emitter   An electron-tube cathode or filament coated with a material, such as thorium oxide, for increased electron emission at low emitter temperatures.

oxide-coated filament   See OXIDE-COATED EMITTER.

oxide film   **1.** The thin film of iron oxide that constitutes the recording surface of a magnetic disk or tape. **2.** The layer of copper oxide formed on the copper plate of a copper-oxide rectifier.

oxide-film capacitor   An electrolytic capacitor, so called because the dielectric is a thin oxide film.

oxide rectifier   A solid-state rectifier using a junction between copper and copper oxide. Also called COPPER-OXIDE RECTIFIER.

oximeter   A photoelectric instrument for measuring the oxygen content of the blood. It operates by passing visible light through the earlobe, and analyzing the color and intensity of the emerging beam. Also called ANOXEMIA TOXIMETER.

oxygen   Symbol, O. Abbreviation, O_2. A gaseous element. Atomic number, 8. Atomic weight, 15.999. Constitutes 21% of Earth's atmosphere. It readily combines with various elements to form compounds (see OXIDATION).

oxygen analyzer   An electronic gas analyzer designed especially to measure oxygen content. The operation of this instrument is based on the paramagnetic properties of oxygen.

oxygen recombination   In nickel-cadmium (NICAD) cells and batteries, a process in which oxygen is generated in the vicinity of the positive electrode, and is reduced with water in the vicinity of the negative electrode. This produces battery heating.

oz   **1.** Abbreviation of OUNCE. **2.** Abbreviation of OZONE.

oz-in   Abbreviation of OUNCE-INCH.

ozocerite   An insulating mineral wax. Dielectric constant, 2.2. Dielectric strength, 4 to 6 kV/mm. Also spelled OZOKERITE.

ozone   Symbol, O_3. An allotropic form of oxygen. Its formula indicates that each molecule has three atoms. Produced by the action of ultraviolet rays (or electrical discharge) on oxygen, its characteristic odor (somewhat like weak chlorine) can often be detected around sparking contacts or in the air after a thunderstorm.

ozone layer   In the earth's atmosphere, a layer of ozone gas in the upper troposphere and lower stratosphere. It is produced by ultraviolet radiation from space, mainly from the sun. The ozone layer tends to block ultraviolet radiation, reducing the amount that reaches the surface of the earth.

ozone monitor   An instrument for measuring the concentration of ozone in the atmosphere. One version measures the extent to which ultraviolet radiation is absorbed by a sample of air; the greater the absorption, the higher the ozone concentration in the sample.

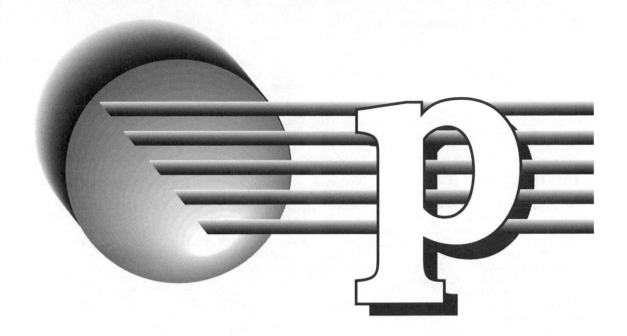

P **1.** Symbol for POWER. **2.** Symbol for PLATE (of a vacuum tube). **3.** Symbol for PHOSPHORUS. **4.** Abbreviation of PRESSURE. **5.** Symbol for PRIMARY. **6.** Abbreviation for prefix PETA-. **7.** Symbol for PERMEANCE. **8.** Abbreviation of POINT.

p **1.** Abbreviation of prefix PICO-. **2.** Subscript for PEAK. **3.** Abbreviation of POUND. **4.** Abbreviation of POINT (often capitalized). **5.** Subscript for PRIMARY. **6.** Subscript for PLATE (of a vacuum tube). **7.** Abbreviation of PITCH. **8.** Abbreviation of PER.

PA **1.** Abbreviation of POWER AMPLIFIER. **2.** Abbreviation of PULSE AMPLIFIER. **3.** Abbreviation of *particular average.* **4.** Abbreviation of *pilotless aircraft.* (Also, P/A.) **5.** Abbreviation of PUBLIC ADDRESS (as in PA system).

Pa **1.** Symbol for PROTACTINIUM. **2.** Symbol for PASCAL.

pA Abbreviation of PICOAMPERE.

pacemaker See CARDIAC STIMULATOR.

pacer See CARDIAC STIMULATOR.

Pacific Standard Time Abbreviation, PST. Local mean time at the 120th meridian west of Greenwich. Also see GREENWICH MEAN TIME, STANDARD TIME, TIME ZONE, and COORDINATED UNIVERSAL TIME.

pack A technique for maximizing a computer memory device's storage capacity, wherein more than one information item is stored in a single storage unit. Also called *crowd.*

package **1.** The enclosure for an electronic device or system. This includes a wide range of housings, from the simple encapsulation of miniature transistors to forced-air-cooled enclosures for heavy power units. **2.** To assemble and house an electronic equipment, or to design a housing for it, in accordance with good engineering techniques. **3.** A computer program of general use for an application (e.g., *payroll package*).

package count The number of discrete packaged circuits in a system.

packaging density **1.** See VOLUMETRIC EFFICIENCY. **2.** Computer storage capacity in terms of the number of information units that can be contained on a given segment of a magnetic medium. Also called PACKING DENSITY. **3.** Within a given integrated circuit, the capacity in terms of the number of active devices that can be contained on a single silicon chip.

packet **1.** A unit of digital information in PACKET COMMUNICATIONS. It consists of a header followed by a certain number of data bits or bytes. **2.** See WAVE PACKET. **3.** See PACKET COMMUNICATIONS. **4.** See PACKET RADIO.

packet communications A method via which data can be exchanged between or among computers. Information is sent and received in units called *packets*, which are routed from the source to the destination automatically through a network.

packet radio The transmission and reception of PACKET COMMUNICATIONS data via radio.

packet switching In data communications, a standard for transmission of information units in grouped segments.

packing In the button of a carbon microphone, bunching and cohesion between the carbon granules.

packing density The number of discrete package circuits within a given surface area or volume.

packing factor **1.** See VOLUMETRIC EFFICIENCY. **2.** In computer operations, the number of bits that can be recorded in a given length of magnetic memory surface. Also called PACKING DENSITY.

pack transmitter   A portable transmitter that can be strapped to the operator's back.

pack unit   A portable transceiver that can be strapped to the operator's back or carried on an animal's back.

PACM   Abbreviation of *pulse-amplitude code modulation.*

pad   **1.** An attenuator network (usually a combination of resistors) that reduces the amplitude of a signal by a desired amount while maintaining constant input and output impedance. **2.** In computer operations, to make a record a fixed size by adding blanks or dummy characters to it. **3.** To lower the frequency of an inductance-capacitance (LC) circuit by adding capacitance to an already capacitively tuned network.

padder   See OSCILLATOR PADDER.

padding capacitor   See OSCILLATOR PADDER.

padding character   In a digital communications system, a character that is inserted solely for the purpose of consuming time while no meaningful characters are sent. The insertion of such characters maintains the synchronization of the system.

paddle-handle switch   A toggle switch the lever of which is a flattened rod. Compare BAT-HANDLE SWITCH, ROCKER SWITCH, and SLIDE SWITCH.

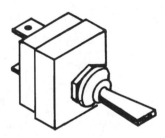

paddle-handle switch

PADT   Abbreviation of POST-ALLOY-DIFFUSED TRANSISTOR.

page   A display of text data on a computer display that completely fills the screen.

page printer   A computer peripheral that prints a message in lines on a page, according to an established format, rather than in a single line.

pager   **1.** A public-address system used for summoning purposes. **2.** See BEEPER, 2.

page turning   The successive display of pages (see PAGE).

pair   **1.** Two wires, especially two insulated conductors in a cable. **2.** A set of two particles or charge carriers (e.g., *electron-hole pair*). **3.** A set of two

transistors or vacuum tubes, operating together in push-pull or parallel in a power amplifier.

paired cable   A cable consisting of separate twisted pairs of conducting wires.

paleomagnetism   The study of certain rocks and minerals to determine the nature of the earth's magnetic field at the time the rocks were formed. When the age of the rock is determined by means of radioactive dating, and numerous rock samples are found covering many different eras, the nature of the earth's magnetic field can be graphed over time.

palladium   Symbol, Pd. A metallic element of the platinum group. Atomic number, 46. Atomic weight, 106.42.

palletizing   In industrial robots, the automatic placing of objects in a tray according to a computer program.

Palmer scan   In radar, a method of simultaneously scanning the azimuth and the elevation.

PAM   Abbreviation of PULSE-AMPLITUDE MODULATION.

Pan   In radiotelephony, a spoken word indicating that an urgent message is to follow. It is equivalent to the XXX of radiotelegraphy.

pan   **1.** To make a panoramic sweep [e.g., to sweep a wide area with a beam (as from an antenna), or to sweep a wide band of frequencies with a suitable tuning circuit]. **2.** A panoramic sweep made as defined in **1**. **3.** In audio engineering, to gradually shift from one audio channel to another or from one reproducer to another.

pan and tilt   **1.** An azimuth-elevation mounting for a television camera. **2.** The simultaneous movement of a television camera in the vertical and horizontal directions.

pancake coil   See DISK WINDING.

panel   A flat surface on which are mounted the controls and indicators of an equipment, for easy access to the operator.

panel lamp   **1.** See ELECTROLUMINESCENT PANEL. **2.** See PANEL LIGHT.

panel light   A pilot light for illuminating the front panel of a piece of equipment.

panel meter   A usually small meter for mounting on, or through an opening in, a panel.

panic button   In a security system, a button or switch that immediately triggers an alarm when it is closed.

panoramic adapter   An external device that can be connected to a receiver to sweep a frequency band and indicate carriers on the air as pips on a screen at the corresponding frequency points. Also called *pan adapter.*

panoramic display   **1.** A wide-angle display. **2.** A spectrum-analyzer display that shows a wide range of frequencies, from zero to well above the maximum frequency in the monitored system.

panoramic radar   An omnidirectional radar (i.e., one that transmits wide-beam signals in all directions without scanning).

panoramic receiver A receiver that displays pips on a screen to show carriers on the air in a given frequency band. All frequencies in the band are presented along the horizontal axis of the screen.

panpot A potentiometer with which panning can be achieved (see PAN, **3**).

pan-range A form of radar display in which target motion can be ascertained.

pantography The transmission of radar information to a distant location for observation or recording.

Papa Phonetic alphabet code word for the letter P.

paper advance mechanism In a data-processing system, the part of a printer that moves (sometimes by computer control) the paper through the printer.

paper capacitor A fixed capacitor whose dielectric is a thin film of paper. The paper is usually impregnated with wax or oil to waterproof it and to increase its dielectric constant and dielectric strength.

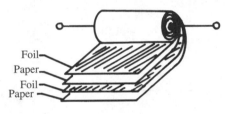

Foil
Paper
Foil
Paper

paper capacitor

PAR Abbreviation of PRECISION APPROACH RADAR.

par Abbreviation of PARALLEL.

parabola A plane curve that is the locus of points that are equidistant from a fixed point (the focus) and a fixed straight line (the directrix). In the Cartesian xy-plane, the general equation is $y = ax^2 + b$, where a and b are constants.

parabola control See VERTICAL-AMPLITUDE CONTROL, **2**.

parabola generator A circuit for generating a parabolic-waveform signal.

parabolic microphone A directional microphone mounted at the principal focus of a parabolic sound reflector; the front of the microphone faces the inside of the parabola. It is useful for detecting sounds from great distances.

parabolic reflector Also called *paraboloidal reflector*. A reflector having the shape of a paraboloid. It is particularly useful for focusing or directing radiation. For example, if a radiator, such as an antenna rod, is placed at the focus of the paraboloid, a beam of parallel rays will be emitted by the reflector.

paraboloid The surface generated by a PARABOLA rotated about its axis of symmetry.

paraffin A relatively inexpensive, easily available, solid, white petroleum wax. At one time, it was used to impregnate capacitors and coils and to waterproof paper used for insulating purposes.

parallax The apparent shift in the position of a relatively nearby object when the observer moves or alternately blinks either eye. Thus, a pointer-type meter will seem to give different readings when viewed from different angles. Some meters have mirrored scales to eliminate this effect.

parallel **1.** Pertaining to the type of operation in a computer when all elements in an information item (e.g., bits in a word) are acted upon simultaneously, rather than serially (one at a time). **2.** The condition in which two comparably sized objects or figures are equidistant at all facing points. **3.** Pertaining to the shunt connection of components or circuits.

parallel access In computer operations, inputting or outputting data to or from storage in whole elements of information items (a word, rather than a bit at a time, for example).

parallel adder In a computer or calculator, an adder in which corresponding digits in multibit numbers are added simultaneously. Also see PARALLEL, **1**.

parallel antenna tuning Antenna-feeder tuning in which the tuning capacitor is connected in parallel with the two feeder wires. Compare SERIES ANTENNA TUNING.

parallel arithmetic unit See PARALLEL ADDER.

parallel capacitance **1.** A capacitance connected in parallel (shunt) with some other component. **2.** The capacitance between the turns of a coil. Also see DISTRIBUTED CAPACITANCE.

parallel capacitors Two or more capacitors connected in parallel (shunt) with each other. The total capacitance is equal to the sum of the individual capacitances. Also see PARALLEL CIRCUIT.

parallel circuit A circuit in which the components are connected across each other (i.e., so that the circuit segment could be drawn showing component leads bridging common conductors as rungs would across a ladder). Compare SERIES CIRCUIT.

parallel-component amplifier An amplifier stage in which the active devices (transistors or vacuum tubes) are connected in parallel with each other for increased power output. Also see PARALLEL CIRCUIT.

parallel-component oscillator An oscillator stage in which transistors are connected in parallel with each other for increased power output. Also see PARALLEL CIRCUIT.

parallel computer A computer equipped to handle more than one program at a time, but not through the use of multiple programming or time-sharing.

parallel-cut crystal See Y-CUT CRYSTAL.

parallel-diode half-wave rectifier See PARALLEL LIMITER.

parallel-fed amplifier An amplifier circuit in which the direct-current operating voltage is applied in parallel with the alternating-current output voltage. Also see PARALLEL FEED.

parallel-fed oscillator An oscillator circuit in which the direct-current operating voltage is applied in parallel with the alternating-current output voltage. Also see PARALLEL FEED.

parallel feed **1.** The presentation of parallel alternating-current (ac) and direct-current (dc) voltages to a device. **2.** The presentation of a dc operating voltage in parallel with the ac output voltage of a device (as in a parallel-fed amplifier or oscillator). Also see SHUNT FEED.

parallel gap welding A welding technique using two electrodes separated by a gap.

parallel gate circuit **1.** A gate circuit using two bipolar transistors with parallel-connected collectors and emitters, and a common collector resistor. The input signal is applied to one base, and the control signal to the other. **2.** A gate circuit using two field-effect transistors with parallel-connected drains and sources, and a common drain resistor. The input signal is applied to one gate, and the control signal to the other.

parallel inductance An inductance connected in parallel (shunt) with some other component.

parallel inductors Inductors connected in parallel and separated or oriented to minimize the effects of mutual inductance. Also see PARALLEL CIRCUIT.

parallel inverse feedback In a single-ended audio amplifier circuit, a simple system for obtaining negative feedback: A high resistance is connected from the output-transistor collector or drain to the driver-transistor collector or drain.

parallel limiter A limiter (clipper) circuit in which the diode is in parallel with the signal. Compare SERIES LIMITER.

parallel-line tuning At ultra-high frequencies (UHF) and microwave frequencies, the use of two parallel wires or rods for tuning. A straight short-circuiting bar is slid along the wires to accomplish tuning.

parallelogram A two-dimensional geometric figure that has four sides. Opposite pairs of sides are parallel. Opposite interior angles have equal measure.

parallelogram of vectors A graphic device for finding the sum of two vectors. A parallelogram is constructed for which the two vectors are adjacent sides. The sum of the vectors is represented by the diagonal of the parallelogram.

parallel operation In computer operations, the simultaneous transmission of all bits in a multibit word over individual lines, as compared with the serial transmission of a word bit by bit.

parallel output A digital output consisting of two or more lines, all of which carry data at the same time.

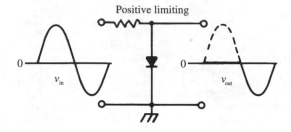

Positive limiting

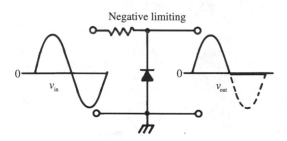

Negative limiting

parallel limiter

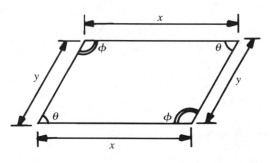

parallelogram

parallel processing In computer operations, the simultaneous processing of several different programs through separate channels. Compare SERIAL PROCESSING.

parallel Q Symbol, Q_p. The figure of merit of a parallel circuit of inductance, capacitance, and resistance.

parallel resistance **1.** A resistance connected in parallel (shunt) with some other component. **2.** The resistance between the plates of a capacitor. **3.** The resistance across a coil.

parallel resistors Resistors connected in parallel. If the individual resistances are represented by R_1, R_2, R_3, ..., R_n, then total resistance R_t is equal to $1/(1/R_1 + 1/R_2 + 1/R_3 + ... + 1/R_n)$. Also see PARALLEL CIRCUIT.

parallel resonance Resonance in a circuit consisting of a capacitor, inductor, and alternating-current source connected in parallel. At the resonant frequency, the inductive reactance is equal in magnitude, but opposite in effect, to the capacitive reactance. The capacitor current and inductor current are maximum, the line current is minimum, and the circuit impedance is maximum. Compare SERIES RESONANCE.

parallel-resonant circuit A resonant circuit in which the capacitor, inductor, and alternating-current source are connected in parallel. Compare SERIES-RESONANT CIRCUIT.

parallel-resonant trap A wavetrap consisting of a parallel-resonant inductance-capacitance (LC) circuit. Compare SERIES-RESONANT TRAP.

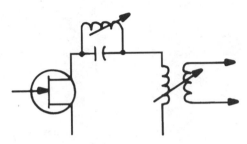

parallel-resonant trap

parallel-resonant wavetrap See PARALLEL-RESONANT TRAP.

parallel-rod oscillator An ultra-high-frequency (UHF) oscillator tuned by means of two straight, parallel quarter- or half-wave rods, one rod connected to the base or gate of a transistor, and the other rod connected to the collector or drain.

parallel-rod tuning Adjustment of the resonant frequency of a section of open-wire transmission line. A movable shorting bar allows quarter-wave resonance. The impedance at resonance is very high.

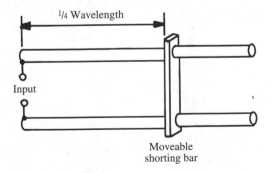

¼ Wavelength

Input

Moveable
shorting bar

parallel-rod tuning

parallel-series Also called *series-parallel.* Pertaining to an arrangement of components, usually similar (e.g., resistances), consisting of parallel circuits connected in series with each other, or of series circuits connected in parallel with each other. Usually, the component values or ratings are all identical, so currents and/or voltages are equally shared among them. Also see PARALLEL CIRCUIT and SERIES CIRCUIT.

parallel-series capacitors Capacitors connected in PARALLEL-SERIES, usually to obtain higher voltage and/or current ratings than an individual capacitor can provide.

parallel-series inductors Inductors connected in PARALLEL-SERIES and separated or oriented to minimize the effects of mutual inductance.

parallel-series resistors Resistors connected in PARALLEL-SERIES, usually to obtain a higher power rating than an individual resistor can provide.

parallel storage In a computer, storage in which all information items can be made available in the same amount of time.

parallel-tee amplifier A bandpass amplifier having a parallel-tee network in its negative-feedback path. The null frequency of the network determines the pass frequency of the amplifier.

parallel-tee measuring circuit A parallel-tee network used for measuring circuit constants. Also called TWIN-TEE MEASURING CIRCUIT.

parallel-tee network A resistance-capacitance (RC) network containing two tee sections (with R and C elements opposite in the tees) connected in parallel. The network produces a null at one frequency. Also called TWIN-T NETWORK.

parallel-tee oscillator A resistance-capacitance tuned oscillator having a parallel-tee network in its negative-feedback path. The null frequency of the network determines the oscillator frequency.

parallel transfer A form of digital information transfer, consisting of two or more lines that carry data at the same time.

parallel-wire line A transmission line consisting of two parallel wires whose separation is kept constant by dielectric rods (open-wire line) or a solid dielectric web (ribbon line).

parallel-wire tank In an ultra-high-frequency (UHF) amplifier or oscillator, a resonant circuit consisting of two separate parallel wires connected to the transistor(s) or tube(s) at one end, and short-circuited or tuned at the other end.

paramagnet A paramagnetic substance (see PARAMAGNETISM). Compare DIAMAGNET.

paramagnetic Possessing PARAMAGNETISM. Compare DIAMAGNETISM.

paramagnetism The state of having a magnetic permeability slightly greater than **1**. Compare DIAMAGNETISM.

parameter **1.** An operating value, constant, or co-efficient that can be either a dependent or an independent variable (e.g., a transistor-electrode current or voltage). **2.** The ratio of one coefficient to another, where both are either fixed or variable (e.g., transconductance of a vacuum tube).

parameter word In a computer memory, a place having a capacity of a word (bit group) in which is stored a parameter for a program.

parametric amplifier A radio-frequency power amplifier based on the action of a voltage-variable capacitor in a tuned circuit.

parametric amplifier diode See VARACTOR.

parametric converter A frequency converter in which a parametric device, such as a varactor, is used to change a signal of one frequency to a signal of another frequency. Also see PARAMETRIC DOWN-CONVERTER and PARAMETRIC UP-CONVERTER.

parametric diode A variable-capacitance diode (see VOLTAGE-VARIABLE CAPACITOR, **1**).

parametric down-converter A parametric converter in which the output signal is of a lower frequency than the input signal. Compare PARAMETRIC UP-CONVERTER.

parametric equalizer A set of audio filters similar to a GRAPHIC EQUALIZER, except that the center frequencies are adjustable, rather than fixed. The center frequencies are selected by the operator; then the attenuation level (in decibels) is set for each frequency. It is used in audio recording studios.

parametric modulation Modulation in which either the inductance or capacitance of a tank circuit or coupling device is varied at the modulation frequency.

parametric oscillator An oscillator that generates visible light energy by means of a parametric amplifier and a tunable cavity.

parametric up-converter A parametric converter in which the output signal is of a higher frequency than the input signal. Compare PARAMETRIC DOWN-CONVERTER.

parametron See PHASE-LOCKED OSCILLATOR.

paramistor A device consisting of several digital circuit elements that use parametric oscillators.

paramp Abbreviation of PARAMETRIC AMPLIFIER.

paraphase inverter A single-transistor phase inverter in which the two out-of-phase output signals are obtained by taking one output from the collector or drain, and the other output from the emitter or source. Thus, the 180-degree phase difference between collector/drain and emitter/source is exploited.

parasitic See PARASITIC OSCILLATION.

parasitic antenna An antenna that is not directly driven but, rather, is excited by energy radiated by another antenna.

parasitic capacitance Stray capacitance. It can be internal or external to a circuit and can introduce undesirable coupling or bypassing.

parasitic choke A small radio-frequency choke coil (with or without a shunting resistor) that suppresses or eliminates parasitic oscillation in a power amplifier.

parasitic director In a multielement directional antenna, a parasitic element acting as a direc-

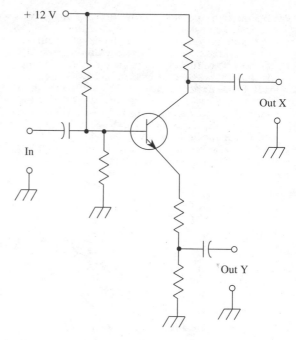

paraphase inverter

tor; usually, it is a few percent shorter than the driven element.

parasitic element In a multielement directive antenna, an element to which no direct connection is made; it receives excitation from a nearby driven element in the antenna array.

parasitic-element directive antenna A directional antenna whose forward gain, front-to-back ratio, and front-to-side ratio are the result of the action of parasitic elements, not phasing of multiple driven elements. Power is applied to a single driven element. Compare DRIVEN-ELEMENT DIRECTIVE ANTENNA.

parasitic eliminator See PARASITIC SUPPRESSOR.

parasitic excitation Excitation of a beam-antenna element without a direct connection to the transmitter. Thus, a director or reflector element can be excited by the field of the radiator element.

parasitic inductance Stray inductance (e.g., the internal inductance of a wirewound resistor).

parasitic oscillation Extraneous, useless oscillation present as a fault in an electronic circuit, particularly a radio-frequency power amplifier.

parasitic reflector In a multielement beam antenna, a parasitic element acting as a reflector; usually, it is a few percent longer than the driven element.

parasitic resistance Stray resistance (e.g., the inherent, internal resistance of a multilayer coil).

parasitic suppressor A small resistor, coil, or parallel combination of the two, connected in series with the plate or collector of a vacuum tube or transistor to eliminate parasitic oscillations in a radio-frequency power amplifier.

PARD Abbreviation of PERIODIC AND RANDOM DEVIATION.

parity 1. At par (with respect to the even-or-odd state of the characters in a group). 2. Having the quality that the number of bits (or the number of similar bits) are even or odd, as intended.

parity bit 1. In computer operations, a logic 1 added to a group of bits so that the number of 1s in the group is, according to specification, even or odd. 2. In computer operations, a check bit that can be a logic 1 or 0, depending on the parity (see PARITY, 1) of the total of 1s in the bit group being checked.

parity check A check of the integrity of data being transferred by adding the bits in, for example, a word, and then determining the parity bit needed and comparing that with the transmitted parity bit.

parity error An error disclosed by a parity check.

parity tree A digital device used to check parity.

parsec Abbreviation, pc. The distance at which the mean radius of the earth's orbit around the sun subtends an angle of 1 second of arc; 1 pc = 3.0857×10^{13} kilometers or 3.2616 light years.

part See CIRCUIT COMPONENT, 1.

part failure The usually destructive breakdown of a circuit component.

partial One of the frequencies in a complex musical tone. It might be a harmonic of the fundamental frequency, although this is not always the case.

partial carry The temporary storage of some or all of the carry information in a digital calculation.

particle 1. A tiny, discrete bit of matter. 2. A unit of matter smaller and lighter than an atom. See, for example, ANTIPARTICLE, ELECTRON, MESON, NEUTRETTO, NEUTRINO, NEUTRON, NUCLEON, POSITRON, and PROTON.

particle accelerator See ACCELERATOR, 1.

particle theory of radiation In physics, a model that explains the nature of electromagnetic radiation (radio waves, infrared, visible light, ultraviolet, X rays, and gamma rays) in terms of discrete particles. Each particle, called a PHOTON, carries a certain amount of energy that depends on the wavelength of the radiation.

particle velocity 1. The speed and direction of the particles from a source of atomic radiation. 2. The speed and direction of the molecules in the medium of an acoustic disturbance.

partitioning In computer operations, breaking down a large block of data into smaller blocks that can be better handled by the machine.

parton model A model for atomic nuclei, in which protons and neutrons are made up of smaller particles called *partons*. Subparticles have been found, commonly called *quarks*.

Pascal A high-level computer programming language, similar to BASIC or FORTRAN in structure. It is used in some schools to teach computer programming.

pascal Symbol, Pa. The SI (derived) unit of pressure; $1\ Pa = 1\ N/m^2 = 1.4503 \times 10^{-4}\ lb/in^2$.

Paschen-Back effect See ZEEMAN EFFECT.

Paschen's law For a two-element, parallel-plate, gas-discharge tube, the plate-to-plate sparking potential is proportional to Pd, where P is the gas pressure, and d is the distance between plates.

pass amplifier A tuned amplifier having the response of a bandpass filter. Like the filter, the amplifier passes one frequency (or a narrow band of frequencies) readily while rejecting or attenuating others. Compare REJECT AMPLIFIER.

passband The continuous spectrum of frequencies transmitted by a filter, amplifier, or similar device. Compare STOPBAND.

passband ripple Multiple low-amplitude attenuation variations within the passband of a filter or tuner, resulting in a ripple pattern on the nose of the response curve.

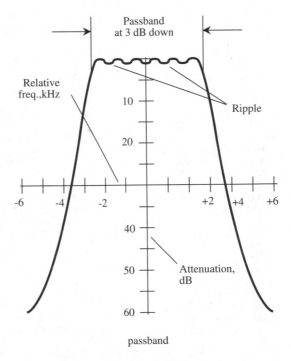

passband

passband ripple

passivation The process of growing a thin oxide film on the surface of a planar semiconductor device to protect the exposed junction(s) from contamination and short circuits. See, for example, PLANAR EPITAXIAL PASSIVATED TRANSISTOR and PLANAR TRANSISTOR.

passive absorber   A substance that reflects minimal sound energy. Examples include acoustical ceiling tile and thick carpeting.

passive circuit   A circuit consisting entirely of nonamplifying components, such as capacitors, resistors, inductors, and diodes.

passive communications satellite   A communications satellite that reflects electromagnetic waves, but does not contain a transponder; that is, it does not receive and retransmit the signals. Also called *passive comsat*. Compare ACTIVE COMMUNICATIONS SATELLITE.

passive component   A device that is basically static in operation (i.e., it is ordinarily incapable of amplification or oscillation and usually requires no power for its characteristic operation). Examples: conventional resistor, capacitor, inductor, diode, rectifier, and fuse. Compare ACTIVE COMPONENT, **1**.

passive comsat   See PASSIVE COMMUNICATIONS SATELLITE.

passive decoder   A decoder that responds to only one signal code, rejecting all others.

passive detection   In reconnaissance, detecting a target without betraying the location of the detector.

passive electric network   See PASSIVE NETWORK.

passive infrared sensor   A device that detects infrared directly, such as that given off by humans because of their body heat. It does not generate energy of any kind. It is used in some intrusion detection systems.

passive mixer   A signal mixer using only passive components (diodes, nonlinear resistors, and nonlinear reactances) (i.e., one without active components, such as transistors). Passive mixers introduce some loss. Compare ACTIVE MIXER.

passive modulator   A modulator using only passive components (diodes, nonlinear resistors, and nonlinear reactances) (i.e., one without active components, such as transistors). Passive modulators introduce some loss. Compare ACTIVE MODULATOR.

passive network   A network composed entirely of passive components (i.e., one containing no generators and providing no amplification).

passive radiator   See DRONE CONE.

passive reflector   A metal surface used to reflect electromagnetic energy at ultra-high and microwave frequencies.

passive transponder   A device that allows a machine, such as a computer or robot, to identify an object. A bar-code reader is a common example. Magnetic labels, such as those on credit cards and bank cash cards, are another example. It is so named because it does not transmit data; it requires a sensor for data detection.

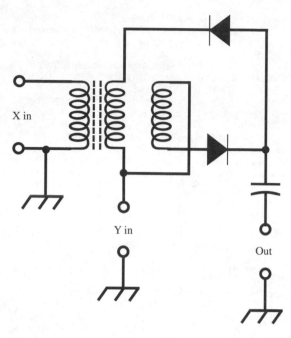

passive mixer

password   As a security device in computer operations, a group of characters upon whose presentation to the system via a terminal the user is allowed access to memory or control of information.

paste   In "dry" batteries and electrolytic capacitors, a gelatinous electrolyte.

patch   **1.** A temporary signal path, as between a radio receiver and a telephone or, conversely, between a telephone line and a radio transmitter. **2.** To make quick, usually temporary connections, as with a patch cord. **3.** Instructions entered by an unconditional branch to a computer program for the purpose of correction.

patch bay   **1.** See PATCH PANEL. **2.** A set of patch panels.

patch cord   A flexible line of one or more conductors with a jack or connector at each end, used to interconnect (patch) circuit points exposed for the purpose on a panel or breadboard.

Patchett tone control   A dual tone-control circuit using a variable series resistance-capacitance (RC) filter for treble boost, and a variable shunt RC filter for bass boost. The input signal is applied in parallel to both filters. The outputs are combined in an audio mixer.

patching   The interconnection of two or more signal media or lines.

patch panel   A panel on which the terminals of a system are accessible for interconnection, tests, etc. It is used especially in high-fidelity audio recording systems. It was once commonly used in manual telephone-switching applications.

patch up **1.** To replace faulty or damaged parts in an electronic system with roughly appropriate surrogates to restore operation quickly (usually under emergency conditions). Also see DOCTOR. **2.** To wire a circuit quickly using patch cords for preliminary test and evaluation.

patent **1.** A document awarded by a government body, giving to an inventor the exclusive right to exploit an invention for a specified number of years. Formally called *letters patent.* **2.** The monopoly granted by a document, as defined in **1**.

path **1.** The route over which current flows. **2.** In radio and navigation, the imaginary line extending directly between transmitter and receiver (or target). **3.** In a computer program, the logical order of instructions.

pathometer A form of lie detector that indicates changes in the electrical resistance of the human body.

pattern **1.** An established sequence of steps in a process. **2.** An arrangement of terms in a matrix. **3.** The graphical representation of a varying quantity (e.g., an alternating-current wave pattern). **4.** The image on the screen of an oscilloscope, or the record traced by an oscillograph. **5.** The graphic polar representation of the radiation field of an antenna. **6.** The arrangement of bits in a word or field.

pattern recognition In machine-vision systems, a method of identifying an object or decoding data according to geometric shape. Optical character recognition (OCR) is an example. The machine recognizes combinations of shapes, and deduces their meanings via a computer program.

pause editing In the editing of audio tape recordings, the use of a "pause" switch to temporarily stop the tape when necessary.

PAV Abbreviation of PHASE-ANGLE VOLTMETER.

pawl In a mechanical stepping device, as in a nonelectric clock, a device made to engage the sloping sprockets on a wheel to ensure shaft rotation in one direction only.

PAX Abbreviation of PRIVATE AUTOMATIC EXCHANGE.

pay-per-view Abbreviation, PPV. Television service in which each subscriber pays only for individually selected programs.

pay TV See SUBSCRIPTION TV.

Pb Symbol for LEAD.

P band A radio-frequency band extending from 225 to 390 MHz.

PBX Abbreviation of PRIVATE BRANCH EXCHANGE.

PC **1.** Abbreviation of PERSONAL COMPUTER. **2.** Abbreviation of PRINTED CIRCUIT. **3.** Abbreviation of PHOTOCELL. **4.** Abbreviation of POSITIVE COLUMN. **5.** Abbreviation of POINT-CONTACT.

6. Abbreviation of PERCENT (also, pct.). **7.** Abbreviation of PROGRAM COUNTER.

pc **1.** Abbreviation of PICOCOULOMB. Also, pC (preferred). **2.** Abbreviation of PICOCURIE. Also, pCi (preferred). **3.** Abbreviation of PARSEC.

pC Abbreviation for PICOCOULOMB.

PCB Abbreviation of PRINTED-CIRCUIT BOARD.

PC board See PRINTED-CIRCUIT BOARD.

PC diode See POINT-CONTACT DIODE.

p-channel JFET See P-CHANNEL JUNCTION FIELD-EFFECT TRANSISTOR.

p-channel junction field-effect transistor Abbreviation, PFET. A junction-type FET in which the gate junction has been formed on a bar or die of p-type semiconductor material. Compare N-CHANNEL JUNCTION FIELD-EFFECT TRANSISTOR.

p-channel MOSFET A metal-oxide semiconductor field-effect transistor in which the channel is composed of p-type silicon. Also see DEPLETION-TYPE MOSFET, DEPLETION-ENHANCEMENT-TYPE MOSFET, and ENHANCEMENT-TYPE MOSFET.

pCi Symbol for PICOCURIE.

PCL Abbreviation of PRINTED-CIRCUIT LAMP.

PCM Abbreviation of PULSE-CODE MODULATION.

PCM-FM Pertaining to a carrier that is frequency modulated by information that is pulse-code modulated. Also see FREQUENCY MODULATION and PULSE-CODE MODULATION.

PCM-FM-FM Pertaining to a carrier that is frequency modulated by one or more subcarriers that are frequency modulated by information that is pulse-code modulated. Also see FREQUENCY MODULATION and PULSE-CODE MODULATION.

PCM level In a pulse-code-modulated signal, one of several different possible signal conditions.

PCM-PM Pulse-code modulation that is accomplished by varying the phase of the carrier wave.

PC relay See PRINTED-CIRCUIT RELAY.

PC transistor See POINT-CONTACT TRANSISTOR.

PD **1.** Abbreviation of PLATE DISSIPATION. **2.** Abbreviation of PULSE DURATION. **3.** Abbreviation of PROXIMITY DETECTOR. **4.** Abbreviation of POTENTIAL DIFFERENCE.

Pd Symbol for PALLADIUM.

PDA Abbreviation of *predicted drift angle.*

PDAS Abbreviation of *programmable data acquisition system.*

P display See PLAN POSITION INDICATOR.

PDM Abbreviation of PULSE-DURATION MODULATION.

PDM-FM Pertaining to a carrier that is frequency modulated by one or more subcarriers that are frequency modulated by pulses that are pulse-duration modulated. Also see FREQUENCY MODULATION and PULSE-DURATION MODULATION.

PDM-FM-FM Pertaining to a carrier that is frequency modulated by one or more subcarriers that are frequency modulated by pulses that are pulse-duration modulated. Also see FREQUENCY MODULATION and PULSE-DURATION MODULATION.

PDM-PM Pertaining to a carrier that is phase modulated by pulse-duration-modulated information. Also see PHASE MODULATION and PULSE-DURATION MODULATION.

PDT Abbreviation of PACIFIC DAYLIGHT TIME.

PDVM Abbreviation of PRINTING DIGITAL VOLTMETER.

PE 1. Abbreviation of POTENTIAL ENERGY. 2. Abbreviation of PROFESSIONAL ENGINEER. 3. Abbreviation of PROBABLE ERROR.

peak 1. The maximum value of a quantity. 2. In an alternating-current cycle, the maximum positive or negative current or voltage point. 3. The frequency at which the transmission by a bandpass circuit or device is maximum (attenuation is minimum), evidenced by a maximum in the frequency-response curve.

peak amplitude 1. The maximum positive or negative current or voltage of a wave. 2. The maximum instantaneous power of a signal.

peak anode (plate) current The maximum instantaneous current flowing in the anode (plate) circuit of a vacuum tube.

peak anode (plate) voltage The maximum instantaneous voltage applied to the anode (plate) of a vacuum tube.

peak chopper See PEAK CLIPPER.

peak current Abbreviation, I_p. The highest value reached by an alternating-current half-cycle or a current pulse. Also called MAXIMUM CURRENT.

peak detector See PEAK PROBE.

peak distortion 1. The maximum instantaneous distortion in a signal, generally expressed as a percentage. 2. Distortion of a modulated signal at envelope peaks.

peaked sawtooth A wave composed of a sawtooth and peaking-pulse components. The deflection voltage of a magnetic-deflection cathode-ray tube requires this waveform to produce a current sawtooth in the deflecting coils.

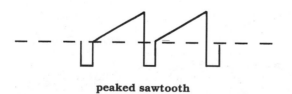

peaked sawtooth

peaked waveform An alternating-current waveform having nearly pointed positive and negative half-cycles. Such a wave contains appreciable third-harmonic energy.

peak envelope power Abbreviation, PEP. For a linear radio-frequency (RF) power amplifier handling a modulated signal, the average RF output power during a single RF cycle at the highest peak of the modulation envelope.

peaker 1. See PEAK FILTER. 2. See PEAKING TRANSFORMER.

peaker-notcher See NOTCHER-PEAKER.

peak factor For an alternating-current wave, the ratio E_m/E_{rms} or I_m/I_{rms}, where E_m is the maximum voltage, E_{rms} is the effective (root-mean-square) voltage, I_m is the maximum current, and I_{rms} is the effective current.

peak filter A frequency-selective circuit, such as a bandpass filter, for producing a peak response (see PEAK, 3).

peak inductor current In a switching regulator, the maximum instantaneous current through the inductor when the device is switching at its fully rated duty cycle.

peaking The adjustment of a control or device for maximum indication on a meter or other display.

peaking coil A small inductor used to compensate the frequency response of a circuit, such as a video amplifier or video detector. Both series and shunt peaking coils are used.

peaking transformer A transformer whose output waveform is sharply peaked (of short duration, with respect to a cycle). The effect is obtained by means of a special core that, because it contains little iron, saturates easily.

peak inverse voltage Abbreviation, PIV. Often used interchangeably with the term PEAK REVERSE VOLTAGE. 1. The peak value of the voltage applied to a rectifier diode in the reverse direction. 2. The maximum value of reverse voltage that a rectifier diode will tolerate according to its specifications.

peak level lamp In audio recording and reproduction, a bulb or light-emitting diode (LED) that illuminates when sound peaks exceed a predetermined amplitude.

peak limiting 1. A method of limiting the maximum amplitude of a signal. When the instanta-

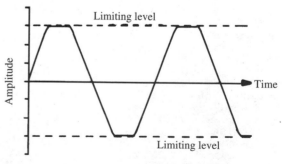

peak limiting

neous peak amplitude, either positive or negative, exceeds a certain value, the output is clipped at that value. **2.** In pulse-code modulation, the effect resulting from the application of an input signal in excess of the virtual decision value.

peak modulated power In an amplitude-modulated wave, the maximum instantaneous signal power (including the carrier and sidebands). In 100-percent sinusoidal modulation, the peak modulated power is four times the unmodulated carrier power.

peak point The highest current point in the current-voltage response curve of a tunnel diode. Immediately beyond this point, the current decreases as the applied voltage is increased, indicating a negative-resistance region. Compare VALLEY POINT.

peak power **1.** Symbol, P_p. Unit, watt. Alternating-current power that is the product of the peak voltage (E_p) and the peak current (I_p). For E_p in volts and I_p in amperes, the peak power in watts is given by $P_p = E_p I_p$. **2.** The highest output power that an amplifier or device can produce without excessive distortion. **3.** The maximum instantaneous power that a speaker can handle without risk of damage.

peak probe A voltmeter test probe containing a diode circuit whose direct-current output voltage is close to the peak value of the applied alternating-current test voltage.

peak recurrent forward current For a semiconductor diode, the maximum repetitive instantaneous forward current as measured under specified conditions of operation.

peak reverse voltage Abbreviation, PRV. In semiconductor operations, the peak value of the voltage applied in reverse polarity across the junction. It is often used interchangeably with the term PEAK INVERSE VOLTAGE.

peak signal level The maximum instantaneous signal power or voltage specified for particular operating conditions.

peak-to-peak Abbreviations, p-p or pk-pk. For an alternating-current waveform, pertaining to the arithmetic difference between the positive peak and negative peak values of current or voltage.

peak-to-peak probe A voltmeter test probe containing a diode circuit whose direct-current output voltage is close to the peak-to-peak value of the applied alternating-current test voltage.

peak-to-peak voltage The arithmetic sum of positive and negative peak voltages in an alternating-current (ac) wave. Thus, a symmetrical sine-wave ac voltage of 115.0 V rms has a peak value of 162.63 V and a peak-to-peak value of 325.3 V. Also see PEAK VOLTAGE.

peak torque Symbol, T_p. For a torque motor, the maximum useful torque at maximum recommended input current.

peak voltage Abbreviation, E_p. The highest value reached by an alternating-current voltage half

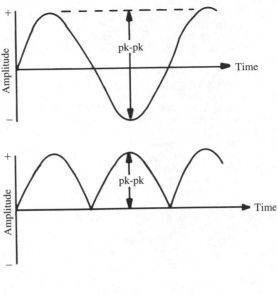

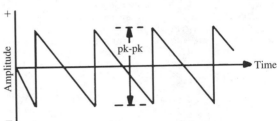

peak-to-peak voltage

cycle, or by a voltage pulse. Also called MAXIMUM VOLTAGE.

peak voltmeter **1.** An alternating-current (ac) voltmeter that responds to the peak value of the applied voltage. **2.** An ac voltmeter that responds to the average value of the applied voltage—even though its scale reads in peak volts.

pea lamp A miniature incandescent bulb, sometimes used as a control-panel or meter light.

PEC Abbreviation of PHOTOELECTRIC CELL.

pedestal See BLANKING PEDESTAL.

pedestal level See BLANKING LEVEL.

pel See PIXEL.

Peltier effect A drop below ambient temperature at the junction between two dissimilar metals when an electric current is passed through the junction.

PEM Abbreviation of *photoelectromagnetic*.

pen-and-ink recorder A graphic recorder in which a fountain-pen-type stylus inscribes an ink line on a paper chart. Also called *pen recorder*.

pencil **1.** A beam of electrons or other particles or rays that either converges to, or diverges from, a specific point. **2.** A pair of geometric entities sharing a property (e.g., lines intersecting at a single point).

pendulum switch A device that closes a circuit when subjected to physical shock. One type consists of a dangling element resembling a pendulum, with one or more nearby contacts.

penetrating frequency For a particular layer of the ionosphere, the lowest high frequency at which a vertically propagated wave penetrates the layer (i.e., it is not reflected back to earth). Also called CRITICAL FREQUENCY.

penetrating radiation Ionizing radiation that passes through otherwise opaque materials. A relative term; low-energy X rays are less penetrating than high-energy X rays, which, in turn, are less penetrating than gamma rays.

penetrating rays See COSMIC RAYS.

penetration depth See DEPTH OF PENETRATION.

pent Abbreviation of PENTODE.

pentavalent element An element whose atoms have five valence electrons (e.g., antimony or arsenic).

pentode A five-electrode vacuum tube in which the electrodes are an anode, cathode, control grid, screen grid, and suppressor grid.

pentode field-effect transistor A field-effect transistor with three separate gates.

pentode transistor A bipolar transistor with three emitters.

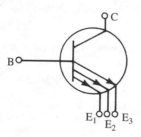

pentode transistor

penumbra **1.** That part of a shadow in which the light source is not fully obscured by the eclipsing object. **2.** In a sunspot, the outer part of the spot; it is less dark than the inner portion.

PEP **1.** Abbreviation of PLANAR EPITAXIAL PASSIVATED. **2.** Abbreviation of PEAK ENVELOPE POWER.

PEP diode See PLANAR EPITAXIAL PASSIVATED DIODE.

PEP reading wattmeter A wattmeter that shows the peak envelope power output of a transmitter.

PEP transistor See PLANAR EXPITAXIAL PASSIVATED TRANSISTOR.

perceived level The level of a disturbance, particularly sound, as sensed by a person. It is generally expressed in decibels, with respect to a

certain threshold value. The threshold is assigned an intensity of 0 dB.

percent An expression of a fraction, in terms of hundredths. A quantity of x percent indicates a fraction of $x/100$. Percent is usually abbreviated by the symbol %.

percentage error The amount by which a measured value differs from the true value, expressed as a percentage (the number of parts per 100 that the measurement is in error).

percentage-modulation meter An instrument that provides direct readings of the modulation percentage of an amplitude-modulated signal. The meter scale or dial is graduated in increments from 0 to somewhat more than 100 percent.

percentage uncertainty The maximum possible error in a measurement, expressed as a percentage of the measured value. Also see UNCERTAINTY IN MEASUREMENT.

percent distortion Symbol, %D. In the determination of harmonic distortion, the total harmonic voltage expressed as a percentage of the fundamental voltage, plus total harmonic voltage; $\%D = 100E_h/E_t$, where E_h is the total voltage of the harmonic components, and E_t is the total signal voltage (fundamental plus harmonics).

percent modulation See MODULATION PERCENTAGE.

percent modulation meter See PERCENTAGE-MODULATION METER.

percent ripple The amount of ripple voltage in the direct-current (dc) output of a rectifier or generator, expressed as a percentage of the nominal dc output voltage.

perfect crystal A crystal without defects or impurities. The atoms are arranged in a regular pattern with no faults.

perforated board A plastic panel provided with a number of small holes in orderly columns and rows for the insertion of the pigtails of components, or of push-in terminals to facilitate quick assembly of prototype circuits. Also called *perfboard.*

performance curve A curve depicting the behavior of a component or circuit under specified conditions of operation. Such a curve, for example, might display the variation of output power with input power, the variation of frequency with voltage, etc. Compare CHARACTERISTIC CURVE.

performance test A test made primarily to ascertain how a system behaves. The test is concerned with normal operation, whereas a diagnostic test is a troubleshooting procedure. Compare TROUBLESHOOTING TEST.

perimeter protection The use of a security system to restrict or prevent access to a designated area, using sensors and/or barriers around the boundaries of the area.

period Symbol, T. Unit, second. The duration of a complete alternating-current cycle or of any cyclic event; $T = 1/f$, where f is the frequency in Hertz. Also see CYCLE, FREQUENCY, and HERTZ.

periodic and random deviation Abbreviation, PARD. In the direct-current output of a rectifier, the combined PERIODIC DEVIATION, including ripple, noise, hum, and transient spikes.

periodic curve A curve that repeats its shape in each period (e.g., a sine curve).

periodic deviation Repetitive deviation of a quantity from its normal value (e.g., ripple in the direct-current output of a rectifier).

periodic function A mathematical function that is represented by a periodic curve (e.g., the sine function $y = \sin x$).

periodicity In a transmission line, the tendency for power to be reflected at a point or points where the diameter of the line changes.

periodic law The observation that when the chemical elements (see ELEMENT, **3**) are arranged in increasing order of atomic number, their physical and chemical properties recur periodically. Also see PERIODIC TABLE.

periodic table A table in which the chemical elements (see ELEMENT, **3**) are arranged according to the periodic law. The vertical columns in the table, labeled groups, contain elements possessing related properties (e.g., silicon and germanium in group IV). The rows, labeled periods, depict the periodic shift in the properties of the elements.

peripheral **1.** Pertaining to equipment accessory to a central system (e.g., peripheral input/output devices online or offline to computers, data recorders, and indicators). Also see ANCILLARY EQUIPMENT. **2.** Peripheral equipment in a computer system (e.g., printers, modems, external disk drives, tape drives, etc.).

peripheral buffer As part of a peripheral in a computer system, a storage unit in which data temporarily resides on its way to or from the central processing unit. Also called INPUT/OUTPUT BUFFER.

peripheral electron See VALENCE ELECTRON.

peripheral equipment See PERIPHERAL, **1, 2**.

peripheral interface adapter Abbreviation, PIA. An integrated circuit that acts as an input/output port to interface a microprocessor with peripheral devices.

peripheral transfer In a computer system, the transfer of a unit of data between peripherals, or between a peripheral and the central processing unit.

Permalloy A high-permeability alloy of iron and nickel.

permamagnetic speaker See PERMANENT-MAGNET SPEAKER.

permanent magnet A body that is always magnetized (i.e., without the application of electricity and without requiring the presence of another magnet). Compare TEMPORARY MAGNET.

permanent-magnet erase Erasure of magnetic tape by the field of a permanent magnet. Typically, it is a two-step process: a magnet erases what it can of the signal, leaving any residual magnetization for erasure by a second magnet.

permanent-magnet focusing In a cathode-ray tube, the focusing of the electron beam by means of permanent magnets.

permanent-magnet generator An electromechanical generator in which the field (either stationary or rotating) is provided by a multipole permanent magnet. Also called *magneto*.

permanent-magnet loudspeaker See PERMANENT-MAGNET SPEAKER.

permanent-magnet magnetizer A magnetizer using a permanent magnet as the magnetic-field source.

permanent-magnet meter An indicating meter in which a movable coil rotates between the poles of a permanent magnet. Compare ELECTRODYNAMOMETER and IRON-VANE METER.

permanent-magnet motor A motor having a permanent-magnet field.

permanent-magnet relay A polarized relay using a permanent magnet.

permanent-magnet speaker An acoustic loudspeaker in which the core is a strong permanent magnet (as opposed to a direct-current electromagnet). Also see MAGNETIC SPEAKER.

permanent storage See NONVOLATILE MEMORY.

permeability Unit, H/m. A quantitative indicator of the extent to which a material concentrates magnetic flux: for a given constant magnetic-field intensity, the ratio of magnetic flux density in the material to the magnetic flux density in air.

permeability curve See B-H CURVE.

permeability-tuned oscillator A radio-frequency oscillator in which the frequency is varied or adjusted by moving a ferromagnetic core in and out of the coil of an inductance-capacitance (LC) tuned circuit.

permeability tuning Variation of the resonant frequency of an inductance-capacitance LC circuit by changing the position of a magnetic core within the inductor. This type of tuning is used in amplifiers, oscillators, filters, and wavetraps.

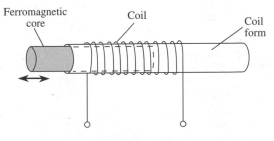

permeability tuning

permeameter   An instrument for measuring permeability.

permeance   Unit, Wb/A. In a magnetic circuit, the ease with which a magnetic field is established. The reciprocal of RELUCTANCE.

Permendur   A high-permeability magnetic alloy containing equal parts of iron and cobalt. At saturation, the flux density of this material can be 2 teslas (20,000 gauss).

Perminvar   A high-permeability magnetic alloy of cobalt, iron, and nickel. At saturation, the flux density of this material can approach 1.2 teslas (12,000 gauss).

permittivity   See DIELECTRIC CONSTANT.

permutation   A selection of several factors or objects from a group, in a specific ordered sequence. For example, one of the permutations of the elements of the set (1, 2, 3, 4, and 5) is the ordered sequence 4, 1, 3, 5, 2.

permutation modulation   A method of modulation accomplished by varying the sequence of digital bits.

peroxide of lead   In a lead-acid cell or battery, a compound of lead and oxygen that composes the positive electrode or electrodes.

persistence   **1.** The effect whereby the retina of the eye continues to register a projected scene for approximately 0.05 second after the scene disappears. This allows perception of a sequence of video frames as a continuous moving image. **2.** The tendency of certain phosphors to glow after the excitation has been removed. Thus, after the electron beam in a cathode-ray tube has passed over the screen, the phosphor might continue to glow for a certain time along the path traced by the beam. Some phosphors, such as those used in high-speed oscilloscopes, have virtually no persistence, whereas others have long persistence.

persistent oscillations   Successive oscillations of constant amplitude. Also called CONTINUOUS WAVE.

persistor   A device used at low temperatures for temporary memory storage that operates between superconducting and normal conditions.

personal computer   A small computer equipped with a keyboard, display, hard disk, diskette drive(s), a modem or fax/modem, one or more serial data ports, and one or more parallel data ports. They are used extensively by individuals and businesses for record keeping, data processing, communications, word processing, graphics, etc.; they are also used in schools as an educational aid.

personal equation   The value of systematic error for a person observing specific phenomena or making measurements.

personality   Characteristics that make an intelligent computer or robot human-like. In general, the more powerful the computer, the more personality it can have, depending on the installed software. In some cases, certain malfunctions in a computer can produce personality quirks.

personal robot   A usually autonomous robot intended for use by individuals. The most common examples are robot toys, programmable with a PERSONAL COMPUTER, intended for the education and entertainment of children. More sophisticated devices can perform domestic tasks, such as cleaning floors and mowing lawns.

peta-   Abbreviation, P. A prefix meaning 10^{15}.

petagram   Abbreviation, Pg. A large unit of mass or force, equal to 10^{15} grams or 10^{12} kilograms.

petameter   Abbreviation, Pm. A large unit of (astronomical) distance, equal to 10^{15} meters or 10^{12} kilometers.

pF   Abbreviation of PICOFARAD.

pf   Symbol for POWER FACTOR.

PFET   Abbreviation of P-CHANNEL JUNCTION FIELD-EFFECT TRANSISTOR.

PFM   Abbreviation of PULSE-FREQUENCY MODULATION.

PG   Abbreviation of POWER GAIN.

Pg   Abbreviation of PETAGRAM.

pH   **1.** Symbol for *hydrogen-ion concentration*. Numerically, pH is the negative logarithm of the effective hydrogen-ion concentration in gram equivalents per liter. The scale runs from zero to 14, on which 7 denotes neutrality relative to acidity vs. alkalinity; values between zero and 7 denote acidity, and values between 7 and 14 denote alkalinity. **2.** Abbreviation of PICOHENRY.

phantom   Radio interference in the form of a beat note (heterodyne), resulting from interference between two strong carriers, often from local radio stations. When the phantom frequency lies within the tuning range of a receiver, the phantom can be tuned in as a separate signal. But when the phantom corresponds to the intermediate frequency (IF) of the receiver, it will ride into the IF amplifier and be present as an untunable interferential signal.

phantom channel   In a properly phased high-fidelity stereo sound system, the apparent sound source centered between the left- and right-channel loudspeakers.

phantom circuit   In wire telephony, a third circuit that has no wires; it results from a method (using repeating coils) of making two other circuits do the work of (this third) one.

phantom signal   Also called *bogey*. In a radar system, a signal that does not correspond to an actual target. The origin of the phantom signal or echo cannot be readily determined.

phantom target   See ECHO BOX.

phase angle   Unit, degree or radian. In an alternating-current (ac) circuit, the lag or lead between the instant that one alternating quantity reaches its maximum value and the instant that another alternating quantity reaches its maximum value. It is usually given in degrees (a complete cycle being 360 degrees) along the horizontal axis of the time-versus-magnitude graph of the ac quantity.

phase-angle voltmeter An instrument that indicates both the magnitude and phase of a voltage.

phase compensation In an operational amplifier, compensation for excessive phase shift in the feedback.

phase compressor A push-pull phase-inverter circuit in which a capacitor is connected between each collector or drain and the opposite output terminal to attenuate in-phase components, such as even-numbered harmonics.

phase constant A figure providing the rate (in degrees of phase per unit length) at which the phase lag of the current or voltage field component in a traveling wave increases linearly in the propagation direction.

phase corrector A circuit that returns a signal to a certain phase after the signal has passed through a circuit or medium that has caused phase distortion.

phased antennas Separate antennas (or antenna elements) excited directly or parasitically, in or out of phase with each other. The radiation pattern changes according to phasing.

phase-delay equalizer See DELAY EQUALIZER.

phase detector See PHASE-SENSITIVE DETECTOR.

phase diagram A graphical representation of waves having equal frequency, but differing in phase. The phase difference for two identical waveforms is greater than or equal to zero degrees, but less than 360 degrees.

phase difference **1.** The difference (in time, angle, or fractional cycle) between the instants at which two alternating quantities reach a given value. **2.** For a dielectric, the complement of PHASE ANGLE; that is, 90 degrees minus the phase angle in degrees.

phase discriminator See DISCRIMINATOR, FOSTER-SEELEY DISCRIMINATOR, RATIO DETECTOR, and TRAVIS DISCRIMINATOR.

phase distortion Distortion characterized by input/output phase shift between various components of a signal passed by a circuit or device.

phase inverter A resistance-capacitance-coupled amplifier with a single-ended input and a push-pull output. This circuit enables a push-pull amplifier to be driven without an input transformer.

phase-locked loop Abbreviation, PLL. A circuit containing an oscillator whose output phase is automatically adjusted to keep it in sync with the signal from a local oscillator. It is used in frequency-synthesized radio transmitters and receivers. It can also act as a detector in a frequency-modulation (FM) or phase-modulation (PM) receiver. Also see PHASE-SENSITIVE DETECTOR.

phase-locked oscillator An oscillator in which the inductance or the capacitance is varied periodically at half the driving frequency.

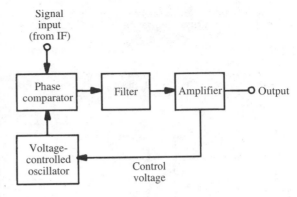

phase-locked loop

phase margin In an integrated-circuit amplifier, the extent to which the device shifts the phase of a signal more or less than one-half cycle (180 degrees) for a certain signal voltage.

phase modulation Abbreviation, PM. A method of modulation in which the phase of the carrier current is varied in accordance with the instantaneous modulating-signal voltage. The result is similar to FREQUENCY MODULATION.

phase modulator A circuit or stage that produces PHASE MODULATION.

phase multiplier A circuit used for the purpose of phase comparison between signals. The frequency of the measured signal is multiplied, resulting in multiplication of the phase difference. This improves the sensitivity of the measuring apparatus.

phase resonance See VELOCITY RESONANCE.

phase reversal **1.** The inversion of an alternating-current (ac) signal. The instantaneous amplitude (current or voltage) is multiplied by a negative constant. Thus, the positive half-cycles become negative, and the negative half-cycles become positive. **2.** A phase shift of ±180 degrees (±½ cycle) in an ac signal.

phase-rotation relay See PHASE-SEQUENCE RELAY.

phase-rotation system A system for producing single-sideband signals without using selective filters. In one such system, two balanced modulators are used. One of these receives carrier and modulating voltages that are 90 degrees out of phase with voltages that are fed to the other balanced modulator.

phase-sensitive detector Abbreviation, PSD. A detector for frequency modulation (FM) and phase modulation (PM). It delivers a direct-current output voltage whose value is proportional to the difference in phase between a reference signal and the signal from a local oscillator.

phase-sequence relay In a polyphase system, a relay or relay circuit that is actuated by voltages reaching maximum positive amplitude in a predetermined phase sequence. Also called PHASE-ROTATION RELAY.

phase shift **1.** A change in the displacement, as a function of time, of a periodic disturbance having constant frequency. **2.** The magnitude of a change, as defined in **1**, measured in fractions of a wavelength or in electrical degrees.

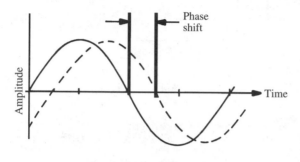

phase shift

phase-shift bridge A four-arm-bridge circuit for shifting the phase of an alternating-current signal. Such a circuit is often used (with one arm variable) to shift the phase of the firing voltage for a thyratron.

phase-shift discriminator See FOSTER-SEELEY DISCRIMINATOR.

phase shifter A circuit, such as an inductance-capacitance (LC) or resistance-capacitance (RC) network, or a device, such as a Helmholtz coil or phase-shifting capacitor, that introduces a phase shift between input and output signals.

phase-shifting capacitor A special four-stator, one-rotor variable capacitor that, with a transformer-coupled resistance-capacitance (RC) circuit, provides 360 degrees of continuously variable phase shift for one rotation of the rotor. The rotor plate turns like a cam under the stators because of the off-center insertion of the rotor shaft.

phase-shift oscillator A single-stage oscillator in which the required 180-degree phase shift in the signal (fed back from output to input) is obtained by passing the output through a phase-shifting network.

phase-shift-type distortion meter A distortion meter in which the output signal of a device under test is compared with a distortion-free input test signal. The output signal phase is shifted 180 degrees, with respect to the input, and the two amplitudes are made equal. If there is no distortion, the signals cancel each other, and the result is zero. Any remaining signal is proportional to the total harmonic distortion (THD).

phase-splitting circuit A circuit that produces, from a single input signal, two output signals differing in phase.

phase-splitting driver A PHASE INVERTER used as the driver of a push-pull amplifier.

phase velocity The velocity of a wave, provided by the product of the frequency and the wavelength.

phase windings In an alternating-current generator, windings that deliver voltages that differ in phase.

phasing capacitor In a crystal filter, a small variable capacitor that constitutes one arm of a four-arm bridge in which the crystal is another arm. Adjustment of this capacitor balances the bridge, thus preventing the undesirable passage of a signal through the capacitance of the crystal holder.

phenol-formaldehyde plastics A family of plastic insulating materials made with phenolic resin, and occasionally used as dielectrics and air-core coil forms. Some of the trade names for these materials include *Bakelite, Catalin, Durez, Durite, Formica,* and *Micarta.*

phenolic insulants See PHENOL-FORMALDEHYDE PLASTICS.

phenolic resin A synthetic resin made by condensing phenol (carbolic acid) with formaldehyde.

phenomenon An event or circumstance that can be verified by the senses, as opposed to one subject to theory or speculation (e.g., the phenomenon of magnetic attraction).

Phillips gate A device that allows measurement of the gas pressure in a confined chamber. A current is passed through the gas. The magnitude of the current, for a given gas, is a function of the gas pressure and temperature.

Phillips screw A screw with a pair of slots in its head. The slots are arranged like an x. Phillips screws are available in many different sizes, as are ordinary screws. The x-shaped pair of slots reduces the tendency for the screwdriver to slip out of the screw head as the screw is rotated.

Phi phenomenon The illusion of motion resulting from the rapid presentation to the eye of pictures showing objects in a succession of different positions. Television and motion pictures exploit this illusion. Also see PERSISTENCE.

pH meter An instrument used to measure the acidity or alkalinity of solutions. Also see PH, **1**.

phon A unit of apparent change in loudness discerned by a listener. Unlike the decibel, the phon includes compensation for the ear's nonlinear response to attendant frequency changes. At a frequency of 1 kHz, a change in loudness of 1 phon is the equivalent of 1 decibel.

phone **1.** Telephone (wire or radio). **2.** To establish communication via telephone. **3.** Colloquialism for voice communication (radiotelephone), particularly via amateur-radio single sideband on the high-frequency bands (160 through 10 meters). **4.** A minimal, unique speech sound. Also called SOUND UNIT.

phoneme An individual sound or syllable in the human voice, with a characteristic amplitude-vs.-frequency spectral pattern. It is important in speech recognition and speech synthesis. Computers can be programmed to identify and transcribe these sounds; computers can also be programmed to generate the sounds from text data.

phone jack   The female mating device for a PHONE PLUG.

phone monitor   A simple device for listening to amplitude-modulated radio transmissions to test their quality. In its most rudimentary form, it consists of a pickup antenna, semiconductor-diode detector, and high-resistance headphones.

phone patch   A device for establishing a connection (patch) between radio and wire-telephone facilities. Also see PATCH.

phone plug   A type of plug originally designed for patching telephone circuits, now widely used in electronics and instrumentation. In its conventional form, it has a rod-shaped neck that serves as one contact, and a ball on the tip of the neck, but insulated from it, that serves as the other contact. Typical diameters are ⅛ inch and ¼ inch.

phone plug

phone test set   An instrument for checking the performance of a radiotelephone transmitter. The set combines the functions of field-strength meter, modulation indicator, and aural monitor. Sometimes it includes a volt-ohm-milliammeter for troubleshooting the transmitter.

phonetic alphabet   Words whose initial letters are used to identify the letters of the alphabet for which they stand. These words are spoken in radiotelephony to identify letters that, if spoken by themselves, might not be clearly heard.

Phonetic alphabet

Letter	Phonetic (Capitals indicate emphasis)
A	AL-fa
B	BRAH-vo
C	CHAR-lie
D	DEL-ta
E	ECK-o
F	FOX-trot

Phonetic alphabet continued

Letter	Phonetic (Capitals indicate emphasis)
G	GOLF
H	ho-TEL
I	IN-dia
J	Ju-li-ETTE
K	KEE-low
L	LEE-ma
M	Mike
N	No-VEM-ber
O	OS-car
P	pa-PA
Q	Que-BECK
R	ROW-me-oh
S	see-AIR-ah
T	TANG-go
U	YOU-ni-form
V	VIC-tor
W	WHIS-key
X	X-ray
Y	YANK-key
Z	ZOO-loo

phonetic alphabet code word   In radio and wire telephony, a word chosen for its easy recognition by ear to identify the letter of the alphabet with which it begins. For example: *Golf* for G, *Juliet* for J, *X-ray* for X.

phonics   See ACOUSTICS, 1.

phonocardiogram   The record made by a PHONO-CARDIOGRAPH.

phonocardiograph   An instrument that makes a graphic record of heart sounds.

phono cartridge   The vibration-to-electricity transducer (pickup) of a phonograph; it is actuated by the stylus (needle). Common types are ceramic, variable-inductance, and variable-reluctance. See PHONOGRAPH and PHONOGRAPH DISC.

phonocatheter   A microphone that can be inserted into the body for the purpose of listening to the functions of internal organs.

phonograph   A device for reproducing sound recorded on disc. It consists of a turntable, an amplifier, and one or more speakers.

phonograph cartridge   See PHONO CARTRIDGE.

phonograph disc   A thin, lightweight disc, usually made of vinyl or similar plastic, on which audio-frequency signals are recorded as irregularities in a spiral groove. In reproduction, these irregularities cause vibration in a PHONO CARTRIDGE as the turntable rotates.

phonograph oscillator   See PHONO OSCILLATOR.

phono jack   Also called *RCA jack*. A jack similar to a PHONE JACK, designed especially for the quick connection and disconnection of coaxial cables used with audio and low-frequency devices.

phonon   A unit of energy resulting from vibration, as of a piezoelectric crystal.

phono oscillator A small radio-frequency (RF) oscillator modulated by the audio-frequency (AF) voltage from a phonograph. The modulated RF signal is picked up by a remote radio receiver (usually in the same room), and the sound is reproduced through a loudspeaker connected to the receiver.

phono plug Also called *RCA plug.* A plug similar to a PHONE PLUG, designed especially for the quick connection and disconnection of coaxial cables used with audio and low-frequency devices.

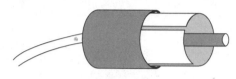

phono plug

phonoreception The hearing of high-frequency sounds.

phonorecord A PHONOGRAPH disc.

phonoselectroscope A special type of stethoscope, in which the main heartbeat is attenuated. This makes abnormal sounds more audible. The device can be adjusted in various ways to listen for abnormalities characteristic of various heart diseases.

phosphor A substance that glows when an electron beam strikes it. Such a substance is used as a coating on the screens of cathode-ray tubes. See also BEAT ZINC SILICATE; CADMIUM BORATE, SILICATE, and TUNGSTATE; CALCIUM PHOSPHATE, SILICATE, and TUNGSTATE; MAGNESIUM FLUORIDE, SILICATE, and TUNGSTATE; ZINC ALUMINATE; ZINC BERYLLIUM SILICATE; ZINC BERYLLIUM ZIRCONIUM SILICATE; ZINC BORATE; ZINC CADMIUM SULFIDE; ZINC GERMANATE; ZINC MAGNESIUM FLUORIDE; ZINC ORTHOSILICATE; ZINC OXIDE; ZINC SILICATE; and ZINC SULFIDE.

phosphor bronze A form of bronze whose elasticity, hardness, and toughness have been greatly improved by the addition of phosphorus. The metal is used for brushes, springs, switch blades, and contacts.

phosphor copper An alloy of copper and phosphorus used in the manufacture of PHOSPHOR BRONZE.

phosphorescence The property of some materials that ordinarily fluoresce to continue to glow after the stimulus (light or an electron beam) has been removed. Compare FLUORESCENCE.

phosphorescent screen A viewing screen coated with a phosphor (e.g., oscilloscope screen).

phosphorous Exhibiting the properties of phosphor (e.g., glowing after stimulation with light). Not to be confused with PHOSPHORUS.

phosphorus Symbol, P. A nonmetallic element of the nitrogen family. Atomic number, 15. Atomic weight, 30.974. It is used as a dopant in semiconductor processing.

phot The cgs unit of illumination: The direct illumination produced upon a one-centimeter-distant surface by a uniform point source of one international foot-candle. Equivalent to one lumen per square centimeter.

photocathode **1.** The photomosaic of a video camera tube. **2.** The light-sensitive cathode in a phototube.

PhotoCD Trade name for an image-recording system developed by Kodak, in which photographs can be stored on compact discs. Viewing is accomplished using personal computers.

photocell See PHOTOELECTRIC CELL.

photocell amplifier An amplifier used to boost the output of a photocell. With respect to the nature of the input signal, it can be an alternating-current (ac) or direct-current (dc) amplifier, depending on whether the output of the photocell is modulated dc or pure dc.

photochemical effect The phenomenon whereby certain substances undergo chemical change when exposed to light or other radiant energy. An example of such a substance is the silver bromide, silver chloride, or silver iodide on photographic film.

photoconductive cell A photoelectric cell, such as the cadmium-sulfide type, whose resistance is proportional to the intensity of light impinging upon it. The photoconductive cell acts as a light-sensitive variable resistor in a current path. Also see PHOTOCONDUCTIVE MATERIAL.

photoconductive effect The tendency for the electrical resistance of a substance to change when infrared radiation, visible light, or ultraviolet radiation strikes it. Different substances exhibit different degrees of this effect.

photoconductive material A substance that exhibits decreased electrical resistance when exposed to infrared rays, visible light, or ultraviolet. Some photoconductive substances are cadmium selenide, cadmium sulfide, germanium, lead sulfide, selenium, silicon, and thallous sulfide. Also see ACTINOELECTRIC EFFECT.

photoconductivity The phenomenon whereby the electrical resistance of certain materials (such as cadmium sulfide, cadmium selenide, germanium, selenium, and silicon) is lowered upon exposure to infrared rays, visible light, or ultraviolet. Also see PHOTOCONDUCTIVE MATERIAL.

photoconductor **1.** See PHOTOCONDUCTIVE MATERIAL. **2.** See PHOTOCONDUCTIVE CELL.

photocurrent See PHOTOELECTRIC CURRENT.

photo-Darlington Also, *photodarlington.* **1.** A phototransistor fabricated as a Darlington amplifier for high output current. **2.** A combination of photodiode (see LIGHT-SENSITIVE DIODE) and Darlington amplifier.

photodecomposition Chemical breakdown by the action of radiant energy. Also called *photolysis.*

photodetachment The removal of an electron from an atom or ion, resulting from the impact of a PHOTON.

photodetector 1. An illumination meter that uses a PHOTOCELL. **2.** See OPTOELECTRONIC COUPLER.

photodielectric effect The tendency for the dielectric constant of a substance to change when infrared radiation, visible light, or ultraviolet radiation strikes it. Different substances exhibit different degrees of this effect.

photodiffusion effect See DEMBER EFFECT.

photodiode See LIGHT-SENSITIVE DIODE.

photodisintegration In the nucleus of an atom, disintegration resulting from PHOTON bombardment.

photoelasticity The tendency for the light-transmission characteristics of a substance to change with externally applied forces.

photoelectric alarm An alarm actuated when a light beam impinging on a photocell is interrupted.

photoelectric amplifier 1. An amplifier for boosting the output of a photosensitive device. **2.** An OPTOELECTRONIC COUPLER possessing gain.

photoelectric cell A device that converts infrared, visible-light, or ultraviolet energy into electricity or electrical effects. It can function by producing a voltage (see PHOTOVOLTAIC CELL, SELENIUM CELL, SILICON CELL, SOLAR CELL, and SUN BATTERY) or by acting as a light-sensitive resistor (see LIGHT-SENSITIVE DIODE, PHOTOCONDUCTIVE CELL, and SELENIUM CELL).

photoelectric constant The quantity h/e, where h is Planck's constant and e is the unit electron charge.

photoelectric counter A counting device (electromechanical or fully electronic) that counts objects as they interrupt a light beam impinging upon a photocell.

photoelectric disintegration See PHOTODISINTEGRATION.

photoelectric effect The phenomenon whereby temporary changes occur in the atoms of certain substances under the influence of infrared, visible light, or ultraviolet radiation. Some of these materials undergo a change in their electrical resistance, whereas others generate electric current (see, for comparison, PHOTOCONDUCTIVE MATERIAL and PHOTOVOLTAIC MATERIAL).

photoelectric efficiency See QUANTUM YIELD.

photoelectric field-effect transistor See PHOTOFET.

photoelectricity Electricity produced by the action of light on certain materials, such as cesium, selenium, and silicon. Also see PHOTOEMISSION and PHOTOVOLTAIC CELL.

photoelectric material See PHOTOCONDUCTIVE MATERIAL and PHOTOEMISSIVE MATERIAL.

photoelectric multiplier A device that internally amplifies the current resulting from bombardment by infrared, visible light, or ultraviolet radiation. A PHOTOMULTIPLIER TUBE is an example of such a device.

photoelectric photometer An instrument that uses a photoelectric device for the purpose of measuring the intensity of infrared radiation, visible light, or ultraviolet radiation.

photoelectric proximity sensor A device that uses a light-beam generator, a photodetector, an amplifier, and a microprocessor to detect the presence of nearby objects. It is useful in robot guidance systems.

photoelectric pyrometer An optical pyrometer in which a photocell and appropriate filters act instead of the human eye.

photoelectric relay A relay actuated directly by a photocell or a photocell and amplifier. This type of relay is the basis of some PHOTOELECTRIC ALARM devices.

photoelectric sensor 1. See ELECTRIC EYE. **2.** See PHOTOELECTRIC PROXIMITY SENSOR. **3.** See PHOTOELECTRIC CELL.

photoelectric smoke alarm An alarm that is tripped by a PHOTOELECTRIC SMOKE DETECTOR when the density of smoke exceeds a safe level.

photoelectric smoke control A system for making automatic adjustments to a burning process when the smoke density exceeds a prescribed level. The initial element in the system is a PHOTOELECTRIC SMOKE DETECTOR.

photoelectric smoke detector A smoke detector in which a photocell, photodiode, phototransistor, or phototube is excited by a light beam passing through the air. The cell output current decreases when smoke fills the air. This current change trips an alarm or deflects an indicating meter when the density of the smoke exceeds a prescribed level.

photoelectric tape reader A punched-tape reader using a photocell, photodiode, phototransistor, or phototube to sense light passing through the holes.

photoelectric transducer A photocell, photodiode, phototransistor, or phototube used as a sensor.

photoelectric tube See PHOTOTUBE.

photoelectric wattmeter A power-measuring instrument useful for the approximate measure-

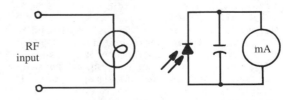

photoelectric wattmeter

ment of radio-frequency power. It consists of an incandescent lamp sharing an opaque enclosure with a photovoltaic cell. The power to be measured is applied to the lamp, which glows proportionately. The light excites the cell, causing it to deliver a direct current proportional to the power. This current deflects a milliammeter or microammeter. The meter can be calibrated to read directly in watts.

photoelectromotive force   The electromotive force (voltage) produced by a photovoltaic cell.

photoelectron   An electron displaced within, or ejected from, an atom, as the result of infrared, visible light, or ultraviolet radiation striking the atom.

photo-emf   See PHOTOELECTROMOTIVE FORCE.

photoemission   The ejection of electrons from certain materials, such as cesium, when these materials are exposed to infrared, visible light, or ultraviolet radiation. Also see PHOTOEMISSIVE MATERIAL.

photoemissive material   A substance that emits electrons when exposed to infrared, visible light, or ultraviolet radiation. A typical use of such a material is in the coating of the light-sensitive cathode of a phototube. The metals cesium, potassium, rubidium, and sodium are photoemissive.

photofabrication   1. A method of circuit-board manufacturing. The etching pattern is placed over the circuit-board material, the board is placed in a special solution, then the assembly is exposed to visible light. The light interacts with the solution to dissolve the metal in areas exposed to the light, but not in areas covered by the etching pattern. 2. The technique in 1, applied to the manufacture of integrated circuits.

photoFET   A FIELD-EFFECT TRANSISTOR that exhibits properties similar to those of a bipolar PHOTOTRANSISTOR.

photoflash   See ELECTRONIC FLASH, 1.

photoglow tube   See DISCHARGE LAMP.

photogram   The permanent shadow produced by an object placed between a light source and photographic paper.

photographic exposure meter   See EXPOSURE METER, 1.

photographic recorder   A graphic recorder that uses a light beam, deflected by galvanometer movement, that moves across photographic film or paper to produce a trace representing a varying quantity.

photographic sound recording   See OPTICAL SOUND RECORDING.

photograph reception   1. The use of FACSIMILE to print photographs transmitted in analog form via wire or radio. 2. The use of a computer, equipped with a modem and graphics software, to display and/or store photographs transmitted in digital form via wire or radio.

photograph transmission   1. The use of FACSIMILE to scan and send photographs in analog

form via wire or radio. 2. The use of a computer, equipped with a modem and video camera or optical scanner, to digitize and send photographs via wire or radio.

photoionization   The ejection of electrons from atoms or molecules by the action of infrared, visible light, or ultraviolet radiation.

photoisolator   See OPTOELECTRONIC COUPLER.

photojunction cell   A photocell consisting of a semiconductor pn junction. The cell is useful mainly for its photoconductivity, although infrared, visible light, or ultraviolet energy striking the junction produces a small amount of photovoltaic action.

photokinesis   Light-induced motion, as in a RADIOMETER.

photolithographic process   A method of producing integrated circuits and printed circuits by photographing (often at considerable reduction) an enlarged pattern of the circuit on a suitable light-sensitized surface of metal or semiconductor, and chemically etching away unwanted portions of the surface.

photolysis   See PHOTODECOMPOSITION.

photomagnetic effect   Light-sensitive magnetic susceptibility in some materials.

photomap   A photo taken of terrain from a high altitude and usually overlaid with a reference grid.

photomask   In PHOTOFABRICATION, the transparent film or template on which the etching pattern is drawn.

photometer   An instrument used to compare the luminous intensity of two light sources.

photometric measurement of power   See PHOTOELECTRIC WATTMETER.

photometry   The science of visible-light measurement. The response of the human eye is used as the basis for preferred sensors (those used with photometric instruments, which have spectral

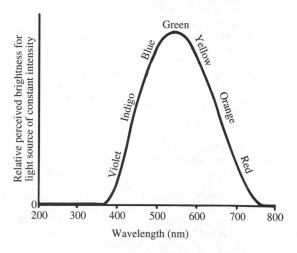

photometry

sensitivity curves resembling those of the eye). Compare RADIOMETRY.

photomosaic In a television camera tube, the flat photocathode screen on which the image is projected by the lens system and scanning electron beam. The surface of the screen is covered with tiny light-sensitive droplets. Also see DISSECTOR TUBE, ICONOSCOPE, and ORTHICON.

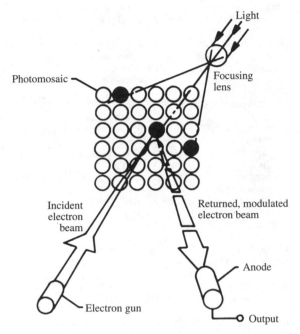

photomosaic

photomultiplier tube A type of PHOTOTUBE that delivers high output current for a given light intensity by utilizing the secondary emission of electrons. The initial light-sensitive cathode emits electrons; these strike a specially placed metal plate with a force that dislodges more electrons. These electrons, together with the initial emission, are reflected to a second plate, where they dislodge still more electrons. This process continues from deflection plate to deflection plate through the tube. The final plate deflects the accumulated electrons to the anode (collector electrode).

photon A quantum of radiant energy whose energy constant W (in joules) is equal to hf, where h is the PLANCK CONSTANT and f is the frequency in Hertz.

photoneutron A neutron released by PHOTODISINTEGRATION.

photophone **1.** A telephone-type communication system using a modulated light beam transmitted between stations. **2.** A process for recording sound on motion-picture film (see OPTICAL SOUND RECORDING).

photorelay See PHOTOELECTRIC RELAY.

photoresistive cell See PHOTOCONDUCTIVE CELL.

photoresistive material See PHOTOCONDUCTIVE MATERIAL.

photoresistivity See PHOTOCONDUCTIVITY.

photoresistor See PHOTOCONDUCTOR, **1**, **2**.

photosensitive device A light-sensitive electronic device. See, for example, PHOTOCONDUCTIVE CELL, PHOTODIODE, PHOTOFET, PHOTOMULTIPLIER TUBE, PHOTOTRANSISTOR, PHOTOTUBE, and PHOTOVOLTAIC CELL.

photosphere The luminous layer at the surface of a star.

photoswitch A light-activated switch. Some photoswitches contain an electromechanical relay; others, such as the light-activated silicon-controlled switch, have no moving parts.

phototimer An electronic timer for timing photographic processes.

phototransistor A transistor in which current carriers emitted as a result of illumination constitute an input-signal current. This current is amplified by the transistor. The output signal delivered by the transistor, accordingly, is larger than the output of an equivalent photodiode.

phototube An electron tube that converts light energy into electrical energy by acting as a light-sensitive resistor. Characteristically, the tube contains an illuminated cathode coated with a photoemissive material, and an anode wire situated nearby. Light energy causes electrons to be emitted from the cathode in amounts proportional to light intensity; the electrons are attracted by the anode, which is connected externally to a positive direct-current voltage.

photovoltaic cell A semiconductor junction that generates a voltage when illuminated. The principal photovoltaic cell is the silicon cell; the selenium cell is also photovoltaic (to a somewhat lesser extent). Also see PHOTOVOLTAIC MATERIAL.

photovoltaic material A substance that generates a voltage when exposed to light. The principal substances exhibiting this effect are silicon, selenium, and germanium. Also see ACTINOELECTRIC EFFECT.

photran A light-sensitive, four-layer semiconductor device, used for switching purposes.

physical properties The distinguishing characteristics of matter, apart from its chemical properties. Included are *boiling point, density, ductility, elasticity, electrical conductivity, hardness, heat conductivity, index of refraction, malleability, melting point, specific heat,* and *state* (solid, liquid, gaseous, or plasma).

physical quantity A quantity expressing the actual number of physical units under consideration, as compared with a dimensionless number.

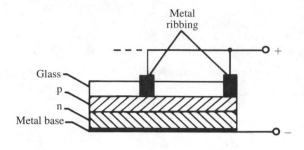

Metal ribbing

Glass
p
n
Metal base

+
−

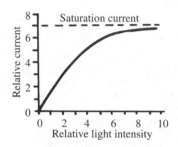

photovoltaic cell

Examples: 50 volts, 39 kilometers, and 30 picofarads. Compare DIMENSIONLESS QUANTITY.

physics   The science of energy and matter and their interactions. Physics is subdivided into several fields, including *mechanics, thermodynamics, acoustics, optics,* and *electricity/magnetism.* Many subdivisions are within the traditional fields.

P_i Symbol for INPUT POWER.

picket fencing   An effect often observed at very-high frequencies (VHF) and ultra-high frequencies (UHF), in which movement of the transmitting station antenna, the receiving station antenna, or both antennas causes rapid fading. The fading is the result of phase effects between the direct wave and indirect wave(s). These effects are most pronounced with vertically polarized antennas.

PIA   Abbreviation of PERIPHERAL INTERFACE ADAPTER.

pickoff   **1.** To monitor a voltage, current, or other characteristic in an active circuit, without disturbing the operation of the circuit. **2.** A device for electronically monitoring linear or angular displacement.

pickup   **1.** A device that serves as a sensor of a signal or quantity. This covers a wide variety of items, including *temperature sensors, vibration detectors, microphones, phonograph pickups,* etc. **2.** Collectively, energy or information that is received (e.g., *sound pickup*).

pickup arm   The pivoted arm that holds the cartridge and stylus of a phonograph.

pickup cartridge   See PHONO CARTRIDGE.

pickup current   **1.** The current required to close a relay. **2.** Current flowing through, or generated by, a pickup.

pickup pattern   The directional pattern of a microphone or other transducer that converts acoustic energy into electrical signals.

pickup voltage   **1.** The voltage required to close a relay or circuit breaker. **2.** The voltage delivered by a pickup.

pico-   **1.** Abbreviation, p. A prefix meaning 10^{-12}. **2.** A prefix meaning extremely small.

picoammeter   A usually direct-reading instrument used to measure current in the picoampere range. Also see CURRENT METER.

picoampere   Abbreviation, pA. A small unit of current equal to 10^{-12} ampere.

picocoulomb   Abbreviation, pC. A small unit of electrical quantity equal to 10^{-12} coulomb.

picocurie   Abbreviation, pCi. A small unit of radioactivity equal to 10^{-12} curie.

picofarad   Abbreviation, pF. A small unit of capacitance equal to 10^{-12} farad.

picohenry   Abbreviation, pH. A small unit of inductance equal to 10^{-12} henry.

picosecond   Abbreviation, ps or psec. A small unit of time equal to 10^{-12} second.

pi coupler   See COLLINS COUPLER.

picovolt   Abbreviation, pV. A small unit of voltage equal to 10^{-12} volt.

picovoltmeter   A usually direct-reading electronic instrument used to measure electromotive force in the picovolt range.

picowatt   Abbreviation, pW. A small unit of power equal to 10^{-12} watt.

pictorial   See PICTORIAL WIRING DIAGRAM.

pictorial diagram   See PICTORIAL WIRING DIAGRAM.

pictorial wiring diagram   A wiring diagram in the form of a drawing or photograph of the components, as opposed to one of circuit symbols. The components are shown in their positions in the finished equipment, and the wiring as lines running between them.

picture black   In facsimile or television, the signal condition resulting from the scanning of a black portion of the image.

picture detector   See VIDEO DETECTOR.

picture diagram   See PICTORIAL WIRING DIAGRAM.

picture element   See PIXEL.

picture information   In a television signal, the variable-amplitude component (i.e., the one carrying energy corresponding to the picture elements) that fills the space between blanking pulses.

picture-in-picture   Abbreviation, PIP. In some television receivers, a feature that allows simultaneous viewing of two programs. One program occupies the full screen, and another program appears in a small portion of the screen.

picture reception **1.** See PHOTOGRAPH RECEPTION. **2.** The reception of television signals.

picture transmission **1.** See PHOTOGRAPH TRANSMISSION. **2.** The transmission or broadcasting of television signals.

picture tube The cathode-ray tube used in a television receiver to display the image. Also called KINESCOPE.

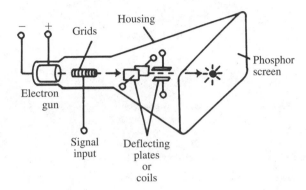

picture tube

pie chart See CIRCLE GRAPH.

Pierce oscillator A simple crystal oscillator in which the crystal is connected directly between the input and output terminals of the active device (usually a bipolar or field-effect transistor). A tuned inductance-capacitance (LC) circuit might be included, but is not required.

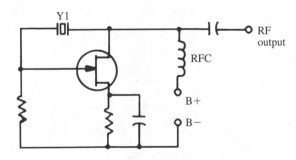

Pierce oscillator

pie winding A method of coil winding in which two or more separate, multilayer coils are connected in series and placed along a common axis. It is sometimes used in radio-frequency chokes to minimize capacitance among the windings.

piezo- A prefix meaning *pressure* (see PRESSURE, **2**).

piezodielectric A substance that, when stretched or compressed, exhibits a change in dielectric constant.

piezoelectric accelerometer An accelerometer using a piezoelectric crystal, whose voltage output is proportional to acceleration.

piezoelectric ceramic A ceramic material that delivers a voltage when deformed, or that changes in shape when a voltage is applied to it.

piezoelectric crystal A crystal (such as quartz, Rochelle salt, tourmaline, or various synthetics) that delivers a voltage when mechanical force is applied between its faces, or that changes its shape when a voltage is applied between its faces.

piezoelectric earphone See CRYSTAL EARPHONE.

piezoelectric filter See CRYSTAL FILTER and CRYSTAL RESONATOR.

piezoelectricity Electricity produced by deforming (squeezing, stretching, bending, or twisting) certain crystals, such as those of quartz, Rochelle salt, or tourmaline.

piezoelectric loudspeaker See CRYSTAL LOUDSPEAKER.

piezoelectric microphone See CERAMIC MICROPHONE and CRYSTAL MICROPHONE.

piezoelectric oscillator See CRYSTAL OSCILLATOR.

piezoelectric pickup See CRYSTAL PICKUP.

piezoelectric resonator See CRYSTAL FILTER and CRYSTAL RESONATOR.

piezoelectric sensor See CRYSTAL TRANSDUCER.

piezoelectric transducer See CRYSTAL TRANSDUCER.

piezoid A complete piezoelectric crystal device.

piezoresistance In certain substances, the tendency of the resistance to change with stretching or compression.

piezo tweeter A tweeter of the piezoelectric type (see CRYSTAL LOUDSPEAKER).

pi filter An unbalanced filter section having one series arm and two shunt arms; its schematic representation has the general shape of the uppercase Greek letter pi.

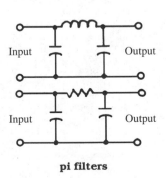

pi filters

piggyback component See OUTBOARD COMPONENT.

piggyback control See CASCADE CONTROL.

piggyback tuner A separate ultra-high-frequency (UHF) television tuner operated in conjunction with the very-high-frequency (VHF) tuner of the receiver.

pigtail **1.** A usually long and sometimes flexible lead, such as the pigtail of a fixed capacitor. **2.** Descriptive of a device containing a long lead or leads, and usually mounted by such leads.

pile **1.** See VOLTAIC PILE. **2.** See NUCLEAR REACTOR. **3.** A battery of electrochemical cells. **4.** Any packed group of particles or granules.

pillow speaker A small, flat loudspeaker intended for use under a pillow.

PILOT Acronym for *programmed inquiry learning or teaching.* A straightforward high-level computer programming language, used in computer-assisted instruction (CAI).

pilot lamp See PILOT LIGHT.

pilot light A usually small, incandescent or neon lamp. When glowing, it serves as a signal that a piece of equipment is in operation.

pilot model A preliminary model of a circuit or device constructed primarily to test the efficacy of a production process. The pilot model usually follows the PROTOTYPE.

pilot production The often small-scale production of a device in a special assembly line apart from the main line in a factory.

pilot regulator A variable-gain circuit that maintains a constant output—even if the input amplitude changes.

PIM Abbreviation of PULSE-INTERVAL MODULATION.

pi mode In a vane-anode magnetron, the mode of operation in which adjacent vanes have radio-frequency voltages of opposite polarity.

pin **1.** A semiconductor junction consisting of a layer of instrinsic semiconductor material situated between n and p layers. **2.** A slender, straight, stiff prong used as a terminal or locking device (see, for example, BASE PIN and BAYONET BASE).

pinchoff In a junction field-effect transistor, the condition in which the gate voltage causes the two depletion regions to meet and close the channel to obstruct drain-current flow.

pinchoff voltage In a junction field-effect transistor, the lowest value of gate voltage that will produce pinchoff.

pinch roller In a tape recorder, a rubber-tired, rotating cylinder that helps to pull the tape past the recording and/or playback heads.

pincushion A type of television picture distortion in which each side of the raster sags toward center screen. Also see ANTIPINCUSHIONING MAGNETS.

pincushion-correction generator A circuit for generating a deflection signal to correct pin-

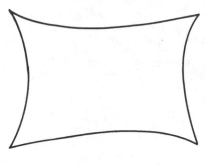

pincushion

cushion distortion (see PINCUSHION). One form consists of a parabola generator and op-amp-type differentiator.

pin diode A silicon junction diode having a lightly doped intrinsic layer serving as a dielectric barrier between p and n layers.

pi network See COLLINS COUPLER.

ping An acoustic pulse; it can be audible sound or ultrasound.

pinhole **1.** A tiny hole present as a defect in a film of dielectric, semiconductor, or metal. **2.** A tiny aperture that acts as a universal lens by permitting the passage of a very small bundle of light rays. The smaller the aperture, the greater the depth of field.

pinhole detector An electronic device for finding pinholes in materials. Also see PINHOLE, 1.

pin jack A jack into which a pin plug is inserted for quick connection.

pink noise Acoustical noise whose amplitude is inversely proportional to the frequency within a limited frequency spectrum. In the extreme, it creates a hissing sound. Compare WHITE NOISE.

pinout A diagram of an integrated circuit depicting the locations of the pins for various functions. It generally takes the form of a rectangle for the circuit itself, and short lines for the pins with designators printed next to the lines.

pin plug A plug consisting of a slender metal pin inserted between the blades of a PIN JACK for a quick connection. The plug usually has a small insulated back for convenient handling.

pin straightener A device for straightening the pins of a transistor, integrated circuit, or other electronic component.

pin switch A switch that changes state when a small pin is pushed or pulled.

pin-usage factor For an integrated circuit, the number of gate equivalents per package pin. Also see GATE EQUIVALENT.

PIO Abbreviation of *parallel input/output.*

pion A subatomic particle consisting of one quark and one antiquark.

PIP Abbreviation of PICTURE-IN-PICTURE.

pip   See BLIP.

pi pad   A resistance-type attenuator having a series arm, a shunt input arm, and shunt output arm; its name is derived from its resemblance to the Greek letter pi. Also see PAD.

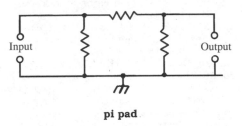

pi pad

pipe radiator   A waveguide having an open end from which microwave energy is radiated.

Pirani gauge   A type of vacuum gauge in which a heated filament, composing one arm of a four-arm resistance bridge, is sealed into the vacuum system. The bridge is balanced before evacuation starts. As evacuation progresses, the heat removed from the filament becomes proportional to the pressure in the system, and the resistance of the filament changes accordingly. The bridge is then rebalanced, and the difference between initial and subsequent null conditions indicate the extent of the vacuum when the bridge has been appropriately calibrated.

pi section   An unbalanced filter or tuner section whose schematic representation has the general shape of the uppercase Greek letter pi.

pi-section coupling   Use of a PI SECTION for coupling a radio transmitter to an antenna. Also see COLLINS COUPLER and PI-SECTION TANK.

pi-section filter   A pi section used as either a low-pass or high-pass filter, depending on the position of the capacitors in the circuit.

pi-section tank   A pi section used as the collector, drain, or plate tank circuit of a radio-frequency power amplifier, and also serving as an antenna coupler.

piston   1. The movable element (cone) of a loudspeaker. 2. The movable, solid plunger of a trimmer capacitor that consists of a plug within a cylinder.

piston directivity   Directivity of sound emitted by the piston of a loudspeaker (see PISTON, **1**). As the frequency of the audio signal increases, radiation from a loudspeaker tends to be concentrated along the axis of the piston.

pit   1. A microscopic depression in a compact disc; scatters and/or absorbs light from the laser, rather than reflecting it. Compare LAND, **1**. 2. In a printed-circuit board, a pockmark in a component or foil run. 3. A pockmark in a metallic substance, resulting from corrosion.

pitch   1. The frequency of a sound, either in general terms (e.g., low, midrange, and high) or as a specific quantity (e.g., 2450 Hz). 2. The distance between the peaks of adjacent grooves on a phonograph disc. 3. The distance between adjacent threads of a screw. 4. The distance between centers of turns in a coil (see PITCH OF WINDING) 5. The number of teeth or threads per unit length. 6. The distance along its axis a propeller moves in a revolution. 7. Up-and-down motion of a robot end effector or other electromechanical device. 8. The extent or range of movement, as defined in **7**.

pitch of winding   In a coil, the distance from the center of one turn to the center of the adjacent turn in a single layer of winding.

PIV   Abbreviation of PEAK INVERSE VOLTAGE.

pivot   The sometimes jeweled, stationary member of the bearing in an analog meter movement.

pi-wound choke   A choke coil consisting of several series-connected sections, mounted on a single core and separated to reduce internal capacitance.

pix   Abbreviation of PICTURE.

pixel   Contraction of *picture element*. The smallest bit of data in a video image. Also called *pel*. The smaller the size of the pixels in an image, the greater the resolution for a given image area.

pixel aspect ratio   In a video image, the ratio of PIXEL height to pixel width.

pix tube   See PICTURE TUBE.

PL   Abbreviation for PRIVATE LINE.

place effect   An apparent change in the perceived pitch of a sound, caused by variations in the way the waves interact inside the human ear.

planar diffusion   In the production of a semiconductor device, the diffusion of all the elements into one face of a wafer. Consequently, connections to the elements all lie in one plane. Also see EPITAXIAL PLANAR TRANSISTOR and PLANAR TRANSISTOR.

planar diode   A semiconductor diode, having a pn junction that lies entirely within a single plane.

planar epitaxial passivated diode   A junction diode that, like the planar epitaxial transistor, has been manufactured by planar diffusion, then passivated to protect the junction. Also see EPITAXIAL GROWTH, EPITAXY, PASSIVATION, and PLANAR DIFFUSION.

PL/1   A computer programming language that is a hybrid of scientific and commercial types (like ALGOL and COBOL), the combined features being powerful problem-solving and mass-data-handling abilities.

planar epitaxial passivated transistor   A planar epitaxial transistor that has been passivated to protect the exposed junctions. Also see EPITAXIAL PLANAR TRANSISTOR, PLANAR TRANSISTOR, EPITAXIAL TRANSISTOR, PASSIVATION, and PLANAR TRANSISTOR.

planar transistor   A transistor in which the emitter, base, and collector elements terminate on

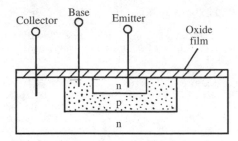

planar transistor

the same face (plane) of the silicon wafer. A thin film of silicon dioxide is grown on top of the wafer to insulate the exposed junctions after the leads have been attached (i.e., the transistor is passivated).

Planck constant   Symbol, h. Unit, joule-second. The constant of proportionality in the fundamental law of the quantum theory, stating that radiant energy is composed of quanta proportional to the frequency of the radiation; $h = q/f =$ 6.62608×10^{-34} J•s, where q is the value of the quantum and f is the frequency in Hz.

plane of polarization   The plane containing the direction of propagation and the electric field vector of a plane-polarized wave (see POLARIZATION, **3** and POLARIZED LIGHT).

plane-polarized light   See POLARIZATION, **3** and POLARIZED LIGHT.

plane-reflector antenna   A directive antenna in which the reflector is a sheet of metal or a metal screen. In a corner-reflector antenna, the reflector is a folded sheet, or two sheets joined along one edge.

planetary electron   See ORBITAL ELECTRON.

planimeter   A mechanical instrument for measuring the area of a closed figure. The outline of the figure is traced with the pointer of the device, and the area is read from a pair of dials. In this application, the planimeter does the work of integral calculus.

PLANNER   A high-level computer programming language sometimes used in artificial intelligence. It is a "goal-oriented" language in that it seeks a solution to a problem using various schemes, as necessary.

plan position indicator   Abbreviation, PPI. A radar display on whose screen small spots of light reconstruct the scanned vicinity, revealing objects, such as buildings, boats, aircraft, etc. The distance from the center of the screen to a spot depicts the range of an object, and the radial angle reveals its bearing.

plant   In computer operations, to put the result of an operation specified by a routine in a storage location from which it will be taken for implementation of an instruction further on in the program.

plaque resistor   A flat, noninductive, power resistor, often used as a dummy load during high-frequency power measurements.

plasma   A usually high-temperature gas that is so highly ionized that it is electrically conductive and susceptible to magnetic fields; it is recognized as one of the states of matter. Also see PHYSICAL PROPERTIES.

plasma diode   A diode in which a plasma substance produces conduction in one direction, but not in the other.

plasma length   See DEBYE LENGTH.

plasma oscillation   In a plasma, a form of electric-field oscillation of the rapidly moving electrons.

plasma torch   A torch, used for such high-heat applications as melting metal, in which a gas is heated by electricity to the high temperature at which it becomes a plasma.

plasmatron   A form of amplifier tube sometimes used at ultra-high and microwave frequencies. It is similar to a thyratron. An inert gas is excited until it becomes a plasma, producing amplification under certain operating conditions.

Plastacele   See CELLULOSE ACETATE.

plastic   A synthetic material usually made from various organic compounds through polymerization (see POLYMERIZE). Plastics can be molded into solid shapes and are available as films. Examples: *celluloid, cellulose acetate, cellulose nitrate, polyethylene,* and *polystyrene.* Also see THERMOPLASTIC MATERIAL and THERMOSETTING MATERIAL.

plasticizer   A substance added to a plastic to make it softer or more flexible.

plastic-leaded chip carrier   Abbreviated PLCC. A surface-mounted package for an integrated circuit. It is small in size and has high electrical and mechanical reliability.

plate   **1.** The anode of an electron tube. **2.** One of the electrodes of a primary or secondary battery cell. **3.** One of the electrodes of a capacitor.

plateau   In a response curve, a region in which an increase in the independent variable produces no further change in the dependent variable. Example: the saturation region in a common-base transistor collector-current curve.

plate blocking capacitor   A capacitor connected between the plate of an electron tube and the plate tank. It allows the direct-current supply voltage to be applied directly to the plate without it passing through the tank coil, while at the same time preventing the tank coil from short-circuiting the plate power supply. The capacitor freely transmits alternating-current signal energy to the tank.

plate capacitance   See PLATE-CATHODE CAPACITANCE.

plate-cathode capacitance   Symbol, C_{PK}. Unit, pF. The internal capacitance between the plate and cathode of an electron tube. Also called OUTPUT CAPACITANCE.

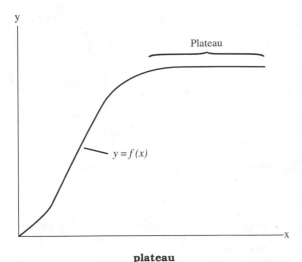

plateau

plate characteristic For an electron tube, the family of plate current-vs-plate voltage curves for various grid-bias voltages.

plate circuit The external circuit associated with the plate of an electron tube.

plate-circuit relay A direct-current relay operated in series with the plate of an electron tube.

plate conductance Symbol, g_P. Unit, siemens. Conductance of the internal plate circuit of an electron tube. The value of static g_P is equal to the plate current divided by the plate voltage (I_P/E_P). The value of dynamic g_P is equal to the derivative of the static g_P: dI_P/dE_P. Plate conductance is the reciprocal of PLATE RESISTANCE.

plate current Symbol, I_P. Direct current flowing in the plate circuit of an electron tube.

plate-current shift A change in the plate current of a radio-frequency power amplifier during amplitude modulation. The action discloses faulty operation because the average plate current should remain constant during modulation.

plate dissipation Abbreviation, *PD*. Unit, watt. Power expended in the plate of an electron tube. For an unloaded tube, $PD = E_P I_P$, where E_P is the direct-current (dc) plate voltage in volts, and I_P is the dc plate current in amperes. For a loaded tube, $PD = P_o - P_i$, where P_o is the alternating-current (ac) power output of an amplifier or oscillator in which the tube operates, and P_i is the dc plate power input.

plated magnetic wire A wire with a ferromagnetic outer coating on a core that is not magnetic.

plated-wire memory See WIRE MEMORY.

plate-grid capacitance Symbol, C_{PG} or C_{GP}. Unit, pF. The internal capacitance between the plate and control grid of an electron tube. Also called INTERELECTRODE CAPACITANCE and FEEDBACK CAPACITANCE.

plate load The power-consuming load into which the plate circuit of an electron tube operates. In an intermediate stage of a multistage amplifier, this load is the grid circuit of the following tube.

plate load impedance Symbol, Z_{LP}. Unit, ohm. In a tube circuit, the (output) impedance that is ac-connected between the plate and ground, or dc-connected between the plate electrode and dc plate power supply.

plate meter A direct-current ammeter or milliammeter that indicates the plate current of an electron tube.

plate modulation A method of AMPLITUDE MODULATION in which a modulating voltage is superimposed on the direct-current plate voltage of a higher-frequency amplifier or oscillator.

platen The "roller" in a teletypewriter or impact printer. It supports the paper against impact by the print head; it also helps to move the paper through the machine.

plate-neutralized amplifier A vacuum-tube radio-frequency power amplifier in which a neutralizing capacitor is connected between the control grid and the free end of a center-tapped plate-tank coil.

plate power Symbol, P_P. Unit, watt. Power in the plate circuit of an electron tube; $P_P = E_P I_P$, where E_P is the plate voltage in volts and I_P is the plate current in amperes.

plate power input See PLATE POWER.

plate power output The output signal power delivered by the plate circuit of an electron tube. Compare PLATE POWER INPUT.

plate power supply The (usually direct current) power supply that furnishes energy to the plate of an electron tube.

plate pulse modulation A method of obtaining pulse modulation by injecting high-voltage pulses into the plate circuit of a vacuum-tube amplifier.

plate relay A relay operated in series with the plate of an electron tube.

plate resistance Symbol, r_P. Unit, ohm. Resistance of the internal plate circuit of an electron tube. The static value of r_P is equal to E_P/I_P, where E_P is the plate voltage in volts, and I_P is the plate current in amperes. The dynamic value is dE_P/dI_P.

plate saturation In an electron tube, the point at which, while plate voltage is increasing, the plate attracts all the electrons emitted by the cathode (i.e., the point beyond which no further significant increase in plate current results from a further increase in plate voltage).

plate-screen capacitance Symbol, C_{PS}. Unit, pF. The internal capacitance between the plate and screen grid of an electron tube.

plate-screen modulation A method of AMPLITUDE MODULATION in which the modulating voltage is superimposed simultaneously on the direct-current plate and screen voltages of a higher-frequency amplifier or oscillator.

plate series compensation   In an audio amplifier, the use of a plate decoupling circuit to obtain a fixed amount of bass boost.

plate shunt compensation   The addition of a network to the plate-output circuit of a tube to boost the bass response of an amplifier.

plate spacing   **1.** The distance between plates in a fixed capacitor. This dimension is usually the same as dielectric thickness. **2.** The distance between plates in a variable capacitor. Also called *capacitor air gap.*

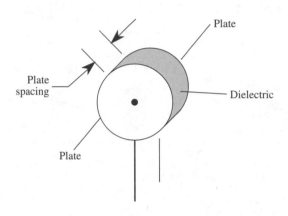

Plate
Plate spacing
Dielectric
Plate

plate spacing, 1

plate supply voltage   Symbol, E_{BB}. The output voltage of a plate power supply.

plate tank   A resonant inductance-capacitance (LC) circuit operated from the plate of an electron tube.

plate tank capacitance   The capacitance required to tune a PLATE TANK to resonance.

plate tank inductance   The inductance of the coil in a PLATE TANK.

plate tank Q   Figure of merit (see *Q*) of a plate tank, a function of the load resistance and the tank inductance-to-capacitance (L/C) ratio.

plate tank voltage   The audio-frequency or radio-frequency voltage developed across the plate tank of an electron-tube circuit.

plate tuning   Tuning an electron-tube circuit by varying the capacitance, inductance, or both in the plate tank.

plate tuning capacitance   See PLATE TANK CAPACITANCE.

plate tuning inductance   See PLATE TANK INDUCTANCE.

plate-type capacitor   A capacitor having flat metal plates, rather than concentric cylinders, a cylinder and rod, etc.

plate voltage   Symbol, E_P. The direct-current voltage applied to the plate of an electron tube.

plate winding   **1.** An inductor connected in series between the plate of a vacuum tube and the

positive power-supply voltage. **2.** The primary winding of a plate-circuit output transformer.

platiniridium   A natural alloy of PLATINUM and IRIDIUM.

platinotron   A form of traveling-wave vacuum tube used as an amplifier at ultra-high and microwave frequencies. There are two output connections.

platinum   Symbol, Pt. A precious metallic element. Atomic number, 78. Atomic weight, 195.08. It is sometimes used for plating of relay and switch contacts, and for certain parts of vacuum tubes.

platinum metals   The rare metals IRIDIUM, OSMIUM, PALLADIUM, PLATINUM, RHODIUM, and RUTHENIUM. They do not react readily with other elements.

platinum-tellurium thermocouple   A thermocouple using the junction between platinum and tellurium wires; it is used in thermocouple-type meters.

platter   **1.** One of the individual disks in a computer HARD DISK drive. **2.** The rotating turntable in a PHONOGRAPH.

playback   The reproduction of recorded material in audio-tape, audio-disc, video-tape, or video-disc systems.

playback computer system   A personal computer and associated peripherals, equipped for reproducing multimedia that has been recorded on CD-ROM.

playback head   In a magnetic recorder/reproducer, the head that picks up the signal from the tape or disc for reproduction. Also called *read head* and *play head.*

playback loss   In disc recording, the difference (at a particular point on the disc) between the recorded level and the reproduced level.

player   A semiconductor layer that is doped to provide current carriers that are predominantly holes. Compare N LAYER.

player   A device or system that reproduces (plays back) data from a tape or disc, but cannot be used to record data onto the tape or disc.

play head   See PLAYBACK HEAD.

playthrough   The condition in which an amplifier delivers a small output signal when the gain control is set to zero.

PLC   Abbreviation of POWER-LINE COMMUNICATION.

PLCC   Abbreviation of PLASTIC-LEADED CHIP CARRIER.

plethysmograph   A medical-electronic device that allows the monitoring of the amount of blood in different parts of the body.

PLL   Abbreviation of PHASE-LOCKED LOOP.

PLM   Abbreviation of *pulse-length modulation* (see PULSE-DURATION MODULATION).

PLO   Abbreviation of PHASE-LOCKED OSCILLATOR.

plot   **1.** A curve depicting the variations of one quantity, with respect to another. **2.** To generate, print, or display a curve of the type defined in **1.**

plotter A machine that plots (see PLOT, **2**) automatically, often by the direction of a computer.

PL tone encoder An audio oscillator and modulator that cause a subaudible-tone modulation of a signal for use in restricted communications systems.

plug A usually male quick-connect device that can be inserted into a JACK to make a circuit connection, or be pulled out of the jack to break the connection. See, for example, MALE PLUG, PHONE PLUG, POWER PLUG, and POLARIZED POWER PLUG.

plug-and-jack connection A connection made by inserting a PLUG into a JACK.

plug fuse A fuse provided with an Edison base for screwing into a socket.

pluggable Capable of being completely removed from the rest of the system without the need for removing any wiring. Pluggable components and circuit boards simplify the servicing of electronic equipment.

plug-in See PLUG-IN COMPONENT and PLUG-IN UNIT.

plug-in capacitor A capacitor with pins or ferrules that can be quickly inserted into, or removed from, a socket.

plug-in coil A coil wound on a form having pins that can be quickly inserted into, or removed from, a socket.

plug-in coil form An insulating form with base pins that mate with socket terminals so that a coil wound on the form can be quickly inserted into, or removed from, a circuit.

plug-in component A component or module, such as a transistor, capacitor, coil, lamp, etc., provided with pins, clips, or contacts for easy insertion into, or removal from, a circuit. See, for example, PLUG-IN CAPACITOR, PLUG-IN COIL, PLUG-IN FUSE, PLUG-IN LAMP, PLUG-IN METER, PLUG-IN RESISTOR, PLUG-IN TRANSFORMER, and PLUG-IN UNIT.

plug-in fuse A cartridge fuse having a metal ferrule on each end for insertion into a matching clip for easy installation and removal.

plug-in fuse

plug-in lamp A lamp with base pins for quick insertion into, or removal from, a socket.

plug-in meter A meter with pins or banana plugs for quick insertion into, or removal from, a circuit.

plug-in resistor A resistor with pins or ferrules for quick insertion into, or removal from, a socket.

plug-in transformer A small transformer with pins for quick insertion into, or removal from, a socket.

plug-in unit A unit, such as a tuned circuit, amplifier, or meter, that has pins or contacts for easy insertion into, or removal from, a larger piece of equipment.

plumber's delight An antenna whose construction, including that of the mast, is entirely of metal rods or tubing, with no insulating parts. Short circuits and grounds are prevented by making all attachments and joints at points that are at zero voltage, with respect to the standing-wave pattern.

Plumbicon A television camera tube, similar to the VIDICON, with a lead-oxide target. It is noted for high sensitivity. The image lag time is shorter than in the conventional vidicon.

plumbing Collectively, the waveguides, tees, elbows, and similar pipelike devices and fixtures used in microwave setups.

plunger-type meter A meter in which an iron or steel plunger is pulled into a coil by the magnetism produced by a current flowing in the coil. The plunger is attached to a pointer that moves over the scale.

plutonium Symbol, Pu. A radioactive metallic element that is artificially produced. Atomic number, 94. Atomic weight, approximately 244.

PM **1.** Abbreviation of PERMANENT MAGNET. **2.** Abbreviation of PULSE(D) MODULATOR. **3.** Abbreviation of *post meridian*. **4.** Abbreviation of PHASE MODULATION.

Pm **1.** Symbol for PROMETHIUM. **2.** Abbreviation of PETAMETER.

P_m Symbol for MAXIMUM POWER.

PME Abbreviation of *photomagnetoelectric*.

PMG Abbreviation of PERMANENT-MAGNET GENERATOR.

PMM Abbreviation of PERMANENT-MAGNET MAGNETIZER.

PMOS Abbreviation of P-CHANNEL METAL-OXIDE SEMICONDUCTOR.

PMU Abbreviation of *portable memory unit*.

PN **1.** Abbreviation of POLISH NOTATION. **2.** Abbreviation of POSITIVE-NEGATIVE (often lowercase).

pn Abbreviation of POSITIVE-NEGATIVE.

pn boundary See PN JUNCTION.

pnip transistor A junction transistor having an intrinsic layer between an n-type semiconductor base and one of the p-type semiconductor layers.

pneumatic computer A computer that uses fluid logic [i.e., one in which information is stored and transferred by the flow of a fluid (gas or liquid) and pressure variations therein].

pn junction The boundary between p-type and n-type semiconductor materials in a single block or wafer of the materials. The junction cannot be duplicated by merely touching two pieces of material (one n-type and one p-type) together, however smooth their mating faces.

pn-junction diode A diode consisting of the junction between p-type and n-type regions in the same wafer of semiconductor material.

PNM Abbreviation of PULSE-NUMBERS MODU-LATION.

pnpn device See NPNP DEVICE.

pnp transistor A bipolar junction transistor in which the emitter and collector layers are p-type semiconductor material, and the base layer is n-type semiconductor material. Compare NPN TRANSISTOR.

Po Symbol for POLONIUM.

P_o Symbol for OUTPUT POWER or POWER OUT-PUT.

POGO Abbreviation of *polar orbiting geophysical observatory*.

point **1.** A dot indicating the place of separation between the integral and fractional parts of a number (e.g., *decimal point*). Also called RADIX POINT. **2.** A precisely defined location in three-dimensional space that has theoretically zero length, zero width, and zero depth (e.g., *focal point*). **3.** The place on a graph in any number of dimensions, at which two or more curves or co-ordinates intersect. **4.** A set of operating condi-tions for a component, device, or system (e.g., *cutoff point, operating point*). **5.** A defined condi-tion at which some specific physical phe-nomenon occurs (e.g., *melting point*).

point charge An electric charge imagined to oc-cupy a single point in space; thus, it has neither area nor volume.

point contact The point at which the sharply pointed tip of a wire or rod conductor touches a second conductor (e.g., the contact between a "cat whisker" and a semiconductor wafer).

point-contact diode A semiconductor diode hav-ing a fine wire ("cat whisker"), whose point is in permanent contact with the surface of a wafer of semiconductor material, such as germanium or silicon.

point-contact junction The pn junction electro-formed under the point at which the "cat whisker" touches the semiconductor wafer in a point-contact diode or transistor.

point-contact transistor A transistor having two fine wires ("cat whiskers") that serve as the emitter and collector electrodes. The pointed tips of the wires are nearly in contact with (a few mils apart from) the surface of a wafer of semi-conductor material, such as germanium. The semiconductor serves as the base electrode. This device was a predecessor of the JUNCTION TRANSISTOR.

point counter A Geiger counter tube in which the central electrode is a pointed, fine wire. Also see PROPORTIONAL COUNTER.

point defect **1.** In a semiconductor substance or piezoelectric crystal, the absence of an atom from its place in the lattice structure. **2.** The presence of an extra atom in the lattice structure.

point effect The tendency of an electrical dis-charge to occur more readily at a sharp point than at a blunt surface (as of an electrode).

pointer A pointed blade, stiff wire, or inscribed line on a transparent blade; it moves over a scale to indicate a setting or the value of a quan-tity. Also called NEEDLE.

pointer-type meter An analog meter in which a pointer moves over a calibrated scale.

point impedance **1.** The impedance observed at a given point in a circuit. **2.** In a transmission line, the intensity of the electric field divided by the intensity of the magnetic field at a given point.

points of saturation For a magnetic core, satu-ration as evidenced by a leveling-off of the posi-tive and negative halves of the magnetization curve.

point source A source from which electromag-netic radiation emanates, and that appears as a geometric point from a great distance.

point mode Descriptive of cathode-ray-tube dis-play operation (in a computer system), in which data is portrayed as plotted dots.

point-to-point communication Communication between two stations whose location can be pre-cisely specified.

point-to-point motion A method of robot arm movement in which the device can attain only certain positions. The coordinates of each stop-ping point are stored in the robot controller (computer) memory.

point-to-point station A radio station that pro-vides POINT-TO-POINT COMMUNICATION.

point-to-point wiring A method of wiring an electronic circuit in which wires are run directly between the terminals or components, usually by the shortest practicable route. It is used mainly in high-voltage circuits, such as power amplifiers. Compare CABLED WIRING.

poise The cgs unit of absolute viscosity; 1 poise is the absolute viscosity of a fluid that requires a shearing force of 1 dyne to move a 1-sq-cm area of one of two parallel layers of the fluid (1 cm apart) with a velocity of 1 cm per second, with respect to the other layer. The comparable SI unit is the *newton-second per meter squared* ($N \cdot s/m^2$); 1 poise = 0.1 $N \cdot s/m^2$.

polar axis **1.** In a crystal, the axis of rotation not perpendicular to a reflection plane. **2.** The straight line connecting epicenters of electric, magnetic, or gravitational poles in a system. **3.** The axis about which the earth or another planet rotates.

polar coordinate conversion See POLAR COOR-DINATE TRANSFORMATION.

polar-coordinate geometry A two-dimensional system for movement of industrial-robot arms. It is based on a system of POLAR COORDI-NATES, in which a radius and a direction angle are assigned to each point in the working plane.

polar coordinates The magnitude and direction of a vector in a defined plane, listed as a radius (magnitude) in combination with an angle (di-rection) between the vector and the polar axis.

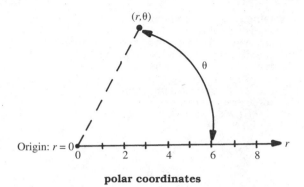

polar coordinates

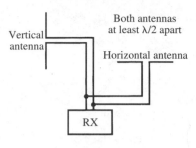

polarization diversity

polarimeter An instrument for measuring the amount of polarized light in a ray that is only partially polarized.

polariscope An instrument used in the observation or testing of materials under POLARIZED LIGHT.

polarity **1.** The condition of being electrically positive or negative. **2.** The condition of being magnetically north or south. **3.** The orientation of the positive and negative poles in a battery or power supply relative to a circuit. **4.** The orientation of a magnetic field, relative to the surrounding environment.

polarity blanking See POLARITY INHIBIT.

polarity inhibit In some instruments, especially those having automatic polarity, the automatic blanking of the polarity sign.

polarity-sensitive relay A direct-current relay actuated only when coil current flows in one direction. One of the simplest versions is a relay having a semiconductor diode connected in series with its coil.

polarity shifter A potentiometer connected to two direct-current sources so that a pair of output terminals has plus and minus polarities at one extreme of potentiometer adjustment, and minus and plus at the other extreme. At the center of the range, the output voltage is zero.

polarity switch A double-pole, double-throw switch connected between a pair of direct-current input terminals so that the polarity of a pair of output terminals can be interchanged.

polarization **1.** In a radio wave, the orientation of the electric lines of flux, with respect to the surrounding environment (e.g., *horizontal polarization* and *vertical polarization*). **2.** The disabling of a battery cell by the formation of insulating gas on one of the plates. **3.** The condition in which transverse waves of light are confined to a specific (e.g., horizontal or vertical) plane.

polarization diversity A form of reception in which two separate receivers, tuned to the same signal, are connected to independent antennas. One antenna is vertically polarized and the other is horizontally polarized. The result is a reduction in fading caused by ionospheric effects on the polarization of the incoming signal.

polarization error In the operation of a loop antenna (e.g., that of a direction finder), null error caused by waves arriving with polarization opposite that of the loop (thus, vertically polarized waves at a horizontal-plane loop, and vice-versa).

polarization fading In radio reception, a form of fading that results from changes in the polarization of the arriving signal with respect to the receiving antenna. When the polarization of the arriving signal coincides with that of the receiving antenna, the received signal strength is maximum. When the received-signal polarization is at right angles to the receiving antenna, the signal strength is minimum.

polarization modulation A method of impressing information on a signal by changing the polarization of the radiated electromagnetic field.

polarization selectivity For a photoemissive surface, the condition in which the ratio of photocurrents for two different angles of plane polarization of the light incident to the surface differs from the ratio of the corresponding amounts of light absorbed by the surface. Also see PHOTOEMISSION; PHOTOEMISSIVE MATERIAL; and POLARIZATION, **3.**

polarized capacitor A conventional electrolytic capacitor, so called because one particular terminal must be connected to the more positive of the two connection points. Compare NONPOLARIZED ELECTROLYTIC CAPACITOR.

polarized light Visible light waves whose electric lines of flux are confined more or less to a single plane. This effect can be obtained via filtering; it also occurs naturally under certain conditions. Scattered sunlight is polarized to some extent by the atmosphere. Light is polarized to some extent when it reflects from a plane surface. Also see POLARIZING FILTER.

polarized plug A plug that can be inserted into a socket or receptacle in only one way to ensure safe and foolproof operation.

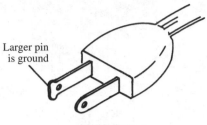

polarized plug

polarized power plug   A polarized plug for connection of equipment to an alternating-current utility power source.

polarized reactor   A saturable reactor in which the lines of flux produced in the three-leg core by the coils on the two outer legs are added in the center leg. Consequently, the flux can reinforce or oppose the controlling current in the coil on the center leg, depending on the direction of the current. Compare NONPOLARIZED REACTOR.

polarized receptacle   A receptacle constructed so that it can receive a plug in only one way, thus preventing incorrect connections.

polarized receptacle

polarized relay   A relay actuated by one polarity of direct current, or by one particular phase of alternating current. Such a relay sometimes contains an armature-centering permanent magnet.

polarized socket   See POLARIZED RECEPTACLE.

polarized X rays   X-ray waves whose electric lines of flux are more or less oriented in a specific plane, as when they are scattered by carbon blocks. See, for illustration, POLARIZATION, **3** and POLARIZED LIGHT.

polarizing filter   A light filter that consists essentially of microscopic heraphathite plastic plate. The plate can be rotated to cause light passing through it to be polarized in any particular plane between horizontal and vertical, depending on the degree of rotation. Also see POLARIZED LIGHT.

polarography   In chemistry, a form of qualitative or quantitative analysis utilizing IE curves ob-

tained when the voltage is gradually increased across a solution in ELECTROLYSIS.

polar orbit   An orbit that carries a satellite over the geographic polar regions of the earth. This type of orbit is oriented at, or nearly at, 90 degrees with respect to the equator, and can have a period ranging from about 90 minutes to several weeks or even months. Low-earth-orbit (LEO) satellites generally have such orbits.

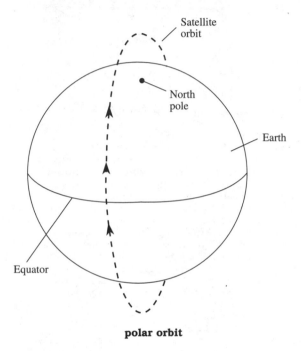

polar orbit

polar-orbiting satellite   Any satellite in a POLAR ORBIT.

polar planimeter   See PLANIMETER.

polar relay   See POLARIZED RELAY.

polar response   The horizontal-plane directional response of an antenna or other transducer.

pole   **1.** An extremity or terminus that possesses POLARITY. Examples: *magnetic pole* and *electric pole*. **2.** The movable member of a switch. **3.** One of the frequencies at which a transfer function becomes infinite.

pole face   The smooth end surface of a pole piece.

pole piece   **1.** A section of specially shaped iron or steel that is attached to a magnetic core. **2.** Half of a two-piece magnetic core that terminates in a pole.

pole shoe   In an electric motor, the section of the field pole nearest the armature.

poles of impedance   For a reactive network, the frequencies at which the impedance is infinite. Compare ZEROS OF IMPEDANCE.

poles of network function The values at which a network function is infinite. Compare ZEROS OF NETWORK FUNCTION.

poles of transfer function The frequencies at which a transfer function becomes infinite. Compare ZEROS OF TRANSFER FUNCTION.

police robot A proposed robotic machine, either autonomous or remotely controlled (teleoperated), that would be used to assist in law enforcement, particularly in dangerous operations.

poling The deliberate adjustment of electromagnetic-field polarity.

Polish notation In Boolean algebra, a form of notation wherein the variables in a statement are preceded by the operators.

polling In data transmission, a technique in which channels being shared by more than one terminal are tested to find one over which data is coming in, or to ascertain which is free for transmission.

polonium Symbol, Po. A radioactive metallic element. Atomic number, 84. Atomic weight, approximately 209.

polychromatic radiation **1.** Visible-light radiation having more than one wavelength; in particular, covering a broad range of wavelengths. **2.** Electromagnetic radiation over a broad band of wavelengths.

polycrystalline material A substance, such as a semiconductor, of which even a very small sample consists of a number of separate crystals bound tightly together. Compare SINGLE-CRYSTAL MATERIAL.

polydirectional microphone See OMNIDIRECTIONAL MICROPHONE.

polyelectrolyte An ELECTROLYTE having high molecular weight.

polyester A resin made by reacting a dihydroxy alcohol with a dibasic acid.

polyester backing A polyester tape on the surface of which iron oxide is deposited to yield a magnetic recording tape.

polyethylene A plastic insulating material. Dielectric constant, 2.2. Dielectric strength, 585 V/mil.

polyethylene disc A phonograph disc made of polyethylene.

polygonal coil A coil wound on a form having a polygonal, rather than circular cross section. Some polygonal forms have as many as 12 sides in cross section.

polygraph An instrument for measuring and recording electrical signals proportional to blood pressure, skin resistance, breathing rate, and other reactions that vary under emotional stress. Also called LIE DETECTOR. Compare PATHOMETER.

polymer A compound that is the product of *polymerization*, resulting from the chemical union of monomers. Also see POLYMERIZE.

polymerize To unite monomers or polymers of the same kind to form a molecule having a higher molecular weight.

polyphase In alternating-current circuits, pertaining to the existence or generation of two or more specific electrical phases. Compare SINGLE PHASE.

polyphase antenna An antenna consisting of two dipole radiators mounted perpendicular to each other at their midpoint and excited 90 degrees out of phase. The radiation pattern is approximately circular in the plane of the elements. Also called TURNSTILE ANTENNA.

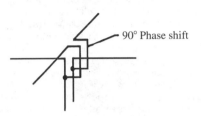

90° Phase shift

polyphase antenna

polyphase generator **1.** A dynamo-type generator of polyphase power (two-phase, three-phase, etc.). **2.** See POLYPHASE OSCILLATOR.

polyphase oscillator An oscillator circuit that generates polyphase alternating current. The circuit contains separate oscillators for each phase. A three-phase circuit, for example, has three symmetrical oscillators with matched inductance and capacitance values.

polyphase power **1.** The total dissipated power in a polyphase alternating-current circuit. **2.** Polyphase alternating current provided for utility purposes.

polyphase rectifier A rectifier of polyphase alternating current generally obtained from a three-phase power line through a transformer. The several common circuits usually contain a diode for each phase. Such rectifiers offer the advantage of higher ripple frequency than is obtainable by single-phase operation. For a three-phase rectifier, for example, the ripple frequency is three times the line frequency; for a six-phase rectifier, it is six times the line frequency.

polyphase system An alternating-current circuit in which voltages or currents are normally out of phase with each other by some fixed amount. Familiar types are two-phase and three-phase.

polyphase transformer An alternating-current transformer specifically designed for use in circuits that have two or more simultaneous current phases.

polypropylene A plastic material commonly used as an electrical insulator. Dielectric constant, 2.0. Dielectric strength, 600 V/mil.

polyrod antenna A tapered dielectric antenna, usually made of polystyrene, for directional microwave transmission.

polysilicon A polycrystalline form of silicon (see POLYCRYSTALLINE MATERIAL).

polystyrene A clear, colorless thermosetting-type plastic. It is widely used as an insulating material in radio-frequency circuits and, to some extent, as a dielectric film in fixed capacitors. Dielectric constant, 2.4 to 2.9. Dielectric strength, 20 to 28 kV/mm.

polystyrene capacitor A high-Q capacitor in which the dielectric film is polystyrene.

polyvinyl chloride Abbreviation, PVC. A plastic insulating material. Dielectric constant, 3.6 to 4.0. Dielectric strength, 800 V/mil.

pool cathode In an industrial electron tube, a cathode consisting of a pool of mercury.

pool-cathode tube An industrial electron tube using a pool cathode. Examples: excitron, ignitron, and mercury-arc rectifier.

popcorn noise A temperature-dependent, random-shot electrical noise. In a radio receiver or audio circuit, this noise resembles the sound of popping corn. It occurs in some operational amplifiers.

population In statistical analysis, the total group of items, quantities, or values under consideration. Sometimes called *universe*.

porcelain A hard, white, usually glazed ceramic used as a dielectric and insulant. Dielectric constant, 6 to 7.5. Dielectric strength, 40 to 100 V/mil. Also called *china*.

porcelain capacitor A ceramic-dielectric capacitor in which the dielectric is composed of porcelain or a related substance.

porcelain insulator An electric insulator fabricated from porcelain.

porch See BACK PORCH and FRONT PORCH.

port 1. In a circuit, device, or system, a point at which energy or signals can be introduced or extracted in a particular manner (e.g., *two-port circulator* and *I/O port*). 2. An aperture in a loudspeaker enclosure.

portable-mobile station See MOBILE STATION.

portable station A communications station that can be carried from one location to another. A portable station differs from a mobile station in that a portable station does not usually operate while in motion, whereas a mobile station does.

ported reflex enclosure A loudspeaker cabinet with openings that facilitate bass (low-frequency) sound reproduction.

pos 1. Abbreviation of POSITIVE. 2. Abbreviation of POSITION.

position 1. The location of a point or object with respect to one or more (usually fixed) references. 2. The setting of an adjustable device, such as a potentiometer, rotary switch, or variable capacitor.

positional notation A method of representing numbers in which the number is indicated by the positions and value of the component digits.

The decimal number system belongs in this category (e.g., the decimal number 1284.67 is equal to $1 \times 10^3 + 2 \times 10^2 + 8 \times 10^1 + 4 \times 10^0 + 6 \times 10^{-1} + 7 \times 10^{-2}$).

positional number system See POSITIONAL NOTATION.

positional representation See POSITIONAL NOTATION.

position-control potentiometers In an oscilloscope, potentiometers used to control the voltage applied to the horizontal and vertical deflecting plates to position the spot on the screen. Also see CENTERING CONTROL.

position controls See POSITION-CONTROL POTENTIOMETERS.

position feedback In a servo or other control system, feedback current, or voltage that is proportional to the position assumed by a member.

position fixing The determination of a position from the intersection on a map of two lines derived from the direction-finding pickups of two transmitting stations. Also see DIRECTION FINDER.

position indicator In a tape recorder, a counter whose numbered wheels revolve when the reels do, thus aiding in locating a desired spot on the tape. Also called *tape counter*.

positioning circuit The circuit associated with a horizontal or vertical centering control (see CENTERING CONTROL).

position sensing 1. In robotics and navigation systems, a method of determining location, relative to the surrounding environment. 2. Any method via which a robot can accurately determine the location(s) of its end effector(s).

position sensor An electronic circuit that detects physical displacement, and transmits a signal proportional to the displacement.

positioning control See CENTERING CONTROL.

positive 1. Possessing positive (plus) direct-current electrical polarity. 2. Pertaining to real numbers greater than zero. 3. A photographic image whose shadings are the same as those in the scene.

positive angle 1. In a system of rectangular coordinates, an angle in the first or second quadrant. 2. In rectangular coordinates, an angle measured counterclockwise from the positive x-axis. Compare NEGATIVE ANGLE.

positive bias A positive voltage or current applied continuously to an electrode of a device (as to a transistor base) to maintain the device's operating point. Compare NEGATIVE BIAS.

positive bus See POSITIVE CONDUCTOR.

positive charge An electrical charge characterized by having relatively fewer electrons than a negative charge. Also see CHARGE, 1; ELECTRIC CHARGE; and UNIT ELECTROSTATIC CHARGE. Compare NEGATIVE CHARGE.

positive conductor The conductor or line connected to the positive terminal of a current, voltage, or power source. Compare NEGATIVE CONDUCTOR.

positive electricity See POSITIVE CHARGE and POSITIVE ELECTRIFICATION.

positive electrification Electrification characterized by a deficiency of electrons. For example, when a glass rod is rubbed with a silk cloth, the rod becomes positively charged because electrons are rubbed off the glass onto the silk. Similarly, when an atom loses an electron, it becomes electrified positively because it has a deficiency of electrons. Compare NEGATIVE ELECTRIFICATION.

positive electrode **1.** An electrode connected to the positive terminal of a current, voltage, or power source. **2.** The positive terminal of a current, voltage, or power source, such as a battery or generator.

positive electron See POSITRON.

positive element See POSITIVE ELECTRODE, **1.**

positive error of measurement An error of measurement in which the difference between a measured value and the true or most probable value is positive. Compare NEGATIVE ERROR OF MEASUREMENT.

positive exponent A positive superscript indicating that a number (x) is to be raised to the positive nth power. Thus, in the expression x^n, the value of n is greater than zero. Compare NEGATIVE EXPONENT.

positive feedback Feedback that is in phase with an input signal. Also called REGENERATION and REGENERATIVE FEEDBACK. Compare NEGATIVE FEEDBACK.

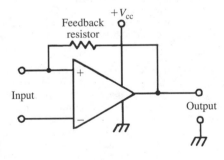

positive feedback

positive function A function having the positive sign. In the rectangular coordinate system, the trigonometric sine function is positive in the first and second quadrants, the cosine in the first and fourth, and the tangent in the first and third. Compare NEGATIVE FUNCTION.

positive ghost In a television picture, a ghost with positive shading (see POSITIVE, **3**). Also see GHOST.

positive-going Pertaining to a signal whose value is changing in a positive direction. This is not restricted to signals of actual positive polarity; a decreasing negative voltage, for example, is positive-going as it falls in the direction of zero—even if it never crosses the zero line.

positive grid In an electron tube, a control grid whose bias or signal voltage is positive, with respect to the cathode.

positive-grid oscillator A microwave oscillator circuit in which the control grid of a triode tube is operated at a positive direct-current potential, and the plate at a negative potential. Electrons move back and forth between cathode and plate, through the grid, and thus give rise to an oscillating current.

positive ground A direct-current electrical system in which the positive power-supply terminal is connected to the common ground. It is not generally used in North America.

positive half-alternation See POSITIVE HALF-CYCLE.

positive half-cycle That half of an alternating-current cycle in which the current or voltage increases from zero to maximum positive and returns to zero.

positive image **1.** A picture in which the blacks, whites, and grays correspond to those in the actual scene (see POSITIVE, **3**). **2.** A normal television picture (i.e., one that has the shading described in **1**).

positive ion An atom that has a deficiency of electrons and, consequently, exhibits a net positive charge. Also called CATION.

positive lead See POSITIVE CONDUCTOR.

positive light modulation In television transmission, the condition in which transmitted power increases as the light intensity increases. Compare NEGATIVE LIGHT MODULATION.

positive line See POSITIVE CONDUCTOR.

positive logic **1.** Binary logic in which a low positive state represents logic 0, and a high positive state represents logic 1. **2.** Binary logic in which a high negative state represents logic 0, and a low negative state represents logic 1. Compare NEGATIVE LOGIC.

positive magnetostriction A form of MAGNETOSTRICTION in which the physical size of a substance is directly proportional to the intensity of the surrounding magnetic field.

positive measurement error See POSITIVE ERROR OF MEASUREMENT.

positive modulation In amplitude-modulated television transmission, the increase in transmitted power when the brightness of the scene increases. Compare NEGATIVE MODULATION.

positive modulation factor For an amplitude-modulated wave having unequal positive and negative peaks, a ratio expressing the maximum positive deviation (increase) from the average value of the envelope. Compare NEGATIVE MODULATION FACTOR.

positive number A real number, whose value is greater than zero. Compare NEGATIVE NUMBER.

positive peak The maximum amplitude of a positive half-cycle or positive pulse.

positive-peak clipper A peak clipper that levels off the positive half-cycle of an alternating-current wave to a predetermined level.

positive-peak modulation Amplitude modulation of the positive peaks of a carrier wave.

positive-peak voltmeter An electronic voltmeter for measuring the amplitude of the positive peak of an alternating-current (ac) wave. In its simplest form, it consists essentially of a direct-current (dc) microammeter with a diode oriented to pass the positive half-cycle. A series capacitor in the circuit is charged to approximately the peak value of the applied ac voltage. Compare NEGATIVE-PEAK VOLTMETER.

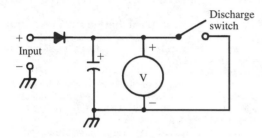

positive-peak voltmeter

positive phase-sequence relay A phase-sequence relay that responds to the positive phase sequence in a polyphase circuit. Compare NEGATIVE PHASE-SEQUENCE RELAY.

positive picture modulation See POSITIVE MODULATION.

positive picture phase In a television signal, the swinging of the picture-signal voltage from zero to positive, in response to an increase in brightness in the scene. Compare NEGATIVE PICTURE PHASE.

positive plate 1. The positive member of an electrochemical cell or battery. Electrons flow to this plate from the negative plate, through the external circuit. 2. A vacuum-tube plate that is biased positively, as in a conventional tube circuit.

positive pole See POSITIVE ELECTRODE, 1, 2.

positive potential 1. The voltage at a positive electrode (with respect to the negative electrode). 2. Voltage greater than that at ground as a reference.

positive power See POSITIVE EXPONENT.

positive resistance Ohmic resistance (see OHMIC RESPONSE). Compare NEGATIVE RESISTANCE.

positive resistor A resistor whose value does not change with current or voltage changes. Compare NEGATIVE RESISTOR.

positive temperature coefficient Abbreviation, PTC. A number expressing the amount by which a quantity (such as the value of a component) increases when temperature is increased. The coefficient is stated as a percentage of the rated value per degree, or in parts per million per degree. Compare NEGATIVE TEMPERATURE COEFFICIENT and ZERO TEMPERATURE COEFFICIENT.

positive transmission In facsimile or television, a form of amplitude modulation in which the picture brightness is directly proportional to the signal strength at any given instant of time.

positive valence The valence of a positive ion.

positron A positively charged particle having the same mass as that of the electron, and the same magnitude of electric charge, but positive (instead of negative). Sometimes called *positive electron.*

post See BINDING POST.

post- Prefix meaning "following," "subsequent to," or "behind."

post-accelerating electrode In a cathode-ray tube, the high-voltage electrode that produces POST-DEFLECTION ACCELERATION of the electron beam. Also called INTENSIFIER ELECTRODE.

postacceleration See POST-DEFLECTION ACCELERATION.

post-alloy-diffused transistor Abbreviation, PADT. A transistor in which electrodes are diffused into the semiconductor wafer after other electrodes have been alloyed.

post-conversion bandwidth The bandwidth of a signal after it has been converted from one frequency to another.

post-deflection accelerating electrode See POST-ACCELERATING ELECTRODE.

post-deflection acceleration In a cathode-ray tube, the intensification of the electron beam following beam deflection. Also see POST-DEFLECTION CRT.

post-deflection CRT An oscilloscope tube provided with a high-voltage intensifier electrode in the form of a ring encircling the inside flare of the tube, between the deflecting plates and the screen. The deflected electron beam is accelerated by this electrode. This arrangement allows the beam to be deflected at low velocity and high sensitivity, then to be accelerated for a brighter image.

post edit The editing of data in a computer output.

postemphasis See DEEMPHASIS.

post-equalization 1. In sound recording and reproduction, equalization during playback. Compare PREEQUALIZATION. 2. See DEEMPHASIS.

postmortem An investigation into the cause of failure of a circuit, device, or system.

postmortem dump At the end of a computer program run, a dump to supply information for debugging purposes.

post office box A type of wheatstone bridge that contains resistance coils in a special box. The coils are connected so that they can be replaced by shorting connectors.

pot **1.** See POTENTIOMETER. **2.** See DASHPOT. **3.** Abbreviation of POTENTIAL. **4.** To encapsulate a circuit in a potting compound, such as epoxy resin.

potassium Symbol, K. A metallic element of the alkali-metal group. Atomic number, 19. Atomic weight, 39.098.

potassium chloride Formula, KCl. A compound used as a phosphor coating on the screen of a nearly permanent-persistence cathode-ray tube. The fluorescence is magenta or white, as is the phosphorescence.

potassium cyanide Formula, KCN. A highly toxic salt that is an electrolyte in some forms of electroplating.

potassium dihydrogen phosphate Abbreviation, KDP. An inorganic ferroelectric material.

pot core A magnetic core for a coil, made of ferrite or of powdered iron, consisting of a central rod, a surrounding potlike enclosure, and a lid. The rod passes through the center of the coil, and the pot and lid completely enclose the coil. This arrangement provides a completely closed magnetic circuit and coil shield.

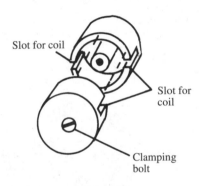

Slot for coil

Slot for coil

Clamping bolt

pot core

potential See ELECTROMOTIVE FORCE.

potential barrier The electric field produced on each side of a semiconductor junction by minority carriers (i.e., by holes in the n-layer and electrons in the p-layer) that face each other across the junction, but cannot diffuse across the junction and recombine.

potential coil The shunt coil in a conventional wattmeter.

potential difference See ELECTROMOTIVE FORCE and VOLTAGE.

potential divider See VOLTAGE DIVIDER.

potential drop **1.** A voltage difference between two points in a circuit. **2.** The voltage across a resistor in a direct-current circuit.

potential energy Energy resulting from the position of a body or particle (e.g., the energy stored

in something lifted against gravity and held in its new position) or from the position of charges (e.g., the energy stored in a charged capacitor). Compare KINETIC ENERGY.

potential gradient See VOLTAGE GRADIENT.

potential profile A rectangular-coordinate display of the VOLTAGE GRADIENT across a body (e.g., the cross section of a transistor).

potential transformer A small step-up transformer for increasing the range of an alternating-current voltmeter.

potentiometer **1.** A variable resistor used as a voltage divider. The input voltage is applied across the entire resistance element and the output voltage is taken from the wiper, relative to one end of the element. One end is usually grounded (at zero potential). **2.** A null device whose operation is based on a variable resistor, and is used for precise voltage measurements. The unknown voltage is applied to the input of a variable resistor whose settings are known with great accuracy; the resistance is adjusted for an output voltage that exactly equals the voltage of a standard cell (as indicated by a null between the two voltages). The unknown voltage is then determined from the resistance and the standard-cell voltage.

potentiometer noise In a current-carrying potentiometer, electrical noise generated when the wiper blade rubs against the resistance element, or by contact between the blade and element.

potentiometric recorder A type of graphic recorder. It consists essentially of a resistance-calibrated potentiometer, a standard cell, and a galvanometer. When an unknown voltage (E_x) is applied to the input terminals of the potentiometer and the potentiometer is set for null, $E_x = E_s (R_2/R_1)$, where E_s is the voltage of the standard cell, R_1 is the input resistance of the potentiometer, and R_2 is the output resistance of the potentiometer.

Potier diagram An illustration of the phase relationship between current and voltage in an alternating-current circuit that contains reactance.

POTS Acronym for *plain old telephone service*, meaning basic service without optional features (such as call waiting, conference calling, call forwarding, etc.).

potted circuit A circuit embedded in plastic or wax to protect it against the environment, and/or to minimize the effects of physical vibration (see POTTING).

potted component An electronic part embedded in a suitable plastic or wax to protect it against the environment, and/or to minimize the effects of physical vibration (see POTTING).

potting A process of embedding a component or circuit in a solid mass of plastic or wax held in a container. The process is similar to encapsulation, except that in potting, the container (envelope) remains as part of the assembly. Compare ENCAPSULATION.

potting material A substance, such as a resin or wax, used for potting electronic gear. Also called *potting compound*.

pound **1.** Abbreviations, lb, p. A unit of weight equal to 16 avoirdupois ounces. **2.** Abbreviation, lbf. A unit of force approximately equal to 4.448 newtons. **3.** Abbreviation, lbm. A unit of mass approximately equal to 0.4536 kilogram.

poundal A unit of force equal to approximately 13825.5 dynes or 0.138255 newton. One poundal is the force that, when acting for one second, will impart a speed of one foot per second to a one-pound mass.

pound-foot Abbreviation, lb-ft. A unit of torque equal to the product of a force of one pound and a moment arm of one foot. Compare OUNCE-INCH.

pounds per square inch absolute Abbreviation, psia. Absolute pressure (i.e., the sum of atmospheric pressure and the pressure indicated by a gauge). Compare POUNDS PER SQUARE INCH GAUGE.

pounds per square inch gauge Abbreviation, PSIG. The value of pressure indicated by a gauge, without correction for atmospheric pressure. Compare POUNDS PER SQUARE INCH ABSOLUTE.

powdered-iron core A magnetic core consisting of minute particles of iron, each coated with a film to insulate it from others, molded into a solid mass. Because of its low eddy-current loss, this type of core is usable in radio-frequency transformers and coils, where it increases the inductance of the winding.

power **1.** Symbol, *P*. Unit, watt. The rate of doing work, or producing or transmitting energy. In direct-current circuits, and in alternating-current circuits containing no reactance, power is the product of the root-mean-square current and voltage. See, for example, AC POWER, APPARENT POWER, DC POWER, KILOVOLT-AMPERE, POWER FACTOR, REACTIVE KILOVOLT-AMPERE, REACTIVE VOLT-AMPERE, TRUE POWER, VOLT-AMPERE, WATT, and WATTLESS POWER. **2.** The product obtained by multiplying a quantity *x* by itself *n* times, written x^n. For example, $2^4 = 2 \times 2 \times 2 \times 2 = 8$; here, 8 is the *fourth power* of 2. Compare ROOT, **1**. **3.** The exponent in an expression, as defined in **2**.

power amplification **1.** The amplification of a signal having a certain power (wattage) to produce a signal having greater power. **2.** The signal power increase, expressed as a ratio or as a figure in decibels, resulting from the process defined in **1**. Also called POWER GAIN.

power amplification ratio See POWER AMPLIFICATION, **2** and POWER GAIN.

power amplifier An amplifier that delivers useful amounts of power to a load, such as one or more speakers. Compare CURRENT AMPLIFIER and VOLTAGE AMPLIFIER.

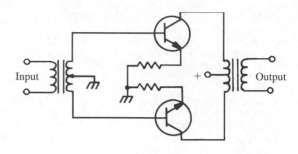

power amplifier

power-amplifier device A high-current tube or transistor designed especially for high power output. Such a device does not always provide significant voltage amplification, but always provides power amplification. Compare VOLTAGE-AMPLIFIER DEVICE.

power at peak torque Symbol, P_p. For a torque motor, the input power in watts needed for peak torque at stall at a winding temperature of 25 degrees Celsius.

power attenuation **1.** A reduction of power level. **2.** See POWER LOSS.

power bandwidth For a high-fidelity audio amplifier, the difference between the maximum and minimum frequencies at which the amplifier can produce at least 50 percent of its maximum power output, with less than a certain amount of total harmonic distortion (usually 10 percent).

power blackout A situation in which all electric power is lost to utility subscribers in a defined region.

power consumption **1.** For a direct-current device, the normal operating voltage multiplied by the normal drawn current. **2.** For an alternating-current circuit, the root-mean-square voltage multiplied by the root-mean-square current.

power control The adjustment of the output voltage of a power supply, usually by means of a variable autotransformer, silicon-controlled rectifier, thyratron, or similar device.

power cutoff frequency Symbol, f_{co}. The frequency at which the power gain of a transistor drops 3 dB below its low-frequency value.

power derating For a temperature higher than the specified ambient temperature, a deliberate reduction of the power dissipated by a component or device. This is done to prevent failure of the component or device. Also see DERATING, DERATING CURVE, and DERATING FACTOR.

power difference An expression of the power lost in a circuit when power is absorbed by a dielectric material.

power diode A heavy-duty diode that is usually used in power-supply service. Also called *rectifier diode*.

power dissipation Abbreviation, PD. The power consumed by a device during normal operation. This power is not available in the electrical output of the device. An example is the direct-current power dissipated in the collector circuit of a high-fidelity audio amplifier.

power divider A circuit that distributes power, in a predetermined manner, among various loads.

power drain The amount of power drawn by a device. It can be operating power or standby power.

power dump See DUMP, 2.

power equations Variations of the basic power equation: $P = EI = E^2/R = I^2R$, where P is the power in watts, E is the voltage in volts, I is the current in amperes, and R is the resistance in ohms.

power factor Abbreviation, PF. In an alternating-current circuit, the ratio (expressed either as a decimal or a percentage) of true power (power actually consumed) to apparent power (simple product of voltage and current). The power factor is equal to the cosine of the phase angle. Also see AC POWER.

power-factor balance In a capacitance bridge, a separate null adjustment for the internal resistance component of a capacitor under measurement. The dial of the variable component for this adjustment reads directly in percent power factor in some bridges.

power-factor correction To raise the power factor of an inductive circuit by inserting a parallel capacitance. In power circuits, this affords improved economy of operation because the current drain is brought more in line with that of a resistive circuit.

power-factor meter An instrument that gives direct readings of power factor (lead or lag). One such meter uses a dynamometer-type movement (see ELECTRODYNAMOMETER) in which the rotating element consists of two coils fastened together at right angles.

power-factor regulator A device that regulates the power factor of an alternating-current line.

power-factor relay An alternating-current relay actuated by a rise or fall in power factor, with respect to a predetermined value.

power frequency 1. See POWER-LINE FREQUENCY. 2. The frequency of an alternating-current generator. 3. The output frequency of a power inverter (see INVERTER, 1).

power-frequency meter An instrument for measuring power-line frequency. It can use electromechanical devices, or can directly count the number of alternations per second.

power gain Abbreviations, PG or PG_{dB}. The extent to which power is increased by a power amplifier. It can be expressed as the ratio of power output to power input as $PG = P_o/P_i$, or in decibels as $PG_{dB} = 10 \log_{10}(P_o/P_i)$.

power grid An aggregation of power-generating stations, transmission lines, and associated equipment, usually extending over hundreds of miles and embracing several communities, so operated that individual members can deliver power to the system or draw power from it, according to local demand.

power ground The power-supply ground for a circuit or system.

power-handling capacity 1. The amount of power that a device can dissipate, either continuously or intermittently, without suffering damage. 2. The maximum input power that can be tolerated by an amplifier transistor or tube without overheating.

power hyperbola For a semiconductor device or vacuum tube, a curve plotted from the device's current and voltage values, which provide the power value when multiplied (e.g., a 2-watt curve for the direct-current collector input of a power transistor).

power input See INPUT POWER.

power-input control The adjustment of the output of a power supply by varying the alternating-current input to the power transformer. Usually, a variable autotransformer is operated ahead of the power transformer. See, for example, VARIABLE TRANSFORMER and VARIAC.

power-level indicator 1. See DB METER. 2. See OUTPUT POWER METER.

power line The line through which electrical energy is received by a subscriber.

power-line communication Abbreviation, PLC. Carrier-current telephony or telegraphy over power lines that are common to transmitting and receiving stations. Also see WIRED WIRELESS.

power-line filter 1. A heavy-duty radio-frequency (RF) filter inserted in the power line close to a device that generates RF energy, such as a radio transmitter. It prevents transmission of RF energy via the power line. 2. An RF filter inserted in the power line, where it enters the power supply of a sensitive electronic device, such as a computer or high-fidelity audio amplifier. It prevents RF energy on the power line from entering the device via the power supply.

power-line frequency The frequency of the alternating current and voltage available over commercial power lines. In the United States, it is 60 Hz; in some countries, it is 50 Hz.

power-line monitor An expanded-scale alternating-current voltmeter for the continuous monitoring of power-line voltage.

wer-line pickup The interception of radio-frequency energy by utility power lines acting as receiving antennas. This energy can enter a sensitive electronic device, such as a computer or a high-fidelity audio amplifier, via the power supply.

power loss The power dissipated in a component. It generates heat while doing no useful work. Represents energy loss, except when the generation of heat is the end purpose.

power-loss factor Symbol, F_p. In interstage coupling, the ratio of available power (with the coupling network in place) to the available power when the network is disconnected.

power meter   See WATTMETER.

power modulation factor   In amplitude modulation, the ratio of the peak power to the average power.

power oscillator   A heavy-duty oscillator delivering useful power output.

power output   See OUTPUT POWER.

power-output meter   See OUTPUT POWER METER.

power pack   An external power-line-operated unit supplying alternating or direct current for the operation of electronic equipment.

power pentode   A heavy-duty pentode vacuum tube designed to deliver relatively high output power.

power plug   A plug for insertion into a power-line outlet.

power programmer   A device that adjusts radar output power, in accordance with the target distance.

power rating   **1.** The specified power required by an equipment for normal operation. **2.** The specified power output of a generator or amplifier.

power reactive   See REACTIVE VOLT-AMPERE.

power rectifier   A heavy-duty semiconductor diode used to rectify alternating current for power-supply purposes.

power relay   A heavy-duty relay designed to switch significant amounts of power. The heavy contacts and armature require high actuating current; this necessitates a larger coil than is used in lighter-duty relays.

power resistor   A heavy-duty resistor (i.e., one designed to carry large currents without overheating).

power stack   A selenium rectifier consisting of a number of rectifier plates stacked in series for higher voltage handling.

power supply   **1.** A device, such as a generator or a transformer-rectifier-filter arrangement, that produces the power needed to operate an electronic equipment. **2.** A reserve of available power (e.g., the power line, an installation of batteries, etc.).

power-supply filter   A low-pass filter that is used to remove the ripple from the output of a power-supply rectifier. See, for example, BRUTE-FORCE FILTER.

power-supply rejection ratio   The ratio of the output-voltage change for an amplifier, oscillator, or other circuit, to the change in power-supply voltage. It is determined on an instantaneous basis.

power-supply sensitivity   In an operational amplifier, sensitivity of the offset to variations in the power-supply voltage.

power surge   **1.** A momentary increase in the voltage on a utility line. **2.** An abnormally high voltage that sometimes exists for the first several milliseconds after utility power is restored following a blackout.

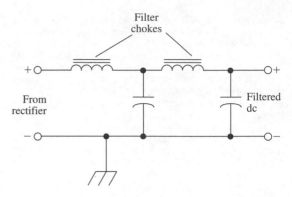

power-supply filter

power switch   The switch for controlling power to a piece of equipment. Also see ON-OFF SWITCH.

power switching   Switching operating power on and off. There are two principal methods: One involves making and breaking the connections between equipment and the power line; the other involves making and breaking the output of a line-operated or battery-type power supply.

power tetrode   A heavy-duty tetrode vacuum tube designed to deliver relatively high output power.

power-to-decibel conversion   Abbreviation, P_{dB}. Power expressed in decibels, with respect to a reference power level. Determined by the formula $P_{dB} = 10 \log_{10}(P_x / P_{ref})$, where P_x is the given power level and P_{ref} is the reference power level.

power transfer   **1.** The passage of power from a generator to a load. **2.** The passage of power from one circuit to another.

power transfer theorem   See MAXIMUM POWER TRANSFER THEOREM.

power transformer   A transformer designed solely to supply operating power to electronic equipment—either directly or through a rectifier-filter circuit. Because a power transformer is used at low (power-line) frequencies, its core does not require the high-grade iron used in audio transformers, nor are special winding techniques needed to reduce the leakage inductance and interwinding capacitance.

power transistor   A heavy-duty transistor designed for power-amplifier and power-control service.

power triode   A heavy-duty triode vacuum tube designed to deliver relatively high output power.

power tube   A heavy-duty electron tube designed to deliver useful amounts of power. See, for example, POWER PENTODE, POWER TETRODE, and POWER TRIODE.

power unit   **1.** A power supply (see POWER SUPPLY, 1). **2.** A unit of power measurement. See, for example, KILOWATT, MEGAWATT, MICROWATT, MILLIWATT, PICOWATT, and WATT.

power user   In personal or business computing, a serious user who has extensive, up-to-date knowledge of hardware and software.

power winding   In a magnetic amplifier or saturable reactor, the output winding (i.e., the winding through which the controlled current flows).

Poynting vector   In an electromagnetic wave, the vector product of instantaneous electric intensity and magnetic intensity.

PP   Abbreviation of *peripheral processor.*

PP   **1.** Symbol for PLATE POWER. **2.** Symbol for PEAK POWER.

ppb   Abbreviation of *parts per billion.*

PPI   Abbreviation of PLAN POSITION INDICATOR.

pp junction   In a semiconductor wafer, the boundary between two p-type regions that have somewhat different properties.

PPM   Abbreviation of PULSE-POSITION MODULATION.

ppm   **1.** Abbreviation of *parts per million.* **2.** Abbreviation of *pulses per minute.*

pps   Abbreviation of *pulses per second.*

ppt   Abbreviation of *parts per thousand.*

PPV   Abbreviation of PAY PER VIEW.

Pr   Symbol for PRASEODYMIUM.

practical component   A circuit component considered in proper combination with the stray components inherent in it. Thus, a resistor has residual inductance and capacitance, an inductor has residual capacitance and resistance. Compare IDEAL COMPONENT.

practical units   A set of physical/electrical units especially suited to a particular application. For example, in direct-current electrical applications, practical units are the AMPERE, OHM, VOLT, and WATT.

praetersonics   See ACOUSTOELECTRONICS; ACOUSTIC DELAY LINE; SURFACE-WAVE AMPLIFIER; SURFACE-WAVE FILTER.

pragilbert   The unit of MAGNETOMOTIVE FORCE in the absolute mks (Giorgi) system.

pragilbert per weber   The unit of RELUCTANCE in the absolute mks (Giorgi) system.

praoersted   The unit of MAGNETIZING FORCE in the absolute mks (Giorgi) system.

praseodymium   Symbol, Pr. A metallic element of the rare-earth group. Atomic number, 59. Atomic weight, 140.908.

preaccelerating electrode   In the electron gun of a cathode-ray tube, the high-voltage electrode that provides initial acceleration to the electron beam.

pre-alarm signal   An audio and/or visual indicator that an alarm will sound if an area is not cleared within a short time. An example is a voice recording in a car alarm system (e.g., "Stand back!").

preamplifier   **1.** A high-sensitivity, low-noise amplifier that usually uses a high-gain field-effect transistor (FET) and is used to enhance the sen-

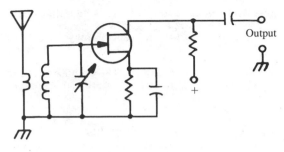

preamplifier

sitivity of a radio communications receiver. They are especially used at frequencies above approximately 15 MHz, where most of the noise comes from the receiver, rather than from outside sources. **2.** A low-noise amplifier used for boosting weak signals for television reception. **3.** A low-noise, low-level amplifier used for boosting signal levels from transducers, such as microphones or photocells.

prebiased relay   A relay through which is maintained a steady current that is just lower than that needed to close the relay. The actuating signal, then, need only be a small amount of additional current.

precedence effect   See FUSION, **1.**

precipitation   **1.** Water falling from the atmosphere in some form (rain, snow, hail, or sleet). See PRECIPITATION STATIC. **2.** The amount of precipitation occurring in a given period of time at a specific location. **3.** Separation of a solid material from a solution, as a result of a chemical or physical action.

precipitation static   **1.** Radio noise that sometimes occurs when it rains or snows. It can be mistaken for artificially generated noise. **2.** Radio noise caused by atmospheric electricity arising from rain, snow, ice crystals, hail, or dust clouds, through which an aircraft carrying the radio flies.

precipitator   See DUST PRECIPITATOR.

precipitron   See DUST PRECIPITATOR.

precision   **1.** Pertaining to electronic hardware, especially test instruments and measuring devices, designed and built to function with a high degree of accuracy. **2.** The relative accuracy of a meter or other indicating device. **3.** The accuracy of the results of an experiment, test, or measurement.

precision approach radar   A radar aimed along the approach path to guide an aircraft during approach.

precision instrument   An instrument possessing high accuracy and stability (i.e., one capable of reproducing readings or settings for various trials under set circumstances).

precision potentiometer 1. A POTENTIOME-
TER possessing highly accurate resistance calibration, linearity, and repeatability of settings.
2. A potentiometer-type voltage-measuring instrument.

preconduction current 1. The cutoff current in
a transistor. **2.** In a thyratron, the small (anode)
current flowing before the tube is fired.

predetermined counter A counter programmed
to count to a desired number and stop.

predistortion See PREEMPHASIS.

pre-Dolby 1. To record a tape with DOLBY compression. **2.** A tape that has been recorded with
Dolby compression.

preemphasis In frequency modulation, the introduction of a rising-response characteristic (response rises as modulation frequency increases).
Compare DEEMPHASIS.

preequalization 1. In sound recording and reproduction, equalization during recording. **2.**
See PREEMPHASIS.

preferred values of components A number
system used by the Electronics Industries Association (EIA) for establishing the values of
composition resistors and small fixed capacitors.

prefix multiplier See MULTIPLIER PREFIX.

prefix notation As used with complex expressions involving many operators and operands, a
type of notation in which the expressions,
rather than containing brackets, are given a
value, according to the relative positions of operators and operands.

preform 1. A small wafer, usually dry-pressed
from powdered plastic, from which the body of a
component, such as a capacitor or resistor, is
heat-molded. Also called a *pill* or *biscuit.* **2.** The
preformed slab used in molding a phonograph
disc. **3.** To shape a moldable circuit before fixing
the final configuration or package.

preliminary information For manufactured
electronic components, data that is released
prior to the actual availability of the device.
Subject to change when units are produced.

premix A molding compound of reinforced plastic.

prerecorded disc A phonograph disc on which a
recording has been made (i.e., a recorded disc).

prerecorded tape Magnetic tape on which a program or data has been recorded. Also called
RECORDED TAPE.

p region See P LAYER.

prescaler A device operated ahead of a counter to
establish a new, usually higher-frequency,
range over which frequency measurements can
be made.

preselector A tuned or untuned radio-frequency
amplifier operated ahead of a radio or television
receiver to boost the sensitivity of the receiver.

presence 1. In sound reproduction, the quality of
being true to life. **2.** The effect of boosted upper-
midrange frequencies in music.

preset counter A pulse counter that delivers one
output pulse for a number of successive input
pulses, determined by the settings of counter-
circuit controls. Thus, a preset counter might
give an output pulse for each train of 125 input
pulses.

preset element In automation and control, an element that can be preset to a given level or
value, and to which other elements can then be
referred.

preset switch In the circuit of a PRESET COUNT-
ER, a multiposition rotary switch that can be
set to determine the number of input pulses
that must be received for the circuit to deliver
one output pulse.

preshoot A downward-moving transient pip that
sometimes precedes the rise of a pulse.

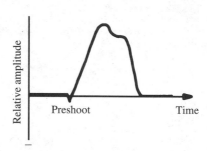

preshoot

preshoot amplitude The peak voltage of a PRE-
SHOOT, measured from the zero line to the valley of the preshoot.

preshoot time The width of a PRESHOOT, measured along the horizontal base line (time axis).

pressing 1. A process by which phonographic
discs are fabricated from plastic. **2.** A disc
pressed from plastic.

press-to-talk microphone A microphone that
uses a PRESS-TO-TALK SWITCH for actuation.

press-to-talk switch A switch in a microphone or
on the end of a control cord. It is used to actuate a transmitter, telephone, or recorder when
the operator wishes to speak.

pressure Abbreviation, P or p. **1.** Force per unit
area. It can be expressed in any appropriate
units of force and area (e.g., newtons per square
meter, pounds per square inch, grams per
square centimeter, etc.). **2.** The application of
force over part or all of a surface. **3.** Compression. **4.** See TENSION, **1.**

pressure amplitude The pressure caused by an
acoustic disturbance. It is usually measured in
dynes per square centimeter.

pressure capacitor An enclosed fixed or variable
capacitor, whose breakdown voltage increases
when the air pressure rises inside the container.

pressure contact   1. Electrical contact made by pressing two conducting surfaces together (to complete a circuit). **2.** A contact for obtaining the condition described in **1**.

pressure-gradient microphone   See PRESSURE MICROPHONE.

pressure microphone   A microphone that receives sound waves at only one side of its diaphragm. This one-sided exposure results in the displacement of the diaphragm by an amount proportional to the instantaneous pressure of the sound waves.

pressure pad   In a tape recorder, a small pad that holds the tape against one of the heads.

pressure pickup   See PRESSURE TRANSDUCER.

pressure roller   In a tape recorder, a rubber-tired roller that presses the tape against the capstan.

pressure sensor   A device that detects the presence of, and/or measures, physical force within a specific area. One simple device uses two metal plates separated by electrically resistive foam. Pressure compresses the foam and reduces the resistance between the plates. This resistance change can be detected and measured.

pressure switch   A switch that is opened or closed by a change in pressure within a system.

pressure transducer   A sensor for converting pressure into proportionate current or voltage. Some use strain gauges; others use piezoelectric crystals, potentiometers, and other variable elements.

pressure zone   A region of high air pressure that is immediately adjacent to a surface reflecting an acoustic (sound) wave.

pressure-zone microphone   A microphone equipped with a deflector that helps to guide acoustic energy toward the diaphragm.

prestore   To place data in memory before it is intended for use.

pretuned stage   A stage, such as one in an intermediate-frequency amplifier or single-frequency receiver, that is preset to a frequency, rather than being continuously tuned.

prf   Abbreviation of PULSE REPETITION FREQUENCY.

pri   Abbreviation of PRIMARY.

primaries   See PRIMARY COLORS.

primary   1. See PRIMARY WINDING. **2.** See PRIMARY STANDARD.

primary battery   A battery composed of primary cells.

primary block   A fundamental group of channels in pulse-code modulation, combined by means of time-division multiplexing.

primary capacitance   1. The distributed capacitance of the primary winding of a transformer whose secondary winding is unloaded. Compare SECONDARY CAPACITANCE, **1**. **2.** A series or shunt capacitance used to tune the primary coil of a radio-frequency transformer. Compare SECONDARY CAPACITANCE, **2**.

primary cell   An electrochemical cell that does not require, and generally will not accept, an electrical charge in order to function. Once it has been discharged, the cell must usually be thrown away. Compare STORAGE CELL. Also see CELL, DRY CELL, and STANDARD CELL.

primary circuit   1. The circuit associated with the primary winding of a transformer. **2.** The circuitry associated with the input to a device or system.

primary coil   See PRIMARY WINDING.

primary colors   See COLOR PRIMARY.

primary current   The current flowing in the primary winding of a transformer. Also called TRANSFORMER INPUT CURRENT. Compare SECONDARY CURRENT.

primary electron   The electron possessing the greater energy after a collision between two electrons. Compare SECONDARY ELECTRON.

primary emission   Emission arising directly from a source, such as the cathode of an electron tube. Compare SECONDARY EMISSION.

primary frequency standard   A device that generates unmodulated signals at precise frequencies. It generally uses a highly stable crystal oscillator that can be referred to a time standard and periodically corrected. A string of multivibrators, together with harmonic amplifiers and buffers, divide, and multiply the fundamental crystal frequency. The resulting signals provide markers for calibrating receivers and test equipment. Compare SECONDARY FREQUENCY STANDARD. Also see PRIMARY STANDARD.

primary impedance   1. The impedance of the primary winding of a transformer whose secondary winding is unloaded. Compare SECONDARY IMPEDANCE, **1**. **2.** An external impedance presented to the primary winding of a transformer. Compare SECONDARY IMPEDANCE, **2**.

primary inductance   The inductance of the primary winding of a transformer whose secondary winding is unloaded. Compare SECONDARY INDUCTANCE.

primary kVA   The kilovolt-amperes in the primary circuit of a transformer. Compare SECONDARY KVA.

primary measuring element   A detector, sensor, or transducer that performs the initial conversion in a measurement or control system. Such an element converts a phenomenon into a signal that can be transmitted to appropriate instruments for translation and evaluation.

primary power   Power in the primary circuit of a transformer. Also see PRIMARY KVA and PRIMARY VA. Compare SECONDARY POWER.

primary radiator   1. The driven element of a directive antenna system that incorporates parasitic elements. **2.** The driven element of a directive antenna that uses a reflector, such as a screen or dish.

primary resistance The direct-current resistance of the primary winding of a transformer. Compare SECONDARY RESISTANCE.

primary standard A usually stationary source of a quantity (e.g., capacitance, frequency, time, inductance, resistance, etc.). This source is so precise, and is maintained with such care, that it can be used as a universal reference. Compare SECONDARY STANDARD.

primary turns Symbol, N_p. The number of turns in the primary winding of a transformer. Compare SECONDARY TURNS.

primary utilization factor Abbreviation, UF_p. For a transformer in a rectifier circuit, the ratio of direct-current power output to primary volt-amperes. Numerically, the primary utilization factor is higher than the secondary utilization factor, but is less than 1. Also see SECONDARY UTILIZATION FACTOR and UTILITY FACTOR.

primary VA The volt-amperes in the input circuit of a transformer. Compare SECONDARY VA.

primary voltage The voltage across the primary winding of a transformer. Also called *transformer input voltage*. Compare SECONDARY VOLTAGE.

primary winding The normal or usual input winding of a transformer. Also called *primary coil*. Compare SECONDARY WINDING.

prime meridian See ZERO MERIDIAN.

prime mover A machine, such as a gas engine, steam engine, or water turbine, that converts a natural force or material into mechanical power.

primitive oscillation period In a complex oscillation waveform, the shortest period for which a definite repetition occurs; the highest fundamental frequency.

principal axis The line passing through the center of the spherical part of a lens, mirror, or dish reflector.

principal focus The focal point of rays arriving parallel to the principal axis of a lens, mirror, or dish reflector.

principal mode See DOMINANT MODE.

principal ray The path described by an electron entering an electron lens parallel to the lens' axis, or by an electron leaving this lens parallel to the axis.

print 1. The material transferred from a typewriter onto paper. 2. The command, in a computer system, that causes data to be placed on paper or onto the output screen. 3. The alphanumeric output of a computer or data terminal.

printed capacitor A two-plate capacitor formed on a printed circuit.

printed circuit A pattern of conductors (corresponding to the wiring of an electronic circuit) formed on a board of insulating material, such as a phenolic, by photo-etching, silk-screening of metallic paint, or by the use of pressure-sensitive preforms. The leads or pins of discrete components are soldered to the printed metal lines at the proper places in the circuit, or the

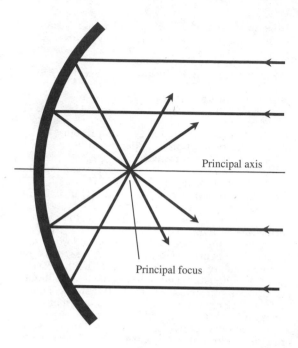

Principal axis

Principal focus

principal focus

components can be formed along with the conductors. Also see ETCHED CIRCUIT.

printed-circuit board A usually copper-clad plastic board used to make a printed circuit.

printed-circuit lamp A baseless lamp having flexible leads for easy soldering or welding to a printed circuit.

printed-circuit relay A usually small relay provided with pins or lugs for easy solder connection to a printed circuit.

printed-circuit switch A rotary switch whose contacts and contact leads are printed on a substrate.

printed-circuit template Also called *etching pattern*. A drawing for the purpose of making printed-circuit boards by photographic means.

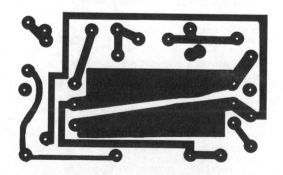

printed-circuit template

printed coil   A flat, spiral coil formed on a printed circuit.

printed component   A component formed on the substrate of a printed circuit. See, for example, PRINTED CAPACITOR, PRINTED COIL, and PRINTED RESISTOR.

printed display   See DATA PRINTOUT, 2.

printed element   See PRINTED COMPONENT.

printed inductor   See PRINTED COIL.

printed resistor   A resistor printed or painted on a printed circuit.

printed wiring   The printed or etched metal lines that serve as the conductors in a printed circuit.

printer   In computer and calculator operations and in measurement procedures, a readout device that prints a permanent record of output data. There are several types, including the *dot-matrix printer*, the *daisy-wheel printer*, the *inkjet printer*, and the *laser printer*. Some printers, such as the daisy-wheel type, can render only text data; others, such as the laser type, can print high-resolution graphic images, sometimes in color.

printing calculator   1. An electronic calculator that supplies a printed record of the results of a calculation. 2. For a programmable calculator, the results, a record of program steps, and plots of curves.

printing digital voltmeter   Abbreviation, PDVM. A digital voltmeter that delivers a printed record of a voltage reading, in addition to the usual digital readout of the voltage.

printing telegraph   1. A telegraph that prints the received message on a tape or page. 2. See TELETYPEWRITER.

printing wheel   See PRINT WHEEL.

print format   The form of data transmitted by a computer program to a printer (e.g., plain text, graphics, color graphics, etc.).

printout   See DATA PRINTOUT, 1, 2.

print-through   In prerecorded magnetic tape on a reel or cassette, the transfer of magnetism between layers of the rolled-up tape.

print wheel   In a daisy-wheel printer, the rotatable wheel on whose rim the letters, numbers, and other symbols are inscribed in relief.

priority indicator   In data transmission, a code that specifies the order of importance of a message in a group of messages to be sent.

priority processing   In multiple programming operations, a system for ascertaining the order of processing for different programs.

privacy code   1. A subaudible tone used in cordless telephone systems to reduce the chances of interference between phones operating on the same channel in close proximity. 2. A subaudible tone used in radio transmissions, especially in conjunction with repeaters, to allow only those stations with the proper code to be received. 3. A tone-burst sequence at the beginning of a transmission that actuates a receiver, allowing only those stations with the proper code to be received.

privacy equipment   Devices, such as speech scramblers and digital encryption programs, that provide some measure of secrecy in communications.

privacy switch   In a telephone amplifier, a switch (usually a pushbutton) for muting outgoing messages.

private automatic exchange   Abbreviation, PAX. A dial telephone system for use within an organization and having no connection to the central office. Compare PRIVATE BRANCH EXCHANGE.

private branch exchange   Abbreviation, PBX. A telephone system, complete with a private manually operated switchboard and individual telephone sets, installed and operated on private premises but having trunk-line connection to the central office. Compare PRIVATE AUTOMATIC EXCHANGE.

private line   1. A communication circuit in which the use is limited, by electronic means, to certain subscribers. 2. A subaudible-tone system used to restrict access to a communications system. The tone frequency is predetermined. For access to the system, a transmitted signal must contain the tone of the appropriate subaudible frequency, in addition to the voice or other information.

probability   1. The branch of mathematics concerned with the likelihood of an event's occurrence. It has many applications in quality control and physics. 2. The mathematical likelihood that an event will occur.

probable error   Abbreviation, PE. The value of error above and below which all other error values are equally likely to occur.

probe   1. A usually slender pencil-like implement with a pointed metal tip and a flexible, insulated lead. It is used to contact live points in a circuit under test (e.g., *voltmeter probe* and *oscilloscope probe*). 2. A device used to sample a radio-frequency voltage or current at a desired point (e.g., WAVEGUIDE PROBE). 3. A pickup device shaped like a probe for insertion into close quarters (e.g., PROBE THERMISTOR).

probe meter   See PROBE-TYPE VOLTMETER.

probe thermistor   A thermistor of slender construction for insertion into an area in which the temperature is to be monitored or controlled.

probe thermocouple   A thermocouple in the form of a slender probe for insertion into close quarters for temperature sensing or temperature control.

probe tip   See PROD.

probe-type voltmeter   A voltmeter installed in a long probe or wand. Kilovoltmeters are sometimes constructed in this fashion, with a long multiplier resistor housed in the probe.

probing   A process for locating, or determining the existence of, external artificial interference (e.g., power-line noise) in a radio communications circuit.

problem-oriented language   Any high-level computer programming language that allows the user to write programs as statements in terms applicable to the field of interest (e.g., COBOL's statements in English for problems relating to business).

problem reduction In artificial intelligence, a process in which problems are made easier by breaking them down into smaller logical parts.

process control The control of a process, such as one of manufacturing, by means of computers.

processor **1.** A circuit or device used to modify a signal in response to certain requirements (e.g., *clipper* and *waveshaper*). **2.** See DATA-PROCESSING MACHINE. **3.** See CENTRAL PROCESSING UNIT. **4.** See MICROPROCESSOR.

prod The metal tip of a probe (see PROBE, 1).

product **1.** The result of mixing or heterodyning of two or more signals. **2.** The result of modulating one signal with another. **3.** The result of combining or processing a signal or signals in a specified manner. **4.** The saleable end result of a manufacturing process. **5.** The result obtained when two or more quantities are multiplied by each other.

product detector A detector circuit whose output is the product of two signals applied simultaneously to the circuit. In a single-sideband receiver, for example, one of the signals is the incoming signal; the other, the signal from the local beat-frequency oscillator.

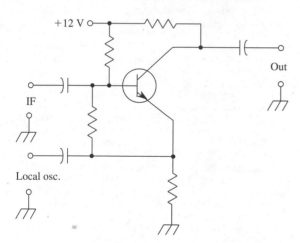

product detector

production lot A manufactured set of components, circuits, or systems, intended for sale. All of the units in the lot are identical. The finished product is suitable (presumably) for consumer use.

production unit One unit in a production lot; a finished unit, ready for use by a consumer.

product modulator A modulator whose output is equal or proportional to the product of carrier voltage and modulating voltage.

product of sine waves The result of multiplying one sine wave by another with attention being paid to the power factor. In the case of a resistive circuit, where the power factor is equal to 1, all voltage-current (EI) products are positive, and are equal to the true power. A product wave has negative half-cycles when the circuit contains reactance.

professional engineer A person licensed by a state board of examiners to work independently as an engineering. Also see PE and REGISTERED PROFESSIONAL ENGINEER.

program **1.** In computer operations, a detailed sequence of instructions representing an algorithm (the necessary steps in solving a problem) that can be implemented by a computer. **2.** The content of a radio or television broadcast during a specified period of time. **3.** In audio recording, the composite output from the mixer, used to make the master tape or disc.

program address counter See INSTRUCTION REGISTER.

program amplifier A broadcast preamplifier used at the studio or a remote location.

programatics The study of computer programming.

program circuit In wire telephony, a circuit capable of handling music and other audio data that covers a wide band of frequencies.

program compatibility The condition in which a program written for one computer can be used with another computer having a different architecture.

program controller In a central processor, a unit that controls the sequence and execution of program instructions.

program counter See CONTROL REGISTER.

program file A flexible reference system for software library maintenance.

program flowchart A representation of a computer program in the form of a flowchart. Each function and transition point is indicated by a box in the chart. A user can follow the flowchart and determine the outcome of the program for any given set of input parameters.

program library A collection of computer or programmable-calculator programs. Usually, it means the collection of programs used in a given computer system, often a software package supplied by the hardware vendor. It might also be a catalog of programs with instructions for their use.

programmable calculator A calculator that can be programmed to perform a chain of operations in a given order repetitively.

programmable read-only memory In a computer, a read-only memory (ROM) that can store a program.

program maintenance The ongoing correcting, updating, and modification of computer programs belonging to a system.

programmed dump A dump that occurs during a program run, according to a program instruction.

programmed halt During a computer program run, a temporary cessation resulting from an interrupt or halt instruction.

programmed instruction See MACRO INSTRUCTION.

programmed timer See CYCLE TIMER.

programmer A person who writes computer programs.

program modification 1. In computer programming operations, a change in the effect of instructions and addresses during a program run by performing arithmetic and logical operations on them. 2. Rewriting, or adding a patch to, a computer program. Also see PATCH, 3.

program register See CONTROL REGISTER.

program segment A unit within a computer program that is stored with others in memory at the time of the program's execution, or sometimes, as overlays loaded individually when the entire program exceeds memory capacity.

program specification A description of the steps involved in the solution of a problem, from which a programmer devises a computer program.

program step An instruction in a computer program.

program tape In computer operations, a magnetic or paper tape that contains programs for a system or application.

program timer 1. A programmed timer (see CYCLE TIMER). 2. A timing unit that controls the duration of a program.

progressive scanning Non-interlaced television raster scanning, in which the lines are traced from top to bottom in succession. Conventional television broadcasting uses INTERLACED SCANNING.

progressive wave A wave disturbance that travels through a theoretically perfect homogeneous medium. This can be a compression (longitudinal) wave, a transverse wave, or an electromagnetic wave.

projected cutoff For an amplifier circuit, the operating point at which crossover distortion vanishes. The direct-current bias voltage (grid or gate) required for projected cutoff is somewhat lower than the value corresponding to conventional cutoff of plate or drain current.

project engineering A field of engineering dealing with the coordination of a complete project.

projection television Large-screen television for viewing by a relatively large group, usually accomplished via a projection tube and optical system.

projection tube A cathode-ray tube, especially a television picture tube, capable of producing a bright image that can be projected onto a large screen by means of a lens system.

projector 1. A device that transmits a visible image onto a surface for reproduction. 2. In general, any device that transmits a signal into space.

PROLOG Acronym for *programming in logic*. A high-level computer programming language, similar to LISP, used in artificial intelligence.

The operator inputs facts and rules; the computer, in effect, derives theorems from the facts by following the logical rules.

PROM Abbreviation of PROGRAMMABLE READ-ONLY MEMORY.

promethium Symbol, Pm. A metallic element of the rare-earth group, produced artificially. Atomic number, 61. Atomic weight, approximately 145. Formerly called *illinium*.

promethium cell A radioactive battery cell using an isotope of promethium. Radioactive particles from this substance strike a phosphor, causing it to glow. Self-generating photocells then convert this light into electricity.

PROM programmer An electronic device that can store a computer program in a PROGRAMMABLE READ-ONLY MEMORY (PROM). It uses a built-in keyboard.

prompt In computer operations, a message received by an operator from an operating system or an individual program. For example, in disk operating system (DOS), it could be the statement "Bad command or file name."

prompting In computer or programmed-calculator operations, the entry of a special, required variable when the machine halts and awaits such entry.

prong See PIN.

prony brake An arrangement for measuring the mechanical power output of a rotating machine. It is a special form of friction brake consisting of a band passed around a pulley on the rotating shaft of the machine under test and held at each end by a spring balance.

propagation 1. The extension of energy into and through space. Thus, radiant energy is *propagated* from and by its source. 2. A phenomenon resulting from the extension of energy into and through space. Thus, radio waves can be spoken of as a *propagation*.

propagation constant For waves transmitted along a line, a number showing the effect the line has on the wave. This is a complex figure [i.e., one containing a real-number component (the attenuation constant) and an imaginary-number component (the phase constant)].

propagation delay 1. Symbol, t_{pd}. In an integrated-circuit logic gate, the time taken for a logic signal to be propagated across the gate. 2. In digital-circuit operation, the time required for a logic-level change to be transmitted through one or more elements.

propagation delay-power product See DELAY-POWER PRODUCT.

propagation factor The ratio E/E_o, where E is the complex electric-field strength at a point to which a wave has been propagated, and E_o is the complex electric-field strength at the point of origin. Also called *propagation ratio*.

propagation loss The path loss of an electromagnetic disturbance between the transmitting and receiving antennas.

propagation mode   See WAVEGUIDE MODE.

propagation ratio   See PROPAGATION FACTOR.

propagation time   In digital-circuit operation, the time required for a binary bit to be transferred from one point to another in the system.

propagation velocity   See VELOCITY OF PROPAGATION.

proportional action   An action, such as amplification or conversion, that produces an output signal proportional to the input signal.

proportional amplifier   An amplifier in which the instantaneous output amplitude is proportional to the instantaneous input amplitude.

proportional control   A voltage-regulation system in which the feedback correction voltage is proportional to the output-voltage error.

proportional counter   A Geiger tube having a pointed-wire (or ball-tipped-wire) anode. The voltage developed across the load resistor is proportional to the number of ions created by the radioactive particles entering the tube.

proprioceptor   A set of transducers and associated circuitry that allows a computerized robot to constantly sense the positions of its end effectors, and use this data in carrying out programmed tasks.

prosodic features   Variations in voice tone and emphasis that lend meaning and implication to spoken statements. It is important in advanced computer speech recognition and speech synthesis systems. Two sentences with identical wording can have greatly different meanings, depending on these factors (e.g., "*You* are!" versus "You *are?*").

prosthesis   An electromechanical artificial human limb or body part. Examples: artificial legs, artificial hands, and artificial respirators. Some such devices are computer-controlled; others can be manipulated by nerve impulses.

protactinium   Symbol, Pa. A relatively short-lived radioactive metallic element. Atomic number, 91. Atomic weight, 231.04 Formerly called *protoactinium.*

protected area   A region to which access is restricted, and that is secured by an alarm system, surveillance cameras, or other intrusion-prevention systems.

protected location   In computer storage, a location whose contents are protected from mutilation or erasure by making the location usable only by following a special procedure (e.g., using a password).

protection   In a multiple processing computer system, preventing interference between data or programs.

protective bias   In the final power amplifier of a radio transmitter, external direct-current bias applied to the base, gate, or grid. Prevents runaway in collector, drain, or plate current when the bias caused by the driving signal is lost.

protective capacitor   A power-line bypass capacitor.

protective device   **1.** A component that breaks a circuit in the event of excessive voltage or current from the power supply. **2.** A device that prevents excessive power from being delivered to a load by a driving circuit.

protective gap   **1.** A spark gap connected in parallel with a component, or between a line and ground as protection against high-voltage transients and surges. **2.** A spark-gap-type lightning arrester.

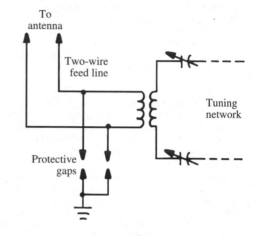

protective gap

protective resistor   **1.** A bleeder resistor connected in parallel with a filter capacitor in a high-voltage direct-current power supply to discharge the capacitor automatically, thus preventing electric shock. **2.** A series resistor that limits the current going through a device.

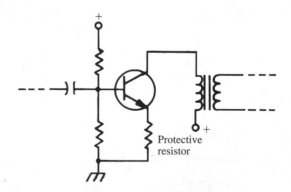

protective resistor, 2.

protector   **1.** A fast-acting power-disconnect device, such as a circuit breaker or fuse, that acts to protect electronic equipment. **2.** A device or connection, such as a safety ground or ground-fault interrupter, that protects an operator from electric shock. **3.** See CONTACT PROTECTOR.

protium The light isotope of hydrogen, having an atomic mass of 1.

protoactinium See PROTACTINIUM.

protocol 1. A set of parameters for a digital communications signal. **2.** The method by which a procedure is followed; a uniform set of governing regulations. It ensures proper operation of a system or network.

proton A positively charged particle in the nucleus of an atom. The mass of a proton is approximately 1840 times the mass of an electron.

proton rest mass See MASS OF PROTON AT REST.

proton-synchrotron A synchrotron that uses frequency modulation of the radio-frequency accelerating voltage. It can accelerate protons to energies of several billion electronvolts.

prototype The preliminary design or model of a device or system. It is often modified numerous times before the final design is attained. Compare PILOT MODEL.

proustite Crystalline silver arsenide trisulfide. Artificial crystals of this compound are used in tunable infrared-ray instruments.

proximity alarm A capacitance relay used to actuate an alerting-signal device when an area is intruded upon or a person is too close to a protected object. Also called INTRUSION ALARM.

proximity detector See PROXIMITY SENSOR.

proximity effect 1. The influence of high-frequency current flowing in one conductor on the distribution of current flowing in an adjacent conductor. **2.** In an audio system, the result of placing a microphone too close to a person's mouth. Under these conditions, some spoken consonants (e.g., B, F, P, and T) produce clapping or booming sounds.

proximity fuse An electronic device situated in the nose of a missile. When the missile is near the target, the fuse transmits a signal that is reflected back from the target; this reflected signal detonates the missile.

proximity relay See CAPACITANCE RELAY.

proximity sensing The ability of a machine, especially a robot, to detect when an object is near. This is an aid in robot navigation because it prevents collisions. Some devices can measure the distance from a robot, or from a robotic end effector, to a nearby object.

proximity sensor A device that indicates the presence of a nearby body. Such a device uses some form of circuit, such as that of a CAPACITANCE RELAY, that changes its operating characteristics when an object enters its field.

proximity switch See CAPACITANCE RELAY.

PRR Abbreviation of PULSE REPETITION RATE.

PRV Abbreviation of PEAK REVERSE VOLTAGE.

PS Abbreviation of POWER SUPPLY.

ps Abbreviation of PICOSECOND. (Also, psec.)

PSD Abbreviation of PHASE-SENSITIVE DETECTOR.

psec Abbreviation of PICOSECOND. (Also, ps.)

pseudocode In a computer system, an instruction or code symbol that affects the operation of the programming in an indirect manner.

pseudo-instruction In computer programming operations, data representing an instruction and requiring translation by a compiler or assembler.

pseudo-offlining During input/output operations in a computer system, maximizing hardware by disconnecting slow devices from the process in question.

pseudo-operation In computer operations, an operation that, rather than being performed by hardware, is carried out by special software or by macroinstruction.

pseudo-random numbers Numbers that, although produced by a computer operating on an algorithm for their generation, are useful for an application requiring random numbers.

pseudo-stereophonic effect A somewhat heightened binaural effect obtained when two loudspeakers are situated, relative to the listener, so that a transit-time difference of 1 to 30 milliseconds results.

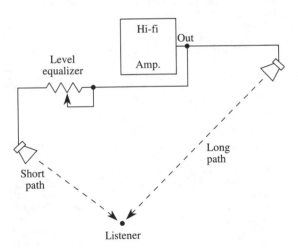

pseudo-stereophonic effect

psf Abbreviation of *pounds per square foot.* (Also, lb per sq ft, lb/ft².)

psi 1. Abbreviation of *pounds per square inch.* (Also, lb per sq in, lb/in².)

psia Abbreviation of POUNDS PER SQUARE INCH ABSOLUTE.

psig Abbreviation of POUNDS PER SQUARE INCH GAUGE.

psi particle A massive elementary particle that represents a resonance in an electron-positron interaction.

PSK   Abbreviation of PHASE-SHIFT KEYING.

PSM   Abbreviation of *pulse-spacing modulation*, more commonly called PULSE-INTERVAL MODULATION.

psophometer   A device used to measure noise in a wire communications system. It provides quantitative readings based on typical human observations.

psvm   Abbreviation of *phase-sensitive voltmeter*.

PSWR   Abbreviation of *power standing-wave ratio*.

psychoacoustics   A field of acoustics, overlapping with psychology, concerned with the effects of sounds on human beings.

PT   Abbreviation of *Pacific Time*.

Pt   Symbol for PLATINUM.

PTC   Abbreviation of POSITIVE TEMPERATURE COEFFICIENT.

PtIr   Symbol for PLATINIRIDIUM.

PTM   Abbreviation of PULSE-TIME MODULATION.

PTO   Abbreviation of PERMEABILITY-TUNED OSCILLATOR.

PTT   Abbreviation for *press-to-talk*. See PRESS-TO-TALK MICROPHONE; PRESS-TO-TALK SWITCH.

PTV   Abbreviation of *public television*.

p-type conduction   In a semiconductor, current flow consisting of the movement of holes. Compare N-TYPE CONDUCTION.

p-type material   Semiconductor material that has been doped with an acceptor-type impurity and, consequently, conducts current mainly via hole migration. Germanium, for example, when doped with indium, becomes p-type. Compare N-TYPE MATERIAL.

p-type semiconductor   An acceptor-type semiconductor (i.e., one containing an excess of holes in its crystal lattice).

PU   Abbreviation of PICKUP.

Pu   Symbol for PLUTONIUM.

public-address amplifier   A high-gain, high-power audio amplifier designed especially for the reproduction of speech and music at large gatherings.

public-address system   A system of sound reproduction especially designed for use at large gatherings indoors or outdoors. The system includes microphones, a public-address amplifier, loudspeakers, and sometimes recorders and playback devices. Also called *PA system*.

puck drive   In a tape recorder, a speed-reduction system for driving the flywheel from the shaft of the (high-speed) motor. In some machines, a rubber tire mounted on the flywheel is driven, through friction, by the motor shaft. In others, an intermediate rubber-tired wheel is placed between the motor shaft and the rim of the flywheel.

puffer   A meter or bridge for measuring small values of capacitance. The name comes from the spoken sound of *pF*, the abbreviation of PICOFARAD.

pulldown   Descriptive of a circuit, device, or individual component used to lower the value (e.g., impedance) of a circuit to which it is connected.

pull-in current   The current required to close a relay.

pulling   **1.** The abnormal tendency of one circuit to cause another to slip into tune with it. This often results from coupling (intended or accidental) that is too tight. Thus, when two oscillators feed a common circuit, such as a mixer, one might pull the other into tune with itself. **2.** Lowering of a crystal frequency by an external reactance.

pull-in voltage   The voltage required to close a relay.

pull switch   A mechanical switch actuated by a pulling action.

pullup   Descriptive of a circuit or component used to raise the value (e.g., impedance) of a circuit to which it is connected.

pulsar   An extremely dense, rapidly rotating collapsed star that produces radio signals at regular intervals. The pulse frequency varies from less than one hertz to several tens or hundreds of hertz.

pulsating direct current   A direct current that periodically rises and falls between zero and a maximum value (or between two positive or negative values) without changing polarity. Thus, it is possible to have either a pulsating positive current or a pulsating negative current. Also see DIRECT CURRENT.

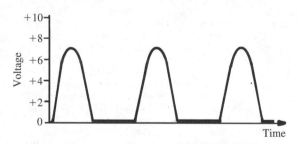

pulsating direct current

pulsating wave   See PULSATING DIRECT CURRENT.

pulse   A transient signal that is usually of short duration, constant amplitude, and one polarity. A typical example is a narrow positive or negative spike.

pulse amplifier   An amplifier having wide frequency response and low distortion, used for amplifying steep-sided pulses of short duration.

pulse-amplitude modulation   Abbreviation, PAM. A type of pulse modulation in which a pulse carrier is amplitude modulated by the modulating signal.

pulse bandwidth   For an amplitude pulse, the minimum bandwidth occupied. The faster the rise and/or decay times of a pulse, the greater the bandwidth. The greater the pulse frequency, the greater the bandwidth.

pulse code   A code in which groups of pulses represent digits.

pulse-code modulation   Abbreviation, PCM. A type of pulse modulation in which a signal is periodically sampled, each sample being subdivided into increments transmitted as a binary code.

pulse-code-modulation binary code   A pulse code used in communications not in the form of line transmission. Individual values are denoted by binary numbers.

pulse-code modulation multiplex equipment   A multiplexer/demultiplexer for signal conversion between a single signal and multiple-channel signals. It uses both pulse-code modulation and time-division multiplexing.

pulse-count divider   A circuit or device that receives an input of a certain number of pulses (or pulses per second) and delivers an output that is a function of that quantity. See, for example, DIVIDE-BY-SEVEN CIRCUIT and DIVIDE-BY-TWO CIRCUIT.

pulse counter   A circuit or device that indicates the number of pulses presented to it in a given time interval.

pulse counting   Counting pulses in a sequence. At low speed (pulse repetition rate), this can be done with an electromechanical dial-type counter. At high speed, a fully electronic circuit is required.

pulse delay circuit   A monostable multivibrator adapted to deliver its single output pulse a predetermined time after the input pulse has been applied.

pulse dialing   A form of telephone dialing in which each digit is formed by a series of pulses, usually at 10 to 20 Hz. The pulses are the equivalent of disconnecting the line for a few milliseconds. Each digit has the corresponding number of pulses, except digit 0, which is formed by 10 pulses.

pulse droop   Distortion observable as a downward-sloping top on the oscilloscope trace of a pulse. It

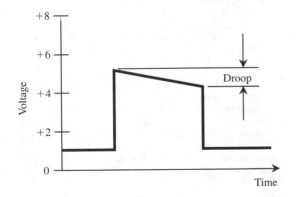

pulse droop

can be quantified in volts, millivolts, microvolts, amperes, milliamperes, or microamperes.

pulsed laser   A laser in which flashes (pulses) of high-intensity light excite the lasing medium.

pulse duration   The time period during which a pulse exists (i.e., its width on an oscilloscope display).

pulse-duration modulation   Abbreviation, PDM. A type of pulse-time modulation in which the pulse duration (width) is varied by the modulation. Also called *pulse-length modulation* and *pulse-width modulation*.

pulse equalizer   A MONOSTABLE MULTIVIBRATOR adapted to deliver pulses of equal amplitude, shape, and width—even when it receives trigger pulses of different kinds.

pulse fall time   The time required for the trailing edge of a pulse to fall from 90 to 10 percent of its peak amplitude. Compare PULSE RISE TIME.

pulse-forming line   A circuit used in radar for producing high-intensity pulses. Inductances and capacitances are combined in a long string, and the effect is to generate high-amplitude radio-frequency pulses.

pulse-frequency modulation   Abbreviation, PFM. Modulation of the repetition rate of a train of pulses.

pulse generator   A signal generator that produces pulses. A general-purpose generator of this sort will produce pulses of adjustable amplitude, duration, shape, and repetition rate.

pulse-height discriminator   A circuit or device that passes only pulses whose amplitudes exceed a predetermined level.

pulse interval   The interval between successive pulses.

pulse-interval modulation   Abbreviation, PIM. Modulation of the spacing (time interval) between pulses.

pulse inverter   A single-stage, wideband, low-distortion, common-emitter, or common-source amplifier. The output-pulse waveforms are therefore inverted, with respect to the input-pulse waveforms.

pulse jitter   In a pulse train, a disturbance characterized by random changes in the spacing between pulses.

pulse-length modulation   See PULSE-DURATION MODULATION.

pulse load   The load impedance for a pulse generator.

pulse mode   See PULSE MODULATION.

pulse modulation   **1.** Modulation using pulses as the modulating signal. **2.** Modulation of a "carrier" consisting of pulses. See, for example, PULSE-AMPLITUDE MODULATION, PULSE-CODE MODULATION, PULSE-DURATION-MODULATION, PULSE-NUMBERS MODULATION, PULSE-POSITION MODULATION, and PULSE-TIME MODULATION.

pulse modulator   **1.** A modulator that delivers power or voltage pulses for modulating a carrier.

2. A device that modulates pulses (see PULSE MODULATION, **2**).

pulse narrower A circuit or device that reduces the duration (width) of a pulse.

pulse-numbers modulation Abbreviation, PNM. A type of modulation of a pulse carrier based upon variation of pulse density (i.e., pulses per unit time).

pulse operation Intermittent operation of a circuit, in the form of discrete pulses.

pulse oscillator Any oscillator with an output that consists of a series of pulses.

pulse-position modulation Abbreviation, PPM. Modulation of the time position of pulses.

pulse rate See PULSE REPETITION RATE.

pulse ratio The ratio of pulse height (amplitude) to pulse width (duration).

pulse regeneration Restoration of the original waveform and frequency to a pulse. It eliminates distortion caused by circuits or propagation conditions.

pulse repetition frequency Abbreviation, PRF. See PULSE-REPETITION RATE.

pulse-repetition rate Abbreviation, PRR. The number of pulses per unit time; usually pulses per second (pps).

pulse rise time The time required for the leading edge of a pulse to rise from 10 to 90 percent of its maximum amplitude. Compare PULSE FALL TIME.

pulse scaler A circuit actuated by the reception of a definite, predetermined number of input pulses.

pulse-shaping circuit **1.** A circuit for producing a pulse from a wave of some other shape (e.g., sine wave). **2.** A circuit for tailoring a pulse to desired shape, amplitude, and duration.

pulse spacing The interval between successive pulses.

pulse-spacing modulation Abbreviation, PSM. See PULSE-INTERVAL MODULATION.

pulse-steering diode In a flip-flop circuit, a diode through which the trigger pulse must pass to switch the circuit. Because of the unidirectional conductivity of a diode, pulses of only one polarity are passed.

pulse stretcher **1.** A shaping circuit that widens a pulse (i.e., increases its duration). **2.** A circuit, such as a special monostable multivibrator, that generates a pulse that is wider than the trigger pulse.

pulse stuffing See JUSTIFICATION, **2**.

pulse tilt The sloping of the normally flat top of a pulse either up or down. Also see PULSE DROOP.

pulse time See PULSE DURATION.

pulse-time modulation See PULSE-POSITION MODULATION.

pulse train A series of successive pulses of usually one kind.

pulse transformer A transformer designed to accommodate the fast rise and fall times of pulses

and similar nonsinusoidal waveforms. Such transformers often use special core materials and are made using special winding techniques.

pulse transmitter **1.** A device that transmits a series of pulses. **2.** A pulse-modulated transmitter. **3.** See PULSE MODULATOR.

pulse waveform The general shape of a pulse as it appears on an oscilloscope display. The various forms range from positive or negative half-sinusoids, through rectangles, to thin-line spikes.

pulse width The horizontal dimension of a pulse (i.e., its duration).

pulse-width modulation Abbreviation, PWM. A form of pulse modulation in which the width of the pulses is varied in accordance with the modulating waveform.

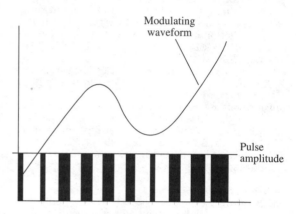

pulse-width modulation

pump **1.** In a parametric amplifier, the oscillator that supplies the signal that periodically varies the reactance of the varactor. **2.** The pumping signal in **1**. **3.** To perform the operation (pumping) described in **1**. **4.** To increase the energy level of an atom or molecule (by exposing it to electromagnetic radiation) to such an extent that oscillation or amplification occurs. A ruby laser, for example, produces its intense, coherent beam as a result of pumping. **5.** The radiation used to pump an atom or molecule. **6.** The device producing the radiation required to pump an atom or molecule.

pump frequency The frequency of a PUMP voltage.

pumping A method of laser actuation. A series of pulses, at the resonant frequency of the lasing material, is injected to cause laser output.

pump oscillator An oscillator for producing a pump voltage.

pump voltage The voltage of a pumping signal. Also see PARAMETRIC AMPLIFIER and PUMP, **1, 2**.

punch **1.** A tool for cutting holes in metal chassis, panels, and boxes for electronic equipment. **2.** High signal strength. **3.** A machine for punching cards or tape for data processing. **4.** To perform the operation in **3**.

punched tape Plastic or paper tape punched with holes, according to a code to record data or Morse-code characters. During playback, the tape is run through a reader in which contact fingers sense the holes.

punched-tape reader A device for reading punched tape. In an optoelectronic type of reader, a light beam passing through the holes as they pass a lamp actuates the circuit through a photocell. In an electromechanical type of reader, a metal feeler reaches through a passing hole and touches a metal contact to close the circuit.

punched-tape recorder A device that records data in the form of holes punched into a paper tape. Also called *reperforator.*

punch-in editing In audio recording, a feature that allows convenient insertion of new material on a tape. The tape recorder can be switched instantly from Play to Record, and back again, whenever the operator wants to add material.

punchthrough In a bipolar transistor, the potentially damaging condition resulting when the reverse bias of the collector is increased to a voltage high enough to spread the depletion layer entirely through the base. This tends to effectively connect the emitter to the collector.

punchthrough region The conduction region associated with higher-than-punchthrough voltage, in which bipolar-transistor current is excessive. Also see PUNCHTHROUGH.

punchthrough voltage The voltage that causes PUNCHTHROUGH in a given bipolar transistor.

puncture voltage See BREAKDOWN VOLTAGE, **1**.

Pupin coil One of several loading coils that can be inserted at intervals in series with a telephone line to cancel line-capacitance effects and, thus, improve the clarity of speech.

pure tone An audio-frequency (AF) tone having essentially no harmonic content; a sine-wave AF tone.

pure wave A wave containing no distortion products.

purging The removal of an undesired gas or other substance from a system by introducing a material to displace it.

purifier A power-line operated alternating-current electromagnet that can be manually rotated in front of a color-television picture tube to demagnetize the tube. Also called a DEGAUSSER.

purity **1.** In color television, complete saturation of a hue. **2.** In a waveform, complete freedom from distortion. **3.** The extent to which spurious signals are attenuated in the output of a radio or television transmitter. Also called *spectral purity.*

purity adjustment In a color-television picture tube, adjustment of each purity control for pure color.

purity coil A variable-current coil around the neck of a color-television picture tube that is used to adjust color purity.

purity control For a purity coil, the variable resistor that controls the current for color correction.

purity magnet A ring-magnet collar around the neck of a color-television picture tube to adjust, by rotation, color purity.

purple plague Corrosion that occurs when aluminum and gold are placed in contact.

pushbutton tuner A radio or television tuner utilizing pushbutton tuning.

pushbutton tuning The tuning of a circuit to various frequencies in single steps by means of pushbutton switches.

pushdown list In data processing, a method of amending a list. A new item entered at the top moves each existing item one position down.

pushdown stack Also called *first-in/last-out.* A digital read-write memory in which data bits emerge in reverse sequence from the order they go in. If data bit x enters the pushdown stack before data bit y, then x will come out after y. Compare FIRST-IN/FIRST-OUT.

push-in terminal A circuit contact or tie point, usually of thin, springy material, that can be inserted into a hole in a perforated board.

push-pull Pertaining to a circuit in which two active devices are used, with the inputs and outputs both placed in phase opposition. In the output circuit, even harmonics are canceled, and odd harmonics are reinforced.

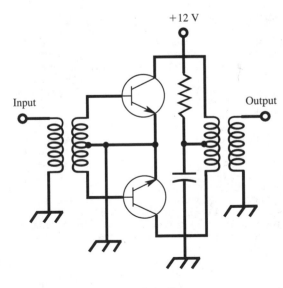

push-pull

push-pull amplifier An amplifier stage in which, for increased power output, two active devices are operated 180 degrees out of phase with each other in opposite halves of a symmetrical circuit. Also see PUSH-PULL CIRCUIT.

push-pull circuit A symmetrical circuit in which two active devices operate on separate halves of the input-signal cycle and deliver a combined output signal.

push-pull deflection In an oscilloscope, the application of deflection voltage to a pair of deflecting plates 180 degrees out of phase with each other. For this purpose, the output amplifier in the horizontal or vertical deflection channel is a push-pull stage.

push-pull doubler See PUSH-PULL MULTIPLIER.

push-pull microphone A set of two microphones, in which the audio-frequency outputs are in phase opposition.

push-pull multiplier A push-pull amplifier with its output circuit tuned to an odd-numbered multiple of the input frequency. This circuit is unsuitable for even-harmonic operation, but has some merit as an odd-harmonic multiplier (e.g., a *tripler* or *quintupler*). Also see PUSH-PUSH MULTIPLIER.

push-pull oscillator An oscillator stage in which, for increased power output, two active devices are operated 180 degrees out of phase with each other in opposite halves of a symmetrical circuit. Also see PUSH-PULL CIRCUIT.

push-pull/parallel amplifier An amplifier stage in which tubes or transistors are connected in push-pull/parallel for increased power output. Also see PARALLEL-COMPONENT AMPLIFIER, PUSH-PULL AMPLIFIER, and PUSH-PULL/PARALLEL CIRCUIT.

push-pull/parallel circuit A push-pull circuit in which two or more active devices are connected in parallel on each side of the circuit. This arrangement gives increased power output over that of the conventional push-pull circuit. See, for example, PUSH-PULL/PARALLEL AMPLIFIER and PUSH-PULL/PARALLEL OSCILLATOR.

push-pull/parallel oscillator An oscillator stage in which active devices are connected in push-pull/parallel for increased power output. Also see PARALLEL-COMPONENT OSCILLATOR, PUSH-PULL OSCILLATOR, and PUSH-PULL/PARALLEL CIRCUIT.

push-pull recording A type of film sound track consisting of two side-by-side images 180 degrees out of phase with each other.

push-pull transformer A transformer having a center-tapped winding for operation in a push-pull circuit.

push-push Pertaining to a circuit in which two active devices are used, with the inputs connected in phase opposition, and the outputs

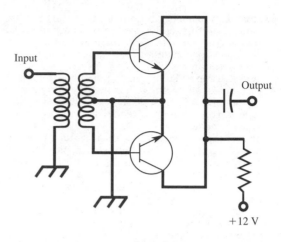

push-push

connected in parallel. The result is reinforcement of the even harmonics, and cancellation of the fundamental frequency and all odd harmonics.

push-push circuit See PUSH-PUSH MULTIPLIER.

push-push multiplier An amplifier circuit containing two active devices with their inputs connected in phase opposition and their outputs connected in parallel. This circuit is unsuitable for fundamental-frequency and odd-harmonic operation, but has some merit as an even-harmonic multiplier (e.g., a *doubler* or *quadrupler*). Also see PUSH-PULL MULTIPLIER.

push-to-talk switch See PRESS-TO-TALK SWITCH.

pushup list In data processing, a method of amending a list, whereby new items are added at the end of the list; all other items retain their original positions. Compare PUSHDOWN LIST.

pV Abbreviation of PICOVOLT.

PVC Abbreviation of POLYVINYL CHLORIDE.

pW Abbreviation of PICOWATT.

PWM **1.** Abbreviation of PULSE-WIDTH MODULATION. **2.** Abbreviation of PLATED-WIRE MEMORY.

pwr Abbreviation of POWER.

Pyralin See CELLULOSE NITRATE.

pyramidal horn antenna A rectangular horn antenna that is flared in two dimensions. The horn width and height both increase linearly with increasing distance (in the direction of maximum radiation/response) from the feed point.

pyramidal wave See BACK-TO-BACK SAWTOOTH.

Pyrex A heat-resistant glass having numerous applications in electronics and chemistry.

pyrheliometer An instrument used to measure infrared radiation.

pyroelectricity In certain crystals, electricity generated by temperature change, and in particular, by the application of heat.

pyroelectric lamp See NERNST LAMP.

pyroelectric material A crystalline material that generates an output voltage when it is heated.

pyrolysis The process whereby heat changes a substance into one of several different substances by rearranging its atoms.

pyromagnetic effect In a material or circuit, the combined effect of heat and magnetism.

pyrometer An instrument, other than a thermometer, used for the measurement of temperature. See, for example, OPTICAL PYROMETER.

Pythagorean scale A sound scale defining a specific type of relationship among audio tones. If x and y are related by the Pythagorean scale and are adjacent in frequency, then a specific frequency (f) exists, so $x = f^2$ and $y = f^3$.

Pythagorean theorem A theorem of plane geometry. For a right triangle, with sides of lengths a, b, and c, where c is the side opposite the right angle, it is always true that $a^2 + b^2 = c^2$.

p-zone See P LAYER.

PZM Abbreviation of PRESSURE-ZONE MICROPHONE.

PZT Abbreviation of LEAD ZIRCONATE TITANATE.

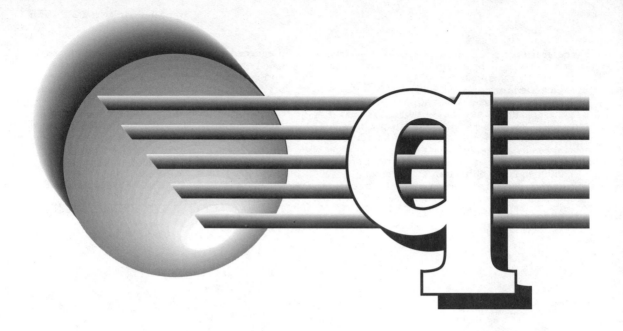

Q **1.** The figure of merit of a capacitor, inductor, or inductance-capacitance (LC) circuit, equal to the reactance divided by the resistance. **2.** Symbol for electrical charge. **3.** Occasional symbol for SELECTIVITY. **4.** See Q BAND. **5.** See *Q* OUTPUT.

q **1.** Symbol for quantity of electricity (in coulombs). **2.** Symbol for the charge carried by an electron (the charge carried by a hole is represented by –q). **3.** Symbol for the value of a quantum.

QA Abbreviation of QUALITY ASSURANCE.

Q adjustment The separate null adjustment for the *Q* value of a component being tested in an impedance bridge having separate resistive and reactive balances.

Q-antenna An antenna in which the transmission line (feeder) is matched in impedance to the center of the radiator by means of a *Q*-matching section.

QAVC Abbreviation of QUIET AUTOMATIC VOLUME CONTROL.

Q band The radio-frequency band 36 to 46 GHz. It is subdivided as follows: Q_a, 36 to 38 GHz; Q_b, 38 to 40 GHz; Q_c, 40 to 42 GHz, Q_d, 42 to 44 GHz; and Q_e, 44 to 46 GHz.

Q bar One of the parallel metal tubes in a *Q*-matching section. Also see *Q* ANTENNA.

Q booster See *Q* MULTIPLIER.

Q bridge An alternating-current bridge used principally to determine the *Q* of capacitors and inductors. Bridges are usually used for audio-frequency *Q* determinations; resonant-type *Q* meters are generally used for measurement of radio-frequency *Q*.

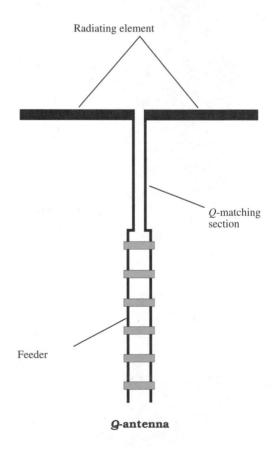

Radiating element

Q-matching section

Feeder

Q-antenna

QC Abbreviation of QUALITY CONTROL.

QCE Abbreviation of QUALITY-CONTROL ENGINEERING or QUALITY-CONTROL ENGINEER.

Q channel In American (NTSC) color television, the 508-kHz-wide green-magenta color information transmission band.

QCT Abbreviation of QUALITY-CONTROL TECHNICIAN.

QCW In the local oscillator and associated circuitry of a color television receiver, a 3.85-MHz CW signal of Q PHASE.

QCW signal In a color television receiver, the component of the chrominance signal that is 90 degrees out of phase with the in-phase component.

Q demodulator In a color television receiver, the demodulator that combines the chrominance signal and the color-burst oscillator signal to recover the Q signal (see Q SIGNAL, **2**).

QED **1.** Abbreviation of QUANTUM ELECTRODYNAMICS. **2.** Abbreviation of *quod erat demonstrandum*, Latin for "which was to be demonstrated." Also, Q.E.D. Often written at the conclusions of valid logical proofs and derivations.

Q factor See *Q*.

QFM Abbreviation of QUADRATURE MODULATION.

QM Abbreviation of QUADRATURE MODULATION.

Q-matching section A linear radio-frequency impedance-matching transformer consisting of two straight, rigid, parallel metal conductors that are used to match a feeder to an antenna. The section is ¼ wavelength long at the operating frequency. The diameters and center-to-center spacing of the conductors are such that the characteristic impedance of the matching section is equal to the geometric mean of the feeder characteristic impedance and the radiation resistance of the radiator. Also see *Q* ANTENNA and QUARTER-WAVELENGTH MATCHING STUB.

Q meter A usually direct-reading instrument for determining the *Q* of a capacitor, inductor, or inductance-capacitance (LC) circuit. Most *Q* meters are operated at radio frequencies, but audio-frequency instruments are available.

Q modulation Amplitude modulation obtained by varying the effective *Q* of a radio-frequency tank circuit in step with a modulating component. See ABSORPTION MODULATION.

QMQB Abbreviation of *quick make/quick break*.

Q multiplier A positive-feedback (regenerative) amplifier that increases the effective *Q* of a tuned circuit, and thereby sharpens its response, when its input is connected across the tuned circuit.

Q output The reference output of a flip-flop.

Q phase A color-television carrier signal that is 147 degrees out of phase with the color subcarrier.

Q point The point or points at which a load line intersects a device characteristic (such as the collector curve of a transistor or plate curve of a tube) and that identifies the quiescent operating point.

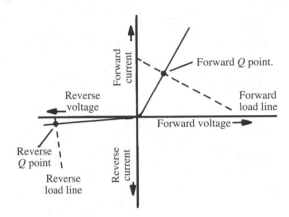

Q points on diode characteristic

QRD Abbreviation of QUADRATIC RESIDUE DIFFUSOR.

Q-section transformer See *Q*-MATCHING SECTION.

Q signal In color television, the quadrature component of the chrominance signal, equal to +0.48(R-Y) and to +0.41(B-Y), where B is the blue camera signal, R is the red camera signal, and Y is the luminance signal.

Q signals A set of three-letter groups, each beginning with the letter Q, used for simplified telegraph and radiotelegraph communication, and sometimes rapid voice communication (in radiotelephony). Each signal represents a commonly used phrase or message.

QSL card A card verifying communication with, or the reception of signals from, the station sending the card. Such verification is common in the amateur radio service and with some shortwave broadcast and CB stations.

QSO Amateur radiotelegraph abbreviation for TWO-WAY COMMUNICATION.

Q spoiler A device or circuit that produces Q SPOILING in a laser.

Q spoiling The technique of inhibiting laser action during an interval when an ion population excess is pumped up. When the laser is subsequently triggered by Q switching, a more powerful pulse of light results than would be otherwise obtained.

Q switching A laser-switching action obtainable with Kerr cells or rotating reflecting prisms, which consists of holding the Q of the laser cavity to a low value during an ion-population buildup, then abruptly switching the Q to a higher value.

Q transformer See Q-MATCHING SECTION.

qty Abbreviation of QUANTITY.

quad **1.** A combination of four components, such as diodes, transistors, etc., in a single housing. The components are usually carefully matched. **2.** In a cable, a combination of four separately insulated conductors (sometimes, two twisted pairs) twisted together. **3.** Abbreviation of QUADRANT. **4.** See QUAD ANTENNA. **5.** See QUADROPHONIC.

quad antenna An antenna consisting of two square loops. One loop is driven, and has a perimeter of one wavelength. The other loop acts as a parasitic reflector, and has a perimeter slightly greater than one wavelength. Also called *cubical quad antenna.*

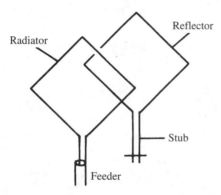

quad antenna

quadded cable See QUAD, 2.

quadding Redundancy obtained by connecting components in series-parallel for enhanced reliability and/or increased power-handling capacity.

quad latch A set of four interconnected flip-flops that is used for digital data storage.

quadrant **1.** A specific 90-degree arc of a circle. **2.** One of the four parts formed on a plane surface by rectangular coordinates and designated I, II, III, and IV in a counterclockwise direction, starting with the upper-right quadrant. **3.** An altitude-measuring instrument.

quadrantal deviation The part of magnetic-compass deviation caused by the induction of transient magnetism into the horizontal soft iron of a vessel by the horizontal component of terrestrial magnetism.

quadrantal error See QUADRANTAL DEVIATION.

quadrant electrometer An electrometer whose principal parts are quadrants (a pillbox-shaped

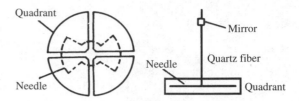

quadrant electrometer

brass chamber split into four parts) and a needle (a flat, bowtie-shaped aluminum vane) suspended by a platinized quartz fiber between the quadrants.

quadraphonic sound Sound recording and reproduction involving four channels.

quadraphony Music recording or playback in which four distinct information channels are used. Also called *four-channel stereo.*

quadratic equation A second-degree equation [i.e., one in which the highest exponent is 2 (the square of an unknown) (e.g., $ax^2 + bx + c = 0$)].

quadratic residue diffusor Abbreviation, QRD. In acoustics, a sound-reflection grating that scatters (diffuses) sound waves almost uniformly in all directions. The depths of the indentations in the grating are determined according to a QUADRATIC EQUATION.

quadrature The state of (cyclic events or points) being 90 degrees out of phase.

quadrature amplifier An amplifier circuit that introduces a 90-degree phase shift. Such amplifiers are used in control devices, test instruments, transmitters, and color television receivers.

quadrature axes The vertical axes in the complex-number plane (i.e., the $+j$ and $-j$ axes).

quadrature carrier See Q PHASE.

quadrature component **1.** The reactive component of an alternating current or voltage. **2.** A vector perpendicular to a reference vector. **3.** The imaginary-number component in a complex-number expression.

quadrature current Reactive current in an alternating-current circuit.

quadrature modulation In-phase modulation of two carrier components having a 90-degree phase difference.

quadrature number See IMAGINARY NUMBER.

quadrature-phase subcarrier signal See QCW SIGNAL.

quadrature portion In color television, the portion of the chrominance signal having the same (or opposite) phase as that of the Q-signal-modulated subcarrier, and that is 90 degrees out of phase with the in-phase portion.

quadrature sensitivity The sensitivity of a transducer to motions in a direction that is perpendicular to the normal axis of response.

quadrature voltage A voltage 90 degrees out of phase with another (reference) voltage.

quadrilateral **1.** Pertaining to an object having four sides. **2.** A four-sided plane polygon.

quadrillion The number 1,000,000,000,000,000 (10^{15}).

quadripartite Having four parts.

quadripole network A four-terminal network, usually with input- and output-terminal pairs.

quadrivalent Having a valence of 4. Tin, for example, is quadrivalent. Also called TETRAVALENT.

quadruped robot A robot with four legs that can move independently. It offers better stability than three-legged designs. Functions well in mobile machines that must navigate irregular terrain.

quadrupler **1.** A rectifier circuit that delivers a direct-current output voltage approximately equal to four times the peak value of the alternating-current input voltage. **2.** An amplifier or other circuit that delivers an output signal of four times the frequency of the input signal.

quadruplex circuit A data circuit in which two messages are carried in each direction simultaneously.

quadrupole **1.** A combination of two dipoles, producing a force that varies inversely with the fourth power of distance. **2.** A four-pole magnet used in some synchrotrons and linear accelerators to focus and bend a particle beam. **3.** A system consisting of two dipoles of equal and opposite direct moment.

qualification The quality-control or quality-assurance scheme used in the production of components, circuits, or systems. Certain minimum requirements must be met for a device to obtain qualification.

qualitative test A test performed to determine the general mode of operation or the presence of certain factors, without regard to numerical values. Compare QUANTITATIVE TEST.

quality **1.** In audio-frequency applications, fidelity of transmission or reproduction. **2.** The degree of conformity of a product to specifications.

quality assurance The outcome of measures taken to bring performance into conformity with specifications. See QUALITY, **2**.

quality control The surveillance of selection, manufacturing, and testing operations to ensure conformity of a product to specifications.

quality-control engineering The branch of engineering concerned principally with the technical methods of quality control and statistical methods of assessing quality (see QUALITY, **2**).

quality-control technician A technician whose principal duty is the performance of operations in the areas of incoming inspection, manufacturing support, and product testing. Sometimes statistical evaluations are required.

quality engineering A field of engineering that deals with quality assurance and quality control in the production of components, circuits, and systems.

quality factor See *Q*.

quality-factor bridge See *Q* BRIDGE.

quality-factor meter See *Q* METER.

quanta Plural of QUANTUM.

quantimeter An instrument used to measure the quantity of X rays to which a body has been exposed.

quantitative test A test performed to determine the numerical values (and their relationships) connected with observable phenomena. Compare QUALITATIVE TEST.

quantity **1.** A parameter (e.g., collector current, grid voltage, etc.). **2.** In calculations, a positive or negative real number. **3.** Electrical charge, usually specified or measured in coulombs (see COULOMB). Also called *electrical quantity*.

quantization The conversion of a quantity having infinitely many possible values or levels (such as an analog signal) into one that can attain only a finite number of defined values or levels (such as a digital signal). The number of levels is usually some integral power of 2 (i.e., 2, 4, 8, 16, 32, etc.). This allows the levels to be represented as binary numbers.

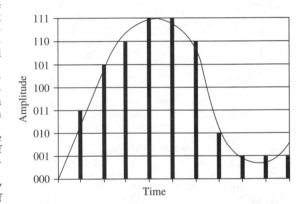

quantization

quantization distortion Distortion introduced by the process of QUANTIZATION in a communications or broadcast signal.

quantization distortion power The level of the distortion in a signal resulting from QUANTIZATION. It is expressed in microwatts, milliwatts, or watts. It can also be expressed as a percentage, or as a level in decibels, relative to the power level of the input signal.

quantization error The difference between the actual values of quantities and their quantized values.

quantization noise Noise introduced by the process of QUANTIZATION in a communications or broadcast signal.

quantize **1.** To perform the process of QUANTIZATION. **2.** To split a quantitative commodity, such as energy into its smallest measurable incremental units.

quantized pulse modulation Pulse modulation involving QUANTIZATION. Examples are PULSE-CODE MODULATION and PULSE-NUMBERS MODULATION.

quantizer A circuit or device that selects the digital subdivision into which an analog quantity is placed (e.g., an analog-to-digital converter).

quantizing See QUANTIZATION.

quantometer An instrument for measuring magnetic flux.

quantum **1.** Abbreviation, Q. Plural, *quanta.* In physics, the elemental unit or particle of electromagnetic energy. The energy contained in one such particle is directly proportional to the frequency, and inversely proportional to the wavelength. **2.** See PHOTON. **3.** Any discrete unit derived by QUANTIZATION.

quantum chromodynamics A term coined by Professor Murray Gell-Mann for the theory of *quarks* and *gluons.*

quantum counter A radiation-counter tube with a window for the admission of light to the cathode.

quantum efficiency See QUANTUM YIELD.

quantum electrodynamics A branch of quantum mechanics that involves the motions of electrons, photons, and muons caused by electromagnetic action. Quantum electrodynamics takes relativistic effects into account.

quantum electronics The branch of electronics concerned with energy states in matter.

quantum equivalence The principle that one electron is emitted for each photon absorbed by a material (when the photon has the necessary energy).

quantum jump The abrupt movement of a particle from one discrete energy state to another.

quantum level The orbit or ring occupied by an electron in an atom.

quantum mechanics A branch of physics concerned with the behavior of matter and energy, on the basis of observable data.

quantum noise A noise signal arising from random variations in the average rate at which quanta impinge upon a detector.

quantum number A number that describes the energy level, or change in energy level, for a particle.

quantum statistics A branch of QUANTUM MECHANICS concerned with the distribution of elementary particles through various quantized energy levels.

quantum theory The theory that the emission or absorption of energy by atoms or molecules occurs in discrete packages or units, rather than continuously. Each unit is the emission or absorption of an energy packet called a QUANTUM. Thus, radiant energy is thought to be divided into *quanta.*

quantum transition The movement of an electron from one energy level to another within an atom.

quantum yield The photoelectric efficiency of a light-sensitive surface in terms of the number of electrons emitted for each absorbed quantum of light.

quark A hypothetical particle having a fractional electrical charge; quarks are thought to be constituents of other subatomic particles.

quarter-deflection method A method of measuring high-frequency resistance, involving the use of a sine-wave signal source, a standard noninductive variable resistor, and a square-law radio-frequency ammeter.

quarter-phase See TWO-PHASE.

quarter wave **1.** The length of time corresponding to 90 electrical degrees in a wave disturbance. **2.** The distance in space, or along a wire or feed line that corresponds to 90 electrical degrees in a wave disturbance.

quarter-wave antenna An antenna in which the radiator is an electrical quarter-wavelength long at the operating frequency.

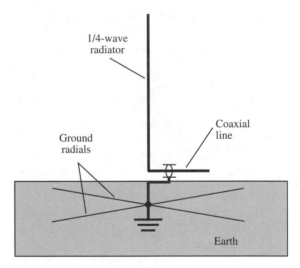

quarter-wave antenna

quarter-wave attenuator In a transmission line or waveguide, two energy-absorbing structures separated by an odd number of quarter wavelengths so that the reflection from one structure is canceled by that from the other.

quarter-wave balun A balun using quarter-wave elements. One form of this device consists of a grounded quarter-wavelength-long cylinder closed at one end and open at the other, for matching an unbalanced low-impedance line to a balanced high-impedance line.

quarter wavelength **1.** In free space, the distance corresponding to 90 electrical degrees of phase (¼ wavelength) at a specified radio frequency. This distance, in meters, is equal to $75/f$, where f is the frequency in MHz. **2.** In or along a medium, such as a transmission line, the distance corresponding to 90 electrical degrees of phase (¼ wavelength) at a specified radio frequency. This distance, in meters, is equal to $75v/f$, where v is the velocity factor of the medium, and f is the frequency in MHz.

quarter-wavelength line A transmission line or feeder that is a quarter-wavelength long at the operating frequency. Also called *quarter-wave line*.

quarter-wavelength matching stub An arrangement consisting of a quarter-wavelength-long parallel-wire section of transmission line, used for matching the impedance of a nonresonant feeder to that of an antenna. It is similar to a Q-MATCHING SECTION, except that flexible transmission line (e.g., ladder line) is used, rather than rigid metal rods or tubing.

quarter-wave monopole A nondirectional UHF vertical antenna requiring no ground. The radiator is ¼ wavelength long, and is an enlarged-diameter outer sleeve connected to the outer conductor of the coaxial feeder. The two sections simulate a half-wave antenna.

quarter-wave plate A plate of double-refracting crystalline material whose thickness allows the introduction of a quarter-cycle phase difference between the ordinary and extraordinary components of light transmitted by it.

quarter-wave resonance Resonance at the operating frequency in a quarter-wave antenna.

quarter-wave resonant line A section of transmission line (such as open-wire line or coaxial cable) that is a quarter-wavelength long at the operating frequency. Such a section is useful in impedance matching and in various radio-frequency tests and measurements.

quarter-wave stub See QUARTER-WAVE TRANSFORMER.

quarter-wave support In a coaxial line, a quarter-wave metal stub that can be used, instead of an insulator, to separate the inner and outer conductors.

quarter-wave termination In a waveguide, a set of two metal barriers separated by 90 electrical degrees. One barrier totally reflects the energy striking it. The other barrier allows some energy to pass through. Resonance occurs in the space between the barriers.

quarter-wave transformer A quarter-wave resonant line short-circuited at one end by an adjustable slider. This arrangement is useful for radio-frequency impedance matching.

quarter-wave transmission line See QUARTER-WAVE LINE.

quartic equation A fourth-degree equation of the form $ax^4 + bx^3 + cx^2 + dx + e = 0$, where a, b, c, d, and e are constants. Also called BIQUADRATIC EQUATION.

quartz A mineral that is a variety of natural silicon dioxide, or an artificially grown material of the same sort. In the natural state, quartz occurs in hexagonal crystals having pyramidal ends. It has various uses in electronics; one of the most common is the manufacture of piezoelectric crystals.

quartz bar A comparatively large, thick piezoelectric quartz plate used in standard-frequency oscillators and in sharply tuned low-frequency filters. Common resonant frequencies are 50 kHz, 100 kHz, and 1000 kHz.

quartz crystal A natural or artificial piece of quartz cut to specific dimensions, usually self-contained in a solder-in or plug-in enclosure. The device acts as a highly stable selective circuit. It exhibits a sharp resonance at the frequency for which it is cut, and at harmonics of this frequency. It is used as the frequency-determining element in precision oscillators.

quartz-crystal oscillator See CRYSTAL OSCILLATOR.

quartz-crystal resonator See CRYSTAL RESONATOR.

quartz delay line An acoustic delay line using quartz to transmit the sound waves.

quartz-fiber electroscope An electroscope using a gold-plated quartz fiber, instead of gold leaves.

quartz-halogen lamp An incandescent, usually low-voltage lamp used in automotive headlights, and in some home and office lighting appliances. It provides greater efficiency than conventional incandescent lamps.

quartz lamp A mercury-vapor lamp with a transparent quartz (instead of glass) envelope. Unlike glass, quartz readily passes the ultraviolet rays generated by the mercury discharge.

quartz lock A circuit that uses a CRYSTAL OSCILLATOR to regulate frequency, timing, or speed. It is used in electronic clocks and watches, television receivers, synthesized radio receivers, transmitters, transceivers, high-fidelity turntables, etc.

quartz oscillator See CRYSTAL OSCILLATOR.

quartz plate A piezoelectric plate cut from a quartz crystal. The plate is itself often called a *crystal*. Also see CRYSTAL AXES and CRYSTAL CUTS.

quartz resonator See CRYSTAL RESONATOR.

quartz timepiece A watch or clock having as its control element a time-determining quartz crystal.

quasi- A prefix meaning "to some extent" or "similar to," as in *quasi-optical radio wave* (a radio wave that behaves like a light ray).

quasi-bistable circuit A trigger-operated multivibrator. It operates as a flip-flop when the trigger frequency is sufficiently high.

quasi-instruction In a computer program, a data item appearing as an encoded instruction, but that is not acted upon.

quasi-linear feedback system A system in which the feedback elements are nearly linear, but not entirely linear.

quasi-negative Pertaining to a voltage that is negative, with respect to some other voltage, but whose absolute polarity is positive. For example, +0.5 volt is quasi-negative, with respect to +5.5 volts.

quasi-optical Behaving like light. The term is used to describe certain extremely short radio waves or other radiations that, like light rays, follow line-of-sight paths and can be directed, reflected, refracted, or diffused.

quasi-optical path A line-of-sight path followed by very short radio waves, such as microwaves.

quasi-positive Pertaining to a voltage that is positive, with respect to some other voltage, but whose absolute polarity is negative. For example, –0.5 volt is quasi-positive, with respect to –5.5 volts.

quasi-random A set of numbers considered to be random, but chosen according to an algorithm.

quasi-rectangular wave A wave whose shape approaches that of a rectangular wave, but that possesses a small amount of tilt and/or curvature.

quasi-scientific A term that is sometimes applied to the design of electronic systems or to the appraisal of circuit behavior, using an intuitive, rather than analytical approach.

quasi-sine wave A waveform that is not a perfect sine curve, but is close enough to be considered sinusoidal, for all practical purposes.

quasi-single sideband A modulated waveform that somewhat resembles single sideband, in which parts of both sidebands are present.

quasi-square wave A waveform that is not a perfect square, but is close enough to be considered square for all practical purposes. It is sometimes applied to a rectangular wave when a square wave is desired.

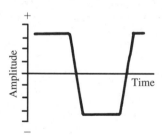

quasi square wave

quasi-technical A term sometimes applied to qualitative tests, as opposed to quantitative tests.

quaternary 1. Pertaining to a base-4 number system. 2. Of an atom, joined to carbon atoms for four bonds. 3. The fourth member of a 4-unit set.

Quebec Phonetic alphabet code word for the letter Q.

quench 1. To suddenly bring to an end (e.g., to quench an oscillation). 2. To cool quickly, as in the quenching of a heated metal object. 3. To extinguish the discharge in a gas tube.

quench capacitor A capacitor that prevents a spark from arcing across an inductor when current flow abruptly stops.

quenched gap See QUENCHED SPARK GAP.

quenched-gap converter A radio-frequency power generator comprising a low-frequency alternating-current source, a quenched spark gap, and a resonant inductance-capacitance circuit.

quenched spark gap A spark gap in which conduction is abruptly stopped by rapid deionization through quick cooling of the gap. It consists of a number of small gaps in series, each being between electrodes, such as metal disks, which are good radiators of heat.

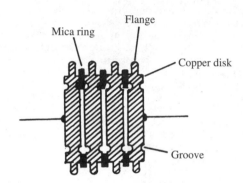

**quenched spark gap
(Remaining disk not shown.)**

quench frequency See QUENCHING FREQUENCY.

quenching action Typical operation of a superregenerative circuit, in which regeneration is increased to nearly the point of oscillation and then reduced; this action is repeated at an ultrasonic frequency and results in very high sensitivity. Also see QUENCHING FREQUENCY, QUENCH OSCILLATOR, and SUPERREGENERATIVE CIRCUIT.

quenching frequency The frequency at which regeneration in a superregenerative circuit is increased and decreased.

quench oscillator In some superregenerative circuits, the separate ultrasonic oscillator that produces the required quenching action.

quench resistor A resistor in a quenching network that prevents a spark from occurring across an inductor when current flow stops.

queue A list of data, steps in a process, or commands awaiting execution in a specific order.

queuing theory A branch of mathematical electronics, dealing with the optimum order in which steps should be executed to obtain a particular end result.

quibinary code In computer operations, a binary-coded decimal system in which each decimal digit is represented by seven bits occupying places whose values are 8, 6, 4, 2, 0, 1, and 0.

quibinary decade circuit A decade counter consisting of a ring-of-5, followed by a single binary stage.

quick break An operating characteristic of a switch, relay, or circuit breaker whereby the contacts open rapidly—even when the actuating current or mechanical force is slow-acting.

quick-break fuse A fuse in which the wire melts and breaks almost instantly when the current rating is exceeded. Also called *quick-blow fuse.* Compare SLOW-BLOW FUSE.

quick-break switch A switch that opens rapidly—even if its handle or lever is moved slowly by the operator. This action minimizes arcing and prevents chatter. Compare QUICK-MAKE SWITCH.

quick charge The process of charging a battery, such as a nickel-cadmium (NICAD) or nickel-metal-hydride (NiMH) type, at a relatively rapid rate, at high charging current. It is sometimes used to charge a battery from a state of almost total discharge. Compare TRICKLE CHARGE.

quick-disconnect The characteristic of a connector that enables its mating halves to be separated quickly and simply, to break the circuit in which it is situated.

quickening liquid A solution of mercuric cyanide or mercuric nitrate, into which objects can be dipped prior to electroplating with silver. The process ensures good adhesion of the silver to the object.

quick make An operating characteristic of a switch, relay, or circuit breaker, whereby the contacts close rapidly—even when the actuating current or mechanical force is slow acting.

quick-make switch A switch that closes rapidly—even if its handle or lever is moved slowly by the operator. Compare QUICK-BREAK SWITCH.

quick printer A high-speed printer, used with a data terminal or computer. A relative term, depending on the user and the application.

quicksilver See MERCURY.

quick-stop control A control on tape recorders and some dictating machines that allows the operator to stop the tape, but keep the machine in the play or record mode. Also called *pause control.*

QuickTime Trade name (Apple Computer, Inc.) for system software commonly used in MULTIMEDIA applications with personal computers.

QUICKTRAN For multiaccess computer systems, a computer programming language based on FORTRAN and offering facilities, through the use of remote terminals, for running, testing, debugging, and compiling programs.

quiescent carrier operation A modulation system in which the carrier is present only during modulation (i.e., it is suppressed at all other times). Also called *controlled-carrier transmission.*

quiescent-carrier telephony A carrier-current (wired-wireless) telephone system in which the carrier is suppressed when there is no voice or alerting signal.

quiescent component In an electronic device, a component that is momentarily nonfunctional.

quiescent current Operating current (usually a direct current) flowing in a circuit or component during zero-signal or no-drain intervals. Also called IDLING CURRENT.

quiescent operation Zero-signal operation of a device, such as a transistor, diode, magnetic amplifier, or similar component.

quiescent period The no-signal interval during which equipment is not operating—even though it is energized.

quiescent point The point on the characteristic curve of a transistor, diode, or similar device, denoting the zero-signal operating conditions.

quiescent push-pull Denoting a push-pull stage, especially an audio power-output amplifier, in which the direct-current signal is essentially zero.

quiescent state The inactive, or resting, state of an active component, such as a transistor or vacuum tube.

quiescent value The zero-signal value of current or voltage for any component supplied with operating power.

quiet AGC See DELAYED AUTOMATIC GAIN CONTROL.

quiet automatic gain control See DELAYED AUTOMATIC GAIN CONTROL.

quiet automatic volume control See DELAYED AUTOMATIC GAIN CONTROL.

quiet AVC See DELAYED AUTOMATIC GAIN CONTROL.

quiet battery A direct-current source specially designed and filtered to minimize noise components in its output.

quieting Noise-voltage reduction in the output of a frequency-modulation (FM) receiver when an unmodulated carrier is received. Also called *noise quieting.*

quieting level In a frequency-modulation (FM) receiver, the limiter threshold point.

quieting sensitivity In a frequency-modulation (FM) receiver, the lowest input-signal amplitude at which the output signal-to-noise ratio is below the specified limit.

quiet tuning A system of tuning in which the output of a receiver is muted until a station is tuned in properly.

quinary code See BIQUINARY CODE.

quinary counter A decade counter consisting of a five-stage ring.

quinhydrone electrode   A pH meter electrode consisting of a platinum wire in a solution of quinhydrone ($C_{12}H_{10}O_4$). Also see PH METER.

quintillion   The number 1,000,000,000,000, 000,000 (10^{18}).

quintupler   **1.** A rectifier circuit that delivers a direct-current output voltage equal to about five times the peak value of the alternating-current input voltage. **2.** A circuit that delivers an output signal at the fifth harmonic of the input signal.

QWERTY   The standard typewriter and computer keyboard layout. The name is derived from the first several letters in the top letter row: Q, W, E, R, T, and Y.

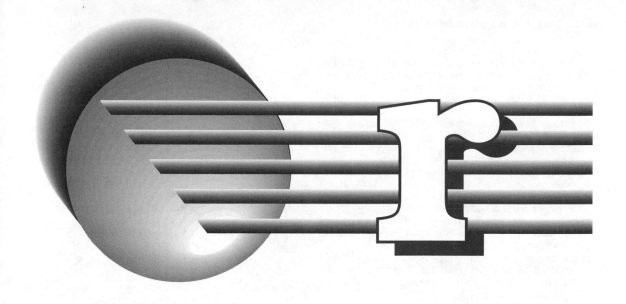

R **1.** Symbol for RESISTANCE. (Also, r.) **2.** Radiotelegraph abbreviation for ROGER. **3.** Symbol for RELUCTANCE. **4.** Abbreviation of RADIUS.

r **1.** Symbol for ROENTGEN. **2.** Symbol for *correlation coefficient.* **3.** Abbreviation of RADIUS. (Also, abbreviated R.)

r_e Symbol for CLASSICAL ELECTRON RADIUS.

RA **1.** Abbreviation of *right ascension.* **2.** Abbreviation of RANDOM ACCESS.

rabbit ears An indoor antenna, sometimes used with a television receiver, consisting of two vertical whips (usually telescoping), the angle between which is adjustable.

RAC Abbreviation of RECTIFIED ALTERNATING CURRENT.

R_{ac} Symbol for AC RESISTANCE. (Also, r_{ac}.)

race Incorrect interpretation of the clock pulses by a digital circuit. Also called *racing.* The circuit improperly attempts to do many operations during one clock pulse, rather than a single operation.

RACES Abbreviation of *Radio Amateur Civil Emergency System.*

raceway See WIRE DUCT and WIREWAYS.

rack An upright frame for holding equipment of RACK-AND-PANEL CONSTRUCTION.

rack-and-panel construction A method of building electronic equipment on a chassis attached horizontally or vertically to a vertical panel. After completion of a unit, the panel is fastened in place on a RACK. Several such panels fill the rack.

rack and pinion A device used for mechanical adjustment of a control, such as the tuning control in a radio receiver. A gear engages a serrated rod. As the gear is turned, the rod moves lengthwise.

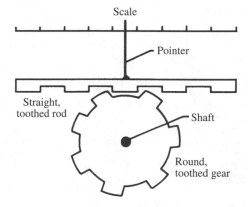

rack and pinion

rack up In computer operations, a way of displaying data, in which a new line added to the already completely occupied screen bumps up what has forgone, thus eliminating the top line.

racon Acronym for *radar beacon.*

rad **1.** A unit of ionizing radiation received by a body (dose) equal to 0.001 J/kg. **2.** Abbreviation of RADIAC. **3.** Abbreviation of RADIAN. **4.** Abbreviation of RADIO. **5.** Abbreviation of RADIX.

radar **1.** A microwave system for detecting objects and determining their distance, direction, heading, speed, and other characteristics. Signals from the transmitter are reflected back to the transmitter site by the object, and the reflection (sometimes along with the transmission) is displayed on a cathode-ray screen. The name is an acronym for *radio detection and ranging*. **2.** The theory and application of radio detection and ranging systems as defined in **1**.

radar altitude   The distance of an aircraft above the surface of the earth, as determined by radar. This value varies with the terrain over which the aircraft passes.

radar antenna   Any antenna used for transmitting and/or receiving radar signals.

radar astronomy   The use of radar equipment to observe and map planets, moons, and asteroids, and to measure their distance from the earth or from a spacecraft.

radar beacon   A radar transceiver that, on receipt of radar signals, transmits encoded signals from which the operator can take a bearing.

radar beam   The cone-shaped main lobe of energy emitted by a radar antenna. The narrower the beam, the greater the resolution of the radar system.

radar clutter   Visual interference on a radar screen caused by reflections from ground or sea.

radar countermeasures   Abbreviations, RCM and rad CM. In wartime, any method of interfering with enemy radar, such as jamming or use of decoys.

radar detector   **1.** A device used in automobiles and trucks to detect the proximity of police or highway-patrol radar. **2.** A device used in military applications, especially aviation, to indicate the presence of radar.

radar homing   A method of missile homing in which radar is used to track a target.

radar speed trap   A radar system used by traffic police to spot speeding vehicles.

radar telescope   The transmission and reception unit used in radar astronomy. Compare RADIO TELESCOPE.

RadCM   Abbreviation of RADAR COUNTERMEASURES. (Also, RCM.)

radial   **1.** Extending outward from a single point. **2.** One of at least two straight conductors extending outward from the base of a vertical antenna, for the purpose of providing a radio-frequency ground.

radial ground   An earth connection composed of radials buried in the ground.

radial lead   A lead (pigtail) attached perpendicular to the axis of a component, such as a resistor or capacitor.

radian   Abbreviation, rad. The angle at the center of a circle subtended by an arc whose length is equal to the radius. Equal to approximately 57.2958 degrees.

radiance   The radiant flux emitted by an object. Radiance is measured in terms of the amount of energy contained in a unit solid angle (steradian) with the source at the apex.

radians-to-degrees conversion   The conversion of radian angular measure into degrees. To change radians to degrees, multiply the number

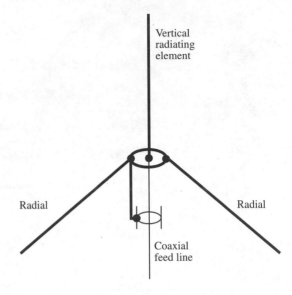

radials

of degrees by 57.2958. Thus, 0.7854 radian = 45 degrees. Compare DEGREES-TO-RADIANS CONVERSION.

radiant efficiency   The ratio of the radiant energy emitted by a source to the energy consumed by the source. The radiant energy is generally specified within a certain range of wavelengths. An example is the incandescent light bulb, which has relatively low radiant efficiency in the visible spectrum between about 750 and 390 nanometers.

radiant energy   **1.** Any form of energy emitted by a source and propagated through space as an electromagnetic disturbance. Included are radio waves, infrared, visible light, ultraviolet, X rays, and gamma rays. **2.** Electromagnetic disturbances at infrared and shorter wavelengths.

radiant flux   The rate at which radiant energy is emitted.

radiation   **1.** The emission of energy or particles (e.g., waves from an antenna, X rays from an X-ray tube, energy from a radioactive material, heat from a body, etc.). **2.** Radio waves, infrared, visible light, ultraviolet, X rays, or gamma rays. **3.** Ionizing emissions from radioactive substances (e.g., alpha particles, beta particles, neutrons, gamma rays, etc.).

radiation angle   The horizontal or vertical angle at which electromagnetic waves are radiated from an antenna. Measured between the central axis of the main lobe and the horizon, or between the central axis of the main lobe and geographic north.

radiation belts   See VAN ALLEN RADIATION BELTS.

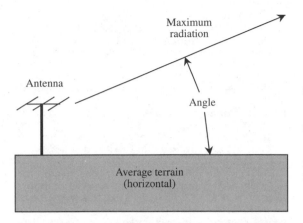

radiation angle

radiation counter An instrument used for determining the intensity of atomic-particle radiation, X rays, or gamma rays. It operates by means of ionization of a gas in a sealed tube.

radiation field The portion of the electromagnetic field that is propagated by a radiator, as opposed to the induction field.

radiation intensity For a directional radio transmitting antenna, the radiated power per steradian in a given direction.

radiation loss Loss of energy through radiation from a conductor. Also see LOSS.

radiation pattern A graphical representation of the intensity of the electromagnetic field in various directions from a radiator, such as a transmitting antenna. It is usually shown in either the horizontal plane or a specific vertical plane containing the antenna. Also see LOBE.

radiation physics The study of radiation and its effects on matter. Radiation physics is especially concerned with ionizing radiation, but it can involve any kind of particle or electromagnetic energy.

radiation pressure Pressure exerted on a surface by impinging electromagnetic radiation.

radiation resistance The inherent resistance at the feed point of a resonant radio antenna.

radiation sickness General physiological symptoms resulting from a short-term overdose of X rays, gamma rays, or atomic-particle radiation.

radiator **1.** The element of an antenna from which radio energy is directly radiated, as opposed to the transmission line, lead-in, reflector, or director. **2.** See LOUDSPEAKER.

radio **1.** Wireless electrical communication, i.e., by means of electromagnetic waves. **2.** See RADIO RECEIVER. **3.** See RADIO TRANSCEIVER. **4.** See RADIO TRANSMITTER. **5.** To communicate by radio.

radio- **1.** A prefix meaning "pertaining to wireless electrical communication." Examples: *radiotele-*

phone and *radiotelegraph.* **2.** A prefix meaning "using radio waves." Examples: *radiosonde, radiolocator,* and *radiothermics.* **3.** A prefix meaning "pertaining to using or possessing radioactivity," or "pertaining to X rays." Examples: *radiograph, radioisotope,* and *radiologist.*

radioactive Having the property of emitting alpha, beta, and (sometimes) gamma rays as the result of nuclear disintegration. Also see HALF-LIFE.

radioactive element A chemical element that is RADIOACTIVE (e.g., uranium). Also called *radioelement.*

radioactive isotope See RADIOISOTOPE.

radioactive tracer A quantity of radioactive material put into a system so that its path can be monitored by means of a radiation detector. An example is the introduction of radioactive barium into the large intestine. The flow and concentration of the barium gives an indication of the functioning of the lower intestine.

radioactive transducer A pickup device for detecting and measuring radioactivity (e.g., *Geiger-Mueller tube*).

radioactivity counter See GEIGER COUNTER and SCINTILLATION COUNTER.

radio altitude See RADAR ALTITUDE.

radio amateur An electronics hobbyist licensed to operate two-way wireless communications stations in various assigned frequency bands, without receiving payment for services rendered.

Radio Amateur Civil Emergency System Abbreviation, RACES. A civil-defense organization of licensed amateur radio stations. Also see RADIO AMATEUR.

radio astronomy The observation, study, and analysis of radio-frequency electromagnetic emissions from bodies or points in space, and the study of these bodies through their radiations.

radioautograph See AUTORADIOGRAPH.

radio beacon **1.** A radio transmitter of direction-finding or guidance signals. **2.** Also called *radio beam.* The signals transmitted by a radio beacon, as defined in **1.**

radio beam **1.** Antenna radiation focused in one direction. **2.** See RADIO BEACON, **2.**

radiobiology A field of biology concerned with the influence of radiant energy or radioactivity on living organisms.

radio broadcast A radio transmission directed to numerous, nonspecific receivers—especially by a station in the *broadcast service.* Also called RADIOCAST. Also see BROADCAST SERVICE, **1, 2.**

radio car An automobile equipped with a two-way radio.

radio carbon Radioactive carbon (i.e., carbon 14).

radiocast See RADIO BROADCAST.

radio channel A single, usually narrow radio-frequency band within a larger band, in which stations are authorized to transmit signals of a specified type. Also see CHANNEL, **1**; CHANNEL SEPARATION; and CHANNEL WIDTH.

radiochemistry   The chemistry of radioactive substances.

radio communication   Wireless communication carried on by means of radio-frequency electromagnetic waves.

radio compass   See DIRECTION FINDER.

radioconductor   A substance or body whose electrical conductivity is affected by radio waves, and that can be used as a sensor of such waves.

radio control   See REMOTE CONTROL.

radio direction finder   See DIRECTION FINDER.

radio Doppler   **1.** A change in the frequency of a radio signal emitted by a source having radial motion, with respect to the receiver. **2.** An electronic device used to measure radial speed by means of the Doppler effect at radio frequencies.

radio-electronics   The branch of electronics specifically involved with wireless communications.

radioelement   See RADIOACTIVE ELEMENT.

radio engineer   A trained professional skilled in the physics and mathematics of radio communications, and in the theory and application of basic electronics engineering and related subjects. Also see RADIO ENGINEERING.

radio engineering   The branch of electronics engineering devoted to the theory and operations of radio communication.

radio field strength   The intensity of radio waves at a given point. Also see FIELD INTENSITY, **2** and RADIO MAP.

radio frequency   Abbreviation, RF. **1.** Consisting of, or pertaining to, alternating currents at frequencies above about 9 kHz (the lowest allocated radio communications frequency). **2.** Consisting of, or pertaining to, electromagnetic fields whose wavelengths are longer than those of infrared, but shorter than about 33 kilometers (corresponding to a frequency of 9 kHz). Also see RADIO SPECTRUM.

radio-frequency amplifier   **1.** In a superheterodyne circuit, the channel in which the incoming

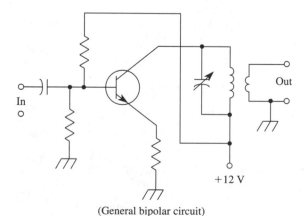

(General bipolar circuit)

radio-frequency amplifier, 2

signal is amplified. Compare INTERMEDIATE-FREQUENCY AMPLIFIER. **2.** Broadly, an amplifier of radio-frequency signals.

radio-frequency choke   Abbreviation, RFC. A low-inductance coil used to block radio-frequency (RF) alternating currents. Many RF chokes have air cores; some have cores of ferrite or powdered iron.

radio-frequency current   Symbol, I_{RF}. **2.** The intensity of a generated radio-frequency (RF) signal, usually expressed in microamperes. **2.** Loosely, any measurable RF signal.

radio-frequency heating   The generation of heat in an object by an intense radio-frequency electromagnetic field. See, for example, DIATHERMY, **1**; DIELECTRIC HEATING; and INDUCTION HEATING.

radio-frequency interference   Abbreviation, RFI. **1.** Annoying electrical noise in radio-frequency (RF) amplifiers, detectors, and instruments. **2.** Undesired RF signals that compete with desired ones in amplifiers, receivers, and instruments. **3.** The unwanted interception and demodulation of a strong RF signal by an audio-frequency (AF) device, such as a telephone set or high-fidelity stereo amplifier.

radio-frequency meter   An instrument for measuring signals of RADIO FREQUENCY (9 kHz and above).

radio-frequency oscillator   Abbreviation, RFO. An oscillator (self-excited or crystal-controlled) for operation at radio frequencies. In such an oscillator, stray components, efficiency, and general losses are of primary concern. Also see RADIO FREQUENCY.

radio-frequency power   Symbol, P_{RF}. Alternating-current power at radio frequencies.

radio-frequency resistance   The total in-phase resistance exhibited by a conductor at radio frequencies. This opposition to current includes direct-current resistance and the in-phase components caused by skin effect, shielding, and the presence of dielectrics.

radio-frequency selectivity   The selectivity of a radio-frequency (RF) channel, such as the RF amplifier and first detector of a superheterodyne circuit.

radio-frequency transformer   A transformer designed for efficient operation at radio frequencies. It can be an air-core type or have a core of low-eddy-current material, such as powdered iron. It has windings designed for low distributed capacitance and low radio-frequency resistance.

radio-frequency transistor   **1.** A transistor capable of providing significant amplification at radio frequencies. **2.** A transistor operable at frequencies above 100 kHz.

radiogenic   Produced by radioactivity.

radiogoniometer   A radio compass (see DIRECTION FINDER and GONIOMETER, **1**).

radiogram   A (usually printed out) message transmitted and received via radiotelegraphy or radioteletype. The term is an acronym for *radio telegram.*

radiograph 1. To contact by sending a RADIOGRAM. **2.** An X-ray photograph.

radio homing 1. A method of homing that uses the tracking of a target on the basis of a radio signal emitted by that target. **2.** A method of keeping a missile on track via radio remote control.

radio interference 1. Interference to radio communication, from whatever cause. **2.** See RADIO-FREQUENCY INTERFERENCE.

radioisotope A radioactive isotope (natural or artificial) of a normally nonradioactive chemical element (e.g., radioactive carbon). Also see ISOTOPE.

radio jamming See JAMMING.

radio knife A surgical instrument consisting essentially of a needle that forms a high-frequency arc. The arc simultaneously cuts and cauterizes tissue.

radiolocation The use of radio and/or radar to locate an object or vessel, or to determine its course.

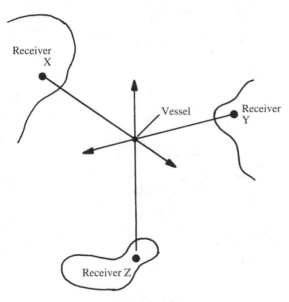

radiolocation

radiolocator See RADAR.

radiological system See X-RAY THERAPY SYSTEM.

radiologist A specialist skilled in RADIOLOGY.

radiology The science embracing the theory and use of X rays and radioactive substances in the diagnosis and treatment of diseases and ailments.

radiolucency 1. The property of a material that allows ionizing radiation to pass through it with little or no absorption. **2.** The extent to which a material transmits ionizing radiation.

radioluminescence Visible light emitted from a radioactive material. A good example is radium; it was once used on wristwatch dials so that they could be seen in the dark.

radiolysis Chemical decomposition brought about by radiation.

radioman A radio technician or operator.

radio map A map of a geographic area, on which lines are drawn connecting measured points of equal field strength for signals from a radio station at the approximate center of the area.

radiometeorograph See RADIOSONDE.

radiometer A device for detecting and measuring the strength of radiant energy. One form consists of a set of vanes blackened on one side and mounted on pivots in a partially evacuated glass bulb. Visible light or infrared causes the vane assembly to rotate, the speed being proportional to the intensity of the light.

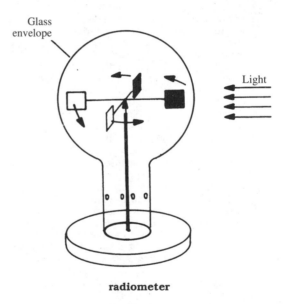

radiometer

radiometry The science and art of measuring radiation in the infrared, visible, and ultraviolet regions of the electromagnetic frequency spectrum. Compare PHOTOMETRY.

radio micrometer See MICRORADIOMETER.

radio net A group of radio stations operating together in an organization, often on or near the same frequency.

radio network See RADIO NET.

radio operator A technician licensed to operate a transmitter in the radio, television, or radar services.

radiopaque Opaque to X rays or other ionizing radiation. Compare RADIOPARENT.

radioparent Transparent to X rays or other ionizing radiation. Compare RADIOPAQUE.

radiophone See RADIOTELEPHONE.

radiophoto A photograph transmitted and received by radio. Also see FACSIMILE.

radio pill See ENDORADIOSONDE.

radio prospecting The use of radio-frequency devices to locate underground or underwater metals and mineral deposits. Also see METAL LOCATOR.

radio range A radio station providing navigational aid to airplanes.

radio receiver The complete apparatus that selects, amplifies, demodulates, and reproduces a radio signal for purposes of communication, as distinct from *facsimile receiver, remote-control receiver, telemetry receiver, television receiver,* etc.

radiosensitivity **1.** The property of being sensitive to ionizing radiation. Most photographic films have this property. **2.** The extent to which a substance or device is sensitive to ionizing radiation.

radio service technician An electronics technician skilled in the repair and maintenance of radio equipment—especially receivers.

radiosonde A balloon-carried combination of radio transmitter and transducers, for sending to a ground monitoring station signals revealing such atmospheric conditions as temperature, humidity, and pressure. It is used mainly for gathering meteorological data at high altitudes.

radiosonobuoy See SONOBUOY.

radio spectroscope A device used by radio astronomers to obtain the radio-frequency profile of a distant star or galaxy. It generally consists of a graph, obtained by scanning the radio spectrum and plotting signal intensity as a function of frequency or wavelength.

radio spectrum The continuum of frequencies useful for radio communication and control. Classified in the following manner: *Very low frequency (VLF),* 9 to 30 kHz; *low frequency (LF),* 30 to 300 kHz; *medium frequency (MF),* 300 to 3000 kHz; *high frequency (HF),* 3 to 30 MHz; *very high frequency (VHF),* 30 to 300 MHz; *ultrahigh frequency (UHF),* 300 to 3000 MHz; *super high frequency (SHF),* 3 to 30 GHz; *extremely high frequency (EHF),* 30 to 300 GHz.

radiostat See CRYSTAL FILTER.

radio station **1.** The location at which a radio transmitter and/or receiver is/are installed. **2.** The complete set of equipment for a radio receiving and/or transmitting installation, including the studio, linking apparatus, and antennas. **3.** A standard broadcast station.

radio technician A professional skilled in the construction, testing, repair, and maintenance of radio equipment, and sometimes in its design, and who usually works under the supervision of a radio engineer. Also see RADIO SERVICE TECHNICIAN.

radiotelegram See RADIOGRAM.

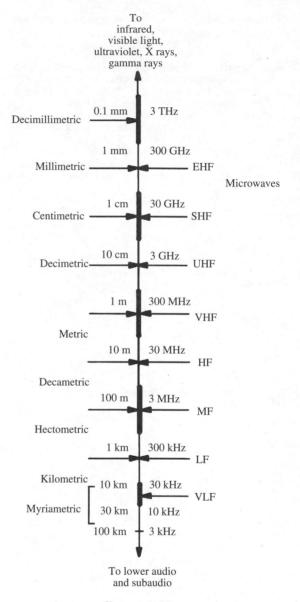

radio spectrum

radiotelegraph **1.** Pertaining to the theory and application of, and the equipment for, Morse code transmission and/or reception via radio. **2.** An installation for Morse code transmission and/or reception via radio. **3.** The transmission and/or reception of Morse code signals via radio.

radiotelegraph code See CONTINENTAL CODE.

radiotelegraph distress signal See SOS.

radiotelegraph monitor See KEYING MONITOR.

radiotelegraphy The transmission and/or reception of telegraphic communications, usually Morse code, by means of radio.

radiotelephone 1. Pertaining to the theory and application of, and the equipment for, voice transmission and/or reception via radio. 2. An installation for voice transmission and/or reception via radio. 3. The transmission and/or reception of voice signals via radio.

radiotelephone distress signal See MAYDAY.

radio/telephone patch See PHONE PATCH.

radiotelephony The transmission and/or reception of audio signals, usually human voices, by means of radio.

radio telescope A directional antenna and associated equipment for receiving and evaluating the radio-frequency electromagnetic radiation from space—especially from celestial objects (such as the sun, planets, stars, nebulae, galaxies, quasars, etc.). See RADIO ASTRONOMY.

radioteletype 1. Pertaining to the theory and application of, and the equipment for, text data transmission and/or reception via radio. 2. An installation for text data transmission and/or reception via radio. 3. The transmission and/or reception of text data signals via radio.

radioteletypewriter A teletypewriter adapted to radio, rather than wire service; it is used in some RADIOTELETYPE installations. In recent years, personal computers and terminals have largely replaced adapted teletypewriters for this purpose.

radiotherapy The use of X rays and/or radioactive substances in the treatment of disease and disorders.

radiothermics The science of the generation of heat by means of radio-frequency current.

radiothermy See DIATHERMY.

radio thorium Radioactive THORIUM.

radiotracer See TRACER.

radio transceiver A RADIO RECEIVER and RADIO TRANSMITTER built into a single unit, and generally intended for use in two-way communication.

radio transmitter The complete apparatus that generates radio-frequency power, modifies it with the data needed for communication, and delivers the product to an antenna for radiation into space. Here, the radio transmitter is distinguished from similar equipment: *facsimile transmitter*, *remote-control transmitter*, *telemetry transmitter*, *television transmitter*, etc.

radio-transparent material 1. A substance through which radio waves pass with little or no attenuation. 2. A substance through which X rays, gamma rays, or high-speed subatomic particles can pass with little or no attenuation.

radiotrician Acronym for *radio electrician*. See RADIO SERVICE TECHNICIAN.

radio tube 1. A VACUUM TUBE used at radio frequencies. 2. A vacuum tube used as an amplifier, local oscillator, detector, or mixer in an early radio receiver.

radiovision See TELEVISION.

radio watch See WATCH.

radio waves Electromagnetic waves in the RADIO SPECTRUM.

radio window That portion of the radio-frequency electromagnetic spectrum that passes through the atmosphere, rather than being refracted or absorbed. The wavelength range is about 20 meters to 5 millimeters, or 15 MHz to 60 GHz. The lower limit of this range is affected by ionospheric conditions. The upper frequency limit depends on various factors, including relative humidity and dust content of the air.

radium Symbol, Ra. A rare radioactive metallic element. Atomic number, 88. Atomic weight, 226.025.

radius The straight-line distance from the center of a circle or sphere to its periphery.

radius vector In spherical or polar coordinates, a line segment drawn from the pole, or origin, and representing the vector magnitude.

radix The number indicating the number of symbols in a system of numerical notation, and the powers of which give the place values of the system. Thus, 10 is the radix of the decimal system, and 2 is the radix of the binary system. Also called BASE.

radix point In a number, the point (dot or period) separating the integral and fractional digits. Its specific name depends on the system of notation involved: *binary point*, *decimal point*, etc.

radome A plastic shell housing a radar antenna—especially aboard an aircraft.

radon Symbol Rn. A gaseous radioactive element that results from the disintegration of radium. Atomic number, 86. Atomic weight, 222.

rad/s Abbreviation of *radians per second*, the SI unit of angular velocity.

rad/s² Abbreviation of *radians per second squared*, the SI unit of angular acceleration.

radux A continuous-wave, low-frequency radionavigation system. Position is determined by comparing the phase of two signals sent from different locations.

RAID Acronym for REDUNDANT ARRAY OF INDEPENDENT DISKS.

rainbow generator A test-signal generator that produces a full color spectrum, a pattern resembling the successive coloration of a rainbow, on the screen of a color-television receiver. Also see RAINBOW PATTERN.

rainbow pattern A test pattern for servicing a color-television receiver. It consists of a full color spectrum, thus taking its name from its resemblance to a rainbow. Also see RAINBOW GENERATOR.

RAM Abbreviation of RANDOM-ACCESS MEMORY.

ramp   A sawtooth wave with a linear rise and a practically instantaneous decay; its name was derived from its resemblance to an incline.

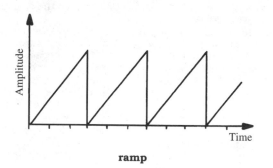

ramp

ramp generator   A test-signal generator that produces sawtooth-wave signals. Also see RAMP.

R and D   Abbreviation of research and development or research and design. (Also, R&D.)

random access   Abbreviation, RA. In computer and data-processing operations, pertaining to storage or memory in which data can be recovered in any order.

random-access memory   In computer and data-processing systems, a memory providing access time that is independent of the address.

random deviation   Irregular RIPPLE.

random-fed antenna   An antenna that uses RANDOM FEED.

random feed   A method of connecting a transmission line to an antenna, wherein the feed point is not necessarily at the center and not necessarily at a current loop or voltage loop. This technique is rarely used; it generally results in some radiation from the feed line.

random noise   Electrical noise in which the pulses or fluctuations have no discernible pattern of occurrence (i.e., they are haphazard in frequency and amplitude).

random number   A number derived by chance. It is used in statistical analysis for various purposes.

random number generator   Hardware or software that provides a sequence of numbers or digits that are random for the purpose of a given statistical application.

random occurrence   See CHANCE OCCURRENCE.

random variable   In statistics, a variable that can have a number of values, each of the same probability.

random winding   A coil winding in which the turns are wound haphazardly to reduce distributed capacitance.

range   1. The limits within which a circuit or device operates (i.e., the territory defined by such limits). Examples: *current range, frequency range,* and *voltage range.* 2. The difference between the upper and lower limits of deflection of a meter. 3. The distance over which a transmitter operates reliably. 4. A clear area for testing antennas. 5. The distance between a radar station and a target. 6. The possible values for a quantity or function that lie between given limits.

range capacitor   See TRIMMER CAPACITOR.

range-height indicator   Abbreviation, RHI. A radar display in which the horizontal axis shows distance to the target, and the vertical axis shows elevation of the target.

range mark   See DISTANCE MARK.

range plotting   The creation of a graph of the distance (range) to objects, as a function of direction or orientation in two or three dimensions. Commonly used in robot guidance systems.

range resistor   See TRIMMER RESISTOR.

range sensing   The measurement of distances to objects via electronic methods such as radar, sonar, vision systems, etc. Commonly used in robot guidance systems.

rank   1. To arrange in a specific sequence according to significance. 2. A place in such a sequence.

Rankine scale   A temperature scale on which the freezing point of water is 491.69 degrees, and the boiling point 671.69 degrees. Absolute zero is represented by 0 degrees. For conversion to kelvins, multiply degrees Rankine by 5/9.

rapid drift   A fast change of a quantity or setting (usually in one direction) with time.

rapid printer   See QUICK PRINTER.

raser   A device that produces coherent electromagnetic waves at radio frequencies; the radio-frequency equivalent of a LASER.

raster   The rectangle of light (composed of unmodulated lines) seen on the screen of a television picture tube when no signal is present.

ratchet circuit   See COMMUTATOR, 2 and ELECTRONIC RATCHET.

rate action   See DERIVATIVE ACTION.

rate effect   In a four-layer semiconductor device, the tendency for the switch to conduct undesirably as a result of a transient spike.

rate-grown transistor   See GRADED-JUNCTION TRANSISTOR.

rate gyro   A special gyroscope for measuring angular rates.

rate of change   1. The extent to which the value of a dependent variable changes in accordance with a specified change in an independent variable (usually time). 2. A quantitative expression of the speed with which a dependent variable changes, with respect to an independent variable (usually time).

rate signal   A signal whose amplitude is proportional to the derivative of a variable, with respect to time.

rate time   In automatic-control operations, the time over which the addition of DERIVATIVE ACTION advances PROPORTIONAL ACTION.

ratio-arm bridge   A simple four-arm bridge in which the balancing potentiometer supplies the

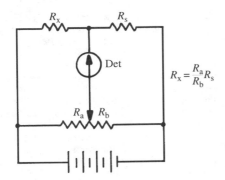

$$R_x = \frac{R_a}{R_b} R_s$$

ratio-arm bridge

two arms, one on each side of the slider at all settings.

ratio arms Two impedance arms serving to establish the numerical ratio of a bridge circuit.

ratio control In automatic-control operations, a system in which the controlled variable is in a prescribed ratio to another variable.

ratio detector A frequency-modulation (FM) second detector resembling the FOSTER-SEELEY DISCRIMINATOR, except that one of the two diodes is reversed and the junction point of the load resistors is grounded. In an FM circuit using a ratio detector, no limiter is required. The ratio of the direct-current outputs is proportional to the ratio of the instantaneous signal voltages applied to the two diodes.

ratio meter An instrument that compares two different signals (and indirectly their sources) and delivers a reading of their ratio.

rational number A number that can be expressed in the form a/b, where a and b are integers and b is not equal to zero.

rational operation Any of the conventional arithmetic operations: multiplication, division, addition, or subtraction.

ratio of geometric progression In a geometric progression, the ratio of one value to the next.

ratio of similitude The ratio of the lengths of corresponding sides in similar geometric figures.

rat race See HYBRID RING.

raven red A variety of red oxide of iron, a commercial red paint used as the magnetic coating of early recording tapes.

raw ac Unrectified alternating current (ac) or voltage.

raw data Data that has not been processed in any way.

rawinsonde A RADIOSONDE tracked by a radio direction finder to determine wind velocity. The name is an acronym from *radar wind radiosonde*.

raw tape See BLANK TAPE.

ray **1.** A line of radiant energy. Such a line (e.g., the path of a single photon of visible light) is imagined to arise from a point source and have zero width. **2.** A thin beam of radiant energy (e.g., the beam of electrons in a cathode-ray tube). **3.** A quantity of radiant energy or ionizing radiation (e.g, *gamma ray*). **4.** One of numerous lines converging toward, or emanating from, a specific point. **5.** A vector representing the direction in which an electromagnetic field or acoustic disturbance travels. **6.** Also called *half line*. The set of points on a line consisting of a defined origin and all the points on one side of the origin. Example: the positive reactance axis in an ARGAND DIAGRAM.

Raydist A continuous-wave, medium-frequency radionavigation system. The position is determined according to the phase difference between two signals transmitted from different locations.

Rayleigh-Carson theorem An expression of the reciprocal relationship between the transmitting and receiving properties of an antenna. If voltage E applied to antenna A causes current I to flow at a given point in antenna B, then the same voltage (E) applied at that point in antenna B will produce identical current I (same magnitude and phase) at the point in antenna A, where voltage E originally was applied. Also see RECIPROCITY THEOREM.

Rayleigh distribution A probability-density function, used to describe the behavior of sky-wave electromagnetic signals.

Rayleigh's law The hysteresis loss in a magnetic material varies in proportion to the cube of the magnetic induction.

Rb Symbol for RUBIDIUM.

R_B Symbol for BASE RESISTANCE. (Also, r_B.)

RC **1.** Abbreviation of RESISTANCE-CAPACITANCE. **2.** Abbreviation of RADIO-CONTROLLED. **3.** Abbreviation of REMOTE CONTROL.

R_c **1.** Symbol for COLLECTOR RESISTANCE. (Also, r_C.) **2.** Symbol for COLD RESISTANCE.

RCA jack See PHONO JACK.

RCA plug See PHONO PLUG.

RC circuit See RESISTANCE-CAPACITANCE CIRCUIT.

RC-coupled amplifier See RESISTANCE-CAPACITANCE-COUPLED AMPLIFIER.

RC coupling See RESISTANCE-CAPACITANCE COUPLING.

RC filter See RESISTANCE-CAPACITANCE FILTER.

RCL **1.** Abbreviation of RECALL. **2.** Abbreviation of RESISTANCE-CAPACITANCE-INDUCTANCE.

RCM Abbreviation of RADAR COUNTERMEASURES. (Also, radCM.)

RC phase shifter See RESISTANCE-CAPACITANCE PHASE SHIFTER.

RC time constant See RESISTANCE-CAPACITANCE TIME CONSTANT.

RCTL Abbreviation of RESISTOR-CAPACITOR-TRANSISTOR LOGIC.

RC tuning See RESISTANCE-CAPACITANCE TUNING.

RCV   Abbreviation for *receive*. (Also, rcv.)

RCVR   Abbreviation for RECEIVER. (Also, rcvr, rx.)

rd   Abbreviation for *rutherford*.

R & D   See R AND D.

R_D Symbol for DRAIN RESISTANCE.

R_d **1.** Symbol for DIODE RESISTANCE. (Also, r_d.) **2.** Symbol for DISTRIBUTED RESISTANCE.

R-DAT   Abbreviation of ROTARY DIGITAL AUDIO TAPE.

R_{dc} Symbol for DC RESISTANCE. (Also, r_{dc}.)

RDF   Abbreviation of RADIO DIRECTION FINDER.

Re   Symbol for RHENIUM.

R_e Symbol for EMITTER RESISTANCE. (Also, r_E.)

REA   Abbreviation of *Rural Electrification Administration*.

reachthrough   See PUNCHTHROUGH.

reachthrough region   See PUNCHTHROUGH REGION.

reachthrough voltage   See PUNCHTHROUGH VOLTAGE.

reactance   Symbol, *X*. Unit, ohm. The opposition offered to the flow of alternating current by pure capacitance, pure inductance, or a combination of the two. Reactance introduces phase shift. Also see CAPACITIVE REACTANCE and INDUCTIVE REACTANCE. Compare RESISTANCE.

reactance chart   A nomograph for capacitance, inductance, and frequency.

reactance factor   The ratio of the alternating-current resistance of a conductor to the direct-current resistance. The reactance factor generally increases as the frequency increases because of skin effect and because the length of the conductor might be a sizable part of the wavelength of the transmitted energy.

reactance modulator   A frequency modulator using a variable reactance, usually a varactor diode in the oscillator.

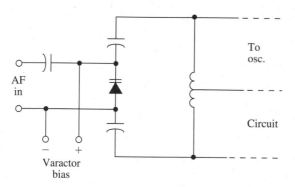

To osc.

AF in

Circuit

−   +
Varactor bias

reactance modulator

reactance transistor   A transistor used as a REACTANCE MODULATOR.

reaction-time meter   See NEOMATACHOGRAPH and NEOMATACHOMETER.

reactive absorber   In acoustics, a device that dissipates impinging sound waves by means of reflection, resonance, and other effects, besides dissipation in the form of heat.

reactive attenuator   An attenuator that functions by means of reactance, rather than by means of resistance.

reactive current   The component of alternating current that is not in phase with the voltage. Compare RESISTIVE CURRENT.

reactive kilovolt-ampere   Abbreviation, kVAR. A unit of high apparent power; it is the product of kilovolts and amperes in a reactive component of a circuit. Also see APPARENT POWER, KILOVOLT-AMPERE, REACTIVE VOLT-AMPERE, and VOLT-AMPERE.

reactive load   **1.** A load device that is capacitive or inductive, rather than resistive. **2.** A load device that contains reactance as well as resistance.

reactive power   See REACTIVE KILOVOLTAMPERE and REACTIVE VOLT-AMPERE.

reactive volt-ampere   Abbreviation, VAR. A unit of apparent power; it is the product of volts and amperes in a reactive component of a circuit. Also see APPARENT POWER, KILOVOLT-AMPERE, REACTIVE KILOVOLT-AMPERE, and VOLT-AMPERE.

reactor   **1.** An inductor, especially one having very low internal resistance, used principally for its inductive reactance. **2.** A chamber in which the nuclei of atoms are split to provide atomic energy. Also see NUCLEAR REACTOR. **3.** In industrial chemistry, a vat in which reactions take place.

read   **1.** In computer operations, to extract data from memory or a storage medium and (usually) transfer it to another area of memory or other medium. Compare WRITE. **2.** In digital communications, to transcribe data into printed form. **3.** In radiotelegraphy, to listen to Morse-code signals and comprehend the text without necessarily writing it down. **4.** To observe and note the indication of an instrument, such as a meter.

readability   In electronic communications, the degree to which a desired signal can be recognized and interpreted in a given context.

readback   In a multiplexer, a feature that facilitates inspection of the contents of the control latch.

reader   A device that transcribes digital signals or markings into meaningful data. Examples: *Morse-code reader* and *bar-code reader*.

read head   In a magnetic memory or in a tape recorder or wire recorder used for data recording, the head that picks up the magnetic pulses from the drum, tape, disk, or wire. Compare WRITE HEAD.

reading rate   The number of input characters per second that a computer or other data-processing device handles.

read-only memory   Abbreviation, ROM. In a computer or calculator, a memory unit in which instructions or data are permanently stored for use by the machine or for reference by the user. The stored information is read out nondestructively.

readout lamp An electron tube containing several cathodes, filled with a gas (such as neon), and used as a numeric or alphanumeric display device. Each cathode is connected to a separate pin on the base. A single anode is common to all cathodes. The cathode(s) to which a voltage is applied glow(s), showing the shape of a numeral, letter of the alphabet, or other symbol. In recent years, this type of display has been replaced by light-emitting diodes (LEDs) and liquid-crystal displays (LCDs).

readout pulse In a random-access memory (RAM), a pulse applied to the word line, facilitating readout of the information in a certain storage slot.

read pulse In computer operations, a pulse that activates the read function (see READ). Compare WRITE PULSE.

read rate The number of data units an input read device can transcribe per unit of time [e.g., *bits per second (bps)* and *words per minute (wpm)*].

readthrough **1.** The reception of signals between transmitted pulses at the same frequency. **2.** The continuous monitoring of a signal being jammed. Any change in the frequency, modulation, or other characteristics of the signal can then be detected, and the jamming signal adjusted accordingly.

read time The period during which data is being transferred from a computer storage unit.

read-write channel In computer operations, a channel over which activity between a central processing unit and a specific peripheral occurs.

read-write head An electromagnetic transducer used for both reading and writing data. See READ and WRITE.

read-write memory **1.** A small data storage bank for short-term use. The contents of the memory are easily changed. **2.** See RANDOM ACCESS MEMORY.

real address See ABSOLUTE ADDRESS.

real axis The axis of the real-number component of a COMPLEX NUMBER (i.e., the horizontal axis in an ARGAND DIAGRAM).

real component The real-number part of a COMPLEX NUMBER.

real image The image formed on a screen when rays from the object converge on passing through a lens. Compare VIRTUAL IMAGE.

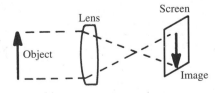

real image

real number A number in the category that includes zero, all rational numbers, and all irrational numbers. Also see COMPLEX NUMBER, IMAGINARY NUMBER, IRRATIONAL NUMBER, and RATIONAL NUMBER.

real power The apparent power multiplied by the power factor in an alternating-current circuit containing reactance. Real power is the difference between the apparent power and the reactive power. Actual radiated or dissipated power cannot exceed the real power.

real time Pertaining to the operation of a computer, communications, or data processing system in which events are represented or acted on as they occur. Data is processed as it becomes available, usually through the use of time-sharing, direct-access storage devices, and remote terminals.

real-time clock A device that produces periodic signals that reflect the interval between events. It is sometimes used to indicate time of day.

rear end The low-frequency portion of a superheterodyne receiver (i.e., the intermediate-frequency amplifier, second detector, and audio-frequency amplifier). Compare FRONT END.

rear projection A method of big-screen television picture reproduction. The image is focused onto a translucent, flat surface. The viewer is positioned on the side of the screen opposite to the projecting beam.

Reaumur scale A thermometer scale on which zero is the freezing point of water and 80 degrees is the boiling point of water. Compare ABSOLUTE SCALE, CELSIUS SCALE, FAHRENHEIT SCALE, and RANKINE SCALE.

rebecca The airborne interrogator in the British REBECCA-EUREKA SYSTEM.

rebecca-eureka system A British 90-mile-hovering radar navigation system that consists of an airborne interrogator (rebecca) and a ground transponder beacon (eureka).

rebroadcast The retransmission of a radio broadcast simultaneously by a station other than the originator. Also see AUTOMATIC RELAY STATION.

rebroadcast station See AUTOMATIC RELAY STATION.

recalescence During the cooling of a metal, the sudden release of heat. Also see RECALESCENT POINT. Compare DECALESCENCE.

recalescent point In a metal whose temperature is being lowered from a higher value, the temperature at which heat is suddenly released. Compare DECALESCENT POINT.

recall Abbreviation, RCL. In computers and calculators, an instruction that brings material from the memory for examination or use. The opposite instruction is STORE.

receiver **1.** A device or system operated at the destination end of a communication link; it accepts a signal and processes or converts it for local use. Also see specific entries for various types of receiver. **2.** The earpiece of a telephone. **3.** A radio broadcast-band tuner integrated with a general-purpose preamplifier and power amplifier, and containing standard jacks for input and output of audio signals to and from peripheral equipment.

receiver muting   See MUTING, **1.**

receiver primaries   See DISPLAY PRIMARIES.

receiver selectivity   The intermediate-frequency and/or audio-frequency channel bandwidth in a broadcast or communications receiver. It can be expressed qualitatively (e.g., sharp or broad) or quantitatively (e.g., 500 Hz or 2.7 kHz). Also see SELECTIVITY.

receiver sensitivity   The degree to which a broadcast or communications receiver will respond to weak signals; it is generally expressed as the input-signal voltage (at the antenna terminals) required to produce a certain signal-to-noise ratio at the speaker or headphone output.

receiving set   RADIO RECEIVER.

receiving station   A station that ordinarily only receives signals (i.e., it makes no type of transmission). Compare TRANSMITTING STATION.

receptacle   **1.** See SOCKET. **2.** The half of a connector that is mounted on a support, such as a panel, and that is therefore stationary.

recharge   In certain cells and batteries, the restoration of chemical energy following use so that the device is ready to deliver its full rated electric current. Also see RECHARGEABLE.

rechargeable   Pertaining to a secondary cell or battery that can accept a restoration of chemical energy following use, and thus can be completely charged and discharged numerous times. Examples: *nickel-metal-hydride (NiMH) battery* and *lead-acid battery.*

reciprocal impedances   See INVERSE IMPEDANCES.

reciprocal ohm   See SIEMENS and MHO.

reciprocation   **1.** The determination of a mathematical reciprocal value from a given value. **2.** The transmission of a message in response to a received message.

reciprocity in antennas   See RAYLEIGH-CARSON THEOREM.

reciprocity theorem   When a voltage E across branch A of a network causes a current I to flow in branch B of the network, the voltage can be applied across branch B to cause the same value of current to flow in branch A. Compare COMPENSATION THEOREM, MAXIMUM POWER TRANSFER THEOREM, NORTON'S THEOREM, SUPERPOSITION THEOREM, and THEVENIN'S THEOREM.

recombination   The refilling of holes by electrons in a semiconductor.

recombination current   In a transistor circuit, base current resulting from recombination.

recombination rate   In a semiconductor material, the speed at which the electrons and holes

recombine. It can be expressed as the time required for a certain proportion of charge carriers to recombine.

recompile   In computer operations, to COMPILE again, usually according to program amendments following debugging, or to create a different form of a program so that it will be compatible with other hardware.

record   **1.** See PHONOGRAPH DISC. **2.** A chart delivered by a graphic recorder. **3.** To make one of the foregoing. **4.** In data processing, a constituent of a file. **5.** In data processing, a data unit portraying a specific transaction.

record blocking   In data processing operations, making data blocks from groups of records so that the blocks can, in a single operation, be transferred to a nonvolatile storage medium, such as diskette or tape.

record count   A usually running total of a file's records.

recorded disc   A phonograph disc on which a recording has been made. Also called PRERECORDED DISC.

recorded tape   Magnetic tape containing recorded material. Also called PRERECORDED TAPE. Compare BLANK TAPE.

recorder   **1.** A machine for preserving sound, video, or data signals in the sequence in which they occur (e.g., DISC RECORDER, TAPE RECORDER, and WIRE RECORDER). **2.** A machine for making a permanent visual record (photographically or by stylus) of an electrical phenomenon. Examples: DRUM RECORDER and OSCILLOGRAPH.

record head   See RECORDING HEAD.

recording density   In a magnetic storage medium, the number of information units (bits, bytes, etc.) represented by magnetized areas, per unit area or length.

recording disc   A phonograph record on which material has not been recorded, or from which recorded material has been removed. Compare PRERECORDED DISC.

recording head   In a magnetic recorder/reproducer, the head that magnetizes the medium in accordance with sounds or other signals. Also called RECORD HEAD and WRITE HEAD. Compare PLAYBACK HEAD.

Recording Industry Association of America   Abbreviation, RIAA. An organization that sets standards for audio recording and reproduction in the United States.

recording instrument   A measuring instrument, such as a voltmeter or ammeter, that makes a permanent record of its deflections. Also see RECORDER, **2.**

recording loss   **1.** Loss of data during a recording process. **2.** Loss resulting from recording efficiency of less than 100 percent; audio power loss.

recording tape   Magnetic tape on which nothing has been recorded, or from which all data has been erased. Compare PRERECORDED TAPE.

recovery time **1.** Symbol, t_r. The time required for a semiconductor pn junction to attain its high-resistance state when the bias voltage is suddenly switched from forward to reverse. **2.** The time required for a circuit to recover from momentary overdrive. **3.** The time required for a computer system to stabilize following a degenerative operation. **4.** The time required for switching a memory from the write to the read mode. It is measured as the length of time from switching out of the write mode until meaningful signals occur at the output. **5.** In a transceiver, the time required from the completion of a transmitted signal until the receiver is activated.

rect Abbreviation of RECTIFIER.

rectangular coordinates See CARTESIAN CO-ORDINATES.

rectangular scan **1.** A method of beam scanning in a cathode-ray tube, in which the beam moves sequentially in parallel lines to cover a rectangular region. Used in television. **2.** In radar, a two-dimensional scan, covering a specific rectangular region.

rectangular wave An alternating or pulsating current or voltage whose rise and decay times are essentially zero, and whose maxima and minima are essentially flat, but not necessarily of equal duration. The SQUARE WAVE is a special type of rectangular wave.

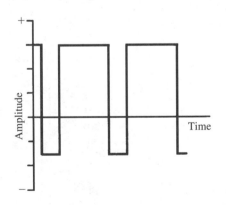

rectangular wave

rectangular waveguide A waveguide having a rectangular cross section.

rectification The conversion of alternating current into pulsating direct current by any means other than the use of a motor-generator. Also see RECTIFIER.

rectification efficiency The ratio (expressed as a percentage) of the direct-current output voltage to the peak alternating-current input voltage of a rectifier.

rectified alternating current The unfiltered, pulsating direct-current output of a rectifier. It con-

sists of the unidirectional half-cycles passed by the rectifier (one per cycle for half-wave rectification, and two per cycle for full-wave rectification).

rectifier Abbreviation, rect. An electronic or electromechanical device that converts alternating current into pulsating direct current.

rectifier diode A heavy-duty tube or semiconductor diode designed primarily to change alternating current to pulsating direct current in power supplies.

rectifier-filter system The rectifier plus power-supply-filter combination for converting alternating current into direct current.

rectifier photocell A photovoltaic cell consisting of two layers of material with a semiconductor junction between them. The device produces direct current when exposed to visible light, infrared, or ultraviolet radiation.

rectifier probe A diode-type probe used with a direct-current (dc) voltmeter to measure radio-frequency (RF) voltage. The diode rectifies the RF signal and presents to the meter a dc voltage proportional to the peak RF voltage.

rectifier stack An assembly of separate rectifier disks or plates in series on a central bolt, as in most selenium rectifiers.

rectifier tube A two-element electron tube, once commonly used for converting alternating current into pulsating direct current in high-voltage, high-current power supplies.

rectifier-type meter See DIODE-TYPE METER.

rectilinear chart A graphic-recorder chart in which the crossing coordinates are arcs, rather than straight lines, to correspond to the swing of the pen. Also see STRIP CHART.

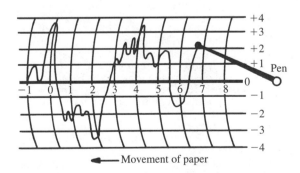

rectilinear chart

rectilinear scan See RECTANGULAR SCAN, **1.**

recurrent network A circuit in which several sections of identical configuration (e.g., L sections) are cascaded.

recurrent phenomenon A phenomenon that repeats itself periodically.

recurrent sweep In an oscilloscope, a repetitive horizontal sweep of the beam occurring at a frequency determined by the settings of the sweep controls. Also called REPETITIVE SWEEP. Compare NONREPETITIVE SWEEP.

recursion   **1.** Generating a complete sequence of functions or numbers by applying an algorithm to initial values in the sequence. **2.** In computer programming and artificial intelligence, a logical process containing loops in calculation or reasoning.

recursive   Relating to a procedure or set of steps that repeat endlessly.

Red Book   The first format developed for compact-disc data storage media, developed by Sony and Philips. It is commonly used in digital audio systems. See also CD-ROM, GREEN BOOK, ORANGE BOOK, and YELLOW BOOK.

red-green-blue   Abbreviation, RGB. In video applications, the three primary colors from which all other colors are derived. Also see COLOR TELEVISION.

red gun   In a three-gun color-television picture tube, the electron gun whose (correctly adjusted) beam strikes only the red phosphor dots on the screen.

red oxide of iron   An iron oxide of the general formula Fe_2O_3, used as the magnetic coating of recording tape. Also see IRON OXIDE.

red oxide of zinc   See ZINCITE.

red-tape operation   An operation or function needed for organizational purposes, but that does not directly contribute to the completion of the task at hand.

reduced instruction set computer   Abbreviation, RISC. A computer architecture in which program instructions are simplified to obtain enhanced processing speed. It is useful especially in complex graphics, animation, multimedia, and scientific work requiring many calculations.

reductio ad absurdum   A method of obtaining a conclusion by proving that its negation results in a contradiction. It is sometimes used in computer programming involving mathematical proofs.

reduction   In an electrochemical cell or battery, a transfer of electrons to the active chemical.

reductionism   The theory that all human thought processes, including emotion and intuition, can be reduced to digital logic, and thus can be duplicated by a sufficiently powerful computer. It is of interest to researchers in artificial intelligence.

reductionist   A person who subscribes to the theory of REDUCTIONISM.

redundancy   **1.** The repetition of components in a circuit (e.g., series or parallel connection of them) so that one will be available for circuit operation if the other fails. **2.** Having available more than one method for performing a function. **3.** Having on hand several copies of data as a safeguard against data loss.

redundancy check   A check for the integrity of digitized data to which extra bits have been added for the purpose (e.g., *parity check*).

redundant   **1.** Pertaining to any two units of data that resemble each other in such a manner that

if either unit is removed, no information is lost from the system. **2.** A unit of data that contains information already present in the system.

redundant array of independent disks   Acronym, RAID. A set of data storage media used to store video programs.

red video voltage   In a three-gun color-television circuit, the red-signal voltage that actuates the red gun.

reed   A usually thin metal blade, leaf, or strip used in vibrators, reed-type relays, reed-type oscillators, and similar devices.

reed oscillator   See REED-TYPE OSCILLATOR.

reed relay   See DRY-REED SWITCH and MERCURY-WETTED REED RELAY.

reed-relay logic   Logic circuits using reed relays. Also see RELAY LOGIC.

reed switch   **1.** A frequency-sensitive switch in which the movable contact is mounted on the tip of a thin, metal strip (reed). The reed is actuated by an alternating-current (ac) coil. The reed closes the contacts when the ac excitation is at its natural frequency. **2.** See DRY-REED SWITCH.

reed-type oscillator   An electromechanical audio-frequency oscillator whose frequency is controlled by a vibrating metal strip (reed) instead of a tuning fork. Also see HUMMER.

reed-type switch   See REED SWITCH.

reel   **1.** The spool around which a magnetic tape or video film is wound. **2.** A spool containing magnetic tape or video film.

reentrant cavity   A resonant cavity in which one or more sections are directed inward to confine the electric field to a small volume.

Cross section

reentrant cavity

reentrant winding   A winding of wire that returns to its starting point—especially in a motor armature.

ref   Abbreviation of REFERENCE.

reference address   As a point of reference, an address for instructions having relative addresses.

reference amplifier   A voltage-regulation device consisting of a transistor and Zener diode in the same envelope.

reference angle   In radar, the angle of incidence of the beam against a target surface, measured with respect to the normal (perpendicular) line at the surface.

reference antenna   A standard antenna, such as an isotropic radiator or a half-wave dipole, used to establish a reference for determining the relative gain of another antenna.

reference bias current   In a reference amplifier, the input current that subtracts from the reference current. It is generally measured in microamperes.

reference current range   In a digital-to-analog converter, the difference between the maximum and minimum reference current for which the device is within specifications for resolution.

reference diode   A Zener diode whose constant voltage drop is used as a direct-current reference potential in calibrator circuits and voltage regulators.

reference dipole   See REFERENCE ANTENNA.

reference electrode   For use with a pH meter, an electrode that provides a reference potential.

reference input slew rate   In a digital-to-analog converter, the average rate of change in output for a given change in the reference input. It is expressed in milliamperes or microamperes per microsecond.

reference level   A specific value of a quantity (e.g., current, frequency, power, or voltage) to which other values of the same quantity are referred.

reference time   The point at which a trigger pulse attains 10 percent of its maximum amplitude.

reference tone   A standard audible tone of known frequency [e.g., 440 Hz (representing A below middle C)]. Sometimes the intensity as well, as the frequency, is specified.

reference white level   The television picture signal value representing the uppermost limit for peak white signals.

R_{eff} Symbol for EFFECTIVE RESISTANCE.

reflectance   **1.** See MISMATCH FACTOR. **2.** The reflected part of the radiant flux striking a surface. It is expressed as a fraction of the total incident radiation.

reflected binary code   See CYCLIC CODE.

reflected electromagnetic field   In a transmission line, the electromagnetic energy not absorbed by the load when an impedance mismatch exists between the load and the line. See INCIDENT POWER and REFLECTED POWER.

reflected impedance   In a coupled circuit, the impedance in the secondary that appears in the primary circuit, or vice-versa, as if it were reflected through the coupling transformer.

reflected power   In a transmission line not perfectly matched to a load at the feed point, an expression of the amount of electromagnetic field reflected from the feed point, rather than absorbed by the load. In general, this can be expressed in watts or as a percentage of the incident power. It is not a true indicator of the loss caused by the mismatch because the reflected field is usually all returned again when it arrives back at the transmitter.

reflected-power meter   A radio-frequency instrument, connected between a source and a load, that can measure INCIDENT POWER and REFLECTED POWER.

reflected ray   The ray that is reflected by the surface of a body or region it strikes. Compare INCIDENT RAY and REFRACTED RAY.

reflected resistance   **1.** In a transformer, the effective resistance across the primary winding when a resistive load is connected to the secondary. **2.** In a transmission line, the resistance at the input end when a load is connected to the output end.

reflected wave   **1.** An electromagnetic wave reflected by the ionosphere or by the surface of the earth. Compare INCIDENT WAVE and REFRACTED WAVE. Also see IONOSPHERE and IONOSPHERIC PROPAGATION. **2.** A wave that is bounced off an obstruction, such as a building or mountain.

reflecting galvanometer   A galvanometer having a light-beam pointer.

reflecting shell   See IONOSPHERE.

reflection   **1.** The turning back of a ray by a surface it strikes. Examples of reflecting media are the surface of the earth, the polished surface of a material, and a layer of the ionosphere. Compare REFRACTION. **2.** The return of energy to the source by the mismatched end of a transmission line or by the end of a radiator.

reflection error   In a radar, radionavigation, or radiolocation system, an error in the reading caused by reflections of the signal from objects other than the intended signal source or object.

reflection factor   See MISMATCH FACTOR.

reflection law   When a ray strikes a smooth reflecting surface, the angle of incidence is equal to the angle of reflection.

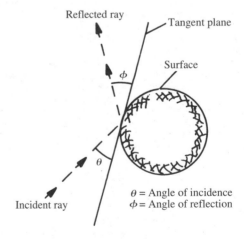

reflection law

reflection loss   **1.** Loss caused by the reflection of an electromagnetic field at a discontinuity in a transmission line. **2.** Loss that occurs when an electromagnetic wave is reflected from a surface or object.

reflection phase grating A device that diffuses sound waves by diffraction effects. The acoustic equivalent of an electromagnetic-wave DIFFRACTION GRATING.

reflective code See GRAY CODE.

reflectivity 1. See MISMATCH FACTOR. 2. The degree to which a point, plane, or surface reflects the radiation (light, for example) that strikes it.

reflectometer 1. See REFLECTED-POWER METER. 2. A type of photometer used to measure reflection.

reflector 1. A smooth, metal surface or wire screen for reflecting radio waves. See, for example, PARABOLIC REFLECTOR. 2. A length of wire, rod, or tubing used in a parasitic antenna to reflect radio waves. Compare DIRECTOR and RADIATOR. 3. A polished surface for reflecting visible light or infrared rays (i.e., a mirror). 4. See REPELLER.

reflector element See REFLECTOR, 2.

reflector satellite A satellite whose skin reflects radio waves.

reflector voltage In a reflex Klystron, the reflector-to-cathode voltage.

reflex baffle A loudspeaker BAFFLE constructed so that some of the sound radiated to the rear of the diaphragm is transmitted forward (after phase shift) to boost acoustic radiation at some frequencies.

reflex bunching In a Klystron, electron bunching following direct-current-field-induced reversal of the velocity-modulated electrons. Also see REFLEX KLYSTRON.

reflex circuit A radio receiver circuit in which a single transistor is used successively for different functions. For example, one active device can act as a mixer and as a radio-frequency amplifier.

reflex Klystron A Klystron having only one cavity. This cavity serves first as the buncher and then, as the electrons are turned around and caused to pass through again, as the catcher.

refracted ray The ray that is refracted by a body or region through which it passes. Compare INCIDENT RAY and REFLECTED RAY.

refracted wave An electromagnetic wave that is refracted by the ionosphere. Compare INCIDENT WAVE and REFLECTED WAVE. Also see IONOSPHERE and IONOSPHERIC PROPAGATION.

refraction The bending of an energy ray as it passes through media that cause a change in the speed of propagation. It can occur with radio waves, infrared, visible light, ultraviolet, X rays, gamma rays, and sound waves.

refractive index See INDEX OF REFRACTION.

refractivity The extent of the ability to refract, given as the quantity $(v_1/v_2) - 1$, where v_1 is the phase velocity in free space, and v_2 is the phase velocity in the medium through which a wave passes.

refractory A heat-resistant, nonmetallic ceramic material.

refrigerator A chamber used to maintain a circuit or component at a constant temperature that is lower than the ambient temperature. This device is analogous to the oven, which maintains a higher temperature than the surrounding medium. A refrigerator can be used to maintain precise frequency for a reference oscillator.

regeneration 1. The processing of a distorted signal so that it has its original characteristics. 2. Positive feedback generally used for the purpose of causing oscillation, or for detection in a regenerative receiver. See POSITIVE FEEDBACK.

regeneration period The period during which the electron beam scans a cathode-ray tube screen to restore changes to the screen surface.

regenerative amplifier An amplifier that uses regeneration to increase its gain and/or selectivity.

regenerative detector A detector provided with regenerative feedback. Although such a detector is sensitive, it can be unstable. Compare NONREGENERATIVE DETECTOR.

regenerative feedback Feedback producing regeneration (i.e., positive feedback). Compare DEGENERATIVE FEEDBACK.

regenerative IF amplifier An intermediate-frequency amplifier in which regeneration is introduced to boost sensitivity and, sometimes, selectivity.

regenerative reading A method of reading data (see READ) so that it is automatically restored, by writing, to locations from which it came.

register In computer systems, an arrangement of several storage devices, such as flip-flops, for storing a certain number of digits (a two-bit register, for example, requires two flip-flops).

register capacity The range of values for quantities that can be handled by a register.

registered professional engineer A title granted by a state board of examiners to a person licensed to work as an engineer.

register length The number of characters or bits that can be held in a register, according to its capacity.

registration The accurate alignment of terminals or other points on different components or on opposite sides of a board so that when the surfaces containing those points are overlaid, all points mate precisely.

regulated power supply A power supply whose output is held automatically to a constant level or within a narrow range, regardless of loading variations.

regulating transformer See VOLTAGE-REGULATING TRANSFORMER.

regulation 1. In general, the adjustment or control of a component, device, or system. 2. Automatic control. See, for example, SELF-REGULATION. 3. See CURRENT REGULATION. 4. See VOLTAGE REGULATION.

regulator 1. A device that automatically holds a quantity to a constant value (e.g., a voltage regulator). 2. A device via which a quantity can be varied (e.g., *potentiometer*, *rheostat*, and *variable autotransformer*).

regulator diode A semiconductor diode—especially a Zener diode used as a two-terminal voltage regulator.

reinitialization The setting of all lines in a microcomputer or microprocessor to logic zero automatically when power is removed, then reapplied.

reject amplifier A tuned amplifier having the response of a band-suppression filter. Like the filter, the amplifier rejects or severely attenuates one frequency (or band of frequencies) while readily passing lower and higher frequencies. Compare PASS AMPLIFIER.

reject filter See REJECTION FILTER.

rejection circuit A circuit performing the function of a REJECTION FILTER.

rejection filter A filter that suppresses one frequency (or band of frequencies) while passing all other frequencies.

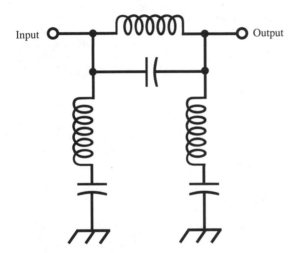

rejection filter

rejection notch A sharp dip in the transmission characteristic of a crystal filter. It provides rejection-filter action at the notch frequency. Also see CRYSTAL RESONATOR and REJECTION FILTER.

rejectivity The degree to which a selective circuit rejects an unwanted signal. Compare TRANSMITTIVITY.

rejuvenation See REACTIVATION.

rel Symbol, R. The cgs unit of reluctance, equivalent to gilberts per maxwell.

relative accuracy In a measuring instrument, the error determined as a percentage of the actual value; the difference between the actual and measured values, divided by the actual value, then multiplied by 100.

relative address In the address part of a computer program instruction, a number specifying a location relative to a BASE ADDRESS. When the base address is added to the relative address, it yields the ABSOLUTE ADDRESS.

relative error The ratio of the absolute error to the exact value of a quantity.

relative gain The current, voltage, or power gain, measured, with respect to a reference standard.

relative humidity Abbreviation, rh. The ratio, as a percentage, of the amount of moisture in the air to the amount the air could contain at a given temperature. Compare ABSOLUTE HUMIDITY.

relative luminosity Luminosity measured with respect to a reference level.

relative permeability The ratio of the permeability of a given material to the permeability of another material (or of the same material under different conditions).

relative power Power level specified with respect to another (often reference) power level.

relative uncertainty The uncertainty of a measurement divided by the measured value. The maximum value that this quotient can have is 1. Also see UNCERTAINTY IN MEASUREMENT.

relative visibility Response of the human eye to light. This is relative because the eye does not see equally well throughout the visible spectrum. The peak response of the human eye is around 5.4×10^{14} Hz; this represents yellow-green light. Photoelectric devices have peak responses that can differ considerably from this value.

relativity theory See EINSTEIN'S THEORY.

relaxation A delayed change in circuit conditions, as a result of change in the input.

relaxation inverter An inverter circuit in which the direct-to-alternating-current conversion device is a RELAXATION OSCILLATOR.

relaxation oscillator An oscillator whose operation results from the buildup of a charge in a capacitor, followed by sudden discharge of the capacitor, the sequence being repeated periodically. In one circuit, a capacitor is connected in series with a resistor and a direct-current power supply, and a neon bulb is connected in parallel with the capacitor. The output is a sawtooth wave.

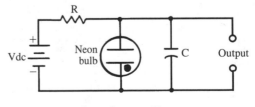

relaxation oscillator

relaxation time **1.** The time required for an exponentially decreasing variable to fall to $1/e$ (approximately 36.8 percent) of its initial value, where e is the natural-logarithm base (approximately 2.71828). **2.** For a gas, the time required for it to return to its original state after having been disturbed.

relay **1.** A signal-actuated switching device. In most instances, a relatively weak current or voltage is used to make the relay switch a higher current or voltage. A relay can be electromechanical or fully electronic (no moving parts). See, for example, ELECTROMECHANICAL RELAY and ELECTRONIC RELAY. **2.** A repeater station. **3.** In communications, to receive a message and retransmit it en route from a source to a destination.

relay amplifier See RELAY DRIVER.

relay booster See RELAY DRIVER.

relay driver A direct-current amplifier (usually one stage) used to actuate an electromechanical relay in response to a low-powered signal.

relay flip-flop See BISTABLE RELAY.

relay logic Abbreviation, RL. In computer and industrial-control operations, a logic system using electromechanical relays as flip-flops (see BISTABLE RELAY).

relay transmitter See AUTOMATIC REPEATER STATION.

release time **1.** The interval between the instant power is removed from a relay and the instant the armature is released sufficiently to operate the contacts. **2.** The time between one control input becoming inactive and another becoming active. **3.** The time required for reception to resume in a transceiver, once transmission has stopped. **4.** An expression for the rapidity with which an automatic gain control reverts to maximum sensitivity following the reception of a strong signal.

reliability **1.** The dependability of operation of a device or circuit under specified conditions. **2.** The proportion of units that still work after a set of units has been in use for a specified length of time.

reliability engineering The branch of engineering devoted to the theory and application of reliability; based on fundamental engineering and advanced statistical concepts.

reluctance Symbol, R. SI unit, A/Wb; cgs unit, rel. In a magnetic circuit, the opposition to the establishment of a magnetic field; it is analogous to resistance in electric circuits.

reluctance motor An electric motor having a squirrel-cage rotor with some of its teeth ground down, and a shaded-pole or split-phase type of stator that supplies a rotating magnetic field. When starting, this motor comes up to speed like an induction motor, but the protruding teeth of the rotor then follow the field in the manner of the poles of a hysteresis motor.

reluctivity Specific reluctance (i.e., the reluctance of a sample of magnetic material one centimeter long and one square centimeter in cross section). Reluctivity is the reciprocal of permeability.

rem Acronym for *roentgen equivalent man*, an amount of ionizing radiation having the same effect on the body as a one-roentgen dose of gamma or X radiation.

remagnetizer A magnetizer used principally to restore weakened permanent magnets.

remainder **1.** The result of subtracting one quantity (the subtrahend) from another (the minuend). Also called DIFFERENCE. **2.** In division, the numerical value left over after the integral part of the quotient has been determined; it becomes the fractional part when divided by the divisor. For example, in 25/3, the remainder is 1.

remanence See RESIDUAL MAGNETISM.

remanent flux density See REMANENCE.

remodulator Any device that changes the modulation of a signal from one form to another, such as from frequency modulation to amplitude modulation, without loss of intelligence.

remote alarm In security systems, an alarm that occurs at a location different from where an intrusion occurs (e.g., at the headquarters of a security company).

remote control Control of distant devices by mechanical means or by radio-frequency signals sent from a transmitter especially designed for the purpose; in the latter case, it is sometimes called *radio control*.

remote-control receiver The complete device that selects, amplifies, and demodulates or rectifies a radio signal for control of a circuit or mechanism at a distance from the transmitter of the control signal. Some receivers have self-contained antennas.

remote-control transmitter The complete device that generates radio-frequency power, adds to it the signals needed for remote control, and radiates the modified power.

remote-control system The complete set of hardware units and software programs facilitating the operation of a computer or robot from a distance.

remote data terminal In a computer system, a terminal connected to the central processor by a telephone line or radio link. It is used for the transfer of data without providing control of the system. Also called *remote data station*.

remote error sensing A method of regulation used in some power supplies. The voltage across the load, or the current through the load, is determined by remote control. The power-supply output is adjusted to compensate for losses in the system.

remote job entry In computer operations, the keying-in of input data at a site physically distant from the central processor.

remote tuning The electrical or radio tuning of a circuit or device from a distance.

rendering In three-dimensional computer animation, the software process in which all the aspects of the model are combined to obtain the presentation.

rep 1. Acronym for *roentgen equivalent physical*, an amount of ionizing radiation that, upon absorption by body tissue, will develop the energy of a one-roentgen dose of gamma or X radiation. **2.** Colloquial abbreviation for *repetition*, as in *rep rate*. **3.** Colloquial abbreviation for *representative*, as in *service representative*.

repeatability The ability of an instrument, system, or method to give identical performance or results in successive instances.

repeater A receiver/transmitter device that retransmits a signal it receives from another source, often simultaneously. In this way, a signal can be transmitted on several frequencies, or the service area of the original station can be extended. Also see ONE-WAY REPEATER and TWO-WAY REPEATER.

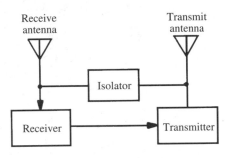

repeater

repeater station See AUTOMATIC REPEATER STATION and REPEATER.

repeating decimal A decimal fraction in which groups of digits recur endlessly (e.g., $25/99 = 0.252525...$).

repeller An electrode, especially in a velocity-modulated tube, for reversing the direction of an electron beam.

repertoire The instruction set for a particular object or source computer programming language.

repetition instruction In a loop in a computer program, an instruction that causes the repetitive implementation of one or more instructions.

repetitive phenomenon See RECURRENT PHENOMENON.

repetitive sweep See RECURRENT SWEEP.

replication In an electronic system, especially in a computer, the redundancy of hardware units to provide standby facilities in case of failure.

replacement A component or circuit that can be substituted directly for another; it fits exactly into place and functions exactly like the component it replaces, without modification to the equipment.

report 1. The results of testing and evaluation of a device, organized into a written document. **2.** The output of a computer, printed on paper for permanent reference.

report program generator Abbreviation, RPG. A computer programming language with which programs can be produced for the generation of business reports.

reproduce head See PLAYBACK HEAD.

reproducing stylus A stylus for the playback of material from a phonograph disc.

reproduction 1. The recovery of data from storage, and its presentation in original form. **2.** Data obtained by the process defined in **1**. **3.** See PLAYBACK.

reproduction loss See PLAYBACK LOSS.

repulsion A force that pushes objects away from each other, as between similar electric charges or similar magnetic poles. Compare ATTRACTION. Also see LAW OF REPULSION.

repulsion-induction motor An alternating-current motor arranged to start as a REPULSION MOTOR and run as an INDUCTION MOTOR, but with better regulation than that of the latter.

repulsion motor An alternating-current motor having an armature and commutator similar to those of a direct-current motor, and a stator similar to that of a split-phase motor, without the auxiliary starting winding. Repulsion caused by the negative half-cycle of torque is utilized to drive the armature, by placing the brushes in such a way that they close the coils only when the latter are in position to receive this repulsive action.

repulsion-start motor An alternating-current motor that starts as a REPLUSION MOTOR but at approximately 75 percent of full speed. Its commutator is automatically short-circuited and the motor runs as an INDUCTION MOTOR. Also see REPULSION INDUCTION MOTOR.

request slip In computer operations, peripheral and memory needs for a program given in a written statement.

reradiation Radiation of energy by a body that has been exposed to radiation, as when a receiving antenna retransmits a signal.

rerecording A recording of played-back material.

reroute 1. In computer operations, to establish new channels between peripherals and main memory. **2.** To establish new circuit paths, physically (as by changing conductor orientation) or electronically (as by selecting an alternate signal bus).

rerun See ROLLBACK.

res 1. Abbreviation of RESISTANCE or RESISTOR. (Also, R and r.) **2.** Abbreviation of RESEARCH. **3.** Abbreviation of RESOLUTION.

reset 1. The clearing of a flip-flop of data in storage (i.e., the setting of the flip-flop to its zero state). **2.** In a computer program, an instruction to initialize the value of a variable. **3.** In a security system, a function that terminates an alarm signal following an intrusion, and renders the system operational again so that it can detect subsequent intrusions should they occur.

reset action   1. The return of a circuit or device to its normal operating condition. **2.** A method of adjusting a circuit to compensate for the severity of an abnormal condition. The extent of readjustment is determined by the extent of the departure from normal conditions.

reset generator   A circuit or device that generates a pulse for resetting a flip-flop or counter. Also see RESET and RESET TERMINAL.

reset pulse   A pulse that resets (see RESET, **1**) a storage cell in a computer memory.

reset terminal   In a flip-flop, the zero-input terminal. Compare SET TERMINAL.

reset time   The elapsed time between a malfunction and the completion of the reset action.

reset timer   A device that returns a circuit or device to its initial state after a specified time delay.

reserve   In multiple programming computer operations, to allocate memory areas and peripherals for a program.

reserve battery   A battery in which the electrolyte is in a special standby chamber outside of the interelectrode section while the battery is on the shelf. When the battery is readied for service, the electrolyte is caused to flow into position between the electrodes, either by heating the battery, shocking it mechanically, or inverting it.

residual amplitude modulation   See INCIDENTAL AM.

residual charge   The electric charge remaining in a capacitor after it has been initially discharged. It results from dielectric absorption.

residual current   A current that continues to flow in a circuit after removing power. The duration is measured in nanoseconds or microseconds.

residual frequency modulation   1. See INCIDENTAL FM. **2.** Frequency modulation of the fundamental frequency of a Klystron by noise or alternating-current heater voltage.

residual gas   Minute quantities of gas remaining in a vacuum tube after evacuation.

residual magnetism   Magnetism remaining in a material, such as iron, after the magnetizing force has been removed.

residual modulation   1. Modulation of a signal by hum or noise. **2.** See INCIDENTAL AM. **3.** See INCIDENTAL FM.

residual voltage   In the output of a null device, such as a bridge, a usually small voltage still present at null and preventing zero balance.

residue check   In computer operations, the verification of the result of an arithmetic operation using the remainders generated when each operand is divided by a special number; the remainder is transmitted along with the operand as a check digit.

resilience   Also called *fault resilience.* The ability of an electronic device or system, especially a

computer, to keep functioning after part of it has failed.

resin   A natural or synthetic organic substance that is polymeric in structure and largely amorphous. Various plastics are made from synthetic resins.

resistance   1. Symbol, R or r. Unit, ohm. In a device, component, or circuit, the simple opposition to current flow. Resistance by itself causes no phase shift. In a purely resistive circuit, $R = E/I$, where R is the resistance in ohms, E is the voltage in volts, and I is the current in amperes. **2.** A property of circuits, devices, or substances that causes impinging energy to be dissipated by conversion to heat. Compare REACTANCE.

resistance

Per kilometer of solid copper wire for American Wire Gauge (AWG) 1 through 40.

AWG	ohms/km	AWG	ohms/km
1	0.42	21	43
2	0.52	22	54
3	0.66	23	68
4	0.83	24	86
5	1.0	25	110
6	1.3	26	140
7	1.7	27	170
8	2.1	28	220
9	2.7	29	270
10	3.3	30	350
11	4.2	31	440
12	5.3	32	550
13	6.7	33	690
14	8.4	34	870
15	11	35	1100
16	13	36	1400
17	17	37	1700
18	21	38	2200
19	27	39	2800
20	34	40	3500

resistance alloys   Metallic alloys used in the manufacture of resistance wire and resistance elements. Such alloys include CONSTANTAN, GERMAN SILVER, MANGANIN, MONEL METAL, and NICHROME.

resistance balance   A device used to balance a circuit, by means of the insertion of resistances.

resistance brazing   A method of brazing in which metal is heated by passing a current through it. The I^2R loss, or dissipated power, occurs in the form of heat.

resistance bridge   A bridge (see BRIDGE, **2**) for measuring resistance only.

resistance-capacitance   Abbreviation, *RC.* Pertaining to a combination of resistance and capacitance (e.g., RESISTANCE-CAPACITANCE CIRCUIT).

resistance-capacitance bridge   1. A four-arm null circuit containing only resistors and capacitors. Also see BRIDGE, **1. 2.** An alternating-current bridge (see BRIDGE, **2**) for measuring resistance and capacitance.

resistance-capacitance circuit A circuit containing only resistors and capacitors. There are no inductors.

resistance-capacitance-coupled amplifier A multistage amplifier circuit in which RESISTANCE-CAPACITANCE COUPLING is used between stages and at the input and output points of the circuit.

resistance-capacitance coupling Coupling, especially between stages in a circuit, using blocking capacitors and supply-path resistors.

resistance-capacitance filter A power-supply filter or wave filter containing only resistors and capacitors. The resistors are in the positions occupied by inductors in inductance-capacitance filters.

resistance-capacitance-inductance Abbreviation, *RCL*. Pertaining to a combination of resistance, capacitance, and inductance.

resistance-capacitance phase shifter A phase shifter containing only resistors and capacitors to obtain the desired shift.

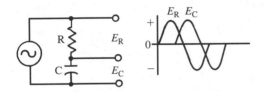

resistance-capacitance phase shifter

resistance-capacitance time constant Symbol, *t*. The time constant (see ELECTRICAL TIME CONSTANT) of a circuit containing (ideally) only resistance and capacitance; $t = RC$, where *t* is in seconds, *R* is in ohms, and *C* is in farads. Compare RESISTANCE-INDUCTANCE TIME CONSTANT.

resistance-capacitance tuning Tuning of a circuit, such as that of an amplifier or oscillator, by means of a variable resistor or ganged units of this type. See, for example, PARALLEL-TEE AMPLIFIER, PARALLEL-TEE OSCILLATOR, and WIEN-BRIDGE OSCILLATOR.

resistance-coupled amplifier See RESISTANCE-CAPACITANCE-COUPLED AMPLIFIER.

resistance drop The voltage drop across a resistor, or across the inherent resistance of a device.

resistance-inductance Abbreviation, *RL*. Pertaining to a combination of resistance and inductance (e.g., RESISTANCE-INDUCTANCE CIRCUIT).

resistance-inductance bridge 1. A four-arm null circuit containing only resistors and inductors. Also see BRIDGE, **1. 2.** An alternating-current bridge (see BRIDGE, **2**) for measuring resistance and inductance only.

resistance-inductance circuit A circuit containing only resistors and inductors. There are no capacitors.

resistance-inductance phase shifter A phase shifter containing only resistors and inductors to obtain the desired phase shift.

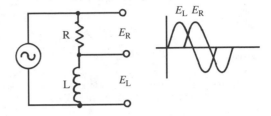

resistance-inductance phase shifter

resistance lamp An incandescent bulb inserted in series with a circuit to provide a dropping resistance. Such a lamp is capable of dissipating a large amount of power, shows very little reactance at low frequencies, and is inexpensive.

resistance magnetometer A magnetometer whose operation is based upon the change of electrical resistance of a material (such as bismuth wire) placed in the magnetic field under test.

resistance material A substance, such as carbon or German silver, whose resistivity is high enough to enable its use as a lumped resistor. See, for example, RESISTANCE ALLOYS and RESISTANCE METAL.

resistance metal A metal, such as iron, whose resistivity is high enough to enable its use as a lumped resistor. Also see RESISTANCE ALLOYS.

resistance pad An attenuator composed of noninductive resistors.

resistance standard A highly accurate and stable resistor used in precision measurements of resistance. Also see PRIMARY STANDARD and SECONDARY STANDARD.

resistance strain gauge An electrical strain gauge in which the stressed element is a thin resistance wire.

resistance strip A strip of metallic or nonmetallic resistance material. Also see RESISTANCE ALLOYS and RESISTANCE METAL.

resistance temperature detector A transducer consisting of a specially made resistor whose resistance varies linearly with temperature.

resistance thermometer An electronic thermometer whose operation is based on the change of resistance of a wire as it is heated or cooled.

resistance transducer See RESISTIVE TRANSDUCER.

resistance tuning See VARIABLE-RESISTANCE TUNING.

resistance welding An electrical or electronic welding process in which the workpieces are heated by current flowing through the inherent resistance of their junction.

resistance wire Wire made of a metal or alloy that exhibits significant resistivity. See, for example, RESISTANCE ALLOYS and RESISTANCE METAL.

resistance-wire sensor A specific length of resistance wire, properly mounted, whose resistance is proportional to a sensed phenomenon (such as strain, temperature, presence of gas, pressure, etc.). See, for example, ELECTRICAL STRAIN GAUGE, GAS DETECTOR, and PRESSURE TRANSDUCER.

resistive current The component of alternating current that is in phase with voltage. Also called WATT CURRENT. Compare REACTIVE CURRENT.

resistive cutoff frequency Symbol, f_{rco}. The frequency beyond which a tunnel diode ceases to exhibit negative resistance.

resistive load A load device that is essentially a pure resistance.

resistive losses Losses resulting from the resistance of a circuit or device, and usually appearing as heat.

resistive transducer A transducer in which the sensed phenomenon causes a change in resistance, which in turn produces a corresponding change in output current or voltage. Compare CAPACITIVE TRANSDUCER, CRYSTAL TRANSDUCER, INDUCTIVE TRANSDUCER, MAGNETIC TRANSDUCER, and PHOTOELECTRIC TRANSDUCER.

resistive trimmer See TRIMMER RESISTOR.

resistive voltage The voltage across the resistance component in a circuit. In an alternating-current circuit, the resistive voltage is in phase with the current.

resistivity Symbol, r. Resistance per unit volume or per unit area. It can be expressed in terms of ohms per cubic meter or ohms per square meter. Also see MICROHM-CENTIMETER and OHM-CENTIMETER.

resistor A device having resistance concentrated in lumped form. Also see RESISTANCE and RESISTIVITY.

resistor-capacitor-transistor logic Abbreviation, RCTL. A form of RESISTOR-TRANSISTOR LOGIC in which capacitors are used to enhance switching speed.

resistor color code See COLOR CODE.

resistor core A form around which a resistance wire can be wound for the purpose of constructing a high-power resistor.

resistor decade See DECADE RESISTOR.

resistor diode A usually forward-biased semiconductor diode that acts as a VOLTAGE-DEPENDENT RESISTOR.

resistor FET See ELECTRONIC RESISTOR.

resistor fuse See FUSIBLE RESISTOR.

resistors in parallel See PARALLEL RESISTORS.

resistors in parallel-series See PARALLEL-SERIES RESISTORS.

resistors in series See SERIES RESISTORS.

resistors in series-parallel See SERIES-PARALLEL RESISTORS.

resistor substitution box A self-contained assortment of common-value resistors arranged to be switched one at a time to a pair of terminals. In troubleshooting and circuit development, any of several useful fixed resistance values can thus be obtained.

resistor transistor See ELECTRONIC RESISTOR.

resistor-transistor logic Abbreviation, RTL. A circuit in which the logic function is performed by resistors, and an inverted output is provided by transistors.

resnatron A form of vacuum tube that is used as an oscillator and amplifier at ultra-high and microwave frequencies. It is essentially a cavity resonator.

resolution 1. The degree to which closely adjacent parts of an image can be differentiated. 2. The reduction of a problem by means of logical analysis. 3. The ability of a vision or ranging system to distinguish between objects that are close together in terms of radial distance, direction, or absolute separation.

resolution ratio In a television image, the ratio of horizontal resolution to vertical resolution.

resonance 1. The state in which the natural response frequency of a circuit coincides with the frequency of an applied signal, or vice versa, yielding intensified response. 2. The state in which the natural vibration frequency of a body coincides with an applied vibration force, or vice versa, yielding reinforced vibration of the body.

resonance bridge An alternating-current bridge (see BRIDGE, 2) in which one or two arms are series-resonant or parallel-resonant, the other arms being resistances. Also see SERIES-TYPE RESONANCE BRIDGE and SHUNT-TYPE RESONANCE BRIDGE.

resonance curve A graph depicting the response of a resonant circuit over a band of frequencies

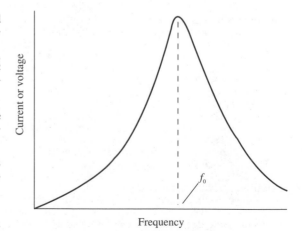

resonance curve

containing the resonant frequency. Current through, or voltage across, the circuit is the dependent variable (vertical axis), and frequency is the independent variable (horizontal axis).

resonance theory of hearing The theory that sound waves pass down the *auditory canal* and cause the *eardrum* to vibrate. Behind the eardrum is a system of three bones leading to the *cochlea.* The cochlea consists of fibers that resonate. Therefore, they vary in length and tension. Various groups of fibers are activated by different sounds, and the vibrations are transmitted to nerves leading to the brain.

resonance radiation Electromagnetic radiation from an energized substance, resulting from movement of electrons from a higher to lower energy level. When an electron moves from a higher to a lower orbit, a photon, having a definite wavelength, is emitted.

resonant cavity A chamber whose size reinforces energy injected into it at a natural frequency, which is determined by the chamber's dimensions. Such cavities can be used with acoustic or electromagnetic waves.

resonant circuit A circuit whose constants are chosen for maximum circuit response at a given frequency. Examples: *parallel-resonant circuit* and *series-resonant circuit.* Also see RESONANCE and RESONANT FREQUENCY.

resonant current Current flowing in a tuned circuit at resonance.

resonant feeder An antenna feeder that is resonant at the operating frequency.

resonant filter A filter containing at least one series- or parallel-resonant arm for sharp response. Thus, a power-supply filter of this kind might have a parallel-resonant arm acting as a wavetrap at the ripple frequency.

resonant frequency Symbol, f_r or f_o. The natural frequency at which a circuit oscillates or a device vibrates. In an inductance-capacitance circuit (series-resonant or parallel-resonant), the reactances cancel at the resonant frequency, leaving only resistance.

resonant-gate transistor A transistor embodying a tiny tuning fork for resonance at low frequencies, thus eliminating bulky coils and capacitors.

resonant line A transmission line that is resonant at the operating frequency.

resonant-line amplifier See LINE-TYPE AMPLIFIER.

resonant-line circuit A circuit using resonant lines as a tank. See, for example, LINE-TYPE AMPLIFIER and LINE-TYPE OSCILLATOR.

resonant-line oscillator See LINE-TYPE OSCILLATOR.

resonant-line wavemeter See LECHER WIRES.

resonant rise See VOLTAGE RISE.

resonant-slope amplifier See DIELECTRIC AMPLIFIER.

resonant-slope detector See SLOPE DETECTOR.

resonant suckout The drawing of radio-frequency energy out of the energized part of a coil or

transmission line by the part not intended to be energized, when the latter resonates at the same frequency.

resonant-voltage rise See VOLTAGE RISE.

resonant-voltage stepup See VOLTAGE RISE.

resonate 1. To exhibit RESONANCE—either electrically or acoustically. 2. To adjust a variable-frequency electrical or acoustical device so that it exhibits RESONANCE at a specific frequency.

resonator A device that produces or undergoes resonance. See, for example, HELMHOLTZ RESONATOR and RESONANT CAVITY.

resource A part of a computer system that can be used for a specific application as a unit (e.g., printer, PCMCIA standard adapter card, tape drive, etc.).

responder The transmitting section of a transponder.

response The behavior of a circuit or device (especially in terms of its dependent variables), in accordance with an applied signal (e.g., *frequency response* and *current-vs.-voltage response*).

response curve A graph depicting the performance of a circuit or device. Examples: *attenuation-vs.-frequency curve* and *current-vs.-voltage curve.*

response time The interval between the instant a signal is applied to or removed from a circuit or device and the instant that the circuit acts accordingly.

restart Following a malfunction or error occurring during a computer program run, to go back to an earlier point in the program.

resting state See QUIESCENT STATE.

restore See RESET.

resultant 1. The vector that results from the addition of two or more vectors. 2. A quantity that results from mathematical operations performed on other quantities.

retarding magnet See DRAG MAGNET.

retentivity 1. The property whereby a material retains magnetism imparted to it. 2. A quantitative measure of the extent to which a material retains magnetism imparted to it.

retention period In computer operations, the time during which the data on a magnetic medium (disk or tape) must be kept intact.

retrace 1. In a cathode-ray tube, the return of the scanning beam to its starting point. 2. In a cathode-ray tube, a line traced on the screen by the scanning beam as it returns to its starting point, if RETRACE BLANKING is not used.

retrace blanking Obliteration of the RETRACE of the electron beam in a cathode-ray tube. It renders the retrace line invisible on the screen so that it will not interfere with the display.

retrace line See RETRACE, 2.

retrace ratio For the swept beam in a cathode-ray tube, the ratio of the scanning velocity in the trace direction to the scanning velocity in the RETRACE direction.

retrace time In a cathode-ray tube, the amount of time required for the scanning beam to move from the end of one trace or line to the beginning of the next.

retrofit To supply something with specially designed or adapted parts that were not available when it was made.

retrograde orbit For an artificial earth satellite, an orbit whose direction is east-to-west, relative to the earth's surface.

return 1. See RETRACE. 2. See RETURN CIRCUIT. 3. See RETURN POINT. 4. In an electronic circuit, the electrical ground and ground current path.

return circuit The circuit through which current returns to a generator.

return instruction In a computer program, an instruction in a subroutine directing operation back to a specific point in the main program.

return interval See RETRACE TIME.

return line See RETRACE, 2.

return point 1. The point to which circuits are returned (e.g., a common ground point). 2. The terminal point of a return circuit.

return ratio See FEEDBACK FACTOR.

return time See RETRACE TIME.

return to zero 1. Abbreviation RZ or RTZ. In the magnetic recording of data, a method in which the write current returns to zero following the write pulse. Compare NONRETURN-TO-ZERO. 2. A logic system in which the zero and one states are represented by zero voltage and a discrete voltage.

return trace See RETRACE, 1, 2.

REV 1. Abbreviation of REENTRY VEHICLE. 2. Abbreviation of REVERSE.

rev 1. Abbreviation of REVOLUTION. 2. To quickly and substantially increase the angular velocity of a motor.

reverberation 1. Multiple reflections of sound waves from the inside surfaces of an enclosed chamber. 2. The dying-out of sound waves in an enclosed chamber as the waves reflect repeatedly from the inside surfaces. 3. In sound recording and/or reproduction, an electronically produced echo. It is used for special effects—especially in electronic music systems. 4. See RESONANCE, 2.

reverberation chamber A room in which the walls, floor, and ceiling absorb very little sound, resulting in echoes. To avoid standing waves, the room is designed so that no two surfaces are exactly parallel.

reverberation system A system of devices operated with an electronic organ to simulate the effect of reverberation in a large room, such as a church auditorium.

reverberation time In an enclosed chamber, the time required for a sound to die down to a specified level (usually -60 dB) after the disturbance has stopped.

reverberation unit A device for producing artificial echoes—especially in the operation of electronic music systems.

reverse 1. To alter the direction of a current or process or motion of an object so that the new direction is exactly opposite the previous direction. 2. In a directional wattmeter, the reflected-power indication or switch position.

reverse AGC Automatic gain control in which a signal-dependent voltage is fed back to an earlier stage to adjust its gain automatically. Compare FORWARD AGC.

reverse bias Reverse voltage or current in a transistor or a semiconductor diode. Compare FORWARD BIAS.

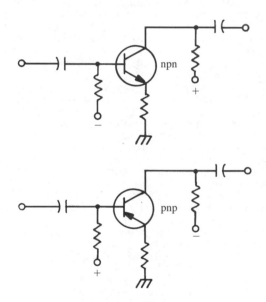

reverse bias

reverse breakdown See AVALANCHE.

reverse breakdown voltage See AVALANCHE VOLTAGE.

reverse characteristic The current-vs.-voltage response of a semiconductor junction that is biased in the reverse (low-conduction) direction. Compare FORWARD CHARACTERISTIC.

reverse conduction The very small current conduction through a pn junction when it is reverse-biased. Compare FORWARD CONDUCTION.

reverse current Symbol, I_r. The current that flows through a pn junction when it is reverse-biased. Also called *back current*. Compare FORWARD CURRENT.

reverse engineering A design process in which a specific device or system is copied functionally, but not literally.

reverse Polish notation Abbreviation, RPN. A system of notation for expressing mathematical operations in which the operators follow the operands being manipulated. It is a mode of entry for some calculators (e.g., the operation 7×2

might be entered by pressing keys in this order: 7, ENTER, 2, ×).

reverse recovery time See RECOVERY TIME, **1**.

reverse resistance Symbol, R_r. The resistance of a reverse-biased pn junction. Also called BACK RESISTANCE. Compare FORWARD RESISTANCE.

reverse voltage Symbol, E_r or V_r. Direct-current voltage applied to a pn junction so that the p-type material is electrically more negative than the n-type material. Also called BACK VOLTAGE. Compare VOLTAGE.

reverse-voltage capacitance The internal capacitance of a reverse-biased semiconductor pn junction.

reverse voltage drop The voltage drop across a semiconductor pn junction that is biased in the reverse (low-conduction) direction.

reversible counter A counter that, by a control signal, can have the value it is holding either increased or decreased.

reversible permeability The permeability of a ferromagnetic substance when the magnitude of the alternating-current field is arbitrarily small.

reversing switch **1**. A switch that reverses the polarity of a direct-current voltage. **2**. A switch that reverses the direction of motor rotation.

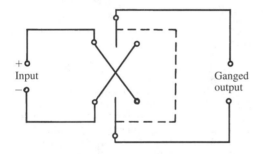

reversing switch

revolute geometry A method by which a robot arm can move freely in three dimensions. The entire assembly rotates from the base in a horizontal plane through a complete circle (360 degrees). An elevation joint at the base moves the arm from horizontal to vertical (90 degrees). A joint in the middle of the arm can bend through about 180 degrees.

revolution Abbreviation, r or rev. One complete rotation (i.e., 360 degrees of circular travel).

revolving field See ROTATING FIELD.

rewind To run a magnetic tape on a transport at a high speed, in the direction opposite to that associated with the play mode.

rewrite In computer operations, to return information read from a storage location to that location by recording.

R_F Symbol for FILAMENT RESISTANCE.

RF Abbreviation of RADIO FREQUENCY.

RF amplifier See RADIO-FREQUENCY AMPLIFIER.

RFC Abbreviation of RADIO-FREQUENCY CHOKE.

RF heating See RADIO-FREQUENCY HEATING.

RFI Abbreviation of RADIO-FREQUENCY INTERFERENCE.

RF inverse feedback A negative-feedback system for radiophone transmitters, in which a portion of the modulated radio-frequency (RF) signal is rectified, and the resulting direct-current voltage is filtered and applied as bias to one of the audio stages in the proper polarity for degeneration.

RF lamp A lighting lamp, used with radio-frequency (RF) alternating current, rather than the conventional 60-Hz utility current. This results in better efficiency, and allows much more light to be generated with a given filament lamp, as compared with 60-Hz current.

RF motion detector In security systems, an intrusion detection and alarm system that senses Doppler-effect-induced changes in the frequency or phase of a radio-frequency (RF) electromagnetic field. The Doppler effect results from motion of objects in the secured area.

RFO Abbreviation of *radio-frequency oscillator*.

RF power supply See OSCILLATOR-TYPE POWER SUPPLY.

RF probe See RECTIFIER PROBE.

RF resistance See RADIO-FREQUENCY RESISTANCE.

RF selectivity See RADIO-FREQUENCY SELECTIVITY.

RF transistor See RADIO-FREQUENCY TRANSISTOR.

R_g Symbol for GRID RESISTANCE.

R_G Symbol for GATE RESISTANCE.

RGB Abbreviation of RED-GREEN-BLUE.

RGT Abbreviation of RESONANT-GATE TRANSISTOR.

Rh Symbol for RHODIUM.

R/h Abbreviation of ROENTGENS PER HOUR.

R_H **1**. Symbol for HEATER RESISTANCE. **2**. Symbol for HOT RESISTANCE.

rh Abbreviation of RELATIVE HUMIDITY.

rhenium Symbol, Re. A metallic element. Atomic number, 75. Atomic weight, 186.207. It is used in some thermocouples.

rheostat A wirewound variable dropping resistor of the rotary type or slider type.

R_{HF} Symbol for *high-frequency resistance* (see RADIO-FREQUENCY RESISTANCE).

RHI Abbreviation of RANGE-HEIGHT INDICATOR.

rhodium Symbol, Rh. A metallic element. Atomic number, 45. Atomic weight, 102.906.

rhombus A four-sided geometric plane figure, in which all four sides have equal length, and opposite angles have equal measure.

rhombic antenna See DIAMOND ANTENNA.

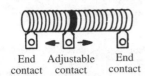

End   Adjustable   End
contact   contact   contact

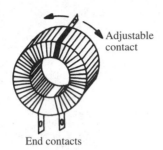

Adjustable
contact

End contacts

rheostat

rho-theta A radio-navigation system in which a single transmitting station is used, and the position is determined, according to polar coordinates (distance and direction).

rhumbatron A RESONANT CAVITY—especially one in a KLYSTRON.

RI Abbreviation of RADIO INTERFERENCE.

R_i Symbol for INPUT RESISTANCE. (Also, R_{in}.)

RIAA Abbreviation of RECORDING INDUSTRY ASSOCIATION OF AMERICA.

RIAA curve The amplitude-versus-frequency function used in recording and reproduction of long-playing (33.3 rpm) phonograph discs, and specified by the Recording Industry Association of America (RIAA). The RIAA curve takes advantage of the sensitivity of the human ear at various frequencies to reduce the level of audible noise.

ribbon microphone See VELOCITY MICROPHONE.

ride gain In broadcasting, the operations of constantly adjusting the audio modulation of the transmitter for optimum operation.

Rieke chart A visual aid, similar to the SMITH CHART, used with traveling-wave tubes in the ultra-high-frequency (UHF) and microwave frequency bands for determining the optimum load impedance.

rig Colloquialism for a radio communications installation—especially a transmitter or transceiver. It is commonly used among amateur radio operators.

right-angle line section See ELL.

right-hand lay See DIRECTION OF LAY.

right-hand polarized wave See CLOCKWISE-POLARIZED WAVE.

right-hand rule for induced emf See FLEMING'S RIGHT-HAND RULE.

right-hand rule for wire A simple rule for indicating the direction of the magnetic field surrounding a straight wire that carries current. When the wire is grasped in the right hand with the thumb pointing in the direction of current flow, the fingers curl in the direction of the magnetic field.

right-hand taper Potentiometer or rheostat taper in which most of the resistance is in the clockwise half of rotation, as viewed from the front. Compare LEFT-HAND TAPER.

right justified In a computer memory location, a data item that takes up consecutive bit positions, from right to left.

Right-Leduc effect A phenomenon somewhat analogous to the Hall effect. When a metal strip conducting heat is placed in a magnetic field perpendicular to the plane of the strip, a temperature difference develops across the strip.

right shift In computer operation, a shift whereby word bits are displayed to the right; the effect is division in a right arithmetic shift.

rim drive **1.** In a tape recorder, a driving method in which the motor shaft is provided with a smooth pulley that transfers motion directly to the rubber-tired rim of the flywheel. **2.** A driving method for a phonograph turntable in which a rotating wheel contacts the outer edge of the platter.

R_{in} Symbol for INPUT RESISTANCE. (Also, R_i.)

ring **1.** The core of a toroidal coil. **2.** See HYBRID RING. **3.** See RING MODULATOR. **4.** See RING INDUCTOR. **5.** See RING MAGNET. **6.** See RINGING.

ring armature A motor or generator armature having a ring winding.

ringback In a telephone system, the signal sent from the receiving (destination) telephone set back to the sending (source) set, indicating that the signal is being received. This consists of a tone, interrupted by pulses at intervals of about 0.05 second. The signal stops when the destination set is taken off the hook. Also see RINGDOWN.

ring circuit **1.** See RING MODULATOR. **2.** A waveguide hybrid-tee resembling a ring having radial branches. **3.** In amateur radio operations, a circuit connected to a telephone line and radio transmitter. The radio transmitter is energized and modulated with an identifiable signal each time the telephone rings, so the telephone can be answered via remote control.

ring counter An electronic counter in which successive cascaded stages form a ring (i.e., the last stage in the chain is connected to the first stage so that the counter advances through the cycle, stage by stage, repetitively).

ringdown In a telephone system, the signal sent from the transmitting (source) set to the receiving (destination) set, causing the destination set to ring. Also see RINGBACK.

ring head   In tape recorders, a recording and playback head that consists essentially of a metal ring with a gap at one point, and on which the coils are wound.

ring inductor   1. An inductor consisting of a single turn of wire, or of a conductor bent into a loop. 2. See SHADING COIL.

ringing   Self oscillation in a pulsed inductance-capacitance circuit, sustained by the circuit's flywheel action (hysteresis), and usually producing a damped wave.

ringing coil   In the horizontal oscillator in a television circuit, a small, adjustable coil (shunted by a capacitor) used to produce a sharp rise in input-signal voltage.

ringing current   In wire telephony, an alternating current superimposed on the direct operating current. Produces RINGDOWN.

ringing time   See RING TIME, 1.

ring magnet   A permanent magnet in the shape of a ring or donut.

ring main   An electric power main that is closed to form a ring. This results in two independent electrical paths between any two points in the circuit. If one path is interrupted, power can still be transmitted to any other point in the circuit from a power station.

ring modulator   A double-balanced diode-type modulator circuit; its name is derived from the ring-like arrangement of the four diodes.

ring oscillator   A self-excited oscillator in which two sets of two transistors are operated in push-pull/parallel.

ring shift   In computer operation, the cyclic shifting of digits from one end of a register to the other.

ring time   1. The period of a damped oscillation—especially one set up in an inductance-capacitance circuit by a pulse. 2. The time required for an ECHO BOX signal to decay below the display level.

ring winding   A winding in which the turns of the coil are laid on the outside of a ring-shaped core and passed through its center, resulting in a donut coil with a core.

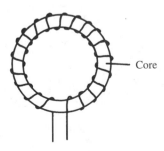
Core

ring winding

ripple   1. A small alternating-current component in the output of a direct-current power supply with inadequate filtering. 2. In computer and data-processing operations, the serial transmission of data.

ripple amplitude   The peak or peak-to-peak value of ripple in a power supply (see RIPPLE, 1).

ripple counter   A binary counter consisting of flip-flops cascaded in series. A pulse must pass sequentially from the input, through each stage, to the output of the chain.

ripple current   Current flowing in a circuit as the result of ripple voltage (see RIPPLE AMPLITUDE).

ripple factor   The ratio of the RIPPLE AMPLITUDE to the direct-current voltage output of a power supply.

ripple frequency   The frequency of a ripple component (see RIPPLE, 1). In power supplies using half-wave rectification, this frequency is normally 60 Hz (the line frequency); in full-wave supplies, it is normally 120 Hz (twice the line frequency).

ripple percentage   See PERCENT RIPPLE.

ripple torque   Symbol, T_R. In a torque motor, the small fluctuation in torque resulting from commutator switching action.

ripple voltage   See RIPPLE AMPLITUDE.

RISC   Abbreviation of REDUCED INSTRUCTION SET COMPUTER.

rise   1. See VOLTAGE RISE. 2. See RISE TIME. 3. An increase in the amplitude of a pulse or wave.

rise cable   1. A vertical feeder cable. 2. A vertical section of a feeder cable.

rise time   The time required for a pulse to rise from 10 percent to 90 percent of its peak amplitude. Compare FALL TIME.

RJE   Abbreviation of REMOTE JOB ENTRY.

R_k   Symbol for cathode resistance.

RL   1. Abbreviation of RESISTANCE-INDUCTANCE. 2. Abbreviation of RELAY LOGIC.

R_L   Abbreviation of LOAD RESISTANCE.

RL bridge   See RESISTANCE-INDUCTANCE BRIDGE.

RL circuit   See RESISTANCE-INDUCTANCE CIRCUIT.

R_{LF}   Symbol for low-frequency resistance.

RL phase shifter   See RESISTANCE-INDUCTANCE PHASE SHIFTER.

R_m   Symbol for METER RESISTANCE.

r_m   Symbol for *emitter-collector transresistance* of a bipolar transistor.

rms   Abbreviation of ROOT MEAN SQUARE.

rms converter   See ROOT-MEAN-SQUARE CONVERTER.

rms current   See EFFECTIVE CURRENT.

rms meter   A current meter or voltmeter whose deflection is proportional to the root-mean-square (rms) value of current or voltage. In most meters, the deflection is proportional to either the peak value or the average value, but the scale of an rms unit is graduated on the basis of sine-wave input.

rms value   See EFFECTIVE VALUE.

rms voltage   See EFFECTIVE VOLTAGE.

Rn   Symbol for RADON.

R_n   **1.** Symbol for NEGATIVE RESISTANCE. (Also, –R.) **2.** Symbol for *null resistance.*

R_o   Symbol for OUTPUT RESISTANCE. (Also, R_{out}.)

robot   **1.** An electromechanical device or system capable of reliably performing complex and/or repetitive tasks. It can be controlled by a human operator or by a computer. **2.** A usually autonomous device, as defined in **1**, built to physically resemble a human being, with a head, two arms, and some form of locomotion.

robot generations   Agreed-on milestones or criteria in the evolution of robots and smart machines. *First generation:* Before 1980. Mainly mechanical, stationary, physically rugged, no external sensors, no artificial intelligence. *Second generation:* 1980–1990. Tactile sensors, vision systems, position sensors, pressure sensors, microcomputer control, programmable. *Third generation:* After 1990. Mobile, autonomy or group control, artificial intelligence, speech recognition/synthesis, teleoperation, navigation systems. *Fourth generation:* In conceptual stages. Highly intelligent, capable of building other robots, capable of doing many human tasks.

robot gripper   A robotic END EFFECTOR designed specifically to grasp objects. The two basic designs are: hand-like and specialized. Hand-like grippers are engineered according to the notion that the human hand has evolved to near perfection, and should be mimicked in robots. Specialized grippers are built by trial-and-error methods and often bear little resemblance to human hands.

robotics   The science and art of robot design, construction, operation, and maintenance.

Rochelle salt   Sodium potassium tartrate, a substance whose crystals are piezoelectric. Such crystals are used in some microphones, loudspeakers, and transducers. Also called SEIGNETE SALT.

rock   Slang for QUARTZ CRYSTAL.

rockbound   Pertaining to an oscillator or radio transmitter whose frequency is determined by a quartz crystal, and is, therefore, not variable over a significant range.

rocker switch   A toggle switch whose lever is a specially shaped bar. The bar is rocked back

rocker switch

and forth to operate the switch. Compare BAT-HANDLE SWITCH, PADDLE SWITCH, and SLIDE SWITCH.

rod   **1.** A unit of length or distance; 1 rod = 5.029 meters. **2.** A bar of material with special properties.

rod antenna   See FERRITE-ROD ANTENNA.

rod magnet   A permanent magnet in the shape of a rod with circular or elliptical cross section.

roentgen   Abbreviation, r. A unit of ionizing radiation; 1 r is the quantity of radiation that produces 1 esu of electricity (positive or negative) per cubic centimeter of air at standard temperature and pressure. In average tissue, 1 r produces ionization equivalent to an energy concentration of 2.58×10^{-4} C/kg (93 ergs per gram). Also see MILLIROENTGEN.

roentgen equivalent man   See REM.

roentgen equivalent physical   See REP.

roentgen ray   See X RAY.

roger   A communications signal meaning "Acknowledged."

Roget spiral   A spring-like wire device that contracts in proportion to the magnitude of the current flowing through it.

role indicator   In computer operations, a code classifying a keyword as a part of the speech (e.g., noun).

roll   **1.** In a display terminal having a line length of less than the standard 80 characters, an operating feature that allows the operator to follow the text along. The cursor remains fixed near the center of the displayed line, while the text moves from right to left. **2.** Vertical movement of a television picture, resulting from lack of vertical synchronization.

rollback   In computer operations, the running again of a computer program or portion of the program. Also called RERUN.

roller inductor   A variable inductor, usually of the air-core type, with a shaft attached that allows the whole assembly to be rotated; a wheel contact provides a movable tap. Such an indicator is continuously variable and is often used in such devices as antenna-tuning networks.

rolling   In television, the apparent continuous upward or downward movement of the picture, resulting from lack of vertical synchronization between the transmitter and receiver.

rolloff   **1.** The rate at which a dependent variable (e.g., output amplitude) diminishes above or below a certain critical value of the independent variable (e.g., frequency). It pertains especially to frequency response in audio devices and systems. **2.** Attenuation of the bass and/or treble response or output in an audio system.

ROM   Abbreviation of READ-ONLY MEMORY.

Romeo   Phonetic alphabet code word for the letter R.

Romex cable   A form of wire cable with a covering that is highly resistant to the environment.

roof mount   A metal bracket for fastening an antenna mast to a roof.

room noise   Ambient acoustic noise in a room.

room resonance   Acoustic resonance caused by the geometry and contents of a room.

room temperature   Abbreviation, RT. **1.** The temperature of the chamber in which a test or fabrication is carried out. It is commonly used to distinguish between operations that can be performed at the ambient temperature and those that require an oven or a cold chamber. **2.** A temperature typical of an indoor environment, approximately 21 degrees Celsius (70 degrees Fahrenheit).

room tone   A qualitative expression for the suitability or behavior of an enclosed area for a given acoustic application. It affected by factors (such as resonances or lack thereof, echoes or lack thereof, overall room size and proportions, and background noise).

root mean square   Abbreviation, rms. The square root of the arithmetic mean (average) of the squares of a set of values.

root-mean-square converter   A device that converts an input signal of any waveform into a direct-current signal of the same value as the EFFECTIVE VALUE of the input signal.

root-mean-square current   See EFFECTIVE CURRENT.

root-mean-square value   See EFFECTIVE VALUE.

root-mean-square voltage   See EFFECTIVE VOLTAGE.

ROP   Abbreviation of *record of production*.

rosin   A substance derived chemically from an extract of pine wood, and used in some solders.

rotameter   A fluid flow gauge consisting of a float within a glass tube having incremental markings.

rotary amplifier   See AMPLIDYNE.

rotary antenna   See ROTATABLE ANTENNA.

rotary beam   A beam antenna, such as a Yagi, that can be rotated in a (usually horizontal) plane to allow transmission and/or reception in various directions. Also see ROTATABLE ANTENNA.

rotary-beam antenna   See ROTARY BEAM.

rotary converter   A dynamo (electric machine) having a direct-current armature connected to a commutator on one end of the shaft and to slip rings on the other end. When the machine is operated as a direct-current motor, it delivers an alternating-current output, and vice versa. Also called DOUBLE-CURRENT GENERATOR.

rotary dialing   An older style of telephone dialing in which a rotary pulse generator is used to dial the digits.

rotary digital audio tape   Digital audio tape used with a recording/playback system that uses a rotating head or heads.

rotary encoder   An optical analog-to-digital (A/D) converter that operates by passing a light beam through a rotating disk. The amplitude of the analog input signal at any moment causes a certain angular rotation of the disk, cutting off the light beam, according to the nature of the pattern on the disk. The resulting modulated light beam has digital characteristics and can be detected using photocells.

rotary inverter   A motor-generator used to change a direct-current input voltage into an alternating-current output voltage.

rotary-motion sensor   A transducer that delivers an output voltage proportional to the arc over which its shaft has been turned.

rotary power amplifier   See DC GENERATOR AMPLIFIER.

rotary relay   An electromechanical relay in which a pivoted armature rotates to open or close the contacts. The *meter relay* is an example.

rotary selector switch   See ROTARY SWITCH.

rotary stepping relay   See STEPPING SWITCH.

rotary stepping switch   See STEPPING SWITCH.

rotary switch   A switch in which a blade moves in a circle or in arcs over the contacts.

rotary transformer   A motor-generator used to change an input voltage into a lower or higher output voltage.

rotatable antenna   An antenna that can be turned to change the orientation of its main lobe (direction of greatest forward gain) in a specific plane (usually horizontal).

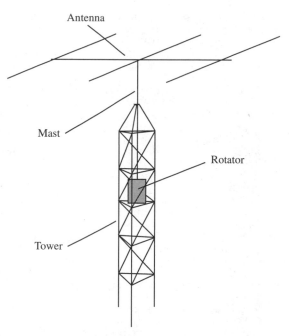

rotatable antenna

rotating amplifier   See DC GENERATOR AMPLIFIER.

rotating antenna An antenna that constantly turns to scan a given area (e.g., a RADAR ANTENNA).

rotating-capacitor modulator A frequency modulator consisting of a motor-driven variable capacitor. Also see WOBBULATOR.

rotating field An alternating-current electric or magnetic field, such as that generated by the stators of some motors, that revolves between poles.

rotating interrupter A commutator (see COMMUTATOR, **1**).

rotating machines Electromechanical devices (such as motors, generators, amplidynes, rotary converters, etc.) that utilize magnetic flux to convert angular motion or displacement into electrical energy, or vice-versa.

rotating memory See DISK MEMORY and DRUM MEMORY.

rotating voltmeter See GENERATING VOLTMETER.

rotator A motor-driven, remotely controlled mechanism for turning a directional antenna in a specific plane.

rotor **1.** A rotatable coil—especially in a motor or generator. Compare STATOR, **1**. **2.** The rotating member of a motor or generator. Compare STATOR, **2**. **3.** The rotating-plate assembly of a variable capacitor. Compare STATOR, **3**.

rotor blade The wiper arm of a rheostat or potentiometer.

rotor coil See ROTOR, **1**.

rotor plate The rotating plate(s) of a variable capacitor. Compare STATOR PLATE.

roulette pattern A circular pattern for frequency identification with an oscilloscope, consisting of loops around the screen's circumference. Compare GEAR-WHEEL PATTERN, LISSAJOUS FIGURE, and SPOT-WHEEL PATTERN.

rounding **1.** A method of approximating a quantity by reducing the number of significant digits. For example, rounding 3.44 to two significant digits yields 3.4; rounding 3.46 to two significant digits yields 3.5. Compare TRUNCATION. **2.** The approximation of a value to a specified number of decimal places or significant digits. **3.** Smoothing of the corners of a square wave or sawtooth wave, resulting in lengthening of the transition time from one state to another.

rounding error The error resulting from the rounding of a number (see ROUNDING, **1**, **2**).

round off To shorten an otherwise lengthy number by replacing numerical digits with zeros and increasing the final nonreplaced digit by 1 if the leftmost replaced digit is 5 or greater. Thus, 3.141592653 can be rounded off to 3.1416 or 3.14.

round-up A form of numerical approximation, in which a number with a value of $n.5$ or greater is assigned the value $n + 1$. This is a feature of many calculators using scientific notation or a fixed number of decimal places.

R_{out} Symbol for OUTPUT RESISTANCE. (Also, R_o.)

route **1.** To physically position wires or conducting circuit paths by planning and deliberation. **2.** The path over which conductors are positioned. **3.** A path over which signals or information can be carried.

routine **1.** In computer operations, the complete sequence of instructions for performing an operation (i.e., a program or program segment). **2.** A test or measurement procedure. **3.** An assembly or manufacturing procedure. **4.** A standard troubleshooting procedure.

row In a matrix, a horizontal arrangement or set of values.

R_P **1.** Symbol for PLATE RESISTANCE. (Also, r_P.) **2.** Symbol for POSITIVE RESISTANCE. **3.** Symbol for PARALLEL RESISTANCE. (Also, R_{par}.) **4.** Symbol for PRIMARY RESISTANCE. (Also, R_{pri}.)

R_{par} Symbol for PARALLEL RESISTANCE. (Also, R_P.)

r parameters **1.** Device or network parameters expressed as resistances. **2.** Transistor parameters in terms of resistance values in the equivalent tee network. Compare G PARAMETERS and H PARAMETERS.

RPG Abbreviation of REPORT PROGRAM GENERATOR.

rpm Abbreviation of *revolutions per minute*.

rpm meter See ELECTRONIC TACHOMETER and STROBOSCOPE.

RPN Abbreviation of REVERSE POLISH NOTATION.

R_{pri} Symbol for PRIMARY RESISTANCE. (Also, R_P.)

rps Abbreviation of *revolutions per second*.

RPT Radiotelegraphic abbreviation of *repeat*.

R_{req} **1.** Symbol for REQUIRED RESISTANCE. **2.** Symbol for SCREEN RESISTANCE.

R_{RF} Symbol for RADIO-FREQUENCY RESISTANCE.

R_S Symbol for SOURCE RESISTANCE in a field-effect transistor.

R_s **1.** Symbol for SERIES RESISTANCE. (Also, R_{ser}.) **2.** Symbol for SECONDARY RESISTANCE. (Also, R_{sec}.)

R_{sec} Symbol for SECONDARY RESISTANCE. (Also, R_s.)

R_{ser} Symbol for SERIES RESISTANCE. (Also, R_s.)

RST flip-flop A conventional flip-flop subject to the operations of reset, set, and trigger.

RST system In the amateur radio service, a method of reporting signal quality in terms of *readability*, *strength*, and *tone*.

R sweep In an oscilloscope or spectrum analyzer, an expanded portion of the trace produced by a long triggered sweep. It permits detailed analysis of a small portion of a displayed waveform or frequency band.

RT **1.** Abbreviation of RADIOTELEPHONE. **2.** Abbreviation of ROOM TEMPERATURE.

rt Abbreviation of RIGHT.

R_T **1.** Symbol for THERMAL RESISTANCE. **2.** Symbol for *total resistance*. (Also, R_t.)

R_t Symbol for *total resistance.*

RTD   Abbreviation of RESISTANCE TEMPERATURE DETECTOR.

RTL   Abbreviation of RESISTOR-TRANSISTOR LOGIC.

RTTY   Abbreviation of RADIOTELETYPE.

RTZ   Abbreviation of RETURN TO ZERO. (Also, RZ.)

Ru   Symbol for RUTHENIUM.

rubber   A natural insulating material; an elastomer exhibiting rapid elastic recovery. Dielectric constant, 2 to 3.5. Dielectric strength, 16 to 50 kV/mm. Also called *India rubber.* Compare HARD RUBBER.

rubber-covered wire   Wire insulated with a jacket of rubber.

rubidium   Symbol, Rb. A metallic element. Atomic number, 37. Atomic weight, 85.468.

ruby laser   A laser using a ruby rod as the resonant element.

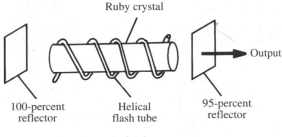

Ruby crystal

Output

100-percent reflector

Helical flash tube

95-percent reflector

ruby laser

ruby maser   A maser in which the resonant material is ruby.

Ruhmkorff coil   See INDUCTION COIL.

rumble   **1.** Low-frequency acoustical noise of a frequency below about 50 Hz. **2.** Low-frequency electrical noise in an audio circuit of a frequency below about 50 Hz. **3.** Vibrations that can occur in a poorly designed or malfunctioning phonograph turntable.

rumble filter   An audio high-pass filter having sharp cutoff below 50 Hz, for eliminating rumble arising from irregularities in the rotation of a phonograph turntable. Also see RUMBLE, **3.**

run   **1.** The execution of a computer routine or program. **2.** To execute a routine or program. **3.** To cause a routine or program to be executed. **4.** A command that causes a routine or program to be executed.

runaway   In a current-carrying circuit or device, especially a semiconductor, a rapid increase in current that causes the temperature to rise, in turn resulting in a further increase in current. Unless preventive measures are taken, this will ultimately damage or destroy the component.

run chart   In computer operations, a flowchart showing the organization and order of pertinent programs to be run.

running accumulator   A computer storage unit having registers linked so that data is transferred unidirectionally from one to the other, and in which only one register is accessible from the outside.

running open   **1.** The condition of a mechanical teleprinter running continuously in the absence of a signal. The teleprinter operates, but nothing is printed; this keeps the machine in synchronization. **2.** Operation of a transmitter at the maximum rated level of input or output power.

running-time meter   See ELAPSED-TIME METER.

run time   **1.** The period of time during which a computer program is executed. **2.** The length of time required for a computer program to be executed.

rupture   **1.** The usually rapid and violent tearing apart, or breaking through, of an insulating material subjected to excessive voltage. **2.** The clean opening of relay, circuit-breaker, or switch contacts to interrupt a current-carrying circuit.

rush   Broadband audio background noise, such as that arising from superheterodyne receivers and high-gain amplifiers. Its name is derived from resemblance to the gentle rushing of wind. Compare HISS, **1, 2.**

ruthenium   Symbol, Ru. A rare metallic element. Atomic number, 44. Atomic weight, 101.07.

rutherford   Abbreviation, rd. A unit of radioactivity equal to 10^6 disintegrations per second (2.7×10^{-5} curie). Also see KILORUTHERFORD, MEGARUTHERFORD, MICRORUTHERFORD, and MILLIRUTHERFORD.

Rutherford atom   An early concept of the nature of the atom, proposed by Rutherford in 1912. In this model, negatively charged electrons orbit a central, positively charged nucleus in a manner similar to the way planets orbit the sun. Compare BOHR ATOM.

RW   Abbreviation of *radiological warfare.*

R_x Symbol for unknown resistance.

RY   Abbreviation of RELAY.

ryotron   A form of inductive semiconductor switch, operated at cold temperatures to maximize conductivity.

R-Y signal   In a color-television circuit, the signal representing primary red (R) minus luminance (Y). A primary red signal is obtained when the R-Y signal is combined with the luminance (Y) signal. Compare B-Y SIGNAL and G-Y SIGNAL.

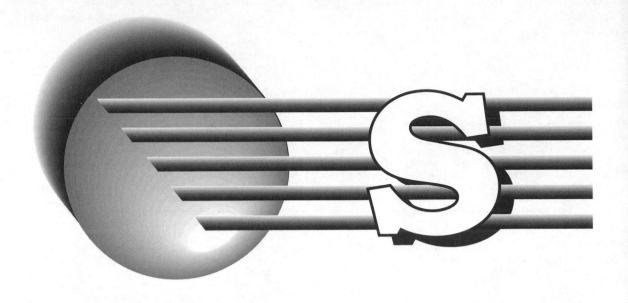

S **1.** Symbol for SCREEN GRID of a vacuum tube. **2.** Symbol for SHELL of a tube or semiconductor device. **3.** Symbol for SULFUR. **4.** Symbol for DEFLECTION SENSITIVITY. **5.** Symbol for SWITCH. **6.** Symbol for ELASTANCE. **7.** Abbreviation of SYNC. **8.** Symbol for SECONDARY. **9.** Abbreviation for SIEMENS. **10.** Abbreviation of SINE. **11.** Symbol for ENTROPY.

s **1.** Symbol for distance or DISPLACEMENT. **2.** Symbol for SCREEN GRID of a vacuum tube. **3.** Symbol for STANDARD DEVIATION. **4.** Abbreviation for SECOND.

SA Abbreviation of SUBJECT TO APPROVAL.

S_A band A section of the S band, extending from 3100 to 3400 MHz.

sabin A unit of sound absorption; 1 sabin represents a surface that can absorb sound at the same rate as 1 square foot of a perfectly absorbent surface.

SADT Abbreviation of *surface alloy diffused-base transistor.*

SAE **1.** Abbreviation of SHAFT-ANGLE ENCODER. **2.** Abbreviation of *Society of Automotive Engineers.*

safe noise level A level of acoustic intensity equal to 85 dB above the threshold of hearing. At sound levels higher than this, eardrum damage is possible.

safety factor A figure denoting the extent of overload that a device can withstand before breaking down.

safety ground A connection made between equipment (usually the metal chassis, panel, case, or B-minus circuit) and the earth as a protective measure against fire and electric shock.

safety switch See ELECTRICAL INTERLOCK.

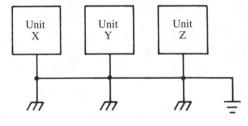

safety ground

sal ammoniac Formula, NH_4Cl. Ammonium chloride, the principal ingredient in the gelatinous electrolyte of some dry cells and batteries.

salient pole A pole, such as the polepiece of a motor or generator, that projects from the rest of the structure (rotor assembly or motor frame).

Salisbury chamber A radio-frequency test chamber in which the walls are non-reflective at various frequencies, thus simulating free space.

salt-spray test A test to assess the life and performance of electronic equipment in a marine environment. The equipment is sprayed, usually with a saltwater mist, and various electrical parameters are measured at prescribed time intervals.

samarium Symbol, Sm. A metallic element of the rare-earth group. Atomic number, 62. Atomic weight, 150.36.

sample **1.** A selection of quantities, events, or objects, taken at a specific time or time interval for analysis or testing. **2.** To take a sample, as defined in **1. 3.** To test a quantity (current, voltage, temperature, pressure, etc.) or a material (electrolyte, insulant, corrosion, rust, etc.) taken from a larger group or body.

sample and hold A method of storing a variable signal for detailed examination.

sampled data system A system that can be either analog or digital, and that works from samples of the input signals.

sampler In audio systems, a device that digitizes and stores sound for a brief interval of time.

sample size In statistics, the number of items in the sample space chosen for analysis.

sample space In statistics, the set of events, numbers, or other items chosen for analysis.

sampling **1.** Observation of a signal at various points in a circuit, without affecting the operation of the circuit. **2.** The conversion of analog signals to binary signals—especially for use in digital communications systems and in computers. **3.** In statistics and probability, a set of function values corresponding to specifically chosen points in the domain.

sampling rate The frequency with which samples are taken [e.g., 1/hr (one sample per hour) or 10/min (10 samples per minute)].

sampling window See WINDOW, **2.**

sand load A microwave power dissipator in which the absorptive material is a mixture of sand and carbon.

sapphire needle See SAPPHIRE STYLUS.

sapphire stylus A jewel-tipped stylus for disc recording and playback. It is noted for durability.

sat **1.** Abbreviation of *saturate.* **2.** Abbreviation of SATURATION. **3.** Abbreviation of SATELLITE.

satd Abbreviation of *saturated.*

satellite An artificial object sent into orbit around the earth or another planet. See, for example, ACTIVE COMMUNICATIONS SATELLITE and PASSIVE COMMUNICATIONS SATELLITE.

satellite communication Communication via one or more satellite transponders. Usually both stations are on the ground, although sometimes one or both stations are airborne or in space.

satellite processor **1.** In a computer, a microprocessor that is subsidiary to the central processing unit (CPU). **2.** In a data-processing system, a CPU used to handle the running of programs of secondary importance to the system's main application.

satisfy To make a statement of inequality or an equation true (e.g., $x = 2$ satisfies the equation $2x = x^2$).

saturable capacitor A voltage-variable ceramic or semiconductor capacitor in which variations in capacitance stabilize at a reasonably constant value after a particular voltage level is reached.

saturable-core magnetometer A MAGNETOMETER in which the sensor is a saturable magnetic core with a winding. The readout is proportional to the change in permeability of the core produced by the magnetic field under test.

saturable reactor An inductor consisting essentially of a coil wound on a core of magnetic material whose magnetic flux can easily reach saturation level. The inductance and, accordingly, the reactance of the device can be varied by passing a direct current through the coil simultaneously with the alternating current to be controlled.

saturable transformer A transformer having a saturable core that permits automatic regulation of an alternating-current voltage.

saturated color A visible color whose energy is concentrated at a single wavelength or in a narrow band of wavelengths. Also called *pure color.*

saturated logic Any form of digital-logic circuit in which the transistors are either completely cut off or completely saturated. It is characterized by relative immunity to noise, high speed, and high input-level requirements.

saturated operation **1.** The operation of a magnetic core at or beyond its saturation point (i.e., in the region where an increase in coil current produces no change in core magnetization). **2.** The operation of a transistor or vacuum tube beyond its saturation point (i.e., in the region where an increase in voltage produces no change in current, or vice versa). Compare UNSATURATED OPERATION.

saturated solution A solution, such as an electrolyte, that contains all of the solute that it ordinarily will hold at a given temperature and pressure. Compare SUPERSATURATED SOLUTION. Also see SOLUTE; SOLUTION, **1** and SOLVENT, **2.**

saturating current See SATURATION CURRENT.

saturation **1.** See SATURATION POINT. **2.** The state of purity of a color. In general, the greater the saturation, the narrower the bandwidth of the electromagnetic energy. The highest possible saturation is represented by energy at a single wavelength [e.g., light of 700 nanometers (nm) appears as highly saturated red, and light of 400 nm appears as highly saturated violet]. Compare HUE. **3.** The condition of a ferromagnetic material in which it can accommodate no additional magnetic flux. **4.** The condition of a dielectric material in which it can accommodate no additional electric flux.

saturation current In a device, the current flowing at and beyond the SATURATION POINT.

saturation flux **1.** The magnetic flux density that will saturate a given sample of magnetic material. **2.** The electric flux density that will saturate a given sample of dielectric material.

saturation flux density See SATURATION INDUCTION.

saturation induction For a magnetic material, the maximum possible flux density.

saturation limiting Output peak clipping that occurs when a transistor or vacuum tube is driven into saturation during part of the input cycle. Compare CUTOFF LIMITING.

saturation point On a voltage-current conduction curve, the point beyond which a further in-

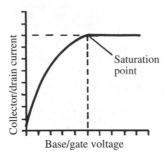

saturation point

crease in voltage produces no appreciable increase in current.

saturation resistance　The voltage-to-current ratio for a saturated semiconductor.

saturation switching　The on/off switching operation in which a transistor is in its saturated state when conducting.

saturation value　**1.** In a transistor, field-effect transistor, or vacuum tube, the lowest level of the input current, voltage, or power that results in saturation. **2.** The maximum obtainable output level for a given circuit. **3.** In a magnetic material, the smallest level of magnetizing force that results in the maximum possible flux density.

saturation voltage　The (usually direct-current output) voltage appearing across a device operating in its saturation region (e.g., the collector voltage of a switching transistor in its switched-on state).

SAVOR　Abbreviation of SIGNAL-ACTUATED VOICE RECORDER.

sawtooth　An alternating or pulsating wave of current or voltage that is characterized by a gradual rise in amplitude followed by a rapid fall, or vice versa; its name is derived from its graphic resemblance to the teeth of a saw.

sawtooth

SB　**1.** Abbreviation of SIDEBAND. **2.** Abbreviation of SIMULTANEOUS BROADCAST.

Sb　Symbol for ANTIMONY.

S band　A radio-frequency band extending from 1550 to 5200 MHz. For subdivisions of this band, see S_A BAND, S_C BAND, S_D BAND, S_F BAND, S_G BAND, S_H BAND, S_Q BAND, S_S BAND, S_T BAND, S_W BAND, S_Y BAND, and S_Z BAND.

SBC　Abbreviation of SINGLE-BOARD COMPUTER.

SBDT　Abbreviation of SURFACE-BARRIER DIFFUSED TRANSISTOR.

SBT　Abbreviation of SURFACE-BARRIER TRANSISTOR.

SC　**1.** Abbreviation of SUPPRESSED CARRIER. **2.** Abbreviation of SHORT CIRCUIT. **3.** On drawings, the abbreviation for *silk-covered*.

Sc　Symbol for SCANDIUM.

sc　**1.** Abbreviation of SINGLE CRYSTAL. **2.** Abbreviation of SCALE. **3.** Abbreviation of *sine-cosine*. **4.** Abbreviation of *science*.

SCA　Abbreviation of SUBSIDIARY COMMUNICATION AUTHORIZATION.

SCA adapter　An auxiliary tuner unit for separating the SCA subcarrier from a main frequency-modulated signal on which it is superimposed. Also see SCA SUBCARRIER and SUBSIDIARY COMMUNICATIONS AUTHORIZATION.

scalar quantity　A quantity having magnitude, but for which direction is not specified. Compare VECTOR QUANTITY.

scale　**1.** A graduated line or curve for indicating values of a quantity. **2.** An ordered set of values. **3.** An ordered series of quantities, such as tones, frequencies, voltages, etc. (e.g., *musical scale*).

scale division　The space between consecutive graduations on a scale (see SCALE, **1**).

scale down　In computer operations, to adjust a group of quantities according to a fixed factor so that it can be accommodated by hardware or software.

scale expansion　Spreading out the divisions in part of a scale (see SCALE, **1**).

scale factor　**1.** A figure by which the readings from a particular scale must be multiplied or divided to give the true values of measured quantities. **2.** A figure via which values in one system of notation are converted to those in another system. **3.** In scaling down (see SCALE DOWN), the factor by which a group of quantities is adjusted. **4.** The ratio of output frequency to input voltage for a voltage-to-frequency converter.

scale-factor adjustment　In some meters, an adjustment that allows full-scale deflection to be set at any desired value (within certain limits) of applied-signal amplitude.

scale-factor error　The absolute value of the difference between the actual scale factor and the ideal scale factor for a multiplier circuit.

scale-factor tolerance　The extent to which a measured value for the scale factor differs from the computed value. It is generally given as a percentage.

scale length　The end-to-end dimension of a scale (see SCALE, **1**), in inches, centimeters, geometric degrees, or number of divisions.

scale multiplier　See SCALE FACTOR, **1**.

scale-of-two counter　A circuit that delivers one output pulse for two successive input pulses.

scale-of-10 counter　A circuit that delivers one output pulse for 10 successive input pulses.

scale-of-ten scaler See SCALE-OF-10 COUNTER.

scaler A circuit or device for extending the frequency range of another device (e.g., a circuit that extends the range of a 1-MHz counter to 100 MHz).

scale range The difference between the lowest and highest values on a scale.

scale span See SCALE RANGE.

scaling The fact, and the implications of the fact, that the mechanical strength of a structure increases in proportion to the square of linear dimension while the weight increases, according to the cube of linear dimension. Thus, weight increases more rapidly than strength as a structure, composed of a given material, is made larger. It is important in the design of large antennas and support structures.

scaling adder An inverting OPERATIONAL AMPLIFIER used to weight and sum multiple voltages.

scaling circuit A circuit, such as one or more flip-flops, that will deliver one output pulse after a predetermined number of input pulses have been received; therefore, it will provide pulse or frequency division. See, for example, SCALE-OF-TWO COUNTER.

scaling factor For a scaler, the number of input pulses required for one output pulse.

scaling ratio See SCALING FACTOR.

scan 1. To traverse a range, field, or dimension. 2. The amount of traversal in 1. 3. See SWEEP. 4. To sample or reproduce an image in a single-line element, as in facsimile or television. 5. A single line resulting from 4. 6. In information retrieval operations, to inspect each record in a file or constituent of a list. 7. To check communications or data channels for availability.

scan conversion In television reception, the scanning of each line twice to convert a conventional image into one that can be displayed on a high-definition picture tube.

scan-converter tube A face-to-face assembly of a cathode-ray tube and a vidicon in one envelope.

scandium Symbol, Sc. A metallic element. Atomic number, 21. Atomic weight, 44.956.

scan frequency See SCANNING FREQUENCY.

scanner A device, especially a radio receiver, equipped with a circuit that searches communications or data channels for signals.

scanner amplifier An amplifier for boosting a scanning signal. Also see SCAN, 1, 3, 4.

scanning 1. In a cathode-ray tube or camera tube, the synchronized movement of the electron beam (or other marker) from right to left and/or from top to bottom. 2. The intermittent, but repetitive, monitoring of two or more communications channels in rotating sequence. 3. The movement of a radar beam for the purpose of obtaining coverage over a specified area.

scanning antenna A transmitting or receiving antenna (such as a rotating one) that covers a generally circular region.

scanning beam The deflected electron beam in a cathode-ray tube. Also see SCAN, 1, 2, 3, 4, 5.

scanning circuit A circuit for producing a scan (see SCAN, 2, 4).

scanning frequency The number of scans per unit time, usually expressed in lines, sweeps, or channels per second or per minute. Also called SCANNING RATE.

scanning line A single line sampled or produced by a scanning process, as in facsimile, television, and graphic recording.

scanning line frequency See SCANNING FREQUENCY.

scanning linearity Uniformity of scanning rate. In a linear scan, for example, scan speed is the same at all points along a line.

scanning loss The effective reduction in radar sensitivity that occurs as the beam scans a given area, rather than remaining in a fixed orientation.

scanning rate See SCANNING FREQUENCY.

scanning receiver A receiver whose tuning is automatically and continuously swept through a frequency band to detect all signals in the band.

scanning sonar A form of distance-measuring or depth-finding sonar, in which the receiving transducer scans to find the direction of the echo or echoes.

scanning speed The rate at which a line, region, or quantity is scanned or at which samples are taken.

scanning yoke See YOKE, 2.

scan rate 1. The rate at which a controlled quantity is checked periodically by a control computer. 2. See SCANNING FREQUENCY.

scan tuning Repetitive, automatic sweeping of a frequency band by a tuned circuit containing a varactor, whose capacitance is periodically varied by a sawtooth voltage.

SCARA Abbreviation of SELECTIVE COMPLIANCE ASSEMBLY ROBOT ARM.

SCA subcarrier An auxiliary carrier (commonly 67 kHz) superimposed on a main frequency-modulated carrier to convey subsidiary communications, such as music without commercials. Also see SUBSIDIARY COMMUNICATION AUTHORIZATION.

scatter To disperse or diffuse transmitted electromagnetic radiation.

scattering 1. The tendency of a concentrated beam of energy to be spread out when it passes

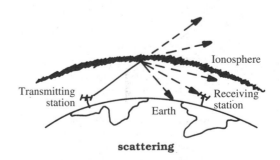

scattering

through a given medium or substance. **2.** The spreading out of radio waves as they pass through the ionosphere or troposphere.

scatter read   In data processing, to distribute data from an input record to several storage areas.

scatter transmission   See BACK SCATTER and FORWARD SCATTER.

S_C band   A section of the S BAND extending from 2000 to 2400 MHz.

scc   Abbreviation of SINGLE-COTTON-COVERED (WIRE).

SCDSB   Abbreviation of SUPPRESSED CARRIER DOUBLE-SIDEBAND (see DOUBLE-SIDEBAND SUPPRESSED CARRIER).

SCE   Abbreviation of *saturated calomel electrode.*

sce   Abbreviation of SINGLE-COTTON-ENAMELED (WIRE).

SCEPTRON   Acronym for SPECTRAL COMPARATIVE PATTERN RECOGNIZER.

schedule   In computer operations, to establish the order of importance of jobs to be run, and assign the necessary resources for those jobs.

schedule method   A method of waveform analysis involving the evaluation of instantaneous amplitudes at numerous points in time. The values are obtained at specific intervals from the image of one complete wave cycle, as displayed on an oscilloscope or plotted on a graph.

schematic diagram   An electronic circuit diagram. Also called WIRING DIAGRAM and *schematic.*

schematic symbol   A graphic symbol used to represent electronic components in a circuit diagram.

Schering bridge   A four-arm capacitance bridge in which the unknown capacitance is compared with a standard capacitance. This bridge is frequently used in testing electrolytic capacitors, to which a direct-current polarizing voltage is applied during the measurement.

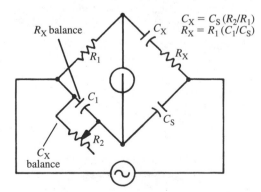

$$C_X = C_S (R_2/R_1)$$
$$R_X = R_1 (C_1/C_S)$$

Schering bridge

Schmidt optical system   In projection television, a lens system used between the bright-image picture tube and the screen.

Schmitt limiter   See SCHMITT TRIGGER.

Schmitt trigger   A multivibrator that produces uniform-amplitude output pulses from a variable-amplitude input signal. This circuit has many applications, one being the conversion of a sine wave into a square wave.

Schottky diode   A solid-state diode in which a metal and a semiconductor form the pn junction. Electrons injected into the metal have a higher energy level than the charge carriers in a semiconductor, and energy storage at the junction is low because current flow is not accompanied by hole movement. Also known as HOT-CARRIER DIODE.

Schottky logic   A form of integrated-injection logic with enhanced operating speed.

Schottky noise   The random noise resulting from the emission of charged particles, usually electrons or holes, from an electrode in an amplifying device. This noise is usually of a wideband nature.

scientific language   Any computer programming language used primarily for mathematical or scientific applications.

scientific notation   The expression of very large and very small numbers as a fixed-point part (mantissa) and a power of the radix (usually 10). Generally, the mantissa is greater than or equal to 1, but less than 10; the power of 10 is adjusted accordingly. Thus, for example, $203,700 = 2.037 \times 10^5$; $0.000533 = 5.33 \times 10^{-4}$. See also SIGNIFICANT FIGURES.

scintillating crystal   A crystal, such as one of sodium iodide, that sparkles or flashes when exposed to radioactive particles or rays.

scintillation   **1.** In radar operations, the apparent rapid displacement of a target from its mean position. **2.** A momentary flash of light produced in a phosphor or scintillating crystal when a high-velocity particle strikes it. **3.** A small fluctuation in radio field intensity at a receiving point.

scintillation counter   A radiation counter consisting essentially of a scintillating crystal in combination with a photomultiplier tube. Flashes from the excited crystal cause the tube to deliver output pulses that are totaled and indicated.

scintillator material   A substance, such as crystalline sodium iodide, that scintillates under certain stimuli.

scissoring   A method of interrupting the electron beam in a cathode-ray tube when the beam would not land on the phosphor screen.

SCLC   Abbreviation of SPACE-CHARGE-LIMITED CURRENT.

sco   Abbreviation of SUBCARRIER OSCILLATOR.

scope   Colloquialism for OSCILLOSCOPE.

Scott oscillator   See PARALLEL-TEE OSCILLATOR.

scp   Abbreviation of SPHERICAL CANDLEPOWER.

SCR   Abbreviation of SILICON-CONTROLLED RECTIFIER.

scrambled signal Any signal in which (for secrecy or exclusivity) the elements are disarranged according to an encryption algorithm. Thus, intelligent reception is possible only if the signal is processed via a suitable decryption algorithm. Example: SCRAMBLED SPEECH.

scrambled speech Voice transmission in which the frequencies have been inverted to prevent eavesdropping. It is automatically unscrambled (by reinversion) at the receiver to restore intelligibility.

scrambler circuit A circuit containing filters and frequency inverters for scrambling speech.

scratch filter An audio-frequency low-pass filter that suppresses high-frequency noise caused by friction between a phonograph disc and the needle.

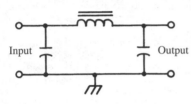

scratch filter

scratchpad memory In computers, a low-capacity memory that stores an intermediate result of a calculation.

scratch tape Magnetic data tape that can be overwritten for any purpose.

screen **1.** See SCREEN GRID. **2.** See SHIELD. **3.** The front surface of a cathode-ray tube. **4.** The surface of a computer or terminal display.

screen angle In radar, the angular difference between the actual horizon and the plane perpendicular to the line connecting the radar set with the center of the earth.

screen current Symbol, I_S or I_{SG}. The current flowing in the screen circuit of an electron tube.

screen grid In a vacuum tube, a grid element between the control grid and plate. It reduces the internal grid-plate capacitance, and consequently prevents self-oscillation when the tube is used in a straight-through amplifier.

screen-grid neutralization Neutralization of an amplifier that uses a tetrode vacuum tube. Such circuits require smaller neutralizing capacitances than those used in triode amplifiers because of the lower interelectrode capacitance of the screen-grid tube.

screen illumination Edge lighting of the transparent screen of an oscilloscope, to make the lines of the graticule more clearly visible.

screen material See PHOSPHOR.

screen resistance Symbol, R_S or R_{SG}. The internal resistance presented by the screen-grid/cathode path of an electron tube.

screen room See CAGE.

screen voltage Symbol, E_S or E_{SG}. The voltage at the screen grid of an electron tube.

scribing The etching of a semiconductor wafer to facilitate breaking the wafer into smaller pieces.

ScriptX A high-level programming language used in the writing of software for personal computers—especially in multimedia. Developed by Kaleida Laboratories.

SCS Abbreviation of SILICON-CONTROLLED SWITCH.

SCT Abbreviation of SURFACE-CHARGE TRANSISTOR.

S curve **1.** The voltage-versus-current curve for a negative-resistance device. Compare N CURVE. **2.** The response curve for a frequency-modulation discriminator or ratio detector.

SD Abbreviation of STANDARD DEVIATION.

S_D band A section of the S BAND extending from 4200 to 5200 MHz.

SDF Abbreviation of static direction finder.

Se Symbol for SELENIUM.

sea clutter Collectively, the radar echoes that the sea reflects.

seal **1.** The point at which a lead or electrode enters or leaves an envelope, case, or housing and is secured to an envelope, case, or housing. Such a point is often tightly closed against the passage of air in or out of the envelope. **2.** To close off a circuit or component from tampering.

sealed dry battery A set of electrochemical dry cells that can be installed without concern for orientation or position. Example: 9-volt "transistor battery."

sealed meter **1.** A meter that is tightly closed against the entry of moisture and foreign materials. **2.** A meter that is locked or otherwise protected against tampering.

sealing compound A substance (such as wax, pitch, or plastic) used to enclose and protect electronic devices.

search **1.** To scan or sweep through a range of quantities or through a region of interest. **2.** To examine (usually in some prescribed order) items of information in a computer memory to find those satisfying a given criterion.

search coil An inductive probe (exploring coil) used to sample magnetic fields.

search oscillator A variable-frequency oscillator used to locate and identify signals by the heterodyne method.

search probe **1.** See SEARCH COIL. **2.** A capacitive probe used to sample electric fields.

search radar A radar that displays a target almost immediately after that target enters a scanned area.

search time The time needed to test items during a search (see SEARCH, **2**).

sea return See SEA CLUTTER.

seasonal effects In ionospheric propagation, the changes produced as a result of the revolution of the earth around the sun. The path of the sun across the sky, and the length of the day, are primarily responsible for such effects.

seasonal static Atmospheric electrical interference, most prevalent during the summer.

S$_E$ band A section of the S BAND extending from 1550 to 1650 MHz.

sec 1. Abbreviation of SECOND. **2.** Abbreviation of SECTION. (Also, sect.) **3.** Abbreviation of SECONDARY. **4.** Abbreviation of SECANT.

secant Abbreviation, sec. The trigonometric function representing the ratio of the hypotenuse of a right triangle to the adjacent side (c/b). The secant is the reciprocal of the cosine; sec x = $1/\cos x$.

second 1. Abbreviation, s and sec. A unit of time. The mean solar second is 1/86,400 of a mean solar day, and is 1/60 minute or 1/3600 hour. **2.** Symbol ("). A unit of arc measure. 1" = 1/3600 geometric degree.

secondaries See SECONDARY COLORS.

secondary 1. See SECONDARY WINDING. **2.** See SECONDARY STANDARD.

secondary battery See STORAGE BATTERY.

secondary calibration The calibration of an instrument, based on a reference instrument calibrated against an absolute source.

secondary capacitance 1. The distributed capacitance of the secondary winding of a transformer whose primary winding is unloaded. Compare PRIMARY CAPACITANCE, 1. **2.** A series or shunt capacitance used to tune the secondary coil of a radio-frequency transformer. Compare PRIMARY CAPACITANCE, 2.

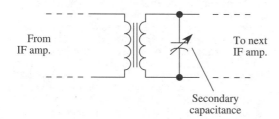

From IF amp.

To next IF amp.

Secondary capacitance

secondary capacitance, 2

secondary cell See STORAGE CELL.

secondary circuit 1. The circuit associated with the secondary winding of a transformer. **2.** See OUTPUT CIRCUIT.

secondary coil See SECONDARY WINDING.

secondary color 1. A color prepared by mixing two primary colors. **2.** In television operations, any displayed color composed of two or more color primaries.

secondary current The current flowing in the secondary winding of a transformer. Also called TRANSFORMER OUTPUT CURRENT. Compare PRIMARY CURRENT.

secondary electron 1. The electron possessing the lesser energy after a collision between two electrons. Compare PRIMARY ELECTRON. **2.** An electron ejected by secondary emission.

secondary emission The action whereby electrons in the atoms at the surface of a target are ejected as a result of bombardment by a beam of (primary) electrons. Thus, in an electron tube, electrons from the cathode strike the plate with a force that drives secondary electrons out of the plate, into the surrounding space.

secondary emitter A source of secondary electrons (e.g., the plate of an electron tube or a dynode in a photomultiplier tube).

secondary failure The failure of a component or circuit, resulting from the failure of some other component. For example, the pass transistor in a power supply might burn out, causing the output voltage to increase; this increased voltage can damage equipment connected to the supply.

secondary frequency standard A device for generating signals of accurate frequency, but that does not possess the very high stability and extreme accuracy of a primary frequency standard. The secondary standard is periodically checked against a PRIMARY FREQUENCY STANDARD and appropriately corrected.

secondary impedance 1. The impedance of the secondary winding of a transformer whose primary winding is unloaded. Compare PRIMARY IMPEDANCE, 1. **2.** An external impedance presented to the secondary winding of a transformer. Compare PRIMARY IMPEDANCE, 2.

secondary inductance The inductance of the secondary winding of a transformer whose primary winding is unloaded. Compare PRIMARY INDUCTANCE.

secondary kVA The kilovolt-amperes in the secondary circuit of an operating transformer. Compare PRIMARY KVA.

secondary power The power in the secondary circuit of a transformer. Also see SECONDARY KVA and SECONDARY VA. Compare PRIMARY POWER.

secondary radiation 1. The (sometimes random) reradiation of electromagnetic waves, as from a receiving antenna. **2.** Rays emitted by atoms or molecules when the latter are struck by other radiation.

secondary rays Rays emitted by atoms or molecules that have been bombarded by other rays of the same general nature. Examples: *secondary X rays* and *secondary beta rays*.

secondary resistance The direct-current resistance of the secondary winding of a transformer. Compare PRIMARY RESISTANCE.

secondary standard An accurate source of a quantity (capacitance, frequency, inductance, resistance, etc.), that is referred periodically to a primary standard for correction.

secondary storage In computer and data-processing operations, storage that is auxiliary to the main storage. Also called *backing storage*.

secondary turns The number of turns in the secondary winding of a transformer. Compare PRIMARY TURNS.

secondary utilization factor For a transformer in a rectifier circuit, the utility factor of the secondary winding (ratio of direct-current power output to secondary volt-amperes).

secondary VA The volt-amperes in the secondary circuit of a transformer. Compare PRIMARY VA.

secondary voltage The voltage across the secondary winding of a transformer. Also called TRANSFORMER OUTPUT VOLTAGE. Compare PRIMARY VOLTAGE.

secondary winding The normal output winding of a transformer. Also called SECONDARY COIL. Compare PRIMARY WINDING.

second breakdown In a large-area power transistor, a destructive breakdown caused by thermal runaway.

second-breakdown voltage The collector voltage at which second breakdown occurs in a transistor.

second-channel attenuation See SELECTANCE, **2**.

second-channel interference In a given channel, interference arising from authorized signals two channels removed.

second detector In a superheterodyne receiver, the intermediate-frequency detector. Compare FIRST DETECTOR.

second-level address In a computer program instruction, an address giving the location of the address of a required operand. Also called *indirect address*.

sect Abbreviation of SECTION. (Also, sec.)

section **1.** A subcircuit or stage of a larger circuit (e.g., the *oscillator section* of a receiver). **2.** The smaller unit described in **1**, when self-contained and operated independently (e.g., *filter section*). **3.** See PROGRAM SEGMENT.

sectionalized antenna A set of collinear radiating elements, placed end-to-end with reactances between them, for the purpose of modifying the radiation pattern.

sectionalized winding **1.** A method of winding a coil in complete, multilayer sections that are stacked side by side or top to bottom, a technique that reduces distributed capacitance. **2.** A coil wound, as defined in **1**.

sector On a magnetic disk, a specific portion of a track.

sectoral horn antenna An (usually sheetmetal) antenna with the shape of a horn of rectangular cross section. It is flared in one dimension only.

sector display In a radar, a display that allows the continuous observation of a portion of the scanned area.

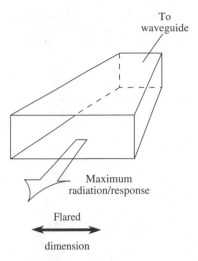

To waveguide

Maximum radiation/response

Flared

dimension

sectoral horn antenna

secular equilibrium The state in which a radioactive substance changing into another substance is decaying as fast as the second substance is being formed.

secular variation A slow change in the intensity of the terrestrial magnetic field.

secure mode In a security system, the condition of being fully activated.

securite In radiotelephony, a spoken word (pronounced say-kyoor-ee-tay) identifying a transmission concerning safety. Equivalent to TT in radiotelegraphy.

security code **1.** A set of alphanumeric characters (letters and/or numbers) or switch settings that activates or deactivates a security system. **2.** See PASSWORD.

security robot Any robot that assists in the protection of people or property—especially against crime.

security system A set of electronic (and sometimes also electromechanical) devices designed to do one or more of the following: restrict access to a premises or computer system, detect abnormal conditions, detect unauthorized entry, alert human operators of abnormal conditions, alert owners and/or authorities of unauthorized entry to a premises, and (in some cases) provide physical protection of property.

Seebeck effect The development of an electromotive force in a junction of two dissimilar metals (a thermocouple) when the temperature of the junction is different from that of the rest of the metal.

Seebeck emf The electromotive force resulting from the Seebeck effect.

seed crystal A small single crystal from which a larger single crystal (e.g., germanium or silicon) is grown. Also see CZOCHRALSKI METHOD.

seeing-eye robot A robot that serves in the capacity of a seeing-eye dog, to help visually impaired people in their daily activities.

seek See SEARCH.

seek area An area of direct-access storage to which are assigned specific records and from which the records can be accessed quickly.

segment 1. The portion of a line or curve lying between two points. 2. See PROGRAM SEGMENT.

segmental meter An expanded-scale meter (see SCALE EXPANSION).

segmented encoding law An approximation of a smooth encoding law, done by means of linear partitions or segments. The greater the number of segments, the more accurate the approximation.

segmenting See PARTITIONING.

segment mark A character indicating the division between tape file sections.

segue (Pronounced SEG-way.) A smooth transition from one sound or channel to another (e.g., between musical selections in a radio broadcast). The first selection decreases in volume as the second selection increases. There is some overlap.

Seignette salt See ROCHELLE SALT.

seismic detector A vibration sensor used in some types of intrusion-detection systems.

seismogram A record produced by a SEISMOGRAPH.

seismograph An instrument for detecting and recording earth tremors. Indicates the direction, magnitude, and time of a quake.

seismometer See SEISMOGRAPH.

seismoscope An instrument that shows the occurrence and time of an earthquake. Compare SEISMOGRAPH.

select To accept or separate a unit, quantity, or course of action from all those available (in a group, mixture, or series).

selectance 1. For a resonant circuit, the ratio Er/Ex, where Er is the voltage at resonance, and Ex is the voltage at a specified nonresonant frequency. 2. For a receiver, the figure $S2/S1$, where $S1$ is the sensitivity of the receiver in a given frequency channel, and $S2$ is the sensitivity in another specified channel.

selected mode In an encoder, a mode in which one output is read and the others are ignored.

selective Pertaining to a device or system, such as a radio receiver, with a high degree of SELECTIVITY.

selective absorption The attenuation or absorption of some frequencies or bands of frequencies, with little or no attenuation at other frequencies or bands of frequencies.

selective amplifier An amplifier that can be tuned, with the desired degree of sharpness, to a single frequency or band of frequencies. Radio-frequency amplifiers are generally tuned by means of inductance-capacitance (LC) circuits; audio-frequency amplifiers are usually tuned by means of resistance-capacitance (RC) circuits.

selective calling The calling, alerting, or alarming of a desired station without interfering with other stations.

selective compliance assembly robot arm Abbreviation, SCARA. An electromechanical device designed especially for use in assembly lines. It uses cylindrical coordinate geometry to allow precise, programmable movements in three dimensions.

selective dump In computer operations, a dump (see DUMP) affecting a small, specific memory area.

selective fading Fading caused by propagation conditions, whose effects differ at slightly different frequencies. In an amplitude-modulated signal, this effect causes the sidebands and carrier to arrive in various phase relationships, with resulting distortion in the received signal.

selective interference Interference confined to a narrow band of frequencies.

selective polarization See POLARIZATION SELECTIVITY.

selective reflection In the reflection of electrons directed into a crystal by means of an electron gun, the tendency of the electrons to be reflected more readily when they strike the crystal at certain speeds.

selective relay 1. A relay or relay circuit tuned to open or close at one signal frequency. 2. A relay or relay circuit adjusted to open or close at one value of current or voltage.

selective trace In computer operations, a diagnostic program used to analyze certain areas of memory or specific kinds of program instructions, for debugging purposes.

selectivity 1. The ability of a circuit or device to pass signals of one frequency and reject signals at other frequencies. 2. The degree to which a circuit or device passes signals of one frequency and rejects signals at other frequencies.

selectivity control In some equipment (such as receivers, crystal filters, wave analyzers, and vibration meters) an adjustment that permits variation of selectivity.

Selectoject A fully electronic, continuously tunable, notcher-peaker that is resistance-capacitance tuned. The name is an acronym for *select or reject*.

selector 1. A channel switch in a radio or television receiver. 2. See SELECTOR SWITCH.

selector channel In data-processing and computer systems, a data transmission channel controlling the information flow between peripherals and a central processing unit.

selector pulse In digital communications, an identifying pulse that represents a certain group of bits or data.

selector relay A device, such as a stepping switch, that actuates one of a number of available circuits on receipt of a predetermined number of pulses.

selector switch A (usually rotary) multiposition switch that allows an operator to select from among several options (such as frequency channels, frequency bands, or selective filters).

selenium Symbol, Se. A nonmetallic element. Atomic number, 34. Atomic weight, 78.96. It is used in the manufacture of some diodes, rectifiers, and photocells.

selenium cell A photoelectric cell that uses specially processed selenium as the light-sensitive material. It can be operated as a photoconductive cell or a photovoltaic cell.

selenium diode A junction diode in which the semiconductor material is specially processed selenium. Also see JUNCTION DIODE.

selenium photocell See SELENIUM CELL.

selenium rectifier A disk- or plate-type power rectifier utilizing the junction between selenium and aluminum or selenium and iron.

self-bias For a transistor or vacuum tube, input-electrode bias voltage resulting from the flow of output-electrode current through a resistor common to both circuits. Also called AUTOMATIC BIAS.

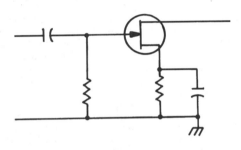

self-bias

self-capacitance The inherent internal capacitance of a device other than a capacitor.

self-checking number A number whose digits have a value that determines the check digit attached to it; thus, it can be verified following its transfer between storage locations or peripherals.

self-cleaning contacts Switch or relay contacts that clean themselves automatically by means of wiping action.

self-contained device A device containing all parts and sections (e.g., main circuit, power supply, meter, loudspeaker, etc.) needed for full operation (i.e., no auxiliary equipment is needed).

self-controlled oscillator See SELF-EXCITED OSCILLATOR.

self discharge The tendency of an electrochemical cell or battery to gradually lose stored energy when not in use.

self-discharge rate A quantitative expression of the speed with which SELF DISCHARGE occurs in an electrochemical cell or battery when it is stored without being used.

self-energy Symbol, E. The energy mc^2, in joules, of a particle traveling at the speed of light c (2.9979×10^8 meters per second) and whose mass is m kilograms.

self erasing In a magnetic tape, the unwanted erasing of data near a highly magnetized region.

self-excited generator An alternating-current generator in which the field coils are supplied with direct current produced by the machine itself. Compare SEPARATELY EXCITED GENERATOR.

self-excited oscillator An oscillator consisting of an amplifier that supplies its own input signal through positive feedback, and whose oscillation frequency depends entirely on circuit constants, such as the capacitance and inductance in a tank circuit. Compare CRYSTAL OSCILLATOR, FORK OSCILLATOR, HUMMER, and MAGNETOSTRICTION OSCILLATOR.

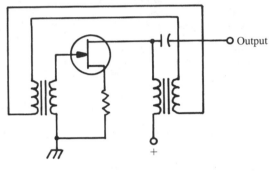

self-excited oscillator

self-focus picture tube A television picture tube in which the electron gun has an automatic, electrostatic focusing arrangement.

self-generating photocell See PHOTOVOLTAIC CELL.

self-generating transducer A voltage-producing transducer, such as a piezoelectric pickup or dynamic microphone.

self-healing capacitor A capacitor, such as a wet electrolytic unit, in which the dielectric is restored to its normal condition after a high-voltage breakdown.

self-heated thermocouple A thermocouple in which the passage of an applied current produces the heat necessary for the activation of the thermocouple.

self-heating thermistor A thermistor heated to above ambient temperature by the current passing through it. Also called DIRECTLY HEATED THERMISTOR. Compare INDIRECTLY HEATED THERMISTOR.

self impedance The effective or measured impedance at a circuit point.

self-inductance   1. The inductance of an inductor. **2.** The inherent internal inductance of a device other than an inductor.

self-induction   Induction that occurs in a single circuit. An instance is the generation of an opposing voltage across a coil by an alternating current flowing through it. Compare INDUCTION. Also see INDUCTANCE.

self-latching relay   A relay that remains in the state that it has been switched (i.e., locked open or closed) until a subsequent signal is received.

self-modulated oscillator   A circuit, such as a blocking oscillator, in which oscillation occurs simultaneously at two frequencies, one modulating the other.

self-organizing   Pertaining to a computer or system that can change the arrangement of data files for particular purposes.

self-powered device   A device that requires no external source of power (i.e., it is equipped with a self-contained battery or a generator).

self-pulsing blocking oscillator   A blocking oscillator that produces a train of radio-frequency pulses. Compare SINGLE-SWING BLOCKING OSCILLATOR.

self-quenching detector   A super-regenerative detector (see SUPER-REGENERATIVE CIRCUIT) in which the low-frequency quenching voltage is supplied by the regenerative detector itself. Also see QUENCHING ACTION and QUENCH OSCILLATOR. Compare SEPARATELY QUENCHED DETECTOR.

self-quenching oscillator   A circuit, such as a blocking oscillator, in which oscillation is periodically switched off automatically, resulting in a self-interrupted wave train.

self-rectifying vibrator   A vibrator-type power supply in which one vibrator reed chops the direct-current input to the primary winding of the transformer, and a second vibrator reed rectifies the alternating-current output delivered by the secondary winding. Also see VIBRATOR RECTIFIER.

self-rectifying X-ray tube   An X-ray tube operated with alternating-current anode voltage.

self-regulation   The ability of a circuit or device to control its output automatically, according to some predetermined plan, by using output error to correct operation or to vary the input.

self reset   1. The action of a circuit breaker to reapply power after a certain elapsed time. **2.** The action of any device, returning a circuit or system to normal automatically.

self-resetting loop   In a computer program, a loop in which instructions cause locations used in the loop to assume their condition prior to the loop's execution.

self-resistance   The inherent internal resistance of a device other than a resistor.

self-resonant frequency   The frequency at which a device will resonate naturally (without external tuning). Thus, an inductor will self-resonate with its distributed capacitance; similarly, a capacitor will resonate with its stray inductance.

self-saturation   In a magnetic amplifier, saturation resulting from rectification of the saturable-reactor output current.

self-starting motor   An alternating-current motor that starts running as soon as voltage is applied (i.e., no external mechanical force is needed). Also see SHADING COIL.

self-sustained oscillations   Oscillations maintained by means of positive feedback (inductive or capacitive) from the output to the input of a circuit. See, for example, SELF-EXCITED OSCILLATOR.

self-test   Any arrangement whereby a device or system determines, without the aid of an external operator, whether or not it is operating correctly.

self-ventilated motor   See OPEN MOTOR.

self-wiping contacts   See SELF-CLEANING CONTACTS.

selsyn   See AUTOSYN and SYNCHRO.

SEM   1. Abbreviation of SINGLE-ELECTRON MEMORY. **2.** Abbreviation of SCANNING ELECTRON MICROSCOPE.

semantic network   A reasoning scheme sometimes used in artificial intelligence. Logical statements or sentences are broken down into nodes (generally nouns) and relationships (generally verbs and modifiers). This allows statements to be mapped in a way that is easy for computers to store and modify.

semiautomatic key   Also called *bug*. A telegraph key that mechanically produces a string of Morse-code dots (short pulses) when its lever is pressed to one side (usually toward the right), and continuous circuit closure when the lever is pressed to the opposite side (usually toward the left). Dashes are manually sent by the operator.

semiconductor   A material whose natural resistivity lies between that of conductors and insulators (e.g., GERMANIUM, SILICON, SELENIUM, and GALLIUM ARSENIDE).

semiconductor counter   A device for measuring the intensity of ionizing radiation (such as alpha particles, beta particles, or gamma rays) using a photodiode and sensing circuit.

semiconductor device   A component (such as a diode, photocell, rectifier, or transistor) that exploits the properties of a semiconductor.

semiconductor diode   A solid-state diode, as opposed to a vacuum-tube diode or gas-tube diode. Examples: *germanium diode*, *selenium diode*, and *silicon diode*.

semiconductor junction   Within a body of semiconductor material, the area of physical contact between two regions (usually n and p) having opposite electrical properties.

semiconductor laser   See LASER DIODE.

semiconductor material   See SEMICONDUCTOR.

semiconductor-metal junction The area of physical contact between a metal and a semiconductor.

semiconductor photosensor A semiconductor photodiode or phototransistor, as opposed to a phototube.

semiconductor rectifier A heavy-duty semiconductor diode (or assembly of such diodes) designed primarily to change alternating current to direct current in power-supply units. Rectifiers commonly are made from copper oxide, germanium, magnesium-copper sulfide, selenium, or silicon. Also see JUNCTION DIODE and METER RECTIFIER.

semidirectional Pertaining to a transducer that exhibits different directional characteristics at different frequencies.

semiduplex operation A two-frequency communication system that operates in duplex at one end of the link, and in simplex at the other end. Also see DUPLEX OPERATION and SIMPLEX TELEGRAPHY.

semilogarithmic graph Also called *semilog graph.* A graph in which one axis is logarithmic and the other axis is linear.

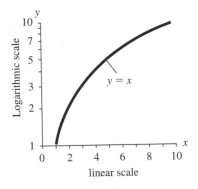

semilogarithmic graph

semimetal An elemental substance that exhibits some, but not all, of the properties of a metal (e.g., antimony and arsenic). Also called METALLOID.

semiresonant line An open-wire transmission line cut approximately to resonant length at the frequency of operation.

semitone See HALF STEP.

sender See TRANSMITTER, **1**, **3**.

sending-end impedance See DRIVING-POINT IMPEDANCE.

sending set **1.** See RADIO TRANSMITTER. **2.** An equipment for transmitting electromagnetic waves. Also see TRANSMITTER, **1**.

sensation level The level of sound that produces a tingling or noticeable sensation in the ear.

sense **1.** To check the condition of a switching device, such as a gate. **2.** See READ.

sense amplifier A device that produces a control signal when some characteristic of the input signal changes.

sense determination In a direction finder that provides an ambiguous indication (two readings 180 degrees apart), the process of deducing, or the ability of the apparatus to deduce, the true direction from which the signal is coming.

sense resistor A (usually low-value) resistor used to sense current in a circuit without introducing a significant loss. The voltage drop across this resistor is proportional to the current and can be applied to a voltmeter, oscilloscope, or other instrument for measurement or observation.

sensing circuit **1.** A circuit that samples a quantity. **2.** In a voltage regulator, the circuit that monitors the output voltage and delivers a control voltage proportional to the output-voltage error.

sensing window See WINDOW, **2**.

sensitive communications Two-way communications of an emergency or priority nature, or involving the security of government operations.

sensitive device A device that responds to a signal of low amplitude.

sensitivity **1.** The ability of a circuit or device to respond to a low-level applied stimulus. **2.** For a receiver, the input-signal (in microvolts or millivolts) required for a specified output level. **3.** For a galvanometer, microamperes or milliamperes per scale division. **4.** The ohms-per-volt rating of a voltmeter. Also see VOLTMETER SENSITIVITY.

sensitivity adjustment **1.** An input gain control in an amplifier circuit. **2.** The radio-frequency gain control of a receiver. **3.** A control or switch that is used to select the range or threshold of a piece of test equipment.

sensitivity control A manual or automatic device for adjusting the sensitivity of a circuit or device.

sensitometer An instrument used to measure the sensitivity of certain materials to light.

sensor **1.** A device that samples a phenomenon, and delivers a proportionate current or voltage in terms of which the intensity of the phenomenon can be measured, or with which control action can be initiated. **2.** An electronic device that detects abnormal conditions (e.g., smoke and heat) and delivers a warning signal to human operators and/or computers. **3.** An electronic device that detects intrusion to a premises and delivers a warning signal to human operators and/or computers.

sentry robot A simple form of SECURITY ROBOT that alerts people or computers to abnormal or potentially dangerous conditions.

separately excited generator An alternating-current generator whose field coils are supplied with direct current from another generator or from a battery. Compare SELF-EXCITED GENERATOR.

separately quenched detector A superregenerative detector (see SUPERREGENERATIVE CIRCUIT) in which the quenching voltage is supplied by a separate low-frequency oscillator. Also see QUENCHING ACTION and QUENCH OSCILLATOR. Compare SELF-QUENCHED OSCILLATOR.

separation See CHANNEL SEPARATION.

separation energy The energy required to remove a proton or neutron from the nucleus of an atom. The separation energy depends on the atomic number.

separator **1.** See FILTER, **1. 2.** A perforated or porous plate of insulating material (usually plastic or wood) for holding active plates apart in a storage cell. **3.** In computer operations, a character marking the division between logical data units. Also called *data delimiter*.

septate cavity A coaxial cavity containing a SEPTUM between the inner and outer conductors.

septate waveguide A waveguide containing one or more septa (see SEPTUM) to control power transmission.

septum A thin metal vane used as a reflector in a waveguide or cavity.

sequence **1.** A succession of objects, parameters, or numbers. **2.** An ordered set of numbers—each of which is related to its predecessor by a specific mathematical function.

sequence checking routine In computer operations, a routine that verifies the order of items of data.

sequence control register In a computer memory, a register whose contents determine the instruction to be implemented next.

sequence programmer A timing device that can be preset to start or stop various operations at predetermined times.

sequencer A device that initiates or terminates events in a desired sequence.

sequence relay A relay whose several contacts close in a predetermined order.

sequence timer A timer in which separate delay circuits are actuated in a predetermined sequence.

sequential In computer operations, a term denoting operations on data items in which the items (e.g., records in a file) are taken in an order determined by key values, rather than in the order in which the items are physically arranged.

sequential access memory Any semiconductor memory in which data can be recalled or addressed only in a certain specified order.

sequential analysis In statistics, using an unspecified number of observations as samples from which a result is derived. Each observation is accepted or rejected, or another observation is made.

sequential color television The successive transmission of the three primary colors in a television system, and their reproduction at the receiver in the same order. Also see DOT-SE-QUENTIAL SYSTEM, FIELD-SEQUENTIAL SYSTEM, and LINE-SEQUENTIAL SYSTEM.

sequential control Computer operation in which the order of instruction implementation is the same as the order of instruction storage.

sequential relay See SEQUENCE RELAY.

sequential scanning Rectilinear television scanning in which the center-to-center distance between successive lines is the same as the nominal line width.

sequential switch **1.** A switch that provides selection of two or more ports in a rotating succession. **2.** In a television system, a switch that allows the monitoring technician to select any of the cameras for viewing.

sequential timer See SEQUENCE TIMER.

ser **1.** Abbreviation of SERIES. **2.** Abbreviation of SERIAL.

serial **1.** Pertaining to the performance of steps, or the occurrence of elements (such as data items on magnetic tape), in succession. **2.** An order, row, or sequence in which one item follows another (as opposed to parallel).

serial access Access to data file records in their order in a storage medium.

serial adder See SERIAL ARITHMETIC UNIT.

serial arithmetic unit In computer operations, an arithmetic unit in which digits are handled in order. Compare PARALLEL ADDER.

serial bit Data in which the bits of each byte or word are sent or received one at a time.

serial memory A register in which the input and output data is stored and retrieved one bit at a time.

serial-parallel **1.** Pertaining to data transfer that is serial in one sense and parallel in another sense. For example, entire words might be serially transmitted within a system, but the constituent bits of each word might be transferred in parallel. **2.** See PARALLEL-SERIES.

serial processing In computer operations, the sequential processing of several different programs through a single channel. Compare PARALLEL PROCESSING.

serial storage In computer operation, storage in which elements are entered in order and are available only in the same order. Compare PARALLEL STORAGE.

serial transfer The propagation of information along a single path, in which data bits are sent one after the other.

series **1.** The sum of a mathematical sequence (see SEQUENCE, **2**). **2.** Pertaining to the connection of elements or components end-to-end (see SERIES CIRCUIT).

series addition See SERIES-AIDING.

series-aiding The condition in which two series voltages or magnetic fields are added together. Compare SERIES-BUCKING.

series antenna tuning Antenna-feeder tuning in which a separate tuning capacitor is connected

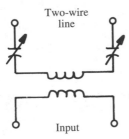

series antenna tuning

in series with each wire. Compare PARALLEL ANTENNA TUNING.

series bucking   The condition in which two series voltages or magnetic fields oppose each other. Compare SERIES-AIDING.

series capacitance   Capacitance acting, or connected, in series with another capacitance or other quantity.

series capacitors   Capacitors connected in series. If the individual capacitors have values $C1$, $C2$, ..., Cn, then the total capacitance Ct is equal to $1/(1/C1 + 1/C2 + ... + 1/Cn)$. Also see SERIES CIRCUIT.

series circuit   A circuit whose components are, in effect, connected in a string (i.e., end-to-end). Compare PARALLEL CIRCUIT.

series-diode half-wave rectifier   See SERIES-DIODE RECTIFIER.

series-diode rectifier   A rectifier circuit in which the diode is connected in series with the source and load. Compare SHUNT-DIODE RECTIFIER.

series dropping resistor   See DROPPING RESISTOR.

series equivalent impedance   A series impedance that will draw the same current (magnitude and phase) drawn by a given parallel circuit connected across the same single-phase source.

series equivalent of parallel circuit   See SERIES EQUIVALENT IMPEDANCE.

series-fed amplifier   An amplifier circuit in which the operating voltages are applied in series with the alternating-current signal voltages. Also see SERIES FEED.

series-fed oscillator   An oscillator circuit in which the direct-current operating voltage is applied in series with the alternating-current output voltage. Also see SERIES FEED.

series feed   The application of alternating-current (ac) and direct-current (dc) voltages in series to a device. Example: the presentation of the dc operating voltages for an amplifier in series with the ac signal voltages (see SERIES-FED AMPLIFIER).

series feedback   A feedback system in which the feedback signal is presented to the input point in series with the input signal. Compare SHUNT FEEDBACK.

series field   A magnetic field produced by a series winding in a motor or generator.

series generator   An electric generator in which the armature and field windings are connected in series. Compare SHUNT GENERATOR.

series inductance   1. Inductance acting, effectively, in series with some other quantity (e.g., the inherent inductance of a wirewound resistor). **2.** An inductance connected in series with other inductances, or with some other quantity (e.g., capacitance and resistance).

series inductors   Inductors connected in series, and separated or oriented in a way that minimizes the effects of mutual inductance. Assuming zero mutual inductance, if the individual inductors have values $L1$, $L2$, ..., Ln, then the total inductance Lt is equal to $L1 + L2 + ... + Ln$. Also see SERIES CIRCUIT.

series limiter   A limiter (clipper) circuit in which the diode is essentially in series with the signal. Compare PARALLEL LIMITER.

series loading   The series insertion of reactances in a circuit for the purpose of impedance matching.

series magnetic circuits   A combination of several magnetic paths in line so that flux extends through each path in sequence; this is analogous to the passage of electric current successively through series-connected resistors.

series motor   An electric motor whose armature and field windings are connected in series. Compare SHUNT MOTOR.

series operation   The operation of units in succession, necessitating sequential current flow through each. Also see SERIES CIRCUIT.

series opposition   See SERIES BUCKING.

series-parallel   See PARALLEL-SERIES.

series-parallel capacitors   See PARALLEL-SERIES CAPACITORS.

series-parallel inductors   See PARALLEL-SERIES INDUCTORS.

series-parallel resistors   See PARALLEL-SERIES RESISTORS.

series regulator   A voltage regulator circuit in which the controlled device is in series with the load. Compare SHUNT REGULATOR.

series resistance   1. Resistance acting in series with another resistance or with another quantity (e.g., capacitance and inductance). **2.** The inherent resistance that acts effectively in series with the plates of a capacitor. **3.** The resistance of the wire in a coil, acting effectively in series with the inductance.

series resistors   Resistors connected in series with each other. If the individual resistors have values $R1$, $R2$, ..., Rn, then the total resistance Rt is equal to $R1 + R2 + ... + Rn$. Also see SERIES CIRCUIT.

series resonance   Resonance in a circuit consisting of a capacitor, inductor, and an alternating-current generator in series. At the resonant frequency, the inductive reactance and the capacitive reactance cancel, so the net reactance is zero. The capacitor current and inductor current are maximum and equal, and the circuit impedance is minimum. Compare PARALLEL RESONANCE.

series-resonant circuit A resonant circuit in which the capacitor, inductor, and generator are connected in series. Also see SERIES RESONANCE. Compare PARALLEL-RESONANT CIRCUIT.

series-resonant trap A wavetrap consisting of a series-resonant inductance-capacitance (LC) circuit. Compare PARALLEL-RESONANT TRAP.

series-resonant wavetrap See SERIES-RESONANT TRAP.

series-shunt circuit See PARALLEL-SERIES.

series tee junction See E-PLANE TEE JUNCTION.

series tracking capacitor See OSCILLATOR PADDER.

series-type frequency multiplier A varactor frequency-multiplier circuit in which the varactor is in series with the input and output. Compare SHUNT-TYPE FREQUENCY MULTIPLIER.

series-type resonance bridge A resonance bridge in which the impedance arm is a series-resonant circuit. Compare SHUNT-TYPE RESONANCE BRIDGE.

series winding 1. In a motor or generator, a winding connected in series with the armature. 2. A method of motor or generator construction in which the field winding is connected in series with the armature.

series-wound generator See SERIES GENERATOR.

series-wound motor See SERIES MOTOR.

serrated pulse A pulse having a notched or slotted top. An example is the vertical sync pulse in television.

serrated rotor plate In a variable capacitor, an external rotor plate that is slotted radially. This alters the capacitance-variation curve of the capacitor to allow alignment of sensitive apparatus (e.g., the tracking of radio-frequency tuned circuits in a radio receiver).

serrated vertical sync pulse In television, the vertical sync pulse notched at twice the horizontal sweep frequency.

service 1. To maintain or repair electronic equipment. 2. To provide maintenance or repair of electronic equipment.

serviceability ratio For a device or system, the ratio $ts/(ts + td)$, where ts is serviceable (operational) time, and td is downtime (non-operational time).

serviceable time The cumulative time during which an operator-monitored (but not necessarily operated) device or system is capable of normal operation.

service area For a broadcast or communications station, the useful coverage area.

service band 1. For a communications system, the band of frequencies in which operation is normally carried out. 2. A band of frequencies specifically assigned, by government regulation, to a certain communications service or services.

service channel The band of frequencies that a particular broadcast or communications station occupies, when the carrier frequency is held constant.

service charge The amount charged by a technician for installation, maintenance, or repair of equipment. It is often performed on a per-hour basis.

service maintenance For a cell or battery, the relative amount of energy capacity (percentage of full-charge capacity) available at a given time, or after a certain length of time in normal use.

service meter 1. An energy ("power") meter. Also see KILOWATT-HOUR METER. 2. A rugged multimeter used by a service technician.

service oscillator A signal generator designed expressly for troubleshooting and repair service.

service switch 1. The main switch controlling the electric service to a building or other place of installation. 2. In television repair, a switch on the rear of a chassis. The switch facilitates adjustment of screen controls by removing vertical deflection temporarily.

service-type instrument An instrument having reasonable accuracy and a degree of ruggedness so that it is suitable for field or shop use. Examples: SERVICE METER and SERVICE OSCILLATOR. Compare LABORATORY-GRADE INSTRUMENT.

servo amplifier A highly stable amplifier designed expressly for use in a SERVOMECHANISM.

servo loop In a control system (particularly a servo amplifier), the output-to-input feedback loop, through which automatic control is performed.

servomechanism Also called *servo*. A self-correcting, closed-loop control system. It usually uses an electromechanical device, such as a motor, that controls some electronic device. Error signals, supplied by the controlled electronic device, cause the motor to run in such a way as to optimize or stabilize the system.

servomotor A motor operated by the output signal of a servo amplifier. Depending on the end application of the servo system, the motor signal might or might not be corrected.

servo oscillation In a servo system, a back-and-forth movement or fluctuation, relative to the optimum setting or position. It Results from improper system adjustment. Sometimes the system stabilizes at the optimum after a short period of oscillation; in some cases, the oscillation continues indefinitely.

servo robot A (usually industrial) robot whose motion sequence is programmed into a computer. The robot follows the instructions given by the computer, and makes precise, timed movements on that basis. Different computer programs allow different motion sequences, so a single robot can be used for various tasks.

servo system An automatic control system using one or more servomechanisms.

set 1. A piece of equipment or a system (e.g., *radio set*). 2. In a flip-flop circuit, an input that is not controlled by the clock. 3. To adjust a circuit or device, such as a flip-flop, to a desired operating point or condition. 4. A class of numbers, things, or events. 5. In computer programming, to initialize a variable (i.e., to assign a label to a location).

set analyzer A combination test instrument designed originally for troubleshooting radio receivers. It consists of a multimeter and transistor tester or vacuum-tube tester.

set noise Electrical noise arising inside a radio or television receiver, as opposed to that picked up from the outside.

set pulse A pulse used to adjust a device to a certain state (see SET, 3).

set terminal In a flip-flop, the one-input terminal. Compare RESET TERMINAL.

setting The position or value to which an adjustable device is set for a particular purpose.

settling time 1. In a digital voltmeter, the time required between the application of a test voltage and the final display of an accurate readout. 2. In a digital-to-analog converter, the time between half of the level change over all inputs and the arrival of the output to a level within a certain tolerance of its specified final level. It is defined for either full-scale to zero or zero to full-scale.

set up To arrange and prepare equipment for operation.

setup See SET, 1.

set-up time 1. The time required to install and test an electronic system, and to ready the system for operation. 2. In a digital gate, the length of time that a pulse must be held to produce a change of state.

sexadecimal number system See HEXADECIMAL NUMBER SYSTEM.

sexagesimal number system A number system whose radix is 60.

SF 1. Abbreviation of SAFETY FACTOR. 2. Abbreviation of SINGLE FREQUENCY. 3. Abbreviation of STANDARD FREQUENCY. 4. Abbreviation of STABILITY FACTOR.

SFA Abbreviation of SINGLE-FREQUENCY AMPLIFIER.

S_F band A section of the S BAND extending from 1650 to 1850 MHz.

SFO 1. Abbreviation of SINGLE-FREQUENCY OSCILLATOR. 2. Abbreviation of STANDARD-FREQUENCY OSCILLATOR.

SFR Abbreviation of SINGLE-FREQUENCY RECEIVER.

SFR-Chireix-Mesny antenna See CHIREIX-MESNY ANTENNA.

SG Abbreviation of SCREEN GRID.

S_G band A section of the S BAND extending from 2700 to 2900 MHz.

SGCS Abbreviation of *silicon gate-controlled switch* (see SILICON-CONTROLLED SWITCH).

shaded-pole motor An induction-type alternating-current motor using shading coils on the field poles for self-starting with a single-phase supply.

shading Electronic enhancement of a television picture, resulting in a different brightness over various portions of the background, as compared with the actual situation. It can be used, for example, to make certain subjects stand out from the background.

shading coil 1. A single, short-circuited turn (copper ring) encircling the tip of the core of a coil that carries alternating current (ac), such as the field pole of a motor. Current induced in the coil causes a momentary flux shift that approximates a rotating field that self-starts a simple single-phase induction motor. 2. A coil used in a simple ac relay to prevent chatter.

shading ring See SHADING COIL.

shading signal In a television camera, a signal that increases the gain of the amplifier while the beam scans a dark part of the image.

shadow area A region in which signal attenuation or the absence of a signal results from the SHADOW EFFECT.

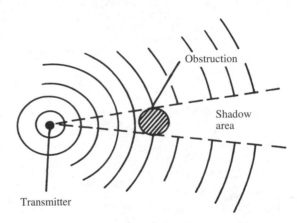

shadow area

shadow attenuation 1. The attenuation of electromagnetic energy caused by an obstacle. It is generally measured in decibels. 2. The attenuation of electromagnetic energy produced by the curvature of the earth.

shadow effect The obstruction of radio waves by objects in their path.

shadow mask See APERTURE MASK.

shadow meter See SHADOW TUNING INDICATOR.

shadow region See SHADOW AREA.

shadow tuning indicator A tuning meter in which the indicating medium is a shadow whose width is proportional to meter current.

shaft   The rodlike part of an adjustable component (such as a potentiometer or variable capacitor) to which a rotating (or turning) member is attached.

shaft-angle encoder   An electronic system for converting shaft rotation into direct binary or decimal readings.

shaft lock   A device for fastening the shaft of an adjustable component (such as a potentiometer, rotary switch, or variable capacitor) in position at a particular setting.

shaft-position encoder   See SHAFT-ANGLE ENCODER.

shaft-position indicator   A device that delivers an analog or digital output signal proportional to the arc of rotation of a shaft.

shaker   See VIBRATOR, 2.

shake table   A platform, actuated by a vibrator, on which components can be mounted for a vibration test.

shallow-diffused junction   A pn junction made by diffusing the impurity material for a short distance into the semiconductor wafer. Compare DEEP-DIFFUSED JUNCTION.

shape factor   1. For a tuned circuit, the ratio of the 60-dB bandwidth to the 6-dB bandwidth. 2. For a filter, the ratio of bandwidth at high attenuation to that at low attenuation.

shaping network   A combination of components for changing the natural response of a circuit to a desired response (i.e., a curve-changing circuit).

shared file   A data file that is available for use by more than one system simultaneously.

shared files system   A data-processing system having one direct-access storage device from which information can be accessed by more than one computer.

sharpener   1. A circuit or device for increasing the selectivity of another circuit or device. 2. A circuit or device for decreasing the rise or fall time of a pulse or square wave. 3. A circuit or device for steepening the response of a filter.

sharpness   See SELECTIVITY.

sharp pulse   A pulse having extremely fast rise and fall times and narrow width (i.e., a spike).

shaving   The physical modification of a phonograph disc, or other permanent recording surface, in preparation for rerecording.

S_H band   A section of the S BAND extending from 3700 to 3900 MHz.

sheath   See POSITIVE-ION SHEATH.

shelf corrosion   In a dry cell in storage, deterioration of the negative electrode because of local action in the zinc.

shelf life   1. The longest period of time that electronic equipment can be continuously kept in storage before deterioration of materials or degradation of performance occurs. 2. The longest period of time that a battery can be stored without use before it must be discarded or recharged.

shell   1. An electronic orbit (imaginary shell) in an atom. 2. The envelope of a component (e.g., the outer casing of a power transistor or the housing of a plug). 3. The rigid case in an audio or video tape cassette.

shell-type choke   See SHELL-TYPE INDUCTOR.

shell-type core   A core that completely surrounds the coil(s) of a choke or transformer.

shell-type inductor   An inductor in which the core completely surrounds the coil.

shell-type transformer   A transformer in which the core completely surrounds the coils.

shf   Abbreviation of SUPERHIGH FREQUENCY.

shield   A metallic partition or box for confining an electric or magnetic field.

shield baffle   A sheet-type shield. Also see BAFFLE, 2 and SHIELD PARTITION.

shield box   A shield having a general box shape, and which is usually enclosed on all sides.

shield braid   Tubing woven from wire, through which an insulated wire is passed and thus shielded.

shield can   A cylindrical shield, usually enclosed on all sides.

shield disk   A flat shield having a disk shape. Also see BAFFLE, 2; SHIELD BAFFLE; and SHIELD PARTITION.

shielded cable   Cable completely enclosed within a metal sheath that is either flexible or rigid.

shielded wire   A single strand of insulated wire completely enclosed in a flexible or rigid shield.

shield partition   A wall-type shield usually consisting of a single, flat sheet of metal, sometimes bent into an angle. Also called BAFFLE SHIELD (see BAFFLE, 2).

shield plate   See BAFFLE, 2; SHIELD BAFFLE; SHIELD DISK; and SHIELD PARTITION.

shield room   See CAGE.

shield wire   A (usually grounded) wire, near and parallel to another wire that it shields.

shift   1. To move from one operating point to another in a characteristic curve, or in the operation of an equipment. 2. To transfer data from one point to another in a system, or move it left or right in a register.

shift flip-flop circuit   A flip-flop designed especially as a stage in a shift register.

shift pulse   In a shift register, a drive pulse that initiates the shifting of characters.

shift register   In computers, calculators, and storage systems, a circuit (usually composed of flip-flops in cascade) in which pulses can be shifted from stage to stage and finally out of the circuit.

shingle-type photocell   A device in which several separate photocells are series connected by slightly overlapping the ends of adjacent cells.

ship station   A radio or radar station installed aboard a ship that is not in port.

ship-to-shore communication   Radio communication between a ship at sea and a land-based station.

shock **1.** See ELECTRIC SHOCK. **2.** A signal applied momentarily to a circuit, as in the *shock excitation* of a tank. **3.** A sudden, dramatic change in an environmental variable (such as temperature). **4.** Physical blows or vibration.

shock absorber Any object or device intended for reducing physical vibration of a component, set of components, circuit, or system.

shock device **1.** A device for administering shock therapy (see ELECTROSHOCK, **1**). **2.** An induction coil and associated primary supply for applying high voltage to a wire fence.

shock excitation Driving an inductance-capacitance (LC) tuned circuit into damped oscillation by momentarily applying a pulse.

shock-excited oscillator A type of self-excited oscillator in which the transistor is suddenly cut off by applying a cutoff voltage to the gate or base electrode. This abrupt interruption of steady drain or collector current shocks the tank into damped oscillations.

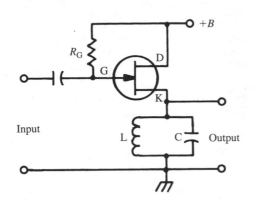

shock-excited oscillator

shock hazard **1.** Any situation that presents the danger of electric shock to attendant personnel. **2.** The existence of a potential difference that will cause a current of at least 5 mA to flow through a resistance of 500 ohms or more, for a prolonged period of time.

Shockley diode See FOUR-LAYER DIODE.

shock mount A structure that secures a microphone while minimizing the pickup of vibrations through the table, floor, or other surface on which the microphone is placed.

shock therapy See ELECTROSHOCK, **1**.

shoran Contraction of SHORT-RANGE NAVIGATION.

shore effect The tendency of radio waves traveling along a shore to be bent either toward or away from the shore. It can occur because of differences in surface conductivity and/or atmospheric temperature over land, as compared with water.

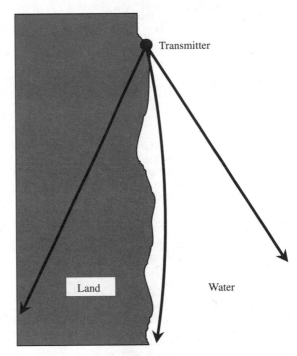

shore effect

shore station A fixed, land-based radio station that communicates with ships at sea.

shore-to-ship communication See SHIP-TO-SHORE COMMUNICATION.

short circuit An often unintended low-resistance path through which current bypasses a component or circuit.

short-circuit current In a power supply, the current that flows when the output is directly shorted. Many power supplies have shutdown devices that cause the current to stop flowing when the output terminals are short-circuited; other supplies effectively insert resistance in series with the load, if necessary, to limit the current.

short-circuiting switch A rotary selector switch in which unused contacts are automatically short-circuited.

short-circuit parameter A parameter for which zero resistance is assumed in the part of the circuit under consideration. The current amplification factor (alpha) of a common-base-connected transistor is such a parameter because its collector load resistance is assumed to be zero.

shorted-stub tuning Tuning a stub to match a feeder to an antenna by sliding a short-circuiting bar along the two wires of the feeder.

shorting bar A thick, metal strap for short-circuiting two binding posts.

shorting link A sheet-metal strip for connecting together two binding posts.

shorting loop In a telephone system, a device that short-circuits two specified points for the purpose of testing or line fault location.

shorting stick A metal rod with an insulating handle, used to short-circuit a charged capacitor to remove the shock hazard.

shorting switch See SHORT-CIRCUITING SWITCH.

short-line tuning Use of a parallel capacitance to tune a transmission line that is less than a quarter-wave long.

short-range navigation Contraction, shoran. Navigation by means of SHORT-RANGE RADAR.

short-range radar A radar having a 50- to 150-mile maximum line-of-sight range for a 1-square-meter reflecting target that is perpendicular to the radar beam.

short skip Skip of only a few hundred miles range. Also see SHORT-SKIP COMMUNICATION.

short-skip communication Radio communication via the ionosphere over relatively short distances (400 to 1300 miles). See, for example, SPORADIC-E SKIP.

short-term drift The gradual change in the value of a quantity, such as frequency or voltage, observed over a comparatively brief interval, as opposed to change occurring over a long period. Compare LONG-TERM DRIFT.

short-term effect The variation of any electrical parameter over a relatively brief time interval. Example: frequency drift over a short time period. Also called *short-time effect*.

short-term stability Stability reckoned over a comparatively brief time interval, as opposed to stability for a long period. Compare LONG-TERM STABILITY.

short-time effect See SHORT-TERM EFFECT.

shortwave **1.** Pertaining to wavelengths shorter than 200 meters (i.e., frequencies higher than 1.50 MHz). **2.** Pertaining to the frequencies above the standard amplitude-modulation broadcast band (above 1.605 MHz), but below 30 MHz.

shortwave converter A superheterodyne converter for adapting a longwave receiver (such as a broadcast receiver) for shortwave reception.

shortwave listener Abbreviation, SWL. A radio hobbyist who receives, but does not transmit, shortwave signals.

shortwave receiver Any radio receiver capable of intercepting and demodulating signals in the range 1.705 MHz to 30 MHz.

shortwave transmitter Any radio transmitter capable of producing energy in the range 1.705 MHz to 30 MHz.

shot-effect noise Electrical noise caused by random fluctuations in a current, as in a diode or transistor. Also see EQUIVALENT NOISE RESISTANCE. Compare THERMAL NOISE.

shotgun microphone A highly directional microphone sensitive only to sounds coming from a specific direction; the response pattern has a narrow main lobe. It name results from its long, cylindrical configuration.

shot noise Electrical noise arising from intermittent impulses, such as those produced by spark discharges, make-and-break contacts, etc. Its name results from its resemblance to pistol shots.

shrink The amount by which a material being measured with an electronic instrument decreases in surface dimension. Compare STRETCH.

shrink tubing Plastic sleeving placed over a conductor or at a conductor/connector joint, and made to shrink tightly with the application of heat.

shunt Synonym, *parallel*. **1.** Pertaining to the connection of one component across (in parallel with) another (e.g., *shunt resistor*). **2.** Pertaining to connection of components in such a manner that they each (or all) are subjected to identical voltages. **3.** A deliberately produced short circuit between two specific points in a device or system. **4.** To deliberately bypass some part of a system by means of a short circuit.

shunt circuit See PARALLEL CIRCUIT.

shunt-diode rectifier A rectifier circuit in which the diode is connected in parallel with the source and load. Compare SERIES-DIODE RECTIFIER.

shunt-fed **1.** Pertaining to a circuit or device in which the direct-current operating voltage and alternating-current signal voltage are applied in parallel to an electrode. **2.** Pertaining to a base-grounded vertical antenna excited at some point above ground.

shunt feed See PARALLEL FEED.

shunt feedback A feedback system in which the fed-back signal is presented to the input of the network in parallel with the input signal. Compare SERIES FEEDBACK.

shunt generator An electric generator in which the armature and field windings are connected in parallel. Compare SERIES GENERATOR.

shunting effect The condition in which a quantity, such as stray capacitance or resistance, acts in parallel with another quantity. Example: the shunting (parallel) resistance of an electrolytic capacitor.

shunt leads Interconnecting wires used for the purpose of attaching a shunting component to a test instrument.

shunt limiter See PARALLEL LIMITER.

shunt loading The parallel insertion of reactance in a circuit, for the purpose of impedance matching.

shunt motor An electric motor whose armature and field windings are connected in parallel. Compare SERIES MOTOR.

shunt regulator A voltage-regulator circuit in which the controlled transistor or vacuum tube is in parallel with the output (load) terminals. Compare SERIES REGULATOR.

shunt resistor **1.** A resistor connected in parallel with a meter or recorder to increase its current range. **2.** A resistor connected in parallel with a voltmeter to convert it into a current meter. Compare MULTIPLIER RESISTOR.

shunt-series circuit See PARALLEL-SERIES CIRCUIT.

shunt tee junction A waveguide H-PLANE TEE JUNCTION.

shunt-type frequency multiplier A varactor frequency multiplier circuit in which the varactor is in parallel with the input and output. Compare SERIES-TYPE FREQUENCY MULTIPLIER.

shunt-type resonance bridge A resonance bridge in which the impedance arm is a parallel-resonant circuit. Compare SERIES-TYPE RESONANCE BRIDGE.

shunt-wound generator See SHUNT GENERATOR.

shunt-wound motor See SHUNT MOTOR.

SI Abbreviation of (Standard) INTERNATIONAL SYSTEM OF UNITS.

S/I Abbreviation of *signal-to-intermodulation ratio*.

Si Symbol for SILICON.

sibilants **1.** High-frequency (hissing) components of speech. **2.** High-frequency sounds or audio signals.

SIC Abbreviation of *specific inductive capacity* (see DIELECTRIC CONSTANT).

SiC Formula for SILICON CARBIDE.

sideband **1.** With respect to a carrier, one of the additional frequencies generated by the modulation process. In simple amplitude modulation, the two sidebands are $fc + fm$ and $fc - fm$, where fc is the carrier frequency, and fm is the modulation frequency. **2.** Pertaining to sidebands as defined in **1**.

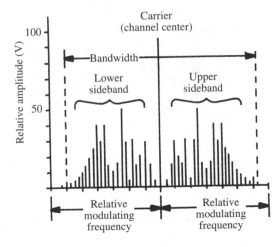

sideband

sideband attenuation See SIDEBAND CUTTING.

sideband cutting Elimination or attenuation of the sidebands of a modulated signal by a circuit having insufficient bandwidth.

sideband frequency The frequency of the modulation-generated signal accompanying a carrier. One sideband frequency is that of the carrier minus that of the modulating signal; another is the sum of the carrier and the modulation frequency. See also SIDEBAND, **1**.

sideband interference **1.** Interference arising from one or both of the normal sidebands of a modulated signal. **2.** Interference caused by spurious sidebands, resulting from overmodulation.

sideband power The power contained in the sideband(s) of a signal.

sideband slicing See SIDEBAND CUTTING.

sideband splatter In an amplitude-modulated or single-sideband signal, the emission of sideband energy at frequencies other than within the designated channel. Also simply called splatter.

sideband technique A method of using, for communications or other purposes, one or both of the sidebands of a modulated signal without the carrier.

side-chain amplifier An auxiliary amplifier that is external to a main amplifier. Such an amplifier might be used, for example, in a feedback channel or in a volume-compression or volume-expansion channel.

side frequency See SIDEBAND.

sidelobe In an antenna directional pattern, a lobe other than the main lobe(s)—especially one at, or nearly at, right angles, with respect to the main lobe(s).

sidelobe suppression Elimination of the sidelobe(s) from the radiation pattern of an antenna.

sidestacked antennas Antennas mounted in a horizontal line, parallel to each other, and connected by a common coupler to a transmitter or receiver.

sideswiper A manual telegraph key operated by moving the lever sideways, rather than up and down.

sidetone **1.** In wire telephony, the reproduction by the receiver of sounds picked up by the transmitter of the same telephone. **2.** In radiotelegraphy, an audible tone actuated when the carrier is transmitted. It allows the sending operator to hear Morse code elements as they are sent.

sidetone telephone A telephone set with no provision for canceling the sidetone.

siemens Symbol, S. The SI unit of conductance. The conductance of a component or medium in siemens is equal to the reciprocal of the resistance in ohms.

Siemen's electrodynamometer A spring-tension meter that operates by means of torque, with zero current through the device representing zero torque. It can be used for measurements of current, voltage, or power.

Sierra   Phonetic alphabet code word for the letter S.

sig   Abbreviation of SIGNAL.

sign   **1.** Any indicator denoting whether a value is positive or negative. **2.** A graphic device indicating an operation. Examples: + (addition), × (multiplication). **3.** Any symbol. An ampersand, for example, is an "and" sign. **4.** A characteristic symptom of malfunction or improper operation (e.g., a high standing-wave ratio in an antenna system is a sign of an impedance mismatch).

signal   An electrical quantity, such as a current or voltage, that can be used to convey information for communication, control, calculation, etc.

signal-actuated voice recorder   Abbreviation, SAVOR. A recorder that goes into operation automatically when the speaker starts talking and stops when the speaker finishes.

signal amplitude   The intensity of a signal quantity (see SIGNAL).

signal booster   See PREAMPLIFIER.

signal channel   In a system, a channel through which only signals flow, control and modifying impulses being accommodated by other channels.

signal circuit   A circuit handling signal currents and voltages to the exclusion of control and operating currents and voltages.

signal conditioner   Any accessory device (such as a peak probe, demodulator probe, current shunt, etc.) used to modify or change the function of a basic instrument (such as an electronic voltmeter).

signal converter   See CONVERTER, **1**.

signal current   The current component of a signal, as opposed to operating current in a system.

signal diode   A diode designed primarily for light-duty signal applications (detection, demodulation, modulation, curve changing), as opposed to the heavy-duty applications of power diodes and rectifiers.

signal distance   In two words (bit groups) of the same length, the number of corresponding bit positions whose states differ. For example, the signal distance between 01001 and 10011 is 3.

signal-flow analysis   A graphic method of analyzing circuits, particularly those using feedback, through the use of diagrams in which straight arrows represent transmission paths, dots represent nodes, and curved arrows represent feedback paths.

signal-flow diagram   The transmission-path diagram used in SIGNAL-FLOW ANALYSIS.

signal gain   The gain of an amplifier circuit—especially if used in small-signal applications. See also AMPLIFICATION, and GAIN.

signal generator   An instrument that produces signals of precise frequency and amplitude, usually over a wide range.

signal ground   **1.** Any circuit point that remains at zero signal potential. **2.** A connection to a point that is deliberately maintained at zero signal potential.

signal/image ratio   See SIGNAL-TO-IMAGE RATIO.

signaling   In a communications system, the exchange of data in electrical form, either analog or digital.

signaling rate   In data communications, the speed at which data is transmitted. It is commonly expressed in bits per second (bps). Also, it is sometimes expressed in baud or in words per minute (wpm).

signaling time slot   In a communications signal, a specified interval of time, starting at a certain instant in each signal frame. This interval is used exclusively for the purpose of signaling.

signal injection   **1.** The introduction of a signal into a circuit. **2.** A method of troubleshooting in communications receivers. A signal generator is used to introduce a test signal into each stage, starting with the output and proceeding stage-by-stage toward the input, until the defective stage or component is located.

signal injector   A simple (usually single-frequency) signal generator used in troubleshooting to introduce a test signal at selected points in a circuit, to locate malfunctioning stages or components. Also see SIGNAL INJECTION, **2**.

signal intensity   See SIGNAL STRENGTH.

signal inversion   Phase reversal of a signal passing through a circuit, device or medium.

signal level   At a given point in a circuit, the strength of a signal, with respect to a reference amplitude.

signal loss   **1.** A reduction in the amplitude of a signal as it passes through a system. **2.** The complete disappearance of a signal. **3.** See FRACTIONAL GAIN.

signal mixer   See MIXER.

signal/noise ratio   See SIGNAL-TO-NOISE RATIO.

signal notcher   See NOTCH FILTER.

signal peaker   See PEAK FILTER.

signal power   The amplitude of a signal expressed in watts, milliwatts, or microwatts, as opposed to amplitude expressed as a current or voltage.

signal processor   Any device, (e.g., preamplifier, expander, amplitude limiter, delay network) inserted into or added onto a system to modify an input or output signal.

signal rectification   The conversion of an alternating-current signal into a proportionate di-

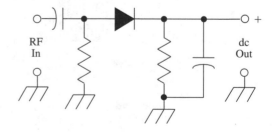

signal rectification

rect-current signal, usually by means of a diode circuit.

signal rectifier   See SIGNAL DIODE.

signal regeneration   See SIGNAL RESHAPING.

signal reshaping   1. The processing of a signal so that it acquires its original waveform. Also called *signal regeneration.* 2. Passing a digital signal of any type through a circuit that delivers a uniform output pulse on a real-time one-to-one basis.

signal shifter   1. A device used for quickly changing the frequency of a transmitted signal. 2. A device that automatically causes a transmitted signal to be sent on a frequency that differs from the receiver frequency by a known and predetermined amount. 3. See MIXER, 1. 4. See CONVERTER, 1.

signal squirter   See SIGNAL INJECTOR.

signal strength   The amplitude of a signal, usually in terms of voltage. Current or power is specified in some applications.

signal-strength meter   1. See FIELD-STRENGTH METER. 2. See S-METER.

signal synthesizer   A special signal generator delivering signals whose frequency, amplitude, and waveshape can be adjusted at will.

signal time delay   The time required for an element of a signal to be transmitted through a circuit or network. This delay results in phase shift in an amplifier.

signal-to-distortion ratio   In a receiver, the ratio of the desired signal to the level of distortion other than the specified signal. Usually expressed in decibels (dB).

signal-to-image ratio   Abbreviation, S/I. In a receiver, the ratio of signal amplitude to image amplitude, both being measured in the same units. It is usually expressed in decibels (dB).

signal-to-noise-plus-noise ratio   Abbreviation, (S+N)/N. In a receiver, the ratio of the combined signal and noise amplitude to the amplitude of the noise alone. It is usually expressed in decibels (dB). Peak voltages are used to determine this ratio in the case of pulse noise; root-mean-square (rms) voltages are used in the case of random noise.

signal-to-noise ratio   Abbreviations: S/N, SNR. In a receiver, the ratio of signal amplitude to noise amplitude. It is usually expressed in decibels (dB). Peak voltages are used to determine this ratio in the case of pulse noise; root-mean-square (rms) voltages are used in the case of random noise.

signal-to-noise-and-distortion ratio   Abbreviation, SINAD. In a receiver, the ratio of the desired signal to the level of noise and distortion, other than the specified signal. It is usually expressed in decibels (dB).

signal tracer   A tuned or untuned detector/amplifier having an input probe and an output indicator (meter, loudspeaker, or both), for following a test signal through a circuit.

signal voltage   The voltage component of a signal, as opposed to the operating voltage of the circuit generating or passing the signal.

signal wave   1. Any electromagnetic disturbance of a periodic nature that is modulated to convey information. 2. The visual illustration or rendition of an electromagnetic disturbance that is modulated to convey information.

signal winding   In a magnetic amplifier or saturable reactor, the coil that receives the control current.

signal window   See WINDOW, 2.

signal wobbulator   A frequency modulator used with an unmodulated signal generator to provide sweep signals for visual alignment. Also see WOBBULATOR.

sign bit   A one-bit SIGN DIGIT.

sign digit   A character indicating the sign (positive or negative) of the value of the field or word to which it is attached (usually at the end).

signed field   In a computer record, a field having a number whose sign is indicated by a SIGN DIGIT.

significant digits   See SIGNIFICANT FIGURES.

significant figures   In a numerical quantity, especially one expressed in scientific (power of 10) notation, those figures (digits) that depict a quantity to a required, relevant, or justifiable degree of precision. For example, 173,201 expressed to three significant figures is 1.73×10^5; 0.00477583 expressed to four significant figures is 4.776×10^{-3}. See also SCIENTIFIC NOTATION.

silencer   See AUTOMATIC NOISE LIMITER.

silent alarm   In security systems, the transmission of a warning signal to attendant human operators and/or computers, without producing an audible or visible warning to intruders.

silent alignment   See VISUAL ALIGNMENT.

silent piano   See ELECTRONIC PIANO.

silica pencil   A rod of silicon dioxide heated to emit infrared rays.

silicon   Symbol, Si. A metalloidal element. Atomic number, 14. Atomic weight, 28.086. Silicon is abundant in the earth's crust. It is used in many semiconductor devices, including integrated circuits, diodes, photocells, rectifiers, and transistors.

silicon capacitor   See VOLTAGE-VARIABLE CAPACITOR.

silicon carbide   Formula, SiC. A compound of silicon and carbon valued as a semiconductor, an abrasive material, and a refractory substance. The commercial product is made by heating carbon and sand to a high temperature in an electric resistance furnace. Also called CARBORUNDUM.

silicon cell   A type of photovoltaic cell using specially processed silicon as the light-sensitive material. This cell has a comparatively high voltage output.

silicon-controlled rectifier   Abbreviation, SCR. A four-layer semiconductor device commonly used in power control applications (e.g., light dimmers and motor-speed controls). The electrodes are called the anode, the cathode, and the gate. The control signal is applied to the gate.

silicon-controlled switch Abbreviation, SCS. A four-terminal semiconductor switching device similar to the SILICON-CONTROLLED RECTIFIER. It is used for light-duty switching.

silicon crystal detector **1.** See SILICON JUNCTION DIODE. **2.** See SILICON POINT-CONTACT DIODE. **3.** A point-contact diode in which a lump of silicon is contacted by either a fine wire (cat whisker) or a blunt-tipped steel screw under pressure.

silicon detector See SILICON CRYSTAL DETECTOR.

silicon-diffused transistor A silicon bipolar transistor fabricated by diffusion techniques. It is characterized by high power-dissipation tolerance.

silicon diode A semiconductor diode in which the semiconductor material is specially processed silicon. Also see SILICON JUNCTION DIODE and SILICON POINT-CONTACT DIODE.

silicon dioxide Formula, SiO_2. A compound of silicon and oxygen. In the passivation of transistors and integrated circuits, a thin layer of silicon dioxide is grown on the surface of the wafer to protect the otherwise exposed junctions.

silicone A polymeric material characterized by a recurring chemical group containing oxygen and silicon atoms in the main chain as links. Various silicone compounds have numerous uses in electronics.

silicon junction diode A semiconductor diode using a pn junction in a silicon wafer. Compare SILICON POINT-CONTACT DIODE.

silicon on sapphire Abbreviation, SOS. Pertaining to integrated-circuit fabrication in which a silicon epitaxial layer is grown on a sapphire substrate.

silicon oxide A compound containing both silicon monoxide and silicon dioxide, and having dielectric properties. It is used in the manufacture of metal-oxide-semiconductor (MOS) devices.

silicon photocell A photocell using a silicon pn junction as the light-sensitive medium.

silicon point contact The contact between a pointed metal wire (cat whisker) and a silicon wafer.

silicon point-contact diode A diode in which a tungsten wire (cat whisker) contacts a wafer of single-crystal silicon. It is useful at ultra high frequencies (UHF). Compare SILICON JUNCTION DIODE.

silicon rectifier A semiconductor rectifier consisting essentially of a junction between n- and p-type silicon inside a specially processed wafer or plate of single-crystal silicon.

silicon resistor See CRYSTAL RESISTOR.

silicon solar cell A relatively heavy-duty photovoltaic cell using specially processed silicon as the light-sensitive material.

silicon steel A high-permeability, high-resistance steel containing 2 to 3 percent silicon. It is used as core material in transformers and other electromagnetic devices.

silicon transistor A transistor in which the semiconductor material is single-crystal silicon.

silk-enameled wire Wire whose insulation is a layer of silk on top of an enamel coating.

silver Symbol, Ag. A precious metallic element. Atomic number, 47. Atomic weight, 107.87. It is used in circuits where low resistance and high Q are mandatory.

silver arsenide trisulfide See PROUSTITE.

silver-dollar construction Printed-circuit assembly on a disk-shaped board, about the size of a U.S. silver dollar.

silver-mica capacitor A fixed capacitor made by painting or depositing a silver layer (capacitor plate) on both faces of a thin mica film (dielectric separator).

silver migration The undesirable tendency of silver to be removed from one location and deposited in another under adverse environmental conditions.

silver solder A solder consisting of an alloy of silver, copper, and zinc. It has a comparatively high melting temperature. Also see HARD SOLDER.

silverstat A multiconductor device used to adjust the balance of a resistance or reactance bridge.

similar decimals Two or more decimal numbers that have the same number of digits to the right of the radix point (e.g., 3.14 and 6.39, or 1.234 and 1.000).

simple quad A combination of two parallel paths—each containing two elements in series.

simple tone A pure sine-wave tone (i.e., one having negligible harmonic content).

simplex channel An information channel for unidirectional transmission.

simplex system **1.** In data communications, a system that transmits data in only one direction. Compare FULL DUPLEX SYSTEM and HALF DUPLEX SYSTEM. **2.** In voice communications via radio, a direct path over a single channel, used alternately for transmitting and receiving at each station.

simplex telegraphy Wire telegraphy in which only one message at a time can be sent over a line.

simplification of circuits See CIRCUIT SIMPLIFICATION.

simulation **1.** Imitation of the performance of a process, device, or system. **2.** The use of a mathematical model to represent a physical process, device, or system. **3.** The use of a computer, sometimes with virtual reality hardware and software, to mimic a real-life situation.

simulator **1.** A software or hardware system capable of simulation (see SIMULATION, **2**). **2.** A computer program whose implementation allows programs written for one computer to be compatible with another computer. **3.** A system of equipment for simulation (see SIMULATION, **1**).

simulcast **1.** To broadcast a program over two or more different channels at the same time. **2.** To broadcast a program over two or more different types of mode, for example, television and radio, at the same time. **3.** A program broadcast over two or more channels or modes at the same time.

simultaneous access See PARALLEL ACCESS.

simultaneous broadcasting See SIMULTANE-OUS TRANSMISSION.

simultaneous computer See PARALLEL COM-PUTER.

simultaneous transmission The transmission of the same information in two or more channels, or by means of two or more processes, at the same time.

sin Abbreviation of SINE.

sin⁻¹ Symbols for the inverse of the sine function, also called the *arc sine*.

sine Abbreviation, sin. The trigonometric function a/c, the ratio of the opposite side of a right triangle to the hypotenuse.

SINAD See SIGNAL-TO-NOISE-AND-DISTORTION RATIO.

sine galvanometer A galvanometer in which the sine of the angle of deflection is proportional to the current. Compare TANGENT GAL-VANOMETER.

sine law The variation in radiation intensity in any direction from a linear source is proportional to the sine of the angle between the axis of the source and the direction of interest.

sine potentiometer A POTENTIOMETER whose output is proportional to the sine of the angle through which the shaft has rotated.

sine wave A periodic wave that can be represented by a sine curve (i.e., its amplitude is directly proportional to the sine of a linear quantity, such as displacement or time). Compare COSINE WAVE.

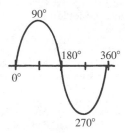

sine wave

singing Audible oscillation in a circuit or device, such as the low-level buzz emanating from the filament of a lamp dimmed with a phase-control circuit.

single-address coding In computer programming, the use of instruction words that contain the address for the location of the data to be operated on, and no other addresses.

single-board computer Abbreviation, SBC. A computer built entirely on one circuit board.

single-button microphone A carbon microphone having only one button attached to the diaphragm. Also see BUTTON MICROPHONE.

single-channel codec A form of CODEC intended for operation on a single signal source, rather than in a multiplexed system.

single-chip codec An integrated circuit contained entirely on one chip and in one package that can accomplish all CODEC functions. It can be a single-channel device or multiplexed.

single-cotton-covered wire Wire insulated with one layer of cotton.

single cotton enameled wire Wire insulated with one layer of cotton on top of an enamel coating.

single-crystal Pertaining to the internal structure of a crystalline material, in which the characteristic lattice is continuous throughout any size piece of the material. Also called MONOCRYS-TALLINE.

single-crystal material A substance, such as a semiconductor, of which a sample, regardless of size, consists of only one crystal (i.e., there are no grain boundaries). Also see SINGLE-CRYS-TAL. Compare POLYCRYSTALLINE MATERIAL.

single-crystal pulling See CZOCHRALSKI METHOD.

single-dial control Adjustment of a multistage system via one rotatable, calibrated control attached to a ganged arrangement that tunes all stages simultaneously.

single-diffused transistor A transistor in which only one diffusion of an impurity substance is made. Thus, in a diffused-base transistor, a single diffusion provides the base region and at the same time creates the emitter-base and collector-base junctions. Compare DOUBLE-DIF-FUSED TRANSISTOR.

single-electron memory Abbreviation, SEM. A computer memory in which the movement of one electron can change a logic bit from 1 (high) to 0 (low) or vice-versa.

single-element rotary antenna See ONE-ELE-MENT ROTARY ANTENNA.

single-ended circuit A circuit that has one end grounded, as opposed to a double-ended circuit and push-pull circuit.

single-ended deflection In an oscilloscope or similar device, horizontal or vertical deflection provided by a single-ended deflection channel. Compare PUSH-PULL DEFLECTION.

single-ended input An input circuit with one terminal grounded (or the equivalent ungrounded input circuit). Also called *unbalanced input*. Compare BALANCED INPUT.

single-ended multiplexer A group of analog switches that selects from several analog signals.

single-ended output An output circuit with one terminal grounded (or the equivalent ungrounded output). Also called *unbalanced output*. Compare BALANCED OUTPUT.

single-ended push-pull circuit An arrangement, such as a complementary symmetry circuit, that provides push-pull output with single-ended input, but does not require transformers.

single-frequency Also called *fixed-frequency*. Pertaining to circuits or devices that normally operate at one frequency only (e.g., *single-frequency oscillator*).

single-frequency amplifier An amplifier that normally operates at only one frequency (or within a very narrow band of frequencies) (e.g., an intermediate-frequency amplifier, or a selective audio-frequency amplifier used for harmonic analysis or bridge balancing).

single-frequency duplex Two-way communications over one medium or frequency. Voice-actuated (VOX) or break-in devices are used at both ends of the circuit.

single-frequency oscillator An oscillator that normally delivers a signal at only one frequency until it is switched to another frequency (e.g., *crystal-controlled oscillator*).

single-frequency receiver A radio or television receiver that normally operates at one carrier frequency, rather than being tunable. Such receivers are used in monitoring specific programs, picking up standard-frequency signals, and in similar applications.

single-gun color picture tube A color-television picture tube in which the image is produced by a single beam that scans the red, green, and blue color-phosphor dots sequentially.

single-hop propagation Long-distance radio-wave propagation involving only one encounter with the ionosphere, and involving no intermediate reflections from the earth's surface.

single-hop return distance The return distance, as a function of the angle of departure from a radio transmission, from a layer of the ionosphere. The illustration shows the maximum possible distance under average conditions and assuming an angle of departure of zero degrees.

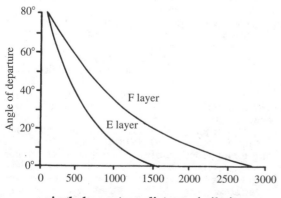

single-hop return distance (miles)

single-image response In an oscilloscope presentation, a single pattern, as opposed to a double-trace pattern.

single-inline package Abbreviation, SIP. A flat, molded component package having terminal pins along one edge. All the pins lie along a common line.

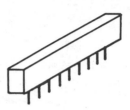

single-inline package

single-junction transistor See UNIJUNCTION TRANSISTOR.

single-layer coil A coil whose turns are wound side by side in one layer.

single-layer solenoid See SINGLE-LAYER COIL.

single-line tap In a telephone system, a connection that provides or designates a separate line (e.g., to serve a single household).

single-loop feedback Feedback through only one path.

single phase Pertaining to the presence or generation of one alternating-current phase only. Compare POLYPHASE.

single-phase full-wave Pertaining to a rectifier operated from a single-phase alternating-current (ac) power line, and rectifying both half-cycles of ac voltage. Compare SINGLE-PHASE/HALF WAVE.

single-phase/full-wave bridge A bridge rectifier operated from a single-phase alternating-current supply, usually from the untapped secondary winding of a transformer. Compare SINGLE-PHASE/FULL-WAVE CIRCUIT and SINGLE-PHASE/HALF-WAVE CIRCUIT.

single-phase/full-wave circuit A rectifier circuit in which each half-cycle of single-phase alternating current is rectified by a separate diode supplied from the ends of a center-tapped winding of a transformer. Compare SINGLE-PHASE/FULL-WAVE BRIDGE and SINGLE-PHASE/HALF-WAVE CIRCUIT.

single-phase/half-wave Pertaining to a rectifier operated from a single-phase alternating-current (ac) power line, and rectifying only one half-cycle of ac voltage.

single-phase/half-wave circuit A rectifier circuit in which a diode, output load, and single-phase alternating-current supply are connected in series, only one half-cycle of the cycle being passed by the diode. Compare SINGLE-PHASE/

FULL-WAVE CIRCUIT and SINGLE-PHASE/FULL-WAVE BRIDGE.

single-phase rectifier See SINGLE-PHASE/FULL-WAVE BRIDGE, SINGLE-PHASE/FULL-WAVE CIRCUIT, and SINGLE-PHASE/HALF-WAVE CIRCUIT.

single-point ground One ground connection to which all channels of a circuit are returned. Such a common connection eliminates or greatly minimizes the common coupling often encountered when separate ground points are used.

single-pole double-throw Abbreviation, SPDT. Descriptive of an electrical, electronic, or mechanical switch with a pole that can be connected to either of two adjacent poles, but not to both.

single-pole single-throw Abbreviation, SPST. Descriptive of an electrical, electronic, or mechanical switch with a pole that can be connected to an adjacent pole (or disconnected from it) at will. It is used to provide the make and break function in a single circuit.

single rail 1. A one-conductor communications medium with a ground return. 2. A one-conductor data line, with a ground return.

single shot Also called *one shot*. Pertaining to circuit operation in which a single input pulse applied to a switching device (such as a multivibrator) causes it to deliver a single output pulse, rather than switch to a stable "on" state. A MONOSTABLE MULTIVIBRATOR operates in this mode.

single-shot multivibrator See MONOSTABLE MULTIVIBRATOR.

single sideband Abbreviation, SSB. Pertaining to a system of modulation in which one of the sidebands from an amplitude-modulated signal is attenuated or canceled out, leaving only one sideband. The carrier is generally suppressed also.

single-sideband suppressed-carrier Abbreviation, SSSC or SSBSC. Pertaining to a system of modulation in which the carrier and one sideband from an amplitude-modulated signal are suppressed; only the remaining sideband is transmitted. Sometimes this mode is simply called SINGLE SIDEBAND.

single signal Pertaining to a mode of reception in which signals appear on only one side of zero beat, enhancing selectivity and reducing interference among received signals. Most superheterodyne receivers have this feature; most direct-conversion receivers do not.

single-signal receiver A superheterodyne receiver that achieves high selectivity via a selective filter in the intermediate-frequency amplifier chain. Signals appear on only one side of zero beat, in a band whose width can be adjusted or selected for various values from about 200 Hz to 3 kHz.

single silk-covered wire Wire insulated with one layer of silk.

single-skip propagation See SINGLE-HOP PROPAGATION.

single-step operation See STEP-THROUGH OPERATION.

single sweep In an oscilloscope, a single time-axis deflection of the electron beam. Also see SWEEP, 1, 2. Compare RECURRENT SWEEP.

single-sweep blocking oscillator A blocking oscillator that cuts off after generating a single cycle or pulse.

single-throw switch A single-action switch with two or more poles.

single-tone keying Modulated continuous-wave keying. A single audio-frequency tone is used to amplitude-modulate or frequency-modulate the carrier.

single-track recorder A recorder, such as a magnetic-tape recorder or a graphic recorder, that permits recording along only one track.

single-trip multivibrator See MONOSTABLE MULTIVIBRATOR.

single-tuned circuit A circuit tuned by varying only one of its components [e.g., an intermediate-frequency transformer in which only the secondary coil (rather than both primary and secondary) is tuned].

single-turn coil 1. A coil consisting of a single turn of wire, tubing, or strip. 2. See RING INDUCTOR. 3. See SHADING COIL.

single-turn potentiometer A potentiometer that can be adjusted through its entire resistance range by no more than one full rotation of the shaft. Usually, the turning range is somewhat less than a full circle (e.g., 300 degrees).

single-wire-fed antenna See WINDOM ANTENNA.

single-wire line 1. See SINGLE-WIRE TRANSMISSION LINE. 2. A single wire used for communication or control purposes. The earth furnishes the return path.

single-wire transmission line An antenna transmission line or feeder consisting of one wire only (see, for example, WINDOM ANTENNA).

sink 1. A device or circuit into which current drains. 2. See HEATSINK.

sink circuit The circuit associated with a load or other sink. Compare SOURCE CIRCUIT, 2.

sinker A piece of semiconductor material used to reduce the base-collector junction resistance in a bipolar transistor.

sintering A process in which various solid bodies are formed from fusible powders at temperatures below their melting points. Example: *sintered magnetic core*.

sinusoidal Having the shape and properties of a SINE WAVE.

SIO Abbreviation of *serial input/output*.

SIP Abbreviation of SINGLE-INLINE PACKAGE.

six-phase rectifier A polyphase rectifier circuit operated from a three-phase supply. The output ripple frequency is six times the supply frequency.

SJD Abbreviation of SILICON JUNCTION DIODE.

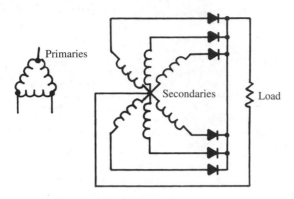

six-phase rectifier

skating In a phonograph turntable, the tendency of the tone arm to swing toward the spindle during record play, independent of the action produced by the stylus following the groove.

skeletal code A generalized computer routine needing only certain parameters to be usable for a specific application.

skeleton bridge A bridge consisting of an adjustable arm (potentiometer) and a pair of binding posts for each of the other three arms. Suitable resistors, capacitors, or inductors are connected to the binding posts to set up the bridge circuit desired.

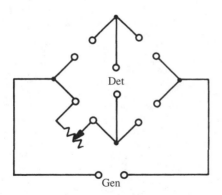

skeleton bridge

skeleton-type assembly 1. A method of electronic-equipment construction in which a minimum of supporting members is used. An example is the use of an open framework, instead of a chassis, to support components. 2. An assembly of electronic equipment, consisting essentially of a foundation unit (containing the basic circuitry) and plug-in units for setting up various complete equipments.

skew 1. A condition resulting from failure of the horizontal synchronization in facsimile or television. The picture appears distorted, and appears as a non-rectangular parallelogram. 2. In a print display, nonalignment of columns resulting from an incorrect number of line spaces in each line. 3. In a probability function, an accumulation of values toward either side of center.

skewing 1. The bending of a curve away from its normal shape. 2. In a differential amplifier, the offset between two signals. Also see OFFSET.

Skiatron A special form of cathode-ray tube, with the fluorescent coating replaced by a screen of halide crystals that darken, instead of glow, when exposed to the electron stream.

skin depth The depth to which current penetrates below the surface of a conductor, as a result of the SKIN EFFECT.

skin effect The tendency of high-frequency alternating current to travel along the surface of a conductor; the high-frequency reactance is lower along the outside than at the center of a conductor. This tends to increase the resistivity of solid conductors at high alternating-current frequencies, as compared with low frequencies and direct current.

skip 1. Ionosphere-reflected radio transmissions. 2. In a computer program, an instruction whose sole function is that of causing a jump to the next instruction.

skip distance For a signal propagated via the ionosphere, the distance from the transmitter to the point at which the returned skywave strikes the earth.

skip fading For a signal propagated via the ionosphere, changes in signal strength caused by fluctuations in the altitude and/or contour of the ionized layer(s).

skip zone See ZONE OF SILENCE.

skirt selectivity 1. The bandwidth between points of high attenuation (usually 30 dB or 60 dB) on the selectivity curve in a communications receiver. 2. The relative steepness of the attenuation-vs.-frequency curve in a communications receiver.

SKM Abbreviation of *sine-cosine multiplier.*

skyhook 1. Colloquialism for ANTENNA. 2. A wire antenna supported by a captive balloon or kite.

sky noise Radio noise originating in outer space.

skywave A radio wave propagated by ionospheric reflections and/or refractions. Compare GROUND WAVE.

skywave correction A factor applied to long-range radionavigation signals to account for the time delay resulting from ionospheric propagation.

skywire See OUTSIDE ANTENNA.

slab 1. A relatively thick body of quartz, ceramic, semiconductor, or dielectric. 2. See SUBSTRATE.

slap back The return of sounds by an acoustically reflective object or surface a short distance away, resulting in almost immediate echoes.

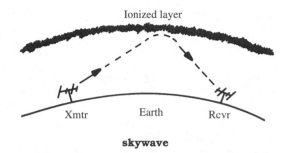

skywave

slashed-field-gun CRT A straight-gun television picture tube (see STRAIGHT-GUN CRT). Because the gap between the anodes in this tube is slanted, the electrostatic field is diagonal, causing the electron and ion beams to be diverted at an angle.

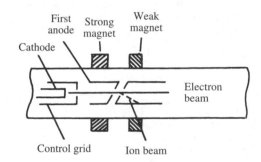

slashed-field-gun CRT

slave flash A photoflash operated by the light flash from another such unit.

slave relay A relay operated by, and whose action follows, a MASTER RELAY.

SLC Abbreviation of STRAIGHT-LINE CAPACITANCE.

sleeping sickness A gradual increase in transistor leakage current.

sleep machine An electronic device sometimes used as an aid for relaxation or sleeping. It consists of a wideband audio-frequency noise generator that produces low-level sounds similar to the noise of waves on a beach or a light wind through trees.

sleeve antenna A vertical antenna in which the upper half is a quarter-wave rod connected to the inner conductor of a coaxial feeder, and the lower half is a quarter-wave metal sleeve connected to the outer conductor of the feeder. Also called COAXIAL ANTENNA.

sleeving A material in tubular form that can be slipped over another material [e.g., insulating sleeving for wires (spaghetti)].

slew rate In an operational amplifier, the rate at which the output can be driven between its limits.

SLF Abbreviation of STRAIGHT-LINE FREQUENCY.

slice A semiconductor wafer cut from a single-crystal ingot.

slicer See CLIPPER-LIMITER.

slide-back meter An electronic voltmeter in which an unknown alternating-current signal voltage applied to the input of an amplifier stage is bucked by an internal, adjustable, accurately known signal voltage. The internal voltage is adjusted until a null occurs, indicating that its magnitude is equal to that of the unknown voltage.

slider A flat-spring contact that slides along the turns of a resistance or inductance coil to vary the coil's resistance or inductance. Also called a WIPER.

slide-rule dial A dial mechanism having a straight scale that resembles a slide rule.

slide switch A switch actuated by sliding a block-shaped button. Compare BAT-HANDLE SWITCH, PADDLE SWITCH, and ROCKER SWITCH.

slide switch

slide wire A simple potentiometer consisting of a single, straight piece of resistance wire with a sliding contact. Also see SLIDE-WIRE RESISTOR.

slide-wire bridge A simple four-arm bridge in which the adjustable element is a single, straight resistance wire along which a clip or slider is moved, and that supplies two arms of the bridge (one on each side of the slider).

slide-wire resistor A variable resistor consisting of a single wire (straight or coiled) along whose length a slider is moved to vary the resistance.

sliding contact A contact that mates with another contact, or moves along a contacted surface, with a sliding motion. Also called SELF-CLEANING CONTACT and WIPING CONTACT.

slip 1. In an eddy-current brake, coupling, or drive, the difference in speed between the field magnets and the iron eddy-current ring. 2. In a synchronous motor, the difference between rotor speed and stator speed.

slip clutch In a gear or rack-and-pinion drive system, a device that releases the load if the torque becomes excessive. The gears then slip instead of being damaged.

slip ring   See COLLECTOR RING, **1**.

slip speed   See SLIP, **2**.

slope   **1.** The slant of a line (graph) in rectangular coordinates, depicted as the ratio of the change in the dependent variable y to the change in the independent variable x. If (x_1, y_1) and (x_2, y_2) are two points on the line, then slope m is determined by $m = (y_2 - y_1)/(x_2 - x_1)$. **2.** The slant of a line in rectangular coordinates as defined in **1**, when the line is tangent to a curve (graph) at a specified point. **3.** The skirt(s) of a selectivity curve, particularly in a communications receiver, where a small change in frequency results in a significant change in gain or attenuation. **4.** The ratio of the extent of change in a quantity to the extent of change in some other quantity, when a causal relation exists between the magnitudes of the quantities. Example: See SLOPE RESISTANCE.

slope detector   An amplitude-modulation (AM) receiving circuit detuned to one side of resonance (i.e., to a point along the skirt of the selectivity curve) to detect a frequency-modulated (FM) signal. The FM swing occurs along the slope of the resonance curve. Slope detection is useful in narrowband FM when conventional FM circuitry is not available.

slope resistance   The ratio of a small change in voltage to a small change in current at an electrode or in a component.

slop-jar capacitor   See WATER CAPACITOR.

slop-jar rectifier   See ELECTROLYTIC RECTIFIER.

slot   **1.** In the armature of a motor or generator, a groove in which the windings are laid. **2.** The notch in the response curve of a crystal filter.

slot antenna   A microwave antenna that radiates energy through a slot cut in a surface, such as the metal skin of an aircraft.

slot cell   A reinforcing, dielectric material (such as plastic) placed in the slot of a ferromagnetic core.

slot coupling   Coupling microwave energy between a waveguide and a coaxial cable by means of two slots, one in the waveguide and the other in the outer conductor of the cable.

slot-discharge resistance   See CORONA RESISTANCE.

slot insulation   **1.** Insulation of wires in the slots of the armature of a motor or generator (see SLOT, **1**). **2.** A material in the form of tape or sheets, used for the purpose defined in **1**.

slot radiator   See SLOT ANTENNA.

slotted line   A device consisting of a section of air-dielectric coaxial line arranged for microwave measurements. The outer conductor is a metal cylinder, and the inner conductor is a concentric metal rod. The cylinder is provided with a lengthwise slot through which a small pickup probe extends for sampling the electromagnetic field inside the device. The probe is attached to a carriage that slides along a graduated scale on the outside of the cylinder. Radio-frequency energy is injected into one end of the line through a coaxial cable; as the probe moves along, response points are indicated by an external detector connected to the probe. The scale is read at these points to determine frequency, standing-wave ratio, impedance, and power. An alternate form of slotted line uses a section of slotted waveguide, instead of a section of coaxial line.

slotted rotor   See SERRATED ROTOR PLATE.

slotted section   See SLOTTED LINE.

slotted waveguide   See SLOTTED LINE.

slot width   **1.** The width of a slot in the armature of a motor or generator (see SLOT, **1**). **2.** The bandwidth of the notch in the response curve of a band-suppression filter of any kind. See, for example, NOTCH FILTER.

slow-acting relay   Any relay designed to operate at some finite period following the application of the actuation voltage.

slow-blow fuse   A fuse in which the melting wire breaks apart slowly. The time delay allows the fuse to withstand momentary current surges that do not damage the protected equipment, but that would cause a fast-blow fuse to break the circuit needlessly.

slow-break, fast-make relay   A relay that opens slowly and closes rapidly.

slow-break, slow-make relay   A relay that opens slowly and closes slowly.

slow charge   Storage-battery charging in which a low current is passed through the battery over a long period of time. It ensures that the rated ampere-hour capacity will be restored to the battery.

slow death   **1.** The gradual deterioration of transistor performance. **2.** The gradual deterioration in the performance of a component, circuit, device, or system.

slow drift   The gradual change of a quantity or setting (usually in one direction). Compare FAST DRIFT.

slow-make, fast-break relay   A relay that closes slowly and opens rapidly.

slow-make, slow-break relay   A relay that closes slowly and opens slowly.

slow-operate, fast-release relay   See SLOW-MAKE-FAST-BREAK RELAY.

slow-operate, slow-release relay   See SLOW-MAKE-SLOW-BREAK RELAY.

slow-release, fast-operate relay   See SLOW-BREAK-FAST-MAKE RELAY.

slow-release, slow-operate relay   See SLOW-BREAK-SLOW-MAKE RELAY.

slow storage   A form of memory with long storage and recovery time.

slow time scale   An extended time scale, i.e., one larger than the time unit of the system under consideration.

SLS   Abbreviation of SIDELOBE SUPPRESSION.

slug   **1.** A movable core of ferromagnetic material, used to tune (varying the inductance of) coil by changing its position along the axis of the coil. Also see SLUG-TUNED COIL. **2.** A copper ring attached to the core of a relay for time-delay purposes (see SLUG-TYPE DELAY RELAY).

slug-tuned coil A coil whose inductance is varied by means of a ferromagnetic slug that slides in and out of the coil.

slug tuner A tuner for a radio or television receiver or test instrument, using slug-tuned coils.

slug-type delay relay A delayed-response relay that achieves time delay through the action of a heavy copper slug on the core. The slug forms a low-resistance, short-circuited single turn in which a current is induced by the magnetic flux, resulting from energizing the relay. The resulting flux of the slug opposes the buildup of relay-coil flux.

slumber switch An alarm-reset switch on an electronic clock radio. If the alarm activates, the slumber switch (usually a pushbutton device) can be pressed to turn off the alarm for a predetermined length of time. Also called *snooze button.*

SLW Abbreviation of STRAIGHT-LINE WAVELENGTH.

Sm Symbol for SAMARIUM.

small-current amplifier **1.** A direct-current (dc) amplifier for low-level input currents (i.e., currents of 1 milliampere or less). **2.** An amplifier (such as a silicon-transistor unit) requiring very low dc operating current.

small-scale frequency response For an analog circuit, the output frequency at which the level is –3 dB, relative to the maximum level, with a small signal at the input, normally 1 volt peak-to-peak.

small signal A low-amplitude signal. Such a signal covers so small a part of the operating characteristic of a device that operation is essentially linear. Compare LARGE SIGNAL.

small-signal analysis Analysis of circuit or component operation in which it is assumed that the signals deviate from (fluctuate to either side of) the steady bias levels by only a small amount. Also see SMALL SIGNAL.

small-signal bandwidth The frequency at which the output signal of an analog circuit decreases to –3 dB, relative to the value for direct current. The output voltage is generally set at 0.1 volt peak-to-peak for testing this value so that the circuit is not overdriven.

small-signal component **1.** A coefficient or parameter (such as amplification, transconductance, dynamic resistance, etc.) calculated or measured under conditions of small-signal operation. Also see SMALL SIGNAL and SMALL-SIGNAL EQUIVALENT CIRCUIT. **2.** A device designed for operation at low signal levels.

small-signal diode See SIGNAL DIODE.

small-signal equivalent circuit For a given transistor circuit, the equivalent circuit for low signal levels (i.e., at amplitudes lower than saturation and cutoff levels). Also see EQUIVALENT CIRCUIT.

small-signal operation Operation at low signal amplitudes (i.e., at signal levels that do not extend into the saturation or cutoff levels of a transistor, diode, or other component).

small-signal transistor A transistor designed for low-level applications, such as the amplification of small voltages and currents and low-voltage switching. Compare POWER TRANSISTOR.

SmallTalk A high-level computer programming language that uses a graphical user interface (GUI). It is used in complex design and research, and in robotics.

smartness The ability of an electronic system, especially a computer or control system, to perform a complete series of operations, substituting alternative steps, where necessary—all with a minimum of instructions from, and supervision by, human operators.

smearing In television or facsimile, a form of picture distortion caused by an excessively narrow receiving bandpass. The image appears fattened and horizontally blurred. Contrast might also be lost.

smectic crystal A liquid crystal in which the molecules are arranged in parallel layers and cannot slide past each other.

S meter In a radio communications receiver, a meter graduated in S units and/or decibels to indicate the strength of a received signal.

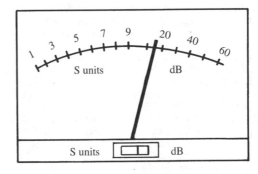

S meter

Smith chart A curvilinear graph on which complex-number impedance values can be plotted. It is useful in evaluating the behavior of radio-frequency circuits, transmission lines, and antenna systems—especially with regard to impedance mismatches and standing-wave ratio.

smoke alarm A device that produces audible and/or visible signals in the presence of smoke or unusual gases in the air. Also see PHOTOELECTRIC SMOKE ALARM.

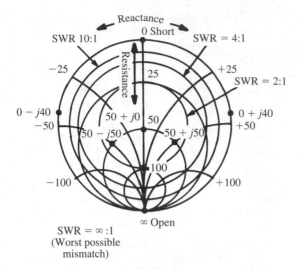

Smith chart

smoke control See PHOTOELECTRIC SMOKE CONTROL.

smoke detector Any circuit or device used to sense the presence of smoke or noxious gases. Some types detect changes in the ionization potential of the air; others sense changes in the dielectric constant of the air. Also see PHOTOELECTRIC SMOKE DETECTOR.

smoke sensor See SMOKE DETECTOR.

smooth **1.** Relatively free from surface irregularity. **2.** To reduce or eliminate irregularities in the voltage or current from a direct-current power source. **3.** To reduce or eliminate irregularities in data or signal amplitude.

smoothing choke A power-supply filter choke having a core with an air gap that prevents saturation at maximum rated direct current. Compare SWINGING CHOKE.

smoothing factor For a power-supply filter, a quantity approximately equal to $6.28fRC$, where f is the alternating-current frequency in Hertz, R is the filter resistance (in an RC filter) or the series reactance of the choke (in an LC filter) in ohms, and C is the filter capacitance in farads.

smoothing filter **1.** A filter for smoothing the alternating-current ripple component of a direct-current power supply following rectification. It can consist of one or more parallel capacitors of large value, and one or more series chokes of large inductance. **2.** A low-pass filter used at the output of a digital-to-analog (D/A) converter for eliminating high-frequency components generated by sampling.

SMPTE Abbreviation of SOCIETY OF MOTION PICTURE AND TELEVISION ENGINEERS.

smudge See SQUEEZEOUT.

SN Abbreviation of semiconductor network.

S/N Abbreviation of SIGNAL-TO-NOISE RATIO.

Sn Symbol for TIN.

snake **1.** A long, strong, flexible wire or strip used to pull other wires through electrical conduits. **2.** To route wires or cables through a group of circuits, components, or boards.

snap-action switch A switch that snaps quickly into the on or off position to prevent arcing and consequent premature contact deterioration.

snap diode A semiconductor diode in which switch-off time after carrier storage is extremely short (e.g., under 1 nanosecond).

snap magnet A magnet that reduces the tendency for arcing in relay-control instruments, thereby minimizing electromagnetic interference and prolonging contact life.

snap-on connector An electrical connector that locks in place, reducing the chance that it will detach unless it is deliberately removed.

snapshot dump During a computer program run, a dump, for debugging purposes, of certain storage areas.

snap switch See SNAP-ACTION SWITCH.

sneak current Unintended current flow through a path that is auxiliary to a main circuit.

sneak path A path through which current is accidentally detoured; it is usually a leakage path.

Snell's law A rule of physics that applies to visible light passing from air (or a vacuum) to some medium with an index of refraction c. If the light ray strikes the medium at an angle u, relative to a line normal (perpendicular) to the surface, and passes into the medium at angle v relative to the normal, then $(\sin u)/(\sin v) = c$.

sniffer See EXPLORING COIL.

sniperscope A telescope, snooperscope, or starlight scope for a carbine or rifle.

(S+N)/N Abbreviation of SIGNAL-PLUS-NOISE-TO-NOISE RATIO.

SNOBOL Acronym for *string-oriented symbolic language*, a computer-programming language for manipulating character strings.

snooperscope **1.** An infrared-sensitive device that permits viewing objects and surroundings in total darkness. It presents the image on a fluorescent screen. **2.** A rifle-mounted starlight scope.

snow A type of television picture interference that typically occurs when the signal-to-noise ratio is low (the reception is marginal or poor). Characterized by countless tiny out-of-focus light spots, whose rapid, random motion mimics the appearance of falling snow.

SNR Abbreviation of SIGNAL-TO-NOISE-RATIO.

soak value The smallest value of current that will cause saturation of a relay core.

Society of Motion Picture and Television Engineers Abbreviation, SMPTE. A group that decides on various procedures in video recording and reproduction, both on magnetic media (tape or disk) and on film.

socket A (usually female) fixture into which a plug, integrated circuit, or other component is inserted for easy installation in, or removal from, a circuit.

socket punch   See PUNCH, **2**.

sodium   Symbol, Na. A metallic element of the alkali-metal group. Atomic number, 11. Atomic weight, 22.9898.

sodium silicate   See WATER GLASS.

sodium-vapor lamp   A gas-discharge lamp containing neon and a small amount of sodium. After the filaments of the lamp are lighted for a short time, the heat vaporizes the sodium, and the filaments are disconnected by an automatic switch. Under the influence of the voltage across the lamp, the sodium vapor glows with a characteristic yellow light.

sofar   A system for pinpointing the source of underwater sounds (coming from as far away as 2000 miles) through triangulation. The name is an acronym for *sound fixing and ranging.*

soft-drawn wire   Wire that is highly malleable, and is therefore easily bent and unbent. Compare HARD-DRAWN WIRE.

soft iron   A grade of iron, used in some cores, that is easily demagnetized.

soft solder   A low-melting-point solder.

software   **1.** Vendor-supplied or user-generated programs or groups of programs for a computer or computer system. **2.** The detailed instructions for performing a particular operation with a calculator or a computer.

soft X rays   Low-frequency (long-wavelength) X rays. Such radiation has relatively poor penetrating power. Compare HARD X RAYS.

sol   **1.** Abbreviation of SOLUTION. **2.** Abbreviation of SOLUBLE.

solar access   For a specific property or location, the availability of direct exposure to the sun's rays as a source of energy.

solar absorption index   A quantitative measure of the effect of the sun on the ionospheric absorption of radio waves.

solar activity   See SOLAR RADIATION and SUNSPOT cycle.

solar battery   A battery composed of solar cells connected in series and/or parallel for increased output.

solar cell   A photovoltaic power transducer that converts visible light to electricity. It is called a cell because its output is a low direct-current voltage. Such cells can be connected in series and/or parallel to provide useful electric power output.

solar cycle   See SUNSPOT CYCLE.

solar energy   **1.** The total energy arriving from the sun, over a given period of time and within a specific surface area, at a given location on the surface of the earth. **2.** Any energy derived entirely from the sun.

solar-energy conversion   Any process that changes solar radiant energy into another useful form.

solar flare   An eruption on the sun, visible as a bright spot or streak on the solar disk. These events result in the emission of high-speed, charged subatomic particles. These particles reach the earth in a few hours following the first appearance of the flare, and cause changes in the earth's magnetic field and ionosphere. This can disrupt radio communications—especially at medium and high frequencies (about 300 kHz to 30 MHz).

solar flux   An indicator of general solar activity. The solar noise level is measured at a particular frequency, such as 2800 MHz. The solar flux tends to be highest during periods of the greatest sunspot activity and immediately following a solar flare.

solar laser   See SUNLIGHT-POWERED LASER.

solar panel   An array consisting of a number of series-connected or series-parallel-connected solar cells mounted on a flat plate.

solar power   Useful amounts of electricity obtained from suitable arrays of solar cells.

solar radiation   Electromagnetic energy of various wavelengths originating in the sun. Such radiation, after passing through the earth's atmosphere, consists mostly of infrared rays and visible light. Some ultraviolet rays also reach the earth's surface.

solar relay   See SUN SWITCH.

solar switch   See SUN SWITCH.

solar wind   Continuous emission of high-speed subatomic particles by the sun. It causes distortion of the lines of flux in the earth's magnetic field. It becomes more intense following a solar flare.

solder   **1.** A metal alloy (usually of tin and lead) that is melted to electrically and mechanically join pieces of other metals. Also see HARD SOLDER and SOFT SOLDER. **2.** To join metals with solder.

solder

Solder type	Melting point (°F/°C)	Principal uses
Tin-lead 50:50, rosin-core	430/220	Electronic circuits
Tin-lead 60:40, rosin-core	370/190	Electronic circuits, low-heat
Tin-lead 63:37, rosin-core	360/180	Electronic circuits, low-heat
Tin-lead 50:50, acid-core	430/220	Non-electronic metal bonding
Silver	600/320	High-current, high-heat

soldering Joining (usually nonferrous) metal parts with solder, a lead-alloy substance. Compare BRAZING.

soldering gun An electric soldering iron having the general shape of a handgun. The element heats and cools more rapidly than the element in a typical soldering iron. The element is heated by pressing a device similar to the trigger on a pistol.

soldering iron An electric or nonelectric tool having a heated tip for melting solder.

solderless breadboard A foundation (see BREADBOARD, **1**) on which a circuit can be assembled by plugging components into tiny jacks without the use of solder.

solderless connection A connection between leads, or between leads and terminals, accomplished entirely through crimping, pinching, splicing, or wire wrapping. Solder is not used. Also see WIRE-WRAP CONNECTION.

solderless terminal A terminal to which a solderless connection can be made. Also see WRAP POST.

solenoid **1.** A coil of wire having a single layer, wound on a cylindrical form. **2.** A multilayer coil used as an electromagnet, and usually having a straight, iron core.

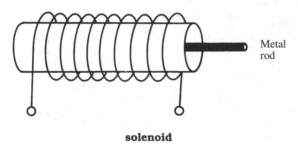

Metal rod

solenoid

solenoid switch A switch consisting of a solenoid coil (see SOLENOID, **2**) into which a core is pulled by the magnetic field to close a pair of contacts.

solid **1.** One of the states of matter. It is characterized by a definite shape and volume, and by atoms that maintain a fixed position, relative to each other. Compare GAS, LIQUID, and PLASMA. **2.** An enclosed, defined volume of three-dimensional space. **3.** In communications, descriptive of error-free reception of a series of coded signals. **4.** In printing and data transmission, a large print area whose entire surface is of equal and maximum intensity (of ink, light, or darkness).

solid angle Unit, steradian. The angle within the apex of a cone formed by all line segments between the center of a sphere and a defined circle on the surface of the sphere.

solid circuit Any circuit consisting of a single piece of hardware that is not normally separated into smaller parts.

solid conductor See SOLID WIRE.

solid electrolyte A solid substance affording ionic action similar to that in a liquid electrolyte.

solid electrolytic capacitor A capacitor using a solid electrolyte.

solid ground See DIRECT GROUND.

solid-state Pertaining to devices and circuits in which the flow of charge carriers (electrons and holes) is controlled in specially prepared blocks, wafers, rods, or disks of solid materials. Semiconductor devices, such as transistors and integrated circuits, are solid-state components.

solid-state battery An atomic battery consisting essentially of a photovoltaic cell in combination with a quantity of radioactive material, whose radiation causes the cell to generate electricity.

solid-state camera A video camera device that makes use of solid-state technology. The target is a matrix of charge-coupled devices (CCDs). When light strikes these devices, charge carriers are separated in a manner similar to that in a photovoltaic cell. The matrix is scanned according to a particular scheme, and the voltages developed in each CCD combine to produce the video signal output.

solid-state capacitor See SOLID ELECTROLYTIC CAPACITOR.

solid-state chronometer Any semiconductor device to indicate or measure time.

solid-state circuit See MONOLITHIC INTEGRATED CIRCUIT.

solid-state lamp **1.** See LIGHT-EMITTING DIODE. **2.** See LASER DIODE. **3.** See ELECTROLUMINESCENT CELL.

solid-state maser A device, such as the ruby maser, in which the stimulated medium is a solid material.

solid-state photosensor A semiconductor photodiode or phototransistor, as opposed to a phototube.

solid-state physics The branch of physics concerned with the nature and applications of such solids as electronic semiconductors.

solid-state relay **1.** A sensitive relay consisting of a conventional electromagnetic relay preceded by a transistorized amplifier. **2.** A completely electronic relay (i.e., one without moving parts) in which switching transistors provide the on and off states. **3.** See THYRISTOR.

solid-state thermometer An electronic thermometer utilizing one or more solid-state components, such as transistors, integrated circuits, or thermistors.

solid-state thyratron See SILICON-CONTROLLED RECTIFIER and SILICON-CONTROLLED SWITCH.

solid-state tube A semiconductor device (diode, rectifier, transistor, SCR, etc.) whose housing and base allow it to replace directly an electron tube.

solid tantalum capacitor A capacitor using tantalum as a solid electrolyte.

solid wire Wire consisting of a single strand of metal. Compare STRANDED WIRE.

solute A substance that is dissolved in some other substance. Also see SOLUTION, **1**.

solution **1.** A well-diffused mixture of two or more substances. It can consist of a gas in a liquid, a gas in a solid, a gas in a gas, a liquid in a solid, or a solid in a solid. A solution, typically, is molecular (i.e., there is no chemical reaction between its constituents). Also see SATURATED SOLUTION; SOLUTE; SOLVENT, **1**; and SUPERSATURATED SOLUTION. **2.** The result of solving a problem or making a calculation. Also called *answer* or *result.*

solution conductivity The electrical conductivity of a solution, such as an electrolyte. The conductivity (and conversely, the resistance) depends on the number and mobility of ions in the solution.

solution-conductivity bridge A direct-current bridge specially designed and calibrated to measure the conductivity of chemical solutions.

solution pressure In an electrolyte into which a metal body is immersed, the force that causes the metal to tend to pass into solution as positive ions and to form a Helmholtz double layer.

solvent **1.** A fluid that dissolves other materials. **2.** The constituent of a solution that dissolves one or more other constituents. Thus, in a salt-water solution, water is the solvent and salt the solute. Also see SOLUTION, **1**.

SOM Abbreviation of *start of message.*

Sonalert Tradename for a small, but loud, sound reproducer used with solid-state circuits for alarm purposes.

sonar A system of detection and ranging by means of sonic and ultrasonic signals. In this system of echo ranging, the distance to an underwater object is determined from the time it takes a sound signal to reach the object and be reflected back to the transmitter. The name is an acronym for *sound navigation and ranging.*

sonde A device for automatically gathering meterological data at high altitudes. An example is the *radiosonde.*

sone A unit of loudness for an individual listener. The level of 1 sone is the loudness of a 1000-Hz tone that is 40 dB above the particular listener's threshold of hearing.

sonic altimeter An altimeter (see ABSOLUTE ALTIMETER) using sound waves. The time required for a transmitted wave to reach a target and be reflected back to the transmitter is proportional to the distance between the transmitter and the target.

sonic boom An explosive sound occurring when the shock wave produced by an aircraft flying at supersonic speed strikes the earth.

sonic delay line A delay line using electroacoustic transducers and an intervening medium through which a sound wave is transmitted.

sonic depth finder See ACOUSTIC DEPTH FINDER.

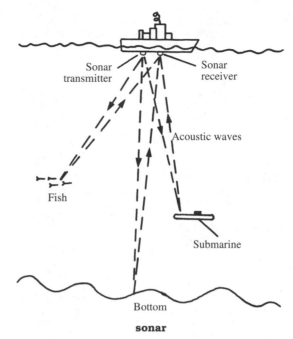

sonar

sonic thermocouple A thermocouple whose heat-absorbing properties are enhanced by subjecting it to acoustic vibrations.

sonobuoy A buoy equipped with an acoustic receiver and radio transmitter. The device is parachuted into the water, where it receives submarine sounds and transmits them to a monitoring station. Several sonobuoys communicating with a computer will track the path of a submarine.

sonovox An electronic device used to produce special sound effects when it is held against the throat of the operator. The special sounds are formed into words by the operator's mouth.

SOP Abbreviation of *standard operating procedure.*

sophisticated electronics Advanced electronics theory and operations, usually dealing with complex devices or systems and requiring rigorous analysis to describe their operation and devise applications. Compare UNSOPHISTICATED ELECTRONICS.

sorption processes Processes whereby certain substances (e.g., activated charcoal) occlude and retain gases and vapors. A chamber containing such a substance is often useful in the production of a vacuum. Sorption includes both absorption and adsorption.

sort **1.** To group information items using their keys. Also see KEY. **2.** To group information items according to some system of classification, as to print an alphabetical list of words stored in a random sequence.

sorting routine A computer program for sequencing data items according to key words (values in specific fields) of the different records.

SOS 1. The international radiotelegraph distress signal; equivalent to *mayday* in radiotelephony. It consists of three dits ("dots"), followed by three dahs ("dashes"), followed by three more dits. **2.** Abbreviation of SILICON ON SAPPHIRE.

sound The vibratory or wave phenomenon to which the sense of hearing is responsive. Conducted by waves in solids, liquids, and gases; not propagated through a vacuum.

sound absorption The nonreflection and nontransmission of acoustic energy by a body or medium, and the attendant conversion of the acoustic energy into another form of energy (usually heat).

sound absorption coefficient A quantitative expression of the extent to which a surface absorbs acoustic energy (as opposed to reflecting, transmitting, diffusing, or scattering it).

sound amplifier 1. An audio amplifier—especially the sound channel of a television system. **2.** A device, such as a horn or reflector, that directly boosts the intensity of sound at a given listening point.

sound analyzer An instrument, often a wave analyzer equipped with a microphone, for measuring such characteristics of sound as amplitude, frequency (pitch), and harmonic content (timbre).

sound articulation See ARTICULATION.

sound bars In a television picture, horizontal bars resulting from interference between the audio and video channels of the receiver.

sound carrier In a television signal, the frequency-modulated carrier that transmits the audio part of the program. Compare VIDEO CARRIER.

sound chamber An air enclosure, usually a box or can, for modifying the acoustic qualities of sound or of an audio signal.

sound detector The discriminator or ratio detector that demodulates the sound signal in a television receiver circuit.

sound-energy density Sound energy per unit volume, expressed in joules per cubic meter or ergs per cubic centimeter.

sound-energy flux The average rate of flow of sound energy through a specified area, as expressed in ergs or joules per second.

sound field A volume of space or material containing sound waves.

sound film Motion-picture film on which a sound track is recorded. Also see OPTICAL SOUND RECORDING.

sound flux The rate of flow of sound energy, usually expressed in terms of sound pressure at a point or over a unit area normal to the direction of sound propagation.

sound gate An optical device used to convert the sound track of a movie film into electrical impulses.

sound generator Any combination of oscillator, amplifier, and transducer (loudspeaker or headphones) for producing sound waves.

sound-hazard integrator An instrument used to measure cumulative noise exposure received by persons in noisy environments. One such instrument provides direct readings in percent of permissible exposure.

sound IF amplifier In a television receiver circuit, the separate amplifier for the sound intermediate frequency. See, for illustration, INTERCARRIER RECEIVER and SPLIT-SOUND RECEIVER.

sound-level meter See SOUND SURVEY METER.

sound marker A marker indicating the sound-carrier point on a television alignment curve displayed on an oscilloscope screen.

sound-marker generator A special radio-frequency signal generator (or a special circuit in a television-alignment generator) for the production of a sound marker.

sound mirage See ACOUSTIC MIRAGE.

sound mix In sound recording or reproduction, the composite output from an audio mixer circuit.

sound-on-film recording See OPTICAL SOUND RECORDING.

sound-on-sound recording The simultaneous recording (on a single track on magnetic tape) of new material with previously recorded material. The old recording is not erased.

sound-operated relay 1. A relay operated indirectly from sound, through the medium of a

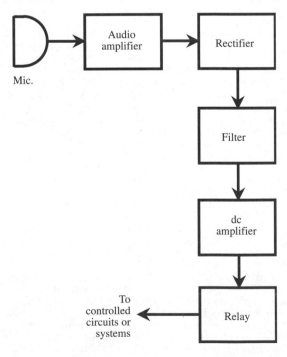

sound-operated relay

pickup microphone and amplifier. **2.** A relay having a delicately poised armature that operates directly from sound vibrations.

sound power The total sound energy per unit time produced by a sound source, as expressed in ergs per second or in watts.

sound power level The extent, in decibels, by which SOUND POWER exceeds one picowatt (10^{-12} watt).

sound pressure **1.** The force exerted by sound waves on a surface area, expressed in dynes per square centimeter (as an rms value over 1 cycle). The sound pressure is proportional to the square root of sound-energy density. **2.** The instantaneous difference between actual air pressure and average air pressure at a given point.

sound pressure level The extent, in decibels, via which SOUND PRESSURE exceeds 20 micropascals (2.0×10^{-5} pascal).

sound probe A transducer used to receive acoustic vibrations for detection or measurement purposes.

sound recording The ' electrical recording of sound, using cylinder, disc, tape, wire, or other comparable storage medium.

sound-recording system A complete, integrated array of equipment for recording sound, including such components as microphones, amplifiers, pickups, filters and other shaping networks, attenuators, level indicators, and recording mechanisms. Compare SOUND-REPRODUCTION SYSTEM.

sound reinforcement Intensification of sound by horns, resonant chambers, or other acoustical devices.

sound relay See SOUND-OPERATED RELAY.

sound reproduction The electrical reproduction of sound from recordings on vinyl discs, magnetic tapes, magnetic discs, compact optical disbs, etc.

sound-reproduction system A complete, integrated array of equipment for the playback of recorded sound, including such components as tape or record players, amplifiers, filters and other shaping networks, attenuators, level indicators, loudspeakers, and headphones. Compare SOUND-RECORDING SYSTEM.

sound spectrograph A device that produces a display of sound amplitude vs. frequency. Similar to a SPECTRUM ANALYZER, except that it operates at audio frequencies (about 20 Hz to 20 kHz) and is actuated by acoustic disturbances, rather than by electromagnetic signals.

sound spectrum The continuous band of frequencies (about 20 Hz to 20 kHz) constituting audible sounds, and sometimes the immediately adjacent (subaudible and superaudible) frequencies.

sound stage The apparent dimensions of a sound source.

sound survey meter A portable instrument for measuring the intensity and other characteristics of sound.

sound sweetening In audio recording or reproduction, the modification of the sound to achieve some desired effect.

sound system A sound-recording system, sound-reproduction system, or a combination of the two.

sound takeoff In a television receiver circuit, the point at which the frequency-modulated sound signal is extracted from the complex signal.

sound track The variable-density or variable-width recording on one side of the film in sound-on-film recording and reproduction. Also see OPTICAL SOUND RECORDING.

sound transducer See ACOUSTIC TRANSDUCER.

sound-transmission coefficient See ACOUSTICAL TRANSMITTIVITY.

sound trap In a television receiver circuit, a wavetrap that prevents the sound signal from entering the picture channels.

sound unit See PHONE, **2**.

sound wave The vibratory phenomenon produced in a medium by acoustic energy. A sound wave in air consists of alternate compressions and rarefactions of the air. Also see ACOUSTIC WAVE.

source **1.** The origin of a signal or electrical energy (e.g., a transmitting station). **2.** In a field-effect transistor, the electrode that is equivalent to the emitter of a common-emitter-connected bipolar transistor, or the cathode of a vacuum tube. **3.** That which is being transcribed to magnetic tape. **4.** Manufacturer, wholesaler, or retailer.

source circuit **1.** The circuit associated with the source electrode of a field-effect transistor. **2.** A generator circuit. Compare SINK CIRCUIT.

source code See SOURCE LANGUAGE.

source computer A computer for compiling a source program.

source-coupled multivibrator A multivibrator circuit using field-effect transistors, in which feedback coupling is achieved with a common source resistor for the two FETs. This circuit is equivalent to the emitter-coupled bipolar-transistor-type multivibrator.

source data automation A means of storing a master data file for easy duplication, whenever necessary.

source deck An audio or video tape player that reproduces original recordings in the editing process.

source follower A field-effect-transistor circuit in which the output is taken across a resistor between source and ground. This circuit is equivalent to the emitter follower, and is a unity-gain stage whose impedance-transformation characteristics make it ideal in signal conditioning, buffering, and impedance-matching applications.

source impedance **1.** The impedance of a generator in a circuit. **2.** The impedance of the source electrode of a field-effect transistor.

source language A computer programming language from which is derived (by a compiler) the machine (object) language on which the computer operates.

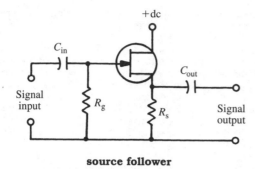

source follower

source program A computer program written in a source language.

south magnetic pole The south pole of the equivalent bar magnet constituted by earth's magnetic field (see EARTH'S MAGNETIC FIELD). The south magnetic pole lies close to the geographic south pole. Compare NORTH MAGNETIC POLE.

south-seeking pole Symbol, S. The so-called south pole of a magnet. When a bar magnet is suspended horizontally, this pole points to earth's south magnetic pole. Compare NORTH-SEEKING POLE.

SP Abbreviation of STACK POINTER.

sp **1.** Abbreviation of *single pole.* **2.** Abbreviation of *special.*

space-charge field **1.** The electric field existing within a group of charged particles. **2.** The electric field existing in a plasma.

space diversity See DIVERSITY RECEPTION.

space-diversity reception See DIVERSITY RECEPTION.

space division A method of data transfer in which different paths are used for the transmission of different signals.

space-division switch A switch having two or more ports and different paths connecting the ports.

space lattice The three-dimensional, redundant pattern formed by atoms and molecules in a crystal and having a shape that is characteristic of a particular crystalline material.

spacer An insulating rod or bar that serves to hold apart the conductors of a two-wire, four-wire, or coaxial air-dielectric transmission line.

space suppression Following the printing of a line by a printer, the prevention of normal paper travel.

space-time-space switch Abbreviated STS switch or STSS. A large switching array with two space switch blocks and a time switch block between them.

space wave One of the components of an electromagnetic ground wave. The space wave, unlike the *surface wave,* is not earth-guided. It has two components: the *direct wave* and the *ground-reflected wave.*

spaghetti Slender, varnished-cambric tubing used as slipover insulation for wires and busbars.

span On an instrument scale, the difference between the highest value and the lowest value.

spark See ELECTRIC SPARK.

spark absorber **1.** See SPARK SUPPRESSOR. **2.** See KEY-CLICK FILTER.

spark coil A small induction coil. Its name is derived from its initial purpose of supplying the high voltage for spark plugs in gas engines.

spark energy The energy dissipated by an electric arc or spark.

spark gap A device consisting essentially of two metal points, tips, or balls that are separated by a small air gap. A high voltage applied to the electrodes causes a spark to jump across the gap.

sparking distance The maximum separation of the electrodes of a spark gap at which a given voltage will produce a spark.

sparking voltage The lowest voltage that will cause a spark to jump across a gap of a given width.

spark killer See SPARK SUPPRESSOR.

sparkover A discharge in air, a vacuum, or a dielectric. It is characterized by sparking between electrodes in the medium.

spark plate In some automobile radios, a noise-interference-eliminating bypass capacitor in which the chassis is one plate.

spark-plug suppressor A small resistive device connected in series with a spark plug to suppress electrical noise arising from the ignition in an internal combustion engine.

spark quencher See SPARK SUPPRESSOR.

spark suppressor A resistor, capacitor, and/or diode used to eliminate or minimize sparking between make-and-break contacts.

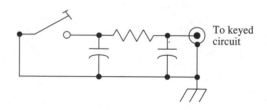

spark suppressor

spark-suppressor diode See SUPPRESSOR DIODE.

spatial distribution The three-dimensional directional pattern of a transducer (such as an antenna, microphone, or speaker).

spc **1.** Abbreviation of *silicon point contact.* **2.** Abbreviation of *silver-plated copper.*

SPDT Abbreviation of SINGLE-POLE/DOUBLE-THROW (switch or relay).

speaker   See LOUDSPEAKER.

speaker damping   See DAMPED LOUDSPEAKER.

speaker-level audio   In a sound reproduction system, radio receiver, or other audio circuit, an audio-frequency signal of sufficient amplitude to drive a speaker or speaker system directly, without the need for additional amplification.

speaking arc   A method of modulated-light transmission. An electric arc is modulated by audio-frequency signals.

special character   A printed, displayed, or encoded character other than a numeral or letter, such as an ampersand (&) or a pound sign (#). Also called SYMBOL.

special effects   Various techniques used in film-making, computer animation, and videotape recording for achieving certain visual scenes or images.

special-purpose computer   A computer designed to handle problems or be suitable for applications of a specific category; a dedicated computer.

special-purpose calculator   An electronic calculator intended for essentially "nonmathematical" purposes, such as biorhythm data, astrological information, metric conversions, musical composing, etc.

specific address   See ABSOLUTE ADDRESS.

specification   **1.** For an electronic device, a statement of performance over specific parameters. Example: for a high-fidelity stereo amplifier, 50 watts per channel over a frequency range of 10 Hz to 30 kHz, with less than 1 percent total harmonic distortion. **2.** A precise listing of requirements or expectations.

specific conductivity   Conductance per unit volume. In SI units, this is expressed in siemens per cubic centimeter (S/cm^3).

specific dielectric strength   For an insulant, the dielectric strength per millimeter of thickness.

specific gravity   Abbreviation, sp gr. The ratio of the density of a material to the density of a substance accepted as a standard (usually water at 4 degrees Celsius or 39.2 degrees Fahrenheit).

specific inductive capacity   See DIELECTRIC CONSTANT.

specific resistance   See RESISTIVITY.

specific sound-energy flux   See SOUND INTENSITY.

spectral comparative pattern recognizer   Acronym, SCEPTRON. Equipment used to classify automatically complex signals obtained from information that has been converted into electrical signals.

spectral density   For a complex signal, the amount of energy contained within a given band of frequencies.

spectral energy distribution   The occurrence of different amounts of energy in different areas of a spectrum (as in a visible-light spectrum, sound spectrum, or radio-frequency spectrum).

spectral response   The characteristic of a device, such as a photocell or the human eye, that describes the device's sensitivity to radiations of various frequencies in a given spectrum.

spectral sensitivity   The color response of a light-sensitive device.

spectrograph   A recording SPECTROMETER.

spectrometer   **1.** An instrument used to measure spectral wavelengths. **2.** An instrument used to measure the index of refraction. **3.** See MASS SPECTROMETER.

spectrophotometer   A photoelectric instrument for chemical analysis. In the device, light passing through the material under analysis is broken up into a spectrum that is examined with a photoelectric circuit, which, in turn, plots a spectrogram.

spectroscope   An instrument that resolves a radiation into its various frequency components and permits measurement of each.

spectrum   A band of frequencies or wavelengths (e.g., *radio spectrum*, *visible-light spectrum*, and *sound spectrum*).

spectrum analyzer   **1.** An automatic wave analyzer with a visual display (oscilloscope). **2.** A scanning receiver with a screen that shows a plot of signals and their bandwidths over a specific frequency band.

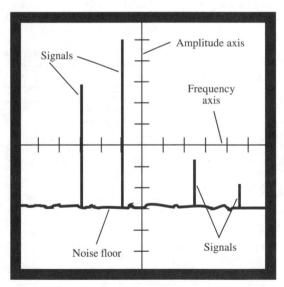

spectrum analyzer, 2.

specularity   A qualitative or experimentally derived expression of the efficiency with which a DIFFRACTION GRATING works.

specular reflection   Reflection in which the reflected ray is in the same plane as the incident ray, as in reflection from an extremely smooth surface.

speech amplifier A (usually low-level) audio amplifier designed especially for speech frequencies. It is generally used to amplify the signals from a microphone.

speech clipper A device, such as a biased diode, (see POSITIVE PEAK CLIPPER) for holding speech signals to a constant amplitude. Compare SPEECH COMPRESSOR. Also see SPEECH CLIPPING.

speech clipping The use of a limiting circuit to maintain the output-signal amplitude of a speech amplifier against fluctuations in the intensity of speech input. The resulting signal requires filtering to remove harmonics generated by the process. Compare SPEECH COMPRESSION.

speech compression Automatic regulation of the gain of a speech amplifier to maintain its output-signal amplitude against speech-input fluctuations. Compare SPEECH CLIPPING.

speech compressor A circuit or device, such as an automatic-gain-control (agc) system, for performing speech compression. Compare SPEECH CLIPPER.

speech digit signaling A method of digital signaling, where time slots generally used for encoded audio or video are used alternately for signaling.

speech frequencies See VOICE FREQUENCIES.

speech intelligibility The quality of reproduced speech that makes it easily understood by a reasonably proficient user of the language. For good speech intelligibility, a circuit should transmit frequencies between 300 Hz and 3000 Hz with minimal distortion. Increased bandwidth improves fidelity, but does not provide a significant increase in intelligibility for normal speech.

speech inverter See SCRAMBLER CIRCUIT.

speech power 1. The alternating-current power in an electric wave corresponding to speech, as opposed to that in a sine wave. 2. Sound power in a speech transmission.

speech recognition The ability of a device to translate audible spoken words, phrases, or sentences into binary digital signals that can be used by machines, such as computers and robots.

speech recognizer An electronic device that translates audible spoken words, phrases, or sentences into binary digital signals that can be used by machines, such as computers and robots.

speech scrambler See SCRAMBLER CIRCUIT.

speech synthesis The ability of a device to translate binary digital signals from a machine, such as a computer or robot, into audible, coherent spoken words, phrases, or sentences.

speech synthesizer An electronic device that translates binary digital signals from a machine, such as a computer or robot, into audible, coherent spoken words, phrases, or sentences.

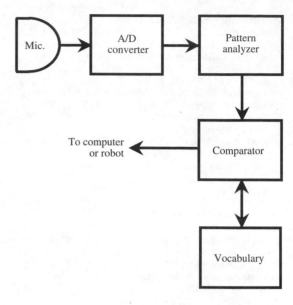

speech recognizer

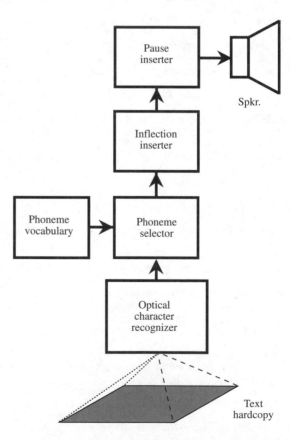

speech synthesizer

speed key **1.** A semiautomatic key for manual generation of Morse code characters. **2.** A similar, fully automatic key used especially for high-speed telegraphy.

speed of light Symbol, *c.* The speed at which electromagnetic waves propagate in a vacuum; approximately 299,792 kilometers per second (186,282 miles per second).

speed of sound The speed at which acoustic waves propagate. It depends on the nature of the medium. In air, at ordinary temperatures, it is approximately 344 meters (1129 feet) per second. In fresh water, it is approximately 1463 meters (4800 feet) per second.

speed of transmission The amount of data sent in a given unit of time. It is generally measured in bits per second (bps), characters per second (cps), characters per minute (cpm), or words per minute (wpm). It is used primarily for digital codes.

speedup capacitor See COMMUTATING CAPACITOR.

SPFW Abbreviation of SINGLE-PHASE FULL-WAVE.

sp gr Abbreviation of SPECIFIC GRAVITY.

sphere **1.** A closed surface in three-dimensional space, represented by the set of all points equidistant from a specified center point. **2.** A solid in three-dimensional space, represented by the set of all points on or within a closed surface, as defined in **1.**

sphere gap A spark gap in which the spark passes between two polished metal spheres. When the air gap is adjustable, unknown high voltages can be measured in terms of the largest gap width at which sparking occurs. Compare NEEDLE GAP.

sphere-gap voltmeter See SPHERE VOLTMETER.

sphere voltmeter A gap voltmeter using a SPHERE GAP.

spherical aberration In a spherical lens, mirror, or reflecting dish, distortion as a result of the spherical (as opposed to paraboloidal) shape of the surface. This causes the focus to be elongated into a short line segment along the principal axis.

spherical angle An angle formed by the intersection of two arcs on the surface of a sphere.

spherical coordinate geometry A scheme for guiding a robot arm in three dimensions via SPHERICAL COORDINATES. The length (radius) of the arm can be varied, as can the elevation (latitude) and azimuth (longitude).

spherical coordinates A method of defining a point (*P*) in three-space using two angles (latitude and longitude) and a radial distance (*r*) from the origin.

spherical degree A unit equal to ¹⁄₇₂₀ of the surface area of a sphere.

spherical distance The length of the shortest arc (lying on a great circle) connecting two specified points on a sphere.

spherical divergence The manner in which energy normally propagates from a fixed point source in three dimensions. Wavefronts expand from the source in the form of spheres, whose centers are at the point source.

spherical reflector A microwave reflector (dish) whose contour is that of a sphere, rather than that of a paraboloid.

spherical wave A wave characterized by wavefronts that are concentric spheres.

spheroidal antenna A sheetmetal or wire-mesh antenna having the cross section of a sphere that is flattened at the ends of one axis.

SPHW Abbreviation of SINGLE-PHASE HALF-WAVE.

spider **1.** The flat, round, springy part that holds the apex of the vibrating cone of a dynamic speaker. **2.** A quickly assembled, chassisless hookup in which the pigtails of components form the wiring and the mechanical support for a circuit.

spiderweb antenna A set of dipole antennas for different frequencies, arranged in a common (usually horizontal) plane. The result is a broadband antenna.

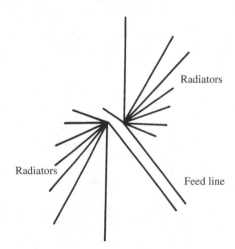

spiderweb antenna

spiderweb coil A flat, single-layer coil in which a strand of wire is woven over and under the spokes of a wheel-like form, and having the general appearance of a spiderweb. The criss-cross winding reduces distributed capacitance by breaking up the parallelism of adjacent turns.

spike **1.** A current or voltage pulse of extremely short duration. **2.** A sharp transient, such as an overshoot on a pulse or square wave.

spike suppressor A clipper or similar device for removing a spike from a signal voltage.

spin A quantity of angular momentum possessed by a subatomic particle. It can be positive, negative, or zero, but it always exists in integral multiples of ½.

spindle **1.** The pivoted shaft that carries the movable element and rotates between the pivots in a meter movement. **2.** The rotor of an alternator—especially when the rotor is a permanent magnet. **3.** The rotating shaft in a motor, generator, or similar electric machine.

spinning electron An electron having nonzero angular momentum.

spinthariscope An optical device for observing the effect of alpha particles emitted by a radioactive substance, from the scintillations they produce upon striking a small, fluorescent screen.

spiral coil See DISK WINDING.

spiral distortion A form of television camera-tube distortion caused by spiraling of the electrons as they are emitted from the photocathode. The result is a twisted image.

spiral-rod oscillator A parallel-line-type oscillator in which the lines are rods that are rolled up into spirals to conserve space. Also see LINE-TYPE OSCILLATOR.

spiral sweep **1.** A means of sweeping the electron beam in a cathode-ray tube to produce a spiral trace on the screen. **2.** The circuit for producing such a sweep.

spiral trace See SPIRAL SWEEP.

spiral winding See DISK WINDING.

spkr Abbreviation of *speaker* (see LOUD-SPEAKER).

splatter See SIDEBAND SPLATTER.

splatter-suppression filter In an amplitude-modulated (AM) or single-sideband (SSB) radio transmitter, a low-pass filter inserted between the output of the audio amplifier and the audio input of the modulator. It suppresses high-frequency audio components that would otherwise cause sideband splatter.

splaying The construction of a room or auditorium so that the walls do not meet at right angles. It is useful in optimizing the acoustic characteristics of the enclosure because it tends to reduce acoustic resonant effects.

splice **1.** A physical or electrical connection between two wires, made by tightly winding the ends together. Solder is often applied for additional mechanical strength and electrical continuity. **2.** A physical connection between two lengths of magnetic tape, made in such a way as to cause minimal disturbance in reproduced audio, video, or data. **3.** To prepare a joint, as defined in **1** or **2**.

splicer A device for making a SPLICE.

splicing block A device specifically designed to facilitate easy splicing of audio, video, or digital magnetic tape.

splicing tape A durable, flexible adhesive designed to hold a magnetic-tape splice together.

spline-based modeling In video animation and advanced computer graphics, a scheme that uses curve-generating formulas (e.g., Bezier curves) to create lifelike images.

split-anode magnetron A magnetron in which the plate (anode) consists of two semicylinders with the cathode at their axis.

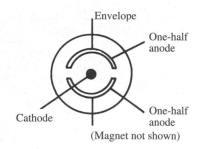

Envelope

One-half anode

Cathode

One-half anode

(Magnet not shown)

split-anode magnetron

split-load phase inverter See PARAPHASE INVERTER.

split-phase motor A fractional-horsepower, alternating-current motor that starts like a two-phase motor and runs like a single-phase motor. After the machine approaches approximately 75 percent of full speed, a centrifugal switch cuts out the starting winding.

split projector An acoustic transmission device with several independently operated transducers.

split-reed vibrator See SELF-RECTIFYING VIBRATOR.

split-rotor plate See SERRATED ROTOR PLATE.

split-stator capacitor A variable capacitor having two separate stator sections and a common rotor section.

split-sound receiver A television receiver circuit in which the sound signal is separated from the composite signal shortly after pickup by the antenna, and is amplified separately from the video signal. Compare INTERCARRIER RECEIVER.

splitter A device used to couple two or more television receivers to a single antenna.

spool See REEL.

sporadic-E layer ionization Occasional, scattered ionization in the E-layer of the ionosphere.

sporadic-E propagation Skywave radio-wave transmission via intermittently ionized regions in the E-layer of the ionosphere. It is often responsible for communications over paths of several hundred miles in the 28-MHz and 50-MHz amateur-radio bands. It can also affect the lower television broadcast channels, usually channels 2 and 3.

SPOT Abbreviation of *satellite position and tracking*.

spot brightness In a cathode-ray tube, the relative brilliance of the glowing dot or trace produced on the screen by the electron beam.

spot check **1.** To take a random sample or to make a random test by arbitrarily selecting a single item from a run of similar items and subjecting it to analysis, examination, performance, or parametric evaluation, etc. **2.** A random sample or test.

spot frequency **1.** A single frequency or signal to which other frequencies can be referred. **2.** A frequency or signal that acts as a limit marker (e.g., to define the edges of an allocated frequency band).

spot jamming Deliberate interference to a radio signal at some frequency and at some specific time.

spot modulation In a cathode-ray tube, modulation of the brightness of the spot (and, accordingly, of the image) produced on the screen by the electron beam. Also see INTENSITY MODULATION.

spot welding A method of electrical welding in which the parts to be joined are held together, overlapping, between the points of two electrodes, between which a current is passed to heat the parts at the spot of contact.

spot-wheel pattern A frequency-identifying wheel pattern produced on an oscilloscope screen by intensity-modulating a circular trace. The circular trace is produced by applying a standard-frequency signal to the horizontal and vertical input terminals 90 degrees out of phase. A square-wave signal of unknown frequency is applied to the intensity-modulation (z-axis) input terminals. The square wave chops the circle into a number of bright sectors or spots. The unknown frequency (fx) equals Nfs, where N is the number of spots in the circle, and fs is the standard frequency. Compare GEAR-WHEEL PATTERN.

sprat Acronym for *small portable radar torch*. A portable radar unit that uses a Gunn diode to generate microwave energy. The range is about 500 meters (⅛ mile).

spray coating **1.** Applying a protective coat of insulating material to a conductor or component by spraying it with a liquid substance and allowing it to dry. Compare DIP COATING. **2.** The coat applied, as defined in **1**.

spreader **1.** An insulator used to separate the wires of an air-spaced transmission line. **2.** Any of the rods composing the supporting structure in a cubical quad antenna.

spreading current In a semiconductor, current caused by the movement of charge carriers by circuitous routes, that is, in paths that deviate significantly from straight lines.

spreading loss Energy lost during the transmission of radiation.

spreading resistance In a semiconductor device, the resistance that is a consequence of electrical paths through material that is not along straight lines between electrodes.

spread spectrum **1.** A method of transmission in which the occupied bandwidth of the signal is deliberately increased, or spread out, over a much wider range than it would normally oc-

cupy with conventional modulation. **2.** A signal transmitted, as defined in **1**.

spring coil See SOLENOID, 1.

spring contact See FLEXIBLE CONTACT.

sprite In video and animated computer graphics, a brief insert, such as a little insect that scurries across the screen, or a face that pops in and smiles. It is used primarily for effect.

SPST Abbreviation of SINGLE-POLE/SINGLE-THROW (switch or relay).

spurious emission From a radio or television transmitter, an unintended and unwanted output signal on a frequency other than the fundamental signal frequency. It can be generated by faulty modulation, amplification, and/or oscillation.

spurious oscillation **1.** Oscillation in a normally nonoscillatory circuit. **2.** In an oscillator, simultaneous oscillation at a frequency other than the normal one.

spurious response In a communications receiver, a signal that appears to be on a certain frequency, when, in fact, the received signal is not on that frequency. It often results from inadequate image rejection.

spurious-response ratio The ratio of the transmission (or gain) of a circuit of a desired signal to its transmission (or gain) for a spurious signal at the same setting of the circuit (e.g., *signal-to-image ratio*).

spurious sidebands In an amplitude-modulated (AM) or single-sideband (SSB) radio signal, sideband energy at frequencies outside the nominal signal band, usually resulting from improper modulation, inadequate filtering, improper envelope clipping, or nonlinear amplification.

Sputnik The first orbiting artificial earth satellite. It was launched by Russia (then known as the Union of Soviet Socialist Republics) in 1957.

sputter **1.** A layer of material obtained by sputtering (see SPUTTERING, 1). **2.** To carry out the process of sputtering (see SPUTTERING, 1).

sputtering **1.** A technique for electrically depositing a film of metal on a metallic or nonmetallic surface. In a vacuum chamber, the piece of metal to be deposited is made the cathode of a high-voltage circuit, with respect to a nearby anode plate. The high voltage causes atoms to be ejected from the surface of the cathode and strike the surface of an object placed in their path, becoming deposited on it as a film of cathode metal. Compare EVAPORATION, 1. **2.** The disintegration of a vacuum-tube cathode through ejection of surface atoms from the cathode by impinging positive ions.

sq Abbreviation of SQUARE.

S$_9$ band A section of the S BAND, from 2400 to 2600 MHz.

SQC Abbreviation of STATISTICAL QUALITY CONTROL.

SQR **1.** Abbreviation of SQUARE ROOTER. **2.** In the BASIC computer-programming language, a function that computes the square root of a positive number.

S quad   See SIMPLE QUAD.

square-law demodulator   See SQUARE-LAW DETECTOR.

square-law detector   A detector whose output is proportional to the square of the root-mean-square (rms) value of the input. Also called WEAK-SIGNAL DETECTOR.

square-law meter   **1.** A meter whose deflection is proportional to the square of the quantity applied to it. Also see CURRENT-SQUARED METER. **2.** A high-impedance electronic voltmeter, whose deflection is proportional to the square of the applied voltage.

square-law modulator   A circuit or device that accomplishes amplitude modulation of one signal current by another, by simultaneously passing the two currents through a component, such as a nonlinear resistor, having a square-law response.

square-law response   Circuit or component operation that results in an output signal, proportional to the square of the input.

square rooter   An analog or digital device used to extract the square root of a number.

square wave   An alternating or pulsating current or voltage whose rise and decay times are essentially zero, and whose maxima and minima are essentially flat. The duration of the maxima is equal to the duration of the minima. A special form of RECTANGULAR WAVE.

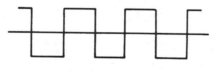

square wave

square-wave amplifier   An amplifier designed to operate with square waves.

square-wave converter   See SQUARING CIRCUIT.

square-wave generator   A signal generator delivering an output signal that has a square waveform. Compare SQUARING CIRCUIT, **1.**

square-wave testing   Testing the response of a circuit or device, such as an amplifier, by observing the extent to which it distorts a square-wave signal passing through it (a measure of high-frequency response).

squaring circuit   **1.** A circuit (such as a twin-diode clipper, overdriven amplifier, or Schmitt trigger) that converts a sine wave or pulse into a square wave. **2.** A circuit whose instantaneous output-signal amplitude is equal to the square of the instantaneous input-signal amplitude.

squarish wave   **1.** A signal whose oscilloscope trace is nearly, but not exactly, the same as that of a square wave. **2.** A rectangular wave that is

not a square wave; that is, whose maxima and minima are not of the same duration. See RECTANGULAR WAVE and SQUARE WAVE.

squawker   **1.** In a three-way speaker system, the midrange speaker. **2.** Any slave station in a multistation intercom network.

squeal   A high-pitched interferential sound, such as that encountered in spuriously oscillating systems.

squeezeout   In optical character recognition (OCR), a condition in which errors occur because the printed characters have excessive ink at the edges. Also called *smudge*.

squegging   A choking-type cutoff action in a circuit caused by an excessively strong signal.

squegging oscillator   An oscillator that starts and stops oscillating intermittently as a result of SQUEGGING.

squelch   See SQUELCH CIRCUIT.

squelch amplifier   An amplifier that can be controlled by a squelch signal. Also see SQUELCH CIRCUIT.

squelch circuit   One of several circuits that automatically disable a receiver or amplifier, except when incoming signals exceed a predetermined threshold amplitude. This action mutes the equipment, eliminating annoying background noise and unwanted signals. Also called MUTING CIRCUIT.

squelch signal   The activating or deactivating signal delivered by a SQUELCH CIRCUIT.

squiggle   See BLIP, **2.**

squint   **1.** The angular resolution of a radar antenna. **2.** The angular difference between the antenna axis and the major lobe of a radar transmitter.

squirrel-cage induction motor   See SQUIRREL-CAGE MOTOR.

squirrel-cage motor   An induction-type alternating-current motor using a squirrel-cage rotor.

squirrel-cage rotor   In an alternating-current motor, a rotor composed of straight copper bars embedded in a laminated soft-iron core and short-circuited at the ends by rings. Its name is derived from its resemblance to a revolving squirrel cage.

squirter   See SIGNAL INJECTOR.

SR   **1.** Abbreviation of SILICON RECTIFIER. **2.** Abbreviation of *silicone rubber* (see SILICONE). **3.** Abbreviation of SHIFT REGISTER.

S-R   Abbreviation of SEND-RECEIVE.

Sr   Symbol for STRONTIUM.

sr   Abbreviation of STERADIAN.

SRAM   Abbreviation of *static random-access memory.*

S-rays   See SECONDARY RAYS.

SRF   Abbreviation of SELF-RESONANT FREQUENCY.

S-RF meter   A dual-function meter in a radio transceiver. In the receiving mode, the meter indicates S units. In the transmit mode, the meter indicates relative output power.

SRR Abbreviation of SHORT-RANGE RADAR.

SS **1.** Abbreviation of SOLID STATE. **2.** Abbreviation of SINGLE SHOT. **3.** Abbreviation of *small signal.* **4.** Abbreviation of SINGLE SIGNAL. **5.** Abbreviation of *same size.* **6.** Abbreviation of *stainless steel.*

SSB Abbreviation of SINGLE SIDEBAND.

S_S band A section of the S BAND extending from 2900 to 3100 MHz.

SSBSC Abbreviation of SINGLE-SIDEBAND SUPPRESSED CARRIER.

ssc Abbreviation of *single-silk-covered* (wire).

S scale A scale of numbers used in radio communications, and especially in amateur radio, to report the approximate strength of signals: S1, faint signals; S2, very weak signals; S3, weak signals; S4, fair signals; S5, fairly good signals; S6, good signals; S7, moderately strong signals; S8, strong signals; S9, extremely strong signals. Also see S METER.

sse Abbreviation of *single-silk-enameled* (wire).

SSI Abbreviation of SMALL-SCALE INTEGRATION.

SSL Abbreviation of SOLID-STATE LAMP.

SSSC Abbreviation of SINGLE-SIDEBAND SUPPRESSED CARRIER. (Also, SSBSC.)

ST Abbreviation of SINGLE THROW.

sta **1.** Abbreviation of STATION. (Also *stn.*) **2.** Abbreviation of STATIONARY.

stab Abbreviated form of stabilizer (see STABILIZER, 4).

stability **1.** The condition in which an equipment or device is able to maintain a particular mode of operation without deviation. **2.** The condition in which the setting or adjustment of a device remains at a particular point without movement. **3.** The condition in which a quantity remains constant, with respect to time, temperature, or another variable. **4.** The ability of inks used in optical character recognition to retain their color after exposure to light or heat.

stability factor Abbreviation, SF. For a bipolar transistor, the derivative dI_c/dI_{co}, where I_c is the steady-state collector current and I_{co} is the collector cutoff current.

stabilized platform See STABLE PLATFORM.

stabilizer **1.** See DAMPING DIODE. **2.** See DAMPING RESISTOR. **3.** A device or circuit for the self-regulation of current or voltage. **4.** A chemical used to control or arrest a reaction.

stabilizing windings Auxiliary field windings used to prevent speed runaway in shunt motors.

Stabistor Trade name for a type of voltage-regulating semiconductor diode.

stable device A device whose characteristics and performance remain substantially unchanged with time or variations in temperature, applied power, or other quantities.

stable element **1.** A component that maintains its value or ratings, despite widely variable environmental conditions. **2.** A navigational instrument that maintains its orientation at all times.

stable platform A gyro-type device used to stabilize objects in space, and to provide accurate information regarding attitude (pitch, roll, and yaw).

stable state A stable condition, such as the high and low states of a flip-flop. The flip-flop has two stable states and will remain in one until it is switched to the other, whereupon it will then remain in that latter state until switched back to the former. Compare UNSTABLE STATE.

stack **1.** A piled assembly of capacitor plates and separating dielectric films. **2.** An assembly of selenium rectifier plates (see POWER STACK). **3.** To assemble a stacked array. **4.** A temporary storage area consisting of a small group of registers in a computer memory.

stacked array An antenna system in which two or more identical antennas, such as dipoles, Yagis, or halos, are placed one above the other or side-by-side. It provides additional forward gain, and, in some cases, enhances the front-to-back ratio and/or front-to-side ratio.

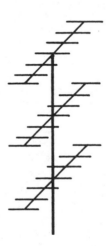

stacked array

stacked-dipole antenna A stacked array of half-wave dipole antennas.

stacking The combination of two or more identical antennas, such as dipoles, Yagis, or halos, in a STACKED ARRAY to provide enhanced forward gain. It can also enhance the front-to-back ratio and/or front-to-side ratio. Stacking can be done vertically or horizontally.

stack pointer Abbreviation, SP. A register indicating the last data item to be entered in a stack (see STACK, 4).

stage A complete functional unit of a system (e.g., *amplifier stage, oscillator stage, modulator stage,* etc.).

stage-by-stage elimination See SIGNAL INJECTION.

stage gain   The amplification provided by a single stage in a system.

stage loss   The loss introduced by a single stage in a system.

stagger   **1.** An error in facsimile reception, occurring as a constant discrepancy in the position of the received dot. **2.** To deliberately tune a set of resonant circuits, especially in a bandpass filter, to one side or the other of the center frequency.

staggered tuning   The tuning of the input and output circuits of a single stage, or the tuning of successive stages to slightly different frequencies to obtain flat-top response.

stagger tuning   See STAGGERED TUNING.

stagger-wound coil   See BASKET-WEAVE COIL and SPIDERWEB COIL.

staircase circuit   See STAIR-STEP CIRCUIT.

staircase generator   A circuit or device for generating a STAIR-STEP WAVE.

staircase wave   See STAIR-STEP WAVE.

stair-step circuit   A circuit that converts a series of equal-amplitude pulses into a stair-step wave.

stair-step wave   A nonsinusoidal wave characterized by a multistep rise and a steep fall. It is so called from its resemblance to the cross section of a staircase.

stair-step wave

stall torque   The torque produced when a motor shaft is prevented from turning.

stalo   Acronym for *stabilized oscillator*.

standard   **1.** A precise specification governing the dimensions and characteristics of a device or system (e.g., *military standard*). **2.** A highly accurate physical or electrical quantity to which similar quantities can be compared (e.g., *standard frequency*). **3.** The device or system that produces a standard quantity as defined in **2** (e.g., *frequency standard*). **4.** Having conventional and widely accepted characteristics.

standard atmosphere   Abbreviation, atm. Air pressure at sea level (1.013 Pascals, or about 14.7 pounds per square inch). Also called ATMOSPHERE.

standard broadcast band   Any of numerous frequency bands allocated to conventional broadcast stations. In the United States, the amplitude-modulation (AM) radio broadcast band extends from 535 to 1705 kHz, and the frequency-modulation (FM) radio broadcast band extends from 88 to 108 MHz. The television (TV) broadcast bands range from 54 MHz to 806 MHz in several sections, designated in channels from 2 through 69. Also see BROADCAST SERVICE, **1.**

standard candle   See CANDELA.

standard cell   A highly refined primary cell used to supply a precise direct-current voltage for electronic measurements. The *Weston standard cell* contains a mercury positive electrode, cadmium amalgam negative electrode, and cadmium sulfate electrolyte, and delivers 1.0183 volts at 20 degrees Celsius. Also see ZINC STANDARD CELL.

standard deviation   In statistical analysis, the square root of the mean of squares of deviation from the mean.

standard frequency   A highly precise frequency to which other frequencies can be compared for identification or measurement.

standard-frequency oscillator   A stable, precise oscillator that delivers a standard frequency. Also see PRIMARY FREQUENCY STANDARD and SECONDARY FREQUENCY STANDARD.

standard-frequency signal   A calibration and reference signal that is broadcast on a standard frequency, such as those transmitted on 2.5, 5, 10, and 15 MHz by the National Bureau of Standards.

standard pitch   The tone corresponding to the frequency 440 Hz (in music, the note A above middle C).

standard signal generator   A (usually continuously variable) high-grade generator of modulated and unmodulated radio-frequency test signals. A general-purpose instrument of this type usually covers a wide range (e.g., 15 kHz to 100 MHz) in several tuning bands. For calibration, a standard signal generator is referred to a primary frequency standard or secondary frequency standard.

standard subroutine   A usually vendor-supplied computer program segment applicable to more than one program and used as needed as a subroutine.

standard temperature and pressure   The condition where the temperature is zero degrees Celsius and the pressure is one atmosphere. Abbreviated STP.

standard time   Official civil time in a particular region. See TIME ZONE.

standby   **1.** The state in which equipment is out of operation, but can be immediately activated. Also called IDLING. **2.** A state of readiness on the part of personnel, equipment, or systems.

standby battery   An emergency power source for a battery-powered installation.

standby current   The CURRENT DRAIN of a circuit, device, or system when in the standby condition.

standby equipment   See EMERGENCY EQUIPMENT.

standby operation   Keep-alive operation during a standby interval (see STANDBY).

standby power The power drawn by an equipment connected to the power supply, but out of operation.

standby power supply A circuit containing a battery, an automatic switch, and sometimes a power inverter. When utility power fails, the switch actuates the supply, and the battery supplies power to essential devices or systems. Similar to an UNINTERRUPTIBLE POWER SUPPLY.

standing wave A stationary distribution of current or voltage along a line because of the interactions between a wave transmitted down the line and a wave reflected back; it is characterized by maximum-amplitude points (loops) and minimum-amplitude or zero points (nodes).

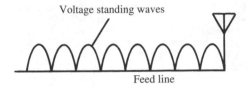

Voltage standing waves

Feed line

standing wave

standing-wave distortion Distortion of current or voltage caused by standing waves on a transmission line terminated in an impedance that contains reactance, and/or that differs from the characteristic impedance of the line.

standing-wave indicator **1.** A device, such as a lamp or meter, used to detect standing waves. **2.** Standing-wave meter (see SWR BRIDGE).

standing-wave loss The additional loss, over the matched-line loss, that occurs in a transmission line when the standing-wave ratio (SWR) is not 1.

standing-wave meter See SWR BRIDGE.

standing-wave ratio Abbreviation, SWR. **1.** The ratio between the maximum and minimum voltage along a transmission line. This quantity is sometimes specifically called *voltage standing-wave ratio (VSWR)*. **2.** The ratio between the maximum and minimum current along a transmission line. **3.** The ratio of load impedance to feed-line characteristic impedance or vice-versa, whichever is greater than or equal to 1. Ideally, the SWR is equal to 1 or 1:1, representing a load impedance that is purely resistive and has the same value as the characteristic impedance of the feed line. A high standing-wave ratio causes increased loss in the line and can also result in excessive conductor heating or dielectric breakdown.

standoff insulator An insulator (usually of the post type) that is used to hold a wire or component away from a chassis or base.

star **1.** In a gravity-battery cell, the copper electrode. The name is derived from its star shape.

2. A star-shaped circuit of three-phase components. Also see WYE CONNECTION.

star connection See WYE CONNECTION.

Stark effect The influence of a strong transverse electric field on the spectrum lines of a gas.

starlight scope A device capable of viewing in apparent total darkness. Its operation depends on its ability to provide high amplification of extremely low light levels, such as that of objects reflecting the light from a moonless, but starlit, sky.

star rectifier See WYE RECTIFIER.

starter **1.** An ignitor electrode in an ignitron (see IGNITOR). **2.** See STARTING BOX.

starting box A special rheostat for starting a motor gradually in steps. The device is provided with an electromagnet for holding the arm in the maximum-speed position and releasing it when power is interrupted.

starting rod An ignitor electrode in an ignitron (see IGNITOR).

starting voltage **1.** For a gas tube, the minimum voltage that will initiate the glow discharge. **2.** In appropriate solid-state devices (e.g., a diac), the voltage at which conduction between electrodes occurs.

start lead The lead attached to the first turn of a coil. Also called *inside lead*. Compare FINISH LEAD.

start/stop multivibrator See MONOSTABLE MULTIVIBRATOR.

stat- A prefix denoting ELECTROSTATIC.

statampere The cgs electrostatic unit of current; 1 statampere = 3.335640×10^{-10} ampere.

statcoulomb The cgs electrostatic unit of charge; 1 statcoulomb = 3.335640×10^{-10} coulomb.

state **1.** The present condition (i.e., on or off, true or false, 1 or 0, high or low) of a bistable device, such as a flip-flop. **2.** The physical or electrial condition or status of a component, device, circuit, or system.

statement The contents of a line in a source-language computer program.

state of charge The amount of charge, measured in coulombs or ampere hours, in a storage cell or battery at a given time. A measure of the available remaining energy in the cell or battery.

statfarad The cgs electrostatic unit of capacitance; 1 statfarad = 1.112650×10^{-12} farad.

stathenry The cgs electrostatic unit of inductance; 1 stathenry = 8.987554×10^{11} henry.

static **1.** Pertaining to that which is constant in quantity (e.g., *static collector current* of a transistor). **2.** Pertaining to that which is at rest (e.g., *static electricity*). **3.** The radio noise (sferics) produced by electric discharges in the atmosphere, usually lightning. **4.** Pertaining to a test-and-measurement mode for a unit or device, without subjecting the unit or device to regular operation. Compare DYNAMIC.

static base current See DC BASE CURRENT.

static base resistance See DC BASE RESISTANCE.

static base voltage   See DC BASE VOLTAGE.

static cathode current   See DC CATHODE CURRENT.

static cathode resistance   See DC CATHODE RESISTANCE.

static cathode voltage   See DC CATHODE VOLTAGE.

static characteristic   An operating characteristic determined from constant, rather than alternating or fluctuating, values of independent and dependent variables. Examples: the direct-current (dc) characteristics of diodes, transistors, and integrated circuits. Compare DYNAMIC CHARACTERISTIC.

static charge   Energy stored in a stationary electric field; electricity at rest.

static collector   A device that grounds the rotating wheels of a motor vehicle, thereby removing the static electricity generated by the friction of the tires on the roadway.

static collector current   See DC COLLECTOR CURRENT.

static collector resistance   See DC COLLECTOR RESISTANCE.

static collector voltage   See DC COLLECTOR VOLTAGE.

static convergence   In a color-television picture tube, the convergence of the three undeflected electron beams at the center of the aperture mask.

static device   A device with no moving parts.

static discharge resistor   A fixed resistor connected between the earth and the high side of the power line in a television receiver to drain off atmospheric electric charge.

static drain current   See DC DRAIN CURRENT.

static drain resistance   See DC DRAIN RESISTANCE.

static drain voltage   See DC DRAIN VOLTAGE.

static dump   In computer operations, a dump occurring at a predetermined point in a program run or at the end of the run.

static electricity   Energy in the form of a stationary electric charge, such as that stored in capacitors or produced by friction or induction.

static emitter current   See DC EMITTER CURRENT.

static emitter resistance   See DC EMITTER RESISTANCE.

static emitter voltage   See DC EMITTER VOLTAGE.

static flip-flop   A flip-flop (see BISTABLE MULTIVIBRATOR) using direct-current operating voltages. A single pulse switches the unit from on to off, and vice versa. Compare DYNAMIC FLIP-FLOP.

static frequency multiplier   A magnetic-core device, similar to a magnetic amplifier or peaking transformer, that provides harmonics by distorting a sine-wave signal.

static gate current   See DC GATE CURRENT.

static gate resistance   See DC GATE RESISTANCE.

static gate voltage   See DC GATE VOLTAGE.

static grid current   See DC GRID CURRENT.

static grid voltage   See DC GRID VOLTAGE.

static hysteresis   The condition in which the magnetization of a material (when it has the same intensity as the magnetizing force) is different when the force is increasing than when the force is decreasing, regardless of the time lag. Compare VISCOUS HYSTERESIS.

static induction   See ELECTROSTATIC INDUCTION.

static machine   See ELECTROSTATIC GENERATOR.

static memory   Also called *nonvolatile memory*. In a computer, a data memory medium (such as programmable read-only memory, or PROM) in which information is stored until it is altered or erased. It does not require a source of power to maintain the integrity of the data. Compare VOLATILE MEMORY.

static mutual conductance   See STATIC TRANSCONDUCTANCE.

static plate current   See DC PLATE CURRENT.

static plate resistance   See DC PLATE RESISTANCE.

static plate voltage   See DC PLATE VOLTAGE.

statics   The study of forces, bodies, poles, charges, or fields at rest or in equilibrium. Compare DYNAMICS.

static skew   In magnetic tape recording or playback, the amount of lead or lag time of one track, with respect to another. Ideally, the static skew should be zero or practically zero.

static source current   See DC SOURCE CURRENT.

static source resistance   See DC SOURCE RESISTANCE.

static source voltage   See DC SOURCE VOLTAGE.

static storage   Also called *nonvolatile storage*. In a computer, a data storage medium (such as magnetic or optical disk) in which information is stored until it is altered or erased. It does not require a source of power to maintain the integrity of the data. Virtually all data storage media are of this type, as contrasted with memory, which is often volatile (see STATIC MEMORY and VOLATILE MEMORY).

static stability   The ability of a robot to maintain its balance while standing still. A robot with two legs is generally poor in this respect. This is one of the reasons why humanoid robots (androids) are difficult to engineer. A minimum of three legs is necessary for good static stability.

static subroutine   In computer programming, a subroutine that always serves the same purpose [i.e., it does not need to be tailored (according to parameters) for a specific application].

station   **1.** An installation consisting of a transmitter, receiver, or both. **2.** A test-equipment installation or position. **3.** A computer installation including peripherals.

stationary battery   A (usually wet storage) battery not normally moved when in use.

stationary state   A particular energy state for an atom represented by its electrons being in shells at specific energy levels.

stationary wave   See STANDING WAVE.

station authorization   The legal privilege assigned to a broadcast or communications station, allowing that station to be used for the purpose of transmitting electromagnetic signals.

station license   See STATION AUTHORIZATION.

statistical quality control   Quality control based upon the techniques of probability and statistics in analyzing findings, making predictions, and formulating procedures for sampling.

statmho   The cgs electrostatic unit of direct-current conductance; 1 statmho = 1.112650×10^{-12} siemens.

statoersted   The cgs electrostatic unit of magnetizing force; 1 statoersted = 265.458 A/m (3.33585×10^{-11} oersted).

statohm   The cgs electrostatic unit of direct-current resistance; 1 statohm = 8.987554×10^{11} ohm.

stator   **1.** A stationary coil. Compare ROTOR, **1.** **2.** The stationary member of a motor or generator. Compare ROTOR, **2.** **3.** The stationary-plate section of a variable capacitor. Compare ROTOR, **3.**

stator coil   A stationary coil (see STATOR, **1**, **2**).

stator plate(s)   The stationary plate(s) of a variable capacitor. Compare ROTOR PLATE.

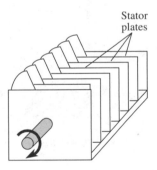

Stator plates

stator plate

stator section   See STATOR, **3.**

statoscope   An aircraft altimeter that shows small changes in altitude.

statvolt   The cgs electrostatic unit of electromotive force; 1 statvolt = 299.7925 volts.

statweber   The cgs electrostatic unit of magnetic flux; 1 statweber = 299.7925 webers (2.997925×10^{10} maxwells).

S_T band   A section of the S BAND, extending from 1850 to 2000 MHz.

std   Abbreviation of STANDARD.

steady-state component   A quantity whose value remains constant during normal operation of a circuit or device, as opposed to an alternating, fluctuating, or transient component.

steerable antenna   A directional antenna having a rotatable major lobe.

steering diode   See DIRECTIONAL DIODE.

Stefan-Boltzmann constant   Value, 5.67051×10^{-8} Wm^{-2}K^{-4}.

Stefan-Boltzmann law   The thermal-radiation law that shows the total emissive power of a blackbody to be proportional to the fourth power of the absolute temperature of the body.

stenode   See CRYSTAL FILTER.

step   **1.** A computer program instruction. **2.** A single action in the operation, maintenance, or troubleshooting of equipment. **3.** A specific increment in a quantity (such as frequency, voltage, current, etc.). **4.** A sharp or rapid change in the value of a quantity.

step-by-step operation   See STEPTHROUGH OPERATION.

step change   A single-increment change in a value.

step circuit   A circuit that produces a step (sharp change of slope) in the response curve of an amplifier.

step counter   **1.** A stair-step circuit arranged to count input pulses. The output capacitor of the circuit discharges when a predetermined number of input pulses has raised the capacitor voltage to the level required to trigger a counter. **2.** In a computer or calculator, a circuit or device that counts the steps in an operation (such as division, multiplication, or shifting) called for by an instruction.

step-down ratio   In a circuit or device, such as a step-down transformer or cathode follower, the ratio of the low output voltage to the high input voltage. Compare STEP-UP RATIO.

step-down transformer   A transformer delivering an output voltage that is lower than the input voltage. In such a transformer, the secondary (output) winding contains fewer turns than the primary (input) winding. Compare STEP-UP TRANSFORMER.

step function   See UNIT FUNCTION.

step generator   **1.** A signal generator that delivers a step function (see UNIT FUNCTION). **2.** A circuit or device that generates a STAIR-STEP WAVE.

stepped leader   The probing flow of electrons through the atmosphere preceding a lightning stroke. Once the path has been established, the discharge takes occurs along the ionized path determined by the stepped leader. It is so called because the electrons move in hesitations, jumping several meters with each advance or step.

stepper motor   A motor in which the shaft advances in uniform angular steps, instead of rotating continuously. These motors are extensively used in robotic devices. When such a motor is stopped and its coils are carrying current, the shaft resists turning.

stepping relay   See STEPPING SWITCH.

stepping switch   A multiposition rotary switch in which an electromechanical ratchet mechanism advances to the next contact position each time that a pulse of current is received.

step-through operation   A way of operating a computer, usually during a debugging operation, in which program instructions are executed one at a time by direction of the user. Also called *single-step operation* and *step-by-step operation*.

step-up ratio   In a circuit or device, such as a step-up transformer or voltage amplifier, the ratio of the high output voltage to the low input voltage. Compare STEP-DOWN RATIO.

step-up transformer   A transformer delivering an output voltage that is higher than the input voltage. In such a transformer, the secondary (output) winding contains more turns than the primary (input) winding. Compare STEP-DOWN TRANSFORMER.

steradian   A unit of solid-angle measure. A cone-shaped solid angle that has a vertex at the center of a sphere (of radius *r*), that cuts off a portion of the sphere's surface whose outer perimeter is a circle, and that has an area (as measured on the sphere's surface) of r^2. Also see SOLID ANGLE.

Sterba array   See BARRAGE ARRAY.

Sterba curtain   See BARRAGE ARRAY.

stereo   1. Contraction of STEREOPHONIC. **2.** General term for a two-channel high-fidelity audio reproduction system.

stereo-adaptable   Pertaining to a television receiver or videocassette recorder (VCR) that requires a special circuit to obtain stereo sound from Multichannel Television Sound signals. Compare STEREO-READY.

stereo amplifier   A two-channel amplifier for binaural reproduction (see BINAURAL).

stereophonic   Pertaining to equipment or techniques for producing a (somewhat) three-dimensional perspective of sound reproduction.

stereophonic sound system   See STEREO SYSTEM.

stereo-irrelevant   Pertaining to sound components in a stereo system that are of equal magnitude in both (or all) channels. Thus, these components sound the same whether the system is reproducing stereophonic sound or monaural sound.

stereo phono cartridge   A phono cartridge capable of reproducing sound from stereo discs.

stereo-ready   Pertaining to a television receiver or videocassette recorder (VCR) that can deliver stereo sound from Multichannel Television Sound signals without the need for a decoding circuit. Compare STEREO-ADAPTABLE.

stereo recording   A method of recording in which two independent sound channels are trans-

ferred to some medium simultaneously, with the intention that the two channels be reproduced at the same time.

stereoscopic television   Television in which the reproduced image appears three-dimensional.

stereo system   A multichannel, high-fidelity sound reproduction system including an amplifier and various other components, such as a radio receiver, compact-disc (CD) player, tape player, turntable, and speakers.

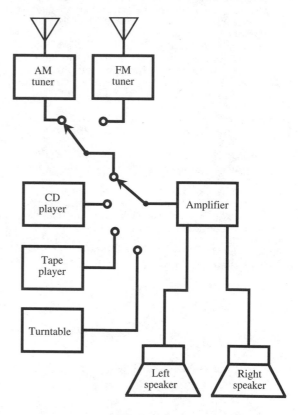

stereo system

stereotape   Magnetic tape bearing more than one channel (usually two channels) for the recording and reproduction of stereophonic sound.

sterilizer   Any electronic device, such as an ultraviolet generator, used to kill germs.

stethoscope   An electronic or nonelectronic instrument used by physicians to listen to the heartbeat and other body sounds, and by technicians to listen to mechanical sounds.

still   1. A stationary picture on television. **2.** A picture transmitted or received by means of facsimile. **3.** A print on photographic paper of a negative.

still television See FACSIMILE.

stinger A brief, loud sound burst, such as a musical chord, sometimes used for effect in recorded audio or audio-visual presentations.

stn Abbreviation of STATION. (Also, sta.)

STO Abbreviation of STORAGE FUNCTION.

stochastic The condition in which, at any instant, a given variable can assume a state dependent on previous states, as well as chance elements (e.g., words uttered extemporaneously by a speaker are random in that they cannot be predicted), while also being dependent, by the application of grammar, on previously spoken words (i.e., previous states).

stop amplifier See REJECT AMPLIFIER.

stopband The continuous spectrum of frequencies rejected by a filter, selective amplifier, or other band-suppression device.

stopband ripple Single or multiple attenuation peaks within the stopband of an elliptic filter, where the frequency of the attenuation peak(s) is/are associated with the resonant circuit(s) in the filter.

stop code See HALT INSTRUCTION.

stop element In digital transmission, a bit or set of bits indicating the end of a character, and serving to inform the receiving device of the end of the character.

stop filter See BAND-SUPPRESSION FILTER.

stopper resistor See STOPPING RESISTOR.

stopping capacitor See BLOCKING CAPACITOR.

stopping coil See CHOKE COIL.

stopping resistor A parasitic-suppressing resistor, usually inserted in series with the input and/or output of a power amplifying device. Also called *stopper resistor.*

storage 1. In computer operations, a medium on which data can be kept for an extended period of time. Examples: magnetic disk, magnetic tape, optical disk. 2. The transferring of data from memory to a more permanent medium. Compare MEMORY. 3. The retention of data of any kind, such as an oscilloscope image or video display, for use at a later time. 4. The retention of electric energy or charge, as in a capacitor or electrochemical cell. 5. The retention of energy in the form of a magnetic field, as in an inductor. 6. The retention of potential energy in any form.

storage allocation The assignment of computer memory areas to certain kinds of information, as outlined in a source program and implemented by a compiler.

storage battery A rechargeable battery; the technical term is *secondary battery.* Also see STORAGE CELL.

storage capacity 1. The amount of data that can be stored in a specific medium, such as a hard disk, diskette, or tape. Generally measured in bytes, kilobytes, megabytes, gigabytes, or terabytes. 2. The energy-delivering capability of a storage battery in terms of ampere-hours, mil-liampere-hours, or other current-time units for a specific rated voltage.

storage cell 1. An electrochemical cell whose potential can be restored by charging it with electricity. Compare PRIMARY CELL. Also see CELL. 2. The smallest part of a computer storage medium. 3. In computer data storage, the part that can hold a data unit (e.g., a bit).

storage CRT See STORAGE TUBE.

storage cycle In computer operation, the period during which a location of a cyclic storage device cannot be accessed.

storage density The number of data units (e.g., bytes, kilobytes, or megabytes) that can be stored in a given length or area of a storage medium.

storage device A medium into which data can be placed and kept for later use. Examples: magnetic disk, magneto-optical disk, optical disk, and magnetic tape.

storage dump See DUMP.

storage function Abbreviation, STO. The so-called "memory" function of a microcomputer chip. It causes data to be inserted into memory or storage for later use. It is commonly used in programmable calculators, automatic-dialing telephones, and radio receivers. Also called *memory function.*

storage laser A laser that stores intense energy before flashing.

storage life See SHELF LIFE.

storage mesh In the cathode-ray tube (CRT) of a storage oscilloscope, a fine metal mesh electrode that serves as the target on which the image is electrostatically stored. Also see STORAGE TUBE.

storage oscilloscope An oscilloscope that retains a displayed image until the display is erased. Also see STORAGE TUBE.

storage register In computers and calculators, a storage unit composed of flip-flops. In computers, it is independent of the central processing unit (CPU).

storage temperature 1. The recommended temperature for storing specified electronic components. 2. The particular temperature at which electronic components have been stored.

storage time 1. The interval during which carriers remain in a semiconductor-junction device after the bias has been removed. Also see DIODE RECOVERY TIME. 2. For a switching semiconductor device, the time required for the amplitude of the output pulse to fall from maximum to 90% of maximum after the input pulse has fallen to zero. 3. In a computer, the time required for data to be transferred from random-access memory (RAM) to nonvolatile storage (e.g., hard disk).

storage tube A cathode-ray tube that retains information in the form of images on a special electrode until erased by a signal.

store **1.** To place data in a nonvolatile medium (such as a hard disk, diskette, optical disk, magnetic tape, etc.). **2.** To place in the memory of a calculator or computer. **3.** In computing, a command that causes data to be placed in a nonvolatile medium. In some applications, this is called *save*. **4.** A nonvolatile medium on which data has been placed for future use or for archival purposes.

stored base charge The carriers that remain in the base layer of a bipolar transistor immediately after the forward bias has been interrupted. This charge maintains collector current momentarily.

stored-energy welding A method of electric welding in which electrical energy is stored slowly, then released at the rate required for the welding.

STP See STANDARD TEMPERATURE AND PRESSURE.

straight adapter An inline coaxial fitting for joining two fixture-terminated coaxial lines in series.

straight angle An angle measuring 180 degrees.

straight dipole A (usually center-fed) dipole antenna having only one radiator. Also see DIPOLE ANTENNA.

straightforward Pertaining to data transmission in one direction only.

straight-gun CRT A cathode-ray tube (CRT) in which the electron gun projects the beam in a straight line through the deflecting elements to the screen. Compare BENT-GUN CRT.

straight-line capacitance Abbreviation, SLC. Pertaining to a variable capacitor for which the setting-vs.-capacitance curve is a straight line; the capacitance variation is linear. Compare STRAIGHT-LINE FREQUENCY and STRAIGHT-LINE WAVELENGTH.

straight-line coding See STRAIGHT-LINE PROGRAMMING.

straight-line frequency Abbreviation, SLF. Pertaining to a variable capacitor in a tuned circuit for which the setting-vs.-frequency curve is a straight line; the frequency variation is linear. Compare STRAIGHT-LINE CAPACITANCE and STRAIGHT-LINE WAVELENGTH.

straight-line programming During the writing of a computer program, avoiding the creation of loops by repeating a series of instructions to reduce execution time.

straight-line tracking In a phonograph turntable, linear lateral stylus movement (as opposed to motion along an arc) as the disc is played. This ensures that the stylus is always at the optimum angle in the disc groove. The result is improved sound reproduction, and longer disc and stylus life because of minimal friction between the stylus and groove.

straight-line wavelength Abbreviation, SLW. Pertaining to a variable capacitor in a tuned circuit for which the setting-vs.-wavelength curve is a straight line; the wavelength variation is linear.

Compare STRAIGHTLINE CAPACITANCE and STRAIGHT-LINE FREQUENCY.

straight-through amplifier An amplifier in which the input and output circuits are tuned to the same frequency. Compare MULTIPLIER AMPLIFIER.

strain A force that compresses or squeezes a body. Compare TENSION, **1.**

strain gauge See ELECTRIC STRAIN GAUGE.

strain-gauge bridge A four-arm resistance bridge in which an ELECTRIC STRAIN GAUGE forms one arm. The resistance of the gauge changes because of strain. The amount of strain can be determined by balancing the bridge.

strain-gauge transducer A transducer, other than a strain sensor, that uses strain gauges to convert values of pressure into their electrical analogs (e.g., *pressure transducer* and *strain-gauge phonograph pickup*).

strain pickup A phonograph pickup using a strain gauge to convert sound vibrations into a varying electric current.

strand A single solid conductor in a STRANDED WIRE.

stranded wire A conductor composed of several non-insulated wires twisted together to provide mechanical flexibility. Compare SOLID WIRE.

stratosphere The portion of earth's upper atmosphere beginning at a height of approximately 10 miles and extending to the ionosphere.

stray capacitance Inherent capacitance in a place where it can be detrimental, such as that between the turns of a coil or between adjacent areas in a circuit. Also see STRAY COMPONENT.

stray component An electrical property that exists as an inherent, and usually undesirable, side effect in a circuit or device. Thus, for example, STRAY CAPACITANCE unavoidably exists between parallel conductors, and STRAY INDUCTANCE is present in all wiring.

stray field The portion of an electric or magnetic field that extends beyond the immediate vicinity of the circuit with which it is associated, and which is, therefore, capable of interfering with other circuits or devices.

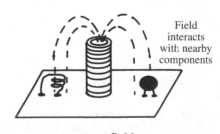

Field interacts with nearby components

stray field

stray inductance Inherent inductance in a place where it can be detrimental (e.g., inductance in the coil of a wirewound resistor). Also see STRAY COMPONENT.

stray resistance   Inherent resistance in a place where it can be detrimental, such as leakage resistance in a dielectric, and wire resistance in an inductor.

streaking   In television or facsimile, a form of distortion in which the image appears enlarged in the horizontal, but not the vertical.

stress   **1.** See STRAIN. **2.** See TENSION, **1. 3.** The force per unit area that produces STRAIN or TENSION on a body.

stretch   The amount by which a material being measured with an electronic device increases in surface dimensions. Compare SHRINK.

stretched string   A long, thin wire or string that vibrates at a certain frequency, causing standing waves. It generally exhibits a specific fundamental frequency and integral harmonics of this frequency. As the wavelength is cut in half, the frequency doubles.

strike   To initiate a discharge, as in striking a gas tube.

striking voltage   See STARTING VOLTAGE.

string   **1.** In computer operations, a set of items in a sequence determined by the order of keys. **2.** In a computer memory, a sequence of bits or characters. **3.** Any group of series-connected components or circuits.

string electrometer   See BIFILAR ELECTROMETER.

string variable   A string of characters, usually forming a word or phrase, represented by a variable name and character string symbol (BASIC's $, for example) in a computer program.

strip chart   A longitudinal, as opposed to circular, chart for graphic recording. In a rectilinear chart, both coordinates are straight; in a curvilinear chart, the crosswise coordinates are arcs.

strip core   A ferromagnetic core material made from a strip of the substance. The method of manufacture results in superior ferromagnetic qualities, but also imparts a polarization to the material.

strip fuse   A fuse in which the fusible element is a flat strip of low-melting-point metal. Compare WIRE FUSE.

strobe   **1.** See ELECTRONIC FLASH, **1. 2.** See STROBOSCOPE.

strobe light   **1.** See ELECTRONIC FLASH, **1. 2.** See STROBOSCOPE.

Strobolume   Trade name for a type of high-output stroboscope.

stroboscope   **1.** An instrument that emits bright, adjustable-rate flashes of light. When this light illuminates an object that is rotating or vibrating at a fixed period, and the flash rate is made to match that period, the object seems to stand still and can be examined for flaws or faulty operation (and its speed can be measured). **2.** A rotatable, slotted disk for producing the effect defined in **1.**

stroboscopic disk   A rotatable disk with alternating white and black radial regions, used in conjunction with a strobe light for precise measurement of the speed of a phonograph turntable.

strobotron   A gas tetrode tube used as the flashing light source in a stroboscope.

stroke speed   See SCANNING FREQUENCY.

strong coupling   See CLOSE COUPLING.

strontium   Symbol, Sr. A metallic element of the alkaline-earth group. Atomic number, 38. Atomic weight, 87.62. It is used in some ceramic dielectrics, such as *barium-strontium titanate.*

Strowger exchange   A telephone system incorporating Strowger switches.

Strowger switch   A switch with one input and 100 individually selectable outputs. It is used with telephone switching networks. The telephone dial code causes a contact to move vertically and horizontally in such a way that a particular output is connected to the input. Each output has a unique dial code and each dial code has a unique output.

structured programming   Computer programming using a limited number of procedural sets, while minimizing branches to make the program as forward-going as possible. This allows it to be easily modified or debugged.

STS switch   See SPACE-TIME-SPACE SWITCH.

stub   A (usually short) section of transmission line that is patched onto a longer line for tuning or impedance matching.

Stubs gauge   See BIRMINGHAM WIRE GAUGE.

stub tuner   A tuning unit consisting of a stub with a short circuit that can be moved along the stub.

stub trap   See INTERFERENCE STUB.

stub-type wavetrap   See INTERFERENCE STUB.

stuffing bits   In a digital communications system, extra bits inserted into some words so that all the words are the same length.

styli   Plural of STYLUS.

stylus   **1.** The "needle" that conveys vibrations to or from the disk in phonograph-disc recording or playback. **2.** One of the pins in the print head of a dot-matrix printer.

stylus drag   See NEEDLE DRAG.

stylus friction   Rubbing of the stylus against the record groove in phonograph-disc playback.

stylus pressure   See VERTICAL STYLUS FORCE.

stylus printer   See WIRE PRINTER.

stylus scratch   See NEEDLE SCRATCH.

sub   Abbreviation of *subtract.*

sub-   Prefix denoting *under, below, less than,* or *lower than,* with respect to size, value, or rank. Compare SUPER-.

subassembly   A completely fabricated unit that forms part of a larger unit into which it easily fits.

subatomic particle   **1.** Any of various particles that comprise atoms of matter. **2.** A particle smaller than an atom. See, for example, ANTIPARTICLE, ELECTRON, MESON, NEUTRETTO,

NEUTRINO, NEUTRON, NUCLEON, POSITRON, and PROTON.

subaudible **1.** Pertaining to any frequency falling below the limit of human hearing, that is, less than about 20 Hz. **2.** Any sound that is too low in amplitude to be heard.

subaudible tone A signal, usually a steady, sine-wave tone, sent along with a radio signal. The tone frequency varies from about 20 Hz to 200 Hz, below the audio cutoff frequency of most voice communications systems. Subaudible tones are used mainly for privacy. The receiver is programmed to receive only signals having the correct subaudible tone frequency.

suballocation A portion of a radio-frequency broadcast or communications band that is legally set aside for specific purposes or users, e.g., the Extra-class segment of the 40-meter amateur-radio band.

subband **1.** A portion of a frequency band with specific characteristics. **2.** A portion of a radio-frequency broadcast or communications band that is set aside, legally or by convention, for specific purposes [e.g., the single-sideband (SSB) portion of the 20-meter amateur-radio band].

subcarrier A modulated carrier wave that composes the modulating signal for another carrier wave.

subcarrier band The band of frequencies in which a subcarrier signal is transmitted.

subcarrier frequency modulation In a system in which a carrier frequency is obtained by beating a low-frequency radio-frequency (RF) signal with a high-frequency RF signal, the application of frequency modulation to the low-frequency component. The technique is sometimes used in sweep-frequency signal generators.

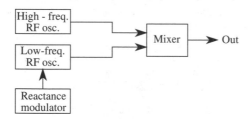

subcarrier frequency modulation

subcarrier oscillator In a color-television receiver, the oscillator operating at the burst (chrominance-subcarrier) frequency of 3.579545 MHz.

subchassis An auxiliary chassis on which one section of a larger piece of equipment is completely assembled and wired.

subfrequency See SUBHARMONIC.

subharmonic An integral submultiple of a fundamental frequency. Thus, for example, the 10th subharmonic of 15 MHz is 1.5 MHz.

submarine cable An underwater cable designed to withstand continuous immersion.

submarine robot A robot designed for underwater operation. It can be operated via telepresence or by simple remote control, usually using a conventional or fiberoptic cable. Some underwater robots have manipulators attached; others are equipped only with cameras, lights, and propulsion devices.

subminiature jack A female connector with an inside diameter of $\frac{3}{32}$ inch.

subminiature plug A male connector with an outside diameter of $\frac{3}{32}$ inch.

submultiple A fractional multiple, usually in reference to a frequency. For example, 7.2 MHz is a submultiple of 14.4 MHz. See SUBHARMONIC.

subpanel The front panel of a removable unit or module that forms a part of a larger unit.

subroutine In a computer program, a sequence of instructions for carrying out a section of the program's function. It is usually entered (led to) by a conditional branch (jump) instruction in the main program.

subscriber An individual user of a communications network or service.

subscript A small number or letter written to the lower right (and occasionally to the lower left) of another number or letter to identify the latter from others of the same designation (e.g., a_5, S_n). Compare SUPERSCRIPT.

subscription TV A television (TV) service paid for by subscribing viewers. The signals are scrambled so as to be useless to nonsubscribers, and legitimate subscribers are provided with a decoder to unscramble the telecasts.

subset **1.** In statistics and set theory, a set whose members are all contained in a larger set. **2.** A telephone handset or deskset (subscriber's set). **3.** A modulator/demodulator for making business machines compatible with telephone circuits.

subsidiary communication authorization Abbreviation, SCA. An authorization provided by the Federal Communications Commission (FCC) for a frequency-modulation (FM) broadcast station to transmit, in addition to its main program, a second program within the assigned bandwidth usually consisting of commercial-free background music on a subcarrier that can be detected only with a special receiver or with a special adapter attached to a standard FM receiver.

subsidiary feedback Feedback other than the main feedback in a system.

subsonic frequencies Frequencies below the range of hearing, that is, less than about 20 Hz. Also called ULTRALOW FREQUENCIES and SUBAUDIBLE FREQUENCIES.

substation An intermediate electricity-distributing location from which electrical energy is transformed and transmitted to users within a given geographical area.

substitution capacitor A capacitor used temporarily in place of another of usually the same value, as in troubleshooting. Also see CAPACI-TOR SUBSTITUTION BOX.

substitution inductor An inductor used temporarily in place of another of usually the same value, as in troubleshooting. Also see INDUCTOR SUBSTITUTION BOX.

substitution method **1.** A method of measuring a quantity (such as capacitance, inductance, or resistance) in which the value of the unknown quantity is determined in terms of the amount of a standard quantity that must be removed to restore the test circuit to its original state of balance. **2.** A method of troubleshooting in which good components are substituted for bad ones in a circuit (see, for example, SUBSTITUTION CAPACITOR, SUBSTITUTION INDUCTOR, SUBSTITUTION RESISTOR, SUBSTITUTION SPEAKER, and SUBSTITUTION TRANSFORMER).

substitution resistor A resistor used temporarily in place of another of usually the same value, as in troubleshooting. Also see RESISTOR SUBSTITUTION BOX.

substitution speaker A loudspeaker used temporarily in place of another, as in troubleshooting.

substitution transformer A transformer used temporarily in place of another having the same characteristics, as in troubleshooting.

substrate A plate, wafer, panel, or disk of suitable material on (or in) which the components of a unit, such as an integrated or printed circuit, are deposited or formed.

subterranean **1.** Pertaining to components, systems, or devices installed underground. It is applicable especially to cables. **2.** Pertaining to a phenomenon, such as the propagation of electric currents or acoustical waves, that occurs underground.

subterranean acoustical communication A method of communication that uses low-frequency sound waves, such as SONAR, to communicate via conduction through earth or water.

subtracter See ELECTRONIC SUBTRACTER.

subtractive color A color formed by mixing subtractive primary pigments.

subtractive primaries Broad-spectrum pigments used in printing to produce a wide variety of colors through filtering. These primaries are cyan (blue-green), magenta (pink-red), yellow, and sometimes black. They are used to print images that have been filtered through additive-primary lenses.

subtrahend In the process of subtraction, the quantity that is subtracted from another (the minuend) to produce the remainder or difference.

subwoofer A speaker designed to effectively reproduce extremely low audio frequencies, in some cases, subaudible (below 20 Hz).

successive derivatives Successive repetition of the operation of differentiating a function, which yields the first derivative, second derivative, and so on to the nth derivative.

successive integration The operation of double or triple integration.

Suhl effect A reduction in hole life that occurs in a semiconductor material in the presence of a magnetic field.

suite **1.** A group of computer programs run successively as a job. **2.** A bundled, high-end software package used especially in business computing.

sulfate Contraction of lead sulfate.

sulfation In a lead-acid storage cell, the formation of disabling lead sulfate during discharge of the cell.

sulfur Symbol, S. A nonmetallic element. Atomic number, 16. Atomic weight 32.06.

sulfur hexafluoride A gas used as a coolant and insulant in some power transformers.

sulfuric acid Formula, H_2SO_4. An acid used in dilute solution as the electrolyte of a lead-acid battery. This highly corrosive fluid also has many industrial uses.

sum The result obtained by adding two or more terms. Compare SUMMATION.

sumcheck See SUMMATION CHECK.

sum frequency **1.** In an amplitude-modulated carrier, the upper sideband frequency (i.e., the sideband equal to the carrier frequency plus the modulating frequency). Compare DIFFERENCE FREQUENCY. **2.** In superheterodyne operation, an intermediate frequency equal to the signal frequency plus the local-oscillator frequency.

summation **1.** The sum of a finite number of terms. Thus, the total resistance of n resistors connected in series is the summation of all R (resistance) terms. **2.** A frequency equal to the sum of two other frequencies.

summation check In computer operations, a check carried out on a group of digits. The result of adding the digits, and disregarding any overflow, is a check digit that can be compared with a standard value for the operation to verify the integrity of data.

summer **1.** See ADDER. **2.** See SUMMING AMPLIFIER.

summing amplifier An operational amplifier whose output is the sum, or is proportional to the sum, of several inputs.

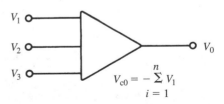

summing amplifier

sun battery A set of photovoltaic cells connected in series, parallel, or series-parallel to produce useful output voltages and currents.

S units   In radio (especially amateur radio), gradations reflecting the strength of received signals. Typically, a value of S9 (9 s-units), representing "extremely strong signals," is equal to a strength of 50 microvolts. The next lower S unit (S8) is 6 dB lower in voltage (i.e., 25 microvolts); S7 is 12 dB below S9 (i.e., 12.5 microvolts), etc.

sun lamp   An incandescent or fluorescent lamp with high ultraviolet output, used in medicine for the treatment of certain skin disorders. It can also be used for skin tanning; most physicians discourage habitual use of the lamps for this purpose.

sunlight lamp   A lamp that produces visible light whose spectral distribution is similar to that of typical daylight. It generally produces more blue and violet light than a conventional lamp. It is sometimes used for indoor lighting in winter at high latitudes, and/or to enhance plant growth.

sunlight-powered laser   A laser whose action is stimulated by sunlight collected by a system of mirrors and lenses. The life of the device is long, compared with that of conventional lasers.

sun-pumped laser   See SUNLIGHT-POWERED LASER.

sun relay   See SUN SWITCH.

sunspot   An area on the sun's surface that is visible as a dark, irregular region of variable size, generally several thousand miles across. Sunspots are believed to be comparatively cool regions associated with solar magnetic disturbances. The number of sunspots is correlated with the frequency and intensity of solar flares (see SOLAR FLARE).

sunspot cycle   Regular periodic variation of sunspot activity. The time between peaks in activity is approximately 11 years.

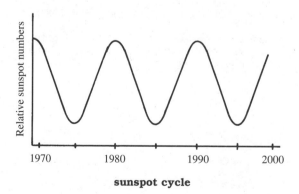

sunspot cycle

sun switch   A photoelectric switch or relay actuated by sunlight and used for various domestic and industrial purposes, such as switching lights, operating window shades, etc.

sup   Abbreviation of SUPPRESSOR.

super   Contraction of *supersonic*.

super-   Prefix denoting *over*, *above*, *greater than*, or *higher than*, with respect to size, value, or rank. Compare SUB-.

superaudible frequency   See ULTRASONIC FREQUENCY.

superbeta transistor   A transistor or transistor combination, such as a Darlington pair (see COMPOUND CONNECTION), that provides a very high current amplification factor (beta).

supercardioid microphone   A microphone that is highly sensitive in one direction and insensitive in all other directions. The directional pattern is similar to a CARDIOID PATTERN, but is exaggerated along the axis of optimum response.

superconducting cable   A cable in which superconductivity is achieved by surrounding the cable with liquid helium to lower its temperature to near absolute zero.

superconductivity   The virtual disappearance of resistance in some metals cooled to temperatures in the vicinity of absolute zero. Also see CRYOGENICS, CRYOSTAT, and CRYOTRON.

superconductor   A material or device that displays superconductivity.

super flatpack   An integrated-circuit package of the flatpack type having considerably more components and leads than those in the conventional flatpack.

superhet   Contraction of *superheterodyne*.

superheterodyne circuit   A circuit in which the incoming signal in a first detector (or mixer) beats with the signal of a local oscillator, resulting in a lower (intermediate) frequency, which then is amplified by an intermediate-frequency (IF) amplifier. This IF signal is detected by a second detector whose output is amplified by an audio-frequency (AF) amplifier. Because the IF amplifier operates at a single (fixed) frequency, it can be adjusted for optimum selectivity and gain. Also called *superhet circuit*.

superheterodyne receiver   A radio or television receiver using a SUPERHETERODYNE CIRCUIT.

superhigh frequency   See RADIO SPECTRUM.

Supermalloy   An alloy having a maximum permeability of 10^6.

supermodulation   A type of amplitude modulation (AM) in which one radio-frequency (RF) power stage continuously generates the carrier, and a second (usually identical) RF power stage is gated into full operation at the proper instant by the audio modulation to add additional RF power (corresponding to 100% modulation) to the signal. At the same time, the carrier amplitude is decreased by the proper amount to fulfill the conditions of a signal amplitude swing between zero and twice maximum for 100% modulation.

superposition   In a complex wave, the manner in which the constituent waves combine. The instantaneous value of the complex wave is equal to the vector sum of the instantaneous values of all the constituent waves.

superposition theorem In a network of linear elements, if a voltage E_1 in branch A causes a current I_1 to flow through branch C, and if a voltage $E2$ in branch B (which might be identical with branch A) causes a current I_2 to flow through branch C, then E_1 in branch A and E_2 in branch B applied simultaneously will cause a current equal to $I_1 + I_2$ to flow through branch C. Compare COMPENSATION THEOREM, MAXIMUM POWER TRANSFER THEOREM, NORTON'S THEOREM, RECIPROCITY THEOREM, and THEVENIN'S THEOREM.

superpower An arbitrary term denoting very high power. In the rating of standard broadcast stations, it has come to signify 1,000,000 watts (one megawatt) radio-frequency (RF) power output.

superradiance In a laser, a rapid increase in intensity of fluorescent-line emission with increasing excitation power.

superregenerative circuit A regenerative detector circuit in which regeneration is periodically increased almost to the point of oscillation, then decreased. This quenching action takes place at a supersonic rate (typically at 50 or 100 kHz) so that the quenching is inaudible. The result is that much more regeneration is afforded, without the detector going into oscillation, than is possible by simply increasing the regeneration manually. An extremely sensitive detector is the result.

supersaturated solution A solution that contains more solute than it normally would hold. Supersaturated solutions are obtained through special techniques and are extremely unstable. Compare SATURATED SOLUTION. Also see SOLUTE; SOLUTION, 1; and SOLVENT, 2.

superscript A small number or letter written to the upper right of another number or letter, the BASE, to indicate the power to which the base must be raised. Example: 10^5, e^x, y^2. Also called EXPONENT. Compare SUBSCRIPT.

supersensitive relay A relay that operates with a current of less than one milliampere, or with a voltage of less than one millivolt.

supersonic flow In a gas or liquid, movement of the medium at a speed greater than the speed of sound in that medium. Supersonic flow results in a greatly increased resistance or drag because of shock waves that form in the medium.

supersonic frequency See ULTRASONIC FREQUENCY.

supersonics See ULTRASONICS.

supervised line In a security system, a wire or foil strip that carries electrical current. If the current changes in such a line, an alarm is actuated.

supervisor 1. In a computer, a set of routines that oversees the operation of the system. The supervisor routines are coordinated by the central processing unit. 2. The execution of such a set of routines. 3. A microcomputer that oversees the operation of a security system.

supervisory circuit In a security system, a link between a sensor and the central computer or control device. This link can be via electric current through a wire or cable, but other methods can be used, such as fiberoptics, line-of-sight optics, infrared, ultrasonic, or radio.

supply 1. See CURRENT SUPPLY. 2. See POWER SUPPLY. 3. See VOLTAGE SUPPLY.

supply current Alternating or direct current available for operating a circuit, device, or system.

supply frequency The frequency of an alternating-current power supply.

supply power The maximum power that can be reliably delivered by an alternating-current or direct-current power supply.

supply reel In a reel-to-reel tape recorder or player, the reel that is initially full, and that gradually empties as the tape moves through the machine.

supply voltage The voltage of an alternating-current or direct-current power supply.

suppressed carrier A carrier that has been canceled or filtered out of a carrier/sideband combination.

suppressed-carrier double sideband See DOUBLE-SIDEBAND and SUPPRESSED CARRIER.

suppressed-zero instrument A meter or graphic recorder in which the zero point is off-scale or upscale, but has been brought to scale-zero by means of mechanical adjustment or use of a bucking voltage.

suppressor 1. A filter used to suppress radio interference. 2. See AUTOMATIC NOISE LIMITER. 3. See SPARK SUPPRESSOR. 4. In a pentode vacuum tube, a gridlike element between the screen grid and the plate, used to suppress secondary emission. Also see GRID, 2 and PENTODE.

suppressor circuit The circuit associated with the suppressor electrode of a vacuum tube.

suppressor diode A semiconductor diode used to prevent inductive kickback in circuits, to eliminate or reduce transients, or to prevent arcing between make-and-break contacts.

suppressor grid See SUPPRESSOR, 4.

suppressor modulation A method of modulation in which a modulating voltage is superimposed on the suppressor voltage of a pentode radio-frequency power amplifier tube.

suppressor pulse A pulse that prevents electron flow.

surface analyzer A device designed for the measurement of surface flatness or uniformity.

surface-barrier diffused transistor See MICROALLOY DIFFUSED TRANSISTOR.

surface-barrier transistor Abbreviation, SBT. A pnp transistor made by means of electrolysis and electroplating: Two fine streams of indium sulfate solution are placed on axially opposite points on the faces of an n-type wafer. At the same time, a direct current is passed through the wafer and solution in such a direction as to remove semiconductor material electrolytically from the faces; the tiny sprayed areas are etched away. When the desired wafer thickness is

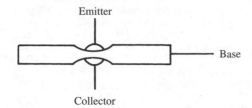

Emitter

Base

Collector

surface-barrier transistor

reached at the points of impact, the etching process is arrested by reversing the direction of current flow. This reversal causes an indium dot to be plated on each opposite face in the etched-out pit. Leads are attached to the collector and emitter dots and to the wafer (base).

surface-charge transistor A semiconductor device consisting essentially of two narrowly separated plates (source electrode and receiver electrode) deposited on the film-insulated surface of a silicon chip, and a third, overlapping electrode (the transfer gate) deposited on, but insulated from, the other electrodes. An input signal stores a charge in the capacitor formed by the source electrode and chip. A subsequent trigger signal applied to the transfer gate transfers the charge to the receiver electrode, where it becomes an output signal (often amplified, with respect to the input signal).

surface effect An effect (such as current, resistance, or resistivity) observed on the surface of a sample of material, rather than throughout the body of the material. Compare BULK EFFECT.

surface insulation A coating applied to the surfaces of core laminations to prevent the passage of currents between laminations.

surface leakage Leakage of current over the surface of a dielectric material, as opposed to leakage through the interior of the material.

surface noise See NEEDLE SCRATCH.

surface recombination rate For a semiconductor, the rate at which electrons and holes recombine at the surface. Compare VOLUME RECOMBINATION RATE.

surface resistivity The resistance of a unit area of a material, measured between opposite edges. Compare VOLUME RESISTIVITY. Also see RESISTIVITY.

surface tension The tendency of the surface of a liquid to "shrink." This property varies with different liquids and is caused by a net molecular force directed inward from the surface.

surface wave **1.** The earth-guided component of a ground wave. (The other component is the SPACE WAVE.) **2.** An acoustic wave traveling along the surface of a plate in a surface-wave amplifier or surface-wave filter.

surface-wave amplifier An amplifying device consisting essentially of a surface-wave filter to which has been added a direct-current-biased

n-type silicon electrode, which is separated from the crystal substrate of the filter by a very thin oxide layer. Amplification is produced by interaction between the electron current in the silicon and the piezoelectric field of the filter. Also see ACOUSTOELECTRONICS.

surface-wave filter An acoustoelectronic device consisting essentially of a crystal plate having electrodes at each end. An alternating-current (ac) input signal applied to one electrode sets up acoustic waves that travel along the surface of the plate to the other electrode, where they generate an ac output voltage by piezoelectric action. The resonant frequency of the device is governed by the dimensions of the crystal plate. Also see ACOUSTOELECTRONICS.

surge A sudden rise or flow of current or voltage.

surge absorber See SURGE SUPPRESSOR.

surge arrester See SURGE SUPPRESSOR.

surge current A heavy current that flows initially into a capacitor when a charging voltage is applied.

surge impedance Symbol, Z_o. The impedance seen by a pulse applied to a transmission line; $Z_o = L/C$ (approximately), where L and C are the inductance and capacitance, in microhenrys and microfarads, per unit length of the line. Also called CHARACTERISTIC IMPEDANCE.

surge protector Misnomer for SURGE SUPPRESSOR.

surge suppressor A semiconductor device used to absorb potentially destructive transients or overvoltages on a utility power line. It has a three-wire cord for plugging into a 117-volt outlet, a power switch, and several three-wire outlets for connection to sensitive electronic equipment (such as personal computers, videocassette recorders, television sets, hi-fi amplifiers, etc.).

surround See SUSPENSION, **1.**

Surround Sound The trade name for a multichannel sound system for use with television receivers and videocassette players. Some televised movies, especially on cable and satellite networks, deliver multichannel sound through receiving/recording systems equipped with special decoders.

surveillance **1.** A method of monitoring a specific area or volume for intrusion or other disturbance. **2.** A means of monitoring a specified portion of the electromagnetic spectrum for unauthorized signals.

surveillance radar An air-traffic-control radar that supplies continuous information regarding the azimuth and distance of aircraft inside a selected radius around an airport.

susceptance Symbol, B. Unit, siemens. The reactive component of admittance, as distinguished from conductance.

susceptibility The capacity of a substance to become magnetized, expressed as the ratio of magnetization to the strength of the magnetizing force.

suspension   1. In a speaker, the flexible, circular or elliptical structure via which the cone is attached to the frame. **2.** The wire or metallized fiber supporting the movable coil of a galvanometer. **3.** Particles of a substance and the liquid in which it is mixed, but not dissolved. **4.** The substance, as defined in **3**.

suspension galvanometer   A meter with a light-beam apparatus for lengthening the arc through which the pointer travels. When the beam of light is cast a long distance, a tiny movement of the coil will cause considerable movement of the image.

sustained oscillations   Oscillations that continue as long as power is supplied to the oscillation generator. Also see CONTINUOUS WAVE. Compare DAMPED OSCILLATIONS.

sustaining voltage   The voltage at which second-collector breakdown occurs in a transistor (see SECOND BREAKDOWN).

S video   In animation, a scheme that separates brightness and color. It can enhance the video in some applications.

SW   Abbreviation of SHORTWAVE.

sw   Abbreviation of SWITCH. (Also, S or s.)

swamping resistor   1. A noninductive resistor connected in parallel with the input circuit of a class-B linear amplifier for automatic regulation of the excitation. **2.** A resistor connected in series with the emitter of a bipolar transistor to minimize the effects of temperature-induced variations in junction resistance.

swarf   The string of material that threads off a disc during sound recording.

S_W band   A section of the S BAND, extending from 3400 to 3700 MHz.

sweep   1. To deflect the electron beam in a cathode-ray tube, usually horizontally, to provide a time base. **2.** The circuit for achieving the particular deflection described in **1**.

sweep circuit   A circuit, such as a deflection generator (e.g., a sawtooth oscillator), for producing a sweep signal. Also see SWEEP.

sweep delay   In an oscilloscope, the process of initiating the sweep of the electron beam at some selected instant after the signal has started.

sweep-delay circuit   In an oscilloscope or radar, the circuit for delaying the sweep until the start of the signal. Also see DELAYED SWEEP.

sweeper   1. See SWEEP GENERATOR. **2.** See SWEEP-SIGNAL GENERATOR.

sweep frequency   1. The frequency at which the electron beam in a cathode-ray tube is deflected along the reference axis. **2.** The frequency at which the carrier frequency is increased and decreased by a sweep-signal generator. **3.** In an oscilloscope, the number of times that the trace moves across the screen in one second. It is equal to the reciprocal of the SWEEP PERIOD.

sweep generator   1. A device that causes the electron beam in a cathode-ray tube to scan at a known speed. **2.** An oscillator that generates a signal that rapidly varies in frequency. It is used

for the testing and adjustment of bandpass filters and other selective circuits.

sweeping receiver   See SCANNING RECEIVER.

sweep magnification   In an oscilloscope, increasing or multiplying the sweep frequency, thus reducing the time per horizontal division. This increases the maximum frequency of waveforms that can be analyzed, and allows closer inspection of high-frequency signal components.

sweep magnifier   In an oscilloscope, a circuit for achieving sweep magnification.

sweep oscillator   See SWEEP GENERATOR.

sweep period   The duration, in seconds, of one complete cycle of sweep signal in an oscilloscope. It is equal to the reciprocal of the SWEEP FREQUENCY.

sweep signal   The (usually linear, sawtooth) signal used to sweep the beam of an oscilloscope tube. Also see SWEEP, **1, 2**.

sweep-signal generator   A signal generator that supplies a signal whose frequency varies automatically and periodically throughout a given band.

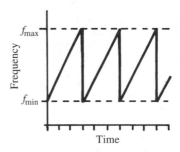

sweep-signal generator

sweep test   A method of testing the attenuation-vs.-frequency characteristics of a selective circuit, using a radio-frequency sweep generator.

sweep time   The actual time required for a single sweep by a deflecting signal; $t = 1/f$, where t is sweep time in seconds, and f is sweep frequency in hertz.

sweep voltage   The peak voltage amplitude of the sweep signal.

SWG   Abbreviation of *standard wire gauge*.

swing   The maximum change exhibited by a varying quantity (e.g., *amplitude swing* and *frequency swing*).

swinging choke   A filter choke that exhibits relatively high inductance when low current flows through it, and lower inductance when high current flows through it. This inductance, which swings under conditions of varying load current, permits the use of a high-resistance bleeder resistor. Compare SMOOTHING CHOKE.

Swiss-cheese packaging   A method of packaging an electronic circuit, in which components are inserted into the assembly through holes drilled or punched in parallel, stacked printed-circuit boards.

switch **1.** A circuit or device (electronic, electromechanical, or mechanical) for opening and closing a circuit or for connecting a line to one of several different lines (e.g., *rotary selector switch*). **2.** To change the logic state of a circuit or device. **3.** In a computer program, a branch instruction directing the program to a line number dependent on the value of a variable or result (e.g., BASIC's GOTO). **4.** To cause an electrical circuit to change state, as from low to high or vice-versa.

switch current **1.** The current flowing through a switch. **2.** The current flowing through a switching diode or transistor. **3.** The minimum current necessary to produce switching of a transistor, specified in milliamperes or microamperes.

switchgear Collectively, devices and systems for making and breaking circuits—either automatically or manually.

switchhook In a telephone set, the spring-and-switch device that engages the line when the receiver is lifted.

switching characteristics Technical data describing the performance and capabilities of switching devices and circuits.

switching circuit An on-off type of circuit containing electronic or mechanical switches.

switching diode See COMPUTER DIODE.

switching frequency The frequency at which a repetitive switch operates. Also see SWITCHING RATE.

switching mode Operation in which a device, such as a transistor or diode functions as a binary digital device, rather than as an analog device. The current is generally either zero (cutoff or pinchoff) or some value that depends on the bias and on the applied voltage.

switching rate The rate (e.g., closures per second) at which a repetitive switch operates. Also see SWITCHING FREQUENCY.

switching speed The time required for a switch to open or close or for a switching device to change states (as from cutoff to saturation). Also see SWITCHING TIME.

switching time The time required, after the application of a pulse, for an electronic switch to change state. Also see SWITCHING SPEED.

switching transistor A transistor designed especially for on-off operation. Such units exhibit short recovery time and low capacitance.

switching voltage The largest voltage that a switching device can handle without malfunctioning.

switch leakage current **1.** The current flowing through a switching device when it is supposed to be nonconducting. **2.** In a switching transistor, for a given voltage, the leakage current between the emitter and collector when the device is supposed to be nonconducting.

SWL Abbreviation of SHORTWAVE LISTENER.

SWR Abbreviation of STANDING-WAVE RATIO.

SWR bridge A four-arm resistance bridge for measuring voltage standing-wave ratio. This radio-frequency bridge has noninductive resistors in three of its arms and the device under test in the fourth arm. The bridge is balanced first with an equivalent noninductive resistor that replaces the device, and the output voltage is noted. Then the device is substituted for the test resistor, and the change in voltage is noted. The standing-wave ratio is determined from the voltage ratio.

SWR meter See SWR BRIDGE.

S_Y band A section of the S BAND, extending from 2600 to 2700 MHz.

syllable compandor A device that compresses or expands the amplitude of an audio signal. The time constant is fast enough to allow response to individual syllables. Compression is generally used at the transmitting station, and expansion at the receiving station.

sym **1.** Abbreviation of *symmetrical*. **2.** Abbreviation of SYMBOL.

symbol **1.** A letter or graphic device representing a quantity or term [e.g., I (current), f (frequency), etc.]. **2.** A conventional device denoting a mathematical operation (e.g., +, /). **3.** In a circuit diagram, a pictorial device representing a component.

symbolic address An address in a source-language computer program (i.e., the arbitrary label used by the programmer).

symbolic language See SOURCE LANGUAGE.

symbolic logic A system for representing logical relationships, such as those acted upon by computer and switching circuits, by means of symbols that are usually nonnumerical. Also see BOOLEAN ALGEBRA.

symmetrical circuit A circuit having identical configurations on each side of a dividing line, such as the ground bus. A push-pull circuit is an example.

symmetrical conductivity Identical conductivity for both positive and negative electricity. Compare ASYMMETRICAL CONDUCTIVITY.

symmetrical FET See SYMMETRICAL FIELD-EFFECT TRANSISTOR.

symmetrical field-effect transistor A field-effect transistor whose source and drain terminals can be interchanged without affecting circuit operation. Also called BIDIRECTIONAL TRANSISTOR. Compare UNILATERAL FIELD-EFFECT TRANSISTOR.

symmetrical input See BALANCED INPUT.

symmetrical output See BALANCED OUTPUT.

symmetrical transistor See BIDIRECTIONAL TRANSISTOR.

symmetrical wave A wave whose positive and negative half-cycles are identical in shape and peak amplitude.

symmetry **1.** The condition of having the same shape on each side of an axis. **2.** The condition of conducting positive and negative currents equally well. **3.** The condition in which a circuit is identical on both sides of a reference line, such as the ground line.

sympathetic vibration Resonant vibration of one body in response to the vibration of another body.

sync 1. Contraction of SYNCHRONIZATION. **2.** Contraction of SYNCHRONISM.

sync amplifier In a television circuit, the amplifier used to increase the amplitude of the sync pulses after they are separated from the composite video signal.

sync generator A circuit that produces the synchronization pulses in a television transmitter.

synchro A dynamo-electric-control device that, when connected to a similar device and the alternating-current power line, permits remote control. Thus, when the rotor of one synchro is turned to a certain position, the rotor of the other assumes the same position. Also see AUTOSYN and SELSYN.

synchrocyclotron A type of cyclotron in which the variation in mass, because of increased velocity, of the charged particles is compensated, resulting in higher energy for the particles.

synchro differential A synchro that receives two input signals and delivers a single output signal. The inputs can be two electrical signals, or one electrical signal and one mechanical signal.

synchrodyne receiver A direct-conversion receiver in which the local oscillator frequency or phase is locked into synchronism with the incoming signal carrier frequency or phase.

synchroflash A flash that is synchronized with the shutter of a camera.

synchro generator The transmitting member of a synchro system.

synchro motor The receiving member of a synchro system.

synchronism 1. The condition of being in step, as when two motors are running in synchronism with each other and the power frequency, or when two relays open and close in step. **2.** The condition of being in phase, as when two pulses occur simultaneously.

synchronization The coincidence of one process or operation with another, as in the synchronization of an oscillator frequency by means of an applied standard-frequency voltage, in which case the oscillator frequency becomes that of the standard signal.

synchronized clamping A type of clamping in which an output voltage is maintained at a predetermined fixed value until a synchronizing pulse is applied, whereupon the output follows the input.

synchronized multivibrator See DRIVEN MULTIVIBRATOR.

synchronizer A computer storage device used between two devices transmitting data at different speeds, to counteract this differential (as a buffer).

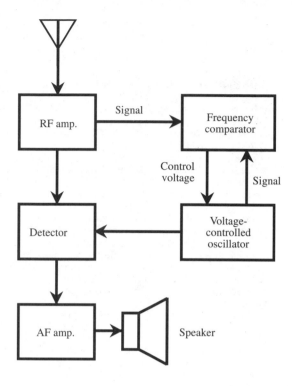

synchrodyne receiver

synchronizing signal A signal used to synchronize another signal, usually in frequency.

synchronous The condition of operating in step (phase) with some reference signal.

synchronous clock 1. An alternating-current clock driven by a synchronous motor. Although 60-Hz models are common, such clocks are not restricted to low-frequency ac operation; 1-kHz types, for example, are used in some primary frequency standards. **2.** The timing source in a synchronous computer.

synchronous computer A computer whose operations are timed by single-frequency clock signals.

synchronous contacts The rectifying contacts of a synchronous vibrator (see VIBRATOR-TYPE RECTIFIER).

synchronous converter A synchronous machine that can run on alternating current and generate direct current, or vice versa. Also called ROTARY CONVERTER.

synchronous gate A gate whose output is synchronized, according to the input signal.

synchronous generator An alternator operating in synchronism with one or more other alternators. Also see SYNCHROSCOPE, **2.**

synchronous induction motor An alternating-current motor that is intermediate between the fractional-horsepower reluctance motor and the multiple-horsepower three-phase, synchronous motor. The synchronous induction machine starts like an induction motor and runs like a synchronous motor.

synchronous inputs In a computer flip-flop, inputs that accept pulses only at the command of the clock.

synchronous machine See SYNCHRONOUS INDUCTION MOTOR.

synchronous motor See SYNCHRONOUS INDUCTION MOTOR.

synchronous network A communications network in which all clocks are set so that they run at the same rate, their increments are identical in duration, and transitions occur simultaneously or with a specified phase difference. Such a system allows for greatly enhanced signal-to-noise ratio for a given amount of transmitter power, and also reduces the bandwidth necessary for a single signal so that many more signals can be placed in a given frequency band.

synchronous orbit See GEOSTATIONARY ORBIT.

synchronous satellite See GEOSTATIONARY SATELLITE.

synchronous speed For an alternating-current (ac) machine, the speed corresponding to the ac frequency.

synchronous transmission A method of signal transmission in which individual symbols are sent at a specified rate, according to a clock that also governs the receiver.

synchronous vibrator See VIBRATOR-TYPE RECTIFIER.

synchroscope **1.** An oscilloscope having a high-speed sweep triggered by a synchronizing signal. Such an instrument is valuable for viewing high-speed pulses. **2.** A pointer-type instrument used to indicate the synchronism between two power alternators.

synchro system A circuit or system using synchros for the transmission and reception of positioning signals. Also see SYNCHRO.

synchrotron A particle accelerator that uses a high-frequency electrostatic field and a low-frequency magnetic field to impart very high velocity to the particles.

sync pulse **1.** A pulse used to control the frequency or repetition rate of an oscillator or other generator. **2.** In a television system, a pulse transmitted as part of the composite video signal to control scanning. Also see HORIZONTAL SYNC PULSE and VERTICAL SYNC PULSE.

sync separator In a television receiver circuit, a stage used to separate and deliver the sync pulses from the composite video signal. See, for example, DIODE SYNC SEPARATOR.

sync signal See SYNCHRONIZING SIGNAL.

sync takeoff The point in the video amplifier circuit of a television receiver at which the composite video signal is sampled to extract the sync pulses.

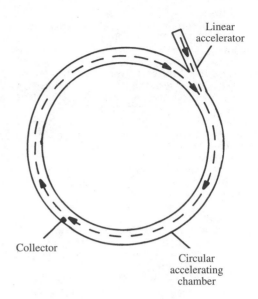

Linear accelerator

Collector

Circular accelerating chamber

synchrotron

syntax **1.** The rules by which computer program statements are structured. **2.** The way that a written or spoken sentence is constructed. It is important in speech recognition and speech synthesis.

synthesis The rigorous (usually mathematical) design of an electronic circuit or device and the accurate prediction of its performance. Compare ANALYSIS.

synthesizer **1.** See SIGNAL SYNTHESIZER. **2.** A circuit synthesizer (i.e., a device that allows a wide variety of circuits to be set up temporarily or simulated, for testing and evaluating). Sometimes, a specially programmed computer serves this purpose. **3.** A keyboard on which music can be played, and whose output can be adjusted to simulate the sounds of various musical instruments. **4.** See MOOG SYNTHESIZER.

synthetic bass An apparent accentuation of bass notes resulting from intermodulation distortion in an amplifier.

synthetic crystal An artificially produced crystal, such as synthetic quartz.

synthetic resin An artificially produced resin. Also see THERMOPLASTIC MATERIAL and THERMOSETTING MATERIAL.

syntony See RESONANCE.

syst Abbreviation of SYSTEM.

system **1.** An integrated assemblage of hardware and/or software elements operating together to accomplish a prescribed end purpose (e.g., *servo system*, *operating system*, and *communications system*). **2.** A methodology incorporating fixed and ordered procedures for accomplishing an end purpose. **3.** A self-contained computer workstation.

systematic error   See CUMULATIVE ERROR.

system engineering   See SYSTEMS ENGINEERING.

system of units   A set of fundamental units for defining the magnitudes of all physical variables. The most common system of units is the standard international (SI) system.

systems analysis   In computer system operation, analyzing the way something is done and devising a better alternative by isolating the problem area, scrutinizing the system as it stands, studying what is thereby disclosed, devising the alternate application of software and/or hardware, disseminating the revised operational procedure, and overseeing the implementation of the new method.

systems engineering   The branch of engineering devoted to the design, development, and application of complete systems. The approach takes into consideration all elements in a system or process and their integration.

systems flowchart   A flowchart showing the interrelationship of activities in a system.

S$_z$ band   A section of the S BAND, extending from 3900 to 4200 MHz.

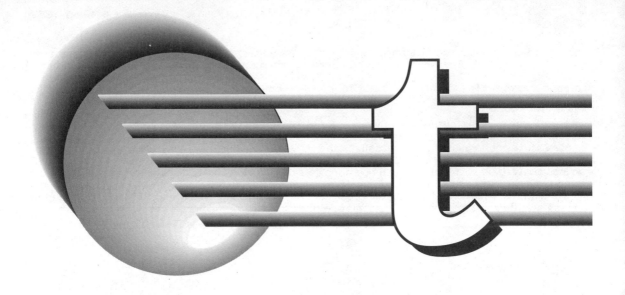

T **1.** Symbol for TRANSFORMER. **2.** Abbreviation of prefix TERA-. **3.** Symbol for *thermodynamic temperature.* **4.** Symbol for TRITIUM. **5.** Abbreviation of TON. (Also, t and tn.) **6.** Abbreviation of TESLA. **7.** Symbol for KINETIC ENERGY. **8.** Symbol for PERIOD. **9.** Symbol for *true.*

t **1.** Symbol for TIME. **2.** Abbreviation of TON. (Also, T and tn.) **3.** Symbol for CELSIUS TEMPERATURE. (Also, T.) **4.** Abbreviation of TARGET. **5.** Abbreviation of *technical.* **6.** Abbreviation of TENSION.

Ta Symbol for TANTALUM.

tab On the keyboard for a computer, typewriter, terminal, or word-processing system, a key that moves the cursor a specified number of spaces toward the right. It also performs various other functions in menu-driven or graphical computer interfaces.

table In an internal or external computer memory, an array (i.e., a list or matrix) of data that can be recalled using keys (e.g., single- or double-subscripted variables).

table look-at Abbreviation, TLA. In computer operations, finding the position of a data item in a table by implementing an algorithm.

table look-up Abbreviation, TLU. In computer operations, locating items in a table by inspecting what is in the table, key by key.

tabulate In data processing, to combine the totals for data item groups having the same key.

tabulation **1.** The printout of what has been tabulated (see TABULATE). **2.** The computer-program-directed movement of the cursor on a cathode-ray-tube display, or of a typewriter carriage, to certain positions in a line.

tabulator See TAB.

tacan A pulse-type UHF air navigation system in which a station is interrogated by signals from an aircraft to provide bearing and range information. The name is an acronym for *tactical air navigation.*

tach Abbreviated form of *tachometer.*

tachometer See ELECTRONIC TACHOMETER.

tachometer generator A small, dynamo-type electric generator that delivers a voltage proportional to the rotational speed of a shaft to which it is attached.

tachyon A high-speed subatomic particle thought to move faster than the speed of light.

tactical air navigation See TACAN.

tactical radar A radar system used in military operations.

tactile sensor A device that provides an intelligent machine with a sense of "touch": temperature, pressure, force, texture, and torque. It is important in robotics, and also in some computer applications, such as virtual reality (VR).

T-adapter See TEE-JUNCTION.

tag **1.** In data-processing and computer operations, the identification of digits or characters forming part of a record. **2.** An encoded price tag (i.e., a passive transponder or barcode strip). It is commonly used in retail stores.

tag converter A device that senses the information on tags (see TAG, **2**) and transfers it to a computer system.

tail **1.** The decay of a waveform from maximum amplitude to zero amplitude. **2.** Any pulse that follows a main pulse as a result of the main pulse.

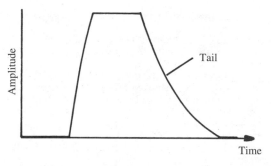

tail

taillight monitor   An electronic device for warning a motorist of taillight failure.

tail pulse   **1.** A pulse with a fast rise time, but a slow decay time. **2.** See TAIL, **2**.

takedown   In computer operations, the process of clearing output peripherals for upcoming program runs.

take-down time   The duration of the TAKEDOWN process.

take-up reel   In a reel-to-reel tape recorder/reproducer, the reel on which the tape accumulates during recording or reproduction.

talk-back circuit   See INTERPHONE.

talk-listen switch   A transmit-receive switch in an intercommunication system (see INTERCOM).

talk power   See SPEECH POWER.

tally   **1.** To obtain a sum or total. **2.** The rows of operands, subtotals, and totals that an adding machine prints.

tally reader   A device that, via optical character recognition (OCR), can read the digits and symbols on a tally (see TALLY, **2**).

tamper switch   A device that closes a circuit or actuates an alarm when a certain set of conditions is altered.

tan   Abbreviation of TANGENT.

tan⁻¹   Arc tan (inverse tangent function).

tandem transistor   An assembly of two series-connected transistors in the same envelope.

tangent   **1.** Abbreviation, tan. The ratio of the side opposite to the side adjacent to an acute angle in a right triangle. **2.** A line that intersects a curve at a single point without crossing the curve. **3.** A plane that intersects a curved surface at a single point.

tangent galvanometer   A galvanometer in which the current is proportional to the tangent of the angle of deflection. Compare SINE GALVANOMETER.

tangential mode   In acoustics, the reflection of sound waves from four surfaces in a room having six interior surfaces.

tanh   Abbreviation of HYPERBOLIC TANGENT.

tank   **1.** A parallel-resonant inductance-capacitance circuit in the output of a radio-frequency amplifier. **2.** A circuit in which is stored electri-cal energy of frequencies in a range whose midpoint is resonance for the circuit. **3.** See MERCURY DELAY LINE.

tantalum   Symbol, Ta. A metallic element of the vanadium family. Atomic number, 73. Atomic weight, 180.95. Tantalum is used in the elements of some electron tubes and in some electrolytic capacitors.

tantalum capacitor   See TANTALUM-FOIL ELECTROLYTIC CAPACITOR.

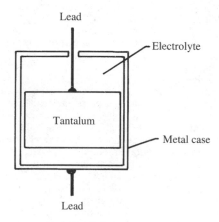

tantalum capacitor

tantalum detector   A radio-frequency contact detector consisting essentially of a fine tantalum wire whose point lightly touches the surface of a small pool of mercury.

tantalum-foil electrolytic capacitor   An electrolytic capacitor whose anode and cathode are tantalum foils, the anode foil being oxide-coated. Compare TANTALUM-SLUG ELECTROLYTIC capacitor.

tantalum-nitride resistor   A resistor consisting of a thin film of tantalum nitride deposited on a substrate. Also see THIN FILM.

tantalum-plug capacitor   See TANTALUM-SLUG ELECTROLYTIC CAPACITOR.

tantalum-slug electrolytic capacitor   An electrolytic capacitor whose anode is a sintered tantalum slug. Compare TANTALUM-FOIL ELECTROLYTIC CAPACITOR.

T-antenna   See TEE-ANTENNA.

tap   A connection made to an intermediate point on a coil, resistor, or other device. See, for example, CENTER TAP and TAPPED COMPONENT.

tap changer   A device that facilitates adjustment of the turns ratio of a transformer by changing the tap on the primary winding, the secondary winding, or both. It also facilitates the adjustment of the impedance-transfer ratio. It can be used for power supplies or audio- or radio-frequency transformers.

tape **1.** Magnetic tape. **2.** Insulating tape. **3.** To make a magnetic tape recording (audio, video, and/or digital data).

tape cable **1.** A form of cable in which all of the conductor centers lie in the same plane. **2.** A flat cable, commonly used in situations, where repeated flexing occurs.

tape cartridge A holder and the reel of blank or prerecorded magnetic (⅛-inch audio or wider video) tape it contains, which can be inserted into a recorder/reproducer without having to thread or otherwise handle the tape for either playing or rewinding.

tape comparator In a data-processing or computer system, a machine that compares tapes generated from the same input, for differences in the data thereon; it is a character-by-character process.

tape core A ring-type magnetic core made by tightly winding metal tape in several layers for the desired thickness.

tape counter See POSITION INDICATOR.

tape deck In a tape recorder/reproducer, the complete tape-transport mechanism (drive, heads, equalization circuitry, and preamplifiers).

tape drive **1.** See TAPE TRANSPORT. **2.** See TAPE DECK. **3.** A tape recorder/reproducer for computer data, used for backup and/or archiving.

tape file A data file recorded on magnetic tape.

tape group An assembly of two or more tape decks.

tape label On a reel or cassette of magnetic tape containing a data file, a record at the beginning or end that contains information about the file.

tape loop An endless loop of magnetic tape.

tape magazine See TAPE CARTRIDGE.

tape mark **1.** A character that subdivides the magnetic tape file on which it is recorded. Also called CONTROL MARK. **2.** A character marking the end of a length of magnetic tape on a reel. Also called END-OF-TAPE MARK.

tape plotting system In computer operations, a system for operating a digital incremental plotter using the information on magnetic tape.

taper In a potentiometer or rheostat, the rate of change in resistance during uniform rotation of the shaft. See, for example, LINEAR TAPER and LOG TAPER.

tape recorder A machine for recording audio, video, or data signals on magnetic tape; it can usually also play back the recorded material.

tapered potentiometer A potentiometer having a tapered resistance winding (see TAPERED WINDING).

tapered winding A resistance winding (in a rheostat or potentiometer) in which the resistance change per unit length of winding is nonuniform (see, for example, LOG TAPER). However, a winding having uniform resistance change is often called LINEAR TAPER.

tape skew A condition in which a magnetic tape passes between the recording or playback heads in an irregular way. The result is that the vari-

ous channels, or tracks, are not always perfectly aligned.

tape sort The (computer) operation of sorting data in a magnetic tape file into a record-key-determined sequence.

tape splicer A mechanism that aligns and secures the overlapping ends of broken magnetic tape so that they can be cut (often with an integral cutter) to form butted ends, and taped into a splice.

tape station See TAPE DECK.

tape-to-head contact See HEAD-TO-TAPE CONTACT.

tape transmitter A transmitter that receives its signal input from a recorded tape.

tape transport In a tape deck or reproducer, the device that moves the tape past the heads.

tape unit **1.** See TAPE DECK. **2.** See TAPE GROUP.

tape verifier In computer operations, a device that checks the integrity of data on paper tape through comparison with an original document.

tape width In magnetic tape, the dimension perpendicular to tape travel; in general, the greater the tape width, the more tracks the tape can contain.

tape-wound core See TAPE CORE.

tapped coil An inductor to which one or more intermediate connections (taps) are made at appropriate turns to provide intermediate values of inductance.

tapped component A coil, transformer, choke, resistor, or other component in which an intermediate connection is made. See, for example TAPPED COIL.

tapped inductor See TAPPED COIL.

tapped resistor A resistor in which one or more intermediate connections (taps) are made to appropriate parts of the resistance element to provide steps of resistance.

tapped transformer A transformer having one or more tapped windings.

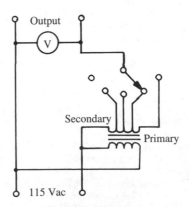

tapped transformer

tapped winding A transformer or choke winding with one or more taps. Also see TAP and TAPPED COIL.

tap switch A multiposition switch used to connect an external circuit to various taps on a component. Also see SELECTOR SWITCH and TAP.

target **1.** The bombarded electrode in an X-ray tube. **2.** The scanned storage element in a television camera tube. **3.** In radar operations, the scanned object. **4.** An object intended for nuclear-particle bombardment. **5.** A goal—especially in a production process (deadline, desired number of units, etc.).

target acquisition **1.** The moment at which a target comes within the range of a radar system. **2.** The observation of a new target on a radar screen.

target discrimination The extent to which a radar system can distinguish between two targets that are close together. Also called *target resolution.* It is specified in linear units (such as meters, kilometers, or miles).

target identification Any method by which the identity of a radar target is determined.

target voltage In a television camera tube, the backplate-to-cathode voltage.

task environment The characteristics of the space in which an autonomous robot works. It depends on such factors as the intended application(s), the required speed at which the robot(s) must work, and the human/robotic or computer/robotic interface.

task-level programming In robotics, the writing of programs to perform sequences of actions. A complex process, it is a primitive level of artificial intelligence (AI). An example is a program that directs a robot to prepare and serve a meal.

taut-band meter A movable-coil meter in which the conventional spiral springs of the coil are replaced by two tightly stretched, thin, straight metal ribbons, whose twist provides torque that returns the pointer to zero after a deflection.

Tb Symbol for TERBIUM.

BS Abbreviation of *talk between ships.*

Tc Symbol for TECHNETIUM.

TCCO Abbreviation of TEMPERATURE-CONTROLLED CRYSTAL OSCILLATOR.

T circuit See TEE NETWORK.

T circuit parameters See R PARAMETERS.

T circulator See TEE CIRCULATOR.

TCL Abbreviation of TRANSISTOR-COUPLED LOGIC.

TCM Abbreviation of *thermocouple meter* (see THERMOCOUPLE-TYPE METER).

TDM Abbreviation of TIME-DIVISION MULTIPLEX.

TDR **1.** Abbreviation of TIME-DELAY RELAY (see DELAY RELAY). **2.** Abbreviation of TIME-DOMAIN REFLECTOMETRY.

TDS Abbreviation of TIME-DELAY SPECTROMETRY.

TE Abbreviation of *transverse electric* (see, for example, TRANSVERSE ELECTRIC MODE).

Te Symbol for TELLURIUM.

teach box A robot-control device via which an operator can program the machine to carry out specific movements. The operator manipulates controls, and the robot's computer stores the data. When the data is accessed, the robot reproduces the motions.

tearing In a television picture, the abnormal condition in which poor synchronization causes the horizontal lines to be irregularly displaced. The effect resembles cloth being torn.

technetium Symbol, Tc. A metallic element produced artificially. Atomic number, 43. Atomic weight, 98. Formerly called *masurium.*

technician **1.** A person who repairs faulty electronic equipment. **2.** A person who assists with the design and debugging of a system prototype. **3.** A person who operates an electronic system.

technocentrism Overdependence on, and/or obsession with, the products of technology, particularly computers.

tee Pertaining to a network, connection, or configuration whose geometric shape or schematic representation resembles an uppercase letter T.

tee adapter See TEE JUNCTION.

tee antenna An antenna consisting of a horizontal radiator with a vertical lead-in or feeder connected to its center point.

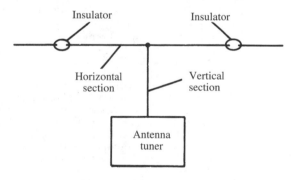

tee antenna

tee circuit See TEE NETWORK.

tee circulator In microwave systems, a tee-shaped junction of three waveguides with a ferrite post at the junction.

tee-equivalent circuit An equivalent circuit in which the components are arranged in the form of a tee. See, for example, TEE NETWORK and R PARAMETERS.

tee junction **1.** A tee-shaped splice between two wires. **2.** A tee-shaped fixture for splicing one coaxial line perpendicularly to another. **3.** A tee-shaped section for joining one waveguide perpendicularly to another. Also called WAVE GUIDE TEE.

tee junction

tee network   A three-terminal network resembling a tee.

tee pad   A three-resistor pad in which two series resistors and a shunt resistor are arranged to form a tee.

tee switch   A combination of three switches arranged to form a tee; two switches are in series with a shunt switch in between. If the series switches are open and the shunt switch is closed, isolation is greatly improved, compared to a single series switch.

Teflon FEP   A plastic insulating material. Dielectric constant, 2.1. Dielectric strength, 2800 V/mil.

Teflon TFE   A plastic insulating material. Dielectric constant, 2.2. Dielectric strength, 600 V/mil.

tel   **1.** Abbreviation of TELEPHONE. **2.** Abbreviation of TELEGRAPH. **3.** Abbreviation of TELEGRAM.

telautograph   A device that transmits and receives handwriting, drawings, and similar material. At the receiver, a pen follows the movements of a similar pen at the transmitter.

teleammeter   A TELEMETER for measuring current generated at a remote point.

telecamera   See TELEVISION CAMERA.

telecast   A television program for general reception. The term a contraction of *television broadcast.*

telechir   A remotely controlled, autonomous robot. See TELEOPERATION and TELEPRESENCE.

telecommunication   Communication, usually between widely separated points, by electrical or electronic means.

telecontrol   See REMOTE CONTROL and TELEOPERATION.

telefacsimile   See FACSIMILE.

telegram   Abbreviation, tel. A (usually printed-out) message transmitted and received via telegraph or teletypewriter. Compare CABLEGRAM and RADIOGRAM.

telegraph   Abbreviation, tel. An instrument for transmitting and receiving messages by means of telegraphy. In its simplest form, it consists of a key and a sounder powered by a battery. Also see PRINTING TELEGRAPH, **1, 2.**

telegraph channel   **1.** The frequency band assigned to a particular telegraph station. **2.** The frequency band occupied by a telegraph signal.

telegraph code   Broadly, Morse code. Wire telegraphy often uses a special version, such as the American Morse code.

telegraph key   See KEY, **1.**

telegraph sounder   See SOUNDER.

telegraph system   A complete, integrated, coordinated arrangement of equipment for communication by means of telegraphy. Included are telegraph keys or keyers, sounders or printers, relays, switchboards, wire lines and cables, and power supplies.

telegraphy   The branch of electrical communications that deals with the transmission and reception of messages by means of prearranged codes—especially over wires. Also see MORSE, **1, 2, 3**; MORSE CODE; and WIRE TELEGRAPHY.

telemeter   **1.** An indicating instrument that measures the value of a quantity generated at a distant point or measures and transmits the value. **2.** The action afforded by the device in **1.**

telemetering   See TELEMETRY.

telemeter receiver   See TELEMETRIC RECEIVER.

telemeter transmitter   See TELEMETRIC TRANSMITTER.

telemetric receiver   A system that selects, amplifies, and demodulates or rectifies a radio signal, and actuates indicating instruments, recorders, or data processors.

telemetric transmitter   A specialized transmitter that generates radio-frequency (RF) power, adds to it signals delivered by data transducers, and delivers the modulated power to an antenna for transmission to a distant telemetric receiver.

telemetry   The transmission of data signals over a distance, either by radio or wire, and the reception and application of the signals to indicating instruments, recorders, etc.

teleoperation   The remote control of autonomous robots. A human operator can control the speed, direction, and other movements of a robot from some distance away. See also TELEPRESENCE.

telephone   Abbreviation, tel. An instrument for transmitting and receiving messages by means of telephony. In its simplest form, it consists of a microphone, earphone, switching and ringing devices, wire line or cable, and power supply. Also see HANDSET.

telephone accessories   Devices (such as answering machines, speaker phones, facsimile machines, etc.) used in conjunction with a telephone set.

telephone amplifier   A small audio amplifier, usually with a self-contained loudspeaker, for increasing the sound volume of a telephone output. Some amplifiers of this kind are connected to the telephone line, and others receive sound from the telephone receiver.

telephone-answering machine   See ANSWERING MACHINE.

telephone bypass capacitors   A set of fixed capacitors installed between each wire in a telephone line and an electrical ground to bypass radio-frequency energy. It can reduce or prevent radio-frequency interference (RFI) to telephone sets and data terminals.

telephone data set A device that converts signals from a data terminal for passage over a telephone circuit to a data-processing center.

telephone dialer In a security system, a circuit that automatically dials one or more telephone numbers, alerting the recipient(s) that an emergency exists at a given location.

telephone induction coil A small telephone-to-line impedance-matching transformer used in telephone systems.

telephone patch See PHONE PATCH.

telephone pickup A device for receiving conversations from a telephone to which it isn't directly connected.

telephone plug See PHONE PLUG.

telephone-radio patch See PHONE PATCH.

telephone receiver The handheld part of a telephone set, containing the microphone and earphone, and, in some cases, the dialing keypad.

telephone repeater An amplifier and associated equipment used to boost the amplitude of a telephone signal at an appropriate point along the line.

telephone service entrance The point at which the telephone wiring in a house or building connects to the outside telephone line.

telephone silencer A device for muting a telephone or its bell.

telephone system A complete, integrated, and coordinated arrangement of equipment for communication by means of telephony. Included are telephones, switchboards and associated equipment, wire lines and cables, and power supplies. Also see DIAL TELEPHONE SYSTEM, HANDSET, PRIVATE AUTOMATIC EXCHANGE (PAX), PRIVATE BRANCH EXCHANGE (PBX), and TELEPHONE.

telephone test set See PHONE TEST SET.

telephone transmitter The sound pickup unit (microphone) of a telephone. Also see TRANSMITTER, **2**.

telephony The branch of electrical communication dealing with the transmission and reception of sounds—especially over wires. Also see WIRE TELEPHONY.

Telephoto **1.** The transmission and/or reception of photographs by means of FACSIMILE. **2.** A photograph transmitted and/or received by means of FACSIMILE.

telephoto lens A camera lens providing a telescopic effect.

Telephoto receiver See FACSIMILE RECEIVER.

Telephoto transmitter See FACSIMILE TRANSMITTER.

telepresence An advanced form of robotic TELEOPERATION, in which a human operator has the impression of being at the robot's location. It includes vision systems, pressure sensors, sound sensors, tactile sensors, and electromechanical control devices. The operator uses, or wears, equipment similar to that used for VIRTUAL REALITY (VR).

teleprinter A terminal telegraph printing machine. Also see PRINTING TELEGRAPH, **1**, **2**.

TelePrompTer A device that presents a running display on a screen before a television announcer, performer, or speaker, of dialogue.

teleran A ground-to-air communications system. Ground-based radar pictures are transmitted, via television, to aircraft.

telescoping antenna A vertical antenna consisting of separate lengths of metal tubing of progressively smaller diameter so that one can slide into another. The antenna can be pulled out to full length or compressed to the length of the largest-diameter section.

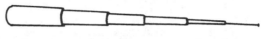

telescoping antenna

teletext A method of communication in which a video image is sent of a page of printed material.

telethermoscope A device for measuring the temperature of distant objects.

Teletorque See AUTOSYN and SYNCHRO.

Teletype **1.** The transmission and/or reception of text messages in digital form, displayed or printed at a distant location. **2.** See TELETYPEWRITER.

teletype grade A term descriptive of a circuit having the quality necessary for communication via telegraphy.

Teletypesetter An electronic system for operating a distant Linotype.

teletypewriter A variety of printing telegraph using electric typewriters and associated equipment. The message is typed on the keyboard at the transmitting station and is typed out in corresponding letters at the receiving station. The same typewriter is able to send and receive messages. Also see RADIOTELETYPEWRITER.

teletypewriter exchange Abbreviation, TWX. A center for switching and routing teletypewriter communications. Also see TELETYPEWRITER.

teleview To observe a scene or program via television.

televise **1.** To convert a scene into a television signal. **2.** To broadcast a scene or program via television.

television **1.** Abbreviation, TV. The transmission and/or reception, via electromagnetic fields, wire cable, and/or fiberoptic cable, of images, usually with sound. **2.** A system for receiving signals, as defined in **1**. **3.** Video programs or data, with or without sound, transmitted via electromagnetic fields, wire cable, and/or fiberoptic cable.

television band See UHF TELEVISION CHANNELS and VHF TELEVISION CHANNELS.

television camera The pickup device that scans a scene and delivers a series of electrical signals that can be used to reconstruct the image on the screen of a picture tube.

television-camera tube See CAMERA TUBE, ICONOSCOPE, and ORTHICON.

television channel A radio-frequency band allocated exclusively for the transmission of a television signal. In conventional broadcasting, this band is usually 6 MHz wide. See, specifically, UHF TELEVISION CHANNELS and VHF TELEVISION CHANNELS.

television engineer A trained professional skilled in video electronics engineering, as well as in basic engineering and associated subjects.

television engineering The branch of electronics engineering devoted to the theory and application of television.

television interference Abbreviation, TVI. Interference to the reception of television signals, usually occasioned by signals from radio services or computers, or by electrical noise.

televisor 1. A television transmitter or receiver. **2.** A person or entity responsible for the broadcast of television programs or signals.

televoltmeter A TELEMETER for measuring voltage generated at a remote point.

telewriter See TELAUTOGRAPH.

Telex 1. A teleprinter system that operates via the telephone lines, and was once commonly used by businesses for sending and receiving short messages. It has largely been supplanted by computerized data communications systems. **2.** A hard-copy message sent or received by such a system.

telluric currents Also called *terrestrial currents.* A flow of electrical charge carriers, primarily electrons, in the earth.

tellurium Symbol, Te. A rare, metalloidal element related to selenium. Atomic number, 52. Atomic weight, 127.60.

TE mode See TRANSVERSE ELECTRIC MODE.

temp 1. Abbreviation of *temperature.* (Also, T.) **2.** Abbreviation of *temporary.* **3.** Abbreviation of TEMPLATE.

temperament The tuning of a keyboard-type musical instrument to produce a nearly perfect diatonic scale.

temperature Symbol, T. A quantitative measure of the heat exhibited by an object or phenomenon. Also see THERMOMETER SCALE.

temperature coefficient A figure that states the extent to which a quantity drifts or varies under the influence of changing temperature. It is generally expressed in percent per degree (%/°C) or in parts per million per degree (ppm/°C).

temperature-compensated crystal oscillation Oscillation in a crystal oscillator, in which the crystal and/or circuit is automatically compensated against frequency drift caused by temperature change.

temperature-compensating component A circuit component, such as a capacitor or resistor, whose temperature coefficient is equal in magnitude and opposite in sign to that of a conven-

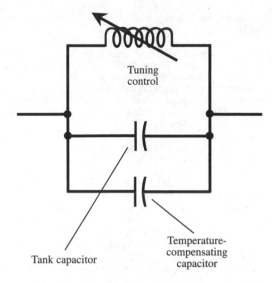

Tuning control

Tank capacitor

Temperature-compensating capacitor

temperature-compensating component

tional component to which it is connected to cancel temperature-induced variation in the latter's value.

temperature compensation The use of a device, such as a temperature-compensating component, to correct a temperature-induced deviation in the value of a conventional component.

temperature control 1. The adjustment of temperature. **2.** The automatic maintenance of temperature at a desired level, as in a temperature-controlled oven. **3.** A device for controlling temperature, as defined in **1** or **2.**

temperature-controlled crystal oscillator Abbreviation, TCCO. A high-precision crystal oscillator in which the crystal plate (and sometimes the circuitry, as well) is held at constant temperature.

temperature degree See DEGREE, **2** and THERMOMETER SCALE.

temperature derating Deliberate reduction of operating current and/or voltage of a device to a specific temperature to ensure proper operation. Also see DERATING, DERATING CURVE, and DERATING FACTOR.

temperature gradient A range of temperature variation, such as the rate of change of temperature, with respect to change of power dissipation, or the rate of change of temperature with spatial displacement.

temperature inversion See INVERSION, **1.**

temperature meter An indicator (usually a direct-current voltmeter or millivoltmeter) whose scale reads directly in degrees.

temperature scale See THERMOMETER SCALE.

temperature-sensitive resistor See THERMISTOR.

temperature shock See THERMAL SHOCK.

temperature-to-voltage converter A circuit or device, such as a thermocouple, that delivers an output voltage proportional to an applied temperature.

template **1.** A diagram, usually drawn on paper, to show the locations at which components should be placed or tasks should be performed. It is taped or cemented temporarily to the work, and the points are transferred to the latter by prick-punching. **2.** A stencil-like plate with alphanumeric and circuit symbols, used as a drafting aid. Sometimes called "drafting stencil."

temporary magnet **1.** A body that exhibits magnetism only briefly after it has been exposed to another magnet. Compare PERMANENT MAGNET. **2.** See ELECTROMAGNET.

temporary storage **1.** In computer and data-processing operations, the storage of data or instructions only until they are needed. Also called INTERIM STORAGE. **2.** Locations in a computer memory set aside during a program run for holding intermediate results of operations.

TEM wave See TRANSVERSE ELECTROMAGNETIC WAVE.

ten code A set of abbreviations used by two-way radio operators. Each "ten signal" represents a specific statement or query.

tension **1.** A force that tends to stretch, pull tight, or pull apart. Compare STRAIN. **2.** A term referring to VOLTAGE—especially in a utility power transmission line.

ten-turn potentiometer A precision potentiometer whose shaft must be turned through 10 complete revolutions to cover the entire resistance range. Also see HELICAL POTENTIOMETER and MULTITURN POTENTIOMETER.

T-equivalent circuit See TEE-EQUIVALENT CIRCUIT.

tera- Abbreviation, T. **1.** A prefix meaning trillion(s), (i.e., 10^{12}). **2.** A prefix meaning 2^{40}.

tera-electronvolt Abbreviation, TeV. A large unit of energy; 1 TeV = 10^{12} electronvolts. Also see ELECTRONVOLT.

terahertz Abbreviation, THz. A unit of extremely high frequency equal to 10^{12} Hz. Also called *Fresnel.*

teraohm A unit of high resistance, reactance, or impedance equal to 10^{12} ohms.

terawatt Abbreviation, TW. A large unit of power; 1 TW = 10^{12} W.

terbium Symbol, Tb. A metallic element of the rare-earth group. Atomic number, 65. Atomic weight, 158.93.

terbium metals A group of rare-earth metals, including *europium, gadolinium, terbium,* and occasionally *dysprosium.*

term In an algebraic expression, constants, variables, or combinations of these, separated by operation signs (e.g., the expression $4xy + z$ has two terms).

terminal **1.** A connection point at the input, output, or an intermediate point of a device, or a point at which a voltage is to be applied. **2.** A metal tab or lug attached to the end of a lead for connection purposes. **3.** Pertaining to the end of a series of events, etc. (e.g., terminal tests). **4.** In a data-communications system, a point of data input or output. Also called *data terminal.* If it does not have computing capability of its own, it is often called a *dumb terminal.*

terminal block A group of several terminals, intended for interconnection of circuits, mounted on a solid insulating block.

terminal board An insulating board carrying several lugs, tabs, or screws as terminals (see TERMINAL, **2**). Also see TERMINAL STRIP.

terminal guidance The navigation of a missile or aircraft to help it reach its target or destination.

terminal impedance The internal impedance of a device measured at the input or output terminals.

terminal point of degradation The point at which degradation of a circuit or component is complete. Also see DEGRADATION FAILURE.

terminal repeater A telephone repeater operated at the end of a line.

terminal strip A strip of insulating material, such as plastic or ceramic, on which are mounted one or more screws, lugs, or other terminals. Also see TERMINAL, **2**.

terminal strip (lug-type)

terminal voltage The voltage at the output terminals of an unloaded battery or generator.

ternary code See TRINARY NUMBER SYSTEM.

ternary fission The splitting of an atomic nucleus into three nuclear pieces. Also see FISSION.

ternary number system See TRINARY NUMBER SYSTEM.

terrain echoes Radar images caused by reflections from hills, mountains, and other natural terrestrial surface features. Also see GROUND CLUTTER.

terrestrial magnetism See EARTH'S MAGNETIC FIELD.

tertiary coil A third winding (see TERTIARY WINDING).

tertiary winding A third winding on a transformer or magnetic amplifier.

tesla Symbol, T. A unit of magnetic flux density; 1 T = 1 weber per square meter = 10^4 gauss.

Tesla coil A special type of air-core step-up transformer for developing high voltage at radio frequencies. It consists essentially of a low-turn primary coil, through which radio-frequency (RF) current flows, and a multiturn secondary coil, across which the high voltage, is developed.

test   A procedure consisting of one or several steps, in which (1) the mode of operation of a circuit or device is established, (2) the value of a component is ascertained, or (3) the behavior of a circuit or device is observed.

test bench   An equipment installation intended for the testing, repair, or debugging of electronic devices by a technician.

test data   Data used to test a computer program, including samples within limits that might be encountered during the program's implementation.

tester   1. See TEST INSTRUMENT. **2.** A technician who primarily makes tests and measurements.

testing window   See WINDOW, **2**.

test instrument   A device for checking the operation of a circuit or the value of a component. This class of instrument is usually less accurate than measurement instruments. Also see TEST SET.

test lead   The flexible, insulated wire attached to a test prod.

test pattern   A picture-and-line display on the screen of a television picture tube, used to check such features as aspect ratio, linearity, contrast, etc.

test point   A terminal intended for connection of test equipment in the repair or debugging of a circuit. Often, test points are labeled by the letters TP followed by numerals (such as TP1, TP2, etc.).

test probe   See PROBE, **1**.

test prod   A stick-type probe (see PROBE, **1**) with a flexible, insulated lead terminating in a plug or lug for attachment to an instrument.

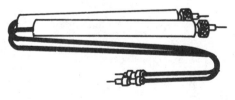

test prods

test program   In computer operations, a program devised to check the functioning of hardware. Also called *utility* and *test routine.*

test run   In computer operations, using test data to check the operation of a program, by comparing the results obtained thereby with what should ideally result.

test set   A combination of instruments assembled on a single panel, and usually enclosed in a carrying case, for convenience in making tests.

test signal   1. A signal used for conducting a test of a component, circuit, or system. **2.** In radiotelegraphy, a special signal signifying that

the transmitting station is testing equipment. Also see VEE SIGNAL.

test-signal generator   A device, such as an oscillator, for producing a signal for testing equipment (see TEST SIGNAL, **1**).

test tape   A magnetic tape containing signals for testing equalization, frequency response, head adjustment, stereo balance, etc. in an audiotape recorder, high-fidelity sound system, computer tape drive, or videocassette recorder.

tetravalent   See QUADRIVALENT.

tetrode   An electron tube in which the principal electrodes are cathode, control grid, screen, and plate.

tetrode transistor   1. A bipolar transistor with two emitters. **2.** A dual-gate field-effect transistor.

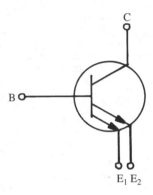

tetrode transistor

TeV   Abbreviation of TERA-ELECTRONVOLT.

T_e **value**   The temperature at which a centimeter cube of glass or ceramic exhibits 1 megohm of resistance.

TE wave   See TRANSVERSE ELECTRIC MODE.

text editor   A computer program for finding and changing data in a file.

texture map   In computer graphics, the topographical qualities of the surface of a three-dimensional rendition. For example, the image of an orange would have a "bumpy" texture map; the image of a peach would have a "fuzzy" texture map.

texture sensing   The ability of a robotic end effector to determine the relative smoothness or roughness of a surface. One common scheme uses reflected light or infrared. Scattered reflections indicate a rough or matte surface.

tgt   Abbreviation of TARGET.

TH   Abbreviation of *true heading.*

Th   Symbol for THEORIUM.

T_H Symbol for *heater temperature.*

thallium   Symbol, Tl. A metallic element. Atomic number, 81. Atomic weight, 204.38.

thalofide cell   An evacuated photoconductive cell using thallium oxysulfide as the light-sensitive material.

THD Abbreviation of TOTAL HARMONIC DISTORTION.

theory A reasonable proposition put forth to account for the behavior of, or the relationships between, bodies and forces, or to explain concepts and their relations. When a theory has stood up under exhaustive tests, it might reveal a scientific law.

therm A gas heating unit. 1 therm = 100,000 British thermal units (10^5 Btu).

thermal agitation Random movement of particles (such as electrons) in a substance, because of heat.

thermal-agitation noise See THERMAL NOISE.

thermal ammeter See HOT-WIRE AMMETER.

thermal anemometer See HOT-WIRE ANEMOMETER.

thermal conductivity The heat-conducting ability of a material. Compare electrical conductivity (see CONDUCTIVITY).

thermal conductivity

Element	Thermal conductivity (mW/m/°C)
Aluminum	22.0
Carbon	2.4
Chromium	6.9
Copper	39.0
Gold	30.0
Iron	7.9
Lead	3.5
Magnesium	16.0
Mercury	0.8
Nickel	8.9
Platinum	6.9
Silicon	8.4
Silver	41.0
Thorium	4.1
Tin	6.4
Tungsten	20.0
Zinc	11.0

thermal-conductivity device An instrument or control unit using a heated filament whose temperature and, accordingly, conductivity is varied by some sensed phenomenon. See, for example, GAS DETECTOR, HEATED-WIRE SENSOR, HOT-WIRE ANEMOMETER, HOT-WIRE FLOW-METER, and HOT-WIRE MICROPHONE.

thermal-conductivity gasmeter See GAS DETECTOR.

thermal detector 1. See BOLOMETER. 2. In a security or fire-protection system, a device that closes a circuit or actuates an alarm if the temperature rises to a specific level.

thermal emf See SEEBECK EFFECT.

thermal gasmeter See GAS DETECTOR.

thermal imaging See THERMOGRAPHY.

thermal instrument See HOT-WIRE METER and THERMOCOUPLE-TYPE METER.

thermally sensitive resistor See THERMISTOR.

thermal meter See HOT-WIRE METER and THERMOCOUPLE-TYPE METER.

thermal neutron A neutron that is essentially in thermal equilibrium with the surrounding medium or environment.

thermal noise Frequency-independent electrical noise caused by the agitation of particles (e.g., atoms and electrons) in a material by heat. Thermal noise is proportional to bandwidth, resistance, and absolute temperature.

thermal radiation See HEAT.

thermal recorder A graphic recorder in which a strip of paper coated with a thin layer of opaque wax is drawn between a knife-edge platen and a heated writing stylus that melts the wax beneath its point, exposing the underlying black paper as a fine line.

thermal resistance Symbol, R_T. For a semiconductor device, the rate of change of junction temperature, with respect to power dissipation; $R_T = dT/dP$, where R_T is in degrees Celsius per milliwatt, T is the temperature in degrees Celsius, and P is the power in milliwatts.

thermal resistor A resistor that is sufficiently temperature-sensitive to be used as a heat sensor. Examples: thermistor and germanium diode.

thermal response time For a power-dissipating component, the elapsed time between the initial change in power dissipation and the moment at which the temperature has changed by a specified percentage (usually 90%) of the total value.

thermal runaway A destructive process resulting from cumulative temperature effects. In bipolar transistors, this can occur if the collector current increases as the temperature rises. As the unit gets hotter, the collector-base junction dissipation increases, generating still more heat. The ultimate result, if the process continues unchecked, is destruction of the component. The process can also occur in certain batteries when they are charged too rapidly or at excessively high temperatures.

thermal shock The effect of applying heat or cold to a device so rapidly that abnormal reactions occur, such as rapid (often catastrophic) expansions and contractions.

thermal switch A switch actuated by a temperature change. Types vary from the simple thermostat to complex servosystem switches with a temperature-transducer input.

thermal time-delay relay A delay relay utilizing the slow-heating and slow-cooling property of one of its components.

thermion An ion or electron emitted by a hot body, such as the heated cathode of a vacuum tube.

thermionic Pertaining to thermions and their applications.

thermionic cathode A heated cathode, in contrast to a cold cathode, used as an emitter of electrons or ions. Also see THERMION.

thermionic current Current caused by thermionic emission—especially in an electron tube.

thermionic detector A vacuum-tube detector. Also see THERMION and THERMIONIC EMISSION.

thermionic diode A hot-cathode diode tube.

thermionic emission The emission of electrons by a hot body, such as the filament or cathode of a vacuum tube. Also see THERMION and HOT CATHODE.

thermionics The study of electron emission from objects or materials at high temperature.

thermionic tube An electron tube (i.e., one in which electrons or ions are emitted by a heated cathode). Also see THERMION, THERMIONIC CURRENT, and THERMIONIC EMISSION.

thermionic work function The energy required to force an electron from inside a heated cathode into the surrounding space (in thermionic emission). Also see WORK FUNCTION.

thermistor A temperature-sensitive resistor, usually made from specially processed oxides of cobalt, magnesium, manganese, nickel, uranium, or mixtures of such substances. Thermistors are available with either a positive or negative temperature coefficient of resistance. The name is a contraction of *thermally sensitive resistor*.

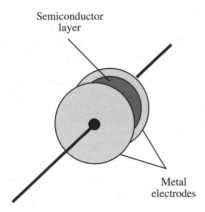

Semiconductor layer

Metal electrodes

thermistor

thermistor bridge A four-arm bridge (see BRIDGE, **1**) in which one arm is a thermistor and, therefore, is temperature sensitive.

thermistor power meter A radio-frequency power-measuring instrument based on a thermistor bridge.

thermistor probe A temperature probe containing a thermistor as the sensing element.

thermistor thermometer An electronic thermometer in which the temperature-sensitive element is a thermistor.

thermoammeter See THERMOCOUPLE-TYPE METER.

thermocouple A device consisting essentially of a bond between two wires or strips of dissimilar metals (such as antimony and bismuth). When the bond is heated, a direct-current voltage appears across it.

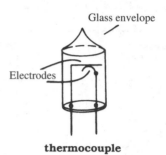

Glass envelope

Electrodes

thermocouple

thermocouple bridge A four-arm bridge (see BRIDGE, **1**) in which one arm is a thermocouple; therefore, it is temperature sensitive, as well as being voltage-productive.

thermocouple meter See THERMOCOUPLE-TYPE METER.

thermocouple-type meter A radio-frequency (RF) meter consisting of a thermocouple and direct-current (dc) ammeter, milliammeter, or microammeter, connected in series. The thermocouple is heated, directly or indirectly, by an applied RF current, and the resulting dc output deflects the meter pointer.

thermodynamics The science dealing with the relationships between heat and mechanical energy and their interconversion. Also see CARNOT THEOREM, FIRST LAW OF THERMODYNAMICS, SECOND LAW OF THERMODYNAMICS, and THIRD LAW OF THERMODYNAMICS.

thermoelectric cooler A cooling device based on the Peltier effect.

thermoelectric effect The production of thermoelectricity by certain materials.

thermoelectricity Heat-produced electricity, as in thermocouple operation.

thermoelectric junction A junction between two conductors that exhibits variable characteristics under conditions of changing temperature.

thermoelectric series A series of conducting metals, sequenced so that if a thermocouple is made from two of the metals, current flows at the hot junction from the metal occurring earlier in the series.

thermoelectron An electron emitted by a hot cathode. Also see THERMION and THERMIONIC EMISSION.

thermoelement A thermocouple, especially a miniature one, used in a THERMOCOUPLE-TYPE METER.

thermogalvanometer See THERMOCOUPLE TYPE METER.

thermography A means of locating or mapping by detecting infrared images. It can be in the form of live video, similar to television, or in the form of photographs, using infrared film. Many common cameras can be used with infrared film to make infrared photographs (thermographs).

thermojunction The junction of the two metals in a thermocouple. A voltage appears when the dissimilar metals are heated.

thermoluminescence Luminescence resulting from the moderate heating of certain materials.

thermomagnetic effect The effects of temperature on the magnetism of a body, or vice-versa.

thermometer A (usually direct reading) device for measuring temperature. Also see ELECTRONIC THERMOMETER and THERMOMETER SCALE.

thermometer scale The scale on a thermometer, graduated in degrees, from which temperature is read. For a description of different scales, see ABSOLUTE SCALE, CENTIGRADE SCALE, FAHRENHEIT SCALE, REAUMUR SCALE, and RANKINE SCALE. The Kelvin scale is the same as the absolute scale, and the Celsius scale is the same as the centigrade scale.

thermonuclear reaction A nuclear reaction in which energy is released when lighter atoms are converted into heavier atoms at temperatures in the millions of degrees Celsius. Also see FISSION, FUSION, and NUCLEAR REACTOR.

thermopile A device consisting of two or more thermocouples connected in series for increased voltage output.

thermoplastic material A plastic that can be resoftened by applying heat after having been molded into a desired shape. Example: polystyrene. Compare THERMOSETTING MATERIAL.

thermorelay See THERMOSTAT.

thermosensitivity Sensitivity of a circuit or device to heat.

thermosetting material A plastic that cures chemically (will not ordinarily soften again when heat is applied) after having been heat-molded into a desired shape. Example: Bakelite. Compare THERMOPLASTIC MATERIAL.

thermostat A temperature-sensitive switch. In one common form, a movable contact is carried by a strip of bimetal and the stationary contact is mounted nearby.

thermostatic switch See THERMOSTAT.

thermoswitch See THERMOSTAT.

theta wave A form of brain wave that occurs at extremely low frequencies, and is associated with sleep or mental incoherence.

Thevenin's theorem The proposition that, with reference to a particular set of terminals, a network containing a number of generators and constant impedances can be simplified to a single generator in series with a single impedance. The equivalent circuit will deliver to a given load, the same current, voltage, and power delivered by the original network. Compare COMPENSATION THEOREM, MAXIMUM POWER TRANSFER THEOREM, NORTON'S THEOREM, RECIPROCITY THEOREM, and SUPERPOSITION THEOREM.

thick film A film of selected material (conductive, resistive, dielectric, etc.) applied to a substrate by painting, photography, or similar process. See, for example, PRINTED CIRCUIT. Compare THIN FILM. Typically, thick films are 1 mil or more in thickness.

thick-film component A unit, such as a capacitor or resistor, fabricated by thick-film techniques. See, for example, PRINTED COMPONENT. Also see THICK FILM. Compare THIN-FILM COMPONENT.

thick-film resistor A resistor fabricated by thick-film techniques. See, for example, PRINTED RESISTOR. Also see THICK FILM. Compare THIN-FILM COMPONENT.

thick magnetic film See MAGNETIC THICK FILM.

thin film An extremely thin layer (less than 1 mil) of a selected material (conductive, resistive, semiconductive, dielectric, etc.) electrodeposited or grown on a substrate. Compare THICK FILM.

thin-film capacitor A capacitor made by electrodepositing a thin film of metal on each side of a grown layer of oxide, as in an integrated circuit. Also see THIN FILM.

thin-film component A unit (such as a capacitor, resistor, diode, or transistor), fabricated by thin-film techniques. Also see THIN FILM. Compare THICK-FILM COMPONENT.

thin-film integrated circuit An integrated circuit in which the components and "wiring" are produced by depositing (or growing) and processing materials on a semiconductor slab or wafer (the substrate). Compare HYBRID INTEGRATED CIRCUIT and MONOLITHIC INTEGRATED CIRCUIT.

thin-film memory In a computer, a storage medium that is a magnetic thin film (see THIN FILM) on a nonmagnetic substrate (often glass) and that can be magnetized to represent digital data.

thin-film microelectronic circuit An integrated circuit that occupies (essentially) two dimensions; that is, a very thin integrated circuit.

thin-film resistor A resistor fabricated by thin-film techniques (see THIN FILM) (e.g., TANTALUM-NITRIDE RESISTOR). Compare THICK-FILM RESISTOR.

thin-film semiconductor A very shallow layer of semiconductor material, such as single-crystal silicon, electrodeposited on a substrate. Also see THIN FILM.

thin-film transistor A transistor fabricated by thin-film techniques. Also see THIN FILM and THIN-FILM COMPONENT.

thin magnetic film See MAGNETIC THIN FILM.

third-generation computer   A computer in which the active discrete components are integrated circuits.

Third Law of Thermodynamics   As the temperature of absolute zero is approached in an isothermal process involving a solid or liquid, the change in entropy approaches zero; and the entropy of a substance is zero at absolute zero.

third-octave band   See ONE-THIRD-OCTAVE BAND.

thirty-channel multiplex   A form of pulse-code-modulated (PCM) multiplex using eight digits and the A-law. There are 30 speech channels and two utility channels.

Thomson bridge   See KELVIN BRIDGE.

Thomson effect   The liberation or absorption of heat (depending on the material of interest) when an electric current flows from a warmer to a cooler part of a conductor.

Thomson heat   The amount of thermal energy transferred because of Thomson effect.

Thomson voltage   The voltage drop between two points on a conductor that are at different temperatures.

thoriated-tungsten filament   In a vacuum tube, a filament made of tungsten to which thorium oxide has been added to increase the emission of electrons. Also see THERMION and THERMIONIC EMISSION.

thorium   Symbol, Th. A radioactive metallic element. Atomic number, 90. Atomic weight, 232.04. Thorium, when heated, is a copious emitter of electrons, so the filaments or cathode cylinders of some electron tubes are coated with one of its compounds.

thoron   Symbol, Tn. A radioactive isotope of RADON.

three-address instruction   A computer program instruction having three addresses, two for operands and one for the result (of the operation called for).

three-channel stereo   A form of stereophonic sound recording and reproduction in which three distinct channels are used; these are usually designated the left, right, and center channels.

three-coil meter   See ELECTRODYNAMOMETER.

three-conductor jack   A female connector in which two separate conductors are provided, in addition to the ground conductor.

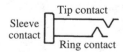

three-conductor jack

three-conductor plug   A male connector in which two separate conductors are provided, in addition to the ground conductor.

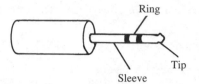

three-conductor plug

three-dimensional television   See STEREOSCOPIC TELEVISION.

three-electrode tube   See TRIODE.

three-element tube   See TRIODE.

three-gun picture tube   A color-television picture tube having a separate gun for each primary color (red, green, and blue).

three-halves-power law   See CHILD'S LAW.

three-junction transistor   A pnpn or npnp transistor. Also see NPNP DEVICE.

three-phase bridge rectifier   A bridge-rectifier circuit for three-phase alternating current. Two diodes are provided for each phase. The ripple frequency is six times the line frequency. Also see BRIDGE RECTIFIER, POLYPHASE RECTIFIER, and THREE-PHASE CIRCUIT.

three-phase circuit   The circuit of a three-phase system. See THREE-PHASE SYSTEM and, specifically, DELTA CONNECTION and WYE CONNECTION.

three-phase current   Current in a three-phase circuit. The currents in the three legs differ in phase by 120°.

three-phase four-wire system   See FOUR-WIRE WYE SYSTEM.

three-phase generator   A (usually dynamo-type) generator of three-phase current or voltage. See THREE-PHASE SYSTEM.

three-phase half-wave rectifier   A half-wave rectifier circuit for three-phase alternating current. One diode is provided for each phase. The ripple frequency is three times the line frequency. Also see HALF-WAVE RECTIFIER, POLYPHASE RECTIFIER, and THREE-PHASE CIRCUIT. Compare THREE-PHASE BRIDGE RECTIFIER.

three-phase motor   An alternating-current motor operating on three-phase power. Above fractional-horsepower size, the three-phase motor is smoother running and more simply structured than the single-phase counterpart.

three-phase power   The total power dissipated or delivered in a three-phase alternating-current circuit.

three-phase rectifier   A rectifier for three-phase alternating current. At least one diode is included for each phase. Also see POLYPHASE RECTIFIER, THREE-PHASE BRIDGE RECTIFIER, THREE-PHASE CIRCUIT, and THREE-PHASE HALF-WAVE RECTIFIER.

three-phase system   An alternating-current electrical system in which three currents or voltages exist simultaneously. They are of equal amplitude, but are 120° out of phase with each other.

three-phase, three-wire system An electrical system having three conductors, with an alternating-current phase difference of 120° between conductor pairs.

three-phase-to-single-phase transformer An alternating-current transformer with three-phase input and single-phase output (one terminal is grounded).

three-phase-to-two-phase transformer An alternating-current transformer with three-phase input and two-phase output, the output currents are 180° out of phase with each other.

three-phase voltage Voltage in a three-phase alternating-current circuit. The voltages across the three legs differ by 120°.

three-quarter bridge A bridge rectifier having diodes in three arms and a resistor in the fourth.

three-space A mathematical continuum in which each point is uniquely defined by three variables in an ordered triple, such as (x,y,z), and each ordered triple corresponds to exactly one point in the space. A common coordinate system is the Cartesian system consisting of three axes, x, y, and z—each mutually perpendicular and intersecting at the origin $(0,0,0)$.

three-space coordinates Any set of coordinates used for locating points or plotting graphs in three dimensions.

three-state logic See TRI-STATE LOGIC.

three-way speaker A set of three individual speakers contained in a single cabinet: a woofer (low-frequency speaker), a midrange speaker, and a tweeter (high-frequency speaker). It is common in high-fidelity music reproduction systems. Compare TRIAXIAL SPEAKER.

three-wire system **1.** An electric-power feed system using three wires, the center one (neutral) being at a potential midway between the potential across the other (outer) two. **2.** See THREE-PHASE and THREE-WIRE SYSTEM. **3.** See TWO-PHASE and THREE-WIRE CIRCUIT.

threshold **1.** The initial (observable) point of an effect (e.g., *threshold of hearing*). **2.** A predetermined point, such as of minimum current or voltage, for the start of operation of a circuit or device.

threshold component A value of current, voltage, sound intensity, etc., selected as the minimum level at which a circuit or device is to operate in some prescribed manner, or beyond which a certain condition will prevail. Also see THRESHOLD, **1**, **2**.

threshold current **1.** The minimum value of current at which a certain effect takes place. **2.** The smallest amount of forward current that flows through a diode. **3.** In a gas, the smallest level of current for which a discharge will maintain itself under variable conditions.

threshold detector A device that prevents a signal from passing until its peak amplitude reaches a certain value.

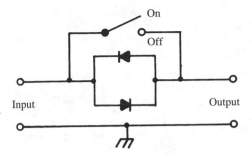

threshold detector

threshold frequency **1.** The cutoff frequency or frequencies in a band-pass, band-rejection, low-pass, or high-pass filter. **2.** The lowest frequency for a metal or semiconductor junction at which incident radiation gives rise to the photoelectric effect.

threshold of hearing The minimum intensity level at which sounds are audible in an environment containing essentially no background acoustic noise.

threshold of pain The intensity level at which hearing a sound causes physical discomfort. This is approximately 120 dB above the THRESHOLD OF HEARING for most people.

threshold signal The weakest signal that can be detected in a receiving system.

throat See HORN THROAT.

throat microphone A small microphone operated in contact with the user's throat.

throttle The feedback control device in a regenerative detector or amplifier.

throughput In computer operations, an overall quantitative indicator of processing power, expressed in terms of the amount of data processed in a given period of time.

throw-out spiral On a phonograph disc, a lead-out groove.

thulium Symbol, Tm. A metallic element of the rare-earth group. Atomic number, 69. Atomic weight, 168.93.

thumbwheel potentiometer A potentiometer operated by means of a knurled knob (usually protruding perpendicularly through a panel) that is turned with the thumb or with a finger.

thumbwheel switch A switch operated by means of a knurled knob (usually protruding perpendicularly through a panel) that is turned with the thumb or with a finger.

thy Abbreviation of THYRATRON.

thyratron A gas triode or gas tetrode used principally for switching and control purposes. Thyratron action differs from that of the vacuum tube in the unique behavior of the thyratron control electrode (grid): Anode current starts to flow abruptly when grid voltage reaches a particular value, at which point the grid provides no further control; anode current continues to flow until the anode voltage is either interrupted or reversed.

thyratron inverter An inverter circuit (see INVERTER, **1**) using thyratrons as the switching devices. Also see THYRATRON.

Thyrector A silicon diode exhibiting very high resistance (approaching that of an insulator) up to a certain voltage, beyond which the unit switches to a low-resistance conducting state.

thyristor **1.** A pnpn-type bistable semiconductor device having anode, cathode, and gate terminals that is used as an electronic switch. **2.** The generic term for all thyratronlike solid-state devices, such as the silicon-controlled rectifier.

Thyrite Ceramic silicon carbide, a nonlinear resistance material, or a resistor made of this material. The resistance of Thyrite decreases sharply as the applied voltage is increased. Thyrite resistors are used in voltage regulators, equipment protectors, lightning arresters, curve changers, and similar devices.

THz Abbreviation of TERAHERTZ.

Ti Symbol for TITANIUM.

tickler A (usually small) coil, through which energy is inductively fed back from the output to the input of a circuit to induce oscillation.

tickler coil See TICKLER.

tickler-coil regeneration Positive feedback obtained via inductive coupling between a small coil (tickler) in the output circuit of an amplifier, and a (usually larger) coil in the input circuit. Also see TICKLER.

tickler-coil regeneration

tickler oscillator An oscillator circuit in which positive feedback is obtained through inductive coupling between an output (tickler) coil and an input coil.

tie A bracket, clamp, clip, ring, or strip for holding several wires tightly as a cable or bundle.

tie cable **1.** A cable that connects two distributing points in a telephone system. **2.** Any cable that interconnects two circuits.

tie point A lug, screw, or other terminal to which wires are connected at a junction.

tie-point strip A terminal strip with lugs to which conductors can be soldered.

tight coupling See CLOSE COUPLING.

tilt switch A device, such as a mercury switch, that is actuated by tilting it to a certain angle.

timbre The quality that distinguishes the sound of one voice or instrument from that of another, largely because of harmonic content.

time Symbol, t. **1.** The instant at which an event occurs. **2.** The instant at which a time-base variable reaches a given value. **3.** The interval between two instants, commonly called *duration* or *length of time*. Also see STANDARD TIME, TIME BASE, TIME ZONE, and ZERO TIME.

time base Time as the independent variable in a physical relation or function. It appears in expressions such as *pulses per second, feet per minute, watts per hour*, etc.

time compressor In audio recording and reproduction, a device that speeds up or slows down the tempo without changing the audio frequencies. It is used for special effects.

time constant See ELECTRICAL TIME CONSTANT and MECHANICAL TIME CONSTANT.

time delay See DELAY, **1**, **2**.

time-delay relay See DELAY RELAY.

time-delay spectrometry In acoustics, a method of simulating an echo-free environment within an enclosure that is actually not echo-free.

time-division multiplexing Abbreviation, TDM. In data and computer communications, a time-sharing technique in which several terminals use the same channel by transmitting data at regular, staggered intervals (i.e., one is active while the others are idle). This gives the appearance of simultaneous real-time operation.

time-division-multiplex switch A switch with multiple ports—each port corresponding to a certain time slot in a time-division-multiplex scheme. The input and output (send and receive) ports are connected by selecting the same TIME SLOT for each.

time-domain reflectometry Abbreviation, TDR. Measuring the reflective characteristics of a device or system by superimposing the direct and reflected components of a step-formed test signal on a time-calibrated oscilloscope screen.

time duration See TIME, **3**.

time-duration modulation See PULSE-DURATION MODULATION.

time factor The ratio t_a/t_r, where t_a is analog time (the relativistic duration of an event as simulated by a computer), and t_r is real time (the actual duration of the event). Also called TIME SCALE.

time-interval mode In computer operations, operation that allows a number of events to be counted between two points on a waveform.

time modulation Any form of modulation in which the instantaneous characteristics of a signal are varied.

timeout The expiration of an allotted time period for a given operation.

timer **1.** A device for automatically controlling the duration of an operation. See ELECTRONIC TIMER. **2.** A device for measuring the duration of an operation.

time sharing In computer operations, a method for interlaced (i.e., nearly simultaneous) use of a machine or facility by two or more persons or agencies. As the cost of computers diminishes, so does the need for time sharing. Also see TIME-DIVISION MULTIPLEXING.

time-sharing dynamic allocator In computer storage, a program that allocates memory areas and peripherals to programs being entered into a time-sharing system; it also controls program execution.

timeshift **1.** To receive a message at a significantly later time than when it was sent. **2.** To use a videocassette or videodisc recorder to view a television program at a later time than when it was transmitted.

time-shifting communications Any form of communications in which the recipient reads or views the message(s) at a significantly later time than the message is sent from the source. A common example is electronic mail (e-mail) using online computer networks.

time signals Special radio transmissions made under the auspices of the National Bureau of Standards, for indicating Coordinated Universal Time (UTC).

time slot A specifically defined time interval in a data signal. It is of importance primarily in digital communications, where a given time interval can be high or low or at some discrete value.

time-space-time switch A large switch consisting of a space block between two time blocks.

time zone One of the 24 zones into which the global map is divided for the purpose of standardizing time. Within these zones, mean solar time is determined in terms of distance east or west of the zero meridian at Greenwich (near London, England). Each zone is equal to 15 degrees of longitude, or 1 hour. Four zones fall within the continental United States: Eastern Standard Time (zone of the 75th meridian), Central Standard Time (zone of the 90th meridian), Mountain Standard Time (zone of the 105th meridian), and Pacific Standard Time (zone of the 120th meridian). Also see MERIDIAN, ZERO MERIDIAN, and ZONE TIME.

timing extraction The retrieval of a timing signal from incoming data.

timing pin current Measured in microamperes. The current that generates a timing waveform in an integrated-circuit voltage regulator.

timing signal A repeating signal sent along with data to control the synchronization of transmitter and receiver.

tin **1.** Symbol, Sn. A metallic element. Atomic number, 50. Atomic weight, 118.71. Tin is widely used in electronics as a structural mate-rial, a constituent of solder, and (in foil form) as the plates of some fixed capacitors. **2.** To prepare the tip of a soldering gun or iron, or the stripped end of a wire or cable, by applying a coat of solder.

tin-oxide resistor See METAL-OXIDE RESISTOR.

tinsel Metal film strips interwoven with fabric threads to provide a flexible cord, particularly for headphones.

tint control In a color-television receiver, the control for changing color hue.

tip jack The mating connector for a tip plug.

tip plug **1.** A prod terminating in a phone tip. **2.** A plug-type connector terminating in a phone tip.

tip plug, 2

titanium Symbol, Ti. A metallic element. Atomic number, 22. Atomic weight, 47.88. Titanium enters into some dielectric compounds (e.g., titanium dioxide).

titanium dioxide Formula, TiO_2. A ceramic dielectric material. Dielectric constant, 90 to 170. Dielectric strength, 100 to 210 V/mil.

T junction See TEE JUNCTION.

Tl Symbol for THALLIUM.

T^2L Abbreviation of TRANSISTOR-TRANSISTOR LOGIC. (Also, TTL.)

TLA Abbreviation of TABLE LOOK-AT.

TLC Abbreviation of *thin-layer chromatography*.

TLU Abbreviation of TABLE LOOK-UP.

TM **1.** Abbreviation of TRANSVERSE MAGNETIC. **2.** Abbreviation of *technical manual*.

Tm Symbol for THULIUM.

TM mode See TRANSVERSE MAGNETIC MODE.

TM wave See TRANSVERSE MAGNETIC MODE.

T network See TEE NETWORK.

TNS Abbreviation of TRANSCUTANEOUS NERVE STIMULATOR.

toggle A bistable device.

toggle switch A switch having a mechanism that snaps into the on or off position at the opposite extremes to which a lever is moved.

tolerance The amount by which error is allowed in a value, rating, dimension, etc. It is usually expressed as a percent of nominal value, plus

toggle switch

and minus so many units of measurement (or parts per million).

toll call   In a telephone system, a call that is charged on a per-minute or per-second basis.

ton   Abbreviation, T, t, or tn. A unit of avoirdupois weight; in the United States, it is usually taken to mean *short ton,* a unit equal to 907.20 kilograms (2000 lb). Compare METRIC TON.

tone   **1.** The pitch (frequency) and timbre (relative harmonic content) of a sound other than noise. **2.** A sound consisting of a periodic waveform having constant frequency; also called *note.*

tone arm   See PICKUP ARM.

tone burst   A test signal consisting of a single-frequency sine wave sustained for a brief period of time, usually having a rectangular envelope (rapid rise and decay).

tone-burst entry   In repeater systems, a technique whereby a short tone signal is used at the start of a transmission to trigger a particular repeater so that all repeaters in the system will not go into operation simultaneously.

tone-burst generator   An oscillator and associated circuitry for producing a tone burst.

tone control   An adjustable device or circuit for modifying the frequency response of an amplifier (i.e., for emphasizing bass, treble, or midrange pitches).

tone dialing   A method of telephone dialing that uses standard tone pairs actuated via a keypad with 12 keys representing digits 0 through 9 and symbols # and *. Some keypads have four additional keys: A, B, C, and D.

tone generator   An oscillator for producing simple audio-frequency signals for communications, control, or testing.

tone keying   In wire and radio telegraphy, the representation of code characters by audio-frequency tones. Also see MODULATED CONTINUOUS WAVE.

tone localizer   A localizer that provides lateral guidance for an aircraft by comparing the amplitudes of two modulating frequencies.

tone modulation   **1.** The transmission of Morse, Baudot, or ASCII signals by audio-frequency modulation of a radio-frequency carrier. **2.** Any rapid variation of the amplitude or frequency of an audio tone.

top cap   A small metal cap on top of some electron tubes, serving as a direct, low-capacitance connection to one of the internal elements—usually the control grid, but sometimes the plate.

top loading   A method of feeding a vertical antenna at or near the top.

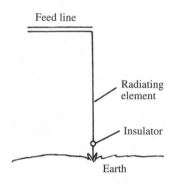

top loading

topology   **1.** A branch of mathematics concerned with the properties of surfaces and spaces. **2.** The details of layout of an integrated circuit. **3.** The characteristics of a surface.

toroid   See TOROIDAL COIL.

toroidal coil   A coil wound on a form that is shaped like a donut. The form is made of powdered-iron or ferrite. Toroidal coils have certain advantages over solenoidal coils: greater inductance for a given physical size, better isolation properties, and higher Q factor. A disadvantage is that an air core is not practical.

toroidal coil

torque   **1.** The force that tends to produce a rotating motion. **2.** Rotation of the plane of polarization of light by some crystals.

torque amplifier   A device having rotating input and output shafts and that delivers greater torque at the output shaft than that required to turn the input shaft.

torque sensitivity Symbol, K_T. For a torque motor, torque output per ampere of input current.

torr A unit of pressure equal to the pressure required to support a column of mercury 1 millimeter high at 0°C and standard gravity; 1 torr = 133.322 Pa (1333.2 microbars).

torsion The effect on an object by torque applied to one end while the other is being held fast or torqued in the opposite direction.

torsion delay line A delay line in which the delay is manifested in a material that is torqued by mechanical vibrations.

torsion waves Waves that travel by means of torque, instead of displacement or compression. The velocity of propagation depends on the modulus of rigidity and the density of the propagating medium.

tot 1. Abbreviation of *total*. 2. To derive a sum or total.

total breakaway torque For a torque motor, the sum of magnetic retarding torque and brush-commutator friction.

total harmonic distortion Abbreviation, THD. The distortion caused by the combined action of all the harmonics present in a complex waveform. An important specification in high-fidelity audio amplifiers.

total distortion See TOTAL HARMONIC DISTORTION.

total internal reflection 1. The reflection of visible light from a boundary between two substances having different indices of refraction. When the angle of incidence, relative to the tangent to the boundary, is smaller than a certain value, as light travels through the more dense medium total reflection occurs at the boundary. 2. Reflection of electromagnetic waves from an ionized layer in the atmosphere. This occurs at angles smaller than a certain angle, relative to the tangent of the plane of the ionizing layer. In some cases, total internal reflection does not occur. Actually, most ionospheric reflection is really refraction; the electromagnetic waves are bent by the ionized layer rather than reflected.

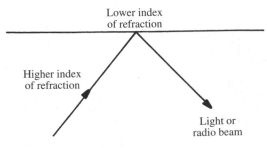

total internal reflection

total reflection Full return of a ray by a reflector, none of the energy being transmitted by or absorbed in the reflecting material.

touchplate relay A capacitance relay in which the pickup element is a small, metal plate that actuates the relay when it is touched.

tough dog A malfunctioning circuit that seemingly defies all attempts to diagnose and correct its trouble. Also see DOG.

tourmaline crystal A piezoelectric and pyroelectric crystal; a transparent plate of tourmaline has the ability to polarize light passing through it. Also see POLARIZATION, **3**; POLARIZED LIGHT; and POLARIZER.

tower 1. A usually tall and self-supporting openwork structure used to support an antenna, and usually having three or four sides. 2. A metal structure, as defined in **1**, used as a vertical antenna.

Townsend discharge In a glow-discharge tube, the discharge that begins after the applied voltage reaches a given level. It is a low-current, non-self-sustaining discharge. Compare ABNORMAL GLOW and NORMAL GLOW DISCHARGE.

touch screen A special cathode-ray tube (CRT) or video display unit that allows input of data via physical contact with the screen surface. Items are selected by simply touching the appropriate spot ("button" or icon) on the screen.

TP Abbreviation of TRANSACTION PROCESSING.

T pad See TEE PAD.

TR Abbreviation of transmit-receive.

t_r 1. Symbol for RECOVERY TIME. 2. Symbol for RISE TIME.

trace 1. A tiny or insignificant quantity. 2. The movement of the electron beam across the face of a cathode-ray tube. 3. A routine used for testing of, or for locating a fault in, a circuit or computer program. 4. The process of implementing such a routine.

trace element See MICROELEMENT.

tracer A suitable substance or object introduced into the human body and whose progress through the body can be followed (or its state monitored) by means of electronic equipment. Tracers are sometimes used also in nonbiological systems, such as pipelines.

track 1. A discrete information band on a magnetic disk or tape. 2. To follow, as by a stylus, a phono disc groove. 3. To follow, as by radar, a target.

trackability An expression of the accuracy with which a phonograph stylus follows the irregularities in a disc.

trackball A device for guiding the cursor or pointer in a computer. It is often used in laptop (notebook) computers. It resembles a ball bearing; the operator moves the cursor or pointer by pushing on the bearing with a finger.

track-drive locomotion A method of robotic locomotion using two or more wheels that drive a belt (track). It uses the same principle as a military tank.

tracking Following in step, as when ganged circuits resonate at the same frequency (or some frequency difference) at all settings, or when a missile closely follows its guiding signal.

tracking force See VERTICAL STYLUS FORCE.

track label On a magnetic storage medium, a record that identifies a track.

tracking mode In tracking supplies, the usual manner of operation in which the output of each of the separate supplies automatically follows that of the one being adjusted. Compare INDEPENDENT MODE.

tracking supplies Adjustable power supplies, packaged two or more to the unit, in which the output of each will automatically follow adjustment made to one of them.

track pitch The distance between tracks (see TRACK, **2**).

traffic **1.** Collectively, messages handled by a communications station. **2.** Collectively, data and instructions handled by a computer system in continual use.

trailer label At the end of a magnetic-tape or floppy-disk file, a record signaling the end of the file and often giving such information as the number of records in the file.

trailer record At the end of a group of computer records, a record containing information relevant to the group's processing.

trailing edge The falling edge of a pulse. Compare LEADING EDGE.

trans Abbreviation of TRANSVERSE.

transaction The exchange of activity that occurs between a computer, via a terminal, and the user, including any processing required (e.g., that involved in adding records to, or deleting them from, a file).

transaction file In data processing, a group of records used to update a master file.

transaction processing In computer operations, the use of a central processor for handling, modifying, or otherwise acting on information by transactions.

transaction tape Magnetic tape on which a transaction file has been recorded.

transadmittance For an active device, the ratio dI_2/dE_1, where I_2 is the alternating-current (ac) component of the current in a second electrode (such as the drain), and E_1 is the ac component of voltage on a first electrode (such as the gate), with constant direct-current operating voltages.

transceiver **1.** A combination radio transmitter-receiver, usually installed in a single housing and sharing some components. Compare TRANSMITTER-RECEIVER. **2.** In computer operations, a read/write data terminal capable of transmitting and receiving information to and from a channel.

transcendental functions Nonalgebraic functions. These include logarithmic functions, exponential functions, trigonometric functions, and inverse trigonometric functions.

transconductance **1.** Symbol, g_m. Unit, micromho. In an electron tube, the extent to which plate current (I_P) changes in response to a change in grid voltage (E_G); $g_m = dI_P/dE_G$. **2.** Symbol, g_{fs}. Unit, micromho. In a field-effect transistor, the extent to which drain current (I_D) changes in response to a change in gate-to-source voltage (V_{GS}); $g_{fs} = dI_D/dV_{GS}$.

transconductance amplifier An amplifier in which the output current is a linear function of the input voltage.

transcribe **1.** To record material, such as a radio program, for future transmission. **2.** In computer operations, the intermedia transfer of data, as from tape to disk.

transcriber A device used for intermedia data transfer (e.g., one that can move the data on magnetic tape to magnetic or optical disc).

transcription A recording of material, such as a record or tape of a radio program, for later use in a transmitter. See ELECTRICAL TRANSCRIPTION.

transcutaneous nerve stimulator Abbreviation, TNS. An electronic device for the temporary relief of pain. In its use, electrodes taped to the skin over the painful area are connected to a portable generator of suitable pulse energy.

transducer A device that converts one quantity into another quantity, specifically when one of the quantities is electrical. Thus, a loudspeaker converts electrical impulses into sound, a microphone converts sound into electrical impulses, a photocell converts light into electricity, a thermocouple converts heat into electricity, etc.

transducer amplifier An amplifier used expressly to boost the output of a transducer.

transducer efficiency For a transducer, the ratio of the output power to the input power.

transductor See MAGNETIC AMPLIFIER.

transfer **1.** To move a signal from one point to another—especially through a modifying circuit or device. **2.** To transmit information or data from one point or device to another, inside or outside a system.

transfer characteristic A figure or plot expressing the output-input signal relationship in a circuit or device. Also see TRANSFER, **1**.

transfer efficiency In a charge-coupled device, the proportion of charge that is transferred under given conditions.

transfer function **1.** See TRANSFER CHARACTERISTIC. **2.** An expression that mathematically shows how two entities or events occurring in different places or at different times are related.

transfer rate The speed at which data can be moved between a computer's internal memory and a peripheral.

transferred charge In a circuit containing a capacitor, the net electric charge that moves around the external circuit from one plate of the capacitor to the other.

transform **1.** See LAPLACE TRANSFORM. **2.** To change the voltage or nature of an electrical parameter (e.g., high to low voltage and alternating to direct current). **3.** To change the form, but not the content, of data.

transformation constant   See DISINTEGRATION CONSTANT.

transformer   **1.** A device using electromagnetic induction to transfer electrical energy from one circuit to another (i.e., without direct connection between them). In its simplest form, a transformer consists of separate primary and secondary coils wound on a common core of ferromagnetic material, such as iron. When an alternating current flows through the primary coil, the resulting magnetic flux in the core induces an alternating voltage across the secondary coil; the induced voltage can cause a current to flow in an external circuit. Also see AIR-CORE TRANSFORMER, INDUCTION, INDUCTIVE COUPLING, IRON-CORE TRANSFORMER, and TURNS RATIO. **2.** A section of radio-frequency (RF) transmission line used to match impedances. Also see LINEAR TRANSFORMER.

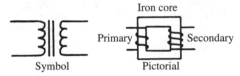

transformer, 1

transformer-coupled amplifier   An amplifier using coupling transformers between its stages or at its input and output points. Compare RESISTANCE-CAPACITANCE-COUPLED AMPLIFIER.

transformer coupling   The inductive coupling of circuits through a transformer. Also see COEFFICIENT OF COUPLING; INDUCTIVE COUPLING; MUTUAL INDUCTANCE; and TRANSFORMER, 1.

transformer equivalent circuit   An equivalent circuit depicting the various parameters of a transformer (such as primary and secondary resistances, primary and secondary reactances, core losses, etc.) and their relationship to each other.

transformer feedback   Inductively coupled feedback (positive or negative) through a transformer.

transformer input current   See PRIMARY CURRENT.

transformer input voltage   See PRIMARY VOLTAGE.

transformer iron   See SILICON STEEL.

transformer loss   The expression (in decibels) 10 $\log_{10} (P_1/P_2)$, where P_1 is the calculated power that a given transformer should deliver to a particular load impedance, and P_2 is the actual power delivered.

transformer oil   A petroleum product in which high-voltage, high-current transformers are sometimes immersed. The oil protects the windings from environmental damage.

transformer output current   See SECONDARY CURRENT.

transformer output voltage   See SECONDARY VOLTAGE.

transformer-type voltage regulator   See VOLTAGE-REGULATING TRANSFORMER.

transformer utilization factor   See UTILITY FACTOR.

transient   **1.** A sudden, high-voltage spike in an alternating-current system, caused by arcing or lightning. **2.** A spurious signal in a hardcopy-receiving system. **3.** Any short pulse attributable to external causes. **4.** Existing for a short period of time, or intermittently for short periods of time.

transient absorber   See SURGE ARRESTER.

transient arrester   See SURGE ARRESTER.

transient-based amplifier   See CRYSTAL AMPLIFIER, 2.

transient current   A momentary pulse of current. Also see TRANSIENT.

transient response   The response of a circuit to a transient, as opposed to its steady-state response, usually evaluated in terms of its ability to reproduce a square wave.

transient suppressor   See SURGE ARRESTOR.

transient voltage   A momentary pulse of voltage. Also see TRANSIENT.

transient voltmeter   An instrument that indicates the voltage of momentary signals. Usually, a peak-reading meter in the instrument displays the highest positive or negative value the transient attains (sometimes holding the deflection for reading later) and can respond to pulses of 1 microsecond in duration.

transistor   An active (commonly three-terminal) semiconductor device capable of amplification, oscillation, and switching action. The name is a contraction of *transfer resistor*. Also see ALLOY-DIFFUSED TRANSISTOR, ALLOY TRANSISTOR, BIPOLAR TRANSISTOR, DIFFUSED-BASE TRAN-SISTOR, DIFFUSED EMITTER-AND-BASE TRANSISTOR, DIFFUSED-JUNCTION TRANSISTOR, DIFFUSED MESA TRANSISTOR, DIFFUSED PLANAR TRANSISTOR, DIFFUSED TRANSISTOR, DIFFUSION TRANSISTOR, DOUBLE-BASE JUNCTION TRANSISTOR, FIELD-EFFECT TRANSISTOR, FIELDISTOR, GERMANIUM TRANSISTOR, GROWN-DIFFUSED TRANSISTOR, GROWN-JUNCTION TRANSISTOR, JUNCTION TRANSISTOR, MESA TRANSISTOR, METAL-OXIDE-SEMICONDUCTOR FIELD-EFFECT TRANSISTOR, MICROALLOY DIFFUSED TRANSISTOR, MICROALLOY TRANSISTOR, PHOTOTRANSISTOR, PLANAR EPITAXIAL PASSIVATED TRANSISTOR, PLANAR TRANSISTOR, POINT-CONTACT TRANSISTOR, POWER TRANSISTOR, SILICON TRANSISTOR, SURFACE-BARRIER TRANSISTOR, SURFACE-CHARGE TRANSISTOR, TANDEM TRANSISTOR, THIN-FILM TRANSISTOR, THREE-JUNCTION TRANSISTOR, and UNIJUNCTION TRANSISTOR.

transistor amplifier An amplifier containing only transistors as the active components. Also called *transistorized amplifier.*

transistor analyzer An instrument for measuring the electrical characteristics of transistors. Compare TRANSISTOR TESTER.

transistor-coupled logic Abbreviation, TCL. In computer and automatic-control operations, logic circuitry and systems using multi-emitter-coupled transistors. Also see RESISTOR-TRANSISTOR LOGIC and TRANSISTOR-TRANSISTOR LOGIC.

transistor current meter An ammeter, milliammeter, or microammeter circuit containing an amplifier using only transistors. Also see ELECTRONIC CURRENT METER.

transistorized voltmeter See TRANSISTOR VOLTMETER.

transistorized voltohmmeter An electronic voltmeter-ohmmeter combination using a transistorized circuit similar to that of a vacuum-tube voltohmmeter.

transistor keyer A power transistor acting as a keying device.

transistor oscillator An oscillator using only transistors as the active components. Also called *transistorized oscillator.*

transistor power supply A high-current, well-filtered, direct-current power supply for operating transistor circuits.

transistor radio Any small, portable, battery-powered radio receiver whose active components are transistors and/or other semiconductor devices.

transistor-resistor logic See RESISTOR-TRANSISTOR LOGIC.

transistor tester An instrument for checking the condition of transistors (i.e., whether good or bad). Compare TRANSISTOR ANALYZER.

transistor tetrode See DOUBLE-BASE JUNCTION TRANSISTOR.

transistor thyratron See SOLID-STATE THYRATRON.

transistor-transistor logic Abbreviation, TTL or T²L. In computer operations, a circuit in which the multiple-diode cluster of the diode-transis-

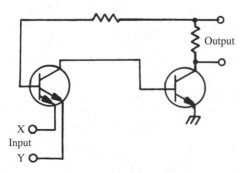

transistor-transistor logic

tor logic circuit has been replaced by a multiple-emitter transistor.

transistor voltmeter Abbreviation, TVM. A voltmeter containing an amplifier that uses only bipolar transistors. Also called *transistorized voltmeter.* Also see ELECTRONIC VOLTMETER. Compare FET VOLTMETER and VACUUM-TUBE VOLTMETER.

transistor VOM See TRANSISTORIZED VOLT-OHMMETER.

transit angle For an electron, the angular frequency multiplied by the time required to travel from one point to another.

transit time The time taken by an electron to travel from one electrode to another—especially from the cathode to the plate in a vacuum tube.

transistor element A metallic element whose atoms have valence electrons in two shells. Examples: chromium, iron, and nickel.

transition factor See MISMATCH FACTOR.

transition region See BARRIER, 1.

translation loss See PLAYBACK LOSS.

translator 1. See COMPILER. 2. See ASSEMBLER.

transliteration 1. To change the characters in one alphabet or code system to the characters in a different system. 2. The function that maps the characters in one alphabet or code system to those in another.

translucence 1. The transmission of radiation, especially visible light, through a material. 2. The extent to which a substance can transmit radiation—especially visible light. 3. Pertaining to a material that partially or totally transmits radiation—especially visible light.

transmission gain Current amplification, power amplification, or voltage amplification.

transmission line 1. A single conductor or group of conductors for carrying electrical energy from one point to another. 2. A correctly dimensioned conductor or pair of conductors for carrying radio-frequency energy from a transmitter to an antenna or coupling device.

transmission mode 1. In a transceiver, the condition in which the transmitter is enabled and the receiver is disabled. 2. In a waveguide, propagation via transverse waves.

transmission speed The number of information elements (words, code groups, data symbols, bits, and bytes) that can be generated or received per unit time (second or minute) by a system or operator.

transmission wavemeter A (usually simple) inductance-capacitance-tuned wavemeter that provides peak response when tuned to the frequency of a signal passing through it; also, the comparable microwave device. Compare ABSORPTION WAVEMETER.

transmit-receive switch A manually or electrically operated switch for transferring a single antenna between a transmitter and receiver.

transmittancy The relative ability of a substance to transmit radiation. Transmittancy depends on the frequency of the radiation, as well as the substance.

transmitter **1.** An equipment for producing and sending signals or data. **2.** See MICROPHONE. **3.** One who originates signals or data.

transmitter-receiver A separate transmitter and receiver housed together. Compare TRANSCEIVER.

transmitting antenna An antenna designed expressly for the efficient radiation of electromagnetic energy into space.

transmitting station A station that only transmits signals (i.e., it engages in no official form of reception). Compare RECEIVING STATION.

transmittivity The degree to which a selective circuit transmits a desired signal. Compare REJECTIVITY.

transmultiplexer A device that changes a signal from one multiplexed form to another while maintaining all of the information contained in the signal. For example, a transmultiplexer might convert time-division-multiplex data to frequency-division multiplex or vice-versa.

transonic Equal to, or approximating, the speed of sound in air (approximately 1100 feet per second).

transparence The practically unimpeded transmission of radiation, such as light, through a material. Compare OPACITY and TRANSLUCENCE.

transponder **1.** A combination transmitter-receiver that automatically transmits an identification signal whenever it receives an interrogating signal. The term is an acronym for *transmitter and responder.* **2.** A frequency channel or band transmitted by a communications or television satellite.

transport See TAPE TRANSPORT.

transportable equipment Portable electronic equipment. See, for example, PORTABLE TRANSMITTER.

transuranium An element whose atomic number is higher than that of uranium.

transverse Occurring in a direction or directions perpendicular to the direction of propagation.

transverse electric mode In a waveguide, the condition in which the electric lines of flux are perpendicular to the direction of propagation. Compare TRANSVERSE MAGNETIC MODE. Also see WAVEGUIDE MODE.

transverse electromagnetic wave An electromagnetic wave having electric-field vectors and magnetic-field vectors perpendicular to the direction of propagation.

transverse magnetic mode In a waveguide, the condition in which the magnetic lines of flux are perpendicular to the direction of propagation. Compare TRANSVERSE ELECTRIC MODE. Also see WAVEGUIDE MODE.

trap **1.** See WAVETRAP. **2.** In a semiconductor crystal, an imperfection capable of trapping current carriers.

trapezoid **1.** A polygon having four sides, of which only two are parallel. **2.** See TRAPEZOIDAL PATTERN. **3.** See TRAPEZOIDAL WAVE.

trapezoidal distortion In television or facsimile, a form of distortion in which the frame is wider at the top than at the bottom, or vice-versa.

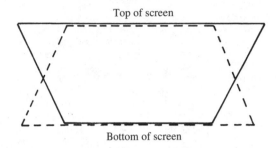

Top of screen

Bottom of screen

trapezoidal distortion

trapezoidal pattern An oscilloscope pattern used to check the percentage of modulation of an amplitude-modulated wave. Its name is derived from its trapezoidal shape.

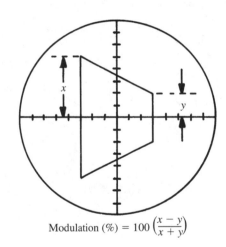

$$\text{Modulation (\%)} = 100 \left(\frac{x - y}{x + y} \right)$$

trapezoidal pattern

trapezoidal wave A nonsinusoidal wave that is a combination of a rectangular component and a sawtooth component. It is the required waveform of the voltage applied to a magnetic deflecting coil (oscilloscope or television) to ensure a sawtooth wave of current in the coil.

traveling-wave amplifier Abbreviation, TWA. An amplifier based on the unique operation of the traveling-wave tube.

traveling-wave tube Abbreviation, TWT. A microwave tube containing an electron gun, helical transmission line, collector, and input and output couplers. A microwave signal is coupled into the helix, through which it travels while the gun projects an electron beam through the helix. When wave and electron velocities are equal, a power gain is obtained in the signal coupled out of the helix. Also see BACKWARD-WAVE OSCILLATOR.

Travis discriminator A discriminator circuit in which the diodes are operated from separately tuned halves of the secondary winding of the input transformer. Compare FOSTER-SEELEY DISCRIMINATOR.

treasure locator See METAL LOCATOR.

treble The higher portion of the sound spectrum—especially the upper end of the musical scale (middle C and above). Compare BASS.

treble boost **1.** Amplification of high audio frequencies (the treble notes) in an audio system—especially in high-fidelity music reproduction. **2.** The extent of amplification of high audio frequencies in audio applications—especially in music reproduction. **3.** A control that allows adjustment of the relative treble gain in an audio system.

treble control See TREBLE BOOST, **3**.

tree **1.** A cause-and-effect chain with two or more independent branches. **2.** A circuit with two or more branches but no meshes.

TRF Abbreviation of *tuned radio frequency*.

TRF amplifier See TUNED RADIO-FREQUENCY AMPLIFIER.

TRF receiver See TUNED RADIO-FREQUENCY RECEIVER.

triac A three-terminal, gate-controlled, semiconductor switching device. Compare DIAC.

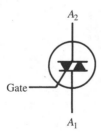

triac

triangular wave See BACK-TO-BACK SAWTOOTH.

triangulation A method of radiolocation in which directional bearings are obtained for the signals from two transmitters whose positions are accurately known. The position of the receiver is indicated by the intersection of two lines on a map, drawn emanating from the transmitter locations 180 degrees opposite their respective bearings.

Triax A double-shielded coaxial cable. A center conductor is surrounded by two concentric, independent shield conductors.

triaxial connector A male or female connector having three concentric contacting surfaces. By contrast, the coaxial jack and coaxial plug have only two such surfaces.

triaxial speaker A dynamic loudspeaker containing three coils and three cones, for high-, low-, and middle-frequency ranges. It is, in effect, three speakers in one. It is commonly used in high-fidelity music reproduction systems. Also called *triaxial driver*. Compare THREE-WAY SPEAKER.

triboelectric Pertaining to frictional electricity.

triboelectric series See ELECTROSTATIC SERIES.

triboluminescence Luminescence produced by means of friction.

trickle charge A continuous slow charge of a storage battery, in which the charging rate is just sufficient to compensate for internal losses or normal discharge.

trickle charger A light-duty unit for charging a battery gradually at low current.

tricorner reflector A device that reflects a ray of incident energy at a 180-degree angle, regardless of the direction from which the ray approaches. Thus, the ray will return to its source, unless some obstruction intervenes. It consists of three mutually perpendicular reflecting plane surfaces that intersect in a common point. The geometry is identical to that in a typical room, where the ceiling meets two walls. It is useful at microwave, infrared, visible, and ultraviolet wavelengths.

triethanolamine An amino alcohol that precipitates metallic silver from a silver-nitrate solution in the deposition of a silver surface on a substrate, such as glass or a ceramic.

trig Abbreviation of TRIGONOMETRY.

trigatron A form of electrically operated switch. The circuit is closed by the breakdown of an electrical gap.

trigger **1.** A pulse used to start or stop the operation of a circuit or device, such as a flip-flop. **2.** To place a circuit or device into or out of operation with a start or stop pulse, as defined in **1**.

trigger diode See DIAC and FOUR-LAYER DIODE.

triggered multivibrator See DRIVEN MULTIVIBRATOR.

triggered sweep In an oscilloscope or similar device, a driven sweep.

triggering point The voltage level at which the action of an electronic switching device is initiated. Also see BREAKOVER POINT.

trigistor A three-junction semiconductor device that exhibits two-state operation, and is useful as a flip-flop or switch. Also see NPNP DEVICE.

trigonometric functions See CIRCULAR FUNCTIONS and HYPERBOLIC FUNCTIONS.

trigonometry The branch of mathematics devoted to the application of CIRCULAR FUNC-

TIONS in a plane. It is useful in electronics for determining impedance and phase.

trim To make a fine adjustment, as of a tuning control, balance control, output adjustment, etc.

trimmer A low-valued variable capacitor, inductor, or resistor operated in conjunction with a main unit (usually of the same sort) for vernier adjustment or range setting. See, for example, HIGH-FREQUENCY TRIMMER and OSCILLATOR TRIMMER.

trimmer capacitor A variable capacitor used as a trimmer.

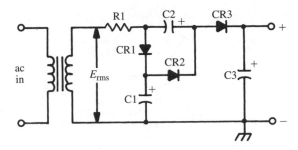

tripler, 1

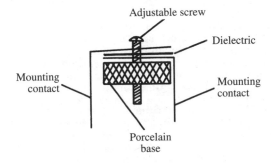

trimmer capacitor

trimmer coil See TRIMMER INDUCTOR.

trimmer inductor A variable inductor used as a trimmer.

trimmer resistor A variable resistor used as a trimmer.

trinary number system The base-3 system of notation. This system uses the digits 0, 1, and 2, the positional values being successive powers of 3 (e.g., decimal 14 equals trinary 112). Also called *ternary number system.*

Trinitron **1.** A single-gun color-television picture tube developed by Sony. **2.** A television set using this tube. The gun has three cathodes that modulate the three color beams (red, green, and blue). The beams are accelerated by common grids and are focused at different angles by convergence plates.

Trinoscope See TRINITRON.

triode A three-electrode tube or transistor, embodying an anode, cathode, and a control electrode as the principal elements.

triple-diffused transistor A diffused transistor in which the base and emitter are diffused into the top face of the chip, and the collector into the bottom face.

triple diode An assembly of three (often closely matched) semiconductor diodes in a single housing.

tripler **1.** A rectifier that delivers a direct-current output voltage at approximately triple the peak value of the alternating-current input voltage. **2.** An amplifier or other circuit that delivers an output signal at triple the frequency of the input signal.

triplexer In radar, a device that facilitates the use of two receivers at the same time.

Tri-state logic Digital logic in which there are three possible states, rather than the usual two. The conditions are defined as 0, 1, and undecided. Trade name of National Semiconductor.

tritium Symbol, T or H_3. An isotope of hydrogen whose nucleus contains two neutrons and one proton. Compare DEUTERIUM.

TRL Abbreviation of *transistor-resistor logic* (see RESISTOR-TRANSISTOR LOGIC).

Trojan horse A program written with the malicious intent of sabotaging the operating system and/or files in a computer. It is somewhat similar to a VIRUS; it is occasionally spread via software whose origin is questionable or unknown.

troposphere The portion of the atmosphere in which virtually all weather phenomena occur. It extends from the surface to an altitude of 8 to 12 miles above sea level.

tropospheric propagation A form of electromagnetic-wave propagation in which over-the-horizon communication is made possible because of effects in the lower atmosphere.

tropospheric scatter Scattering of electromagnetic waves at certain frequencies, resulting

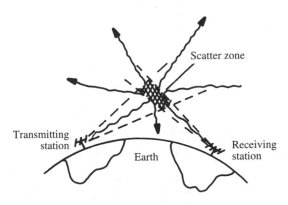

tropospheric scatter

from irregularities in the troposphere. Also see FORWARD SCATTER.

troubleshoot **1.** To look for the cause of equipment failure. **2.** To look for flaws in computer software or to debug a program.

troubleshooting test A test that is part of the procedure for finding the cause of faulty electronic equipment operation. Also see DIAGNOSTIC TEST. Compare PERFORMANCE TEST.

trough value The minimum amplitude of a composite current or voltage.

true complement See RADIX COMPLEMENT.

true ground The earth, as opposed to an artificial ground, such as that provided by the radials of a ground-plane antenna or an equipment chassis.

true power In an alternating-current (ac) circuit, the power actually dissipated in the resistive component; the reactive component consumes no power. In ac circuits containing reactance, the true power is less than the product of the voltage and current. Also see AC POWER and POWER FACTOR.

truncation A method of approximating a quantity by cutting off its digits beyond a certain point. For example, 3.44 and 3.46, when truncated to two significant digits, both become 3.4. Compare ROUNDING.

trunk **1.** A communications link between two points, one usually being external. **2.** The interface between a central processing unit and a peripheral device.

trunk link In computer systems, an interface permitting access to main storage via a peripheral.

truth table In logic analysis and logic circuit design, a table in which are listed all combinations of input values and the corresponding output values for a given logic function.

truth table

$$(x + y)' + xz$$

x	y	z	x + y	(x + y)'	xz	(x + y)'+xz
0	0	0	0	1	0	1
0	0	1	0	1	0	1
0	1	0	1	0	0	0
0	1	1	1	0	0	0
1	0	0	1	0	0	0
1	0	1	1	0	1	1
1	1	0	1	0	0	0
1	1	1	1	0	1	1

ts Abbreviation of tensile strength.

Tschebyscheff filter See CHEBYSHEV FILTER.

TSS Abbreviation of TIME-SHARING SYSTEM.

T switch See TEE SWITCH.

TST switch See TIME-SPACE-TIME SWITCH.

TTL Abbreviation of TRANSISTOR-TRANSISTOR LOGIC. (Also, T^2L.)

TTT In radiotelegraphy, a signal indicating that a message concerning safety is to follow (equivalent to *securite* in radiotelephony).

TTY Abbreviation of TELETYPE.

T-type antenna See TEE ANTENNA.

T-type attenuator See TEE PAD.

tube **1.** Generic term for any electron tube (e.g., vacuum tube, gas tube, cathode-ray tube, X-ray tube, etc.). **2.** Glow lamp: argon bulb, neon bulb, mercury-vapor lamp, etc.

tube capacitances The internal capacitances between the elements of an electron tube.

tube diode A two-element (cathode and anode) electron tube for current rectification. Also see DIODE.

tube of flux A group of flux lines within a circular cross section. It can vary in diameter as the density of the flux lines changes.

tube parameters Operating coefficients of electron tubes (e.g., plate current, grid voltage, screen current, transconductance, amplification factor, etc.).

tube tester An instrument for checking one or more of the parameters of an electron tube.

tubular capacitor A fixed capacitor consisting of a wound section enclosed in a cylindrical can.

tune **1.** To adjust a selective circuit to accept or reject a signal. **2.** To correct the natural frequency of vibration of a body. **3.** To adjust a radio transmitter for optimum output. **4.** To adjust the frequency of an oscillator—especially in a radio transmitter or receiver. **5.** To adjust the resonant frequency of an antenna, antenna coupler, or antenna system.

tuned AF amplifier **1.** An audio amplifier that is continuously tunable over a band of frequencies. **2.** An audio oscillator that is set to a fixed, precise frequency. See, for example, PARALLEL-TEE AMPLIFIER.

tuned-base oscillator A self-excited, common-emitter connected, bipolar-transistor oscillator in which the tuned tank is in the base circuit.

tuned circuit A (usually series-resonant or parallel-resonant) circuit adjusted to accept or reject a signal. Also see RESONANCE.

tuned-collector oscillator A self-excited, common-emitter connected, bipolar-transistor oscillator in which the tuned tank is in the collector circuit.

tuned coupler An antenna coupler (transmatch) that can be adjusted independently of the transmitter or receiver with which it is used.

tuned dipole A half-wave, center-fed, resonant antenna.

tuned feeders An antenna feed line that is adjusted or trimmed so that the entire system (feeders and radiating element) is resonant at the transmitted-signal frequency.

tuned headphones Headphones used in radiotelegraphy that are fix-tuned to a single audio frequency (e.g., 1 kHz) by means of a small parallel capacitor.

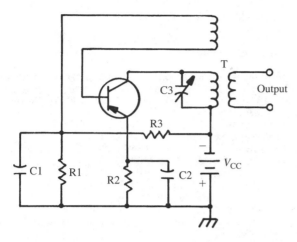

tuned-collector oscillator

tuned line An antenna wire or transmission line that provides a resistive load at a specific resonant frequency.

tuned pickup A pickup circuit or device (such as a radio-frequency sampling coil) that is tuned to the signal frequency.

tuned radio-frequency amplifier An amplifier circuit that is continuously tunable over a specific band of radio frequencies.

tuned radio-frequency receiver A radio receiver consisting only of a tuned-radio-frequency amplifier, detector, and audio amplifier. Compare SUPERHETERODYNE RECEIVER.

tuned reed A vibrating reed whose length, width, and/or thickness have been adjusted so that it vibrates naturally at a desired frequency.

tuned-reed frequency meter An audio frequency meter using tuned metal reeds as the indicators. Also see POWER FREQUENCY METER, **2**.

tuned relay An electronic or electromechanical relay that closes at one frequency. See, for example, REED SWITCH, **1**.

tuned signal tracer A signal tracer that can be tuned sharply to the frequency of the test signal being traced.

tuned transformer An audio-frequency or radio-frequency transformer tuned via a capacitor in parallel with its primary winding and/or a capacitor in parallel with it secondary winding.

tuner A circuit or device that can be set to select one signal from a number of signals in a frequency band.

tungsten Symbol, W. A metallic element. Atomic number, 74. Atomic weight, 183.85. Also called *wolfram*. It is used in switch and relay contacts, in the elements of some electron tubes, and in incandescent-lamp filaments.

tuning **1.** Adjustment of the frequency of a receiver to intercept a signal on a given fre-

quency. **2.** Adjustment of a transmitter oscillator to a desired frequency. **3.** Adjustment of an inductance-capacitance circuit for resonance on a desired frequency. **4.** Adjustment of an antenna or antenna system to a desired frequency. **5.** Adjustment of a radio-frequency amplifier for optimum performance. **6.** Alignment of a musical instrument for correct tone frequency.

tuning capacitor A variable capacitor used to tune an inductance-capacitance circuit (series-resonant or parallel-resonant).

tuning coil A variable inductor used to tune an inductance-capacitance circuit (series-resonant or parallel-resonant).

tuning core See TUNING SLUG.

tuning diode See VOLTAGE-VARIABLE CAPACITOR, **1**.

tuning fork A metal device that vibrates at a precise audio frequency when struck physically. It usually has two prongs and looks something like a fork.

tuning-fork oscillator See FORK OSCILLATOR.

tuning indicator **1.** A meter or display that indicates when a receiver is properly tuned to the frequency of an incoming signal. **2.** Sometimes, a bridge null detector.

tuning meter A meter-type resonance indicator.

tuning potentiometer A single or ganged potentiometer (depending on the circuit in which it is used) used to vary the frequency response of a resistance-capacitance-tuned circuit, such as the bridge-tee, parallel-tee or Wien-bridge circuit.

tuning slug A powdered-iron core that slides or screws in and out of a coil to vary the inductance.

tuning voltage An adjustable direct-current voltage used to vary the capacitance of a varactor diode (serving as the capacitor in a tuned circuit).

tuning wand See NEUTRALIZING TOOL.

tunnel diode A specially processed junction diode whose forward conduction characteristic displays negative resistance.

tunnel-diode amplifier A circuit that uses the negative-resistance properties of a tunnel diode to produce gain. It is used primarily at ultra-high and microwave frequencies.

tunnel-diode oscillator A circuit that uses the negative-resistance properties of a tunnel diode to produce oscillation at a specific frequency. It is used primarily at ultra-high and microwave frequencies.

turbidimeter A device used to measure the turbidity (relative opaqueness) of liquids.

turbidity meter See TURBIDIMETER.

Turing machine A hypothetical model, conceived by Alan Turing in the 1930s, devised as an exercise in problem solving. In effect, it was a computer programming language with a limited instruction set, operating in a computer with infinite memory and storage capacity.

Turing test   A scheme devised by Alan Turing, designed to test computers for artificial intelligence (AI). If the machine can fool a person into thinking it is another person most of the time, then the machine in effect "passes" the test, indicating that it has some AI.

turn   One complete loop of a coil.

turnaround time   **1.** The length of time required for a repair to be performed. **2.** The length of time required for a computer program to be completed. **3.** The time required for a transceiver to switch from the full-transmit to the full-receive condition.

turn factor   For a given inductor core, the number of turns (in a standard configuration) that results in an inductance of 1 H.

turn-off time   The time required for the operation of a circuit or device to cease completely after a signal or operating power has been removed. Compare TURN-ON TIME.

turn-on time   The time required for a circuit or device to come up to full (normal) operation after application of a trigger or operating power. Compare TURN-OFF TIME.

turnover pickup   See DUAL PICKUP.

turns ratio   For a transformer, the ratio of the number of turns in the primary winding to the number of turns in the secondary winding.

turnstile antenna   A polyphase antenna that resembles a turnstile gate.

turntable   **1.** The motor-driven, rotating platter on which a phonograph disc rests during recording or reproduction. **2.** In a high-fidelity phonograph system, the assembly containing the platter, as defined in **1**.

turret tuner   A television front-end tuner having a separate tuned-circuit section for each channel. Turning a knob rotates a desired section into position against switch contacts. Also called DETENT TUNER.

TV   **1.** Abbreviation of TELEVISION. **2.** Abbreviation of *terminal velocity*.

T/V   Abbreviation of *temperature to voltage*.

TV decoder   A device for unscrambling a television broadcast that has been intentionally encrypted to prevent its use by unauthorized viewers. See SUBSCRIPTION TV.

TV ghost   See GHOST.

TVI   Abbreviation of TELEVISION INTERFERENCE.

TVL   Amateur radio abbreviation of *television listener* (looker).

TVM   Abbreviation of TRANSISTORIZED VOLTMETER.

TVO   Abbreviation of TRANSISTORIZED VOLT-OHMMETER. (Also, TVOM.)

TVOM   Abbreviation of TRANSISTORIZED VOLT-OHMMETER. (Also, TVO.)

TV projector   A combination electronic and optical device for projecting television images on a large screen.

TV sound marker   See SOUND MARKER.

TVT   Abbreviation of *television terminal* (computer peripheral).

TW   Abbreviation of TERAWATT.

TWA   Abbreviation of TRAVELING-WAVE AMPLIFIER.

tweeter   A loudspeaker that favors the extreme treble (high) audio frequencies, ranging from 4000 or 5000 Hz to more than 20,000 Hz. Compare WOOFER.

twin diode   See DUAL DIODE.

twinlead   See FLAT-RIBBON LINE.

twin line   See FLAT-RIBBON LINE.

twin meter   See DUAL METER.

twin-T measuring circuit   See PARALLEL-TEE MEASURING CIRCUIT.

twin-T network   See PARALLEL-TEE NETWORK.

twisted pair   A simple wire line used for communications. It consists of two wires twisted together to form a helix.

twister   A piezoelectric crystal, such as one of Rochelle salt, that generates a voltage when torqued.

twistor   A magnetic-memory element consisting of a winding of magnetic wire on a length of nonmagnetic wire.

two-channel amplifier   See DUAL-CHANNEL AMPLIFIER.

two-channel recorder   See DOUBLE-CHANNEL RECORDER.

two-electrode amplifier   See DIODE AMPLIFIER.

two-electrode tube   See TUBE DIODE.

two-element amplifier   See DIODE AMPLIFIER.

two-element beam   A Yagi antenna consisting of a driven element and one parasitic element. The parasitic element can be either a reflector, about 5% longer than the resonant half wavelength at the operating frequency, or it can be a director, about 5% shorter than a half wavelength at the operating frequency.

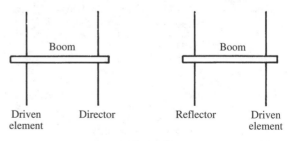

two-element beam

two-element tube   An electron tube having two principal electrodes (i.e., a tube diode).

two-five code   See BIQUINARY CODE.

two-phase   Pertaining to circuits or devices in which two components (two voltages, two currents, or a current and a voltage) are 90° out of phase with each other.

two-phase system   See QUARTER-PHASE SYSTEM.

two-phase, three-wire circuit   A circuit using three conductors, one of which (the common return) is 90° out of phase with the other (outer) two.

two-pincher gripper   A simple robotic end effector using two tongs, and resembling large tweezers or needle-nosed pliers. It grasps objects by "pinching" them.

two-point tuning   See DOUBLE-SPOT TUNING.

two-space   A two-dimensional mathematical continuum in which each point is uniquely defined by two variables in an ordered pair, such as (x,y), and each ordered pair corresponds to exactly one point in the continuum. A common scheme is the Cartesian coordinate system; another scheme is the polar coordinate system. See CARTESIAN COORDINATES and POLAR COORDINATES.

two-space coordinates   A coordinate system for defining points in two-space. See CARTESIAN COORDINATES and POLAR COORDINATES.

two-state device   A device having two stable states (e.g., a flip-flop).

two-state logic   Digital logic in which there are two possible conditions (called high and low, true and false, or 1 and 0).

two-tone keying   See FREQUENCY-SHIFT KEYING.

two-track recording   Recording on two adjacent tracks on magnetic tape. The separate recordings can be in the same direction (as in stereo) or in opposite directions.

two-way amplifier   An amplifier whose input and output terminals can be used interchangeably.

two-way communication   The exchange of messages between two or more stations that transmit as well as receive. Compare ONE-WAY COMMUNICATION, **1**.

two-way radio   **1.** Any form of TWO-WAY COMMUNICATION using electromagnetic waves. **2.** A radio transceiver—especially one used for voice communication at very-high or ultra-high frequencies.

two-way repeater   In telephony, a device that amplifies and retransmits a signal in either direction. Also see TWO-WAY AMPLIFIER.

two-way speaker   A woofer/midrange speaker and a tweeter occupying the same enclosure, and interconnected by a crossover network for wideband frequency response.

TWT   Abbreviation of TRAVELING-WAVE TUBE.

TWX   Abbreviation of TELETYPEWRITER EXCHANGE.

Twystron   A form of microwave-oscillator tube, similar to the Klystron.

Type A telephone line   A telephone line serving one subscriber (as opposed to a party line).

U **1.** Symbol for URANIUM. **2.** Abbreviation of UNIT.

u Symbol (ital.) for UNIFIED ATOMIC MASS UNIT.

Ua Abbreviation of *unit of activity* (electro-encephalography).

UAM Abbreviation of *underwater-to-air missile.*

ubiquitous carrier A current carrier (especially an electron) whose velocity is so high, or mechanism of transfer so subtle, that it appears to be in two places simultaneously. Thus, in the tunnel diode, during the interval of tunneling a single electron, appears to be on both sides of the barrier at the same time.

Ubitron A tube in which a periodic magnetic field causes an electron beam to undulate. Through its transverse velocity component, the beam interacts with a radio-frequency wave, and its kinetic energy is converted into radio-frequency energy. The ubitron can be used as an amplifier or oscillator.

UCT Abbreviation of UNIVERSAL COORDINATED TIME.

UDC Abbreviation of *universal decimal classification.*

UDOP Abbreviation of *ultra-high-frequency Doppler.* A 440-MHz phase-coherent tracking system used to determine the velocity and position of missiles and space vehicles.

UEP Abbreviation of *underwater electric potential.*

UFET Abbreviation of unipolar field-effect transistor. (Also, UNIFET.) See UNIPOLAR TRANSISTOR.

UFO See UNIDENTIFIED FLYING OBJECT.

UG Abbreviation of underground.

UHF Abbreviation of ULTRAHIGH FREQUENCY.

UHF adaptor See UHF CONVERTER, **1.**

UHF capacitor A button-type capacitor. Because of its unique design, it is an efficient bypass capacitor at ultrahigh frequencies.

UHF converter **1.** A circuit, usually consisting of a radio-frequency amplifier and mixer, for converting ultra-high-frequency (UHF) signals to a lower band of frequencies. **2.** A circuit for converting UHF television signals to very-high-frequency (VHF) signals so that they can be accommodated by an older (VHF only) television receiver. See UHF TELEVISION CHANNELS and VHF TELEVISION CHANNELS.

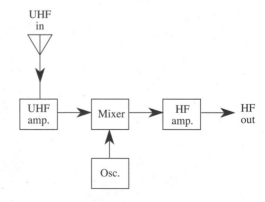

UHF converter, 1

UHF diode A semiconductor diode whose rectification efficiency is good at ultra-high frequencies.

UHF generator   1. An oscillating device (such as a transistor, tunnel diode, Klystron, or magnetron) used to produce radio-frequency energy at ultra-high frequencies (UHF). 2. The equipment in which such a device is used. 3. An ultra-high-frequency test-signal generator.

UHF loop   A (usually single-turn) loop antenna with a toroidal radiation pattern perpendicular to the loop; the antenna has a natural wavelength in the ultra-high-frequency (UHF) range.

UHF receiver   A receiver tunable to frequencies in any band in the range 300 MHz to 3000 MHz.

UHF television channels   Television channels 14 through 69, whose frequencies lie in the ultra-high range.

UHF transistor   A transistor specially designed and fabricated for ultra-high-frequency (UHF) operation. It is characterized by extended beta cutoff frequency, low junction capacitance, and fast recovery time.

UHF translator   A television broadcast translator station transmitting in an ultra-high-frequency (UHF) channel.

UHF transmitter   A transmitter that is specially designed for operation at ultra-high frequencies. In such a transmitter, stray parameters are minimized and special tubes or transistors are required.

UHF tube   A vacuum tube specially designed for ultra-high-frequency operation. It is characterized by low interelectrode capacitance, low input and output capacitances, short electron transit time, and low lead inductance.

UHF tuner   1. A superheterodyne receiver front end tunable in the ultra-high-frequency (UHF) range. It is usually arranged to deliver the mixer output to a lower-frequency receiver. 2. A television receiver front end tunable to the UHF channels.

UHR   Abbreviation of ULTRA-HIGH RESISTANCE.

U index   The difference between consecutive daily mean values of the horizontal component of the geomagnetic field.

UJT   Abbreviation of UNIJUNCTION TRANSISTOR.

UL   1. Abbreviation of UNDERWRITERS LABORATORIES. 2. Abbreviation of ULTRALINEAR.

ULD   Abbreviation of ULTRA-LOW DISTORTION.

ULF   Abbreviation of ULTRA-LOW FREQUENCY.

U-line section   A short section of coaxial cable or hardline having the shape of a squared U.

ULSI   See ULTRA-LARGE-SCALE INTEGRATION.

ultimate attenuation   The maximum attenuation in a circuit or device when it is operated outside its passband, or within its stopband.

ultimately controlled variable   In an automated system, the quantity or operation (e.g., liquid level, temperature, pressure, precision drilling, etc.), whose control is the end purpose of the system.

ultimate-range ballistic missile   A ballistic missile whose range is greater than half the earth's circumference (approximately 12,000 miles).

ultimate ratio   The limiting value of a ratio (i.e., the value approached by a ratio).

ultimate sensitivity   1. In an instrument or system, the maximum degree of perception of, or response to, a quantity or condition. 2. In a graphic recorder, half the deadband.

ultimate threshold   See ULTIMATE SENSITIVITY, 2.

ultimate trip current   For a specified set of environmental conditions, the lowest value of current that will trip a circuit breaker.

ultimate trip limits   For a circuit breaker, the maximum and minimum current at which the breaker trips and drops out.

ultor anode   The second anode of a television picture tube or oscilloscope tube.

ultor element   In a television picture tube, the element that receives the highest direct-current voltage. Also called *ultor electrode*. Also see ULTOR ANODE.

ultor voltage   The high direct-current voltage applied to the second anode of an oscilloscope tube or television picture tube. Also see ULTOR ANODE.

ultra-   A prefix meaning *above, larger than, greater than*, or *higher than*. See the following several definitions for examples.

ultra-atomic   Pertaining to particles smaller than atoms (i.e., SUBATOMIC).

ultra-audible frequency   A frequency higher than the highest audible frequency. Also called ULTRASONIC FREQUENCY and *supersonic frequency.*

ultra-audion oscillator   See ULTRAUDION OSCILLATOR.

ultracentrifuge   A centrifuge that spins at a very high speed.

ultrafast switch   An electronic switch capable of microsecond operation.

Ultrafax   A system for high-speed transmission of printed matter by facsimile, radio, or television.

ultra-high frequency   A radio frequency in the range 300 MHz to 3000 MHz, corresponding to free-space wavelengths between 1 meter and 10 centimeters.

ultra-high-frequency band   See UHF BAND.

ultra-high resistance   Resistance of 100 megohms or higher.

ultra-large-scale integration   An integrated-circuit process that goes several orders of magnitude beyond VERY-LARGE-SCALE INTEGRATION. More than 4×10^6 transistors could be on a single chip.

ultra-linear   Pertaining to the most linear operation obtainable with state-of-the-art electronic equipment.

ultra-linear amplifier   A high-fidelity audio-frequency power amplifier having wide frequency response and very low distortion.

ultra-low distortion   Total harmonic distortion (THD) of less than 0.1 percent.

ultra-low frequencies **1.** Radio frequencies between 300 Hz and 3 kHz, pertaining to wavelengths between 1000 kilometers and 100 kilometers. **2.** Audio frequencies lower than those in the human hearing range.

ultramicrometer An electronic instrument for extremely small linear measurements.

ultramicroscope An optical microscope using refracted light to illuminate minute particles.

ultramicrowave Pertaining to wavelengths in the range 10^{-3} to 10^{-6} meter (300 GHz to 300 THz).

ultraminiature See SUBMINIATURE.

ultraphotic rays Collectively, infrared and ultraviolet rays.

ultrared rays See INFRARED RAYS.

ultra-short waves Waves whose length correspond to ultra-high frequencies (i.e., wavelengths between 0.1 and 1 meter).

ultrasonic Of higher frequency than those that are audible (supersonic). See, for example, ULTRASONIC FREQUENCY.

ultrasonic bonding A method of bonding metal by means of physical vibration at frequencies above the human hearing range.

ultrasonic brazing Forming a nonporous bond between metal parts through the use of ultrasonic energy and a second, different metal (or alloy) having a lower melting point.

ultrasonic cleaning A method of cleaning delicate or intricately structured items (such as dentures, contact lenses, or jewelry) in which the soiled items are immersed in a fluid that is agitated by ultrasonic transducers; the foreign particles are shaken away.

ultrasonic cleaning tank A thick-walled stainless-steel tank with ultrasonic transducers mounted within its walls and used for ultrasonic cleaning.

ultrasonic coagulation The coagulation of a substance through ultrasonic agitation.

ultrasonic communication Underwater telegraphic communication between ships and/or submarines by keying the echo-ranging sonar equipment.

ultrasonic delay line A delay line, such as the mercury type, through which an ultrasonic signal is propagated. The delay results from the relatively slow propagation of the ultrasonic wave through the substance in the line.

ultrasonic densitometer A density-measuring apparatus whose operation is based on the time required for an ultrasonic signal to penetrate the material under test, or for the signal to penetrate the material and be reflected back to the transmitter.

ultrasonic depth finder See ACOUSTIC DEPTH FINDER.

ultrasonic detector A device that responds to ultrasonic waves by indicating their presence, intensity, and/or frequency.

ultrasonic diagnosis The medical determination of the condition of tissues or structures within the body, in terms of reflection of ultrasonic waves by those tissues or structures. The technique is useful in situations where other techniques, such as radiology or the use of catheter probes, are risky. Also see ULTRASOUND.

ultrasonic disintegrator In biology and related fields, a device that uses ultrasonic energy to rupture or shatter cells, tissues, or foreign bodies, such as kidney stones.

ultrasonic drill A drill running at speeds corresponding to ultrasonic frequencies. The tool is valuable in drilling hard or brittle materials and in dentistry.

ultrasonic filter **1.** A bandpass filter whose operation is based on the natural (ultrasonic) vibration frequency of small disks or rods of magnetostrictive metal. See MAGNETOSTRICTION. Also called *mechanical filter*. **2.** Generally, a filter operating at ultrasonic frequencies.

ultrasonic flaw detector A system analogous to radar, in which an ultrasonic wave is transmitted through a solid material and is reflected back to a detector and display device to reveal flaws, cracks, and strain in the material.

ultrasonic frequency For an acoustic disturbance, any frequency above the limit of human hearing (higher than 20 kHz).

ultrasonic generator **1.** An oscillator that operates at frequencies above the range of human hearing, and the output of which is intended for coupling to an electroacoustic transducer. **2.** Any device that produces ultrasonic waves.

ultrasonic grating constant For a sound wave producing a diffraction spectrum, a figure indicating the distance between diffracting centers of the wave.

ultrasonic heating The production of heat in a specimen by means of ultrasonic energy directed into or through it.

ultrasonic image converter A device that makes visible acoustic field patterns.

ultrasonic inspection The use of ultrasonic waves to detect internal flaws in solid materials, such as metals. It is valued particularly because it is nondestructive. Also see ULTRASONIC FLAW DETECTOR.

ultrasonic intrusion alarm A security system activated when an intruder disturbs a pattern of ultrasonic waves in the protected area; a sensitive relay closes, setting off an alarm.

ultrasonic level detector A level-monitoring system in which an ultrasonic transmitter and detector are mounted together on one wall of a tank or chamber. When the tank is empty, the transmitted signal is reflected by the opposite wall back to the detector. When the liquid rises, the reflection time is reduced; this change is used to operate a device that indicates that the tank has been filled to a desired level.

ultrasonic light diffraction Diffraction resulting from the periodic variation of light refraction when a beam of light passes through a longitudinal sound-wave field.

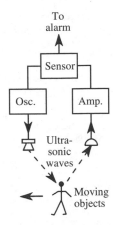

ultrasonic intrusion alarm

ultrasonic light modulator A device that modulates a light beam passing transversely through a fluid agitated by sound waves.

ultrasonic material dispersion The use of the agitative action of high-intensity ultrasonic waves to disperse or emulsify one substance in another.

ultrasonic plating The use of ultrasonic energy to deposit or bond one material onto the surface of another.

ultrasonic probe A rodlike director of ultrasonic energy.

ultrasonic relay An electronic relay actuated by ultrasound.

ultrasonics 1. The use of high-frequency acoustic energy in industry, medicine, research, and the home. See ULTRASONIC FREQUENCY. 2. The use of high-frequency acoustic energy for medical diagnosis and treatment. 3. The branch of physics dealing with the effects and behavior of acoustic disturbances at frequencies above the range of human hearing.

ultrasonic soldering See ULTRASONIC BRAZING.

ultrasonic sounding Determining the depth of a body of water in terms of the time taken for a transmitted ultrasonic signal to be reflected back to a transmitting point on the surface of the water.

ultrasonic space grating A periodic variation in the index of refraction when acoustic waves are present in a light-transmitting medium. Also see ULTRASONIC LIGHT DIFFRACTION.

ultrasonic storage cell See ULTRASONIC DELAY LINE.

ultrasonic stroboscope A stroboscope that uses an ultrasonically modulated beam of light.

ultrasonic switch An electronic switch actuated by ultrasound.

ultrasonic therapy The use of ultrasonic energy in medicine for treatment of certain disorders.

ultrasonic thickness gauge An instrument that determines the thickness of a specimen in terms of the propagation time (or echo time) of ultrasonic waves through the specimen.

ultrasonic transducer A transducer that converts electrical energy into ultrasonic energy, or vice-versa. Common types are the quartz crystal, ceramic crystal, and magnetostrictive disk.

ultrasonic waves Acoustic waves whose length corresponds to ultrasonic frequencies (i.e., frequencies above 20 kHz).

ultrasonic welding A below-melting-point technique of joining two metallic bodies by clamping them tightly together and applying ultrasonic energy, rather than heat, in the plane of the desired weld. Compare ULTRASONIC BRAZING.

ultrasonic whistle A whistle whose pitch is beyond the range of human hearing. Although some are of the simile (blown) type, others are (usually miniature) electronic sound generators. These devices can be used for the remote control of television receivers, garage-door openers, and other equipment.

ultrasonography A method of examining human tissues or organs by transmitting ultrasonic waves into the body and receiving the echoes.

ultrasound 1. Acoustic disturbances at frequencies above 20 kHz. 2. See ULTRASONIC FREQUENCY. 3. See ULTRASONOGRAPHY.

ultraviolet 1. Electromagnetic radiation at wavelengths somewhat shorter than those of visible light. Longwave or *near ultraviolet* extends from approximately 390 nanometers (nm) down to 50 nm. Shortwave or *far ultraviolet* extends from 50 nm down to 4 nm. 2. Pertaining to the behavior and effects of electromagnetic radiation in the range of approximately 390 nm to 4 nm.

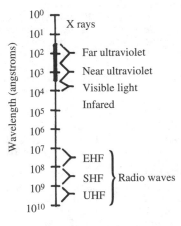

ultraviolet

ultraviolet altimeter An altimeter that uses ultraviolet rays instead of radio waves to determine the altitude of an aircraft or spacecraft.

ultraviolet lamp   A lamp that delivers ultraviolet rays. Common types are arc lamps and mercury-vapor lamps.

ultraviolet light   See ULTRAVIOLET RAYS.

ultraviolet power   The power (in watts) of ultraviolet radiation.

ultraviolet rays   Radiation at frequencies in the ultraviolet region (i.e., between the highest visible-light frequencies and the lowest X-ray frequencies).

ultraviolet therapy   The use of ultraviolet rays by physicians and other health personnel in the treatment of certain disorders.

ultraviolet wavelength   The wavelength range of ultraviolet radiation [e.g., 390 nanometers (nm) to 4 nm].

ultraviolet waves   See ULTRAVIOLET RAYS.

umbilical cord   1. A cord through which missiles and rockets are controlled and powered until they are launched. 2. A cord connecting an astronaut to his space vehicle during extravehicular activity (e.g., during a space "walk").

umbilical tower   The vertical tower supporting the umbilical cords extending to a rocket in the launch position.

umbra   1. The region of total (conical) shadow behind an object situated in the path of a radiation. 2. The comparatively dark central region in a sunspot.

umbrella antenna   An antenna consisting of a number of wires, extending from the top of a vertical mast to points on a circle below, at the center of which the mast is mounted. The wires are usually fed in parallel from the top.

Umklapp process   A process responsible for thermal resistance in nonconducting materials. It results from collision between phonons, or phonons and electrons.

UMW   Abbreviation of ULTRAMICROWAVE.

unabsorbed field strength   The field strength with no absorption between transmitter and detector. The unabsorbed field strength is an ideal quantity; the actual field strength over a given distance is always less. It is expressed in volts per meter.

unamplified back bias   A negative-feedback voltage developed across a fast-time-constant circuit within a single amplifier stage.

unamplified feedback   A positive or negative current or voltage taken from the output of a system and presented to the input without being boosted through auxiliary amplification.

unamplified ALC   Automatic level control (ALC) in which the control-signal voltage is taken from a point in the circuit and fed to the controlled point without being boosted by an auxiliary amplifier. Compare AMPLIFIED ALC.

unattended operation   Operation, as of an electronically programmed machine, with minimal (or no) human supervision.

unattended time   The period, excluding down time for repair or checkout, during which a computer is unpowered.

unattenuated   Not reduced in intensity of amplitude. Thus, an unattenuated signal is one that has retained its original strength during its transmission through a system.

unavailable energy   The difference between the quantity of heat energy supplied to a system and the available energy of the system.

unbalance   1. Lack of balance or symmetry in a circuit, line, or system. 2. The condition in which a bridge (or the equivalent) is not nulled.

unbalanced circuit   See SINGLE-ENDED CIRCUIT.

unbalanced delta system   A three-phase circuit in which the elements are connected in a triangular (delta) configuration, but are of unequal impedance. In an unbalanced delta system, no definite relationship exists between line and phase currents. Compare BALANCED DELTA SYSTEM.

unbalanced input   See SINGLE-ENDED INPUT.

unbalanced line   1. A transmission line in which one side (conductor) is grounded (e.g., a coaxial line). 2. A normally balanced transmission line in which the currents in the two halves are out of balance (i.e., they are not equal in amplitude and opposite in phase).

unbalanced multivibrator   A multivibrator in which the time constant of one base or gate circuit differs from that of the other base or gate circuit. The asymmetry results in short-duration output pulses separated by long time periods.

unbalanced output   See SINGLE-ENDED OUTPUT.

unbalanced two-phase system   A two-phase circuit in which the load elements are of unequal impedance.

unbalanced wire circuit   A wire line whose (two) sides are dissimilar.

unbalanced-wye system   A three-phase circuit in which the elements are connected in the familiar wye, or star, configuration, but are of unequal impedance.

unbalanced-Y system   See UNBALANCED-WYE SYSTEM.

unbalance-to-balance transformer   A transformer for matching an unbalanced transmission line to a balanced line (e.g., a coaxial line to a parallel-wire line).

unbiased limiting   Peak limiting that results from overdriving an unbiased active device.

unbiased unit   A device or circuit operated without bias [e.g., a transistor without base bias (common emitter and emitter follower) or emitter bias (common base)].

unblanking   Removal of the blanking pulse in a cathode-ray-tube circuit (i.e., turning on the beam).

unblanking generator   A (usually pulse-type) signal source for turning on the beam of a blanked cathode-ray tube.

unblanking interval   The period during which the beam of a cathode-ray tube is turned on. Compare BLANKING INTERVAL.

unblanking pulse A pulse that turns on the beam of a blanked cathode-ray tube. Compare BLANKING PULSE.

unblanking time 1. See UNBLANKING INTERVAL. **2.** The instant at which unblanking begins.

unbonded strain gauge A strain gauge that is not directly attached (by cement, for example) to the strained surface.

unbound electron A free electron (i.e., an electron not confined to a shell within an atom).

unbuffered output An output (signal, power, etc.) that is delivered directly from the generating device without the benefit of an isolating stage, such as a buffer amplifier. Compare BUFFERED OUTPUT.

unbypassed emitter resistor In a common-emitter transistor circuit, an emitter resistor without a bypass capacitor. The flow of output-signal current through the resistor produces negative feedback within a single stage.

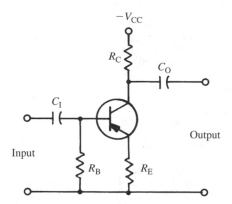

unbypassed emitter resistor (R_E)

unbypassed source resistor In a common-source field-effect transistor circuit, a source resistor without a bypass capacitor. The flow of output-signal current through the resistor produces negative feedback within a single stage.

uncage In a displacement gyroscope system, to disconnect the erection circuit.

uncalibrated unit A component, circuit, or instrument that has never been calibrated or has not recently been calibrated and, hence, is of questionable accuracy.

uncanny valley According to a theory put forth by certain Japanese roboticists, a phenomenon that can occur among people as technology advances. As machines rapidly get more sophisticated, a point is reached at which their human users become unnerved, partially offsetting the advantages the technology has to offer.

uncased choke See UNSHIELDED CHOKE.

uncased transformer See UNSHIELDED TRANSFORMER.

uncertainty in computation The degree of doubt concerning the exactness of computations. This uncertainty is always greater than that of the roughest measurement used in obtaining data for the computation. Uncertainty is closely related to the tolerance of the instruments and formulas used.

uncertainty in measurement The estimated maximum amount whereby the numerical value of a measured quantity can differ from the true value.

uncertainty principle The observation that high precision in the location of an electron is obtainable only at a sacrifice in the accuracy with which the momentum of the electron can be determined, and vice-versa.

uncharged Without an electric charge, as opposed to discharged (depleted of a charge).

unclamp To switch off clamping action in a circuit. See CLAMPER and CLAMPING.

uncoated filament 1. A plain filament (i.e., one without a coating of electron-increasing material). **2.** A stripped filament (i.e., one from which the electron-increasing coating has been burned off).

uncompensated Not modified to produce a desired type of performance, such as increased bandwidth or reduced temperature sensitivity. Example: an uncompensated amplifier put into service in the (wide) video band. Compare COMPENSATED AMPLIFIER, COMPENSATED CAPACITOR, and COMPENSATED DIODE DETECTOR.

uncompensated amplifier An amplifier without a provision for the automatic or manual modification or correction of its response. Compare COMPENSATED AMPLIFIER.

uncompensated capacitor A fixed or variable capacitor without a provision for the automatic or manual correction or modification of its capacitance or range or the improvement of its temperature coefficient. Compare COMPENSATED CAPACITOR.

uncompensated inductor A fixed or variable inductor without a provision for the automatic or manual correction or modification of its inductance or range or the improvement of its temperature coefficient.

uncompensated resistor A fixed or variable resistor without a provision for the automatic or manual correction or modification of its resistance or range or the improvement of its temperature coefficient.

unconditional branch See UNCONDITIONAL JUMP.

unconditional jump In computer operations, a program instruction that interrupts, without a relational test being made, the normal, ordered sequence of instructions and gives the address of (usually) the first instruction in a subroutine [e.g., BASIC's GOTO (line number)]. Also called *unconditional branch.* Compare CONDITIONAL JUMP.

unconditional stability Stability of a system at all frequencies and ages. Also called *absolute stability*.

unconditional transfer See UNCONDITIONAL JUMP.

uncontrolled multivibrator A multivibrator that is not synchronized with a signal source. Also called ASTABLE MULTIVIBRATOR and FREE-RUNNING MULTIVIBRATOR.

uncontrolled oscillator See SELF-EXCITED OSCILLATOR.

uncorrected power In an alternating-current circuit, a power value calculated without regard for power factor (i.e., the volt-ampere product).

uncorrected time Local standard time that has not been corrected in terms of the distance of the locality from the nearest standard-time meridian.

uncorrected tube A television picture tube operated without antipincushioning magnets.

uncoupled mode A mode of vibration existing in a system concurrent with (but independent of) other modes.

undamped galvanometer A galvanometer for which no provision has been made to limit overswing or prevent oscillation.

undamped meter **1.** A meter for which no provision has been made to limit overswing or prevent oscillation. **2.** A meter that is unprotected by a short circuit for limiting vibratory movement of the pointer during transport.

undamped natural frequency In the absence of damping, the oscillation frequency of a system having one degree of freedom when a transient force displaces the system momentarily from its position of rest.

undamped oscillation Continuous-wave oscillation. Also see CONTINUOUS WAVE.

undamped output circuit An audio power-amplifier output circuit that has not been designed so that overswing of the loudspeaker cone is prevented.

undamped speaker enclosure A loudspeaker cabinet for which provision has not been made to deaden resonances and other undesired vibration.

undamped wave See CONTINUOUS WAVE.

undeflected beam A cathode-ray beam or a light beam in its normal position of rest (quiescence).

underbiased unit A component, such as a transistor or vacuum tube, whose bias voltage or current is lower than the prescribed value. Compare OVERBIASED UNIT.

underbunching Less-than-optimum bunching of electrons in a velocity-modulated tube because of lowered buncher voltage.

undercompounded generator A generator in which the output voltage varies inversely with load resistance.

undercoupling Loose coupling, usually of an amount insufficient for optimum signal transfer.

undercurrent A current of lower than specified strength. Compare OVERCURRENT.

undercurrent relay A relay that is actuated when coil current falls below a predetermined level.

undercut The removal of the metal under the edge of the resist in a printed circuit by the etchant; thus the cross section of the conductor is reduced.

undercutting A phonograph-disc groove that is cut too shallow or with reduced internal movement of the recording stylus.

underdamping Insufficient damping of a system (i.e., not enough to prevent output oscillation following application of a transient force).

underdriven unit An amplifier, oscillator, or transducer whose driving signal (current, voltage, power, or other quantity) is lower than the prescribed value. Compare OVERDRIVEN UNIT.

underexcited Receiving lower-than-normal excitation, as in an underdriven final amplifier of a radio transmitter. Compare OVEREXCITED.

underflow In computer operations, the condition in which a quantity entered into storage is shorter than the space provided for it (e.g., a 12-digit quantity in a 16-position register).

underground antenna A transmitting or receiving antenna installed and operated below ground. Included are buried antennas and antennas on equipment operated in tunnels, cellars, and similar areas.

underground cable A cable that is buried in the earth.

underground communication Communication between a transmitter and receiver, both below the surface of the earth.

underground image The below-ground mirror image of an antenna; it combines with the actual antenna to form the complete radiation pattern.

underground line A power line laid below the surface of the earth.

underground receiver **1.** A receiver situated completely below the surface of the earth. **2.** A clandestine receiver.

underground reception Reception of an above-ground station's transmissions by an underground receiver. Compare UNDERGROUND COMMUNICATION.

underground transmitter **1.** A transmitter situated completely below the surface of the earth. **2.** A clandestine transmitter.

under insulation The insulation (usually a strip of tape) laid under a wire brought up from the center of a coil.

underinsulation Inadequate or insufficient insulation.

underlap In a facsimile or television picture, a crowding of the scanned lines.

underload circuit breaker See CIRCUIT BREAKER.

underloaded amplifier 1. An amplifier whose load resistance (impedance) is less than the prescribed value. **2.** A power amplifier delivering less than its rated output power. Compare OVERLOADED AMPLIFIER.

underload relay A relay actuated when circuit current drops below a predetermined value. Compare OVERLOAD RELAY.

undermodulation Incomplete modulation of a carrier wave. Compare COMPLETE MODULATION and OVERMODULATION.

underpass The crossing of two conductors on a semiconductor wafer, without an electrical connection.

underpower relay A relay actuated when power drops below a predetermined level. Compare OVERPOWER RELAY.

underrate To assign a rating (e.g., current or power) lower than the quantity of the rating an equipment can handle, or tolerate. For safety or reliability, apparatus sometimes is deliberately underrated—especially in power output and maximum current or voltage.

undershoot On an oscilloscope screen or graph, a momentary swing of a current or voltage below the reference axis. Compare OVERSHOOT.

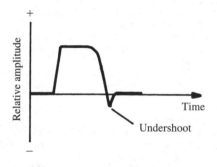

undershoot

undershoot distortion Distortion caused by reduction of the maximum amplitude of a signal wavefront below the steady-state amplitude that would be reached by a prolonged signal wave.

understudy See BACKUP.

underthrow A form of signal distortion that occurs when the modulating-waveform frequency is too high in proportion to the frequency of the wave itself.

undervoltage A voltage of lower than specified value. Compare OVERVOLTAGE.

undervoltage protection The automatic disconnection of a load device from its driving source when the driving voltage falls below a predetermined (threshold) level. This action is sometimes accomplished with a Zener diode (whose breakdown voltage is equal to the threshold voltage) in series with a disconnect relay.

undervoltage relay A relay actuated when voltage drops below a predetermined level. Compare OVERVOLTAGE RELAY.

underwater antenna A transmitting or receiving antenna normally operated in a body of water. It is usually associated with a submarine.

underwater sound projector A hydroacoustic transducer that converts audio-frequency power into sound waves, which it radiates through a body of water to a receiver.

Underwriters Code The advisory National Electrical Code adopted by the National Fire Protection Association; it is often enforced by courts of law and inspection agencies.

Underwriters Laboratories Abbreviation, UL. A private corporation that issues standards of safety for electrical components and equipment, and for their operation.

undistorted power output For active amplifier devices, a specified maximum audio power output level at which the total distortion does not exceed a specified low value (i.e., at which operation is practically distortionless).

undistorted wave 1. A sine wave that contains essentially no harmonic energy. **2.** A nonsinusoidal wave whose shape corresponds exactly to the equation for the wave.

undisturbed-one output In digital-memory operations, the one-output of a magnetic cell or other memory unit that has received a full, rather than partial, read pulse. Compare UNDISTURBED OUTPUT SIGNAL.

undisturbed output signal In digital-memory operations, the output of a magnetic cell or other memory unit previously set to one or zero, and that has received a full, rather than partial, read pulse. Also called *undisturbed response voltage.*

undisturbed response voltage See UNDISTURBED OUTPUT SIGNAL.

undisturbed-zero output In digital-memory operations, the zero-output of a magnetic cell or other memory unit that has received a full, rather than partial, read pulse. Compare UNDISTURBED OUTPUT SIGNAL.

Universal Truth Machine (UTM) A hypothetical computer capable of proving any logically true statement. According to the Incompleteness Theorem proved in 1930, such a machine cannot exist for a first-order logical system.

undoped Pertaining to a pure semiconductor material (i.e., one containing no lattice-altering additives).

undulating current A current, such as an alternating or composite current, whose value oscillates in the manner of a wave.

undulation A wavelike alternation.

undulatory theory The theory that light is transmitted by means of an undulating (wavelike) movement between the luminous object and the eye.

unequal alternation In an alternating-current waveform, a form of asymmetry in which the positive and negative half-cycles are not exact mirror images; they might vary in peak amplitude, duration, shape, etc.

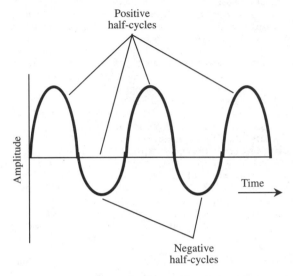

unequal alternation

unexpected halt During a computer program run, an undirected (unplanned) halt (e.g., one caused by a machine fault or program bug).

unfiltered Not having been subjected to filtering action. An example is the pulsating-direct-current output of an alternating-current-operated rectifier circuit.

unfocused light source In a photoelectric system, a light source that delivers diffused light.

unformed rectifier A newly fabricated semiconductor rectifier (especially selenium) or an electrolytic rectifier before it has been electroformed for improved characteristics.

unfurlable antenna An antenna that can be unrolled to increase its length, thereby lowering its fundamental resonant frequency; it can also be rolled up to decrease its length and increase its fundamental resonant frequency.

ungrounded item A component, circuit, or circuit point having no connection to ground, except an inadvertent one through common impedances or leakage paths.

ungrounded system A system operated entirely above ground, any path to ground being accidental.

unguided Without electronic guidance (pertaining to missiles, rockets, satellites, etc.).

uni- A prefix (combining form) meaning *one* or *single* and appearing in a number of electronic terms. See the following several definitions for examples.

uniaxial **1.** Having one axis. **2.** Referred to one axis.

uniaxial crystal A crystal having one optical axis.

unibivalent electrolyte An electrolyte, such as sodium carbonate (Na_2CO_3), that dissociates into two univalent ions and one bivalent ion.

uniconductor cable A cable having a single conductor, usually of braided or twisted wires.

uniconductor waveguide A waveguide consisting of a metal sheath deposited on a solid dielectric of cylindrical or rectangular cross section.

unidentified flying object Abbreviation, UFO. An object claimed to have been seen in flight, but not identified by reliable authorities as any known type of vehicle.

unidirect To commutate (see COMMUTATOR).

unidirectional **1.** Flowing or acting in one direction only. **2.** Having a radiation or response sensitivity that is maximum in primarily one direction in space.

unidirectional antenna See UNIDIRECTIONAL ARRAY.

unidirectional array A beam antenna that radiates in one direction only, or principally in one direction, unless rotated.

unidirectional conductivity Electrical conductivity in only one direction; it characterizes an ideal diode.

unidirectional coupler A directional coupler sampling only one direction of transmission.

unidirectional current A current that flows always in the same direction, although it might fluctuate in intensity.

unidirectional elements Circuit elements, such as diodes or transistors, that transmit energy in only (or best in) one direction.

unidirectional field-effect transistor See UNILATERAL FIELD-EFFECT TRANSISTOR.

unidirectional hydrophone An underwater unidirectional microphone.

unidirectional loudspeaker A loudspeaker that radiates sound substantially in one direction.

unidirectional microphone A microphone that receives sound waves from one direction, usually from the front, minimum response usually being from the sides and back.

unidirectional network A network that transmits signals in only one direction (i.e., the input and output terminals are not interchangeable).

unidirectional pattern For a transducer (such as an antenna, speaker, or microphone), a radiation or response pattern that shows a pronounced maximum in one direction only.

unidirectional pulse A single-polarity pulse.

unidirectional pulse train A series of unidirectional pulses.

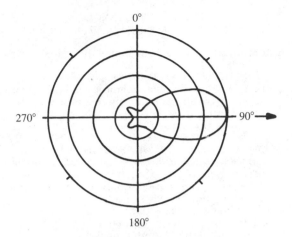

unidirectional pattern

unidirectional response For a receiving transducer, such as an antenna or microphone, a response pattern that shows a pronounced maximum in one direction only.

unidirectional speaker See UNIDIRECTIONAL LOUDSPEAKER.

unidirectional transducer A transducer that operates in one direction only (i.e., its input and output cannot be interchanged).

unidirectional voltage A voltage that never changes polarity, although it might fluctuate in value.

UNIFET Abbreviation of UNIPOLAR FIELD-EFFECT TRANSISTOR. (Also, UFET.)

unified-field theory A theory, as yet unproved, that all forces in nature are interrelated and are controlled by the same causes and factors. Albert Einstein worked on this theory after he successfully developed the theories of relativity.

unifilar Having (or wound as) one fiber, wire, filament, or thread.

unifilar magnetometer A magnetometer in which a bar is suspended at its center of gravity by a single thread.

unifilar suspension A method of meter construction in which the moving part is suspended by a single filament. The torque might be provided by this filament or by a spring or other resisting device; the greater the displacement, the greater the torque.

uniform circular motion Motion at a uniform rate and describing a circle (e.g., a motor armature rotating at a constant speed).

uniform electric field An electric field in which all the lines of flux are straight and parallel, and in which the electrostatic force has the same value at all points (e.g., the field between two oppositely charged, flat, parallel plates).

uniform field See UNIFORM ELECTRIC FIELD and UNIFORM MAGNETIC FIELD.

uniform frequency response Frequency response that is flat throughout a specified range. Such response is characterized by the transmission of a signal with no introduced amplitude or phase distortion.

uniform line A transmission line having identical electrical properties over its entire length.

uniform magnetic field A magnetic field in which all the lines of flux are straight and parallel, and in which the magnetic force has the same value at all points.

uniform plane wave A free-space plane wave at an infinite distance from the generator, having constant-amplitude electric and magnetic field vectors over the equiphase surfaces.

uniform precession In regions of the uniform magnetic field of a sample of material, the state in which the magnetic moments of all atoms are parallel and precess in phase around the magnetic field.

uniform waveguide A waveguide having constant electrical and physical characteristics along its axis.

uniground 1. The grounding of a circuit at one point to reduce susceptibility to hum and noise. 2. The point at which such a connection is made.

unijunction transistor A semiconductor device consisting of a thin silicon bar on which a single pn junction acting as an emitter is formed near one end. Two bases are provided—each an ohmic connection made to one end of the bar. Also called *double-base diode*.

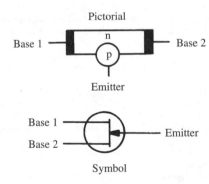

unijunction transistor

unilateral area track A film sound track having modulation on only one edge of the opaque area.

unilateral bearing In radio direction finding, a bearing obtained with a finder that produces unilateral response and thereby eliminates 180-degree error.

unilateral conductivity See UNIDIRECTIONAL CONDUCTIVITY.

unilateral element See UNIDIRECTIONAL ELEMENTS.

unilateral field-effect transistor A field-effect transistor whose source and drain terminals cannot be interchanged. Also called ASYMMETRICAL FIELD-EFFECT TRANSISTOR. Compare SYMMETRICAL FIELD-EFFECT TRANSISTOR.

unilateralization A system of neutralization used in transistor amplifiers at very-high and ultra-high frequencies, in which the internal capacitive and resistive components are compensated by the neutralization feedback.

unilateralized amplifier A transistor amplifier in which both the internal resistive and capacitive components are compensated by the neutralizing circuit. Also see UNILATERALIZATION.

unilateral network See UNIDIRECTIONAL NETWORK.

unilateral transducer See UNIDIRECTIONAL TRANSDUCER.

uninterruptible power supply Abbreviation, UPS. A device that provides a continuous utility current to electronic devices in the event of a utility power dip or blackout. It contains a battery and a power inverter. These devices are used extensively in personal computing to prevent loss of data that could otherwise result from a utility power failure.

union **1.** The logical inclusive-OR operation. **2.** See BOND, 1.

union catalog In computer operations, the compiled list of the contents of two or more tape or disk libraries.

unionic material A material having no ions (i.e., one in which all atoms are neutral).

uniphase antenna See COLLINEAR ANTENNA.

UNIPOL Acronym for *universal problem-oriented language*, a high-level computer-programming language.

unipolar **1.** Having or using a single pole or polarity. **2.** Operating with one class of current carrier.

unipolar armature An electric-motor armature that maintains its polarity throughout a complete revolution.

unipolar field-effect transistor See UNIPOLAR TRANSISTOR.

unipolar induction Induction by only one pole of a magnet.

unipolar input The input circuit of an instrument or device designed for input signals of one polarity only.

unipolar pulse A pulse in which the current flows in only one direction, or in which the voltage occurs with only one polarity.

unipolar transistor A field-effect transistor (FET). It utilizes only one kind of carrier (electrons in the n-channel FET, holes in the p-channel FET). Compare BIPOLAR TRANSISTOR.

unipolar winding The winding of a UNIPOLAR ARMATURE.

unipole **1.** An all-pass filter having one pole and for which there is one zero. Also see ALL-PASS FILTER, POLES OF IMPEDANCE, and ZEROS OF IMPEDANCE. **2.** A hypothetical, omnidirectional antenna.

unipotential cathode An indirectly heated tube cathode. Also called *equipotential cathode.* See INDIRECTLY HEATED CATHODE.

unit **1.** A named, single magnitude adopted as a standard by physical measurement. Thus, the unit of current is the ampere, the unit of frequency is the hertz, the unit of capacitance is the farad, etc. Also see ABSOLUTE SYSTEM OF UNITS, INTERNATIONAL SYSTEM OF UNITS, and CENTIMETER-GRAM-SECOND. **2.** A single piece or assemblage of equipment, such as amplifier, converter, power supply, etc. **3.** A quantity of 1 implied when unit is the adjective describing a quantity (e.g., *unit length* means a distance of 1 meter, 1 foot, etc.).

unitary code In computer operations, a code based on one digit. The number of times the digit is repeated indicates a given number.

unit cell In crystals, the simplest polyhedron exhibiting all the structural features and which is repeated to form the crystal lattice.

unit charge See UNIT ELECTROSTATIC CHARGE.

unit electric charge See UNIT ELECTROSTATIC CHARGE.

unit electrostatic charge An electrostatic point charge that will attract or repel a point charge of equal strength 1 centimeter away in a vacuum, with a force of 1 dyne (10^{-5} newton).

unit function Symbol, H or 1. A time-dependent quantity that is zero before the start of a period (when time t is zero) and 1 for all values of t greater than zero. It is approximated by a square wave, and is useful in solving problems involving transients.

unit length **1.** A fundamental unit of distance or time, used for reference in a measuring system. For example, in the mks (meter-kilogram-second) system, the distance unit length is the meter, and the time unit length is the second. **2.** The duration of a fundamental element, or bit, in a binary-code transmission system.

unitized construction The fabrication of an electronic equipment in subassemblies (such as modules) that can be tested separately, and that can be easily replaced (plugged in) in the event of individual failure.

unit line A line of electric or magnetic flux.

unit magnetic pole See UNIT POLE.

unit matrix A matrix whose main diagonal terms (all) are all at unity, the other terms being zero.

unitooth Pertaining to the use in electrical machinery of one slot per pole per phase.

unitor See OR GATE.

unit pole The strength (magnetic flux) of a (hypothetical) magnetic pole that will attract or repel a pole of equal strength 1 centimeter away in a vacuum, with a force of 1 dyne; 1 unit pole = 1.257×10^{-7} weber.

unit-ramp function A function whose value is zero before time t, and becomes equal to the time measured from t at all other instants. The integral of the UNIT FUNCTION.

unit record In computer operations, a complete record consisting of many data elements and contained within one storage medium, such as a magnetic disk.

unitrivalent electrolyte An electrolyte, such as sodium phosphate (Na_3PO_4), that dissociates into three univalent ions and one trivalent ion.

units position In a numbering system, the rightmost position in a multidigit whole number; or, if the number contains a radix point, the digit immediately to the left of the radix point.

unit-step function See UNIT FUNCTION.

unitunnel diode A special form of semiconductor diode, used as an oscillator at ultra-high and microwave frequencies.

unit vector A vector that is 1 unit long in terms of the scale representing a factor of interest, and has the same direction as the vector of interest. For example, if u is a unit vector, then $5u$ represents a vector having the same direction and five times the magnitude of u.

unity **1.** The figure 1 implied. **2.** A ratio of 1:1. **3.** A gain of 0 dB.

unity coupling Tight coupling between two coils, the turns ratio often being 1 to 1 and the coils always being closely interwound.

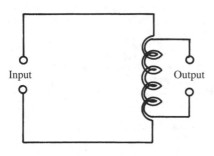

unity coupling

unity gain The condition in which the output amplitude is the same as the input amplitude; that is, a gain factor of 1, or 0 dB.

unity-gain bandwidth **1.** For an active filter, the bandwidth between the frequencies at which the gain is 0 dB. **2.** For an operational amplifier having a rolloff of 6 dB per octave, the frequency at which the open-loop gain is 0 dB.

uni-univalent electrolyte An electrolyte that dissociates into two univalent ions [e.g., sodium chloride (NaCl)].

univ Abbreviation of *universal.*

UNIVAC The name given to a family of digital computers and data-processing systems. The name is an acronym for *Universal Automatic Computer.*

univalent Having a valence of 1. For example, in the compound sodium chloride (NaCl), the sodium ion (Na+) and the chlorine ion (Cl–) are univalent.

universal bridge A bridge for the measurement of capacitance (C), inductance (L), and resistance (R). Such a bridge often is a skeletal foundation circuit with a provision for plugging L, C, or R standards in the various arms, as required. Also called *general-purpose bridge.*

universal coordinated time Abbreviation, UTC. Greenwich mean time coordinated by the International Time Bureau for broadcast as signals (on WWV, for example).

universal coupler **1.** An arrangement of one or more inductors and variable capacitors for matching a transmitter to virtually any antenna. One such device is the Collins coupler. **2.** A device for matching numerous generator output impedances to numerous load impedances.

universal filter An active filter that is continuously tunable over a wide frequency range and that offers low-pass, high-pass, bandpass, and band-suppression functions.

universal frequency counter A digital frequency meter usable at radio and audio frequencies.

universal motor A small series-wound motor that runs on direct current or single-phase alternating current. This type of motor is used in many household appliances and in motor-driven tools, such as portable electric drills, polishers, etc.

universal output transformer An output transformer having a number of taps on its primary and secondary windings for use with a wide variety of impedances.

universal product code Abbreviation, UPC. The variable-width-bar code appearing on price tags or product labels, and yielding such information as cost, size, and color when read by supermarket (or other retailer) optical character-recognition equipment. Also called *universal vendor marking (UVM).*

universal receiver A radio receiver that can be operated either from alternating current or direct current (i.e., from utility power or battery power).

universal shunt See AYRTON-MATHER GALVANOMETER SHUNT.

universal time See GREENWICH MEAN TIME.

universal transformer See UNIVERSAL OUTPUT TRANSFORMER.

universal transmitter A radio transmitter that can be operated either from alternating current or direct current (i.e., from utility power or battery power).

universal Turing machine In computer theory, a TURING MACHINE capable of simulating other Turing machines.

universal vendor marking See UNIVERSAL PRODUCT CODE.

universal winding A zigzag winding used to reduce the distributed capacitance of multilayer coils. Also called *lattice winding* and *honeycomb winding.*

universal-wound coil A coil using a universal winding. Such coils are common in intermediate-frequency (IF) transformers and in radio-frequency (RF) chokes.

univibrator See MONOSTABLE MULTIVIBRATOR.

unknown quantity Any variable quantity sought in calculations; it is usually represented by lowercase italic letters from the second half of the alphabet (e.g., x, y, z).

unlike charges Dissimilar electric charges (i.e., positive and negative).

unlike poles Dissimilar poles, such as the north and south poles of a magnet.

unload **1.** To remove data from a file. **2.** To disconnect the load from a circuit.

unloaded amplifier See UNTERMINATED AMPLIFIER.

unloaded antenna An antenna operated without added inductance or capacitance.

unloaded-applicator impedance In dielectric-heating operations, the unloaded impedance of applicator electrodes placed in their normal working position without the dielectric-material load in place.

unloaded battery **1.** A battery in the standby condition. **2.** A battery tested for open-circuit terminal voltage (i.e., with no load, except the voltmeter).

unloaded generator See UNTERMINATED GENERATOR.

unloaded line See UNTERMINATED LINE.

unloaded potentiometer A potentiometer or voltage divider with an open-circuited output.

unloaded Q The Q factor (degree of selectivity) of a coil or tuned circuit that is activated by a signal, but that delivers no output to a load.

unloaded transmitter A transmitter operated under open-circuit conditions (i.e., without an external load, such as an antenna or dummy resistor).

unmanned factory A manufacturing plant run largely by robots and computers. There must generally be at least one human being, whose job(s) is/are to oversee and maintain the operation of the machines.

unmatched elements **1.** Components (such as resistors, capacitors, semiconductors, etc.) having different values. **2.** Mating elements or devices not having the same impedance. Also called MISMATCH.

unmodulated carrier See CONTINUOUS WAVE.

unmodulated current A current whose characteristics (amplitude, phase, or frequency) are not varied by a signal or by noise.

unmodulated voltage A voltage whose characteristics (amplitude, phase, or frequency) are not varied by a signal or by noise.

unmodulated wave See CONTINUOUS WAVE.

unode See MONODE.

unpack In computer operations, to remove data from a storage location into which, with other data, it has been packed (as a memory-conservation measure).

unpolarized light Light in which the wave orientation is random around the axis of the beam.

unpolarized plug A plug that can be inserted into a socket in two or more different ways, thus increasing the likelihood of a wrong connection. Compare POLARIZED PLUG.

unpolarized receptacle A receptacle into which a plug can be inserted in two or more different ways, thus increasing the likelihood of a wrong connection. Also called UNPOLARIZED SOCKET. Compare POLARIZED RECEPTACLE.

unpolarized relay A relay that always closes in the same direction, regardless of the direction of current in its coil. Also called *nonpolarized relay.*

unpolarized socket A socket into which a component or plug can be inserted in two or more different ways, thus increasing the likelihood of wrong connections. Also called UNPOLARIZED RECEPTACLE.

unprotected antenna An outside antenna operated without a lightning arrester or grounding switch. Increases the risk of damage to equipment, such as radio receivers and transmitters, connected to the antenna. It also increases the danger to personnel using the equipment.

unrationalized systems of units Collectively, the absolute centimeter-gram-second (cgs) electrostatic system of units, the absolute cgs electromagnetic system of units, and the absolute meter-kilogram-second (mks) system of units.

unreflected ray See UNREFLECTED WAVE.

unreflected wave **1.** See DIRECT WAVE. **2.** See GROUND WAVE. **3.** An electromagnetic wave that penetrates the ionosphere and passes into space.

unregulated Not held to a constant value. For example, an unregulated voltage is free to fluctuate in value.

unregulated power supply A power supply whose output current or voltage is not automatically held to a constant value. Compare CONSTANT-CURRENT SOURCE and CONSTANT-VOLTAGE SOURCE.

uns Abbreviation of UNSYMMETRICAL.

unsaturated core A magnetic core operated below the point of saturation (i.e., below the point at which an increase in coil current produces no further increase in magnetization of the core).

unsaturated logic A digital-logic scheme in which the switching devices operate between the saturated and cut-off conditions during either or both of the high and low states.

unsaturated operation Operation of a device at a point below saturation [i.e., below the point at which (1) an increase in voltage produces no

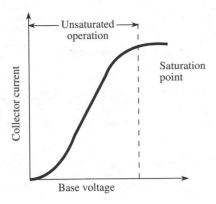

unsaturated operation

further increase in current, or vice versa, or (2) an increase in coil current produces no further increase in magnetization of a core]. Compare SATURATED OPERATION.

unsaturated standard cell   See STANDARD CELL.

unshielded cable   A cable, such as a twisted pair or a multiwire twist, lacking a shielding jacket. Unless special precautions are taken, such as transposing conductors, such a cable is susceptible to stray pickup and is capable of radiation.

unshielded choke   An uncased choke (i.e., one without a protective and shielding metal housing).

unshielded coil   An inductor without a field-confining enclosure.

unshielded probe   An instrument probe that has no shielding enclosure. Such a probe is desirable for some tests, but it is subject to antenna-pickup effect, body capacitance, and stray-field pickup.

unshielded stage   In electronic equipment, a stage operating entirely in the open (i.e., without electrostatic or magnetic shielding enclosures). It is, therefore, susceptible to stray pickup and is capable of radiation.

unshielded transformer   **1.** An uncased transformer (i.e., one without a protective and shielding metal housing). **2.** A transformer having no electrostatic shield between its windings.

unshift   The mechanical action in a teletypewriter when the carriage moves from the figures position to the letters position.

unshunted current meter   A single-range D'Arsonval milliammeter or microammeter that has no shunt resistor. The resistance of the instrument is, therefore, equal to the resistance of the movable coil.

unsolder   To separate wires, contacts, or fastenings by melting the solder that holds them together. Also called DESOLDER.

unsophisticated electronics   Electronics theory and operations of the simplest kind, involving little or no mathematics. It is generally intended for a hobbyist audience. Compare SOPHISTICATED ELECTRONICS.

unstable oscillation   **1.** Relaxation oscillation. **2.** The periodically interrupted oscillation characteristic of a blocking oscillation.

unstable region   The negative-resistance portion of an N- or S-shaped response curve.

unstable servo   A servo having unlimited output drift.

unstable state   A condition, such as a negative-resistance region, that is difficult to maintain and often results in oscillation. The negative-resistance region of the tunnel diode forward-conduction curve is evidence of such a state. Compare STABLE STATE.

untapped winding   A winding having two terminals, one at either end, and no intermediate terminals or connections. Also called *untapped coil.*

unterminated amplifier   An amplifier operated without a load device (i.e., under open-circuit output conditions).

unterminated generator   A generator operated without a load device (i.e., under open-circuit output conditions).

unterminated line   A transmission line that is not terminated with an impedance (i.e., an open-ended line).

untriggered flip-flop   A flip-flop that, at a particular instant, receives no actuating pulse, and that, therefore, does not change state.

untuned amplifier   A radio-frequency amplifier that is not tuned to a single frequency, but has useful gain over a wide band of frequencies. Examples are the *distributed amplifier* and the *video amplifier.*

untuned filter   See ALL-PASS FILTER.

untuned line   An aperiodic transmission line (i.e., one that is only tuned to a particular frequency by its own distributed characteristics).

untuned transformer   A transformer having simple primary and secondary windings and no tuning devices (such as capacitors in series or parallel with the windings), and designed so that its natural resonant frequency (because of distributed capacitance) lies outside the specified range of operation.

unused time   See UNATTENDED TIME.

unweighted average   In the statistical analysis of data, an average calculated from terms not weighted by a factor. Compare WEIGHTED AVERAGE. Also see UNWEIGHTED TERM.

unweighted term   In the statistical analysis of data, a term not operated upon by a weighting factor. Therefore, it has no extraordinary influence on a final result, such as an average. Compare WEIGHTED TERM.

unwind   To eliminate all redundant or unnecessary operations in a computer system.

up-and-downer amplifier   In broadcasting and sound amplification, an auxiliary amplifier that allows the level of sound effects and background music to be controlled automatically without disturbing the dialogue levels.

UPC Abbreviation of UNIVERSAL PRODUCT CODE.

upconv Abbreviation of UP CONVERTER.

up convert In superheterodyne conversion, to heterodyne a signal to an intermediate frequency higher than the signal frequency. Compare DOWN CONVERT.

update In data-processing operations, to make a file reflect the current status of pertinent information by using transactions for its modification.

up-down counter See BIDIRECTIONAL COUNTER.

uplink 1. The signal sent up to a satellite transponder. **2.** The frequency of the signal sent up to a satellite transponder.

uplink frequency 1. The specific frequency of a given signal sent up to a satellite transponder. **2.** The band of frequencies sent up to a satellite transponder. There can be many signals in an uplink; there can also be many different stations sending uplink signals within the band.

uplink power 1. The power output of the transmitter sending the signal up to a satellite transponder. **2.** The effective radiated power of the station sending the uplink signal.

uplink station Any station that transmits a signal, or group of signals, up to a satellite transponder.

upper atmosphere See IONOSPHERE, STRATOSPHERE, and TROPOSPHERE.

upper sideband Abbreviation, USB. In an amplitude-modulated wave, the component whose

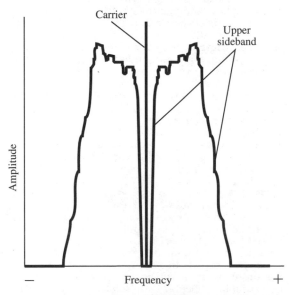

upper sideband

frequency is the sum of the carrier frequency and the modulation frequency. Compare LOWER SIDEBAND.

upper sideband, suppressed carrier Abbreviation, USSC. A single-sideband transmission technique in which the upper sideband is transmitted, the lower sideband is suppressed, and the carrier is suppressed. Compare DOUBLE SIDEBAND, SUPPRESSED CARRIER, LOWER SIDEBAND, and SUPPRESSED CARRIER.

UPS Abbreviation for UNINTERRUPTIBLE POWER SUPPLY.

upside down 1. In radioteletype, a signal in which the MARK and SPACE signals are reversed in frequency. **2.** In single sideband, reception of a signal on the wrong sideband, resulting in "monkey chatter."

up time See SERVICEABLE TIME.

upturn A usually sudden rise in a performance curve. Compare DOWNTURN.

upward modulation Modulation in which the output current of the modulated circuit increases during modulation. Compare DOWNWARD MODULATION.

UR Abbreviation of ULTRARED.

uranium Symbol, U. A radioactive metallic element. Atomic number, 92. Atomic weight, 238.03.

uranium 235 Symbol, U-235. An isotope of uranium of mass number 235, used in atomic bombs and atomic power plants.

uranium 238 Symbol, U-238. An isotope of uranium of mass number 238, which, under fast-neutron bombardment, decays to become neptunium and then plutonium (of mass number 239).

uranium metals The group of heavy, radioactive elements of atomic numbers 89 through 103. Also called the *actinide series*.

uranium rays The ionizing radiation emitted by uranium. In 1896, Antoine Henri Becquerel observed that uranium salts emit rays (later identified as alpha, beta, and gamma) that can pass through bodies opaque to light and are capable of exposing a photographic plate. Also called *Becquerel rays*.

urea formaldehyde resin A thermosetting, synthetic resin used in the manufacture of a number of plastic dielectric bodies and formed by the reaction of urea with formaldehyde.

urea plastic Any of several thermosetting plastics having a urea base and used as a dielectric and as a molding material in electronics (e.g., *urea formaldehyde resin*).

URSI Abbreviation of *Union Radio Scientifique Internationale (International Radio Scientific Union)*.

ursigram A broadcast message giving information on sunspots, radio propagation, terrestrial magnetism, and related subjects. Also see URSI.

usable frequency 1. Any frequency at which communications can be maintained between two points via ionospheric propagation. **2.** Any frequency at which a communications system is operational.

usable sample **1.** The portion of an oscilloscope or monitor display that is visible on the screen. **2.** In statistics, a sample that is considered valid for calculation purposes.

USB Abbreviation of UPPER SIDEBAND.

user friendliness **1.** For electronic equipment and systems, the quality of being easy for people to operate. **2.** The relative ease with which a machine, especially a computer, can be operated by people.

useful life The elapsed time between the installation of an expendable component, circuit, or system, and the time it must be replaced.

useful line In television, the portion of a scanning line that can be used for picture signals. Also called AVAILABLE LINE.

user group A group of hobbyists or company representatives having in common the ownership and/or use of a specific brand of computer, and who meet or otherwise interact to share their expertise with, or programs for, the machine. Also applicable to similar groups of programmable-calculator owners.

user's library A compilation of programs supplied to (by the vendor) or generated by a user group.

USM Abbreviation of *underwater-to-surface missile.*

USSC Abbreviation of UPPER SIDEBAND, SUPPRESSED CARRIER.

UTC Abbreviation of UNIVERSAL COORDINATED TIME.

utility **1.** An organization providing a public service, such as electric power or electronic communications. **2.** In computer operations, a program or set of programs intended for diagnosing and/or correcting hardware and software problems.

utility box A general-purpose aluminum or steel box, supplied in various convenient sizes (painted or unpainted), used as a housing or shield for electronic equipment.

utility factor For a transformer used in a direct-current (dc) power supply, the ratio of dc output to required kilovolt-ampere (kVA) capacity.

utilization factor See UTILITY FACTOR.

UTL Abbreviation of *unit transmission loss.*

UUM Abbreviation of *underwater-to-underwater missile.*

UV **1.** Abbreviation of ULTRAVIOLET. **2.** Abbreviation of UNDERVOLTAGE.

Uvicon A television camera tube in which a conventional vidicon scanning section is preceded by an ultraviolet-sensitive photocathode, an electron-accelerating section, and a special target.

Uviol lamp An ultraviolet lamp using uviol glass—a special glass that is transparent to ultraviolet rays.

UVM Abbreviation of UNIVERSAL VENDOR MARKING.

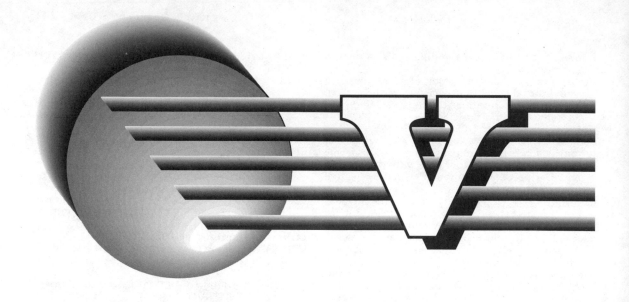

V **1.** Abbreviation of VOLT. **2.** Symbol (ital) for VOLTAGE or POTENTIAL. **3.** Symbol for VANADIUM. **4.** Symbol for VOLUME. **5.** Symbol (ital) for RELUCTIVITY. **6.** Abbreviation of VERTICAL. (Also, vert.)

v **1.** Abbreviation of VELOCITY. **2.** Abbreviation of VECTOR.

VA Abbreviation of VOLT-AMPERE.

V/A Abbreviation of *volts per ampere* (ohms).

VAC Abbreviation of *vector analog computer*.

vac Abbreviation of VACUUM.

V_{ac} Symbol for AC VOLTS. (Also, Vac.)

vacancy In a crystal lattice, a position not occupied by a nucleus.

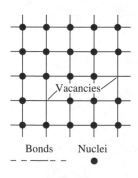

Vacancies

Bonds   Nuclei

– – –   ●

vacancy

vacuum A space from which all air and other gases have been removed to the greatest practicable extent. Some electronic parts, such as the elements of an electron tube, are housed in an evacuated space to protect them from the deterioration that would result from open-air operation.

vacuum capacitor A plate- or concentric-cylinder-type capacitor sealed in an evacuated glass tube or bulb. The vacuum acts as the dielectric and provides a dielectric constant of 1 and very high voltage breakdown.

vacuum deposition The electrical application of a layer of one material (such as a metal) to the surface of another (the substrate), carried out in a vacuum chamber (e.g., evaporation and sputtering). Also see DEPOSITION and EVAPORATION, **1.**

vacuum envelope The shell or tube of an electron tube, X-ray tube, or other electron device that requires a vacuum.

vacuum evaporation A method of manufacturing thin-film circuits by vaporizing a substance, and letting it accumulate or condense on a base.

vacuum gauge An instrument for measuring the vacuum in a device being evacuated. One of the several varieties of this gauge uses the elements of a triode, which are sealed in part of the vacuum system, some characteristic of the tube being continuously monitored as the vacuum pumping progresses. Another uses a thermistor sealed in part of the system; the resistance of the thermistor changes proportionately during the vacuum pumping.

vacuum impregnation The impregnation of a device (such as a capacitor, transformer, or choke coil) in a vacuum chamber. The process causes the pores in the device and its insulating materials to be completely filled with the impregnant.

vacuum level 1. The pressure, in millimeters of mercury (mm/Hg). Normal atmospheric pressure is 760 mm/Hg. A perfect vacuum would be represented by 0 mm/Hg. 2. The proportion, or percentage, of normal atmospheric pressure in a given environment.

vacuum phototube A phototube enclosed in an evacuated envelope, as opposed to one that is gas-filled.

vacuum pump A pump for removing air and gases from electron tubes, X-ray tubes, lamp bulbs, etc. Such pumps include mechanical types, diffusion types, and combinations of these. Also see DIFFUSION PUMP.

vacuum range The range of a communications system if propagation takes place through a perfect-vacuum (theoretical) medium.

vacuum seal An airtight seal between adjoining parts in an evacuation system.

vacuum switch A switch that is enclosed in a vacuum bulb or tube to reduce contact sparking.

vacuum thermocouple A thermocouple enclosed in a vacuum bulb with a small heater element. Radio-frequency current passed through the heater raises its temperature and causes the thermocouple to generate a proportional direct-current voltage.

vacuum tube An electron tube from which virtually all air and gases are removed. Also see ELECTRON TUBE.

vacuum-tube amplifier An amplifier using one or more vacuum tubes, rather than semiconductor devices.

vacuum-tube bridge A special bridge for determining vacuum-tube characteristics by null methods.

vacuum-tube characteristics The operating parameters of a vacuum tube, such as plate current, grid voltage, input resistance, interelectrode capacitances, amplification factor, transconductance, etc., that describe tube performance.

vacuum-tube coefficients See VACUUM-TUBE CHARACTERISTICS.

vacuum-tube current meter An ammeter, milliammeter, microammeter, or nanoammeter embodying an amplifier that uses one or more vacuum tubes. Also see ELECTRONIC CURRENT METER.

vacuum-tube modulator A circuit using one or more vacuum tubes to impress a modulating signal on a carrier.

vacuum-tube rectifier 1. An alternating-to-direct-current converter circuit using one or more vacuum tubes, rather than gas tubes or semiconductor devices. 2. A rectifier tube.

vacuum-tube sweep A sweep oscillator using a vacuum tube, rather than a gas tube. Also called HARD-TUBE SWEEP.

vacuum-tube voltmeter Abbreviation, vtvm. A voltmeter using a tube-type amplifier. Also see ELECTRONIC VOLTMETER.

val Abbreviation of VALUE.

valence A unit showing the degree to which elements or radicals (replaceable atoms or groups of atoms) will combine to form compounds.

valence band In the energy diagram for a semiconductor, the band of lowest energy. This band lies below the forbidden band (energy gap), which is below the conduction band. Also see ENERGY BAND DIAGRAM.

valence bond In a semiconductor material, an interatomic path over which shared electrons travel.

valence electrons Electrons in the outermost orbits of an atom. These electrons determine the chemical and physical properties of a material. Also see FREE ELECTRON.

valence shells See ELECTRON SHELLS.

validate To check data for correctness.

validity 1. Correctness or accuracy of data. 2. The logical truth of a derivation or statement, based on a given set of propositions.

valley A dip between adjacent peaks in a curve or wave.

valley current In a tunnel diode, the current at the valley point.

valley point The lowest point of finite current on the current-voltage response curve of a tunnel diode. Immediately before this point, current decreases with increasing applied voltage (an indication of negative resistance). Beyond this point, however, the current again increases with increasing voltage. Compare PEAK POINT.

valley voltage In a tunnel diode, the voltage at the valley point.

value 1. The level or magnitude of a quantity (e.g., voltage value). 2. The worth of a system, procedure, device, etc. in terms of goal fulfillment or other criterion.

valve Variation (Brit.) of ELECTRON TUBE. The term was applied to the first tube, a diode (the Fleming valve), and is descriptive of the action of a tube (a controller of electric current), rather than its appearance.

vanadium Symbol, V. A metallic element. Atomic number, 23. Atomic weight, 50.94.

Van Allen radiation belts Two high-altitude zones that surround the earth and consist of high-energy subatomic particles. These belts were once thought to preclude space travel by humans beyond the immediate vicinity of the earth.

Van de Graaff generator See BELT GENERATOR.

vane-anode magnetron A magnetron having plane parallel walls between adjacent cavities.

vane attenuator A waveguide attenuator consisting essentially of a slab (vane) of resistive material that slides laterally through the waveguide.

vane instrument See IRON-VANE METER.

vane-type magnetron See VANE-ANODE MAGNETRON.

vane-type meter See IRON-VANE METER.

V antenna See VEE ANTENNA.

vapor lamp   A discharge lamp consisting essentially of a glass tube filled with a small amount of gas under low pressure and some element, such as mercury or sodium. A high voltage is applied between electrodes sealed into each end of the tube. The voltage causes the element to vaporize. This, in turn, ionizes the gas, causing it to glow.

vapor pressure   In a confined medium, the pressure of a gas, measured in atmospheres, pounds per square inch, or millimeters of mercury.

VAR   Abbreviation of VOLT-AMPERES REACTIVE.

var   Abbreviation of VARIABLE.

varactor   A semiconductor-type voltage-variable capacitor. Sometimes called a *varactor diode*.

varactor amplifier   A dielectric amplifier using a varactor as the voltage-variable capacitor.

varactor flip-flop   A bistable multivibrator based on the nonlinear performance of one or two varactors.

varactor frequency multiplier   A frequency multiplier (doubler, tripler, etc.) in which multiples of a fundamental frequency result from the nonlinear action of a varactor.

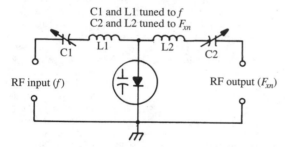

C1 and L1 tuned to f
C2 and L2 tuned to F_{xn}

C1   L1   L2   C2

RF input (f)   RF output (F_{xn})

varactor frequency multiplier

varactor tuning   A method of tuning a circuit or adjusting the frequency of an oscillator, using an inductor and a varactor to obtain the desired frequency. The varactor acts as a variable capacitor.

VAR-hour   Abbreviation, VARh. Short for *volt-ampere-reactive-hour*, a unit of reactive energy; 1 VARh can be represented by 1 VAR for 1 hour, 2 VAR for 0.5 hour, 0.5 VAR for 2 hours, etc.

VAR-hour meter   An instrument that measures reactive energy.

variable   Abbreviation, var. A quantity whose value changes at some stated or calculable rate, and is given names in expressions or equations, such as x, y, or z. Compare CONSTANT. Also see DEPENDENT VARIABLE and INDEPENDENT VARIABLE.

variable-area sound track   See VARIABLE-WIDTH SOUND RECORD.

variable block   In computer operations, a unit of data, such as a group of records, whose size is dependent on data requirements (i.e., it is not fixed).

variable-capacitance diode   See VARACTOR.

variable-capacitance transducer   See CAPACITIVE TRANSDUCER.

variable capacitor   A capacitor that can be adjusted from a low value (practically zero) to some maximum value. A step-type unit contains a number of fixed capacitors that can be switched in parallel with each other until, at the last step, all are in parallel. A continuously variable unit has a provision for moving one plate or set of plates, relative to another plate or set of plates; or one plate might be moved, with respect to another, so that the distance between them is changed. In a voltage-variable capacitor (such as a varactor), capacitance varies in accordance with an applied direct-current voltage.

variable-carrier modulation   See QUIESCENT-CARRIER OPERATION.

variable connector   In a flowchart, a path leading from a box in which a decision is made, to a number of other points on the diagram.

variable coupling   Coupling that is adjustable. In an inductively coupled circuit, the distance or angle between the coils is usually the adjustable factor. In a capacitively coupled circuit, a variable capacitor is generally used.

variable-density sound record   In photographic sound-on-film recording, a sound track made by varying, in sympathy with the sound frequency, the amount of light reaching the film. Compare VARIABLE-WIDTH SOUND RECORD.

variable-depth sonar   A sonar device that can be placed far below the surface, for the purpose of detecting objects or terrain at greater depths than would be possible with a surface-located sonar device.

variable-efficiency modulation   See EFFICIENCY MODULATION.

variable-erase recording   In magnetic-tape operations, recording a signal by selectively erasing a previously recorded signal.

variable field   **1.** Any field with an intensity that changes with time. An electromagnetic field is a common example. **2.** In a computer record, a field that is a variable block with a terminal symbol at the end.

variable-frequency oscillator   Abbreviation, VFO. An oscillator (usually self-excited) whose frequency is continuously variable.

variable-inductance pickup   A phonograph pickup in which vibration of the stylus causes the inductance of a small coil to vary in sympathy with the sound frequency.

variable-inductance transducer   A transducer in which a monitored quantity causes the inductance of a coil to vary proportionately. The coil thereby offers a varying impedance to an alternating-current supply voltage.

variable inductor An inductor whose value can be adjusted from zero to a certain maximum. The variability might be in steps, provided by taps on the inductor, or a sliding contact can be used. Several different inductors can be connected in series and parallel combinations, with switches to facilitate variability. One type of variable inductor uses a roller contact to allow continuous adjustment. See ROLLER INDUCTOR. Another method of varying inductance is to change the permeability of the core, such as by moving a rod of ferrite or powdered iron in and out of the coil. See VARICOUPLER and VARIOMETER.

variable-pitch indication An audible signal used in lieu of, or in conjunction with, a meter to indicate voltage, current, logic state, etc. The higher the value of the measured quantity, the higher the pitch.

variable-reluctance microphone A microphone in which the impinging sound waves cause corresponding variations in the reluctance of an internal magnetic circuit.

variable-reluctance pickup A phonograph pickup in which the stylus causes an armature to vibrate in a magnetic field, and consequently the reluctance of the magnetic circuit varies in sympathy with the audio frequency.

variable-reluctance transducer A transducer in which the monitored quantity causes the reluctance of an internal magnetic circuit to vary proportionately.

variable-resistance pickup A phonograph pickup in which the vibration of the stylus causes the resistance of an internal resistive element to vary in sympathy with the sound frequency.

variable-resistance transducer A transducer in which a monitored quantity causes the resistance of an internal resistive element to vary proportionately.

variable-resistance tuning Tuning of a selective resistance-capacitance (RC) circuit, such as a Wien bridge or parallel-tee network, by varying one or more of its resistance arms.

variable resistor A resistor whose value can be varied either continuously or in steps. Also see POTENTIOMETER and RHEOSTAT.

variable selectivity In a circuit or device, selectivity that is adjustable. Example: a variable-selectivity intermediate-frequency (IF) amplifier.

variable-speed motor Any motor whose speed is adjustable, smoothly or in steps, under load.

variable transformer A transformer (often an autotransformer) whose output voltage is adjustable from zero (or some minimum value) to maximum. For this purpose, one winding (usually the secondary in a two-winding transformer) can have a number of taps. Smooth variation can be provided by a wiper arm that slides over the turns of the winding.

variable-width wound record In photographic sound-on-film recording, a sound track made by varying the width of the track in sympathy with the sound variations. Compare VARIABLE-DENSITY SOUND RECORD.

Variac See VARIABLE TRANSFORMER.

Varicap A voltage-variable capacitor of the semiconductor-diode type. Also see VOLTAGE-VARIABLE CAPACITOR.

varicoupler An adjustable radio-frequency transformer consisting of a primary coil (usually the rotor) and a secondary coil (usually the stator), the former being rotatable to vary the coupling between the coils. The inductance of the stator is varied via a set of taps.

varindor A coil having a special core and whose inductance varies with the amount of direct current flowing through the winding. Also see SATURABLE REACTOR.

variocoupler A radio-frequency transformer in which one winding is rotatable, for the purpose of adjusting the mutual inductance between the primary and secondary. It is used in certain antenna-coupling applications.

variolosser A variable attenuator.

variometer A continuously variable inductor consisting of two coils connected in series or parallel and mounted concentrically—one rotating inside the other. Inductance is maximum when the coils are perpendicular to each other, and minimum when they are parallel.

varioplex A time-sharing method of transmitting and receiving wire telegraph signals. It allows the optimum usage of available lines.

varistor See VOLTAGE-DEPENDENT RESISTOR.

Varley-loop bridge A four-arm, direct-current bridge circuit in which one of the arms, a two-wire line, is accidentally grounded at a distant point. By adjustment of the bridge, the resulting resistance indicates the distance to the fault.

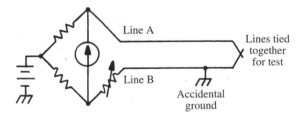

Varley loop bridge

VAR meter An instrument for measuring the apparent (VAR) power in a reactive circuit.

varnished cambric Cotton or linen fabric in sheets, tape or tubes, that has been varnish-impregnated and baked. A common form of this insulating material, the slender tubing known as *spaghetti*, has largely been replaced by plastic tubing.

varnished-cambric tubing Slender tubes of varnished cambric slipped over bare wires and busbars to insulate them. Also called *spaghetti*.

VATE Abbreviation of VERSATILE AUTOMATIC TEST EQUIPMENT.

V_B Symbol for BASE VOLTAGE of a bipolar transistor.

V_{BB} Symbol for *base-voltage supply* for a bipolar transistor.

V beam system See VEE BEAM SYSTEM.

V_C Symbol for COLLECTOR VOLTAGE of a bipolar transistor.

VCA Abbreviation of VOLTAGE-CONTROLLED AMPLIFIER.

V_{CC} Symbol for *collector-voltage supply* of a bipolar transistor.

VCCO Abbreviation of VOLTAGE-CONTROLLED CRYSTAL OSCILLATOR. (Also, lowercase.)

VCD Abbreviation of VARIABLE-CAPACITANCE DIODE.

VCG Abbreviation of VOLTAGE-CONTROLLED GENERATOR.

VCO Abbreviation of VOLTAGE-CONTROLLED OSCILLATOR.

V connection of transformers See VEE CONNECTION OF TRANSFORMERS.

VCR Abbreviation of VIDEO CASSETTE RECORDER.

VCSR Abbreviation of *voltage-controlled shift register*.

V-cut crystal See VEE-CUT CRYSTAL.

VCXO Abbreviation of VOLTAGE-CONTROLLED CRYSTAL OSCILLATOR. (Also, lowercase.)

VD **1.** Abbreviation of VOLTAGE DROP. **2.** Abbreviation of *vapor density*.

V_D Symbol for drain voltage of a field-effect transistor.

Vdc Symbol for DC VOLTS.

VDU Abbreviation of VISUAL DISPLAY UNIT.

vdcw Symbol for DC WORKING VOLTAGE. (Also, dcwv.)

VDIG Abbreviation of VIDEO DIGITIZER.

VDR **1.** Abbreviation of VOLTAGE-DEPENDENT RESISTOR. **2.** Abbreviation of VIDEODISC RECORDER.

V_{drive} Abbreviation for DRIVING VOLTAGE or OUTPUT VOLTAGE.

VE Abbreviation of value engineering.

V_E Symbol for EMITTER VOLTAGE of a bipolar transistor.

vectograph A graphic three-dimensional representation of a scene composed of superimposed images photographed through polarizing filters of different orientation, and reconstructed by a similar viewing technique.

vector **1.** A quantity having direction (in two or three dimensions) and magnitude. **2.** A graphical representation of a quantity, as defined in **1**. It consists of a straight arrow indicating the direction, and whose length is proportional to the magnitude.

vector addition The summation of two vectors, determined by adding their corresponding component values. In two dimensions, for example, suppose $\mathbf{A} = (x_1, y_1)$ and $\mathbf{B} = (x_2, y_2)$. Then $\mathbf{A} + \mathbf{B} = [(x_1 + x_2),(y_1 + y_2)]$. The sum can be found geometrically by constructing a parallelogram from the vectors, corresponding to the two known sides, as determined by the vectors. The sum is the vector originating at the point where the two vectors originate, and extending the diagonal of the parallelogram.

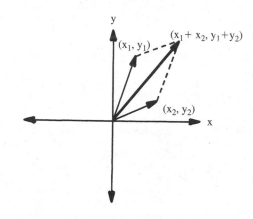

vector addition

vector admittance The reciprocal of VECTOR IMPEDANCE.

vector cardiograph An electrocardiograph that indicates the magnitude and the direction of a heart signal.

vector components **1.** The Cartesian coordinates of a vector, or its component angle and radius (polar coordinates). **2.** Quantities that can be represented by means of vectors (e.g., impedance and velocity).

vector diagram A graphical representation of vector quantities.

vector function A function having both magnitude and direction. Also see VECTOR; VECTOR COMPONENTS, **2**; and VECTOR QUANTITY.

vector generator A device that graphically illustrates vectors.

vectorial angle **1.** The angle between a vector and the horizontal axis. **2.** The angle between two vectors.

vector impedance Complex impedance (i.e., an impedance of the form $R + jX$, where R is resistance, X is reactance, and j is an operator indicating that the reactance is 90 degrees out of phase, relative to the resistance).

vector-mode display On a cathode-ray-tube display, the data representation in which points on the screen are connected by straight lines.

vector power   The vector quantity $(P_a^2 + P_x^2)^{1/2}$, where P_a is the active power and P_x is the reactive power.

vector power factor   The ratio $P_a/(P_a^2 + P_x^2)^{1/2}$, where P_a is the active power and P_x is the reactive power. In sine-wave situations, this ratio (of active power to vector power) produces a figure identical to the conventional power factor.

vector quantity   A quantity having both magnitude and direction, and that can, therefore, be represented by a vector.

vectorscope   A special oscilloscope for visual adjustment of a color-television receiver by means of a color-phase diagram.

vector sum   The resultant of two nonparallel vectors; therefore, the resultant of the forces or quantities represented by them. For example, reactance and resistance can be represented by two perpendicular vectors.

vector voltmeter   A voltmeter that indicates the phase as well as the amplitude of an alternating-current voltage.

V_{EE} Symbol for *emitter-voltage supply* of a bipolar transistor.

vee antenna   A center-fed antenna in which the two halves of the radiator form an angle considerably less than 180 degrees.

vee-beam system   An elevation-measuring radar system in which fan-shaped vertical and inclined beams, intersecting at ground and rotating continuously around the vertical axis, are radiated by one antenna. Target elevation is determined from the interval between successive echoes from the target.

vee connection of transformers   In a three-phase system, a method of connecting two transformers so that the line current and voltage equal the phase current and voltage. Also called *open-delta connection.*

vee-cut crystal   A piezoelectric plate cut from a quartz crystal so that its faces are not parallel to the *x, y,* or *z* axis of the crystal. Also see CRYSTAL AXES and CRYSTAL CUTS.

vee particle   A short-lived elementary particle that results when high-energy neutrons or protons collide with nuclei. The particle can be positive, negative, or neutral, and gets its name from its cloud-chamber track.

vee signal   In radiotelegraphy, the letter V (di-di-di-dah) transmitted as a test signal, usually three times in rapid succession. It is used during on-the-air transmitter tests, followed by the station's call letters.

vehicle   An inert substance, usually a liquid, that acts as a solvent, carrier, or binder for some other, more active substance. Thus, shellac can be the vehicle for the metallic powder in a silver paint used in silk-screening electronic circuits.

vehicle smog-control device   See COMPUTER-CONTROLLED CATALYTIC CONVERTER and EXHAUST ANALYZER.

vel   Abbreviation of VELOCITY.

velocimeter   **1.** An instrument for measuring the velocity of sound in various materials. **2.** An electronic velocity meter—especially a radial-velocity meter using Doppler radar. **3.** An electronic flow meter.

velocity   Symbol, *v.* Abbreviation, vel. Unit, distance per unit time [e.g., meters per second (m/s)]. **1.** The change in the position of a body over a specified period of time. **2.** The derivative of displacement with respect to time. Compare ACCELERATION.

velocity constant   See VELOCITY FACTOR.

velocity error   For a servomechanism in which the input and output shafts rotate at the same speed, the angular displacement between them.

velocity factor   Abbreviation, v. For a transmission line, the ratio of the speed of electromagnetic wave propagation in the line to the speed of electromagnetic waves in a vacuum (299,792 kilometers per second). It can be expressed as a number between 0 and 1, or as a percentage between 0 and 100. In practical feed lines, v ranges from about 0.66 (for coaxial line with a solid polyethylene dielectric) to about 0.95 (for open-wire line with widely separated spacers).

velocity hydrophone   A hydrophone whose output, like that of the velocity microphone, is proportional to the instantaneous particle velocity in the sound wave impinging on the device.

velocity-lag error   A lag (proportional to the input-variation rate) between the input and output of a device, such as a servomechanism.

velocity level   For a sound, the ratio v_0, expressed in decibels:

$$v_0 = 20 \log_{10}(v_s/v_r)$$

where v_s is the particle velocity of the sound, and v_r is a reference particle velocity.

velocity microphone   A microphone in which the vibratory element is a thin, aluminum or Duralumin ribbon suspended loosely between the poles of a strong permanent magnet. Vibration of the corrugated ribbon in the magnetic field causes an audio-frequency voltage to be induced across the ribbon. The microphone is so called because its output is proportional to the instantaneous particle velocity in the sound wave impinging on the ribbon. Also called *ribbon microphone.*

velocity-modulated amplifier   A circuit in which radio-frequency amplification is obtained by velocity modulation.

velocity-modulated oscillator   A vacuum-tube device in which an electron stream is velocity-modulated (see VELOCITY MODULATION) as it passes through a resonant cavity (the buncher); the subsequent energy, of a higher intensity, is extracted from the bunched stream as it passes through another resonant cavity (the catcher). Feedback from catcher to buncher sustains oscillations. See, for example, KLY-STRON OSCILLATOR.

velocity-modulated tube A vacuum tube utilizing velocity modulation. See, for example, KLYSTRON.

velocity modulation The process in which the input signal of a vacuum tube varies the velocity of the electrons in a constant-current electron beam in sympathy with the input signal.

velocity resonance A state of resonance in which a 90-degree phase difference is between the fundamental frequency of oscillation of a system and the fundamental frequency of the applied signal.

velocity sorting Selecting and separating electrons, according to their velocity.

velocity spectrograph A device that uses electric or magnetic deflection to separate charged particles into various streams, according to their velocity.

velocity variation See VELOCITY MODULATION.

velocity-variation amplifier See VELOCITY-MODULATED AMPLIFIER.

velocity-variation oscillator See VELOCITY-MODULATED OSCILLATOR.

velometer An instrument used to measure the velocity of air (e.g., to determine wind speed).

venetian-blind effect A television-display malfunction in which the picture seems to appear through horizontal slits.

Venn diagram A method of illustrating the relationship among various subsets within a specified universal set. The subsets are shown as geometric figures, usually circles.

air. **2.** In an electrolytic capacitor, a lightly covered blowout hole for the relief of gas pressure in the event of severe overload. **3.** A small opening for relieving gas pressure in an automobile battery. **4.** In a loudspeaker enclosure, such as the bass-reflex type, an auxiliary opening that extends the low-frequency range of the speaker.

vented baffle A loudspeaker enclosure having the proper auxiliary opening(s) for coupling the speaker to the surrounding air.

vented-baffle loudspeaker See ACOUSTICAL PHASE INVERTER and BASS-REFLEX LOUD-SPEAKER.

vent mount A metal bracket for fastening an antenna mast to a (plumbing) vent pipe on a roof.

ventricular fibrillation See FIBRILLATION.

verification **1.** The process of ensuring that two sets of data are identical. **2.** The process of validating (see VALIDATE).

vernier **1.** An auxiliary scale along which a regular, linear scale (such as that of a tuning dial) slides. The vernier scale is graduated so that when the main scale is set to an unmarked point between two of its graduations, and the "0" point on the vernier scale is used as the index, "1" on the vernier scale will exactly coincide with "1" on the main scale. The corresponding number on the vernier scale indicates the exact number of subdivisions between two points on the main scale. Vernier arrangements are provided with the dials of some precision analog instruments. **2.** See VERNIER CAPACITOR. **3.** See VERNIER DIAL. **4.** See VERNIER RESISTOR.

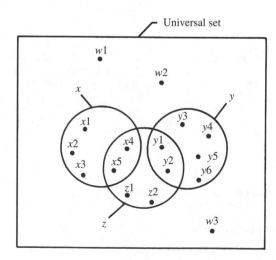

Venn diagram

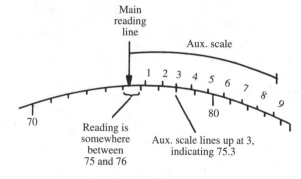

vernier, 1

vent **1.** An opening in an equipment enclosure for the entry of cool air or the escape of warm

vernier capacitor A low-capacitance variable capacitor connected in parallel with a higher-capacitance fixed or variable capacitor for precise adjustment of the total capacitance.

vernier dial **1.** A slow moving dial for fine tuning an adjustable device. The required reduction ratio is obtained with gears, friction wheels, or a belt-and-pulley combination. **2.** A dial provided with an accessory vernier scale.

vernier resistor A low-resistance variable resistor connected in series with a higher-resistance fixed or variable resistor to precisely adjust the total resistance.

vernier rheostat See VERNIER RESISTOR.

vers Abbreviation of VERSED SINE.

versatile automatic test equipment Abbreviation, VATE. For troubleshooting the electronic systems of missiles, a computer-controlled tester that isolates faults through logical operations.

versed sine Abbreviation, vers. A trigonometric function equal to the difference between the cosine of an angle and one; vers $x = 1 - \cos x$.

vert Abbreviation of VERTICAL.

vertex **1.** The terminal point at which two or more branches of a network meet. Also see NODE, 1. **2.** The point of intersection of two lines that form an angle.

vertex plate In the reflector of a microwave antenna, a matching plate mounted at the vertex.

vertical **1.** The direction indicated by a line perpendicular to the plane of the horizon (e.g., a vertical axis). **2.** In the 45-45 recording process, the signal resulting from sound that arrives simultaneously and 180 degrees out of phase at the two microphones and causes up-and-down movement of the cutting stylus.

vertical amplification Gain provided by the vertical channel of a device, such as an oscilloscope, cathode-ray electrocardiograph, or television receiver. Compare HORIZONTAL AMPLIFICATION.

vertical amplifier The circuit or device that provides gain in the vertical channel of a device. Compare HORIZONTAL AMPLIFIER.

vertical-amplitude control **1.** See VERTICAL-GAIN CONTROL. **2.** In a color television receiver, one of the three controls by which the amplitude of the parabolic voltages applied to the coils of the magnetic-convergence assembly are adjusted.

vertical angle of radiation The angle, with respect to the plane of the horizon, at which radio-frequency energy is propagated from a transmitting antenna.

vertical antenna **1.** An antenna that consists essentially of a single, straight, vertical conductor. **2.** An antenna that is mounted vertically, instead of horizontally.

vertical blanking See VERTICAL RETRACE BLANKING.

vertical-blanking pulse In a television signal, the pulse at the end of each field that accomplishes vertical retrace blanking. Compare HORIZONTAL-BLANKING PULSE.

vertical-centering control See CENTERING CONTROL.

vertical channel The system of amplifiers, controls, and terminations that constitutes the path of the vertical signal applied to a device, such as an oscilloscope. Compare HORIZONTAL CHANNEL.

vertical compliance In disc sound reproduction, the ease with which the stylus can move vertically while it is in position on the disc.

vertical coordinates See CARTESIAN COORDINATES.

vertical deflection **1.** In an oscilloscope or television receiver, the movement of the spot up and down on the screen. Compare HORIZONTAL DEFLECTION. **2.** In a direct-writing recorder, up or down deflection of the pen.

vertical deflection coils In a cathode-ray tube, the pair of coils in a deflection yoke that provides the electromagnetic field for the vertical deflection of the electron beam. Compare HORIZONTAL DEFLECTION COILS.

vertical deflection electrodes See VERTICAL DEFLECTION COILS and VERTICAL DEFLECTION PLATES.

vertical deflection plates In an oscilloscope (and in some early television picture tubes), a pair of plates that provides the electrostatic field for vertical deflection. Compare HORIZONTAL DEFLECTION PLATES.

vertical dipole An antenna consisting of a straight, center-fed, half-wave conductor oriented vertically.

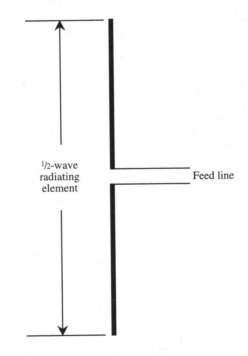

½-wave radiating element

Feed line

vertical dipole

vertical dynamic convergence During the scanning of points along a vertical line through the center of a color-television picture tube, the convergence of the electron beams at the aperture mask. Compare HORIZONTAL DYNAMIC CONVERGENCE.

vertical field strength   The field strength of signals in a vertical plane passing through an antenna. Compare HORIZONTAL FIELD STRENGTH.

vertical-field-strength diagram   A plot of vertical field strength.

vertical frequency response   The gain-frequency characteristic of the vertical channel of an instrument, such as an oscilloscope. Compare HORIZONTAL FREQUENCY RESPONSE.

vertical gain   The overall amplification (gain) provided by the vertical channel of an instrument, such as an oscilloscope, graphical recorder, or television receiver. Compare HORIZONTAL GAIN.

vertical-gain control   A control, such as a potentiometer, for adjusting vertical amplification. Compare HORIZONTAL-GAIN CONTROL.

vertical-hold control   In a television receiver, the control for adjusting the frequency of the vertical oscillator so that the picture can be locked to prevent vertical roll. Compare HORIZONTAL-HOLD CONTROL.

vertical-incidence transmission   Transmission of a wave vertically to the ionosphere and the subsequent reflection of the wave to the earth.

vertical-lateral recording   In stereophonic disc recording, the recording of one signal vertically (see VERTICAL RECORDING) and the other laterally (see LATERAL RECORDING).

vertical linearity   Linearity of response (gain and deflection) of the vertical channel of an oscilloscope or television receiver. A linear picture is neither contracted nor expanded vertically in any part of the screen. Compare HORIZONTAL LINEARITY.

vertical-linearity control   In an oscilloscope or television receiver, the control whereby vertical linearity is adjusted. Compare HORIZONTAL-LINEARITY CONTROL.

vertically polarized wave   An electromagnetic wave whose electric lines of flux are perpendicular to the plane of the horizon. Compare HORIZONTALLY POLARIZED WAVE.

vertical-metal-oxide semiconductor field-effect transistor   Abbreviation, VMOSFET. A metal-oxide semiconductor field-effect transistor fabricated so that the current flow within the device is vertical, instead of the usual horizontal, affording several advantages over the conventional MOSFET.

vertical oscillator   In a television receiver, the oscillator that generates the vertical sweep signal. Compare HORIZONTAL OSCILLATOR.

vertical-output regulator   In a television receiver, a voltage-dependent resistor used to stabilize the sweep voltage across the horizontal deflection coils—especially during warmup.

vertical output stage   In a television receiver, an output amplifier following the vertical oscillator. Compare HORIZONTAL OUTPUT STAGE.

vertical polarization   Pertaining to an electromagnetic wave whose electric lines of flux are perpendicular to the plane of the horizon. In general, when the radiating element of an antenna is vertical, the electric lines of flux in the transmitted waves are vertical, and the antenna is most sensitive to incoming signals whose electric lines of flux are vertical. Compare HORIZONTAL POLARIZATION.

vertical positioning control   See CENTERING CONTROL.

vertical quantity   The quantity measured along the y-axis of a graph, or represented by the vertical deflection of an electron beam. Compare HORIZONTAL QUANTITY.

vertical radiator   See VERTICAL ANTENNA.

vertical recording   Disc recording in which the depth of the groove is varied in sympathy with the sound. Also called HILL-AND-DALE RECORDING. Compare LATERAL RECORDING.

vertical redundance   In computer operation, the error state when a character has an odd number of bits in an even-parity system, or vice versa.

vertical resolution   The number of horizontal wedge-lines that can be easily seen in a television test pattern before they blend. Compare HORIZONTAL RESOLUTION.

vertical retrace   In a cathode-ray device, such as an oscilloscope or television receiver, the rapid return of the beam to its starting point at the top of the screen after completely traversing the screen from top to bottom. Compare HORIZONTAL RETRACE.

vertical retrace blanking   In a television receiver, the automatic shutoff of the electron beam during a vertical retrace period, to prevent an extraneous line being traced on the screen during this period. Also see BLACKOUT, **2**; BLANKING INTERVAL, **1**, **2**; BLANKING PEDESTAL; BLANKING TIME; VERTICAL RETRACE; and VERTICAL RETRACE PERIOD. Compare HORIZONTAL RETRACE BLANKING.

vertical retrace period   In a television receiver, the interval during which the spot returns from the bottom to the top of the screen after having traced all horizontal lines from top to bottom. Compare HORIZONTAL RETRACE PERIOD.

vertical sensitivity   The signal voltage required at the input of a vertical channel to produce full vertical deflection. Also see VERTICAL GAIN. Compare HORIZONTAL SENSITIVITY.

vertical signal   A signal serving as a vertical quantity (e.g., one that deflects the beam in a cathode-ray tube upward and/or downward). Compare HORIZONTAL SIGNAL.

vertical-speed transducer   A transducer whose electrical output is proportional to the vertical speed of an aircraft or missile carrying the transducer.

vertical stylus force   In disc sound reproduction, the downward force (in grams or ounces) that the stylus exerts on the disc.

vertical sweep   **1.** In a cathode-ray tube, especially a television picture tube, the movement of the spot up or down on the screen. Compare HORIZONTAL SWEEP. **2.** The circuit that produces this sweep.

vertical sweep frequency   The frequency at which vertical sweep occurs. In a television receiver, it is 60 Hz. Also called *vertical sweep rate.* Compare HORIZONTAL SWEEP FREQUENCY.

vertical sweep rate   See VERTICAL SWEEP FREQUENCY.

vertical synchronization   In a television receiver, synchronization of the vertical component of scanning with that of the camera. Also see VERTICAL SYNC PULSE. Compare HORIZONTAL SYNCHRONIZATION.

vertical sync pulse   In a video signal, the pulse that synchronizes the vertical component of scanning in a television receiver with that of the camera, and that triggers vertical retrace and blanking. Compare HORIZONTAL SYNC PULSE.

vertical wave   See VERTICALLY POLARIZED WAVE.

vertical width control   See WIDTH CONTROL, **1, 2.**

very high frequency   Abbreviation, VHF. Radio frequencies in the range 30 MHz to 300 MHz, corresponding to free-space wavelengths of 10 meters to 1 meter. It is sometimes divided into *VHF low band* (30 MHz to 50 MHz) and *VHF high band* (50 MHz to 300 MHz). Also see RADIO SPECTRUM, **1.**

very high resistance   Abbreviation, VHR. Large values of resistance; usually expressed in megohms, gigohms, or teraohms.

very-high-resistance voltmeter   Abbreviation, VHRVM. A voltmeter using a low-range microammeter or picoammeter and a very high value of multiplier resistance (see VOLTMETER MULTIPLIER).

very-high-speed integrated circuit   An integrated circuit used for switching or other digital functions at thousands, millions, or billions of changes of state per second.

very-large-scale integration   Abbreviation, VLSI. The inclusion of several complete systems, such as computers, on a single integrated-circuit chip. This can extend several orders of magnitude beyond large-scale integration (LSI).

very long range   Abbreviation, VLR. Pertaining to ground radar sets having a maximum slant range of over 250 miles. Compare VERY SHORT RANGE.

very low frequency   Abbreviation VLF. A radio frequency in the range 10 kHz to 30 kHz, corresponding to wavelengths between 30 kilome-

ters and 10 kilometers. Also see RADIO SPECTRUM, **1.**

very low resistance   Abbreviation, VLR. Values of resistance less than 1 ohm, usually expressed in milliohms or microhms.

very short range   Abbreviation, VSR. Pertaining to ground radar sets having a maximum slant range of less than 25 miles. Compare VERY LONG RANGE.

vestigial   **1.** An effect that remains as a by-product, but that serves no directly applicable purpose. See, for example, VESTIGIAL SIDEBAND. **2.** Unnecessary; extraneous.

vestigial sideband   **1.** A portion of one sideband in an amplitude-modulated signal, remaining after passage through a selective filter. **2.** An amplitude-modulated signal in which one sideband has been partially or largely suppressed. **3.** The small amount of energy emitted in the unused sideband in a single-sideband transmitter.

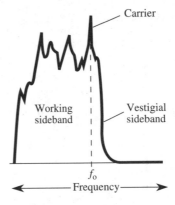

vestigial sideband, 2

vestigial-sideband filter   A filter operated between an amplitude-modulated transmitter and an antenna to obtain a vestigial-sideband signal.

vestigial-sideband signal   An amplitude-modulated signal in which one of the sidebands has been partially suppressed.

vestigial-sideband transmission   Transmission of a signal containing a vestigial sideband. In television, for example, the upper sideband is transmitted fully, while the lower sideband is almost completely suppressed. The lower sideband is, therefore, a vestigial sideband.

vestigial-sideband transmitter   An amplitude-modulated transmitter equipped with the filters or other subcircuits necessary for emitting a vestigial-sideband signal.

VF   Abbreviation of VIDEO FREQUENCY.

V$_{FB}$ Abbreviation for *feedback voltage* in an integrated circuit device. The term applies especially to operational amplifiers.

VFO Abbreviation of VARIABLE-FREQUENCY OSCILLATOR.

V_g Abbreviation of GENERATOR VOLTAGE. (Also, E_g.)

VGA Abbreviation of VARIABLE-GAIN AMPLIFIER.

V_{GD} Symbol for GATE-DRAIN VOLTAGE of a field-effect transistor.

V_{GS} Symbol for GATE-SOURCE VOLTAGE of a field-effect transistor.

VHF Abbreviation of VERY HIGH FREQUENCY.

VHF high band See VERY HIGH FREQUENCY.

VHF low band See VERY HIGH FREQUENCY.

VHF omnirange Abbreviation, VOR. A very-high-frequency radionavigation system that provides radial lines of position.

VHF oscillator A radio-frequency oscillator specially designed to operate in the range 30 MHz to 300 MHz.

VHF receiver 1. A radio receiver specially designed to operate in the range of 30 MHz to 300 MHz. 2. A television receiver for the VHF channels (see VHF TELEVISION CHANNELS).

VHF television channels Twelve 6-MHz-wide channels (television channels 2 through 13) between 54 and 216 MHz.

Channel	Frequency (MHz)
2	54.0–60.0
3	60.0–66.0
4	66.0–72.0
5	76.0–82.0
6	82.0–88.0
7	174–180
8	180–186
9	186–192
10	192–198
11	198–204
12	204–210
13	210–216

**VHF television channels
(United States)**

VHF transmitter A radio or television transmitter specially designed to operate in the range 30 MHz to 300 MHz.

VHR Abbreviation of VERY HIGH RESISTANCE.

VHRVM Abbreviation of VERY-HIGH-RESISTANCE VOLTMETER.

VHS videocassette recorder A popular scheme for videocassette recording, used in millions of households in the United States alone. Typical VHS cassette play times range from about two hours to more than eight hours.

VHSIC Abbreviation for VERY HIGH SPEED INTEGRATED CIRCUIT.

VI 1. Abbreviation of VOLUME INDICATOR. 2. Abbreviation of VISCOSITY INDEX.

V_i Symbol for INPUT VOLTAGE. (Also, V_{in}.)

vibrating bell A bell with a striking mechanism that oscillates, causing a continuous ringing sound.

vibrating-reed frequency meter See POWER-FREQUENCY METER, 2.

vibrating-reed oscillator An audio-frequency oscillator in which an iron, steel, or alloy reed vibrating in a magnetic field acts like a tuning fork to control the oscillation frequency.

vibrating-reed relay An electromechanical relay in which the movable contact is carried by the end of a thin, metal strip (reed) of iron or magnetic alloy. The strip is supported within the magnetic field of a coil carrying an alternating control current; when the frequency of this current corresponds to the natural (resonant) frequency of the reed, it vibrates vigorously enough to close the contacts. Such a relay, consequently, is frequency selective.

vibrating-wire oscillator An oscillator similar to the vibrating-reed oscillator, but using a wire, instead of a reed.

vibrating-wire transducer A transducer in which the fluctuating tension of a thin wire suspended in a magnetic field frequency-modulates the operating voltage.

vibration 1. The changing of the position or dimensions of a body back and forth, usually at a rapid rate, an action seen in the repetitive movement of a musical string, headphone diaphragm, loudspeaker cone, loose machine, etc. 2. See OSCILLATION.

vibration analyzer See VIBRATION METER.

vibration calibrator A device that generates a standard vibration, usually at a fixed frequency, for calibrating vibration meters, pickups, transducers, etc.

vibration galvanometer A type of alternating-current galvanometer. The natural frequency of the movable element of the instrument is made equal to that of the alternating current under test, to obtain a reading.

vibration isolator In an electronic-equipment assembly, a cushioning support that protects the equipment from vibration.

vibration machine See VIBRATOR, 2.

vibration meter An instrument for measuring the amplitude and frequency of vibration (see VIBRATION, 1). It consists essentially of a vibration pickup followed by a selective amplifier and an indicating voltmeter graduated in vibration units.

vibration pickup A transducer that senses mechanical vibration and converts it into a proportionate output voltage, or changes resistance in sympathy with the vibration.

vibrato In electronic musical instruments, a circuit or device that modulates a note by varying its frequency, amplitude, or both, at an extremely low frequency (a few hertz).

vibrator 1. See INTERRUPTER. 2. See VIBRATING-REED RELAY. 3. A device for shaking something under test at selected frequencies and amplitudes.

vibrator-type power supply   A battery-operated, high-voltage power supply in which one vibrator (see INTERRUPTER) makes and breaks direct current flowing from the battery into the primary winding of a step-up transformer, and another vibrator rectifies the high voltage delivered by the secondary winding.

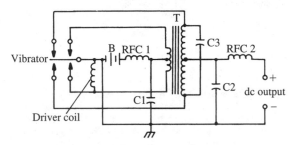

vibrator-type power supply

vibrator-type rectifier   A vibrator (see INTERRUPTER) that connects one terminal of the secondary winding of a transformer to an output terminal each time that terminal is positive. When the negative half-cycle appears at the transformer terminal, the vibrator is open. In this way, the alternating-current output of the transformer is rectified.

vibrocardiography   A method of monitoring and recording the movement of the chest cavity as a result of the beating of the heart.

vibrograph   A device for observing and recording vibration.

vibrometer   See VIBRATION METER.

vibroscope   An instrument for observing (and sometimes recording) vibration.

Victor   Phonetic alphabet communications code word for the letter V.

Victron   A brand of polystyrene, a low-loss plastic insulant that is especially useful at high radio frequencies.

video   **1.** Pertaining to television—especially to its picture circuitry or to circuits and devices related to television, but used for other purposes. **2.** The picture portion of a television broadcast, as opposed to the sound (audio) portion. **3.** Sometimes, a cathode-ray-tube terminal or display. **4.** Generally, television in adjective sense (e.g., *video play*). **5.** The images on a computer display or monitor.

video amplifier   **1.** In television, the wideband stage (or stages) that amplifies the picture signal and presents it to the picture tube. **2.** A similar wideband amplifier, such as an instrument amplifier or preamplifier having at least a 4-MHz bandwidth.

video animation   Movement of graphic images on a cathode-ray-tube display by the use of computer-manipulation through special software, under the direction of an operator using a keyboard, joystick, or digitizer.

video buffer   A unity-gain circuit that minimizes loading effects caused by having several video multiplexer inputs connected to the same signal source.

video carrier   The television carrier amplitude-modulated by the picture information, synchronization pulses, and blanking pulses.

videocassette recorder   Abbreviation, VCR. A machine for recording television programs on magnetic-tape cassettes (see CASSETTE, 1).

videocast   **1.** Television broadcast. Also called TELECAST. **2.** To make a television broadcast.

videocaster   See TELECASTER.

video CD-ROM   A digital optical VIDEODISC, resembling an audio or computer compact disc. A typical disc can store more than an hour's worth of conventional television programming.

video correlator   A device used with radar to locate and identify a target with high precision.

video detector   In a television receiver, the demodulator for the video signal. This detector follows the video intermediate-frequency amplifier and precedes the video amplifier. It usually embodies a relatively simple, wideband diode circuit.

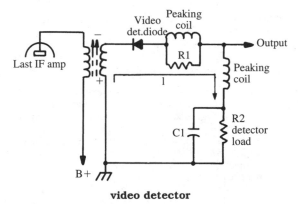

video detector

Video Digitizer   Abbreviation, VDIG. A program developed for multimedia video in personal computer systems.

videodisc   A flat magnetic or optical disc on which audio-visual programs are recorded, and from which they can be played back into a television receiver or multimedia personal computer.

videodisc recorder   Abbreviation, VDR. A machine for recording television programs on discs comparable to those used for sound or data recording.

video discrimination   In radar, the use of a circuit or device to decrease the width of the video-amplifier passband.

video frequency 1. Pertaining to signals in the wide passband of a video amplifier: 30 Hz to 4 MHz. **2.** Pertaining to a device capable of operating over the wide passband of a video amplifier (e.g., a video-frequency alternating-current voltmeter).

video-frequency amplifier An amplifier capable of handling signals of a wide frequency range (e.g., direct current to 4 MHz). Also see VIDEO FREQUENCY, **1.**

video gain control In a television receiver, a gain control for adjusting the video signal amplitude. In a color-television receiver, a pair of these controls permits adjustment of the three color signals to the proper amplitude ratio.

video game A game, such as football, basketball, slot machine, tic-tac-toe, etc., played on the screen of a television receiver or on a computer.

videogenic Suitable for television.

video IF amplifier In a television receiver, the broadband intermediate-frequency (IF) amplifier of the video signal. In modern receivers, this IF amplifier also handles the sound signal.

video mapping A system of surveillance or mapping in which, for reference, the outlines of the area being surveyed are superimposed electronically on the radar display of the area.

video masking A form of radar signal processing in which ground clutter and other unwanted echoes are removed, making the desired targets more readily visible.

video mixer A circuit or device for mixing the signals from two or more television cameras.

video modulation In television transmission, amplitude modulation of the carrier wave with pulses and waves corresponding to the picture elements.

video on demand Television service in which subscribers can choose the programs they want to watch, and also the specific times for viewing.

video random-access memory Abbreviation, VRAM. In computer systems, RANDOM-ACCESS MEMORY used primarily for enhancing the performance of the display.

video recording 1. Recording wideband material (such as a video signal) on a tape or disc. **2.** The recording made of a telecast. Also see VIDEOTAPE RECORDER.

video signal 1. In television, the amplitude-modulated signal containing picture information and pulses. Also see VIDEO, **2** and VIDEO MODULATION. **2.** Broadly, a telecast signal, including sound.

video stretching In some electronic navigation systems, increasing the duration of a video pulse.

video synthesizer A computerized device that produces graphical renditions of objects or circuits in three dimensions.

videotape 1. A special magnetic tape for video recording (see VIDEO RECORDING, **2**). **2.** To make a video recording.

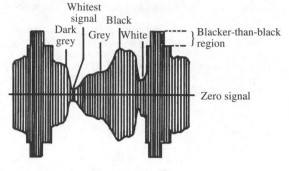

video signal

videotape recorder Abbreviation, VTR. A wideband, magnetic-tape recorder for producing video recordings with a camera, or for making a record of television programs, for subsequent reproduction (playback).

videotape recording 1. Abbreviation, VTR. The technique of recording video signals on magnetic tape. Also see VIDEO RECORDING, **1, 2** and VIDEOTAPE. **2.** A tape on which a video signal has been recorded.

videotext A system that allows television viewers to dial up special material, such as stock market quotations, weather data, sports scores, etc.

vidicon A television camera tube in which the electron beam scans a charged-density pattern that has been formed and stored on the surface of the photoconductor. It is commonly used in camcorders, closed-circuit television systems, and robot vision systems. Its assets include compactness and sensitivity.

viewfinder An accessory or integral device in which an image (formed optically or electronically) corresponds to the image viewed by the camera with which it is used.

viewing mesh In a cathode-ray storage tube, the mesh on which the image is presented for viewing by the operator. Also see CHARGE-STORAGE TUBE.

viewing mirror In an oscilloscope-camera assembly, a flat, slant-mounted mirror that reflects the image on the oscilloscope screen to the viewer's eye.

viewing screen In a cathode-ray device, such as an oscilloscope tube or television picture tube, the face on which the image appears.

viewing time In a storage type cathode-ray tube, the length of time for which the image persists.

viewing window See WINDOW, **2.**

Villard circuit 1. A voltage-doubler circuit using only one diode and two capacitors. The open-circuit direct-current output voltage is approximately twice the peak value of the alternating-current input voltage. Also see VOLTAGE DOUBLER. **2.** See SELECTOJECT.

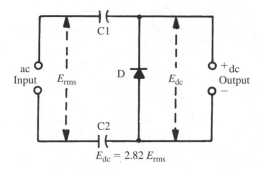

$$E_{dc} = 2.82\, E_{rms}$$

Villard circuit, 1

Villari effect   In certain magnetostrictive materials, the change in magnetic induction that accompanies the application of a mechanical stress in a given direction. Also see MAGNETOSTRICTION.

vinyl   A general name for *vinyl copolymer resins*.

vinylidene chloride   A plastic insulant. Dielectric constant, 3 to 5. Dielectric strength, 20 kV/mm.

Vinylite-A   A brand of the plastic *polyvinyl acetate*.

Vinylite-Q   A brand of the plastic *polyvinyl chloride*.

vinyl resin   A synthetic resin resulting from the polymerization of compounds that contain the group $CH_2 = CH–$.

violation   In a security system, a condition that results in the actuation of an alarm. Example: an intruder breaks the light beam in an electric eye.

virgin magnetic material   Core or shield material that has never been magnetized. When virgin material is first subjected to magnetization, the hysteresis loop starts at zero, but never returns to zero (see BOX-SHAPED LOOP).

virgin neutron   Any neutron that has not been involved in a collision with another particle subsequent to its initial generation.

virgin record   See BLANK RECORD.

virgin tape   See BLANK TAPE.

virtual address   In computer operations, an address that must be modified to refer to a location in main memory.

virtual decision value   In quantizing or encoding, a method of expressing the maximum input amplitude. Two values are extrapolated from actual decision values—one at either end of the working range used.

virtual height   The altitude that a vertically propagated electromagnetic wave would reach before reflection if its path in the ionosphere were a straight line. The actual distance at which the wave penetrates the ionosphere before reflection is less than the virtual height.

virtual image   The image formed when rays from a scene diverge after passing beyond the focal point of a convex lens. The scene appears inverted to an observer. Compare REAL IMAGE.

virtual memory   **1.** In a computer system, a means of using two or more memory stores simultaneously. **2.** Auxiliary memory used in conjunction with the main, or core, memory.

virtual ppi reflectoscope   A device used to superimpose a virtual image of a chart or map onto a plan-position indicator (ppi) radar display. Also see VIDEO MAPPING.

virtual reality   Abbreviation, VR. A general term for any of various high-level computer simulation or remote-control programs. The user often wears a head-mounted display that provides vivid, three-dimensional imagery and binaural sound. It can be used in robotic telepresence systems for precision remote control.

virus   See COMPUTER VIRUS.

vis   **1.** Abbreviation of *visibility*. **2.** Abbreviation of *visual*.

viscometer   An instrument for measuring viscosity. There are several electronic versions of this device. In one, a steel ball falls through a material (such as an oil) under test and distorts the magnetic field of a pickup coil, causing the deflection of a meter by an amount proportional to the speed of the ball and, consequently, to the viscosity of the fluid.

viscosimeter   See VISCOMETER.

viscosity   The resistance offered by a fluid (liquid or gas) to objects passing through it. The viscosity of pure water is low; that of heavy oil is high. Expressed in newton-seconds per meter squared.

viscosity index   Abbreviation, VI. A number indicating how well an oil retains its viscosity with temperature changes; larger indexes are assigned to oils that are little influenced by variations in temperature.

viscous-damped arm   A phonograph pickup arm with an oil dashpot to prevent arm resonance and to slow the descent of the arm to the disc.

viscous damping   The use of a viscous fluid in the dashpot of a device (such as a relay, timer, or pickup arm) to provide damping. See, for example, DASHPOT RELAY.

viscous hysteresis   A slow, slight increase in the magnetization of a material when the magnetizing field is constant. Compare STATIC HYSTERESIS.

visibility factor   See DISPLAY LOSS.

visible radiation   Electromagnetic radiation that is perceptible to the eye. Also see VISIBLE SPECTRUM.

visible spectrum   The band of electromagnetic wavelengths that the human eye perceives as visible light. For most people, this band extends from approximately 750 nanometers (nm), representing red light, down to 390 nm, representing violet light. The visibility curve peaks in the yellow-green region at about 560 nm; 1 nm = 0.000 000 001 meter = 10^{-9} m. Also see ELECTROMAGNETIC THEORY OF LIGHT.

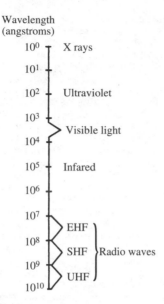

Wavelength (angstroms)

10^0 — X rays

10^1

10^2 — Ultraviolet

10^3

10^4 — Visible light

10^5 — Infared

10^6

10^7

10^8 — EHF

SHF — Radio waves

10^9 — UHF

10^{10}

visible spectrum

vision system   A set of devices that allows a machine (computer or robot) to observe and respond to visual stimuli. Typically, it includes a camera [such as a vidicon or charge-coupled device (CCD)], a cable, electromagnetic or fiberoptic link, a receiver, and software for interpreting the images.

visual alignment   Optimization of a circuit (such as a radio receiver) with the aid of meter deflections, rather than with audible indications. Also called *silent alignment.*

visual-aural radio range   A radio aid to air navigation (characterized by an audible signal, meter deflection, or both) used by the pilot of an aircraft to determine if the course is being followed.

visual-aural range   See VISUAL-AURAL RADIO RANGE.

visual-aural signal tracer   A troubleshooting instrument for following a signal through a circuit by sensing it at successive points in the circuit. The signal strength is indicated by a meter and a loudspeaker.

visual carrier frequency   See VIDEO CARRIER and VIDEO-FREQUENCY, **1.**

visual communication   **1.** Transmission and reception of signals by visible-light means, such as modulated beams of flashing lights. **2.** Transmission and reception of messages by direct visual observation, such as signal lights.

visual display unit   Abbreviation, VDU. **1.** A computer peripheral consisting of a cathode-ray tube, a keyboard, and often a pointing device. **2.** A dumb terminal for operation of a computer from a remote site.

visual horizon   **1.** The distance from a given point to the farthest visible point on the surface of the earth in a particular direction. **2.** The enclosed geometric plane figure on the surface of the earth, representing the set of farthest-visible points for a particular location.

visual telegraphy   Telegraphy in which the received signals are read from a visual device, such as a blinking light, meter, or swinging pen.

visual transmitter   The equipment used to transmit the picture portion of a television broadcast.

visual transmitter power   The peak power output of a visual transmitter during normal operation.

vitreous   Pertaining to a material or surface resembling, or related to, glass (e.g., the *vitreous enamel* on certain types of resistors).

VLF   Abbreviation of VERY LOW FREQUENCY.

VLR   **1.** Abbreviation of VERY LOW RESISTANCE. **2.** Abbreviation of VERY LONG RANGE.

VLSI   Abbreviation of VERY-LARGE-SCALE INTEGRATION.

V/m   Abbreviation of VOLTS PER METER (a unit of electric field strength).

VMOS   Abbreviation of *vertical-metal-oxide semiconductor.*

VMOSFET   Abbreviation of VERTICAL-METAL-OXIDE SEMICONDUCTOR FIELD-EFFECT TRANSISTOR.

V_o Symbol for OUTPUT VOLTAGE. Also, V_{out}.

VOA   Abbreviation of VOLT-OHM-AMMETER.

vocabulary   In computer-programming operations, a list of available operating codes and instructions for the computer. Also called INSTRUCTION SET.

Vocoder   A device for reducing speech to frequencies low enough for efficient transmission through a limited-bandwidth channel. The term is a contraction of *voice coder.*

Voda   In a telephone system that utilizes a radio link (using the same frequency for transmission in both directions) and land-line links, an automatic, voice-operated switching system for enabling the transmitter and disabling the receiver, and vice versa. The name is an acronym for *voice-operated device, antising.*

Vodacom   Contraction of *voice data communications.*

Voder   An electronic device that synthesizes speech. The term is an acronym for *voice operation demonstrator.*

vogad   A type of automatic gain control for audio amplifiers and modulators. In a radio transmitter, it maintains 100% modulation of the carrier—even when the speaker's voice level varies widely. The name is an acronym for *voice-operated gain adjusting device.*

voice actuation   See VOICE-OPERATED CONTROL.

voice analyzer   A circuit that evaluates the characteristics of human voices, such as the amplitude-vs.-frequency function or the amplitude-vs.-time function.

voice band See VOICE FREQUENCIES.

voice coil The moving coil of a dynamic microphone or dynamic speaker.

voice-controlled break-in A type of break-in operation for radiotelephony, in which the transmitter automatically switches on and the receiver switches off immediately when the operator starts talking; the transmitter switches off and the receiver switches on a moment after the operator stops talking.

voice-controlled relay An electronic relay that is actuated by the human voice.

voice filter **1.** A filter for passing, suppressing, or modifying voice frequencies. **2.** A parallel-resonant circuit inserted into a line that feeds several loudspeakers, to trap certain frequencies and thereby improve the sound of the reproduced voice.

voice frequencies **1.** The audio-frequency range of human speech, from about 60 Hz to 8000 Hz. **2.** The frequencies within the audio passband of a typical single-sideband voice transmitter or receiver. The lower limit is generally 200 Hz to 300 Hz; the upper limit is about 2500 Hz to 3000 Hz.

voice-frequency carrier telegraphy A type of carrier-current telegraphy (see WIRED WIRELESS) in which the modulated carrier can be transmitted over a telephone line having a voice-frequency bandwidth.

voice-frequency dialing A system of telephone dialing involving the conversion of direct-current pulses into voice-frequency alternating-current pulses.

voice-frequency telephony Wire telephone communication in which the frequencies of the electric waves are identical to the frequencies of the sound waves (or very nearly so).

voice grade Pertaining to a communications system having a bandpass capable of transferring a human voice with reasonable intelligibility. See VOICE FREQUENCIES, **2.**

voice-grade channel **1.** A telephone line and attendant equipment suitable for the transmission of speech and certain other information, such as control signals, digital data, etc. **2.** In a radiotelephone transmitter, a speech amplifier-modulator channel suitable only for voice frequencies.

voice-operated control Abbreviation, vox. Pertaining to a device (such as a relay, automatic modulation control, transmit-receive switch, etc.) that is actuated when the operator speaks into a microphone.

voice-operated device, anti-sing See VODA.

voice-operated gain-adjusting device See VOGAD.

voice-operated loss control and suppressor In wire telephony, a device that switches the loss from the transmitting line to the receiving line when the subscriber speaks, and vice versa.

voice-over The simultaneous recording of a human voice (such as that of a narrator) along with other sounds (such as music, children playing, wind in trees, ocean waves, chirping birds, etc.). The voice is generally louder than the other sounds.

voice print A graphic recording of the speech frequencies produced by an individual and used as a means of identifying that individual.

voice-recognition device See SPEECH RECOGNIZER.

voice security In voice communications system, the use of encryption and decryption, usually in the form of digital algorithms, to "scramble" speech at the source and "unscramble" it at the destination.

voice-stress analyzer Abbreviation, VSA. An instrument that samples the spoken voice and produces a display from which the relative amount of stress experienced by the speaker can be determined, and from which, in turn, probable truth or falsity of statements or answers can be inferred.

voice synthesis device See SPEECH SYNTHESIZER.

void space See VACUUM.

vol Abbreviation of VOLUME.

volatile **1.** Capable of evaporating (e.g., *volatile solvents* used in the encapsulation of electronic equipment). **2.** Explosive (noun and verb). **3.** Pertaining to a state which is difficult to maintain (e.g., a VOLATILE MEMORY).

volatile memory In computer operations, memory whose contents are lost when there is a loss of power [e.g., random-access memory (RAM)].

volatile storage See VOLATILE MEMORY.

volatile store See VOLATILE MEMORY.

Voldicon A form of semiconductor logic device used for analysis of analog signals. Trade name of Adage, Inc.

volt Abbreviation, V. The basic practical unit of difference of potential (i.e., of electrical pressure); 1 volt is the difference of potential produced across a resistance of 1 ohm by a current of 1 ampere. Also see KILOVOLT, MEGAVOLT, MICROVOLT, MILLIVOLT, NANOVOLT, and PICOVOLT.

Volta effect See VOLTA'S PRINCIPLE.

voltage Symbols, E, e, V, v. Electromotive force, or difference of potential; $E = IR$, where I is current and R is resistance. Also see VOLT.

voltage-actuated device An electronic device, such as a field-effect transistor, that amplifies a voltage signal or is controlled by a voltage, and draws virtually no signal current or control current. The opposite is a current-actuated device, such as a bipolar transistor.

voltage amplification **1.** Abbreviation, A_v. Amplification of an input-signal voltage to provide a higher output-signal voltage. **2.** Abbreviation, A_v. The signal increase (V_{out}/V_{in}) resulting from this process. Also called *voltage gain*.

voltage-amplification device A low-current device designed especially for voltage amplification. It provides little or no power amplification.

voltage amplifier An amplifier operated primarily to increase a signal voltage. Compare CURRENT AMPLIFIER and POWER AMPLIFIER.

voltage at peak torque Symbol, V_p. For a torque motor operated at 25°C, the voltage required to produce peak torque at standstill.

voltage attenuation 1. The reduction in voltage at a given point in a circuit. 2. For a device, the ratio of input voltage to output voltage when the output voltage is the lower quantity.

voltage-balance relay A relay actuated by a voltage differential.

voltage breakdown See BREAKDOWN VOLTAGE.

voltage-breakdown test 1. A test in which the measured voltage applied to an insulating material is continuously increased until the breakdown point is reached. 2. A test in which the measured reverse voltage applied to a semiconductor junction is continuously increased until the reverse breakdown point is reached (see AVALANCHE BREAKDOWN).

voltage burden The voltage drop across a CURRENT SHUNT.

voltage calibrator A device used to calibrate, in terms of voltage, a meter scale, oscilloscope screen, graphic-recorder chart, etc.

voltage-capacitance curve A plot depicting the variation of capacitance with applied voltage for a voltage-variable capacitor. For a varactor (variable-capacitance diode), capacitance varies inversely with reverse direct-current voltage.

voltage coefficient A figure that shows the extent to which a quantity drifts under the influence of voltage. It is generally expressed in percent per volt or in parts per million per volt (ppm/V).

voltage coefficient of capacitance For a voltage-dependent capacitor, the capacitance change per unit change in applied voltage.

voltage coefficient of resistance For a voltage-dependent resistor, the resistance change per unit change in applied voltage.

voltage coil See POTENTIAL COIL.

voltage comparator A device for comparing (usually only two) voltages. The various types range from simple, manually balanced potentiometers to analog or digital devices that automatically compare the applied voltages and provide a direct readout of either their difference or the percent of unbalance.

voltage control 1. A component or circuit that allows the adjustment of the output voltage of a power supply within a given range. 2. The adjustment of the output voltage of a power supply to optimize the performance of a circuit connected to the supply. 3. Any form of circuit control that is accomplished by the adjustment of the voltage at a given circuit point.

voltage-controlled amplifier Abbreviation, VCA. An amplifier in which gain is controlled by means of a voltage applied to a control terminal.

voltage-controlled attenuator An attenuator circuit in which a transistor serves as a voltage-variable resistor. The output resistance of the transistor varies inversely with the direct-current bias voltage applied to the input electrode (base, emitter, or gate).

voltage-controlled capacitor See VOLTAGE-DEPENDENT CAPACITOR.

voltage-controlled crystal oscillator Abbreviation, VCCO or VCXO. A voltage-controlled oscillator of the crystal-stabilized type.

voltage-controlled generator Abbreviation, VCG. Any signal-generating device whose output frequency is varied by changing one of the direct-current operating voltages of the device.

voltage-controlled oscillator Abbreviation, VCO. An oscillator whose output frequency varies with an applied dc control voltage.

voltage-controlled resistor See VOLTAGE-DEPENDENT RESISTOR.

voltage corrector See VOLTAGE REGULATOR.

voltage crest See VOLTAGE PEAK.

voltage-current characteristic See VOLTAGE-CURRENT CURVE.

voltage-current crossover The point at which a voltage-regulated supply becomes a current-regulated supply.

voltage-current curve For a circuit or device, the plot of the interrelationship of current and voltage, with voltage as the independent variable.

voltage-current feedback See CURRENT-VOLTAGE FEEDBACK.

voltage decay The exponential decrease of voltage across a discharging capacitor. Also see EXPONENTIAL DECREASE.

voltage-dependent capacitor A capacitor (such as a varactor) whose capacitance varies with applied voltage.

voltage-dependent resistor A nonlinear resistor whose value varies inversely with the voltage drop across it. Also called *varistor*.

voltage detector A circuit or device that delivers an output voltage only when the input voltage is of a prescribed value. Compare VOLTAGE DISCRIMINATOR.

voltage-determined property A property (capacitance, current, frequency, or resistance) whose magnitude depends on the value of an applied voltage. See, for example, VOLTAGE-DEPENDENT CAPACITOR, VOLTAGE-DEPENDENT RESISTOR, and VOLTAGE-CONTROLLED OSCILLATOR.

voltage differential Symbol, dE or dV. An infinitesimal change in voltage. Compare VOLTAGE INCREMENT.

voltage-directional relay 1. A relay that is actuated when voltage exceeds a certain value in a given direction. 2. A relay that closes only when the applied voltage is in a specific direction.

voltage discriminator A circuit or device whose output voltage is zero when the input voltage is of a prescribed value. When the input voltage is greater than this value, the output is positive; when it is less, the output is negative.

voltage distribution   1. The delivery of operating voltage throughout a circuit (e.g., high and low direct-current voltages in the various stages of a control circuit). **2.** Sometimes, the distribution of electrical energy ("power" distribution).

voltage divider   A resistive or capacitive potentiometer or network used to divide an applied voltage by a desired amount.

voltage doubler   A power-supply circuit that supplies a direct-current output voltage of about twice the peak value of the alternating-current input voltage.

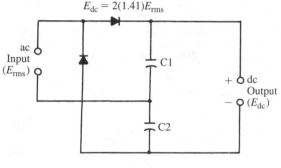

$$E_{dc} = 2(1.41)E_{rms}$$

voltage doubler

voltage drift   See DRIFT VOLTAGE.

voltage drop   Abbreviation, VD. The voltage (E) set up across a resistance (R) carrying a current (I); $E = IR$. For alternating current, reactance X and impedance Z can be substituted for resistance, where applicable.

voltage-equalizing resistors   In a power-supply filter, resistors connected across each capacitor in a string of electrolytics connected in series to withstand a high voltage. The resistors protect the capacitors by equalizing the voltage across them.

voltage-fed antenna   An antenna in which the feeder is attached to the radiator at a voltage loop (current node). Compare CURRENT-FED ANTENNA.

voltage feed   The delivery of voltage to a device or circuit at a point where voltage, rather than current, is dominant. Compare CURRENT FEED.

voltage feedback   A feedback signal consisting of voltage fed from the output to the input circuit of an amplifier or other device. Compare CURRENT FEEDBACK and CURRENT-VOLTAGE FEEDBACK.

voltage-frequency transducer   1. A device whose output voltage is a function of the frequency of a signal at the input. **2.** A device whose output frequency is a function of the voltage at the input.

voltage gain   See VOLTAGE AMPLIFICATION.

voltage generator   See VOLTAGE SUPPLY.

voltage gradient   The voltage per unit length along a defined path.

voltage increment   A change in voltage represented by $E_2 - E_1$, where E_2 and E_1 are the voltages at two defined points on a curve, and the difference is finite (nonzero). Compare VOLTAGE DIFFERENTIAL.

voltage input encoder   An analog-to-digital encoder for which the input is an analog voltage. See, for example, VOLTAGE-TO-SHAFT-POSITION ENCODER.

voltage inverter   A circuit or device whose voltage output has the sign opposite that of the input voltage. The device might or might not provide amplification.

voltage jump   1. An upward transient in voltage. **2.** In a glow-discharge tube, a sudden break or increase in voltage drop across the tube.

voltage lag   The condition in which voltage changes occur after corresponding current changes. Compare CURRENT LAG and VOLTAGE LEAD.

voltage lead   The condition in which voltage changes precede corresponding current changes. Compare CURRENT LEAD and VOLTAGE LAG.

voltage level   1. A prescribed reference value of voltage (e.g., the black level in a television picture signal). **2.** The discrete value of a steady voltage, or the average value of a fluctuating voltage, as observed or measured in a circuit.

voltage limit   The maximum or minimum level in a voltage range.

voltage loop   In a standing-wave system, such as an antenna or transmission line, a maximum-voltage point. Compare VOLTAGE NODE.

voltage loss   1. Reduction of a voltage across a load, occurring because of a series resistance. **2.** The ratio, in decibels, between the input voltage to a transmission line and the output voltage at the load end of the line, assuming that the impedance is the same at both points.

voltage maximum   See VOLTAGE PEAK.

voltage minimum   See VOLTAGE TROUGH.

voltage-mode switching circuit   A resistor-transistor-logic (RTL) NAND or NOR circuit in which (in the off state) the transistor is cut off by the V_{BB} bias voltage. The output is then approximately equal to the collector supply voltage, V_{CC}. The proper combination of input pulses overrides the cutoff bias, and the transistor switches on. The output then drops to a level equal to V_{CC} minus the voltage drop across the external collector resistor.

voltage multiplier   A special type of rectifier circuit that delivers a direct-current output voltage that is a multiple of the peak value of the alternating-current input voltage, thus affording voltage step-up without a transformer. See, for example, VOLTAGE DOUBLER; VOLTAGE QUADRUPLER; QUINTUPLER, **1**; and VOLTAGE TRIPLER.

voltage node In a standing-wave system, such as an antenna or transmission line, a minimum-voltage point. Compare VOLTAGE LOOP.

voltage of self-induction The voltage drop across an inductor, resulting from the flow of alternating current through the inductor; it is caused by self-induction.

voltage peak The highest value attained by a voltage during an excursion. Also called *voltage crest* or *voltage maximum*. Compare VOLTAGE TROUGH.

voltage-power directional relay A relay system in which two circuits are connected when their voltage difference exceeds a predetermined value in one direction, and are disconnected when the voltage in the opposite direction exceeds a predetermined level.

voltage quadrupler A special rectifier circuit that supplies a direct-current output voltage of approximately four times the peak alternating-current input voltage.

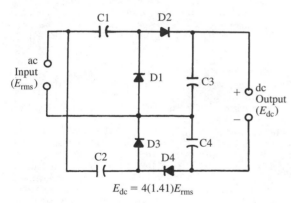

$$E_{dc} = 4(1.41)E_{rms}$$

voltage quadrupler

voltage quintupler See QUINTUPLER, **1**.

voltage-range multiplier **1.** A multiplier resistor (see VOLTMETER MULTIPLIER) connected in series with a voltmeter that has an internal multiplier, to increase the range of the instrument. **2.** For an alternating-current voltmeter, an input amplifier used to increase the sensitivity of the instrument.

voltage rating **1.** For a circuit or device, the recommended maximum voltage that can be applied, or the recommended working voltage, as specified. **2.** For a generator, the specified output voltage.

voltage ratio The quotient of the voltages, E_1/E_2, at two specific points in a circuit, device, or system. Examples: ratio of input voltage to output voltage and ratio of primary voltage to secondary voltage.

voltage-ratio box See VOLT BOX.

voltage reference See STANDARD CELL and ZENER-DIODE VOLTAGE REFERENCE.

voltage-reference cell See STANDARD CELL.

voltage-reference diode A Zener diode biased into its Zener region. The voltage drop across the diode is comparatively constant. Under proper conditions, it can be used for reference purposes. Also see ZENER-DIODE VOLTAGE REFERENCE.

voltage reflection coefficient In a reflected-wave situation, the ratio E_r/E_i, where E_i is the field-strength voltage of the incident wave, and E_r is the field-strength voltage of the reflected wave.

voltage-regulated supply See CONSTANT-VOLTAGE SOURCE.

voltage-regulating transformer A special transformer in which a resonant circuit and core saturation (see SATURATED OPERATION, **1**) are used to provide a constant output voltage.

voltage regulation The stabilization of a voltage against fluctuations in source or load.

voltage-regulation constant Symbol, K_v. For a voltage-regulated power supply, the ratio dE_L/dE_i, where dE_i is a change in input voltage, and dE_L is the corresponding change in load voltage.

voltage regulator A circuit or device that holds an output voltage constant during variations in the output load or input voltage.

voltage-regulator diode See ZENER-DIODE VOLTAGE REGULATOR.

voltage-regulator transformer See VOLTAGE-REGULATING TRANSFORMER.

voltage relay A relay or relay circuit that is actuated by a discrete voltage, rather than by current or power.

voltage-responsive device See VOLTAGE-ACTUATED DEVICE.

voltage rise The normal condition in a series-resonant circuit, in which the voltage across the coil or capacitor is higher than the voltage applied to the circuit.

voltage saturation In a current-actuated device, such as a bipolar transistor, the situation in which an increase in current provides no increase in voltage drop beyond a certain point (the saturation point).

voltage-sensitive bridge A bridge having a nonlinear element (such as a voltage-dependent resistor) as one of the arms. Because of this element, the bridge can be balanced (with a given set of other arms) at only one value of applied voltage. At lower voltages, the bridge becomes unbalanced in one direction; at higher voltage, in the opposite direction.

voltage-sensitive capacitor See VOLTAGE-DEPENDENT CAPACITOR.

voltage-sensitive resistor See VOLTAGE-DEPENDENT RESISTOR.

voltage sensitivity **1.** Particular responsiveness of a circuit or device to voltage, rather than cur-

Nonlinear element (varistor,
semiconductor diode, thermistor,
tungsten-filament lamp, etc.)

Adjustable
voltage
input

Output

voltage-sensitive bridge

rent or power. See, for example, VOLTAGE-DE-
PENDENT CAPACITOR, VOLTAGE-DEPENDENT
RESISTOR, and VOLTAGE RELAY. **2.** See VOLT-
METER SENSITIVITY.

voltage-spectrum function The voltage-vs.-fre-
quency curve at the output of a circuit or transducer.

voltage-stabilized supply See CONSTANT-VOL-
TAGE SOURCE.

voltage stabilizer See VOLTAGE REGULATOR.

voltage-stabilizing diode See ZENER-DIODE
VOLTAGE REGULATOR.

voltage standard A device that delivers a voltage
of accuracy and stability so that it can be used
to calibrate other voltage generators and test instruments. See, for example, STANDARD CELL
and ZENER-DIODE VOLTAGE REFERENCE.

voltage standing-wave ratio Abbreviation, VSWR.
In a standing-wave system, the ratio of the maximum voltage to the minimum voltage.

voltage supply A power supply whose usable
output is voltage, rather than current or power.
When such a supply is not voltage-regulated, it
can only be used reliably with a very light load.

voltage to chassis In electronic equipment
mounted on a metal chassis, the voltage between
the chassis and a given point in the circuit.

voltage-to-frequency converter A device or
circuit that delivers an output frequency proportional to an input voltage (usually direct
current). Compare FREQUENCY-TO-VOLT-
AGE CONVERTER.

voltage to ground **1.** In a circuit, the voltage
measured between a given point and the ground
point. **2.** The voltage measured between the
earth and a line or piece of equipment.

voltage to panel In electronic equipment mounted
on a metal panel, the voltage between the panel
and a given point in the circuit.

voltage-to-shaft-position encoder An encoder for
which the output is the rotation of a motor shaft
over an arc proportional to an input voltage.

voltage transformer **1.** A transformer used primarily to supply voltage with little or no current.
2. A small step-up transformer for increasing
the sensitivity of an alternating-current voltmeter. Also called POTENTIAL TRANSFORMER.

voltage tripler A rectifier circuit that, without a
transformer, supplies a direct-current output
voltage of approximately three times the peak
value of the alternating-current input voltage.

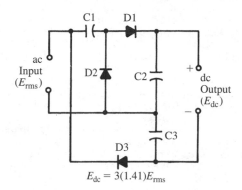

$$E_{dc} = 3(1.41)E_{rms}$$

voltage tripler

voltage trough The lowest value reached by a
voltage during an excursion. Compare VOLT-
AGE PEAK.

voltage tuning A method of adjusting the frequency of an oscillator or resonant circuit by
means of a variable, direct-current voltage.

voltage-tunable magnetron A magnetron oscillator in which the output frequency is varied by
adjusting the direct-current voltage on the tube.

voltage-tunable oscillator See VOLTAGE-CON-
TROLLED OSCILLATOR.

voltage-turns ratio The turns ratio of a transformer, indicated by the ratio of primary voltage
to secondary voltage, or vice-versa.

voltage-type telemetry Telemetry based upon
the variation of a single voltage in sympathy
with the changes in a sensed phenomenon.

voltage-variable capacitor **1.** A specially processed semiconductor diode of which the voltage-variable capacitance of the junction is
utilized. Also called VARACTOR. **2.** A capacitor
having a specially processed nonlinear dielectric, such as barium strontium titanate, whose
capacitance varies inversely with the applied
direct-current bias voltage.

voltage-variable resistor See VOLTAGE-DEPEN-
DENT RESISTOR.

voltage vector In a vector diagram, a vector
showing the magnitude and phase of a voltage.
Compare CURRENT VECTOR.

voltaic Pertaining to chemically produced direct current. Sometimes interchangeable with
galvanic.

voltaic cell For the generation of a direct-current voltage, a primary cell consisting of two electrodes made of different metals and immersed in an electrolyte. Also called GALVANIC CELL. Also see CELL, ELECTROMOTIVE SERIES, and PRIMARY CELL.

voltaic couple A pair of dissimilar metals (or other substances) that generate a direct-current voltage when they contact an electrolyte.

voltaic pile A rudimentary primary battery consisting of a series of disks made of two different metals, stacked alternately with electrolyte-soaked cloth or paper disks.

voltaic series See ELECTROMOTIVE SERIES.

voltameter An electrolytic cell for determining the value of an unknown current, or of an unknown quantity of electricity, from the weight of metal deposited out of an electrolyte onto the cathode by the passage of current over an accurately timed interval.

volt-ammeter A combination meter for measuring electrical voltages and currents.

volt-ampere Symbol, VA. Unit, watt. The simple product of voltage and current in volts and amperes, yielding the true power in a direct-current circuit and the apparent power in an alternating-current circuit. Also see APPARENT POWER and TRUE POWER.

volt-ampere-hour meter See VAR-HOUR METER.

volt-ampere meter See VAR METER.

volt-amperes reactive Abbreviation, VAR. The product of volts and amperes for a purely reactive circuit. This product does not produce the true power because the power factor is neglected; it produces only the apparent power. A true reactance absorbs power during one half-cycle of alternating current, and returns it to the generator during the next half-cycle.

Volta's law See VOLTA'S PRINCIPLE.

Volta's pile See VOLTAIC PILE.

Volta's principle Two dissimilar metals brought into contact (even in air) will generate a difference of potential whose value is characteristic of the metals. Also see ELECTROMOTIVE SERIES.

volt box A precision, potentiometer-type voltage divider used in the calibration of meters and other instruments. The device is usually provided with a set of terminal posts for selecting various ratios of output voltage to input voltage.

volt-electron See ELECTRONVOLT.

voltmeter A usually direct-reading instrument used to measure voltage. Also see ELECTRONIC VOLTMETER, FET VOLTMETER, TRANSISTOR VOLTMETER, and VACUUM-TUBE VOLTMETER.

voltmeter-ammeter See VOLT-AMMETER.

voltmeter amplifier A wideband, flat-frequency-response, low-distortion preamplifier used to boost the sensitivity of an alternating-current voltmeter.

voltmeter-millivoltmeter A voltmeter that provides several low ranges, as well as several high ones. A familiar example is an alternating-current voltmeter, which has various full-scale ranges from about 1 millivolt to about 1000 volts.

voltmeter multiplier A resistor connected in series with a current meter (usually a milliammeter or microammeter) to convert it into a voltmeter.

voltmeter sensitivity Unit, ohm per volt. For a voltmeter, the total resistance of the instrument (multiplier resistance plus the resistance of the meter movement) divided by the full-scale deflection of the meter. Thus, a 0-to-10 direct-current voltmeter with an input resistance of 100 kilohms has a sensitivity of 10,000 ohms per volt.

volt-milliammeter A combination meter for measuring volts and milliamperes.

volt-ohm-ammeter A multimeter for measuring voltage, resistance, and current (in amperes).

volt-ohmmeter A combination meter for measuring voltage and resistance.

volt-ohm-milliammeter Abbreviation VOM. A multimeter for measuring voltage, resistance, and current (in milliamperes and microamperes).

voltsensor See VOLTAGE DETECTOR.

volts per meter Abbreviation, V/m or Vpm. The unit of electric field strength.

volume 1. Intensity of sound. Also called LOUDNESS. 2. A circumscribed portion of space, either imaginary or actually occupied, and described by three dimensions (e.g., sphere, ellipsoid, cube, pyramid, etc.). 3. In a computer system, a unit of magnetic storage medium (e.g., a diskette.)

volume compression The automatic reduction of the gain of an audio amplifier. The process differs from clipping (which "slices off" the tops of waves) in that compression (ideally) reduces the amplitude while preserving the waveform. Compare VOLUME EXPANSION.

volume compressor A circuit or device (such as an automatic-gain-control amplifier) for achieving volume compression. Compare VOLUME EXPANDER.

volume conductivity The reciprocal of VOLUME RESISTIVITY.

volume control A variable resistor (usually a potentiometer) or a network of resistors (such as a pad) for adjusting the gain, and, consequently, the output-signal loudness, of an amplifier.

volume equivalent In wire telephony, speech loudness throughout the system, expressed in terms of the trunk loss in a reference system and adjusted for equal loudness.

volume expander A circuit or device for automatically boosting the volume of an audio-frequency signal. Also see EXPANDER. Compare VOLUME COMPRESSOR.

volume expansion The technique of automatically increasing the gain, and consequently the output-signal volume, of an audio amplifier. Also see VOLUME EXPANDER. Compare VOLUME COMPRESSION.

volume indicator A fast-acting alternating-current meter used to monitor the volume level in

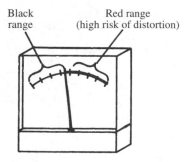

Black range

Red range (high risk of distortion)

volume indicator

an audio channel in which the signal level is fluctuating. The scale is graduated in VOLUME UNITS. Also called *VU meter*.

volume lifetime In a homogeneous semiconductor, the interval between minority-carrier generation and recombination.

volume limiter A circuit or device that automatically holds the volume level of an audio channel to a predetermined maximum. Also see VOLUME COMPRESSION and VOLUME COMPRESSOR.

volume-limiting amplifier An amplifier that functions as a volume limiter through the action of volume-limiting subcircuits.

volume magnetostriction **1.** The decrease in the total volume of certain ferromagnetic substances under the influence of a magnetic field. **2.** The increase in the total volume of certain ferromagnetic substances under the influence of a magnetic field.

volume range Unit, decibel (dB). The difference between the maximum and minimum volume levels that a device or system can accommodate.

volume recombination rate Within the volume of a semiconductor, the rate at which electrons and holes recombine.

volume resistance The effective resistance, through a given medium, between two electrodes placed within that medium.

volume resistivity The resistance of a specific volume of a material (e.g., the resistance between opposite faces of a 1-centimeter cube of the material). Also see MICROHM-CENTIMETER; OHM-CENTIMETER; RESISTIVITY.

volumetric efficiency In an electronic assembly, the ratio of the volume of parts to the total volume of the assembly.

volumetric radar A radar providing a three-dimensional display.

volumetric sensor In security systems, a device that detects effects in a specifically defined three-dimensional region, such as an entire room (from floor to ceiling).

volume unit Abbreviation, VU. The unit of measurement of fluctuating alternating-current power, such as that of speech or music. Zero VU corresponds to a reference power of 2.51 milli-

watts, or +4 dBm (four decibels above 1 milliwatt). Volume units are measured with a VOLUME INDICATOR.

volume-unit indicator See VOLUME INDICATOR.

volunteer examiner In amateur radio, a person who works with the Federal Communications Commission (FCC) to administer license examinations. Such a person is not actually an employee of the FCC, but serves on an independent, volunteer basis.

VOM Abbreviation of VOLT-OHM-MILLIAMMETER.

von Hippel breakdown theory The theory that, assuming no electron-energy distribution, breakdown occurs at field intensities for which the recombination rate of electrons and holes is lower than the rate of ionization by collision.

von Neumann architecture In computer systems, a design scheme in which the bits are transmitted serially (one by one) along a single line or bus.

VOR Abbreviation of *very-high-frequency omnirange* (see VHF OMNIRANGE).

voter See MAJORITY LOGIC.

vox Abbreviated form of VOICE-OPERATED CONTROL.

V_P **1.** Symbol for GATE-SOURCE PINCHOFF VOLTAGE of a field-effect transistor. **2.** Symbol for PLATE VOLTAGE.

V_p Symbol for VOLTAGE AT PEAK TORQUE.

V particle See VEE PARTICLE.

Vpm Abbreviation of VOLTS PER METER. (Also, V/m.)

VR **1.** Abbreviation of VIRTUAL REALITY. **2.** Abbreviation of VOLTAGE REGULATOR.

VRAM Abbreviation of VIDEO RANDOM-ACCESS MEMORY.

V_{ref} Abbreviation of *reference voltage.*

vrr Abbreviation of *visual radio range.*

V·s Abbreviation of *volt-seconds* (webers).

V·s/A Abbreviation of *volt-seconds per ampere* (henrys).

VSA Abbreviation of VOICE-STRESS ANALYZER.

VSB Abbreviation of VESTIGIAL SIDEBAND.

VSF Abbreviation of VESTIGIAL-SIDEBAND FILTER.

V signal See VEE SIGNAL.

vsr Abbreviation of VERY SHORT RANGE.

VSWR Abbreviation of VOLTAGE STANDING-WAVE RATIO.

vt **1.** Abbreviation of VACUUM TUBE. **2.** Abbreviation of *variable time.*

VT fuse See PROXIMITY FUSE.

VTL Abbreviation of VARIABLE-THRESHOLD LOGIC.

vtm Abbreviation of VOLTAGE-TUNABLE MAGNETRON.

VTO Abbreviation of VOLTAGE-TUNABLE OSCILLATOR.

VTR Abbreviation of VIDEOTAPE RECORDER or VIDEOTAPE RECORDING.

VTVM   Abbreviation of VACUUM-TUBE VOLT-METER.

vt voltmeter   See VACUUM-TUBE VOLTMETER.

VU   Abbreviation of VOLUME UNIT.

vulcanized fiber   A tough insulating material derived from cellulose. Dielectric constant, 5 to 8.

VU meter   See VOLUME INDICATOR.

VVCD   Abbreviation of *voltage-variable capacitor diode* (see VOLTAGE-VARIABLE CAPACITOR, 1).

VVV signal   See VEE SIGNAL.

VW   Abbreviation of *volts working* (see WORKING VOLTAGE).

vy   Abbreviation for *very*.

W **1.** Symbol for WORK. **2.** Abbreviation of WATT. **3.** Symbol for TUNGSTEN. **4.** Symbol for ENERGY. **5.** Abbreviation of *west.* **6.** Abbreviation of WIDTH.

w **1.** Abbreviation of WEIGHT. (Also, wt.) **2.** Abbreviation of *week.*

WAC Amateur radio abbreviation of *Worked All Continents*, an award given to operators who have engaged in verified two-way communication with stations on all continents.

wafer **1.** Semiconductor die. **2.** A thin, flat disk, ring, or plate around which the contacts of a rotary switch are spaced. **3.** A thin square or rectangle of dielectric material used as the dielectric member in a fixed capacitor. **4.** A plate cut from a crystal (e.g., a quartz wafer).

wafer fabrication The various processes used in the manufacture of semiconductor integrated circuits.

wafer slicing Cutting plates from a mother crystal, as when piezoelectric plates are cut from a quartz crystal.

wafer socket A component socket consisting of a plastic or ceramic wafer with spring-type contacts for gripping the pins.

wafer switch A rotary switch whose contacts are arranged around the periphery of a plastic or ceramic wafer.

Wagner ground A circuit (often a single potentiometer) that facilitates cancellation of stray reactance in an alternating-current bridge. The bridge is balanced alternately with the bridge-balance control and the Wagner control, until there is no further shift of null point when changing from one to the other.

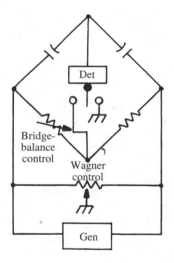

Wagner ground
(with capacitance bridge)

waiting time **1.** See WARMUP TIME. **2.** The delay between the time a data transfer to or from a computer memory is called for and the actual transfer of the data. Also called LATENCY.

walkie-lookie A portable combination camera and transmitter for remote television pickup. At sports events and other gatherings, the unit is strapped to the shoulder of the camera operator.

walkie-talkie A portable, compact transceiver (or transmitter-receiver).

wall absorption Diminished radioactive emission (especially of beta and gamma rays) because of absorption by the radiating substance.

wall box A wall-mounted (usually metal) box enclosing circuit breakers, fuses, switches, etc.

wall effect In an ionization chamber, the rise in ionization because of electrons being released by the walls of the chamber.

wall energy In a ferromagnetic substance, the energy per unit area stored in a domain wall between two regions of opposite magnetization.

Wallman amplifier A cascode amplifier (see CASCODE).

wall mount A metal bracket for fastening an antenna to a wall.

wall outlet A plug or socket, usually mounted in a protective box or can and recessed in a wall that can be accessed from the front. It is commonly used for supplying alternating-current power to appliances at 117 volts or 234 volts. It is also used in telephone and cable-television systems.

wall plaque A loudspeaker so thin that, mounted in a frame (sometimes behind grill cloth), it can be hung on a wall.

wall plate A (usually rectangular) plate of metal or plastic for holding a wall outlet or wall switch.

wall plug A male or female plug usually mounted in a protective box or can and recessed in a wall. Such a device can provide easy access to an antenna, telephone line, or load; or it can deliver alternating-current, direct-current, or radio-frequency power.

walls The sides of the groove cut into a record disc.

wall socket A male or female socket usually mounted in a protective box or can and recessed in a wall. Such a device can provide easy access to an antenna, telephone line, or load; or it can deliver alternating-current, direct-current, or radio-frequency power.

wall speaker See WALL PLAQUE.

wall switch A switch usually mounted in a protective box or can and recessed in a wall.

wall telephone A wall-mounted telephone set. It generally fits over the jack, so the only cord is between the main unit and the receiver.

wall-through tube See LEAD-IN TUBE.

Walmsley antenna A phased array consisting of several full-wavelength loops.

wamoscope A radar display tube that performs several microwave-receiver functions (detection, oscillation, amplification, etc.) as well as displaying an image. The name is an acronym for *wave-modulation oscilloscope.*

wander See SCINTILLATION, **1**.

warble **1.** A periodic rise and fall in the pitch of a musical tone or combination of tones. **2.** To rise and fall in pitch with a definite period.

warble-tone generator An audio-frequency oscillator whose frequency is varied at a subaudible rate over a fixed frequency range.

warm junction The heated junction in a two-junction thermocouple circuit. Also called HOT JUNCTION. Compare COLD JUNCTION.

warmup The process of stabilizing an electronic equipment by allowing its temperature to rise to the optimum level.

warmup time The time required for an electronic circuit to become fully operational, or to stabilize, after the power has been switched on.

warning bell (buzzer) A bell (or buzzer) used as an audible alarm in a WARNING DEVICE.

warning device A device, such as an electronic signaler, for alerting a person to an emergency (intrusion on premises, danger to life and safety, etc.) or to the existence of an intrusion into a secured area.

warning lamp See WARNING LIGHT.

warning light A lamp used as a visual alarm in a warning device.

warpage Distortion of the normally straight sides of a triangular wave.

warping In multimedia computer graphics, a change in the shape of an object that occurs smoothly over a period of time.

WAS Amateur radio abbreviation of *Worked All States*, an award given to operators who have engaged in verified two-way communication with stations in all states of the United States.

washer capacitor A very thin donut capacitor.

washer resistor A resistor made in the general shape of a washer or ring and having a center hole for a mounting screw or stacking rod.

washer thermistor A thermistor made in the general shape of a washer and having a center hole for a mounting screw or stacking rod.

washer varistor A varistor made in the general shape of a washer and having a center hole for a mounting screw or stacking rod.

washout process A method of fabricating bipolar transistors. The contact metal is deposited in the diffusion hole.

waste instruction In a computer program, an instruction not meant to be acted upon (e.g., one used to take up space in the listing for some reason). Also called *null instruction* and *dummy instruction.*

watch A work shift, as of electronic personnel (e.g., radio station operators).

watchcase receiver An earphone enclosed in a small, round case with a screw-on cap. Its is derived from its resemblance to a large pocket watch.

water absorption For a solid material, such as a dielectric, the ratio of the weight of water absorbed by the material to the weight of the material.

water-activated battery A battery that contains all the ingredients of its electrolyte, except water, which must be added when the battery is put into service.

water adsorption   The formation of a thin layer of water molecules on the surface of normally dry material, but not by absorption. Also see ADSORPTION.

water analogy   The useful, but not wholly accurate, teaching device of comparing an electric current with the flow of water. In such a comparison, voltage is shown equivalent to water pressure, and current to the quantity (e.g., gallons) of water flowing in unit time.

water battery   A primary battery or cell using water as the electrolyte.

water calorimeter   A calorimeter used to measure power in terms of the increase in temperature of water heated by the electrical energy.

water capacitor   An emergency capacitor made by setting one glass of water in another larger jar of water so that the two bodies of water are separated by the walls of the smaller jar. The bodies of water, in which an electrolyte has been dissolved, form the "plates" of the capacitor, and the wall of the smaller jar serves as the dielectric between them.

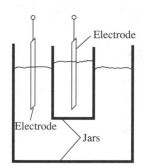

Electrode

Electrode

Jars

water capacitor

water-cooled tube   A power tube, such as a large radio transmitting tube, cooled by the circulation of water in the space between the outside of the tube envelope and a surrounding jacket.

water cooling   A method of cooling components by pumping water through pipes surrounding them.

water-flow alarm   An electronic circuit that actuates an alarm when the flow of water through pipes or other channels changes from a predetermined rate.

water-flow control   A servo system for automatically maintaining or adjusting the flow of water through pipes or other channels.

water-flow gauge   See WATER-FLOW METER.

water-flow indicator   See WATER-FLOW METER.

water-flow meter   An instrument used to monitor the flow of water through pipes or other channels, sometimes showing its direction as well as its rate.

water-flow switch   In water-cooled systems (e.g., water-cooled tubes), a switch that actuates an alarm when the water slows or stops.

water glass   Sodium silicate, a substance used as a fireproofing agent and protective coating.

water ground   An earth connection made by dropping a weighted wire into a body of water.

water jacket   In a water-cooled device, the outer jacket that, along with the outer wall of the cooled component, forms a space through which the cooling water flows.

water-level control   A servo system that automatically maintains or adjusts the level of water inside a tank or other container.

water-level gauge   An electronic system that gives direct water level readings inside a tank or other container.

water-level indicator   See WATER-LEVEL GAUGE.

water load   1. A makeshift, power-dissipating resistive load (see DUMMY LOAD) consisting of a container of tap water or saltwater into which two wires are immersed. 2. A waveguide termination containing water heated by the microwave energy. It is usable as a water calorimeter.

water monitor   A sensitive electronic instrument for checking radioactivity in a water supply.

water-pipe ground   An earth connection made by running a wire to the nearest cold-water pipe. This scheme works only with metal pipes devoid of insulating joints or splices.

water power   Hydroelectric power (i.e., electrical energy produced by generators driven by water).

water-pressure alarm   An electronic circuit that actuates an alarm when water in pipes or other channels changes from a predetermined level.

water-pressure control   A servo system for automatically maintaining or adjusting water pressure in pipes or other channels.

water-pressure gauge   See WATER-PRESSURE METER.

water-pressure indicator   See WATER-PRESSURE METER.

water-pressure meter   An instrument that directly indicates water pressure in a pipe or tank.

water-pressure switch   A switch that actuates an alarm when water pressure rises or falls.

water pump   In a water-cooled electronic system, the (usually rotary) pump that circulates the water.

water resistor   An electrolytic resistor in which the electrolyte is tap water or dilute saltwater.

water rheostat   A variable water resistor. Usually, the resistance is varied by moving the immersed electrodes closer together or farther apart.

water tester   An instrument for checking pH, electrical resistance, and other properties of water.

water witching   Locating underground water by electronic methods.

WATS   Acronym for *Wide Area Telephone Service.* A form of long-distance telephone service. Rates are charged on a different basis than normal long-distance service. The system is especially favored by businesses because it saves money for subscribers making a large number of calls in each billing period.

watt   Abbreviation, W. The practical unit of electric and other power. One watt is dissipated by a resistance of 1 ohm through which a current of 1 ampere flows. See also KILOWATT, MEGAWATT, MICROWATT, and MILLIWATT.

wattage   Electrical power, especially when expressed in watts.

wattage rating   **1.** The recommended output power of a device. **2.** The recommended power dissipation of a device.

watt current   The component of alternating current that is in phase with voltage. Also called RESISTIVE CURRENT. Compare REACTIVE CURRENT.

watt-decibel conversion   The conversion of a power level, such as the power output of an amplifier, in watts to the corresponding power level in decibels, with respect to a reference level. Thus, n dB = 10 $\log_{10}(P/P_{ref})$, where P is the power of interest (watts), and P_{ref} is the reference level (e.g., one milliwatt).

watt-hour   Abbreviation, WH. The unit of electrical energy or work; 1 WH = 3600 joules = 10^{-3} kWH. Also see ENERGY, KILOWATT-HOURS, POWER, and WATT-SECOND.

watt-hour capacity   The number of watt-hours that a storage battery can deliver reliably and safely under specified operating conditions.

watt-hour-demand meter   A combination watt-hour meter and demand meter.

watt-hour efficiency   For a storage battery, the ratio of watt-hours output to watt-hours of recharge.

watt-hour constant   In an electric-energy meter, the number of watt-hours in one revolution of the indicating disk.

watt-hour meter   An instrument for measuring electrical energy in watt-hours. One well-known type consists essentially of a small motor geared to a row of four dial indicators. An eddy-current disk keeps the motor speed proportional to the watt-hours consumed by a load, a value which is the sum of the readings of the dials. Also called SERVICE METER and KILOWATT-HOUR METER.

wattless current   The component of alternating current that is out of phase with voltage. Also called REACTIVE CURRENT. Compare RESISTIVE CURRENT.

wattless power   The apparent power in a reactive circuit, indicated by the product of volts and amperes. There is no actual power consumption because the power taken by a reactance during a half-cycle is returned to the generator during the next half-cycle. Also see AC POWER, APPARENT POWER, REACTIVE KILOVOLT-AMPERES, and REACTIVE VOLT-AMPERES.

wattless volt-amperes   See WATTLESS POWER.

wattless watts   See WATTLESS POWER.

wattmeter   Abbreviation, WM. An instrument used to measure electrical power. The scale usually reads directly in watts, kilowatts, milliwatts, or microwatts. Also see ELECTRONIC WATTMETER.

watt-second   Abbreviation, Ws. A small unit of electrical energy or work; 1 watt-second = 1 joule = 1/3600 watt-hour. Also see ENERGY and POWER.

watt-second constant   In an electric-energy meter, the number of watt seconds in one revolution of the indicating disk.

wave   **1.** A single oscillation of some property of matter or space, such as density, displacement, or field strength. It moves outward from a point of disturbance and grows weaker as it travels farther. Wave motion is associated with mechanical vibration, sound, radio, heat, light, X rays, gamma rays, and cosmic rays. See SOUND and WAVELENGTH. **2.** A single cycle of alternating or pulsating current or voltage. Also see AC VOLTAGE, ALTERNATING CURRENT, PULSATING DC VOLTAGE, and PULSATING DIRECT CURRENT.

wave absorption   The removal of energy from electromagnetic waves as they pass through certain media, such as solid bodies, water, and the atmosphere. Compare POLARIZATION, WAVE REFLECTION, and WAVE REFRACTION.

wave amplitude   The peak value of a wave. Also see WAVE CREST and WAVE TROUGH.

wave analyzer   An instrument consisting essentially of a continuously tunable bandpass filter and an electronic alternating-current voltmeter. As the filter is tuned successively to the fundamental frequency of a complex wave and to its various harmonics, the voltmeter shows the amplitude of each of the components. Also see HETERODYNE WAVE ANALYZER.

wave angle   The angle, measured with respect to the horizon, at which a radio wave is transmitted or received.

wave antenna   See BEVERAGE ANTENNA.

wave attenuation   The reduction of wave amplitude, with respect to distance from the source.

waveband   A band of radio frequencies. Also called FREQUENCY BAND.

waveband switch   See BANDSWITCH.

wave beam   Unidirectional radiation from a directive antenna.

wave bounce   See WAVE REFLECTION.

wave clutter   Radar interference caused by waves on a body of water, particularly large swells on the ocean.

wave converter   A waveguide part, such as a baffle-plate or grating, that changes a wave pattern from one type to another.

wave crest   The maximum value of a wave envelope. Compare WAVE TROUGH.

wave cycle   A complete single alternation of a wave.

wave direction   The direction in which an electromagnetic wave travels. It is perpendicular to the wave front and depends (whether it is forward or backward) upon the direction of the electric and magnetic components. If either is reversed, wave direction reverses; if both are reversed, the direction remains unchanged.

wave duct   **1.** See DUCT, **1**. **2.** A tubular waveguide in which wave propagation is concentrated.

wave envelope   The outline described by the various amplitude peaks of the cycles in an amplitude-modulated wave. The envelope frequency is equal to the modulating frequency.

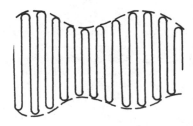

wave envelope

wave equation   A second-degree partial differential equation whose solution describes wave phenomena.

wave filter   A circuit or device that offers different amounts of attenuation to signals of different frequencies. See BANDPASS FILTER, BAND-SUPPRESSION FILTER, HIGH-PASS FILTER, and LOW-PASS FILTER.

waveform   The shape of a wave described in terms of its resemblance to some well-known figure or to its conformity to the curve of the applicable wave equation (e.g., sinusoidal, square, sawtooth, cosine, rectangular, and triangular).

waveform-amplitude distortion   See AMPLITUDE DISTORTION.

waveform analyzer   See WAVE ANALYZER.

waveform converter   A circuit or device for changing a signal of one waveform (such as a sine wave) into one of another waveform (such as a pulse or square wave).

waveform distortion   The malfunction evidenced by a change of the waveshape of a signal passing through a circuit.

waveform error   In a quantity displayed by an alternating-current test instrument, an error caused by the waveform of the measured signal. Thus, a voltmeter calibrated with a sine-wave voltage is subject to error when a measured signal is nonsinusoidal. Also called *waveform effect*.

waveform generator   See FUNCTION GENERATOR.

waveform influence   See WAVEFORM ERROR.

waveform monitor   In television operations, an oscilloscope that continuously displays the video waveform.

waveform synthesizer   A variable-frequency signal generator that allows the tailoring of waveshape to suit individual applications. A *function generator* (see FUNCTION GENERATOR, **1**) is such an instrument, but it usually provides only a choice of common waveshapes.

wave front   For a radio wave, the plane that is parallel to the perpendicular electric and magnetic lines of flux. The wave propagates at right angles to this plane.

wave function   A point function in a wave equation, specifying wave amplitude.

wave group   The resultant of several different-frequency waves traveling over a common path.

waveguide   A carefully dimensioned, usually rectangular, hollow, metal pipe through which microwave energy is transmitted.

waveguide apparatus   See WAVEGUIDE COMPONENTS.

waveguide attenuator   A device, such as an interposed energy-absorbing plate, for signal attenuation in a waveguide.

waveguide choke flange   A waveguide flange that presents no impedance to the signal, and which need not be metallic for continuity.

waveguide component   A device adapted for connection to, or insertion into, a waveguide system. Such components include waveguide parts and accessories (e.g., splicing hardware, attenuators, loads, wavemeters, etc.).

waveguide connector   A fitting for joining waveguides for the efficient propagation of a signal.

waveguide coupling   See WAVEGUIDE CONNECTOR.

waveguide critical dimension   The cross-sectional dimension that determines the cutoff frequency for a waveguide.

waveguide cutoff   In a waveguide, the highest or lowest frequency that can be propagated with less than a specified amount of attenuation per unit length.

waveguide directional coupler   A directional coupler made of two parallel waveguides with a common wall. Two slots cut in the wall allow part of the microwave energy propagated in one direction in the main waveguide to be extracted, and energy traveling in the opposite direction to be rejected.

waveguide dummy load   A waveguide section that dissipates the microwave energy entering it.

waveguide elbow   **1.** A curved bend in a waveguide. **2.** A waveguide connector with a bend.

waveguide flange   A flat, liplike fitting at the end of the pipe of a waveguide. It fastens waveguide sections together or attaches a waveguide component, equipped with an identical flange, to the end of a waveguide.

waveguide frequency meter   See WAVEGUIDE WAVEMETER.

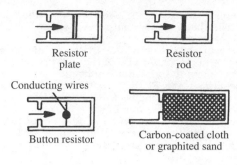

Resistor plate

Resistor rod

Conducting wires

Button resistor

Carbon-coated cloth or graphited sand

waveguide dummy load

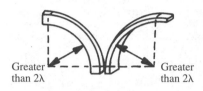

Greater than 2λ

Greater than 2λ

waveguide elbow

waveguide gasket A gasket that provides electrical continuity between mating waveguide sections.

waveguide grating An array of wires mounted inside a waveguide, and that passes signals at some frequencies while obstructing others.

waveguide impedance Where the power P is known, and voltage E and current I are defined, with respect to a type of wave and waveguide, the value is either E^2/P or P/I^2.

waveguide junction A fitting that allows one waveguide section to be joined at an angle to another section. See, for example, WAVEGUIDE TEE and WAVEGUIDE WYE.

waveguide lens A microwave lens consisting of waveguide sections that provide the required phase shifts.

waveguide load See WAVEGUIDE DUMMY LOAD.

waveguide mode The form of propagation indicated by the field pattern in a plane transverse to the direction in which energy is propagated through a waveguide. Common modes are TRANSVERSE ELECTRIC MODE, also called *TE mode*, and TRANSVERSE MAGNETIC MODE, also called *TM mode*.

waveguide mode suppressor A filter that suppresses undesired propagation modes in a waveguide.

waveguide phase shifter A shifter for adjusting the phase of waveguide output energy, with respect to input energy.

waveguide plunger A plunger-like device that reflects incident microwave energy in a waveguide.

waveguide post A transverse rod inside a waveguide that acts as a parallel susceptance.

waveguide probe A pickup probe (tip or loop, as required) for sampling the field inside a waveguide, or a similar injection probe for introducing energy into a waveguide. Also see WAVEGUIDE SLOTTED LINE.

waveguide propagation 1. The transmission of microwave energy through a waveguide by successive reflections between the inner walls. 2. Propagation of very-high-frequency (VHF), ultra-high-frequency (UHF), or microwave electromagnetic fields through an atmospheric duct (see DUCT, 1), as if through a waveguide. 3. Propagation of very-low-frequency (VLF) electromagnetic fields through a waveguide-like duct between the ionosphere and the earth's surface.

waveguide radiator An antenna consisting of an open-ended waveguide with or without a horn. It radiates microwave energy into space or to a reflector.

waveguide resonator A waveguide section used as a cavity resonator (see RESONANT CAVITY).

waveguide seal A protective cover for the end of a waveguide. The seal introduces very little microwave attenuation, while preventing entry of moisture and debris.

waveguide shim A thin, pliable metal sheet inserted between mating waveguide components for electrical continuity. Also see WAVEGUIDE GASKET.

waveguide shutter An adjustable mechanical barrier, such as a rotatable vane, inserted into a waveguide to block or divert microwave energy.

waveguide slotted line A section of waveguide having a slot that accommodates a movable probe or coupling element.

waveguide slug tuner A quarter-wave dielectric slug inserted into a waveguide so that its amount of penetration and position can be adjusted for tuning purposes.

waveguide stub A stub consisting of a waveguide section joined to a main waveguide at an angle and provided with a nondissipative termination.

waveguide stub tuner An adjustable piston in a waveguide stub for tuning purposes.

waveguide switch A switch consisting of a movable section of waveguide that can be positioned for coupling to one of several other waveguide sections; it thus passes the energy it receives to any of the other sections.

waveguide system Microwave "plumbing" consisting of waveguides, their fittings and accessories, and associated components (such as attenuators, loads, wavemeters, etc.).

waveguide taper A connector that is flared to allow coupling between two waveguide sections having different cross-sectional sizes.

waveguide tee In a waveguide assembly, a tee-shaped junction used to connect a section of waveguide in series or parallel with another section.

waveguide transformer A waveguide component that functions as an impedance transformer.

waveguide tuner In a waveguide system, an adjustable tuner providing impedance transformation.

waveguide twist A length of waveguide whose cross section is rotated around the longitudinal axis (e.g., from vertical to horizontal).

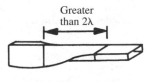

Greater than 2λ

waveguide twist

waveguide wavelength In a uniform waveguide operating at a given frequency and in a particular mode, the distance between similar points for 360° phase shift.

waveguide wavemeter A waveguide component that acts as an absorption wavemeter or transmission wavemeter for identifying microwave frequencies.

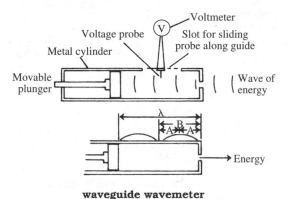

waveguide wavemeter

waveguide wedge See WEDGE, 1.

waveguide window A thin metal opening mounted transversely inside a waveguide for impedance-matching purposes. The edges of the slit in a capacitive window are perpendicular to the electric field; in an inductive window, they are parallel to the electric field.

waveguide wye In a waveguide assembly, a wye-shaped junction for joining three waveguide sections.

wave heating Heating a material by energy absorbed from traveling electromagnetic waves.

wave interference Interaction between two or more waves, resulting in reinforcements and cancellations of energy.

wavelength Unit, meter. The displacement in one complete wave of an alternating or vibrating phenomenon, generally measured from crest to crest or from trough to trough of successive waves. For electromagnetic waves in free space, the wavelength in meters is equal to 3×10^8 divided by the frequency in Hertz. Also see WAVELENGTH-PERIOD-FREQUENCY RELATIONSHIPS.

wavelength constant The imaginary-number component of the propagation constant.

wavelength shifter **1.** A frequency shifter whose performance is indicated in units of wavelength, rather than in units of frequency. **2.** In certain photosensitive cells and tubes, a photofluorescent substance that raises the efficiency of the device by absorbing photons and then releasing ones of longer wavelength.

wave mechanics A theory of matter that views subatomic particles as complex wave patterns, and attempts to account for all physical processes in terms of wave phenomena.

wavemeter An instrument for measuring the wavelength or frequency of radio waves. One form consists of a series-resonant circuit containing an inductor, variable capacitor, and diode-type meter. The dial of the capacitor is calibrated to read in MHz. The inductor picks up energy from the radio-frequency source of unknown frequency, the capacitor is tuned for peak deflection of the meter, and the unknown frequency is read from the dial. This instrument is often called an *absorption wavemeter* because it absorbs a certain amount of power from the signal source under test. See also CAVITY WAVEMETER, COAXIAL WAVEMETER, LECHER WIRES, and SLOTTED LINE.

wave motion Undulating motion (e.g., up and down, and side to side). An electromagnetic wave has undulating electric and magnetic components that are both in phase and perpendicular to each other and to the direction of propagation of the wave.

wave normal **1.** The direction of propagation of an electromagnetic wave. **2.** A unit vector directed at a right angle to both the electric and magnetic lines of flux in an electromagnetic wave.

wave number The reciprocal of wavelength. This number denotes the number of waves per unit distance.

wave packet A short pulse composed of waves.

wave packets Radiant energy resulting from a number of wave trains of different wavelength.

wave path The line along which a WAVE TRAIN is propagated.

wave polarization The direction (horizontal or vertical) of wave undulations (i.e., the plane of the undulations, with respect to the direction of propagation). In general, a vertical antenna radiates a vertically polarized wave, and a horizontal antenna radiates a horizontally polarized wave.

wave propagation The movement of waves through space or through some medium. Electromagnetic waves travel through space at the speed of light (approximately 3×10^8 meters, or 186,000 miles, per second) and, like light, can be reflected and refracted.

wave reflection The reflection of electromagnetic waves by an obstruction, such as a solid body or a layer of the ionosphere. Compare WAVE ABSORPTION, WAVE POLARIZATION, and WAVE REFRACTION.

wave refraction Bending of the line of propagation of electromagnetic waves as they pass through various media, such as the troposphere or the ionosphere. Compare WAVE ABSORPTION, WAVE POLARIZATION, and WAVE REFLECTION.

waveshape The overall contour of a wave—especially as revealed by a curve plotted for the particular wave equation. Also see WAVEFORM.

waveshaping circuit A circuit that receives an input signal having a certain waveshape, and delivers an output signal having a different waveshape. For example, a squaring circuit converts a sine wave into a square wave at the same frequency.

wave surface See WAVE FRONT.

wave tail In a decaying pulse or signal envelope, the interval between the beginning of the decay and the point at which the amplitude reaches zero.

wave telegraphy See RADIOTELEGRAPHY.

wave telephony See RADIOTELEPHONY.

wave theory of matter A physical theory that the charge of an electron is distributed in space, rather than being focused at a point. Also see WAVE MECHANICS.

wave tilt A slight forward tilt of the electric flux lines in a radio wave radiated at the surface of the earth by a vertical antenna.

wave train A series of identical electromagnetic wave cycles propagated at equal intervals; an electromagnetic energy burst lasting at least several cycles.

wavetrap A resonant circuit consisting of an inductor and capacitor, either or both of which can be adjustable for tuning, used to remove (trap) a signal at the resonant frequency from a signal mixture.

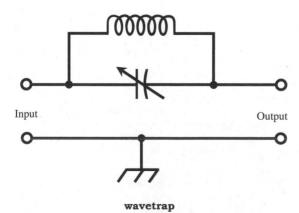

wavetrap

wave trough The minimum value of a wave envelope. Compare WAVE CREST.

wave velocity The distance per unit time traversed by a wave passing through a given medium.

wave winding See DRUM WINDING.

wa-wa pedal A foot-operated device used with an electronic musical instrument to produce a "wah-wah" sound fluctuation.

wax **1.** Any of a series of organic materials having important uses as dielectrics, impregnants, sealers, and lubricants in electronics. They are usually solid or semisolid, waterproof, and easily melted. **2.** In certain phonograph record discs, a blend of wax (see **1**, above) and metallic soaps. Also see WAX MASTER, **2**.

wax cake See WAX MASTER, **1, 2**.

wax capacitor A fixed capacitor that has been dipped in or impregnated with a wax, such as halowax.

wax-dipped capacitor A fixed capacitor that has been dipped in a wax for sealing against moisture.

waxed paper See WAX PAPER.

wax-filled capacitor A fixed capacitor impregnated with a wax for enhancing the properties of its dielectric (usually paper) and sealing the capacitor unit.

wax master **1.** In disc-recording operations, the original recording made on a wax-surface disc. **2.** To make an original recording on a wax-surface disc.

wax original See WAX MASTER.

wax paper Wax-saturated paper used as a dielectric film in fixed capacitors and as an insulator.

way-operated circuit A single or duplex circuit shared by three or more party stations.

way point An important point selected on a radionavigational course line.

way station A station consisting of a teletypewriter connected at an intermediate point in a line (i.e., between, and in series with, other teletypewriter stations).

WAZ Amateur radio abbreviation of *Worked All Zones*, an award given to operators who have carried on verified two-way communication with stations in all communications zones of the world.

WB Abbreviation of *weather bureau*.

W_B Abbreviation of *base-region width* (in a transistor).

Wb Symbol for WEBER.

Wb/m^2 Abbreviation of *Webers per square meter* (see TESLA).

W_C Abbreviation of *collector-region width* (in a transistor).

WCEMA Abbreviation of *West Coast Electronic Manufacturers' Association.*

W/cm^2 Abbreviation of *watts per square centimeter.*

WE Abbreviation of write enable.

W_E Abbreviation of *emitter-region width* (in a transistor).

weak battery **1.** A battery that has been depleted to the point that its output (no-load or full-load) is too low to be useful. **2.** A battery specially designed for low-voltage output.

weak color Lack of color vividness or poor contrast between colors in a color-television picture. The condition is often caused by some malfunction in the chroma demodulator(s).

weak contrast In a television picture, poor differentiation of adjacent tonal areas.

weak coupling See LOOSE COUPLING.

weak current An extremely small electric current. The term is relative; generally, it refers to currents of a few microamperes or less.

weak magnet **1.** A magnet whose power has deteriorated considerably below a prescribed level. **2.** A body that normally is only slightly magnetic.

weak signal A signal whose amplitude is very low compared with that of signals considered satisfactory in a given application. Although the term is relative, it usually implies a signal that is noncompetitive with other signals in a given environment.

weak-signal detector A detector in which, at low input-signal amplitudes (weak-signal levels), the direct-current output is proportional to the square of the root-mean-square (rms) value of the input-signal voltage.

wearout The complete deterioration of a component or system (i.e., beyond restoration to useful service).

wearout failure Failure because of wearout, which can be predicted on the basis of known lifetime and the deterioration characteristics of components and equipment.

wearout point The instant of wearout, in terms of power output, watt-hour capacity, or some other specification.

weather antenna An antenna dimensioned for reception exclusively in the 162.4- to 162.55-MHz weather band. See WEATHER TRANSMISSION.

weathering Deterioration of electronic equipment as a result of exposure to outdoor heat, cold, moisture, wind, and similar conditions.

weather-protected machine A machine (usually a generator or motor) whose vent holes are designed to prevent entry of dust, water, and debris.

weather protection The coating, sealing, or treating of electronic equipment for protection against corrosion, humidity, and temperature changes in outdoor use.

weather satellite A satellite designed to photograph weather systems in infrared and/or visible light, and relay the pictures to earth via facsimile or television.

weather sonde See RADIOSONDE.

weather transmission The radio transmission of meteorological reports. Sometimes the transmissions are combined with guidance transmissions, from which they can be separated by means of a filter in the receiver.

weber Abbreviation, Wb. The SI unit of magnetic flux and of the magnetic flux quantum; 1 Wb = 10^8 maxwells = 1.257×10^{-7} unit pole.

Weber-Fechner law The law expressing the relationship between a stimulus and the physiological reaction it produces: The sensation is proportional to the logarithm of the stimulus.

weber per square meter Symbol, Wb/m². See TESLA.

weber turn A unit of magnetic flux linkage equal to 10^8 maxwell turns.

wedge **1.** In a waveguide, a termination consisting of a tapered block or plate of carbon (or other dissipative material). **2.** In a television test pattern, convergent, equally spaced lines for checking resolution.

wedge bonding In integrated-circuit fabrication, a method of bonding in which a thermocompression bond (see COLD-COMPRESSION WELDING) is obtained through pressure from a wedge-shaped tool.

Wehnelt cathode An oxide-coated cathode in an electron tube.

Wehnelt cylinder In a cathode-ray tube, the cathode-enclosing cylinder that concentrates the electrons emitted by the cathode.

weight **1.** The amount of gravitational pull on a body or particle. **2.** Extra significance given to a term or value. See, for example, WEIGHTED TERM. **3.** The dot-to-space ratio in a Morse-code signal.

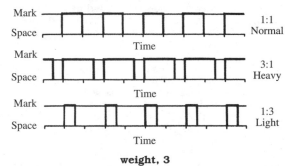

weight, 3

weight-density Symbol, d. Unit, kg/m³. The weight per unit volume of a liquid, such as an electrolyte or insulating oil; also called *density*.

weighted distortion factor In the measurement of harmonic distortion, a factor whose use allows the harmonics in the complex waveform to be weighted in proportion to their relationship.

weighted noise level Unit, dBm. The noise level weighted with respect to the 70-dB equal-loudness contour of hearing.

weighting **1.** Adjustment of a parameter to compensate for some imbalance in a system. **2.** Adjustment of the dot-to-space ratio in a Morse code signal. **3.** Adjustment of the mark-to-space ratio in a digital communications signal.

weighting filter A filter used in a communications network to represent the characteristics of the transmission passband.

weighting network A network that weights differently (in a prescribed ratio) the frequency components appearing in an output signal by offering unequal attenuation to those frequencies.

weightlessness switch See ZERO-GRAVITY SWITCH.

Weir circuit In frequency-modulated signal transmission, a circuit used to stabilize the carrier wave. It compares the average carrier frequency with the frequency of a standard crystal oscillator, obtaining a direct-current compensating voltage (proportional to frequency deviation) that is applied to the frequency modulator. Also called *Weir stabilization circuit*.

Weiss constant In paramagnetism, a constant also known as *paramagnetic Curie temperature*. It can be positive or negative, depending on the particular paramagnetic material. It is important in defining the behavior of certain paramagnetic substances.

weld A strong bond of materials (usually metals) obtained by applying heat to areas to be joined while they are held or pressed together. No foreign metal is used, as is the case in brazing and soldering. The required heat is sometimes obtained by passing a high electric current through the materials.

welder **1.** An electrical device, often electronically controlled, for welding materials. **2.** A person who operates a device, as defined in **1**.

weldgate pulse In a welding device, the pulse that affects the arc current; therefore, it also affects the intensity of the heat produced by the device.

welding control An electronic system for controlling the interval during which current is passed through a workpiece in spot welding or seam welding. In this system, an electronic timer circuit determines the conduction time of thyratrons, ignitrons, or silicon-controlled rectifiers in the welding circuit. The control system can also regulate the welding current.

welding current The high electric current passed through a workpiece to produce the heat required for welding.

welding cycle The required sequence of steps (and the time required) in making a weld electronically.

welding time See WELD TIME.

welding transformer For electronic welding, a special very-high-current step-down transformer.

weld junction See WELD.

weld polarity The polarity of welding current. Some materials require a certain direction of current flow for a good weld.

weld time The interval during which welding current flows through the bodies to be bonded together.

well counter A radiation-counter setup in which a radioactive sample and detector are enclosed together in a thick-walled (usually lead) cylinder to minimize background count.

well-structured language An advanced form of high-level computer programming language. It is used in graphical and control applications.

Wenner element An adjustable, dual-slidewire balancing resistor used in constant-current, laboratory potentiometers to eliminate the necessity for sliding contacts in the measuring circuit.

Wenner winding A low-capacitance, low-inductance winding for high-frequency wirewound resistors in which the direction of the wire is reversed by looping alternate turns along the form.

Wertheim effect The tendency for a potential difference to develop between opposite ends of a length of wire, when the wire is placed parallel to magnetic lines of flux and rotated.

Western Union joint A strong splice of two wires made by tightly twisting a short portion of the tip of each wire along the body of the other. For increased ruggedness, the joint is often soldered. Also called *Western Union splice*.

Weston cell See STANDARD CELL.

Westrex system A system of sound recording in which signals from two separate microphone channels are recorded on opposite walls of a groove on a disc.

wet battery A battery of cells having a liquid electrolyte.

wet Liquid, especially pertaining to the electrolyte material in an electrochemical cell.

wet cell A battery cell having a liquid electrolyte. Compare DRY CELL.

wet-charged stand The length of time that a fully charged, wet storage cell can stand idle before its capacity drops by a specified amount.

wet electrolytic capacitor An electrolytic capacitor in which the electrolyte is a liquid. The leakage current in this type is higher than in the dry electrolytic, but it is self-healing after momentary voltage breakdown. Compare DRY ELECTROLYTIC CAPACITOR.

wet grab The adherence of a pressure-sensitive tape or sheet to a surface when very little pressure is used.

wet rectifier See ELECTROLYTIC RECTIFIER.

wet shelf life The specified shelf life of a discharged, wet storage cell. Compare DRY SHELF LIFE.

wetted-contact relay See MERCURY-WETTED REED RELAY.

wetting Applying a mercury coating to a contact surface.

wetting agent A substance (such as an alcohol or ester) that promotes the spreading and adhesion of a liquid or its absorption by a porous material.

WG Abbreviation of WIRE GAUGE.

WH Abbreviation of WATT-HOUR.

wh Abbreviation of WHITE.

Wheatstone bridge A four-arm balancing circuit (see BRIDGE), having resistors in each

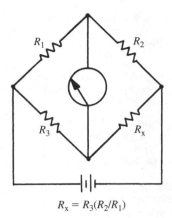

$$R_x = R_3(R_2/R_1)$$

Wheatstone bridge

arm and used to measure an unknown resistance in terms of a standard resistance. The bridge supply is usually direct current, but alternating current can be used if all four resistances are nonreactive.

wheel-drive locomotion The use of wheels for moving mobile apparatus such as robots. Offers simplicity and low cost. The main disadvantage is the inability to negotiate irregular terrain.

Wheeler's formula A formula for calculating the inductance of a multilayer air-core coil:

$$L = (0.8a^2n^2)/(6a + 9l + 10b)$$

where L is in microhenrys, a is the mean radius (inches) of the winding (axis to center of cross section), b is the depth of winding (inches), l is the length of winding (inches), and n is the number of turns.

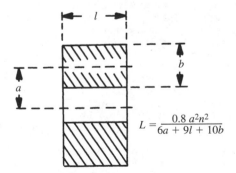

$$L = \frac{0.8\,a^2n^2}{6a + 9l + 10b}$$

**Wheeler's formula
(dimensions illustrated)**

wheel pattern A frequency test pattern produced on an oscilloscope screen by z-axis modulation of a circular trace. A sinusoidal axis signal pro- duces a *gear-wheel pattern*, and a square-wave or pulse z-axis signal produces a *spot-wheel pattern*.

wheel printer A printout device for computers and calculators. It consists essentially of a rotating metal wheel around whose rim letters and numbers stand in relief. When the desired character comes into position, a hammer strikes it through the recording paper and carbon paper, printing the character on the recording paper. Also called *daisy-wheel printer*.

wheel static Static electricity (and the resulting radio interference) generated by friction between automobile tires and the road.

whiffletree switch In computer operations, a multiposition electronic switching circuit, so called from its circuit configuration, which resembles the contrivance used between a wagon and the horse team pulling it.

whip antenna A small-diameter, vertical rod (often telescoping) used as an antenna—especially in mobile communications, portable radio and television receivers, field-strength meters, etc.

whirl One of the circular, magnetic lines of flux around a straight wire carrying current.

whisker 1. The pointer-wire electrode of a point-contact diode, point-contact transistor, or crystal detector. 2. A slender filament of metal or ceramic, having high purity and high tensile strength.

whisker resistance In a semiconductor material, the resistance of a whisker component (see WHISKER, **1**).

Whiskey Phonetic alphabet code word for the letter W.

whistle A high-pitched tone (e.g., a beat note or acoustic feedback).

whistle filter A notch filter used to eliminate a whistle in an amplifier or other audio-frequency circuit. This filter can be of several versions, ranging from a simple resistance-capacitance (RC) null circuit tuned to remove the offending frequency to a feedback-type band-suppression amplifier.

whistle interference The appearance of extraneous whistles in audio-frequency circuits. In some equipment, whistles result from oscillating amplifiers; in radio receivers, they are usually audible beat notes (heterodynes) produced by interfering carriers.

whistler A type of very-low-frequency (VLF) radio noise. They are thought to be caused by electromagnetic fields from distant lightning strokes, circulating in the earth's magnetic field. The name is derived from the peculiar sound the noise makes in a VLF radio receiver.

whistler mode propagation Radio transmission from the northern hemisphere to the southern hemisphere along the flux lines of earth's magnetic field.

whistlestop See WHISTLE FILTER.

whistling atmospheric See WHISTLER.

white   The color that results from mixing all the additive primary colors: red, green, and blue.

white acid   Hydrofluoric acid. Formula, HF. Used as an etchant, especially of glass.

white brass   Brass that is more than 49% zinc.

white compression   In television transmission, reduction of gain at highlight levels in the picture.

white-dot pattern   In color-television tests with a dot generator, the one-white-dot pattern obtained when beam convergence has been secured.

white lamp   See DAYLIGHT LAMP.

white level   The lower-voltage point in a video signal, corresponding to full brilliance of the line on the screen (i.e., to the condition of whiteness in the picture).

white light   See WHITE RADIATION, 2.

white noise   Random noise (acoustic or electric) equally distributed over a given frequency band, an example being the noise resulting from the random motion of free electrons in conductors and semiconductors.

white-noise generator   A test device that generates electrical noise over a wide frequency spectrum. A simple type uses a reverse-biased silicon diode, the output of which is useful for testing audio amplifiers and radio receivers.

white-noise record   A phonograph record containing recorded bands of white noise, each accompanied by voice announcements (e.g., instructions), and used to test the frequency response of a sound system.

white object   A body that reflects and diffuses light of all wavelengths equally well.

white peak   In a television picture signal, the maximum excursion in the white direction.

white radiation   1. See WHITE NOISE. 2. Visible light radiated with more or less equal intensity throughout the visible spectrum; seen as gray or white.

white raster   See CHROMA-CLEAR RASTER.

white recording   1. In amplitude modulation, recording characterized by a correspondence of maximum received power to minimum recording-medium density. 2. In frequency modulation, recording characterized by a correspondence of lowest received frequency to minimum recording-medium density.

white room   See CLEAN ROOM.

white saturation   See WHITE COMPRESSION.

white signal   The facsimile signal (see FACSIMILE) corresponding to scanning the copy area having maximum density.

white-to-black amplitude range   1. At a point in a positive amplitude-modulated (AM) facsimile system (see FACSIMILE), the ratio (in dB) of signal current or voltage corresponding to white in the picture to that for black in the picture. 2. At a point in a negative AM facsimile system, the ratio (in dB) of signal current or voltage corresponding to black in the picture to that for white in the picture.

white-to-black frequency swing   At a point in a frequency-modulated facsimile system, the frequency difference $fw - fb$, where fb is the frequency corresponding to black in the picture, and fw is the frequency corresponding to white.

white transmission   A system of picture or facsimile transmission in which the maximum copy darkness corresponds to the smallest amplitude (in an amplitude-modulated transmitter) or the highest instantaneous frequency (in a frequency-modulated transmitter). The opposite of BLACK TRANSMISSION.

white X radiation   X rays of the continuous, or general, type.

whizzer   An attachment that can improve the high-frequency reproduction in some audio loudspeakers.

whole-number division   Arithmetic division (as in the division of binary numbers) in which the quotient is a whole number (i.e., division in which the divisor is contained in the dividend an integral number of times).

whorl   See WHIRL.

WHP   Abbreviation of *water horsepower*.

wick action   1. The absorption of a liquid by, and its flow through, a cloth or thread, such as a lamp wick or lubricating wick. 2. The flow of molten solder along and under the insulation of a wire.

wicking   See WICK ACTION.

wide-angle diffusion   A form of diffusion characterized by the wide-angle scattering of light; causes the source to have the same brightness at all viewing angles.

wide-area network   A group of computers linked together, but separated by large geographic distances. Links can be made via telephone lines or radio.

wide-area service   A teletype network that operates over long-distance wire lines.

Wide Area Telephone Service   See WATS.

wideband   1. Having a bandwidth greater than the minimum necessary to transmit a signal with acceptable intelligibility. 2. For a voice signal, having a bandwidth greater than 6 kHz. 3. Having the capability to operate, without adjustment, over a broad and continuous range of frequencies or wavelengths.

wideband amplifier   An amplifier that exhibits reasonably flat response to a broad band of frequencies. The term is relative, depending on the application.

wideband antenna   An antenna that transmits or receives signals over a broad frequency range, usually without the need for tuning.

wideband axis   In a color-television signal, the direction of the fine chrominance primary phasor.

wideband communications   1. Communications carried out over a band of frequencies wider than the minimum necessary for effective transfer of the information. 2. A method of transmitting and receiving signals by deliberately varying the channel frequency over a wide range. Also called *spread-spectrum communications.*

wideband generator A signal generator covering a wide frequency range. Typical coverage in a laboratory-type instrument is 10 kHz to 1000 MHz.

wideband oscilloscope An oscilloscope whose horizontal, vertical, and sweep channels operate over a wide band of frequencies. Although the term wideband is relative, a wideband oscilloscope is usually assumed to be capable of displaying both radio and audio frequencies.

wideband ratio The ratio $B1/B2$, where $B1$ is frequency bandwidth and $B2$ is intelligence bandwidth.

wideband receiver A radio receiver that can tune in signals over a broad range of frequencies. An example is a communications receiver that can cover 10 kHz to 30 MHz continuously.

wideband repeater A repeater capable of operating over a wide range of input and output frequencies. Such repeaters are used in active communications satellites handling many different channels at the same time.

wideband signal generator See WIDEBAND GENERATOR.

wideband sweep 1. In the operation of an oscilloscope, a repetitive sweep of the electron beam, the frequency of which is adjustable to any desired point within a wide range. The basic sweep rate in simple oscilloscopes is restricted to the audio-frequency spectrum (up to about 20 kHz), but a wideband sweep extends to much higher frequencies, typically several tens of MHz. 2. A sweep circuit that produces the wideband sweep action described in 1.

wideband test meter An alternating-current (ac) meter that can measure quantities over a wide frequency range in its basic form (i.e., without special external probes or converters). An example is an electronic ac voltmeter with a range extending from 10 Hz to 2.5 MHz.

wide-base diode A junction diode in which the p region is considerably wider than the n region.

wide-open 1. Pertaining to wideband, untuned response. 2. Pertaining to maximum-gain operation (e.g., a wide-open amplifier or receiver).

wide-range reproduction High-fidelity audio-frequency reproduction.

width 1. The horizontal dimension of a pulse, usually corresponding to its effective duration; also called PULSE DURATION. 2. The horizontal dimension of an image, such as a television picture.

width coding The modification of pulse duration according to a code.

width coil See WIDTH CONTROL, 1.

width control 1. In a television receiver, the variable component for adjusting the swing of the horizontal deflection voltage and, therefore, the width of the picture. It is often a slug-tuned coil connected in parallel with a portion of the secondary winding of the horizontal output trans-

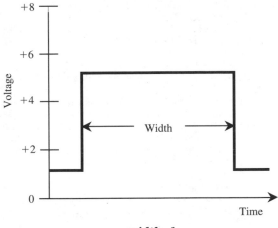

width, 1.

former. 2. Sometimes, the horizontal gain control in an oscilloscope.

width mode In electronic-counter operations, a time-interval mode in which the signal is measured.

width modulation Modulation of the interval during which a gate circuit is open.

Wiedemann effect See DIRECT WIEDEMANN EFFECT.

Wiedemann-Franz law For metals that are good electrical conductors, the ratio of thermal conductivity to electrical conductivity is nearly constant, and is proportional to the absolute temperature.

Wien bridge A frequency-sensitive bridge in which two adjacent arms are resistances and the other two adjacent arms are resistance-capacitance (RC) combinations. One of the latter contains resistance and capacitance in series; the other contains resistance and capacitance in parallel. Because the bridge can be balanced at only one frequency at a time, it is useful as a

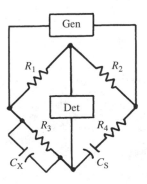

Wien bridge

simple audio frequency meter (see BRIDGE-TYPE AF METER). It is used also for capacitance and resistance measurements. When inductors are substituted for the capacitors, the Wien bridge can be used for inductance measurements (see WIEN INDUCTANCE BRIDGE).

Wien-bridge audio frequency meter   See WIEN-BRIDGE FREQUENCY METER.

Wien-bridge distortion meter   A distortion meter in which a Wien bridge circuit is used to remove the fundamental frequency from the complex waveform. The bridge is inserted between amplifier stages, and its notch response is sharpened by means of overall negative feedback.

Wien-bridge equivalent   A resistance-capacitance null circuit, such as the parallel-tee (twin-tee) network, which has the same balance equation as the Wien bridge.

Wien-bridge filter   A Wien bridge used as a band-suppression filter (notch circuit).

Wien-bridge frequency meter   A bridge-type audio frequency meter in which the continuously variable frequency-selective circuit is a Wien bridge. Also see BRIDGE-TYPE AF METER.

Wien-bridge heterodyne eliminator   A notch filter composed of a continuously variable Wien-bridge circuit (see WIEN BRIDGE). The device is connected in the audio-frequency channel of a radio receiver, and is tuned to remove a troublesome heterodyne whistle.

Wien-bridge oscillator   An oscillator in which the frequency-selective feedback network is a Wien-bridge circuit (see WIEN BRIDGE). Also see BRIDGE-TYPE OSCILLATOR.

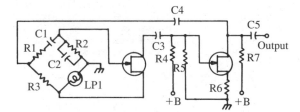

Wien-bridge oscillator

Wien capacitance bridge   A Wien bridge arranged for the measurement of unknown capacitance.

Wien effect   For an electrolytic substance, an increase in conductivity (decrease in resistivity) that occurs when a very large voltage is placed across the material. This voltage must be greater than approximately 1 megavolt per 50 cm.

Wien inductance bridge   A Wien bridge containing inductors in place of capacitors and used for the measurement of unknown inductance.

Wien's displacement law   The wavelength of maximum radiation of a black body is inversely proportional to the absolute temperature.

Wien's first law   See WIEN'S DISPLACEMENT LAW.

Wien's laws   See WIEN'S FIRST LAW, WIEN'S SECOND LAW, and WIEN'S THIRD LAW.

Wien's radiation law   See WIEN'S SECOND LAW.

Wien's second law   The emissive power of a black body is proportional to the fifth power of the absolute temperature.

Wien's third law   An empirical law for the spectral distribution of energy radiated from a black body at a specified temperature. The distribution is a curve with a peak (maximum) at a wavelength that depends on the temperature. The higher the temperature, the shorter the wavelength at which maximum radiation occurs.

willemite   See ZINC ORTHOSILICATE PHOSPHOR and ZINC SILICATE PHOSPHOR.

Williams tube   A type of electrostatic cathode-ray storage tube.

Wilson chamber   See WILSON CLOUD CHAMBER.

Wilson cloud chamber   An airtight chamber containing water vapor or alcohol vapor at low pressure, and provided with a viewing window. Radioactive particles penetrating the chamber are made visible as droplets form trails when the vapor condenses on them.

Wilson effect   Electric polarization of a dielectric material being moved in a magnetic field.

Wilson electroscope   A leaf-type electroscope (see ELECTROSCOPE) using a single leaf hanging vertically.

Wilson experiment   An experiment demonstrating the WILSON EFFECT. It consists of rotating about its axis a hollow dielectric cylinder (whose inner and outer surfaces are metallized) in a magnetic field parallel to the axis. The result: An alternating voltage appears between the metallized surfaces.

Wimshurst machine   A rotating machine used to produce high-voltage static electricity. The machine contains two glass disks, each having separate sectors of metal foil spaced around its face. The disks rotate in opposite directions, and the foil sectors passing each other form variable capacitors. Metal brushes pick up charges from the sectors passing under them and deliver this energy to one or more Leyden jars for storage.

wind charger   A wind-driven generator used specifically to supply direct current for charging storage batteries.

wind-driven generator   A dynamo-type generator, either stationary or mobile, powered by a windmill-like device.

wind gauge   See ANEMOMETER.

winding   1. A coil in an inductor or transformer (e.g., *primary winding, secondary winding, output winding*, etc.). 2. A coil in a motor or generator.

winding arc The winding length of a coil, expressed in degrees.

winding cross section The cross section of a multilayer coil.

winding depth The depth of a multilayer coil, measured from the outermost layer to the innermost layer.

winding factor For a transformer or choke coil (or for a toroidal coil), the ratio of the total area of wire in the window to the window area.

winding length The length of a coil from the first turn to the last in a single-layer coil, or from the first turn to the last in one layer of a multilayer coil when all layers are identical.

winding space The window area of the core of a transformer or choke (see WINDOW, 3).

wind loading **1.** The total wind pressure on an antenna system, generally measured in pounds or kilograms. The greater the wind speed, the greater the wind loading for a given antenna. The greater the exposed surface of the antenna, the greater the wind loading for a given wind speed. **2.** The highest wind speed, in miles per hour or meters per second, that an antenna system can safely withstand, assuming no accumulation of ice on the antenna structure.

Windom antenna **1.** A multiband antenna in which a single-wire feeder is attached to a horizontal half-wave radiator wire somewhat off center, at a point about ⅙ wavelength from one end of the radiator. The antenna operates with reasonable efficiency at the first several harmonics of the frequency at which it measures ½ wavelength. **2.** A similar antenna using a parallel-wire feeder.

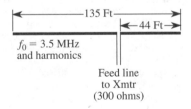

$f_0 = 3.5$ MHz and harmonics

135 Ft
44 Ft
Feed line to Xmtr (300 ohms)

Windom antenna, 2

window **1.** Radar-interference material (see CHAFF). **2.** An interval during which a circuit is gated open to permit signal sampling. During this interval, a window is figuratively open to the signal. **3.** The open spaces between the legs of an iron core for a transformer or choke coil. **4.** An electromagnetic frequency band easily transmitted by earth's atmosphere. **5.** The period during which conditions are ideal for a complex operation, such as a rocket or spacecraft launch. **6.** An application space in a computer program that uses a graphical interface.

window area See WINDOW, 3.

window comparator A comparator that detects voltage levels within a certain range of values, rather than simply indicating whether a voltage is more or less than a certain specified value.

window corridor An area where window (see WINDOW, 1) has been dispersed.

window jamming The disturbance of electronic communications, especially radar, by dumping reflective material, such as metal foil, from an aircraft. Also see CHAFF; JAMMING; and WINDOW, 1.

Windows Trade name (Microsoft) for a personal-computer interface scheme. The several versions all use selectable icons and menus.

window strip An insulated, flat, metal strip for bringing an antenna lead-in through a window. The window can be closed on the strip.

wind screen A foam covering that can minimize the roar caused by wind blowing against or across a microphone.

wind shield A radio-transparent cover placed over a radar antenna to protect it against damage from high winds. It is used especially in radar systems aboard aircraft.

wing In an antenna or other radiator, a (usually flat) member attached to, and sticking out from, another member. Its name is derived from its characteristic shape.

winterization The protective treatment and preparation of electronic equipment for winter storage or for operation in frigid regions.

wipeout Severe interference that obliterates all desired signals.

wipeout area An area in which WIPEOUT occurs.

wiper **1.** A thin metal blade or strip in sliding contact with a coil or other element over which it is turned to vary some quantity (such as resistance, inductance, voltage, current, etc.). **2.** A brush in a motor or generator.

wiper arm See WIPER, 1.

wiper blade See WIPER, 1.

wiping action The movement of contacts against each other when they slide as they mate or withdraw.

wiping contact A contact that makes and breaks with a sliding motion.

wire **1.** A metal strand or thread serving as a conductor of electricity. **2.** To connect wires between points in a circuit. **3.** See TELEGRAM. **4.** To send a TELEGRAM.

wire bonding **1.** The interconnection of components within a discrete package, by means of fine wire conductors welded to the individual components. **2.** A method of temporarily splicing the outer conductors of two coaxial cables. **3.** In general, any solderless method of splicing between two conductors.

wire broadcasting Broadcasting by means of carrier-current communication (see WIRED RADIO).

wire cloth A net of fine wire, used as an electrical shield when air circulation is necessary.

wire communication Communication carried on by means of signals transmitted over wire lines, as opposed to wireless (radio) communication.

wire control The control of remote devices by means of signals transmitted over wire lines, as opposed to radio control.

wire core A magnetic core consisting of a bundle of iron (or magnetic alloy) wires.

wired AND See DOT AND.

wired-in component A component to which wires are permanently connected in a circuit, as opposed to a plug-in component.

wired OR See DOT OR.

wired-program computer A computer in which instructions are wired-in by making appropriate connections to a panel with patch cords.

wired radio The transmission and reception of voice and other sounds, telegraph signals, pictures, control signals, telemetry signals, and the like by means of radio-frequency energy conducted by wire lines. Usually, the lines are used primarily for some other purpose (e.g., power lines or telephone lines).

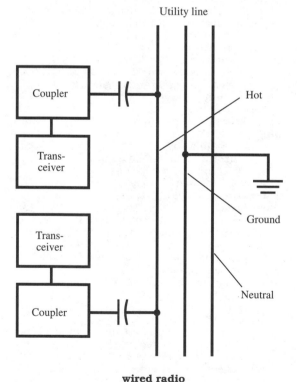

Utility line

Coupler

Trans-ceiver

Trans-ceiver

Coupler

Hot

Ground

Neutral

wired radio

wired-radio receiver The complete device or system that selects, amplifies, and demodulates or rectifies a radio signal picked up from wires that conduct it from a transmitting station.

wired-radio transmitter The complete device or system that generates radio-frequency power, adds signals (for communication, remote control, telemetry, etc.), and delivers the power to wires or to a cable for reception at a distant point.

wire drawing In the manufacture of wire, pulling metal through special dies to form wire of selected diameter.

wire dress The careful arrangement of wires in a chassis to ensure optimum performance. Also called *lead dress* (see DRESS).

wire duct A conduit through which wires are run. Such ducts have several shapes, but generally are rectangular.

wired wireless See WIRED RADIO.

wire fuse A fuse in which the fusible element is a wire of low-melting-point metal. Compare STRIP FUSE.

wire gauge 1. A system for specifying the characteristics of wire. See AMERICAN WIRE GAUGE and BIRMINGHAM WIRE GAUGE. 2. A wire number governed by diameter (e.g., 18-gauge wire for #18 wire). 3. A tool or instrument for measuring wire diameter or for determining wire number.

wire gauze A fine screen of thin wires.

wire grating See WAVEGUIDE GRATING.

wire-guided Pertaining to guiding a machine, such as a robot, by means of signals sent by wire from the control point.

wire leads Leads that are (usually thin, flexible) wires, rather than pins, bars, strips, etc. An example is the wire leads of some transistors (as opposed to terminal pins).

wireless 1. Pertaining to data communications and control systems that operate without wires (e.g., an infrared link between a notebook computer and a desktop computer). 2. An early name for radio; it is still used in some countries. Sometimes for specificity, radio is referred to as *wireless telegraphy* or *wireless telephony*. See RADIOTELEPHONY.

wireless broadcaster See WIRELESS MICROPHONE.

wireless compass A radio compass (see DIRECTION FINDER).

wireless device A device that operates over a distance, without the use of interconnecting wires.

wireless intercom An intercom using wired-radio for transmission and reception over the power line from which it is operated. Also see WIRED RADIO.

wireless microphone A device consisting of a small radio-frequency oscillator modulated by the microphone to which it is attached, and provided with a tiny antenna. The modulated signal is picked up and reproduced by a radio receiver.

wireless telegraphy See RADIOTELEGRAPHY.

wireless telephone 1. A radio transceiver interconnected with the telephone lines. 2. A telephone in which a short-range radio link replaces the cord between the receiver and the base unit. It normally has a range of several hundred feet.

wireless telephony See RADIOTELEPHONY.

wire line One or more wires or cables conducting currents for communication, control, or measuring purposes.

wire link A line for wire communication or wire control.

wire-link telemetry Telemetry carried on over a wire link.

wireman **1.** An electrician who specializes in the installation and servicing of electrical wiring. **2.** See LINEMAN.

wire mile A unit of measure equal to the product *ns*, where *n* is the number of separate, equal-length conductors in a line, and *s* is the length of a conductor in miles.

Wirephoto **1.** A system for transmitting and receiving photographs over wire lines. Also called *Telephoto.* See FACSIMILE. **2.** A photograph transmitted and/or received, as defined in **1. 3.** A trademark for a photograph transmitted and received over telephone lines.

wire printer A printout device consisting of a wire array in which each wire is activated by an electromagnet. When a wire is selected (electrically), it is pushed against, and makes a dot on the recording paper. The letters and figures, then, are dot patterns. Compare WHEEL PRINTER.

wire radio See WIRED RADIO.

wire recorder In audio applications and data recording, a machine that records sounds or data pulses in the form of magnetized spots on a thin wire.

wiresonde A system for transmitting weather information data through a cable that holds a captive balloon. Compare RADIOSONDE.

wire splice A strong, low-resistance joint between (usually two) wires. See, for example, WESTERN UNION JOINT.

wire stripper A hand tool or power machine for cutting the insulating jacket on a wire and removing it without cutting or nicking the wire.

wiretap **1.** An instance of wiretapping. **2.** A wiretapping device.

wiretapper **1.** A device for wiretapping. **2.** A person who practices wiretapping.

wiretapping The act of making direct or indirect connections to a communications line to overhear or record a conversation.

wire telegraphy Telegraphic communication carried on by means of signals transmitted over wire lines, as opposed to wireless (radio) telegraphy.

wire telephony Voice communication carried on by means of signals transmitted over wire lines, as opposed to wireless (radio) telephony.

wire tie See TIE.

wire wave communication See WIRED RADIO.

wireways Hinged-cover metal troughs for containing and protecting wires and cables. Also see WIRE DUCT.

wirewound potentiometer A potentiometer in which the resistance element is a coil of resistance wire wound on a cord bent into a cylinder, or on a rigid, circular core.

wirewound resistor A resistor consisting essentially of resistance wire (such as one of Manganin or Nichrome) wound into a coil on a card or slab or on a cylindrical core.

wirewound rheostat A rheostat in which the resistance element is a coil of resistance wire wound on a card bent into a cylinder, or on a rigid, circular core.

wire wrap A method of circuit-board wiring in which components are interconnected by individual wire conductors, the ends of which are wrapped around terminal posts using a special tool.

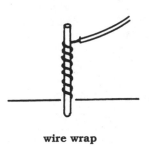

wire wrap

wire-wrap connection An electrical connection made by tightly wrapping a bare wire around a special terminal.

wire-wrapping tool A device used to make a wire-wrap connection.

wiring **1.** The system of wires or similar conductors connected between circuit components. **2.** Connecting and dressing such wires, as in wiring a circuit. **3.** Collectively, the connections (either actual wire or printed metal lines or processed semiconductor paths) between terminals and components in an electronic circuit. **4.** The process of installing or making such connections.

wiring board The control panel of a computer (i.e., a plugboard).

wiring capacitance Unavoidable capacitance between wires in a circuit, or between the wires and nearby metal bodies.

wiring connector A small (usually metal) fitting used to tie wires together.

wiring diagram See CIRCUIT DIAGRAM.

wiring impedance Unavoidable impedance in the wires in a circuit, and in associated terminals and hardware conducting alternating current. This impedance is the vector sum of WIRING REACTANCE and WIRING RESISTANCE.

wiring inductance Unavoidable inductance in the wires in a circuit, and in associated terminals and other hardware, through which alternating currents flow.

wiring reactance Unavoidable reactance in the wires in a circuit, and in associated terminals and other hardware, conducting alternating current. This reactance is caused by WIRING CAPACITANCE and/or WIRING INDUCTANCE.

wiring resistance Unavoidable resistance in the wires in a circuit and in associated terminals and other hardware.

Witka circuit A voltage-tripler circuit using only two diodes and two capacitors. Its no-load direct-current output voltage is approximately three times the peak value of the alternating-current input voltage. Also see VOLTAGE TRIPLER.

wk 1. Abbreviation of WORK. 2. Abbreviation of *week*.

WL 1. Abbreviation of WAVELENGTH. 2. Abbreviation of *waterline*.

WM Abbreviation of WATTMETER.

Wm² Symbol for *watt square meter* (unit of the first radiation constant).

W/(MK) Symbol for *watts per meter kelvin* (unit of thermal conductivity).

WMO Abbreviation of *World Meteorological Organization*.

wobbulator A device that sweeps the frequency of an oscillator. There are several types, from a motor-driven, rotating, tank capacitor to sophisticated, fully electronic variable capacitors or variable inductors.

wolfram See TUNGSTEN.

Wolf's equation A sunspot-number equation used to forecast maximum usable frequency: $R = k(10G + N)$, where R is relative sunspot number, k is a constant for the telescope used, G is the number of sunspot groups observed, and N is the total number of sunspots.

Wollaston wire An extremely fine wire made by coating platinum with silver, drawing it thinner, and dissolving the silver coat.

womp A sudden surge in amplitude that causes a flare up of brightness in a television picture.

woodpecker A slang term used to describe the sound of the signal from over-the-horizon radar. Operating in the high-frequency part of the spectrum and changing in wavelength, roughly following the maximum usable frequency, the signal consists of repeated "spikes" that can interfere with routine communications.

woodpecker filter A special type of blanking filter used to quiet a shortwave receiver during strong, brief "spikes." It is similar to a noise blanker, but is designed to filter out the longer peaks characteristic of the over-the-horizon radar, known as the WOODPECKER.

Wood's alloy See WOOD'S METAL.

Wood's metal A low-melting-point (159.8°F) alloy containing bismuth (50%), cadmium (12.5%), lead (25%), and tin (12.5%). The alloy looks like lead and is used to mount rectifying crystals (such as galena) whose electrical sensitivity would be destroyed by the high temperatures required to melt most soft metals.

woofer A large loudspeaker, often a foot or more in diameter, designed specifically to reproduce very low (bass) audio frequencies. It is commonly used in high-fidelity stereo sound systems. Compare TWEETER.

word 1. In computer operations, a group of bits or characters treated as a unit. 2. In telegraphy, a data unit consisting of five characters plus one space

word-address format A method of addressing a word by means of a single character, such as the first letter of the word.

word code 1. A cipher in which word meanings are interchanged, rather than letter symbols. 2. A word having an altered meaning in a cipher system, as defined in 1. For example, "word" might mean "code."

word format The specific sequence of characters that forms a word of data.

word generator A special signal generator that delivers pulses in selected combinations corresponding to digital words (see WORD, 1). It is used in testing computers and digital systems.

word length 1. In computer operations, the number of bits in a word. 2. In telegraphic communications (radio or wire), the average number of letters in a word.

word pattern The shortest meaningful word (see WORD, 1, 2) that can be recognized by a machine.

word processor 1. An electronic device, similar to a typewriter, used for writing. Words, phrases, sentences, or paragraphs can be changed, replaced, or deleted prior to the final printout. 2. A computer used for writing, as defined in 1. 3. Software that allows a computer to be used for writing, as defined in 1.

word rate In a communications or computer system, the number of words per unit time (e.g., WORDS PER MINUTE).

word size See WORD LENGTH.

words per minute In telegraphy, a measure of data speed. It is approximately equal to the number of characters (including spaces) per minute divided by 6.

word time In computer operations, the time required to process one word that is in storage.

work 1. Symbol, W. Units: joule, erg, foot-pound, kilogram-meter. That which is accomplished by the transfer of energy from one body to another, as when an exerted force causes a displacement. The amount of work performed is equal to force times distance: $W = Fd$. 2. An amateur radio term meaning to engage in two-way communication with another station.

work area In computer operations, a temporary area of memory for data items being processed. Also called INTERMEDIATE STORAGE, WORKING MEMORY, and WORKING STORAGE.

work coil The alternating-current-carrying coil that induces energy in the workpiece in induction heating.

work envelope The range of motion over which a robot arm can move. It can be two-dimensional or three-dimensional.

work function Unit, eV. The energy required to bring an internal particle to the surface of a material and out into space, as when an electron is emitted by the hot cathode of a vacuum tube. The work function is the voltage required to extract 1 electrostatic unit of electricity from the material.

working data file A temporary accumulation of data sets that is erased or otherwise discarded after its transferal to another medium.

working life The expected or guaranteed lifetime of a material, device, or system in actual operation or use. Compare SHELF LIFE.

working memory See WORK AREA.

working point The operating point of an active device (i.e., the point along one of the characteristic curves around which operation is fixed).

working Q The Q of a loaded circuit or device (e.g., tank-circuit Q of a radio transmitter loaded with an antenna or dummy load).

working range 1. The usable maximum distance between a transmitter and receiver in a wireless communications circuit. 2. The allowed range over which specified parameters can vary in a particular system while facilitating normal operation, or operation within rated specifications.

working storage See WORK AREA.

working voltage The (usually maximum) voltage at which a circuit or device can be operated continuously with safety and reliability.

workout 1. A dry run; a test. Example: checking a computer's processing power using a set of benchmark programs. 2. An exacting test of equipment; a burn-in procedure.

workpiece The object heated by an induction or dielectric heater.

worm A cylindrical gear whose spiral "teeth" resemble a screw thread.

worm drive A mechanism for transferring motion from a tuning-knob shaft through a right angle

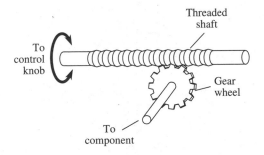

worm drive

to the shaft of an adjustable component, such as a potentiometer or variable capacitor. The knob turns a threaded shaft that mates with a gear wheel.

worst-case circuit analysis Analysis that seeks the worst possible effects of variations in circuit parameters on circuit performance—especially variations in component characteristics.

worst-case noise pattern See DOUBLE-CHECKERBOARD PATTERN.

worst-case design The design of electronic equipment in such a way that normal operation is obtained—even though the characteristics of circuit components might vary widely.

woven resistor A resistance element made of strands of resistance material woven in the form of gauze.

wow Slow, periodic variations in the pitch of reproduced sound because of variations in the speed of the drive mechanism. Its name is derived from its characteristic sound. Compare FLUTTER.

wow meter An instrument that indicates the amount of wow produced by a turntable or other moving part.

Wpc Abbreviation of *watts per candle.*

wpm Abbreviation of *words per minute.*

wrap See WIRE-WRAP CONNECTION.

wrap-around 1. The extent of curvature in magnetic tape passing over the heads during recording or playback. 2. An enclosure that resembles a sheet (wrapped around a piece of electronic equipment). 3. In computer and data-processing operations, a technique in which the display is cleared of data once it is filled (all available lines are occupied) and additional data is traced from top to bottom.

wrap joint See WIRE-WRAP CONNECTION.

wrapper A paper or tape wound around a component, such as a coil or capacitor, for insulation and protection.

wrapping 1. See WRAPPER. 2. Insulating a wire or other conductor by wrapping insulating tape around it.

wrap post A terminal post, tip, pin, or lug used in a wire-wrap connection.

wrap-up The (usually successful) completion of a design, fabrication, test, or investigation.

Wratten filter A light filter for separating colors. It is available in transparent sheets of various colors and is useful in photography and in several phases of electronics, including the operation of color meters and color matchers.

wrinkle finish A pattern of fine wrinkles created by special paint when it dries on a surface, such as that of a metal cabinet for a piece of electronic equipment.

wrist-force sensor In robotics, a set of strain gauges that detects the various forces in the joint connecting an end effector to an arm, and sends signals back to the robot controller. The controller can use the signals to direct the movements of the arm and end effector.

write **1.** In computer operations, to transfer data from one form of memory or storage to another form. Example: To transfer data in a computer from random-access memory (RAM) to the hard disk. Compare READ. **2.** To produce an image on the storage mesh in the cathode-ray tube of a storage oscilloscope.

write enable ring   See WRITE PERMIT RING.

write gun   See WRITING GUN.

write head   In a magnetic memory or in a tape recorder or wire recorder used for recording data, the head that magnetizes the drum, tape, disk, or wire. Compare READ HEAD.

write pulse   In computer operation, the pulse that causes information to be recorded in a magnetic cell, or sets it to the one-state. Compare READ PULSE.

write time   The time taken to write data to a storage device.

writing gun   In a storage oscilloscope, the electron gun that produces the image electronically on the storage mesh. It is mounted in the rear of the cathode-ray tube. Compare FLOOD GUN.

writing head   See WRITE HEAD.

writing rate   In photographing the image on a cathode-ray tube screen, the highest spot speed at which an acceptable picture can be made.

writing speed   See WRITING RATE.

writing telegraph   See TELAUTOGRAPH.

wrong color   The instance of an undesired color (e.g., purple instead of red) in a color-television picture. The condition is often caused by a malfunction of the chroma demodulator(s).

W/(sr·m²)   Abbreviation of *watts per steradian square meter.*

WT   **1.** Abbreviation of wireless telegraphy. **2.** Abbreviation of WATERTIGHT.

wt   Abbreviation of WEIGHT.

WUI   Abbreviation of *Western Union International.*

Wulf electrometer   See BIFILAR ELECTROMETER.

Wullenweber antenna   An electronically steerable antenna composed of two concentric circular arrays of masts connected to the steering circuitry.

WUX   Abbreviation of *Western Union telegram.*

WVdc   Abbreviation of *direct-current working voltage:* the maximum continuous direct-current voltage that can safely be placed across a component.

ww   Abbreviation of *wirewound.*

W/sr   Abbreviation of *watts per steradian* (unit of radiant intensity).

WWV   The call letters of a standard-frequency/standard-time broadcasting station operated by the National Bureau of Standards and located in the continental United States. Also see WWVH.

WWVH   The call letters of a standard-frequency/standard-time broadcasting station operated by the National Bureau of Standards and located in Hawaii. Also see WWV.

wx   Radiotelegraph abbreviation of weather.

WXD   International Telecommunications Union symbol for *meteorological radar station.*

WXR   International Telecommunications Union symbol for *radiosonde station.*

wye adapter   A connector that provides two outputs for a single input, or vice-versa. It is commonly used in audio applications.

wye box   In a three-phase power-measuring setup, a special arrangement of two impedances, each of which is equal to the impedance of the potential element of the wattmeter used in the setup. The box permits a single wattmeter to be used, which indicates one-third the total power. Without the box, three wattmeters would be needed.

wye connection   A method of connecting three windings in a three-phase system so that one terminal of each winding is connected to the neutral point. It is shaped like the letter Y. Also called *star connection.*

wye current   Current through one of the branches of a three-phase star (wye) connection.

wye delta starter   A starter circuit for a three-phase squirrel-cage induction motor. When the starter switch is thrown in one direction, the stator of the motor is wye-connected for starting; thrown in the opposite direction, the stator is delta-connected for continued operation.

wye equivalent circuit   A wye-connected three-phase circuit equivalent to a delta-connected circuit when the impedance of any pair of corresponding lines for both wye and delta are the same; the third line is unconnected.

wye junction   See WAVEGUIDE WYE.

wye-matched-impedance antenna   An antenna in which the impedance of a nonresonant

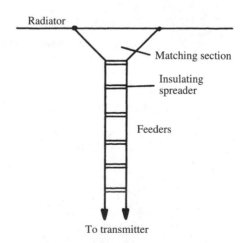

wye-matched-impedance antenna

open-wire feed line is matched to that of the center of the radiator by spreading the end of the feeder wires out into a Y-shaped or delta-shaped matching section. Also called DELTA-MATCHED-IMPEDANCE ANTENNA.

wye point   The star point in a three-phase system. Also see WYE CONNECTION.

wye potential   In a three-phase armature, the voltage between a terminal and the neutral point.

wye rectifier   A three-phase rectifier circuit in which the transformer or generator windings are arranged in a wye connection.

wye-wye circuit   A circuit consisting a wye-connected generator and a wye-connected load.

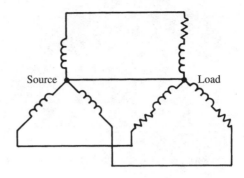

wye-wye circuit

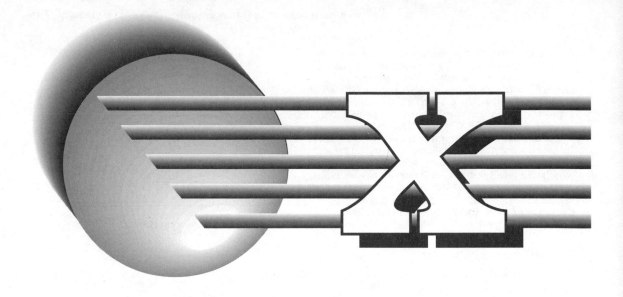

X **1.** Symbol for REACTANCE. **2.** Symbol for *no connection.* (Also, NC.) **3.** Symbol for the HORIZONTAL AXIS of a graph or screen in the rectangular (Cartesian) coordinate system. **4.** Symbol for an unknown quantity.

x **1.** Symbol for number of carriers drawn from collector to base of a transistor, for each carrier collected. **2.** Symbol for an unknown quantity. **3.** Symbol for the HORIZONTAL AXIS of a graph or screen in the rectangular (Cartesian) coordinate system.

x amplifier The horizontal amplifier of an oscilloscope or recorder. Compare Y AMPLIFIER and Z AMPLIFIER.

X and Z demodulation Color television demodulation based on the 60-degree difference between the two reinserted 3.58-MHz subcarrier signals. The R-Y, B-Y, and G-Y voltages derived from the demodulated signals control the three guns of the picture tube. Compare Q MODULATION.

x-axis **1.** The horizontal axis of a chart, graph, or screen in the rectangular (Cartesian) coordinate system. **2.** In a quartz crystal, the axis drawn through the corners of the hexagon.

x-axis amplifier See X AMPLIFIER.

XB Abbreviation of *crossbar.*

X balance The reactance balance (either the variable component or the adjustment of it) in an impedance bridge in which separate resistance (R) and reactance (X) balancing is provided.

X band The frequency band extending from 5.2 to 11 GHz.

X bar A rectangular, piezoelectric quartz bar cut from a Z-section, whose faces are parallel to the X-axis and whose edges are parallel to the X-, Y-, and Z-axes. See CRYSTAL CUTS.

X bridge An alternating-current bridge for measuring reactance.

X_C Symbol for CAPACITIVE REACTANCE.

X channel The horizontal channel of an oscilloscope or recorder. Compare Y CHANNEL and Z CHANNEL.

X-channel gain See X GAIN.

X component In a complex impedance, the reactive component (either inductive or capacitive).

x coordinate See ABSCISSA.

X-cut crystal A piezoelectric plate cut with its faces perpendicular to the X-axis of a quartz crystal. See CRYSTAL CUTS.

xcvr Abbreviation of TRANSCEIVER. Often capitalized.

X deflection Horizontal deflection of the spot on the screen of a cathode-ray tube. Compare Y DEFLECTION.

X diode The decoding diode in each of the X lines of a memory matrix. Compare Y DIODE.

X direction The horizontal direction in deflections and in graphical presentations of data.

X drive The driving source or energy for the X lines of a computer memory matrix.

xducer Abbreviation of TRANSDUCER.

Xe Symbol for XENON.

xenon Symbol, Xe. An inert gaseous element. Atomic number, 54. Atomic weight, 131.29. Xenon is present in trace amounts in the earth's atmosphere and is used in some thyratrons, electric lamps, and lasers.

xenon tube A flash tube filled with xenon.

xerography A system for the reproduction of printed matter, drawings, and other graphic matter. It is an electrostatic process in which a charged photoconductive surface is exposed to an image of the material to be copied. A latent image is formed on the surface and is developed (by dusting with black powder attracted to the charged image) to make the image visible.

xeroradiography   Xerography using X RAYS.

xerothermic   A condition characterized by both heat and dryness.

Xerox   **1.** Name of a company that manufactures a wide variety of office and computer equipment. **2.** Trade name for a XEROGRAPHY machine. **3.** The reproduction obtained by means of XEROGRAPHY (generic term). **4.** To make a xerographic reproduction (generic term).

X factor   **1.** An unknown or unidentifiable quantity or parameter. **2.** See X COMPONENT.

xformer   Abbreviation of TRANSFORMER.

X gain   The gain (or gain control) of the horizontal channel of an oscilloscope or X-Y recorder. Compare Y GAIN and Z GAIN.

X-H array   See LAZY-H ANTENNA.

XHV   Abbreviation of EXTREMELY HIGH VACUUM.

x intercept   The x coordinate of the point at which a line or plane intersects the X-AXIS.

x irradiate   To expose to X RAYS.

xistor   Abbreviation of TRANSISTOR.

X_L   Symbol for INDUCTIVE REACTANCE.

X line   A horizontal line in a memory matrix. Compare Y LINE.

XLR connector   A microphone connector with a locking device to prevent unintentional disconnection. It has three pins and is commonly used with balanced audio systems.

X meter   **1.** An instrument for measuring reactance and phase angle. **2.** A form of simple capacitance meter whose dial is direct-reading in microfarads, although the deflection is actually proportional to the reactance of the capacitor under measurement.

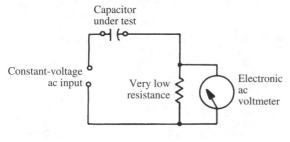

X meter, 2

xmission   Abbreviation of *transmission.*

xmit   Abbreviation of *transmit.* Also, xmt.

xmitter   Abbreviation of TRANSMITTER. Also, xmtr.

XMODEM   In data transmission, an error-correcting mode in which data is sent in blocks of 128 kilobytes (128K), or 131,072 bytes. The source and destination tally up the bytes in each block. If they agree, the next data block is sent. If they do not agree, the current data block is retransmitted. Compare YMODEM and ZMODEM.

xmt   Abbreviation of *transmit.* Also, xmit.

xmtr   Abbreviation of TRANSMITTER. Also, xmitter.

XOR   Abbreviation of EXCLUSIVE-OR.

xover   Abbreviation of CROSSOVER.

X particle   See MESON.

xponder   Abbreviation of TRANSPONDER.

X position   **1.** The alignment of a cathode-ray beam along the horizontal axis of an oscilloscope screen. **2.** The position of a point, with respect to the horizontal axis of a graph in the rectangular (Cartesian) coordinate system.

XR   Abbreviation of INDEX REGISTER.

X radiation   Electromagnetic energy in the form of X rays.

X-ray   **1.** Phonetic alphabet communications code word for the letter X. **2.** Pertaining to, or consisting of, X rays.

X-ray astronomy   The science of observing celestial objects and the sky in the X-ray band of wavelengths. Generally, this must be done from above the earth's atmosphere because the atmosphere absorbs X rays.

X-ray crystallography   The science of observing atomic patterns in a crystal by means of X rays.

X-ray detecting device   **1.** An X-ray instrument for spotting flaws in solid bodies. **2.** A device, such as a fluoroscope, for showing the presence of X rays.

X-ray diagnosis   The use of X rays in the diagnosis of disease and in the observation of internal parts of the body.

X-ray diffraction   The diffraction of X rays by a material into or onto which they are directed. Also see X-RAY DIFFRACTION CAMERA and X-RAY DIFFRACTION PATTERN.

X-ray diffraction camera   A special camera that furnishes a photograph of the pattern created by X rays diffracted by a material. See X-RAY DIFFRACTION and X-RAY DIFFRACTION PATTERN.

X-ray diffraction pattern   The pattern produced on film exposed to X rays diffracted by a material. Also see X-RAY DIFFRACTION and X-RAY DIFFRACTION CAMERA.

X-ray goniometer   An instrument used to find the position of the axes of a quartz crystal. It uses X rays reflected from the atomic planes of the crystal.

X-ray inspection   The use of X rays in the examination and study of the internal features of materials and devices.

X-ray laser   A laser designed to emit coherent X rays in a narrow beam.

X-ray load   **1.** An X-ray tube that is the terminal member of an electronic system. **2.** A body, mass, or material exposed to X rays.

X-ray machine   A device that generates X rays for a specific purpose, such as medical diagnosis.

X-ray photograph A photograph made by exposure to X rays, especially an *X-ray shadowgram*, a picture made without a camera by interposing an object (such as a part of the human body) between an X-ray tube and photographic film.

X-ray radiation See X RADIATION.

X rays Invisible, electromagnetic radiation having wavelengths ranging from approximately 0.01 nanometer (10^{-11} meter) to 0.15 nanometer (1.5×10^{-10} meter). These waves are shorter than ultraviolet, but longer than gamma rays. They can be produced by bombarding a target of heavy metal (such as tungsten) with a stream of high-speed electrons in a vacuum tube. X rays have high penetrating power, can expose photographic film, and cause some substances to fluoresce. Also see X-RAY DIAGNOSIS, X-RAY INSPECTION, and X-RAY THERAPY.

X-ray spectra The continuous band of ionizing electromagnetic radiation having wavelengths ranging from approximately 0.01 nanometers to 0.15 nanometers.

X-ray spectrograph A spectrograph used to disperse and measure the wavelength of X rays.

X-ray spectrometer A spectrometer with which the diffraction angle of X rays reflected from the surface of a crystal can be measured. The device allows the characteristics and composition of almost any material to be studied.

X-ray star A collapsed star that emits high-intensity energy concentrated mainly in the X-ray region of the electromagnetic spectrum.

X-ray system Collectively, an X-ray tube and the associated equipment required for a specific application, such as crystallography, irradiation, or medical therapy.

X-ray technician **1.** A professional skilled in the operation and maintenance of X-ray systems, who usually works under the supervision of an engineer. **2.** A professional skilled in the medical use of X rays, who works under the supervision of a medical doctor.

X-ray therapy The use of X rays in the treatment of certain physiological diseases.

X-ray therapy system An X-ray system designed for X-ray therapy.

X-ray thickness gauge An instrument used to measure the thickness of metal, such as a continuously moving sheet of steel. The measurement is in terms of the amount of absorption of an applied X-ray beam by the metal.

X-ray tube A specialized, very-high-voltage diode in which a high-speed electron beam bombards an anode (target) of heavy metal, such as tung-

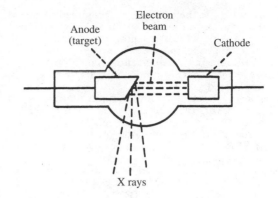

X-ray tube

sten, causing it to emit X rays. The target is tilted to reflect the X rays through the glass wall of the tube.

X section Abbreviation of *cross section*.

X sink The circuit or device into which the X lines of a memory matrix feed. Compare Y SINK.

X_T Symbol for total reactance.

xtal Abbreviation of CRYSTAL.

xtalk Abbreviation of CROSSTALK.

x unit A small unit of length, equal to approximately 10^{-13} meter or 10^{-4} nanometer. Now seldom used, the x unit was once often used in the expression of ultraviolet and X-ray wavelengths.

X wave One (the extraordinary) of the pair of components into which an ionospheric radio wave is divided by the earth's magnetic field. Compare O-WAVE.

XXX In radiotelegraphy, a signal meaning *urgent*.

X-Y counting A technique used with electronic counters to determine the ratio of one frequency (X) to another (Y). When X is the higher frequency, the counter readout shows the number of pulses of X producing one cycle of Y.

XY-cut crystal A piezoelectric plate cut from a quartz crystal at such an angle that its electrical characteristics fall between those of the X-cut and Y-cut crystal.

x-y plotter An output device similar to the x-y recorder. It allows a digital computer to plot graphs. Also called *data plotter*.

x-y recorder An instrument that produces a permanent record (photographic print or directly inked paper) of a variable quantity on a chart having Cartesian (rectangular) coordinates.

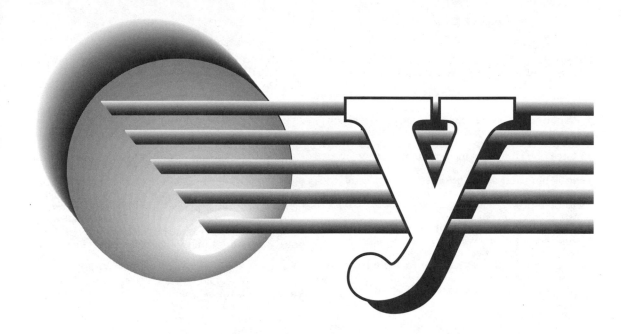

Y **1.** Symbol for ADMITTANCE. **2.** Symbol for YTTRIUM. **3.** Symbol for YOUNG'S MODULUS.

y **1.** Abbreviation of YEAR. (Also, yr.) **2.** Abbreviation of YARD. (Also, yd.) **3.** Symbol for the vertical axis of a graph or screen in the rectangular (Cartesian) coordinate system.

Y adapter See WYE ADAPTER.

YAG Abbreviation of *yttrium-aluminum-garnet*, the stimulated substance in some lasers.

Yagi antenna A directional antenna consisting of several parallel rods or wires. One rod serves as a driven half-wave dipole radiator, one as a parasitic reflector, and one or more as parasitic directors. Also called *yagi*.

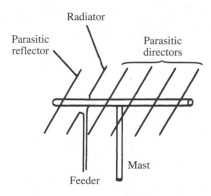

yagi antenna

y amplifier The vertical amplifier of an oscilloscope or recorder. Compare X AMPLIFIER and **Z** AMPLIFIER.

Yankee Phonetic alphabet communications code word for the letter Y.

yard Abbreviation, yd. A unit of linear measure in the English system. 1 yd = 3 ft = 36 inches = 0.9144 meter.

yaw Side-to-side movement in a vehicle or robotic end effector. Essentially horizontal displacement about the vertical axis.

yaw amplifier In an aircraft servo system, the unit that amplifies the yaw signal (the signal proportional to the deviation of the aircraft from the line of flight).

yaw meter An instrument for measuring the angle of yaw of an aircraft.

y-axis **1.** The vertical axis of a chart, graph, or screen in the rectangular coordinate system. **2.** In a quartz crystal, the axis drawn perpendicular to the faces of the hexagon.

y-axis amplifier See Y AMPLIFIER.

Yb Symbol for YTTERBIUM.

Y box See WYE BOX.

Y channel See Y AMPLIFIER.

Y-channel gain See Y GAIN.

Y circulator An interconnection among three waveguides. When power is applied to the junction through one waveguide, the wave is transferred to the adjacent waveguide immediately to the right or left.

Y connection See WYE CONNECTION.

y coordinate See ORDINATE.

Y current See WYE CURRENT.

Y-cut crystal A piezoelectric plate cut from a quartz crystal in such a way that the plane of the plate is perpendicular to the Y-axis of the crystal. See CRYSTAL AXES and Y-AXIS, **2.**

yd Abbreviation of YARD.

Y deflection   Vertical deflection of the spot on the screen of a cathode-ray tube. Compare X DEFLECTION.

Y diode   The decoding diode in each of the Y lines of a memory matrix. Compare X DIODE.

y direction   The vertical direction in deflections and in graphical presentations of data.

Y drive   The driving source or energy for the y lines of a computer memory matrix. Compare X DRIVE.

year   Abbreviation, y or yr. The period of the earth's revolution around the sun, with respect to distant stars: approximately 365.25 days or 3.15576×10^7 seconds.

Yellow Book   A specialized format for *compact-disk read-only memory (CD-ROM)* computer data storage media, developed by Sony and Philips. It is similar to RED BOOK, but it includes superior error correction and storage capacity. See also CD-ROM, GREEN BOOK, ORANGE BOOK, and RED BOOK.

yellow copper ore   See CHALCOPYRITE.

yellow metal   A copper-zinc alloy that is 60% copper.

yellow pyrites   See CHALCOPYRITE.

Y-equivalent circuit   See WYE-EQUIVALENT CIRCUIT.

Y gain   The gain (or gain control) of the vertical channel of an oscilloscope or x-y recorder. Compare X GAIN and Z GAIN.

yield   In a phototube or photocell, the photoelectric current per unit intensity of light.

yield map   A diagram of an integrated circuit showing the locations of faulty components.

yield strength   The lowest stress for plastic deformation of a material, below which the material is elastic and above which it is viscous.

yield value   The amount of physical stress that causes a substance to become stretched permanently out of shape.

YIG   Abbreviation of *yttrium-iron-garnet*, a crystalline material used in certain types of acoustic delay lines, parametric amplifiers, and filters.

YIG crystal   A crystal of yttrium-iron-garnet. See YIG.

YIG filter   A filter using a YIG crystal and tuned electromagnetically.

YIG-tuned parametric amplifier   A parametric amplifier in which tuning is accomplished by continuously varying direct current through the solenoid of a YIG filter.

y intercept   The y coordinate of the point at which a line or plane intersects the y-axis.

ylem   The material from which the primordial fireball is thought to have been made, and from which the entire known universe is believed to have originated approximately 10 billion (10^{10}) years ago.

Y line   A vertical line of a memory matrix. Compare X LINE.

Y-matched-impedance antenna   See WYE-MATCHED-IMPEDANCE ANTENNA.

YMODEM   In data transmission, an error-correcting mode in which data is sent in blocks of one megabyte (1MB), or 1,048,576 bytes. The source and destination tally up the bytes in each block. If they agree, the next data block is sent. If they do not agree, the current data block is retransmitted. Compare XMODEM and ZMODEM.

yoke   **1.** The ferromagnetic ring or cylinder that holds the pole pieces of a dynamo-type generator and acts as part of the magnetic circuit. **2.** The system of coils used for magnetic deflection of the electron beam in cathode-ray tubes.

yoke method   A method of measuring the permeability of a sample of magnetic material. It involves completing the magnetic circuit with a heavy yoke of soft iron.

Young's modulus   Symbol, Y. The ratio of tensile stress to tensile strain.

Y parameters   The admittance parameters of a four-terminal network or device.

Y point   See WYE POINT.

Y position   **1.** On a cathode-ray screen, the vertical position of the beam spot. **2.** On a graph, the position of a point along the vertical axis.

Y potential   See WYE POTENTIAL.

yr   Abbreviation of YEAR. Also, y.

Y rectifier   See WYE RECTIFIER.

Y signal   In color television, the monochromatic signal conveying brightness information.

Y sink   The circuit or device into which the Y lines of a memory matrix feed. Compare X SINK.

ytterbium   Symbol, Yb. A metallic element of the rare-earth group. Atomic number, 70. Atomic weight, 173.04.

ytterbium metals   The rare-earth metals dysprosium, erbium, lutetium, holmium, thulium, and ytterbium.

Yttralox   A transparent polycrystalline ceramic composed primarily of yttrium oxide, which has many applications in electro-optics.

yttria   Formula, Y_2O_3. Yttrium oxide, a white powder used in Nernst lamps.

yttrium   Symbol, Y. A metallic element of the rare-earth-metals group. Atomic number, 39. Atomic weight, 88.906.

yttrium-iron-garnet   See YIG.

yttrium metal   Any of the group of metals, including yttrium, erbium, holmium, lutetium, thulium, ytterbium, and sometimes dysprosium, gadolinium, and terbium.

Yukon Standard Time   Standard time of the ninth time zone west of Greenwich, embracing the Yukon Territory and a portion of southern Alaska.

Y winding   See WYE CONNECTION.

Y-Y circuit   See WYE-WYE CIRCUIT.

Z **1.** Symbol for IMPEDANCE. **2.** Symbol for ATOMIC NUMBER. **3.** Symbol for *zenith distance* (astronomy).

z **1.** Abbreviation of ZERO. **2.** Symbol for ELECTROCHEMICAL EQUIVALENT. **3.** Abbreviation of ZONE. **4.** Symbol for the vertical axis of a three-dimensional Cartesian graph.

zag The short, straight deflection of a point or particle, or of waves along a jagged path in a direction opposite that of a ZIG; one of the components of ZIGZAG DEFLECTION.

Zamboni pile A high-voltage electrochemical cell consisting of an aluminum anode, a manganese-dioxide cathode, and an aluminum-chloride electrolyte.

Z amplifier The intensity-modulation amplifier in an oscilloscope. Compare X AMPLIFIER and Y AMPLIFIER.

Z-angle meter An instrument, commonly of the null-balance type, that indicates the impedance and phase angle of capacitors, inductors, and sometimes of inductance-capacitance-resistance (LCR) combinations.

z-axis **1.** The intensity-modulation input of an oscilloscope, including the associated circuit. **2.** The video-signal input of a television picture tube, including the associated circuit. **3.** The third axis in a three-dimensional coordinate system. **4.** The lengthwise axis of a quartz crystal.

z-axis amplifier See Z AMPLIFIER.

z-axis modulation See INTENSITY MODULATION.

Z bar See Z-CUT CRYSTAL.

z channel See Z AMPLIFIER.

z-channel gain See Z GAIN.

Z-cut crystal A plate cut from a quartz crystal so that the plane of the plate is perpendicular to the Z-axis of the crystal and parallel to the X-axis. See CRYSTAL AXES.

ZD Abbreviation of *zero defects*.

Z deflection Deflection of a cathode-ray beam beyond the (ordinarily defined) deflection area on the tube screen.

Zeeman effect The splitting of a spectral line of a gas into closely spaced, polarized frequency components by an applied magnetic field.

Zenely electroscope A sensitive alpha-ray electroscope (see ELECTROSCOPE) whose leaf is attracted by a metal plate biased at 50 to 200 volts. On touching the plate, the leaf becomes charged and is repelled. But the gas ions around the leaf neutralize the charge, and the leaf returns to the plate to repeat the action. This sequence causes the leaf to oscillate, the number of oscillations per second being proportional to the strength of the ionizing source.

Zener See ZENER DIODE.

Zener breakdown See AVALANCHE BREAKDOWN.

Zener current See AVALANCHE CURRENT.

Zener diode Also sometimes called *avalanche diode* or *Zener*. A semiconductor diode (usually silicon) specially fabricated to take advantage of the effects of avalanche breakdown. It is available in a wide variety of configurations and ratings; it is commonly used as a voltage regulating devices in low-voltage power supplies.

Zener-diode clipper A signal-amplitude clipper that does not require direct-current bias because it uses a Zener diode. Clipping takes place at the avalanche voltage. Zener diodes can be connected back to back for alternating-current clipping.

Zener-diode coupling element A Zener diode used as a direct coupling element between amplifier stages in an electronic system. When no signal is present, the resistance of the diode is extremely high because the direct-current voltages of the diode-coupled amplifier stages reverse-bias the diode to below the avalanche point, and no current flows from one stage to the next. The signal raises the voltage enough to cause avalanche breakdown; the signal is thus readily transmitted from one stage to the following one.

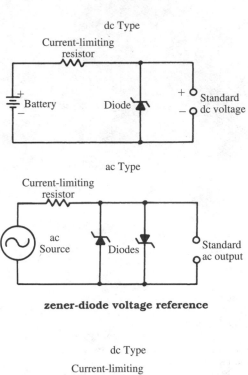

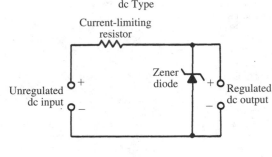

zener-diode voltage reference

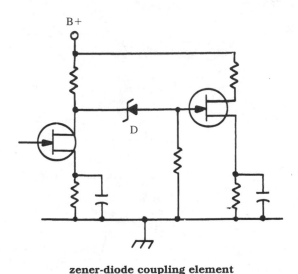

zener-diode coupling element

Zener-diode voltage reference A device that utilizes the constant voltage drop across a Zener diode operated in its breakdown region, to provide a standard voltage for reference purposes. It consists essentially of a direct-current (dc) voltage source, limiting resistor, and Zener diode. For an alternating-current (ac) reference voltage, an ac voltage source, limiting resistor, and two Zener diodes (connected in parallel, back to back) are required. Zener diodes can be connected in series to supply a higher reference voltage than can be delivered by a single diode.

Zener-diode voltage regulator A simple voltage regulator whose output is the constant voltage drop developed across a Zener diode conducting in the reverse breakdown region. The simple regulator circuit consists of a Zener diode and an appropriate limiting resistor connected in series across the output terminals of an unregulated direct-current power supply. For alternating-current voltage regulation, two Zener diodes can be connected in parallel, back to back. Zener diodes can be connected in series to regulate a higher voltage than can be accommodated by a single diode.

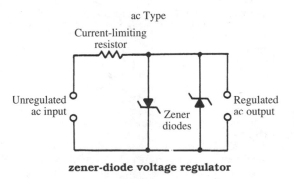

zener-diode voltage regulator

Zener effect See AVALANCHE BREAKDOWN.
Zener knee In the response of a reverse-biased Zener diode, the point of abrupt transition from low current (high resistance) to high current (low resistance). For voltage regulation and volt-

age standardization, the knee should be as sharp as possible.

Zener knee current In a Zener diode, the current that flows when the reverse bias reaches the avalanche voltage.

Zener-protected MOSFET See GATE-PRO-TECTED MOSFET.

Zener voltage The particular value of reverse voltage at which a Zener diode or other reverse-biased pn junction abruptly exhibits the avalanche effect. Depending on the Zener diode, this potential can be less than 10 volts, or as much as several hundred volts.

zenith In the sky, the point directly overhead, exactly 180 degrees opposite the direction of the earth's center.

Zeolite process A method using certain artificial Zeolites (hydrous silicates) to soften water used in some electronic manufacturing and testing operations.

zeppelin antenna **1.** Originally, an antenna designed to be operated from flying blimps or zeppelins, consisting of a quarter-wave, two-wire transmission line terminated on one side by a half-wavelength trailing wire. The intent was to have the antenna function with a balanced tuning network and no direct-current ground. **2.** An antenna in which a wire measuring one-half wavelength is fed with any length of open-wire line and tuned at the transmitter end by means of a transmatch having a balanced output. The antenna can be in line with the feed line or at an angle to the line, most commonly a right angle (90°). The antenna operates at all integral multiples of the design frequency. It is a narrowband antenna and there is some radiation from the

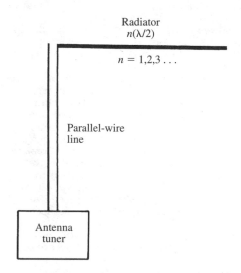

Radiator
$n(\lambda/2)$

$n = 1,2,3 \ldots$

Parallel-wire line

Antenna tuner

zeppelin antenna

line. The standing-wave ratio (SWR) is generally quite high, on the order of 5:1 or greater.

zero **1.** The number represented by the cipher symbol (0). **2.** To set a meter or other instrument to its zero reading or condition. **3.** To align one element of a system precisely with another. **4.** In computer operations, to set a register to zero. **5.** In computer operations, using zero pulses to replace what is in a storage area.

zero-access memory See ZERO-ACCESS STORAGE.

zero-access storage Computer storage requiring negligible waiting time (latency).

zero-address instruction A computer instruction requiring no address; the operation specified by the instruction defines the locations of the operands. Also called *addressless instruction*.

zero adjust In an analog metering device, a mechanical or electrical control that allows precise setting of the reading to zero, when the parameter to be measured is actually zero.

zero adjustment **1.** The act of setting an instrument or circuit to its zero reading or zero-operating condition. **2.** A device or subcircuit used to set a meter to its zero reading. Also see ZERO SET, **1**, **2**.

zero-angle cut An alternate term for *X cut*, as applied to quartz crystal plates. Also see CRYSTAL CUTS.

zero axis In a plot of a variable quantity, the (usually horizontal) reference line that indicates the zero value of the quantity.

zero-axis symmetry The condition in which a waveshape is symmetrical about a zero axis.

zero beat Complete absence of a beat note (i.e., silence), a condition occurring when the frequencies of the beating signals (or their harmonics) are equal. See BEAT NOTE.

zero-beat detector A device or circuit used to sense and indicate the condition of zero beat.

zero-beat indicator See ZERO-BEAT DETECTOR.

zero-beat method A means of adjusting the frequency of one signal exactly to that of another (usually standard) signal by setting the first signal frequency to zero beat with the second signal frequency.

zero-beat reception A system of reception entailing zero beating an incoming signal with the signal from a local oscillator. Also called *homodyne reception*.

zero-bias operation Operation of a transistor or vacuum tube without direct-current base, gate, or grid bias.

zero-bias tube A vacuum tube designed for operation (particularly in a class-B power amplifier) without direct-current grid bias. In such a tube, the zero-signal plate current is very low because of the large amplification factor.

zero capacitance **1.** Absence of capacitance (a theoretically ideal condition). **2.** In some circuits, the lowest capacitance point, to which all other capacitances are referred.

zero compensation   The elimination or minimizing of the zero-signal output of a transducer or similar device.

zero compression   See ZERO SUPPRESSION, **1**.

zero condition   See ZERO STATE.

zero current   **1.** Absence of movement of electrical charge carriers. **2.** In some circuits, the lowest current level, to which all other currents are referred.

zero-cut crystal   A piezoelectric plate cut from a quartz crystal in such a way that the frequency-temperature coefficient is zero.

zero-dB reference level   An agreed-upon zero level for decibel ratings (which are by nature relative). Zero dBm, for example, corresponds to 1 milliwatt. Compare VOLUME UNIT.

zero drift   **1.** The (usually gradual) drift of a zero point, such as the zero setting of an electronic voltmeter. **2.** The condition of no change in the value of a quantity.

zero elimination   See ZERO SUPPRESSION, **1**.

zero energy   The condition in which energy is neither generated, consumed, nor dissipated.

zero error   **1.** In instruments and measurements, an error so small that it can be considered inconsequential. **2.** In a radar system, the inherent delay in the transmitter and receiver circuits.

zero field emission   Thermionic emission from a cathode or hot conductor within a uniform electrostatic field.

zero fill   See ZERO, **5**.

zero gravity   The condition of weightlessness (i.e., the state in which gravitational pull by a celestial body is completely absent or has been nullified).

zero-gravity switch   A switch actuated automatically when the condition of zero gravity is reached.

zero impedance   **1.** Absence of impedance (a theoretically ideal condition). **2.** In some circuits, the lowest impedance level, to which all other impedances are referred.

zero inductance   **1.** Absence of inductance (a theoretically ideal condition). **2.** In some circuits, the lowest inductance level, to which all other inductances are referred.

zero input   **1.** Complete absence of input (signal or noise). **2.** Absence of operating voltage or power to a system. **3.** In a flip-flop, the input terminal that is not receiving a trigger signal.

zero-input terminal   In a flip-flop, the input-signal terminal at which a trigger signal will switch the flip-flop output to zero. Also called *zero terminal* and RESET TERMINAL.

zero instant   See ZERO TIME.

zero level   The reference level for the comparison of quantities. For example, it might be a voltage or current level; in audio measurements, it is the zero-dB reference level.

zero-line stability   In an analog metering device, the ability of the instrument to maintain proper zero adjustment over a period of time.

zero magnet   A permanent magnet used to set the pointer of a meter to zero.

zero magnitude   **1.** For a quantity, the state of being valueless (i.e., a complete absence of the quantity). **2.** In some tests, measurements, or calculations, the lowest value of a quantity, to which all other values are referred.

zero meridian   The meridian at Greenwich (near London), England, from which longitude and standard time are reckoned. Also see TIME ZONE and ZONE TIME.

zero method   A method of measurement entailing adjustment of a circuit or device (such as a bridge, tee network, or potentiometer) for zero response of the detector. Also called *null method*.

zero modulation   The momentary lack of modulation in a communications or broadcast system, as during a pause in speech.

zero-modulation noise   Noise produced by previously erased tape that is run under specified operating conditions.

zero output   **1.** Complete absence of output signal or output power, sometimes disregarding noise output. **2.** In a flip-flop, the normal condition of no signal pulse at a particular output terminal.

zero-output terminal   In a flip-flop, the output terminal that is not delivering an output pulse.

zero phase   In an alternating-current circuit, the condition in which the current and voltage are in step. That is, the current peaks occur at exactly the same times as the voltage peaks; the phase difference between the current and voltage is zero degrees.

zero pole   In a multiconductor line, the common or reference conductor.

zero potential   **1.** Complete absence of voltage. **2.** In some circuits, the lowest voltage, to which all other voltages are referred. **3.** The potential of the earth as a reference point.

zero power   **1.** Complete absence of dissipated power. **2.** In some circuits and systems, the lowest power level, to which all other power values are referred.

zero-power resistance   In a thermistor, the resistance at which power dissipation is zero.

zero-power resistance-temperature characteristic   For a thermistor, a figure that reveals the extent to which zero-power resistance varies with the temperature of the thermistor body.

zero-power temperature coefficient of resistance   A temperature coefficient that reveals the extent to which the temperature of the thermistor body causes the zero-power resistance to change (expressed in ohms per ohm per degree Celsius).

zero reactance   **1.** Absence of reactance (a theoretically ideal condition in alternating-current circuits). **2.** In some circuits, the lowest reactance, to which all other reactances are referred.

zero resistance   **1.** Absence of resistance (a theoretically ideal condition). **2.** In some circuits, the lowest resistance, to which all other resistances are referred.

zero scale current In a digital-to-analog (D/A) converter, the current into the output when all logic inputs are low (off) and the output is at a certain predetermined value, in microamperes or milliamperes.

zero screw The mechanical zero adjuster of a meter.

zero set 1. A (usually screwdriver-adjusted) mechanism for setting the pointer of a meter to zero. 2. An electrical circuit consisting of a resistance bridge or adjustable bucking voltage for setting a meter to read zero under specific conditions.

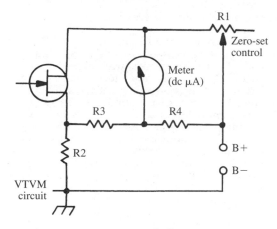

zero set, 2

zero shift See ZERO DRIFT.

zero signal 1. The condition of complete absence of signal. 2. A finite signal level used as a reference point against which all other signal levels are measured.

zeros of impedance For an alternating-current network, the frequencies at which the impedance is zero. Also called *zeros*.

zeros of network function The real or complex values at which the network function is zero. Compare POLES OF NETWORK FUNCTION.

zeros of transfer function The frequencies at which a transfer function becomes zero. Compare POLES OF TRANSFER FUNCTION.

zero stability Constancy of the zero condition in an instrument or system (i.e., absence of zero drift).

zero state The low, zero, off, or false logic state of a bistable device, such as a flip-flop or magnetic cell. It might be actual zero output or a low-voltage output. Compare ONE STATE. In binary notation and calculation, the zero state is represented by a cipher.

zero suppression 1. In computer operation, automatic nonsignificant leading-zero cancellation. 2. Absence or removal of a restraining medium, such as a noise-suppression voltage. 3. In an audio recording system, the introduc-

tion of a voltage to cancel the steady-state component of the input signal.

zero temperature 1. The point from which temperatures are reckoned on a thermometer scale. On the Celsius (centigrade) scale, zero degrees corresponds to the freezing point of pure water at standard atmospheric pressure. On the Fahrenheit scale, zero degrees is 32 degrees colder than the freezing point of pure water at standard atmospheric pressure. On the Kelvin or Rankine scales, zero degrees corresponds to the complete absence of thermal energy; it is the coldest possible temperature. 2. A temperature point relative to which all other temperatures are reckoned.

zero temperature coefficient A temperature coefficient having the value zero (i.e., one that indicates there is no temperature-dependent drift of a given quantity).

zero terminal See ZERO-INPUT TERMINAL and ZERO-OUTPUT TERMINAL.

zero time 1. In some measurements, the first instant of time, to which all other instants are referred. 2. See ZERO PHASE.

zero time reference During one cycle of radar operation, the time reference of the schedule of events.

zero vector A vector whose magnitude is zero.

zero voltage See ZERO POTENTIAL.

zero voltage coefficient A voltage coefficient having the value of zero (i.e., one that indicates there is no voltage-dependent drift of a given quantity).

zero-zero The atmospheric condition in which the ceiling and visibility both are zero (i.e., extremely dense fog).

Z gain The gain (or gain control) of the intensity channel of an oscilloscope. Compare X GAIN and Y GAIN.

zig The short, straight deflection of a point or particle, or of a wave along a jagged path in a direction opposite that of ZAG; a component of ZIGZAG DEFLECTION.

zigzag deflection Deflection of a particle, point, or object in a path that contains side-to-side motion, as well as forward motion. Also see ZAG and ZIG.

zigzag rectifier A special version of the three-phase star (three-phase, half-wave) rectifier circuit. Direct-current (dc) saturation of the transformer secondary is avoided by winding half the turns of each secondary on a separate core (i.e., each core carries two half-windings). The opposing flux resulting from different phases in the half-windings causes cancellation of the dc component of flux in each core.

zigzag reflections Multihop reflections of waves along a zigzag path, resulting from repeated reflections within the ionosphere.

zinc Symbol, Zn. A metallic element. Atomic number, 30. Atomic weight, 65.39. It is used as the negative-electrode material in dry cells and as a protective coating for some metals used in electronics.

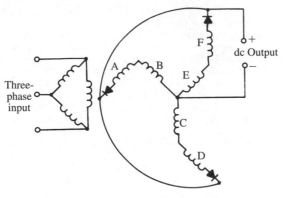

zigzag rectifier

zinc aluminate phosphor   Either of two similar substances used as a phosphor coating for cathode-ray tube screens. One form glows blue; the other form glows red.

zinc beryllium silicate phosphor   A substance used as a phosphor coating for cathode-ray-tube screens. It glows yellow.

zinc beryllium zirconium silicate phosphor   A substance used as a phosphor coating for cath-ode-ray-tube screens. It glows white.

zinc borate phosphor   A substance used as a phosphor coating for cathode-ray-tube screens. It glows yellow-orange.

zinc cadmium sulfide phosphor   Either of two similar substances used as a phosphor coating for cathode-ray-tube screens. One form glows blue; the other form glows red.

zinc-carbon cell   A primary cell in which the negative electrode is zinc and the positive electrode is carbon. It can be either wet or dry. Also see CELL, DRY CELL, and PRIMARY CELL.

zinc germanate phosphor   A substance used as a phosphor coating for cathode-ray-tube screens. It glows yellow-green.

zinc magnesium fluoride phosphor   A substance used as a phosphor coating for cathode-ray-tube screens. It glows orange.

zincolysis   Electrolysis in a cell having a zinc anode.

zinc orthoscilicate phosphor   Also called *Willemite*. A substance used as a phosphor coating for cathode-ray-tube screens. It glows yellow-green.

zinc oxide   A substance used as a phosphor coating for cathode-ray-tube screens. It glows blue-green. It is also used in the manufacture of certain electronic components, such as resistors.

zinc-oxide resistor   A voltage-dependent resistor whose active ingredient is zinc oxide.

zinc silicate phosphor   A substance used as a phosphor coating for cathode-ray-tube screens. It glows blue.

zinc standard cell   A standard cell using zinc and mercury electrodes, and a mercurous sulfate excitant and depolarizer. Produces 1.4322 volts at 15°C. Also called *Clark cell*. Compare WE-STON CELL.

zinc sulfide phosphor   A substance used as a phosphor coating for cathode-ray-tube screens. Glows blue-green or yellow-green.

ZIP   Abbreviation of *zinc-impurity photodetector*.

zip cord   A simple two-conductor, flexible power cord.

zirconia   Preparations of zirconium (especially ZrO_2), valued for their high-temperature dielectric properties.

zirconium   Symbol, Zr. A metallic element. Atomic number, 40. Atomic weight, 91.22.

Z marker   A vertically radiating marker beacon defining the zone above a radio-range station.

Z meter   A device for measuring impedances. Instruments of this kind take four principal forms: (1) a direct-reading meter resembling an ohmmeter; (2) an adjustable circuit manipulated somewhat like a bridge and that compares an unknown impedance with a standard resistance; (3) an impedance bridge for evaluating the reactive and resistive components of an unknown impedance; (4) a section of transmission line used with a signal source and voltmeter for measuring impedance in terms of a standard resistor and/or standing waves.

ZMODEM   In data communications, an error-correction mode similar to XMODEM, except that when an error is found during transmission of a block of data, the source retransmits only that portion of the block following the error. This improves data transmission speed because, when an error occurs, the number of bytes retransmitted is generally fewer than the 128K block size standard in XMODEM. Compare XMODEM and YMODEM.

Zn   1. Symbol for ZINC. 2. Symbol for AZIMUTH.

Z_0   Symbol for CHARACTERISTIC IMPEDANCE.

zone   1. On a magnetic disk, a group of tracks whose associated transfer rate is not the same as that for the rest of the disk. 2. In computer operations, the area of a storage medium containing digits. 3. In a computer system, a main memory area set aside for a particular purpose. 4. In a security system, a specified area or region under surveillance.

zone blanking   In a radar system, a method of extinguishing the cathode-ray-tube beam during a portion of the antenna sweep.

zone candle power   In a given zone, the luminous flux per steradian, emitted by a light source under test.

zoned circuit   In a security system, a circuit in which some areas are protected at all times, while the protection in other areas can be temporarily disabled for entry or exit.

zone leveling   See ZONE REFINING.

zone marker   See Z MARKER.

zone melting   See ZONE REFINING.

zone of silence   The region between alternate reflections of a radio wave, in which no signal is detectable. Also called *skip zone.*

zone plate antenna   A rapid-scan radar antenna having a reflector composed of confocal parabolas arranged in a circle.

zone-position indicator   A radar that reveals the position of an object to a second radar having a restricted field.

zone purification   See ZONE REFINING.

zone refining   A method of purifying semiconductor materials (such as germanium and silicon) in which a molten zone in an ingot of the material moves along the length of the ingot, dissolving impurities as it travels, eventually depositing them at the end of the ingot, which is sawed off. This concentrated and segregated melting is accomplished by means of radio-frequency heating.

zone time   In a given time zone, standard time in terms of the number of hours that must be added to local time to equal the time at the zero (Greenwich) meridian.

zoning   **1.** A method of fabricating a microwave reflector in concentric, flat regions, producing the same practical results as a continuous paraboloid. **2.** In a communications system, the division of the coverage area into different geographic regions for a specific purpose.

zoom   **1.** To rapidly change the focal length of a television or motion-picture camera lens so that the object seems to advance toward or recede from the viewer, remaining in focus as it does so. **2.** See ZOOM LENS. **3.** To magnify the image in a computer graphical user interface. A user can enlarge a specific portion of the display, at the expense of other portions. It is generally measured in percent (e.g., 200% zoom represents a magnification factor of 2).

zoom lens   A continuously adjustable lens system that allows zoom effects to be obtained with a television or motion-picture camera, or a similar arrangement for still cameras that obviates the need for lens interchange when different focal lengths are needed. The lens system, which can be operated electronically, allows either narrow- or wide-angle views to be obtained without losing focus at any time.

Z parameters   Device or network parameters expressed as impedances.

ZPI   Abbreviation of ZONE-POSITION INDICATOR.

Z-plunger   In a waveguide, a combination choke and bucket plunger for radiation leakage reduction.

Zr   Symbol for ZIRCONIUM.

Z signals   A collection of letter groups, each starting with the letter Z, used for simplified telegraphy and radiotelegraphy by the military services.

Zulu   Phonetic alphabet communications code word for the letter Z.

Zulu time   Greenwich mean time. Also see ZEBRA TIME.

zwitterion   An ion that carries both a positive and a negative charge.

Appendix A
Schematic symbols

ammeter		cathode (directly heated)	
amplifier (operational)		cathode (indirectly heated)	
AND gate		cathode (cold)	
antenna (balanced, dipole)		cavity resonator	
antenna (general)		cell	
antenna (loop, shielded)		circuit breaker	
antenna (loop, unshielded)		coaxial cable	
		coaxial cable (grounded shield)	
antenna (unbalanced)		crystal (piezoelectric)	
antenna (whip, or telescopic)		delay line	
attenuator (or resistor, fixed)		diode (field-effect)	
		diode (general)	
attenuator (or resistor, variable)		diode (Gunn)	
battery		diode (light-emitting)	
capacitor (feedthrough)		diode (photosensitive)	
capacitor (fixed, nonpolarized)		diode (photovoltaic)	
capacitor (fixed, polarized)		diode (pin)	
		diode (Schottky)	
capacitor (ganged, variable)		diode (tunnel)	
capacitor (single, variable)		diode (varactor)	
		diode (zener)	
capacitor (split-rotor, variable)		directional coupler (or wattmeter)	
capacitor (split-stator, variable)		exclusive-OR gate	

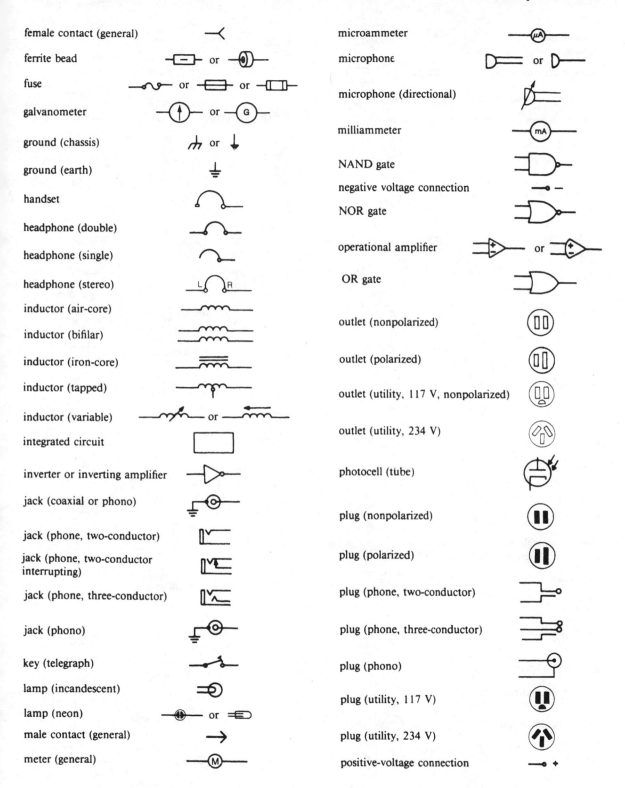

female contact (general)	
ferrite bead	or
fuse	or or
galvanometer	or
ground (chassis)	or
ground (earth)	
handset	
headphone (double)	
headphone (single)	
headphone (stereo)	
inductor (air-core)	
inductor (bifilar)	
inductor (iron-core)	
inductor (tapped)	
inductor (variable)	or
integrated circuit	
inverter or inverting amplifier	
jack (coaxial or phono)	
jack (phone, two-conductor)	
jack (phone, two-conductor interrupting)	
jack (phone, three-conductor)	
jack (phono)	
key (telegraph)	
lamp (incandescent)	
lamp (neon)	or
male contact (general)	
meter (general)	

microammeter	
microphone	or
microphone (directional)	
milliammeter	
NAND gate	
negative voltage connection	
NOR gate	
operational amplifier	or
OR gate	
outlet (nonpolarized)	
outlet (polarized)	
outlet (utility, 117 V, nonpolarized)	
outlet (utility, 234 V)	
photocell (tube)	
plug (nonpolarized)	
plug (polarized)	
plug (phone, two-conductor)	
plug (phone, three-conductor)	
plug (phono)	
plug (utility, 117 V)	
plug (utility, 234 V)	
positive-voltage connection	

potentiometer
(variable resistor, or rheostat)

probe (radio-frequency)

rectifier (semiconductor)

rectifier (silicon-controlled)

rectifier (tube-type)

rectifier (tube-type, gas-filled)

relay (DPDT)

relay (DPST)

relay (SPDT)

relay (SPST)

resistor (fixed)

resistor (preset)

resistor (tapped)

resonator

rheostat (variable resistor,
or potentiometer)

saturable reactor

shielding

signal generator

solar cell

source (constant-current)

source (constant-voltage)

speaker

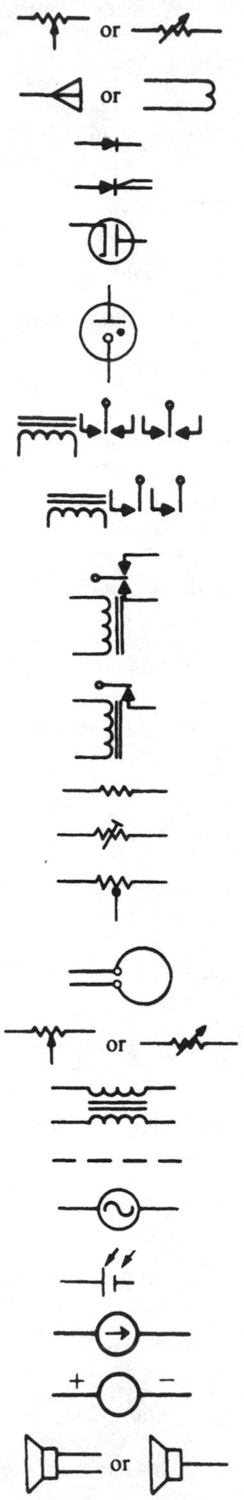

switch (DPDT)

switch (DPST)

switch (momentary-contact)

switch (rotary)

switch (silicon-controlled)

switch (SPDT)

switch (SPST)

terminals (general, balanced)

terminals (general, unbalanced)

test point

thermocouple

thyristor (diac)

thyristor (triac)

transformer (air-core)

transformer (air-core, adjustable)

transformer (iron-core)

transformer (iron-core, adjustable)

transformer (powdered-iron-core)

transformer (tapped-primary)

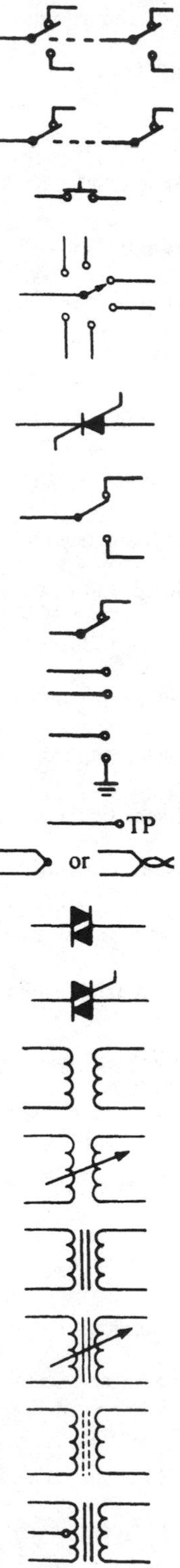

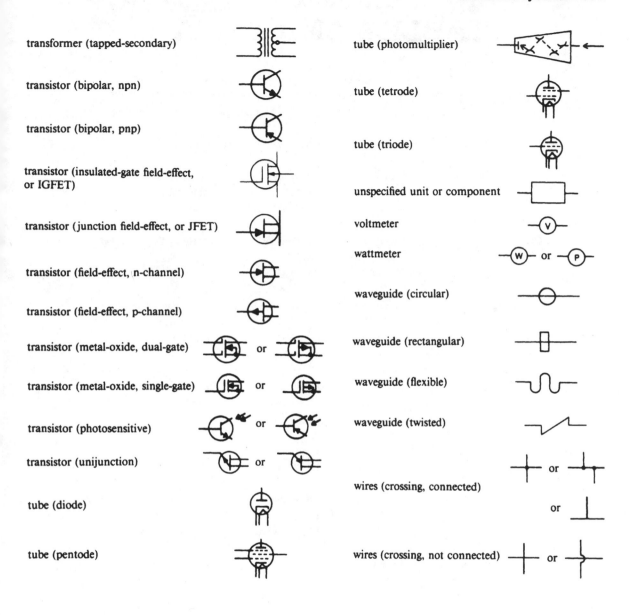

transformer (tapped-secondary)	tube (photomultiplier)
transistor (bipolar, npn)	tube (tetrode)
transistor (bipolar, pnp)	tube (triode)
transistor (insulated-gate field-effect, or IGFET)	unspecified unit or component
transistor (junction field-effect, or JFET)	voltmeter
transistor (field-effect, n-channel)	wattmeter
transistor (field-effect, p-channel)	waveguide (circular)
transistor (metal-oxide, dual-gate) or	waveguide (rectangular)
transistor (metal-oxide, single-gate) or	waveguide (flexible)
transistor (photosensitive) or	waveguide (twisted)
transistor (unijunction) or	wires (crossing, connected) or or
tube (diode)	
tube (pentode)	wires (crossing, not connected) or

TABLES AND DATA

Conversion between Electrical Systems

Property	mks	System cgs electromagnetic	cgs electrostatic
Capacitance	1 farad	10^{-9} abfarad	9×10^{11} statfarad
	10^9 F	1 abF	9×10^{20} statF
	$10^{-11}/9$ F	$10^{-20}/9$ abF	1 statF
Charge	1 coulomb	0.1 abcoulomb	3×10^9 statC
	10 C	1 abC	3×10^{10} statC
	$10^{-9}/3$ C	$10^{-10}/3$aC	1 statC
Charge density	1 coulomb/m^3	10^{-7} abcoulomb/cm^3	3×10^3 statcoulomb/cm^3
	10^7 C/m^3	1 abC/cm^3	3×10^{10} statCcm^3
	$10^{-3}/3$ C/m^3	$10^{-10}/3$ aC/cm^3	1 statC/cm^3
Conductivity	1 siemens/m	10^{-11} absiemens/cm	9×10^9 statSiemens/cm
	10^{11} S/m	1 abS/cm	9×10^{20} statS/cm
	$10^{-9}/9$ S/m	$10^{-20}/9$ abS/cm	1 statS/cm
Current	1 ampere	10^{-1} abampere	3×10^9 statampere
	10 a	1 abA	3×10^{10} statA
	$10^{-9}/3$ a	$10^{-10}/3$ abA	1 statA
Current density	1 ampere/m^2	10^{-5} abampere/cm^2	3×10^5 statampere/cm^2
	10^5 A/m^2	1 abA/cm^2	3×10^{10} statA/cm^2
	$10^{-5}/3$ A/m^2	$10^{-10}/3$ aA/cm^2	1 statA/cm^2
Electric field intensity	1 volt/m	10^6 abvolt/cm	$10^{-4}/3$ statvolt/cm
	10^{-6} V/m	1 abV/cm	$10^{-10}/3$ statV/cm
	3×10^4 V/m	3×10^{10} aV/cm	1 statV/cm
Electric potential	1 volt	10^8 abvolt	$10^{-2}/3$ statvolt
	10^{-8} V	1 abV	$10^{-10}/3$ statV
	3×10^2 V	3×10^{10} aV	1 statV
Electric dipole moment	1 coulomb-m	10 abC-cm	3×10^{11} statC-cm
	0.1 C-m	1 abC-cm	3×10^{10} statC-cm
	$10^{-11}/3$ C-m	$10^{-10}/3$ abC-cm	1 statC-cm

| | | System | |
Property	mks	cgs electromagnetic	cgs electrostatic
Energy	1 joule	10^7 erg	10^7 erg
	10^{-7} J	1 e	1 e
	10^{-7} J	1 e	1 e
Force	1 newton	10^5 dyne	10^5 dyne
	10^{-5} N	1 d	1 d
	10^{-5} N	1 d	1 d
Flux density	1 Weber/m^2	10^4 gauss (or abtesla)	$10^{-6}/3$ electrostatic unit
	10^{-4} Wb/m^2	1 G	$10^{-10}/3$ esu
	3×10^6 Wb/m^2	3×10^{10} G	1 esu
Inductance	1 henry	10^9 abhenry	$10^{-11}/9$ stathenry
	10^{-9} H	1 abH	$10^{-20}/9$ statH
	9×10^{11} H	9×10^{20} abH	1 statH
Inductive capacity	1 farad/m	10^{-11} abfarad/cm	9×10^9 statfarad/cm
	10^{11} F/m	1 abF/cm	9×10^{20} statF/cm
	$10^{-9}/9$ F/m	$10^{-20}/9$ abF/cm	1 statF/cm
Magnetic flux	1 weber	10^8 Maxwell	$10^{-2}/3$ electrostatic unit
	10^{-8} W	1 Mx	$10^{-10}/3$ esu
	3×10^2 W	3×10^{10} Mx	1 esu
Magnetic dipole moment	1 ampere-m^2	10^3 abampere-cm^2	3×10^{13} statampere-cm^2
	10^{-3} A-m^2	1 abA-cm^2	3×10^{10} statA-cm^2
	$10^{-13}/3$ A-m^2	$10^{-10}/3$ abA-cm^2	1 statA-cm^2
Permeability	1 henry/m	10^7 abhenry/cm	$10^{-13}/9$ stathenry/cm
	10^{-7} H/m	1 abH/cm	$10^{-20}/9$ statH/cm
	9×10^{13} H/m	9×10^{20} abH/cm	1 statH/cm
Power	1 watt	10^7 erg/s	10^7 erg/s
	10^{-7} W	1 e/s	1e/s
	10^{-7} W	1 e/s	1e/s
Resistance	1 ohm	10^9 abohm	$10^{-11}/9$ statohm
	10^{-9} ohm	1 abohm	$10^{-20}/9$ statohm
	9×10^{11} ohm	9×10^{20} abohm	1 statohm

GREEK ALPHABET

Capital	Lowercase	Name
A	α	alpha
B	β	beta
Γ	γ	gamma
Δ	δ or ∂	delta
E	ϵ	epsilon
Z	ζ	zeta
H	η	eta
Θ	θ or ϑ	theta
I	ι	iota
K	$\varkappa$	kappa
Λ	λ	lambda
M	μ	mu
N	ν	nu
Ξ	ξ	xi
O	o	omicron
Π	π	pi
P	ϱ	rho
Σ	σ or ς	sigma
T	τ	tau
Υ	υ	upsilon
Φ	ϕ or φ	phi
X	χ	chi
Ψ	ψ	psi
Ω	ω	omega

Mathematical Functions

Signs and symbols

$\cdot$	radix (base) point	$\neq$	not equal to
$\bullet$	multiplication symbol; logic AND function	$\sim$	similar to
∞	infinity	$<$	less than
$+$	plus; positive; logic OR function	$\nless$	not less than
$-$	minus; negative	$<<$	much less than
$\pm$	plus or minus; positive or negative	$>$	greater than
$\mp$	minus or plus; negative or positive	$\ngtr$	not greater than
$\times$	times	$>>$	much greater than
$\div$	divided by	$\leq$	equal to or less than
$/$	divided by (expressive of a ratio)	$\geq$	equal to or greater than
$=$	equal to	$\propto$	proportional to; varies directly as
$\equiv$	identical to; is defined by	$\doteq$ or $\rightarrow$	approaches
$\simeq$ or $\cong$	approximately equal to, congruent to	$:$	is to; proportional to
$\approx$	approximately equal to	$\therefore$	therefore

@	at the rate of; at cost of
e	natural number = 2.71828
π	pi $\approx 3.14159\ldots$
( )	parentheses (use to enclose a group of terms)
[ ]	brackets (use to enclose a group of terms that includes one or more groups in parentheses)
{ }	braces (use to enclose a group of terms that includes one or more groups in brackets.
$\angle$	angle
°	degrees (arc or temperature)
'	minutes; prime
"	seconds; double prime
$\parallel$	parallel to
$\perp$	perpendicular to
. . .	and beyond
∇	(del or nabla) vector differential operator

Operations

$x + y$	x added to y; x OR y
$x - y$	y subtracted from x
$x \cdot y$, $x \times y$, or xy	x multiplied by y; x AND y
$x \div y$	x divided by y
x/y or $\dfrac{x}{y}$	x divided by y
$1/x$	reciprocal of x
x^n	x raised to the indicated power of n
$\sqrt[n]{x}$	indicated root n of x
$x : y$	x is to y
$\lvert x \rvert$	absolute value of x, magnitude of x
$\bar{X}$, $\dot{X}$, or $\mathbf{X}$	vector X

$\bar{x}$	average value of x; x not
$f(x)$ or $F(x)$	function of x
i	$\sqrt{-1}$
j	operator, equal to $\sqrt{-1}$
Δx	increment of x
dx	differential of x
∂x	partial differential of x
$\dfrac{\Delta x}{\Delta y}$	change in x with respect to y
$\dfrac{dx}{dy}$	derivative of x with respect to y
$\dfrac{d}{dy}(x)$	derivative of x with respect to y
$d_y x$	derivative of x with respect to y
$\dfrac{\partial x}{\partial y}$	partial derivative of x with respect to y
Σ	summation
$\displaystyle\sum_{b}^{a}$	summation between limits (from a to b)
Π	product
$\displaystyle\prod_{b}^{a}$	product between limits (from a to b)
$\int$	integral
$\displaystyle\int_{a}^{b}$	integral between limits (from a to b)
$\int x\,dy$	integral of x with respect to y
$\vert a$	evaluated at a
$\vert_{a}^{b}$	evaluated between limits (from a to b)
$n!$	factorial of n

Prefixes

Prefix	Quantity	Symbol
atto-	10^{-18}	a
femto-	10^{-15}	f
pico-	10^{-12}	p
nano-	10^{-9}	n
micro-	10^{-6}	μ
milli-	10^{-3}	m
centi-	10^{-2}	c
deci-	10^{-1}	d
deka-	10	da
hecto-	10^{2}	h
kilo-	10^{3}	k
mega-	10^{6}	M
giga-	10^{9}	G
tera-	10^{12}	T
peta-	10^{15}	P
exa-	10^{18}	E

RESISTOR COLOR CODE

The first three color bands supply the total resistance. The fourth color (if any) gives the tolerance. Example: A 5,600-ohm resistor would have green (first color, 5), blue (second color, 6) and red (third color, 00) bands.

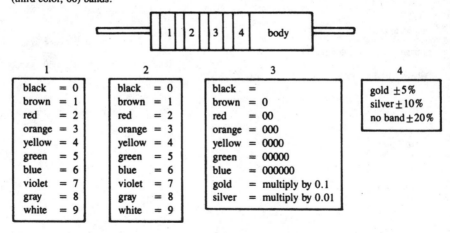

1	2	3	4
black = 0	black = 0	black =	gold ±5%
brown = 1	brown = 1	brown = 0	silver ±10%
red = 2	red = 2	red = 00	no band ±20%
orange = 3	orange = 3	orange = 000	
yellow = 4	yellow = 4	yellow = 0000	
green = 5	green = 5	green = 00000	
blue = 6	blue = 6	blue = 000000	
violet = 7	violet = 7	gold = multiply by 0.1	
gray = 8	gray = 8	silver = multiply by 0.01	
white = 9	white = 9		

Appendix C

Electronics abbreviations

a	atto-; area; acceleration; acre, anode; obsolete for ab
A	ampere; area; gain; anode
Å	angstrom
AAC	automatic aperture control
ab-	prefix for multiple of 10 in cgs system
abA	abampere
abc	automatic bass compensation; automatic bias control; automatic brightness control; automatic brightness compensation
abC	abcoulomb
abF	abfarad
abH	abhenry
abS	absiemens
ABS	absolute value function
abV	abvolt
abW	abwatt
abWb	abweber
ac, AC	alternating current (lowercase preferred); aerodynamic center; attitude control; automatic computer
a/c	aircraft; air conditioning
ACA	automatic circuit analyzer
acc	automatic chrominance control; automatic color compensation; acceleration
ACIA	asynchronous communications interface adapter
acr	audio cassette recorder; audio cassette recording
ACS	automatic control system
ACU	automatic calling unit
A/D, AD, a/d	analog-to-digital; analog-to-digital converter
adc	analog-to-digital converter
ADF	automatic direction finder
ADI	alternate digit inversion
adp	ammonium dthydrogen phosphate; automatic data processing
adu	automatic dialing unit
aF	attofarad (SI); obsolete for abfarad (cgs)
AF	audio frequency
AFC	automatic frequency control
AFPC	automatic frequency/phase control
AFSK	audio-frequency-shift keying
AGC	automatic gain control
Ah	ampere hour
aH	attohenry (SI); obsolete for abhenry (cgs)
AIP	American Institute of Physics
Al	aluminum
alc	automatic level control
ALU	arithmetic and logic unit
Am	americium
AM	amplitude modulation; amplitude modulator
AMI	alternate mark inversion
AMNL	amplitude-modulation noise level
amp	ampere
amp-hr	ampere hour
amu	atomic mass unit
ANSI	American National Standards Institute
ant	antenna

APC	automatic phase control; automatic picture control
APL	average picture level
Ar	argon
ARRL	American Radio Relay League
ARS	Amateur Radio Service; amateur radio station
As	arsenic
ASA	American Standards Association
ASCII	American Standard Code for Information Exchange
ASRA	automatic sterophonic recording amplifier
At	astatine
ATR	antitransmit-receive
ATV	amateur television
AU	astronomical unit
Au	gold
a/v	audio-visual
aV	attovolt (Sl); obsolete for abvolt (cgs)
AVC	automatic voltage control
AWG	American wire gauge
AZ-EL	azimuth-elevation
B	susceptance; magnetic flux density; battery; boron; base (transistor); bass; bel
b	susceptance; base (transistor); bass; barns
B&S	American wire gauge
BA	battery
Ba	barium
BAL	balance
BAT	battery
BC	broadcast
BCD	binary-coded decimal
BCFSK	binary-coded frequency-shift keying
BCI	broadcast interference
BCL	broadcast listener; broadcast listening
BCN	beacon
BCO	binary-coded octal
BCST	broadcast
BDC	binary decimal counter
Be	beryllium
beO	beryllium oxide
BeV	billion electron volts
BFO	beat-frequency oscillator
BG	Birmingham wire gauge
B-H	flux density and magnetizing force
Bi	bismuth
BiMOS	bipolar and metal-oxide-semiconductor
bip	binary image processor
BIPM	International Bureau of Weights and Measures
bit	binary digit
BITE	built-in test equipment
BK	break; break-in
Bk	berkelium
BO	beat oscillator
bp	bandpass
bpi	bits per inch
bps	bits per second
Br	bromine
Btu	British thermal unit
bw	bandwidth; black-and-white
B&W, B/W, b&w, b/w	black and white
BWA	backward-wave amplifier
BWG	Birmingham wire gauge
BWO	backward-wave oscillator

BX	armored and insulated cable
C	capacitance; collector; carbon; Celsius; coulomb
c	centi; capacitance; speed of light in vacuum; colorie, curie, candle; collector
Ca	calcium
CAD	computer-aided design
cal	calorie
CAL	conversional algebraic language
CAM	content-addressable memory; computer-aided manufacturing
cap	capacitance; capacitor
CAT	computerized axial tomography
CATV	community-antenna television
CB	citizens band
Cb	columbium
C_B	base capacitance
C_c	collector capacitance
cc	cubic centimeter
CCA	current-controlled amplifier
CCD	charge-coupled device
CCIS	common-channel interface signaling
CCTV	closed-circuit television
ccw	counterclockwise
Cd	cadmium
cd	candela
cd/m^2	candelas per square meter
Ce	cerium
C_E	emitter capacitance
Cf	californium
C_{GK}	grid-cathode capacitance
C_{GP}	grid-plate capacitance
cgs	centimeter-gram-second
CHIL	current-hogging injection logic
Ci	curie
C_i, C_{in},	input capacitance
circ	circuit; circular
cis	on this side of
ckt	circuit
Cl	chlorine
Cm	curium
cm	centimeter
c.m., cir mil	circular mil
cm^2	square centimeter
cm^3	cubic centimeter
C_{max}	maximum capacitance
C_{min}	minimum capacitance
CML	current-mode logic
CMOS	complementary metal-oxide semiconductor
CMR	common-mode rejection
CMRR	common-mode rejection ratio
Co	cobalt
C_O	output capacitance
COBOL	common business-oriented language
CODEC	coder/decoder
COM	computer output on microfilm
CONTRAN	computer language that uses no compiler
CORAL	high-level, real-time computer language
COS	complementary symmetry
cp	candle power; central processor
cps	cycles per second; characters per second
CPU	central processing unit
Cr	chromium
CRO	cathode-ray oscilloscope

crt, CRT	cathode-ray tube
Cs	cesium
CS	complementary symmetry
C_s	standard capacitance; source capacitance
CTL	complementary transistor logic
Cu	copper
cu ft	cubic foot; cubic feet
cu in	cubic inch; cubic inches
cur	current
CW, cw	continuous wave; clockwise
D	deuterium; displacement; flux density; dissipation factor; dissipation; drain; determinant; diffusion constant
d	deci; differential; distance; density; drain; dissipation; day; degree; diameter; drive
DA, D/A, d/a	digital-to-analog; digital-to-analog converter
da	deka
DAC	digital-to-analog converter
DACI	direct adjacent-channel interference
DAGC	delayed automatic gain control
DAM	data-addressed memory
DART	data-analysis recording tape
DAT	diffused-alloy transistor
DAVC	delayed automatic volume control
DB	diffused base; double break
dB	decibel
dBa	adjusted decibels
dBc	decibels referred to carrier
DBD	double-base diode
dBd	decibels of antenna gain referred to half-wave dipole
dBi	decibels of antenna gain referred to isotropic radiator
dBj	RF signal level relative to 1 mV
dBk	RF signal level relative to 1 kW
DBM	database management
dBm	decibels relative to 1 mW
dBmO	dBm relative to zero transmission level
dBmp	dBm with psophometric weighting
dBmOp	dBm0 with psophometric weighting
dBmV	decibels relative to 1 mV
dBr	decibels relative to zero transmission level
dBrap	decibels above reference acoustic power
dBrn	decibels above reference noise
dBrncO	noise in dBrnc relative to zero level
dBV	decibels relative to 1 V
dBW	decibels relative to 1 W
dBx	decibels above reference coupling
dc, DC	direct current (lowercase preferred); direct-coupled
D/CMOS	combined DMOS and CMOS
DCM	digital capacitance meter
DCTL	direct-coupled transistor logic
dcu	decimal counting unit
dev	dc volts; dc voltage (variation of preferred Vdc)
DDA	digital differential analyzer
DDD	direct distance dialing
DE	decision element
deac	deaccentuator
deca	prefix for 10
deci	prefix for 1/10
deg	degree; degrees
dens	density
df, DF	direction finder; direction finding
dg	decigram
dia, diem	diameter

DIIC	dielectric-isolated integrated circuit
DIP	dual in-line package
dj	diffused junction
DMA	direct memory access; direct memory addressing
DMM, dmm	digital multimeter
DMOS	double-diffused metal-oxide semiconductor
DNL	differential nonlinearity
DP	data processing
dpdt, DPDT	double-pole, double-throw
dpm	digital power meter; digital panel meter; disintegrations per minute
dpst, DPST	double-pole, single-throw
dr	dram
DRO	digital readout
DSB	double sideband
DSBSC	double sideband, suppressed carrier
dsc	double silk covered
DSP	double silver plated
DSR	dynamic spatial reconstructor
DSS	direct station selection
DSSC	double-sideband, suppressed carrier
DT	data transmission
dt	differential of time
DTL	diode-transistor logic
DTn	double tinned
DTS	data transmission system; digital telemetry system
DU	duty cycle
dv	differential of velocity
dvm, DVM	digital voltmeter
dvom , DVOM	digital volt -ohm-milliammeter
DX	distance; duplex
Dy	dysprosium
dyn	dyne
dyna-	power
E	voltage; electric field strength; emitter; exa-; energy
e	voltage; emitter; electron charge; natural log base = 2.71828 . . .; eccentricity; erg
E_o	zero-reference voltage
EAM	electronic accounting machine
E_{avg}	average voltage
E_b	battery voltage
E_{BB}	plate supply voltage
EBI	equivalent background input
EBR	electron beam recording
EBS	electron-bombarded semiconductor
ec	enamel-covered
E_{cc}	grid supply voltage
ECDC, ECDT	electrochemical diffused-collector (transistor)
ECG	electrocardiogram; electrocardiograph
ECL	emitter-coupled logic
ECM	electronic countermeasures
eco	electron-coupled oscillator
ECTL	emitter-coupled transistor logic
EDD	envelope-delay distortion
EDP	electronic data processing
EDT	ethylene diamine tartrate
EDU	electronic display unit
EDVAC	electronic discrete variable automatic computer
EE	electrical engineer; electrical engineering
E_{eff}	effective voltage
EEG	electroencephalogram; electroencephalograph
EEPROM	electrically erasable programmable read-only memory
EFL	emitter-follower logic

E_G	grid voltage; gate voltage; generator voltage
E_H	heater voltage
EHF	extremely high frequency
EHV	extra-high voltage
E_i, E_{in}	input voltage
EIT	engineer in training
E_K	cathode voltage
EKG	electrocardiogram; electrocardiograph
EL	electroluminescent
ELD	edge-lighted display
ELSIE	electronic letter-sorting and indicator equipment
EM	effficiency modulation; electromagnetic; electromagnetics; electromagnetic iron; electromagnetizer; electron microscope; exposure meter; electromotive
E_m	maximum voltage; maximum junction field
e/m_e	ratio of electron charge to electron mass
E_{max}	maximum voltage
EMC	electromagnetic compatibility
emf	electromotive force
ENIAC	electronic numerical integrator and computer
ENIC	voltage negative-impedance converter
E_o, E_{out}	output voltage
EOF	end of file
EOL	end of line
EOLM	electro-optical light modulator
EOR	end of run
EOS	electro-optical system
EOT	end of tape
EOTS	electro-optical tracking system
E_p	plate voltage; peak voltage
ep, EP	extended play
E_{pk}	peak voltage
Epk-pk, Ep-p, Epp	peak-to-peak voltage
EPROM	electrically programmable read-only memory
EPU	electronic power unit; emergency power unit
Eq, eq	equation; equivalent
equiv	equivalent
Er	erblum
ER	voltage drop across a resistance
Erms	root-mean-square voltage
ERP	effective radiated power
ES	einsteinium
Es	screen voltage
ESG	electronic sweep generator
ESS	electronic switching system
esu	electrostatic unit; electrostatic units
E_{sup}	suppressor voltage
ETC	electronic temperature control
Eu	europium
eV	electronvolt; electronvolts
E_X	voltage drop across a reactance; excitation energy
exc	exciter; excitation
exp	exponential; experimental
E_Z	voltage drop across an impedance
F	force, fluorine; Fahrenheit; farad; fermi; focal length; filament; fuse; Faraday constant
f	femto-; frequency; function; factor
F_0	damping factor
F_1	frequency-shift keying
fax	facsimile
fc	foot-candle
f_c	carrier frequency

FCC	Federal Communications Commission
f_{co}	cutoff frequency
FDM	frequency-division multiplex
FDS	Faraday dark space
FE	ferroelectfic
Fe	iron
FE-EL	ferroelectric-electroluminescent
femto-	10^{-15}
ferfi- ferro-	denotes magnetic properties
FET	field-effect transistor
FET VOM	field-effect transistor volt-ohm-milliammeter
FF	flip-flop
FFI	fuel-flow indicator
fig	figure
fil	filament
FIR	far infrared
fL	foot-lambert
Fm	fermium
FM	frequency modulation
f_m	modulation frequency
FORTRAN	formula translation (computer language)
FOSDIC	film optical scanning devices for input to computer
F_p	power-loss factor
FPIS	forward propagation by ionospheric scatter
fps	feet per second; frames per second; footpound-second
Fr	francium
fr	frankline
FRUGAL	fortran rules used as a general applications language
FRUSA	flexible rolled-up solar array
FSK	frequency-shift keying
FSM	field-strength meter
FSR	feedback shift register
ft	foot; feet
ft-L	foot-lambert
ft-lb	foot-pound
G	conductance; giga; deflection factor; perveance; gravitational constant; generator; gate
g	gravity; conductance; gram; gate; generator; grid
GA	go ahead
Ga	gallium
GaAs	gallium arsenide
Gd	gadolinium
gdo	grid-dip oscillator; gate-dip oscillator
Ge	germanium
gen	generator
GeV	gigaelectronvolt
gfi	ground-fault interrupter
g_{fs}	forward transconductance
G/G	ground-to-ground
GHz	gigahertz
G_{in}, G_f, g_{in}, g_i	input conductance
giga	10^9
GJD	germanium junction diode
gm	gram
g_m	transconductance
gcal or gmcal	gram-calorie
gmcm	gram-centimeter
gmm	gram-meter
gnd, GND	ground
G_{out}, G_o, g_{out}, g_o	output conductance
G_P, g_p	plate conductance

gpc	germanium point-contact
GSR	galvanic skin resistance
H	magnetic field strength; magnetizing force; hydrogen; unit function; horizontal; heater; henry; harmonic
h	hecto (100); Planck constant; hour; height
hal	halogen
HCD	hard-copy device
HCM	half-cycle magnetizer
HDB3	high-density bipolar-3
He	helium
He-Ne	helium-neon
Hf	hafnium
HF	high frequency
Hg	mercury
HIC	hybrid integrated circuit
HIDM	high-information delta modulation
hi-fi	high fidelity
hipot	high potential
HLL	high-level language
Ho	holmium
hor, horiz	horizontal
HOT	horizontal output transformer; horizontal output transistor; horizontal output tube
hp	horsepower
h-p	high-pressure
hr	hour
HSM	high-speed memory
HTL	high-threshold logic
HV	high voltage
hy	henry (variation of the preferred H)
Hz	hertz
I	current; iodine; intrinsic semiconductor; luminous intensity
i	$\sqrt{-1}$; instantaneous value; intrinsic semiconductor; angle of incidence; instantaneous current; vector parallel to xaxis; incident ray
I_A	anode current
I_{ac}	ac component current
I_{AF}	audio-frequency current
IAGC	instantaneous automatic gain control
IALC	instantaneous automatic level control
IAVC	instantaneous automatic volume control
I_B	plate power-supply current
I_b	base current; plate current
IC	integrated circuit; internal connection
I_C	collector current; grid current
ICAD	integrated control and display
ICAS	intermittent commercial and amateur service
ICBM	intercontinental ballistic missile
I_{CBO}	static reverse collector current, common-base
ICBS	interconnected business system
I_{CEO}	static reverse collector current, common-emitter
ICET	Institute for the Certification of Engineering Technicians
I_{co}	collector cutoff current
ICW	interrupted continuous wave
ID	inside diameter
I_{dc}	dc component current
$I_{D(off)}$	drain cutoff current
IDOT	instrumentation online transcriber
IDP	industrial data processing; integrated data processing; intermodulation-distortion percentage
I_{DSS}	drain current at zero gate voltage
I_E	emitter current
IEC	integrated electronic component

IKE	Institution of Electrical Engineers
IEEE	Institute of Electrical and Electronics Engineers
IF	intermediate frequency
I_f	filament current
I_{FB}	IC feedback current
I_{FS}	full-scale current
I_G	gate current
1_g	grid current
IGFET	insulated-gate field-effect transistor
I_{GSS}	gate reverse current
I_h	heater current; hold current; holding current
IHF	inhibit flip-flop
I_i	input current; instantaneous current
I_K	cathode current
I^2L	integrated infection logic
IM	intermodulation
I_m	maximum current; meter current
IMPATT	impact avalanche transit time
In	indium
in	input; inch; inches
ind	indicator; inductance; inductor
INV	inverter
inv	inverse
I/0	input/output
I_o	output current
I_P	plate current
I_p	peak current
ipm	inches per minute
ips	inches per second
IR	product of current and resistance; insulation resistance; infrared
Ir	iridium
I_R	current in a resistor
IRE	Institute of Radio Engineers
I_{RF}	radio-frequency current
I_S	source current; screen current
ISCAN	inertialess steerable communications antenna
I_{sup}	suppressor current
$I(t)$	indicial response
I_X	current in a reactance
I_Y	current in an admittance
I_Z	current in an impedance
J	joule; jack; connector; emissive power
j	engineer's symbol for j operator or $\sqrt{-1}$
JEDEC	Joint Electron Device Engineering Council
JFET	Junction field-effect transistor
JHG	joule heat gradient
J/K	joules per kelvin
J/(kg·K)	joules per kilogram-kelvin
J/s	joules per second
JSR	jump to subroutine
K	constant; dielectric constant; potassium; kelvin; go ahead (radiotelegraph); cathode; 1024 bits
k	kilo; Boltzmann constant; constant; dielectric constant
kA	kiloampere
kb, Kb	kilobit
kc	kilocycle (alternate of the preferred kHz); kilocurie
kcal	kilocalorie
kCi	kilocurie
kcs	1000 characters per second; 1000 cycles per second (obsolete)
KDP	potassium dthydrogen phosphate
Kel-f	polymonochlorotrifluoroethylene

keV	kiloelectronvolt
kg	kilogram
kgc	kilogram-calorie
kgm	kilogram-meter
kg/m^3	kilograms per cubic meter
kHz	kilohertz
kJ	kilojoule
km	kilometer
Kr	krypton
kV	kilovolt
kVA	kilovolt-ampere
kVAR	reactive kilovolt-ampere
kVARh	reactive kilovolt-ampere-hour
kW	kilowatt
L	inductance; mean life; low; Laplace transform; lambert
I	length; liter; low; lumen
La	lanthanum
LASCR	light-activated silicon-controlled rectifier
LASCS	light-activated silicon-controlled switch
lb	pound
LC	liquid crystal; inductance-capacitance
LCD	liquid-crystal display
LCR	inductance-capacitance-resistance
L_d	distributed inductance
LED	light-emitting diode
LF	low frequency
Li	lithium
LIY	liquid crystal
LLL	low-level logic
lm	lumen
lm/ft^2	lumens per square foot
lmhr	lumen-hour
lm/m^2	lumens per square meter
lm/W	lumens per watt
ln	natural logarithm
LO	local oscillator
lo	low
log	logarithm
$\log_e$	natural logarithm
$\log_{10}$	base-10 logarithm
loran	long-range navigation
LP	low power; long playing; low pressure
LPB	lighted pushbutton
lpm, l/m	lines per minute
lpW, l/W	lumens per watt
L+R	sum of left and right stereo channels
L–R	difference of left and right stereo channels
LSB	least significlant bit; lower sideband
LSC	least significant character
LSD	least significant digit
LSI	large-scale integration
LSSC	lower-sideband suppressed carrier
LTROM	linear transformer read-only memory
Lu	lutetium
LUF	lowest usable frequency
LV	low voltage
LVDT'	linear variable differential transformer
Lw	lawrencium
lx	lux
LZT	lead zirconate-titanate
M	mega-; mutual inductance; refractive modulus

m	milli-; mass; meter; mile; modulation coefficient
m^2	square meter
m^3	cubic meter
mA	milliampere; milliamperes
MADT	microalloy diffused transistor
MAG	maximum available gain
magamp	magnetic amplifier
MAR	memory-address register
MAT	microalloy transistor
max	maximum
mb	millibar
MBM	magnetic bubble memory
MBO	monostable blocking oscillator
MBS	magnetron beam switching
mc	megacycle; millicurie; meter-candle
Mc	megacurie
MCG	magnetocardiogram; magnetocardiograph
mCi	millicurie
MCi	megacurie
MCW	modulated continuous wave
Md	mendelevium
MDI	magnetic direction indicator
MDS	minimum discernible signal
m_e	electron rest mass
meg	megohm
mega	millions (10^6)
MESFET	combination depletion/enhancement-mode field-effect transistor
MeV	megaelectronvolt
mF	millifarad
mf	medium frequency; mid-frequency
MFSK	multiple frequency-shift keying
Mg	magnesium
MGD	magnetogasdynamics
MHD	magnetohydrodynamics
MHz	megahertz
mi	mile; miles
MIC	microwave integrated circuit
mic; mike	microphone
MICR	magnetic ink character recognition
micro	millionths (10^{-6}); extremely small
MINIDOS	mini disk operating system
min	minimum; minute
MIR	memory-information register
mks	meter-kilogram-second
mL	millilambert
ml	milliliter
mm	millimeter
mmf	magnetomotive force; micromicrofarad (now picofarad)
mmol	millimole
mmv	monostable multivibrator
mu	millimicro- (now nano); millimicron (nanometer)
Mn	manganese
m_n	neutron rest mass
mntr	monitor
MO	master oscillator
Mo	molybdenum
mod	modulator; modulus; modification
mol	mole
MOPA	master oscillator-power amplifier
MOS	metal-oxide semiconductor; metal-oxide silicon
MOSFET	metal-oxide-silicon field-effect transistor

MOSROM	metal-oxide-silicon read-only memory
MOST	metal-oxide-silicon transistor
MOV	metal-oxide varistor
MPG	microwave pulse generator
mph	miles per hour
MPO	maximum power output
mps	meters per second; miles per second
MPT	maximum power transfer
MPX	multiplex
MR	memory register
mrad	milliradian
ms	millisecond
msec	millisecond (alternative of preferred ms)
mea	message
MSI	medium-scale integration
mtr	meter (alternative of preferred m)
mu	Greek letter μ; micro; amplification factor; permeability; micron; electric moment; inductivity; magnetic moment; molecular conductivity
MUF	maximum usable frequency
MUPO	maximum undistorted power output
MUSA	multiple-unit steerable antenna
MV	megavolt; multivibrator
mV	millivolt
MV	medium voltage
MVA	megavolt-ampere
mV/m	millivolts per meter
MVP	millivolt potentiometer
MW	megawatt
mW	milliwatt
MWh	megawatt-hour
mWRTL	milliwatt resistor-transistor logic
Mx	maxwell
μ	micro-; amplification factor; permeability; micron; electric moment; inductivity; magnetic moment; molecular conductivity
μA	microampere
$\mu\mu$	micromicro- (now pico, 10^{-12})
μ_B	Bohr magneton
μCi	microcurie
μ_e	electron magnetic moment
μF	microfarad
μg	microgram
μH	microhenry
μl	microliter
μ_n	nuclear magneton
μ_o	free-space permeability constant
μP	microprocessor
$\mu\upsilon$	micromho (alternative of the preferred microsiemens, mS)
$\mu\Omega$	microhm
$\mu\Omega$-cm	microhm-centimeter
μ_p	proton magnetic moment
μS	microsiemens
μs, msec	microsecond
μV	microvolt
μV/m	microvolts per meter
μW	microwatt
μW/cm^2	microwatts per square centimeter
N	number; natural number; set of natural numbers; nitrogen; newton
n	number (usually integer); nano (10^9); index of refraction; amount of substance
Na	sodium
nA	nanoampere
nano-	billionth(s) (10^{-9})

NAP	nuclear auxiliary power
NAPU	nuclear auxiliary power unit
NARTB	National Association of Radio and Television Broadcasters
NAS	National Academy of Sciences
NAVAiDS	navigational aids
Nb	niobium
nb, n/b	narrowband
NBFM	narrowband frequency modulation
NBTDR	narrowband time-domain reflectometry
nbw	noise bandwidth
NC	normally closed; no connection; numerical control
N/C	numerical control
nc	no connection
NCS	net control station(s)
Nd	neodymium
Ne	neon
NEB	noise equivalent bandwidth
NEC	National Electric Code
NEDA	National Electronic Distributors' Association
NEI	noise equivalent input
NEL	National Electronics Laboratory
NELA	National Electric Light Association
NEMA	National Electrical Manufacturers' Association
NEP	noise equivalent power
NEPD	noise equivalent power density
NESC	National Electrical Safety Code
NET	noise equivalent temperature
NF	noise figure
nF	nanofarad
NFET	n-channel junction field-effect transistor
NFM	narrowband frequency modulation
NG	negative glow; no good
NGT	noise-generator tube
nH	nanohenry
Ni	nickel
NIDA	numerically integrating differential analyzer
NIF	noise improvement factor
NIPO	negative input/positive output
NIR	near infrared
NLR	nonlinear resistance; nonlinear resistor
NLS	no-load speed
N/m^2	newtons per square meter (pascals)
NMOS	N-channel metal-oxide semiconductor
NMR	nuclear magnetic resonance; normal mode rejection
NO	normally open
No	nobelium
No., no.	number
Np	neptunium; neper
N_p	number of primary turns
NPM	counts per minute
NP0	negative-positive-zero
NPS	counts per second
NRD	negative-resistance diode
NRZ	nonreturn-to-zero
N_s	number of secondary turns
ns, nsec	nanosecond
NSPE	National Society of Professional Engineers
NTC	negative temperature coefficient
NTSC	National Television Systems Committee
nu	Greek v; reluctivity
nV	nanovolt

nW	nanowatt
O	oxygen; output
o	output; origin
O_2	oxygen
O_3	ozone
OAT	operating ambient temperature
OBWO	O-type backward-wave oscillator
o/c	open circuit
OCR	optical character recognition
oct	octal
OD	outside diameter
Oe	oersted
OGL	outgoing line
OLRT	online real time
OM	optical microscope; old man (ham radio slang)
op	operate; operator; operational
op amp	operational amplifier
op code	operation code
opt	optical; optional
Os	osmium
osc	oscillator
Os-Ir	osmiridium
OTA	operational transconductance amplifier
OTL	output-transformerless
ox	oxygen
oz	ounce; ounces; ozone
oz-in	ounce-inch; ounce-inches
P	plate; power; phosphorus; pressure; primary; peta; permeance; point
p	pico- (10^{-12}); peak; pound; point; primary; plate; pitch; per
PA	power amplifier; pulse amplifier; particular average; pilotless aircraft; public address
Pa	proactinium; pascal
pA	picoampere
PACM	pulse-amplitude code modulation
PADT	post-alloy-diffused transistor
PAM	pulse-amplitude modulation
PAN	urgent message to follow
PAV	phase-angle voltmeter
PAX	private automatic exchange
Pb	lead
PBX	private branch exchange
PC	photocell; printed circuit; positive column; point contact; percent; program counter; punched card
pc	picocurie; parsec
PCB, pcb	printed-circuit board
PCL	printed-circuit lamp
PCM	pulse-code modulation; punched card machine
PD	plate dissipation; pulse duration; proximity detector; potential difference
Pd	palladium
PDAS	programmable data acquisition system
PDM	pulse-duration modulation
PE	potential energy; professional engineer; probable error
PEM	photoelectromagnetic
PEP	planar epitaxial passivated; peak envelope power
pF	picofarad
pf	power factor
PFET	p-channel junction field-effect transistor
PFM	pulse-frequency modulation
PG	power gain
pH	hydrogen-ion concentration
P_i, P_{in}	input power

PIA	peripheral interface adapter
PIM	pulse-interval modulation
PIO	parallel input/output
PIV	peak inverse voltage
PLC	power-line communication
PLL	phase-locked loop
PLM	pulse-length modulation
PLO	phase-locked oscillator
PM	permanent magnet; pulse(d) modulator; pulse(d) modulation; phase modulation; post meridian
Pm	promethium; petameter
P_m, P_{max}	maximum power
PMOS	p-channel metal-oxide semiconductor
PN	Polish notation; positive-negative
PNM	pulse-numbers modulation
Po	polonium
P_o, P_{out}	output power
pos	positive; position
pot	potentiometer; dashpot; potential
PP	peripheral processor
P_p	plate power; peak power
ppb	parts per billion (10^9)
ppm	parts per million; pulses per minute
pps	pulses per second
ppt	parts per thousand
Pr	praseodymium
prf, PRF	pulse repetition frequency
pri	primary
PROM	programmable read-only memory
PRR	pulse repetition rate
PRV	peak reverse voltage
PS	power supply
ps	picosecond
PSD	phase-sensitive detector
psec	picosecond (alternative of preferred ps)
pef	pounds per square foot
psi	pounds per square inch; angle; flux
psia	pounds per square inch absolute
psig	pounds per square inch gauge
PSK	phase-shift keying
PSM	pulse-spacing modulation
psvm	phase-sensitive voltmeter
PSWR	power standing-wave ratio
Pt	platinum
PTC	positive temperature coefficient
PTM	pulse-time modulation
PTO	permeability-tuned oscillator
PTT	press-to-talk
Pu	plutonium
pV	picovolt
PVC	polyvinyl chloride
pW	picowatt
PWM	pulse-width modulation; plated-wire memory
pwr	power
PZT	lead zirconate titanate
Q	figure of merit; electrical charge; selectivity; Q band; Q output
q	electrical quantity; charge carried by electron; value of quantum; quart
QAVC	quiet automatic volume control
QCW	Q-phase cw signal (television)
QFM	quantized frequency modulation
QM	quadrature modulation

QMQB	quick-make, quick break
QSO	two-way contact (amateur radio)
qt	quart
qty	quantity
qual	qualitative
R	resistance; resistor; message received (roger); radical; reluctance
$R_{(00)}$	Rydberg constant
r	roentgen; correlation coefficient; radius
r_e	classical electron radius
RA	right ascension; random access
rac	rectified alternating current
R_{ac}	ac resistance
racon	radar beacon
red	radiac; radian; radio; radix; radius; radical
RAM	random-access memory
Rb	rubidium
R_B	base resistance
RC	resistance-capacitance; radio-controlled; remote control
R_C	collector resistance; cold resistance
RCL	recall; resistance-capacitance-inductance
RCTL	resistor-capacitor-transistor logic
RCV, rcv	receive
RCVR, rcvr	receiver
R&D	research and development
R_D	drain resistance
R_{dc}	dc resistance
RDF	radio direction finder
Re	rhenium
R_E	emitter resistance
rect	rectifier; rectified; rectification
ref	reference
R_{eff}	effective resistance
rej	reject; rejection
rei	relative
rem	roentgen equivalent man
res	resistance; resistor; research; resolution
rev	revolution: reverse
R_f	filament resistance; feedback resistor
RF	radio frequency
RFC	radio-frequency choke
RFI	radio-frequency interference
RFO	radio-frequency oscillator
R_G	gate resistance
R_g	grid resistance
RGB	red green blue
RGT	resonant-gate transistor
Rh	rhodium
R_{HF}	high-frequency resistance
RI	radio interference
R_i, R_{in}	input resistance
R_K	cathode resistance
RL	resistance-inductance; relay logic
R_L	load resistance
R_{LF}	low-frequency resistance
R_m	meter resistance
r_m	emitter-collector transresistance
RMA	Radio Manufacturers' Association
rms	root mean square
Rn	radon
R_n	negative resistance
R_o, R_{out}	output resistance

ROM	read-only memory
R_P	plate resistance; parallel resistance; primary resistance
RPG	report program generator
rpm	revolutions per minute
R_{pri}	primary resistance
rps	revolutions per second
RPT	repeat
R_{req}	required resistance
R_S	source resistance
R_s	secondary resistance; screen resistance; series resistance
R_{sec}	secondary resistance
RST	readability-strength-tone
R_T	thermal resistance
R_t, R_T	total resistance
RTD	resistance temperature detector
RTL	resistor-transistor logic
RTTY	radioteletype
RTZ	return to zero
Ru	ruthenium
R_x	unknown resistance
RY	relay
RZ	return to zero
S	screen; shell; sulfur; deflection sensitivity; switch; elastance; sync; secondary; siemens; sine; entropy
s	distance; displacement; screen; standard deviation; second
SADT	surface alloy diffused-base transistor
SAE	shaft-angle encoder; Society of Automotive Engineers
sat	saturate; saturation
satd	saturated
SAVOR	signal-actuated voice recorder
SB	sideband; simultaneous broadcast
Sb	antimony
SBC	single-board computer
SBDT	surface-barrier diffused transistor
SBT	surface-barrier transistor
SC	suppressed carrier; short circuit; silk-covered
Sc	scandium
sc	sine-cosine; single crystal; science; scale
SCA	subsidiary communications authorization
scc	single cotton covered
sce	single cotton enameled
SCEPTRON	spectral comparative pattern recognizer
SCLC	space-charge-limited current
sco	subcarrier oscillator
SCR	silicon-controlled rectifier
SCS	silicon-controlled switch
SCT	surface-charge transistor
SD	standard deviation
Se	selenium
sec	second; section; secondary; secant
sech	hyperbolic secant
SELCAL	selective calling
SEM	scanning electron microscope
ser	series; serial
SF	safety factor; single-frequency; standard-frequency; stability factor
SFA	single-frequency amplifier
SFO	single-frequency oscillator; standard-frequency oscillator
SFR	single-frequency receiver
SG	screen grid
SGCS	silicon gate-controlled switch
SHF	superhigh frequency

SI	International System of Units
S/I	signal-to-intermodulation ratio
Si	silicon
SIC	specific inductive capacity
SiC	silicon carbide
sig	signal
sin	sine
SINAD	signal-to-noise-and-distortion ratio
SIO	serial input/output
SIP	single in-line package
Si(x)	sine integal
SJD	silicon junction diode
SKM	sine-cosine multiplier
SLS	side-lobe suppression
Sm	samarium
SN	semiconductor network
S/N	signal-to-noise ratio
Sn	tin
SNOBOL	string-oriented symbolic language
SNR	signal-to-noise ratio
sol	solution; soluble
SOM	start of message
SOP	standard operating procedure
SOS	distress signal (telegraphy)
SP	self-propelled; stack pointer
sp	single-pole; special
spc	silicon point-contact; silver-plated copper
spdt, SPDT	single-pole, double-throw
spec	specification; spectrum
spec an	spectrum analyzer
specs	specifications
SPFW	single-phase, full-wave
sp gr	specific gravity
SPHW	single-phase, half-wave
spkr	speaker
SPOT	satellite position and tracking
spst, SPST	single-pole, single-throw
sq	square
SQR	square rooter; square-root function
SR	silicon rectifier; silicon rubber; shift register
S-R	send-receive
Sr	strontium
SRAM	static random-access memory
SRF	self-resonant frequency
SS	solid-state; single-shot; small-signal; single-signal; same size; stainless steel
SSB	single-sideband
SSBSC	single-sideband, suppressed carrier
ssc	single silk covered
sse	single silk enameled
SSI	small-scale integration
SSL	solid-state lamp
SSSC	single-sideband, suppressed carrier
st, ST	single-throw
sta	station; stationary
stab	stabilizer; stability; stabilization
stalo	standardized oscillator
stat-	electrostatic
statA	statampere
statC	statcoulomb
statF	statfarad
statH	stathenry

statOe	statoersted
statS	statsiemen
statV	statvolt
statWb	statweber
std	standard
stn	station
STO	store; storage
STP	standard temperature and pressure
sup	suppressor; suppression
SW	shortwave
sw	switch
SWG	standard wire gauge
SWL	shortwave listener; shortwave listening
SWR	standing-wave ratio
sym	symmetrical; symmetry; symbol
sync	synchronization; synchronism
T	transformer; tera (10^{12}); thermodynamic temperature; tritium; ton; tesla; kinetic energy; period; true
t	time; ton; Celsius temperature; target; technical; tension
Ta	tantalum
tach	tachometer
tan	tangent
tanh	hyperbolic tangent
Tb	terbium
Tc	technetium
TCCO	temperature-controlled crystal oscillator
TCL	transistor-coupled logic
TCM	thermocouple meter
TDM	time-division multiplex,,
TDR	time-delay relay; time-domain reflectometry
TE	transverse electric; trailing edge
Te	tellurium
tel	telephone; telegraph; telegram
TEM	transverse electromagnetic
tera	trillion (10^{12})
TeV	tera-electronvolt
TGTP	tuned-grid, tuned-plate
TH	true heading
Th	thorium
THD	total harmonic distortion
thy	thyratron
THz	terahertz
Ti	titanium
Tl	thallium
T^2L	transistor-transistor logic
TM	transverse magnetic; technical manual
Tm	thulium
tot	total; to derive a total
TP	transaction processing
TPTG	tuned-plate, tuned-grid
TR	transmit-receive
t_r	recovery time; rise time
trans	transverse; transmit; transmitter; transformer
trf	tuned radio frequency
trig	trigonometry; trigonometric
ts	tensile strength
TSS	time-sharing system
TTL	transistor-transistor logic
TTY	teletype; teletypewriter
TU	terminal unit
TV	television; terminal velocity

T/V	temperature-to-voltage
TVI	television interference
TVL	television listener; television listening
TVM	transistor voltmeter
TVO, TVOM	transistor volt-ohmmeter
TVT	television terminal
TW	terawatt; traveling wave
TWA	traveling-wave amplifier
TWT	traveling-wave tube
U	uranium; unit; universal set; union of sets
u	micro (when symbol μ is not available); unified atomic mass unit
U_a	unit of activity
UDOP	ultra-high-frequency doppler system
UEP	underwater electric potential
UFET	unipolar field-effect transistor
UHF	ultrahigh frequency
uhr	ultrahigh resistance
UJT	unijunction transistor
ULD	ultralow distortion
ULF	ultralow frequency
uni-	single; one
UNIFET	unipolar field-effect transistor
UNIPOL	universal problem-oriented language
UNIVAC	universal automatic computer
uns	unsymmetrical; unstable
UPC	universal product code
upconv	up converter
USB	upper sideband
USSC	upper-sideband, suppressed-carrier
UTL	unit transmission loss
W	ultraviolet; undervoltage
UVM	universal vendor marking
V	volt; voltage; potential; vanadium; volume; reluctivity; vertical
v	velocity; vector; voltage
VA	volt-ampere
V/A	volts per ampere
VAC	vector analog computer
vac	vacuum; volts ac (alternative of preferred Vac)
Vac, V_{ac}, v_{ac}	volts ac
val	value
VAR	volt-amperes reactive
var	variable
V_B	base voltage
V_{BB}	base-voltage supply
V_c	collector voltage
VCA	voltage-controlled amplifier
V_{CC}	collector-voltage supply
VCCO	voltage-controlled crystal oscillator
VCD	variable-capacitance diode
VCG	voltage-controlled generator
VCO	voltage-controlled oscillator
VCR	video-cassette recorder
VCSR	voltage-controlled shift register
VCXO	voltage-controlled crystal oscillator
VD	voltage drop; vapor density
V_D	drain voltage
Vdc, V_{dc}	volts dc
VDU	visual display unit; video display unit
vdcw	dc working voltage
VDR	voltage-dependent resistor; video-disk recorder
V_{drive}	drive voltage

VE	value engineering
V_E	emitter voltage
V_{EE}	emitter-voltage supply
vel	velocity
vers	versed sine
vert	vertical
VF	video frequency
V_{FB}	feedback voltage
VFO	variable-frequency oscillator
v_g, V_g	generator voltage
VGA	variable-gain amplifier
V_{GD}	gate-drain voltage
V_{GS}	gate-source voltage
VHF	very high frequency
VHR	very high resistance
VHRVM	very-high-resistance voltmeter
VI	volume indicator; viscosity index
V_i, V_{in}	input voltage
VLF	very low frequency
VLR	very low resistance; very long range
VLSI	very large scale integration
V/m	volts per meter
VMOS	vertical metal-oxide semiconductor
VMOSFET	vertical metal-oxide-semiconductor field-effect transistor
V_o, V_{out}	output voltage
VOA	volt-ohm-ammeter
vol	volume
VOM	volt-ohm-milliammeter
VOR	very-high-frequency omnirange
vox	voice-operated control
V_p	pinchoff voltage; plate voltage
Vpm, V/m	volts per meter
VR	voltage regulator
V_{ref}	reference voltage
vrr	visual radio range
V•s	volt-seconds (webers)
V•s/A	volt-seconds per ampere (henrys)
VSA	voice-stress analyzer
VSB	vestigial sideband
VSF	vestigial-sideband filter
vsr	very short range
VSWR	voltage standing-wave ratio
vt	vacuum tube; variable time
VTL	variable-threshold logic
vtm	voltage-tuned magnetron
VTO	voltage-tuned oscillator; voltage-tunable oscillator
VTR	video-tape recorder; video-tape recording
VTVM	vacuum-tube voltmeter
VU	volume unit
VVCD	voltage-variable capacitor diode
VVV	test signal (telegraphy)
VW	volts working
W	work; watt; watts; tungsten; energy; west; width
WAC	worked all continents
WAS	worked all states
WATS	wide-area telephone service
WAZ	worked all zones
W_B	base-region width
Wb	weber
Wb/m^2	webers per square meter
W_c	collector-region width

W/cm^2	watts per square centimeter
WE	write enable
W_E	emitter-region width
WG	wire gauge
wgt	weight
WH	watt-hour
WHP	water horsepower
WL	wavelength; waterline
WM	wattmeter
$W \cdot m^2$	watt square meter
$W/(m \cdot K)$	watts per meter kelvin
$W/(m^2 \cdot K^4)$	unit of Stefan-Boltzmann constant
w/o	without
Wpc, W/c	watts per candle
wpm	words per minute
$W/(sr \cdot m^2)$	watts per steradian per square meter
WT	wireless telegraphy; watertight
wt	weight
WVdc	dc working voltage
ww	wirewound
W/wr	watts per steradian
X	reactance; no connection; abscissa; unknown quantity; multiplication
x	number of carriers; abscissa; unknown quantity; multiplication
XB	crossbar
X_C	capacitive reactance
Xe	Xenon
xfmr, xformer	transformer
XHV	extremely high vacuum
xistor	transistor
X_L	inductive reactance
xmission	transmission
xmit	transmit
xmitter	transmitter
XMT, xmt	transmit
XMTR, xmtr	transmitter
XOR	exclusive OR
xover	crossover
xponder	transponder
XR	index register
X-section	cross section
X_T, X_t	total reactance
xtal	crystal
xtaLk	crosstalk
Y	admittance; ordinate; yttrium; Young's modulus
y	year; yard; ordinate
YAG	yttrium-aluminum-garnet
YIG	yttrium-iron-garnet
yT	y-matrix of transistor
yV	y-matrix of vacuum tube
Z	impedance; atomic number; zenith distance
z	zero; electrochemical equivalent; zone
Zn	zinc; azimuth
Z_0	characteristic impedance
Zr	zirconium

Suggested additional reading and reference

American Radio Relay League, *The ARRL Handbook*, ARRL, annual.

Everest, F. Alton, *The Master Handbook of Acoustics*—3rd Edition, TAB/McGraw-Hill, 1994.

Gibilisco, Stan, *McGraw-Hill Encyclopedia of Personal Computing*, McGraw-Hill, 1996.

Gibilisco, Stan, *Teach Yourself Electricity and Electronics*, TAB/McGraw-Hill, 1993.

Gibilisco, Stan, *TAB Encyclopedia of Electronics for Technicians and Hobbyists*, TAB/McGraw-Hill, 1997.

Gibilisco, Stan, *Amateur Radio Encyclopedia*, TAB/McGraw-Hill, 1994.

Graf, Rudolf F., *Encyclopedia of Electronic Circuits*, TAB/McGraw-Hill, 1985.

Graf, Rudolf F., *Encyclopedia of Electronic Circuits*—Volume 2, TAB/McGraw-Hill, 1988.

Graf, Rudolf F., *Encyclopedia of Electronic Circuits*—Volume 3, TAB/McGraw-Hill, 1991.

Graf, Rudolf F. and Sheets, William, *Encyclopedia of Electronic Circuits*—Volume 4, TAB/McGraw-Hill, 1992.

Graf, Rudolf F. and Sheets, William, *Encyclopedia of Electronic Circuits*—Volume 5, TAB/McGraw-Hill, 1995.

Internet and World Wide Web, WWW online computer networks.

Jurgen, Ronald, *Automotive Electronics Handbook*, McGraw-Hill, 1995.

Sams Publishing, *Reference Data for Engineers*, SAMS, Prentice-Hall Computer Publishing, 1993.

About the author

Stan Gibilisco is a professional technical writer who specializes in books on electronics and science topics. He is the author of *The Encyclopedia of Electronics, McGraw-Hill Encyclopedia of Personal Computing,* and previous editions of *The Illustrated Dictionary of Electronics,* as well as over twenty other technical books. His published works have won numerous awards, and *The Encyclopedia of Electronics* was chosen as one of the Best Reference Books of the 1980s by *Booklist.*